New Perspectives on

MICROSOFT®
WINDOWS® XP
PROFESSIONAL

Power Users

HARRY L. PHILLIPS
Santa Rosa Junior College

THOMSON

COURSE TECHNOLOGY

Australia • Canada • Mexico • Singapore • Spain • United Kingdom • United States • Japan

THOMSON
COURSE TECHNOLOGY

New Perspectives on Microsoft Windows XP Professional for Power Users
is published by Course Technology.

Managing Editor:
Rachel Crapser

Senior Editor:
Donna Gridley

Senior Product Manager:
Kathy Finnegan

Technology Product Manager:
Amanda Young

Associate Product Manager:
Brianna Germain

Editorial Assistant:
Emilie Perreault

Developmental Editor:
Lisa Ruffolo

Production Editor:
Elena Montillo

Composition:
GEX Publishing Services

Text Designer:
Meral Dabcovich

Cover Designer:
Efrat Reis

Preface

Course Technology is the world leader in information technology education. The New Perspectives Series is an integral part of Course Technology's success. Visit our Web site to see a whole new perspective on teaching and learning solutions.

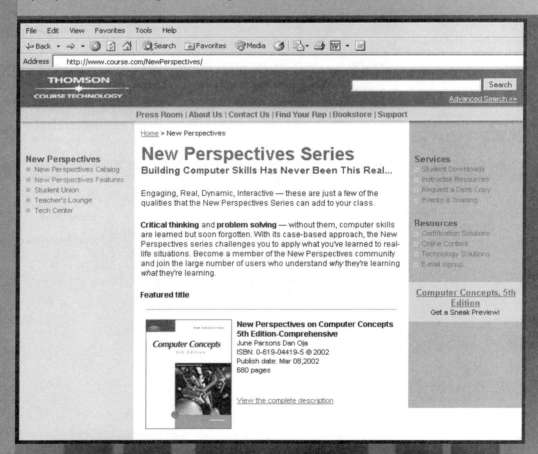

File   Edit   View   Favorites   Tools   Help

← Back ▾ → ▾ ⊗ ⬜ ⌂ | ⚲Search ⬜Favorites ⬜Media ⬜ | ⬜▾ ⬜ ⬜ ▾ ⬜

Address | http://www.course.com/NewPerspectives/

THOMSON
COURSE TECHNOLOGY

[Search]
Advanced Search >>

Press Room | About Us | Contact Us | Find Your Rep | Bookstore | Support

Home > New Perspectives

New Perspectives
- New Perspectives Catalog
- New Perspectives Features
- Student Union
- Teacher's Lounge
- Tech Center

New Perspectives Series
Building Computer Skills Has Never Been This Real...

Engaging, Real, Dynamic, Interactive — these are just a few of the qualities that the New Perspectives Series can add to your class.

Critical thinking and **problem solving** — without them, computer skills are learned but soon forgotten. With its case-based approach, the New Perspectives series challenges you to apply what you've learned to real-life situations. Become a member of the New Perspectives community and join the large number of users who understand *why* they're learning *what* they're learning.

Featured title

New Perspectives on Computer Concepts
5th Edition-Comprehensive
June Parsons Dan Oja
ISBN: 0-619-04419-5 © 2002
Publish date: Mar 08, 2002
680 pages

View the complete description

Services
- Student Downloads
- Instructor Resources
- Request a Desk Copy
- Events & Training

Resources
- Certification Solutions
- Online Content
- Technology Solutions
- E-mail signup

Computer Concepts, 5th Edition
Get a Sneak Preview!

Computer Concepts
5th Edition

New Perspectives—Building Computer Skills Has Never Been This Real

Why New Perspectives will work for you.

Critical thinking and **problem solving**—without them, computer skills are learned but soon forgotten. With its **case-based** approach, the New Perspectives Series challenges students to apply what they've learned to real-life situations. Become a member of the New Perspectives community and watch your students not only **master** computer skills, but also **retain** and carry this **knowledge** into the world.

New Perspectives catalog
Our online catalog is never out of date! Go to the Catalog link on our Web site to check out our available titles, request a desk copy, download a book preview, or locate online files.

Complete system of offerings
Whether you're looking for a Brief book, an Advanced book, or something in between, we've got you covered. Go to the Catalog link on our Web site to find the level of coverage that's right for you.

Instructor materials
We have all the tools you need—data files, solution files, figure files, a sample syllabus, and ExamView, our powerful testing software package.

How well do your students know Microsoft Office?
Experience the power, ease, and flexibility of SAM XP and TOM. These innovative software tools provide the first truly integrated technology-based training and assessment solution for your applications course. Click the Tech Center link to learn more.

Get certified
If you want to get certified, we have the titles for you. Find out more by clicking the Teacher's Lounge link.

Interested in online learning?
Enhance your course with rich online content for use through MyCourse 2.0, WebCT, and Blackboard. Go to the Teacher's Lounge to find the platform that's right for you.

Your link to the future is at
www.course.com/NewPerspectives

What you need to know about this book.

- Student Online Companion takes students to the Web for additional work.

- ExamView testing software gives you the option of generating a printed test, LAN-based test, or test over the Internet.

- New Perspectives Labs provide students with self-paced practice on computer-related topics.

- The step-by-step instructions and screen illustrations guide students as they tour the Windows XP desktop, explore Windows XP online Help, and work with OLE technologies.

- Students will appreciate the contemporary, realistic scenarios ranging from a pharmaceutical company to a home-based graphics business.

- Students will gain confidence with Windows XP by customizing Windows XP, creating shortcuts, optimizing disks, and installing and troubleshooting hardware.

- Web Technology coverage is woven throughout all of the chapters.

- This text provides a comprehensive overview of working with Windows XP. It moves quickly and is suitable for both beginning students and experienced students, who can use it as a review.

CASE	TROUBLE?	SESSION	Power Users Tips	RW
Tutorial Case Each tutorial begins with a problem presented in a case that is meaningful to students. The case sets the scene to help students understand what they will do in the tutorial.	**TROUBLE? Paragraphs** These paragraphs anticipate the mistakes or problems that students may have and help them continue with the tutorial.	**Sessions** Each tutorial is divided into sessions designed to be completed in about 45 minutes each. Students should take as much time as they need and take a break between sessions.	**Power Users Tips** Tips for accomplishing tasks more efficiently or by using an alternate approach are included at key points in each tutorial.	**Reference Windows** Reference Windows are succinct summaries of the most important tasks covered in a tutorial. They preview actions students will perform in the steps to follow.

www.course.com/NewPerspectives

TABLE OF CONTENTS

Tutorial 4   4.01

Creating and Customizing Shortcuts

Customizing a Computer at Delta Oil

Tutorial 5   5.01

Using OLE Technologies

Preparing a Company Logo for Visual Arts, Inc.

Tutorial 13　13.01

Exploring the Windows Registry

Customizing Systems at DGL Communications Group

Tutorial 14　14.01

The Windows XP Command-Line Environment

Working in a Command-Line Environment at The Travis Foundation

Acknowledgments

Many individuals at Course Technology were involved in the planning, development, writing, review, editing, copyediting, testing, and production of this book. Their efforts reflect Course Technology's strong commitment to the highest quality textbooks for both instructors and students.

I would like to thank the following reviewers whose valuable comments and insight helped shape this book:

- Timothy Powers, Associate Professor of Computer Information and Office Systems, The University of Alaska Southeast, Juneau, Alaska
- Eric Salveggio, Program Director, Network Engineering, Palisades Campus Extension, Virginia College, Birmingham, Alabama
- Thomas Trevethan, Networking Instructor, Computer Information Systems, ECPI College of Technology, Virginia Beach, Virginia

I would also like to thank all the members of the New Perspectives team who helped in the development and production of this book. Special thanks go to Lisa Ruffolo of The Software Resource, Madison, Wisconsin, who as Developmental Editor, successfully guided this project and who also contributed her insight and experience as an author to the development and scope of the book. I would like to thank Rachael Crapser, Managing Editor; Donna Gridley, Senior Editor; Elena Montillo, Production Editor; Briana Germain, Associate Product Manager; Emilie Perreault, Editorial Assistant; John Freitas, Bryan Raffetto, Greg Bigelow, and Heather McKinstry, Quality Assurance; Laura Burns, Manufacturing; Mark Goodin, Copyeditor; Trevor Kallop, Customer Service; as well as the student testers, Nick Atlas, Harris Bierhoff, Marianne Broughey, Vitaly Davidovich, Serge Palladino, Chris Scriver, and Danielle Shaw. Thanks once again to Floyd J. Winters, Computer Science Professor, Manatee Community College, Bradenton, Florida, for providing two photos for use in this book.

—Harry L. Phillips

New Perspectives on

MICROSOFT® WINDOWS® XP PROFESSIONAL POWER USERS

Read This Before You Begin

To the Student

This Power Users book is designed for a full semester class and assumes no prior knowledge of Microsoft Windows XP Professional or Microsoft Windows XP Home Edition. The coverage of Windows XP accelerates at a much quicker pace than CT's Comprehensive book on Windows XP, and prepares you for an MCSE (Microsoft Certified Systems Engineers) track or networking track.

Data Disks

To complete the tutorials, Review Assignments, and Case Problems in this book, you need 3 Data Disks. Your instructor will either provide you with Data Disks to copy or ask you to make your own.

If you make your own Data Disks, you will need 3 blank, formatted high-density floppy disks. You will need to copy a set of folders and files from a network or standalone computer onto your floppy disks. Your instructor will tell you which computer, drive, and folder contain the folders and files you need. You could also download the files by going to **www.course.com**, clicking Student Downloads, and following the instructions on the screen. The following table shows you what folders and files go on each of your disks:

Disk 1

Write this on the disk label:
Data Disk #1
Tutorials 3, 5, 6, & 7
Put these folders and files on the disk:
Business Records, Company Documents, Company Projections, Personal Records, Presentations, Resources, and Wallpaper Designs folders plus the files File0000.chk and ~WRC0070.tmp

Disk 2

Write this on the disk label:
Data Disk #2
Tutorials 4, 6, & 7
Put these folders and files on the disk:
Delta Oil folder

Disk 3

Write this on the disk label:
Data Disk #3
Tutorials 5 & 6
Put these folders and files on the disk:
Visual Arts folder

When you begin each tutorial, be sure you are using the correct Data Disk. See the inside front or inside back cover of this book for more information on the Data Disks, or ask your instructor or technical support person for assistance.

Using Your Own Computer

If you are going to work through this book using your own computer, you will need:

■ **Computer System** Microsoft Windows XP Professional or Microsoft Windows XP Home Edition must be installed on your computer. This book assumes a typical installation of Microsoft Windows XP Professional and Microsoft Windows XP Home Edition.

■ **Data Disks** You will not be able to complete certain tutorials or exercises in this book using your own computer until you have the Data Disks.

To the Instructor

To complete the tutorials in this book, your students must use a set of Data Disk files. The files for the Data Disks are available on the Instructor's Resource Kit for this title. Follow the instructions in the Help file on the CD-ROM to copy the Data Disk folders and files to your network or standalone computer. For information on creating Data Disks, see the "To the Student" section above.

Once the folders and files are copied to your network or standalone computer, you can make Data Disks for the students yourself, or tell students where to find the files so they can make their own Data Disks. Make sure the folders and files are copied correctly by following the instructions in the Data Disks section above.

CT Data Files

You are granted a license to copy the Data Disk files to any computer or computer network used by students who have purchased this book.

In this tutorial you will:

- Review the basic functions of an operating system

- Examine important desktop operating systems and their features

- Examine Windows XP's new features

- Switch your desktop view from Web style to Windows Classic style, and vice versa

- Use the new Windows XP Help and Support Center

- Learn about Windows Product Activation

- Create a password reset disk

- Navigate your computer system, and examine its organization

- View properties of your computer system

THE WINDOWS XP OPERATING SYSTEM

Evaluating Windows XP Professional at Energy Technology Group, Ltd.

CASE

Energy Technology Group, Ltd.

Energy Technology Group, Ltd. (ETG) is a rapidly growing business that provides its clients with the latest information on the use of scientific, engineering, and computer technology in energy production. Its clients primarily include utilities that locate and develop new sources of energy for their customers. ETG relies on networked desktop computers for practically every facet of its operation. Michele Edmundson, a network technician at ETG, is currently supervising the upgrade of company computers from Windows 2000 Professional and Windows 98 to Windows XP Professional. Many of the company's employees are also ready to upgrade their home computers to either the Windows XP Professional Edition or the Windows XP Home Edition so that they can take advantage of new features that allow them to work at home or on the road and access their office computers.

In the first session of this tutorial, you examine the importance, role, and functions of operating system software, and then look at specific PC operating systems and their features. This overview provides a historical perspective on the development of the Windows operating system as well as an overview of important features available in different versions of Windows.

The Importance of Operating System Software

After installing Windows XP on the computers at ETG, Michele announces an upcoming workshop to familiarize employees with the important role that operating system software plays in the proper functioning of their computer system and its resources.

An **operating system** is software that manages all the basic processes in a computer, coordinates the interaction of hardware and software so that all the components work together, and supports other software, such as application software. Although specific operating systems vary in the scope of tasks that they manage, all operating systems handle the following tasks:

- **Configuring a computer**. After you power on your computer, a **routine** (or program) stored on a special type of computer chip called the **ROM BIOS (Read Only Memory Basic Input Output System)** on the motherboard locates the operating system software on the hard disk, and starts loading the operating system into memory. After the core operating system files load into memory, the operating system takes control of the computer, loads the remainder of the operating system software, allocates system resources to hardware devices, and completes booting the computer. During the early stages of booting, the operating system detects the type of hardware in your computer, and configures itself by loading the appropriate device drivers, or software, that it needs to operate with the computer's hardware. A **device driver** is a small program file that enables the operating system to communicate with a specific hardware device, and vice versa.

- **Customizing a computer**. Near the end of the booting process, the operating system loads optional programs that you choose to use on your computer. For example, many people wisely choose to use antivirus software on their computers. In those cases, the operating system loads their antivirus software as early as possible during booting, and it in turn checks their computer for computer viruses, and then monitors their computer while they work. **Computer viruses** are programs designed to damage or interfere with the performance of your computer or other computers to which you are connected.

- **Displaying a user interface**. Once your computer boots, the operating system displays a **user interface**, which enables you to interact with your computer. Although most people think of the interface as consisting of the view displayed on their computer by the operating system, the user interface also includes the hardware, such as the monitor, keyboard, and mouse, that enable you to interact with the operating system. The interface presented by the operating system and its ease of use have become increasingly important to users, because they rely on it to simplify the tasks they perform on the computer. The first PC operating systems relied on a command-line interface, whereas present-day operating systems rely on a graphical user interface. Most computer users today are familiar with the graphical user interface included in the various versions of Windows, but not necessarily with the use of a command-line interface. As you see later when you examine the DOS operating system, in a **command-line interface**, you interact with the operating system by entering and executing commands from a command prompt displayed on the screen.

- **Providing support services to applications**. The operating system provides important support services to software applications and other programs that you use. Since every application provides you with an option for saving and retrieving files from disk, the operating system handles this task, so that each application does not need to contain the same program code for the same operations. This approach also provides consistency across different applications, and protects the file system on your computer. Whether you are saving or retrieving a file from disk, you provide the application with three important pieces of information: the names of the drive, folder, and file that contain the document or data you want to use. When saving a document or data to a file on disk, the operating system transfers a copy of the document from RAM to disk. **RAM (Random Access Memory)**, the predominant type of memory within a computer, stores currently used programs, documents, and data, and thereby provides a temporary workspace for the user. Since this memory is **volatile** (dependent on the availability of power), you should periodically save your documents and data to disk. When retrieving a file from disk, the operating system also transfers a copy of the file from disk to RAM so that you can use the document or data in that file within an application.

■ **Handling input and output**. The operating system manages all input and output. In addition to retrieving files from disk (input) and saving files to disk (output), the operating system also interprets signals from the keyboard and mouse (input), and assists with printing (output). For example, when you press a key on the keyboard, the keyboard produces a **scan code**, which the operating system interprets, so that the application you are using displays the correct character on the monitor. When you print a document, the operating system uses a process called **spooling** to store the processed document in a temporary file on disk (a **spool file**) and to transmit the spool file to the printer in the background, so that you can continue to work in your application or perform other tasks, such as connecting to your **ISP (Internet Service Provider)**, and checking e-mail. Also, by spooling documents to disk, the operating system can print a set of documents one after the other while you continue to work. The operating system stores the documents in a **print queue** (a list of print jobs) and prints the documents in the order in which they were received. Without spooling, you would have to wait until each document printed before you could do anything else.

■ **Managing the file system**. Your computer's **file system** consists of the operating system components and data structures that the operating system uses to keep track of all the files on your computer. The operating system organizes and manages all the disks, drives, folders and subfolders (also called directories or subdirectories), and files. In other words, these file system components are organized into a hierarchy, or file system structure, that starts with disks at the top of the hierarchy (or file system structure), and works its way down to the files at the bottom of the hierarchy. Although your computer might only have one physical hard disk drive, that drive might be divided into one or more partitions that are treated as **logical drives**, such as drive C and drive D. Disk management has always been one of the important functions of the operating system.

■ **Managing system resources**. The operating system manages all the hardware and software so that everything works properly together—a major feat because of the wide spectrum of hardware and software products. One especially important resource managed by the operating system is memory. When you open an application, the operating system loads that application from disk into RAM and, in the process, allocates memory to that application. When you exit an application, the operating system reclaims the memory used by that application so it can allocate that memory to the next application you use. If your computer does not have enough RAM for the types of operations you want to perform on your computer, the operating system can set aside unused storage space on the hard disk for use as additional memory (called **virtual memory**), thereby increasing the total amount of memory available to the operating system and applications. Memory management is another of the important functions performed by the operating system.

- **Resolving system errors and problems**. The operating system must handle and, if possible, resolve errors as they occur. For example, if you save a document to a floppy drive, but do not put a diskette into that drive, the operating system informs you of the problem, and you resolve it by inserting a disk and trying again. If you print a document, but forget to turn the printer on, the operating system informs you that the printer is off, off-line, or out of paper.

- **Providing Help**. Operating systems typically include a Help system that provides you with information about the use of the operating system and its features. Some Help systems step you through operations with tutorials and wizards, and include hyperlinks and troubleshooting assistance. A **wizard** is a tool that asks you a series of questions about what you want to do and what settings you want to use, and then completes the operation for you. A **hyperlink** is a link between one object and another on your local computer, network, or the Web.

- **Optimizing system performance**. Operating systems typically include a variety of **utilities**, or programs, for optimizing the performance of your computer. For example, you might use a utility to check the file system and hard disk for errors and, where possible, to repair those errors. You might use another utility to improve the speed of accessing data on disk by rearranging how folders, software applications, and your document files are stored on disk.

- **Providing troubleshooting tools**. In addition to information provided within the Help system, the operating system on your computer also provides you with troubleshooting tools, such as Safe Mode or the ability to make boot disks. Safe Mode, which you examine in Tutorial 9, is a special mode for booting your computer so that you can troubleshoot problems. You might also be able to prepare **boot disks**, or **system disks**, that contain the core operating system files needed to boot your computer from drive A, so that you can troubleshoot problems with the operating system or the hard disk.

As you can see, the operating system is an indispensable component of your computer. You cannot use a computer without an operating system. As you work with application software, or other types of software, such as utilities and games, the operating system manages the moment-to-moment operation of your computer in the background, from when you initially power on the computer until you shut it down. Furthermore, since the operating system handles important operations, such as disk, drive, folder, and file management, as well as all input/output functions, application software can focus on what it is designed to do best, and the operating system can focus on core functions required of all programs. As you examine desktop operating systems in general and Windows XP in particular, you learn about other ways in which the operating system manages your computer and provides you with the tools you need to work effectively.

PC **Operating Systems**

Because of the wide variety of computers and software applications in use today, many companies and their clients rely on more than one operating system. Also, an employee might use one operating system at work, and another one on a home computer. In some cases, individuals might set up a dual-boot configuration or multiple-boot configuration on their computer so that, during booting, they can select an operating system from a list of two or more operating systems installed on their computer. In a **dual-boot configuration**, your computer has two operating systems, such as Windows XP Professional and Windows 2000 Professional, and you can choose the operating system that you want to use during booting. In a **multiple-boot configuration**, your computer has two or more operating systems, such as Windows XP Professional, Windows 2000 Professional, and Windows 98, one of which you can choose during booting. Under Windows XP, you must divide the hard disk drive into partitions and install each operating system on a different partition if you want a dual-boot or multiple-boot configuration.

The predominant operating systems used on PCs today are ones developed by Microsoft Corporation, and they share a common history. Features, concepts, and techniques introduced with earlier operating systems remain important to the effective use of later operating systems. Therefore, you should be familiar not only with the operating system used on your computer, which, for example, might be Windows XP Professional, but also with other operating systems, such as Windows XP Home Edition, Windows 2000 Professional, Windows Me, Windows 98 SE, Windows 98, Windows 95, Windows NT Workstation 4.0, and MS-DOS.

The DOS Operating System

In 1981, IBM contracted with Microsoft Corporation, then a small company in Washington state, to provide the operating system for its first IBM PC. Microsoft developed DOS 1.0, the first version of DOS, for use on those IBM PCs. **DOS**, an abbreviation for Disk Operating System, eventually referred to three related operating systems: PC-DOS, IBM-DOS, and MS-DOS. Over the years, Microsoft and IBM worked cooperatively to develop different versions of PC-DOS or IBM-DOS for use on IBM microcomputers, while Microsoft developed different versions of MS-DOS for use on IBM-compatible computers. An **IBM-compatible** is a personal computer that adheres to standards established by IBM for the IBM-PC. IBM-compatible computers contain similar or identical hardware, function like an IBM-PC, and provide support for the same applications. Eventually, IBM developed its own versions of IBM-DOS for its IBM microcomputers. Although there are subtle differences between PC-DOS, IBM-DOS, and MS-DOS, all manage the hardware and software resources within a computer in similar ways, provide access to similar types of features, and include similar utilities for enhancing the performance of a system. Once you know how to use MS-DOS, then you know how to use IBM-DOS, or vice-versa.

The DOS operating system and other operating systems like it (UNIX , VAX/VMS, and Linux, for example) use a command-line interface that enables you to communicate with the operating system by typing a command after an **operating system prompt**, or **command prompt**. After you power on a computer that uses a version of the DOS operating system, you will see an operating system prompt (usually C:\>) displayed on the screen, unless, of course, someone customized the startup process. See Figure 1-1.

| Figure 1-1 | DOS COMMAND-LINE INTERFACE |

operating system prompt, or command prompt

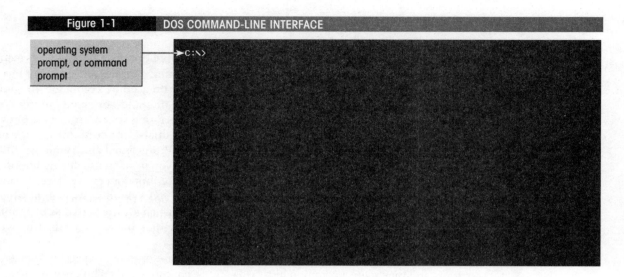

The operating system prompt indicates that the computer booted successfully, that the operating system loaded into memory, and that the operating system is using a specific drive as a reference point. There are no other on-screen clues to help you figure out what to do next. You must not only know what command to use, but you must also know the proper format for entering the command. You must also know what options are available for modifying how each command works.

For example, Figure 1-2 illustrates how you might use the Format command to format a floppy disk for use as a system disk, or boot disk. After you enter the command with the proper syntax and optional switches (or parameters), the MS-DOS operating system locates and loads the program associated with that command. Then the program performs a specific action; in this case, formatting a disk and displaying information about the formatting process. When the program completes its operation (or when you exit an application), the DOS operating system redisplays the command prompt so that you can enter another command to start another program.

| Figure 1-2 | EXECUTING A DOS COMMAND |

operating system prompt, or command prompt

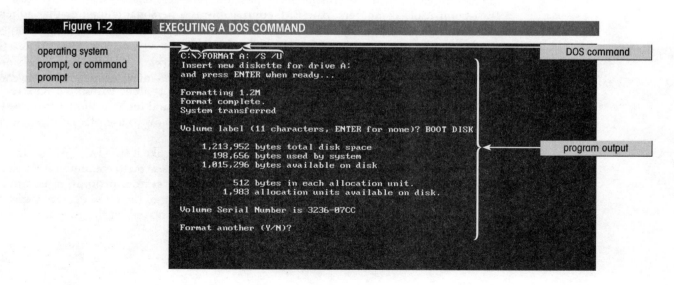

In this figure, the Format command identifies the drive to be formatted (A:, or drive A). The System switch (/S) is an optional switch that modifies the Format command so that it copies the MS-DOS operating system files (Io.sys, Msdos.sys, Command.com, and Drvspace.bin) to the disk after the disk is formatted. The message "System transferred" verifies this step. The Unconditional switch (/U) is an optional switch that formats the disk so that the formatting cannot be reversed.

Not surprisingly, because of the simplicity of the user interface and the need to know operating system commands and their proper syntax, users found it difficult to use the DOS operating system and, as a result, relied on computer technicians to customize their computers so that their version of the DOS operating system automatically loaded Windows 3.1 (for example), or displayed a menu after booting so that the user could select an installed application or perform some common operation, such as formatting a disk. In some cases, users did not realize that the underlying operating system was MS-DOS.

Another important feature of command-line interface operating systems is that they operate in text mode. In **text mode**, the operating system displays only text, numbers, symbols, and a small set of graphics characters, using white, amber, or green characters on a black background. Because text mode does not need to display a user interface with graphics, the DOS operating system was fast and required far less memory and other system resources than present-day computers that rely on a graphical user interface.

Command-line skills that derive from using the DOS operating system are still important today, especially for network administrators, network specialists, network technicians, telecommunication specialists, troubleshooters, computer consultants, tweakers (people who specialize in fine-tuning and optimizing computers), and trainers, to name a few professions. All of these professions find DOS skills an invaluable resource in their jobs. Furthermore, different versions of the Windows operating systems support in part, or in whole, the use of DOS applications, utilities, and games, as well as DOS commands, in a command-line window or in a full-screen mode that emulates the DOS operating environment.

The Windows Operating Environment

In 1985, Microsoft introduced Windows 1.0, the first in a series of Windows operating environments. An **operating environment** is a software product that performs the same functions as an operating system, except for configuring and customizing a computer system, and handling the storage and retrieval of data in files on a disk. Although Windows 3.1, the most commonly used version of the Windows operating environment, required a version of the DOS operating system in the background to handle basic file functions, its interface was completely different from that of a command-line operating system. Instead of displaying a command-line interface in text mode, Windows 3.1 (and previous versions) relied on a graphical user interface originally derived from an interface used on Apple computers. See Figure 1-3.

| Figure 1-3 | WINDOWS 3.1 GRAPHICAL USER INTERFACE |

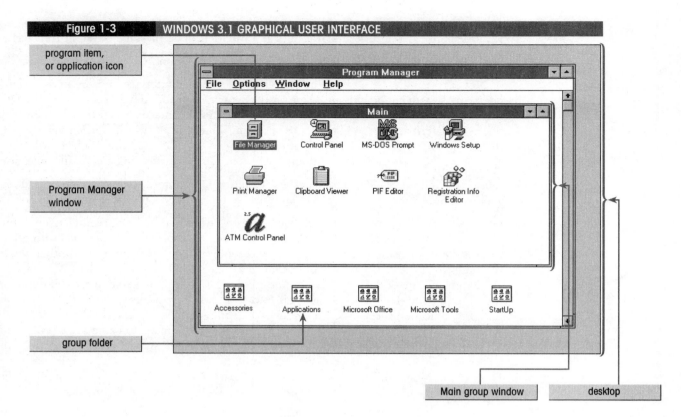

A **graphical user interface**, or **GUI** (pronounced "gooey"), uses a combination of features and screen elements to provide a visually rich working environment, as well as on-screen clues that simplify interaction with the operating system. The graphical user interface in different versions of Windows uses colors, fonts (character styles), and special design elements (such as shading) to provide a more conducive and interesting working environment. Windows also uses **icons**, or pictures, to represent hardware and software components, as well as system tools, that you can open and use. The Windows graphical user interface uses **windows**, or work areas on the screen (usually defined by borders) that are designed to organize your view of applications and documents. Every time you open an application, it appears within an application window. If you open more than one application, then each application operates within its own window. Likewise, each document you open with an application appears within its own document window. Windows uses **menus** to list options for performing different types of command operations. Typical of menu-driven software, you know what your choices are, and you can easily select them from a list displayed on the menu. Once you select a menu option, Windows may display a **dialog box** that includes options and settings for completing that operation. In a graphical user interface, the mouse plays an important role and is a required hardware component. You use it to point to and select icons as well as options in windows, on menus, and in dialog boxes, and to open applications. Unlike a command-line operating system, Windows operates in graphics mode rather than text mode. In **graphics mode**, Windows can display text in a variety of fonts and colors, as well as graphic images; however, the use of graphics mode requires far more memory than text mode.

Although DOS was the predominant PC operating system for 14 years from 1981-1995, the Windows operating environments were important because they eventually led to the development of the Windows operating system. In fact, Microsoft referred to the Windows operating environment as an operating system, anticipating the day when Windows would be a full-fledged operating system that no longer required the DOS operating system and that, in turn, would mark a major change in the use of computers.

The Windows 95 and Windows 98 Operating Systems

Windows 95 (Windows Version 4.00.950), released in the summer of 1995, marked a revolutionary change in Windows. If you installed Windows 95 on a computer that already had an installed version of the DOS operating system, Windows 95 replaced DOS as the operating system. If the computer also included an installed version of Windows, such as Windows 3.1, Windows 95 replaced that as well, unless you specified a dual-boot configuration that included DOS and your previous version of Windows.

Like Windows 3.1, Windows 95 had a graphical user interface; however, Microsoft made significant changes to the Windows 95 graphical user interface to make it easier for you to interact with your computer and focus on accomplishing your tasks. The Windows **desktop** replaced Windows 3.1 Program Manager, resulting in an interface that is simpler in design and use. See Figure 1-4. The desktop icons represented specific components of the Windows 95 operating system, such as My Computer, Network Neighborhood, Recycle Bin, and eventually My Documents, and were designed to help you understand your computer's organization, and to provide quick access to its contents. The **taskbar** at the bottom of the desktop displayed buttons for open applications and windows, letting you quickly locate an open but perhaps hidden application or window. By using the **Start** button on the taskbar, you could access a **Start menu** and **Programs menu** from which you could open any application installed on your computer, plus access other important Windows components, such as the Help system, the Control Panel for configuring your computer, and the Favorites folder with your Internet shortcuts. A **shortcut** is a direct link to a component, or object, on your local computer, a network computer, or the Web. Although the Windows 95 graphical user interface was different in appearance from those of previous versions of Windows, you still interacted with the operating system and other software using icons, windows, menus, and dialog boxes.

| Figure 1-4 | WINDOWS 95 DESKTOP |

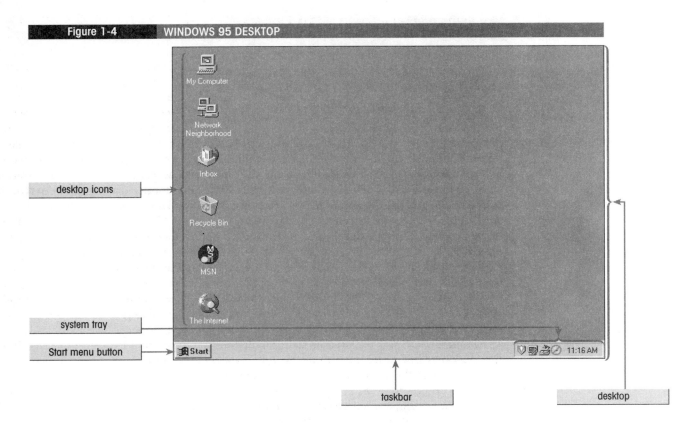

After introducing the original version of Windows 95 in the summer of 1995, Microsoft introduced four other versions, listed in Figure 1-5. The first upgrade, Microsoft Windows 95 Service Pack 1 (also called OSR 1), included fixes to the original version of Windows 95, as well as additional components. OSR 2 (OEM Service Release 2), or Windows 95B, included Internet Explorer 3.0 and support for newer types of hardware, as well as a new file system called FAT32 that was not available in the original version of Windows 95 and Windows 95a. These earlier versions of Windows 95 used the FAT16 file system, which was originally developed for use with the DOS operating system. (You examine these file systems in more detail in Tutorial 3.) The new FAT32 file system used hard disk storage space more efficiently; however, you could not upgrade your computer from the original version of Windows 95 or Windows 95a to Windows 95B. Instead, Windows 95B was only installed on new computers, starting in the fall of 1996. Since some of the components in Windows 95B also worked in Windows 95 and Windows 95a, Microsoft posted those components (called downloadable components) on its Web site. When added to Windows 95, the downloadable components made the Windows 95 interface similar to that of Windows 95B and eventually Windows 98. OSR 2.1, a minor upgrade of Windows 95B, added support for the **USB (universal serial bus)**—a high-speed communications port. OSR 2.5, or Windows 95C, included Internet Explorer 4.0, support for other online services (including an MSN 2.5 upgrade), another USB upgrade, and Internet components now found in Windows 98 and Windows 2000. **MSN (The Microsoft Network)**, originally an online service, is now an Internet Service Provider (ISP).

Figure 1-5	WINDOWS 95 VERSIONS		
WINDOWS 95 VERSION	**POPULAR NAME**	**WINDOWS VERSION**	**RELEASED**
Original	Windows 95	Windows 4.00.950	August, 1995
OSR 1 (Microsoft Windows 95 Service Pack 1)	Windows 95a	Windows 4.00.950a	December, 1995
OSR 2.0 (OEM Service Release 2)	Windows 95B	Windows 4.00.950 B	August, 1996
OSR 2.1	Windows 95B	Windows 4.00.950 B	November, 1996
OSR 2.5	Windows 95C	Windows 4.00.950 C	January, 1998

Microsoft released Windows 98 (Windows Version 4.10.1998) in the summer of 1998, and then Windows 98 Second Edition (SE) (Windows Version 4.10.2222A) a year later. The Windows 98 graphical user interface, shown in Figure 1-6, is obviously very similar to that of Windows 95. Microsoft incorporated all of the service pack/service release upgrades found in prior versions of Windows in Windows 98, and expanded the role and capabilities of the Windows operating system.

Figure 1-6	WINDOWS 98 DESKTOP

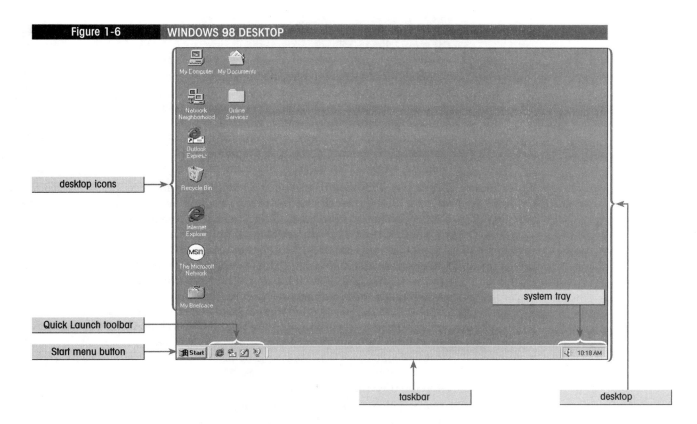

The following important features are found not only in both Windows 95 and Windows 98, but also in later versions of Windows:

- **Docucentric approach**. The redesigned graphical user interface made it easier to use a document-oriented approach rather than an application-oriented approach to opening files that contained documents that you wanted to use. When you use an **application-oriented** approach, you first open the software application, and then you locate and open the document you want to use. This approach was the only one available with the DOS operating system, and the predominant approach used with the Windows operating environment (for example, Windows 3.1). In contrast, when using a **document-oriented**, or **docucentric**, approach, you locate and open the file with the document you want to use, and then the operating system opens the application you originally used to produce that document or the application currently associated with that type of file. Although the docucentric approach was available with the Windows operating environment, it did not come into its own right until the release of Windows 95, and it provided a different and unique way of working with files.

- **Object-oriented interface**. Windows 95 and Windows 98, as well as subsequent versions of Windows, treat components of the graphical user interface and computer as **objects**. Hardware and software components, such as disks, drives, folders, files, and applications, are all objects. Every object has actions and properties. **Actions** are operations you can perform on an object. For example, you can open and explore the contents of your hard disk drive, search its contents, share the drive on your network, format the drive, create a shortcut to the drive, and change the volume label assigned to the drive. Each object has a default action, such as open, associated with it. You can view a list of other actions specific to an object by right-clicking the object and displaying the object's **shortcut menu**, or **context menu** (a feature introduced with Windows 95). **Properties**, on the other hand, are characteristics of an object. You can view and often change the settings of those characteristics by right-clicking the object and selecting Properties on the object's shortcut menu. An object is defined as an element of the user interface that you can right-click. Because every object has a shortcut menu associated with it, you can use the same method of performing actions and examining properties whether the object is a drive, a piece of clip art pasted into a document, an icon in the system tray on the taskbar, a desktop shortcut, a Web page, or the desktop itself.

■ **New system architecture**. Microsoft introduced a new **system architecture** (the internal design and coding of an operating system) in Windows 95. The improved system architecture provided support for newer types of processors and for operating modes of earlier processors. This system architecture also supported **multitasking**, the simultaneous or concurrent use of more than one application; **task-switching**, the ability to switch from one open task to another; and **multithreading**, the execution of multiple units of program code (called **threads**) within the same application. To further increase the effectiveness and reliability of Windows 95 and Windows 98, the system architecture included new design features that increased the **robustness**, or stability, of the operating system, and protected important system resources. These features were designed to ensure that a single malfunctioning application did not crash other running applications or the entire computer.

■ **Backward compatibility**. Both Windows 95 and Windows 98 (and to some degree later versions of Windows) supported the use of DOS applications developed for all processors from the original 8088 to the newest processor. Both also supported application software designed for prior versions of Windows, as well as many older types of hardware devices. The ability to handle hardware and software designed for earlier systems is called **backward compatibility** and enables you to keep your current computer system and its hardware and software without having to purchase a new computer system, or upgrade hardware and software when you install a new version of Windows. However, backward compatibility has hindered the development of the Windows operating system by requiring it to support past technologies wherever possible.

■ **Plug and Play**. Windows 95, Windows 98, and later versions of Windows (except Windows NT Workstation 4.0) support Plug and Play hardware as well as legacy devices. **Plug and Play (PnP)** refers to a set of specifications for automatically detecting and configuring hardware. Once you add a new Plug and Play hardware device to your computer, the operating system automatically detects and configures the hardware device either during booting or (in some cases) when the computer is already on, with little or no intervention on your part. In contrast, **legacy devices** are older types of hardware components that do not meet the Plug and Play specifications and require manual installation by setting jumpers or DIP switches. A **jumper** or **jumper shunt**, is a small metal block that you use to complete a circuit for two pins on a circuit board and, in the process, specify a configuration. See Figure 1-7. A **DIP (dual in-line package) switch** is a set of toggle switches mounted on a chip, which is in turn mounted on an add-in board. See Figure 1-8. You flip a switch to one position or the other (on or off) to specify a configuration setting. In some cases, you have to set a combination of switches to specify a configuration setting, such as the setting for a COM port (or communications port), or an IRQ (Interrupt Request) setting (features that you examine in Tutorial 12). Note that Windows 95, Windows 98, and later versions of Windows do not provide support for all legacy devices and as a result, these operating systems might not detect or might not even be able to work with certain types of legacy hardware devices.

Figure 1-7	DIAGRAMMATIC REPRESENTATION OF A JUMPER SHUNT

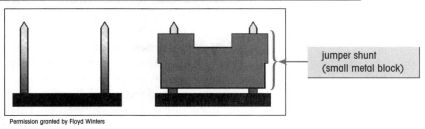

Permission granted by Floyd Winters

Figure 1-8	DIAGRAMMATIC REPRESENTATION OF A DIP SWITCH

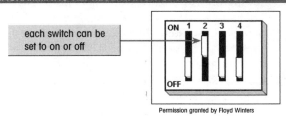

Permission granted by Floyd Winters

- **Multimedia support.** Windows 95 provided increased support for the use of multimedia applications and multimedia hardware (such as CD-ROM drives and sound cards), video and audio recording and playback, and the integration of graphics, video, sound, and animation within documents and the user interface. Windows 98 supported even newer technologies for improving gaming, multimedia, and 3-D rendering. It also included broadcast software to receive television programming via cable, satellite, or the Web.

- **Hardware support.** Both Windows 95 and Windows 98 provided support for hardware in use at the time of their releases, as well as newer types of hardware technologies that were ready to appear in the marketplace. Both provide increased support for display adapters, monitors, printers, modems, and CD-ROM drives, as well as support for new Plug and Play hardware devices, PCMCIA devices (interface cards the size of a credit card), and ECP (enhanced capabilities port) devices, such as modems. Windows 98 supports new features of the Pentium II, Pentium MMX (Multimedia Extensions), Pentium III, and later microprocessors; the accelerated graphics port (AGP) for handling 3-D graphics throughput; the universal serial bus (USB) for connecting multiple devices and for fast data transfer rates; digital video discs (DVDs) for storage and playback of movies; IEEE 1394 ports for connecting multiple devices and for handling throughput of video cameras, VCRs, stereos, and other consumer electronic devices; IrDA (infrared) ports for wireless communication; multi-monitor support (the use of up to nine monitors for a "SurroundView" effect); and improved power management of desktop and portable PCs.

■ **Network support**. Both Windows 95 and Windows 98 are network operating systems that provide enhanced support for connecting to networks and working with network operating software. These operating systems can interact with network application software and hardware (such as printers) and access documents, e-mail, and other types of information on networks. Using Windows 95, Windows 98, and later versions of Windows, you can set up a **peer-to-peer network**, a simple type of network in which each computer can access other computers to which they are connected and share peripherals, hardware devices such as printers, hard disk drives, removable storage devices (such as CD-ROM, Zip, and DVD drives), as well as software, folders, and files. A peer-to-peer network does not require a server. A **server** is a high-performance computer that manages a computer network with the use of network operating system software, such as Windows XP Server or Windows 2000 Server.

■ **Support for portable computers**. Windows 95 and Windows 98 include support for features such as Dial-Up Networking, which let employees connect their portable computers to their company's network when working at home or while traveling on business. They also support Direct Cable Connection to link a portable and desktop computer by means of a parallel or null modem cable, file synchronization between computers using My Briefcase, Advanced Power Management (APM) for managing power on a portable computer, Quick View for viewing the contents of files, Microsoft Exchange (and later Windows Messaging) for e-mail access, Microsoft Fax for sending and receiving faxes, and deferred printing.

■ **Support for online services**. One of the controversial features introduced with Windows 95 (and still available in later versions of Windows) is software that lets you choose The Microsoft Network as your ISP. By joining The Microsoft Network or any other online service, or by setting up an account with an ISP, you gain access to the Internet and the World Wide Web, and to other features and resources such as e-mail, online chats, and file libraries with downloadable software and multimedia files.

■ **Web integration**. Microsoft integrated Internet Explorer 3.0 into the Windows 95B user interface, and later it integrated Internet Explorer 4.0 and 5.0 in the Windows 98 user interface, thereby providing support for a feature called the Active Desktop. **Active Desktop** technology enables you to work on your local computer and network in the same way that you browse the Web. You can make your desktop look and work like a Web page. If you switch the user interface from **Classic view** (the view originally included with the first version of Windows 95) to **Web view** or **Web style** (a Web browser view), objects on your local computer act like links on a Web page. That means that you can open an object on your computer, such as an application, with a single-click instead of a double-click. You can also place the active content of Web pages on the desktop as objects, and then periodically synchronize and update them with new content from their original Web site. For example, you could add an investment channel, or a weather map channel, from the Windows Media Showcase or a page you found on the Web, to the desktop. A **channel** is essentially a dynamic (updateable) connection to active content on a Web site. With Active Desktop technology, you can also right-click, perform actions, and view properties of items listed on the Start menu and Programs menu, customize and create toolbars either on the taskbar or as desktop objects, use JPEG and GIF images as well as Web pages as desktop wallpaper, customize your view of folders as Web pages, and add Active Desktop items to the desktop. When you add an Active Desktop item to the desktop, you create an object that consists of all or part of a Web page, combined with its links and properties. You can view the Web page and its interactive content without connecting to the Web and, if you click a link, Windows dials up your ISP, connects you to the Internet, and displays the Web page from which the Active Desktop item was created. These features were inspired by the realization that the Internet and the World Wide Web would eventually become critical to the everyday needs of almost every profession. While these features are now considered *de facto* standards for ways of working with your computer, when they were introduced, they represented an innovative way to integrate Windows and the Internet, and to extend your desktop to encompass the World Wide Web.

Windows 95 and Windows 98 also included other tools, such as Outlook Express, a new e-mail tool; FrontPage Express, a personal Web page editor; NetMeeting for Internet conferencing; and NetShow for delivering streaming multimedia across the Internet.

Although Windows 95 was introduced as a new desktop operating system, it also was the first Internet-oriented operating system because it enabled millions of users to access the Internet and its benefits for the first time. Windows 95 users were among the first users to access resources available on Internet and Web servers around the world and to exchange e-mail. If you examine statistics on the growth of the Internet and the World Wide Web at Hobbe's Internet Timeline (*www.isoc.org/guest/zakon/Internet/History/HIT.html*), you discover that the rapid increase in Internet use occurred right after the introduction of Windows 95. The line charts in Figure 1-9 and Figure 1-10 were created by plotting information derived from that Web site. The chart in Figure 1-9 measures the growth of the Internet as a function of time. As you can see, the sharp rise in the curve showing the number of computers occurred at the time that Microsoft released Windows 95. The chart in Figure 1-10 measures the growth of the World Wide Web, a component of the Internet, as a function of time. The increase in World Wide Web usage occurred at the time that Microsoft released Windows 95 and at the time of Windows 98's release, it started increasing exponentially. The introduction of the Windows 95 operating system, followed closely by Windows 98, initiated the Internet revolution that we find so indispensable to our work and play today.

Figure 1-9   GROWTH OF THE INTERNET

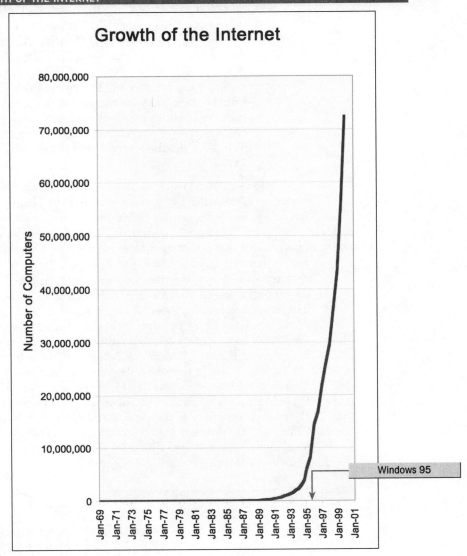

| Figure 1-10 | GROWTH OF THE WORLD WIDE WEB |

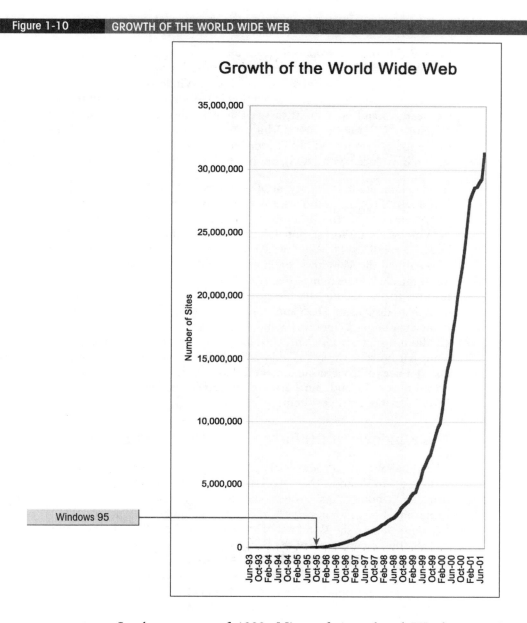

In the summer of 1999, Microsoft introduced Windows 98 Second Edition (or Windows 98 SE) as an upgrade to the original version of Windows 98. Windows 98 SE included Internet Explorer 5.0; **Internet Connection Sharing** for setting up and configuring computer networks at home so that more than one computer can share a single Internet connection through one computer; new and improved support for hardware, such as IEEE 1394 and USB high-speed connections for peripherals; new and improved applications, including a new version of NetMeeting, as well as improved support for WebTV, DirectX, and ACPI (Advanced Configuration and Power Interface).

The diverse range of features in Windows 95 and Windows 98 not only expanded the role of the Windows operating system, but also emphasized the importance of integrating applications and features to optimize the performance of a computer, to integrate the Web with the desktop, to more effectively manage its resources, and to increase productivity.

The Windows NT Workstation 4.0 Operating System

In 1993, Microsoft introduced an advanced network operating system named Windows NT (for "New Technology") that supported computers with different types of processors and file systems. Unlike versions of Windows prior to Windows 95, it did not require DOS. Over the years, Windows NT gained a reputation in corporate and industrial applications for its security features and its stability, as well as its ability to handle multithreading in real time. Windows NT was the first 32-bit operating system, and it provided support for its own native file system (called NTFS, for New Technology File System) as well as FAT16 (a file system introduced with DOS), but not FAT32 (a file system introduced with Windows 98).

In the summer of 1996, a year after the release of Windows 95, Microsoft released the Windows NT Workstation 4.0 network operating system for use on desktop computers. Microsoft included the Windows 95 interface and as many Windows 95 features as possible in Windows NT Workstation 4.0. For example, the Windows NT Workstation 4.0 desktop looks identical to the Windows 95 desktop. However, parts of the user interface look and respond like the Windows 3.1 interface, and are therefore not object-oriented (you could not right-click some items). Because NTFS, the Windows NT file system, contains security features for protecting the file system, such as not permitting DOS applications to write directly to disk, using DOS applications under Windows NT Workstation 4.0 was more difficult than under Windows 95 and Windows 98. Furthermore, Windows NT Workstation 4.0 did not support Plug and Play, had limited multimedia support, and did not support as many hardware devices as Windows 95. However, its release was important because it introduced a network operating system for use on desktop computers that was previously used only on servers and, furthermore, it served as the precursor for the Windows 2000 Professional operating system.

The Windows 2000 Professional Operating System

The Windows 2000 Professional operating system originally started out as Windows NT 5.0, an upgrade to Windows NT Workstation 4.0, but during development, Microsoft changed its name to Windows 2000 Professional Edition (Windows Version 5.00.2195). Windows 2000 Professional incorporates the features of Windows 95, Windows NT Workstation 4.0, and Windows 98 into the Windows NT product line for use on desktop computers. The desktop, and all other components of the Windows 2000 Professional graphical user interface are similar to those of Windows 95, Windows NT Workstation 4.0, and Windows 98. See Figure 1-11. However, the entire user interface is now objected-oriented. Like previous versions of Windows 95 and Windows 98, Internet Explorer 5.0 is integrated into the user interface so that it supports Active Desktop technologies and features.

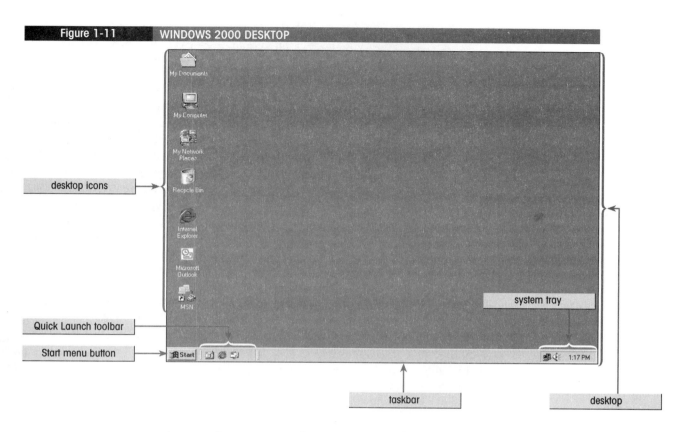

Figure 1-11 WINDOWS 2000 DESKTOP

Among the many new features now available in Windows 2000 Professional are the following:

- **Support for Intel's Pentium III, Pentium III Xeon**, and **Pentium 4 processors**. Windows 2000 Professional provides support for newer processors and other emerging hardware technologies. In fact, over the years, rapid changes in hardware technologies required frequent upgrades to operating systems so that they could support the new hardware technologies.

- **Plug and Play support**. Unlike its predecessor, Windows NT Workstation 4.0, Windows 2000 Professional supports Plug and Play hardware devices.

- **Advanced power management**. Like Windows 98, Windows 2000 Professional allows you to select or define power management schemes that control power to components on your computer, such as the monitor and hard disk. It also supports **Standby** mode, a state in which hardware devices such as the monitor and hard disk are turned off and the computer is placed in a low-power state, as well as **Hibernation**, a power-saving mode that writes the contents of RAM onto the hard disk and then shuts down the computer. Windows 2000 Professional then restores the contents of RAM when you next power on your computer.

- **Device Manager**. Windows 2000 Professional includes Device Manager, a tool for examining, documenting, and troubleshooting the hardware configuration of your computer. Device Manager was originally introduced in Windows 95 and was available in Windows 98, but not in Windows NT Workstation 4.0.

- **Support for different file systems.** Windows 2000 Professional supports NTFS, the Windows NT file system used in Windows NT Workstation 4.0 and previous versions of Windows NT; the FAT16 file system supported by DOS, Windows 95, Windows 98, and Windows NT Workstation 4.0; and the FAT32 file system used in Windows 98 and in the later versions of Windows 95. Windows NT Workstation 4.0 uses NTFS 4.0, and Windows 2000 Professional uses NTFS 5.0, but it also supports the use of NTFS 4.0.

- **Utilities for system maintenance.** While Windows 95 and Windows 98 included the ScanDisk disk analysis and repair utility, Windows 2000 Professional relies on the Check Disk utility, originally developed for use with the DOS operating system, but obviously enhanced for Windows 2000 Professional and its different file systems. Like Windows 95 and Windows 98, Windows 2000 Professional now includes a Disk Defragmenter utility (not included with Windows NT Workstation 4.0) for optimizing the arrangement of programs and data on disks.

- **Windows Update.** Like Windows 98, Windows 2000 Professional includes a Windows Update wizard that connects you to Microsoft's Web site, examines the installed software on your computer, and recommends software updates, device driver updates, and add-on components for your computer.

Windows 2000 Professional proved to be the next important step in operating system technology after Windows 95, Windows NT Workstation 4.0, and Windows 98, and it provided a stable network operating system with enhanced security features for users of desktop computers. The Windows XP operating systems are upgrades to the Windows 2000 Professional operating system.

The Windows Me Operating System

The Windows Me operating system, or Windows Millennium Edition (Windows Version 4.900.3000), was initially designed as an upgrade of Windows 98 that included features of Windows 2000 Professional, and marked the next development in the Windows 9x product line. Windows Me was also initially intended to act as a bridge for upgrading to the Windows NT product line from Windows 95 and Windows 98. Windows 9x refers to the Windows 95 and Windows 98 operating systems, and now includes the Windows Me operating system. See Figure 1-12. This product line was designed for the home user, although businesses also used these operating systems. In contrast, the Windows NT product line includes Windows NT Workstation 4.0 and Windows 2000, network operating systems more commonly used in business environments rather than by home users. Over the years, Microsoft indicated it would eventually combine the two different product lines into one product line. Start with Windows 95 in Figure 1-12 and go from left to right down the table to find the order in which the products in the two lines were released. Also, prior versions of the Windows NT product line were released before Windows NT Workstation 4.0.

Figure 1-12	WINDOWS DESKTOP OPERATING SYSTEM PRODUCT LINES
WINDOWS 9X PRODUCT LINE	**WINDOWS NT PRODUCT LINE**
Windows 95	Windows NT Workstation 4.0
Windows 98	Windows 2000
Windows Me	Windows XP

While continuing to include features found in previous versions of Windows, one of the important new features introduced in Windows Me is the System Restore feature. This feature creates **system checkpoints** where it saves changes to system files, device drivers, and system settings on your computer system so that if you run into a problem later, you can "roll back" your computer system and restore it to an earlier working state. If you install a new application or modify a hardware configuration and then encounter problems, you can roll back your computer to the point just before you made these changes, and restore a previous configuration that worked without any problems, essentially undoing the changes you made.

Another new component in Windows Me is the **Home Networking Wizard** which is designed to step a user through the process of setting up a home network, enabling Internet Connection Sharing (if desired), and choosing which files and printers to share on the network.

One of the areas of emphasis in Windows Me is its enhanced multimedia capability. Windows Me includes **Windows Movie Maker** for editing and enhancing video and home movies; an enhanced **Windows Media Player** for listening to music CDs with on-screen visualizations of sounds, creating music libraries, playing movies, listening to Internet radio stations, and customizing the appearance of Windows Media Player with the use of **skins** (a design scheme for changing the look of Windows Media Player); **WebTV** for viewing television programs broadcast over the Internet with a TV tuner card (a feature originally introduced in Windows 98); and the **Windows Image Acquisition** technology for obtaining images from a scanner or digital camera. Not surprisingly, these technologies are incorporated into the Windows XP operating systems.

The Windows XP Operating System

The Windows XP (for "Experience") operating system marks another important and major change in the development of the Windows operating system. Windows XP supports and enhances many of the features included in all previous versions of Windows, including major changes to the graphical user interface, and introduces many new features.

In October 2001, Microsoft released the following three versions of Windows XP:

- **Windows XP Professional Edition**. (Windows Version 2002, or Windows Version 5.1.2600) for business users, and for advanced users who prefer to use it on their home computer system

- **Windows XP Home Edition**. (Windows Version 2002, or Windows Version 5.1.2600) for home users and for entertainment

- **Windows XP 64-Bit Edition**. For scientific, engineering, business, and other types of resource-intensive applications, such as those required for handling special effects in movies and 3D animation

Windows XP 64-Bit Edition is designed for use with Intel's new Itanium processor. It supports up to 16 GB of RAM, and up to 16 TB (terabytes) of virtual memory. The **Itanium** processor is capable of performing 20 instructions simultaneously, and can preload data into virtual memory for faster access and processing.

For users of prior Windows versions, the most obvious change in the Windows XP Professional and Windows XP Home Editions is the redesign of the graphical user interface, including the desktop. For new installations of Windows XP, Microsoft has simplified the desktop by removing all icons except the Recycle Bin. The Start menu now serves as the primary way you access resources on your computer system. In addition to e-mail and Internet access links, the Start menu lists the five most recently used programs so that you can quickly open a program you commonly use. Also from the Start menu, you can open the My Documents, My Computer, My Pictures, My Network Places, and Control Panel folders, as well as the enhanced Help and Support Center. You access all installed software through the All Programs menu on the Start menu. Control Panel is organized into a new view called **Category view**, which provides links to common tasks for customizing and configuring your computer. When you are working in a folder window, Windows XP uses **dynamic menus** to display options related to your current task, and links to other places on your computer where you might want to work. For example, if you are working in a folder that contains document files, the dynamic menus list options for working with files, such as copying, moving, renaming, and deleting files. Also, the new **Tiles view** organizes the contents of a folder by file type. For example, if a folder contains Microsoft Word and Microsoft Excel files, Windows XP groups all the Word document files together and all the Microsoft Excel files together so that you can easily locate what you need to use. Within the My Pictures folder, **Filmstrip view** displays thumbnail views of images contained within files. Rather than setting aside a taskbar button for each document you open in each application, Windows XP use **taskbar grouping** to provide access to all open documents of a certain type (such as Word documents) under one taskbar button.

Here are some of the new features available in both the Windows XP Professional and Home Editions:

- **Performance enhancements**. Windows XP starts up more quickly, performs better, uses system resources and memory much more efficiently, and shuts down faster than other versions of Windows.

- **Fast User Switching**. Another user can log onto their user account while you remain logged onto your account. After the other user logs off, you can switch back to your user account and your application and document windows, which are still open and available.

- **System Restore**. Windows XP periodically saves information about changes to the configuration of your computer system, operating system files, and device drivers, so that if you make a change to your computer and then encounter a problem, you can "roll back" your computer system to an earlier functioning state.

- **Device Driver Rollback**. This tool replaces a newly installed device driver that does not work properly with a previously working version of that same device driver.

- **Internet Connection Firewall**. You use this feature to protect your computer from intruders and hacker attacks when you are connected to the Internet.

- **Credential Manager**. This tool secures, and also automatically provides, your user name and password to applications (such as e-mail software), services (such as your ISP), and Web sites that request such information so that you do not have to repeatedly specify the same user name and password.

- **Remote Assistance**. A technical support person, colleague, or friend can remotely connect to your computer to assist you with a project or to troubleshoot a problem. (Both systems must use Windows XP.)

- **Network Setup Wizard**. This wizard steps you through the process of creating a home network so your computers can share hardware devices (such as a printer), software, files, and use Internet Connection Sharing to share a single Internet connection.

- **Enhanced multimedia features and capabilities**. With **Windows Movie Maker**, you can capture, edit, and organize video clips derived from a digital video camera or an analog camera so that you can create and share home movies on your computer. You can use the **Scanner and Camera Wizard** to scan images or download images from a camera, and automatically store those images in your My Pictures folder. Within the enhanced **My Pictures** folder, you can organize and preview digital photos as well as order prints using a Web service. You can use the enhanced **Windows Media Player** to play CDs and DVDs, burn CDs, and organize music files in the **My Music** folder.

- **Internet Explorer 6**. This is an enhanced and improved version of Microsoft's Web browser, and **Windows Messenger,** an instant messaging application which you can use to find out who is online, send an instant message, engage a group of friends in an online conversation, invite someone who is online to play a game, dial a contact's computer, send one or more files to someone else, and, if you have a HotMail account, receive a notification when new e-mail arrives.

- **Help and Support Center**. Microsoft has expanded and enhanced the Help system in Windows XP so that you can find information on your local computer or on the Web.

- **Side-by-side DLLs**. Windows XP maintains different versions of the same DLL (dynamic link library) program file used by different applications. This feature prevents problems caused by replacing a DLL file used by several different applications when installing a new application.

- **Dynamic Update**. The Setup program used to install Windows XP can now check Microsoft's Windows Update Web site for important system updates and download them before it installs Windows XP. That in turn guarantees that the operating system files on your computer are up to date.

Here are some additional features and capabilities of Windows XP Professional:

- **Remote Desktop**. This tool allows you to access and use another computer from a computer with Windows 95 or later. For example, you can use Remote Desktop to access your office computer from your home computer, or vice versa.

- **Enhanced processor and memory support**. Window XP Professional (but not Windows XP Home Edition) now supports two symmetric multiprocessors and up to 4 GB of RAM. In a computer that uses **symmetric multiprocessing**, programs or tasks can be processed simultaneously by multiple microprocessors.

- **Wireless 802.1x networking support**. This feature improves performance for wireless networks.

- **Encrypting File System**. This feature, introduced in Windows 2000 Professional, augments the NTFS file system and enables you to encrypt files with a randomly generated key. This feature provides a high level of protection from hackers and other individuals who might attempt to steal data from your computer.

- **Network Location Awareness**. This new Windows XP service allows the operating system and applications to determine when a computer has changed its network location.

- **User State Migration Tool**. Administrators can use this tool to migrate a user's data, operating system settings, and application settings from a previously used computer to another computer with Windows XP Professional.

Not surprisingly, Windows XP Professional provides increased performance and support for setting up, configuring, securing, administering, and troubleshooting networks, as well as Internet and Web technologies, and protection for the Windows XP operating system and operating environment, all important factors in providing the best possible support for businesses.

The Convergence of the Windows 9x and Windows NT Product Lines

As noted earlier, the different versions of the Windows operating systems fall into two major product lines: the Windows 9x and the Windows NT product lines, as shown earlier in Figure 1-12. Each of these product lines reflects real differences in the needs of Microsoft's home user base and its business user base. Over the years Microsoft has worked to merge the two product lines into one Windows operating system. This transition not only requires successfully merging technologies in the different product lines, but also meeting the more complex networking and security needs of businesses, while appealing to home users who want simplicity and access to entertainment-based multimedia technologies. With the development of Windows XP, Microsoft is moving much closer to that goal.

The rapid changes in hardware technologies and in the Internet and the World Wide Web are reflected in a rapid change in operating system technologies. Figure 1-13 shows a line chart that delineates the introduction of operating systems and operating environments over a 20-year period from 1981-2001. As Figure 1-13 shows, the primary operating system used on PCs over this period of time was the DOS operating system, having been used for more than twice as long as the different versions of the Windows operating systems. Also, although there were six major upgrades of the DOS operating system over a 14-year period, the Windows operating system has upgraded six times in a six-year period. The pace of development and change in operating system technology in the future will probably be as rapid as it was in the past, and coincide with rapid changes in the Internet, World Wide Web, and hardware technologies.

Figure 1-13   PC OPERATING SYSTEMS & OPERATING ENVIRONMENTS

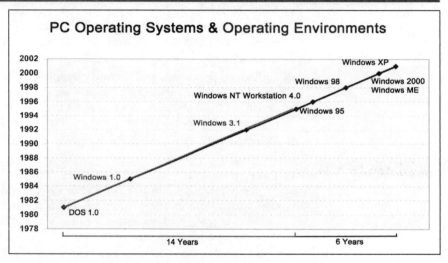

In the next section of the tutorial, you log on your computer and examine the features of the Windows XP desktop and the graphical user interface. Then you compare the use of Web style with Windows Classic view. You open the new Windows XP Help and Support Center and examine three techniques for locating Help information. During this process, you locate Help information on using keyboard shortcuts and Windows Product Activation, and you create a password reset disk. After examining the Help and Support Center, you navigate your computer, examine its folder structure and organization, examine the use of long filenames, and also examine specific types of operating system files. Then you view and print properties of your computer system. Finally, you log off your computer.

Logging On Your Computer

So that your coworkers feel comfortable with Windows XP Professional, Michele asks you to log on your computer and provide a quick tour of Windows XP.

Note that the figures in this book are derived from computers that have the first version of Windows XP Professional, or the first version of Windows XP Home Edition, so you might notice slight differences between your screen views and the figures. For example, on the initial Welcome screen, which you examine in the first step in this section, Windows XP Professional displays the option "Turn off Windows XP System," but Windows XP Home Edition displays the option "Turn off Windows XP Home Edition." Likewise, if you are using a later version of Windows XP Professional or Windows XP Home Edition, you can expect differences between your screen views and the figures.

To log on your computer:

1. If your computer is turned off, power on your computer. During booting, your computer might briefly display information about startup operations and technical specifications on your computer, or you might see a splash logo for your computer's manufacturer. Then you briefly see a progress indicator. The next screen displays the Microsoft Windows XP Professional logo and another progress indicator. Then Windows XP displays a Welcome screen, and prompts you to select your user name. See Figure 1-14. You can either log on under your user name or turn off your computer.

TROUBLE? If you do not see the Welcome screen, this feature is turned off, and you log on your computer using the standard Log On to Windows dialog box.

TROUBLE? If you do not see a Welcome screen or a Log On to Windows dialog box, Windows XP automatically logs you on your computer.

TROUBLE? If you are working on a network domain, you might need to press Ctrl+Alt+Del before you can log onto your computer.

TROUBLE? If you are working in a computer lab, your instructor and lab support staff will tell you what user name and password you should use.

Figure 1-14	WINDOWS XP WELCOME SCREEN

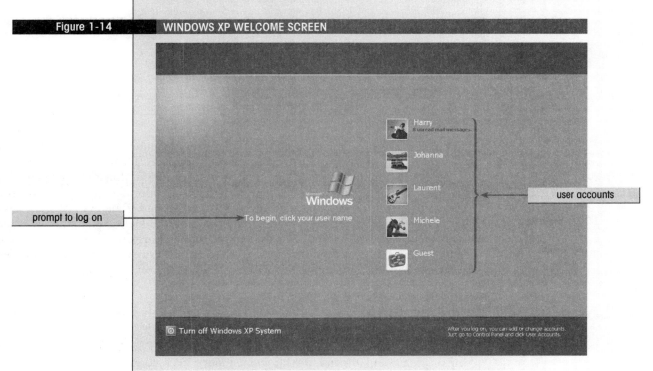

prompt to log on

user accounts

2. If Windows XP displays a Welcome screen, click your **user account** icon, and if Windows XP prompts you for your password, type your **password**, and then press the **Enter** key, or click the **Next** button [→]. If Windows XP displays a Log On to Windows dialog box, enter your **user name** (if necessary), type your **password** (if you use a password), and then press **Enter**, or click the **OK** button. Windows XP loads your personal settings and then displays the desktop. See Figure 1-15. Since either you or your computer dealer might have already customized the Windows XP desktop, your desktop might differ from the one shown in this figure. If you upgraded your computer from a previous version of Windows, your desktop will differ.

TROUBLE? If you do not remember the password for your user account, and if you are logging on your computer from the Welcome screen, you can click the Password Hint button [?], and Windows XP will display a hint to remind you of your password, assuming you have already specified a hint, or provided one to your network administrator.

TROUBLE? If Windows XP displays an MSN Explorer dialog box informing you that no one is set up to use MSN Explorer on your computer and prompting you to click "Add New User" to create a user account, click the Close button (x) in the MSN Explorer dialog box, and then click the Close button [x] in the MSN dialog box. Unfortunately, Windows XP might continue to redisplay these dialog boxes every few seconds or periodically, and you might need to close them to continue working with your computer. If Windows XP displays a "Take a tour of Windows XP" informational Help balloon, click its Close button [X].

Figure 1-15	WINDOWS XP DESKTOP

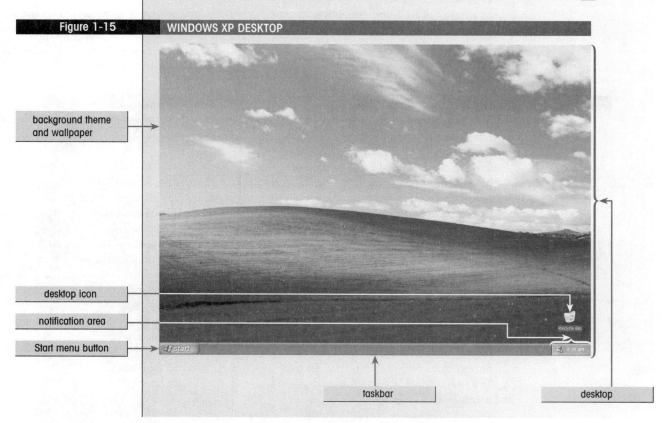

background theme and wallpaper

desktop icon

notification area

Start menu button

taskbar

desktop

If your computer is a member of a network domain, then each user is assigned to a group, which in turn provides each user with any rights and permissions granted to the group by the network administrator. A **domain** consists of a group of computers on a network that share a common directory database. Each domain has a unique name and is administered as a unit with common rules and procedures. A **group** consists of a set of users, computers, contacts, and even perhaps other groups. A **right** is a task that a user can perform on a computer or within a domain. For example, the administrator might grant a user the right to log onto a computer locally. A **permission** is a rule that determines which users can access an object and how they can access that object. For example, a network administrator might grant different users different permissions for use of a printer, such as the right to print, the ability to manage the printer, and the ability to manage documents.

A user can belong to the Administrators, Power Users, Users, Backup Operators, Guests, or Replicator group. A member of the **Administrators** group has full access to the computer, and can install an operating system, update or upgrade the operating system, configure and troubleshoot the operating system, manage the security of the computer system, and back up and restore the computer system. A member of the **Power Users** group can install software that does not modify the operating system, customize or make changes to some system settings and system resources (such as power options), and create and manage local user accounts and groups. A member of the **Users** group cannot modify the operating system, its settings, or data belonging to other users, and therefore is considered the most secure account. A member of the **Backup Operators** group can back up and restore files on a computer, but cannot change security settings. A member of the **Guests** group can log onto a computer and use the computer, but with limits. A member of the **Replicator** group can replicate files across a domain. The same types of user groups are also found in Windows 2000 Professional.

Instead of belonging to a domain, users might belong to a **workgroup**, which consists of a group of computers that provides users with access to printers and other shared resources, such as shared folders, on the network. Or a user might have a user account on a standalone computer that is not connected to other computers within a network. On a workgroup or standalone computer, there are three types of user accounts: Computer Administrator, Limited, and Guest. A **Computer Administrator** account allows a user to make changes to the computer system, including creating and removing other user accounts, as well as installing software. A member with this type of account can also access all files on the computer. Windows XP creates the Computer Administrator account during installation, and uses the Administrator password you provide during setup. Under a **Limited** account, a user cannot install hardware or software, or change his or her account name or account type. A member with this type of account can use software already installed on the computer, and can make some changes to their account, such as changing their password or picture. A **Guest** account, if enabled, allows users who do not have a user account to log onto and use the computer. There is no password for a Guest account.

If you are the only user on a computer, then your user account is also an Administrator account that gives you full access to the computer. If you create multiple accounts when you install Windows XP, each account will be a Computer Administrator account. You should create another account with limited access, and use that account, especially when you connect to the Internet, so as to prevent unauthorized changes to your system. If you log onto your computer as an Administrator and then connect to the Internet, a hacker who gains access to your computer then has full access to your computer system. You are also vulnerable to **Trojan horses**, programs that appear to be *bona fide* programs, but which are designed to retrieve information from your computer, such as user names and passwords, and then transmit that information to others who then can later access your computer via an Internet connection.

To further protect your computer, you should use a password that contains at least seven to 14 characters, and that also contains letters of the alphabet (both uppercase and lowercase), numerals, and symbols. Use at least one symbol as the second through sixth character. Your password should not be a common name or word, and you should not repeat previously used passwords. Although Windows XP supports passwords that are up to 127 characters long, you should use passwords that are seven to 14 characters long if you have other networked computers that are running either Windows 95 or Windows 98, because they do not support longer passwords.

The Windows XP Desktop

Windows XP uses the desktop as the starting point for accessing and using the resources and tools on your computer. Under previous versions of Windows, the desktop contained icons for My Computer, My Documents, My Network Places (called Network Neighborhood in Windows 95, and Network in Windows 98), Internet Explorer, and the Recycle Bin. If you upgrade from a previous version of Windows, your Windows XP desktop contains the same icons as before. If you purchase a new computer with Windows XP Professional or Home Edition, the Recycle Bin is the only icon on the desktop, unless the manufacturer of that computer customized the desktop. However, you can place the standard desktop icons found in previous versions of Windows on the desktop, and you can add shortcuts to the desktop (as you learn in Tutorials 2 and 4). As you install software and hardware, icons for those products might also be placed on the desktop.

Microsoft has reorganized the Start menu in Windows XP so that the Start menu consists of two panels, each separated into groups. See Figure 1-16. On the left panel of the Start menu used for this figure, Internet MSN Explorer and E-mail with Microsoft Outlook are listed above the separator line in an area called the **pinned items list**. Items in this area always remain on the Start menu. Your e-mail option might indicate that you use MSN Explorer instead of Microsoft Outlook. Under the separator line, Windows XP lists your most frequently used programs in an area called the **most frequently used programs list**. At the bottom, you can point to All Programs to display the All Programs menu from which you can choose a system tool, such as Windows Update, or open an installed application. From the right panel, you can open the My Documents, My Pictures, My Music, My Computer, or My Network Places folders, or use My Recent Documents to open a recently used document. You can also open the Control Panel or Printers and Faxes folders, connect to MSN Explorer, or display all connections. In the Windows Home Edition, you might not have a Connect To option (though it can be added to the Start menu). You can open the Help and Support Center, which has been expanded to provide you with access to not only Help but also system settings. Search has been expanded so that you can search for pictures, music, video, documents, files, folders, computers, people, or even information in the Help and Support Center. As in previous version of Windows, you can use Run to open a program, folder, document, or Web site. You also log off and turn off your computer from the Start menu. As you can tell, in Windows XP, the focal point has shifted from the desktop to the Start menu.

Figure 1-16   WINDOWS XP START MENU

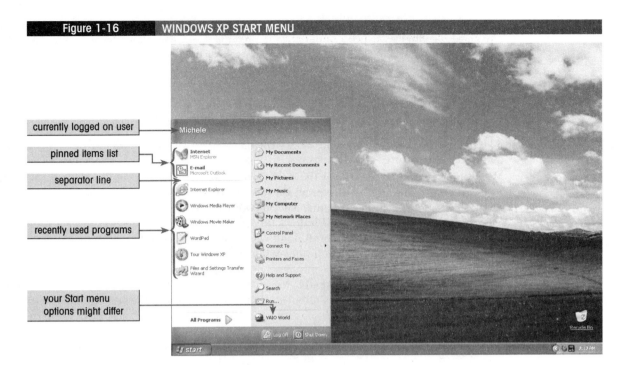

- currently logged on user
- pinned items list
- separator line
- recently used programs
- your Start menu options might differ

In addition to displaying the Start button and **notification area** (formerly called the system tray), the taskbar retains the same features and functions found in earlier versions of Windows. However, Windows XP supports **taskbar grouping**. As noted earlier, this feature groups documents opened with the same application on the same taskbar button. In other words, if you open many different documents with the same application, Windows XP combines all the documents into one taskbar button labeled with the name of the application. When you click this taskbar button, Windows XP displays a pop-up list of the document names so that you can select the document you want to use. Another advantage of taskbar grouping is that you can perform the same operation on all documents opened with the same application. For example, you can right-click a taskbar button, and then close all documents opened with the same application.

As in previous versions of Windows, the notification area contains not only the current time, but also icons for programs loaded in the background. If you have not used an icon in the notification area for a while, Windows XP hides the icon. You can click the Show Hidden Icons button to display icons that are currently hidden from view.

Although Microsoft has redesigned the desktop, Start menu, and taskbar, you should feel at home with Windows XP, because you still have access to the same basic Windows user interface and the same basic features found in previous versions of Windows. As you learn in Tutorial 2, you can customize each of these components to meet your specific needs.

Michele recommends that you compare the Windows Classic and Web styles so that you can decide which style you prefer to use.

Changing to Windows Classic Style

Windows XP uses a view and a way of interacting with your computer called Web style, instead of the Windows Classic style common to earlier versions of Windows. However, the company for which you work might have already set up their workplace computers so that they use Windows Classic style. Your company might prefer that you use the same style as you used in a previous version of Windows so that it is easier for you to initially adapt to

Windows XP. If you, or the company for which you work, prefer that you use the Windows Classic style, you can switch to that style by making four changes to the user interface:

- Apply the Windows Classic theme
- Change the Start menu style to the Windows Classic Start menu
- Apply the Windows Classic folders option
- Switch to the option for double-clicking icons to open objects

As you make these changes in the following tutorial steps, you might discover that your computer already uses certain settings, but not other settings, and your original view of the user interface was therefore a mix of Web style and Windows Classic style. Remember which settings your computer uses so that you can restore those settings later.

If you are working in a computer lab, make sure you have permission to change desktop settings. If necessary, ask your instructor or technical support staff before you continue with this tutorial. If you are not allowed to change desktop settings, read, but do not keystroke, the steps in this section. However, do examine the figures so that you are familiar with the features described in these steps.

If your computer already uses the Windows Classic style, you can still work through the following tutorial steps to determine whether all four types of changes have been made to the user interface.

To apply the Windows Classic theme:

1. Right-click an empty area of the desktop, and then click **Properties** on the short-cut menu. Windows XP opens the Display Properties dialog box. See Figure 1-17. The name of the currently used theme is shown in the Theme list box.

Figure 1-17   CHOOSING A DESKTOP THEME

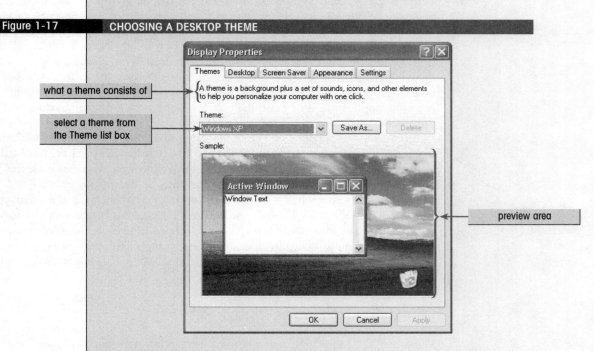

what a theme consists of

select a theme from the Theme list box

preview area

2. On the Themes property sheet, click the **Theme** list arrow, click **Windows Classic**, and after Windows XP displays a preview of the Windows Classic view in the Sample area, click the **OK** button. Windows XP switches to a desktop view that is similar to the Windows Classic style in earlier versions of Windows. See Figure 1-18.

| Figure 1-18 | WINDOWS CLASSIC DESKTOP THEME |

3. Click the **Start** button. Notice that Windows XP has also modified the style of the Start menu, but it's not the Windows Classic Start menu. See Figure 1-19. Instead, it retains the basic structure and layout of the original Windows XP Start menu.

| Figure 1-19 | START MENU AFTER CHANGING TO THE WINDOWS CLASSIC THEME |

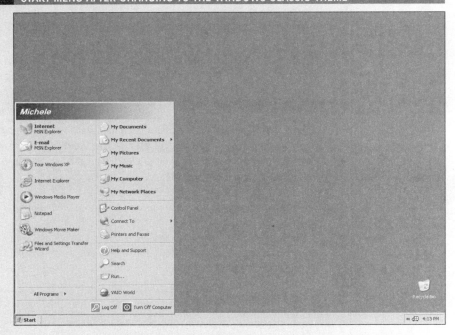

4. Click the **Start** button again to close the Start menu.

The next step is to change the Start menu style to the Windows Classic Start menu.

To change the Start menu style:

1. Right-click the **Start** button, click **Properties**, and after Windows XP opens the Taskbar and Start Menu Properties dialog box, click the **Start Menu** tab if it is not already selected. You can use the Start Menu property sheet to switch between the Windows XP Start menu style and the Windows Classic Start menu, and to also customize the appearance of the Start menu. See Figure 1-20.

Figure 1-20	START MENU PROPERTY SHEET

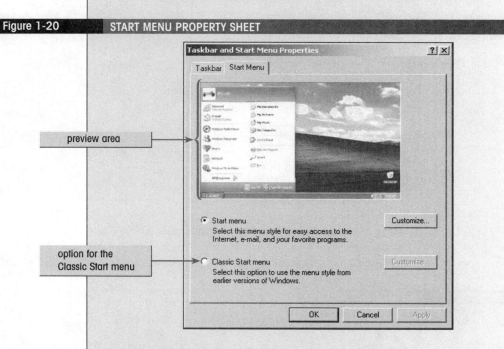

preview area

option for the Classic Start menu

2. Click the **Classic Start menu** option button, and then click the **OK** button. Windows XP adds icons for My Documents, My Computer, and My Network Places on the desktop. In the Home Edition, you also see an icon for Internet Explorer added to the desktop.

3. Click the **Start** button. Notice that the Start menu's appearance, structure, layout, and options appear more like the Start menu found in earlier versions of Windows. See Figure 1-21. The primary difference, however, is the use of the new Windows XP icons.

Figure 1-21	VIEWING THE WINDOWS CLASSIC START MENU

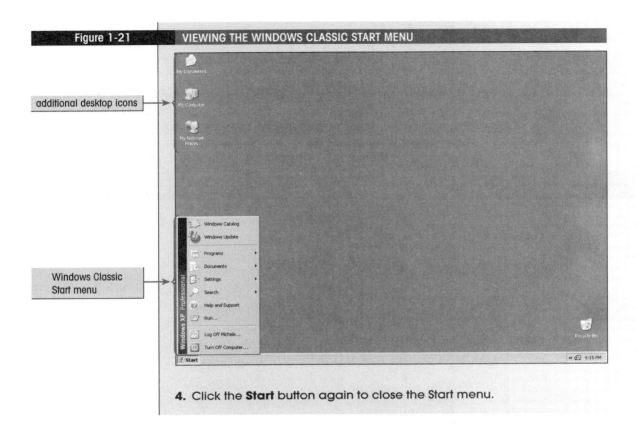

additional desktop icons →

Windows Classic
Start menu →

4. Click the **Start** button again to close the Start menu.

Before you change to the Windows Classic folders view, examine the My Documents folder so that you can compare the task-oriented view found in Web style with the Windows Classic folders view. In **task-oriented view**, Windows XP uses dynamic menus to display links to common folder tasks and other locations on your computer.

To change to Windows Classic folders and enable double-clicking:

1. Double-click the **My Documents** icon on the desktop. Windows XP displays the contents of the folder in task-oriented view. See Figure 1-22. For this folder, Windows XP provides links to common File and Folder Tasks, as well as links to Other Places on your computer.

Figure 1-22	TASK-ORIENTED VIEW WITH DYNAMIC MENUS

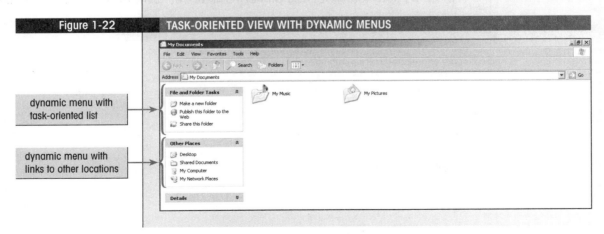

dynamic menu with
task-oriented list →

dynamic menu with
links to other locations →

2. Close the My Documents window.

3. Click the **Start** button, point to **Settings**, and then click **Control Panel**. After Windows XP opens the Control Panel window, click **Switch to Classic View** in the Control Panel dynamic menu. Notice that Windows XP retains the dynamic menus so that you can switch back to Category View.

4. Double-click the **Folder Options** icon. Windows XP opens the Folder Options dialog box. See Figure 1-23.

| Figure 1-23 | FOLDER OPTIONS DIALOG BOX |

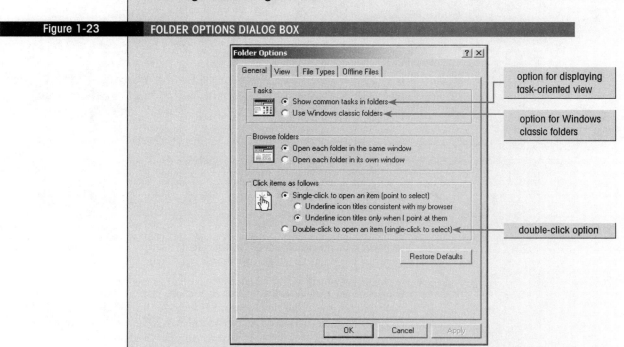

5. On the General property sheet, click the **Use Windows classic folders** option button under Tasks, click the **Double-click to open an item** option button under the "Click items as follows" section if it is not already selected, and then click the **OK** button. You no longer see dynamic menus in the Control Panel.

6. Close Control Panel, and then double-click the **My Documents** folder icon on the desktop. Windows XP no longer displays the task-oriented list and the links to Other Places on your computer in the folder window. See Figure 1-24.

| Figure 1-24 | WINDOWS CLASSIC FOLDERS VIEW |

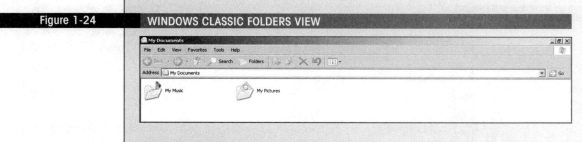

7. Close the My Documents window.

REFERENCE   WINDOW   **RW**

Changing to Windows Classic Style

- Right-click an empty area of the desktop, and then click Properties on the shortcut menu.
- After Windows XP opens the Display Properties dialog box, click the Theme list box arrow on the Themes property sheet, click Windows Classic, and then click the OK button.
- Right-click the Start button, click Properties, and after Windows XP opens the Taskbar and Start Menu Properties dialog box, click the Start Menu tab if it is not already selected.
- Click the Classic Start menu option button, and then click the OK button.
- Click the Start button, point to Settings, and then click Control Panel.
- After Windows XP opens the Control Panel window, click the "Switch to Classic View" link in the Control Panel dynamic menu.
- Double-click the Folder Options icon, and after Windows XP opens the Folder Options dialog box, click the "Use Windows classic folders" option button under Tasks on the General property sheet, click the "Double-click to open an item" option button under the "Click items as follows" section if it is not already selected, and then click the OK button.
- Close Control Panel.

Now you've modified the user interface so that it more closely resembles the Windows Classic view found in Windows 2000. Depending on your individual preferences, you might combine elements of Web style and Classic view so that you can work more easily with your computer.

Changing to Web Style

To change your computer from Windows Classic style to Web style, you have to reverse the changes that you made in the previous section of the tutorial, namely:

- Apply the Windows XP theme
- Change the Start menu style
- Change to a task-oriented view of folders
- Switch to the option for single-clicking to open objects

The remainder of the tutorials in this book uses the default Web style built into Windows XP, and if you are not using Web style, you need to switch to Web style so that your screen views match the figures in the book.

If you are working in a computer lab, make sure you have permission to change desktop settings. If necessary, ask your instructor or technical support staff before you continue with this tutorial. If you are not allowed to change desktop settings, read, but do not keystroke, the steps in this section. However, do examine the figures so that you are familiar with the features described in these steps.

To apply the Windows XP theme:

1. Right-click an empty area of the desktop, and then click **Properties** on the shortcut menu.

2. After Windows XP opens the Display Properties dialog box, click the **Theme** list arrow on the Themes property sheet, click **Windows XP**, and then click the **OK** button. Windows XP applies the Windows XP theme to the desktop.

> TROUBLE? If Windows XP does not display the original desktop wallpaper used on your computer, right-click an empty area of the desktop, click Properties, click the Desktop tab in the Display Properties dialog box, locate and select that desktop wallpaper in the Background list box, and then click the OK button.

Now you can change the Windows Classic Start Menu style back to the Windows XP Web style.

To change the Start menu style:

1. Right-click the **Start** button, click **Properties**, and after Windows XP opens the Taskbar and Start Menu Properties dialog box, click the **Start Menu** tab if it is not already selected.

2. Click the **Start menu** option button, and then click the **OK** button. Windows XP removes the My Documents, My Computer, My Network Places, and Internet Explorer icons (if previously displayed) from the desktop and switches to the Windows XP Start menu style.

Next, change the Windows Classic folders view back to a task-oriented view and enable the use of single-clicking.

To change to a task-oriented view of folders and enable single-clicking:

1. Click the **Start** button, click **Control Panel**, and then double-click the **Folder Options** icon in the Control Panel window. Windows XP opens the Folder Options dialog box.

2. On the General property sheet, click the **Show common tasks in folders** option button under Tasks, click the **Single-click to open an item** option button if it is not already selected, click the **Underline icon titles only when I point at them** option button if it is not already selected, and then click the **OK** button. Notice that Windows XP has restored the dynamic menus in the Control Panel window.

3. Click the **Switch to Category View** link in the Control Panel dynamic menu, and then close Control Panel.

Changing to Web Style

■ Right-click an empty area of the desktop, and then click Properties on the shortcut menu.
■ After Windows XP opens the Display Properties dialog box, click the Theme list arrow on the Themes property sheet, click Windows XP, and then click the OK button. *Note*: If you want to apply a different desktop wallpaper option, choose that wallpaper option from the Background list box on the Desktop property sheet in the Display Properties dialog box before closing it.
■ Right-click the Start button, click Properties, and after Windows XP opens the Taskbar and Start Menu Properties dialog box, click the Start Menu tab if it is not already selected.
■ Click the Start menu option button, and then click the OK button.
■ Click the Start button, click Control Panel, and then double-click the Folder Options icon in the Control Panel window.
■ After Windows XP opens the Folder Options dialog box, click the "Show common tasks in folders" option button under Tasks on the General property sheet, click the "Single-click to open an item" option button if it is not already selected, click the "Underline icon titles only when I point at them" option button if it is not already selected, click the OK button, and then close Control Panel.
■ Click the "Switch to Category View" link in the Control Panel dynamic menu, and then close Control Panel.

Now you've restored your computer to the default Windows XP Web style. As you've already seen, Web style simplifies the way you work with Windows XP, and allows you to use your Web browsing skills within the Windows XP user interface.

Using the Windows Help and Support Center

Michele explains to employees that they should first check Windows XP's Help and Support Center for answers to their questions before contacting her tech support staff, because Microsoft has expanded and improved Windows Help so that it has now become a more comprehensive resource for obtaining Help information. Plus, new users can view tutorials and demonstrations on how to use Windows XP features. Once you open the Help and Support Center, you can view information on specific topics, search for information using a keyword, or use the index to locate information by a keyword.

Viewing Help Topics on Keyboard Shortcuts

If you are working at the keyboard and want to perform a task that would otherwise require the mouse, you can use a **keyboard shortcut**, a key or a combination of keys, to accomplish the same task. Keyboard shortcuts can increase your productivity and make your computer system easier to use because you do not have to keep moving your hand from the keyboard to the mouse.

Keyboard shortcuts are also quite important when you experience problems with Windows. If, for some reason, the mouse stops responding, or if the image on the monitor flickers so fast you cannot see the mouse pointer, then you can still use keyboard shortcut keys to shut down your computer and restart it.

Since your job calls for you to help coworkers troubleshoot problems with Windows XP, Michele suggests that you use the Help and Support Center to locate information on keyboard shortcuts and become familiar with what options are available not only within the Help and Support Center itself, but also within the Windows XP user interface.

To locate information on keyboard shortcuts for Windows XP:

1. Click the **Start** button, click **Help and Support**, and maximize the Help and Support Center window, if necessary. Below the title bar is a navigation bar with the Back button ⊙ · and the Forward button ⊙ · for navigating backwards and forwards from one Help page to another, a Home button ⟳ for returning to the Help and Support Center home page, an Index button ▣ for locating Help information, a Favorites button ☆ for viewing previously saved Help pages, a History button ⊙ for viewing Help pages accessed during a session, a Support button ▦ for obtaining help using Remote Assistance or from a support professional, and an Options button ▢ for customizing the Help and Support Center. See Figure 1-25. Below the navigation bar is a Search box for quickly searching the Help and Support Center. There are also links to specific Help topics, wizards, and tools. Since your computer manufacturer might have customized the Help and Support Center on your computer, your view might vary.

Figure 1-25   **HELP AND SUPPORT CENTER**

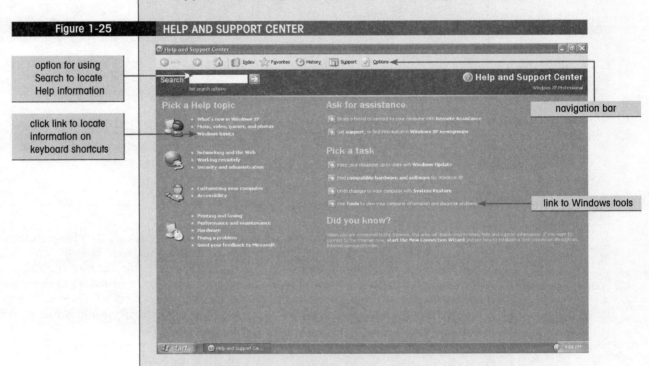

option for using Search to locate Help information

click link to locate information on keyboard shortcuts

navigation bar

link to Windows tools

Using the Options button ▢ , you can change Help and Support Center options, such as choosing whether to display Favorites and History on the navigation bar, specifying the font size, and controlling the display of text labels for navigation bar buttons. You can also set search options, including whether and how to search the Microsoft Knowledge Base at the Microsoft Web site. You can also install Windows Help from another Windows XP system or from a related version of a Windows server operating system, and then switch from one operating system's Help content to another.

After you examine the Help topics, you realize that information on keyboard shortcuts would most likely be found under the Windows basics Help topic.

2. Under the Pick a Help topic, click the **Windows basics** link. Under Windows basics, the Help and Support Center lists links to Help topics that focus on using basic features of Windows XP. See Figure 1-26. Under See Also, the Help and Support Center lists links to the Windows Glossary and to specific Help topics. Note that there is a link for "Tips on using Help." From that Help topic, you can find another shortcut to "Using Help and Support Center keyboard shortcuts," which explains how to navigate and use the Help and Support Center with keyboard shortcuts.

Figure 1-26	SEARCHING FOR INFORMATION ON SHORTCUT KEYS

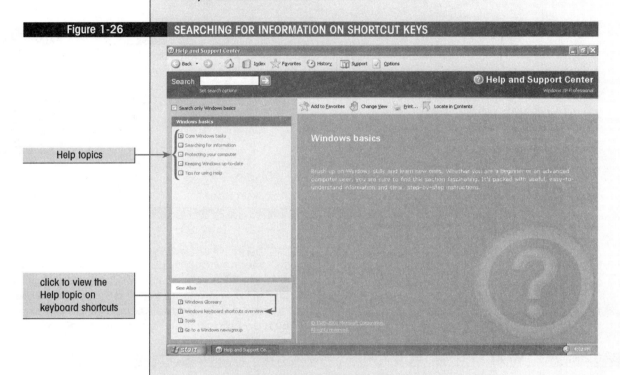

Help topics

click to view the Help topic on keyboard shortcuts

3. Under See Also, click the **Windows keyboard shortcuts overview** link. The Help topic pane on the right describes ways to use shortcut keys, organizes information on keyboard shortcuts by groups, and provides notes and hints on using keyboard shortcuts. See Figure 1-27.

Figure 1-27 **WINDOWS KEYBOARD SHORTCUTS OVERVIEW HELP TOPIC**

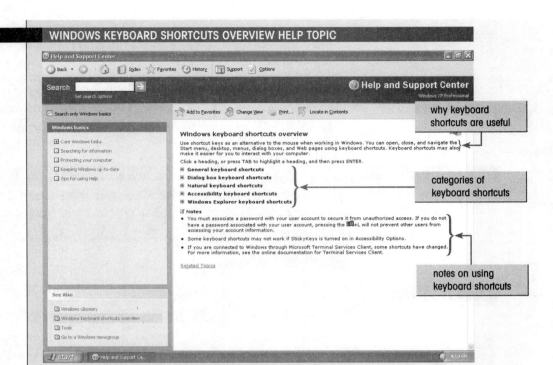

4. Click the **expand view** box ⊞ to the left of the General keyboard shortcuts heading. The Help and Support Center now displays a list of keyboard shortcuts. See Figure 1-28. You can use the F2 keyboard shortcut to rename a folder or file. If you scroll further down through the list of shortcuts, you find that you can use the Ctrl+Esc keyboard shortcut to display the Start menu, and the Esc key to close the Start menu. The Esc key is commonly used to cancel an action.

Figure 1-28 **VIEWING A LIST OF GENERAL KEYBOARD SHORTCUTS**

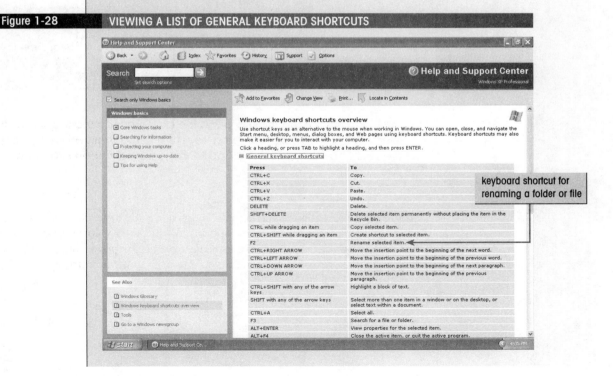

5. Press and hold the **Ctrl** key while you press the **Esc** key, and then release both keys. Windows XP displays the Start Menu.

6. Press the **Esc** key. Windows XP closes the Start menu. The Alt key also closes the Start menu. If you lose the use of the mouse, then you can use the Ctrl+Esc shortcut key to display the Start menu, press the Up arrow key ↑ to choose the "Turn Off Computer" option, press Enter to select this option, use the Right arrow key → to select "Restart," and then press Enter to complete the operation. So that you can quickly return to this Help page for reference, you decide to add it to your list of favorite Help pages.

7. Click the **Add to Favorites** button ☆ on the Help toolbar directly above the topic pane, click the OK button in the Help and Support Center dialog box, and after Windows XP verifies that the page has been added to your Help and Support Favorites list, click the **Favorites** button ☆ on the navigation bar. You now have a bookmark to the "Windows keyboard shortcuts overview" Help page. See Figure 1-29.

Figure 1-29	VIEWING HELP FAVORITES

Help topic on keyboard shortcuts added to your Help Favorites

8. Double-click the **Windows keyboard shortcuts overview** link in the Favorites frame. The Windows keyboard shortcuts overview Help topic appears again. Examine each category of shortcut keys to determine if you might benefit from any other keyboard shortcuts. Under "Natural keyboard shortcuts" you discover that if you have a Microsoft Natural Keyboard, then you can also use the Windows key by itself to display or close the Start menu. If you click the "Related Topics" link on a Help topic page, Windows XP displays a list of related Help topics from which you can choose.

9. After you finish examining information on keyboard shortcuts, click the **Home** button ⌂ on the navigation bar to return to the main Help and Support Center page. Keep the Help and Support Center window open for the next section of the tutorial.

You can use keyboard shortcuts as you work with different components of Windows, such as dialog boxes, accessibility options, Windows Explorer, and a Microsoft Natural Keyboard. Keyboard shortcuts are especially useful for power users, and essential for individuals who provide tech support and troubleshoot computer problems.

Searching the Help and Support Center

After further discussion with Michele, you discover that home users must activate Windows XP on their computer. Since you are considering upgrading your home computer to Windows XP Professional, Michele recommends that you search for information on activating a newly installed version of Windows XP in the Help and Support Center. She notes that one of the fastest ways to locate information is to use the search feature.

To locate information on activating Windows XP:

1. Click inside the **Search** box, type **activation**, and then click the **Start searching** button ➡. Under Search Results, Windows XP displays a list of links to specific tasks, Help page overviews, articles, and tutorials. See Figure 1-30. As you look down the list of topics, you notice it includes an overview of activating Windows XP that might prove useful. The number of items shown in your list might differ from that shown in the figure.

Figure 1-30 · SEARCHING FOR HELP INFORMATION ON ACTIVATING WINDOWS XP

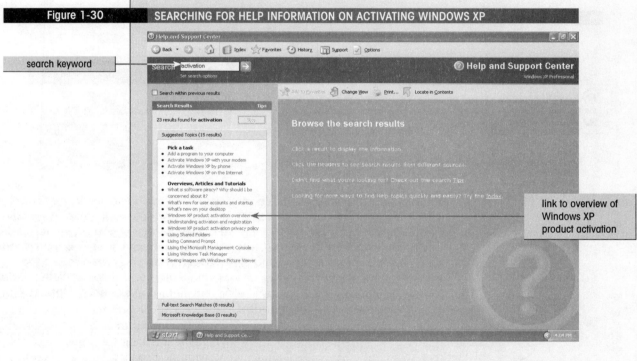

search keyword

link to overview of Windows XP product activation

2. Under Overviews, Articles, and Tutorials, click the **Windows XP product activation overview** link. In the Help topic pane, the Help and Support Center provides detailed information on activating your copy of Windows XP. See Figure 1-31. Note that the word you used for the basis of the search is highlighted wherever it is found in the Help page topic.

Figure 1-31   VIEWING THE HELP PAGE TOPIC ON WINDOWS PRODUCT ACTIVATION

search word
highlighted throughout
Help topic

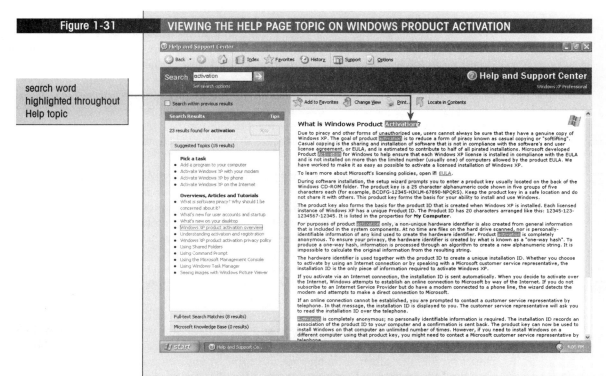

3. After you examine the information on activating Windows XP, click the **Home**
   button ⌂ on the navigation bar to return to the main Help and Support Center
   page, and then keep the Help and Support Center window open for the next
   section of the tutorial.

This overview provides you with some helpful information on understanding why you must activate your version of Windows XP. To prevent home users from installing Windows XP on more than one computer system using the same Windows XP CD, and thereby violating the Windows XP license agreement, Microsoft has implemented a feature called **Windows Product Activation**. During the installation of Windows XP on your computer, Windows XP creates a Product ID code using the Product Key that you provide during installation. Windows XP also creates a nonunique hardware identifier using what is called as a "one way hash" from general information gleaned from the system components on your computer. To produce this hardware identifier, Windows XP uses an **algorithm** (a formula or procedure) to convert that general information to a new alphanumeric **string** (or sequence of characters). Windows XP uses the hardware identifier along with the Product ID code to create a unique ID for your installed version of Windows XP. This information is then conveyed to Microsoft either via modem using an Internet connection or via phone with a customer service representative. Once you have activated your copy of Windows XP, you can use the Product Key to install Windows XP on that computer system an unlimited number of times; however, you might need to contact a Microsoft customer service representative if you want to install Windows on a different computer using that same version of Windows XP and the same Product Key. This feature is designed to prevent software piracy.

Microsoft claims that Windows XP does not scan the files on your hard disk drive, and that it does not use any personal information to create the hardware identifier. Microsoft also notes that it is impossible to reverse the process and calculate the original information from the resulting string.

You have a 30-day period in which to activate your newly installed retail version of Windows XP. At the end of that grace period, all features of Windows XP, except the product activation feature, stop functioning. At any time, you can activate your copy of Windows XP by using the Windows Product Activation Wizard. Just open the System Tools menu under Accessories, and select the Activate Windows menu option.

Activating your version of Windows XP does not automatically register it. That is a separate step, and registration is optional. However, if you register your copy of Windows XP, then you are entitled to product support, update information, and other benefits. Also, note that business users do not need to activate their licensed copies of Windows XP.

Using the Help and Support Center Index

At the end of her overview of Windows XP, Michele describes the importance of having a password reset disk for your user logon on your home computer system. If you forget your password, you can use the password reset disk to create a new password for your user account, and then you can log onto Windows XP under that user account. If you forget your password and do not have a password reset disk, you are locked out of your computer. This feature applies only to local user accounts, not to network accounts. A **local user** is an individual who uses a computer that is not connected to a network. Each user, including a Computer Administrator, can only create a password reset disk for their user account.

Michele suggests you use the Help and Support Center to step you through the process of making a password reset disk. With the Help and Support Center's Index tool, you can quickly pinpoint information on a specific topic by entering a keyword or phrase. When you use the Index feature, Windows searches a list of keywords and phrases that it has compiled from Help files.

To complete the following steps, you need a formatted, but empty, high-density diskette.

To use the Help and Support Center to find Help information on creating a password reset disk:

1. Click the **Index** button ◻ on the navigation bar. Windows XP explains that you can use the Index feature if you know exactly what you are looking for. In the "Type in the keyword to find" text box in the Index frame, you enter the word or phrase for which you want to locate information. See Figure 1-32. The list box displays a list of index entries arranged in alphabetical order. As you start to type a word or phrase, Windows XP automatically locates the first index entry that matches what you type.

Figure 1-32	USING THE HELP INDEX

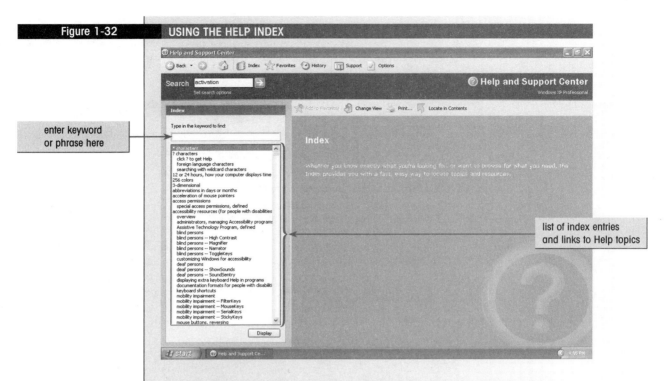

enter keyword
or phrase here

list of index entries
and links to Help topics

2. Type **passwords** and then stop. Windows locates the first entry that starts with the word "passwords". See Figure 1-33.

Figure 1-33	LOCATING INFORMATION ON CREATING A PASSWORD RESET DISK

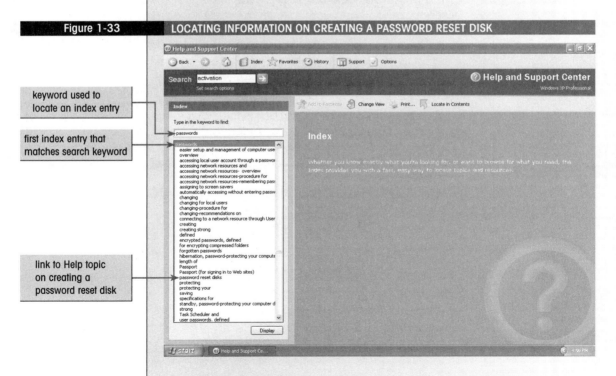

keyword used to
locate an index entry

first index entry that
matches search keyword

link to Help topic
on creating a
password reset disk

3. Under the passwords index entry, click **password reset disks**, and then click the **Display** button in the lower-right corner of the navigation pane. Windows XP explains that every local user should make a password reset disk and keep it in a safe place. See Figure 1-34. If you forget your password, you can use this disk to create a new user password and then access your user account. Help also notes that you can click the Related Topics link and use the Forgotten Password Wizard to create a password reset disk

| Figure 1-34 | PASSWORD RESET DISK OVERVIEW |

why a password reset disk is important

how to locate the Forgotten Password Wizard

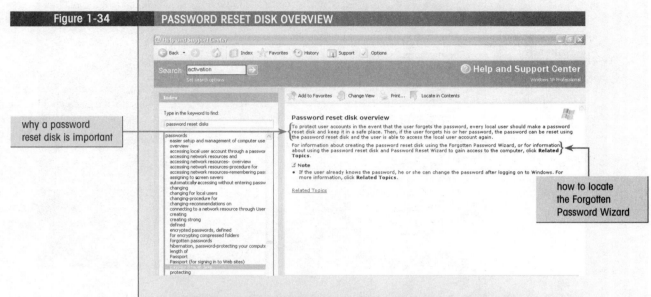

4. Click the **Related Topics** link, click **Create a password reset disk**, and then click the **expand view** boxes ⊞ to the left of "If you have a computer administrator account" and "If you have a limited account." Help now explains how to create a password reset disk depending on your account. See Figure 1-35. Notice that the two processes are similar, and notice that in each case, there are links to the User Accounts tool within Control Panel.

TROUBLE? If the Related Topics link does not include an option for creating a password reset disk, then read, but do not keystroke, the remaining steps in this section of the tutorial so that you are familiar with the process of creating a password reset disk for a local user account.

| Figure 1-35 | STEPS FOR CREATING A PASSWORD RESET DISK |

steps for creating a password reset disk for a computer administrator account

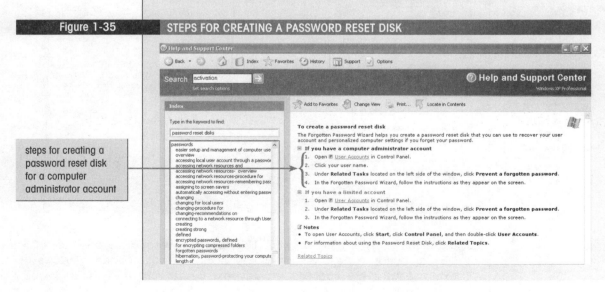

If you are a local user and want to create a password reset disk for your user logon, complete the following steps. If not, read, but do not keystroke, the steps, so that you are familiar with the concept and use of a password reset disk. Examine the figures so that you know how the wizard works.

To create a password reset disk:

1. Click the **Change View** button on the Help bar, click the **User Accounts** link for either a computer administrator account or a limited account (choose the one related to the type of account you have), right-click the **taskbar**, and then click **Tile Windows Horizontally** on the taskbar shortcut menu. You can now use the vertical scroll bars in each window to adjust your view, select options within each window, and view the step-by-step instructions in the Help and Support Center as you create a password reset disk. See Figure 1-36.

Figure 1-36   **WINDOWS TILED HORIZONTALLY**

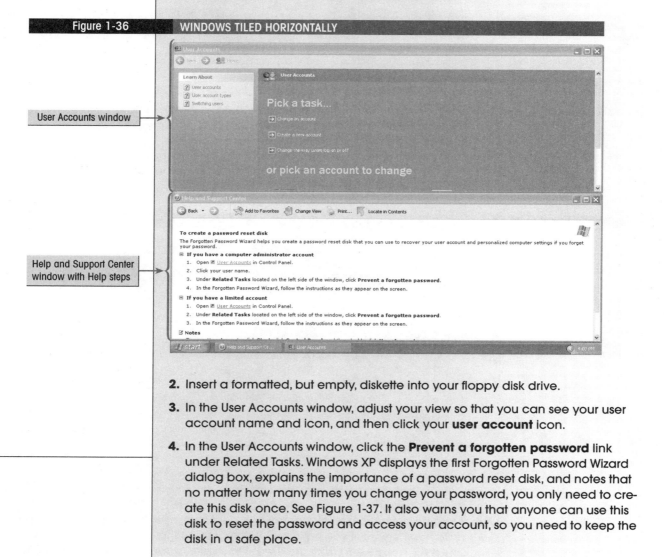

User Accounts window

Help and Support Center window with Help steps

2. Insert a formatted, but empty, diskette into your floppy disk drive.

3. In the User Accounts window, adjust your view so that you can see your user account name and icon, and then click your **user account** icon.

4. In the User Accounts window, click the **Prevent a forgotten password** link under Related Tasks. Windows XP displays the first Forgotten Password Wizard dialog box, explains the importance of a password reset disk, and notes that no matter how many times you change your password, you only need to create this disk once. See Figure 1-37. It also warns you that anyone can use this disk to reset the password and access your account, so you need to keep the disk in a safe place.

Figure 1-37	USING THE FORGOTTEN PASSWORD WIZARD

how to use this
password reset disk

password reset disk
works even if you
change your password

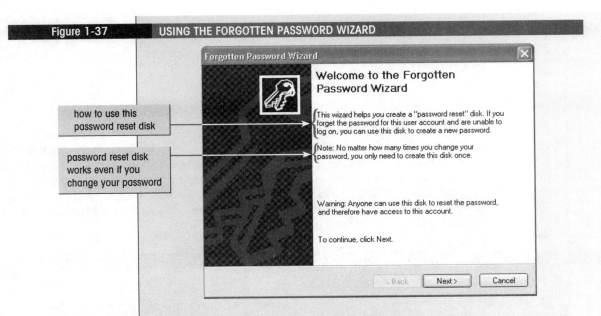

5. Click the **Next** button. In the next Forgotten Password Wizard dialog box, you are prompted to select the drive that contains the disk you want to use as a password reset disk. See Figure 1-38. By default, Windows XP selects the 3½ Floppy (A:) drive; however, if you have another removable disk drive, you can use that drive instead. If you do not have another removable disk drive, the Forgotten Password Wizard automatically prompts you to insert a blank formatted disk into drive A.

Figure 1-38	SELECTING THE DRIVE FOR MAKING A PASSWORD RESET DISK

6. If you do not have another removable disk drive, click the **Next** button to use drive A; otherwise, if you have the option of selecting a removable disk drive, select **3½ Floppy (A:)** from the "I want to create a password key disk in the following drive" list box if it is not already selected, and then click the **Next** button. The Forgotten Password Wizard now prompts you for your current user password. See Figure 1-39. If you do not have a password, leave this box blank.

Figure 1-39 | SPECIFYING YOUR USER ACCOUNT PASSWORD

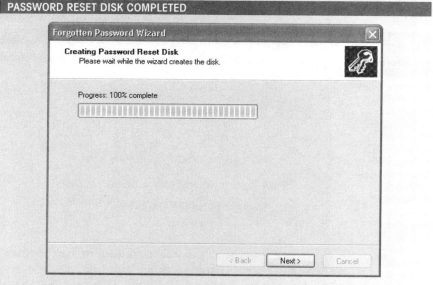

7. If you do not have a password for your user account, click the **Next** button; otherwise, type your user account **password**, and then click the **Next** button. The Forgotten Password Wizard creates a password reset disk. See Figure 1-40.

Figure 1-40 | PASSWORD RESET DISK COMPLETED

TROUBLE? If Windows XP displays a Replace Previous Disk dialog box and informs you that there is already a password reset disk for your user account, click the Yes button to create a new one. Note that your other password reset disk will no longer be usable.

8. After the process is complete, click the **Next** button. The Forgotten Password Wizard verifies that the operation was successful, and tells you to discard any previous disks, label this disk "Password Reset", and store it in a safe place. See Figure 1-41.

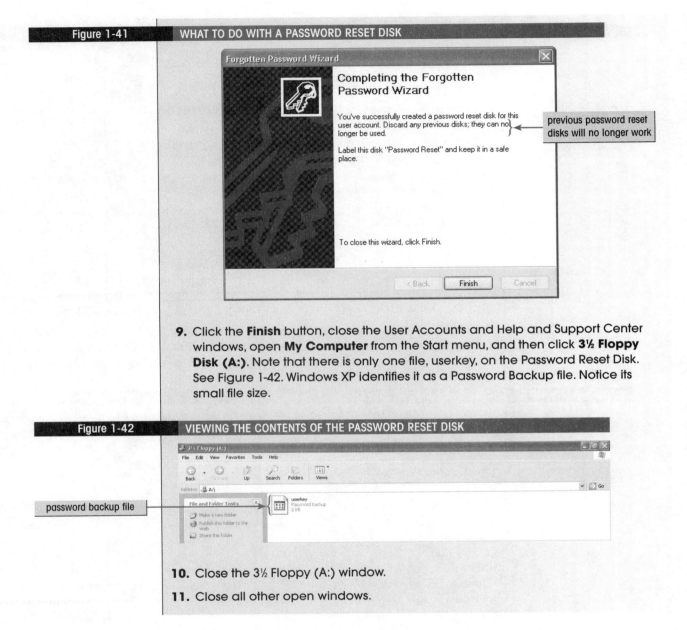

Figure 1-41   WHAT TO DO WITH A PASSWORD RESET DISK

previous password reset disks will no longer work

9. Click the **Finish** button, close the User Accounts and Help and Support Center windows, open **My Computer** from the Start menu, and then click **3½ Floppy Disk (A:)**. Note that there is only one file, userkey, on the Password Reset Disk. See Figure 1-42. Windows XP identifies it as a Password Backup file. Notice its small file size.

Figure 1-42   VIEWING THE CONTENTS OF THE PASSWORD RESET DISK

password backup file

10. Close the 3½ Floppy (A:) window.

11. Close all other open windows.

If you forget your password and need to use the password reset disk to access your user account, enter your user name and password at the Windows XP Welcome screen and then click the Next button ⬛. When Windows XP asks you if you have forgotten your password, click the "Use your password reset disk" link in the Help balloon. Follow the instructions in the Password Reset Wizard to create a new password, click your user account, if necessary, and then log on to your user account with that new password.

REFERENCE WINDOW   **RW**

Using the Help and Support Center
- Click the Start button, and then click Help and Support.
- If you want to locate Help by topic, click a Help category link under "Pick a Help topic", click a more specific Help topic subcategory (if necessary), and then click the Help topic link of interest to you.
- If you want to bookmark a topic you know you frequently need, locate and select the topic, and then click the Add to Favorites button on the Help toolbar.
- To locate a previously saved favorite Help topic, click the Favorites icon on the navigation bar, and then click the Help topic under Favorites.
- If you want to perform a broad-based search using a keyword or phrase, click inside the Search box, type a keyword or phrase, click the Start searching button, and then click a Help topic in the Search Results' list of Suggested Topics.
- If you want to use the Index to locate Help, click the Index button on the navigation bar, type a keyword or phrase in the "Type in the keyword to find" text box, click a topic under the index entry that corresponds to the keyword or phrase you entered, and then click the Display button.
- If you want to return to the Help and Support Center Home Page, click the Home button on the navigation bar.

Windows Help contains both basic Help information for the new user, including tutorials on new features such as Fast User Switching, and information on more advanced topics and new features, such as Remote Assistance. You can also connect to the Web and access online Help.

Navigating Your Computer

Windows XP provides two different ways to navigate, view, and work with the contents and resources of your computer. In prior versions of Windows, you used My Computer and Windows Explorer to display these two different views. Now, in Windows XP, these two tools are integrated, and you can use the Folders button on the Standard Buttons toolbar within folder windows to switch between these two views.

To more effectively use Windows XP, you need to understand some important concepts about the organization of the resources, drives, folders, and files on your computer as well as how you and the operating system designate names for these components.

Computers can contain different types of drives, but most computers have at least a hard disk drive, a floppy disk drive, and either a CD-ROM or DVD-ROM drive. Your computer might also have other types of drives, such as a CD-RW (CD-Rewritable) drive, a Zip disk drive, and perhaps a tape drive. The hard disk drive contains the installed version of the Windows XP operating system, as well as all applications, games, and utilities installed on your computer, and your document files. In some versions of Windows, the floppy disk drive provides one mechanism for gaining access to your computer system if you experience problems with the hard disk drive. You can boot your computer with a system or boot disk specific to that version of Windows, and then either troubleshoot the problem or rebuild your system. Since most software developers distribute their software on CDs, a CD-ROM or DVD-ROM drive has essentially become a required hardware component. On newer computers, the CD-ROM drive also provides an alternate way to gain access to your computer, and either repair, install, or reinstall your operating system software.

The term **drive** refers not only to the physical disk installed in your computer but also to the name assigned by the operating system to all or part of the storage space on a physical disk, such as the hard disk, or a **virtual disk** (such as a RAM drive that you designate as a temporary storage location). A **RAM drive** is a drive created from part of the available RAM on your computer. It functions like a regular drive in that you can create folders and files on the drive; however, it has the added advantage of read and write speeds that far exceed those of other drives. Unlike other drives, it's volatile, and therefore depends on the availability of power. If the power fails, you lose whatever is stored on the RAM drive. The Windows 98 Startup Disk, which allows you to boot your computer from a floppy disk in drive A, creates a RAM drive, and then extracts and copies troubleshooting utilities to the RAM drive. Windows 98 uses a RAM drive because the floppy disk drive does not contain enough storage space for all the operating system files, CD device drivers, and troubleshooting utilities that are needed for this type of disk. So, some of the utilities are stored in a compressed file on the floppy disk, and then extracted to the RAM drive during booting.

According to conventions set by IBM for the first IBM PC, the first floppy disk drive is always named **A:** and called **drive A**, and the second floppy disk drive (if present) is named **B:** and called **drive B**. The first nonremovable media that contains an active, primary partition with the operating system is named **C:** and called **drive C**. Any additional disk drives (whether hard disks or partitions of a single drive) are assigned other names using letters of the alphabet, such as **D:** for **drive D**. Although most people work on computers whose entire physical hard disk is assigned the name C: for drive C, it is possible to divide one physical hard disk into multiple logical drives. For example, a single hard disk might be divided equally into a drive C and a drive D. You might partition, or subdivide, a hard disk into multiple drives if, for example, you want to store all your software on drive C and all your document files on drive D. You can partition your hard disk if you want to install different operating systems on different partitions. Also, it is possible to have more than one physical hard disk in a computer.

On hard disks, software and documents are organized into folders. A **folder** is a file that keeps track of a group of related objects, such as files and perhaps other folders. The term **subfolder** refers to a folder contained within another folder. A **file** consists of a collection of data, such as a program or a document, stored on a disk under a unique filename and file extension (if specified). The operating system allocates a certain amount of disk storage space to each program and document, and associates each file's allocated space with the **filename** assigned to the file. The primary function of folders is to organize related information so that you (and the operating system) can easily find that information. If you have worked with the DOS operating system or a command-line operating system, then you are already familiar with the terms **directory** and **subdirectory**, which correspond to the terms folder and subfolder. If you open a Command Prompt window in Windows XP and work in a command-line environment, you then use the terms directory and subdirectory to refer to the folders and subfolders on the disks in your computer.

Although most people think of a folder as a container for objects, such as other folders and files, the folder itself and the other folders and files are all separate objects stored at different locations on the hard disk. Those other folders and files are not actually stored within that one folder. Since a folder is essentially a **logical** concept, it is common practice to think of files as being stored within folders (and folders stored within other folders), and to describe relationships using this approach. In the future, the Windows file system might change from a file-oriented system to an object-oriented system, and actually store subfolders and files within a folder. The features built into an operating system, and the data structures used by the operating system for naming, organizing, storing, and tracking folders and files on disks constitutes its **file system**. Different operating systems support different types of file systems (the focus of Tutorial 3).

As you work with the operating system and the applications and documents on your computer, you access different drives so that you can work with the folders and files stored in those different locations. You then select different folders and files to view information contained in those objects and, as needed, to move, copy, rename, delete, and change properties of folders and files. If you work primarily on a hard disk drive, these tasks can be complicated by the increasingly greater storage capacities of hard disk drives and the increasing amount of storage space required for installing software products. When you install an operating system or an application, literally thousands of files are copied to folders on your hard disk. For example, a new installation of Windows XP Professional might include 660 folders with over 17,000 files that require approximately 2 GB of storage space on the hard disk. You must therefore develop effective strategies for organizing the many different types of files that you create and work with on a daily basis so that you can locate those files quickly and easily.

Using Long Filenames

Another important operating system feature is the support that it provides for assigning names to files. Most filenames consist of three parts: the main part of the name (sometimes called the "root name"), a period (referred to as a delimiter or separator, and called a "dot"), and the **file extension**, which consists of the characters that follow the period. For example, in the filename Explorer.exe (the program that displays the desktop and the views you see within folder windows), "Explorer" is the main part of the filename, and "exe" is the file extension. The file extension is important in Windows because it identifies the type of file and, in many cases, the application that you use to open and modify the file. The "exe" file extension stands for "executable," and identifies this file as a program file the contents of which can be loaded into memory and executed. The contents of an executable file are stored in a format that the processor can directly execute, and unlike the source code, or program code, from which it is derived, you cannot read the contents of the file. Depending on how your computer is set up, you might or might not see the file extension with filenames.

Like all other versions of Windows, starting with Windows 95, you can use filenames that are up to 255 characters in length. These filenames can include spaces, periods, and symbols; however, the following nine symbols are not allowed because they have special meaning to the operating system:

$$: \quad / \quad \backslash \quad | \quad < \quad > \quad * \quad ? \quad "$$

If you try to use one of these **reserved symbols** in a filename, Windows informs you that the filename is invalid. Figure 1-43 lists examples of valid and invalid filenames. Since a filename might contain multiple periods, the last period in the filename is the one that separates the "main" part of the filename from the file extension. Although the file extension is not required, Windows applications typically assign file extensions to files that contain documents you produce with those applications, and Windows uses those file extensions to determine which application to open when you click (or double-click) a file icon. Also, file extensions serve to organize files by function and type, and when you choose the option to open a file from an application, that application displays a filtered view of the files within a folder, showing you only those filenames that have a certain file extension. If you want to view other file types (in other words, files with a different file extension), you can specify the file type.

Figure 1-43	EXAMPLES OF VALID AND INVALID FILENAMES

VALID FILENAMES	VALID CHARACTERS OR FEATURES
Five Year Sales Projection.xls	Spaces
PerformanceMeasurements.htm	Mixed case
FAT vs. NTFS Comparison.txt	Multiple periods
CASHFLOW.XLS	All uppercase characters
Ntldr	No file extension
Resume #1.doc	Pound sign (#) and numbers
Windows XP's System Requirements.doc	Apostrophe
Windows XP 64-Bit Edition Overview.htm	Dash and numbers
Windows XP Performance_Files	Underscore
Sales Commissions (1st Quarter).xls	Parentheses and numbers
Pilot Project Analysis & Summary.doc	Ampersand (&)
Multi-Booting with Windows XP, Windows 2000, and Windows 98.doc	Commas
@Backup Privacy Policy.doc	@ Symbol
Résumés	Special symbols

INVALID FILENAMES	INVALID CHARACTERS
Drive C: Backup Report.txt	Reserved device name (C:) in filename
Analysis: First Quarter Performance.doc	Colon in filename
File Systems (FAT16/FAT32/NTFS).doc	Slashes (/)
Explorer\Advanced Registry Subkey.txt	Backslash (\)
High Priority Projects.doc	Asterisks (*)
Potential Mergers?.doc	Question mark (?)
"Top-Notch" Sales Staff.doc	Quotation marks
<Client Mailing List>.mdb	Chevrons (< and >)
Level 1	Level 2	Level 3 Rating Systems.doc	Pipe Symbol (|)

You can also use these **long filenames**, as they are called, for folders, but a folder name usually does not have a file extension and, in some cases, files (such as operating system files) do not have file extensions. Note that the **path**, or notation used to identify the location of a folder or file (which you examine in more detail in Tutorial 3), limits the actual number of characters that you can use in a long filename, because you also have to take into account the name of the folder (and perhaps a sequence of folders) that identifies the location of the file.

Because some network operating systems do not recognize long filenames, Microsoft uses names for its program files and other supporting files that follow the DOS rules for naming files. DOS filenames are limited to eight characters for the main part of the filename, followed by a period, and then three characters for the file extension (called an **8.3 filename**). Furthermore, no spaces are allowed in a filename, and you can only use one period to separate the filename from the file extension.

Michele recommends that each employee take the time to explore and become familiar with the components on their computer as well as understand how Windows XP organizes their view of the computer. Because My Computer represents your entire computer system, it is the logical place to start.

Next, you are going to open the Fonts folder and view one of the installed fonts on your computer. As you browse your computer, you examine its folder structure and filenames with different types of file extensions.

The remainder of the instructions and the figures in this tutorial assume you are using Web style. If you are currently using Windows Classic style, then you will need to switch back to the Windows XP Web style using the instructions provided earlier in the tutorial so that your view of the desktop, folder windows, and application windows more closely resembles the views shown in the figures.

If you are working in a computer lab, make sure you have permission to change desktop settings. If necessary, ask your instructor or technical support staff before you continue with this tutorial. If you are not allowed to change desktop settings, read, but do not keystroke, the steps in this section. However, do examine the figures so that you are familiar with the features described in these steps.

To open and explore My Computer:

1. If you have already opened an application, drive, or folder window, close those windows and return to the desktop.

2. From the Start menu, click **My Computer**, and if the My Computer window is not already maximized, click the **Maximize** button ▣. The My Computer window, like every other type of window, contains a **title bar** at the top of the window to identify the name of the window and your location on the computer. See Figure 1-44. **Resizing buttons** on the right side of the title bar let you minimize, maximize, restore, and close a window. A **menu bar** with menu names provides access to commands. The **Standard Buttons** toolbar contains buttons for common tasks, and the **Address Bar** identifies your current location on your local computer or your network, and lets you enter an address for some other location on your local computer or network, or a URL (for **Uniform Resource Locator**) to access a Web site. The My Computer window consists of two frames. The frame on the right displays icons for shared and personal folders, the hard disk drives within your computer, and devices with removable storage. By default, Windows XP uses **Tiles view** to organize the information into the categories or groups that you see. The frame on the left contains dynamic menus with links to System Tasks and to Other Places on your computer, and Details on the folder you've opened or on an object within the folder that you select. Note also in Figure 1-44 that under Details, Windows XP identifies the My Computer folder as a System Folder.

Figure 1-44   VIEWING THE CONTENTS OF THE MY COMPUTER FOLDER

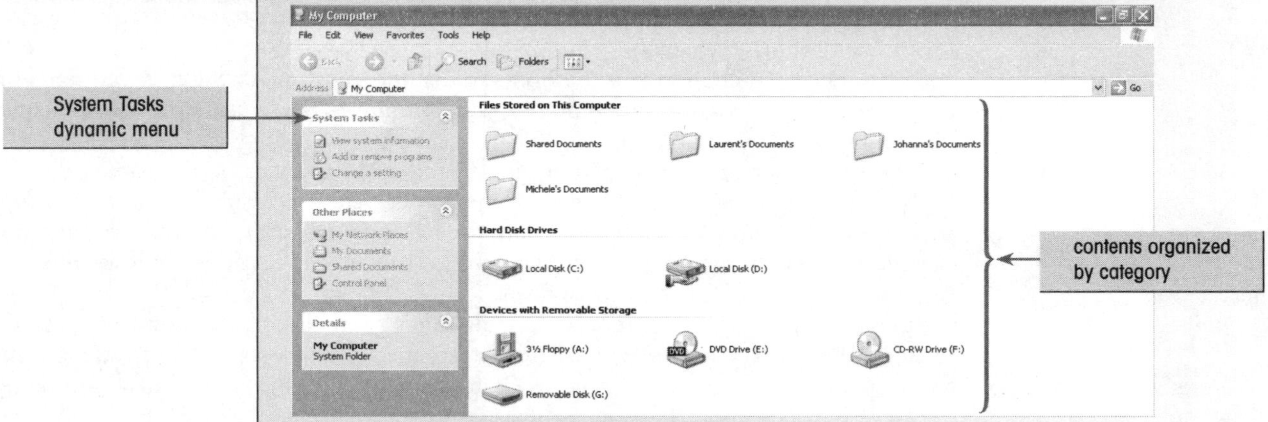

System Tasks dynamic menu

contents organized by category

On the computer shown in the figure, the physical hard disk drive is partitioned into two logical drives (drive C and drive D) that are each identified as a Local Disk, a 3½ Floppy drive (drive A), a DVD drive (drive E), a CD-RW drive (drive F), and another removable disk drive (drive G). The contents of your My Computer window differs from those shown in this figure.

Windows XP displays a Documents folder for each other user on the computer. Windows XP also creates a My Documents, My Pictures, and My Music folder for each user on the computer. Any folders or files copied or moved to the Shared Documents folder are then available to everyone who uses the computer. Likewise, if users want to share pictures or music, they can place pictures in a Shared Pictures folder and music in a Shared Music folder, both of which are found within the Shared Documents folder. If you are connected to a network domain, the Shared Documents, Shared Pictures, and Shared Music folders are not available.

TROUBLE? If you do not see the Standard Buttons toolbar, click View on the menu bar, point to Toolbars, and then click Standard Buttons.

TROUBLE? If you do not see an Address Bar, click View on the menu bar, point to Toolbars, and then click Address Bar. If the Address Bar appears to the right of the Standard Buttons toolbar, right-click the Address Bar, and if there is a check mark next to "Lock the Toolbars," click Lock the Toolbars; otherwise, click the folder background. Then point to the name of the Address Bar, and drag it under the Standard Buttons toolbar.

3. Point to the **Local Disk (C:)** icon, but do not click this drive icon. In the Details area, Windows XP identifies the file system used on this disk (FAT32 on the computer used for this figure), the free space, and the total storage capacity of the disk. See Figure 1-45. Your drive C details might differ.

Figure 1-45 VIEWING DETAILS OF DRIVE C

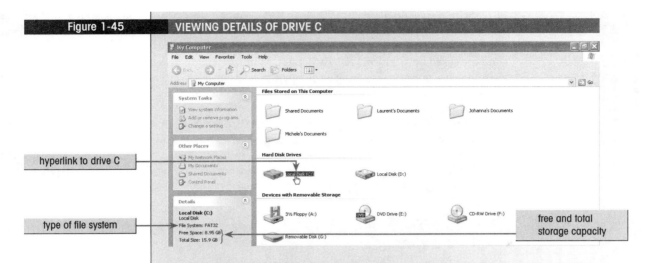

hyperlink to drive C

type of file system

free and total storage capacity

4. Click the **Local Disk (C:)** icon in the My Computer window and if Windows XP informs you that the files on drive C are hidden, click the **Show the contents of this folder** link to view the files. Windows opens the top-level folder of drive C. See Figure 1-46. When a hard disk is first formatted, the operating system (or perhaps even a formatting utility) creates a **top-level folder** on the disk. Once formatting is complete, you can create new folders within the top-level folder of that disk. DOS referred to the top-level folder as the **root directory**.

Figure 1-46 FOLDERS ON DRIVE C

notation for top-level folder of drive C

first level of folders below top-level folder of drive C

dynamic menu for file and folder tasks

Although your folder view might differ from that shown in the figure, you should have a Documents and Settings folder, Program Files folder, and Windows folder (which might have a different name). The Documents and Settings folder provides access to the user account folders for each user on the computer. The Windows folder contains folders and files for your installed version of Windows XP Professional or Home Edition. The Program Files folder contains folders and files for your installed software applications, games, and utilities as well as folders and files for some components of the operating system, such as Internet Explorer.

As you explore your computer, you can collect more information about your system if you display file extensions for known file types. A known file type, or **registered file type**, is a file that is associated with an application on your computer via its file extension. If you click, or double-click (depending on whether you are in Web style or Windows Classic style) the icon of a file with a specific file type, Windows XP automatically opens the associated application and then opens the file. Additionally, as you navigate your computer, you can display all folders and files as well as operating system files so that you can better understand the resources, folders, and files used by Windows XP. By default, Windows XP hides system folders and files in folder windows to prevent you from accidentally deleting, moving, or otherwise altering the files. Likewise, some applications create hidden files for their own use, such as verifying whether the application is registered.

If you are working in a computer lab, make sure you have permission to display hidden files and protected operating system files. If necessary, ask your instructor or technical support staff before you continue with this tutorial. If you are not allowed to change these settings, read, but do not keystroke, the steps in this section. However, do examine the figures so that you are familiar with the features described in these steps.

To view file extensions, hidden and system files, and operating system files:

1. Click **Tools** on the menu bar, click **Folder Options**, and then click the **View** tab. In the Advanced settings box on the View property sheet, you can specify a variety of settings for viewing information on your computer. See Figure 1-47.

Figure 1-47   SPECIFYING ADVANCED DISPLAY SETTINGS

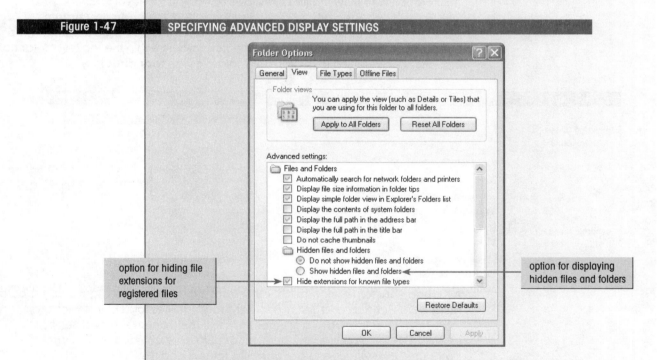

option for hiding file extensions for registered files

option for displaying hidden files and folders

2. Under Hidden files and folders, click the **Show hidden files and folders** option button if it is not already selected, click the **Hide extensions for known file types** check box if it has a check mark (to remove the check mark), click the **Hide protected operating system** files check box if it has a check mark (to remove the check mark), click the **Yes** button in the Warning dialog box when asked to verify that you want to display operating system files marked as hidden and system files, and then click the **OK** button to close the Folder Options dialog box. Windows XP applies the three new settings, and displays additional folders and files in the top-level folder of drive C. See Figure 1-48.

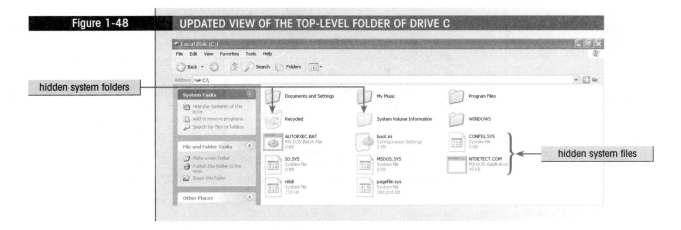

Figure 1-48   UPDATED VIEW OF THE TOP-LEVEL FOLDER OF DRIVE C

The two additional folders displayed in the window are the Recycled folder, which stores files you delete from your hard disk, and the System Volume Information, which contains information on restore points for use with the System Restore utility, so that you can roll back your computer to an earlier functioning state.

Also, you can now see file extensions for those files that have them. For those files with file extensions, Windows XP also identifies the file type associated with that file extension. For example, the Boot.ini file has the "ini" file extension, which stands for "initialization," and the file type for this file extension is "Configuration Settings." "Ini" (pronounced "I-N-I") or initialization files contain configuration settings that are used by the operating system or other programs. In this case, Boot.ini contains a list of operating systems used to boot your computer. If you do not have a dual-boot or multiple-boot configuration, then Microsoft Windows XP Professional is the only operating system file listed in Boot.ini. Ntldr (for "NT Loader") is a system file that starts the process of loading Windows XP when you power on your computer. Ntdetect.com checks the hardware on your computer during booting so that Windows XP can configure and manage that hardware. Ntdetect.com is identified as an MS-DOS Application because it contains the "com" file extension, which stands for "command." Files with the file extension "com" or "exe" are program files that you can load and use. Windows programs typically use the "exe" file extension, and DOS programs typically use the "com" file extension. Io.sys (for Input/Output) and Msdos.sys are operating system files used in prior versions of Windows and retained for compatibility with programs used in those versions of Windows. The "sys" file extension stands for "system" and identifies the file as a system file, configuration file, or a device driver. Config.sys and Autoexec.bat are MS-DOS startup configuration files, again retained for compatibility with programs used in previous versions of Windows. The file extension "bat" stands for "batch," and identifies the file as an MS-DOS Batch File with a set of commands that the operating system can process during booting. Note that Io.sys, Msdos.sys, Config.sys, and Autoexec.bat are all 0 KB in size; in other words, they're empty. The settings in these files are now incorporated into the Windows Registry (covered in Tutorial 13). As noted, Windows XP retains the files for backward compatibility with programs that checked these files for settings. You can specify the use of alternate settings by including those settings in Config.sys or Autoexec.bat. Pagefile.sys is another operating system that provides virtual memory (the focus of Tutorial 10), in effect increasing the amount of memory on your computer.

If you have a multiple-boot configuration, and if Windows XP is not installed on drive C, but rather another drive, such as drive D, the Documents and Settings, Program Files, Recycled, System Volume Information, and Windows folders, as well as Pagefile.sys, are on that other drive. However, Boot.ini, Ntldr, and Ntdetect.com are on drive C.

Michele recommends that you become more familiar with file extensions and file types, so you can better understand how the Windows XP operating system works with applications and documents.

To continue your exploration of your computer:

1. Click the **Documents and Settings** folder. Within this folder, you find a folder for each user as well as other folders used by Windows XP. See Figure 1-49. Each user's account and profile is created initially from a copy of the Default User folder and its contents—a default user profile, or combination of configuration settings. Each user profile uses the common program groups found in the All Users folder.

Figure 1-49	USER FOLDERS

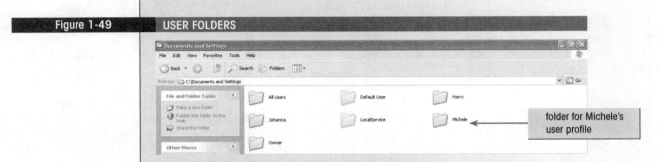

2. Click the **folder** icon with your user name, or if you are working on a computer in your college's computer lab, click the folder icon with the name of the logon account for your class. Each user folder contains an Application Data folder where software vendors store program-specific data; a Cookies folder (explained in the next step); a Desktop folder with your custom desktop shortcuts; a Favorites folder with Internet shortcuts to your favorite Web sites; a Local Settings folder (explained later); a My Documents folder; a My Recent Documents folder with shortcuts to recently opened drives, folders, and files; a NetHood folder with shortcuts to network resources; a PrintHood folder; a SendTo folder with shortcuts to other locations and to applications on your computer (the focus of Tutorial 4); a Start Menu folder (explained later); a Templates folder with document templates with default settings for different applications; and perhaps a UserData folder. See Figure 1-50. The Ntuser.dat file contains information on your user profile and represents the Registry portion of your user profile, Ntuser.data.log is the associated log file for Ntuser.dat, and Ntuser.ini is the associated initialization file with configuration settings. The **Registry** consists of a set of database files that contain all hardware, software, and network configuration settings, as well as security settings and user profile data for your computer.

Figure 1-50	VIEWING FOLDERS WITHIN A USER ACCOUNT'S FOLDER

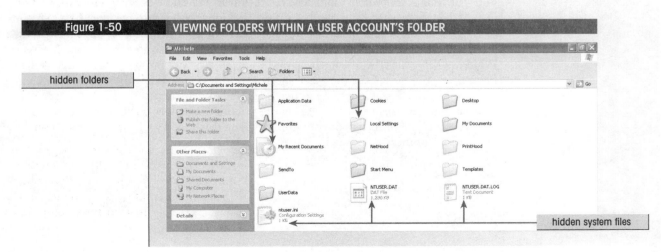

3. Click the **Cookies** folder. The Cookies folder contains an Index file, identified as a DAT (for "data") file, and a set of other files identified as text documents. See Figure 1-51. When you visit a Web site, the Web server for that Web site might put a cookie on your computer. The **cookie** is a text file that contains information about your visit to that Web site.

Figure 1-51	VIEWING THE CONTENTS OF THE COOKIES FOLDER

4. If you have one or more Text Document files, or cookies, in your Cookies folder, click one of the Text Document files to open it in Notepad. Figure 1-52 shows one of the cookies on Michele's computer. Although you might not be able to interpret most of the information stored in a cookie, you should see a reference to the URL of the Web site that created the cookie. On the computer used for this figure, the cookie identifies the domain (yahoo.com) and the path (/) of the Web site that created this cookie. The domain identifies the location and name of the server on the Internet, while the / symbol identifies the path as the entire Web site.

Figure 1-52	VIEWING THE CONTENTS OF A COOKIE

URL and domain from which cookie was derived

A cookie might also contain an expiration date expressed as the number of seconds since January 1, 1970, 00:00:000 GMT (Greenwich Mean Time). This value is called the UNIX time, because the UNIX operating system measures time using this approach. A cookie might also contain a TRUE or FALSE value to indicate that all computers within the domain of the Web site can access the information in the cookie, or to indicate that a secure connection is required, such as in the case of an online purchase in which you are providing your credit card number. Cookies also contain values specific to the Web site you visit.

5. Close the Notepad window, and then click the **Back** button ⊙ on the Standard Buttons toolbar.

Although not all Web sites use cookies, their use by many Web sites has raised the issue of **online privacy** and how information stored in a cookie might be used by the Web site that created the cookie, and perhaps by other Web sites. Advertising agencies are obviously interested in cookies, because they can develop a profile of your interests from the Web sites that you visit and then use this information to develop more effective marketing strategies that promote products you are likely to find interesting and that display that information in customized banner advertising. Cookies, however, can also be useful to you. For example, if you frequently visit the same Web site, and if that Web site requires you to identify yourself, then a cookie stored on your computer the first time you visit the site expedites your access to that same site later. If you visit an interactive gaming site, and advance to different skill levels, that Web site can use a cookie on your computer to identify the skill level you last attained, so that you can pick up where you left off when you return. Cookies are also used to track information an online transaction, such as purchasing products. If you visit a Web site that sells products in different countries, that site might place a cookie on your computer that identifies your country (and therefore your language system).

If you want to control the use of cookies on your computer, you can use your Web browser to prompt you before placing cookies on your computer, or to reject all cookies. In the latter case, you might not be able to access certain Web sites, such as HotMail, which requires the use of cookies. You can also acquire software, such as WebWasher (from *www.webwasher.com*), that can more effectively control cookies than your Web browser, and that offer other features, such as eliminating banner advertising and pop-up windows.

You can delete the cookies (in other words, the Text Document files) in the Cookies folder, but you cannot delete the Index.dat file. Someone with the right program can reconstruct your cookie history from the Index.dat file. If you want to remove the contents of this Index.dat file as well as others created in other folders, you can use a program named Spider (from *www.fsm.nl/ward*), a Hidden URL Inspector.

The Favorites folder contains Internet shortcuts to Web sites that you've visited and that you've chosen to save to this folder. The Local Settings folder contains the Application Data, History, Temp, and Temporary Internet Files folders as well as a Desktop.ini file that contains information about how to display the contents of a folder. The Temporary Internet Files folder (your Internet cache) contains all the files downloaded from every Web site you visit. Over time, the size of this folder increases substantially, and you need to periodically use your Web browser or the Disk Cleanup Wizard (covered in Tutorial 7) to empty this folder. The History folder contains a daily history of the Web sites you visit, the folders that you open on your local computer, files that you open, and the Help topics that you view in the Help and Support Center. You can also use your Web browser to empty the History folder. The program Spider (mentioned in the last paragraph) can not only remove cookies and clean Index.dat files, but also remove all temporary Internet files and History files.

The Temp folder contains temporary files (usually with the "tmp" file extension) created on your computer system by Windows XP or the applications you use. A **temporary file** (covered in more detail in Tutorial 7) is a file created and used by the operating system, an application, or a utility to store a copy of the data that it is processing until it completes the operation.

To continue your exploration of drive C:

1. Click the **Back** button ◎· twice, locate and click the **Windows folder** icon (which might have a name other than Windows, such as WinNT), and if Windows XP informs you that the files in this folder are hidden, click the **Show the contents of this folder** link.

TROUBLE? If you've explored other folders, you might need to use the Up button 🔄 to "step up" the folder structure until you return to the top-level folder of drive C. Then you can open the Windows folder and continue with this step.

2. Click **View** on the menu bar, and then click **Details**. This folder and its subfolders contain the majority of the Windows XP operating system files on your computer. See Figure 1-53. The rest of the software is stored in different folders within the Program Files folder, such as the Internet Explorer folder, and in the top-level folder. In Details view, Windows XP displays a Name column with the name of the folder or file, a Size column that displays file sizes in KB (kilobytes, or thousands of bytes), a Type column that identifies the type of object (such as file folder), and a Date Modified column with the date and time the object was modified. Windows XP is only able to display a small portion of the contents in this folder window.

POWER USERS TIP If you right-click one of the column buttons (such as Name), then you can pick and choose the types of information that you want to display in Details view, including categories such as Artist, Album Title, Track Number, Genre, Duration, and Camera Model.

| Figure 1-53 | VIEWING THE CONTENTS OF THE WINDOWS FOLDER IN DETAILS VIEW |

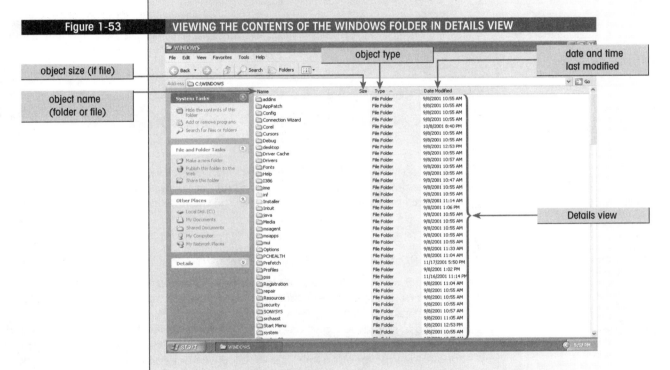

3. Click the **Type** column button (if necessary, click more than once) until Windows XP arranges the contents of this folder in alphabetical order by object type. Folders, identified as File Folders, are then listed first.

4. Adjust your view by scrolling down until you see the last File Folder listed and the beginning of the filenames. See Figure 1-54. The object type for the Downloaded Program Files, Offline Web Pages, and Tasks folders is Folder. Unlike the other folders, these folders contain custom icons and have special properties. Files identified as an Application have the "exe" file extension and are executable programs. Application Extensions have the "dll" file extension and are dynamic link libraries, or files with modules of program code. Files identified as Bitmap Images have the "bmp" file extension and contain graphic images (covered in Tutorial 2). Also listed are "ini" files identified as Configuration Settings. Files with the "log" and "txt" file extensions are log files and text files, and are identified as Text Documents. You will more than likely see other types of folders and files in the Windows folder on your computer.

| Figure 1-54 | VIEWING FILES IN THE WINDOWS FOLDER |

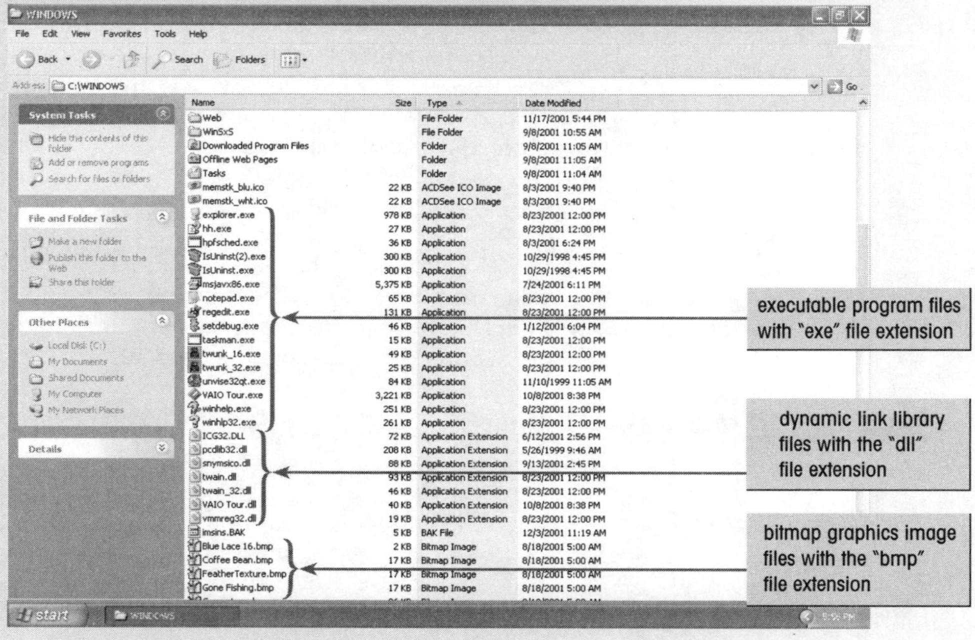

executable program files with "exe" file extension

dynamic link library files with the "dll" file extension

bitmap graphics image files with the "bmp" file extension

The folder structure within the Windows folder is multitiered and fairly extensive, not surprising considering that the 17,000 or more files are organized into over 400 folders.

Next, you're going to open the Fonts folder and examine information about a commonly used font.

To view an installed font on your computer:

1. Locate and click the **Fonts** folder icon. In the Fonts folder window, Windows XP displays icons for the individual font files. See Figure 1-55. Your set of fonts might differ from those shown in the figure. A **font** is a design style for a set of characters. Fonts are used to display text and symbols on the screen as well as on paper. Arial and Times New Roman are two different fonts commonly used by many programs. You see an icon for each font if it is installed on your computer. All the fonts in the Fonts folder are available for use in all your Windows programs. The outlined letter "O" used on the file icon of many of the font files identifies them as OpenType fonts. An **OpenType font** is an outline font that Windows XP creates from commands for drawing lines and curves. Windows XP can scale and rotate these types of fonts. OpenType fonts are an extension of the TrueType (indicated by the "TT" used on the file icon) font technology available in previous versions of Windows. The "A" on the file icon indicates a screen font. A **screen font** is a typeface designed for display on a computer monitor's screen. The operating system relies on the use of screen fonts for components of the GUI. In contrast, TrueType and OpenType fonts are scalable font technologies for rendering fonts both on a printer and on the screen.

| Figure 1-55 | VIEWING THE CONTENTS OF THE FONTS FOLDER |

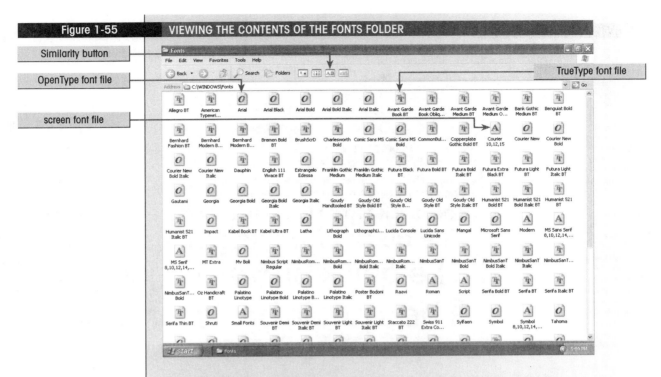

The Standard Buttons toolbar is different from the one in other folder windows. Notice that there is no Views button 🔲▾, but instead you have the following buttons: Large Icons 🔳, List 🗐, Similarity 🅰🅱, and Details 🔳. You can use the Similarity button 🅰🅱 to locate fonts that are similar to, or dissimilar from, a font that you select in this folder.

2. Click the **Arial** file icon, and then maximize the window, if necessary. The Arial (OpenType) window contains information about this font, shows the characters available in this **typeface** (the actual design style), and then illustrates samples of different **point sizes** (the height of characters, where one point = 1/72 of an inch (one inch tall = 72 points), and shown in the window as 12, 18, 24, 36, 48, 60, and 72, for points). See Figure 1-56. When you clicked the Arial file icon, Windows XP automatically opened a program named Fontview to display information about this font.

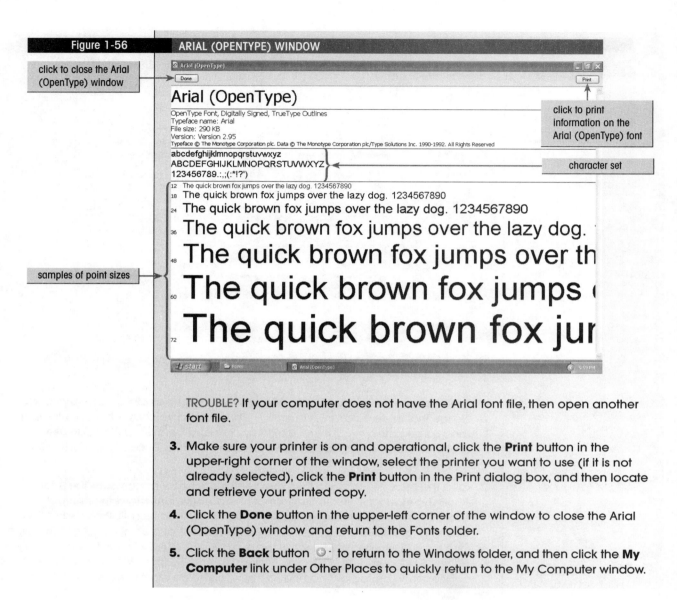

Figure 1-56   ARIAL (OPENTYPE) WINDOW

click to close the Arial (OpenType) window

click to print information on the Arial (OpenType) font

character set

samples of point sizes

TROUBLE? If your computer does not have the Arial font file, then open another font file.

3. Make sure your printer is on and operational, click the **Print** button in the upper-right corner of the window, select the printer you want to use (if it is not already selected), click the **Print** button in the Print dialog box, and then locate and retrieve your printed copy.

4. Click the **Done** button in the upper-left corner of the window to close the Arial (OpenType) window and return to the Fonts folder.

5. Click the **Back** button ⊙· to return to the Windows folder, and then click the **My Computer** link under Other Places to quickly return to the My Computer window.

Notice that, as you navigated drive C, each time you selected a drive or folder to open, you stepped down one level in the folder structure of your computer. When you clicked the Back button ⊙·, you returned to the previous folder. You could have also used the Up button 🗁 to move up one level in the folder structure of your computer. No matter where you are, you can also quickly jump to other locations on your computer using links under Other Places. You can also change your view within a folder window so that you can view the hierarchy, or relationship, of system components, drives, and folders on your computer and, if necessary, quickly jump to another location.

To view the hierarchy of your computer:

1. Click the **Folders** button 🗀 on the Standard Buttons toolbar. Windows XP replaces the dynamic menus with a Folders toolbar. See Figure 1-57. The Folders toolbar shows the hierarchy and relationships among different objects on your computer.

Figure 1-57	CHANGING TO FOLDERS VIEW

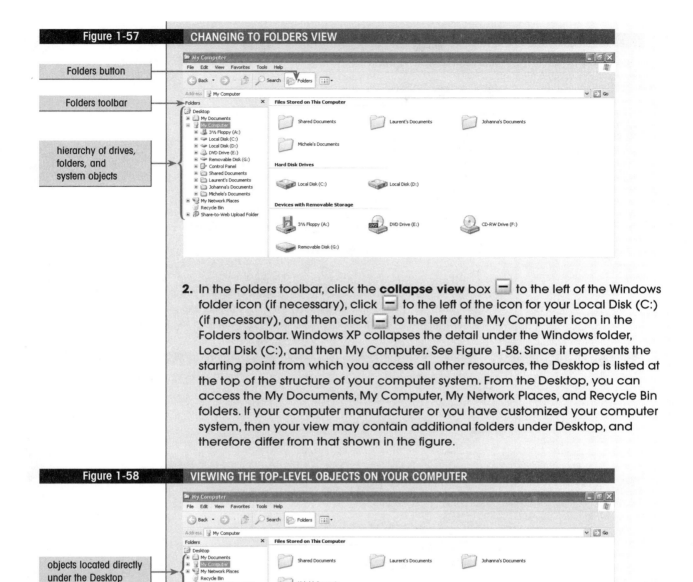

Folders button

Folders toolbar

hierarchy of drives, folders, and system objects

2. In the Folders toolbar, click the **collapse view** box ▬ to the left of the Windows folder icon (if necessary), click ▬ to the left of the icon for your Local Disk (C:) (if necessary), and then click ▬ to the left of the My Computer icon in the Folders toolbar. Windows XP collapses the detail under the Windows folder, Local Disk (C:), and then My Computer. See Figure 1-58. Since it represents the starting point from which you access all other resources, the Desktop is listed at the top of the structure of your computer system. From the Desktop, you can access the My Documents, My Computer, My Network Places, and Recycle Bin folders. If your computer manufacturer or you have customized your computer system, then your view may contain additional folders under Desktop, and therefore differ from that shown in the figure.

Figure 1-58	VIEWING THE TOP-LEVEL OBJECTS ON YOUR COMPUTER

objects located directly under the Desktop

3. In the Folders toolbar, click the **expand view** box ➕ to the left of the My Computer icon. Windows XP expands My Computer to show the drives, system folder (Control Panel), and user folders at the next level in the folder structure on your computer. See Figure 1-59.

| Figure 1-59 | VIEWING THE CONTENTS OF MY COMPUTER IN THE FOLDERS TOOLBAR |

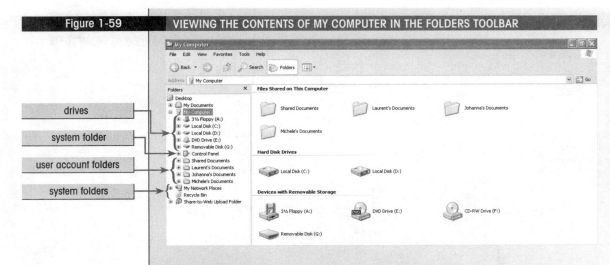

drives

system folder

user account folders

system folders

4. In the Folders toolbar, click ▬ to the left of the icon for Local Disk (C:). Windows XP now displays the first level of folders below drive C or, to think of it a different way, the folders within the top-level folder of drive C. See Figure 1-60.

| Figure 1-60 | VIEWING THE CONTENTS OF DRIVE C |

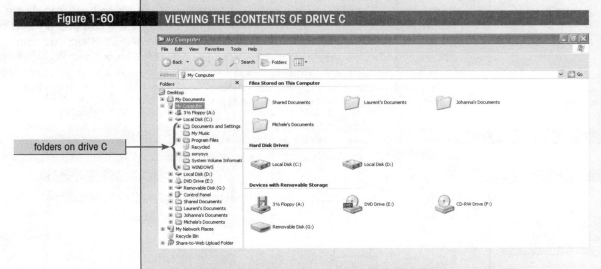

folders on drive C

5. In the Folders toolbar, click ✚ to the left of the Windows folder icon, and then adjust your view within the Folders toolbar by scrolling right. Windows XP expands the folder structure again, and displays the folders below the Windows folder. See Figure 1-61. When you expanded the folder structure below the Windows folder, Windows XP automatically adjusted the view in the Folders toolbar so that the Windows folder is at the top of the pane, and you can view as many folders under the Windows folder as can fit in the Folders toolbar. Your view in the Contents pane on the right has not changed because you have not selected a folder. One advantage of using the Folders toolbar is that you can navigate the folder structure without changing the view in the Contents pane.

Figure 1-61   VIEWING THE CONTENTS OF THE WINDOWS FOLDER

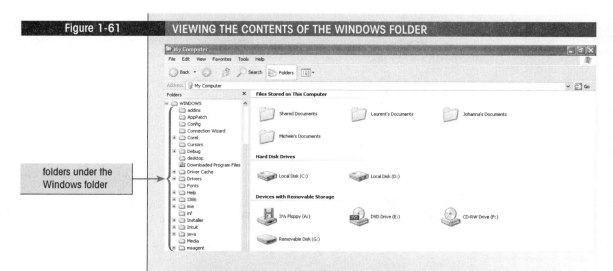

folders under the
Windows folder

If the Folders toolbar is not wide enough for you to see longer filenames for
folders, then you can move your pointer so that it is over the bar that separates
the Folders and Contents pane and, when you see a double-headed black
arrow that points to the left and right (◄─►), drag the bar to the right (or left),
and adjust your view onto the Folders toolbar.

TROUBLE? If you accidentally clicked the Windows folder icon or the
Windows label, then click the Back button ◎· to select My Computer in the
Folders toolbar and then repeat this step.

6. Click the **Fonts** folder icon in the Folders toolbar. Windows XP displays the
contents of the Fonts folder in the Contents pane. See Figure 1-62. Yet another
advantage to using the Folders toolbar is that you can more quickly select
folders and view their contents.

Figure 1-62   VIEWING THE CONTENTS OF THE FONTS FOLDER

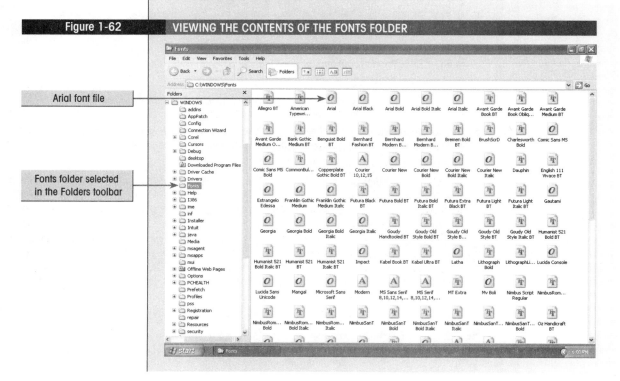

Arial font file

Fonts folder selected
in the Folders toolbar

7. Locate and click the **Times New Roman** file icon in the Contents pane on the right, and then maximize the Times New Roman (OpenType) window. Now Windows XP displays information about this font.

8. Close all open windows to return to the desktop.

If you have a Microsoft Natural keyboard, then you can simultaneously press the Windows key (with the flying windows logo) and the E key to quickly open a My Computer window and also display the Folders toolbar.

REFERENCE WINDOW

Navigating Your Computer

- From the desktop, click the Start button, click My Computer, and if necessary, maximize the My Computer window.
- If you do not see the Standard Buttons toolbar, click View on the menu bar, point to Toolbars, and then click Standard Buttons.
- If you do not see an Address Bar, click View on the menu bar, point to Toolbars, and then click Address Bar.
- Click the drive C icon.
- To display file extensions, all folders and files, and operating system files, click Tools on the menu bar, click Folder Options, and then click the View tab. In the Advanced settings box on the View property sheet, click the "Show hidden files and folders" option button under "Hidden files and folders" if it is not already selected, click the "Hide extensions for known file types" check box if it has a check mark (to remove the check mark), click the "Hide protected operating system files" check box if it has a check mark (to remove the check mark), click Yes in the Warning dialog box when asked to verify that you want to display operating system files marked as hidden and system files, and then click the OK button to close the Folder Options dialog box.
- To view the contents of the folder for your user account, click the Documents and Settings folder, and then click the folder icon with your user name.
- If you explore other folders within the Documents and Settings folder, you can click the Back button on the Standard Buttons toolbar to return to the previous folder or the Up button to "step up" the folder structure.
- If you want to view the contents of the Windows folder, click the My Computer link under Other Places, click Local Disk (C:), and then click the Windows folder icon.
- If you want to switch to Details view, click View on the menu bar, and then click Details.
- If you want to arrange the contents of this folder in alphabetical order by object type, click the Type column button once or twice.
- To display the Folders toolbar and view the hierarchy of your computer, click the Folders button on the Standard Buttons toolbar.
- Use the expand view box and the collapse view box to adjust your view onto the folder structure of your system.
- If the Folders toolbar is not wide enough to see longer filenames for folders, then you can move your pointer so that it is over the bar that separates the Folders and Contents pane and, when you see a double-headed black arrow that points to the left and right, you can drag the bar to the right and adjust your view onto the Folders toolbar.
- If you want to view the contents of a specific folder, click the icon or name of that folder.
- If you want to view dynamic menus, click the Folders button again.

As a power user, you will invariably need to quickly access resources on your computer system. By using Windows XP's object-oriented nature and its reorganized user interface, you can quickly navigate your computer and locate the resources you need—whether it be drives, folders, or files.

Viewing **Properties of Your Computer**

If you need to locate general information about your computer, such as the operating system version and the amount of RAM installed in your computer, you view properties of your computer system. Whether you're a novice or power user, you should know how to find this information, especially if you need to troubleshoot your computer.

Michele recommends that you open the System Display properties dialog box, and then print the information about your computer.

To view properties of My Computer:

1. Click the **Start** Button, right-click **My Computer**, and then click **Properties** on the shortcut menu. Windows displays the System Properties dialog box. See Figure 1-63. The General property sheet displays system information, including the type of operating system and its version number. The property sheet shows that Version 2002 of Microsoft Windows XP Professional is installed on the computer used for this figure. In addition to showing the registered owner, the General property sheet also identifies the type of processor (in this case, a Pentium 4 that operates at approximately 1.5 GHz) and the amount of installed RAM (in this case, 256 MB).

Figure 1-63	VIEWING PROPERTIES OF A COMPUTER

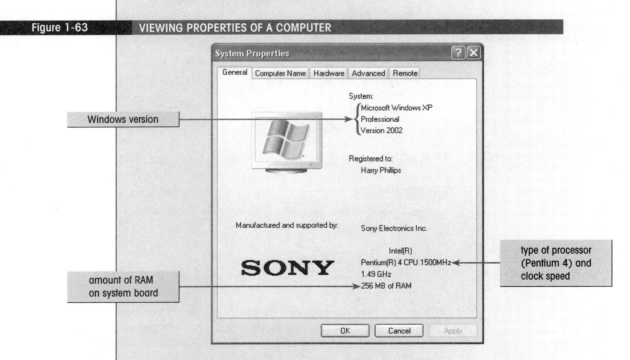

2. Press and hold down the **Alt** key while you press the **Print Scrn** key, release the **Print Scrn** key, and then release the **Alt** key. Although nothing appears to have happened, you just copied the contents of the System Properties dialog box to

the Windows Clipboard, an area of memory for holding copied or cut objects. Alt+Print Scrn copies the active window or the active dialog box (shown with the blue title bar) to the Clipboard. If you press Print Scrn and do not press the Alt key, Windows XP copies the entire desktop to the Clipboard.

3. Click the **Start** button, point to **All Programs**, point to **Accessories**, and then click **WordPad**.

4. After the WordPad application window opens, maximize the window, type your name, your course number (such as CIS 50.91), the course name (such as Exploring Windows), the lab assignment number (such as Lab Assignment #1), and any other information (such as the section number and date) that your instructor requests that you include on lab assignments.

5. Press the **Enter** key a couple of times to insert blank rows.

6. Click **Edit** on the menu bar, and then click **Paste**. Windows XP inserts the copy of the System Properties dialog box stored on the Windows Clipboard as an object into your WordPad document. See Figure 1-64.

   TROUBLE? If Windows XP inserts a copy of your entire desktop instead of just the System Properties dialog box, then more than likely you released the Alt key just before you pressed the Print Scrn key. Press the Delete key to delete the inserted object (which should still be selected), and then repeat Step 2 and this step.

Figure 1-64	SAVING A COPY OF THE SYSTEM PROPERTIES DIALOG BOX

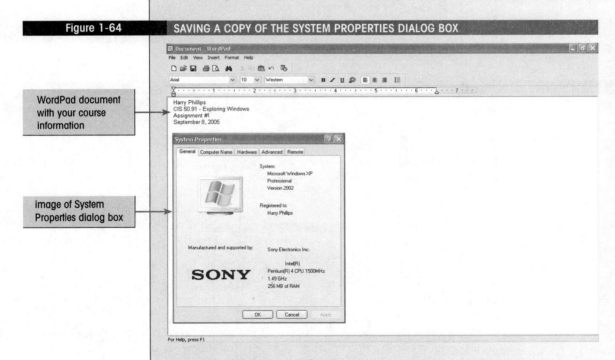

WordPad document with your course information

image of System Properties dialog box

7. If you want to save this document, click **File** on the menu bar, click **Save**, click the **Save in** list arrow, click **3½ Floppy (A:)**, select Document.rtf (the default document name) in the Filename box and replace it with a filename of your own choosing (such as System Properties Dialog Box), and then click the **Save** button.

8. To print this document, click **File** on the menu bar, click **Print**, select the printer you want to use (if it is not already selected) in the Print dialog box, click the **Print** button in the Print dialog box, and then locate and retrieve your printed copy.

9. Close WordPad, and since you did not make any changes to the properties of your computer system (and since it's always preferable to err on the side of caution), click **Cancel** to close the System Properties dialog box.

The Windows Clipboard can only hold one object—such as a character, a paragraph, 50 pages (for example) of a document, a graphics image, a table, or a reference to a folder or file. Whatever you copy or cut to the Windows Clipboard stays there until you copy or cut something new. When you shut down Windows, anything stored on the Windows Clipboard is erased from memory. In contrast, Microsoft Office XP has a feature called **collect and paste** that allows you to store up to 24 different objects from one or more applications, including your Web browser, on the Office Clipboard, which is separate from the Windows Clipboard. You can copy one or more items to the Office Clipboard, and you can choose one or more items on the Office Clipboard to paste into a document.

REFERENCE   WINDOW   **RW**

<u>Copying and Pasting the Image of a Window or Dialog Box into a Document</u>
- Open the window or dialog box that you want to copy to the Clipboard.
- If you want to copy only the active window or active dialog box, press and hold down the Alt key while you press the Print Scrn key, release the Print Scrn key, and then release the Alt key.
- If you want to copy the entire desktop, press and release the Print Scrn key.
- From the Start menu, point to All Programs, point to Accessories, and then click WordPad.
- After the WordPad application window opens, maximize the window, enter a title or any other explanatory text (if necessary), insert blank lines after the title or explanatory text (if necessary), and position the insertion point marker where you want to paste the image.
- Click Edit on the menu bar, and then click Paste.

If you call Microsoft tech support or another tech support line, the person you talk to will more than likely ask you to display the System Properties dialog box and identify the version of Windows XP installed on your computer, the type of processor, and the amount of RAM. Each of these pieces of information might serve as a valuable clue in identifying the source of a problem and solving that problem on your computer. If you need to document an error condition or system settings, you can use Alt+Print Scrn to copy the active window or dialog box to a document so that you can then print the file, or attach the file to an e-mail message (for example, to tech support).

Restoring **Your Computer**

If you are working in a computer lab, or if you want to restore your computer to its original state (prior to starting this tutorial), complete the following steps.

To restore your computer:

1. If you want to restore the default Folder options and view settings, open My Computer, click **Tools** on the menu bar, click **Folder Options**, click the **Restore Defaults** button, click the **View** tab, click the **Restore Defaults** button, click the **OK** button, and then close the My Computer window.

WINDOWS   1.76   TUTORIAL 1   THE WINDOWS XP OPERATING SYSTEM

2. If you want to remove the Favorites bookmark that you created earlier in the Help and Support Center, click **Help and Support** on the Start menu, click the **Favorites** button ☆ on the navigation bar, click **Windows keyboard shortcuts overview** in the Favorites list box, click the **Remove** button, and then close the Help and Support Center window.

3. If your computer originally used Windows Classic view, follow the steps described earlier in the tutorial for switching your computer to Windows Classic style.

Logging Off, or Turning Off, Your Computer

Once you have finished working with Windows XP, you can do one of two things: you can shut your computer down, or if you are connected to a network, you can log off your user account. If you are working on a company network, on a network in a computer lab, or on your own home network, you can use the Log Off option to display the Welcome screen or the Log On to Windows dialog box. Then you or someone else can log onto the computer and network later.

If you are working in a computer lab, do not shut down your computer unless your instructor or technical support staff specifically requests you to shut it down. If you are unsure as to what to do, check with your instructor or technical support staff. *Most computer labs prefer that you do not turn off the computers for any reason.* Usually, the computer lab support staff turns on the computers first thing in the morning when the lab opens, the computers remain on all day long, and the computer lab support staff shuts down the computers when the lab closes at night.

To log off, or turn off, your computer:

1. If you want to log off your own computer, or if you are working in a computer lab and want to log off the computer you are using, click the **Start** button, click the **Log Off** button, and then click the **Log Off** button in the Log Off Windows dialog box. Windows XP then displays the Welcome screen or a Log On to Windows dialog box.

2. If you are using your own computer and want to turn off the computer, open the Start menu, click the **Turn Off Computer** button, and in the Turn off computer dialog box, click the **Turn Off** button.

If you are working on a company network, it is a good idea to log off when you finish your work so that no one else can access files under your account. Also, when you are ready to shut down a computer at the end of the day, it is important to use the Turn Off Computer option so that Windows XP can save important settings to disk and properly shut down your computer.

Michele's coworkers thank her for the information she has shared with them, and they ask her to set aside some time at each weekly staff meeting to describe new features of interest to the staff, answer questions that might arise on the use of Windows XP, and provide them with power tips to help them become more productive.

REVIEW ASSIGNMENTS

Michele has just hired Ryan Poole, a new summer intern, for a special project. Since he is familiar with the use of Windows 98 on computers at his high school, she thinks he can adapt to Windows XP quickly. While she is waiting for the go-ahead to implement the new project, she asks Ryan to explore Windows XP and become comfortable with the operating system. Since he is interested in animation, graphics, and music, and wants to eventually design special effects for movies, she recommends that he explore the new features found in Windows XP's My Pictures and My Music folders.

To complete the steps for working with the My Music folder, you need a computer with speakers, or you need a computer set up to use earphones so that you can hear music.

As you complete each step, record your answers to questions so that you can submit them to your instructor. Use a word-processing application such as Word or WordPad to prepare and then print your answers to these questions. Also, if you change any settings on the computer you are using, make a note of the original settings so that you can restore them later.

1. If necessary, start Windows XP and log on your computer under your user account.

2. Examine the desktop and determine if Windows XP is set up for Web style with single-click activation. If not, switch to Web style.

Explore 3. From the Start menu, open the My Pictures folder, and then open the Sample Pictures folder. What type of view does Windows XP use for the contents of this folder? *Hint*: Check the View menu to determine which view is currently used.

Explore 4. Use the View menu to switch to Thumbnails view, and then back to Filmstrip view. Briefly describe how these two views differ.

Explore 5. In Filmstrip view, use the Next Image button 🔘 and Previous Image button 🔘 to cycle through all the images stored in the files in this folder.

6. Use the mouse pointer to point to and select an image, click Edit on the menu bar, click Copy on the Edit menu, click Edit again, and then click Paste on the Edit menu to create a duplicate copy of the image so that you can experiment with it. How does the name of the new file differ from that of the original file you copied?

Explore 7. Use the mouse pointer to point to and select the copy of the image that you just made, and then use the Rotate Clockwise button 🔄 and Rotate Counterclockwise button 🔄 to examine the image from different perspectives. Why was it a good idea to make a duplicate copy of an existing image, and then use that duplicate copy instead of the original image?

8. Click one of the thumbnail images. What happens, and what program are you currently using?

9. Maximize the window with the image you selected. Explore the use of the following buttons: Zoom In 🔍, Zoom Out 🔍, Actual Size 🔳, and Best Fit 🔲.

Explore 10. Click the Start Slide Show button 🖥️. What happens? Move the mouse. What happens? After you finish, press the Esc key to exit your current view.

11. Click the "closes this program and opens the image for editing (Ctrl + E)" button 🖼️. What happens, and what program are you currently using?

12. Close the program window and return to the My Pictures folder.

13. Examine the Picture Tasks dynamic menu. What types of tasks can you perform on the contents of this folder?

14. From the Tools menu, select Folder Options, and then select the View tab. Choose the option for showing hidden files and folders, and remove the options for hiding extensions for known file types and for hiding protected operating system files. Close the Folder Options dialog box, apply these changes, and examine the contents of this folder. What additional files does Windows XP display? If someone asked you to guess the purpose of each of these files, what would you tell that person?

15. Point to and select a file with a graphic image, and then examine the information in the Details dynamic menu. What is the file's extension and file type?

16. Click the Up button 🔼 on the Standard Buttons toolbar to return to the My Pictures folder. Does Windows XP include a link to the My Music folder in any of the dynamic menus?

17. Click the Folders button 📁 on the Standard Buttons toolbar. Where are you currently located in the folder structure of your computer?

18. Click the Expand View button ➕ to the left of the My Documents folder in the Folders toolbar, click the My Music folder, and then click the Sample Music folder shortcut. Where are you currently located in the folder structure of your computer?

19. What advantage does the use of a view with the Folders toolbar provide over the task-oriented view?

20. What advantage does the task-oriented view provide over the use of a view with the Folders toolbar?

21. Play one of the music files located in this folder. If Windows XP opens a program other than the Windows Media Player, close the program, open the All Programs menu, point to Accessories, point to Entertainment, and then click Windows Media Player. Once Windows Media Player opens, click File on the menu bar, click Open, open the Sample Music folder, and then open of the music files.

Explore

22. Use the Next Visualization button 🔘 or the Select Visualization button ✳️ to change the visualization. (If you don't see the visualization buttons, you can use the Visualizations option on the View menu.) Use the Skin Chooser button to select another skin, and then click the Apply Skin button to open the skin. (If you don't see the taskbar with the option for choosing skins, select Full Mode options on the View menu, and then turn off the option for hiding the taskbar.)

23. Click Help on the Windows Media Player menu bar, and then click Help Topics, or right-click the skin, and choose Help. (You can also click the Show menu bar button, if the menu bar does not appear on your Windows Media Player window.) In the Contents pane, expand the "Customizing the Player" book, click the "Changing how the Player looks with skins" book topic under "Customizing the Player", and then read the information in the Help topic pane. Click the skin link, and then click the skin mode link (shown in green). What is a skin? What is skin mode?

24. In the Contents pane, click "Using visualizations" under "Customizing the Player." What are visualizations? How do skins affect the use of visualizations?

25. In the Contents pane, expand the "Understanding digital media concepts" book, and then click the "Understanding streaming" book topic. What is streaming?

26. In the Contents pane, click the "Understanding buffering" book topic under "Understanding digital media concepts". What is buffering?

27. Close Windows Media Player Help, and after you finished experimenting with Windows Media Player and its options, close the Windows Media Player window, and then close the Sample Pictures folder window.

28. Open the Help and Support Center, and use Search to locate information on the use of digital media. Under Overviews, Articles, and Tutorials, click the "DirectX overview" link, and then read the information about DirectX technology. What does DirectX do? What is the advantage of including DirectX technology within Windows?

29. Close the Help and Support Center, and then log off, or turn off, your computer.

CASE PROBLEMS

Case 1. *Upgrading Computers at Townsend & Sumner Publishing* Townsend & Sumner Publishing is a San Francisco-based firm that contracts with corporate clients to produce employee training manuals on the use of specialized client software. To produce these manuals, employees must work with multiple applications and documents, and copy text, graphics, concept art, and illustrations from one document to another. Mike Lyman, who supervises the production of manuals, wants to upgrade the operating systems used on their computers so that the company's staff can work more effectively and efficiently on the company's intranet. He asks you to examine the software and document support of Windows operating systems on the market—namely, Windows XP, Windows 2000 Professional, Windows Me, and Windows 98—and prepare a written report that analyzes the important factors he should consider prior to recommending a specific product.

Use a word-processing application, such as Word or WordPad, to prepare and print a two-page report on your recommendations. As you work on this case, draw on the information presented in the tutorial and, if necessary, you might also want to use Windows XP's Help and Support Center and Microsoft's Web site (*www.microsoft.com*), which contains information on each operating system.

1. Identify five features of operating system software that would support and simplify the process that employees use to produce training manuals at Townsend & Sumner.

Explore

2. Describe each of the five features, and briefly explain in one paragraph what benefits employees might derive from using each of these features.

3. In your report, include a short section that lists specific operating systems the company should evaluate prior to the proposed operating system upgrade.

4. Include an additional section that describes any hardware features that this company should take into consideration when upgrading to a new operating system.

Case 2. *Upgrading Hardware at Stratton Graphics, Inc.* Eve Stratton, the owner of Stratton Graphics, Inc., and her staff design 3-D models, animation, video, and online presentations for the Web sites of her business clients. All of these features make intensive demands on the hardware used by employees at Stratton Graphics. By upgrading their computers to include new hardware technologies that support the use of multimedia, Eve hopes to more efficiently and effectively meet the needs of all her clients and also to attract new clients. She asks you to examine the hardware support provided by Windows operating systems—namely, Windows 95, Windows 98, Windows NT Workstation 4.0, Windows 2000 Professional, Windows Me, and Windows XP—and prepare a written report that analyzes important hardware support and operating system technologies she should consider.

Use a word-processing application, such as Word or WordPad, to prepare and print a two-page report on your recommendations. As you work on this case, draw on the information presented in the tutorial and, if necessary, you might also want to use Windows XP's Help and Support Center.

1. Identify five new types of hardware technologies that can benefit Eve Stratton's firm.

Explore
2. Describe each of the five hardware and operating system technologies, and briefly explain in a paragraph what benefits employees might derive from using each of these features.

3. Include a short section that lists specific operating systems the company should evaluate prior to the proposed software upgrade.

Case 3. *Exploring the Start Menu Folder at Computers for You!* You have recently been hired as a tech support specialist by Computers for You!, a new downtown business that sells and services computer systems. When customers bring their computers into the store for service, repair, upgrades, and customization, they often ask about customizing their Start menu. Since the Start menu is even more important in Windows XP and provides individuals with access to the different types of resources and applications on their computer, Toby Landucci, the owner of Computers for You!, asks you to explore techniques for opening, viewing, and understanding the organization and contents of the Start menu folder so that you can more effectively help individual clients.

As you complete each step in this case problem, record your answers to questions so that you can submit them to your instructor. Use a word-processing application such as Word or WordPad to prepare and then print your answers to these questions. Also, if you change any settings on the computer you are using, make a note of the original settings so that you can restore them later.

Explore
1. Display the shortcut menu for the Start button, and choose Open. What is the name of the window that opens? What does Windows display in this folder window?

2. From the Tools menu, select Folder Options, and on the View property sheet, choose the option for showing hidden files and folders, and remove the options for hiding extensions for known file types and hiding protected operating system files.

3. After you close the Folder Options dialog box and apply these changes, does Windows XP display any other folders or files in the Start Menu folder? If so, what are their names?

4. Open the Programs folder, and switch to Details view. What three types of objects does Windows XP display in this window?

Explore
5. Click the Start button, point to All Programs, and compare the contents of the All Programs menu with the contents of the Programs folder. How are these two objects similar, and how do they differ?

Explore
6. Point to Startup on the All Programs menu, and view the contents of the Startup menu. What options, if any, are displayed on the Startup menu?

7. Close the Start menu, and then open the Startup folder in the Programs window. Any icons in the Startup folder are shortcuts, or links, to programs that are automatically loaded by Windows XP when you power on, or restart, your computer. What are the names of the programs, if any, that automatically load on your computer?

8. Close the Startup folder window.

9. Open the shortcut menu for the Start button again, but this time, choose the Explore option. How does this Start menu window differ from the previous one when you chose Open on the Start button's shortcut menu?

10. Expand the Programs folder under the Start Menu folder in the Folders toolbar, and then select the Startup folder. What does Windows XP display in the Contents pane?

11. Close the window.

12. If you right-click an object that represents a folder and select Open from the object's shortcut menu, what type of view would you expect Windows XP to display in the window that it opens?

13. If you right-click that same object and choose Explore from its shortcut menu, what type of view would you expect Windows XP to display in the window that it opens?

14. Is there any other way that you can switch between these two different views? If so, explain.

15. Restore your computer's settings that determine what Windows XP displays in a folder window. From the Tools menu, select Folder Options, and on the View property sheet, choose the options for not showing hidden files and folders, for hiding extensions for known file types, and for hiding protected operating system files. Close the Folder Options dialog box, apply these changes, and then close the Start menu window.

Case 4. Using Fast User Switching at Bayview Travel Service Bayview Travel Service is a small business that just upgraded its computers to Windows XP Professional. Since different employees work on the same computers during the day and weekend, Sasha Janowczyk, the owner, asks that employees use a new Windows XP feature called Fast User Switching so that they do not need to close their applications and log off if another employee needs access to a computer. She recommends that you use the Help and Support Center to locate information about Fast User switching so that you can prepare a short training session on its use for all employees.

As you complete each step in this case problem, record your answers to questions so that you can submit them to your instructor. Use a word-processing application such as Word or WordPad to prepare and then print your answers to these questions. Also, if you change any settings on the computer you are using, make a note of the original settings so that you can restore them later.

1. Open the Help and Support Center, and locate information on Fast User Switching.

2. Prepare a one- to two-page report that covers the following topics:

- The benefits of Fast User Switching
- Which versions of Windows XP support this feature?
- The conditions under which you can and cannot use Fast User Switching
- How you can turn on and turn off Fast User Switching
- Why it might be advantageous under certain conditions to turn off Fast User Switching
- How you switch from one user account to another
- An example of a situation in which you might actually use Fast User Switching on your computer

In this tutorial you will:

- Display desktop icons

- Customize the Start menu and taskbar

- Customize and create toolbars on the taskbar

- Change mouse properties

- Use desktop themes, wallpaper, and special display effects

- Adjust screen resolution and color depth

- Customize a screen saver and create a slide show screen saver

- Examine power management features of your computer

CUSTOMIZING WINDOWS XP

Customizing Desktops at Thorsen Pharmaceuticals

CASE

Thorsen Pharmaceuticals

Thorsen Pharmaceuticals is an international company that produces and sells new pharmaceuticals around the world. Over the last 25 years, Thorsen Pharmaceuticals has developed new drugs in its research labs in Great Britain, France, and Sweden. Recently, Thorsen Pharmaceuticals opened a new research facility in the United States that uses gene splicing and recombinant DNA technology to accelerate the process for finding new classes of drugs. To increase the productivity of its staff, Thorsen Pharmaceuticals has purchased 100 state-of-the-art Pentium computers for its scientific, technical, and administrative support staff at this new division. The company from which they purchased these computers has already installed Windows XP Professional on the computers. Over the next several weeks, you will work with Jaime Navarro, a microcomputer systems specialist at the new research facility, to help staff members customize their desktops. As Jaime has discovered from past experience, employees are more productive if they can customize their working environment.

In the first part of the tutorial, you help other employees customize their desktop, Start menu, and taskbar, as well as customize and create toolbars for the taskbar and desktop. You also examine mouse properties, and customize the use of the mouse.

Getting Started

To complete this tutorial, you need to switch your computer to Web style, and you also need to activate the options for showing hidden folders and files and for displaying file extensions. As you complete these steps, you may discover that your computer is already set up for Web style, or you might only need to make a few changes to your computer's settings.

To set up your computer:

1. To change to the Windows XP theme, right-click the **desktop**, click **Properties** on the shortcut menu, and after Windows XP opens the Display Properties dialog box, click the **Theme** list arrow on the Themes property sheet, then click **Windows XP**, if necessary, and then click the **OK** button. On the computer used for Figure 2-1, Windows XP displays the Internet Explorer and Recycle Bin desktop icons, along with an additional icon unique to this computer, and the default background view called "Bliss" on the desktop. If your computer is new, it shows only the Recycle Bin on the desktop. Your icons might otherwise differ.

Figure 2-1	WINDOWS XP DESKTOP THEME

Bliss background wallpaper

2. To switch to the Windows XP Start menu style, right-click the **Start** button, and then click **Properties.** After Windows XP opens the Taskbar and Start Menu Properties dialog box, click the **Start menu** option button on the Start Menu property sheet, if necessary, and then click the **OK** button.

3. To change to a task-oriented view of folders and enable single-clicking, click the **Start** button, click **My Computer**, click **Tools** on the menu bar, click **Folder Options**, and after Windows XP opens the Folder Options dialog box, click the **Show common tasks in folders** option button if it is not already selected, then

> click the **Single-click to open an item** option button if it is not already selected, and then click the **Underline icon titles only when I point at them** option button if it is not already selected.
>
> **4.** Click the **View** tab, click the **Show hidden files and folders** option button if it is not already selected, and if there is a check mark in the "Hide extensions for known file types" check box, click that check box to remove the check mark, click the **OK** button to close the Folder Options dialog box, and then close My Computer.

Now you're ready to customize your computer.

Displaying **Desktop Icons**

Previous versions of Windows displayed desktop icons for My Computer, My Documents, Internet Explorer, and My Network Places so that you could quickly access those components on your computer. However, if you acquire a new computer with Windows XP Professional or Windows XP Home Edition, the only icon on the desktop might be the one for the Recycle Bin. Although you can open My Computer, My Documents, My Pictures, My Music, and My Network Places from the Start menu, you might also want to display the icons for some of these objects on the desktop so that you can open them right after Windows XP displays the desktop.

After new computers arrived at Thorsen Pharmaceuticals with Windows XP Professional preinstalled on them, one of the first questions employees asked Jaime was, "Where are my desktop icons?" Jaime asks you to help him show employees how to add specific icons back to their desktop.

> *To display the My Computer and My Document desktop icons:*
>
> **1.** Right-click the **desktop**, click **Properties** on the shortcut menu, click the **Desktop** tab in the Display Properties dialog box, and then click the **Customize Desktop** button. In the Desktop Items dialog box, you can add icons to or remove icons from the desktop, and change or restore the icon for common desktop objects. See Figure 2-2. Notice that, by default, Windows XP runs the Desktop Cleanup Wizard every 60 days to move any unused desktop items to a folder on the desktop named Unused Desktop Shortcuts.

Figure 2-2   VIEWING DESKTOP SETTINGS IN THE DESKTOP ITEMS DIALOG BOX

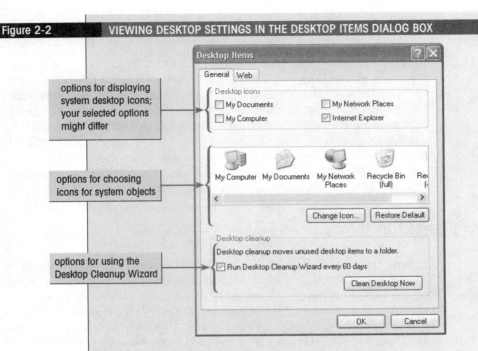

options for displaying system desktop icons; your selected options might differ

options for choosing icons for system objects

options for using the Desktop Cleanup Wizard

2. If the My Documents and My Computer icons are not displayed on the desktop, click the **My Documents** and **My Computer** check boxes (and add a check mark to each), click the **OK** button to close the Desktop Items dialog box, and then click the **OK** button to close the Display Properties dialog box. Windows XP adds icons for My Documents and My Computer to the desktop. See Figure 2-3.

Figure 2-3   MY DOCUMENTS AND MY COMPUTER ADDED TO THE DESKTOP

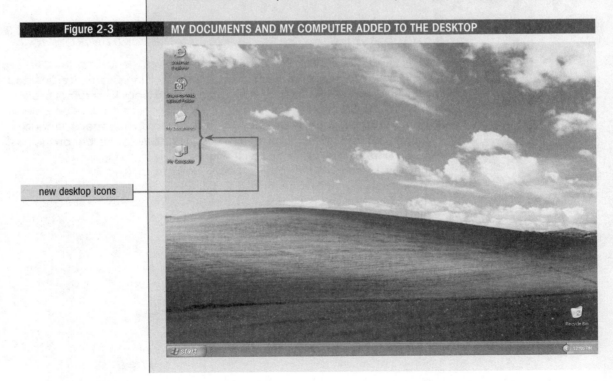

new desktop icons

POWER USERS TIP If you right-click My Documents or My Computer on the Start menu, you can choose "Show on Desktop" to either display or hide these desktop icons.

REFERENCE WINDOW   **RW**

Displaying My Computer and My Documents on the Desktop
- Right-click the desktop, click Properties on the desktop shortcut menu, click the Desktop tab in the Display Properties dialog box, and then click the Customize Desktop button.
- If the My Documents and My Computer icons are not displayed on the desktop, click the My Documents and My Computer check boxes (and add a check mark to each) on the General property sheet of the Desktop Items dialog box, click the OK button to close the Desktop Items dialog box, and then click the OK button to close the Display Properties dialog box.

Now you can access My Computer and My Documents directly from the desktop, and you can still access them from the Start menu.

Customizing **the Start Menu**

Because the Start menu is now the focal point for accessing the contents of a computer, you can customize it to simplify your access to Windows XP tools and installed applications. For example, you can specify:

- **Icon sizes**. You can choose between large or small icons. Small icons are useful if you add more items to the Start menu. Large icons are useful if you have limited vision.

- **Most frequently used programs** (new to Windows XP). If you use many different applications, utilities, and games, and want Windows XP to display them on the most frequently used programs list so you have quick access to these programs, you can adjust the number of programs displayed on the Start menu. You can also periodically clear that list.

- **Pinned items list programs** (new to Windows XP). You can specify which programs Windows XP displays in the pinned items list for Internet access and also for e-mail. For example, if you use MSN Explorer, you can specify whether Windows XP displays MSN Explorer or Internet Explorer on the Start menu. If you have a Hotmail account, you can specify whether Windows XP displays Hotmail, Microsoft Outlook, MSN Explorer, or Outlook Express on the pinned items list for your primary e-mail account.

- **Start menu behaviors** (new to Windows XP). By default, Windows XP highlights newly installed programs on the Start menu in a different color, and also immediately displays the submenu for a menu option when you pause on that menu option. If you prefer, you can turn off one or both of these settings.

- **Start menu items** (some new to Windows XP). You can specify whether Windows XP displays the Control Panel, Favorites, Help and Support, My Computer, My Documents, My Music, My Network Places, My Pictures, Network Connections, Printers and Faxes, Run, Search, and Administrative Tools on the Start menu. For some of these items, you can also specify whether Windows XP displays the item as a link or as a menu. By default, Windows XP displays menu items as links. For example, when you click Control Panel on the Start menu, Windows XP opens the Control Panel folder window so that you can then choose a Control Panel tool. If you display the Control Panel as a menu instead, Windows XP displays the tools within the Control Panel folder window as items on a submenu. These same options are also available for the My Computer, My Documents, My Music, and My Documents folders. If you choose to display the Favorites menu on the Start menu, you have yet another method for locating and opening Web sites that you've bookmarked. If you've organized your bookmarks into folders, then you see those folders on the Favorites menu. If you are a member of the Administrators group, you more than likely want to display Administrative Tools on the Programs menu. From the System Administrative Tools menu, you can open tools for managing your computer and monitoring its performance. If you are not a member of the Administrators group, you can still open options under System Administrative Tools, although you might be restricted from using most options.

- **Start menu items behavior** (some new to Windows XP). By default, drag and drop is enabled for Start menu items. You can use drag and drop to rearrange the placement of items on the Start menu and its submenus in case a different order is more logical for you or provides you with quicker access to tools you commonly use. If you prefer, you can turn this option off. Also, by default, if your All Programs menu contains more menu items than Windows XP can display within the height of the screen, the additional items appear on what are called "horizontal pages." In other words, the All Programs menu appears like a book with two pages of menu items. If you choose the option "Scroll Programs," Windows XP displays only one menu, and you then use a scroll arrow to scroll up or down the menu.

- **Recently used documents**. You can specify that Windows XP lists documents that you recently opened so that you can quickly select a document you've previously used. If you enable this option, Windows XP displays the My Recent Documents menu item on the Start menu, and lists the last 15 documents you've opened. You also have the option of periodically clearing this list if you know that you will no longer work with its documents.

- **Start menu items actions and properties** (some new to Windows XP). Because each item listed on the Start menu is an object, you can right-click a Start menu item, view actions associated with that menu item, and examine its properties. Although actions vary with the Start menu item you select, actions can include opening, exploring, browsing, searching, playing, sharing, copying, renaming, printing, sending, and removing an object as well as making it available offline. You can also, for example, sort the items on the All Programs menu in alphabetical order.

Because the Start menu is an important resource that you access and use many times, you should take a few minutes to customize it so that it meets your needs as you work and play.

Jaime suggests that you also customize your Start menu so that your computer is set up the way in which you want to work.

To check and change Start menu settings:

1. Right-click the **Start** button, click **Properties**, and after Windows XP opens the Taskbar and Start Menu Properties dialog box, click the **Customize** button next to the Start menu option button on the Start Menu property sheet. Windows XP displays the Customize Start Menu dialog box. See Figure 2-4. On the General property sheet, you can adjust icon sizes, specify the number of programs listed in the most-frequently used programs list, clear that list periodically, and decide which options are listed on the pinned items list. On the computer used for this figure, MSN Explorer is listed as the Internet access option, and Microsoft Outlook Express as the e-mail software. Yours may differ.

POWER USERS TIP If you have already opened the Start menu, and then realize that you want to change its properties, you can right-click your user name at the top of the Start menu, and then click Properties.

| Figure 2-4 | BASIC OPTIONS FOR CUSTOMIZING THE START MENU |

options for changing the size of Start menu icons

option for specifying the number of previously used programs to display on the Start menu, and an option for clearing this list

options for displaying programs on the pinned items list

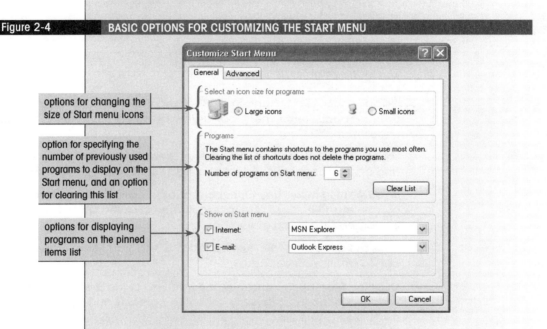

2. Click the **Advanced** tab. On this property sheet, you can specify Start menu settings, choose which options you want to display on the Start menu (and in some cases how the options are displayed), specify Start menu items behaviors (for example, the use of drag and drop), choose whether to display "My Recent Documents" on the Start menu, and periodically clear the list of previously used documents. See Figure 2-5.

Figure 2-5   VIEWING ADVANCED START MENU SETTINGS

option for highlighting newly installed programs on the Start menu

options for choosing what to display on the Start menu, and how to display it

option for displaying My Recent Documents on the Start menu, and an option for periodically removing its contents

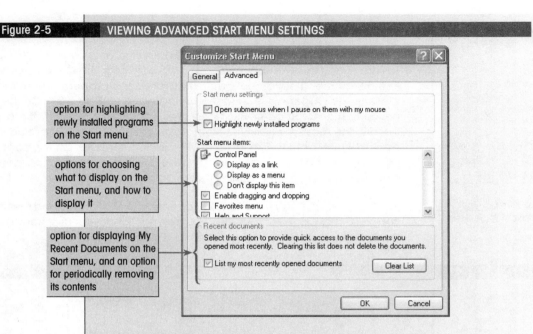

3. If it does not already contain a check mark, click the **List my most recently opened documents** check box under "Recent documents" and add a check mark.

4. Locate and click the **Favorites menu** check box in the "Start menu items" box and add a check mark if it is not already selected.

5. If you want to make any further changes to customize the Start menu on your computer, make those changes, and then click the **OK** button to close the Customize Start Menu dialog box.

6. Click the **OK** button to close the Taskbar and Start Menu Properties dialog box and to apply your changes.

7. Click the **Start** button and view the contents of the Start menu. Notice that Windows XP now displays My Recent Documents and Favorites on the Start menu. See Figure 2-6.

Figure 2-6 VIEWING ADDITIONS TO THE START MENU

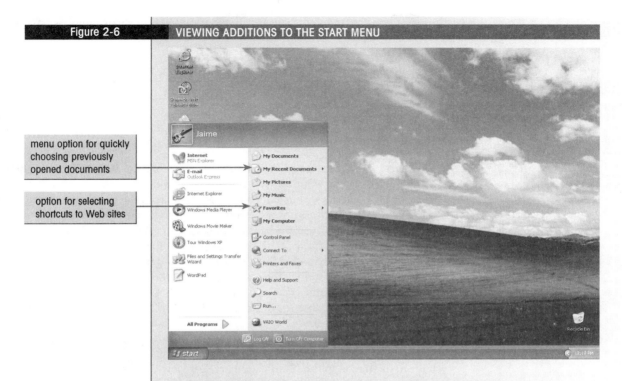

menu option for quickly choosing previously opened documents

option for selecting shortcuts to Web sites

8. Click the **Start** button a second time to close the Start menu

---

REFERENCE WINDOW RW

Customizing the Start Menu
- Right-click the Start button, click Properties, and after Windows XP opens the Taskbar and Start Menu Properties dialog box, click the Customize button next to the Start menu option button on the Start Menu property sheet.
- On the General property sheet of the Customize Start Menu dialog box, you can choose between the use of Large or Small icons, you can increase the number of programs that Windows XP lists in the most frequently used programs list under Programs, or you can also periodically clear that list, and you can decide which options are listed on the pinned items list under "Show on Start menu."
- Click the Advanced tab. On the Advanced property sheet, the "Highlight newly installed programs" option under Start menu settings, if enabled, highlights a newly installed program on the Programs menu in a different color. In the Start menu items list box, you can choose what items are listed on the Start menu (such as Favorites and Administrative Tools) and, in some cases, how they are listed, and you can also choose other options, such as "Enable dragging and dropping." Under "Recent documents," you can choose whether to display "My Recent Documents" on the Start menu for quick access to previously used documents.
- You can use the Help button to display Help information on the use of different options on these property sheets.
- After you choose the options you want to use, click the OK button to close the Customize Start Menu dialog box.
- Click the OK button to close the Taskbar and Start Menu Properties dialog box and to apply your changes.

By customizing your Start menu, you can make life easier and gain quick access to the options you need and frequently use in your line of work.

Customizing the Taskbar

Since the taskbar is an object, and since it's another important desktop resource that you frequently use, you can also customize it. For example, you can specify the following properties of the taskbar:

- **Taskbar appearance**. You can lock the toolbar to prevent it from accidentally being moved (a new Windows XP feature), auto-hide the taskbar to display more of the contents within a document window, keep the taskbar on top of other windows so that it's always visible (thus providing quick access to any other open windows), use taskbar grouping (new to Windows XP), and display the Quick Launch toolbar. When you lock the toolbar, you cannot change the size or position of any toolbar on the taskbar. If you need to move the taskbar or a toolbar, you can unlock the taskbar by right-clicking it and choosing "Lock the taskbar." If you unlock the taskbar, you can dock it on another edge of the desktop, and also increase (or decrease) its height. The "Auto-hide the taskbar" option reduces the taskbar to a thin bar at the bottom of the desktop when you are not using the taskbar. When you point to the thin bar, Windows XP displays the taskbar temporarily so that you can select the Start button, a taskbar button, or an icon in the Notification area, or view the time. If you need to use another computer and notice it doesn't seem to have a taskbar, move the mouse pointer to the bottom of the desktop to redisplay the taskbar. In the case of the taskbar grouping option, if the taskbar buttons shrink below a certain size, Windows XP combines all the taskbar buttons for the same application into one single button.

- **Notification area**. You can choose whether you want to display the clock, and whether you want to hide inactive icons (the latter is new to Windows XP). Because it's not uncommon for many programs to load during startup, and then display icons in the Notification area, hiding inactive icons proves useful because you only see icons for active programs. You can also specify the behavior for active, inactive, and urgent notifications (new to Windows XP). For example, you can choose to hide an icon when it is inactive, always hide an icon, or always show an icon.

Jaime had frequently noticed that under previous versions of Windows, many employees did not realize that they could double-click an icon in the Notification area to open an application window, such as Norton AntiVirus, or that they could right-click an icon to access a shortcut menu of actions that they could perform on that object, such as closing or exiting the program, which then removed the icon from the Notification area. They also were unaware they could use the shortcut menu to display property sheets for the object and change object settings. So, when employees ask how to interpret the contents of the Notification area and use it effectively, Jaime suggests that you demonstrate what options are available and explain when they might use them.

To view taskbar settings and customize the taskbar:

1. Right-click the **taskbar**, and then click **Properties** on the shortcut menu. The Taskbar and Start Menu Properties dialog box opens, the same one that you just used to customize the Start menu; however, this time you're viewing the Taskbar property sheet instead of the Start Menu property sheet. See Figure 2-7. On this property sheet, you can customize the appearance of the taskbar and

the Notification area. Notice that all the options are enabled except those for using Auto-hide and for displaying the Quick Launch toolbar.

POWER USERS TIP The shortcut menu for the taskbar also provides a "Lock the Taskbar" option that you can turn on or off.

Figure 2-7	VIEWING BASIC TASKBAR AND NOTIFICATION AREA SETTINGS

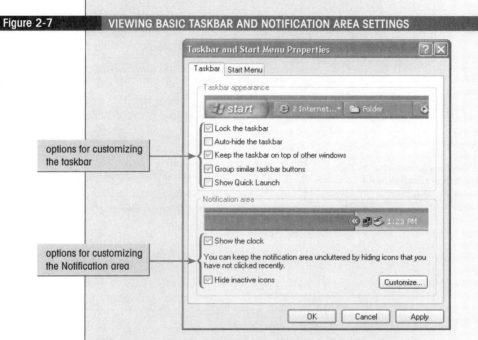

options for customizing the taskbar

options for customizing the Notification area

2. Click the **Customize** button in the Notification area. The Customize Notifications dialog box opens. See Figure 2-8. This dialog box displays information about the icons displayed in the Notification area. Yours may differ. These items are grouped into two categories: Current Items and Past Items. Windows XP also notes that it displays icons only for active and urgent notifications. However, you can select any item in the list and change its behavior.

Figure 2-8	OPTIONS FOR CUSTOMIZING ICONS IN THE NOTIFICATION AREA

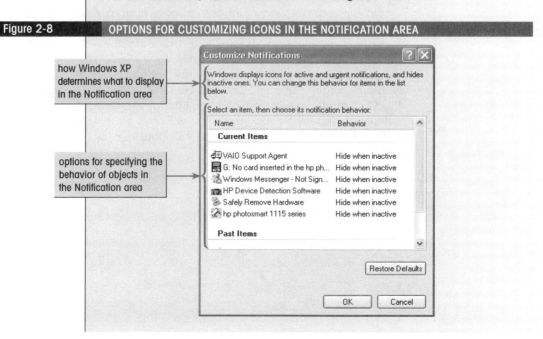

how Windows XP determines what to display in the Notification area

options for specifying the behavior of objects in the Notification area

3. Click an item in the Current Items list, and then click the **Behavior** list arrow for that item. Note that in addition to the default "Hide when inactive" behavior, you can also choose the "Always hide" or "Always show" behavior. See Figure 2-9. You can also display hidden items by clicking the Show hidden icons button ◀ in the Notification area of the taskbar.

Figure 2-9	BEHAVIOR OPTIONS FOR ICONS IN THE NOTIFICATION AREA

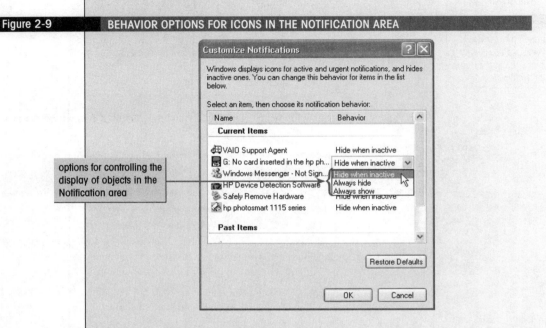

options for controlling the display of objects in the Notification area

4. If you want to change any items now, make those changes, click the **OK** button to close the Customize Notifications dialog box and apply the changes, and then click the **OK** button to close the Taskbar and Start Menu Properties dialog box.

5. In the Notification area, click the **Show hidden icons** button ◀ if you do not see any icons, right-click the **Windows Messenger** icon 👤 (which might have an icon of a red circle with a white "X" within it, indicating that it is not active), the **Volume** icon 🔊, or the **Safely Remove Hardware** icon 📎. Windows XP displays a shortcut menu with one or more options. Figure 2-10 shows the shortcut menu for Windows Messenger. Notice that this menu includes options that are available, such as Exit, Open (the default used by Windows XP when you double-click the icon), and Sign In, as well as options that are not currently available (or appropriate), such as My Hotmail Inbox, Send an Instant Message, My Status, and Sign Out. Yours may differ. For example, you might see the My E-mail Inbox option, or an option for you to sign in under your e-mail address. The default menu option or action is always shown in bold and indicates what Windows XP does when you double-click the icon.

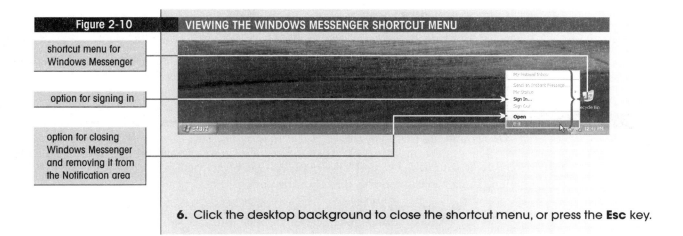

| Figure 2-10 | VIEWING THE WINDOWS MESSENGER SHORTCUT MENU |

shortcut menu for
Windows Messenger

option for signing in

option for closing
Windows Messenger
and removing it from
the Notification area

6. Click the desktop background to close the shortcut menu, or press the **Esc** key.

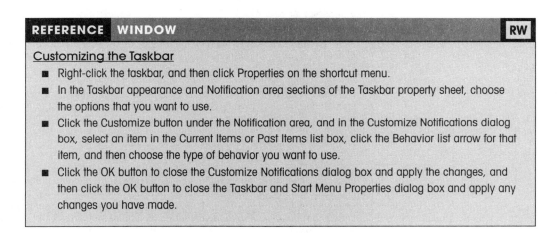

REFERENCE WINDOW   **RW**

Customizing the Taskbar

- Right-click the taskbar, and then click Properties on the shortcut menu.
- In the Taskbar appearance and Notification area sections of the Taskbar property sheet, choose the options that you want to use.
- Click the Customize button under the Notification area, and in the Customize Notifications dialog box, select an item in the Current Items or Past Items list box, click the Behavior list arrow for that item, and then choose the type of behavior you want to use.
- Click the OK button to close the Customize Notifications dialog box and apply the changes, and then click the OK button to close the Taskbar and Start Menu Properties dialog box and apply any changes you have made.

For a power user, these options are quite useful, because you might need to quickly access features in an application or close a background program so that you can back up your computer (covered in Tutorial 6), or use a utility such as ScanDisk or Disk Defragmenter (covered in Tutorial 7).

Customizing **and Creating Toolbars**

In Windows XP, you can add Windows XP toolbars to the taskbar or create new toolbars and place them on the taskbar. Then you can quickly access features or components on your computer system by clicking a single button on a toolbar. You can also customize Windows XP toolbars by adding options, or create a toolbar from the contents of a folder or a Web site. You can drag toolbars from the taskbar onto the desktop, and either work with them as floating toolbars (which you can then move to any location on the desktop), or dock them on one side of the desktop.

Customizing a Toolbar

Like previous versions of Windows that supported the Active Desktop technology, Windows XP includes four Windows XP toolbars that you can add to the taskbar: the Address, Links, Desktop, and Quick Launch toolbars. The Quick Launch toolbar contains three buttons: a Launch Internet Explorer browser button 🄴 for opening Internet Explorer, a Show Desktop button 🄴 for displaying the desktop (after minimizing all open windows), and a Windows Media Player button ▶ for playing digital media, such as music, videos, CDs, DVDs, and Internet Radio.

The Address toolbar contains an Address box in which you can type the URL of a Web site you want to access, and a list arrow you can click to select a previously visited Web site. The Links toolbar contains the following options:

- **Customize Links shortcut**. Takes you to a Microsoft Web site that explains how to add, remove, rearrange, and customize shortcuts (such as changing a shortcut's icon) on the Links Bar.

- **Free Hotmail shortcut**. Takes you to Microsoft's MSN Hotmail Web site where you can sign up for an e-mail account.

- **RealPlayer shortcut**. Takes you to the Real.com Web site where you can download updates, new players, music, games, accessories, and business solutions for digital media.

- **Windows shortcut**. Takes you to Microsoft's Windows Family Home Page where you can obtain information about Windows products and new technology developments.

- **Windows Media shortcut**. Takes you to Microsoft's WindowsMedia.com Media Guide Web site.

When you display the Desktop toolbar, it includes icons for all the objects and shortcuts that currently appear on your desktop. For example, if you have the My Documents, My Computer, My Network Places, Recycle Bin, and Internet Explorer icons on your desktop, the Desktop toolbar displays a menu with each of these items. If you point to My Documents on the Desktop toolbar menu, you see a list of all the folders and files within the My Documents folder. If you point to My Computer, the submenu displays a list of all your drives (including network drives), system folders (such as the Control Panel), and the My Documents folder for different users as well as the Shared Documents folder (just called Documents). If you then point to Local Disk (C:), you see another submenu with a list of folders and files on drive C. You can quickly access the contents, including folders and individual files, from the Desktop toolbar without having to open a window and without having to navigate your computer from window to window.

Coreen O'Hara, a staff scientist new to the use of Windows, wants to set up her computer so that she can easily switch back to the desktop, and also quickly open My Documents from the application window where she records and analyzes her scientific measurements. After talking with you and Jaime, she discovers she can add toolbars to the taskbar, and then customize each toolbar to meet her needs. Jaime points out that one way to quickly switch from an application window to the desktop is to right-click the taskbar, and select "Show the Desktop." If you have already switched to the desktop, you can right-click the taskbar, and select "Show Open Windows" to switch back to your application window. Jaime also notes that an alternate option is to add the Quick Launch toolbar to the taskbar because it has a Show Desktop button that you can click instead of right-clicking the taskbar.

So that she can quickly access the Web and her desktop when she has open application windows, Jaime recommends that you show Coreen how to add the Quick Launch toolbar to the taskbar on her computer, and then customize this toolbar to include an option for quickly opening My Documents.

To add the Quick Launch toolbar to the taskbar and then customize it:

1. If there is no Quick Launch toolbar on the taskbar, right-click the **taskbar**, point to **Toolbars**, and then click **Quick Launch**. Windows XP displays the Quick Launch toolbar to the right of the Start button. See Figure 2-11.

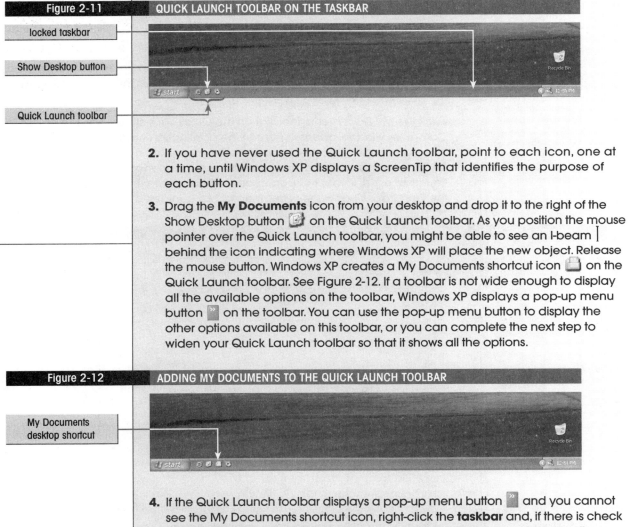

| Figure 2-11 | QUICK LAUNCH TOOLBAR ON THE TASKBAR |

locked taskbar

Show Desktop button

Quick Launch toolbar

2. If you have never used the Quick Launch toolbar, point to each icon, one at a time, until Windows XP displays a ScreenTip that identifies the purpose of each button.

3. Drag the **My Documents** icon from your desktop and drop it to the right of the Show Desktop button on the Quick Launch toolbar. As you position the mouse pointer over the Quick Launch toolbar, you might be able to see an I-beam | behind the icon indicating where Windows XP will place the new object. Release the mouse button. Windows XP creates a My Documents shortcut icon on the Quick Launch toolbar. See Figure 2-12. If a toolbar is not wide enough to display all the available options on the toolbar, Windows XP displays a pop-up menu button on the toolbar. You can use the pop-up menu button to display the other options available on this toolbar, or you can complete the next step to widen your Quick Launch toolbar so that it shows all the options.

| Figure 2-12 | ADDING MY DOCUMENTS TO THE QUICK LAUNCH TOOLBAR |

My Documents
desktop shortcut

4. If the Quick Launch toolbar displays a pop-up menu button and you cannot see the My Documents shortcut icon, right-click the **taskbar** and, if there is check mark to the left of "Lock the Taskbar," click **Lock the Taskbar** and remove the check mark. Point to the right border of the Quick Launch toolbar, and drag the border to the right until Windows XP displays all the icons on the Quick Launch toolbar. If you want to lock the toolbar again, right-click the **taskbar**, and then click **Lock the Taskbar**.

5. Point to the **My Documents** shortcut icon on the Quick Launch toolbar and let the mouse pointer rest on it until Windows XP displays the My Documents ScreenTip for this new button. Although the My Documents icon on the Quick Launch toolbar appears to be a copy of the My Documents object on the desktop, it is actually a shortcut. However, Windows XP does not display the short-cut arrow box because of the small sizes of the icons on the toolbar. The same feature applies to program shortcuts on the All Programs menus or its submenus.

Like any other object, you can customize a toolbar using its shortcut menu. For example, you can change the toolbar view to show large icons instead of small icons (the default), show the title of the toolbar (for example, Quick Launch), and show the title (or text label) of each icon (for example, Show Desktop); however, the latter takes up too much horizontal space to be useful. You can also open the folder that contains the shortcuts on the toolbar, close the toolbar, and move it from the taskbar.

Jaime suggests that you open an application, and then test the use of the My Documents shortcut on the Quick Launch toolbar.

To test the My Documents option on the Quick Launch toolbar:

1. Open the Start menu, point to **All Programs**, and open an application, such as Microsoft Word, or open WordPad from the Accessories menu, and then maximize the application window.

2. Click the My Documents shortcut on the Quick Launch toolbar. The My Computer window opens in front of the application window. See Figure 2-13. You did not need to close or minimize the application window, and then open My Documents using the desktop icon or the Start menu. This feature saves you time and effort. If your My Documents window is maximized, you cannot see the WordPad window; however, the taskbar contains a WordPad taskbar button.

| Figure 2-13 | USING MY DOCUMENTS ON THE QUICK LAUNCH TOOLBAR |

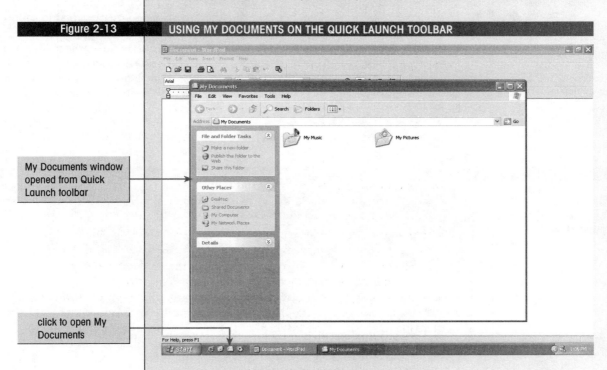

My Documents window opened from Quick Launch toolbar

click to open My Documents

3. Close the My Documents window, and then close the application window.

Even if the desktop icons are hidden behind one or more open windows, the taskbar is always available, and you can quickly open My Documents and access your files by using the My Documents shortcut on the Quick Launch toolbar.

REFERENCE WINDOW **RW**

Displaying and Customizing the Quick Launch Toolbar

- If there is no Quick Launch toolbar on the taskbar, right-click the taskbar, point to Toolbars, and then click Quick Launch.
- If you want to customize the Quick Launch toolbar by adding desktop icons to the toolbar, drag an icon from your desktop and drop it on the Quick Launch toolbar.
- If the Quick Launch toolbar is not wide enough to display the new shortcut for the desktop icon, right-click the taskbar and, if there is a check mark to the left of "Lock the Taskbar," click "Lock the Taskbar" and remove the check mark. Point to the right border ▓ of the Quick Launch toolbar, and drag the border to the right until Windows XP displays all the icons on the Quick Launch toolbar. If you want to lock the toolbar again, right-click the taskbar, and then click "Lock the Taskbar."

Creating a Toolbar for the Control Panel

The Control Panel consists of a set of programs for configuring, customizing, and setting up features, hardware, and software on your computer. The programs available in the Control Panel depend on how you or someone else installed Windows XP and the other software on your computer. The programs you see may differ from the following:

- **Accessibility Options**. Provide accessibility features important to individuals with disabilities or individuals with limited vision, hearing, or mobility
- **Add Hardware**. Install and troubleshoot hardware
- **Add or Remove Programs**. Install or remove software or Windows XP components
- **Administrative Tools**. Configure administrative settings for your computer, such as managing disks, local and remote computers, data sources and their drivers, security policies, and system performance (some of which you examine in later tutorials)
- **Date and Time**. Set the date and time on your computer, as well as select a time zone, and enables an option for automatically adjusting the computer's clock for daylight savings changes
- **Display**. Select a desktop theme, customize the desktop display, choose a screen saver, customize elements of the Windows XP graphical user interface, choose special display effects, change the resolution and color depth, and change or troubleshoot adapter and monitor settings
- **Folder Options**. Customize the display of files and folders, change file associations, and make network files available offline
- **Fonts**. View, install, and remove fonts in the Fonts folder
- **Game Controllers**. Add, remove, and configure game controller hardware, such as joysticks and gamepads
- **Internet Options**. Configure your Internet display and connection settings (also available from Internet Explorer)
- **Keyboard**. Adjust keyboard speed
- **Mouse**. Configure the mouse and choose mouse pointer shapes
- **Network Connections**. Connect to other computers, networks, and the Internet

- **Phone and Modem Options**. Specify telephone dialing rules, and add or remove modems, view modem properties, and run diagnostic tests on a modem
- **Power Options**. Choose a power management scheme and specify power management settings
- **Printers and Faxes**. Add, remove, and configure local and network printers and fax printers
- **QuickTime**. Configure QuickTime settings and hardware
- **RealPlayer**. Configure RealPlayer
- **Regional and Language Options**. Choose numeric, currency, time, and date settings specific to different languages of the world
- **Scanners and Cameras**. Add, remove, and configure installed scanners and digital cameras
- **Scheduled Tasks**. Schedule tasks to run automatically
- **Sounds and Audio Devices**. Control speaker volume, associate sounds with specific system events, specify sound playback and recording settings, and configure audio devices
- **Speech**. Change settings for text-to-speech translation, and for speech recognition
- **System**. View, change, and troubleshoot system properties, performance, and settings
- **Taskbar and Start Menu**. Customize the Start Menu and taskbar
- **User Accounts**. Manage user accounts on a computer

In Tutorial 1, you examined the Fonts folder. In this tutorial, you've already examined the options for configuring the taskbar and Start menu and some display properties as well as Folder Options. As this tutorial progresses, you examine features of the Display, Mouse, and Power Options tools in the Control Panel. In later tutorials, you examine the Performance Monitor, the Add Hardware and Add or Remove Programs tools, the Printers and Scheduled Tasks folders, the System tool, and the Network Connections tool.

Jaime asks you to help him set up, customize, and check the configuration of every new computer so that each employee starts off with the same settings. Then you can show individual employees how to further customize their computers to meet their individual needs. To simplify the process for setting up your computer, Jaime recommends that you create a Control Panel toolbar and place it on the desktop.

Next, you create a custom toolbar that provides quick access to the Control Panel's tools for configuring your computer.

To create a toolbar for the Control Panel:

1. Right-click the **taskbar**, point to **Toolbars**, and then click **New Toolbar**. The New Toolbar dialog box opens and asks you to choose a folder or type an Internet address. See Figure 2-14. This dialog box also shows the folders on your desktop, but not shortcuts.

| Figure 2-14 | CHOOSING THE FOLDER TO USE FOR A NEW TOOLBAR |

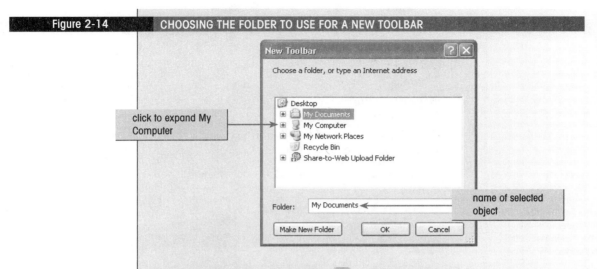

click to expand My Computer

name of selected object

2. Click the **expand view** box ⊞ to the left of the My Computer icon, locate and click the **Control Panel** folder icon (which also displays the folders under Control Panel), and then click the **OK** button. Windows XP adds a Control Panel toolbar to the left of the Notification area on the taskbar. See Figure 2-15. Because the taskbar is not wide enough to display all the options in the Control Panel along with the name of the toolbar and labels for each button, it displays a pop-up menu button ⏵⏵ to the right of the toolbar name.

| Figure 2-15 | CONTROL PANEL TOOLBAR ON THE TASKBAR |

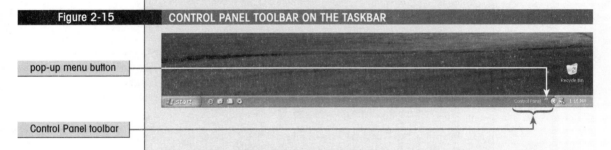

pop-up menu button

Control Panel toolbar

3. Click the **pop-up menu** button ⏵⏵. Windows XP displays a pop-up menu with a list of all the options available in the Control Panel folder. See Figure 2-16.

Figure 2-16   VIEWING THE CONTENTS OF THE CONTROL PANEL TOOLBAR

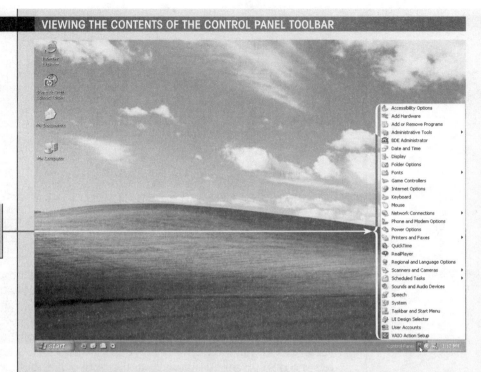

Control Panel toolbar menu showing all the options within the Control Panel folder

4. Click the **pop-up menu** button [»] again to close the pop-up menu. Before you can create a floating toolbar, you must unlock the taskbar.

5. Right-click the **taskbar**, and if there is a check mark next to "Lock the Taskbar," click **Lock the Taskbar** to remove the check mark; otherwise, if you have already unlocked the taskbar and if there is no check mark next to "Lock the Taskbar," click the desktop background to close the taskbar shortcut menu without making any changes. You can now see the borders of the Quick Launch and Control Panel toolbars.

6. Point to the **Control Panel** title on the Control Panel toolbar, and then drag the Control Panel toolbar onto the desktop. Windows XP displays a floating toolbar, as shown in Figure 2-17. Notice that the Control Panel toolbar now has a title bar and a Close button. At the bottom of the toolbar is another pop-up menu button for displaying the other options on this toolbar. If you drag the toolbar near an edge of the desktop, Windows XP docks the toolbar on that side of the desktop.

TROUBLE? If you already docked the Control Panel toolbar on one side of the desktop, point to the Control Panel title on the toolbar, and then drag the Control Panel toolbar onto the desktop so that you can see what a floating toolbar looks like. If you drag the Control Panel toolbar to the edge of the taskbar, Windows XP once again displays the Control Panel toolbar on the taskbar and it is no longer a floating toolbar.

Figure 2-17   FLOATING CONTROL PANEL TOOLBAR

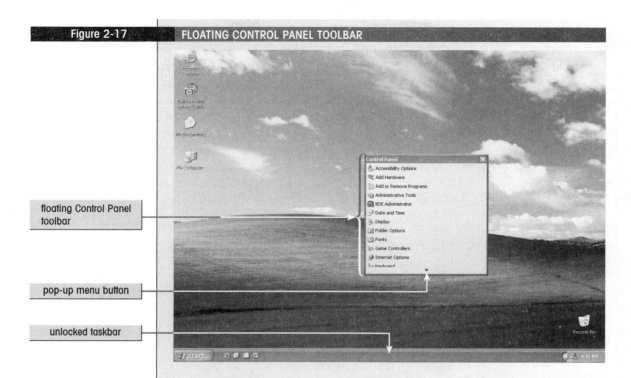

floating Control Panel toolbar

pop-up menu button

unlocked taskbar

7. Drag the **Control Panel** toolbar to the right side of the desktop (unless that is where your taskbar is docked), dock it, point to the left border of the Control Panel toolbar, and when the mouse pointer changes to ←→, drag the left border to widen the Control Panel toolbar so that you can see the longest entry on the toolbar, as shown in Figure 2-18. (Note that some entries are never displayed in their entirety, no matter how wide the column. These end with an ellipsis "…".)

Figure 2-18   DOCKED CONTROL PANEL TOOLBAR

docked Control Panel toolbar

8. Right-click the **Control Panel** title at the top of the Control Panel toolbar, and then click **Auto-Hide** on the shortcut menu for the Control Panel toolbar.

9. Move your mouse pointer to the middle of the desktop and, if Windows XP does not immediately hide the toolbar, click the **desktop** to change the focus from the Control Panel toolbar to the desktop. Windows XP hides the Control Panel toolbar, and only a thin vertical bar hints at the presence of a toolbar. See Figure 2-19. The primary advantage of this feature is that the Control Panel toolbar does not take up valuable desktop space when you do not need to use the toolbar.

| Figure 2-19 | USING THE AUTO-HIDE FEATURE |

Control Panel toolbar automatically hidden when mouse pointer is moved away from the toolbar

10. Move your mouse pointer to the right edge of the desktop. Windows XP displays the Control Panel toolbar. The assumption here is that if you move your mouse pointer to the right edge of the desktop where you originally docked the Control Panel toolbar, you want Windows XP to display the toolbar so that you can use it.

Now as you customize your computer, you can quickly access the tools available in the Control Panel.

REFERENCE WINDOW RW

Creating a New Desktop Toolbar

- Right-click the taskbar, point to Toolbars, and then click New Toolbar.
- In the New Toolbar dialog box, locate and click the folder you want to use to create the new toolbar, or type an Internet address, and then click the OK button.
- If you want to work with a floating or docked toolbar, right-click the taskbar, click "Lock the Taskbar" to turn off this option (if necessary), drag the toolbar off the taskbar, and then place it on the desktop, or dock it at one side of the desktop.
- Adjust the toolbar's width so that you can see the options on the toolbar.
- If you want to use the Auto-Hide feature, right-click the title of the toolbar, and then click Auto-Hide.

As noted earlier, you can also create toolbars for an Internet site, including Web sites and FTP sites. Figure 2-20 shows a floating toolbar for one of Course Technology's FTP servers. The toolbar, which appears similar to a folder window, shows directories within the NPTeam directory on this FTP server. You can work with the directories and files at this FTP site in the same way you work with folders and files in a folder window on your computer.

| Figure 2-20 | TOOLBAR FOR AN FTP SITE |

currently open folder at FTP site

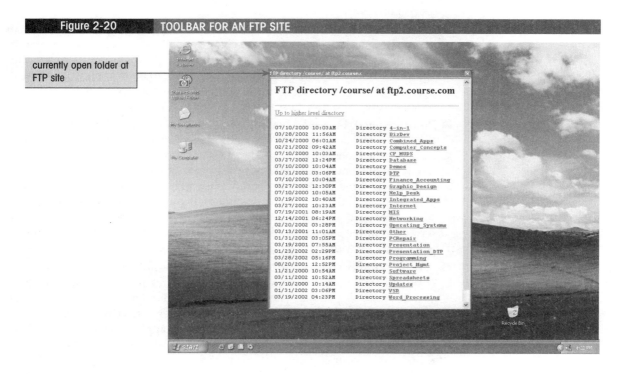

The Control Panel toolbar remains on the desktop or the taskbar until you close it. If you close the Control Panel toolbar, or other toolbars that you create from folders or Web sites, then you have to re-create the toolbar from scratch if you want to use it in the future. However, as you've seen, it's very simple to create a toolbar.

Changing **Mouse Properties**

When you use an operating system, like Windows XP, that relies on the use of the mouse, you will probably want to customize your mouse so that you can work more effectively and reduce the risk of injury from prolonged use of the mouse. No matter what type of mouse you have, you can customize the use of your mouse in these four basic ways:

- **Mouse button configuration**. The default mouse settings assume that you are right-handed and that you use a right-handed mouse; however, if you are left-handed, you can switch the use of the mouse buttons. The **primary mouse button** is the one you use to select, click, and drag objects as well as position an insertion point in a document. The **secondary mouse button** is the one you use to right-click an object. If you are right-handed, you work with the mouse on the right side of your desk, and you use your index finger to click the left mouse button and your middle finger to click the right mouse button. If you are left-handed, you most likely work with the mouse on the left side of your desk, and you need to swap the use of the left and right mouse buttons so you can use the index finger of your left hand to click with the right mouse button and the middle finger on your left hand to "right-click" with the left mouse button. Since each user has a different user account, Windows XP remembers each user's mouse settings.

- **Double-click speed**. Even if you use Web style, you need to double-click in certain instances, such as double-clicking an icon in the Notification area of the taskbar to view and change a program's settings. If you prefer to work in Windows Classic style, you need to double-click to open applications, documents, and other objects. To make double-clicking easier, no matter what style you use, you can adjust and test your double-click speed.

- **Pointer speed**. Depending on the type of work that you do, you can adjust the mouse pointer speed so that it responds in the way that you need. For example, if you set the mouse pointer speed to a faster setting, a small movement of the mouse on the mouse pad or desk creates a greater movement of the mouse pointer across the screen. This feature is useful if you only have a small amount of desk space available for using the mouse. If you change the mouse pointer speed to a slower setting, the mouse pointer moves more slowly across the screen. A slower pointer speed gives you more control of the mouse pointer when working with drawing software.

- **Mouse pointer shapes**. Windows XP uses a set of default mouse pointer shapes to provide visual clues about your use of the mouse. For example, if Windows XP displays ⌖, you know that you can point to an object, select an object, open an object, or display its shortcut menu. If Windows XP displays ⌛, you know that Windows XP and perhaps an application are busy, and that you have to wait until an operation is complete before you can do anything else on your computer. If you prefer, you can select other mouse pointer shapes so that you can more easily identify where the mouse pointer is on the screen, or simply to make using the mouse more interesting.

Although you can access properties of an object by right-clicking the object and choosing Properties on its shortcut menu, you obviously cannot right-click the mouse pointer itself. Instead, you must open the Control Panel, and then open the Mouse tool.

Jan Weiler, a computer graphics artist at Thorsen, relies extensively on the use of a mouse in his job. He asks you and Jaime if Windows XP includes any options that would not only make it easier to use the mouse, but also provide greater control over the movement of the mouse pointer. Jaime tells Jan that the Mouse tool in the Control Panel folder contains a variety of options for customizing a mouse, even including the mouse pointer. You offer to show Jan how to use these features.

To view and change mouse properties:

1. Point to the right edge of the desktop, and when the Control Panel toolbar appears, click the **Mouse** button. The Mouse Properties dialog box opens. See Figure 2-21. On the Buttons property sheet of the computer used for this figure, you can change the Button configuration, Double-click speed, and ClickLock settings.

   TROUBLE? Depending on the type of mouse you use and what type of software support you installed for that mouse, your Mouse Properties dialog box might contain property sheets different from those shown in the figure. If this is the case, you might find the mouse properties that are described in subsequent steps on property sheets different from those described and shown in the accompanying steps and figures. These mouse properties might also have slightly different names, but you can use the Help button 🔹 to help you identify the use of specific features.

Figure 2-21	MOUSE PROPERTIES DIALOG BOX (YOURS MAY DIFFER)

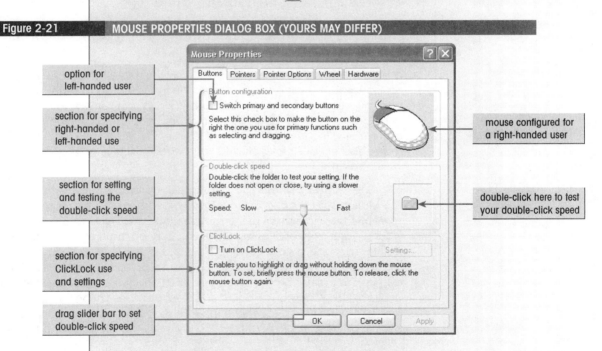

- option for left-handed user
- section for specifying right-handed or left-handed use
- section for setting and testing the double-click speed
- section for specifying ClickLock use and settings
- drag slider bar to set double-click speed
- mouse configured for a right-handed user
- double-click here to test your double-click speed

2. If you are left-handed and want to swap the left and right mouse buttons, click the **Switch primary and secondary buttons** check box under Button configuration. Windows XP applies the setting immediately.

In the Double-click speed section, you can adjust the response recognition time for a double-click. If your property sheet allows you to set the double-click speed with a slider bar, as is the case on the computer used for this figure, you can choose a slower speed setting, and thereby double-click more slowly. A faster speed would require that you double-click more quickly for Windows XP to recognize the double-click. On the Buttons property sheet shown in Figure 2-21, you double-click the folder icon in the test area on the right of the Double-click speed section to test Windows XP's reaction to your double-click speed setting. If Windows XP recognizes the double-click, you see the folder open. If you double-click again, Windows XP closes the folder. If you double-click and you do not see any change in the folder icon, the double-click speed setting is too fast. Adjust it downward and try again.

The ClickLock setting for the mouse on this computer allows you to highlight or drag without having to hold down a mouse button. You press the mouse button briefly, release it, and then move the pointer to select a group of folders or files, for example, or move an object from one location to another. A second click completes the selection or drag. If you start to use this feature, and then change your mind, you can press the Esc key to cancel it. You have to practice the use of this feature because, as you can imagine, it is harder to use with single-click activation. For example, when you click the mouse over a folder icon, does that mean you want Windows XP to open the folder or to select the folder with ClickLock and move it to a different location?

To adjust the double-click speed setting and examine other mouse settings:

1. Drag the **Double-click speed** slider bar to a new position between Slow and Fast, and double-click the folder icon in the test area to determine how this change affects the use of the mouse. Try different settings to find the double-click speed setting that works best for you, and then apply the setting to your computer with the Apply button. If you set the slider bar closer to Slow, you can more leisurely double-click and save wear and tear on the tendons in your wrist and arm.

2. Click the **Pointer Options** tab, or locate the property sheet with a Motion section. The Motion setting controls the relative movement of the mouse pointer on the screen to the movement of the mouse across the desktop. See Figure 2-22. If you want greater control over mouse movement on the screen, adjust the mouse pointer speed to a slower setting. If you have only a limited amount of desktop space for moving the mouse, set the mouse pointer speed to a faster setting to accelerate it faster across the screen. The Enhance pointer precision option, if available for your mouse, and if enabled, provides you with more control of the mouse pointer when you move the mouse a small distance, and the mouse pointer decelerates faster when you slow down or stop moving the mouse.

| Figure 2-22 | EXAMINING MOUSE POINTER OPTIONS (YOURS MAY DIFFER) |

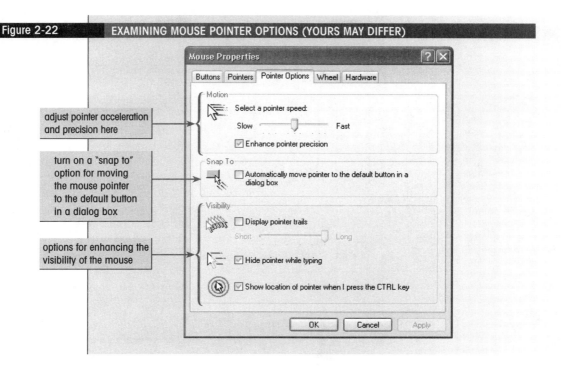

adjust pointer acceleration and precision here

turn on a "snap to" option for moving the mouse pointer to the default button in a dialog box

options for enhancing the visibility of the mouse

A Snap To option (shown under Snap To in the figure), if available for your mouse, moves the pointer to the default button in a dialog box, such as the OK button; however, you have to test this option with the types of programs that you use. In some programs, the mouse pointer moves to the center of the dialog box instead.

If you have an option for displaying mouse trails (shown under Visibility in the figure), and if you are using an LCD (liquid crystal display) or a computer attached to an overhead projector, you might want to enable this option to make it easier to find the mouse pointer. When enabled, Windows XP displays images of previous positions of the mouse pointer as you move the mouse, so that it appears as if there is a trail on the screen.

If available, the option for hiding the mouse pointer when you are typing is useful, because the mouse pointer does not inadvertently block your view of what's displayed on the screen when you type. The pointer disappears when you start typing, and reappears when you move the mouse. If available, you can also enable the option of showing the mouse pointer location when you press the Ctrl key. This feature is useful if you can't find the pointer and need to quickly locate it. This feature displays concentric circles that focus in on the position of the mouse pointer.

To continue your examination of mouse settings:

1. Click the **Wheel** tab (if available). On the Wheel property sheet shown in Figure 2-23, you can adjust the Scrolling setting for the mouse wheel so that moving the wheel on the mouse one notch scrolls either a specific number of lines or one screen at a time. This option simplifies scrolling, because you do not have to click scroll arrows repeatedly or drag a scroll box to adjust your view.

Figure 2-23   VIEWING OPTIONS FOR SCROLLING WITH THE MOUSE WHEEL

set mouse wheel so you
can scroll one or more
lines, or an entire
screen, quickly

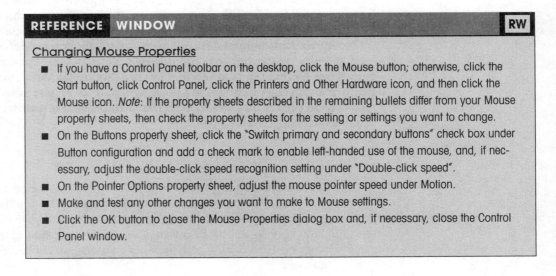

2. Examine your mouse property settings, test different settings that you might find useful (except those for mouse pointer shapes), and then click **Apply**.

3. Keep the Mouse Properties dialog box open for the next section of the tutorial.

As you test different mouse settings, you discover that some settings simplify your use of the mouse while others complicate its use.

REFERENCE WINDOW   RW

<u>Changing Mouse Properties</u>

- If you have a Control Panel toolbar on the desktop, click the Mouse button; otherwise, click the Start button, click Control Panel, click the Printers and Other Hardware icon, and then click the Mouse icon. *Note*: If the property sheets described in the remaining bullets differ from your Mouse property sheets, then check the property sheets for the setting or settings you want to change.
- On the Buttons property sheet, click the "Switch primary and secondary buttons" check box under Button configuration and add a check mark to enable left-handed use of the mouse, and, if necessary, adjust the double-click speed recognition setting under "Double-click speed".
- On the Pointer Options property sheet, adjust the mouse pointer speed under Motion.
- Make and test any other changes you want to make to Mouse settings.
- Click the OK button to close the Mouse Properties dialog box and, if necessary, close the Control Panel window.

By adjusting mouse properties you can make it easier to use your computer at home or at work. Also, companies can reduce the number of workers' compensation claims for carpal tunnel syndrome, a common form of repetitive stress injury (RSI), by helping employees find ways to work more easily with their keyboards and mice. **Carpal Tunnel syndrome** starts with numbness and burning in the fingers and wrists, and can eventually cause permanent and irreversible nerve damage. By using Web style, choosing single-click activation, and adjusting the double-click speed to a lower setting, and by adjusting other mouse settings, you might reduce or eliminate problems that arise from using the mouse for extended periods of time.

Using Animated and Static Cursors

As noted in the previous section, mouse pointer shapes provide a clue about the current status of your system. Although Windows XP uses a set of default mouse pointer shapes, you can choose other mouse pointer shapes.

Windows XP works with two types of pointers: static cursors and animated cursors. A **static cursor** is a mouse pointer shape that does not change. The Normal Select ᐳ pointer shape, the one you see the majority of the time, is an example of a static cursor. In contrast, an **animated cursor** is a mouse pointer shape that plays back a short animation. For example, one of the animated cursors included with Windows XP is an animation of a galloping horse 🐎. You might, for example, choose this animated cursor for the mouse pointer shape that indicates your system is busy. Not only can you select different pointer shapes, but you can also apply a **pointer scheme**, which consists of a set of pointer shapes for common types of mouse operations.

Jaime recommends that you show Jan how he can choose his own mouse pointer shapes, or work with the Windows XP pointer schemes.

To choose pointer shapes and schemes:

1. Click the **Pointers** tab in the Mouse Properties dialog box. On the Pointers property sheet, Windows XP lists the default pointer scheme, Windows Default (system scheme), or whatever you last selected, and displays a list of the pointer shapes included with this scheme. See Figure 2-24. In addition to the Normal Select pointer shape ᐳ, the default pointer scheme includes other pointer shapes that you more than likely recognize, such as Working In Background ᐳ⧖, Busy ⧗, Text Select I, Vertical Resize ↕, Horizontal Resize ↔, and Link Select 👆. You see 👆 in Web style when you point to or click the icon for an object. By default, Windows XP displays shadows for pointers to create a 3D effect.

Figure 2-24   VIEWING DEFAULT SETTINGS FOR MOUSE POINTER SHAPES

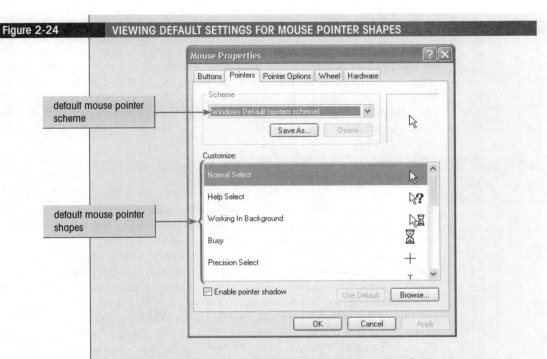

default mouse pointer scheme

default mouse pointer shapes

2. Click the **Working In Background** pointer shape 🔄⌛ in the Customize box, and then click the **Browse** button. Windows XP displays the contents of the Cursors folder, which is located within the Windows folder. See Figure 2-25. The files that contain pointer shapes have one of two file extensions. Static cursor files have the "cur" file extension, while animated cursor files have the "ani" file extension. Since you can download animated cursors from Web sites and place them in this folder for use with Windows XP, your list of cursor files might differ from those shown in the figure.

TROUBLE? If Windows XP displays the contents of drive C or some other folder in the Browse dialog box, open the Windows folder (if necessary), and then open the Cursors folder.

Figure 2-25   BROWSING FOR ANIMATED AND STATIC CURSOR FILES

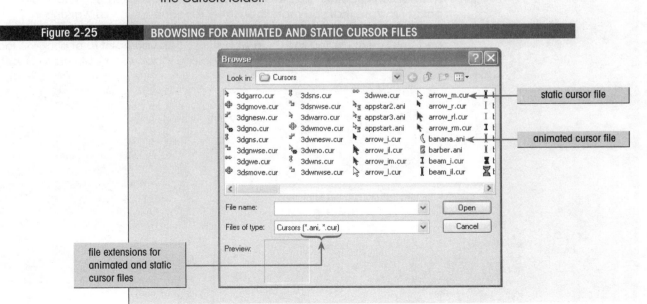

static cursor file

animated cursor file

file extensions for animated and static cursor files

3. In the Browse dialog box, locate **horse.ani**, click the background of the Browse dialog box to change the focus to this box so that you can select the mouse pointer shape without opening it, and then point to **horse.ini** to select it. Windows XP shows a preview of this animated cursor in the Preview box. See Figure 2-26.

TROUBLE? If you do not have the horse.ani file, then choose another animated cursor file.

Figure 2-26   SELECTING AN ANIMATED CURSOR

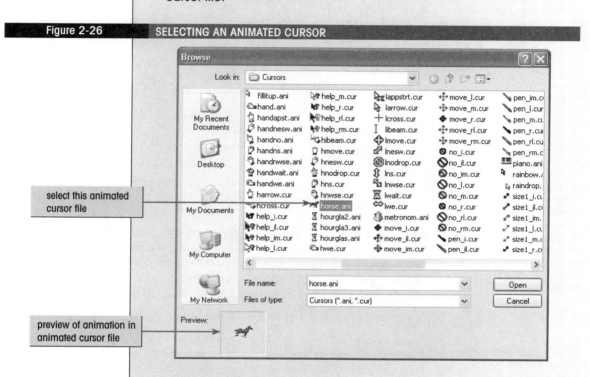

select this animated cursor file

preview of animation in animated cursor file

---

4. Click the **Open** button or click **horse.ani**. The pointer shape you selected replaces the one that Windows XP used, and you see a preview of this pointer shape in the preview box located in the upper-right corner of the Pointers property sheet. See Figure 2-27.

Figure 2-27   NEW POINTER SHAPE SELECTED FOR USE

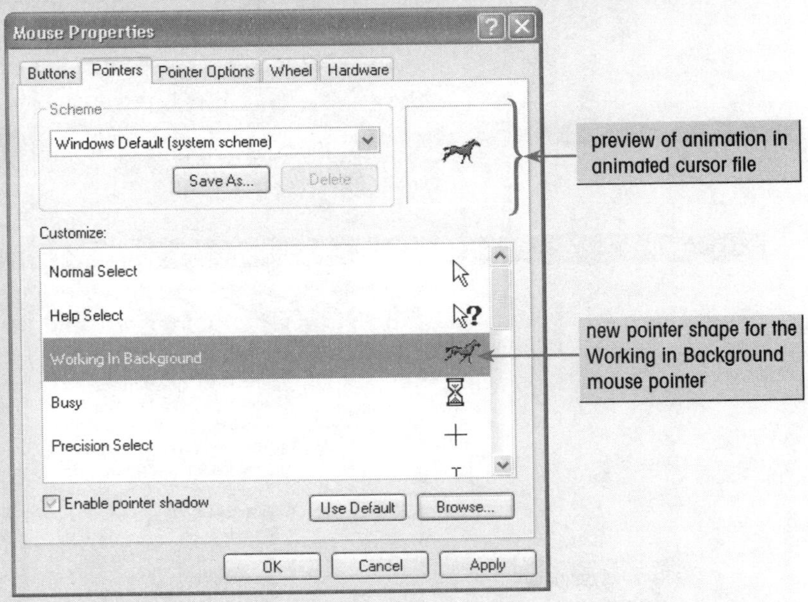

preview of animation in animated cursor file

new pointer shape for the Working in Background mouse pointer

5. Click the **Save As** button and, in the Save Scheme dialog box, type a new name for this pointer scheme. To distinguish your pointer scheme from that of other students, you might want to use your first name as part of the scheme. For example, Jan Weiler might name his pointer scheme "Jan's Pointer Scheme" or you might prefer to use a more generic name, such as "My Pointer Scheme."

6. Click the **OK** button to save the cursor scheme.

7. Click the **Apply** button to apply this change to your computer. If you now open the Help and Support Center or an application that makes demands on system resources, you see the new pointer shape for a split second or so.

8. From the Start menu, click **Help and Support**, and watch the mouse pointer. As the Help and Support Center opens, Windows XP briefly displays the animated cursor (or whatever type of pointer shape you chose).

   TROUBLE? If you did not see the animated cursor, you are probably using a higher performance and faster computer that displays the animated cursor so briefly you do not see it.

9. Close the Help and Support Center window.

As you try different animated pointers, you may discover that some are difficult to use when you need to point to a small object. You might find that the standard pointer shape is the best for pointing and selecting objects. There are two ways to restore the original pointer shape. You can select the Windows Default (system scheme) scheme (or whatever scheme you started with) from the Scheme list box, or you can click the Use Default button on the Pointers tab to restore the original pointer shape.

To restore a pointer shape:

1. Make sure the **Working In Background** pointer shape is selected in the Customize box.

2. Click the **Use Default** button. Windows XP changes the pointer shape back to the default pointer shape. If you now close the Mouse Properties dialog box, your new pointer scheme will contain this default pointer shape.

The Use Default button allows you to restore a pointer shape included in one of the Windows XP pointer schemes in the event you change a pointer scheme and save your changes under the same pointer scheme name. In addition to changing pointer shapes, Windows XP comes with its own pointer schemes from which you can choose an assortment of pointer shapes that are designed to complement each other.

To use another pointer scheme:

1. Click the **Scheme** list arrow. Windows XP displays pointer schemes available on your computer. See Figure 2-28. For the Windows Black, Windows Inverted, and Windows Standard schemes, you can select large and extra large pointer sizes. These larger sizes are obviously useful for people with limited vision.

| Figure 2-28 | VIEWING THE LIST OF POINTER SCHEMES |

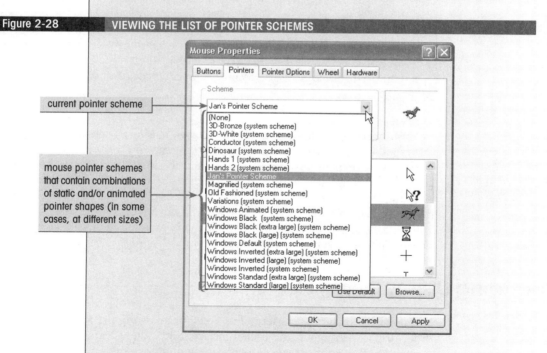

current pointer scheme

mouse pointer schemes that contain combinations of static and/or animated pointer shapes (in some cases, at different sizes)

2. Select different pointer schemes from the Scheme list box, including Old Fashioned, if it is available, and view the pointer shapes within each scheme. Some pointer schemes use a combination of static and animated cursors, such as Hands 1, Hands 2, Old Fashioned, Variations, and Windows Animated.

3. If you do not want to keep the pointer scheme you just created, or if you work in a computer lab, select the pointer scheme that you created and saved from the Scheme list box, click the **Delete** button, and then click the **Yes** button in the Confirm Scheme Removal dialog box.

4. To restore your original pointer scheme, click the **Scheme** list arrow, and choose the pointer scheme that your computer originally used, probably Windows Default (system scheme), and then click the **OK** button to close the Mouse Properties dialog box.

REFERENCE WINDOW **RW**

Choosing Mouse Pointer Shapes and Schemes

- If you have a Control Panel toolbar on the desktop, click the Mouse button; otherwise, click the Start button, click Control Panel, click the Printers and Other Hardware icon, and then click the Mouse icon.
- If you want to use a pointer scheme, click the Pointers tab, and then select a pointer scheme from the Scheme list box.
- If you want to customize individual pointers in the pointer scheme you've selected, click the Pointers tab, click the pointer shape you want to change in the Customize box, click the Browse button, click the mouse pointer shape you want to use in the Cursors folder (or any other folder), and then click the Open button.
- If you want to save your pointer shapes under a new pointer scheme, click the Save As button, and in the Save Scheme dialog box, type a new name for the pointer scheme, and then click the OK button.
- To restore a mouse pointer shape to the default shape, click the mouse pointer shape, and then click the Use Default button, or switch back to the Windows Default (system scheme) pointer scheme, or the original one used on your computer.
- Click the OK button to close the Mouse Properties dialog box.

Customizing your mouse is an important part of using an operating system like Windows XP that relies on a graphical user interface. Not only can you create a more pleasant and interesting working environment for yourself, but you can also implement options that protect the tendons in your hand, wrist, arm, and shoulder, thus making it easier to perform your work.

In the second part of the tutorial, you change display properties of the desktop. You examine the use of Windows XP themes, as well as graphic images for the desktop background, choose visual effects, change the display resolution, and examine the use of color depth settings. You also examine how Windows XP manages power to hardware devices.

Changing Display Properties

Windows XP includes a variety of options for adjusting the appearance of the desktop and other display settings in the user interface. Since these features affect your working environment and the performance of your computer, take the time to explore and choose those that allow you to work more effectively and enjoy the time you spend on a computer.

Using Desktop Themes

Unlike previous versions of Windows, where you had to purchase and install Microsoft Plus! for Windows, Windows XP now includes desktop themes for customizing the appearance of the user interface. Microsoft Plus! is a separate software package, and includes not only new themes and screen savers, but also 3D games and enhancements for the use of Windows Media Player. A **theme** consists of a set of visual elements that are designed to provide a unified look for your desktop and user interface. Each theme determines not only the appearance of the desktop background, but also the types of fonts, colors, and 3D effects used in windows, menus, and dialog boxes, the appearance of icons and mouse pointers, the type of screen saver used by Windows XP, and the sounds that Windows XP uses for system events, such as starting Windows XP. As you have already discovered in Tutorial 1, you can use the Windows Classic scheme if you want to work in Windows Classic view, and the Windows XP theme if you want to work in Web style. You can also further customize the Windows XP theme to suit your needs. Once you create a theme you want to keep, you can save it.

Because of his background and interest in graphic design, Jan asks you to show him how to select a Windows XP desktop theme, and then customize it for use on his computer.

To examine available desktop themes:

1. Point to the right edge of the desktop, click the **Display** button on the Control Panel toolbar, and after Windows XP opens the Display Properties dialog box, click the **Theme** list arrow on the Themes property sheet. In a new installation of Windows XP, you see five options in the Theme list box. In addition to the ones for Windows XP and Windows Classic, you also see an option for My Current Theme, an option for obtaining more themes online, and a Browse option. See Figure 2-29. If you choose the Browse option, Windows XP opens an Open Theme dialog box so that you can browse for themes.

| Figure 2-29 | CHOOSING A DESKTOP THEME |

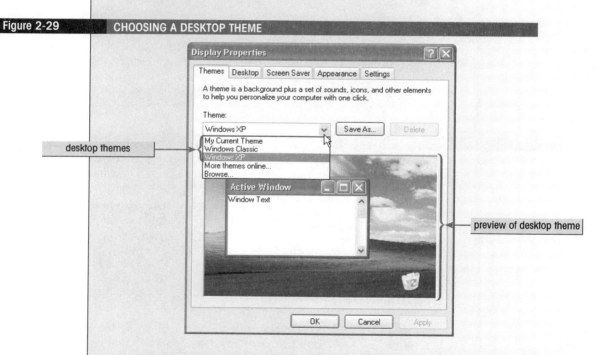

If you choose the "More themes online" option, Windows XP connects you to Microsoft's Web site for Microsoft Plus! for Windows XP. See Figure 2-30.

Figure 2-30   BROWSING AT MICROSOFT'S WEB SITE FOR DESKTOP THEMES

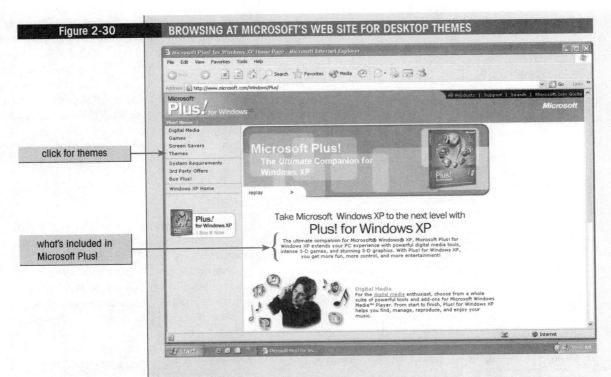

click for themes

what's included in
Microsoft Plus!

If you click the Themes link in the left-hand frame of the Web page, you obtain
a preview of additional themes. See Figure 2-31. To use Microsoft Plus!, Microsoft
recommends a processor that operates at 750 MHz or faster, 128 MB of RAM,
and 300 MB of hard disk space (though the latter might vary depending on
what you install).

Figure 2-31   PLUS! THEMES

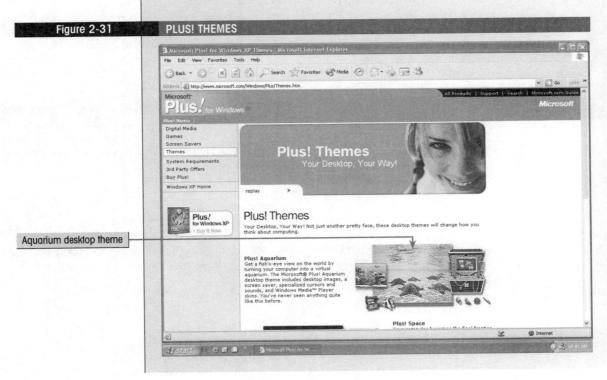

Aquarium desktop theme

2. If you've changed schemes, or modified the Windows XP theme, click **Windows XP** in the Theme list box, click **Apply**, and then keep the Display Properties dialog box open for the next section of the tutorial.

REFERENCE WINDOW **RW**

Choosing a Desktop Theme

- If you have a Control Panel toolbar on the desktop, click the Display button; otherwise, click the Start button, click Control Panel, click the Appearance and Themes icon, and then click the Display icon.
- In the Display Properties dialog box, click the Theme list arrow on the Themes property sheet, and then select a desktop theme
- Click the OK button to close the Display Properties dialog box.

On the Themes property sheet, Windows XP explains that themes allow you to personalize your computer with one click because they combine the use of a variety of settings.

Using Desktop Wallpaper

Background wallpaper is simply an image that you display on the desktop. You can use an image that you create with a graphics application, a scanned photo, an image that you download from a Web site or Web gallery, or even a Web page. You can use images stored in files with the file extension "bmp" for bitmap image, "gif" for Graphics Interchange Format, "jpg" or "jpeg" for Joint Photographic Experts Group, "dib" for Device Independent Bitmap, and "png" for Portable Network Graphics. Each of these types of graphic file formats contains a bitmapped graphic. A **bitmapped graphic** is an image represented by a pattern of pixels, or picture elements, as shown in Figure 2-32. This figure shows the Windows XP logo on the Start button at actual size and magnified 800%. As you can see, the image consists of an array of pixels, each of which consists of a different color. Each **pixel** consists of one or more dots, or points, which are treated as one unit on the monitor. Each dot in turn is composed of Red, Green, and Blue (RGB) components that blend together to form a single color. At your computer's maximum resolution (covered in the next section of the tutorial), one pixel equals one dot. The contents of each pixel are represented by one or more bits, which in turn determine the number of colors or shades of gray available for that pixel. Each pixel can be set to not only a different color, but also a different intensity, or brightness.

Figure 2-32   A BIT-MAPPED GRAPHIC IMAGE

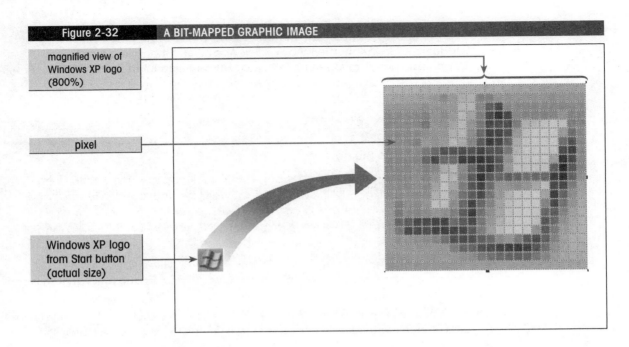

magnified view of
Windows XP logo
(800%)

pixel

Windows XP logo
from Start button
(actual size)

A **Device Independent Bitmap** with the "bmp" or "dib" file extension is a Windows graphics format that Windows XP can render independently of the video hardware in a computer. Bitmap image files ("bmp") are one common type of bitmapped graphic file. If you enlarge a bitmap image, the image becomes distorted. Since information is stored for each pixel in an image, and since bitmap images might be represented by hundreds of thousands or millions of pixels, bitmap image file sizes can be quite large. For example, Bliss.bmp, the bitmap image file that Windows XP uses for the default background wallpaper, is 1.37 MB.

The **GIF** (pronounced "jiff" or "gif") file format stores a bitmapped image at a compression of 1.5:1 to 2:1 without any loss of detail in the image (called **lossless compression**). The actual amount of compression depends on the degree to which the same colors are repeated within the image itself. The standard types of GIF files are limited to a palette of 256 colors or less. A **palette**, or **color palette**, is a set of available colors used either by an application or by the operating system. An **animated GIF** is a GIF file format that contains multiple images through which a Web browser can cycle.

The **JPG** or **JPEG** (pronounced "jay peg") file format achieves higher compression ratios of 10:1 or 20:1, or greater, by removing some of the detail in an image (changes that the human eye typically cannot detect), and therefore is called **lossy compression**. Both GIF and JPG files are commonly used on Web pages and the Internet to reduce transmission times for graphic images as they are downloaded to your Internet cache and then displayed on your monitor.

The **PNG** (pronounced "ping") file format is similar to the GIF file format, although it does achieve a slightly greater compression. It may eventually replace the GIF file format since it improves on the GIF file format in several ways, and is patent free, therefore requiring no license for its use.

If you choose a file that contains a graphic image for wallpaper, you have the option of centering, tiling, or stretching the image. If you choose to center a wallpaper option, the image appears in the center of the desktop. If you choose the tiling option, Windows XP repeats the image across the desktop, starting in the upper-left corner. This option is useful for files that contain a small graphic image. The stretching option stretches a graphic image to fill the desktop. This option is useful if the image is slightly smaller than the desktop. Too much stretching of an image causes distortion.

You can also use HTML document files with the "htm" or "html" file extension as background wallpaper. An **HTML document** is a file that contains HTML (Hypertext Markup Language) code for determining the layout and appearance of a Web page.

In the original versions of Windows 95, you were limited to BMP and RLE (**Run-Length Encoding,** a compressed bitmapped file format) file types for use as wallpaper.

After talking with you, Jan discovers to his delight that he can use graphic images that he has designed on the desktop background.

To view background wallpaper options:

1. Click the **Desktop** tab in the Display Properties dialog box. The Background box of the Desktop property sheet lists the names of files that contain images and HTML document files that you can use as wallpaper. In Figure 2-33, Windows XP displays the Bliss wallpaper, or whatever wallpaper you use, in the preview area (which appears as a monitor).

   The bitmap image files, such as Bliss, and the JPEG files, such as Ascent, are stored in the Wallpaper folder, which is under the Web folder, which in turn is under the Windows folder.

Figure 2-33   VIEWING BACKGROUND WALLPAPER OPTIONS

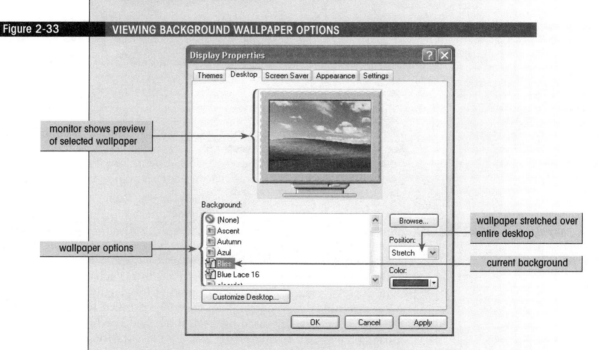

monitor shows preview of selected wallpaper

wallpaper options

wallpaper stretched over entire desktop

current background

2. Note the wallpaper setting for your computer so that you can restore that setting later.

3. Select each of the wallpaper options (such as Ascent, Autumn, Azul, Bliss, Crystal, Follow, Home, Moon flower, Purple flower, Radiance, Red moon desert, Stonehenge, Tulips, Vortec space, Wind, and Windows XP) in the Background box, and either view the images in the preview area, or click the **Apply** button to apply the image to the desktop background to discover some stunningly realistic images.

4. Locate and click the **Windows XP** background wallpaper option, click **Stretch** in the Position list box if it is not already selected, click the **Apply** button, and then click the **Themes** tab. Windows XP applies the Windows XP image to the desktop

background, and the Themes list box shows that you are now working with a modification of the Windows XP theme. See Figure 2-34. The Windows XP wallpaper appears blue in Windows XP Professional and green in Windows XP Home Edition.

Figure 2-34   SELECTING A NEW WALLPAPER AFFECTS THE DESKTOP THEME

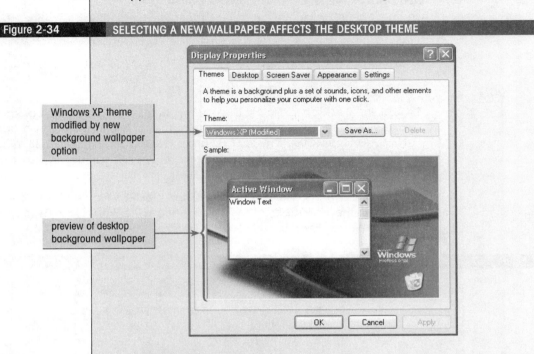

Windows XP theme modified by new background wallpaper option

preview of desktop background wallpaper

5. Click the **Desktop** tab, click the **Customize Desktop** button and, in the Desktop Items dialog box, click the **Web** tab. On the Web property sheet, you can display your home page on your desktop, and you can use the Synchronize button to periodically update the content from your home page so that it appears on the desktop as well. See Figure 2-35.

Figure 2-35   CHOOSING YOUR HOME PAGE FOR USE AS WALLPAPER

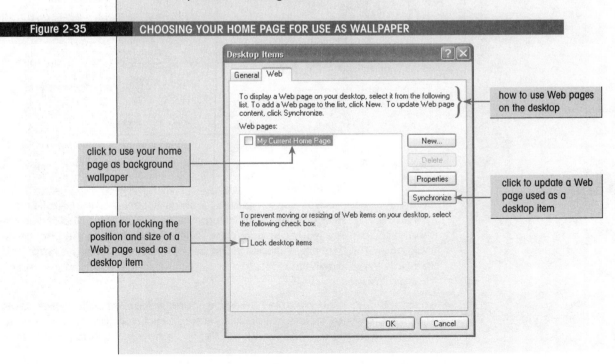

how to use Web pages on the desktop

click to use your home page as background wallpaper

click to update a Web page used as a desktop item

option for locking the position and size of a Web page used as a desktop item

With the New button, you can add new Web sites to your list of Web pages that are available for use as a desktop background. You can also lock a Web page on the desktop so that they remain at their current location and size, and if the Web page does not fit down the length of the desktop, you can scroll to view the remainder of the Web page. If you need to move or resize desktop items, you need to remove the check mark from the "Lock desktop items" check box.

6. Click the **My Current Home Page** check box in the Web pages box, click the **OK** button to close the Desktop Items dialog box, and then click the **OK** button to close the Display Properties dialog box.

On the computer used for Figure 2-36, Windows XP displays the MSN Web page on the desktop background. Notice that Windows XP displays the desktop icons in a frame on the left side of the desktop, and also displays a vertical scroll bar on the right side of the desktop so that you can adjust your view of the Web page. Windows XP also displays the animation associated with any animated objects on the Web page, and all the links are active. That means that the user of the computer shown in Figure 2-36 can go directly to his or her Hotmail account to get e-mail, and quickly access any of the other features available on this home page. If you always use a search engine when you access the Web, you can save a copy of that Web page to a folder on your computer, and then select it as desktop wallpaper. Any links on that Web page are still functional, and you could initiate a Web search directly from your desktop.

TROUBLE? If Internet Explorer cannot display your home page because you are not connected to the Internet, you see the message "Web page unavailable offline" followed by instructions on how to make the content of your home page available offline. Follow the instructions to view your home page on the desktop, and then press the F5 (Refresh) key to update your desktop view.

Figure 2-36	HOME PAGE PLACED ON THE DESKTOP

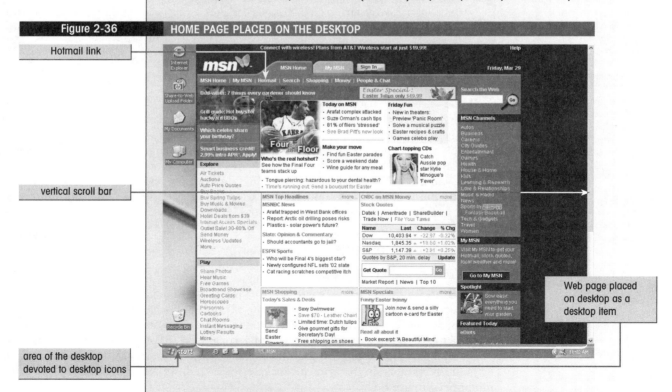

Hotmail link

vertical scroll bar

area of the desktop devoted to desktop icons

Web page placed on desktop as a desktop item

7. Point to the right edge of the desktop, and after Windows XP displays the Control Panel toolbar, click the **Display** button, click the **Desktop** tab, click the **Customize Desktop** button, click the **Web** tab in the Desktop Items dialog box, click the **My Current Home Page** check box to remove the check mark, click the **OK** button to close the Desktop Items dialog box, and then click the **Apply** button. Windows XP removes your home page from the desktop background.

8. Keep the Display Properties dialog box open for the next section of the tutorial.

If you want to remove the background wallpaper all together, choose (None) in the Background box on the Desktop property sheet, and then apply the change, or select the Windows XP theme (or the theme you typically use) from the Themes property sheet, and then apply the change.

REFERENCE WINDOW RW

Choosing Background Wallpaper

- If you have a Control Panel toolbar on the desktop, click the Display button, and then click the Desktop tab; otherwise, right-click the desktop, click Properties, and then click the Desktop tab.
- If you want to apply a background image to a desktop, click a wallpaper option in the Background box, click the Position list arrow, click Center, Tile, or Stretch, and then click the OK button, or click the Browse button, locate and open a folder with graphic images or HTML files, select a file for use as desktop wallpaper, and then click the OK button to close the Display Properties dialog box and apply the wallpaper.
- If you want to use a Web page, such as your home page, as the desktop background, click the Customize Desktop button on the Desktop property sheet, and then click the Web tab in the Desktop Items dialog box. In the Web pages box, click the check box for the Web page you want to use, click the OK button to close the Desktop Items dialog box, and then click the OK button to close the Display Properties dialog box and apply the wallpaper.

If you use an animated GIF as wallpaper, Windows XP displays the animation on the desktop. In other words, the desktop is "alive," and the meaning of Active Desktop becomes immediately obvious.

If you are viewing an image in a graphics application, and if you want to display that image on your desktop, check the File menu to see if it includes a "Set As Wallpaper" option so that you can quickly apply the image directly from the application. Likewise, if you are browsing the Web and find an image you want to use as wallpaper, you can right-click the image, and then choose the option to set it as background wallpaper.

Customizing Elements of the User Interface

You can change and customize the appearance of several different elements of the user interface at one time, thereby changing the visual style of your desktop theme. You can also customize individual components, including 3D objects, active and inactive title bars, active and inactive window borders, the background of an application window, caption buttons, the desktop, desktop icons, horizontal and vertical icon spacing, menus and items that you select on menus, message boxes, scrollbars, ScreenTips, and windows.

Jaime recommends that you investigate the Windows XP color schemes in case you might need to use them.

To examine Windows XP color schemes:

1. Click the **Appearance** tab in the Display Properties dialog box. Windows XP displays the Appearance property sheet. See Figure 2-37.

Figure 2-37	VIEWING OPTIONS ON THE APPEARANCE PROPERTY SHEET

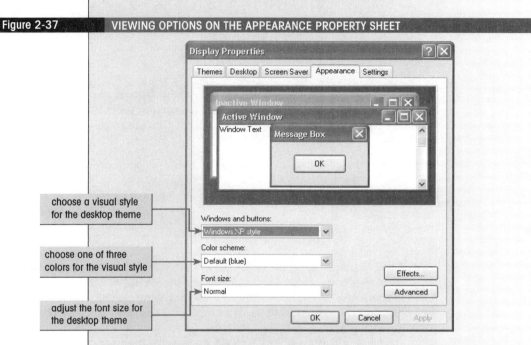

choose a visual style for the desktop theme

choose one of three colors for the visual style

adjust the font size for the desktop theme

Under the preview area, which shows you the design applied to elements of the user interface, you can pick a visual style for your current theme from the Windows and buttons list box. There are two options: Windows XP style, and Windows Classic style. From the Color scheme list box, you can select a color—Default (blue), Olive Green, or Silver—for the visual style you select in the Windows and buttons list box. From the Font size list box, you can choose Normal, Large Fonts, or Extra Large Fonts for the visual style.

2. Choose different options in each of these three list boxes, and examine how they change the user interface in the preview area, but do not apply any changes to your computer unless you want to keep those changes.

3. Click the **Advanced** button. Windows XP displays the Advanced Appearance property sheet. See Figure 2-38. Under the preview area, Windows XP notes that if you select a Windows and buttons style other than Windows Classic, the settings for that visual style override any settings you choose here, except perhaps in some older programs.

Figure 2-38	VIEWING OPTIONS FOR CHANGING ELEMENTS OF THE USER INTERFACE

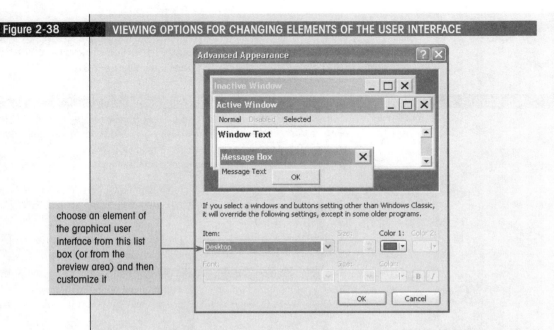

choose an element of the graphical user interface from this list box (or from the preview area) and then customize it

4. Click the **Item** list arrow. Windows XP displays different elements of the user interface that you can customize if you use the Windows Classic style. See Figure 2-39. Depending on which element you select, Windows XP may display options for changing the element's size, color (and in some instances, combinations of colors that you can use), font, font size, and font color, and may activate the Bold and Italics buttons. If you click an element of the user interface in the preview area, Windows XP automatically selects it in the Item list box.

Figure 2-39	SELECTING A COMPONENT OF THE USER INTERFACE

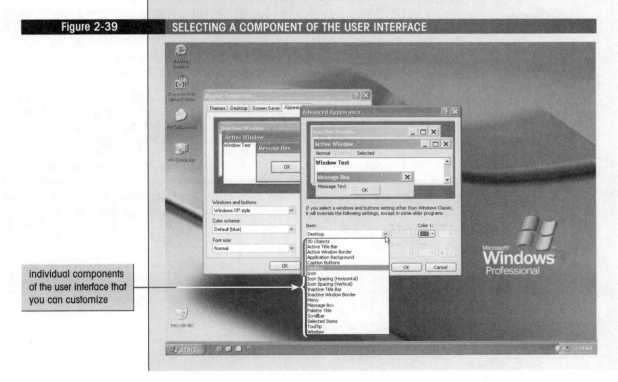

individual components of the user interface that you can customize

> **5.** Click the **Cancel** button to close the Advanced Appearance dialog box without making any changes, and leave the Display Properties dialog box open for the next section of the tutorial.

Visual styles are a new feature of Windows XP not available in earlier versions of Windows. However, the options available in the Advanced Appearance property sheet provide compatibility with earlier versions of Windows in which you customized the user interface by using these options on the Appearance property sheet.

REFERENCE WINDOW   **RW**

Customizing Elements of the User Interface

- If you have a Control Panel toolbar on the desktop, click the Display button, and then click the Appearance tab; otherwise, right-click the desktop, click Properties, and then click the Appearance tab.
- Choose a visual style from the Windows and buttons list box, a color for the visual style from the Color scheme list box, and a font size from the Font size list box.
- If you are using the Windows Classic visual style and want to further customize elements of the user interface, click the Advanced button and, in the Advanced Appearance dialog box, choose an element of the user interface from the Item list box or by clicking it in the preview area, specify its size, color(s), font, font size, font color, apply boldface or italics, and then click the OK button.
- Click the OK button to apply the settings and close the Display Properties dialog box.

In some cases, such as a computer used for a training presentation before a large audience, you might find it useful to customize individual elements of the user interface to make it easier for all participants to see elements of the desktop, as well as options available in other parts of the user interface, such as in windows, menus, and dialog boxes.

Choosing Special Display Effects

To further enhance your use of Windows XP, you can choose the following special display effects:

- **Transition effects**. You can choose from one of two transition effects, or animations, for menus and ScreenTips, namely the Scroll effect or the Fade effect. If you choose the Scroll effect, menus, lists, and ScreenTips slide in and out. If you choose the Fade effect (the default), menus, lists, and ScreenTips fade in when you open them, and dissolve when you close them.

- **Smoothing the edges of screen fonts**. If you magnify the image you see on the monitor, you notice that text characters are formed from dots, or groups of pixels, illuminated together. If the text you see on the monitor consists of diagonal or curved lines, rather than straight lines, you see a "stairstep" effect in which the outline of the characters looks uneven. See Figure 2-40.

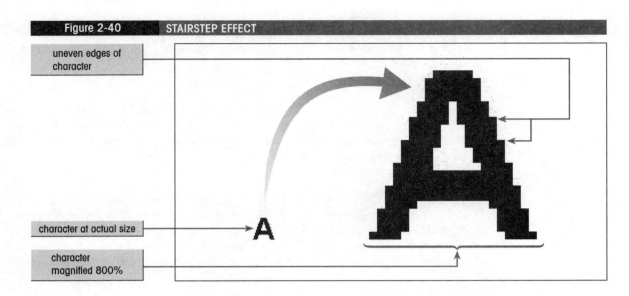

Figure 2-40   STAIRSTEP EFFECT

uneven edges of character

character at actual size

character magnified 800%

If you enable the option for smoothing the edges of screen fonts, Windows XP changes the appearance of characters displayed in large font sizes so that they look smoother, as shown in Figure 2-41. You can select one of two methods for smoothing the edges of screen fonts, namely Standard or ClearType. The Standard setting is designed for use with desktop monitors, whereas the ClearType setting is designed for most laptop computers and other flat screen monitors.

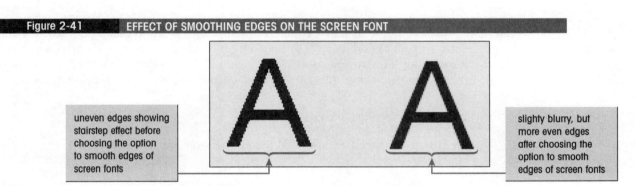

Figure 2-41   EFFECT OF SMOOTHING EDGES ON THE SCREEN FONT

uneven edges showing stairstep effect before choosing the option to smooth edges of screen fonts

slightly blurry, but more even edges after choosing the option to smooth edges of screen fonts

- **Large Icons**. If you enable the option for using large icons, Windows replaces the default view, which relies on small icons, with one that uses large icons so the icons are easier to see.

- **Menu shadows**. Windows XP displays a slight shadow behind menu options to create a three-dimensional look.

- **Showing window contents while dragging**. When you drag a window or dialog box to another location on the desktop, Windows XP displays the window and its contents, or a dialog box and its contents. While helpful, this feature can place heavy demands on some computers. If you turn this option off, and then drag a window or dialog box, you see only a border of the window or dialog box to indicate where the object will appear once you release the mouse button.

■ **Hiding keyboard navigation letters.** If you enable the "Hide underlined letters for keyboard navigation until I press the Alt key" option, Windows XP does not display the underlined characters used as keyboard shortcuts for commands on menus and options in dialog boxes until you press the Alt key on the keyboard. Also, it does not display the **input focus indicator**—the dotted rectangle that appears around the selected object until you start using the keyboard to navigate from object to object.

Some of these special display effects, such as showing the windows contents while dragging, can affect the performance of a computer system.

As you and Jaime discuss the types of support needed by staff, Jaime mentions that some employees might install Windows XP Professional or Windows XP Home Edition on a slightly older computer with a limited amount of memory at home so that they can work in the evenings on special company projects, and then encounter problems with the performance of their computers. If these employees mention that their computers are slow when they need to perform common types of operations, such as moving a window, then you should show them how to locate the special display settings and discuss the pros and cons of using them.

To check the settings for special display effects:

1. Click the **Appearance** tab if it is not already selected, and then click the **Effects** button. In the Effects dialog box, you can choose visual effects that enhance the performance of your computer. See Figure 2-42.

| Figure 2-42 | VIEWING SETTINGS FOR SPECIAL VISUAL EFFECTS |

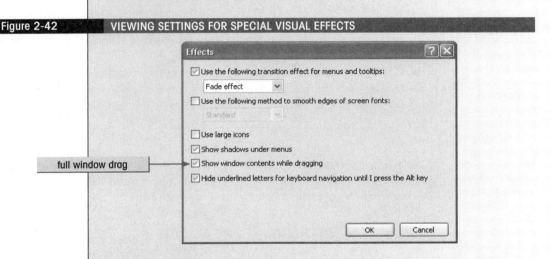

full window drag

2. Note which options are used on your computer so that you can restore them if you make any changes.

3. If the "Show window contents while dragging" check box does not contain a check mark, click this check box, click the **OK** button to close the Effects dialog box, and then click the **Apply** button in the Display Properties dialog box.

4. Drag the Display Properties dialog box around the desktop, and note whether it moves smoothly or more slowly while displaying images of previous positions (similar to pointer trails). On a newer, higher performance computer, the dialog box should move smoothly around the desktop.

5. Click the **Effects** button, remove the check mark from the "Show window contents while dragging" check box, click the **OK** button to close the Effects dialog box, and then click the **Apply** button in the Display Properties dialog box.

6. Drag the Display Properties dialog box around the desktop, and note whether it moves smoothly or more slowly while displaying images of previous positions. As you drag the dialog box, Windows XP only displays an outline of the dialog box so that you know where to position the dialog box. When you release the mouse button, Windows XP displays the contents of the dialog box. If you are using a higher performance computer, you will not note any difference in the movement of the dialog box; however, if you are using an older computer with limited memory, then this change might improve its performance over that which you noticed in Step 4.

7. If your computer used this special visual display setting, or if you want to use this option on your computer, click the **Effects** button, click the **Show window contents while dragging** check box, click the **OK** button to close the Effects dialog box, and then click the **Apply** button.

8. Keep the Display Properties dialog box open for the next section of the tutorial.

REFERENCE WINDOW   RW

Choosing Special Visual Effects

- If you have a Control Panel toolbar on the desktop, click the Display button, click the Appearance tab, and then click the Effects button; otherwise, right-click the desktop, click Properties, click the Appearance tab, and then click the Effects button.
- In the Effects dialog box, choose the special visual effects you want to use.
- Click the OK button to close the Effects dialog box, and then click the OK button to close the Display Properties dialog box and apply the effects to your computer.

So that your computer performs optimally, and so that you have access to the types of special display settings that you want to use, you should test each of these settings, and observe whether they affect your computer's performance.

Adjusting the Resolution, Color Setting, and Refresh Rate

One of the important characteristics of your video display is the sharpness of the image that appears on the monitor, or its **screen resolution**. The **display adapter** (or **video card**, or **video adapter**), a device inside your computer, determines the resolution by controlling the number of pixels displayed on the monitor. For example, at a resolution of 640 by 480, the display adapter produces 640 pixels across the width of the screen and 480 pixels down the screen. If you multiply 640 by 480, you find that an image displayed on the screen at this resolution is composed of 307,200 pixels. A resolution of 640 by 480 is referred to as **standard VGA display mode** (**VGA** stands for video graphics array), and is a low resolution. Most display adapters operate in display modes of 800 by 600 and 1024 by 768, as well as even higher resolutions, such as 1152 by 864, 1280 by 1024, and 1600 by 1200. The resolution of 800 by 600 is a commonly used video display mode, because the image on the monitor is not too small, though 1024 by 768 is becoming more popular.

At higher resolutions, more pixels form the image you see, as shown in Figure 2-43. The more pixels the video adapter displays across the width of the screen and down its length, the greater the resolution (and the more memory Windows XP uses to render the image). As you increase the resolution, the screen image becomes sharper and crisper because the pixels are closer together. Objects and text labels on the desktop also become smaller, and the desktop becomes larger. If you increase your desktop resolution, you might want to also adjust the size of fonts so that icon text labels are easier to read on the desktop, in windows, and on menus. If you are using a computer with a large monitor, a higher resolution, such as 1024 by 768, works well.

Figure 2-43	NUMBER OF PIXELS AT DIFFERENT RESOLUTIONS			
	RESOLUTION	PIXELS	RESOLUTION	PIXELS
standard VGA resolution →	640 × 480	307,200	1152 × 864	995,328
commonly used resolution →	800 × 600	480,000	1280 × 1024	1,310,720
useful resolution for large monitors →	1024 × 768	786,432	1600 × 1200	1,920,000

In addition to controlling resolution, the display adapter determines the number of colors you see. Standard VGA adapters, for example, are 4-bit video display adapters that display 2^4 or 16 colors. The "4-bit" refers to the number of bits used by the video adapter to define individual colors. With four bits, there are a maximum of 16 possible combinations of 0 (zero) and 1 (one). As you may know, the 0 and 1 are the only two digits used in the binary numbering system. By combining these 0s and 1s, you can produce codes that uniquely define a color. Adapters capable of using 8-bit video can display 2^8 or 256 colors; 16-bit video display adapters can display 2^{16} or 65,536 colors, a feature referred to as **High Color**; and 24-bit video display adapters can display 2^{24} or approximately 16.7 million colors, a feature referred to as **True Color**. On some computers, High Color is defined with 15-bits instead of 16 bits, so those video display adapters can display 2^{15} or 32,768 colors. Many systems have another True Color mode that uses 32 bits. This option provides access to 16.7 million colors (just like 24 bits), but also supports an additional feature called transparency.

The resolution you choose may also determine the number of colors that you can view. As you increase the resolution, you might find that you are limited to displaying fewer colors because your video adapter does not have enough memory to display a higher resolution with more colors. For example, to display 16.7 million colors (using 24-bit True Color) at a resolution of 1024 by 768, you need at least 4 MB of video RAM on your video display adapter card. If you increase your resolution to 1600 by 1200, you need 8 MB to display the same number of colors.

As you increase the resolution and the number of colors displayed on the monitor, the quality of the image approaches photo quality. The resolution and color setting that you choose obviously depends on the type of work that you do, the type of documents that you produce, and the type of software that you use. If you work as a graphic designer and need photo quality, choose True Color or High Color along with a resolution of 1024 by 768 or higher. As you change your color settings, pay attention to how your video display adapter updates the image on the screen as you scroll through documents. If the scrolling is uneven and jerky, try another color setting.

You can change the screen resolution and color depth setting "on the fly" (that is, without having to reboot) if you have a video display adapter that supports multiple display modes and colors. When you change the resolution or color setting in Windows XP (as well as earlier versions of Windows), you might need (or want) to reboot your computer to achieve the best possible results.

At the request of another staff scientist who analyzes models of the molecular structure and intramolecular forces of new chemical compounds on his computer, and who now needs to adjust the resolution and colors shown in these models, Jaime asks you to help the scientist determine the best resolution and color setting for his work.

Before you make changes to the screen resolution or color setting, check the documentation for your video display adapter and monitor to make sure that they support the use of those settings. Also make sure your video display and adapter are properly configured so that the options listed for the screen resolution and color quality work properly on your computer. If Windows XP does not display the wallpaper after you change a setting, but does display the desktop, you might be able to update your desktop view by pressing the F5 (Refresh) key.

To document and then change the screen resolution:

1. Click the **Settings** tab in the Display Properties dialog box. The Settings property sheet contains options for adjusting the resolution and the number of colors displayed in the color palette (called the **color depth**). See Figure 2-44. The computer used for this figure has a video adapter card that currently uses a screen resolution of 1024 by 768 and a color setting of Highest (32 bit) for True Color (yours might differ). If you change the resolution, the image in the monitor preview area shows you how the desktop, windows, and desktop icons change in size.

| Figure 2-44 | VIEWING SCREEN RESOLUTION AND COLOR SETTINGS |

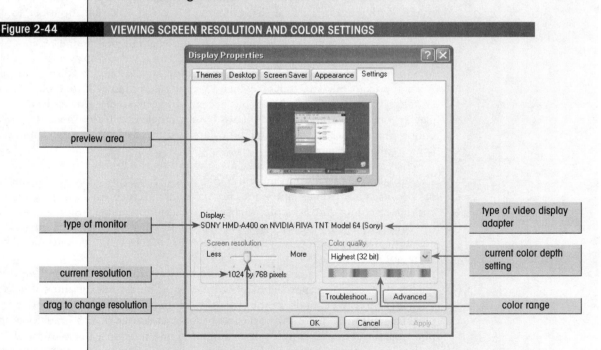

2. Press and hold down the **Alt** key while you press the **Print Scrn** key, release the **Print Scrn** key, and then release the **Alt** key.

3. Open WordPad from the Accessories menu, type your name, your course number, the course name, the lab assignment number, and any other information (such as the section number and date) that your instructor requests that you include on lab assignments. Press the **Enter** key twice to insert blank rows. Click **Edit** on the menu bar, and then click **Paste** to insert the copy of the Display Properties dialog box stored on the Windows Clipboard as an object into your WordPad document.

   POWER USER TIP You can press Ctrl+V to paste the contents of the Clipboard into the document.

4. If you want to save this document, click **File** on the menu bar, click **Save**, click the **Save in** list arrow, click **3½ Floppy (A:)**, select **Document.rtf** (the default document name) in the File name text box and replace it with a filename of your own (such as Display Properties Dialog Box), and then click the **Save** button.

5. To print this document, click **File** on the menu bar, click **Print**, select the printer you want to use (if it is not already selected) in the Print dialog box, click the **Print** button in the Print dialog box, locate and retrieve your printed copy, and then close WordPad.

6. Examine the quality of the image before you make any changes, and then drag the **slider bar** in the Screen resolution area left or right to the next available screen resolution. For example, if you are currently using a screen resolution of 1024 by 768, drag the slider bar right one notch to select 1280 by 1024 pixels (or whatever option is available on your computer). After you make this change, check the image in the preview monitor. Notice that the desktop window and icons are smaller at higher resolutions.

   TROUBLE? If your computer is already set for the highest screen resolution, drag the slider bar to the left one notch to the next lower resolution, and examine the change in the preview monitor.

7. Click the **Apply** button, but *do not click* the Yes or No button in the Monitor Settings dialog box. Windows XP resizes the desktop and displays a Monitor Settings dialog box so that you can choose whether to keep the new setting. If your video display adapter does not support the new resolution and displays an error message, wait 15 seconds for Windows XP to restore your previous screen resolution. On the computer used in Figure 2-45, the screen resolution increased to 1280 by 1024, and the desktop area increased as the size of desktop components decreased. At this point, carefully examine the screen and determine whether there are any potential problems, such as distortion of the image or loss of part of the image.

   TROUBLE? If Windows XP does not display a Monitor Settings dialog box, but instead immediately applies the new setting, open the Display Properties dialog box if Windows XP closed it, click the Settings tab, drag the slider bar to the screen resolution previously used on your computer, click the Apply button to restore your previous screen resolution, and then skip the next step.

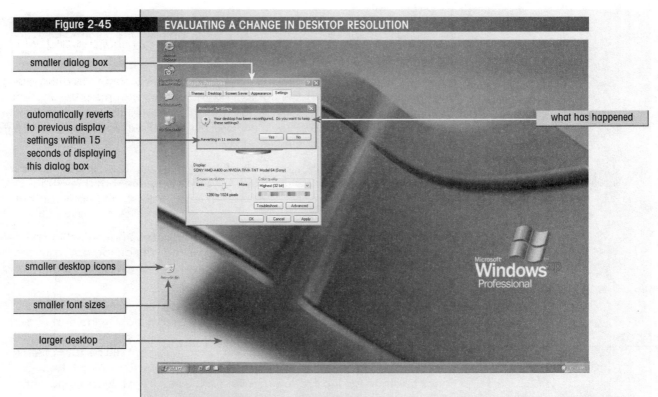

Figure 2-45   EVALUATING A CHANGE IN DESKTOP RESOLUTION

smaller dialog box

automatically reverts to previous display settings within 15 seconds of displaying this dialog box

what has happened

smaller desktop icons

smaller font sizes

larger desktop

8. Wait 15 seconds; *do not click* the Yes or No button in the Monitor Settings dialog box. Windows XP restores the original resolution.

9. Keep the Display Properties dialog box open.

If you decide to permanently use a higher screen resolution on your computer, consider increasing the default font size for displaying icon titles.

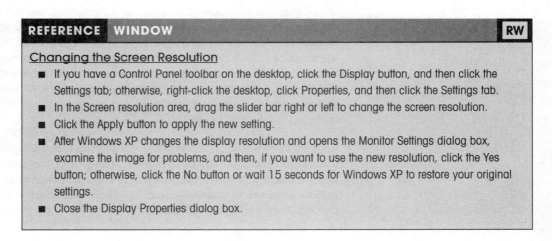

REFERENCE WINDOW   RW

Changing the Screen Resolution
- If you have a Control Panel toolbar on the desktop, click the Display button, and then click the Settings tab; otherwise, right-click the desktop, click Properties, and then click the Settings tab.
- In the Screen resolution area, drag the slider bar right or left to change the screen resolution.
- Click the Apply button to apply the new setting.
- After Windows XP changes the display resolution and opens the Monitor Settings dialog box, examine the image for problems, and then, if you want to use the new resolution, click the Yes button; otherwise, click the No button or wait 15 seconds for Windows XP to restore your original settings.
- Close the Display Properties dialog box.

You can also change your color depth setting using the Color quality list box on the Settings property sheet.

To view and change the color settings:

1. Examine the quality of the image before you make any changes, and note your current color quality setting.

2. Click the **Color quality** list arrow. Windows XP lists the color settings available for your display adapter and monitor. See Figure 2-46. The computer used for this figure has two color depth settings: Medium (16 bit) for High Color, and Highest (32 bit) for True Color. Yours may differ, and might include Medium (16 bit), High (24 bit), and Highest (32 bit), for example.

Figure 2-46   VIEWING COLOR DEPTH SETTINGS

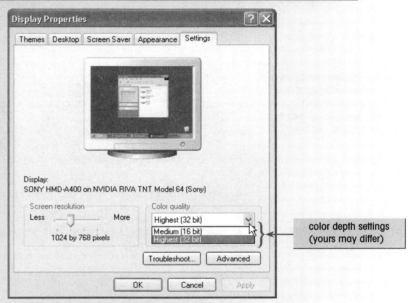

color depth settings
(yours may differ)

3. In the Color quality list box, click the next higher color depth setting (or next lower color depth setting) for your computer, and then click the **Apply** button. Windows XP displays a Monitor Settings dialog box, informing you that the desktop is reconfigured and asking if you want to keep the new setting. If you experience a problem when you change the color setting, wait 15 seconds for Windows XP to restore your previous color setting. On the computer shown in Figure 2-47, there was a noticeable degradation in the quality of the image of the monitor after changing from a higher color setting to a lower one, namely from True Color (32 bit) to High Color (16 bit).

TROUBLE? If Windows XP does not display a Monitor Settings dialog box, but instead immediately applies the new setting, open the Display Properties dialog box if Windows XP closed it, click the Settings tab, select the Color quality setting previously used on your computer, click the Apply button to restore your previous color setting, and then skip the next step.

Figure 2-47 | EFFECTS OF CHANGING TO A LOWER COLOR DEPTH SETTING

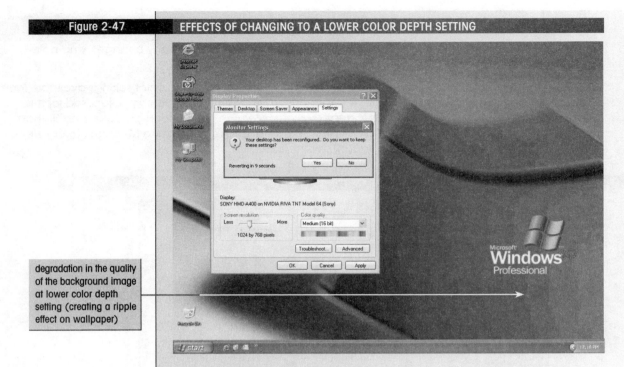

degradation in the quality of the background image at lower color depth setting (creating a ripple effect on wallpaper)

4. Wait 15 seconds; *do not click* the Yes or No button in the Monitor Settings dialog box. Windows restores the original color depth setting.

5. Keep the Display Properties dialog box open for the next section of the tutorial.

If you change the color setting from a lower color depth setting to a higher one, the quality of the image on the monitor improves, in some cases, dramatically. The image may appear sharper and "more alive with color." Furthermore, the three-dimensional depth or perspective of the image may improve remarkably. If you change from a higher color depth setting to a lower one, you more than likely notice that the quality of the image degrades.

Note that increasing the screen resolution and the number of colors that you can see places additional demands on the resources of your computer system, including processing power and memory. As your processor manages more and more pixels *and* colors, you might notice a change in the performance of your system. If you need to operate your system at greater screen resolutions and display more colors, you might be able to add additional memory, called **VRAM** or **video RAM**, to your display adapter for processing multicolored, high-resolution images. When you purchase a new computer, you should consider the amount of RAM included on the video card in your decision as to whether to purchase the computer.

REFERENCE WINDOW | **RW**

Changing the Color Depth Setting

- If you have a Control Panel toolbar on the desktop, click the Display button, and then click the Settings tab; otherwise, right-click the desktop, click Properties, and then click the Settings tab.
- Click the Color quality list arrow, click the color setting you want to use, and then click the Apply button.
- After Windows XP changes the color setting and displays the Monitor Settings dialog box, examine the image, and then, if you want to use the new color depth setting, click the Yes button; otherwise, click the No button or wait 15 seconds for Windows XP to restore your original setting.
- Close the Display Properties dialog box.

Another factor that you can control on some computers is the refresh rate. The **refresh rate** refers to the number of times per second that the image on the screen is redrawn by the video card. If the refresh rate is too low, then you notice the image flicker, and that flicker makes it difficult to work with the monitor. It is generally recommended that you work with a refresh rate of 72 Hz (hertz) or slightly higher. Most people cannot detect flicker at refresh rates above 72 Hz. However, because individual monitors differ, you should test settings in the range of 72 to 85 Hz. It serves no purpose to increase the refresh rate to very high values because it is believed that your eyes cannot detect flicker at these rates. Furthermore, if you increase the resolution, the refresh rate might drop because of the increased demands placed on the video card to display more pixels. You may need to strike a compromise and select a high-enough resolution that permits a refresh rate that does not produce flicker detectable to your eyes.

Your peripheral vision is more sensitive to flicker. To test your monitor for flicker, hold a finger a couple of inches to the side of the screen, look at the finger, and then concentrate on your peripheral vision. If you detect any flicker, you can experience eyestrain if you continue to use the computer, even if the flicker seems to disappear when you view the center of the screen. You should boost the refresh rate, and then test your monitor again. Before you change refresh rates, you should check the documentation for your monitor and find out what refresh rates it supports so that you do not inadvertently boost the refresh rate to a value that physically damages your monitor. If Windows XP does not display a property sheet that allows you to change the refresh rate, you should make sure that it is using the proper device driver for your video card and monitor.

Before he leaves for his next appointment, Jaime decides to show you how to check other video display properties, including the refresh rate.

To check the other video display properties and the refresh rate:

1. On the **Settings** tab in the Display Properties dialog box, click the **Advanced** button. The Properties dialog box for your monitor and display adapter opens. On the General property sheet, you can adjust the DPI setting in the Display area if your screen resolution causes items to appear too small. See Figure 2-48. DPI stands for "dots per inch," and in the DPI setting list box, you can choose Normal size (which is 96 DPI), Large size (120 DPI, or 25% larger), or Custom setting. If you choose Custom setting, you can specify either a percentage of Normal size, or you can set your display for actual size by matching an inch of distance on the monitor to an inch of distance on a ruler held up to the screen.

Figure 2-48   VIEWING GENERAL DISPLAY SETTINGS

option for changing the dots per inch which in turn changes the font size

program compatibility settings

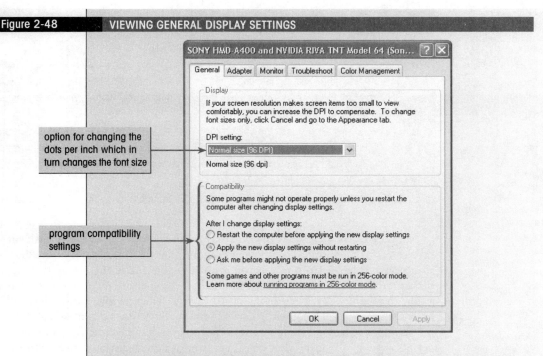

The options in the Compatibility area determine how Windows XP handles changes to display settings. It notes that some programs do not operate properly unless you restart your computer after changing display settings. The default setting is to apply the change without restarting. The warning messages that you see when you change display settings depend on which of these three options is active. Note also that a link to a Help topic in the Help and Support Center provides information about running games and other programs in 256-color mode.

2. Click the **Monitor** tab. On the Monitor property sheet, you can specify the Screen refresh rate, and you can view properties of the monitor. See Figure 2-49. On the computer used for this figure, the refresh rate is set at 75 Hertz. If you change the refresh rate, Windows XP applies the change and then displays the Monitor Settings dialog box so that you can decide whether to keep the change.

| Figure 2-49 | VIEWING MONITOR SETTINGS |

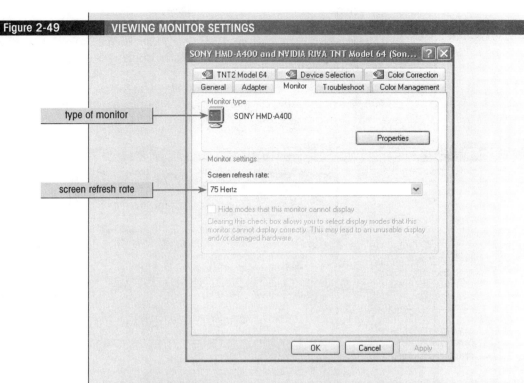

type of monitor

screen refresh rate

3. Click the **Adapter** tab, examine the information about the adapter (including the amount of video memory), and then click the **List All Modes** button. In the List All Modes dialog box, Windows XP lists all combinations of resolutions, color settings, and refresh frequencies available on your computer. See Figure 2-50. Your settings might differ. If you choose an available mode in the List of valid modes box, Windows XP adjusts the screen resolution, color depth, and refresh rate in one step.

| Figure 2-50 | VIEWING ADAPTER DISPLAY MODES |

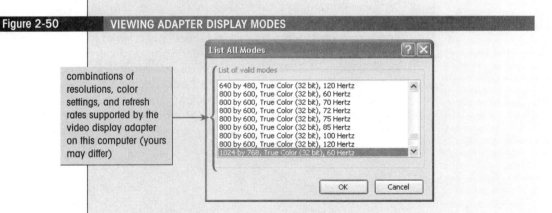

combinations of resolutions, color settings, and refresh rates supported by the video display adapter on this computer (yours may differ)

4. Click the **Cancel** button (to close this dialog box without making changes), and then click the **Troubleshoot** tab. Windows XP notes that if you are having trouble with your graphics hardware, you might be able to resolve the problem by adjusting the hardware acceleration, and thereby disable features of the video display adapter. See Figure 2-51. If the slider bar is set to "Full" hardware acceleration, all accelerations of the video display adapter are enabled. Windows XP recommends you use this setting if your computer has no problems. As you

move the slider bar to the left one notch at a time, you reduce or eliminate accelerator functions to correct problems with the mouse pointer, unexpected program errors, and other severe problems, such as the computer not responding. Windows XP updates the information below the slider bar to show you how a setting might resolve a problem. The settings on this property sheet are usually chosen as a last resort, or as a temporary measure while you try to resolve the problem.

Figure 2-51   VIEWING HARDWARE ACCELERATION SETTINGS

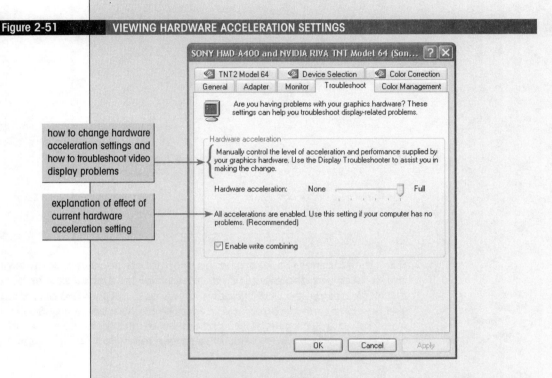

how to change hardware acceleration settings and how to troubleshoot video display problems

explanation of effect of current hardware acceleration setting

5. Click the **Cancel** button to close the Properties dialog box for your monitor and display adapter.

6. Click the **Cancel** button to close the Display Properties dialog box.

If you are having problems with your video display, try the Troubleshoot button on the Settings property sheet. If you click this button, Windows XP opens the Help and Support Center and selects the Video Display Troubleshooter so you can use this wizard to help you analyze and resolve video problems step by step.

REFERENCE WINDOW | RW

<u>Checking Video Display Settings</u>

- If you have a Control Panel toolbar on the desktop, click the Display button, and then click the Settings tab; otherwise, right-click the desktop, click Properties, and then click the Settings tab.
- Click the Advanced button.
- Check the General property sheet for the DPI and Compatibility settings, the Adapter property sheet for all the possible display modes on your computer, the Monitor property sheet for your computer screen's refresh rate, the Troubleshoot property sheet for dealing with video display problems, and the Color Management property for selecting color profiles for use with your video display. Carefully read the documentation for your video adapter and monitor before making changes to any of these settings.
- If you have video display problems that you were unable to resolve, click the Troubleshoot button on the Settings property sheet to open and use the Video Display Troubleshooter.
- To exit the Properties dialog box for your monitor and video display adapter without making changes, click the Cancel button, and then click Cancel to close the Display Properties dialog box. If you have made changes that you know you want to keep, click the OK button to close each of these dialog boxes and apply the changes to your system.

As noted earlier, by clicking Cancel, you can explore property settings so you know what's available if you ever need to locate and change a setting, and you can then gracefully back out of a dialog box without accidentally applying settings to your computer that you do not want or which might create problems that you did not expect.

If you work with desktop publishing, graphics, and digital photography applications, you more than likely want to check and adjust the resolution and color settings on your computer so that you can see a more realistic representation of an image or document on the monitor. You might also need to invest in a higher-performance video display adapter card with ample amounts of video RAM, as well as a computer with a high-performance processor.

Customizing a Screen Saver

A **screen saver** is a program that Windows XP automatically starts if you have not used the mouse or keyboard for a certain period of time, and it usually displays a moving image on the monitor. Although most people use screen savers because they are interesting, originally screen savers were used to prevent burn-in of an image on the monitor. That's not a concern with the monitors in use today. You can also customize screen savers, and if necessary, turn on password protection so that if you are away from your computer after the screen saver becomes active, Windows XP requires that you (or someone else) enter a password to gain access to your computer or, if fast user switching is enabled, require you to log on again under your password.

While optimizing the screen resolution, color setting, and refresh rate on the computer used by one of the staff scientists, you also realize that he would benefit from the use of a password-protected screen saver. If he leaves his workstation to answer the phone, run an errand, or attend a meeting, then he can prevent any changes to the molecular models he's evaluating while he is away. You offer to show him how to select and password-protect a screen saver.

To select and customize a screen saver:

1. Open the Display Properties dialog box, and then click the **Screen Saver** tab. On the Screen Saver property sheet, you can select and customize a screen saver. See Figure 2-52. The default screen saver is Windows XP, which displays a moving Windows XP logo when the screen saver is active.

Figure 2-52	VIEWING SCREEN SAVER PROPERTY SHEET OPTIONS

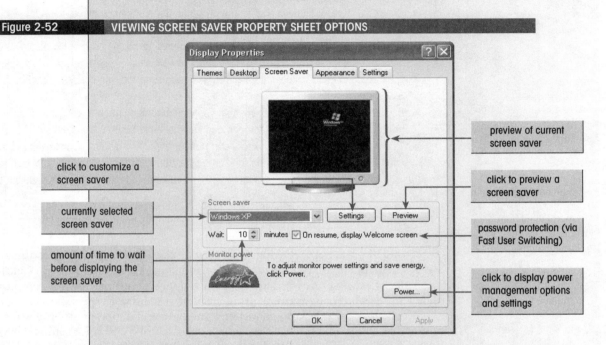

2. Click the **Screen saver** list arrow, and then click **3D Pipes**. Windows XP displays a preview of this screen saver in the preview area represented by a monitor. See Figure 2-53. As you can tell from the preview, this screen saver draws three-dimensional pipes of different colors on the monitor when the screen saver is active.

   TROUBLE? If you do not have the 3D Pipes screen saver, select another screen saver and adapt this step and the remaining steps in this section for the use of that screen saver, or just read, but not keystroke, this step and the remaining steps in this section.

   TROUBLE? If Windows displays the text "No preview available" in the preview area, your 3D Pipes screen saver will probably still work when you preview it full screen in the next step.

Figure 2-53	PREVIEWING ANOTHER SCREEN SAVER

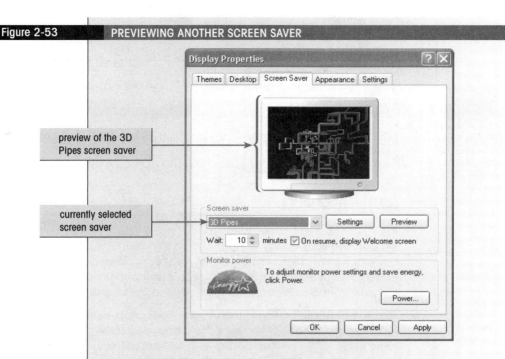

preview of the 3D
Pipes screen saver

currently selected
screen saver

3. Click the **Preview** button, remove your hand from the mouse, and do not touch the keyboard or mouse. Windows XP previews the screen saver in full-screen mode.

4. After you have viewed the screen saver for a short while (you might want to let it cycle through one full set of drawing pipes before the image dissolves and it starts over), move the mouse to turn off the display of the screen saver and return to the Display Properties dialog box.

5. Click the **Settings** button under Screen Saver (not the Settings tab). Windows XP displays the 3D Pipes Settings dialog box. See Figure 2-54. For those screen savers that you can customize, the Settings dialog box contains different options unique to the screen saver you select. For this screen saver, you can specify a single pipe (the default) or multiple pipes, you can specify a solid (the default) or textured surface style, you can select a joint type—Elbow (the default), Ball, Mixed (a mixture of Elbow and Ball), or Cycle (another mix of Elbow and Ball joint types), and you can set the speed with which the screen saver draws the 3D pipes. The textured option allows you to browse and choose a Texture File—a file with the "bmp," "jpg," "tga" (for Targa), or "png" file extension. The **Targa**, or **TGA** file format, is a bitmap file format for 24-bit and 32-bit color images. Once you choose a graphic image, the image is repeated across the surface of the 3D pipes when the screen saver is active.

Figure 2-54   **VIEWING OPTIONS FOR CUSTOMIZING A SCREEN SAVER**

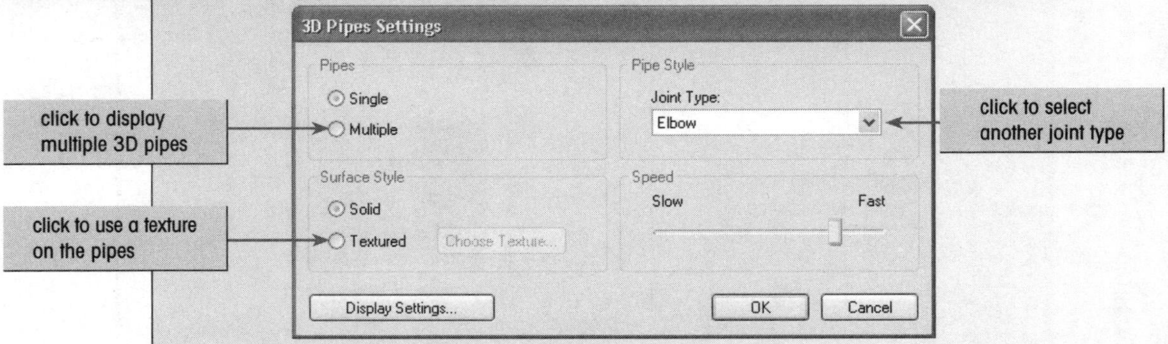

click to display multiple 3D pipes

click to use a texture on the pipes

click to select another joint type

You can use the Display Settings button to determine whether this screen saver supports hardware 3D rendering on your computer, and to choose a display mode for your video adapter that works well with your screen saver settings. However, Windows XP automatically determines these settings.

6. Click the **Multiple** option button in the Pipes area, click the **Textured** option button under Surface Style, click the **Choose Texture** button, click the **View Menu** button on the toolbar in the Choose Texture File dialog box, click **Details**, click the **Size** column button to arrange files in order by file size, scroll down the folder and file list, click **Blue Lace 16.bmp** (or another small bitmap image file), click the **Joint Type** list arrow under Pipe Style, click **Ball**, click the **OK** button, click the **Preview** button, remove your hand from the mouse, and do not touch the keyboard or move the mouse. Windows XP previews your custom screen saver in full-screen mode, and you can see how Windows XP applies a texture to this screen saver.

7. To restore the default settings for the 3D Pipes screen saver, click the **Screen saver** list arrow, click **3D Pipes**, click the **Settings** button under Screen Saver, and after Windows XP opens the 3D Pipes Settings dialog box, click the **Single** option button under Pipes, click the **Solid** option button under Surface Style, click the **Joint Type** list arrow under Pipe Style, click **Elbow** in the Joint Type list, and then click the **OK** button to close the 3D Pipes Settings dialog box and return to the Display Properties dialog box.

Using the Wait list box, you can specify how long you want Windows XP to wait before it displays a screen saver. On the computer used for this figure, notice that there is "On resume, display Welcome screen" check box with a check mark. If Fast User Switching is available and enabled on your computer (in other words, it's part of a workgroup or it's a standalone computer, as is the case for the computer used for this figure), this check box is available. If the screen saver becomes active, and you touch a key or the mouse, Windows XP displays the Welcome screen so that you can log on under your user account.

If your computer is part of a network domain, or if Fast User Switching is turned off, Windows XP instead displays an "On resume, password protect" check box in which you can enable password protection for the screen saver. Your screen saver password is the same as your logon password. If the screen saver becomes active, Windows XP locks your computer. When you touch a key or the mouse, Windows XP prompts you for your password to unlock and gain access to your computer.

Choosing and Customizing a Screen Saver

- If you have a Control Panel toolbar on the desktop, click the Display button, and then click the Screen Saver tab; otherwise, right-click the desktop, click Properties, and then click the Screen Saver tab.
- Click the Screen saver list arrow, and then click the name of the screen saver you want to use.
- To preview the screen saver in full-screen mode, click the Preview button, remove your hand from the mouse, and do not touch the keyboard or mouse.
- After you have viewed the screen saver for a short while, move the mouse to turn off the display of the screen saver and return to the Display Properties dialog box.
- If you want to customize a screen saver (assuming the screen saver includes options for customizing it), click the Settings button under Screen Saver (not the Settings tab), specify the settings you want to use for that screen saver, and then click the OK button to close the Settings dialog box.
- To preview the changes you made to your screen saver, click the Preview button, remove your hand from the mouse, and do not touch the keyboard or move the mouse.
- After you have viewed the screen saver for a short while, move the mouse to turn off the display of the screen saver and return to the Display Properties dialog box and Screen Saver property sheet.
- Close the Display Properties dialog box.

You can also create a custom screen saver that uses your own personal pictures. Before you can use this feature, you must have a folder with two or more pictures contained in it. For the next set of steps, you will use the graphic images in the Wallpaper folder. If you prefer, you can choose another folder and use your own set of pictures as you try this feature.

To create a custom screen saver with your own pictures:

1. Click the **Screen saver** list arrow, click **My Pictures Slideshow**, and then click the **Settings** button under Screen Saver (not the Settings tab). Windows XP opens the My Pictures Screen Saver Options dialog box. See Figure 2-55. You can use slider bars to specify the interval of time between each picture and the size of the pictures relative to the screen, you can browse and locate the folder that contains the pictures you want to use, you can stretch small pictures to fit the setting you specify for the picture size, you can show the filename of each picture displayed on the screen, you can use transition effects between pictures, and you can scroll through pictures using the keyboard without turning off the screen saver.

Figure 2-55   SPECIFYING OPTIONS FOR A SCREEN SAVER SLIDE SHOW

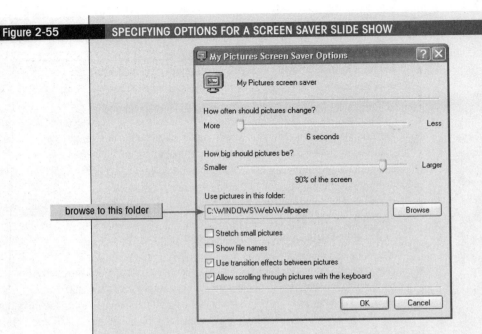

browse to this folder

2. Click the **Browse** button, and in the Browse for Folder dialog box, scroll and locate the Windows folder (it might be named Windows or Winnt), click the **expand view** button ⊞ to the left of the Windows folder icon, scroll and locate the **Web** folder under the Windows folder, click ⊞ to the left of the Web folder icon, click the **Wallpaper** folder icon, click the **OK** button in the Browse for Folder dialog box, click the **Allow scrolling through pictures with the keyboard** check box and add a check mark (if it is not already selected), click the **OK** button in the My Pictures Screen Saver Options dialog box, click the **Preview** button, remove your hand from the mouse, and do not move the mouse. Windows XP previews your custom screen saver in full-screen mode, displays each picture in the Web folder using a different transition effect every six seconds. See Figure 2-56. If you have used Microsoft PowerPoint, then you may recognize the same transition effects that are available in that Office application for preparing presentations.

Figure 2-56   VIEWING AN IMAGE IN A SCREEN SAVER SLIDE SHOW

3. After viewing the slide show for a short while, press the → and ← to scroll from picture to picture.

4. Move the mouse to turn off the slide show and return to the Display Properties dialog box.

5. To restore the default slide show settings, click the **Settings** button under Screen Saver, click the **Browse** button and in the Browser for Folder dialog box, locate and click the default My Pictures folder for your user account under the Documents and Settings folder, and then My Documents folder or the folder that you want to use for your own slide shows, and then click the **OK** button to close the Browse for Folder dialog box, click the **Allow scrolling through pictures with the keyboard** check box and remove the check mark (if it did not originally have a check mark), click the **OK** button in the My Pictures Screen Saver Options dialog box, and return to the Display Properties dialog box.

6. To restore your original screen saver setting or choose the default screen saver option, click the **Screen saver** list arrow, choose your original screen saver or click **(None)**, and then click the **Apply** button.

7. Keep the Display Properties dialog box open for the next section of the tutorial.

REFERENCE WINDOW   **RW**

Creating a Slide Show Screen Saver Using Your Own Pictures

- If you have a Control Panel toolbar on the desktop, click the Display button, and then click the Screen Saver tab; otherwise, right-click the desktop, click Properties, and then click the Screen Saver tab.
- Click the Screen saver list arrow, and then click My Pictures Slideshow.
- Click the Settings button (not the Settings tab), and in the My Pictures Screen Saver Options dialog box, choose the settings that you want to use for your custom slide show, click the Browse button to open the Browse for Folder dialog box so that you can locate the folder that contains two or more pictures for use with the slide show, click the OK button to close the Browse for Folder dialog box, and then click the OK button to close the My Pictures Screen Saver Options dialog box.
- To preview the slide show screen saver, click the Preview button, remove your hand from the mouse, and do not touch the keyboard or move the mouse.
- After you have viewed the screen saver for a short while, move the mouse to turn off the display of the screen saver and return to the Display Properties dialog box and Screen Saver property sheet.
- Close the Display Properties dialog box.

With the new Windows XP My Pictures Slideshow screen saver, you can now use photos that you take with your digital camera or create with your scanner, or pictures that you download from the Web (assuming they are not copyrighted), and create custom slide shows that you can use as screen savers.

Using Power Management

In Windows XP, you can choose a **power scheme**, or combination of settings that manages power usage on your computer and, if necessary, you can customize those settings. If the hardware in your computer supports power management, then Windows XP can conserve power automatically by:

- Turning off your monitor and hard disk(s)
- Placing your computer in standby mode when it is idle (i.e., not being used)
- Placing your computer in hibernation mode

For Windows XP to use standby or hibernation mode, your computer must support the **Advanced Configuration and Power Interface (ACPI)**. ACPI is a set of power-management specifications developed by Microsoft, Intel, and Toshiba that allow the Windows XP operating system to control the amount of power that each device receives. Windows XP monitors the power state of the computer, determines the power needs of applications and hardware devices, and increases or decreases the availability of power as needed by the computer system.

In **Standby mode**, Windows XP turns off your monitor and hard disk, and reduces the computer's power usage. If you press a key or move the mouse, the operating system resumes power to the monitor and hard disk. If you decide to use standby mode, you should manually save your work first. If a power failure occurs in standby mode, you lose whatever information is currently stored in RAM. In **Hibernation mode**, Windows XP turns off your monitor and hard disk, saves everything in memory to a hidden file named Hiberfil.sys in the top-level folder of drive C, and turns off your computer. The next time you start your computer, Windows XP uses Hiberfil.sys to restore your system and the contents of memory to the condition it was in when your computer went into hibernation mode, and you can immediately pick up where you left off in whatever applications and documents you were using prior to hibernation. You do not need to save your work; however, that is always a good precaution against problems you might not anticipate.

If you have a UPS device, then you can also specify settings for that device. A **UPS** is a device that relies on a battery backup to provide power to a computer for a short interval of time (such as a few minutes) so that you can save your work and shut down your computer. The UPS device can signal the operating system via a COM port (or Communications port) about a problem, such as a power failure.

At the urging of environmentally conscious employees, Thorsen Pharmaceuticals recently launched a drive to conserve energy. Jaime wants you to show employees how to use the power-saving features in Windows XP to reduce power consumption when their computers remain idle for any length of time.

The hardware documentation on your computer and its peripheral components tell you whether components in your computer support power management. You should review this information before you make changes to the power-savings features on your computer. Furthermore, the BIOS also contain settings which affect power management, and which might conflict with Windows (you examine the BIOS in Tutorial 8), so you might need to open the BIOS Setup utility and examine the settings for your computer. Also, you must have Administrator privileges to make certain changes to power management settings on a computer.

If you do not want to make changes to the power management settings on the computer you are using, or if you are not permitted to make these changes in your computer lab, read, but do not keystroke, this section.

To select a power management scheme:

1. If the Display Properties dialog box is still open, click the **Power** button on the Screen Saver property sheet; otherwise, point to the right edge of the desktop and then click the **Power Options** button on the Control Panel toolbar. Windows XP opens a Power Options Properties dialog box. See Figure 2-57.

The types of property sheets that you see in the Power Options Properties dialog box, and the options available on each property sheet vary depending on your computer's hardware. At the top of the Power Schemes property sheet, Windows XP recommends that you select a power scheme that is appropriate to how you use your computer. On the computer used for this figure, Windows uses the Home/Office Desk power scheme to turn off the monitor if there is no keyboard or mouse activity for 20 minutes, but Windows XP does not turn off the hard disk.

| Figure 2-57 | VIEWING POWER MANAGEMENT OPTIONS (YOURS MAY DIFFER) |

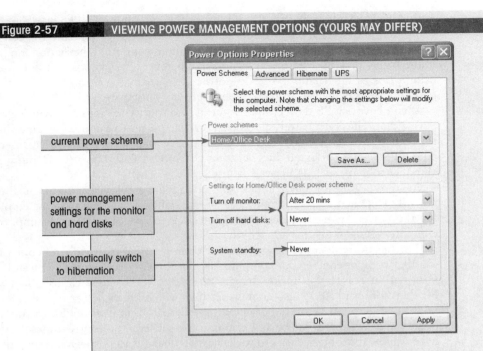

current power scheme

power management settings for the monitor and hard disks

automatically switch to hibernation

2. Click the **Power schemes** list arrow. As shown in Figure 2-58, you see power schemes such as Home/Office, Portable/Laptop, Presentation, Always On, Minimal Power Management, and Max Battery, each of which changes the settings for the monitor, hard disks, and system standby, and each of which is designed to optimize power management under different use conditions.

If System standby is enabled on your computer, in the System standby list box, you can choose an interval of time after which Windows XP places your computer into system standby. If Hibernation is enabled on your computer, Windows XP also displays a System hibernates list box from which you can choose an interval of time before the system hibernates.

Figure 2-58   VIEWING POWER SCHEME OPTIONS

list of power schemes

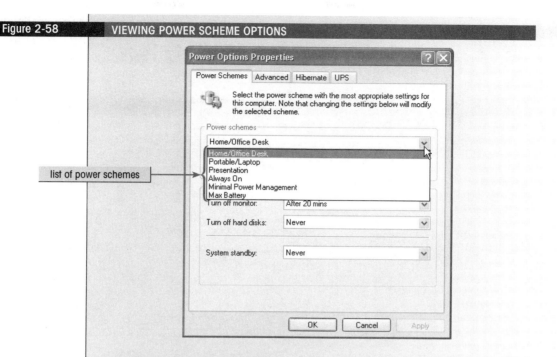

3. Click the **Power schemes** list arrow again to close the power schemes list, and then click the **Advanced** tab. On the Advanced property sheet, you can specify additional power-saving options. See Figure 2-59. The "Always show icon on the taskbar" option in the Options section will display a power icon in the Notification area on the taskbar so that you can quickly open the Power Options Properties dialog box. If your computer supports standby mode, you can also have Windows XP prompt you for a password when your computer comes out of standby mode. In the Power buttons section (if available on your computer), you can specify what action Windows XP should take when you press the power on/off button on your computer: you can specify that Windows XP do nothing, ask you what to do, switch to standby mode, switch to hibernation mode, or shut down the system and turn off all power.

TROUBLE? If power settings are dimmed, you are not logged on your computer under a user account with Administrator privileges.

Figure 2-59   VIEWING ADVANCED POWER OPTIONS

option for showing a power icon in the Notification area

option for controlling how the computer responds to the power button

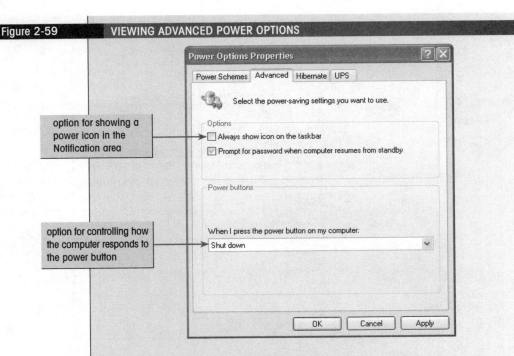

4. Click the **Hibernate** tab. On the Hibernate property sheet, Windows XP explains how Hibernation works. See Figure 2-60. If you enable hibernation on a computer, Windows XP will show how much disk space it will use to store the contents of memory onto the hard disk before shutdown. That amount of disk space matches the amount of installed RAM in your computer.

TROUBLE? If you do not see a Hibernate tab, your computer does not support hibernation. Read this step, and then continue with the next step.

Figure 2-60   VIEWING HIBERNATION OPTIONS

option for enabling hibernation

size of the Hiberfil.sys file in the top-level folder of hard disk (same size as amount of installed RAM)

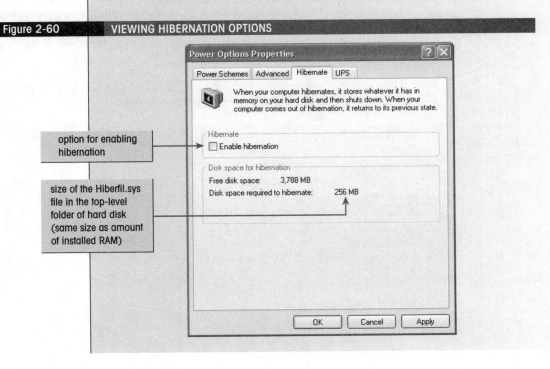

5. Click the **UPS** tab. The UPS property sheet shows settings for your Uninterruptible Power Supply (UPS), if you have one. See Figure 2-61. The UPS settings depend on the specific type of hardware installed on your computer.

   If you have a UPS device connected to a COM port, you can see the current status of that device, and then configure the device. On the computer used for this figure, no UPS device is attached to a COM port (hence, the Status portion of this sheet is dimmed). If a UPS device is attached, the Status area will report the type of power source (AC power or UPS battery power), the estimated UPS runtime, or the number of minutes that the device's battery can support the computer before it must be shut down, the estimated capacity of the UPS (expressed as a percentage of its maximum capacity), and the condition of the battery. In the Details area, you use the Select button (if you have Administrator privileges) to specify the type of UPS device and the COM port to which it is connected, and the Configure button to show how your system is set to respond during critical power events.

Figure 2-61   **VIEWING UPS POWER OPTIONS**

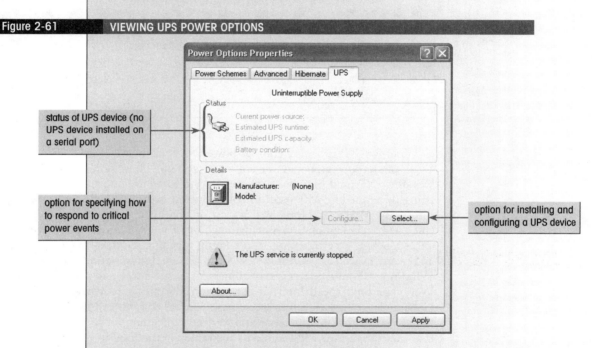

status of UPS device (no UPS device installed on a serial port)

option for specifying how to respond to critical power events

option for installing and configuring a UPS device

6. Click the **Cancel** button to close the Power Options Properties dialog box without inadvertently making any changes.

Power management is particularly important in the case of portable computers, because these features can double or triple the lifetime of the battery in the computer. Furthermore, the use of power-saving features on PCs, now commonplace in offices and homes, can not only significantly reduce the cost of electricity to both business and home users, but can also improve the quality of the environment by reducing the amount of fossil fuel burned.

Checking Power Management Settings

- If you want to change or specify standby or hibernation settings, log on your computer as a member of the Administrators group.
- If you have a Control Panel toolbar on the desktop, click the Power Options button, and then click the Settings tab; otherwise, right-click the desktop, click Properties, click the Screen Saver tab in the Display Properties dialog box, and then click the Power button under Monitor power.
- On the Power Schemes property sheet in the Power Options Properties dialog box, select the power scheme you want to use from the Power schemes list box, or change the settings in the Settings area for turning off the monitor, turning off the hard disks, and activating System Standby, if available.
- Click the Advanced tab, and specify power-saving settings, such as displaying a power icon on the taskbar, prompting for a password when the computer comes out of standby mode, and specifying how Windows XP should respond to the use of the power button on your computer.
- Click the Hibernate tab, and decide whether to enable (or turn off) Hibernation mode.
- Click the UPS tab, use the Select button to select the UPS device attached to a COM port, use the Configure button to specify how Windows XP should respond during critical power events, and use the information in the Status area to view statistics on the UPS device.
- Click the OK button to close the Power Options Properties dialog box and apply your changes, or click Cancel to avoid making any inadvertent changes to power-management settings.

Windows XP can also control power to consumer devices, such as a telephone, TV, VCR, or stereo, connected to a computer system. These power management capabilities of Windows XP (and previous versions of Windows) are a forerunner of newer technologies being developed by Microsoft in collaboration with major appliance manufacturers. In the future, the Microsoft Home will consist of a home network connected to consumer devices (such as your telephone, answering machine, TV, VCR, and DVD player), consumer appliances (such as a refrigerator, dishwashing machine, clothes washing machine, microwave, and oven), as well as your home's security system, temperature control system, and lighting. Windows will be able to control all devices in the home and provide access not only to the Web via a high-speed Internet connection, but also subscriber services such as cable TV. Consumer appliances will essentially be "smart" computers that communicate information, such as scheduled maintenance and warranty information, to Windows. It is even expected that the refrigerator will be able to keep track of the food in your refrigerator, and communicate this information to your computer so that you will have an up-to-date list of what to purchase online. Your Microsoft Home will be able to monitor the activity of children or a newborn baby, provide you with access to your CD and video libraries as well as personal photographs in every room of your home, display an image on your computer of the visitor at your front door (and probably also provide detailed information on that individual), regulate temperature and lighting from room to room to meet your needs at any given moment, manage your sprinkler system, control the lighting, temperature, and humidity in your greenhouse, provide an up-to-date inventory of your home, assist you with bank transactions as well as bill and loan payments, and manage your investments.

Restoring **Your Computer's Settings**

If you work in a computer lab, you need to restore the original settings to the computer you used. If you used your own computer, you might want to restore some or all of the original settings.

To restore your computer's settings:

1. If you want to remain in Web view, but restore your original desktop theme, open the Display Properties dialog box, if necessary, click the **Themes** tab, click the **Theme** list arrow, click **Windows XP** or the desktop theme you want to use, and then click the **Apply** button.

2. If you want to remove the My Documents and My Computer icons from the desktop, click the **Desktop** tab in the Display Properties dialog box, click the **Customize Desktop** button, click the **My Documents** and **My Computer** check boxes (and remove the check mark from each), click the **OK** button to close the Desktop Items dialog box, and then click the **OK** button.

3. If you want to restore the default Folder options and view settings, open My Computer, click **Tools** on the menu bar, click **Folder Options**, click the **View** tab, click the **Do not show hidden files and folders** option button in the Advanced settings box, click the **Hide extensions for known file types** check box to add a check mark and enable this option, click the **OK** button, and then close My Computer.

4. If you want to remove the My Documents icon from the Quick Launch toolbar, drag the My Documents icon to the Recycle Bin. If you want to empty the Recycle Bin, right-click the **Recycle Bin** icon, and then click **Empty the Recycle Bin**. Click the **Yes** button to confirm, if necessary. You may also want to drag the Recycle Bin back to its original position in the lower-right corner of the desktop (Windows XP moved it when you displayed your home page on the desktop).

5. If you want to remove the Quick Launch toolbar from the taskbar, right-click the **taskbar**, point to **Toolbars**, and then click **Quick Launch**.

6. If you want to lock the taskbar, right-click the **taskbar**, and then click **Lock the Taskbar**.

7. If you want to restore your mouse settings, click **Mouse** on the Control Panel toolbar, restore the original settings, and then click the **OK** button to close the Mouse Properties dialog box.

8. If you want to remove My Recent Documents and Favorites from the Start menu, right-click the **Start** button, click **Properties**, click the **Customize** button, click the **Advanced** tab in the Customize Start Menu dialog box, click and remove the check mark from the **Favorites menu** check box under Start menu items, click and remove the check mark from the **List my most recently opened documents** check box under Recent documents, restore any other Start menu settings you changed, click the **OK** button to close the Customize Start Menu dialog box, and then click the **OK** button to close the Taskbar and Start Menu Properties dialog box.

9. Right-click the **Control Panel label** on the Control Panel toolbar, click **Close Toolbar**, and then click the **OK** button in the Confirm Toolbar Close dialog box.

10. If you switched from Windows Classic style to Web style at the beginning of the tutorial and want to switch back to Windows Classic style, open the Display Properties dialog box, click the **Theme** list box arrow on the Themes property sheet, click **Windows Classic**, and then click the **OK** button. Right-click the **Start** button, click **Properties**, click the **Classic Start menu** option button, and then click the **OK** button. Click the **Start** button, point to **Settings**, click **Control Panel**, click **Switch to Classic View** in the Control Panel dynamic menu, and then click the **Folder Options** icon. After Windows XP opens the Folder Options dialog box, click **Use Windows classic folders** under Tasks on the General property sheet, click the **Double-click to open an item** option button under "Click items as follows," click the **OK** button, and then close the **Control Panel**.

As you have discovered with Jaime's help, Windows XP has a wide variety of options for customizing your working environment and simplifying many of your daily tasks. You can adapt Windows XP to the way you work, to the types of applications you use, and to the types of documents you create.

REVIEW ASSIGNMENTS

Thorsen Pharmaceuticals has decided to open another research facility in Brazil. The scientists at that facility will study the flora of the rain forests of South America in an effort to discover new drugs to develop and market. Jaime is responsible for customizing the first set of computers that the company will ship to its new research facility. To meet a short deadline, Jaime enlists your assistance. Jaime has already prepared a list of directions for customizing the computers so that all the computers have the same settings.

As you complete each step, record your answers to questions so that you can submit them to your instructor. Use a word-processing application such as Word or WordPad to prepare and then print your answers to these questions. Also, if you change any settings on the computer you are using, note the original settings so that you can restore them later.

1. If necessary, switch to Web style.

2. Right-click the desktop, select Properties, select the Desktop property sheet, click the Customize Desktop button, and add the My Computer, My Documents, and My Network Places icons to the desktop.

3. Right-click the taskbar, point to Toolbars, and add the Quick Launch toolbar to the taskbar.

4. Right-click the taskbar, and unlock the taskbar by removing the check mark next to "Lock the Taskbar."

5. Drag My Computer, My Documents, and My Network Places from the desktop and add them to the Quick Launch toolbar. Is there any advantage to placing these objects on the Quick Launch toolbar? If so, explain.

6. Right-click the desktop, select Properties, select the Desktop property sheet, click the Customize Desktop button, and remove the My Computer, My Documents, and My Network Places icons from the desktop.

7. Right-click the taskbar, point to Toolbars, and select New Toolbar. Under My Documents, select My Pictures, and then click the OK button. Drag the My Pictures toolbar from the taskbar onto the desktop, dock the toolbar on the right side of the

desktop, and adjust its width so that you can read the options on the toolbar. What types of objects do you see on the My Pictures toolbar? What specific types of files are contained in your My Pictures folder? *Hint*: If you point to an object for a moment, Windows XP displays a ScreenTip that provides information about the object. Is there any advantage(s) to creating a My Pictures and a My Music toolbar on the desktop? If so, explain.

8. Locate and then click a file with a graphic image on the My Pictures toolbar. What happens?

9. Close any open windows.

10. Right-click the My Pictures toolbar title, choose the option to close this toolbar, and then confirm your action.

11. Create a Control Panel toolbar on the taskbar, drag the Control Panel toolbar from the taskbar, dock it on the right side of the desktop, adjust its width, right-click the Control Panel toolbar title, and choose the option for Auto-Hide.

12. Open the Mouse Properties dialog box, pick and test three different mouse settings, and then describe how each of these settings changes your use of the mouse. Restore the original mouse settings.

13. From the Mouse Properties dialog box, choose the Old Fashioned pointer scheme (or another pointer scheme if that one is not available), apply it to your system, and then test the use of the new mouse pointer shape for selecting, opening, and moving objects. Test the select text mouse pointer shape for entering text in a text box (such as when entering a filename for a document), the resize mouse pointer shapes for adjusting the width and/or height of a window, and logging off and then logging back onto your computer system. Was it difficult or easy to work with these mouse pointer shapes? Would you benefit in your work from using a pointer scheme like this one, or from a custom mouse pointer scheme that you design? If so, explain. Restore the original pointer scheme and mouse pointer shapes on your computer. Close the Mouse Properties dialog box.

14. Right-click the desktop, click Properties, and after the Display Properties dialog box opens, choose the Windows XP theme in the Theme list box on the Themes property sheet, if necessary.

15. From the Display Properties dialog box, change the Background wallpaper option to Red moon desert (or another background option of your own choice). From the Position list box, choose the option for centering the wallpaper, and then close the Display Properties dialog box and apply the wallpaper to the desktop. Does the background wallpaper fill the entire desktop? Is there an advantage to centering rather than stretching a wallpaper option that does not fill the entire desktop? If so, explain.

16. Open the Display Properties dialog box, and select the Settings property sheet. What is your current resolution? What is your current color depth setting? Change your screen resolution to the next lower resolution (if available) on your computer, and then view the wallpaper. Did the quality of the background wallpaper improve when you decreased the resolution? If so, explain. Open the Display Properties dialog box again, and increase the screen resolution to the next higher resolution (if available) over the one you typically use. Did the quality of the background wallpaper improve when you increased the resolution? If so, explain.

17. Open the Display Properties dialog box, select the Settings property sheet, and restore your original resolution. What is your current resolution? What is your current color depth setting? Change your color depth setting to the next lower setting (if available) on your computer, and then view the wallpaper. Did the quality of the background wallpaper

improve when you decreased the color depth setting? If so, explain. In the Display Properties dialog box, increase the color depth setting to the next higher setting (if available) over the one you typically use. (If you have only two color depth settings, then use the next available one.) Did the quality of the background wallpaper improve when you increased the color depth setting? If so, explain.

18. In the Display Properties dialog box, select the Settings property sheet, and restore your original resolution and color depth setting.

19. From the Display Properties dialog box, select the Appearance property sheet, and then click the Effects button. Examine how the "Show window contents while dragging" option affects the performance of your computer when you turn this feature on and off. In each case, open the My Computer window, and if the window is maximized, click the Restore Down button ⧉ and then resize the window so that it's somewhat smaller than the desktop. In each case, drag the window to a different location on the desktop. Does this feature adversely affect the performance of your computer? If so, explain. If not, what does this tell you about the quality of your system? Is this a feature that enhances your use of a computer, even if it places demands on the performance of your computer? If so, explain. Restore the original settings on the Effects property sheet.

20. In the Display Properties dialog box, select the Screen Saver property sheet, and then choose 3D Text from the Screen saver list box. Click the Settings button (not the Settings tab), and in the 3D Text Settings dialog box, change the Custom Text from "Microsoft Windows" to "Thorsen" (without the quotation marks). Under Motion, select and then preview each of the four different Rotation Types (Spin, See-saw, Wobble, and Tumble). Restore your original Rotation Type. Under Surface Style, select and preview Solid Color, Texture, and Reflection. Describe how these three options change the appearance of the text when previewed. Then select and preview the Texture and Reflection Surface Styles with a Custom Texture and Custom Reflection using a bitmap image file of your own choice from the Windows folder. Restore the original Custom Text (Microsoft Windows) or text of your own choosing, restore the Rotation Type to Spin, remove the use of a Custom Texture or Custom Reflection under Surface Style, restore the Surface Style to Solid Color, and restore any other settings you changed. Close the 3D Text Settings dialog box, and from the Screen saver list, select (None) or the screen saver you typically use.

21. From the Screen Saver property sheet, click the Power button, or if you closed the Display Properties dialog box, click Power Options on the Control Panel toolbar. View the power-saving features and settings for your computer. What type of power scheme does your computer use? What is the interval of time that Windows waits before it shuts off your monitor and hard disk? Does your computer support the use of Standby or Hibernation? Is Hibernation enabled and, if so, how much disk space does Windows XP require for the hibernation file? Select the Advanced property sheet (if available). What happens when you press the power button on your computer? In other words, does it shut down, switch to Standby, or use Hibernation mode? Close the Power Options Properties dialog box without making any changes to your system.

22. In the Display Properties dialog box, restore the Windows XP desktop theme or the original desktop theme used on your computer, close the Display Properties dialog box, right-click the Control Panel toolbar and choose the option for closing the toolbar, drag the My Computer, My Documents, and My Network Places icons from the Quick Launch toolbar and place them on the desktop or drag them to the Recycle Bin, and then right-click the Recycle Bin, and choose the option for emptying the Recycle Bin.

23. Right-click the taskbar, point to Toolbars, choose the option for removing the Quick Launch toolbar from the taskbar, right-click the taskbar again, and then click "Lock the Taskbar."

CASE PROBLEMS

Case 1. Creating Custom Toolbars at Northbay Computers   Northbay Computers sells and rents computer equipment for homeowners and businesses. It also provides training and troubleshooting support for its customers. Eric Baum, a support technician at Northbay Computers, wants to create custom toolbars that will allow him to quickly access drives, folders, and files on his computer so that he can respond quickly to customer concerns on the telephone.

As you customize Windows XP, keep a record of your original computer settings so that you can restore your computer after you finish. Also, keep a record of the changes and observations you make so that you can prepare a short summary at the end of the case problem.

1. Unlock the taskbar, and then add the Quick Launch and Address toolbars to the taskbar. Adjust the width of the Address toolbar so that you can see the Address box for entering URLs.

2. Display the My Documents and My Computer icons on the desktop, add My Documents and My Computer to the Quick Launch toolbar, and then remove the My Documents and My Computer icons from the desktop.

3. Create floating toolbars for the Windows folder on drive C, the Control Panel, the Printers and Faxes folder, and My Network Places. Adjust the width of the toolbars so that you can see one column, and arrange them on the desktop for easy access. Adjust the height of the toolbars so that you can see as many menu options as possible without, of course, docking the toolbars.

4. Test the use of the buttons on the Quick Launch toolbar, access your home page or another Web site using the Address toolbar, examine some of the options available on the Windows, Control Panel, and Printers and Faxes toolbars to determine if there are any features you might find useful in the future. In the case of the Windows toolbar, you must be careful because many folders store system files critical to the operation of Windows. Examine the contents of the Cursors, Desktop, Fonts, Help, Media, Offline Web Pages, and Web Wallpaper folders. Do not start the Add Network Place, Network Setup Wizard, Connection Wizard, Add Printer Wizard, or any other wizards because you might inadvertently reconfigure your computer.

5. Using a word-processing application such as Microsoft Word or WordPad, prepare a one-page summary that describes at least one feature (or a combination of features) on each toolbar that might prove beneficial to you now or in the future.

6. Restore your computer by removing the floating toolbars from the desktop, drag My Documents and My Computer from the Quick Launch toolbar to the Recycle Bin, and empty the Recycle Bin, close the Address and Quick Launch toolbars, and then lock the taskbar.

Case 2. Customizing Display Settings at Desktop Publishing Unlimited   Desktop Publishing Unlimited is a rapidly growing, New Orleans business that employs graphic artists with skills in different specialties. Marsha Hartman, the owner and senior graphics artist in the firm, recently purchased a new computer system for herself. She wants to compare the effects of using different screen resolutions and color settings on her desktop so that she can choose the best combination to use for her work.

As you customize Windows XP, keep a record of your original computer settings so that you can restore the desktop after you finish. Also, keep a record of the changes and observations you make so that you can prepare a short summary at the end of the case problem.

Before you make changes to the screen resolution or color setting, check the documentation for your video display adapter and monitor to make sure that they support the use of those settings. Also make sure your video display and adapter are properly configured so that the options listed for the screen resolution and color quality work properly on your computer. If Windows XP does not display the wallpaper after you change a setting, or only displays part of the image, but does display the desktop, you might be able to update your desktop view by pressing the F5 (Refresh) key

1. Open the Display Properties dialog box, select the Windows XP theme, if necessary, and then select a background wallpaper image from the Background list box and apply it to the desktop, or use the Browse button to locate and apply an image in the My Pictures folder to the desktop. Stretch the image if it is large enough to stretch without distortion. If the image is relatively small, tile the background wallpaper. What image did you choose, what position option did you choose, and why did you make these choices?

2. Test each of the screen resolutions available on your computer using your current color depth setting. Start with the lowest resolution and increase the resolution to the highest one available on your computer. At each screen resolution, examine the image on the monitor and notice how the resolution affects the image. Prepare a list of each screen resolution that you tested, note the default screen resolution on your computer, and then briefly describe how the quality of the image changed with each change in the screen resolution. Also note your current color depth setting since this setting also affects the quality of the image.

3. Switch back to your default screen resolution. Test each of the color depth settings available on your computer using your current screen resolution. Start with the lowest color depth setting and increase the color depth setting to the highest one available on your computer. At each color depth setting, examine the image on the monitor and notice how the color depth setting affects the image. Prepare a list of each color depth setting that you tested, and then briefly describe how the quality of the image changed with each change in the color depth setting. Also note your current screen resolution setting since this setting also affects the quality of the image. *Note*: If you have only two color depth settings, you might want to test them at two different screen resolutions.

4. Restore your computer to its original desktop resolution, color depth setting, and background wallpaper.

5. Compare the different views, and briefly describe which view you prefer and why you prefer that combination of screen resolution and color depth setting.

Case 3. Preparing a Desktop Design for a Home Computer Windows XP provides a variety of tools, some of which you have examined in this tutorial, for customizing your desktop environment. Using what you have learned, as well as other options for customizing the user interface, design a new desktop using the guidelines that follow. If you need to review, or learn about new display options, use the Windows Help and Support Center.

As you make changes to the desktop, keep a record of the original settings so that you can restore the desktop after you finish. Also, keep a record of the changes and observations you make so that you can prepare a short summary at the end of the case problem.

1. Before you start, print a copy of your desktop, so that you have a "before" picture. Press the Print Scrn key to capture an image of the entire desktop and place it on the Windows Clipboard, open Microsoft Word or WordPad, use the Page Setup option on the File menu to change the page orientation to Landscape and all the margin settings to 0.5 inches, and then enter your name, course title, course name, lab assignment number, and any other information requested by your instructor. Also list the case problem number, resolution, color setting, and date. From the Edit menu, choose Paste to copy

the image from the Clipboard into the document, preview the document with Print Preview on the File menu, and if necessary, adjust the size of the image so that the document prints on one page. To change the size of the image, click the image, point to the handle on the lower-right corner of the image, and then drag up and to the left. Print the document. If you want to keep a copy of the document for future reference, save the document to a Zip drive, or your own computer's hard disk.

2. Use an animated GIF (which you can download from a Web site) or an HTML document (a Web page which you can save from a Web site) as background wallpaper for your new desktop.

3. If possible, increase the display resolution and color depth setting.

4. Select a 3D screen saver, and then customize the screen saver.

5. Test and select different visual effects for use with your new desktop design.

6. Test each of the three Windows color schemes, and choose the one you feel looks the best.

7. Open the Display Properties dialog box, and select the Appearance property sheet.

8. After you finish making all the changes you want to make to the desktop, print a copy of your new desktop view with the Display Properties dialog box open (to show your color scheme).

9. Using a word-processing application such as Microsoft Word or WordPad, prepare and print a short summary of the types of features that you implemented in your desktop design, which features you intend to keep, and which features you do not need. Include a brief paragraph that summarizes what you learned from experimenting with different design features.

10. If you want to restore your desktop settings, use your record of the changes you made to restore each of the settings you changed.

Case 4. Tri-City Community College's Help Desk Lorraine Jeffries works for the Help Desk at Tri-City Community College in Pennsylvania, and assists employees all over the campus with computer problems. Employees use new computers with Windows XP as well as older computers that have a limited amount of RAM and that use previous versions of Windows. As Lorraine works with users to customize their computers and resolve problems, she documents her efforts so that her coworkers can benefit from her experience.

Using what you have learned in this tutorial about customizing Windows XP, record your answers to the following questions so that you can submit them with your lab assignment. Use a word-processing application such as Word or WordPad to prepare and print your answers to these questions.

1. An employee has returned to work after a vacation to discover that his desktop no longer contains the standard icons for My Computer, My Documents, and Internet Explorer. What should he do to correct this problem?

2. Another employee has added the Quick Launch toolbar to the taskbar and then customized it by adding My Documents, My Computer, and Network Places to the toolbar; however, Windows XP does not display buttons for all the items on the toolbar. Although Windows XP does display a pop-up menu button ⟫ from which she can access all the options on the Quick Launch toolbar, she would prefer to view all the options on the toolbar. What would you recommend she do to correct this problem?

3. A new employee wants to customize his Start menu so that he can choose an option from the Control Panel, My Computer, My Documents, My Music, and My Pictures without opening a window for each folder. List the steps this employee should follow to customize the Start menu on his computer.

4. A student working in one of the college's computer labs could not get the mouse to open an object when she double-clicked in Windows Classic view. The network administrator has checked the settings on this computer, but cannot find the source of the problem. What would you recommend that she check to correct this problem?

5. A summer employee uses links on the college's home page and his department's home page to quickly look up information for students. He now wants the option of placing either Web page on his desktop so that he can click a link and quickly access the Web site with the information he needs. Explain what he should do to make both of these Web pages available as desktop items.

6. A new employee complains that the background wallpaper image she's placed on the desktop is not sharp and seems washed out. How can this employee improve the quality of the image on her computer desktop?

7. An intern working on an older computer in the Office of Admissions and Records complains that his computer is unusually slow. After watching him work on the computer, you notice that Windows XP shows the window's contents while he drags the window. What would you recommend that the intern do to improve the performance of his computer?

8. An administrative assistant working in the Enabling Services Department notices a flicker on her screen as she works. She wants to know if there is some way to correct this problem. What would you recommend?

9. A new employee in Health Services complains that his monitor "goes blank" periodically, but he is not using a screen saver. Although the image on the monitor reappears when he touches the keyboard or mouse, he wants to know if the monitor is failing and, if not, what he can do to correct this problem. What is the probable cause, and what would you recommend that he do?

10. An employee in the Graphics department wants to set up her computer so that it automatically displays graphic images designed by students in the department. Explain how this employee can accomplish her objective without purchasing a new software product specifically for this purpose.

WINDOWS XP FILE SYSTEMS

Organizing Client Files at Cressler Graphics

CASE

Cressler Graphics, Inc.

Sharon Cressler operates a home-based business called Cressler Graphics, which provides a wide range of design and graphics services for her clients in the New Orleans area. She designs company logos, brochures, newsletters, annual reports, catalogs, ads, business cards, and expensive wine bottle labels. She scans and restores photos, creates illustrations and cartoons, designs eye-catching Web graphics, and offers contract training on the use of graphic software as well as design principles. She stores the files for her client projects, contracts, proposals, and designs, on the hard disk of a computer on her home network. She also stores her business and personal records on that same computer. Since her business is growing and since turnaround times on projects are always tight, she asks you to help her develop a more effective strategy for organizing documents stored on her hard disk.

In the first part of the tutorial, you examine the importance of, and guidelines for, organizing folders and files on a hard disk. Next, you compare and contrast the FAT16, FAT32, and NTFS file systems. You format a floppy disk, and make a copy of a floppy disk and its contents, or copy files from a network drive. After you view the contents of the floppy disk, you look at the use of long filenames and aliases. Finally, you examine properties of individual folders and files, as well as group properties of a collection of files.

Organizing **Folders and Files**

Whether you work on a desktop computer, a computer connected to a network, or a laptop, one of the most important tasks you face is managing drives, folders, and files. You should periodically analyze your needs and develop a strategy for organizing the contents of your hard disk that simplifies access to your documents and software, improves your productivity, and optimizes your computer's performance.

With the rapid growth in her business, and a corresponding increase in the number of client files she must manage, Sharon wants you to help her reevaluate the organization of her computer and develop a more efficient approach for organizing her folders and files.

Organizing Your Installed Software

The software for the operating system as well as the applications, utilities, and games that you use on your computer are all stored on your hard disk. If you have a single hard disk, and if that hard disk is partitioned into one logical drive (drive C), the operating system, other software, and your document files are all installed on that one drive. If your hard disk is partitioned, or divided, into two drives (a drive C and drive D), or if you have two hard disks (a drive C and a drive D), the operating system, applications, and other software, as well as system files, are probably installed on drive C and your document files are probably stored on drive D. However, in the latter case, if you store your documents in the My Documents folders, the files for those documents are actually stored on drive C unless you specify otherwise.

   When you install an operating system, application, utility, or game on your computer, a Setup program creates folders on the hard disk and then copies the files for that software product to those folders. Most Setup programs allow you to specify the location and name of the folder that will contain the installed software; however, unless there is an overriding reason, most people use the default locations and folder names proposed by the installation program. This organization of software into folders by the installation program is important for several reasons:

■ First, the Setup program stores files for a software product together. For example, most of the software for the Windows XP operating system is installed in a Windows folder. In the Windows 9x product line, the Windows folder is usually named Windows, whereas in the Windows NT product line, it is usually named WinNT. However, Windows XP departs from that tradition, and for new installations of Windows XP, the Windows folder is named Windows. Within your Windows folder, you can find not only program and supporting files, but also close to 500 folders that contain groups of related folders and files. For a full installation of Windows XP, there might be close to 19,000 files that use 2 GB of storage space in 500 folders under the Windows folder, so there is no other choice than to organize them into folders. The Windows XP Setup program also creates a separate Program Files folder in the top-level folder of drive C for folders with other software installed as part of the operating system, such as folders for Internet Explorer, Windows Messenger, Movie Maker, Outlook Express, and Windows Media Player. Other software products, such as Microsoft Office, are also typically installed in folders within the Program Files folder. In fact, that's the primary purpose of the Program Files folder. Microsoft prefers that software developers design their software products so that the Setup program installs a software application into the Program Files folder; however, not all software developers follow that recommendation. Although the Setup program for an application installs most of the files in the folder designated for that application, dynamic link library files for applications are commonly stored in the Windows System32 or System folders. A **dynamic link library** is a file with a "dll" file extension that contains executable program code which provides support to one or more programs.

- Organizing installed software into specific folders makes it easier to update the installed software or, if necessary, uninstall and remove the software.

- Lastly, because of the massive storage capacities of hard disks, you can more easily locate the folders and files that you might need to examine, modify, document, or troubleshoot if the software is organized into folders with groups of logically-related files. Furthermore, the operating system can better manage those files.

Organizing Your Document Files

You can benefit from using folders for your own files. You can organize your files into folders to easily locate a group of files or a specific file. For example, if you create different versions of your résumé, you could store the files that contain those résumés in a single folder (or subfolder) called Resumes. When you need to open one of your résumés, you know exactly where it is. You do not have to search through different folders, trying to figure out where it might be stored on your hard disk. You can also keep those files separate from all other types of files that you use. Furthermore, when you are ready to back up your files, you can quickly locate the folders with your document files.

To assist you with organizing your files, Windows XP provides three important folders: My Documents, My Pictures, and My Music. Many applications save documents to the My Documents folder by default, and save you one important step in the process of selecting the right drive and folder for your document file. If you prefer to store your documents in a folder other than the My Documents folder, you can specify a different folder within each application.

If you store photos and other images in the My Pictures folder rather than an alternate folder, you have access to features specific to the My Pictures folder, such as displaying images in Filmstrip view so that you can quickly locate and preview images, and using dynamic menus with options for viewing the images in the folder as a slide show, ordering prints online, printing a picture, choosing and setting an image as your background wallpaper, and copying images to a CD. You might, for example, store JPEG, GIF, and bitmap image files in this folder, or other types of graphic files that you produce with your scanner or digital camera. Likewise, the My Music folder has a dynamic menu with options for playing all of the music files in the folder (or only selected music files), shopping for music online, and copying music files to an audio CD. You might store Windows Media Player files and other types of audio, or perhaps even video, files in this folder.

If your computer is part of a workgroup or a standalone system, Windows XP also provides a Shared Documents folder, a Shared Pictures folder, and a Shared Music folder where you can store documents, pictures, and music that you want to share with others who also use your computer. If your computer is part of a network domain, the Shared Documents, Shared Pictures, and Shared Music folders are not available.

If you operate a business, you want to plan the organization of folders on your hard disk so that you can find information for your clients and business. For example, suppose you operate a small business like Sharon's where you perform contract work for various clients. On your home computer, you might create a folder named Clients to track all client information, as shown in Figure 3-1. Within that folder, you might create a folder for each client for whom you do contract work. Because you more than likely perform the same type of work for each client, you probably have the same types of folders for each client so that you can track similar information. For example, within each client folder, you probably have folders for contracts, correspondence, invoices, and project information. For certain clients, you might have additional folders where you store records specific to that client. You probably also have a folder for your business records, so that you can track information, such as assets, cash flow, and taxes important to maintaining that business. If you work for just a single client or employer, and then work on multiple projects for that same client, you might prefer to organize the information on your hard disk by project rather than by client.

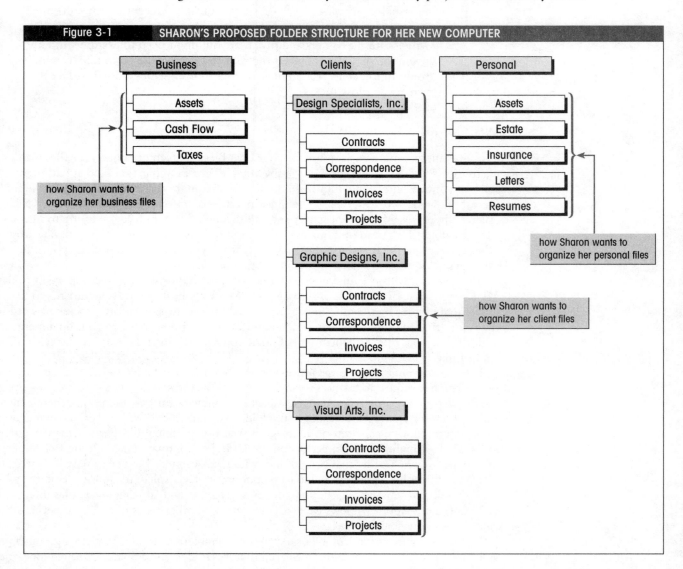

Figure 3-1   SHARON'S PROPOSED FOLDER STRUCTURE FOR HER NEW COMPUTER

You might also have a personal folder for tracking important personal information, such as your personal portfolio, personal assets (useful for bank loans and insurance), investments, estate information (such as a will), insurance information, personal correspondence, and résumés (for use with project proposals where you or your client are seeking outside sources of funding).

If you need to locate a contract for a specific client, you know exactly where to find that document. If you need to print a monthly cash flow report for your business or update your database of personal assets, you know which folders contain those files.

You could take this folder organization one step further, and store all the folders with your personal and business files under one main folder, such as My Documents, as shown in Figure 3-2. Then you can back up your files simply by selecting the My Documents folder.

Figure 3-2   ADAPTING THE FOLDER STRUCTURE TO THE MY DOCUMENTS FOLDER

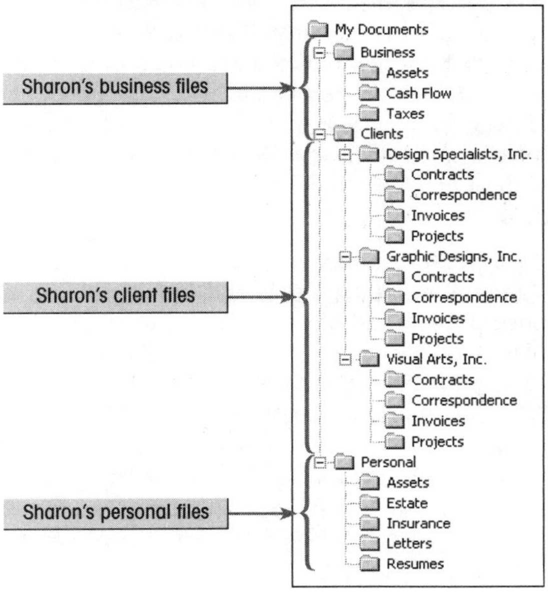

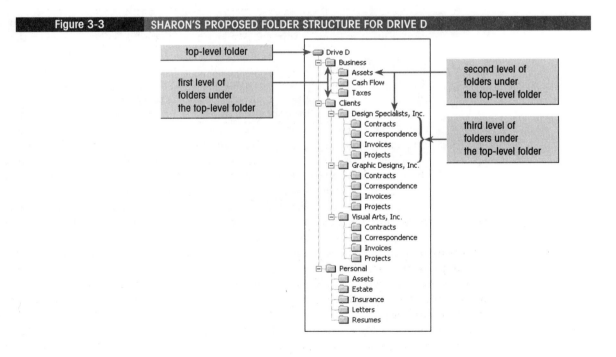

If you've partitioned your computer into two drives and store all your document files on drive D, you can organize your folders below the top-level folder of that drive, as shown in Figure 3-3.

Figure 3-3   SHARON'S PROPOSED FOLDER STRUCTURE FOR DRIVE D

Guidelines for Organizing Folders and Files

As previously noted, when you install software on your computer, the setup or install program creates and names the folders that contain the software files, although you often override this feature and specify the names you want to use. For the folders that contain your business and personal files, you want to assign folder names and filenames that clearly identify the purpose of the folders and the contents of the files.

Consider the following guidelines as you plan the organization of folders and files on your hard disk:

- **Store and organize your document folders and files within the My Documents folder.** As noted earlier, you can simplify access to your document folders and files from applications by using the My Documents folder. That also has the advantage of separating your document folders and files from those the operating system and installed software use. Another advantage is that, even though a user's My Documents folder is located three folder levels below the top-level folder of drive C, you can open this folder with a single click if you display the My Documents icon on the desktop. Also as noted, if you work with images and sound files, you can benefit from the added features associated with the My Pictures and My Music folders.

- **Limit the use of the top-level folder to system folders and files (and perhaps specific document folders).** When you or someone else formats a disk (including a hard disk), the operating system creates a top-level folder or root directory on the disk at the end of the formatting process. The top-level folder constitutes the first part of the file system for that disk and tracks information on the folders and files that you place in that folder. On a hard disk, you should reserve the top-level folder for folders with your installed software and system files as well as any document folders that you do not want to store within the My Documents folder. When you view the folders in the top-level folder of your hard disk, you want that view to look as much like a table of contents of your computer system as is possible. Then, within each of the folders in the top-level folder, you can organize files by subfolder. As noted earlier, you might create a Clients folder in the top-level folder of a drive. In the Clients folder, you would organize your client files by client name, project name, type of file (such as a Projects folder), or whatever category best suits the way in which you work. You should not store your document files in the top-level folder, but rather store them in a folder with other logically related files. The operating system and other software that you install on your computer store or create files in the top-level folder for their own use. You should leave those files there. If you move or delete those files, the operating system might not be able to boot your computer, or load an application.

- **Make sure you store software and document files in different folders.** Under the DOS operating system, it was not uncommon for applications to create a folder for document files below the folder of the application used to produce those files. This approach implies that documents are subordinate to applications—a situation which is no longer the case with document-oriented, or docucentric, operating systems such as Windows XP. As you might expect, this previous approach posed problems. If you removed the folder with the installed software, you ran the risk of removing your document folder or folders as well. If you decided to back up your files on the hard disk, you might have overlooked certain document folders that contain files important to you because they were contained with a software folder.

Furthermore, you might find that you use several applications to produce different types of files for the same general purpose. For example, you might use Microsoft Word to produce a project summary for a client. You might then use Microsoft Excel to create a spreadsheet projection or forecast for that same project, produce a three-dimensional bar chart that visually illustrates the projection or forecast, and then copy the chart into the Word project summary report. Even though you produce these files with two different applications, it makes sense to store the two files together in the same folder because they are logically related to each other. When you are working on one file, you can quickly find and open the other files if they are in the same folder.

■ **Limit your folder structure to no more than three levels below the top-level folder**. If you create a complex folder structure that extends, for example, six or seven folder levels deep, you will likely spend more time navigating from one folder to the next in order to locate files (even when opening files from an Open dialog box or choosing a folder in a Save As dialog box). If you create a folder within another folder, you should stop and evaluate whether it makes more sense to create that new folder at the same level as the other folder, or whether you should create it below the top-level folder. Sharon's folder organization shown in Figure 3-1 follows these guidelines. Although installed software, including both operating system software and other types of software, such as application software, creates a complex, multi-tiered folder structure, you do not need to follow that practice. Also consider that if you burn CDs, the software might report that the folder structure that you are copying is too complex and that it will have to modify it.

■ **Subdivide document folders when the number of files exceeds a reasonable or manageable level**. When the number of files in a folder exceeds a level that proves manageable, such as 50 or 60 files, you should stop and examine the files, and determine whether the files actually fall into two or more logical groups. If so, create new folders for those files and move the files to the new folders. You might also discover files that you thought you had lost because you did not store those files in the correct folder in the first place. If you subdivide a folder, also think about whether it makes sense to create those folders within this same folder or move all the new folders up one level in the folder structure and delete the original (and now empty) folder. *This guideline applies only to folders that contain your own files, not to folders with software. Do not reorganize the structure of folders that contain installed software; otherwise, the software will not work.*

■ **Select folder names carefully**. Windows XP, Windows 2000, Windows Me, Windows 98, Windows NT Workstation 4.0, and Windows 95, as well as applications designed for these operating systems, support long filenames with up to 255 characters. You can now name a folder to clearly identify its contents, such as Visual Arts, Inc. (one of Sharon's clients). If you are working on a network, find out if that network's operating system supports the use of long folder and file names. *If it doesn't, that network operating system will truncate (or chop off part of) and thereby modify a long filename.* You examine the features of long folder and filenames later in the tutorial.

■ **Do not move, rename, or modify folders that contain installed software**. If you move or rename a folder that contains software (for example, the Windows folder or the Microsoft Office folder), Windows XP will not be able to locate and load any of the programs stored in that folder. Although you might periodically clean some program folders of files that you know you no longer need, do not change those folders unless you know what you are doing. For example, you might want to remove bitmap image files that you no longer intend to use from the Windows folder, so that you can free up storage space on the hard disk. As a precautionary measure, if you try to open the top-level folder of drive C, Windows XP (unlike previous versions of Windows) now warns you that this folder contains files that keep your system working properly, and you should not modify its contents. See Figure 3-4.

Figure 3-4	WARNING ABOUT MAKING CHANGES TO THE FOLDERS ON DRIVE C

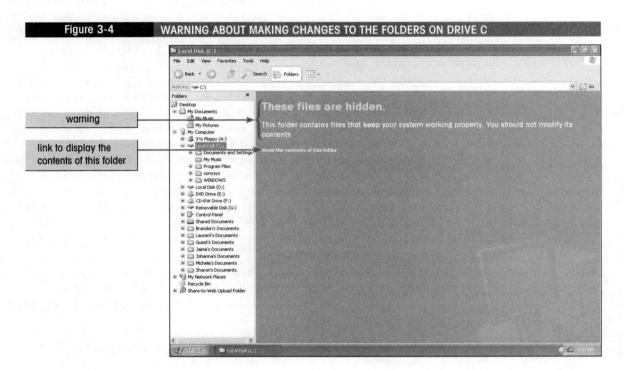

warning

link to display the contents of this folder

■ **Periodically evaluate your current document folder structure**. After you have used your computer for a while, you should reevaluate its folder structure. You might find a more efficient approach to organizing the folders that contain your files. If you do move or rename folders, you also have to update software applications so that they default to these new folders and make sure they do not inadvertently store files in a folder other than the one you expect. For example, if you work with Microsoft Word, you would open the Tools menu, select Options, and after the Options dialog box opens, select the File Locations tab. On the File Locations sheet, Word displays a list of file types (such as Documents and Clipart pictures) and the default locations (the paths to the folders where Word stores these types of files), as shown in Figure 3-5. You can then select a file type and use the Modify button to update the path to point to a new folder or to a folder that you just moved or renamed.

Figure 3-5	DEFAULT FILE LOCATIONS FOR WORD 2002

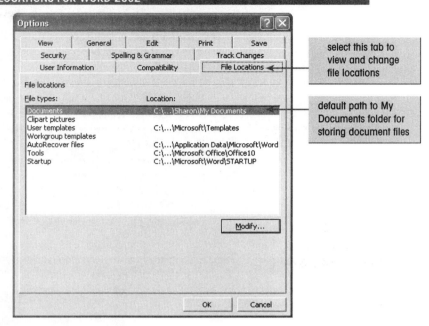

Today, as a result of the greater storage capacities of hard disks and the greater amount of storage space that it takes to install software, computer owners must effectively manage the storage space on their hard disks. Since most people use multiple applications and create a wide variety of files, they must also manage their folders and files. Like Sharon, you learn that it is an ongoing process, and you discover ways to improve the organization of your computer.

The Windows XP File Systems

The term **file system** refers to the data structures that an operating system uses to track information on files stored on a disk. When you format a hard disk or install or upgrade an operating system, you usually decide at that point which type of file system or file systems that operating system will use. Later, you might decide to convert one file system to another so you can take advantage of features available in the other file system.

Before installing Windows XP Professional on her newest computer, Sharon must decide which file system to use for the hard disk. Windows XP supports three file systems: FAT (for FAT16), FAT32, and NTFS. She asks you to research the differences between these file systems and help her choose the one that best suits her needs and optimizes the performance of her computer.

The FAT16 File System

The original version of Windows 95 and Windows 95a used the FAT16 file system (referred to as just FAT) for hard disks for backward compatibility with DOS, which also used the same file system. The FAT16 file system relied on the use of a File Allocation Table (FAT). To illustrate how this file system works, let's look at what happens when you format a floppy disk.

Operating systems that use the FAT file system perform three basic operations when you format a floppy disk. The operating system completes the following tasks:

■ **Subdivides the disk into storage compartments called tracks and sectors.** The operating system creates concentric recording bands, called **tracks**, around the inner circumference of the floppy disk, as shown in Figure 3-6. Then the operating system subdivides each track into equal parts, called **sectors**. Although not all of them are shown in this diagram, there are 80 concentric tracks on a 3½-inch high-density disk, and each track is divided into 18 sectors. Each sector in turn can store 512 bytes of data. A **byte** is the storage space required on a disk (or memory) for one character. A single-spaced page can contain approximately 3,500 characters, and therefore requires 3,500 bytes of storage space on a disk. That means a sector stores approximately one-seventh of a page. If you create a one-page report, the operating system uses at least (and often more than) seven sectors to record the contents of that document in a file on the disk.

| Figure 3-6 | TRACKS AND SECTORS ON A FORMATTED 3½-INCH HIGH-DENSITY DISK |

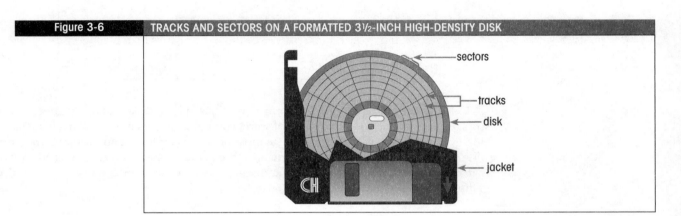

Although the sector is the basic unit of storage on a disk, operating systems that rely on the FAT file system allocate storage space on a cluster-by-cluster basis rather than on a sector-by-sector basis. A **cluster**, now known as an **allocation unit**, consists of one or more sectors of storage space, and represents the minimum amount of space that an operating system allocates when saving the contents of a file to disk. As shown in Figure 3-7, an allocation unit or cluster on a high-density disk consists of one sector. On a double-density disk, an allocation unit or cluster consists of two sectors. On a hard disk, the number of sectors in an allocation unit or cluster varies, depending on the size of the hard disk (and also the file system), but might consist of 8, 16, 32, or 64 sectors. If you create a small file, such as a short note that is no larger than a sector in size, it is assigned a cluster of storage space whether you store it on a floppy disk or a hard disk. However, because the number of sectors per cluster varies on different types of disk, this file would use one sector of storage space on a 3½-inch, high-density disk, two sectors of storage space on a 3½-inch, double-density disk, and up to 64 sectors of storage space on a hard disk close to 2 GB in size. Any space allocated to a file, but not used to actually store the contents of the file, is wasted space and is referred to as **slack**. No other file uses that wasted space. The amount of slack produced by a file system is therefore one important factor in determining which file system to use. Also, this figure illustrates another important fact. Although a hard disk with only 2 GB of storage space is relatively small by today's standards, the FAT16 file system only supports hard disks with up to 2 GB in storage capacity.

Figure 3-7 **CLUSTER SIZES ON DISKS WITH DIFFERENT FILE SYSTEMS**

TYPE OF DISK	FILE SYSTEM	CLUSTER SIZE
High-density diskette (HD or DS/HD)	FAT12	1 sector
Double-density diskette (DS/DD)	FAT12	2 sectors
2 GB hard disk	FAT16	64 sectors
2 GB hard disk	FAT32	8 sectors
(HD = High-Density, DS = Double-Sided, DD = Double-Density)		

- **Checks the surface of the disk for defective sectors**. The operating system records "dummy" data to each sector of the disk and reads that data back to verify that the sector supports read and write operations. If it encounters a problem reading or writing to a sector, it marks the cluster that contains that sector as defective and does not store data in the cluster and the defective sector.
- **Creates four tables in the system area of the disk**. The operating system creates four tables at the outer edge of the disk in an area called the **system area**. Right after the system area is the **files area** where you store your document files. The four tables for the FAT file system are the following:
  - Boot record
  - File Allocation Table #1 (or FAT1)
  - File Allocation Table #2 (or FAT2)
  - Directory table

Each of these tables, or data structures, plays an important role in the FAT file system.

The Boot Record

The **boot record** (sometimes called the **boot sector**) is a table that contains the name and the version number of the operating system used to format the floppy disk, as well as information on the physical characteristics of the disk, such as the following:

- number of bytes per sector
- number of sectors per cluster or allocation unit
- number of FATs (File Allocation Tables)
- maximum number of files allowed in the top-level folder or root directory
- total number of sectors
- media descriptor byte, which identifies the type of disk
- number of sectors for the FAT (File Allocation Table)
- number of sectors per track
- number of sides formatted
- drive number
- volume serial number (calculated from the date and time on the computer)
- volume label (an electronic label)
- type of file system
- number of hidden, reserved, and unused sectors

The boot sector also contains the names of the operating system files needed to start the process of loading the operating system, as well as a **bootstrap loader** program whose sole function is to locate and load the operating system if the floppy disk is a boot disk that contains those operating system files. If the floppy disk is not a boot disk, but rather stores document files, this program displays an "Invalid system disk" error message (or comparable message) if you leave it in drive A and if your computer attempts to boot from that drive.

When the operating system accesses a drive that contains a floppy disk, it reads the boot record so that it knows how to work with and allocate storage space on that disk drive. The boot sector is therefore important because different types of disks (including hard disks) have different storage capacities and allocate storage space differently.

The File Allocation Tables

After the boot sector, the operating system creates two copies of a table called the **File Allocation Table (FAT)** to keep track of which allocation units (or clusters) are available or unused, which ones store the contents of files and are therefore used, which are defective and unusable, and which are reserved for use by the operating system. Figure 3-8 shows a diagrammatic representation of a File Allocation Table. In this figure, you are looking at information on two files that use clusters 1500-1505 and 1506-1508. Each cluster contains the number of the next cluster (called a pointer) for that same file (shown in the column labeled "FAT"). The last cluster of a file contains an **end-of-file (EOF)** code or marker. Since the operating system can determine the cluster number by counting the entries in the table, the File Allocation Table only contains the information shown in the FAT column.

Figure 3-8	PARTIAL VIEW OF CLUSTER USAGE IN THE FILE ALLOCATION TABLE

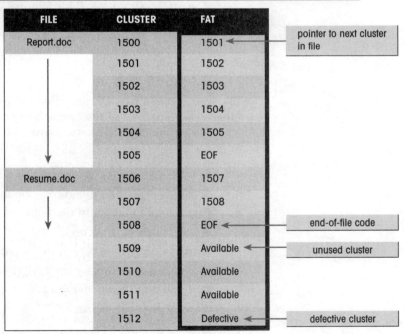

FILE	CLUSTER	FAT	
Report.doc	1500	1501	← pointer to next cluster in file
	1501	1502	
	1502	1503	
	1503	1504	
	1504	1505	
	1505	EOF	
Resume.doc	1506	1507	
	1507	1508	
	1508	EOF	← end-of-file code
	1509	Available	← unused cluster
	1510	Available	
	1511	Available	
	1512	Defective	← defective cluster

Because the File Allocation Table is so important to the operating system's ability to locate files, the operating system places two copies of this table on a disk. One copy is called FAT1, the other, FAT2. Each time the operating system saves a new or modified file to a disk, it updates both tables. FAT2 is therefore a backup of FAT1.

The Directory Table

The **directory table** keeps track of information on the folders and files stored in the top-level folder or root directory. This table contains the names of folders and files, as well as information on their sizes, dates and times of creation, last access dates, dates and times of modification, and any special **attributes**, or characteristics, assigned to the folder or file by the operating system. In Figure 3-9, you see a diagram representing a partial view of the contents of a directory table. The directory table only keeps track of the folders and files located in the top-level folder. This table does not keep track of the folders and files contained within subfolders below the top-level folder. Each subfolder below the top-level folder is actually a directory table, like the one for the top-level folder, and each directory table tracks the folders and files contained within that subfolder. In essence, the operating system divides up the labor of tracking folders and files on a hard disk among different directory tables.

Figure 3-9	DIRECTORY TABLE FOR TOP-LEVEL FOLDER OR ROOT DIRECTORY

FILENAME	EXTENSION	ATTRIBUTES	FILE TIME	FILE DATE	STARTING CLUSTER	SIZE
Resources		D	08:30:02	10/14/2004	156	
Company Brochure	doc	A	10:31:58	10/27/2004	157	75,968
Company Logo	psd		16:32:19	03/21/2005	1890	312,335
Display Ad	psd	A	09:27:43	02/07/2005	536	693,712
Newsletter	doc		14:01:32	11/15/2004	298	121,690

document files

a folder (or directory)

In the FAT file system, the directory table keeps track of the Read-Only, Hidden, System, Archive, and Directory attributes. Files with the **Read-Only** attribute (shown as "R" in the Attributes column of Figure 3-10), such as Ntldr, Io.sys, Ntdetect.com, and Msdos.sys, can be read, but not modified or deleted. Files with the **Hidden** attribute (shown as "H" in the Attributes column of Figure 3-10), such as Boot.ini, which contains boot settings, and Hiberfil.sys, the file Windows XP uses to store the contents of RAM on disk when the computer switches to Hibernation mode, are not displayed in file listings (unless you choose the option to display all files). Files with the **System** attribute (shown as "S" in the Attributes column of Figure 3-10), such as Pagefile.sys and all the other files shown in the top-level folder of the computer used for this figure, are operating system files that play a role in the booting process. Windows XP assigns the **Archive** attribute (shown as "A" in the Attributes column of Figures 3-9 and 3-10) to newly created or modified files so that a backup utility can identify which files should be backed up (covered in detail in Tutorial 6). Files assigned the **Directory** attribute (see Figure 3-9) are folders.

| Figure 3-10 | FOLDERS AND FILES IN THE TOP-LEVEL FOLDER OF DRIVE C |

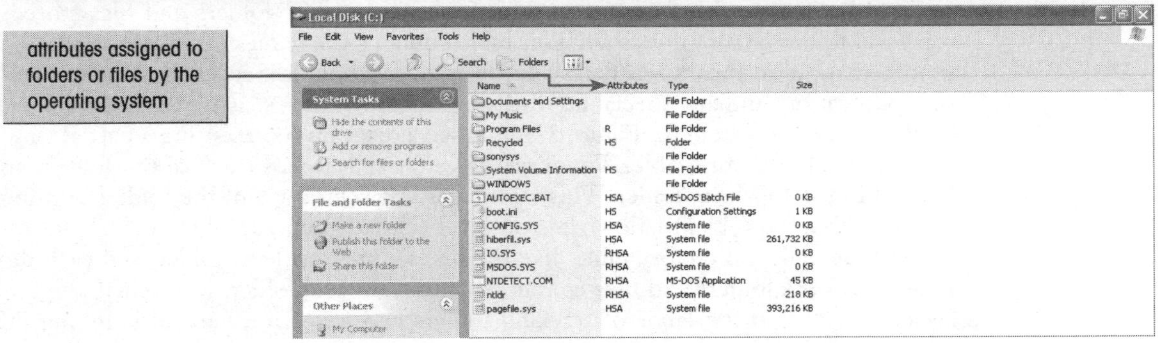

attributes assigned to folders or files by the operating system

Another important feature of the directory table is that it contains the number of the starting cluster for each folder and file on a disk. By using the directory table and the File Allocation Table, the operating system can locate all the clusters used by a folder or file on a FAT volume and reassemble the file so that you can work with the document in that file.

Although the MS-DOS file system for hard disks is called FAT16, the MS-DOS file system for floppy disks is referred to as FAT12 because floppy disks have limited storage capacities. **FAT12** supports a maximum of 4,096 clusters (2^{12}) on a floppy disk. In contrast, FAT16 supports a maximum of 65,536 clusters (2^{16}) clusters on a disk. Since some clusters are reserved, the actual limit is 65,524 clusters. Another feature of the FAT file system is that the boot record, File Allocation Table #1, File Allocation Table #2, and directory table are fixed in size. The size of the File Allocation Tables cannot exceed 128 KB, and that impacts the usage of storage space on hard disks because the File Allocation Table can only track 4,096 clusters, no matter how large the disk. As hard disk storage capacities increase, the number of sectors per cluster must increase because the number of clusters cannot increase. Figure 3-11 shows cluster sizes on different-sized volumes that use FAT16 under Windows XP. For hard disks that range in capacity from 1 GB up to 2 GB, each cluster is 64 sectors in size. Although Windows XP supports FAT16 volumes up to 4 GB, such volumes are actually limited to 2 GB to provide backward compatibility with MS-DOS, Windows 95, Windows 98, and Windows Me.

| Figure 3-11 | CLUSTER SIZES FOR FAT16 VOLUMES |

VOLUME SIZE		CLUSTER SIZE
From	To	
17 MB	32 MB	1 sector
33 MB	64 MB	2 sectors
65 MB	128 MB	4 sectors
129 MB	256 MB	8 sectors
257 MB	513 MB	16 sectors
513 MB	1 GB	32 sectors
1 GB	2 GB	64 sectors

Because the directory table for the top-level folder of a hard disk that uses FAT16 is also fixed in size, it can only track a total of 512 folders and files. That's why it's important to organize files into folders so that the top-level folder or root directory does not become full. That's also why you should limit your use of long filenames for folders and files in the top-level folder, because long filenames take more than one directory entry and therefore use up the available **directory space**. Each folder below the root directory can track as many other folders and files as you want or need, because there is no limit on the size of the directory table for each folder, and you can also use long filenames without any restrictions.

The Master Boot Record and Hard Disk Partition Table

Each drive on a hard disk that uses the FAT file system has a boot record, two copies of the File Allocation Table, and a directory table. However, the very first sector on a hard disk is not the boot sector for drive C, but rather the Master Boot Record. The boot sector for drive C follows the Master Boot Record. The **Master Boot Record (MBR)** contains information on the disk's partitions. A **partition** is all or part of the physical hard disk that is set aside for a drive or set of logical drives. The **primary partition** is the bootable partition that contains the operating system (usually drive C). An **extended partition** does not contain operating system files, but can be divided into additional logical drives, such as drive D, etc. You can have as many as 23 logical drives (drive D through drive Z). Within the Master Boot Record is a table called the **Hard Disk Partition Table** that contains information about the partitions on the hard disk. Figure 3-12 shows the Hard Disk Partition Table for a computer that contains two partitions. The primary partition, labeled HUGE, is the boot drive (drive C) with 2 GB of storage space, and the extended partition, labeled EXTEND, is drive D with 23.5 GB of storage space.

Figure 3-12   HARD DISK PARTITION TABLE

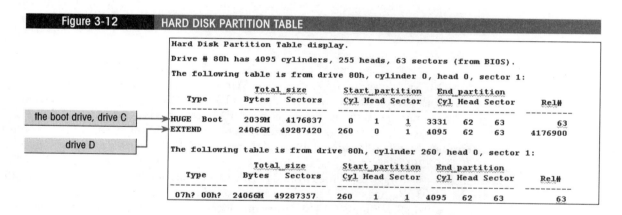

As you can see from the information in the figure, the first table is from cylinder 0, head 0, and sector 1 of drive 80h (a boot indicator value that identifies the partition used to boot the computer). A **head** refers to a side of a disk or platter. Head 0 is the top side of a platter. On a hard disk, you also refer to a combination of tracks as **cylinders**. Each cylinder consists of tracks located at the same position on different sides of each of the platters that constitute the hard disk. See Figure 3-13.

Figure 3-13 | HARD DISK

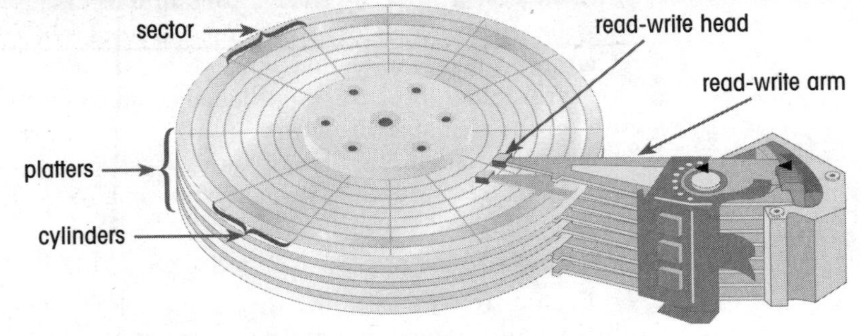

A **platter** is similar to the disk within a floppy disk drive jacket, except that it is made of aluminum or glass, and provides all or part of the storage capacity of a drive.

When your computer finds the hard disk during booting, it reads the Master Boot Record, finds the location of the boot drive (drive C), and then reads the boot record on drive C. The bootstrap loader then locates and loads the operating system from the hard disk.

Windows XP supports FAT16 because it provides backward compatibility with earlier versions of Windows, and thereby enables you to upgrade your operating system. Another advantage of providing support for FAT16 is that it is compatible with most other operating systems. In a multi-boot configuration with MS-DOS, Windows 95 (original version), or Windows 95b, you must use FAT16 for the partition from which one of these operating system boots. On the Windows XP partition, you can use its native file system, NTFS; however, if MS-DOS, Windows 95, Windows 98, Windows Me, or Windows NT Workstation 4.0 is installed on another partition it will not be able to read the contents of the Windows XP partition.

The FAT32 File System

Windows XP, Windows 2000, Windows Me, Windows 98, Windows 95b, and Windows 95c support another type of file system called **FAT32**. FAT32 improves the efficiency with which the operating system uses storage space. FAT32 supports a maximum of 268,435,456 clusters (2^{28}) on a hard disk, so cluster sizes can be smaller. Although FAT32 uses 32 bits for each entry in the File Allocation Table, and therefore would theoretically support a maximum of 4,294,967,296 clusters (2^{32}), the first 4 bits of each entry are reserved. Under FAT32, hard disks with storage capacities from 257 MB to 8 GB have cluster sizes of 8 sectors. On a 2 GB hard disk that uses FAT32, a cluster consists of only 8 sectors (as compared to 64 sectors for FAT16). See Figure 3-14. Another important feature of FAT32 is that it can support much larger hard disks, theoretically up to 8 TB (terabytes); however, FAT32 volumes are limited to 32 GB in size because Windows XP can only format FAT32 volumes up to 32 GB. Above 32 GB, you must use the NTFS file system.

Figure 3-14	CLUSTER SIZES FOR FAT32 VOLUMES	

VOLUME SIZE		CLUSTER SIZE
From	To	
33 MB	64 MB	1 sector
65 MB	128 MB	2 sectors
129 MB	256 MB	4 sectors
257 MB	8 GB	8 sectors
8 GB	16 GB	16 sectors
16 GB	32 GB	32 sectors

Although large files obviously take a lot of storage space on a disk, small files waste a lot of storage space relative to their size and create slack. For example, on a 2 GB hard disk that uses FAT16, a 256-byte shortcut requires only ½ sector of storage space, but actually uses 64 sectors of storage space because the operating system allocates one cluster (or 64 sectors) to the shortcut. So, that shortcut wastes 63½ sectors (which now becomes slack). If that same file were stored on a disk that used FAT32, the operating system would still allocate one cluster (but only 8 sectors) to that shortcut, so only 7½ sectors of storage space would be wasted (and end up as slack).

The boot record on FAT32 drives is larger and contains a backup of critical data structures. Furthermore, a backup of the boot sector is stored elsewhere on the volume. The size of each FAT can now be up to 2 MB. Unlike FAT16, the File Allocation Tables and directory table in the FAT32 file system are not fixed in size, and these system files can "spill over" from the system area to the files area of the disk where you store document folders and files. An added advantage is that FAT32 supports up to 65,536 folders and files in the top-level folder.

The larger size of each FAT does pose a problem, because the FAT is read into RAM. If you have a computer with a limited amount of RAM, only part of the FAT is loaded into memory. Windows XP must return to the hard disk to find information on the location of folders and files, and disk access is far slower than RAM. For example, a computer might have a hard disk with an access time of 6 milliseconds (6 thousands of a second, or 0.006 seconds) and RAM with an access time of 50 nanoseconds (50 billionths of a second, or 0.00000005 seconds). The RAM in this computer is therefore 120,000 times faster than the hard disk access time. **Access time** is the amount of time it takes a device to locate an item of data and make it available to the rest of the computer system.

Microsoft has stated that FAT32 is 10 to 15 percent more efficient in using disk space than FAT16, and that it improves the use of storage space on large drives—drives that range in size from 33 MB to 32 GB. Microsoft also claims that applications load 50 percent faster under FAT32. If you have a smaller 2 GB drive that uses FAT16, you can gain from 200 to 300 MB of additional storage space on the disk by converting the file system to FAT32.

The Virtual File Allocation Table

The adaptation of the FAT file system for Windows 95 (and later versions of Windows) is called **VFAT**, for Virtual File Allocation Table. VFAT provides faster disk access and supports the use of long filenames (up to 255 characters for each folder and file name). To maintain backward compatibility with MS-DOS and Windows 3.x, Windows 95 used the MS-DOS File Allocation Table as the foundation for its file system, but expanded the capabilities of that file system with the use of a virtual device driver. A **device driver** is a program that enables an operating system to communicate with and control a hardware device or software component within a computer. Examples of device drivers include the drivers for your video display adapter, modem, and printer. Under MS-DOS, a device driver managed the use of a system resource for a single application. Under Windows 95 and later versions of Windows, a **virtual device driver** (also referred to as a VxD) managed a hardware or software resource so that more than one application could use that resource at the same time. Virtual device drivers therefore allowed those operating systems to support multitasking.

A virtual device driver is a special type of device driver which Windows uses when it operates in protected mode and exploits the full capabilities of 80386 and later microprocessors. **Protected mode** is a microprocessor operating mode in which the microprocessor can address more than 1 MB of memory, support virtual memory (a technique for supplementing memory by using unused storage space on a hard disk as memory), provide memory protection features for applications (so that one application does not attempt to use the memory space allocated to another application), use 32-bit (rather than 16-bit) processing, and support multitasking.

The NTFS File System

Like its predecessors in the NT product line, Windows XP has its own native file system, called **NTFS** (the **NT File System**). When you install Windows XP, you can choose a file system, and you can also specify a file system when you format a volume. Windows XP can convert a FAT16 and FAT32 volume to an NTFS volume without formatting the volume. Windows XP can also upgrade previous versions of NTFS to the version used in Windows XP. You can use the Windows XP Convert command in a Command Prompt window to convert a FAT or FAT32 volume to NTFS; however, you cannot reverse the process.

NTFS does not use a File Allocation Table with pointers, but instead relies on a **Master File Table (MFT)**, a special file that keeps information about the folders and files on disk, as well as the volume itself. Some of the information in the MFT is also stored in the boot sector, and a duplicate copy of the boot sector is stored in the center of the volume or drive. The MFT contains a transaction log of disk activities so that the NTFS file system can recover files if disk problems occur and even repair itself. Under the NTFS file system, each file stores information about its filename, file size, date and time of modification, and attributes. Like all previous versions of Windows since Windows 95, NTFS supports long filenames and object-oriented applications that treat files as objects with user-defined and system-defined properties. NTFS also supports very large storage media and works the best with such disks.

In addition to the System, Hidden, Read-Only, and Archive attribute, NTFS supports three other attributes—Compress, Encrypt, and Index. The **Compress** attribute, when enabled, compresses a folder or file so that it uses less disk space. If you compress a folder or file, the way that you access and use that folder or file does not change, because NTFS handles the decompression of folders and files transparently. Windows XP displays compressed folders and files in a different color so that you can identify which folders and files are compressed and which are uncompressed. If you compress a file, you cannot encrypt it (discussed in next paragraph). Although you can only apply the Compress attribute to the contents of an NTFS volume, Windows XP now supports a new feature called **Compressed (zipped) Folders** that work on FAT as well as NTFS volumes. Any files you place within a Compressed (zipped) folder are compressed, and you can move these folders to any drive or folder on your local or network computer, as well as the Internet. When you create a Compressed (zipped) folder in a folder window, the folder displays a zipper icon . The Compressed (zipped) folder behaves exactly like a zipped file created with a utility like WinZip. When you copy a Compressed (zipped) folder to another computer that uses a different version of Windows that does not have this feature, the Compressed (zipped) folder appears as a WinZip file with the "zip" file extension. If you open this archive file on another computer with a utility like WinZip, you can view the files contained in the original folder, and you can extract the files from the zipped file. The Compressed (zipped) folder feature, however, is not available in the Windows XP 64-Bit Edition.

The **Encrypt** attribute prevents access to a folder or file by any person other than the user who encrypted the folder or file (and, of course, the Administrator). As with compression, once you encrypt a folder or file, the way that you access and use that folder or file does not change, because Windows XP handles the decryption and encryption transparently. The Encrypting File System (EFS) is the Windows XP component that works in conjunction with NTFS to encrypt and decrypt folders and files.

The **Index** attribute indexes the content of a file and its properties so that you can search for text within a file as well as search for file properties.

You can also set security permissions for files and folders on NTFS volumes. As noted in Tutorial 1, a permission is a rule associated with an object to regulate which users can gain access to the object and in what manner. When you set permissions for a folder or file, you specify what access a group or user has to the folder or file.

NTFS uses disk space more efficiently than either FAT16 or FAT32. Figure 3-15 shows cluster sizes for different volume sizes. Notice that clusters for volumes from 2 GB up to 2 TB (terabytes) are only 8 sectors in size.

Figure 3-15	CLUSTER SIZES FOR NTFS VOLUMES	
VOLUME SIZE		**CLUSTER SIZE**
From	To	
7 MB	512 MB	1 sector
513 MB	1 GB	2 sectors
1 GB	2 GB	4 sectors
2 GB	2 TB	8 sectors

If you compare cluster sizes for FAT16, FAT32, and NTFS volumes that are the same size, the difference immediately becomes apparent. Example #1 in Figure 3-16 compares the space required for a shortcut that is 256 bytes, or ½ sector, in size under NTFS, FAT32, and FAT16 on a 2 GB volume, which is supported by all three file systems. Under NTFS, Windows XP allocates one cluster, or 4 sectors, to that shortcut, and 3½ sectors are wasted space, or slack. However, under FAT32, Windows XP allocates twice as much storage space, or 8 sectors (one cluster) of storage space, which wastes 7½ sectors (which now becomes slack). On a FAT16 volume, Windows XP allocates 16 times as much storage space, or 64 sectors (one cluster), which wastes 63½ sectors (that now become slack).

Figure 3-16	COMPARISON OF CLUSTER USAGE UNDER NTFS, FAT32, AND FAT16

EXAMPLE #1:

Volume Size	File System	Cluster Size	Shortcut Size	Slack
2 GB	NTFS	4 sectors	½ sector	3½ sectors
2 GB	FAT32	8 sectors	½ sector	7½ sectors
2 GB	FAT16	64 sectors	½ sector	63½ sectors

EXAMPLE #2:

Volume Size	File System	Cluster Size	Shortcut Size	Slack
32 GB	NTFS	8 sectors	½ sector	7½ sectors
32 GB	FAT32	32 sectors	½ sector	31½ sectors

Example #2 in Figure 3-16 compares that same shortcut under NTFS and FAT32 on a 32 GB volume, a size that is more typical of a smaller drive on today's computer systems. Under NTFS, Windows XP allocates one cluster, or 8 sectors, to that shortcut, and 7½ sectors are wasted. Under FAT32, Windows XP allocates four times as much storage space, or 32 sectors (one cluster) of storage space, which wastes 31½ sectors (that now become slack).

After examining the three different file systems and after discussing the pros and cons of each file system with Sharon, you recommend that she use the NTFS file system on her new computer. Not only does Windows XP support much larger volume sizes, which is critical to today's operating systems and applications, but it also uses storage space more efficiently than FAT32 and FAT16. Furthermore, it provides enhanced security, a feature important to her home network, and special features, such as encryption and compression, one of which she might choose to implement on her computer.

Getting Started

To complete this tutorial, you need to switch your computer to Web style, and you also need to activate the options for showing hidden folders and files and for displaying file extensions. As you complete these steps, you may discover that your computer is already set up for Web style, or you might only need to make a few changes to your computer's settings.

To set up your computer:

1. To change to the Windows XP theme, right-click the **desktop**, click **Properties** on the shortcut menu, and after Windows XP opens the Display Properties dialog box, click the **Theme** list arrow on the Themes property sheet, click **Windows XP**, and then click the **OK** button.

2. To switch to the Windows XP Start menu style, right-click the **Start** button, click **Properties** on the shortcut menu, and after Windows XP opens the Taskbar and Start Menu Properties dialog box, click the **Start menu** option button on the Start Menu property sheet, if it is not already selected, and then click the **OK** button.

3. To change to a task-oriented view of folders and enable single-clicking, click the **Start** button, click **My Computer**, click **Tools** on the menu bar, click **Folder Options**, and after Windows XP opens the Folder Options dialog box, click the **Show common tasks in folders** option button if it is not already selected. Then click the **Single-click to open an item** option button if it is not already selected, and click the **Underline icon titles only when I point at them** option button if it is not already selected.

4. Click the **View** tab, click the **Show hidden files and folders** option button if it is not already selected, and if there is a check mark in the "Hide file extensions for known file types" check box, click that check box to remove the check mark, click the **OK** button to close the Folder Options dialog box, and then close My Computer.

As you work with files, you can see their file extensions and you gradually become familiar with associating file extensions with specific programs on your computer.

Some tutorials, such as this one, require that you use a Data Disk to complete the steps. You can obtain these Data Disks in one of three ways:

■ Download a self-extracting file with the Data Disk files from Course Technology's Web site, extract the contents of the self-extracting file to a folder on your hard disk, and then copy the files to a floppy disk or Zip disk.

■ Copy the Data Disk files from a network folder to a floppy disk or Zip disk.

■ Make a copy of a floppy disk that contains the Data Disk files.

If you prefer to download the Data Disk files from Course Technology's Web site, follow the instructions included on the inside back cover of this book.

If you are working on a network, your instructor or technical support staff has placed a copy of the Data Disk #1 folders and files for Tutorial 3 in a folder on a network drive so that you can copy the files from the network to a floppy disk or Zip disk. If this is the case, complete the steps in this section of the tutorial. If you need to format your floppy disk, complete the steps in the "Formatting a Floppy Disk" section (covered later in the tutorial), and then return to this section to complete the steps for copying the Data Disk #1 folders and files to your floppy disk.

If your instructor or technical support staff has prepared a floppy disk with the Data Disk #1 folders and files for Tutorial 3, you need to make a copy of that disk. Skip ahead to the "Identifying the File Systems Used on Your Computer" section and continue working through the tutorial. Be sure to complete the steps in the "Copying a Floppy Disk" section even if you already have Data Disk #1, because you should know how to copy a floppy disk.

To copy the Data Disk #1 folders and files for Tutorial 3 from a network:

1. Insert a newly formatted floppy disk or a preformatted floppy disk that does not contain any files into drive A.

2. Open My Computer, and then open the network drive that contains a copy of the Data Disk #1 folders and files for Tutorial 3.

3. Open your class folder, and then open the **Data Disk #1** folder. You should see six folders and two files. *Note*: Do not delete the files named ~WRC0070.tmp and File0000.chk, as you need them later.

4. Click **Edit** on the menu bar, and then click **Select All**. Windows XP selects all the files and folders within the Data Disk #1 folder.

5. Click **File**, point to **Send To**, and then click **3½ Floppy (A:)**. Windows XP displays a Copying dialog box as it copies files from the network drive to your floppy disk.

6. After the copy is complete, close the Data Disk #1 folder, close the network drive window, and then close My Computer.

7. Label the floppy disk "Data Disk #1."

Now you're ready to examine the file system used on your computer.

Identifying the File Systems Used on Your Computer

If you want to find out what file system your computer currently uses for a specific volume, you can examine the information on the General property sheet for that volume. As noted earlier, the file system indicates how much data you can store on a disk, how efficiently Windows XP stores that data, and whether you can compress the disk to save disk space.

Windows XP also uses other file systems for other types of disks, including DVD, CD-RW, and CD disks. To access a DVD, Windows XP uses the **Universal Disk Format (UDF)** file system. UDF is a successor to the **Compact Disc File System (CDFS)**, originally designed for CDs. UDF provides support for long filenames (greater than 64 characters) and a multi-tiered folder structure.

Besides identifying the file system, the General property sheet also provides other information about a selected disk, such as the amount of used space, the amount of free space, and the total capacity of the volume. This information can help you manage your computer resources and improve performance—Windows XP or any operating system works more slowly with a disk that is full or nearly full than one that has plenty of free space.

As you complete the next set of steps, you will be working with the terms "disk," "drive," "volume," and "volume label," so it's important to review and understand what these different terms encompass and how they differ. A **disk** is a physical device, such as a hard disk, DVD, CD, or floppy disk. A **drive**, a logical concept, consists of all or part of a single disk, has its own file system, and is assigned a drive name (such as C: or A:). You also can create a **virtual drive** by assigning a drive name to a folder (such as a network drive). A **volume** is another logical concept, consists of all or part of a hard disk, uses one of three file systems, and is assigned a drive name. A single hard disk can have multiple volumes on that one disk, or a volume can span multiple disks. A **volume label** is a name assigned to a physical disk, such as a hard disk, DVD, CD, or floppy disk.

Sharon's new computer includes a hard disk that is partitioned into two drives, as well as a DVD drive, CD-RW drive, and 3½-inch floppy disk drive. Because you are helping her on some of her client projects, you need to become familiar with her computer features. She asks you to find out which file systems are used on these different drives.

To check the file systems used on your computer:

1. Open My Computer, right-click the **drive C** icon, and then click **Properties** on the shortcut menu. On the General property sheet of the Properties dialog box for drive C of the computer used in Figure 3-17, Windows XP reports that the file system used on drive C is FAT32. Yours may differ. If Windows XP uses FAT16 for drive C, it would report that file system as just FAT. If the drive used NTFS, Windows XP would report it as NTFS.

Figure 3-17	VIEWING PROPERTIES OF A FAT32 VOLUME

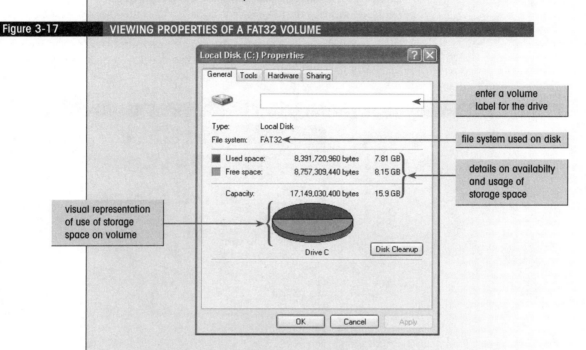

In the text box next to the drive icon, you can enter and assign an electronic label (also called a volume label) to the drive to identify the contents or purpose of the drive, or perhaps even to identify its ownership by using your last name as the volume label. If the drive uses the FAT (for FAT16) or FAT32 file system, you can enter a label with up to 11 characters. If the drive uses NTFS, the label can have up to 32 characters, you can use any symbols you want as part of the volume label, and you can mix different cases (uppercase and lowercase characters). If you or someone else has not assigned a volume label or name to drive C, then Windows XP identifies itself as Local Disk (C:). If you or someone else has assigned a volume name to drive C, then that volume label appears with the designation for the drive, namely (C:). Note also that the drive shown in Figure 3-17 is about half full.

2. Click the **Hardware** tab and, in the All disk drives box, double-click the border after the Type and then the Name columns (in that order) for a best fit of the contents in each column. On the Hardware property sheet, Windows XP lists all the disk drives in your computer. See Figure 3-18. Although Windows XP identifies drives in the My Computer window, this property sheet has the added advantage of identifying the manufacturer and model of each drive, when that information is known. If you select a drive in the All disk drives box, then the Device Properties section identifies the manufacturer, the physical location (such as the bus number or the SCSI ID), and the device status (whether or not the device is working properly). Most importantly, if there is a problem with the device, Windows XP identifies the type of problem and recommends a solution for correcting the problem. It might also display a problem code for use by a Microsoft technical support representative.

Figure 3-18	LIST OF DRIVES ON A COMPUTER

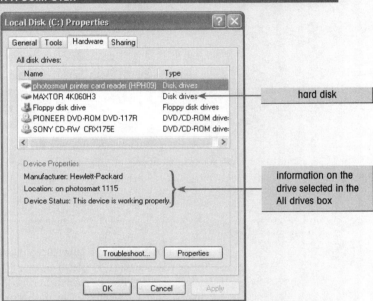

3. Close the drive C Properties dialog box.

4. If you have another drive on your hard disk, right-click the **drive** icon for that volume, and then click **Properties**. On the computer used for Figure 3-19, drive D uses NTFS. The Indexing Service, a Windows XP feature enabled for this drive, indexes the contents and properties of unencrypted document files, so that you can use the Windows XP Search Companion to more quickly locate what you need on this drive. If you choose the compression option at the bottom of this property sheet, Windows XP displays a Confirm Attribute Changes dialog box where you can indicate whether you want to compress only the top-level folder or the top-level folder and every folder and file below the top-level folder.

Figure 3-19   VIEWING PROPERTIES OF AN NTFS VOLUME

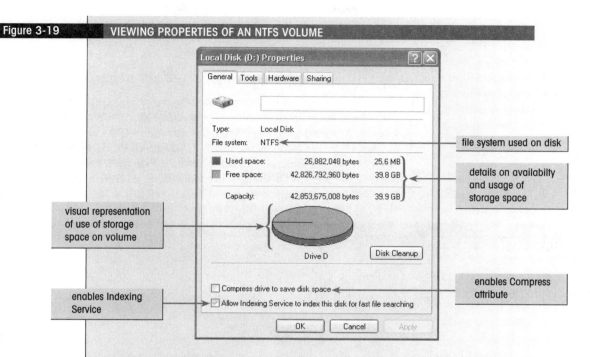

visual representation of use of storage space on volume

enables Indexing Service

file system used on disk

details on availabilty and usage of storage space

enables Compress attribute

5. Close the Properties dialog box for the drive that you selected.

6. If you have a formatted floppy disk (any one works, including Data Disk #1), insert that floppy disk into drive A, right-click the **3½ Floppy (A:)** drive icon, and then click **Properties**. In the 3½ Floppy (A:) Properties dialog box, Windows XP reports the file system as FAT (for FAT12, in this case). See Figure 3-20.

Figure 3-20   VIEWING PROPERTIES OF A FLOPPY DISK

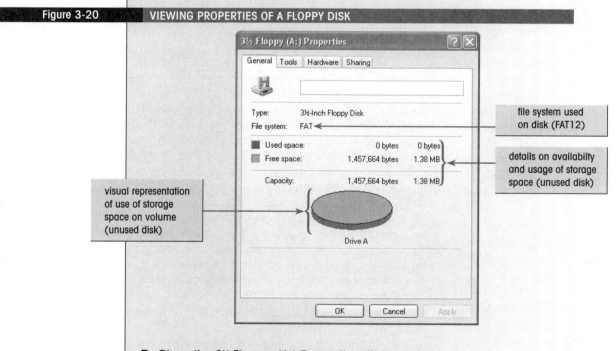

file system used on disk (FAT12)

details on availabilty and usage of storage space (unused disk)

visual representation of use of storage space on volume (unused disk)

7. Close the 3½ Floppy (A:) Properties dialog box.

You can also view the file system used for other types of drives, such as DVD, CD-RW, and CD drives.

To examine the file systems used on other types of drives:

1. If you have a DVD drive on your computer and a DVD, insert the DVD into the DVD drive, wait a moment, and if Windows XP opens a dialog box to ask you what you want it to do with the contents of the DVD, click the **Cancel** button to close the dialog box, right-click the **DVD drive** icon, and then click **Properties**. On the General property sheet for the DVD drive, Windows XP identifies the drive type as a CD Drive, and the file system as UDF. See Figure 3-21. Notice that the total storage capacity of this DVD is just under 8 GB.

Figure 3-21	VIEWING PROPERTIES OF A DVD DRIVE

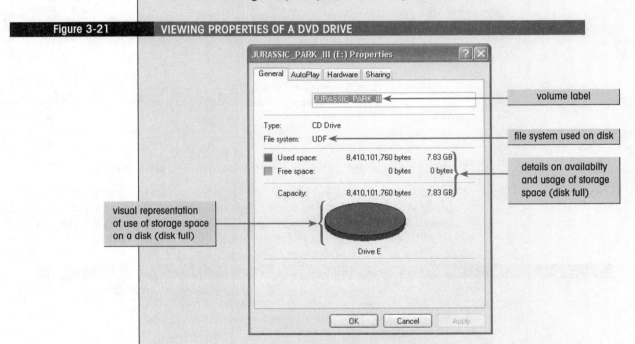

2. Click the **AutoPlay** tab. The AutoPlay property sheet provides you with information on how Windows XP responds if you insert a DVD into the DVD drive on your computer. See Figure 3-22. Your information may differ. You can specify a content type for the drive, such as Music files, Pictures, Video files, Mixed content, Music CD, or DVD movie so that Windows XP responds appropriately when you insert a DVD into the DVD drive. Then, under Actions, you can decide whether you want Windows XP to prompt you each time for the action it should take when you insert a DVD, or you can specify an action to automatically take, saving you time and effort. If you don't specify an action, but use the default option for prompting you, then Windows XP displays a dialog box with a list of all the actions you can take. Examine each of the content types and their corresponding actions, as you might be pleasantly surprised as to what actions are available for each content type.

Figure 3-22	VIEWING AUTOPLAY SETTINGS FOR A DVD DRIVE

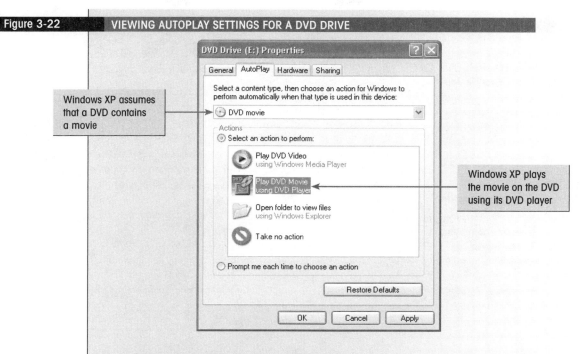

Windows XP assumes that a DVD contains a movie

Windows XP plays the movie on the DVD using its DVD player

3. Close the DVD Drive Properties dialog box.

4. If you have a CD-RW or CD drive on your computer and a CD-RW disc or CD, insert the CD-RW disc or CD into the CD-RW or CD drive, wait a moment, and if Windows XP first displays an AutoPlay dialog box and then opens a dialog box to ask you what you want it to do with the contents of the CD-RW disc or CD, click the **Cancel** button to close the dialog box, right-click the **CD-RW** or **CD drive** icon, and then click **Properties**. On the General property sheet for the CD-RW drive on the computer used for Figure 3-23, Windows XP identifies the file system as CDFS. This CD is the Windows XP Professional CD. Notice that there is an AutoPlay tab also for CD drives so that you can specify the default content type of the types of CDs you use and the corresponding action to take.

Figure 3-23 | **VIEWING PROPERTIES OF A CD-RW DRIVE**

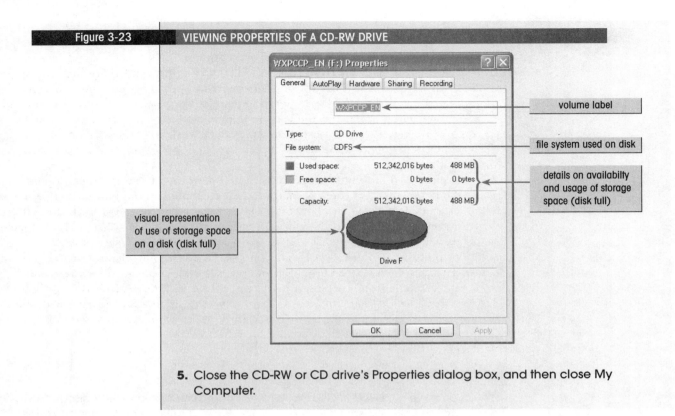

5. Close the CD-RW or CD drive's Properties dialog box, and then close My Computer.

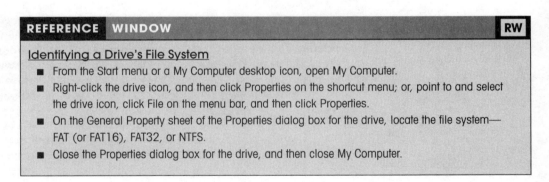

REFERENCE WINDOW   **RW**

Identifying a Drive's File System

- From the Start menu or a My Computer desktop icon, open My Computer.
- Right-click the drive icon, and then click Properties on the shortcut menu; or, point to and select the drive icon, click File on the menu bar, and then click Properties.
- On the General Property sheet of the Properties dialog box for the drive, locate the file system—FAT (or FAT16), FAT32, or NTFS.
- Close the Properties dialog box for the drive, and then close My Computer.

NTFS is considered the optimal file system for use with Windows XP because it supports larger hard disks, uses disk space more efficiently than FAT16 or FAT32, builds security features into the file system, and it offers additional features, such as folder and file compression and folder and file encryption.

Formatting a Floppy Disk

Most floppy disks that you purchase today are preformatted and, in theory, you can immediately use them. If you accidentally or deliberately purchase unformatted floppy disks, you must format them first before the operating system can store files on the disk. If you find that you no longer need the files stored on a disk, you can reformat the floppy disk and erase whatever is stored on it so you can reuse it. In many cases, reformatting is faster than deleting the files.

Even if you purchase preformatted floppy disks, it is a good idea to reformat those disks on the computer that contains the operating system you intend to use with those floppy disks, so that those floppy disks work optimally on your system. Preformatted disks are formatted with an IBM-DOS or MS-DOS utility, and therefore, you might encounter difficulties if you use those preformatted floppy disks on computers that use different versions of the Windows operating system. Because the operating system and other programs check the name and version number of the operating system in the boot record of a floppy disk, certain programs might not work with the disk, the disk might fail far earlier than you would typically expect, or Windows XP might not even be able to work with the disk.

If you reformat preformatted disks, you should perform a full format, not a quick format, of the floppy disk. A **Quick format** erases the contents of the File Allocation Tables and directory table without checking the disk for defective sectors. Although the contents of the files remain on the disk, there is no reference to the files. In contrast, a **full format** (the default) lays down new tracks and sectors and verifies the integrity of each sector on the disk by performing a surface scan. During a **surface scan**, the operating system records dummy data onto each sector of the disk and reads it back. If it is unable to record data in a sector or read data from a sector, it marks the cluster with that sector as defective. The operating system does not attempt to store any data in the defective or bad cluster. Obviously, if you are formatting a brand new (unformatted) floppy disk, you must use the full format option.

Depending on the type of disk you are formatting, you may or may not have a choice as to the file system. In the case of a floppy disk, the only choice is to use the FAT (FAT12) file system. However, if you are formatting a hard disk, you can format it for FAT, NTFS, or FAT32 (assuming you have rights to perform this operation). Whatever type of disk you format, Windows XP sets the size of an allocation unit (or cluster) based on the disk's storage capacity.

When Sharon conducts certain types of hands-on training sessions for her clients, she prepares a set of floppy disks with sample files for the participants so that she can step them through the use of specific features and have everyone work from the same type of file. Like most people, Sharon purchases preformatted floppy disks; however, she has discovered that she has fewer problems with these disks if she reformats them with Windows XP first. She asks you to format a set of floppy disks for her. Later, she copies the sample files to these floppy disks.

To complete the next set of steps, you need a preformatted or unformatted high-density disk—not a double-density disk. If you use a formatted floppy disk with files already stored on the disk, all the files are erased from the disk. Also, make sure the disk is not write-protected. If you examine the back side of a floppy disk, you notice a write-protect notch with a write-protect tab in the lower-right corner of the disk, opposite the metal shutter which slides open when you insert the disk into a drive. If you use your fingernail to move the write-protect tab down to the locked position (which might also be indicated with an impression on the disk of a closed lock), then the disk is write-protected, and you can see through the write-protect notch (a square hole). Once write-protected, you cannot format the disk or record any data onto the disk. If you move the write-protect notch up to the unlocked position (which might also be indicated with an impression on the disk of an open lock), you remove the write-protection on the disk, and you cover the write-protect notch so that you cannot see through the square hole. Now, you can format the disk and record data on the disk. By default, a floppy disk is not write-protected unless you deliberately move the write-protect tab.

To format a floppy disk:

1. Make sure your floppy disk is not write-protected, and then insert it into drive A.

2. Open **My Computer**, right-click the **3½ Floppy (A:)** drive icon, and then click **Format** on the shortcut menu. In the Format 3½ Floppy (A:) dialog box, the Capacity list box shows the format capacity of floppy disks supported by Windows XP. See Figure 3-24. In the Format options area, you can choose the Quick Format option if you are reformatting a disk. The Enable Compression option, which supports compression of folders and files, is only available for disks that use the NTFS file system (not floppy disks). Windows XP, unlike Windows 2000, has an additional option that allows you to create an MS-DOS startup disk (covered in Tutorial 8).

Figure 3-24	CHOOSING FORMATTING SETTINGS

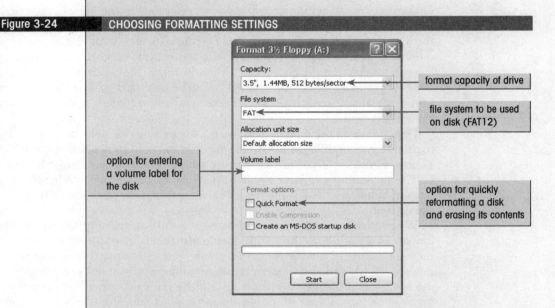

3. Click the **Start** button in the Format 3½ Floppy (A:) dialog box (not the Start button on the taskbar). Another Format 3½ Floppy (A:) dialog box warns you that formatting will erase all the data on the disk.

4. Click the **OK** button to continue. A progress indicator bar appears at the bottom of the Format 3½ Floppy (A:) dialog box to indicate the progress of the formatting process. After a short while, the Formatting 3½ Floppy (A:) dialog box informs you that the format is complete.

5. Click the **OK** button, and then click the **Close** button to close the Format 3½ Floppy (A:) dialog box.

6. Label the newly formatted floppy disk "Copy of Data Disk #1."

7. Keep the My Computer window open for the next section.

It is always a good idea to place a label on a floppy disk, and then identify the disk's contents and write your name on the label. This is especially important if you are working in a computer lab, because it's a common practice for people to inadvertently leave their floppy disks and Zip disks in the drive units.

REFERENCE WINDOW | **RW**

<u>Formatting a Floppy Disk</u>
- Insert the floppy disk you want to format into drive A, open My Computer, right-click the 3½ Floppy (A:) drive icon, and then click Format on the shortcut menu.
- If you want to enter a volume label for the disk, click inside the Volume label box and type a label no longer than 11 characters in length. (You can use a space.)
- In the Format options section, select Quick Format if you want to reformat a disk.
- Click the Start button in the Format 3½ Floppy (A:) dialog box, and then click OK in the Format 3½ Floppy (A:) dialog box to verify that you want to format the disk.
- After formatting is complete, click OK to close the Formatting 3½ Floppy (A:) dialog box, click Close to close the Format 3½ Floppy (A:) dialog box, and then close My Computer.

Formatting a disk determines how Windows XP interacts with the file system on a disk, uses the storage space on the disk, opens and retrieves files, and saves and writes files to the disk. Now that you have a formatted floppy disk, you can use it to make a copy of Sharon's disk containing her client sample files.

Copying a Floppy Disk

When you copy a floppy disk, the operating system makes a sector-by-sector copy of the original disk, called the **source disk**, and records the exact information onto another disk, called the **destination disk** or **target disk**. The source and destination disks must be the same size and same storage capacity. If your computer only has one floppy disk drive (which is the case on most of today's computer systems), you must use the same disk drive for the source and destination disks (for example, A: to A:). You cannot perform a disk copy from drive C to drive A (or to a Zip drive). Since you typically use the same drive for both the source and destination disks, Windows XP asks you for the source disk first, and then copies the contents of the disk. Next it asks you for the destination disk, and then copies the contents of the source disk onto the destination disk.

The disk copy operation replaces any information already stored on the destination disk with the contents of the source disk. After the disk copy is complete, the source and destination disks are identical, except for their serial numbers. If your original disk contains important information you want to protect during the disk copy operation, write-protect it. Otherwise, if the destination disk is newly formatted and not write-protected, and you insert the disks in the wrong order, you end up with two blank disks. After the disk copy operation, you can remove the write protection from the source disk.

Now that you have formatted a set of floppy disks, Sharon asks you to make copies of the floppy disk that contains the sample files she will use in her upcoming client training session.

To view properties and then copy the contents of the source disk:

1. Insert Data Disk #1 into drive A. This is the source disk that you must examine and then copy for Sharon.

2. In the My Computer window, right-click the **3½ Floppy (A:)** drive icon, and then click **Properties** on the shortcut menu. The 3½ Floppy (A:) Properties dialog box shows that Sharon's files use 1.03 MB of storage space, and the disk has 359 KB of unused storage space. See Figure 3-25. If you divide 1,090,048 bytes by 1024

twice (1,024 bytes in a kilobyte, and 1,024 kilobytes in a megabyte), you obtain a value just under 1.04 MB. Its total storage capacity is 1,457,664 bytes, or 1.38 MB (the full capacity of the disk).

Figure 3-25	PROPERTIES OF THE TRAINING DISK

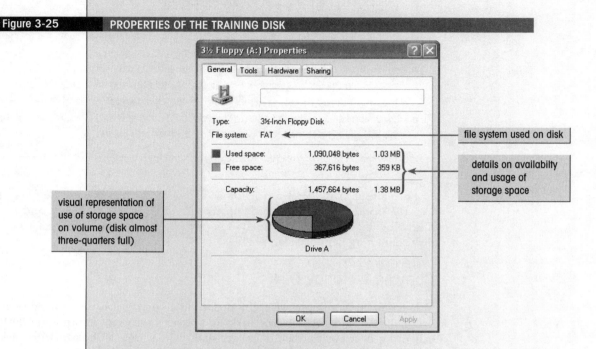

3. Close the 3½ Floppy (A:) Properties dialog box.

4. Right-click the **3½ Floppy (A:)** drive icon, and then click **Copy Disk** (not Copy) on the shortcut menu. In the Copy Disk dialog box, Windows XP highlights the name of the drive that you selected. See Figure 3-26. If you only have one floppy disk drive, as is the case on the computer shown in the figure and also on almost all other computers, that drive name automatically is highlighted in both the Copy from and the Copy to boxes. *Note*: If you right-click the drive C icon, there is no Copy Disk option on the shortcut menu.

   TROUBLE? If you have an Iomega Zip drive, you might see an Iomega Copy Disk dialog box. You can use it to copy a floppy disk or Zip disk.

Figure 3-26	CHOOSING THE SOURCE AND DESTINATION DRIVES

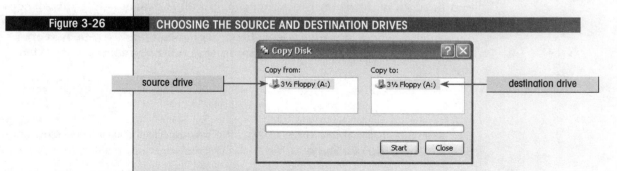

5. Click the **Start** button in the Copy Disk dialog box (not the Start button on the taskbar). Windows XP opens a Copy Disk dialog box asking for the source disk. Make sure you have inserted the disk you want to copy (Data Disk #1), and

then click the **OK** button. Windows XP reads the contents of your source disk, and the progress indicator shows you the progress of the copy operation. After it copies your source disk, Windows XP opens a Copy Disk dialog box and prompts you to insert the destination disk.

6. Remove the source disk from drive A, insert the floppy disk you formatted earlier (the Copy of Data Disk #1), and then click the **OK** button. Windows XP reports that it is writing to the destination disk, and then that the copy is successfully completed.

   TROUBLE? If you do not have the disk that you formatted earlier, you can use any floppy disk that does not contain any files. If the disk is not formatted, Windows XP asks you if you want to format the disk.

   TROUBLE? If Windows XP opens a Copy Disk dialog box to inform you that it cannot write to the destination disk and notes that the disk might be read-only (write-protected), damaged, or in use, click the Cancel button, remove the disk from drive A, click the Cancel button to close the next Copy Disk dialog box, remove the write-protection from the disk and try the step again, or if the disk is not write-protected, try another floppy disk for the copy operation.

7. Close the Copy Disk dialog box and then close My Computer.

REFERENCE   WINDOW   **RW**

Copying a Floppy Disk
- Insert in drive A the source disk you want to copy, open My Computer, right-click the 3½ Floppy (A:) drive icon, and then click Copy Disk on the shortcut menu.
- In the Copy Disk dialog box, select or verify the Copy from and the Copy to drives.
- Click Start and, when prompted for the disk to copy, click OK in the Copy Disk dialog box.
- When prompted, replace the source disk with the destination disk.
- When the copy is complete, close the Copy Disk dialog box and then close My Computer.

 POWER USERS TIP If you need to make multiple copies of the same floppy disk, it is easier to use the Diskcopy command in a Command Prompt window (which you examine in more detail in Tutorial 14). The Diskcopy command makes a sector-by-sector copy of a source disk and creates an identical image on the destination disk. After each disk copy, it asks if you want to make another copy of the same disk. You can just press Y (for Yes), insert a new floppy disk, and then repeat the copy of the same image of the source disk.

Viewing the Contents of a Floppy Disk

After you copy the contents of one floppy disk to another, you should view the contents of the destination disk to make sure that it contains the same files as the source disk and verify that no problems occurred.

Before she leaves for the client training session, Sharon asks you to view the contents of the floppy disk you just copied to make sure it contains the correct set of files and that there are no problems with the disk itself.

To view the contents of a floppy disk:

1. Make sure the Copy of Data Disk #1 is in drive A, open **My Computer**, click the **3½ Floppy (A:)** drive icon, and then, if necessary, maximize the 3½ Floppy (A:) window. Windows XP displays the folders and files in the top-level folder of drive A. See Figure 3-27. Sharon has organized the sample files into six different folders.

| Figure 3-27 | VIEWING THE CONTENTS OF THE TRAINING DISK |

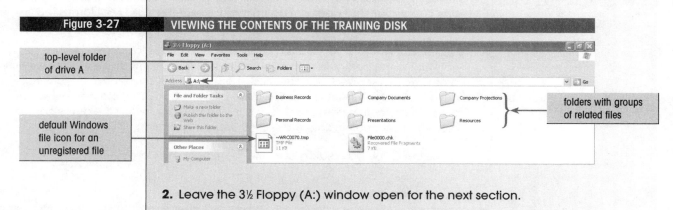

top-level folder of drive A

default Windows file icon for an unregistered file

folders with groups of related files

2. Leave the 3½ Floppy (A:) window open for the next section.

The file named ~WRC0070.tmp is a temporary file that remained on the source disk after a power failure. Temporary files are normally deleted after the operating system or an application no longer needs them; however, if a power failure interferes with that process, you should manually remove the files or use the Disk Cleanup Wizard (covered in Tutorial 7) to locate and remove temporary files. Because the file extension for the temporary file is not associated with an application, Windows XP displays a default Windows icon 🖽 for the file. The Windows XP default Windows icon is different from the one used in previous versions of Windows. The file named File0000.chk is a recovered file that was created by the Scan Disk utility (comparable to the Check Disk utility covered in Tutorial 7). You learn more about file extensions and their associations later in this tutorial.

Using **Long Filenames and Aliases**

As noted in Tutorial 1, if you use applications designed for Windows XP, Windows 2000, Windows Me, Windows 98, Windows NT Workstation 4.0, or Windows 95, you can use long filenames with up to 255 characters to more clearly identify the contents and purpose of a file. You can also include special symbols or characters, such as the ampersand (&), pound sign (#), dollar sign ($), percentage symbol (%), single quotes (' and '), as well as opening and closing parentheses and spaces. You can also assign long filenames to folders so that you can clearly identify the types of files stored within those folders.

If you assign a long filename to a folder or file, Windows XP automatically creates an alias to provide backward compatibility with MS-DOS and Windows 3.x applications (for example, applications designed for Windows 3.1 and 3.11) that do not recognize long filenames. An **alias** is an **MS-DOS filename** (also called a **short filename**) that follows the rules and conventions for **8.3 filenames** (that is, names that allow 8 characters and then a 3-character extension, only one period, and no spaces). An alias consists of the first six characters of the long filename, followed by a tilde (~), a number, a period, and the first three characters after the last period in the long filename. Any spaces in a long filename are not used in the alias.

For example, if you have a folder named Cressler Graphics, Windows XP would assign it the alias CRESSL~1 (assuming no other file has that same alias). If another file in the same folder had already been assigned the alias CRESSL~1, Windows XP would use an **algorithm**, a formula or procedure, to increment the number until it creates a unique filename. To continue with the example, Windows XP would then check to see if another folder (or file if the file has no file extension) used the alias CRESSL~2. If not, it would use this alias as the MS-DOS name for the Cressler Graphics folder. Note that lowercase (which Windows XP recognizes) is converted to uppercase (the default for the DOS operating system).

If a folder contains five or more files whose long filename starts with the same set of characters (for example, Five Year Sales Projection.xls, Five Year Sales Analysis.xls, Five Year Growth Plan.xls, Five Year Growth Plan Template.xls, and Five Year Budget Summary.xls), Windows XP follows the approach just described to create short filenames for the first four files (namely, FIVEYE~1.XLS, FIVEYE~2.XLS, FIVEYE~3.XLS, and FIVEYE~4.XLS). But, for each file after the fourth file, Windows XP uses a different approach to creating the short filename. It uses the first two characters of the long filename, followed by four characters that are mathematically generated from the remainder of the characters in the long filename, and then a tilde followed by a unique number (for example, the fifth file would have the short filename FIB7A5~1.XLS).

Under Windows XP, you might see a folder, shortcut, and file with the same name; however, the file extension (if present) differs, and each has a different short filename. Folders usually do not have a file extension (though temporary folders for installed software might have the "tmp" extension) and no reported size. Shortcuts have the file extension "lnk" (for Link) or, in the case of shortcuts to DOS applications, "PIF" (for Program Information File). *Note*: The first character in the "lnk" file extension is the lowercase character "l", not the number "1."

The alias is important for DOS applications and Windows 3.x applications that you might use under Windows XP because those applications do not recognize long folder names and long filenames. Instead, these applications can only "see" the alias (or MS-DOS name, or short filename) for folders and files. You and the applications that you use cannot specify the alias that Windows XP assigns for long filenames. If you use a filename that follows the 8.3 file-naming convention for DOS and Windows 3.x applications, and also use all uppercase characters, the long filename and alias are the same.

If you use a DOS application or a Windows 3.x application (such as an earlier version of Microsoft Word), you only see the MS-DOS names in Open and Save As dialog boxes. This can make it difficult to know which folder or file to open or which file to replace. For example, Figure 3-28 shows an Open dialog box for Microsoft Office XP. Note that you can see long filenames for folders and files. Also note the long filenames "2003 Sales Summary.xls" and "2004 Sales Summary.xls" are similar, and that the files "Five Year Growth Plan.xls" and "Five Year Plan Template.xls" are similar.

Figure 3-28   VIEWING LONG FILENAMES IN AN OPEN DIALOG BOX

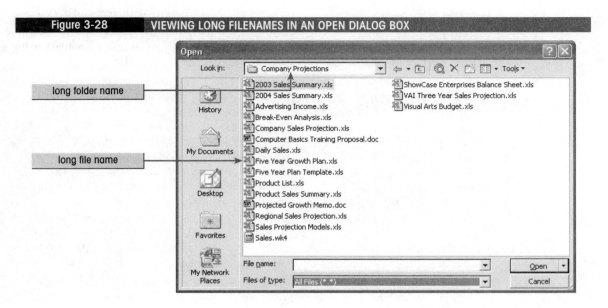

Figure 3-29 shows an Open dialog box for Collage Complete, a pre-Windows 95 application used to create all the screen captures for figures in this book. Notice that you can only see the MS-DOS names for folders and files. 2003SA~1.XLS and 2004SA~1.XLS are the MS-DOS names for "2003 Sales Summary.xls" and "2004 Sales Summary.xls." Likewise, FIVEYE~1.XLS and FIVEYE~2.XLS are the MS-DOS names for the files "Five Year Plan Template.xls" and "Five Year Growth Plan.xls," but you cannot tell them apart. In the Directories box, COMPAN~2 is the alias for the Company Projections folder.

Figure 3-29   VIEWING ALIASES IN AN OPEN DIALOG BOX

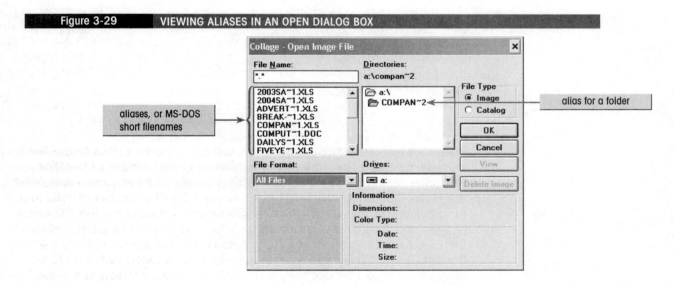

You should understand how Windows XP and other versions of Windows work with long and short filenames if you work with DOS, Windows 3.x, and applications designed for other versions of Windows on the same or different computer systems. You should also understand long and short filenames if you provide support to clients who might have a variety of software configurations on their computers, if you troubleshoot problems, and if you set up, configure, and customize computers for other users. If you find yourself in a situation where you need to create a set of files with similar names, think carefully about how you name those files. You might want to use names that begin with different characters. For example, instead of using the filenames "Five Year Growth Plan.xls" and "Five Year Plan Template.xls," you could use the filenames "Five Year Growth Plan.xls" and "Template for a Five Year Growth Plan.xls." Then you could more easily tell these files apart using their MS-DOS short file names (FIVEYE~1.XLS and TEMPLA~1.XLS).

Viewing **Properties of Folders and Files**

When you view properties of a folder, Windows XP displays the icon for the folder, the folder name, the type of folder (for example, a File Folder), the location of the folder (such as A:\ ), the amount of data contained in the folder in kilobytes (KB) and bytes, the space the folder takes on the disk, the number of files and folders within this folder, the date and time the folder was created, and any attributes assigned to the folder.

When you view properties of a file, Windows XP displays the icon used for this file type, the filename, the file type, the program that Windows XP opens if you click the file icon, a Change button for changing the application associated with this file type (covered later in the tutorial), the path (covered in the next section of the tutorial) for the location of the file, the size of the file in kilobytes and bytes, the amount of storage space it uses on disk, and the date and time the file was created, modified, and last accessed, as well as any attributes assigned to the file.

If you view properties of a folder or file, Windows XP provides more information on the folder or file than you would see by pointing to the folder icon to view a ScreenTip.

If you select a group of folders, or a group of files, then you can view their group properties, and Windows XP provides you with information on the total number of files and folders, their type (for example, "Multiple Types" for a group of files with different file types, or "All of type Microsoft Excel Spreadsheet" for a selection of just Excel spreadsheet files), their common location, their total size in kilobytes and bytes, the total amount of space they require on disk, and their common attributes.

Sharon frequently checks the properties of folders and files to make sure that she has enough storage space on a disk to accommodate whatever she needs to store on that disk. She asks you to check the size of the Company Projections folder, which has the largest number of files, and the files in the Presentations folder, because these files typically are large. Then she can decide whether to remove some of the files in those folders and free up some additional storage space on the disk.

To view properties of a folder:

1. Right-click the **Company Projections** folder icon, and then click **Properties** on the shortcut menu. The General property sheet in the Company Projections Properties dialog box, shows that this folder contains 18 files, but no subfolders. See Figure 3-30. If you divide 434,188 bytes by 1,024 (the number of bytes in a kilobyte), you obtain 424 KB, the total size reported in kilobytes. The difference between the number of bytes for "Size on disk" and "Size," namely, 500 bytes, is the amount of slack, or wasted space, allocated to the files, but not used by the files. The backslash (\ ) next to the drive name (A:) is a notation that refers to the top-level folder, or root directory, on a disk. In this case, it indicates that the Company Projections folder is contained within the top-level folder of the disk in drive A.

   TROUBLE? If you clicked the Company Projections folder icon and opened this folder by mistake, click the Up button 🔼 on the Standard Buttons toolbar, and then repeat Step 1.

TROUBLE? If you copied the data folders and files for Data Disk #1 from a net-work folder, the General property sheet for the folders *only* shows the date and time that you performed the copy and differs from the information shown in the figure. Likewise, if you copied the student data (folders and) files from a floppy disk, and if that floppy disk was created by copying folders and files from a net-work folder, the date and time for the folders (*only*) reflects the date and time the floppy disks were made by the technical support staff or instructor.

Figure 3-30	VIEWING PROPERTIES OF A FOLDER

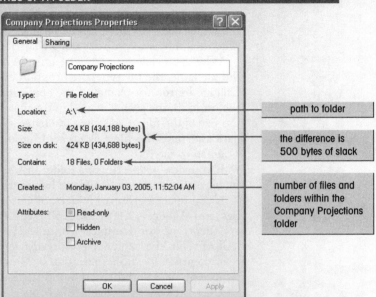

path to folder

the difference is 500 bytes of slack

number of files and folders within the Company Projections folder

2. Close the Company Projections Properties dialog box.

3. Click the **Presentations** folder icon to open this folder.

4. Right-click the **Example of a Memory Leak.ppt** file icon, and then click **Properties**. On the General property sheet of the Example of a Memory Leak.ppt Properties dialog box, Windows XP identifies this file as a Microsoft PowerPoint Presentation, and if you click the file icon, Windows XP opens the file in Microsoft PowerPoint. See Figure 3-31. If Microsoft Office or Microsoft PowerPoint is not installed on your computer, then the "ppt" file extension more than likely cannot be associated with any application. If this is the case, Windows XP identifies the Type of file as "PPT File," and uses the default Windows file icon ⊞. The location of the file is A:\Presentations, indicating that it is located in the Presentations folder, which in turn is under the top-level folder of the disk in drive A. The fact that the number of bytes for "Size" and for "Size on disk" match indicates that there is no wasted space, or slack, for this file.

Figure 3-31 VIEWING PROPERTIES OF A FILE

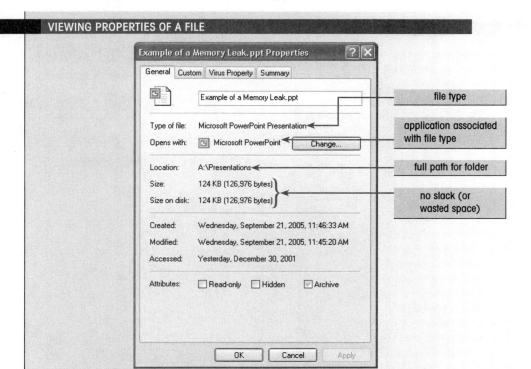

5. Click the **Custom** tab. On the Custom property sheet, you can assign custom properties to this file. See Figure 3-32. From the Name list box, you can select one of 27 properties (such as those shown for Purpose, Department, and Owner) or you can create a new property by entering its name (such as the one shown for Description). In the Type list box, you can specify whether the data is Text, Date, Number, or Yes or No (in other words, logical data). In the Value box, you type the data you want to assign to the property you selected or entered in the Name box. After you fill in the Name, Type, and Value text boxes, you click the Add button to add the custom property to the Properties box. You can also select a custom property and use the Remove button to remove it.

Figure 3-32   VIEWING OPTIONS ON THE CUSTOM PROPERTIES SHEET

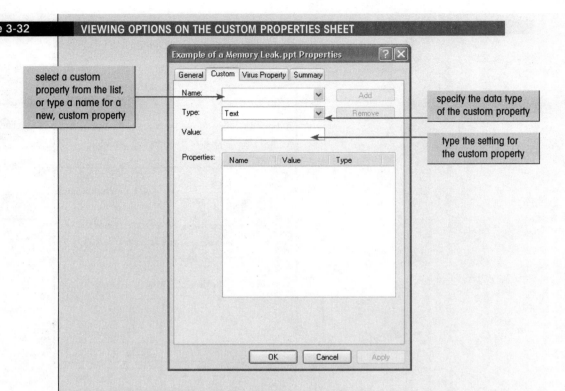

select a custom property from the list, or type a name for a new, custom property

specify the data type of the custom property

type the setting for the custom property

6. Click the **Summary** tab. On the Summary sheet, Windows XP lists information about the file. See Figure 3-33. Within each Office application, you can specify this information by choosing Properties on the File menu. Sharon obtained this document from a friend for use in her workshops.

TROUBLE? If the Summary sheet looks like the one in Figure 3-34 instead of the one in Figure 3-33, click the Simple button to change views.

Figure 3-33   VIEWING SUMMARY PROPERTIES OF A FILE

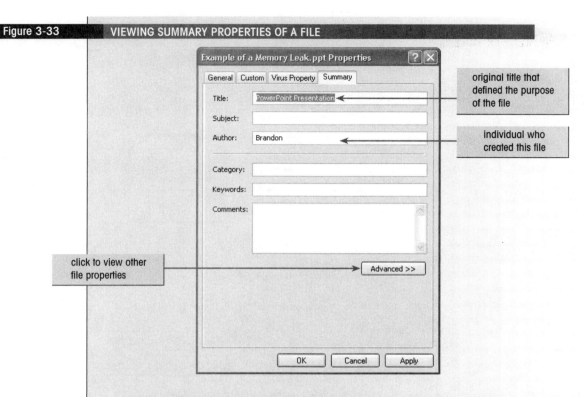

Example of a Memory Leak.ppt Properties

General | Custom | Virus Property | Summary

Title: PowerPoint Presentation ◄—— original title that defined the purpose of the file

Subject:

Author: Brandon ◄—— individual who created this file

Category:

Keywords:

Comments:

click to view other file properties ——► Advanced >>

OK   Cancel   Apply

7. Click the **Advanced** button. The Summary property sheet now displays more detailed information about the file, some of which is specific to the file type (such as the number of slides within the PowerPoint presentation). See Figure 3-34.

POWER USERS TIP The word count of a document is shown under Description.

Under Origin, Windows XP identifies the author of the document, the individual who last saved the document, the number of times the document was revised, the presentation format (On-screen Show), for this PowerPoint presentation, the individual's company, and the date created, last saved, and edit time. If you click the <<Simple button, you return to the previous simple summary.

| Figure 3-34 | VIEWING ADDITIONAL FILE PROPERTIES |

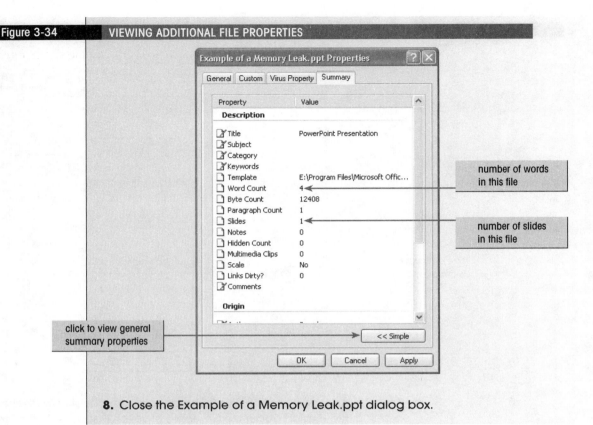

number of words in this file

number of slides in this file

click to view general summary properties

8. Close the Example of a Memory Leak.ppt dialog box.

You can use the Custom property sheet to keep track of important information about a file, and the Summary property sheet to obtain information that might otherwise be more difficult to locate or determine.

Next, Sharon asks you to view the group properties of all the files in the Company Projections folder so that she has a broad overview of the contents of this folder for the upcoming training session.

To view group properties of the files in the Company Projections folder:

1. Click the **Back** button ⊙ on the Standard Buttons toolbar, and then click the **Company Projections** folder icon.

2. After Windows XP opens the Company Projections folder, click **Edit** on the menu bar, and then click **Select All**. Windows XP selects and highlights all the files in the window.

POWER USERS TIP You can also press the Ctrl+A keys to select all files.

3. Click **File** on the menu bar, and then click **Properties**. Windows XP displays a group properties dialog box named 2003 Sales Summary.xls,... Properties. See Figure 3-35. The filename shown in the title bar is the name of the first file in the folder, followed by an ellipsis (...) that indicates you are viewing information on a group of files. There are 18 files in this folder (and no subfolders). The object type, Multiple Types, indicates that you are viewing information on multiple types of objects in this folder; in other words, different types of files associated with different applications. All the files share the same location, namely, All in A:\Company Projections. All the objects take up 424 KB of storage space on the disk, the same value that Windows XP reported for the size of the folder itself. Since the size of a folder is small, Windows XP treats it as being equal to zero. Also, the total slack for all the files is 500 bytes.

POWER USERS TIP You can also right-click one of the selected files, and then click Properties to view group properties.

Figure 3-35 VIEWING GROUP PROPERTIES OF A SET OF FILES

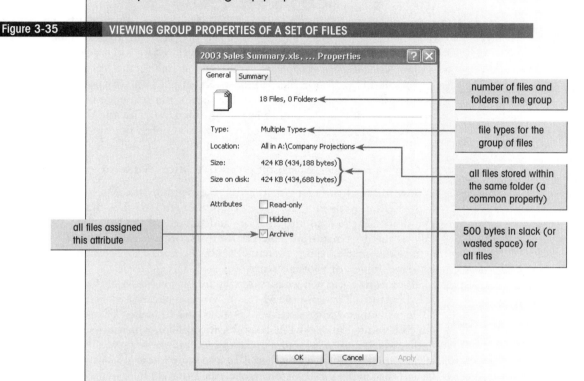

all files assigned this attribute

number of files and folders in the group

file types for the group of files

all files stored within the same folder (a common property)

500 bytes in slack (or wasted space) for all files

4. Close the 2003 Sales Summary.xls,... Properties dialog box, and then close the Company Projections window.

POWER USERS TIP By viewing group properties of selected folders (such as those that contain your business and personal files), you can quickly find out how much storage space they use on your disk and decide how much storage media you would need for a backup of those selected folders and files.

REFERENCE WINDOW RW

Viewing Properties of a Folder or File, or a Group of Folders or Files
- Point to the folder or file for which you want to display properties, or select a group of folders or files. If you want to select all the files within a folder, or all the contents of a folder (both subfolders and files), click Edit on the menu bar, and then click Select All.
- Click File on the menu bar, and then click Properties, or right-click the selected object or objects, and then select Properties on the shortcut menu.
- View object settings in the Properties dialog box for the object or group of objects, and then close the Properties dialog box.

In the next part of the tutorial, you will examine the importance of the full path and examine the elements of a full path for a folder and file. Then you will examine information on a registered file type, including the use of the full path to define actions for a registered file type and thereby associate it with an application.

Understanding **the Importance of the Full Path**

Windows XP uses the full path to locate and load software applications. It also uses the full path to locate and open folders and files. The **full path**, also called the **MS-DOS path**, is a notation that identifies the exact location of a file or folder on a disk. Windows 95 used the term "MS-DOS path" because this feature was introduced in, and used with, the MS-DOS operating system. The different versions of Windows now refer to the MS-DOS path as the full path.

For the full path of a file, Windows XP displays the drive name followed by a backslash (to identify the top-level folder on the drive), the sequence of folder name(s) that identify the location of the file, and then the full filename with the file extension. For example, if Microsoft Office 2002 is installed on your computer, the full path for the Microsoft Word application included with your version of Microsoft Office is:

C:\Program Files\Microsoft Office10\Office\Winword.exe

Winword.exe is the name of the file that contains the Microsoft Word application. Files with the file extension "exe" are **executable** files, or files that contain program code that Windows XP can load into memory and run. All of the backslashes other than the one that follows the drive name are called **delimiters**, because they separate the names of two folders or a folder name from a filename. Only the backslash after the drive name refers to the top-level folder, or root directory.

If someone asked you where the program file for Microsoft Word is stored, you would probably read the full path for the Microsoft Word application from right to left, and you would say, "The program for Microsoft Word is stored in a file called Winword.exe in the Office10 folder, which is located under the Microsoft Office folder, which is located under the Program Files folder, which in turn is located in the top-level folder of drive C." If you read the full path from left to right instead, you would say, "To locate the Microsoft Word program file, first go to drive C, and then in the top-level folder, open the Program Files folder. Next, open the Program Files folder, then the Microsoft Office folder, and finally the Office10 folder. In the Office10 folder you will find the program file named Winword.exe." Basically, the full path describes the route (or path) that you (or Windows XP) navigate in order to locate a specific program file.

In the case of a folder, the full path identifies the drive name followed by a backslash (again, for the top-level folder on the drive), and the sequence of folder names that identify the location of a specific folder on a disk. For example, suppose you want to open the Fonts folder so that you can install new fonts on your computer. If Windows XP is installed in a folder named Windows, the full path for the Fonts folder is:

C:\Windows\Fonts

In a path for a folder, the folder name, subfolder name(s), and target folder (Fonts) are separated from each other by a backslash symbol (\). If someone asks you to describe how to get to the Fonts folder, you would either say, "The Fonts folder is located below the Windows folder, which in turn is located below the top-level folder of drive C," or "To get to the Fonts folder, open a window onto the top-level folder of drive C, locate and open the Windows folder, and then locate and open the Fonts folder."

If you tell someone else that the Fonts folder is located below the Windows folder, that person most likely assumes that you mean the top-level folder of drive C (not drive D, although it is possible to install Windows XP on a partitioned hard disk that has a drive D). In the latter case, you are specifying what is comparable to a relative path, rather than an absolute path. A **relative path** makes assumptions about the location of a folder or file, whereas an **absolute path** spells out the full path. For example, the relative path for the Fonts folder might be \Windows\Fonts or just Windows\Fonts. \Windows\Fonts makes the assumption that the Windows folder is located on the current drive (assume its drive C), and Windows\Fonts assumes that the Windows folder is located below the current folder (whatever folder that might be) of the current drive.

The absolute path would be C:\Windows\Fonts. In the case of an absolute path, you know exactly which drive contains the folders, and you know the names of all the folders that you open to locate the Fonts folder (first the top-level folder then the Windows folder), and you know the exact name of the folder (Fonts). With an absolute path, you need not make assumptions about where a folder or file is located.

When working with the DOS operating system, you use either the absolute or relative path in commands to locate directories and files. The relative path is especially important because it saves time and typing. Under Windows, it is better to use the absolute path when creating or editing links to objects (such as applications, folders, and files), though you can use the relative path if you are working in a command-line window.

If you use long filenames in the full path, you must enclose the entire path in quotation marks so that Windows XP knows it is one specification; otherwise, it might interpret the spaces as delimiters which separate different parts of a command line.

As you discovered in Tutorial 1, in the Windows XP graphical operating environment, the path actually starts with the desktop, and then proceeds to My Computer before it reaches the drives, because there could be (and usually are) several drives available to a computer, including network drives. The Desktop folder is therefore your starting point for gaining access to your computer. Once you are familiar with the use of a path, you can discern what the path is for a user account, which in turn leads to that person's desktop. For example, Sharon logs on to her computer under the account name "Sharon." The full path to her desktop is:

C:\Documents and Settings\Sharon\Desktop

Again, as you saw in Tutorial 1, the folder for a user account (such as "Sharon") in the full path is the name of a folder that contains copies of system folders and files for that specific user. The Desktop folder contains any objects that user decides to put on the desktop. The actual desktop that you see on the monitor is a special view of the contents of the Desktop folder for your user account and also includes system objects, such as Internet Explorer and the Recycle Bin, and My Documents, My Computer, and My Network Places if you choose to place them on the desktop, also.

As you navigate from folder to folder on your computer, Windows XP displays the folder name in the title bar. If your computer is set up to show the Address bar in folder windows, Windows XP displays the full path of the current folder in the Address bar. As you navigate your computer, you can use this information to gradually become acquainted with the path names for different folders and their relative location with respect to each other. If you open the Folder Options dialog box by using the Tools menu in a folder window, you will see an option for displaying the full path in the Address bar and an option for displaying the full path in the title bar. See Figure 3-36. Even though Windows XP will show the full path for a folder with either of these options, it does not display the full path to a file within a folder, even if you point to and select the file.

Figure 3-36   ADVANCED FOLDER SETTINGS

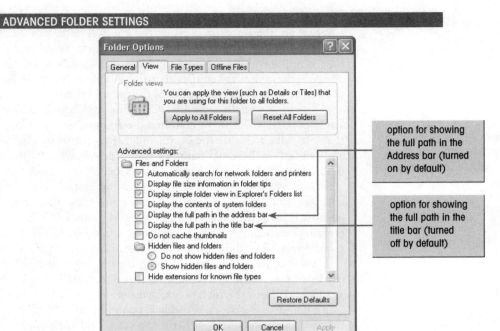

As you work with registered files in the next section of the tutorial, you explore the importance of the full path for defining actions associated with registered file types.

Working with Registered Files

As noted earlier, when you install an application, that application registers certain file types with Windows XP. From that point on, Windows XP associates certain file extensions with that application (assuming the associations do not change when you install another software product). As part of the file association, Windows XP uses the same icon for all files that use a certain file extension. For example, Windows XP uses [W] as the application icon for Microsoft Word, and [W] as the file icon for Microsoft Word document files. If you click a file icon with the "doc" file extension, Windows XP locates and loads your version of Microsoft Word, and then opens the file.

As you work on your computer, you come across many different files and file extensions. Over time, you gradually learn what many of the file extensions stand for and which file extensions are associated with which applications on your computer. Figure 3-37, Figure 3-38, Figure 3-39, Figure 3-40, Figure 3-41, and Figure 3-42 show common file extensions.

Figure 3-37	FILE EXTENSIONS AND FILE TYPES (323-CHS)		
FILE EXTENSION	**FILE TYPE**	**FILE EXTENSION**	**FILE TYPE**
323	H.323 Internet Telephony	AST	Adobe Photoshop Separation Tables
386	Virtual Device Driver (Windows 3.x)	ASV	Adobe Photoshop Selective Color
ABR	Adobe Photoshop Brush (or Brushed)	ASX	Active Streaming Format Metafile; Windows Media Audio/Video Shortcut
ACA & ACF	Microsoft Agent Character File (HTTP Format)	ATF	Adobe Photoshop Transfer Function
ACF	Adobe Photoshop Custom Filter	AU	Audio (Sound Clip); AU Format Sound
ACG	Microsoft Agent Preview File	AUDIOCD	AudioCD
ACO	Adobe Photoshop Colors, or Color Palette	AVI	Video Clip (AVI = Audio Video Interleaved)
ACS	Microsoft Agent Character File	AXT	Adobe Photoshop Replace Color/Color Range
ACT	Adobe Photoshop Color Table	BAK	Backup
ACV	Adobe Photoshop Curves	BAT	Batch (User-Defined Program)
ACW	Accessibility Wizard Settings	BKF	Microsoft Backup File
ADO	Adobe Photoshop Duotone Options	BIN	Binary
AHS	Adobe Photoshop Halftone Screens	BLG	Performance Monitor File
AIF, AIFC, & AIFF	Audio Interchange File Format	BMO	Bluematter Offer
AIFC	AIF Compressed	BMP	Windows Bitmap Graphics
AIS	ACDSee Image Sequence	BMR	Bluematter Reference
ALBM	Photo Album	BMT	Bluematter Song
ALF	Dvgate Assemble List File	CAB	Cabinet (Compressed Program)
ALV	Adobe Photoshop Levels	CAT	Security Catalog
AMP	Adobe Photoshop Arbitrary Map	CCC	Microsoft Chat Conversation
AMS	Adobe Photoshop Monitor Setup	CDA	CD Audio Track
AMU	PhotoAlbum Document	CDF	Channel Definition File
ANI	Animated Cursor; ACDSee ANI Image	CDX	Corel Draw Compressed File
APL	ACD Plugin	CER	Security Certificate
ART	America Online ART File	CFG	Configuration File
ASC	ASCII (DOS, DOS Text, Text, or Print File)	CHK	Check Disk File, Recovered File Fragments
ASF	Active Streaming Format File; Windows Media Audio/Video File	CHM	Compiled HTML Help File
ASP	Adobe Photoshop Separation Setup; Active Server Page	CHS	Corel Presentations 9 Chart Style

Figure 3-38	FILE EXTENSIONS AND FILE TYPES (CIL-INF)

FILE EXTENSION	FILE TYPE	FILE EXTENSION	FILE TYPE
CIL	Clip Gallery Download Package	DOTHTML	Microsoft Word HTML Template
CLP	Clipboard Clip	DQY	ODBC Query File
CNF	SpeedDial Conferencing	DRV	Device Driver
CNT	Contents (Help)	DSN	Data Source Name
COM	Command (DOS Program)	DUN	Dial-Up Networking File
COV	Fax Cover Page File	EML	Internet E-Mail Message; Outlook Express Mail Message
CPD & CPE	Cover Page Editor Document (FAX)	EMM	IBM EMMS Music Track
CPI	Code Page Information	EPS	Encapsulated Postscript
CPL	Control Panel Extension	EXE	Executable (Application)
CRL	Certificate Revocation List	FAV	Outlook Bar Shortcuts
CRT	Security Certificate	FDF	Adobe Acrobat Forms Document
CSS	Cascading Style Sheet Document	FMT	Format (Lotus 1-2-3, dBASE)
CSV	Comma Separated Values (Text)	FND	Saved Search
CUR	Cursor (Static); ACDSee CUR Image	FON	Font File
DAT	Database	FPX	FlashPix Bitmap
DB	Database File	FRM	WordPerfect 9 Document
DBF	Database (dBASE)	GIF	GIF Image (GIF =Graphics Interchange Format)
DIB	Windows Device Independent Bitmap	GRA	Microsoft Graph 2000 Chart
DIF	Data Interchange Format	GRP	Group (Microsoft Program Group)
DER	Security Certificate	HLP	Help File
DESKLINK	DESKLINK File (Show Desktop)	HT	HyperTerminal File
DGF	InterTrust DigiFile	HTA	HTML Application
DIB	Bitmap Image (Device Independent Bitmap)	HTM & HTML	HTML Document
DIR	Macromedia Director Movie	HTT	HyperText Template
DJV	AT&T DjVu Image	ICN	AT&T Multigen
DLL	Dynamic Link Library (Application Extension)	ICO	Icon File; ACDSee ICO Image
DOC	Microsoft Word Document; WordPad Document	IDX	Index (Database)
DOCHTML	Microsoft Word HTML Document	IFF	Amiga Interchange File Format
DOS	DOS Configuration File	III	IntelliPhone Compatible
DOT	Microsoft Word Template	INF	Setup Information File

Figure 3-39	FILE EXTENSIONS AND FILE TYPES (INI-NCS)		
FILE EXTENSION	**FILE TYPE**	**FILE EXTENSION**	**FILE TYPE**
INI	Initialization (Configuration Settings)	M1V	Movie File (MPEG)
INS	Internet Communication Settings	M2A, M2T, M2V	Movie File (MPEG)
IOD	Dvgate Motion IN/OUT List File	MAC	MacPaint Image
IQY	Microsoft Excel Web Query File	MAG	ACDSee MAG Image
ISP	Internet Communication Settings (Internet Signup)	MAPIMAIL	MAPIMail File (MAPI = Messaging API)
ITS	Internet Document Set	MBF	Corel VisualDTD 8.0
IVF	Indeo Video File	MBO, MBOX	Preview Systems MBOX File
JIF, JFIF	JPEG File Interchange Format	MDA	Microsoft Access Add-In
JOB	(Scheduled) Task Object	MDB	Microsoft Access Database
JOD	Microsoft.Jet.OLEB.4.0	MDW	Microsoft Access Workgroup Information
JPE, JPEG, JPG	Joint Photographic Experts Group	MED	a2b Music Download
JS	JScript Script File	MES	a2b Music
JSE	JScript Encoded Script File	MHT & MHTML	Microsoft HTML Document
KBD	Keyboard	MID & MIDI	Musical Instrument Device Interface
KDC	Kodak Photo-Enhancer	MJF	MJuice Music File
LA1	Liquid Audio File	MJV	MJuice Voucher File
LAR	Liquid Audio Passport	MMM	Media Clip
LAV	Liquid Audio Free Download	MOV	Quick Time Movie
LAVS	Liquid Auto Secure Download	MP2 & MP2V	Movie File
LBM	Delux Paint Graphics File; Linear Bitmap	MP3	MP3 Format Sound
LDF	LuraDocument File	MPA, MPE, MPEG, & MPG	Moving Pictures Experts Group; Movie File
LEX	Lexicon	MPJ	MPJ File
LGC	LGC File	MPV2	Movie File (MPEG); Movie Clip
LMU	Label	MSC	Microsoft Common Console Document
LNK	Link (Shortcut)	MSG	Message (Outlook Express Item)
LOG	Log File; Text Document	MSI	Windows Installer Package; Microsoft Installer
LQT	Liquid Music Track	MSP	Windows Installer Patch; Microsoft Patch
LSF	Streaming Audio/Video	MSRCINCIDENT	Microsoft Remote Assistant Incident
LSX	Streaming Audio/Video Shortcut	MSSTYLES	Windows Visual Style File
LWF	LuraWave File	MSWMM	Windows Movie Maker Project
LWV	Microsoft Linguistically Enhanced Sound	NCS	Lotus Notes Content Source

Figure 3-40   FILE EXTENSIONS AND FILE TYPES (NFO-RA)

FILE EXTENSION	FILE TYPE	FILE EXTENSION	FILE TYPE
NFO	MSInfo Document (System Information)	PIX	Inset Systems Graphics
NLU	Norton AntiVirus LiveUpdate	PKO	Public Key Security Object
NMW	Microsoft NetMeeting T126 Compatible Whiteboard; NetMeeting Whiteboard	PMA, PMC, PML, PMR, & PMW	Performance Monitor File
NWS	Internet News Message; Outlook Express News Message	PNG	Portable Network Graphics
OCX	ActiveX Control	PNTG	MacPaint Image
OFT	Outlook Item Template	PPM	Portable PixelMap
OQY	Microsoft Excel OLAP Query File	PPT	Microsoft PowerPoint Presentation
OSS	Office Search	PRF	PICSRules File
OTF	OpenType Font File	PRN	DOS Print File
P10	Certificate Request	PSD	Adobe Photoshop Bitmap
P12	Personal Information Exchange	PSF	PSF File
P7B	PKCS #7 Certificates	PSP	Paint Shop Pro 5 Image
P7C	Digital ID File	PSS	System Configuration Utility Backup (for System Files)
P7M	PKCS #7 MIME Message	PSW	Password Backup
P7R	PKCS #7 Certificates	PWL	Password List
P7S	PKCS #7 Signature	QDAT	QuickTime Install Cache
PBK	Dial-Up Phonebook	QDB	Quicken Data File
PBM	Portable Bit Map	QDF	Quicken Data File
PCD	Kodak Photo CD	QDS	Directory Query
PCT	PC Paint File	QDT	Quicken Data File
PCX	Picture Exchange (PC Paintbrush Graphics)	QFX	Quicken Fax
PDF	Portable Document Format (Acrobat)	QIC	Backup File for MS Backup (Quarter Inch Cartridge)
PDU	PhotoDecor Document	QPX	QuickTime Player Plugin
PDX	IDS_CATALOG_INDEX	QT	Quick Time Movie
PFC	PFC File	QTI or QTIF	Quick Time Image
PFM	Type 1 Font File	QTL	QuickTime Movie
PFX	Personal Information Exchange	QTP	QuickTime Preferences
PGM	Portable Gray Map Bitmap	QTS	QuickTime
PIC or PICT	Macintosh QuickDraw Image	QTX	QuickTime Extension
PIF	Program Information File (DOS Shortcut)	RA	RealAudio Clip

Figure 3-41   FILE EXTENSIONS AND FILE TYPES (RAM-VXD)

FILE EXTENSION	FILE TYPE	FILE EXTENSION	FILE TYPE
RAM	RealPlayer File	SD2	Sound Designer 2
RAS	Sun Raster Graphics	SDP	Scalable Multicast
RAT	Rating System File	SET	Settings (File Set for Microsoft Backup)
RDP	Remote Desktop Connection	SHB	Shortcut into a Document
REG	Registration Entries	SHS	Shell Scrap (Scrap Object)
RF	RealG2 with Flash Clip	SLK	Symbolic Link Data Import Format
RJS	RealSystem Skin	SMI & SMIL	Synchronized Multimedia Integration Language
RJT	RealSystem Track Info Style	SND	AU Format Sound
RLE	Run Length Encoded (Compressed Bitmap)	SNP	Snapshot File
RLF	Dvgate Motion Record List File	SPC	PKCS #7 Certificates
RM	RealMedia File	SPL	Shockwave Flash Object
RMF	Acrobat Rights Management Document	SPOP	InterTrust SPOP
RMI	MIDI Sequence	SSM	Standard Streaming Metafile
RMJ	RealSystem Media Clip	SST	Microsoft Serialized Certificate Store
RMM	RealPlayer File	STL	Certificate Trust List
RMP	Rich Metadata Package	SWF	Shockwave Flash Object
RMX	RealSystem Secure Media Clip	SYS	System File
RNK	Dial-Up Shortcut	TGA	Targa Graphics
RNX	RealPlayer File	THEME	Windows Theme File
RP	RealPix Clip	TIF & TIFF	Tagged Image File Format (Graphics)
RSB	Red Storm Image Format	TMP	Temporary File
RSML	RealSystem ML File	TTC	TrueType Collection Font File
RT	RealText Clip	TTF	TrueType Font File
RQY	Microsoft Excel OLE DB Query	TVPI	TV Program Information
RTF	Rich Text Format (Formatted) Document	TXT	Text Document
RV	RealVideo Clip	ULS	Internet Location Service
RWZ	Office Data File	URL	Internet Shortcut (Uniform Resource Locator)
SC	IBM EMMS Secure Download	VBE	VBScript Encoded Script File
SAM	Ami & AmiPro	VBS	VBScript Script File
SCP	Text Document; Dial-Up Networking Script	VCF	vCard File
SCR	Screen Saver	VIR	Virus Infected File
SCT	Windows Script Component	VXD	Virtual Device Driver

| Figure 3-42 | FILE EXTENSIONS AND FILE TYPES (WAB-ZIP) |

FILE EXTENSION	FILE TYPE	FILE EXTENSION	FILE TYPE
WAB	Address Book File	WSC	Windows Script Component
WAV	Wave Sound	WSF	Windows Script File
WAX	Windows Media Audio Shortcut	WSH	Windows Script Host Settings File
WB1	Quattro Pro for Windows 5.0	WTX	Text Document
WBK	Microsoft Word Backup Document	WVX	Windows Media Audio/Video Shortcut
WDB	Microsoft Works Database	XBM	X Bitmap
WHT	Microsoft NetMeeting Old Whiteboard Document	XIF	Xerox Image Format
WIZ	Microsoft Word Wizard	XLA	Microsoft Excel Add-In
WK1, WK3, WK4	Lotus 1-2-3 Worksheet	XLB	Microsoft Excel Worksheet
WKS	Lotus 1-2-3 & MS Works Worksheet	XLC	Microsoft Excel Chart
WLG	Dr. Watson Log File	XLD	Microsoft Excel DialogSheet
WM	Windows Media Audio/Video File (Streaming Audio/Video)	XLK	Microsoft Excel Backup File
WMA	Windows Media Audio File	XLM	Microsoft Excel 4.0 Macro
WMD	Windows Media Player Download Package	XLS	Microsoft Excel Worksheet
WMF	Windows Metafiles	XLSHTML	Microsoft Excel HTML Document
WMP	Windows Media Player File	XLT	Microsoft Excel Template
WMS	Windows Media Player Skin File	XLTHTML	Microsoft Excel HTML Template
WMV	Windows Media Audio/Video File	XLV	Microsoft Excel VBA Module
WMZ	Windows Media Player Skin Package	XLW	Microsoft Excel Workspace
WPD	WordPerfect Document	XML	Extensible Markup Language Document
WPG	Corel Presentations 9 Drawing	XNK	Exchange Shortcut
WPS	Microsoft Works Word Processing	XSL	Extensible Stylesheet Language
WPT	WordPerfect 9 Document	ZAP	Software Installation Settings
WQ1, WQ2	Quattro Pro	ZIP	Zip (Compressed)
WRI	Write Document; Windows 3.x Write		

Sharon has found that the Windows XP docucentric features have made her life easier. She uses her time more efficiently because she can quickly find and open client files, business records, and personal documents. She has noticed, however, that not all files are associated with specific applications, and she has even accidentally specified the wrong file association for certain types of files.

On her training disk, Sharon has a temporary file with the file extension "tmp", but the file icon used indicates that it is not associated with any application. Before she removes it from her disk, she asks you to find out what is stored in the file.

To open a file not associated with an application:

1. Insert Data Disk #1 in your floppy disk drive, open **My Computer**, and then click the **3½ Floppy (A:)** drive icon to open a window that shows the contents of this disk. In Tiles view, Windows XP identifies ~WRC0070.tmp as a TMP file. See Figure 3-43. Since this file is not associated with an application, Windows XP displays a default file icon rather than a custom file icon, and it identifies the file type as a "TMP File" rather than using a custom description for the file type. When Windows XP lists a file type derived from the file extension, you know that that file type is not associated with any application. Since the file size is not listed as 0 KB, you know that the file contains data.

Figure 3-43   VIEWING INFORMATION ABOUT A TEMPORARY FILE

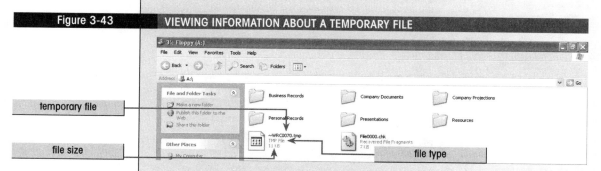

temporary file

file size

file type

2. Click the **~WRC0070.tmp** file icon. The Windows dialog box opens and informs you that it needs to know what program created the file in order to open it. See Figure 3-44. Windows XP also notes that it can go online to look up that information, or you can select the program from a list of programs available on your computer.

Figure 3-44   ATTEMPTING TO OPEN AN UNREGISTERED FILE TYPE

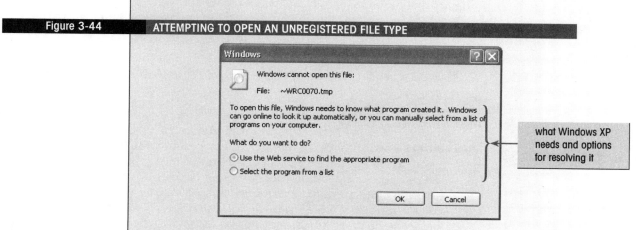

what Windows XP needs and options for resolving it

3. Make sure the **Use the Web service to find the appropriate program** option button is selected, click the **OK** button, and, if necessary, connect to your ISP. In the Microsoft Application Search window with the title "Microsoft Windows .NET File Associations," Windows XP identifies the file type as a "Temporary File" with the file extension .tmp (notice it includes the dot or period), and it explains that applications create this type of file to store information temporarily. See Figure 3-45. This Web page also contains links to Web sites for related software and information. Since this approach did not provide you with the information you need, you now have to search for the information you need by using links to various Web sites from this Web page, or try some other approach.

Figure 3-45	USING MICROSOFT'S WEB SERVICE TO LOCATE A PROGRAM FOR A FILE TYPE

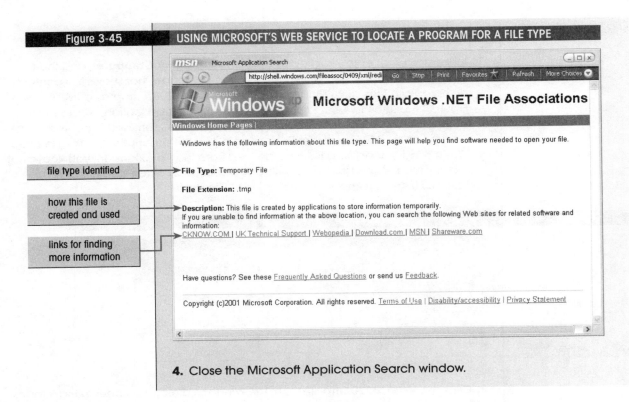

file type identified

how this file is created and used

links for finding more information

4. Close the Microsoft Application Search window.

Because you don't know what type of data is stored in this temporary file, you don't know what application to use to open the file. You can, however, try to open this file in a simple text editor, like Notepad or WordPad, and then attempt to locate information about the original application that produced the data in the file.

You decide to open the file with WordPad. However, you also want to make sure you do not *inadvertently* create a file association until you are sure that WordPad can read the file's contents.

To open this temporary file in WordPad without creating a file association:

1. Click the **~WRC0070.tmp** file icon, and after Windows XP opens a Windows dialog box, click the **Select the program from a list** option button, and then click the **OK** button. The Open With dialog box prompts you to choose a program for opening this file. You can select a program in the Programs box, which displays the programs installed on your computer, or you can use the Browse button to locate a program on your computer. See Figure 3-46. Your list of programs will differ. If you select a program, Windows XP always uses this program to open this kind of file. In other words, it creates an association between this file type and an application based on the file's extension. If you decide to pursue this course of action, you should enter a description for this file type (such as Temporary File) in this dialog box.

Figure 3-46 | OPENING AN UNREGISTERED FILE TYPE

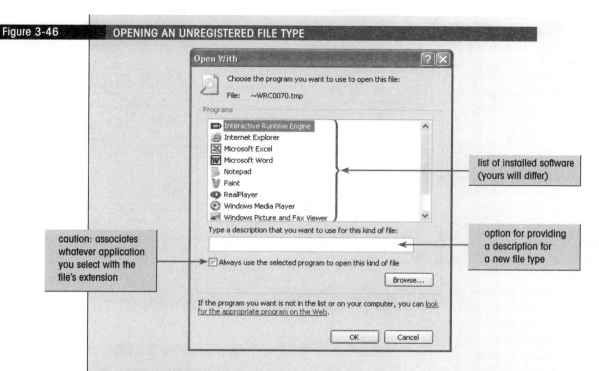

list of installed software (yours will differ)

option for providing a description for a new file type

caution: associates whatever application you select with the file's extension

TROUBLE? If someone has previously attempted to open a file of this same type with one of the programs on the computer you are using, the list of programs is subdivided into two categories—a Recommend Programs category and an Other Programs category. You can still proceed with the steps.

2. Click the **Always use the selected program to open this kind of file** check box and *remove* the check mark from the check box.

3. Double-check to make sure you removed the check mark from the "Always use the selected program to open this kind of file" check box before proceeding to the next step.

4. In the Programs box, locate and click **WordPad**, click the **OK** button, maximize the WordPad application window if necessary, click **View** on the menu bar, and then click **Options**. In the Options dialog box, click the **Text** tab if it is not already selected, click **Wrap to window** under Word wrap, and then click the **OK** button. You can now see part of the contents of this temporary file. See Figure 3-47. Although the file contains uninterpretable formatting codes, you also see the text contained within the document. The document also includes other information, such as the type of document, namely, a Microsoft Word 6.0 Document, which identifies the original application.

Figure 3-47   VIEWING THE CONTENTS OF A TEMPORARY FILE

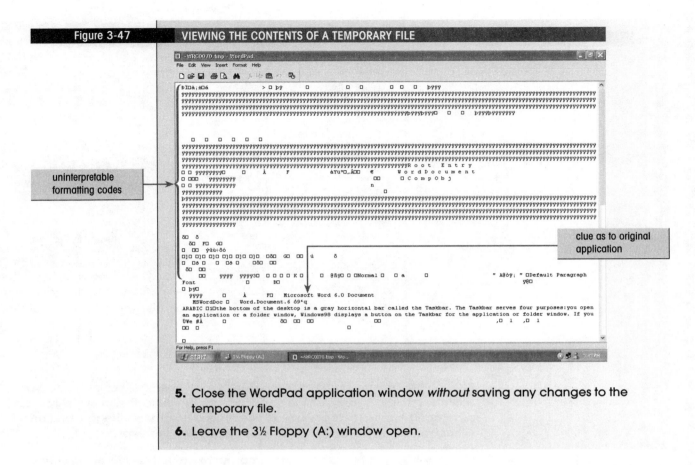

uninterpretable formatting codes

clue as to original application

5. Close the WordPad application window *without* saving any changes to the temporary file.

6. Leave the 3½ Floppy (A:) window open.

You now know that the original file was a Microsoft Word document, and that this file was created to temporarily hold the file's contents while Word worked with the file. This temporary file would normally have been deleted when you closed Microsoft Word; however, more than likely a power problem, system lockup, or nonresponding program prevented that operation, so the temporary file remained on the disk. If you try to open this file in Microsoft Word, you will discover that it cannot open the file, and so there's no point in trying to establish an association with Microsoft Word (but recall that WordPad was able to open it). If, however, you want to permanently associate a file extension with a specific application on your computer, you can choose the option for always opening this file type with the program you select in the Open With dialog box.

For other types of files, such as files with extensions that have been accidentally or deliberately changed, you can open the file in WordPad or Notepad, examine the first part of the document for information or a code that identifies the original type of file (such as GIF) or the original application, and then you can restore the file's original file extension and thereby associate it with the proper application on your computer.

Viewing **Information on Registered Files**

If you open the Folder Options dialog box and then examine file types on your computer, Windows XP lists all your registered file types by file extensions and by file types using the description assigned to each file type. You can create a new file type, delete a registered file type, change the program associated with a specific file extension and file type, or modify the actions (such as Open and Print) associated with a registered file type. If you accidentally assigned a program to a file extension, you can remove that newly registered file type; however, you must be part of the Administrators group, or the Administrator must temporarily provide you with Administrator privileges, to make these changes.

So that you can better understand how Windows XP works with registered files, Sharon encourages you to view information on a simple registered file type, namely, the Text Document file type.

Note: If your account is not an Administrator account, or if you do not have Administrator privileges, you cannot complete all the steps in this section of the tutorial. However, you can read, but not keystroke, those steps, and examine the figures, so that you understand how Windows XP works with registered file types.

To view information on a registered file:

1. In the 3½ Floppy (A:) window, click **Tools** on the menu bar, click **Folder Options**, and after Windows XP opens the Folder Options dialog box, click the **File Types** tab. Windows XP lists file extensions and file types in the Registered file types box. See Figure 3-48. Some registered file types, such as folders, do not have extensions. Yours will differ. In the "Details for" section, Windows XP displays information about the current selection in the Registered file types box.

   TROUBLE? If you are not logged on under an account with Administrator privileges, the New, Delete, Change, and Advanced buttons are dimmed, and you cannot make changes to registered file types. You can, however, view some types of information on registered files.

   TROUBLE? If you are logged on under an account with Administrator privileges, and if the Delete and Change buttons are dimmed, you cannot remove or change the file type selected in the Registered file types box.

Figure 3-48	VIEWING INFORMATION ON REGISTERED FILE TYPES

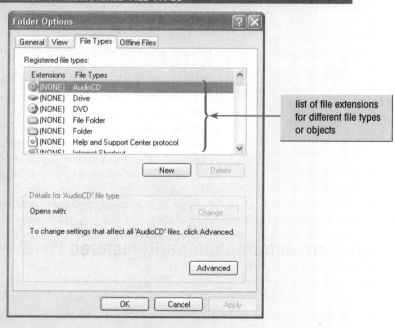

list of file extensions for different file types or objects

2. In the Registered file types list box, double-click the thin border between the Extensions column and the File Types column for a best fit so that you can see the longest file extension, click an **extension** (such as (NONE)), type **u** to locate the first file extension that starts with the letter "u," and then click **TXT** under Extensions to display details about TXT files. See Figure 3-49. In the Details for 'TXT' extension section, Windows XP notes that it uses Notepad to open files with the TXT file extension, and it shows the Notepad application file icon. In the Registered file types box, Windows XP also shows the icon it uses for files with this extension.

Figure 3-49	TEXT DOCUMENT FILE TYPE

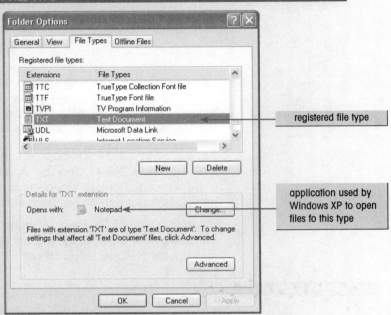

3. Click the **Advanced** button. In the Edit File Type dialog box, Windows XP displays the icon used for files of this type and the description "Text Document" for this file type, and provides a button that you can use to choose a new file icon. See Figure 3-50. When you change your view in a folder window to Tiles view or Details view, or choose the option to arrange files in order by Type (no matter which view you choose), Windows XP uses this description to group files of the same type and then lists them in alphabetical order by the description. In the Actions list box, Windows XP lists actions defined for this file type: open, print, and printto. Your list of options might differ.

TROUBLE? If the Advanced button is dimmed, you cannot complete this step and the remainder of the steps in this section of the tutorial. Read, but do not attempt to keystroke, this step and the remaining steps, and examine the figures.

Figure 3-50	VIEWING INFORMATION ON THE TEXT DOCUMENT FILE TYPE

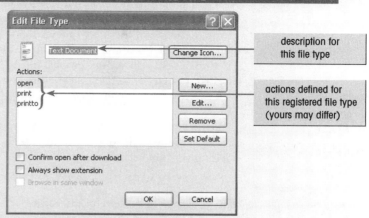

description for
this file type

actions defined for
this registered file type
(yours may differ)

Below the Actions box, you can choose to confirm whether to open the file after you download it from a Web site, to always show the file extension, and in some cases, specify that you want to open files of this type in the existing window rather than in a new window.

4. In the Actions list box, click **open**, and then click the **Edit** button. The Editing action for type: Text Document dialog box opens. See Figure 3-51. In the Application used to perform action box, Windows XP lists the full path for the program file that it opens if you click (or double-click in Windows Classic style) the file icon for this file type. If your Windows folder is named Windows, your full path will be C:\WINDOWS\system32\NOTEPAD.EXE %1 or if your Windows folder name is WinNT, then your full path will be C:\WINNT\system32\NOTEPAD.EXE %1

TROUBLE? If you have a multiple-boot configuration and if Windows XP is installed on another partition, then the drive name is different.

Figure 3-51	COMMAND FOR OPENING A TEXT DOCUMENT

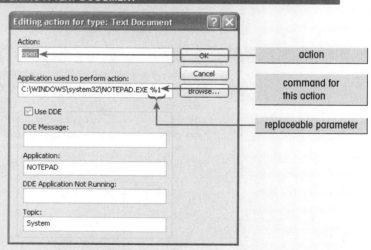

action

command for
this action

replaceable parameter

If you click (or double-click) a file with the "txt" file extension, Windows XP opens Notepad.exe, which is located in the System32 folder under the Windows folder on drive C. The %1 following the full path is a **replaceable parameter** that tells Windows XP to substitute the name of the file you clicked for %1 after the full path of the program. For example, if you click (or double-click) a file named EULA.txt (the file that contains the Windows XP End-User License Agreement) in the Windows System32 folder, Windows XP substitutes EULA.txt for %1 so that the full command for opening the file now becomes:

C:\WINDOWS\system32\NOTEPAD.EXE EULA.txt

Later, if you click (or double-click) a file named License.txt in the Windows System32 folder, Windows XP substitutes the filename License.txt for %1, and the full command for opening this file becomes:

C:\WINDOWS\System32\NOTEPAD.EXE License.txt

The replaceable parameter therefore acts as a placeholder for the filename. By using a replaceable parameter, the command becomes more flexible, and Windows XP can use it to open any text document file, no matter what its name is.

To continue your examination of actions for this file type:

1. Click the **Cancel** button to close the Editing action for type: Text Document dialog box without making any changes.

2. In the Actions list box, click **print**, and then click the **Edit** button. In the Application used to perform action text box, you see the full path for the program file that Windows XP uses if you right-click a file icon for this file type and then choose Print from the shortcut menu. See Figure 3-52. Again, Windows XP opens Notepad.exe and substitutes the filename for the %1 replaceable parameter. The /p switch tells Windows XP to print the document rather than display it. A **switch** is an optional parameter that modifies the way in which a command works. Most switches start with a forward slash (/) and are followed by one or more codes (as you will see in more detail in Tutorial 14). If you right-click a Text Document file type, and then click Print on the shortcut menu, Windows XP quickly opens Notepad, opens the file, prints the file, closes the file, and finally closes Notepad.

| Figure 3-52 | COMMAND FOR PRINTING A TEXT DOCUMENT |

3. Click the **Cancel** button to close the Editing action for type: Text Document dialog box without making any changes, click the **Cancel** button to close the Edit File Type dialog box without making any changes, and click the **Cancel** button to close the Folder Options dialog box.

4. Close the 3½ Floppy (A:) folder window.

If you examine other file types, you discover similar definitions for similar actions, such as opening and printing. You also find information about other types of objects, such as drives and folders.

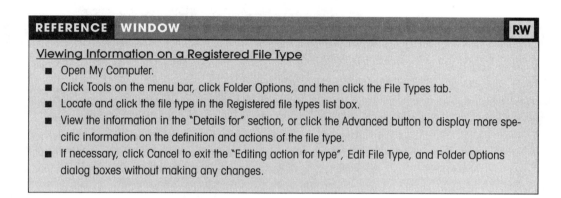

REFERENCE WINDOW   **RW**

Viewing Information on a Registered File Type
- Open My Computer.
- Click Tools on the menu bar, click Folder Options, and then click the File Types tab.
- Locate and click the file type in the Registered file types list box.
- View the information in the "Details for" section, or click the Advanced button to display more specific information on the definition and actions of the file type.
- If necessary, click Cancel to exit the "Editing action for type", Edit File Type, and Folder Options dialog boxes without making any changes.

Windows XP relies on the full path for the name and location of the program file to open a registered file. The full path might also include switches that control the operations Windows XP performs, and a replaceable parameter to indicate where to insert the filename in the command. You also now know how the file type description affects the sorting of files in folder windows.

Registered files are one of the most important features of a docucentric operating system such as Windows XP, and you might find instances where you want to define new file types and associate them with an application so that you can open and print the contents of these files. You might also want the option of defining actions that permit you to open a file using one or more other applications in addition to the default application associated with that file type.

Restoring Your Computer's Settings

If you are working in a computer lab or on a company network, complete the following steps to restore the original display settings on your computer. If you are using your own computer, and want to restore the original settings, also complete the following steps.

To restore your computer's display settings:

1. If your computer was originally set for the Windows Classic style, right-click the desktop, click **Properties** on the shortcut menu, and after Windows XP opens the Display Properties dialog box, click the **Theme** list arrow on the Themes property sheet, click **Windows Classic**, and click the **OK** button.

2. To switch to the Windows Classic Start menu style, right-click the **Start** button, click **Properties** on the shortcut menu, and after Windows XP opens the Taskbar and Start Menu Properties dialog box, click the **Classic Start menu** option button on the Start Menu property sheet, and click the **OK** button.

3. To change to Windows classic folders view, click the **Start** button, point to **Settings**, click **Control Panel**, and after Windows XP opens a Control Panel window, click **Tools** on the menu bar, click **Folder Options**, and after Windows XP opens the Folder Options dialog box, click the **Use Windows classic folders** option button, and click the **Double-click to open an item** option button under "Click items as follows."

4. Click the **View** tab in the Folder Options dialog box. If necessary, restore the original settings for the "Display the full path in the address bar" check box, the "Show hidden files and folders" option, and the "Hide extensions for known file types" check box.

5. Click the **OK** button to close the Folder Options dialog box and restore your original settings, and then close the Control Panel folder window.

Sharon discovered that the time you helped her plan the folder structure of her hard disk has paid off. Her client, business, and personal files are logically organized and easy for her to find and use. Sharon decides to convert the FAT32 file system used on her hard disk to NTFS so that she can enjoy the efficient usage of disk storage space and the additional features available with NTFS. Furthermore, she can now help clients resolve problems with registered file types and file associations on their computers.

REVIEW ASSIGNMENTS

Sharon recently hired another graphics artist, Jacqueline Lyden, to help her with her client projects. On Jacqueline's first day of work, Sharon describes the types of client support that the two of them must provide for the successful completion of their projects. Sharon asks you to show Jacqueline the folder structure and file system used on her computer so that Jacqueline can adapt a similar structure on the computer she uses.

As you complete each step in this Review Assignment, record your answers to questions so that you can submit them to your instructor. Use a word processing application such as Word or WordPad to prepare and then print your answers to these questions. Also, if you change any settings on the computer you are using, note the original settings so that you can restore them later. You need your copy of Data Disk #1 to complete this assignment.

1. Insert Data Disk #1 into drive A, and then open My Computer.

2. From the Tools menu, open the Folder Options dialog box and, if necessary, enable Web style. Also, turn on the options for showing hidden files and folders, file extensions for known file types, and the full path in the Address bar if they are not currently selected. Then close the Folder Options dialog box and apply these new settings.

3. Point to and select the drive C icon, click File on the menu bar, and then click Properties. What is the volume label for this drive (if any)? What type of file system does Windows XP use for this drive? What is the total storage capacity of drive C? Approximately what percentage of the storage capacity of the disk is available, or free?

Explore   4. Click the Hardware tab and, in the All disk drives box, select your first hard disk. Who is the manufacturer, and what is the model? What is the location of the device? What is the device status?

5. Close the Properties dialog box for drive C.

Explore   6. Do you have another drive, for example, a drive D? If so, what type of file system does it use, and what is its total storage capacity? Also, what percentage of the storage capacity of the disk is free? Close the Properties dialog box for this drive.

7. Could you upgrade the file system of each drive and improve the overall performance of your computer? Explain.

8. View the contents of your Data Disk #1.

9. Right-click the Business Records folder and view its properties. What is the size of this folder? How many files does this folder contain? How much storage space is slack? Close the Properties dialog box for this folder.

10. Open the Business Records folder, use the Select All option on the Edit menu to select all the files in the window, and then select Properties from the File menu to display information on the group properties of these files. Does the total size of these files and the amount of storage space that they use on disk match what Windows XP reported in the previous step? When Windows XP reports the size of a folder in that folder's Properties dialog box, what is it actually reporting? Based on this information, what do you conclude is the size of the directory table that tracks the contents of the Business Records folder? What is the path for this folder? Close the Properties dialog box for this group, and return to the top-level folder of drive A.

11. While you hold down the Ctrl key, point to and select the Business Records, Personal Records, and Resources folders. Then choose Properties from the File menu to view the group properties of these folders. How many files and folders are contained within this group selection? What is the combined size of these folders? How much slack do the combined contents of these folders use? Close the Properties dialog box for the group.

Explore   12. Assume Sharon created the Company Documents folder first, and created the Company Projections folder next. When Windows XP creates an alias for the Company Projections folder, would its alias depend on the alias of the Company Documents folder? If so, why? If not, why not? What would be the most likely aliases that Windows XP would use for these two folders?

13. Open the Presentations folder. What does Windows XP report as the file type for the file named File Systems.pps? Is this file type associated with an application on your computer? If so, identify three ways in which you can tell it is associated with an application. What is the full path of this file? Close any open dialog boxes.

14. Select Folder Options from the Tools menu, select the File Types tab, and examine information on the Rich Text Format registered file type. If this file type is not listed as a registered file type on your computer, choose another file type. What registered file type did you examine? What is the default file extension for that registered file type? What application does Windows XP use to open that registered file type?

Explore   15. *Optional*: This step requires that you have Administrator privileges. What types of actions are defined for the Rich Text Format file type? What is the default action, and how can you tell? Choose the Open action for this file type, and examine the command for that action. What command does Windows XP use for that action? Why is the path enclosed within quotation marks? Does the command use any switches or replaceable parameters? If so, what are they? Close all open dialog boxes without making any changes.

16. Restore the original settings used on your computer, and then close the drive A window.

CASE PROBLEMS

Case 1. Evaluating the Organization of Folders at Peninsula Child Care Peninsula Child Care is a nonprofit agency that provides childcare services for parents who are reentering the job market. Federal, state, and county agencies, as well as corporations fund the agency's programs with special grants and donate computer equipment for its administrative staff. The office manager, James O'Connor, checks each donated computer to make sure it is set up for use by other staff members. More often than not, he has to install software, reorganize folders on the hard disk, remove unneeded files, and check system settings. Recently, a staff member in another office acquired a new computer and gave James his old computer so that it could be set up for yet another staff member. After examining the computer, James discovered that:

- The folder structure for document files is complex and extensive and, in some cases, includes five or six levels of folders below the top-level folder of the disk.

- Some document files are stored in folders below software folders.

- Some document folders contain close to 100 files, many of which are relatively small.

- The top-level folder contains document files as well as temporary files and fragments of files probably created by a power failure.

- The hard disk, which uses the FAT32 file system, is almost full.

James asks you to propose a more effective organization for the files and folders on this computer. Using a word-processing application such as Microsoft Word or WordPad, prepare a list of at least six recommendations on how James might improve the organization of information and increase the free storage space on the computer. Assume that James wants to keep most of the document files, because these files contain grant proposals, agency progress reports, annual reports, budget documents, and other types of documents that invariably prove valuable to other staff members.

Case 2. Tracking Case Files at Midland Hospital Marion Tompkins works as an epidemiologist for Midland Hospital. As she analyzes the appearance and spread of contagious diseases, she produces a set of case files and supporting documents. She asks you to develop an easy-to-use method for tracking the information on her hard disk. At the same time, the records are confidential, so she wants you to create a folder system that uses the word Case along with the case number to maintain the confidentiality of her patients. Because she uses Windows XP applications and one older application designed for Windows 3.1 for statistical analyses, she wants to be sure that the folder names easily identify a case by its case number and enable her to locate a given folder no matter what application she uses. She asks you to start by experimenting with her proposed folder-naming system.

As you complete each step in this case, record your answers to the questions so that you can submit them to your instructor. Use a word-processing application such as Word or WordPad to prepare and then print your answers to these questions.

1. On your copy of Data Disk #1, create a new folder named Cases, open the Cases folder, and then create two folders with the long filenames Case 0001 and Case 0002. Create the folders in the order listed.

2. Prepare a table that lists the long filename and the alias for each folder.

3. Create two other folders with the long filenames Case 0005 and Case 0012 (in this order), and then add the names of these folders and their aliases to the table you are preparing.

Explore   4. Would Windows XP use the same process to create a short filename if you added a fifth folder named Case 0015? Explain.

5. If Marion continues to use this method of naming folders, will she run into any problems if she uses her Windows 3.1 application to locate these folders and their files? Explain and provide an example.

Explore   6. What other approach could Marion use for naming these folders so that she can quickly identify the case numbers in the folder name no matter what type of application she uses? As you answer this question, list the folder names you would use in lieu of Case 0001, Case 0002, Case 0005, and Case 0012. Also list their aliases.

Explore   7. Identify which of the following applications display long filenames in an Open and Save As dialog box: Windows XP applications, Windows 2000 applications, Windows Me applications, Windows 98 applications, Windows NT Workstation 4.0 applications, Windows 95 applications, Windows 3.1 applications, and DOS applications.

Explore   8. Identify which of the following applications display only MS-DOS filenames (or aliases) in an Open and Save As dialog box: Windows XP applications, Windows 2000 applications, Windows Me applications, Windows 98 applications, Windows NT Workstation 4.0 applications, Windows 95 applications, Windows 3.1 applications, and DOS applications.

Case 3. Analyzing Registered File Types at A&E Training Specialists Margo McCain works as a trainer for A&E Training Specialists, which offers customized training programs for employees of companies in the greater Los Angeles area. Recently, Financial Management Inc. contracted with A&E Training Specialists for a one-day training session on registered file types for its technical staff. To prepare for this training session, Margo asks you to help her review information about common types of registered file types so that she can quickly answer questions and point out similarities between different file types. She also intends to use the information she compiles in a handout for the training session.

To complete this case problem, you need to log on your computer using an account with Administrator privileges.

As you complete each step in this case, record your answers to the questions so that you can submit them to your instructor. Use a word-processing application such as Word or WordPad to prepare and then print your answers to these questions.

1. Identify five to 10 file types that you frequently use on your computer and their file extensions, and identify the applications associated with these file types. *Hint*: To recall the most common types of files you use, you can look through the Registered File types box on the File Types property sheet in the Folder Options dialog box.

2. Identify the application that Windows XP uses to open each of the file types listed in the previous step. *Hint*: If you cannot see the entire designation for the Opens with option, use the Change button to display an Open With dialog box so that you can view the entire program name or library. Then click the Cancel button to close the Open With dialog box without making any changes to your system.

Explore   3. List the command for the Open action for each of these file types. Why are some full paths enclosed within quotation marks? What does %1 in a command represent, and how does Windows XP use this variable? Give an example using one of the commands for a file type listed in this step.

Case 4. Evaluating Computer File Systems at Straub Design Group Maarten Keresey works as a technical support person at the Straub Design Group in New York City. Many of the employees are graphic designers, and often complete projects on their home computers. Periodically, an employee asks him for advice on the best type of file system to use for their home computer. Describe what Maarten should recommend in each of the following cases.

Use a word-processing application such as Word or WordPad to prepare and then print your answers to these questions.

1. Rhonda has just purchased a new, top-of-the-line computer system for use at home. After she set up the computer, she opened My Computer and noticed that Windows XP reported that she had two drives with different file systems. Drive C is just under 16 GB in size and uses the FAT32 file system, while Drive D is 40 GB in size and uses the NTFS file system. Rhonda wants to know if she would benefit by upgrading FAT32 to NTFS. Would this be possible and advisable? If so, what benefits would Rhonda derive from changing the file system to NTFS? If not, explain why Rhonda should retain the FAT32 file system on drive C.

2. Tim has an older computer system that he has upgraded several times. The hard disk has a storage capacity of almost 4 GB. What file system would you recommend Tim use on his computer, and why?

3. Eva's computer is even older than Tim's; however, she hopes to purchase a new computer system in the near future and let her children have her older computer. Her computer has a hard disk with almost 2 GB of storage space, and it uses the FAT16 file system. Would Eva benefit from upgrading her computer to FAT32 or NTFS? If so, explain what type of upgrade would be possible and describe what advantages each file system would provide. If not, why not?

4. Alex has a fairly new computer with 40 GB of storage space; however, instead of one drive, the hard disk has been partitioned into two drives with 20 GB of storage space, and each drive uses the FAT32 file system. Why did the manufacturer set up this computer with two drives, each of which uses FAT32, rather than partition it into just one drive that uses FAT32? Can Alex upgrade the file system on each drive and, if so, what would you recommend he do?

Explore   5. Maria's home computer has worked like a charm since day one. Her computer has an 18 GB hard disk that uses FAT32. Although her coworkers recommend that she consider upgrading to NTFS, she is reluctant to change her computer and risk creating problems. She would, however, like the option of compressing folders and files on her computer so that storage space was used more efficiently. Is this possible, and if so, how would she do it?

Explore   6. Todd's computer has an 80 GB hard disk partitioned into one drive. Todd would like to repartition his computer and divide the hard disk into two 40 GB drives so that he can store all his document files on one drive and simplify the process of backing up his computer. If Todd made this change, what file system(s) can he use on each 40 GB drive?

OBJECTIVES

In this tutorial you will:

- Create and use desktop and Internet shortcuts

- View shortcut properties

- Customize shortcuts

- Add shortcuts to, and remove shortcuts from, the Start menu

- Customize the Start menu

- Customize the Send To menu

- Create and update a Briefcase

CREATING AND CUSTOMIZING SHORTCUTS

Customizing a Computer at Delta Oil

CASE

Delta Oil Company

Delta Oil is a small oil company with its headquarters in San Diego, California. Delta Oil develops and sells a variety of petroleum-based products, including high-quality motor oils. Like many other small companies, Delta Oil has relied on a minicomputer to handle the majority of its data-processing requirements. However, as the company has grown, employees now use desktop computers to perform many of their job functions, but they still access information stored on the minicomputer to produce management reports and sales projections and analyses.

You work with Jason Kalman, a staff resource specialist who assists employees with the use of their desktop computers. So that employees can work more efficiently and save valuable time, Jason has designed templates for different types of company documents. A **template** is a file that contains the structure, formatting, and some of the actual contents of a specific type of document, such as a slide presentation for use in company training programs, or a spreadsheet for analyzing a company's performance and projected growth. Templates also have the advantage of giving company documents a consistent look. Because you are now responsible for providing employees with the templates and resources they need, Jason wants you to customize your computer with shortcuts so that you can quickly respond to staff requests.

In the first part of the tutorial, you use different techniques to create shortcuts to components on your computer system, such as drives, folders, files, and applications. You also create and use Internet shortcuts. You examine the properties of each of these types of shortcuts so that you understand how shortcuts work. You also step through the process of customizing shortcuts by changing their icons and by changing how they operate.

Using Shortcuts

As you start to handle staff requests, you discover that you need quick access to drives, folders, applications, utilities, and documents on your computer so that you can prepare and assemble templates and other types of resources for employees at Delta Oil. Rather than use the Start menu and My Computer to locate and then open a drive, folder, application, or document, Jason suggests that you create shortcuts that can take you directly to those objects on your computer.

A desktop **shortcut** is a special type of file that contains the full path to an object and, as a result, is a direct link to that object. When you click a shortcut in Web style, or double-click a shortcut in Windows Classic style, Windows XP locates and opens the object referenced by the shortcut. After creating a shortcut, you can go directly to a drive, application, utility, document, or printer in one step. You can also create shortcuts to objects on a network, including another computer, or to Web sites. Figure 4-1 and Figure 4-2 illustrate examples of the types of shortcuts that you can create on your computer.

| Figure 4-1 | | EXAMPLES OF HARDWARE, SOFTWARE, AND FOLDER SHORTCUTS |

Type of Object	Shortcut	Path or Object Name
Hardware Shortcuts		
Drive A		A:\
Drive C		C:\
Drive E (DVD Drive)		E:\
Drive F (CD-RW Drive)		F:\
Drive Z (Mapped Network Drive)		\\Micronpc\Photos
Software Shortcuts		
Windows Explorer		C:\Windows\Explorer.exe
Microsoft Word		"C:\Program Files\Microsoft Office\Office10\Winword.exe"
Microsoft Outlook		"C:\Program Files\Microsoft Office\Office10\Outlook.exe"
Internet Explorer		"C:\Program Files\Internet Explorer\IExplore.exe"
Windows Update		C:\Windows\System32\Wupdmgr.exe
Command Prompt (Command Line)		C:\Windows\System32\Cmd.exe
Folder Shortcuts		
My Documents (or Jason's Documents)		"C:\Documents and Settings\Jason\My Documents"
My Pictures		"C:\Documents and Settings\Jason\My Documents\My Pictures"
Shared Documents		"C:\Documents and Settings\All Users\Documents"
Windows		C:\Windows
Multimedia		D:\Multimedia
Business		D:\Business
Clients		D:\Clients

Figure 4-2   EXAMPLES OF DOCUMENT, NETWORK, AND INTERNET SHORTCUTS

Type of Object	Shortcut	Path or Object Name
Document Shortcuts		
Resume (Word Document)		"C:\Documents and Settings\Jason\My Documents\Resumes\Resume.doc"
Assets (Excel Document)		C:\Documents and Settings\Jason\My Documents\Personal\Assets.xls
Windows XP (Wallpaper)		"C:\Windows\Web\Wallpaper\Windows XP.jpg"
Beethoven's Symphony No. 9		"C:\Documents and Settings\All Users\Documents\My Music\Sample Music\Beethoven's Symphony No. 9 (Scherzo).wma"
Shortcut into a Document		Document Shortcut 'E-Mail Shortcuts...'
Network Shortcuts		
My Network Places		My Network Places
Network Workgroup		Mshome
Network Computer		\\Micronpc
Network Drive		\\Micronpc\Drive E
Network Printer		\\Micronpc\LaserJet
Network Zip Drive		\\Micronpc\Zip Drive
Network Folder		\\Micronpc\Drive E\Photos
Internet & Web Shortcuts		
MSN Explorer		
Microsoft Web Site		www.microsoft.com/ms.htm
Microsoft Knowledge Base		support.microsoft.com/default.aspx?scid=fh;rid;kbinfo
Course Technology Web Site		www.course.com

As you can tell from these figures, the shortcut icon is similar to the icon for a specific object, except for a box with a small arrow in the lower-left corner [icon]. Notice that network paths include two backslash characters at the beginning of the path. For example, \\MicronPC identifies a computer on a network. This path is called the **UNC path** (for Universal Naming Convention), and is a standard approach used to reference servers, printers, and other resources on a network.

Shortcut icons to system objects, such as drives, are identical to the icon that Windows XP uses for the object itself. The same is also true for application shortcuts and document shortcuts. If you create a shortcut to folders, Windows XP uses the same type of folder icon, unless the shortcut is to a system folder such as My Pictures that already has a custom icon. Shortcuts to network drives and folders have the same shortcut icon. The same is true for shortcuts to Web sites.

You can place shortcuts on the desktop, in folders where you frequently work, in documents, and in e-mail messages. For example, you might place a shortcut to your word-processing application, or even to a document that you work on daily, on the desktop or on a taskbar toolbar. You might store copies of the same shortcut in different places, so that you can quickly access the object. Shortcuts are also useful in networked environments, because you do not have to browse the network looking for a network resource; instead, you can go directly to that resource from the desktop or the My Documents folder, for example.

If you store a shortcut in a document, you can double-click the shortcut to go directly to the object in another window. For example, you might produce a report for the marketing director that summarizes marketplace trends important to your company's future growth. In the summary report, you might include one or more shortcuts that link directly to the document with the supporting data that you used as the basis for your analysis. If the Marketing Director wants to examine that original data, all she needs to do is double-click the shortcut to that document. If you are sending an e-mail message to a coworker or friend, you might include a shortcut to a favorite Web site.

Getting Started

To complete this tutorial, you need to switch your computer to Web style, and you also need to activate the options for showing hidden folders and files, displaying file extensions, and displaying the full path in the Address bar. You also need to display the Quick Launch toolbar on the taskbar. As you complete these steps, you may discover that your computer is already set up for Web style, or that other settings are already in place, so you might only need to make a few changes to your computer's settings.

To set up your computer:

1. To change to the Windows XP theme, right-click the **desktop**, click **Properties** on the shortcut menu, and after Windows XP opens the Display Properties dialog box, click the **Theme** list arrow on the Themes property sheet, click **Windows XP**, if necessary, and then click the **OK** button.

2. To switch to the Windows XP Start menu style, right-click the **Start** button, click **Properties**, and after Windows XP opens the Taskbar and Start Menu Properties dialog box, click the **Start menu** option button on the Start Menu property sheet, if necessary, and the click the **OK** button.

3. To change to a task-oriented view of folders and enable single-clicking, click the **Start** button, click **My Computer**, click **Tools** on the menu bar, click **Folder Options**, and after Windows XP opens the Folder Options dialog box, click the **Show common tasks in folders** option button if it is not already selected, click the **Single-click to open an item** option button if it is not already selected, and click the **Underline icon titles only when I point at them** option button if it is not already selected.

4. Click the **View** tab, click the **Display the full path in the address bar** check box if it is not already selected, click the **Show hidden files and folders** option button if it is not already selected, and if there is a check mark in the "Hide extensions for known file types" check box, click that check box to remove the check mark. Click the **OK** button to close the Folder Options dialog box, and then close My Computer.

5. Right-click the **taskbar**, point to **Toolbars**, and then click **Quick Launch**.

Now you're ready to create shortcuts.

Creating **Shortcuts**

If you want to create a shortcut to a drive, application, folder, or file on the desktop, you can use any of the following techniques:

- **Dragging**. If you want to create a shortcut to a drive or system folder, you can open My Computer and drag the drive or folder icon to the desktop. You can also select more than one drive or system folder, and drag them all to the desktop to create several shortcuts at once. However, you should not use this approach to create a shortcut to a folder that contains installed software or to a folder that contains your document files, because Windows XP moves the folder instead of creating a shortcut. To be on the safe side, you should not drag the file icon for an application or another type of program from a window to the desktop.

- **Right-dragging**. If you right-drag the icon for a drive, application, folder, or file to the desktop, Windows XP displays a shortcut menu with an option for creating a shortcut.

- **Right-clicking**. If you right-click the icon for a drive, application, folder, or file, you can choose the option for creating a shortcut. If you perform this operation on a drive or system folder in My Computer, Windows XP places the shortcut on the desktop. However, if you perform this operation in a folder with installed software or a folder with documents, Windows XP creates a shortcut in that folder. You can then move the shortcut to the desktop.

- **Using the File menu**. You can select a drive, application, folder, or file, and then use the option for creating a shortcut on the File menu. If you perform this operation on a drive or system folder in My Computer, Windows XP places the shortcut on the desktop. However, if you perform this operation in a folder with installed software or a folder with documents, Windows XP creates a shortcut in that folder. You can then move the shortcut to the desktop.

- **Using the Send To menu**. If you right-click a drive, application, folder, or file, and then point to Send To on the shortcut menu, you can choose Desktop (create shortcut). Windows XP places the shortcut on the desktop. This approach is the easiest and also the safest one to use.

As you step through the tutorial, you use these techniques and other techniques to create shortcuts. Then, as you work on your computer, you can use the technique or techniques that best suits the situation.

Creating Shortcuts to Drives

If you want to create a shortcut to a drive shown in the My Computer window, you can drag the drive icon onto the desktop, and Windows XP will create the shortcut without prompting you. If you right-click a drive icon, and choose the Create shortcut option on the shortcut menu, Windows XP asks if you want to place the shortcut on the desktop because you cannot create objects within the My Computer window. A simple drag is faster; however, part of the desktop must be visible. If you are working in a maximized My Computer window, you would use the other approach to create the shortcut.

Jason recommends that you start by creating shortcuts to drive A and drive C on your computer. You can then use the drive C shortcut to locate templates quickly and, after you copy the templates a coworker needs to a floppy disk, you can use the drive A shortcut to examine the floppy disk and verify that it has everything the coworker wants. You can also use these shortcuts to quickly back up files at the end of a busy day, and to copy files that you can then work on at home or while traveling on company business.

To complete these steps, you need a copy of Data Disk #2.

To create shortcuts to drive A and then to drive C:

1. Insert your copy of Data Disk #2 into drive A.

2. Open My Computer, click the **Restore Down** button 🗗 if the window is maximized, and adjust the placement and size of the My Computer window so that you can see the 3½ Floppy (A:) icon in the My Computer window and an empty area of the desktop.

3. Drag the **3½ Floppy (A:)** icon in the My Computer window to the desktop, release the left mouse button, and then click the **desktop** to change the focus from the shortcut. Windows XP creates a desktop shortcut to the 3½ Floppy (A:) drive. See Figure 4-3. Your icon might be named "Shortcut to 3½ Floppy (A:)." As you drag the icon, Windows XP displays a shortcut arrow box 🡥 in the drive icon.

Figure 4-3	CREATING A SHORTCUT USING DRAG AND DROP

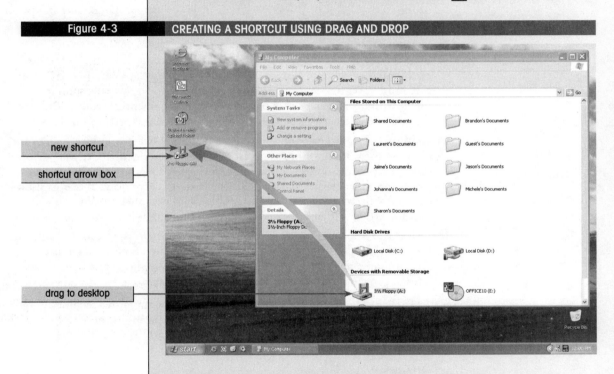

new shortcut
shortcut arrow box
drag to desktop

4. Point to and select the **3½ Floppy (A)** shortcut, press the **F2** (Rename) key, type **Drive A**, and then press the **Enter** key to change the shortcut's name.

5. Maximize the My Computer window, right-click the icon for drive C, and then click **Create Shortcut** on the shortcut menu. The Shortcut dialog box informs you that Windows XP cannot create a shortcut here (meaning the My Computer folder window) and asks if you want to place it on the desktop instead.

6. Click the **Yes** button in the Shortcut dialog box, and then restore the My Computer window so that you can see the desktop. Windows XP has now placed a shortcut to drive C on the desktop. See Figure 4-4. Your shortcut name might differ, and might be preceded by the phrase "Shortcut to."

| Figure 4-4 | SHORTCUT CREATED FROM A SHORTCUT MENU |

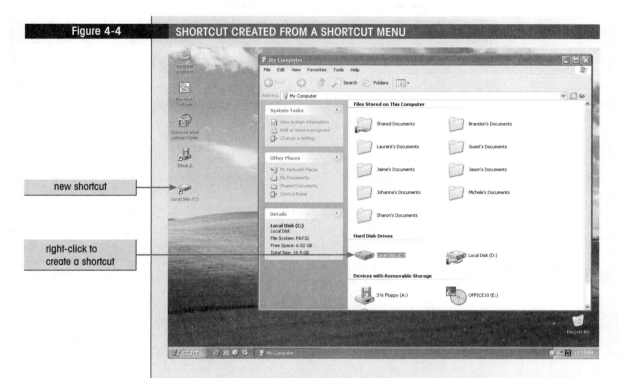

new shortcut

right-click to
create a shortcut

7. Change the name of the drive C shortcut to **Drive C** (using the F2 key or any other method).

TROUBLE? If Windows XP does not highlight the drive C shortcut, click the desktop background to change the focus, and then try this step again.

8. Close the My Computer window.

Because you could see the contents of the My Computer window and the desktop at the same time, the simple left-drag that you used to create the Drive A shortcut was the fastest and simplest approach to use. However, when you created the drive C shortcut, the My Computer window was maximized, so you could not drag the drive C icon to the desktop. You had to use another approach that was both appropriate to the situation and fast.

You can now test the shortcuts to make sure they work.

To test the shortcuts:

1. Click the **Drive A** shortcut, and after Windows XP opens a 3½ Floppy (A:) window onto the contents of your copy of Data Disk #2, close the window.

2. Click the **Drive C** shortcut, and after Windows XP opens a window showing the contents of the top-level folder of drive C, close the window.

If you did not have these shortcuts (and assuming you did not place a My Computer icon on the desktop), you would have had to click the Start button, click My Computer on the Start menu, and then click the drive icon in the My Computer window to get to the top-level folder of each drive (for a total of three steps). Each shortcut requires only one step. Therefore, these shortcuts save you two steps every time you use them. If you use these shortcuts frequently, you might want to put them on the Quick Launch toolbar rather than the desktop so that you can quickly access those drives while working in a maximized application window that covers the desktop.

Creating a Shortcut to a Drive

- Open My Computer.
- If you can see a portion of the desktop, drag the drive icon from the My Computer window to the desktop. If the My Computer window is maximized, right-click the drive icon, click Create Shortcut, and in the Shortcut dialog box, click Yes to verify that you want to put the shortcut on the desktop.
- Close My Computer.

Instead of creating drive shortcuts one at a time, you can select all of the drives for which you want to create shortcuts, and then either drag them to the desktop, or right-click one of the selected drives, click Create Shortcut, and then verify that you want to put the shortcuts on the desktop. To select multiple drives in Web style, hold down the Ctrl key while you point to and select the drive icon for each drive. You can use this technique (Ctrl+Point) to select other types of objects, such as folders, files, and shortcuts. The selected objects constitute a **collection**; in other words, a group of objects that are not adjacent to each other. You select the first object (by pointing to it until Windows XP highlights it), hold down the Ctrl key, point to the next object until Windows XP adds it to the collection (highlights it), and then you repeat this process until you have selected all the objects. If you need to remove an object from the collection, you point to and select it a second time while you are still pressing the Ctrl key.

If you are using Windows Classic style, you must use Ctrl+Click to select objects. Click the first object, and then hold down the Ctrl key while you click the next object, and then repeat this process until you have selected all the objects. Do not click too fast, or Windows XP thinks you want to make duplicate copies of all the objects you've selected.

Viewing Properties of a Shortcut

Like any other type of object, you can right-click a shortcut and choose the option to view its properties. On the Shortcut property sheet, Windows XP displays the shortcut's icon, the shortcut's name, the target type (for example, Local Disk), the target location (for example, My Computer), and the target's path (for example, C:\). You can define a keyboard shortcut for use with the shortcut, specify the type of window to open (normal, maximized, or minimized), enter a shortcut comment, locate the target, or change the shortcut's icon.

Jason wants you to view properties of your drive C shortcut so that you understand how it works.

To view shortcut properties:

1. Right-click the **Drive C** shortcut, and then click **Properties**. The Target type identifies the type of object that the shortcut points to; in this case, a Local Disk. See Figure 4-5. The shortcut actually points to the top-level folder of drive C, as shown by the full path in the Target text box. In the Run list box, Windows XP displays "Normal window," indicating that the window appears at the same size and in the same position as the last time you used the window (not necessarily maximized). You can also choose to open the object in a maximized window (full screen) or a minimized window (as a button on the taskbar). If you always work in a maximized window, adjusting this setting saves you one additional step.

Figure 4-5   VIEWING PROPERTIES OF A DRIVE SHORTCUT

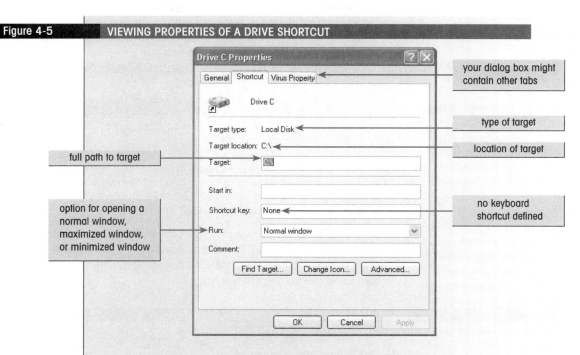

your dialog box might contain other tabs

type of target

location of target

full path to target

option for opening a normal window, maximized window, or minimized window

no keyboard shortcut defined

2. Click the **Help** button [?], and then click the **Shortcut key** text box. Windows XP displays a pop-up Help window that explains how to assign a keyboard shortcut (in other words, a combination of keys) to the shortcut, so that you can use that keyboard shortcut instead of the mouse to activate the shortcut. See Figure 4-6.

Figure 4-6   VIEWING HELP FOR A SHORTCUT SETTING

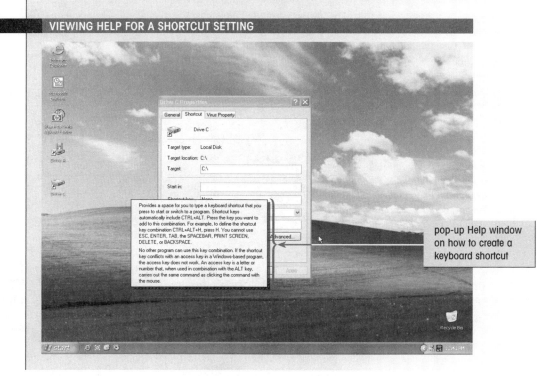

pop-up Help window on how to create a keyboard shortcut

To assign a keyboard shortcut, place your cursor in the Shortcut key text box and type the character (such as "c" for drive C) that you want to use. Windows XP automatically inserts "Ctrl+Alt+" in the Shortcut key text box. When you use a keyboard shortcut, you press and hold the Ctrl and Alt keys while you press and then release the character you assigned to the shortcut key; then you release the Ctrl and Alt keys. If you assign a keyboard shortcut and want to remove it later, click in the Shortcut key text box on this property sheet, and then press the Backspace key. Windows XP displays "None" in the text box. Notice also that the shortcut key takes precedence over the same key combination used within a Windows application.

To locate the target and view other shortcut properties:

1. Click the **pop-up Help window** (or the desktop or dialog box background), or press the **Esc** key to close the pop-up Help window.

2. Click the **Find Target** button. The My Computer window opens and shows you the location of the target. You are now viewing the contents of My Computer. See Figure 4-7. The target (drive C) is contained within My Computer. Notice that Windows XP highlights the target.

| Figure 4-7 | FINDING THE TARGET FOR A SHORTCUT |

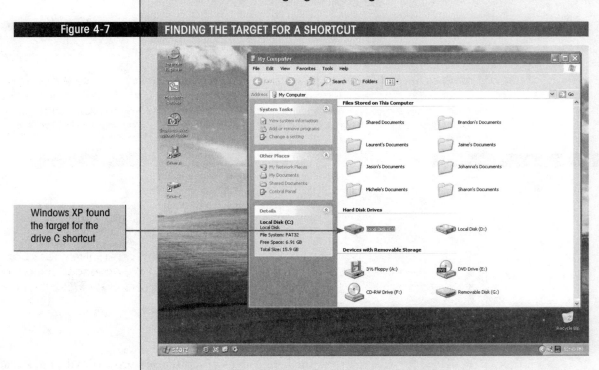

Windows XP found the target for the drive C shortcut

3. Close the My Computer window.

4. Click the **General** tab in the Drive C Properties dialog box. On the General property sheet, you see information on the type of file (a shortcut), the file's location (the path to the folder with the shortcut), the file's size and the amount of storage space it uses on disk, and the dates and times the shortcut was created, last modified, and last accessed. See Figure 4-8. Yours will differ. Windows XP also identifies what attributes, or characteristics, are assigned to the object. Because you just created this shortcut, Windows XP turned on the Archive attribute so that

your Backup software automatically selects it during your next backup (covered in more detail in Tutorial 6). If you create a shortcut on the desktop, the full path for the location of the shortcut points to the folder that contains your user profile for your logon account. On the computer used for this figure, the shortcut is stored in Jason's desktop folder—C:\Documents and Settings\Jason\Desktop. The location of your Desktop folder will differ from that shown in the figure. Note also that shortcuts can waste a disproportionate amount of space compared to their size; however, the tradeoff is that they are very useful. Notice that this shortcut, which is 197 bytes in size, is allocated 4,096 bytes (4.00 KB, or 4 times 1,024 bytes/kilobyte) on the disk, wasting 3,899 bytes of disk space. The size and allocated storage space of your shortcut might differ.

| Figure 4-8 | VIEWING GENERAL SHORTCUT PROPERTIES |

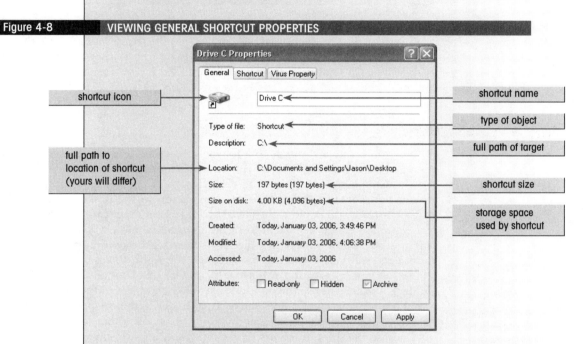

TROUBLE? If your General property sheet does not show an Archive check box, your drive C is an NTFS volume, and you have to click the Advanced button to view the "File is ready for archiving" setting for the Archive and Index attributes.

5. Close the Drive C Properties dialog box.

Windows XP does not show the full filename of shortcuts in Properties dialog box, and it does not show the file extension of the shortcut in a folder window, even when you choose the option to display file extensions for known file types. The filename for the Drive C shortcut is "Drive C.lnk" and the filename for the Drive A shortcut, as you would expect, is "Drive A.lnk" (the first character in the file extension is the letter "l", not the number 1). The "lnk" file extension stands for "link" and emphasizes that the shortcut is a direct link to an object on your computer. The short filenames for these two shortcuts are (most likely) DRIVEC~1.LNK and DRIVEA~1.LNK.

REFERENCE WINDOW   **RW**

Viewing Properties of a Shortcut
- Right-click a shortcut, and then click Properties.
- In the Properties dialog box for the shortcut, use the Shortcut property sheet to view or find a shortcut's target, specify a shortcut key, indicate how to open the target window, and include a comment.
- Click the General tab to view information about the location, size, allocated space, and attributes of a shortcut, or to change the shortcut name and change attribute settings.
- Close the Properties dialog box for the shortcut.

Shortcuts like these for drives A and C simplify many routine tasks that you perform on a daily basis and allow you to work smart. If you frequently work with other drives, such as a Zip drive, DVD drive, CD-RW drive, or CD drive, you can also create shortcuts for those drives, and thereby save yourself time and effort.

Creating Shortcuts to Folders

When you create a shortcut to a folder, you *cannot* drag that folder to the desktop as you dragged the drive icon for drive A, because Windows XP will *move* the folder if the folder is on the same drive (i.e., drive C) as the Desktop folder for your user profile. If you drag a folder that contains software for an application to the desktop, that application will not work. Instead, you could right-click the folder and drag it to the desktop, and then choose the option to create a shortcut from the shortcut menu. Or you could create the shortcut in the folder window where the object is located, and then drag the shortcut to the desktop; however, you must make sure you choose the right object to drag (the shortcut, not the folder). If you are creating a shortcut to a folder that contains software (or even a document folder), it is *safer* to use the option for sending an object to the desktop as a shortcut. Then you do not inadvertently drag the original folder to the desktop. You can use this approach to create a shortcut to your Windows folder as well as other folders and files.

Because the drive shortcuts have proved so useful, Jason asks you to create shortcuts to folders you commonly use on your computer. Both of you constantly need to check information stored in the Windows folder. You also need to quickly access the folder that contains templates and other staff resources on the hard disk so that you can prepare templates and other files and copy them to Zip disks or floppy disks for your coworkers.

First, create a shortcut to the Windows folder on your hard disk. You can watch the process by adjusting the drive C window so that you can see the desktop.

To create a shortcut to the Windows folder:

1. Click the **Drive C** shortcut to open a window onto the top-level folder of drive C, click the **Restore Down** button 🗗 , if necessary, and then adjust the size of the window so that you can also see the desktop.

TROUBLE? If your Windows folder is stored on another drive, open My Computer, open that drive, and then restore the drive window.

2. Locate and right-click the **Windows** folder icon, point to **Send To** on the short-cut menu, and then click **Desktop (create shortcut)**. Windows XP creates a shortcut to the Windows folder on the desktop. See Figure 4-9. Your shortcut name may differ, and might be preceded by the phrase "Shortcut to."

TROUBLE? If your Windows folder has another name, such as WinNT, locate and right-click that folder, point to Send To on the shortcut menu, and then click Desktop (create shortcut).

| Figure 4-9 | CREATING A SHORTCUT TO THE WINDOWS FOLDER |

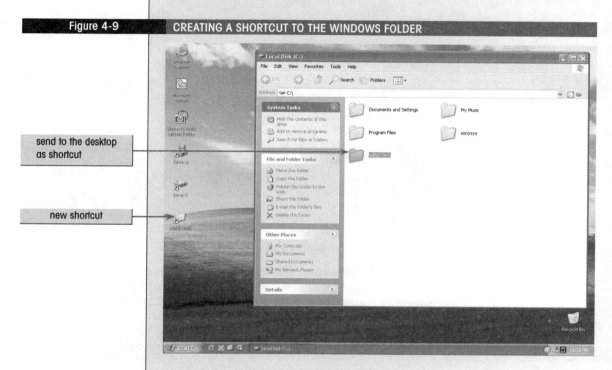

send to the desktop as shortcut

new shortcut

3. Close the drive C window.

4. If your Windows shortcut is named "Shortcut to Windows," or "Shortcut to WinNT," press the **F2** (Edit) key to change the name to **Windows**.

5. Click the **Windows** shortcut on the desktop. Windows XP opens the Windows folder on drive C (or on the drive that contains your Windows folder). See Figure 4-10. Your view will differ, and the contents of the Windows folder might be hidden. If you did not have this shortcut, you would have had to click the Start button, click My Computer, click the drive C icon in the My Computer win-dow, perhaps use the scroll bars to locate the Windows folder in the drive C window, and then click the Windows folder to get to this same point. This short-cut saves you at least four steps every time you use it. Also, you may not have to scroll through a folder window with many objects to locate the object you want. Scrolling is time consuming, and causes unnecessary wear and tear on the tendons in your arm.

Figure 4-10	OPENING THE WINDOWS FOLDER WITH A SHORTCUT

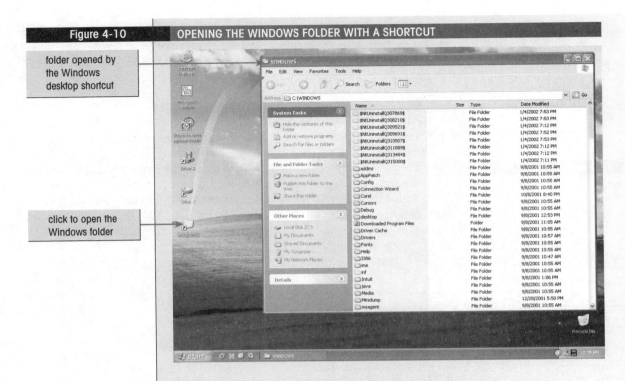

folder opened by
the Windows
desktop shortcut

click to open the
Windows folder

6. Close the Windows folder window.

7. Right-click the **Windows** shortcut, and then click **Properties**. The Target text box on the Shortcut property sheet shows the path for the target. See Figure 4-11. If your Windows folder is named Windows, the path is C:\Windows. Although not shown, the filename is Windows.lnk, and the short filename is WINDOWS.LNK.

Figure 4-11	VIEWING PROPERTIES OF THE WINDOWS DESKTOP SHORTCUT

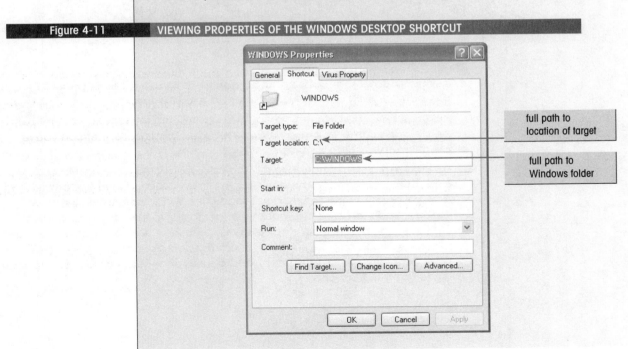

full path to
location of target

full path to
Windows folder

When you create a shortcut to a folder, Windows XP uses the same folder icon for the shortcut. However, you can change the icon and customize it so it more closely identifies the object to which it is linked. That also makes it easier for you to quickly distinguish and pick the desktop shortcut you want to use.

To change the icon for a shortcut:

1. On the Shortcut property sheet, click the **Change Icon** button. The Change Icon dialog box shows the icons in the Shell32.dll system file. See Figure 4-12. Notice that this file is stored in the System32 folder, and that the icons within this file are ones that Windows XP uses for components on your computer system. You can select another icon contained within this file, or you can browse for another file. Icons can be found in files with the "exe," "dll," or "ico" file extension; however, not all "exe" and "dll" files have icons. "Ico" stands for "Icon."

| Figure 4-12 | CHOOSING A NEW ICON FOR THE WINDOWS SHORTCUT |

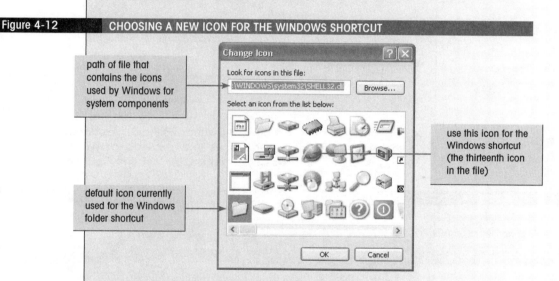

path of file that contains the icons used by Windows for system components

default icon currently used for the Windows folder shortcut

use this icon for the Windows shortcut (the thirteenth icon in the file)

2. Click the **Globe** icon in the fourth column, second row. If you count icons in this dialog box by starting the count with the icon in the upper-left corner, count down each column, count from left to right, and start your count with "0" (zero) rather than "1" (one), then you would be identifying the location of the icon in the file in the same way that Windows XP does. In this case, the icon you're using is number 13 (not number 14).

3. Click the **OK** button in the Change Icon dialog box. Windows XP updates the icon displayed on the Shortcut property sheet to the one you just selected. See Figure 4-13.

Figure 4-13   NEW ICON SHOWN ON SHORTCUT PROPERTY SHEET

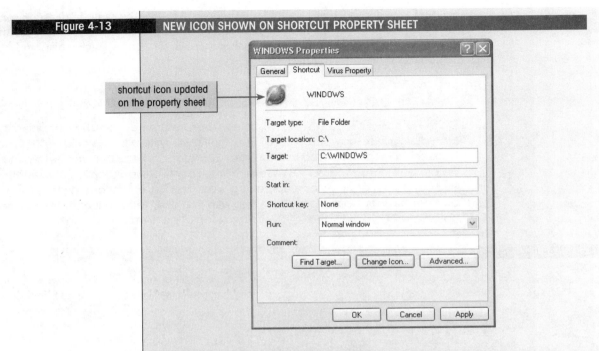

shortcut icon updated
on the property sheet

4. Click the **OK** button to close the Windows Properties dialog box, and then click the **desktop** to change the focus. In a few seconds, Windows XP updates the image of the Windows desktop shortcut icon. See Figure 4-14.

Figure 4-14   VIEWING THE NEW ICON FOR THE WINDOWS SHORTCUT

new icon for the
Windows shortcut

REFERENCE WINDOW **RW**

<u>Creating a Shortcut to a Folder</u>
- Open My Computer, open the drive that contains the folder for which you want to create a short-cut, and then locate the folder itself.
- Right-click the folder icon, point to Send To on the shortcut menu, and then click Desktop (create shortcut).
- Close the drive window (or folder window).
- If you want to change the desktop shortcut's icon, right-click the shortcut, click Properties, and then click the Change Icon button on the Shortcut property sheet. Choose a new icon, or browse for an icon file.
- Click OK to close the Change Icon dialog box, and then click OK to close the Properties dialog box for the shortcut.

Although shortcuts can save steps, you also have to consider that they can take up valuable "real estate" on your desktop or on a taskbar toolbar. Also, as you saw earlier, although shortcuts are relatively small—less than a sector in size—they can also waste storage space on your hard disk because Windows XP must allocate a full cluster to the shortcut even if it only uses a small amount of that cluster. In each instance, you have to decide whether a shortcut helps you work faster and more efficiently.

Creating a Shortcut to a Document Folder

If you store all the files that you use daily in the same folder, and if you open that folder many times during the day, you can save yourself time and effort by creating a shortcut to that folder. Some people move the folder that contains their documents to the desktop for ease of access. However, if you create a shortcut to that folder, you can leave the folder in its original location. That also simplifies backups.

Next, Jason wants you to create a shortcut to the Delta Oil folder within your My Documents folder. The Delta Oil folder contains company templates and other important company files that you need to quickly access.

You need to copy the Delta Oil folder from Data Disk #2 to the My Documents folder on your hard disk. Before you copy this folder to your computer, make sure you do not already have a folder by that name. If you are working in a computer lab, your instructor and technical support staff might designate another folder or drive for you to use.

To check for the presence of a Delta Oil folder and then copy the folder to your computer:

1. Open My Documents, maximize the My Documents folder window, and then check for a folder named Delta Oil.

2. If My Documents already contains a folder named Delta Oil, and if you are working on a computer in a computer lab, someone else has most likely left a copy of the Delta Oil folder on the computer. Point to and select the Delta Oil folder, press the **Delete** key, and then click the **Yes** button in the Confirm Folder Delete dialog box. If you are working on your own computer and have a Delta Oil folder with documents you need, use another name, such as Delta Oil Company, for the Delta Oil folder in this tutorial.

3. Click the **Show Desktop** button 🖳 on the Quick Launch toolbar, and then click the **Drive A** shortcut.

4. Point to and select the **Delta Oil** folder and, after Windows XP highlights the folder icon, click **Copy this folder** on the File and Folder Tasks dynamic menu. The Copy Items dialog box opens so you can select the location for the copy of the Delta Oil folder. See Figure 4-15. You can select a drive or folder, or if you are copying a set of files, you can use the Make New Folder button to create a folder under a drive or another folder first.

| Figure 4-15 | COPYING THE DELTA OIL FOLDER FROM DRIVE A |

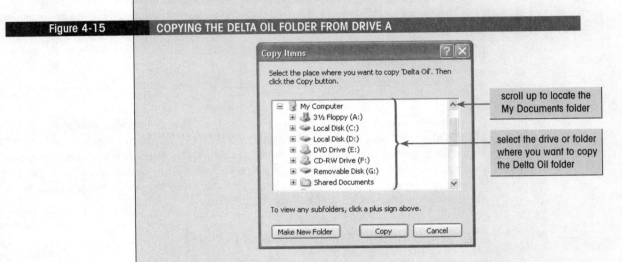

5. Locate and click **My Documents**, and then click the **Copy** button. The Copying dialog box shows you the progress of the copy operation.

6. Click **My Documents** in the Other Places dynamic menu. The My Documents folder now contains a copy of the Delta Oil folder. See Figure 4-16.

| Figure 4-16 | DELTA OIL FOLDER |

7. Leave the My Documents window open for the next section of the tutorial.

REFERENCE WINDOW   **RW**

<u>Copying a Folder from Drive A to Drive C</u>

- Check the destination on your computer to make sure you do not have a folder with the same name as the folder you want to copy.
- Click the Show Desktop button on the Quick Launch toolbar.
- Open My Computer, and then click the 3½ Floppy (A:) icon, or click the drive A desktop shortcut.
- Locate and select the folder you want to copy, click "Copy this folder" on the File and Folder Tasks dynamic menu, and in the Copy Items dialog box, locate and select the drive or folder to where you want to copy the folder, and then click the Copy button.
- Close the 3½ Floppy (A:) window.

Now you are ready to create a shortcut to the Delta Oil folder, and then test the shortcut.

To create a shortcut to a document folder:

1. Right-click the **Delta Oil** folder in the My Documents folder, point to **Send To**, and then click **Desktop (create shortcut)**.

2. Close the My Documents window. You now have a Delta Oil shortcut on your desktop. See Figure 4-17. Your shortcut name might be "Shortcut to Delta Oil."

Figure 4-17	DELTA OIL DESKTOP SHORTCUT

Delta Oil shortcut

3. If your Delta Oil shortcut is named "Shortcut to Delta Oil," use the **F2** (Rename) key to change its name to **Delta Oil**.

4. Right-click the **Delta Oil** shortcut, and then click **Properties**. Although you are not able to see the entire path at once, notice that the path used by the shortcut is:

   "C:\Documents and Settings\Jason\My Documents\Delta Oil"

   Your path will differ.

5. Close the Delta Oil Properties dialog box.

6. Click the **Delta Oil** shortcut. Windows XP opens the Delta Oil folder. See Figure 4-18. This folder contains five folders—Company Templates, Designs, Memos, Overhead Transparencies, and Training.

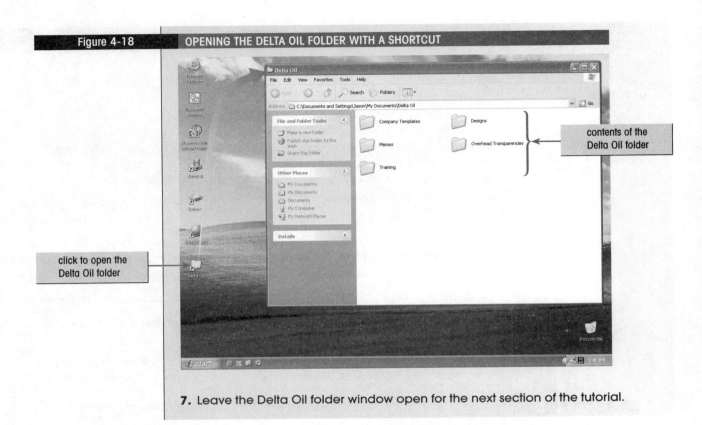

Figure 4-18   **OPENING THE DELTA OIL FOLDER WITH A SHORTCUT**

contents of the
Delta Oil folder

click to open the
Delta Oil folder

7. Leave the Delta Oil folder window open for the next section of the tutorial.

Folder shortcuts can be useful, especially if you store your documents in a few folders, and then repeatedly open and close those folders to access, copy, or back up certain files.

Creating a Shortcut to a File

If you work with the same file every day, or work with a specific file for the duration of a project, you can create a desktop shortcut to that file so that you can immediately open it after your computer boots to the desktop. You can use the same approach as you used to create a shortcut to a folder.

Jason and others in his work group are designing a new logo for Delta Oil. The file that contains the background for that logo is stored in the Designs folder. Jason asks you to open the Designs folder and create a shortcut to this file so that you and others in his workgroup can quickly open and work on the final design of the company logo.

To create a shortcut to a file:

1. Click the **Designs** folder. Since this folder contains a file with an image, Windows XP automatically switches to Filmstrip view. See Figure 4-19.

| Figure 4-19 | VIEWING THE COMPANY LOGO DESIGN BITMAP IMAGE |

image contained in the Company Logo Design.bmp file

right-click this file to create a desktop shortcut

2. Right-click the **Company Logo Design.bmp** file icon, point to **Send To**, click **Desktop (create shortcut)**, and then close the Designs folder window. Windows XP created a shortcut to this bitmap image file on the desktop. See Figure 4-20. Your shortcut name might be Shortcut to Company Logo Design.bmp. Notice that the name of the shortcut includes the file extension, which can be misleading, because you might think this object was the actual file unless you noticed the shortcut arrow box 🔲.

| Figure 4-20 | COMPANY LOGO DESIGN.BMP DESKTOP SHORTCUT |

shortcut for opening a bitmap image file from the desktop

TROUBLE? If you are using Windows XP Home Edition, your shortcut icon will differ from that shown in the figure.

3. Point to and select the **Company Logo Design.bmp** shortcut on the desktop, press the **F2** (Rename) key, press the **End** key to move the insertion point to the end of the label, and use the **Backspace** key to delete the file extension and the period, and then press **Enter**. The new name of the shortcut should be Company Logo Design (without the file extension).

TROUBLE? If your shortcut is named "Shortcut to Company Logo Design.bmp," use the F2 (Rename) key to change the shortcut's name to "Company Logo Design".

4. Click the **Company Logo Design** shortcut. Windows XP opens the file using the Windows Picture and Fax Viewer. See Figure 4-21.

TROUBLE? If Windows opens the file in another application, the "bmp" file extension is associated with that application on your computer, and that's okay. The important point is that the shortcut worked.

Figure 4-21	OPENING A FILE WITH A SHORTCUT

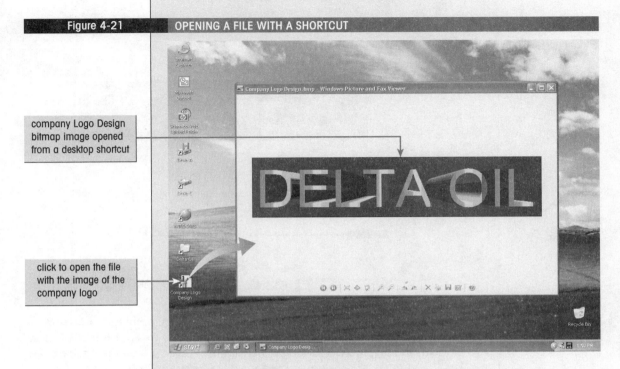

company Logo Design bitmap image opened from a desktop shortcut

click to open the file with the image of the company logo

5. Close the Windows Picture and Fax Viewer window (or the application window) along with the contents of the Company Logo Design file.

6. Right-click the **Company Logo Design** shortcut, and then click **Properties**. Although you are not able to see the entire path in the Target text box, the path on the computer used in Figure 4-22 is "C:\Documents and Settings\ Jason\My Documents\Delta Oil\Designs\Company Logo Design.bmp". Your path will differ. Notice also that the "Start in" folder is "C:\Documents and Settings\Jason\My Documents\Delta Oil\Designs". Your path will differ. The "Start in" text box identifies the folder that contains the object, or related files that an application might need.

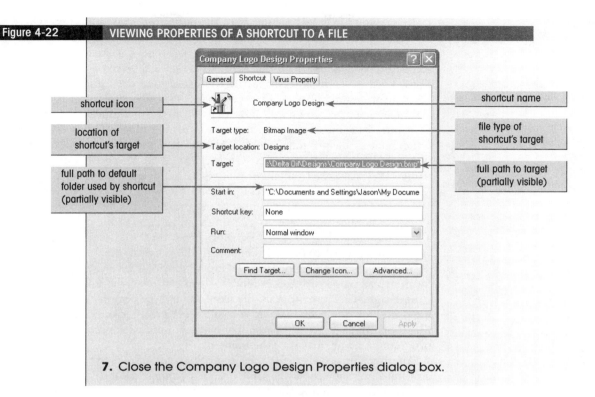

Figure 4-22   **VIEWING PROPERTIES OF A SHORTCUT TO A FILE**

7. Close the Company Logo Design Properties dialog box.

The use of shortcuts and the docucentric nature of Windows XP simplify the process for locating and opening files.

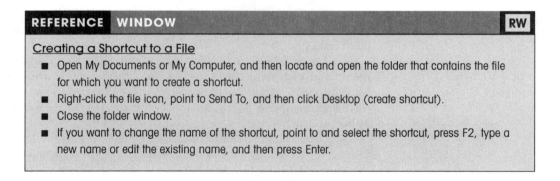

REFERENCE WINDOW   **RW**

Creating a Shortcut to a File
- Open My Documents or My Computer, and then locate and open the folder that contains the file for which you want to create a shortcut.
- Right-click the file icon, point to Send To, and then click Desktop (create shortcut).
- Close the folder window.
- If you want to change the name of the shortcut, point to and select the shortcut, press F2, type a new name or edit the existing name, and then press Enter.

For each project on which you work, you can create a set of shortcuts to folders and files that you need to open. After your computer boots to the desktop, a single click means you are ready to work.

Creating a Shortcut to an Application

Even though you can open all the installed software on your computer from the All Programs menu, using this menu often requires many steps to locate and open a program. Instead, you can create shortcuts to applications, utilities, and games on your computer so that you can open them directly from the desktop. As you've seen, once you create the shortcut, it's a one-step process to open the target.

Before you can create a shortcut to an application, you must know where that application is stored on your computer, so you should become familiar with the folder structure and the locations of installed software products. You also need to identify the program file for each software product for which you want to create a shortcut. The program files for applications, utilities, and games have the file extension "exe" (for executable program file) or "com" (for command file). The main part of the filename for a program file is limited to eight characters, so you might have to use your best judgment in interpreting these shorter filenames. In some cases, you can easily guess the filename. For example, in the Microsoft Office suite, the program file for Microsoft Excel is named Excel.exe. The Microsoft Outlook program file is named Outlook.exe. The Microsoft PowerPoint program file is named Powerpnt.exe (remember there is a limit of eight characters for the main part of the filename). The Microsoft Access program file is named Msaccess.exe, and the Microsoft Word program file is named Winword.exe, not an easy one to guess. Notice that all of these Windows applications have program files with the "exe" file extension. As you can see, with a little understanding of how Microsoft and software developers name their program files, you can usually figure out the filename of the program file.

You can use several approaches to create shortcuts for installed software. If you know the location and name of the program file, you can open the folder where the program file is stored, right-click the program file icon, and use the option on the Send To menu for creating a desktop shortcut—just as you did when creating shortcuts to folders and document files. You can also use the Search Companion, but this approach requires that you know the program filename or part of the filename.

Another approach is to use the Create Shortcut Wizard to browse for the program file and customize the shortcut at the same time. You right-click the desktop, point to New, and click Shortcut on the desktop shortcut menu. The Create Shortcut Wizard then asks you to enter the location of the item (in other words, its full path), or you can browse and locate the program, folder, file, computer, or Web site. Once you've located the object for which you want a shortcut, the Create Shortcut Wizard asks you for a name for the shortcut. After you enter a name, click Finish, and you are done. When you locate the object by browsing, you are providing Windows XP with the full path to that object. The only problem with this approach is that you have to browse your computer looking for the object, and that also can be time-consuming.

A faster and easier way is to copy the shortcut for a program from the All Programs menu, and then send it to the desktop. This approach works only for programs that are listed on the All Programs menu (not all are), but if you've properly installed a program, the All Programs menu is the obvious first place to check for a shortcut for an application, utility, or game.

As he creates and modifies company templates, Jason opens Microsoft Word and Microsoft Excel every day. Rather than open these applications from the Start menu, or display and use the Microsoft Office Shortcut Bar, he creates desktop shortcuts to these applications. He also recommends that you create the same types of shortcuts for your computer, including one for WordPad, so that you can use that shortcut to examine files that might not be associated with an application (such as temporary files or files without file extensions).

To create a shortcut to an application:

1. From the Start menu, point to **All Programs**, point to **Accessories**, and then right-click **WordPad** on the Accessories menu. Windows XP displays the WordPad shortcut menu. See Figure 4-23.

Figure 4-23	CREATING A DESKTOP SHORTCUT FROM AN ACCESSORIES MENU SHORTCUT

use the Send To menu to copy this shortcut to the desktop

right-click to display shortcut menu for this Accessories menu shortcut

2. Point to **Send To**, click **Desktop (create shortcut)**, and then click the **Start** button to close the Start menu (or click the desktop background). Windows XP places a copy of the WordPad shortcut from the Accessories menu on the desktop. See Figure 4-24.

Figure 4-24	WORDPAD DESKTOP SHORTCUT

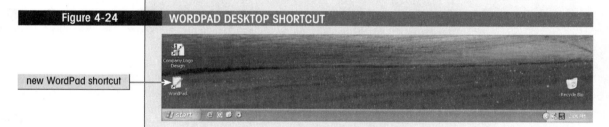

new WordPad shortcut

3. Right-click the **WordPad** desktop shortcut, and then click **Properties**. The Target text box shows that the full path for WordPad is "C:\Program Files\Windows NT\ Accessories\wordpad.exe". See Figure 4-25. Windows XP displays the text in the Comment text box as a ScreenTip when you point to and select the shortcut. You can create a ScreenTip for a shortcut by entering a comment, or if a shortcut already has a comment, you can edit the existing comment and thereby customize the shortcut's ScreenTip.

Figure 4-25   **VIEWING PROPERTIES OF THE WORDPAD SHORTCUT**

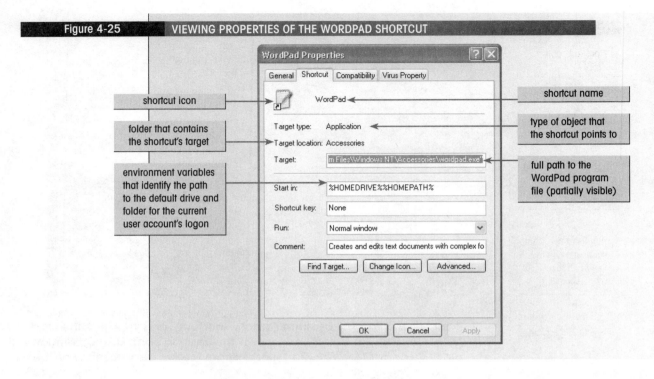

shortcut icon

folder that contains
the shortcut's target

environment variables
that identify the path
to the default drive and
folder for the current
user account's logon

shortcut name

type of object that
the shortcut points to

full path to the
WordPad program
file (partially visible)

%HOMEDRIVE% and %HOMEPATH% in the Start in box are environment variables. An **environment variable** is a name assigned to a system setting. The name of the environment variable and its associated setting are stored in an area of memory called the **Windows environment**. Windows XP and other programs check the Windows environment for settings that they need.

The setting for HOMEPATH is the relative path to the folder that contains the user profile for the currently logged on user, or what could be called the user's **home directory**, and the HOMEDRIVE is the name of the drive containing the user profile folder for the currently logged on user, or that user's home directory. For example, Jason's HOMEPATH is \Documents and Settings\Jason and C: is his HOMEDRIVE. When you substitute this information in the path shown in the Start in text box on the Shortcut property sheet, you discover that the "Start in" path is: C:\Documents and Settings\Jason.

Other users with different user account names have a similar path, but obviously the name of the user profile folder differs. Their HOMEDRIVE and HOMEPATH are assigned when they log on to their computer, and then Windows XP can translate the path defined by environment variables in the Start in box to a real path. When Chet, another member of Jason's workgroup, logs on to his computer, the path to his home directory is C:\Documents and Settings\Chet—also constructed from the same environment variables.

To test your application shortcut:

1. Close the WordPad Properties dialog box.

2. Click the **WordPad** desktop shortcut. Windows XP opens the WordPad application. If you want to create a document, you are ready to work. See Figure 4-26.

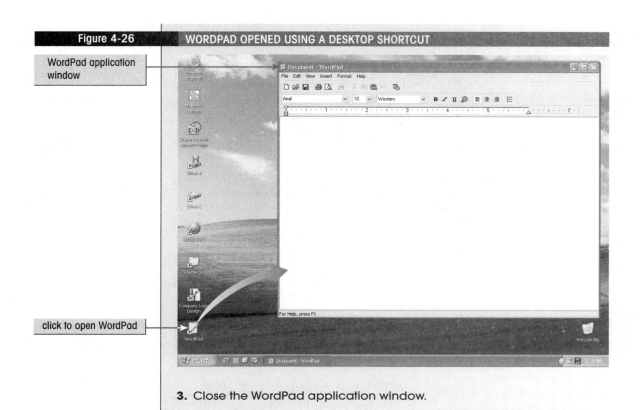

Figure 4-26   WORDPAD OPENED USING A DESKTOP SHORTCUT

WordPad application window

click to open WordPad

3. Close the WordPad application window.

Another important environment variable is %SystemRoot%. This environment variable identifies the path and folder name for the Windows folder, such as C:\Windows or C:\WinNT.

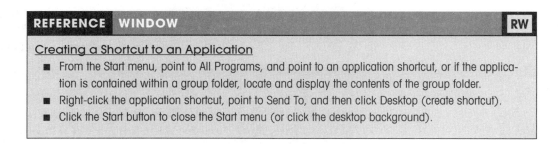

REFERENCE WINDOW   **RW**

Creating a Shortcut to an Application

- From the Start menu, point to All Programs, and point to an application shortcut, or if the application is contained within a group folder, locate and display the contents of the group folder.
- Right-click the application shortcut, point to Send To, and then click Desktop (create shortcut).
- Click the Start button to close the Start menu (or click the desktop background).

As you can tell, the All Programs menu and its submenus are a rich resource for obtaining application, utility, game, and other program shortcuts quickly.

Customizing a Folder Shortcut for Windows Explorer

If you choose the program Windows Explorer from the Accessories menu, Windows XP opens a folder window and display the Folders toolbar by default. In previous versions of Windows, this view was commonly called the Windows Explorer view. (Because of the similarity of names, be careful not to confuse it with Internet Explorer.) If you prefer to work in this type of view, you can copy the Windows Explorer shortcut from the Accessories menu and place it on the desktop. You can also customize shortcuts that open folder windows so that they display a Folders toolbar.

To simplify the type of work you must do, often under tight deadlines, Jason asks you to customize your Delta Oil shortcut so that Windows XP automatically performs the following operations:

■ Displays the Folders toolbar after opening the Delta Oil folder

■ Limits the view of the folder structure in the Folders toolbar to just the Delta Oil folder and its subfolders

■ Displays all the folders below the Delta Oil folder so that you are ready to start work

The shortcut for the Delta Oil folder uses "C:\Documents and Settings\Jason\My Documents\Delta Oil" as the full path. (Your path will differ.) To implement the changes that Jason wants you to make to the Delta Oil shortcut, you must modify the shortcut's path. At the beginning of the path, you must include the path for opening Windows Explorer from the Windows folder:

C:\Windows\Explorer.exe

You do not need to include this path in quotation marks because there are no long filenames with spaces in the path. If your Windows folder is named WinNT, then the path is:

C:\WinNT\Explorer.exe

You must also add switches that change the way the Explorer window opens. Three useful switches are the following:

/n,   This switch opens a *new* Windows Explorer window (with the Folders toolbar).

/e,   This switch *expands* the folder specified in the path to show the subfolders below that folder.

/root,   This switch makes the folder in the full path the *root* folder (the top folder).

The **root folder** is the folder at the top of the folder hierarchy in the Folders toolbar. If you use the /root, switch, you do not see—and cannot choose—any folders above the one specified in the full path. This feature allows you to focus on a branch of the folder structure of a disk where you need to work. Also, unlike the backslash delimiter (\), switches use the forward slash (/) that points in the opposite direction.

You can revise the current path so that it uses all three switches, as follows:

C:\Windows\Explorer.exe   /n,   /e,   /root,   "C:\Documents and Settings\Jason\ My Documents\Delta Oil".

Or if your Windows folder is named WinNT:

C:\WinNT\Explorer.exe   /n,   /e,   /root,   "C:\Documents and Settings\Jason\ My Documents\Delta Oil". (Your path will differ.)

All these switches include a comma at the end of the switch as well as a space after the comma; in fact, if you do not include the comma, Windows XP displays an error message when you attempt to use the shortcut.

When Jason works in the Delta Oil folder window, he frequently switches from the default folder view with dynamic menus to one with a Folders toolbar so that he can see the relationship of one folder to another, quickly select folders, and quickly move and copy files from folder to folder. He suggests that you customize the Delta Oil shortcut for easy access to the same features and ways of working.

To modify the Delta Oil shortcut:

1. Right-click the **Delta Oil** shortcut, and then click **Properties**. Windows XP selects and highlights the path in the Target text box.

2. Press the **Home** key to quickly move to the beginning of the path, type **C:\Windows\Explorer.exe /e, /n, /root,** and then press the **spacebar**. *You have to type the comma and press the spacebar after each of the three switches.*

TROUBLE? If your Windows folder has a different name, substitute that name for "Windows" in the full path for Windows Explorer. For example, if your Windows folder is named WinNT, you type C:\WinNT\Explorer.exe /e, /n, /root, and then press the spacebar.

3. Check your new path, and then, if necessary, make any corrections. Figure 4-27 shows part of the command line. The new path should be similar to that shown on the computer used for this figure:

C:\Windows\Explorer.exe /e, /n, /root, "C:\Documents and Settings\Jason\ My Documents\Delta Oil"

| Figure 4-27 | UPDATING THE PATH FOR THE TARGET OF THE DELTA OIL SHORTCUT |

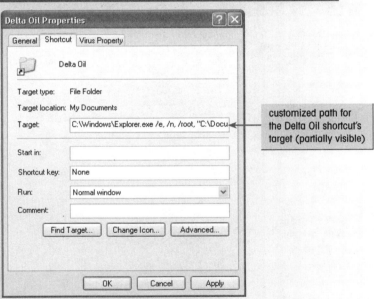

customized path for the Delta Oil shortcut's target (partially visible)

4. Click the **OK** button to close the Delta Oil Properties dialog box, and then look at the desktop icon for the Delta Oil shortcut. Windows XP automatically changes the icon to the one used by My Computer. See Figure 4-28. Explorer.exe is the program that displays the views within folder windows, whether you use My Computer or Windows Explorer. The modifications you made to the shortcut have converted it into a shortcut that opens an application, namely, Explorer.exe, instead of one that opens a folder. The path to the Delta Oil folder in the shortcut is now an argument, or parameter, of the program you open.

Figure 4-28   UPDATED DELTA OIL DESKTOP ICON

icon updated after you customized the path for the shortcut's target

5. Click the **Delta Oil** shortcut. Windows XP opens the Delta Oil folder window with the Folders toolbar. The Delta Oil folder is the root folder in the Folders toolbar, and Windows XP expanded the Delta Oil folder to show the subfolders below the Delta Oil folder. See Figure 4-29. Notice that the Up button 🗁 is dimmed, indicating that you cannot step up one level in the folder structure of the disk.

Figure 4-29   WINDOWS EXPLORER VIEW OF THE DELTA OIL FOLDER

Folders toolbar automatically displayed

root folder

subfolders automatically displayed

click to open the Delta Oil folder

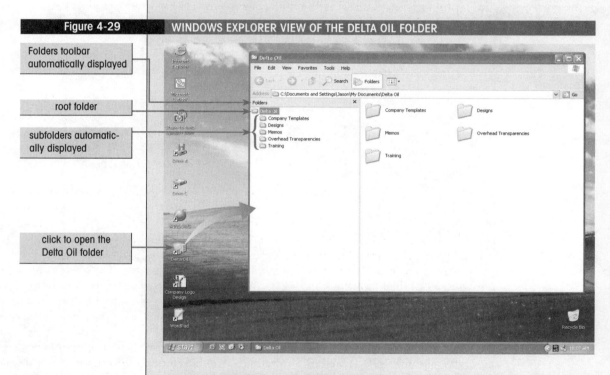

TROUBLE? If Windows XP displays a Windows Explorer dialog box and informs you that the path does not exist or it is not a directory, you did not include the comma after one or more of the switches in the path. Click OK to close the Windows Explorer dialog box, right-click the Delta Oil shortcut, click Properties, and then correct the path in the Target text box, click OK, and then click the Delta Oil shortcut again.

6. Close the Delta Oil window.

You might want to experiment with each of the switches separately and in combination with each other to determine how they affect the operation of folder shortcuts and find what works best for you.

REFERENCE WINDOW **RW**

Customizing a Folder Shortcut for Windows Explorer
- Right-click the shortcut you want to customize, and then click Properties.
- Click before the path in the Target text box, type C:\Windows\Explorer.exe /e, /n, /root, (*you have to type the correct name of the Windows folder and also type commas after the switches and insert the spaces*), and then press the spacebar before the remainder of the line that includes the full path of the target folder.
- Click OK.

You might also want to make similar modifications to the shortcut to your Windows folder. If you frequently open the Windows folder to check settings or make changes, you can modify your Windows shortcut so that it opens in a Windows Explorer window with the Windows folder as the root folder. The folder structure then expands to show you all the subfolders below the Windows folder so you are ready to work. This feature makes it easier to work with folders because it screens out those folders you do not need to see or use, and allows you to focus on where you need to work.

Creating an Internet Shortcut

An Internet shortcut is similar to a desktop shortcut, except that the target is the address of a Web site. When you access a Web site with Internet Explorer, you can use the Favorites button to create an Internet shortcut to the current Web site. That shortcut, like all other Internet shortcuts you create with Internet Explorer, is then stored in your Favorites folder. When you open Internet Explorer, you can select an Internet shortcut for the Web site you want to visit from the Favorites menu, or if you are already in the Favorites folder, you can click an Internet shortcut to open Internet Explorer, and connect your computer to the Web site referenced by the Internet shortcut. If you add the Favorites menu to the Start menu, you can access these same Internet shortcuts via the Start menu. You can also copy an Internet shortcut from the Favorites menu or Favorites folder and paste it onto the desktop so that you have a direct link to a Web site you visit regularly.

The next set of steps assumes you are using Internet Explorer. If you are using another browser, adapt the following steps to your browser. If you are using your own computer, you need to log on to your Internet service provider (ISP). If you are working in a computer lab, follow the procedures provided by your instructor or technical support staff for accessing the Internet.

Because you frequently check Microsoft's Web site for the latest news on product upgrades and features, as well as for technical troubleshooting information, you decide to create an Internet shortcut to Microsoft's Web site.

To create an Internet shortcut to Microsoft's Web site:

1. If necessary, connect to your ISP, and then click the **Internet Explorer** icon on the desktop or on the Quick Launch toolbar.

2. If necessary, maximize the Internet Explorer window, and if your home page is not Microsoft's home page, click inside the **Address bar** to select the address for your home page, type **www.microsoft.com**, and then press the **Enter** key.

3. After Internet Explorer displays Microsoft's home page, right-click the **background** of the Web page shown in the Internet Explorer browser window, click **Create Shortcut**, and in the Microsoft Internet Explorer dialog box that gives you the choice of placing the shortcut on the desktop, click the **OK** button.

4. Close the Internet Explorer window, but do not disconnect from your ISP. On your desktop, you now see an Internet shortcut labeled "Welcome to the Microsoft Corporate Web Site." See Figure 4-30. Since the names of Web sites change periodically, your Internet shortcut name may differ.

Figure 4-30	MICROSOFT INTERNET DESKTOP SHORTCUT

Internet shortcut to the Microsoft home page

5. Change the name of the "Welcome to the Microsoft Corporate Web Site" shortcut to **Microsoft**.

6. Click the **Microsoft** Internet shortcut. Internet Explorer (or your default Web browser) displays Microsoft's home page. See Figure 4-31.

Figure 4-31	USING THE MICROSOFT SHORTCUT TO GO TO MICROSOFT'S HOME PAGE

click to go to Microsoft's home page

Microsoft's home page

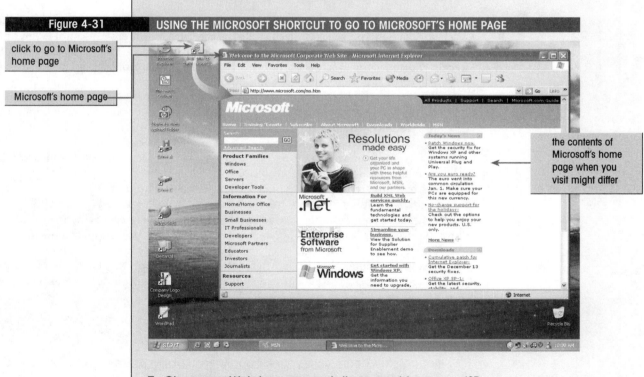

the contents of Microsoft's home page when you visit might differ

7. Close your Web browser, and disconnect from your ISP.

 POWER USERS TIP If your Web browser window does not cover the entire desktop, you can also create an Internet shortcut by dragging the Internet Explorer icon from the Address bar to the desktop.

POWER USERS TIP If you want to create a shortcut to a link on a Web page, drag the link to the desktop.

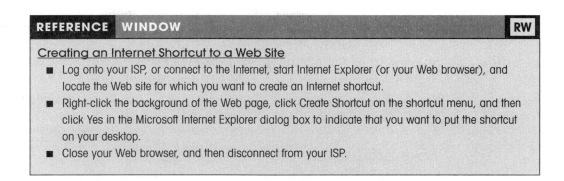

Creating an Internet Shortcut to a Web Site
- Log onto your ISP, or connect to the Internet, start Internet Explorer (or your Web browser), and locate the Web site for which you want to create an Internet shortcut.
- Right-click the background of the Web page, click Create Shortcut on the shortcut menu, and then click Yes in the Microsoft Internet Explorer dialog box to indicate that you want to put the shortcut on your desktop.
- Close your Web browser, and then disconnect from your ISP.

Next, view properties of the Internet shortcut so that you can compare it to other desktop shortcuts.

To view properties of an Internet shortcut:

1. Right-click the **Microsoft** Internet shortcut, and then click **Properties**. Windows XP opens the Microsoft Properties dialog box. See Figure 4-32. On the Web Document property sheet, the URL text box contains the address for Microsoft's home page. Notice that you have the option of changing the icon for the Internet shortcut, you can specify a keyboard shortcut, and you can make the Web page available offline. The property sheet also tracks the number of visits you made to the Web site.

Figure 4-32 VIEWING PROPERTIES OF THE MICROSOFT INTERNET SHORTCUT

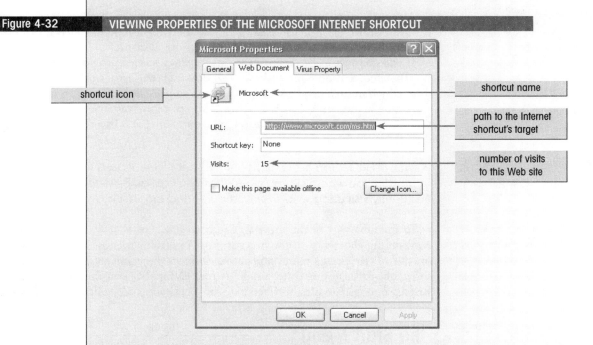

2. Click the **General** tab. On the General property sheet, Windows XP shows the type of file (Internet Shortcut), the location of the file (the Desktop folder for your logon account under the Documents and Settings folder), and other details about the shortcut. See Figure 4-33. Notice that Internet shortcuts, like regular desktop shortcuts, use a disproportionate amount of storage space on disk relative to their size. The size and allocated storage space of your shortcut might vary.

| Figure 4-33 | VIEWING GENERAL PROPERTIES OF THE MICROSOFT INTERNET SHORTCUT |

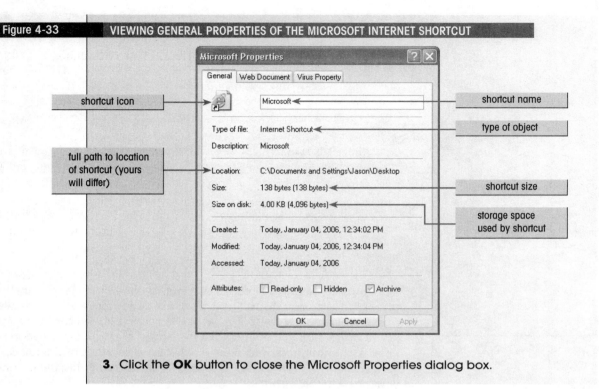

shortcut icon

full path to location of shortcut (yours will differ)

shortcut name

type of object

shortcut size

storage space used by shortcut

3. Click the **OK** button to close the Microsoft Properties dialog box.

Although not shown on any of the property sheets, "url" is the file extension for an Internet shortcut. So, for example, the filename of the Microsoft Internet shortcut is Microsoft.url and MICROS~1.URL is its short filename.

If you connect to the Internet via an Internet service provider, the next time you click an Internet shortcut on your desktop, Windows XP will either open an Internet Explorer window, which in turn displays a copy of the Web page stored in your Temporary Internet Files folder, or Windows XP will display a "Web page unavailable while offline" dialog box, and you can click a Connect button to log on to your ISP. Then the Internet shortcut takes you directly to the Web site.

POWER USERS TIP You can copy your Internet shortcuts to a removable disk and carry them with you wherever you go so that you can quickly access Web sites that you frequently visit using whatever computer and browser is available.

In the next part of the tutorial, you customize the Start menu by adding, removing, and rearranging shortcuts on the Start and All Programs menus. You create a new group folder on the All Programs menu and move desktop shortcuts to this new folder. Then you use shortcuts to customize the Send To menu. Finally, you create a Briefcase and use that Briefcase to update files between a desktop computer and a floppy disk.

Customizing **the Start Menu**

If you are working in a maximized application window such as Microsoft Word or viewing a Web page with Internet Explorer, you might not want to minimize the window just to locate and click a shortcut, and then later maximize the window again. However, the Start button and taskbar are always accessible. If you place a shortcut on the Start menu or on a taskbar toolbar such as the Quick Launch toolbar, as you saw in Tutorial 2, you can leave your application window maximized and still locate and use the shortcut.

If you want to customize the Start menu, you can add new group folders and shortcuts to the Start menu, All Programs menu, and other menus in one of three ways:

- **Using the Taskbar and Start Menu Properties dialog box.** As you saw in Tutorial 2, you can customize the Start menu to include those options that you need for your work, and you can also customize the use of some of those options.
- **Using the Start Menu folder.** You can also open the Start Menu folder, create new group folders and shortcuts, or reorganize the existing group folders and shortcuts. Using this approach you can revamp the All Programs menu so that programs are organized more logically for you and require fewer steps to locate.
- **Using drag and drop.** You can use drag and drop to rearrange, move, or copy group folders and application shortcuts on the Start and All Programs menus and to also drag them from one menu to another. You can even drag desktop shortcuts and drop them on the Start menu.

The approach you use depends on how you prefer to work, the types of changes you want to make, and the degree to which you want to customize the Start and All Programs menus.

Adding Shortcuts to the Start Menu

To add a desktop shortcut to your Start menu, you simply drag it from the desktop and drop it on the Start button. Windows XP then copies the shortcut to the Start menu. The original shortcut remains on the desktop.

Jason invariably finds that he needs to switch to the Delta Oil folder when he is working within an application window or examining a Web site with Internet Explorer. Rather than switch to the desktop to access the Delta Oil shortcut and later reopen the window where he was working, he decides it would be faster to add the Delta Oil shortcut directly to the Start menu so that all he has to do is click the Start button, and then click the Delta Oil shortcut. His application window can remain maximized while he selects the Delta Oil shortcut on the Start menu. He asks you to also add the Delta Oil desktop shortcut to your Start menu.

To add a desktop shortcut to the Start menu:

1. Before you change the Start menu, click the **Start** button and examine the pinned items list in the upper-left corner of the Start menu. On Jason's computer, there are only two items in this area—options for using MSN Explorer to access the Internet, and Microsoft Outlook for composing, sending, and receiving e-mail messages. See Figure 4-34. Your Start menu options might differ.

Figure 4-34 | VIEWING THE PINNED ITEMS ON THE START MENU

options on pinned items list

2. Click the **Start** button a second time to close the Start menu.

3. Drag the **Delta Oil** shortcut from the desktop to the Start button, release the mouse button, and then click the **Start** button if Windows XP does not display the Start menu. Notice that Windows XP added a copy of the Delta Oil shortcut to the pinned items list. See Figure 4-35.

POWER USERS TIP If you want to control the placement of the shortcut on the Start menu, you can hover over the Start button for a moment, and wait for Windows XP to open the Start menu, and then you can choose where you want to drop the shortcut.

Figure 4-35 | DRAGGING A SHORTCUT TO THE START MENU

desktop shortcut added to the Start menu by dragging and dropping on the Start button

4. Click **Delta Oil** on the Start menu. The Delta Oil shortcut on the Start menu works just like the desktop shortcut and opens the Delta Oil folder.

5. Close the Delta Oil window.

As Jason has discovered, you might also find it useful to have the same shortcut in two or more places for quick access from wherever you are working.

Creating a Group Folder on the Programs Menu

You can take the strategy of copying shortcuts to the Start menu a step further. You can create a group folder on the Start menu and copy all of your desktop shortcuts to that group folder so that you can access any of them from the Start menu. As noted earlier, you can modify the Start menu by working directly in the Start Menu folder.

Jason asks you to create a Shortcuts group folder on the Start menu, and then copy your desktop shortcuts to that folder.

To create a group folder and copy shortcuts to it:

1. Right-click the **Start** button, and then click **Open**. Windows XP opens the Start Menu for your user account, as shown in Figure 4-36.

Figure 4-36	VIEWING THE CONTENTS OF THE START MENU FOLDER

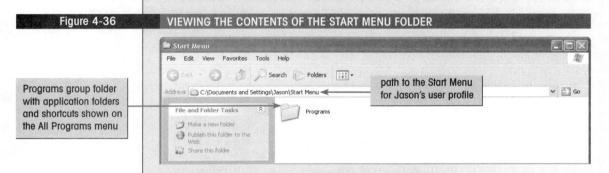

Programs group folder with application folders and shortcuts shown on the All Programs menu

path to the Start Menu for Jason's user profile

2. Click the **Programs** group folder icon. Windows XP displays the group folders and shortcuts found on the All Programs menu. See Figure 4-37. What you see in this folder depends upon what programs have been installed on the computer you are using. The Startup folder includes shortcuts to programs that are loaded when you log on to your computer.

Figure 4-37	VIEWING THE CONTENTS OF THE PROGRAMS FOLDER

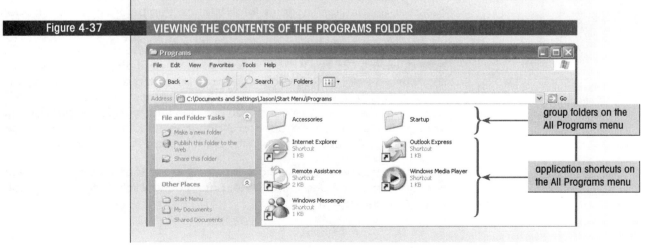

group folders on the All Programs menu

application shortcuts on the All Programs menu

3. Right-click the **background** of the Programs folder window, point to **New**, and then click **Folder** on the New menu. Windows XP creates a new group folder (not the standard file folder), and names it "New Folder". Like other objects, the background of a folder window has actions and properties associated with it. *Note*: You can also create a new group folder by clicking File on the menu bar, pointing to New, and then clicking Folder.

4. Type **Shortcuts,** press **Enter**, and then click the **background** of the Programs folder to change the focus from the new group folder. See Figure 4-38. Note that the group folder has a custom icon.

   TROUBLE? If you already have a group folder called Shortcuts, use a different name for the new group folder that you create. For example, you could use the name "My Shortcuts". Whatever name you choose, use that name instead of "Shortcuts" in the remaining steps.

| Figure 4-38 | CREATING A NEW GROUP FOLDER FOR THE ALL PROGRAMS MENU |

new Shortcuts group folder for the All Programs menu

5. Click the **Shortcuts** group folder icon. Windows XP opens the Shortcuts group folder window. Now you can copy your desktop shortcuts to this folder.

6. Adjust the size and position of the Shortcuts group folder window so that you can see your desktop shortcuts. Read the next step before you copy the desktop shortcuts.

7. Click the **desktop background** to change the focus to the desktop, press and hold down the **Ctrl** key while you point to and select each of the desktop shortcuts you've created, and then, while still holding down the **Ctrl** key, drag the desktop shortcuts into the Shortcuts folder window, release the mouse button, release the **Ctrl** key, and then click the **Shortcuts** folder background to change the focus from the desktop shortcuts in this folder. Windows XP places copies of the desktop shortcuts in the Shortcuts folder. See Figure 4-39.

   TROUBLE? If you accidentally move the desktop shortcuts instead of copying them, right-click the desktop or folder background, click Undo Move, and then repeat this step again.

Figure 4-39 | **VIEWING SHORTCUTS IN THE SHORTCUTS GROUP FOLDER**

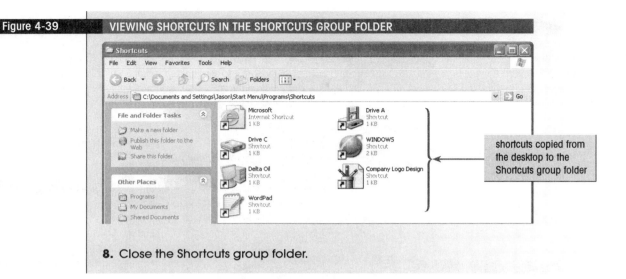

shortcuts copied from the desktop to the Shortcuts group folder

8. Close the Shortcuts group folder.

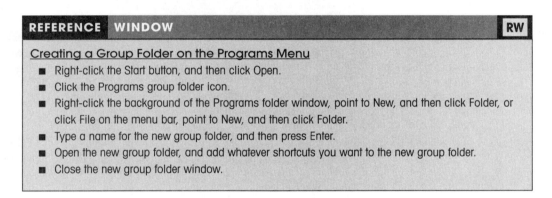

REFERENCE WINDOW RW

Creating a Group Folder on the Programs Menu

■ Right-click the Start button, and then click Open.

■ Click the Programs group folder icon.

■ Right-click the background of the Programs folder window, point to New, and then click Folder, or click File on the menu bar, point to New, and then click Folder.

■ Type a name for the new group folder, and then press Enter.

■ Open the new group folder, and add whatever shortcuts you want to the new group folder.

■ Close the new group folder window.

Now you can test the option for opening the Windows folder from the new Shortcuts group folder on the Programs menu.

To open the Windows folder using the Shortcuts menu:

1. Open the Start menu, point to All Programs, and point to Shortcuts until Windows XP displays a Shortcuts menu with copies of the desktop shortcuts. See Figure 4-40.

Figure 4-40 | VIEWING THE NEW SHORTCUTS GROUP FOLDER

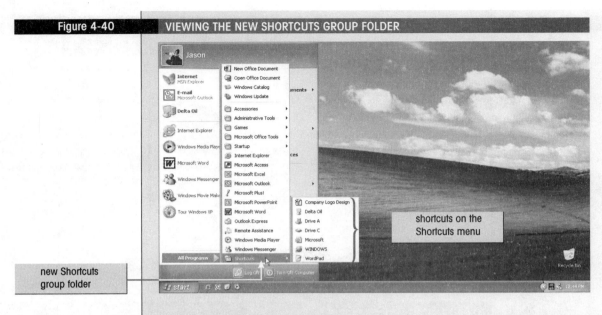

new Shortcuts group folder

shortcuts on the Shortcuts menu

2. If the group folders and shortcuts are not listed in alphabetical order by name, right-click the **All Programs** menu, and then click **Sort by Name**.

3. Point to **Shortcuts** (if necessary), and then click **WINDOWS**. Windows XP opens the Windows folder.

4. Close the Windows folder.

Next, you want to place a copy of the Shortcuts group folder in your My Documents folder.

To copy the Shortcuts group folder to the My Documents folder:

1. Right-click the **Start** button, click **Open**, click the **Programs** folder, point to and select the **Shortcuts** group folder icon, click **Copy this folder** on the File and Folder Tasks dynamic menu, locate and click **My Documents** in the Copy Items dialog box, and then click the **Copy** button.

2. Click **My Documents** on the Other Places dynamic menu. Windows XP creates a copy of the Shortcuts group folder and its contents and places it in the My Documents folder. See Figure 4-41. Note that Windows XP changed the icon for the Shortcuts group folder from a custom icon to a standard folder icon.

Figure 4-41 | VIEWING THE CONTENTS OF THE MY DOCUMENTS FOLDER

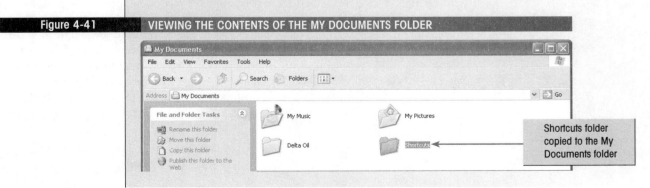

Shortcuts folder copied to the My Documents folder

> **3.** Click the **Shortcuts** folder icon. This folder contains all the shortcuts that you placed in the Shortcuts group folder on the Programs menu.
>
> **4.** Close the Shortcuts folder window.

Now, whenever you are working in the My Documents folder, you can quickly access your commonly used shortcuts. You can also access them from your Start menu or the desktop.

As you've seen in this section, the Start menu that opens when you click the Start button is a special view of a folder on your hard disk. The All Programs menu, Accessories menu, and other menus are simply folders or group folders stored on drive C under your user profile folder. The options for opening applications, utilities, and games are nothing other than shortcuts stored in the Start menu, Programs, and other group folders. By knowing how to navigate the folder structure of your disk; how to create, copy, and move folders; and how to create, copy, and move shortcuts, you can customize the Start menu to suit your needs.

Customizing **the Send To Menu**

The Send To menu lets you quickly copy or move folders and files from one drive to another on your computer. In fact, this option is faster than any other type of drag-and-drop, cut-and-paste, or copy-and-paste operation because you don't have to open multiple windows. Similar to the Start menu, the Send To menu consists of a set of shortcuts stored in a folder named SendTo. You also can add more shortcuts to this folder.

After you install Windows XP, the Send To menu contains shortcuts to your drive(s) that you can write to, and to the My Documents folder. The My Documents option on the Send To menu is a special file named My Documents.mydocs, and its short filename is MYDOCU~1.MYD. (Do not confuse My Documents on the Send To menu with the actual folder by the same name.) Notice that Windows XP adjusts long file extensions to three characters to adhere to the 8.3 file naming conventions.

The Desktop (create shortcut) option, as you've seen, allows you to send an object to the desktop as a shortcut. The Desktop (create shortcut) option is a special file named "Desktop (create shortcut).DeskLink", and its short filename is DESKTO~1.DES.

The Compressed (zipped) Folder option on the Send To menu can copy a file and store it in a new, but compressed (zipped) folder by the same name. In effect, this option provides a simple method for quickly creating a zip file that you then can attach to an email message. The Compressed (zipped) Folder option is a special file named "Compressed (zipped) Folder.ZFSendToTarget", and its short filename is COMPRE~1.ZFS.

The Mail Recipient option on the Send To menu adds a file as an attachment to an e-mail message which you can then address and send. If you send a file with an image, Windows XP offers you the option of "making all your pictures smaller;" in other words, sending files in a compressed format. The Mail Recipient option is useful because, for example, Windows XP can compress a 2 MB bitmap image to 35 KB and reduce the overall size of the attachment to your email message. The Mail Recipient option is a special file named "Mail Recipient.MAPIMail," and its short filename is MAILRE~1.MAP. **MAPI** (Messaging Application Program Interface) is a programming interface for sending e-mail using a Windows application and attaching the current document to the e-mail message.

If you accidentally delete the My Documents, Desktop (create shortcut), Compress (zipped) Folder, or Mail Recipient options on the Send To menu, you can recreate them as follows. (*Note*: The following are not tutorial steps.)

- **Open the SendTo folder**. Right-click the Start button, click Open, click the Up button 🗁, and then click the SendTo folder.

■ **Choose the option to display file extensions**. Click Tools on the menu bar, click Folder Options, click the View tab in the Folder Options dialog box, and under Hidden files and folders in the Advanced settings box, click the Show hidden folders and files option button, and then click the OK button.

■ **Create a new text file by the same name**. Right-click the SendTo folder background, point to New on the shortcut menu, and then click Text Document on the New menu. Change the default name from "New Text Document.txt" to the name of the object you want to create (described above), and press Enter. Windows XP displays a Rename dialog box, warns you that changing a file extension may cause a file to become unstable, and then asks if you want to change the file extension. Click Yes to change the file extension.

After adding shortcuts to your desktop and to the Start menu, Jason asks you to further customize your computer so that you can perform routine operations, such as moving files from one folder to another or opening a document in an application other than the one Windows XP typically associates with that application. Rather than use drag-and-drop or cut-and-paste, Jason suggests that you use the Send To option on an object's shortcut menu.

Use the Send To menu to make a duplicate copy of the Delta Oil folder for use by Jason's summer intern.

To complete the next set of steps, you need a formatted diskette that does not contain any files.

To copy folders and files to a floppy disk using the Send To menu:

1. Remove Data Disk #2 from drive A and insert a formatted floppy disk that does not contain any files.

2. Open the My Documents folder.

3. Right-click the **Delta Oil** folder, point to **Send To**, and then click **3½ Floppy (A:)**. The Copying dialog box shows the name of each file being copied, the source and destination folders, and the amount of time left for the copy operation. See Figure 4-42. After the copy operation is complete, Windows XP closes the Copying dialog box.

Figure 4-42	COPYING THE DELTA OIL FOLDER

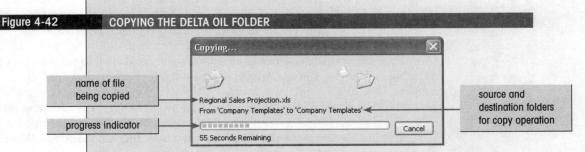

4. Close the My Documents window, and then click your **Drive A** desktop shortcut. The floppy disk now contains a copy of the Delta Oil folder.

5. Click the **Delta Oil** folder in the drive A window. During the copy, Windows XP recreated on drive A the same folders in the Delta Oil folder on drive C.

6. Click the **Overhead Transparencies** folder. Windows XP copied all the files from the Overhead Transparencies folder on drive C to the Overhead Transparencies folder on drive A.

7. Close the Overhead Transparencies window.

This approach is a quick and easy way to make backups of selected folders and files at the end of a busy day.

REFERENCE WINDOW   **RW**

<u>Copying Files to a Floppy Disk Using the Send To Menu</u>
- Insert a floppy disk in your 3½ Floppy (A:) drive.
- Open My Documents (or one of your drives), and select the folder(s) or file(s) you want to copy.
- Right-click the folder(s) or file(s) you want to copy, point to Send To, and then click 3½ Floppy (A:), or after selecting the folder(s) or file(s), click File on the menu bar, point to Send To, and then click 3½ Floppy (A:).
- Close the My Documents (or drive) folder window.

 POWER USERS TIP If you have a set of Internet shortcuts that you rely on, you can store a copy of them in an Internet Shortcuts folder and use the Send To menu to quickly copy the folder and its Internet shortcuts to a floppy disk or Zip disk that you can carry with you to another location and, as noted earlier, then use to quickly access those Web sites you frequently visit.

Adding Shortcuts to the Send To Menu

Jason wants you to copy some of your desktop shortcuts to the SendTo folder, so that these shortcuts appear on the Send To menu. First, you select and copy the desktop shortcuts, and then you paste them into the SendTo folder.

To select and copy desktop shortcuts:

1. Point to and select the **drive C** shortcut on the desktop.

TROUBLE? If Windows XP does not highlight the drive C shortcut, click the desktop background to change the focus, then try this step again.

2. After Windows highlights the drive C shortcut, press and hold down the **Ctrl** key while you point to and select the **Windows**, **Delta Oil**, and **WordPad** shortcuts, and then release the **Ctrl** key. You have selected a collection of shortcuts.

TROUBLE? If you select a collection and accidentally include an object that you realize you do not need, press and hold the Ctrl key while you point to the object a second time. After Windows XP removes it from the collection, release the Ctrl key.

3. Right-click one of the highlighted shortcuts, and then click **Copy** on the shortcut menu.

TROUBLE? If you do anything other than a single right-click, you remove the selection from the desktop shortcuts. You will need to start over, select the shortcuts again, and repeat this step.

4. Right-click the **Start** button, click **Open**, click the **Up** button 🖼, and then click the **SendTo** folder. The SendTo folder contains the objects and shortcuts on your Send To menu. See Figure 4-43. This approach to opening the SendTo folder is the fastest way to locate the SendTo folder for your user account.

   TROUBLE? If you do not see a SendTo folder, click Tools, click Folder Options, click the View tab, and in the Advanced settings box, click the Show hidden files and folders option button, click OK to close the Folder Options dialog box, and then repeat this step.

| Figure 4-43 | VIEWING THE CONTENTS OF THE SENDTO FOLDER |

5. Right-click the **SendTo** folder background, click **Paste**, and then click the **folder background**. Windows XP copies the desktop shortcuts you selected to this folder. See Figure 4-44.

| Figure 4-44 | DESKTOP SHORTCUTS ADDED TO THE SENDTO FOLDER |

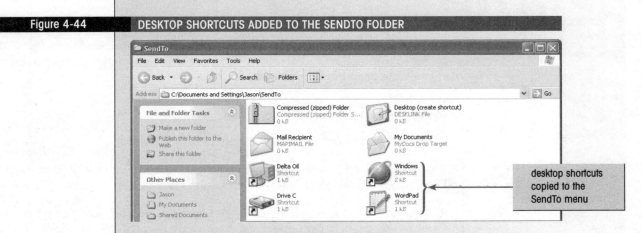

6. Close the SendTo folder window.

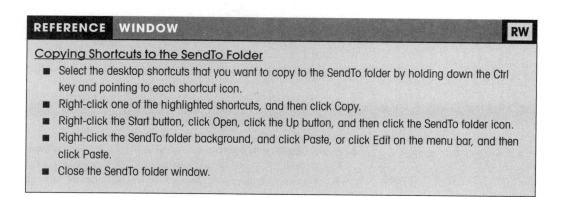

Copying Shortcuts to the SendTo Folder
- Select the desktop shortcuts that you want to copy to the SendTo folder by holding down the Ctrl key and pointing to each shortcut icon.
- Right-click one of the highlighted shortcuts, and then click Copy.
- Right-click the Start button, click Open, click the Up button, and then click the SendTo folder icon.
- Right-click the SendTo folder background, and click Paste, or click Edit on the menu bar, and then click Paste.
- Close the SendTo folder window.

Next, Jason asks you to send a copy of the Company Logo Design bitmap image file to the Windows folder so that you can use it as background wallpaper on your computer.

To copy a bitmap image using the Send To menu:

1. Click the **Delta Oil** desktop shortcut, and after Windows XP opens the Delta Oil folder, click the **Designs** folder icon, right-click **Company Logo Design.bmp**, and point to **Send To**. The Send To menu now contains copies of the desktop shortcuts as menu options. See Figure 4-45.

Figure 4-45   COPYING A FILE USING THE SENDTO MENU

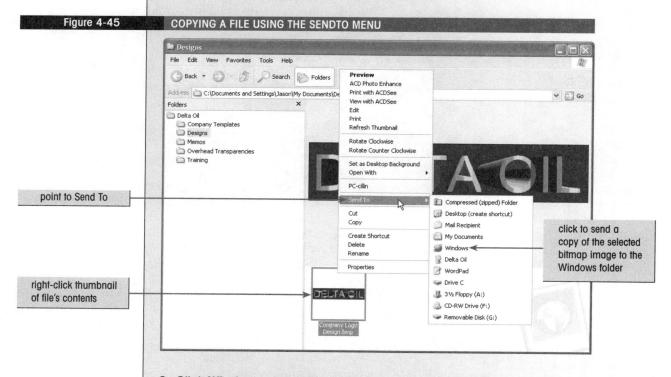

2. Click **Windows** on the Send To menu. Windows XP copies the Company Logo Design.bmp file to the Windows folder.

3. Close the Designs folder window.

Why couldn't you right-click the Company Logo Design shortcut on the desktop, and use its Send To menu to send a copy of this file to the Windows folder? If you did this, you would send a copy of the desktop shortcut, not a copy of the file, to the Windows folder.

Jason now wants you to display the image in the Company Logo Design.bmp as desktop wallpaper.

To view the company logo as wallpaper:

1. Right-click the **desktop**, click **Properties**, click the **Desktop** tab in the Display Properties dialog box, locate and click **Company Logo Design** in the Background box, click **Center** in the Position list box, if necessary, and then click the **OK** button to close the Display Properties dialog box. Windows XP displays the image in this file as wallpaper. See Figure 4-46.

Figure 4-46   USING THE COMPANY LOGO DESIGN AS DESKTOP WALLPAPER

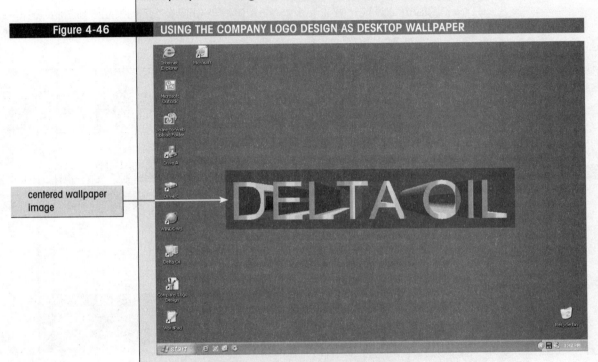

centered wallpaper image

2. To restore the Windows XP wallpaper, right-click the **desktop**, click **Properties**, click **Windows XP** in the Theme list box on the Themes property sheet, and then click the **OK** button to close the Display Properties dialog box.

By viewing the Company Logo Design file as wallpaper, you not only have an idea of how well the design works as wallpaper, but you have also verified that Windows XP copied it to the Windows folder.

REFERENCE WINDOW [RW]

Copying a File to a Folder Using the Send To Menu
- Open the folder that contains the file you want to copy .
- Right-click the file, point to Send To, press and hold the Ctrl key while you click the folder shortcut on the SendTo menu.
- Close the folder window.

 POWER USERS TIP If you want to reorganize your document files on your hard disk and move them to new folders, create the new folders first, then create shortcuts to those new folders, and add the shortcuts to the SendTo folder. Then you can quickly move files from one folder to another with the Send To menu and guarantee that the files end up where you want them.

Using a Briefcase

The **Briefcase** is a special Windows XP folder that is represented by an icon of a briefcase. After you create a Briefcase, you copy files from folders on your computer to the Briefcase. The Briefcase keeps track of the full path and name of the original file(s) that you copied. You can then move the Briefcase to a floppy disk or another type of removable disk and work on those files at home or on a business trip, for example. Later, when you return to work on the computer that has the original copies of these files, you can use the Briefcase to update the original files on that computer. If you then change the files on your office computer, you can use the same Briefcase to update the copies in the Briefcase itself. Likewise, you can use the Briefcase over a network to update copies of the same files stored on two different networked computers.

The Windows XP Briefcase uses the date and time stamp on files to determine whether two copies of the same file are different or identical, so the date and time on your computer and on other computers where you work with a briefcase should be set correctly. When updating two different versions of a file, the Windows XP Briefcase relies on the applications that produced the files to reconcile differences and update the older file so that it matches the most recent file. The Windows XP Briefcase relies on the file extension and file associations defined in Windows XP to determine which application to call upon for the file update.

If you change the original file on your office or home computer, and then later change the copy of that file in the Briefcase without first updating the original file with the Briefcase, the files are "out of sync" and the Briefcase cannot update the files. Instead, it will recommend that you skip any future updates. Therefore, if you change one of the two copies of a file, you should use the Briefcase to update the other file before you work on it and make further changes. You also can split a file in the Briefcase from the original copy of that file, so that you can update both files independently of each other.

Instead of using the Briefcase, why not copy a folder and its files from your office computer to a Zip disk, for example, and after you have changed those files on the Zip disk, just copy the folder and its file back to your office computer? One advantage of using the Briefcase over a simple copy-and-paste operation is that it is much faster. It identifies only the files that need to be updated and then performs the update faster than you could with copy and paste. If you create a Briefcase on a Zip disk to store a copy of a folder with hundreds of files, the Briefcase can quickly identify only those files that need updating, perform the update, and save you literally hours of time. If you do not use the Briefcase, but try to remember which files you need to update, you run the risk of overlooking some files, and eventually you have two or more different versions of those files that you have to manually reconcile. Likewise, if you copy files from different folders into a Briefcase, and then work on them at another location, the Briefcase can update the original files in each of the original folders much faster than you can manually. This is particularly useful if you work on multiple projects and store files for each project in different folders, or if you work for different clients, and store your client files in different folders.

Creating a New Briefcase

To create a Briefcase, open a window onto the drive or folder where you want to store the Briefcase, and then right-click the folder window or desktop, point to New, and then choose Briefcase. Once you create a Briefcase, you use drag and drop or copy and paste to copy the folder, folders, or files you want to store in the Briefcase.

Jason often takes files home so that he can work on them in the evenings and on weekends. When he travels to other offices, he also takes a copy of his files with him. After he revises a file at home or on the road, he needs to copy it to his office computer, so that he has the most recent copy of the file in both locations. Occasionally, he discovers that he has not updated files on his office computer, his home computer, or his portable laptop. As a result, he ends up with two or three versions of the same file. So that you don't encounter the same problems when you take work home, he asks you to create a Windows XP Briefcase for the Delta Oil folder and its files.

In the next set of steps, you are going to create a Briefcase, copy the Delta Oil folder from the My Documents folder on drive C to that Briefcase, change one of the Briefcase files, and then automatically update the corresponding file in the Delta Oil folder on drive C. Then you are going to change one of the files in the Delta Oil folder on drive C, and update the corresponding file in the Briefcase. To accomplish these tasks, you need a floppy disk that does not contain any files. To use the Briefcase, you need Microsoft Office 2000 or a later version installed on your computer, or you need to use another computer with Microsoft Office 2000 or a later version. If you do not have access to a computer with one of these versions, read, but do not keystroke, the following steps so that you are familiar with the use of the Briefcase. Also examine the figures to see how to use the Briefcase.

To create a Briefcase:

1. Insert a blank formatted floppy disk in drive A.

2. From the Start menu, open the **My Documents** folder (or the folder that contains the Delta Oil folder), and then minimize the My Documents folder window.

3. Click the **Drive A** shortcut, and then click the **My Documents** taskbar button.

4. With both windows open, right-click the **taskbar**, and then click **Tile Windows Vertically**. Windows XP places both windows side-by-side. Note that both windows are of equal size, and the last window you selected (My Documents) is placed on the left side of the desktop.

    POWER USERS TIP If you want to reverse this order, select the window you want to appear on the right, and then repeat this step.

5. Right-click the **background** of the 3½ Floppy (A:) window, point to **New**, and then click **Briefcase**. Windows XP creates a new Briefcase called "New Briefcase," as shown in Figure 4-47. *Note*: You can also click File on the menu bar, point to New, and then click Briefcase.

Figure 4-47 | CREATING A NEW BRIEFCASE

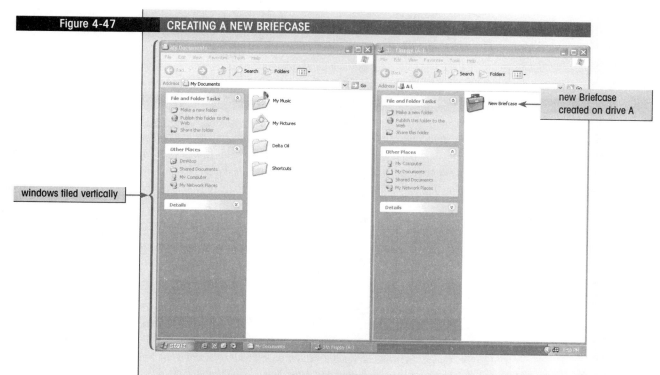

windows tiled vertically

new Briefcase
created on drive A

6. Change the name of the New Briefcase to **Delta Oil Briefcase**.

7. Drag the **Delta Oil** folder from the My Documents window and drop it on the **Delta Oil Briefcase** icon in the 3½ Floppy (A:) window. The Updating Briefcase dialog box shows the progress of folders and files being copied to the Delta Oil Briefcase. See Figure 4-48.

TROUBLE? If the Briefcase utility reports that it was unable to load the merge handlers, you are probably using Microsoft Office 97. You will need to complete these tasks on a computer with Microsoft Office 2000.

Figure 4-48 | COPYING THE DELTA OIL FOLDER TO THE BRIEFCASE

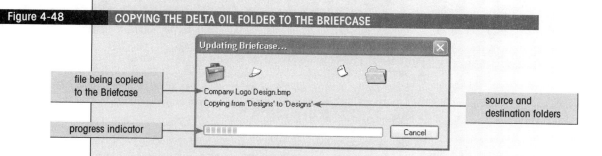

file being copied
to the Briefcase

source and
destination folders

progress indicator

8. Close the My Documents window, maximize the 3½ Floppy (A:) window, click the **Delta Oil Briefcase** icon, and if Windows XP displays a "Welcome to the Windows Briefcase" dialog box, read the information in that dialog box, and then click **Finish** to close the dialog box. The Delta Oil Briefcase contains a copy of the Delta Oil folder. See Figure 4-49. Windows XP displays the full path to the My Documents folder on drive C (yours will differ), and informs you that the copy of the Delta Oil folder in the Delta Oil Briefcase is up to date.

TROUBLE? If the "Sync Copy In" column does not display the entire path to your My Documents folders, point to the thin border that separates this column from the Status column, and double-click that thin border for a best fit of the "Sync Copy In" column.

| Figure 4-49 | VIEWING THE CONTENTS OF THE DELTA OIL BRIEFCASE |

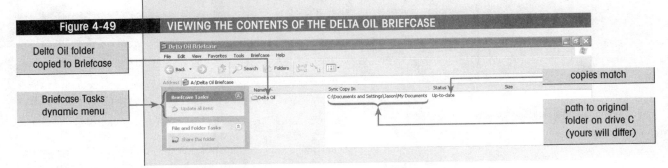

Delta Oil folder copied to Briefcase

Briefcase Tasks dynamic menu

copies match

path to original folder on drive C (yours will differ)

Like any other briefcase, you can now carry it with you.

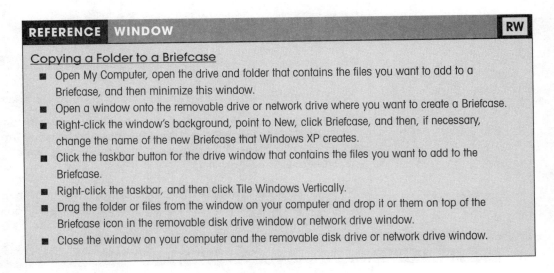

REFERENCE WINDOW | RW

Copying a Folder to a Briefcase

- Open My Computer, open the drive and folder that contains the files you want to add to a Briefcase, and then minimize this window.
- Open a window onto the removable drive or network drive where you want to create a Briefcase.
- Right-click the window's background, point to New, click Briefcase, and then, if necessary, change the name of the new Briefcase that Windows XP creates.
- Click the taskbar button for the drive window that contains the files you want to add to the Briefcase.
- Right-click the taskbar, and then click Tile Windows Vertically.
- Drag the folder or files from the window on your computer and drop it or them on top of the Briefcase icon in the removable disk drive window or network drive window.
- Close the window on your computer and the removable disk drive or network drive window.

You can have as many Briefcases as you need—one for each client or each project, for example—to organize your business and personal files.

Modifying a File in the Briefcase

The Briefcase is similar to other folders you use. If you want to modify a file, you open the Briefcase, open the folder containing the file, and then open, modify, and save the file back to its Briefcase folder. Later, you can update the original copy of this same file stored on another computer.

Jason wants you to update a memo he has prepared for his staff by mentioning that Microsoft's Technical Support can be reached via its Web site.

Although you are going to continue to work on the same computer, imagine that you have taken the floppy disk with the Briefcase from work to home or with you on the road, and then changed the file in the Briefcase.

To modify a Briefcase file:

1. Click the **Delta Oil** folder in the Delta Oil Briefcase, and then click the **Memos** folder.

2. Right-click the **Microsoft's Web Site.doc** file icon, point to **Send To**, and then click **WordPad**. If you have Microsoft Word on your computer, or some other application like Microsoft Word that uses the "doc" file extension for document files, you have just overridden that file association using the Send To menu.

3. After Windows opens the memo in WordPad, insert this sentence before the last sentence: **You can also access Microsoft Technical Support from this Web site.**

4. Click **File** on the menu bar, click **Save**, and then close the WordPad window.

   TROUBLE? If WordPad displays an Unsupported Save Format dialog box and informs you that it cannot save the document in its current format and that it will instead convert the document to Rich Text, click the OK button, and then close WordPad.

5. Close the Memos folder window (and Briefcase).

Recall that you can also place shortcuts to applications in the Send To folder so that you can bypass Windows XP file associations and open a file in another application. For example, you might have several applications installed on your computer, each allowing you to work with bitmap image files, but the file extension for the bitmap file type is only associated with one application. To open a file in another application, add to the Send To folder a shortcut to that application, and then you can send (i.e., "open") that application from the Send To menu.

REFERENCE WINDOW   **RW**

<u>Modifying a File in a Briefcase</u>
- Open My Computer, and then open a window for the drive that contains the Briefcase.
- Click the Briefcase icon, click the folder icon that contains the file you want to modify, and then click the file icon.
- Change the file, save your changes, and then close the application window.
- Close the Briefcase.

As you work at home or travel, you can modify any file in the Briefcase, and then update your original copies when you return to the computer that contains the original files.

Using a Briefcase to Update Files

If you need to update the files in a Briefcase with new versions of the original copies of the files, or if you need to update the original files with copies of the changed files in the Briefcase, you open the Briefcase and click the Update All button. The Briefcase utility then identifies which files need updating. It also identifies the location of the files to be updated (the original files on your desktop computer or the files in the Briefcase itself). You can perform the update, change the direction of the update (restoring a previous copy of a file), or skip the update.

After returning to your office, you need to update the copy of the staff memo stored on your office computer using your copy of the Delta Oil Briefcase.

To update files using Briefcase:

1. Click the **Drive A** shortcut, and then click the **Delta Oil Briefcase** icon. Note that the Briefcase indicates that the Delta Oil folder needs updating. See Figure 4-50.

Figure 4-50   BRIEFCASE NEEDS UPDATING

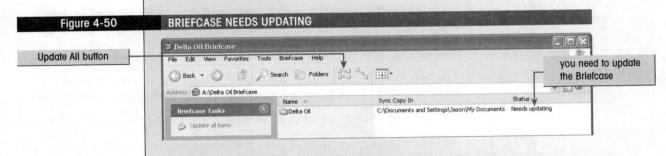

2. Click the **Update All** button on the Standard Buttons toolbar. The Update Delta Oil Briefcase dialog box opens and identifies the file that needs to be updated. See Figure 4-51. The Briefcase recommends that you replace the unmodified version of the Microsoft's Web Site.doc file in the Delta Oil Memos folder on drive C (the one identified on the right) with the more recent version in the Briefcase (the one identified on the left). Notice that the times of the modified and unmodified files are different. If you had modified more than one file, then the Update Delta Oil Briefcase dialog box would list all of the files you had modified. If you right-click the Replace arrow, the Briefcase will display a shortcut menu that allows you to change the direction of the Replace so that you can restore the copy in the Briefcase to its original condition using the original file stored on drive C. If you do not want to update one of the files listed in this dialog box, you can use the shortcut menu to change the Replace action to a Skip action. You can also perform an update by choosing the Update All option on the Briefcase menu.

Figure 4-51   UPDATING THE DELTA OIL FOLDER ON DRIVE C

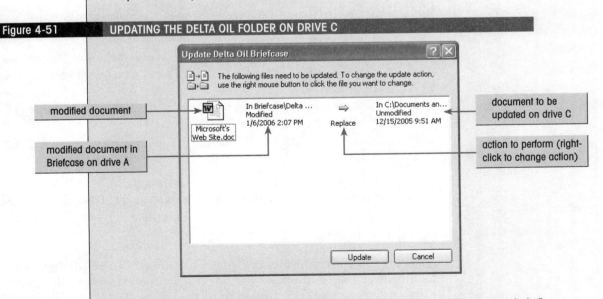

3. Click the **Update** button. The Updating Briefcase dialog box opens briefly as the update occurs, and then the Briefcase shows that the Delta Oil folder is up to date. See Figure 4-52.

Figure 4-52   BRIEFCASE UPDATED

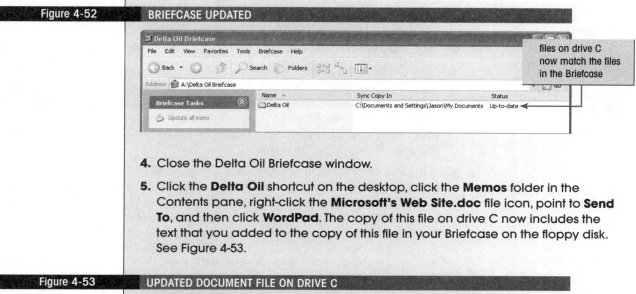

files on drive C
now match the files
in the Briefcase

4. Close the Delta Oil Briefcase window.

5. Click the **Delta Oil** shortcut on the desktop, click the **Memos** folder in the Contents pane, right-click the **Microsoft's Web Site.doc** file icon, point to **Send To**, and then click **WordPad**. The copy of this file on drive C now includes the text that you added to the copy of this file in your Briefcase on the floppy disk. See Figure 4-53.

Figure 4-53   UPDATED DOCUMENT FILE ON DRIVE C

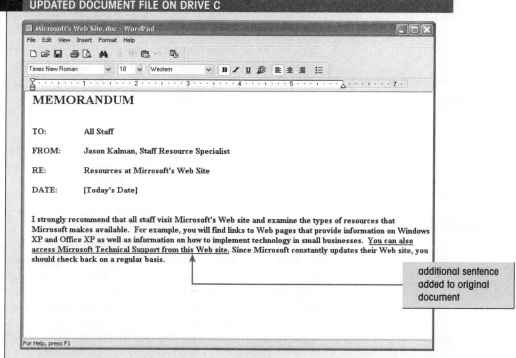

additional sentence
added to original
document

Jason asks you to make a couple of additional changes to the memo, review the design in the Designs folder, and delete a file he no longer needs. So that your copies of these files are up to date, you then want to update your Briefcase.

To make further changes to the memo and to other files in the Delta Oil folder on drive C:

1. Change (Today's Date) to the current date.

2. Insert a second paragraph that reads: **If you need assistance, you can reach me at extension 758.**

3. Click **File** on the menu bar, click **Save**, and then close the WordPad window.

4. Click the **Designs** folder icon in the Folders toolbar, right-click the **Company Logo Design.bmp** icon, point to **Open With**, click **Paint**, and then maximize the Paint application window, if necessary. This time, you used the Open With option on a file's shortcut menu to override the default file association. Earlier, when you clicked the desktop shortcut for this file, Windows XP opened it in the Windows Picture and Fax Viewer.

5. In the Paint application window, click the **Fill With Color** button 🖌 (second column, second row) in the Tool Box on the left side of the Paint window, click the **bright blue** color box in the Color Box (first row, fourth box from right) at the bottom left of the Paint window, and then click the **dark blue** background of the image. Paint changes the background to a bright blue.

   TROUBLE? If you do not see a Tool Box, click View, and then click Tool Box. If you do not see a Color Box, click View, and then click Color Box.

6. Click **File**, click **Save**, and then close the Paint window.

7. Click the **Overhead Transparencies** folder in the Folders toolbar, right-click the **Sales.wk4** file icon, click **Delete** on the shortcut menu, and then click the **Yes** button in the Confirm File Delete dialog box.

8. Close the Overhead Transparencies folder window.

Now you are ready to update the copies in your Briefcase. However, you realize that it might be a good idea to not update the Company Logo Design file in your Briefcase just yet, because you might need the original design in this file.

To update the Briefcase:

1. Click the **Drive A** shortcut, click the **Delta Oil Briefcase** icon, and then click the **Update All** button on the Standard Buttons toolbar. The Update Delta Oil Briefcase window identifies the files that need to be updated. See Figure 4-54. The Briefcase recommends that you delete the copy of the Sales.wk4 file in the Briefcase and replace the unmodified versions of the Company Logo Design.bmp and Microsoft's Web Site.doc files in the Briefcase with the more recent versions from the Delta Oil folder on drive C.

| Figure 4-54 | ACTIONS FOR UPDATING BRIEFCASE FILES ON DRIVE A |

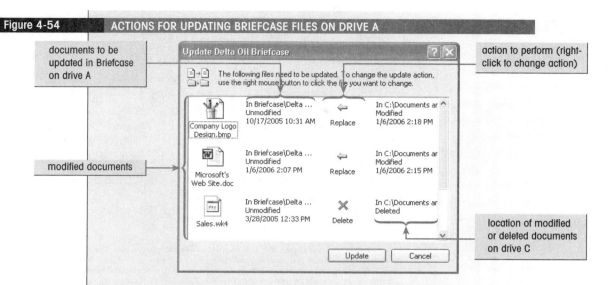

documents to be updated in Briefcase on drive A

modified documents

action to perform (right-click to change action)

location of modified or deleted documents on drive C

2. Right-click the **Replace** action arrow for the Company Logo Design.bmp file, and then click **Skip** on the shortcut menu. The Briefcase updates the action for this file, as shown in Figure 4-55.

| Figure 4-55 | FINAL ACTIONS FOR UPDATING BRIEFCASE FILES |

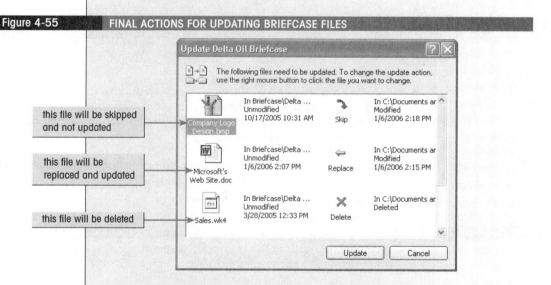

this file will be skipped and not updated

this file will be replaced and updated

this file will be deleted

3. Click the **Update** button. The Updating Briefcase dialog box appears as the updates occur.

4. Click the **Delta Oil** folder icon in the Delta Oil Briefcase window, click the **Memos** folder icon, right-click the **Microsoft's Web Site.doc** file icon, point to **Send To**, and then click **WordPad**. The file in the Briefcase now has the text that you added as a second paragraph in the document file on drive C. See Figure 4-56.

| Figure 4-56 | VIEWING AN UPDATED DOCUMENT IN THE BRIEFCASE |

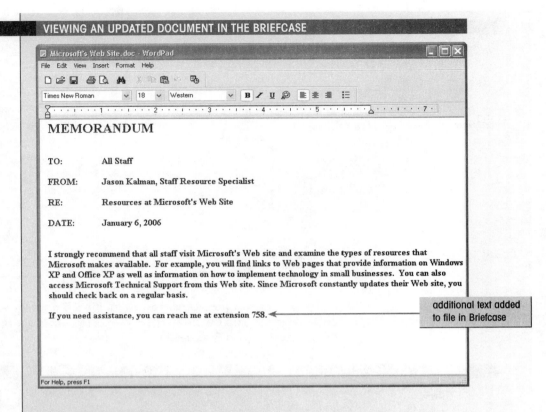

additional text added
to file in Briefcase

5. Close the WordPad window.

6. Click the **Folders** button on the Standard Buttons toolbar, and then click the **Overhead Transparencies** folder icon in the Folders toolbar. The Briefcase removed the Sales.wk4 file that you had previously deleted from the Delta Oil folder on drive C. See Figure 4-57.

TROUBLE? If you cannot see the complete names of the folders in the Folders toolbar, maximize the Memos folder window, adjust the width of the Folders toolbar, and then complete this step.

| Figure 4-57 | FILE REMOVED FROM THE OVERHEAD TRANSPARENCIES FOLDER |

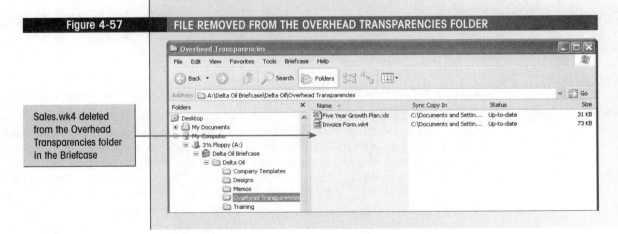

Sales.wk4 deleted
from the Overhead
Transparencies folder
in the Briefcase

7. Click the **Designs** folder icon in the Folders toolbar, right-click **Company Logo Design.bmp**, point to **Open With**, and then click **Paint**. As you requested, the Briefcase skipped the update of this file. You had changed the background to a bright blue, but the background of this image retains the original dark blue color. See Figure 4-58.

Figure 4-58   UPDATE SKIPPED

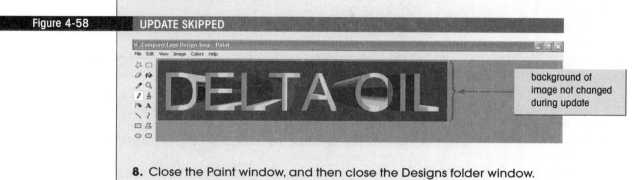

8. Close the Paint window, and then close the Designs folder window.

REFERENCE WINDOW   **RW**

Updating Files in a Briefcase
- Open My Computer, and then open a window for the drive that contains the Briefcase.
- Click the Briefcase icon, and then click the Update All button on the Standard Buttons toolbar.
- Review the files in the Update Briefcase dialog box, and if necessary, right-click the action arrow and change the direction of the replace, or choose the option to skip the replace.
- In the Update Briefcase dialog box, click the Update button.
- Close the Briefcase window.

A Briefcase simplifies the process of reconciling different versions of the same file on different drives or different computer systems so that you have the most recent version of any file that the Briefcase tracks. You can create a Briefcase for each set of folders and files that you use on more than one computer system. You can use a Briefcase on a network. If you change files on one computer, you can immediately update the corresponding files on other computers in the network. You can also use the Briefcase as an option for backing up files.

Restoring Your Computer's Settings

If you are working in a computer lab, or if you want to restore your desktop computer to the settings that existed prior to working on this tutorial, complete the following steps to remove folders, files, and shortcuts.

To remove folders, files, and shortcuts:

1. Open the My Documents folder, point to and select the **Delta Oil** folder, press and hold the **Ctrl** key, point to and select the **Shortcuts** folder, right-click one of the selected folders, click **Delete** on the shortcut menu (or press the **Delete** key), click the **Yes** button in the Confirm Multiple File Delete dialog box, and then close the My Documents window.

2. Right-click the **Start** button, click **Open**, click the **Up** button 🔼, click the **SendTo** folder, point to and select the **Delta Oil** shortcut, press and hold down the **Ctrl** key while you point to and select the **Windows**, **Drive C**, and **WordPad** shortcuts, press the **Delete** key, click the **Yes** button in the Confirm Multiple File Delete dialog box, and then close the SendTo folder window.

3. Open the Start menu, right-click **Delta Oil** in the pinned items list, and then click **Remove from This List**.

4. Point to **All Programs**, right-click **Shortcuts**, click **Delete**, and then click the **Yes** button in the Confirm Folder Delete dialog box.

5. Click the **Windows** shortcut, click **View** on the menu bar, click **Details**, click the **Date Modified** column button twice, point to and select the **Company Logo Design.bmp** file, click **Delete this file** on the File and Folder Tasks dynamic menu, click the **Yes** button in the Confirm File Delete dialog box, and then close the Windows window.

TROUBLE? If Company Logo Design.bmp is not listed as the first file in the Windows folder window, you will have to locate it. You can click the Name column to arrange files in alphabetical order by filename, or you can click the Type column button to arrange files by type. If you choose the latter option, look for the files listed with the file type Bitmap Image. Once you locate the Company Logo Design.bmp file, point to and select this file, click "Delete this file" on the File and Folder Tasks dynamic menu, click Yes in the Confirm File Delete dialog box, and then close the Windows window.

6. Click the **Drive A** desktop shortcut, point to and select the **Delta Oil Briefcase**, press the **Delete** key, click the **Yes** button in the Confirm Folder Delete dialog box, and then close the 3½ Floppy (A:) window.

7. Point to and select the **Drive A** desktop shortcut, press and hold down the **Ctrl** key while you point to and select the **Drive C**, **Windows**, **Delta Oil**, **Company Logo Design**, **WordPad**, and **Microsoft** desktop shortcuts, release the **Ctrl** key, press the **Delete** key, and then click the **Yes** button in the Confirm Multiple File Delete dialog box.

8. Empty the Recycle Bin.

You may also need to restore your computer's settings.

To restore your computer's display settings:

1. If your computer was originally set for the Windows Classic style, right-click the **desktop**, click **Properties** on the shortcut menu, and after Windows XP opens the Display Properties dialog box, click the **Theme** list arrow on the Themes property sheet, click **Windows Classic**, and then click the **OK** button.

2. To switch to the Windows Classic Start menu style, right-click the **Start** button, click **Properties**, and after Windows XP opens the Taskbar and Start Menu Properties dialog box, click the **Classic Start menu** option button on the Start Menu property sheet, and then click the **OK** button.

3. To change to Windows classic folders view, click the **Start** button, point to **Settings**, click **Control Panel**, and after Windows XP opens a Control Panel window, click **Tools** on the menu bar, click **Folder Options**, and after Windows XP opens the Folder Options dialog box, click the **Use Windows classic folders** option button, and then click the **Double-click to open an item** option button under "Click items as follows."

4. Click the **View** tab in the Folder Options dialog box. If necessary, restore the original settings for the "Display the full path in the address bar" check box, the "Do not show hidden files and folders" option button, and the "Hide extensions for known file types" check box.

5. Click the **OK** button to close the Folder Options dialog box and restore your original settings, and then close the Control Panel folder window.

6. To remove the Quick Launch toolbar from the taskbar, right-click the **taskbar**, point to **Toolbars**, and then click **Quick Launch**.

As Jason and you have discovered, shortcuts unlock the power of Windows XP by bypassing many of the intermediate steps that you would otherwise perform as you work on your computer, and by taking you directly to what you need to use, whether it's on your computer, another computer, or the World Wide Web. The Briefcase augments the use of shortcuts, and provides an easy-to-use mechanism for updating versions of the same files on different drives and computers.

REVIEW ASSIGNMENTS

Jason recently hired another graphics artist, Natasha Ellingsen, to help him with client projects. On her first day of work, Jason explains to Natasha how he works with Windows XP and describes the types of support that they must provide for other employees. Because time seems to always be at a premium, Jason asks you to create shortcuts to the drives, applications, folders, and files that Natasha will be using on a daily basis. He also asks you to create a Briefcase for Natasha's document files so that she can carry them with her when she travels to Delta Oil branch offices.

As you complete each step in the Review Assignments, record your answers to questions so that you can submit them to your instructor. Use a word-processing application such as Word or WordPad to prepare and then print your answers to these questions. Also, if you change any settings on the computer you are using, note the original settings so that you can restore them later. If you are using another browser, adapt the instructions to that browser.

To complete the steps for using the Briefcase, you need Microsoft Office 2000 or a later version installed on your computer, or you need to use another computer with Microsoft Office 2000 or a later version.

1. Insert your Data Disk #2 into drive A.

2. If necessary, change to Web style, and choose the option for single-click activation.

3. Open My Computer, and then adjust the size and placement of the window so that you can also see part of the desktop. Click Tools on the menu bar, click Folder Options, and then choose the options for displaying hidden files and folders and for displaying file extensions for known file types.

4. Create a desktop shortcut to your CD-ROM drive, DVD-ROM drive, or some other type of drive that supports removable media (such as a Zip drive) by right-dragging the drive icon to the desktop and selecting Create Shortcuts Here on the shortcut menu. To which drive did you create a shortcut? What type of icon does Windows XP use for the shortcut? What happens when you click the drive shortcut? For what other types of drives on your computer might you want to create desktop shortcuts? Close the window opened by the drive shortcut.

5. Right-click the desktop shortcut that you just created for a removable drive, and select Properties. What is the full path to the folder where the shortcut is stored? What is the full path of the target for the shortcut? What is the size of the shortcut, and how much space does it use on disk? Close the Properties dialog box for the drive shortcut.

6. Open the Start menu, and drag the Control Panel to the desktop. What type of icon does Windows XP use for the Control Panel shortcut? What happens when you click the shortcut? What is the target for this shortcut? Close the window opened by the Control Panel shortcut.

7. From My Computer, open a window onto your copy of Data Disk #2.

8. Right-click the Delta Oil folder, click Copy, click My Documents in the Other Places dynamic menu or, if you have another drive where you prefer to work, click My Computer in the Other Places dynamic menu, open a window onto that drive, right-click the My Documents or drive folder background, and click Paste.

Explore 9. Open the Delta Oil folder, right-click the Training folder icon, and click Create Shortcut. What is the name of the new shortcut? Drag the shortcut to the desktop. What happened to the name of the shortcut? If necessary, change the name of the shortcut to Training. Right-click the Training shortcut, click Properties, click the Change Icon button on the Shortcut property sheet, click the Browse button, locate and open the Pifmgr.dll file in the System32 folder, choose one of the icons contained in this icon library file, apply the changes to your computer, and close the Delta Oil folder. What icon did you pick for this desktop shortcut? What happens when you click the Training shortcut? What is the full path for this shortcut's target? Close the window opened by the Training shortcut.

10. Open the Delta Oil folder, open the Designs folder, hover over and select the "Company Logo Design.bmp" file, click File on the menu bar, and then click Create Shortcut. Drag (and move) the shortcut from the Designs folder to the desktop. Right-click the shortcut, click Rename, and change the name of the shortcut to Logo. What type of icon does Windows XP use for the shortcut? What happens when you click the Logo shortcut? What is the full path for this shortcut's target? Close the window opened by the Logo shortcut.

Explore 11. Open the Start menu, point to All Programs, point to Accessories, right-click Paint, and then click Copy. Right-click the desktop, and then click Paste. What type of icon does Windows XP use for the shortcut? What happens when you click the Paint shortcut? What is the full path to the shortcut's target? Explain the use of the environment variable in the path. Close the window opened by the Paint shortcut.

Explore 12. Drag the Logo desktop shortcut and drop it onto the Paint desktop shortcut. What happens? Close the window that Windows XP opened.

Explore 13. Right-click the Training shortcut, click Copy, right-click the desktop, and then click Paste. What happens? What type of icon does Windows XP use for the new shortcut? Change the name of the new shortcut to Windows. Change the icon for the Windows shortcut to one of the icons in the Shell32.dll file in the System32 folder. Change the command line and path for the shortcut's target so that the shortcut uses the following command to open the Windows folder in a Windows Explorer window, displays the

Windows folder as the root folder, and expands the folders below the Windows folder in the Folders toolbar:

C:\Windows\Explorer.exe /n, /e, /root, C:\Windows

If your Windows folder has another name, such as WinNT, use that name in the path instead of Windows. Test the new Windows shortcut. Describe your view of the Windows window. If Windows XP reports an error, or if the shortcut does not work as you intended, check and correct the command and path in the Target box of the Shortcut property sheet for the Windows shortcut, and then test the shortcut again. Close the window opened by the Windows shortcut.

Explore

14. Connect your computer to the Internet using Internet Explorer (or another Web browser), enter *www.intel.com* (the URL of the Intel Web site) in the Address box, locate this Web site, adjust the size and placement of the Internet Explorer window so that you can see a portion of the desktop, and then drag the Internet Explorer icon located on the left side of the title bar or the one located to the left of the URL in the Address bar to the desktop. What happens? Close Internet Explorer, change the name of the Intel Internet shortcut to Intel, and then click the shortcut. What happens? View properties for this shortcut. What is the target URL for the Intel shortcut? Close the window opened by the Intel shortcut.

15. Drag the Windows shortcut to the Start button, and then examine the Start menu. Where did Windows XP place the Windows shortcut? Test the Windows shortcut on the Start menu, and then close the window opened by the Windows shortcut.

16. Right-click the Start button, click Open, open the Programs folder, click File on the menu bar, point to New, click Folder, and assign the name Training Resources to the new group folder.

17. Open the Training Resources group folder, hold down the Ctrl key, drag your Training desktop shortcut to the Training Resources group folder, and then release the Ctrl key. Why did you need to hold down the Ctrl key during the drag operation? Close the Training Resources window.

Explore

18. From the Start menu, point to All Programs, and then drag the Training Resources folder so that it is above the Accessories group folder near the top of the All Programs menu. Open the Training folder from the Training Resources menu, and then close the Training folder window.

19. Use Ctrl+Point to select the Training, Paint, and Windows desktop shortcuts. Right-click one of the selected shortcuts, and then click Copy. Right-click the Start button, click Open, click the Up button on the Standard Buttons toolbar, open the SendTo folder, right-click the folder background, and then click Paste. What happens? Close the SendTo window.

20. Click the Windows shortcut. In the Folders toolbar, locate and select the Wallpaper folder under the Web folder.

21. Right-click one of the JPG files, press and hold down the Ctrl key, point to Send To, click Training, and then release the Ctrl key. Close the Wallpaper folder window, and click the Training shortcut. Which JPG file did you copy to the Training folder using the Send To menu?

22. Right-click the JPG file, point to Send To, and then click Paint. What happens? Close the Paint window, and then close the Training window.

23. Insert a blank, formatted floppy disk into drive A, open My Computer, open drive A, right-click the folder background, point to New, and click Briefcase. Change the name of the Briefcase to "Training Briefcase" (without the quotation marks).

24. With the 3½ Floppy (A:) window still open, click the Training shortcut on the desktop, click the Up button on the Standard Buttons toolbar, right-click the taskbar, click Tile Windows Vertically, and drag the Training folder from the Delta Oil folder window on drive C and drop it on the Training Briefcase in the 3½ Floppy (A:) window.

25. Open the Training folder under the Delta Oil folder on drive C, and click the Excel Basics.doc file to open it in either Microsoft Word or WordPad (whichever your system uses). Change the title to "EXCEL BASICS TRAINING PROPOSAL" (without the quotation marks and in all uppercase), and then save and close the document. If Microsoft Word prompts you to upgrade the file to the latest Word format, click the No button to save it in the current format. Close the Microsoft Word or WordPad window.

26. Open the Training Briefcase on the 3½ Floppy (A:) drive, click the Update All button on the Standard Buttons toolbar. What does the Training Briefcase propose you update, and how? Perform the update.

27. Open the updated Excel Basics.doc file in the Training Briefcase using either Microsoft Word or WordPad, insert a line below the title that reads "Prepared by: " followed by your name, and then save and close the document.

Explore   28. In the Training Briefcase, point to and select the JPG file that you originally copied from the Windows folder earlier, press the Delete key, and confirm that you want to delete the file.

Explore   29. In the Training Briefcase, click Briefcase on the menu bar, and then click Update All to view which files need to be updated in the Training folder on drive C. What does the Training Briefcase propose you update, and how?

Explore   30. Right-click the action for the JPG file, and click "Don't Delete." Right-click the action for the Excel Basics.doc file, and click the Replace arrow that points in the opposite direction so that the Training Briefcase restores the original, unchanged version on drive C in the Training Briefcase on your 3½ Floppy (A:) drive. Then update these files.

Explore   31. Open the Excel Basics.doc file in the Training Briefcase. How did the Training Briefcase update this file? Close Excel Basics.doc. Did the Training Briefcase delete the JPG file in the Training folder on drive C?

32. To restore your computer, click the Up button twice in the Training window on your 3½ Floppy (A:) drive, select and delete the Training Briefcase, close the 3½ Floppy (A:) window, click the Up button twice in the Training window on drive C, select and delete the Delta Oil folder from drive C, and then close the My Documents or drive window.

33. From the Start menu, right-click the Windows folder shortcut, and then click Remove from This List. On the Start menu, point to All Programs, right-click the Training Resources group folder, click Delete, and then confirm that you want to delete this folder.

34. Right-click the Start button, click Open, click the Up button, open the SendTo folder, select and delete the Windows, Training, and Paint shortcuts from the SendTo folder, and then close the SendTo window.

35. Select and delete the removable disk, Control Panel, Training, Logo, Paint, Windows and Intel desktop shortcuts.

36. Empty the Recycle Bin.

CASE PROBLEMS

Case 1. *Using Shortcuts at Midway College's Reentry Services* Midway College's Reentry Services Department provides resources and assistance to prospective students who are returning to college after many years in the work force so that they can acquire and upgrade their job skills. Joyce St Martin, who manages their college program, wants to create shortcuts on her computer so that she can quickly open the Program Files folder, the Printers folder, and Accessibility Options whenever she needs to verify a software installation, check on the status of print jobs, and adjust accessibility options for staff members who also must use the same computer.

As you complete each step in this case, record your answers to questions so that you can submit them to your instructor. Use a word-processing application such as Word or WordPad to prepare and then print your answers to these questions. Also, if you change any settings on the computer you are using, note the original settings so that you can restore them later.

1. Create a desktop shortcut to the Program Files folder on drive C. Change the icon for the shortcut to an icon in the Shell32.dll or Pifmgr.dll icon library files, and then test the shortcut. What is the full path for the target of this shortcut?

2. Create a shortcut to the Printers and Faxes folder in the Control Panel. *Note:* If you are using Category view, first click the Printers and Other Hardware link to locate Printers and Faxes. How does the icon for this shortcut differ from the default icon Windows XP used for the Program Files folder? Where does Windows XP get the icon for this shortcut? What is the target for this shortcut? What happens when you click this shortcut?

Explore 3. Create a shortcut to the Accessibility Options in the Control Panel. *Note*: If you are using Category View instead of Classic View, you need to open the Accessibility Options category first so that you can create a shortcut to the Accessibility Options tool. Where does Windows XP obtain the icon for this shortcut? What is the target for this shortcut? What happens when you click this shortcut?

4. Customize the Program Files shortcut so that Windows XP opens a window with the Program Files folder at the root of the folder tree and expands the folder to show the folders below the Program Files folder. What command line and path did you specify in the target box? What happens when you click the shortcut? (Describe your view of the Program Files folder.) What advantages do you gain from customizing the Program Files shortcut?

Explore 5. Can you customize the Printers and Faxes and the Accessibility Options in the same way that you customized the Program Files shortcut? Explain.

6. Create a folder with the name Resources within the My Documents folder. Then, create a shortcut to the Resources folder and drag the Resources folder shortcut to the desktop. What is the path for the shortcut's target? Change the icon for the Resources shortcut to one of your own choosing.

7. Drag the Program Files, Printers and Faxes, and Accessibility Options shortcuts and drop them onto the top of the Resources shortcut. Use the Resources shortcut to open the Resources folder. What is stored in the Resources folder? How did this happen? Can you think of a reason why it would be useful to have a Resources folder on drive C for storing desktop shortcuts?

8. Click the Program Files shortcut in the Resources folder. Does this shortcut work in the same way as the desktop shortcut?

9. What new features of shortcuts did you discover from this case?

10. To restore your computer, delete the Resources folder within the My Documents folder and the Resources shortcut on the desktop, and then empty the Recycle Bin.

Case 2. Customizing a Start Menu at Emerging Technologies, Inc. Emerging Technologies, Inc. offers its clients a wide spectrum of services ranging from consulting and training to on-site setup, installation, and configuration of computers. Langston Dunsmore, a PC specialist, relies on utilities to check the status of a computer, identify and document important system settings, pinpoint problems in the configuration of computers, monitor the use of memory, and optimize the performance of the hard disk. To simplify his efforts, Langston wants to create a System Utilities group folder on the Start menu for quick access. Then he wants to add shortcuts to other utilities and programs on his computer to this group folder. Langston asks you to make these changes for him.

As you complete each step in this case, record your answers to questions so that you can submit them to your instructor. Use a word-processing application such as Word or WordPad to prepare and then print your answers to these questions. Also, if you change any settings on the computer you are using, note what the original settings are so you can restore them later.

To complete this case, you need a copy of Data Disk #2.

1. Open the Start menu, and then display the contents of the All Programs, Accessories, and System Tools menus. List the options available on the System Tools menu.

Explore   2. Open the Start Menu folder for your user account, open the Programs folder, and then open the Accessories folder. What is the path to this folder? Does the Accessories folder contain a System Tools folder? Close the Accessories folder window.

Explore   3. Open the Start menu, display the Accessories menu, right-click System Tools, and choose Open (or "Open All Users"). What does this folder contain? What is the path to this folder? What do the last step and this step tell you about the use of the System Tools menu under Windows XP? If you add shortcuts to this folder, does it affect other users? Close the System Tools window.

4. Open the Start Menu folder for your user account again, open the Programs folder, and then open the Accessories folder. Create a new group folder named "System Utilities" (without the quotation marks), and then open this folder.

5. Open the Control Panel, and then tile the Control Panel and System Utilities windows vertically. Using both Category view and Classic view in the Control Panel window, create shortcuts to the following items and place them in your new System Utilities folder: Display, Folder Options, Power Options, Scheduled Tasks, System, Mouse, Printers and Faxes, Date and Time, and Regional and Language Options.

6. Close both windows, open the Start menu, open the Accessories menu, and sort the Accessories menu by name.

7. What menu options are displayed on the System Utilities menu? What other feature is available to you on the System Utilities menu that you might not have expected?

Explore   8. Drag the System Utilities menu from the Accessories menu to the pinned items list, and then click System Utilities in the pinned items list. What happens? What does this tell you about the nature of the System Utilities object on the Start menu? Close the System Utilities folder.

Explore   9. Send a copy of System Utilities from the pinned items list to your copy of Data Disk #2. How did you perform this operation? Open a window onto your copy of Data Disk #2, and then view the contents of the System Utilities folder on this disk. How might you use this copy of the System Utilities folder?

10. Is there a System Utilities group folder under the Accessories menu on the Start menu?

11. What new features of shortcuts did you discover from this case?

12. To restore your computer, remove the System Utilities group folder from the pinned items list on the Start menu and also from the Accessories menu, and then remove the System Utilities group folder from your copy of Data Disk #2.

Case 3. Customizing the Send To Menu at O'Donnell Associates, Inc. O'Donnell Associates, Inc. provides consulting services to major landscaping firms around the state of Minnesota. As she works on specific client projects, Merrill McGill tracks information about each project, conducts research, and prepares documents for her clients. So that she can quickly locate client information, Merrill prepares shortcuts to client document files on her hard disk and stores them on her desktop, along with other desktop shortcuts that she uses for every project. Merrill wants to further customize her computer so that she can move shortcuts for a specific project to a folder on her hard disk when she needs to turn her attention to another project or when she has completed work on a specific project. When she returns to a project, or if a client account becomes active again, she wants to move the shortcuts back to her desktop. Merrill asks you to show her how to complete these shortcut tasks.

As you complete each step in this case, record your answers to questions so that you can submit them to your instructor. Use a word-processing application such as Word or WordPad to prepare and then print your answers to these questions. Also, if you change any settings on the computer you are using, note the original settings so you can restore them later.

To complete this case, you need a copy of Data Disk #2.

1. Create a desktop shortcut to the My Documents folder on drive C, as well as a shortcut to your 3½ Floppy (A:) drive. If you have a second hard disk drive that you prefer to use instead of the My Documents folder, create a desktop shortcut to that drive.

Explore

2. Use your 3½ Floppy (A:) shortcut to open a window onto your copy of Data Disk #2. Drag the Delta Oil folder from the 3½ Floppy (A:) window and drop it onto the desktop shortcut for the My Documents folder or the one for your second hard disk drive. What does Windows XP do? After you are finished, close the 3½ Floppy (A:) window.

3. Open the My Documents folder or the drive that contains the copy of the Delta Oil folder, and then rename the Delta Oil folder to "O'Donnell Associates" (without the quotation marks). Create a desktop shortcut to the O'Donnell Associates folder, and then change the icon of the shortcut to one of your own choosing from Shell32.dll, Pifmgr.dll, or Moricons.dll. What is the full path to the shortcut's target?

4. Open the O'Donnell Associates folder and delete the Overhead Transparencies, Training, and Memos folders. Change the name of the Company Templates folder to "Stafford Client Files" and the name of the Designs folder to "Stafford Designs" (both without the quotation marks).

5. Create a desktop shortcut to the Stafford Client Files and Stafford Designs folders, and then change the icons of the shortcuts to ones of your own choosing from Shell32.dll, Pifmgr.dll, or Moricons.dll. What is the full path of each shortcut's target? After you are finished, close the O'Donnell Associates folder window.

6. If Microsoft Word and Microsoft Excel are installed on your computer, copy the shortcuts for these applications from the Start menu to the desktop. If these applications are not installed on your computer, find out what word-processing and spreadsheet applications are installed, and then copy (or create) shortcuts to those applications, and place the shortcuts on the desktop. What are the names of the applications, you used, and what is the full path to the target of each of these shortcuts?

7. Connect your computer to the Web and search the Web for a landscaping firm that specializes in designing blueprints, and add an Internet shortcut to that site on the desktop. What is the name of the Web site, and what is the target of the Internet shortcut?

Explore

8. Open the O'Donnell Associates folder, create a new folder called O'Donnell Shortcuts, create a shortcut to the O'Donnell Shortcuts folder, send a copy of that shortcut to the desktop, and then move the shortcut to the O'Donnell Shortcuts folder to the SendTo folder. Change the default folder icon to the Tree icon 🌳 in the Shell32.dll file. What is the full path to the target of this shortcut?

9. Close any open windows.

10. Select all of the desktop shortcuts you created for O'Donnell Associates, and use the Send To menu to copy them to the O'Donnell Shortcuts folder. Open the O'Donnell Shortcuts folder using your desktop shortcut, and confirm that Windows XP copied the shortcuts to this folder. Was there any other way that you could have copied the shortcuts to the O'Donnell Shortcuts folder? If so, explain how you would have done it. Name two advantages of having a duplicate copy of these shortcuts in the O'Donnell Shortcuts folder.

Explore

11. When Merrill completes the current project for Stafford Associates, and is ready to start on a new project for another client, what should she do with the desktop shortcuts that she used for the Stafford Associates project? What should she do to prepare her desktop for her next client project? If she returns to the Stafford Associates project again at a later date, what should she do to set up her desktop to continue with that project?

12. What new features of shortcuts did you discover from this case?

13. To restore your computer, delete the O'Donnell Associates folder in the My Documents folder, delete the desktop shortcuts for this case, and then empty the Recycle Bin.

Case 4. Creating a Briefcase for Mikal Zarek's Project Files Mikal Zarek works as a consultant for small businesses, and helps his clients develop more complex types of documents to meet their business needs. He specializes in developing spreadsheet templates, projections, and analyses, as well as PowerPoint presentations for use on his client's Web sites. He travels from one client's office to another so he can meet individually with his clients and discuss their specific business needs. His clients illustrate how they use specific types of files in their business, and provide him with copies of these files so that he can revise them to meet their needs. To keep track of each client's set of files, Mikal uses a Briefcase on a removable disk to update each client's files on his home computer. After he makes changes to those files on his home computer, he uses the same Briefcase to update his copies on his removable disk so that he can carry that disk with him to his client's offices. The Briefcase also acts as a valuable backup of his client files. Mikal has just acquired a new client, and needs to set up a Briefcase for the first set of files he has developed for that client.

As you complete each step in this case, record your answers to questions so that you can submit them to your instructor. Use a word-processing application such as Word or WordPad to prepare and then print your answers to these questions. Also, if you change any settings on the computer you are using, note the original settings so you can restore them later.

To complete this case, you need a copy of Data Disk #2, and a blank, formatted floppy disk. You also need Microsoft Office 2000 or a later version installed on your computer, or you need to use another computer with Microsoft Office 2000 or a later version.

Explore

1. Drag My Documents from the Start menu onto the desktop to create a shortcut to the My Documents folder. Then, open My Computer and create a desktop shortcut to your 3½ Floppy (A:) drive.

2. Insert your copy of Data Disk #2 in your 3½ Floppy (A:) drive, and open a window onto your 3½ Floppy (A:) drive.

3. Drag the Delta Oil folder from the 3½ Floppy (A:) window and drop it on the My Documents desktop shortcut.

4. Close the 3½ Floppy (A:) window, and then open My Documents using your desktop shortcut. Change the name of the Delta Oil folder to "Nolan Associates" (without the quotation marks).

5. Insert a blank, formatted floppy disk in your 3½ Floppy (A:) drive, use your desktop shortcut to open a window on that drive, and then create a new Briefcase named "Nolan Associates" (without the quotation marks).

6. Copy the Nolan Associates folder from the My Documents folder to the new Briefcase on your floppy disk.

7. Open the Nolan Associates folder in the My Documents folder, delete the Training folder, change the name of the "Company Templates" folder to "Business Spreadsheets" (without the quotation marks), and change the name of the "Overhead Transparencies" folder to "Presentations" (without the quotation marks).

8. Open the Business Spreadsheets folder, and then delete the "Break-Even Analysis.xls," "Daily Sales.xls," "Loan Payment Analysis.xls," "Product List.xls," "Regional Sales Projection.xls," "Savings Plan.xls," "Software Quotes.xls," and "Visual Arts Employees.xls" files. Change the filename "ShowCase Enterprises Balance Sheet.xls" to "Nolan Associates Balance Sheet.xls," change "VAI Three Year Sales Projection.xls" to "Nolan Associates Three Year Sales Projection.xls," and change "Visual Arts Budget.xls" to "Nolan Associates Budget.xls" (all without the quotation marks). Open the Presentations folder, and delete the "Invoice Form.wk4" and "Sales.wk4" files. Open the Memos folder and delete the "Microsoft's Web Site.doc" file.

9. In the Memos folder, create a new Microsoft Word or WordPad file named "Business Plan.doc" (without the quotation marks) that you will use to prepare a general business plan for the new client.

10. Open the Nolan Associates Briefcase, choose the option to update the Briefcase, and perform the update. What problems would you have faced if you did not have the Briefcase and had to perform the updates manually?

Explore   11. In the Briefcase, open the Nolan Associates folder, and then open the Business Spreadsheets folder. Select the "Advertising Income.xls" file, and move it to a new folder named Advertising under the Nolan Associates folder. Open the Business Spreadsheets folder, and move the "Company Sales Projection.xls," "Five Year Growth Plan.xls," "Five Year Plan Template.xls," "Nolan Associates Three Year Sales Projection.xls," and "Sales Projection Models.xls" to a new folder named Projections under the Nolan Associates folder.

12. Choose the option to update the Briefcase, change the action for creating a new copy of the Five Year Plan Template.xls on drive C to "Skip," and then perform the update.

Explore   13. In the Briefcase, open the Business Plan.doc file in the Memos folder in either Microsoft Word or WordPad, and enter the title "Proposed Business Plan for Nolan Associates" (without the quotation marks), and then save and close the file.

Explore   14. Switch to the Nolan Associates folder in the My Documents folder on drive C, and then open the Business Plan.doc file in the Memos folder in either Microsoft Word or WordPad, and enter the title "Nolan Associates Business Plan" (without the quotation marks), and then save and close the file.

15. Choose the option to update the Briefcase. What does the Briefcase propose you do with the Business Plan.doc file? Why did this happen? What other options do you have for updating this file? Why is the Briefcase proposing that you create a copy of "Five Year Plan Template.xls" in the corresponding folder on drive C?

16. For the Business Plan.doc file, change the action so that the Briefcase replaces the modified copy stored in the corresponding folder on drive C, change the action for the "Five Year Plan Template.xls" so that the Briefcase does not create this file on drive C, and then perform the update.

17. Prepare a list of the folders in your Briefcase, and list the names of the files that are stored in each folder. Then prepare a list of the folders in the Nolan Associates folder on drive C, and list the names of the files that are stored in each folder.

18. Compare the list of folders and files that you compiled in the previous step. Is there any difference between the two copies of the Nolan Associates folders? If so, what are they?

19. To restore your computer, delete the Nolan Associates folder from drive C and from drive A, delete the Nolan Associates Briefcase from your floppy disk, and then delete the desktop shortcuts for drive A and for the My Documents folder.

In this tutorial you will:

- Explore the features and capabilities of Object Linking and Embedding

- Create a compound document with OLE technology

- Insert and modify embedded and linked objects

- View properties of embedded and linked objects

- Create and use scraps in compound documents

- Examine the use of OLE technology in productivity software

- Use the OLE properties of the taskbar

- Locate objects on your computer with link tracing

USING

OLE

TECHNOLOGIES

Preparing a Company Logo for Visual Arts, Inc.

CASE

Visual Arts, Inc.

Visual Arts, Inc. is one of the largest graphic design companies in the Boston metropolitan area. Over the last five years, the company has experienced a phenomenal rate of growth. Rosemarie Trevino, a graphic artist, has worked at Visual Arts since its inception, and now oversees the work of all the designers at the firm. Many client projects require that designers build documents that include objects from different applications, such as brochures that use text from documents created in a word-processing application and images created in a graphics application. Rosemarie and her staff find that Windows XP simplifies the task of copying information from one document to another, no matter what applications created them.

Renee Bessone, the president of Visual Arts, has asked Rosemarie and her staff to design a new company logo. Renee wants them to develop two designs, then circulate those logo designs among the staff, and obtain staff feedback before she makes the final decision. Rosemarie offers to show you how to use Object Linking and Embedding to simplify these tasks.

In the first part of this tutorial, you examine the features and capabilities of the Microsoft technology known as Object Linking and Embedding (OLE). Then you create a compound document that contains linked and embedded objects. As you create the compound document, you examine properties of both linked and embedded documents and compare and contrast the differences between them.

Object Linking and Embedding

So that all the staff can provide feedback on the design of the company's new logo, Rosemarie decides to prepare a memo that includes the two designs developed by her own graphics design staff. To insert the designs in the memo, she uses **Object Linking and Embedding**, referred to as **OLE** (pronounced "oh lay").

Using this Microsoft technology, you can create compound documents via one of two approaches: object linking or object embedding. The document you produce with this technology is called a **compound document** because it contains information drawn from other documents produced with other applications. The application that provides the data (or object) is called the **server application** (or **OLE server**), and the application that contains the object is called the **client application**. The server application is also called the **source application**. Some applications provide and accept objects, other applications only provide objects, and still others only accept objects.

OLE technology allows you to not only share data among applications but also to maintain a "dynamic" relationship either to the original data or to the original application. For example, Deborah Woods, a financial analyst at Visual Arts, prepares a three-year forecast on projected sales and expenses of the company each year. Using the financial performance of the company for the previous five years, she prepares a most likely case scenario for the next three years so that the president and managers can plan the future growth of Visual Arts more effectively. Deborah uses Microsoft Word to prepare the main body of her yearly report, and then she inserts a table with a financial analysis and a three-dimensional column chart that illustrates the company's projected performance. She produces the table and column chart in Microsoft Excel, a spreadsheet application. The resulting compound document provides three different views to effectively convey the results of her analyses, namely:

- The main body of the report summarizes the information using descriptive text
- The table provides more detail for those managers who want to take a closer look at the basis of the forecast
- The chart provides a broad overview of predicted changes in a visual format

Prior to the introduction of OLE technology, Deborah would have had to produce and print three documents—the report, table, and chart. Then she would have had to use scissors to cut the table and chart from the page on which they are printed, paste them on the page that contains the report, and then copy the page to produce a new copy of the final report. Or she might opt for including the table and chart as attachments to the report. OLE technology now allows her to more easily and efficiently create a document with all three types of information.

To share information among documents, the applications you use must support OLE technology. There are differences in the type of support provided by OLE-aware applications. For example, some applications might support the newer OLE 2.0 (second generation) standards, while others support OLE 1.0 (first generation). Later in the tutorial, you look at differences between OLE 2.0 and 1.0.

When you create a compound document, you insert one or more objects, such as a table or chart, from another document into the current document you are creating or modifying. You can either embed the object or create a link. When you **embed** an object, a copy of an object is pasted into the current document, and there is no further connection with, or relationship to, the original object. Figure 5-1 illustrates how you might create a compound document using object embedding. The document on the left is a Microsoft Excel spreadsheet that contains a table with a three-year financial forecast and a three-dimensional column chart that illustrates the change in net sales over the three-year period. This is your **source document**. It contains the data, or objects, you want to copy. You can copy and paste both the table and the chart from the Excel spreadsheet into a memo that you are producing with Microsoft Word (shown in the center). Windows XP embeds the objects into the destination document to produce the final view of the document that you see on the right side of the figure. The **destination document** is the compound document that contains objects copied from another document.

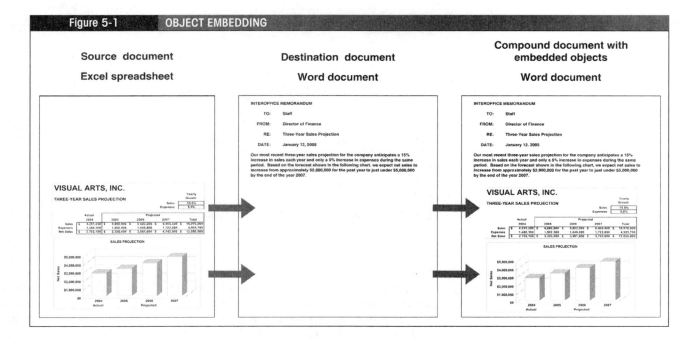

Figure 5-1   OBJECT EMBEDDING

An embedded object is not connected in any way to the original object that you copied. If you change the original object in the source document, the embedded object in the destination document does not change. Likewise, if you change the embedded object in the destination document, the original object in the source document does not change. However, an embedded object does contain information that identifies the application that produced the object so that you can edit the object with the tools of the original application (OLE 2.0) in the current application window, or with the original application itself (OLE 1.0) in a new window.

In contrast, when you create a **link**, the destination document contains a pointer to the file that contains the original object. The **pointer** is the full path of the file that contains the original object. If the link is to an object within a file, such as a chart in a Microsoft Excel spreadsheet, the full path also contains the name of that object. Therefore, a link is similar to a shortcut. The linked object appears identical to the original object.

To create a link, you select the object you want to copy in the source document, just as you do when embedding an object. But when you paste the object, you specify that you want a link to the original object. Each time you open the document that contains the linked object, Windows XP examines the source document with the linked object, and then updates the linked object in the destination document.

Figure 5-2 illustrates how you might create a compound document using object linking. As in the example used for object embedding, the source document on the left is a Microsoft Excel spreadsheet that contains a spreadsheet table and a three-dimensional column chart. Just like embedding, you can copy and paste both the table and the chart from the Excel spreadsheet into a memo that you are producing with Microsoft Word; however, during the paste, you specify that you want to establish links to the original objects. In the destination document on the right, you see the same view of the objects that you see when you embed them; however, the linked objects are connected to the original objects. If you open the source document and change the spreadsheet table and chart, then Windows XP uses the links to update the objects in the destination document the next time you open it.

Figure 5-2   OBJECT LINKING

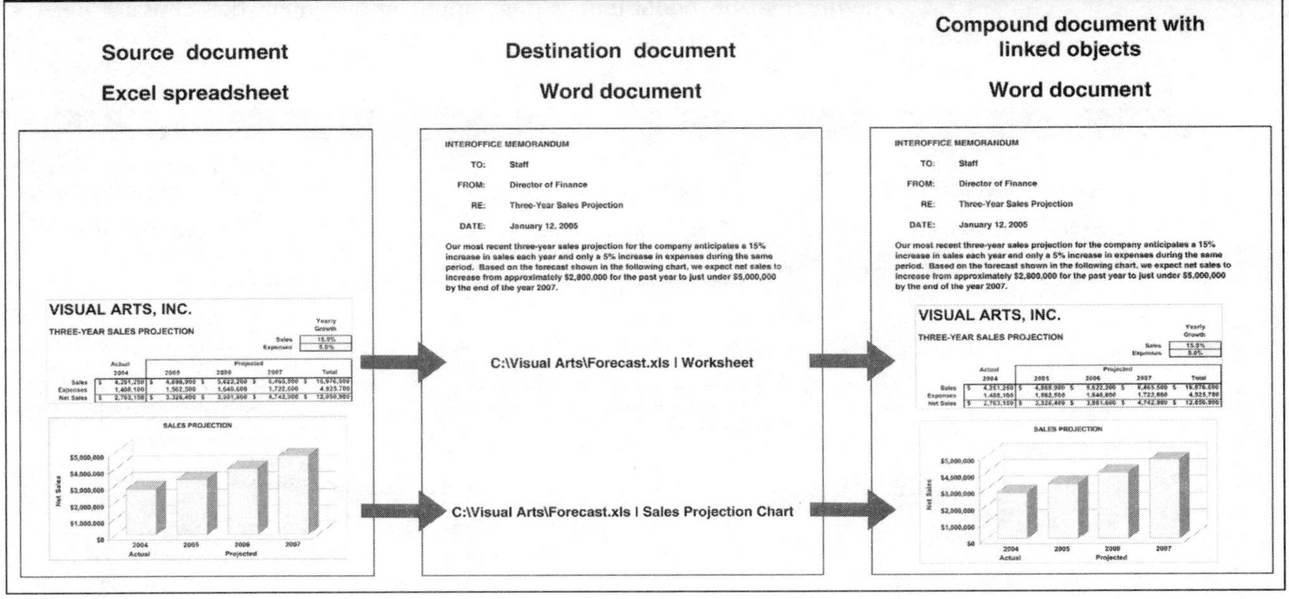

In the Microsoft Excel spreadsheet, the chart is linked to the values in the table. If the values in the table change, Excel automatically updates the chart. If you copy the table and chart to a Word document and create a link, the next time you change the information in the table, Excel updates not only the table but also the chart in the spreadsheet, and Windows XP updates the links to the table and chart in the Word document. If your spreadsheet undergoes frequent or periodic changes, and if you need those changes reflected in a Word document, you would use object linking. On the other hand, if you want the Word document to show values in the table and the chart for a specific point in time, then you would embed the table and chart in the Word document. If you change the spreadsheet later, the table and chart in the Word document does not change. Essentially, you have captured a snapshot of a spreadsheet analysis at a specific point in time.

You can edit both embedded and linked objects in compound documents. To edit an embedded object in an application that supports OLE 2.0, you double-click the object (even in Web style). Windows XP does not open the original application; instead, the current application window changes to display the menus and tools of the application that produced the original object. You can then edit the embedded object in place. This feature is called **visual editing**. In contrast, if you double-click an embedded object in an application that supports OLE 1.0, Windows XP opens the original application that produced that object in a new window and displays a *copy* of the embedded object in that application's window so you can edit it. After you edit the copy of the embedded object, you save the changes and close that application window. Then Windows XP updates the embedded object. This approach to editing embedded objects is one important difference between OLE 2.0 and OLE 1.0.

To edit a linked object (whether using an application with OLE 1.0 or 2.0 support), you double-click it in the destination document. Windows XP opens the application that produced the original object in a new window and *also* opens the source document in that same window. After you edit the object, you save your changes, and return to the destination document. Windows XP automatically updates the link to reflect changes in the original object. In fact, the update usually occurs immediately after you change the original object.

What advantage does embedding have over linking, and vice versa? In other words, when would you use embedding and when would you use linking? If you embed an object, you can modify it with the tools of either the current application or the original application and *not* affect the original object in the source document. Likewise, you can modify the original object without affecting the embedded object in the destination document. You can move a document containing an embedded object from one computer to another without causing any problems. The file is said to be "portable." As long as the application that produced the original object is on the computer to which you move the document, you can open and edit it.

Object linking, on the other hand, requires that the source document be present *on the same computer or on the same network* as the destination document. If you move a document containing a linked object to another computer, but you don't move the source document, then you break the link to the original object. If you break a link, any changes made to the source document are *not* reflected in the destination document. Therefore, the source document and the destination document must "travel" together.

However, linking is ideal when you need to reference the same information or the same object in numerous destination documents. Each destination document would contain a link to the object in the source document. Whenever you update the object in the source document, all documents with links to the source document are automatically updated. For example, assume that each department in a company is responsible for creating its own budget for the upcoming year. Each departmental spreadsheet can contain links to a central document with companywide assumptions for the upcoming year, such as the percent increase in salary for all employees. If this assumption changes during the budgeting process, one person makes that change in the central document. Later, when each department opens its departmental budget spreadsheet, all references to this assumption are immediately updated. Not only does everyone in the company use the same assumption, but the assumption does not have to be manually updated by a different person in each department.

Embedding and linking also differ in how they affect the size of a document. Embedded objects can substantially increase document size. A document with an embedded object contains the data needed to display and print the object (called the **presentation data**), a copy of the original object, the name and version number of the source application, the object's name, the object type, the current document's name, and information about, or copies of, the source application's tools for editing the embedded object (such as the menu bar, toolbars, color palette, and embedded fonts). In some cases, the embedded object might contain a copy of the entire file with the source document attached to it. The original copy of the object, plus all the other data needed to edit and maintain the object, is called the **native data**.

In contrast, a linked object contains the object's presentation data, a pointer to the source object (the full path), the name of the source document, the name of the source object, and the source object's type, but not the native data. Therefore, a linked object is usually only a few percent of the size of the original object.

Note that although Microsoft developed the guidelines for OLE technology, it is up to developers of software applications to decide how to implement this technology in their software products. As such, it is not always implemented consistently.

For OLE technology to work properly on your computer, your computer must meet the following requirements:

- Sufficient amount of RAM
- Functional file system
- Hard disk free of errors
- Properly installed and configured operating system
- Properly installed and configured applications
- Applications that support OLE 2.0 or OLE 1.0 in whole or in part
- A functional Windows Registry

OLE technology places additional demands on your computer. Today, because of the complexity of software applications, if you plan on using OLE, you should have a high-performance processor with a sufficient amount of RAM. As far as memory is concerned, the more you have the better. On a Pentium 4, 512 MB of RAM or more is essential. If you attempt to build compound documents with OLE technology and encounter difficulties, you might not have enough RAM to support these activities, or you might need to close other applications, or even restart your computer. You may also have to check your hard disk for errors, and repair those errors, or even reinstall applications and your operating system. You also need a functional Registry. The Windows XP **Registry** is a database that contains information on all the installed hardware and software on your computer, as well as user settings and information about OLE objects.

In later tutorials, you examine and evaluate the use of memory within your computer so that you can decide whether your computer has enough memory to support the types of operations that you perform (Tutorial 10), use the ScanDisk utility to identify and repair problems with the file system and hard disk (Tutorial 7), examine the process for installing and upgrading the operating systems and applications (Tutorial 11), and learn how to restore a working copy of the Registry using the Last Known Good Configuration (Tutorial 9).

Getting Started

To complete this tutorial, you need to switch your computer to Web style, and you also need to turn on the options for showing file extensions and displaying the full path in the Address bar. You also need to create a WordPad shortcut. As you complete these steps, you may discover that your computer is already set up for Web style, or that other settings are already in place, so you might only need to make a few changes to your computer's settings.

To set up your computer:

1. To change to the Windows XP theme, right-click the **desktop**, click **Properties** on the shortcut menu, and after Windows XP opens the Display Properties dialog box, click the **Theme** list arrow on the Themes property sheet, click **Windows XP**, if necessary, and then click the **OK** button.

2. To switch to the Windows XP Start menu style, right-click the **Start** button, click **Properties** on the shortcut menu, and after Windows XP opens the Taskbar and Start Menu Properties dialog box, click the **Start menu** option button on the Start Menu property sheet, and then click the **OK** button.

3. To change to a task-oriented view of folders and enable single-clicking, click the **Start** button, click **My Computer**, click **Tools** on the menu bar, click **Folder Options**, and after Windows XP opens the Folder Options dialog box, click the **Show common tasks in folders** option button if it is not already selected, click the **Single-click to open an item** option button if it is not already selected, and then click the **Underline icon titles only when I point at them** option button if it is not already selected.

4. Click the **View** tab, click the **Display the full path in the address bar** check box if it is not already selected, click the **Show hidden files and folders** option button if it is not already selected, and if there is a check mark in the "Hide extensions for known file types" check box, click that check box to remove the check mark, click the **OK** button to close the Folder Options dialog box, and then close My Computer.

5. Open the Start menu, point to **All Programs**, point to **Accessories**, right-click **WordPad**, point to **Send To**, and then click **Desktop (create shortcut)**.

6. Click the **Start** button to close the Start menu.

Because the files that you use and create for this tutorial require more space than is available on a floppy disk, you need to copy the contents of Data Disk #3 to the My Documents folder on drive C or, if you have another drive, to that drive instead. If you copy the data files to a drive other than drive C, you need to adapt the tutorial steps for that drive.

To copy the data files to the My Documents folder:

1. Insert your copy of Data Disk #3 into your 3½ Floppy (A:) drive.

2. Open My Computer, and then open a window onto your 3½ Floppy (A:) drive.

3. Point to and select the **Visual Arts** folder (but do not open it).

4. In the File and Folder Tasks dynamic menu, click **Copy this folder** and, after the Copy Items dialog box opens, click the **Up** scroll arrow ⌃, locate and click **My Documents**, and then click the **Copy** button.

5. After the copy operation is complete, click **My Documents** in the Other Places dynamic menu. You should now see a copy of the Visual Arts folder within the My Documents folder.

6. Leave the My Documents window open for the next section of the tutorial.

Now you're ready to examine the process for creating and working with compound documents.

Creating a Compound Document

When you create a compound document, you create a document in one application, and then link or embed objects stored in files produced by other applications so that your final document draws on data from multiple sources.

After her staff prepares two designs for the new company logo using Adobe Illustrator, Rosemarie decides to send a memo to all staff asking for their feedback on these two designs. She asks you to create this memo, and insert copies of the two logos so you can see how OLE technology works.

Before you create a compound document, you examine the images for the logo designs. You also track changes to the sizes of these files so that you can compare object sizes as you create OLE objects from the contents of these files.

To view the bitmapped image files with the logo designs:

1. Click the **Visual Arts** folder in the My Documents folder, click the **Designs** folder, and then maximize the Designs folder window. Since the Designs folder contains two files with graphic images, Windows XP displays the folder contents in Filmstrip view. See Figure 5-3. At the bottom of the Designs folder window, you see thumbnails of the images contained in the files. In the main part of the Designs folder window, Windows XP displays the contents of the first file, Logo Design #1.bmp, at full magnification.

Figure 5-3	VIEWING THE CONTENTS OF THE DESIGNS FOLDER

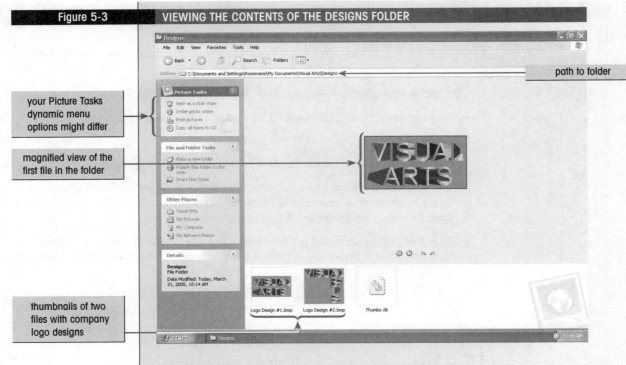

your Picture Tasks dynamic menu options might differ

magnified view of the first file in the folder

thumbnails of two files with company logo designs

path to folder

2. Click **View** on the menu bar, and then click **Details**. Windows XP reports that Logo Design #1.bmp is 94 KB in size, and that Logo Design #2.bmp is 145 KB. See Figure 5-4.

Figure 5-4	VIEWING FILE SIZES

file types

file sizes

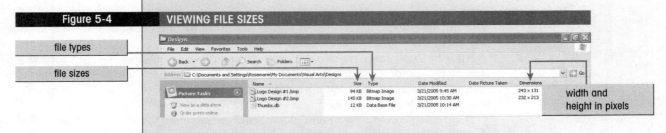

width and height in pixels

3. Click **View** on the menu bar, and then click **Filmstrip**.

4. Right-click **Logo Design #1.bmp**, and then click **Properties** on the shortcut menu. In the Logo Design #1.bmp Properties dialog box, Windows XP reports the file type (a Bitmap Image), the default application for opening this file type (Windows Picture and Fax Viewer), the location of this file (in other words, its path), the size of this file (93.6 KB, or 95,946 bytes), and the amount of space it requires on disk (96.0 KB, or 98,304 bytes). See Figure 5-5.

As is the case on this computer, your Properties dialog box for files might contain additional property sheets. Also, if your drive uses NTFS, this dialog box includes an Advanced button instead of an Archive check box.

Figure 5-5   VIEWING PROPERTIES OF THE FIRST LOGO DESIGN FILE

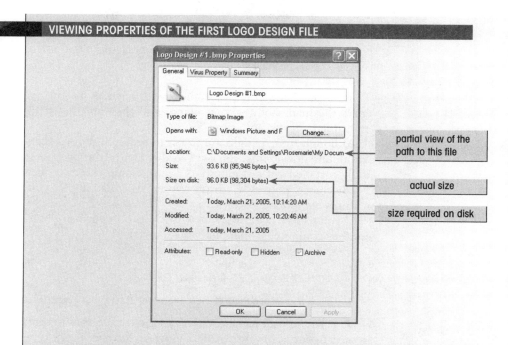

partial view of the path to this file

actual size

size required on disk

5. Close the Logo Design #1.bmp Properties dialog box.

6. Right-click **Logo Design #2.bmp**, and then click **Properties** on the shortcut menu. In the Logo Design #2.bmp Properties dialog box, Windows XP reports the file type (a Bitmap Image), the default application for opening this file type (Windows Picture and Fax Viewer), the location of this file, the size of this file (144 KB, or 148,302 bytes), and the amount of space it requires on disk (148 KB, or 151,552 bytes). See Figure 5-6. Your properties might differ.

Figure 5-6   VIEWING PROPERTIES OF THE SECOND LOGO DESIGN FILE

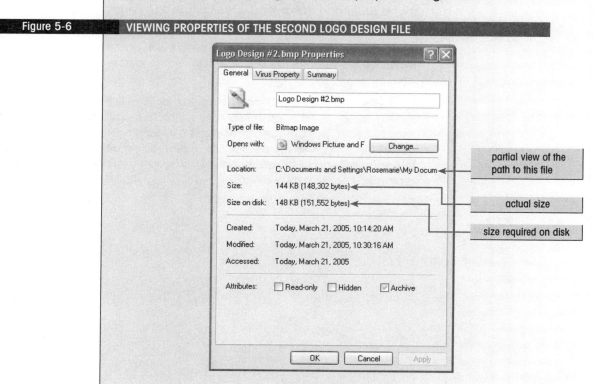

partial view of the path to this file

actual size

size required on disk

7. Close the Logo Design #2.bmp Properties dialog box.

8. Close the Designs folder window and return to the desktop.

To create a compound document, you open WordPad, specify page layout settings, and enter the main body of the memo, and then you insert the logo designs as linked and embedded objects.

Although most people use full-featured applications such as Microsoft Word to create compound documents, you use WordPad and Paint because these applications are automatically installed with Windows XP and should therefore be available on every computer. Furthermore, unlike Microsoft Word, WordPad allows you to examine object properties within a compound document.

If you experience problems with OLE on your computer, you might need to switch to another computer to complete this tutorial.

To open and set up WordPad:

1. Click the **WordPad** desktop shortcut to open WordPad.

2. If you do not see the WordPad Toolbar under the menu bar in the WordPad application window, click **View** on the menu bar, and then click **Toolbar**. The toolbar is comparable to the Standard toolbar found in full-featured applications such as Microsoft Word, and contains buttons for common types of operations, such as saving a file.

3. If you do not see the WordPad Format Bar under the WordPad Toolbar, click **View**, and then click **Format Bar**. The Format Bar is comparable to the Formatting toolbar found in full-featured applications such as Microsoft Word, and contains options for changing the font and font size, applying enhancements (boldface, italics, and underlining), and aligning objects (right, center, and left alignment).

4. If you do not see the WordPad ruler, click **View**, and then click **Ruler**. The ruler marks off the width of the document in inches, and is useful for aligning objects on a page.

5. Click **File**, and then click **Page Setup**. In the Page Setup dialog box, you can specify the paper size, paper source, orientation, and margins for a document. See Figure 5-7. The default paper size is the standard letter-sized sheet of paper (8½ x 11 inches), and the default orientation is Portrait (prints across the width of the page instead of sideways across the length of a page). Your Page Setup dialog box settings may differ.

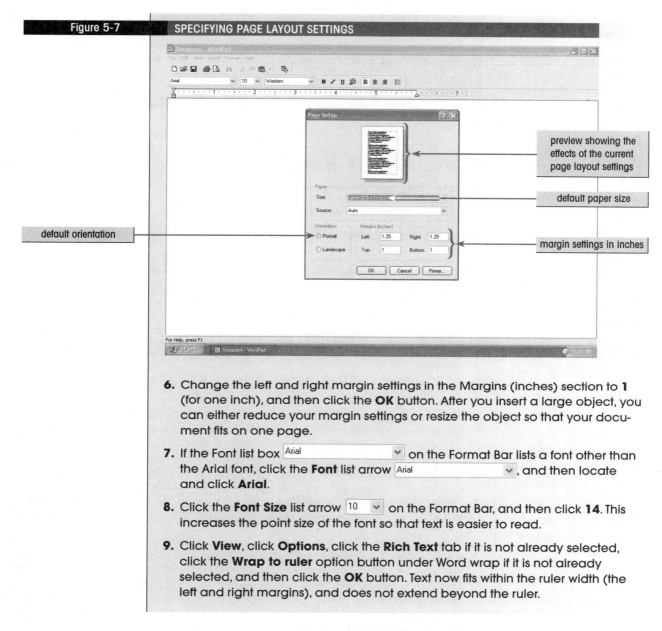

Figure 5-7   SPECIFYING PAGE LAYOUT SETTINGS

preview showing the effects of the current page layout settings

default paper size

default orientation

margin settings in inches

6. Change the left and right margin settings in the Margins (inches) section to **1** (for one inch), and then click the **OK** button. After you insert a large object, you can either reduce your margin settings or resize the object so that your document fits on one page.

7. If the Font list box [Arial] on the Format Bar lists a font other than the Arial font, click the **Font** list arrow [Arial], and then locate and click **Arial**.

8. Click the **Font Size** list arrow [10] on the Format Bar, and then click **14**. This increases the point size of the font so that text is easier to read.

9. Click **View**, click **Options**, click the **Rich Text** tab if it is not already selected, click the **Wrap to ruler** option button under Word wrap if it is not already selected, and then click the **OK** button. Text now fits within the ruler width (the left and right margins), and does not extend beyond the ruler.

Next, enter the text that constitutes the main body of the memo, and then save your work before you insert the new company logo designs as OLE objects.

To create the main body of the memo:

1. Type the text shown in Figure 5-8. Use your name instead of Rosemarie Trevino's, use the current date, and insert three blank lines with the Enter key between the first and second paragraphs of the memo so that you can insert copies of the new company logo designs between those two paragraphs.

Figure 5-8 CREATING A STAFF MEMO

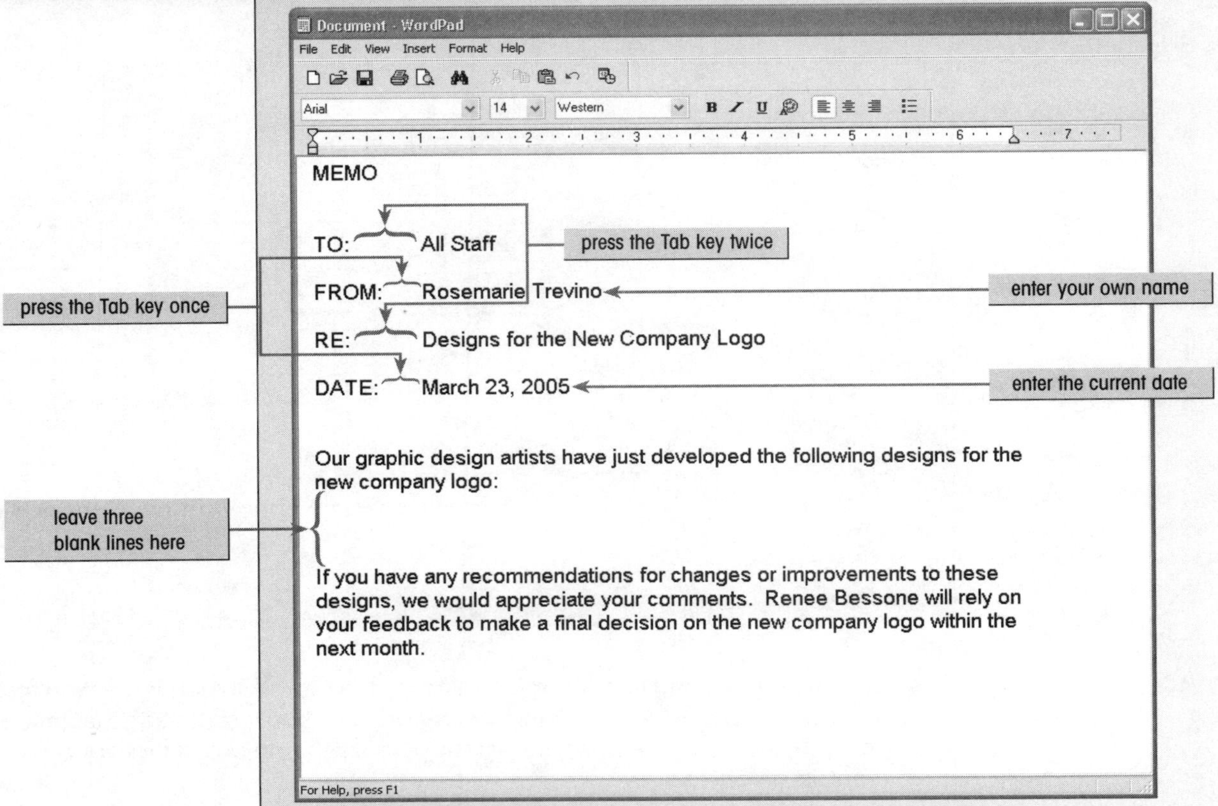
Document - WordPad
File Edit View Insert Format Help
Arial
14
Western
MEMO
TO: All Staff
FROM: Rosemarie Trevino
RE: Designs for the New Company Logo
DATE: March 23, 2005
Our graphic design artists have just developed the following designs for the new company logo:
If you have any recommendations for changes or improvements to these designs, we would appreciate your comments. Renee Bessone will rely on your feedback to make a final decision on the new company logo within the next month.
For Help, press F1
press the Tab key twice
press the Tab key once
enter your own name
enter the current date
leave three blank lines here

2. Click the **Save** button on the Toolbar, and when the Save As dialog box opens, click **Visual Arts**, click the **Create New Folder** button, type **Memos**, press the **Enter** key to assign the name to the new folder, and then press the **Enter** key again to open the Memos folder.
3. Click **Document.rtf** in the File name text box, type **Company Logo Designs** as the filename, and then click the **Save** button in the Save As dialog box.
4. Leave the memo open for the next section of the tutorial.

In previous versions of Windows, you could save a WordPad document as a Word 6 Document with the "doc" file extension; however, that option is not available in Windows XP. Instead, documents are saved in the Rich Text Format (RTF) with the "rtf" file extension. This file format preserves the formatting within the document.

Once you have made your initial save, you can stop briefly as you work and click the Save button on the toolbar to quickly update the contents of the file on disk. If you are working on a large or complex document, then periodic saves are critical. In the event of a power failure, you only have to reconstruct what you've lost since your last save. Full-featured applications such as Microsoft Word include an AutoSave feature so that you can specify how frequently you want the program to save your work for you.

Inserting a Linked Object

When using object linking, you can create and insert a new object using one of the applications installed on your computer or one of the applications provided with Windows XP, or you can insert an object from an existing file. If you insert a new object, Windows XP modifies the current application's window to support the tools and features of the application associated with that object type. Then you can use those tools to create the object from scratch. If you create an object from a file, you can specify the path to the file or you can browse and locate the file you want to insert, and also specify whether you want a link. If you do link the object, Windows XP inserts a picture of a file's contents into your document, and links the picture to the file so that any changes you make to that file are reflected in your document.

Rosemarie wants you to insert a copy of the first logo design into the memo as a linked object. If she needs to make any last minute changes to the design of this logo in the original file, Windows XP not only updates the original logo design, but also the copy of the logo design in this memo.

To insert a linked object:

1. If necessary, adjust your view within the WordPad application window so that you can see the blank lines between the first and second paragraphs of the memo.

2. Click at the beginning of the blank line that is halfway between the two paragraphs.

3. Click **Insert** on the menu bar, and then click **Object**. In the Insert Object dialog box, you can create and insert a new object or insert an object from an existing file. See Figure 5-9. In the Object Type box, Windows XP lists the types of files that you can insert as new objects into the document. The object types listed depend on the types of applications installed on your computer.

Figure 5-9   OPTIONS FOR INSERTING AN OBJECT

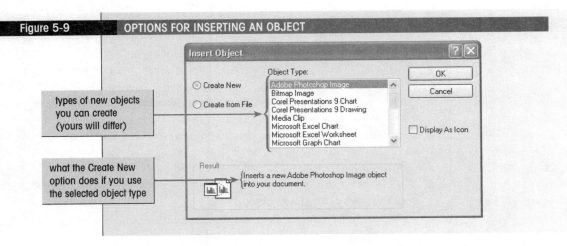

types of new objects
you can create
(yours will differ)

what the Create New
option does if you use
the selected object type

Because you already have the files that contain the images you want to insert into this memo, you choose the option for creating an object from a file.

To create an object from a file:

1. Click the **Create from File** option button. The dialog box changes so that you can specify the path to the file and create a link. See Figure 5-10.

Figure 5-10   CHOOSING THE CREATE FROM FILE OPTION

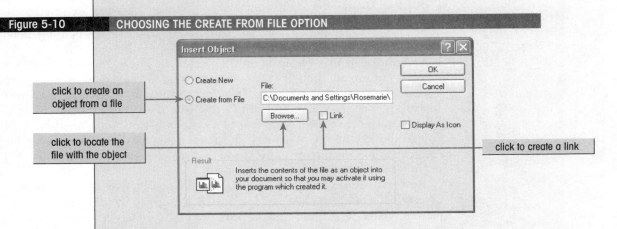

click to create an
object from a file

click to locate the
file with the object

click to create a link

2. Click the **Link** check box. Under Result, Windows XP explains that this option inserts a picture of the file contents into the document, and because the picture is linked to the original file, any changes to that file are then reflected in this document. See Figure 5-11.

Figure 5-11   SPECIFYING A LINK

Figure 5-11   SPECIFYING A LINK

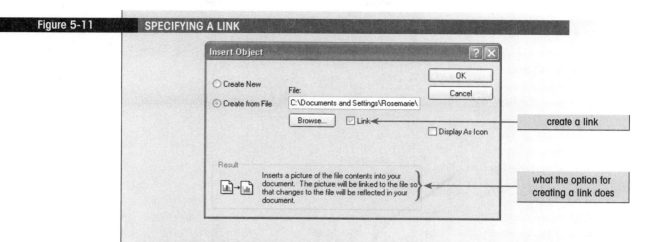

create a link

what the option for
creating a link does

3. Click the **Browse** button. In the Browse dialog box, you can locate the file that contains the image you want to insert into your document as a linked object. The Look in list box shows the last folder you accessed—the Memos folder.

4. Click the **Up One Level** button 🔼 , click **Designs**, and then click **Logo Design #1.bmp**. Now that you've selected the file with the image you want to insert into your memo, Windows XP displays the file type of the object (a Bitmap Image) and the full path to the file with that object. See Figure 5-12.

Figure 5-12   CREATING A LINK TO THE CONTENTS OF A FILE

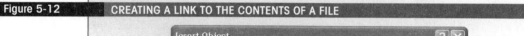

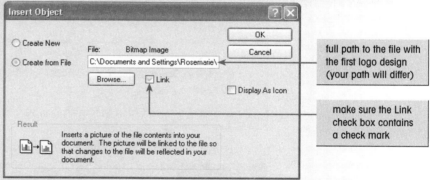

full path to the file with
the first logo design
(your path will differ)

make sure the Link
check box contains
a check mark

5. Click the **OK** button and wait for Windows XP to complete the link. Windows XP inserts a picture of the logo into the document as a discrete object. See Figure 5-13. The red border around the object, and the red selection handles at each corner and midsection indicate that the focus is on this object. In other words, the object is currently selected.

Figure 5-13 | **LINKED OBJECT IN DESTINATION DOCUMENT**

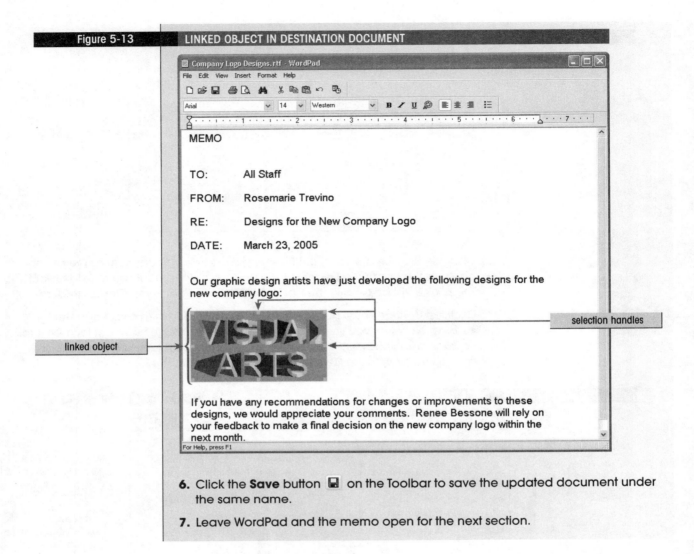

linked object

selection handles

6. Click the **Save** button 🖫 on the Toolbar to save the updated document under the same name.

7. Leave WordPad and the memo open for the next section.

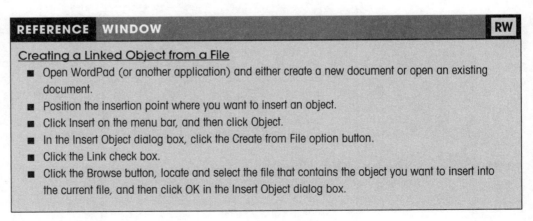

REFERENCE WINDOW | **RW**

Creating a Linked Object from a File
- Open WordPad (or another application) and either create a new document or open an existing document.
- Position the insertion point where you want to insert an object.
- Click Insert on the menu bar, and then click Object.
- In the Insert Object dialog box, click the Create from File option button.
- Click the Link check box.
- Click the Browse button, locate and select the file that contains the object you want to insert into the current file, and then click OK in the Insert Object dialog box.

You have successfully inserted an object into a document and created a link between a source document and a destination document.

Viewing Properties of a Linked Object

You can view properties of a linked object either by using the Edit menu or the object's shortcut menu. Because you just created a linked object, the WordPad Edit menu has three options: Links (for viewing information about all linked objects), Object Properties (for displaying the object's property sheets), and Linked Bitmap Image Object (for editing or opening a linked object). The latter two options are also available from the object's shortcut menu. If the Links option is dimmed, your document does not contain any linked objects.

When you work with other applications, such as Microsoft Word or Microsoft Excel, you find slightly different options. For example, the Microsoft Word Edit menu has a Links option and its Insert menu has an Object option. If you embed an object or create a link, then you see an option on the Microsoft Word Edit menu and the object's shortcut menu to edit, open, or convert the object. While the details of implementing OLE might vary between applications, the same basic features and concepts apply.

By viewing the properties of a linked object, you can determine the object type and size and the path to the original object. The path of a linked object refers to the file that contains the original object, not the current document with the picture of the object. Recall that when Windows XP creates a link to an object, it does not store a copy of the object, but rather maintains a pointer (the full path) to the object. Therefore, linked objects are relatively small and only slightly increase the size of a document.

In the property sheets of a linked object, you can also specify how to view the object in the document. If you display the object as editable information (the default), you see the object as it would appear in the source application, and you can edit the object. If you display the object as an icon, you replace the view of the object with a view of the icon for the object's file type. Doing so compresses the object so that it takes much less space in your document. Because linked objects are relatively small, this feature is more useful for embedded objects. If you like, you can change the icon used for the object, similar to the way you change icons for a shortcut or for a registered file type.

If necessary, you can also change the link by selecting a different source object or by editing the full path to the original object. You can also specify whether you want to update links automatically or manually. Updating automatically means that when you change the original object, the linked object is updated the next time you open the file. Manual updating means that you must choose the option for manually updating the object from one of the object's property sheets. If you no longer want to link the object to the compound document, you can break the link. If you break a link, you are left with only a picture of the object, and you cannot edit it using OLE.

To view properties of a linked object:

1. Right-click the **linked object**, and then click **Object Properties** on the shortcut menu. In the Linked Bitmap Image Properties dialog box, the General property sheet shows that the object is a Bitmap Image with a size of 1.50 KB, or 1,536 bytes. It also shows the path to the original object. See Figure 5-14. Although you cannot see the entire path on this property sheet, you can see the full path on the Link property sheet.

POWER USER TIP If you want to see the rest of the path on the General property sheet, click the path and then press the End key.

Also note that in this instance the file size is only about 1.6% (1.50 KB) of the original file (93.6 KB). Your object size might be different from the size shown in the figure.

Figure 5-14   VIEWING PROPERTIES OF A LINKED OBJECT

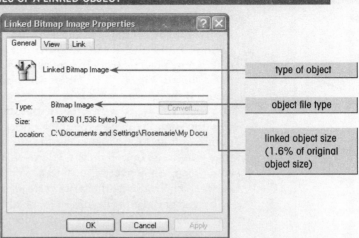

type of object

object file type

linked object size
(1.6% of original
object size)

TROUBLE? If Windows XP (mis)reports the object size (in other words, if it reports the file size close to the original size of 93.6 KB) or reports it as Unknown, you have encountered a problem using OLE. Click the object once to select it (if it is not already selected), press the Delete key to delete the object, and then repeat the steps in the previous section for inserting the image as a linked object again. Make sure you choose the option for creating a link.

TROUBLE? If your dialog box does not contain a Link tab, and if you do not see Linked Bitmap Image Properties on the title bar of the dialog box, you did not create a link to the object in the file. Close the dialog box, press the Delete key to remove the object, and then step through the process in the previous section for inserting the image as a linked object again. Make sure you click the Link check box in the Insert Object dialog box.

TROUBLE? If you right-click the linked object, but no shortcut menu appears, you have encountered a problem using OLE. Save your work, close the application and document, log off your computer, restart Windows XP, and then pick up where you left off and try again.

2. Click the **View** tab. The View sheet allows you to specify how to view the object in the document. See Figure 5-15. The default is to display the object as editable information. To display the object as an icon and compress the object, you use the Display as icon option button.

Figure 5-15   DISPLAY OPTIONS FOR OBJECTS

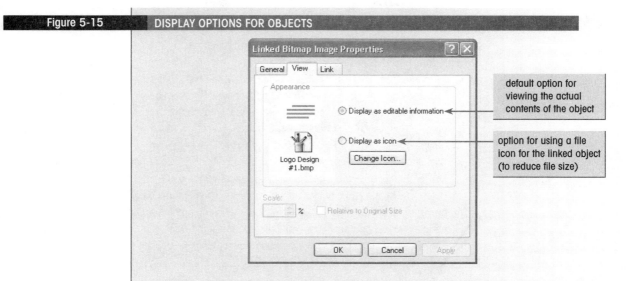

default option for viewing the actual contents of the object

option for using a file icon for the linked object (to reduce file size)

3. Click the **Link** tab. The Link property sheet shows the full path to the original object. See Figure 5-16. You can use the Change Source button to browse for another object in another file and change the link. In the Update section, the default option for updating a link is Automatically. You use the Manually option button to specify that you want to manually update the link with the Update Now button. Use the Open Source button to open the source document, and the Break Link button to break the link.

Figure 5-16   VIEWING OPTIONS ON THE LINK PROPERTY SHEET

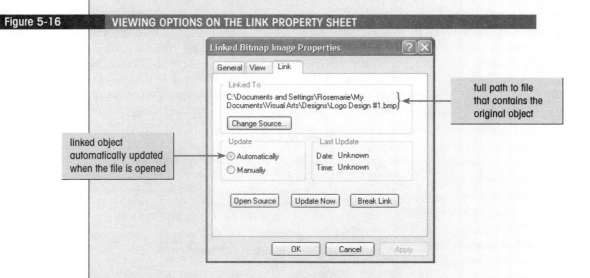

full path to file that contains the original object

linked object automatically updated when the file is opened

4. Click **Cancel** to close the Linked Bitmap Image Properties dialog box without making any changes to the linked object.

You can use the object properties dialog box to verify the type of object (linked or embedded), follow changes in object sizes, and to view or change properties of an object.

Editing a Linked Object

Once you insert a linked object into a document, you can double-click that object to open the application that was used to create the object and the source file. You have to double-click, even in Web style; if you single-click, then you only select the object. After you make changes to the original object, you save your changes, and then exit the application and return to the file that contains the linked object. By default, Windows XP automatically updates the linked object so that it reflects any changes you made to the source document.

After viewing the logo in the memo, Rosemarie asks you to change the background color of this first logo design to a lighter color so that the company name stands out.

To edit the linked object:

1. Double-click the **linked object**. On the computer used for Figure 5-17, Windows XP opens the Paint application, and then opens the document containing the original logo design. You can now arrange the two application windows—the source and destination application windows—to watch how Windows XP updates a link.

TROUBLE? If the application window is not wide enough to show the entire image, adjust the size of the application window.

TROUBLE? If Windows XP opens another application, such as Adobe Illustrator, Photoshop, or CorelDraw, then you can make the changes using tools of that application.

Figure 5-17	EDITING A LINKED OBJECT

file containing
the original object

original object

double-click to
open the file with
the original object

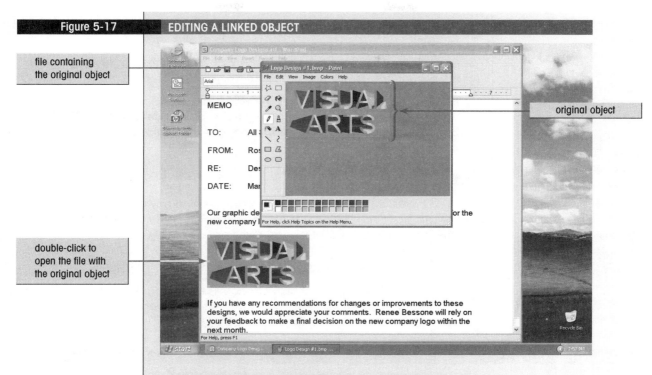

2. Right-click the **taskbar**, and then click **Tile Windows Vertically**. Windows XP
   now displays a view of the Paint and WordPad windows. See Figure 5-18.

Figure 5-18	TILING WINDOWS VERTICALLY

compound document
with linked object

source application
window with
source object

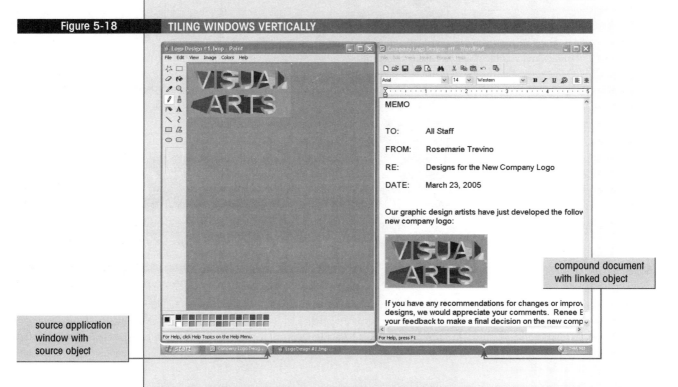

3. If necessary, adjust the view in the Paint and WordPad windows so that you can
   see the original logo design and the linked object at the same time, as shown
   in Figure 5-18.

4. If it is not already selected, click the **title bar** in the Paint window to select this window.

5. In the Color Box (bottom left of Paint window), click the **bright blue** color box in the second row (seventh color box from the left).

   NOTE: Later, you will print this document. If you are using a black and white printer, you might want to use the light blue color box (second row, sixth color box from the left) instead, because the light blue color appears as a light gray when printed.

   TROUBLE? If you do not see a Color Box, click View, and then click Color Box.

6. Click the **Fill With Color** button 🖍 in the second row of the second column of the Tool Box. When you move the mouse pointer onto the canvas, the mouse pointer appears as a paint bucket with paint pouring out of it.

   TROUBLE? If you do not see a Tool Box, click View, and then click Tool Box.

7. Click the **teal background** of the image. Paint changes the background color to the light blue you selected, and Windows XP immediately updates the linked object in the WordPad window. See Figure 5-19.

| Figure 5-19 | UPDATING A LINKED OBJECT |

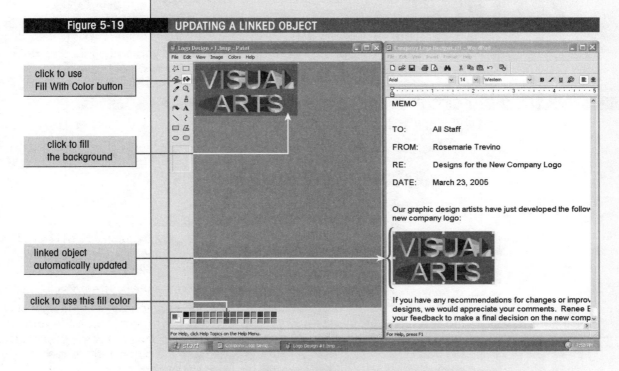

click to use
Fill With Color button

click to fill
the background

linked object
automatically updated

click to use this fill color

TROUBLE? If Windows XP does not update the object immediately, then you need to save your changes to that object (described in the next step), or you might even need to save both documents, close the documents, and then open the memo again for the update to occur.

8. In the Paint window, click **File** on the menu bar, and then click **Save**. If you want to retain this change in the original object, and in all linked objects, you must save your changes to the original object.

9. After the save is complete, close the Paint window, and then maximize the WordPad window.

REFERENCE WINDOW   RW

Editing A Linked Object
- Double-click the linked object.
- Once Windows XP opens the application that was used to create the object (or the application associated with that file type on your computer) and the source file, right-click the taskbar, click Tile Windows Vertically, and then adjust your view in both windows.
- Modify the contents of the original object.
- Save the changes to the source file.
- Exit the application that produced the original object, or that is associated with the original object.

As you can see, creating links to objects in other files is one important way you can build compound documents that draw on resources stored in other files.

Embedding an Object

Now you are ready to insert the second logo design for Rosemarie. Since Rosemarie wants to adapt this particular design in the company's annual report later, she wants you to embed, rather than link, it in the memo. If you embed a copy of the original design, any changes she makes to this copy do not affect the original design. Also, she can still edit the design even though the embedded object is stored in a different type of file.

To insert an embedded object:

1. If necessary, adjust your view so that you can see the blank space between the first and second paragraphs as well as the linked object. You need to position the insertion point where you want to insert the next object.

2. The linked object should still be selected. If it's not, click (*do not double-click*) the **linked object**. Press the **End** key to move the insertion point to the right of the linked object, and thereby remove the selection from the object. Instead of using the End key, you can also click immediately to the right of the object at the next available position on the line. Make sure the object is no longer selected and that you see the insertion point to the right of the linked object.

3. Press the **Tab** key to move the insertion point to the 3-inch mark on the ruler.

4. Click **Insert** on the menu bar, click **Object**, click the **Create from File** option button in the Insert Object dialog box, and click the **Browse** button.

5. In the Browse dialog box, click **Logo Design #2.Bmp**.

6. After you return to the Insert Object dialog box, make sure the Link box does not contain a check mark. Under Result, Windows XP explains that your current settings insert the contents of the file as an object, and you can activate that object using the program that created it. See Figure 5-20.

| Figure 5-20 | SPECIFYING AN EMBEDDED OBJECT |

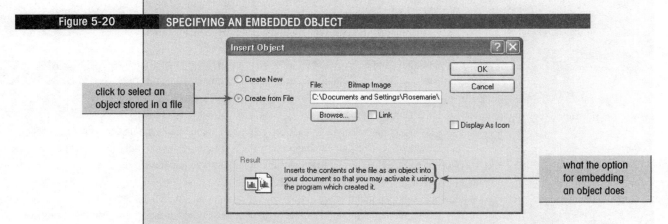

click to select an object stored in a file

what the option for embedding an object does

7. Click the **OK** button. The object is embedded in the memo. See Figure 5-21.

| Figure 5-21 | EMBEDDING AN OBJECT |

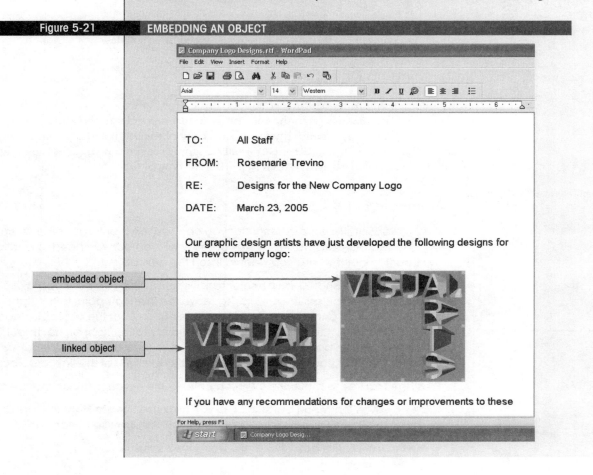

embedded object

linked object

TROUBLE? If the embedded object does not appear on the same line as the linked object, but rather wraps around to the next line so that it's below the linked object, you will need to delete one or more tabs (or whatever spacing you used) between the linked and embedded objects. Just click the blank space between the two objects, and use the Backspace or Delete keys to remove tabs or spaces. You might also need to adjust the size of the object.

8. Click the **Save** button 🖫 on the toolbar.

REFERENCE WINDOW **RW**

Inserting an Embedded Object in a Document
- Open WordPad (or another application) and the document in which you want to embed an object.
- Position the insertion point marker where you want to insert the embedded object.
- Click Insert on the menu bar, and then click Object.
- In the Insert Object dialog box, click the Create from File option button.
- Click the Browse button, locate and click the file that contains the object you want to insert in the current file, and then click OK in the Insert Object dialog box.

Notice that in WordPad, you use the same approach for inserting linked or embedded objects into document. However, for a linked object, you have to remember to choose the option for creating a link.

Viewing Properties of an Embedded Object

You can now view properties of the embedded object in the same way that you viewed properties of the linked object.

Rosemarie asks you to check the size of the embedded object so she can get an idea of how much space this object takes in the memo.

To view properties of an embedded object:

1. Right-click the **embedded object**, and then click **Object Properties** on the shortcut menu. In the Bitmap Image Properties dialog box, the General property sheet shows the object's type (still a Bitmap Image), the object size (149 KB, or 152,576 bytes). See Figure 5-22. The object size is slightly larger than the object in the original file (144 KB), because the embedded object includes not only the object itself, but also all the information needed to edit the object with the tools of the original application within the current application. The Convert button lets you convert an embedded object from its current object type to another object type so you can associate the object with a different application or with a different data format.

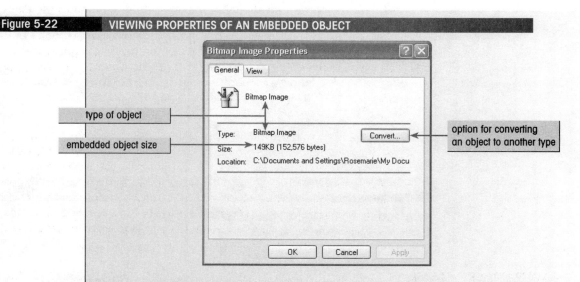

Figure 5-22 — VIEWING PROPERTIES OF AN EMBEDDED OBJECT

2. Click the **path** shown to the right of Location, and then press the **End** key. The location refers to the file that contains the embedded object, not the source file.

3. Click the **View** tab. The View property sheet has the same viewing options as for a linked object. Since this object is an embedded object, and not a linked object, there is no Link property sheet in the Bitmap Image Properties dialog box.

4. Click the **Cancel** button to close the Bitmap Image Properties dialog box without making any changes to the embedded object.

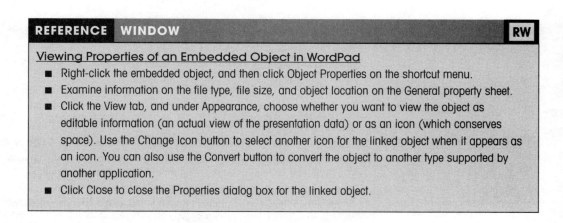

REFERENCE WINDOW   **RW**

Viewing Properties of an Embedded Object in WordPad
- Right-click the embedded object, and then click Object Properties on the shortcut menu.
- Examine information on the file type, file size, and object location on the General property sheet.
- Click the View tab, and under Appearance, choose whether you want to view the object as editable information (an actual view of the presentation data) or as an icon (which conserves space). Use the Change Icon button to select another icon for the linked object when it appears as an icon. You can also use the Convert button to convert the object to another type supported by another application.
- Click Close to close the Properties dialog box for the linked object.

One way to distinguish an embedded object from a linked object is that an embedded object does not have a Link property sheet. Also, the location for a linked object points to another file.

Editing an Embedded Object

Because an embedded object does not contain a link to the original object, you can modify an embedded object without affecting the original object. When you double-click the embedded object, Windows XP displays the object in a special window within the WordPad application window. The WordPad menu bar, toolbar, and Format Bar are replaced with the Paint menu bar, Tool Box, and Color Box. You are still working with the selected object in its actual location within WordPad, but the interface now contains the Paint tools for editing the object. As mentioned earlier, this feature is referred to as **visual editing**, or **in-place editing**, and is available in applications that support OLE 2.0.

Rosemarie also wants you to change the background of the embedded object to the same color you used for the linked object because it improves the appearance of the logo.

To edit an embedded object:

1. Double-click the **embedded object**. The object appears in a **visual editing window** with scroll bars so that you can adjust your view of the object. See Figure 5-23. The gray hatched border around the object and the black handles indicate that the object window has the focus. In other words, the object is selected. Although you are still in the WordPad application window, as shown by the document and application name on the title bar and the text in the document window, you now see elements of the Paint interface, such as the menu bar options, Tool Box, and Color Box.

Figure 5-23   **USING VISUAL EDITING TO MODIFY AN EMBEDDED OBJECT**

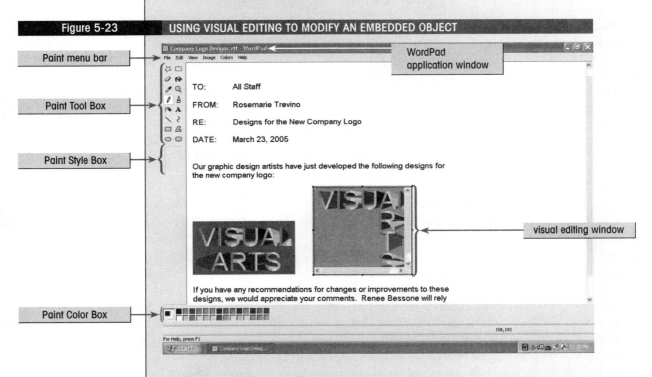

2. In the Color Box, click the **bright blue** color that you selected earlier for the linked object (second row, seventh color box from left), click the **Fill With Color** button 🖌 in the Tool Box, and then click the **teal background** of the embedded object. The background color of the embedded object changes to bright blue. See Figure 5-24.

NOTE: As noted earlier, you will print this document later. If you are using a black and white printer, you might want to use the light blue color box (second row, sixth color box from the left) instead, because the light blue color appears as a light gray when printed.

Figure 5-24   VIEWING CHANGES TO THE EMBEDDED OBJECT

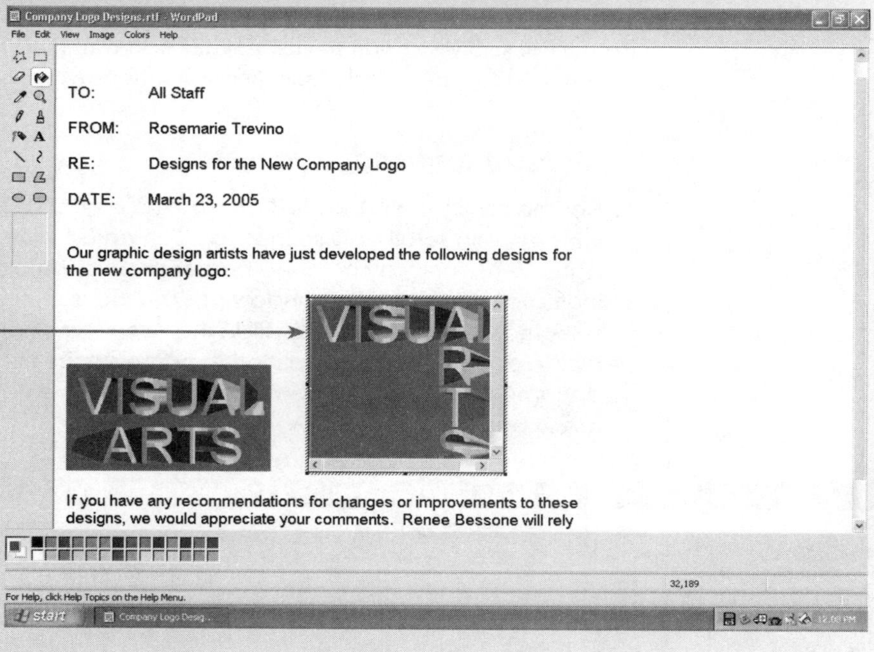

background color
changed with Paint tools

3. Click the **white background** outside the visual editing window. You return to the WordPad window. See Figure 5-25. The WordPad window now has the WordPad menu bar, Toolbar, Format Bar, Ruler, and Status Bar.

Figure 5-25	RETURNING TO THE WORDPAD WINDOW

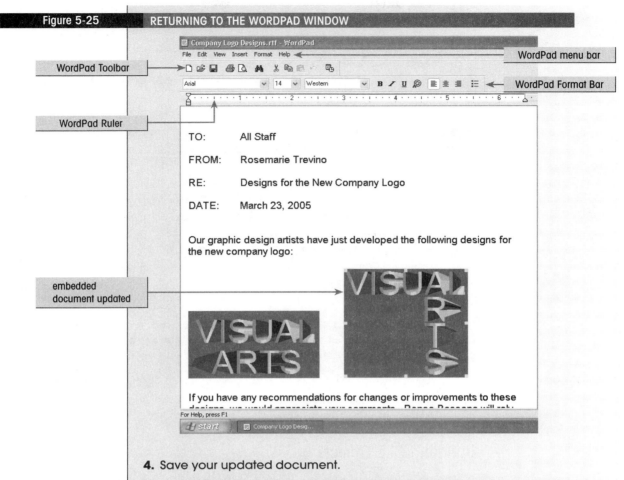

4. Save your updated document.

5. Close the WordPad window, which also closes the Company Logo Designs.rtf document.

6. From the Start menu, open **My Documents**, click the **Visual Arts** folder icon, click the **Memos** folder icon, click **View** on the menu bar, and then click **Details**. Windows XP reports the file size of the Company Logo Designs memo as 981 KB. See Figure 5-26. The file is close to a megabyte, and compared to the sizes of compound documents that you might create with Microsoft Word, it is relatively small. If you open this file and change the object properties of the linked and embedded objects to display icons instead of editable information, Windows XP compresses the objects, and reduces the file size by 68% to 329 KB.

Figure 5-26	VIEWING THE SIZE OF THE FILE WITH THE EMBEDDED AND LINKED OBJECTS

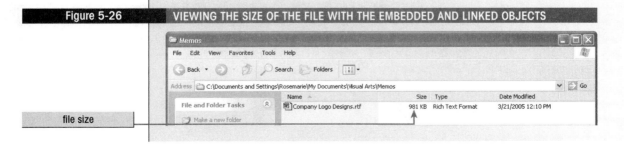

7. Close the Memos folder window.

POWER USER TIP Another way to quickly distinguish an embedded object from a linked object in OLE 2.0 (the standard today) is to double-click on the object. If the object is an embedded object, you see a visual editing window.

REFERENCE WINDOW   **RW**

Editing an Embedded Object
- Double-click the embedded object.
- After Windows XP displays a visual editing window for the object and the tools and menus of the application that produced the object (or that is associated with the object), use those tools to modify the object.
- After you finish editing the object, click the background outside the visual editing window to return to the window of the open application.

Visual editing, an OLE 2.0 feature, simplifies the process of updating objects in a document because you can see the object and its placement within the document as you make changes. It is also revolutionary in that the tools for editing an embedded object are incorporated into the interface of the open application. Under OLE 1.0, Windows would open a copy of the object in a separate application window, so that you could edit the document. When you saved your changes and closed that window, Windows updated the embedded object in the compound document.

Updating OLE Objects

Rosemarie needs to turn to another task that has suddenly become high priority. While she completes that task, she wants you to open and print an original for photocopying.

To update OLE objects:

1. Using your WordPad desktop shortcut, open WordPad.

2. Click the **Open** button 📂 on the Toolbar and, in the Open dialog box, click the **Up One Level** button 🔼, click **Memos**, and then click **Company Logo Designs.rtf**. The Updating ActiveX objects dialog box shows the progress of updating the linked object in the WordPad document. See Figure 5-27.

TROUBLE? If the Look in list box does not display the name of the last folder you opened (the Designs folder), use the Look in list box to select the disk that contains the Visual Arts folder, open the Visual Arts folder, open the Memos folder, and then open Company Logo Designs.rtf.

Figure 5-27   UPDATING A LINKED OBJECT

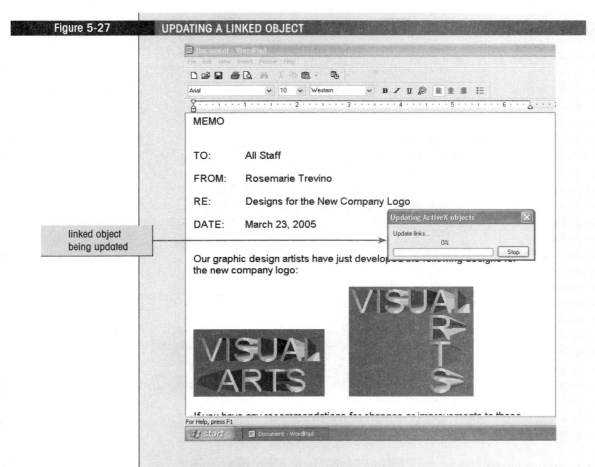

linked object being updated

3. Leave the Company Logo Designs.rtf open for the next section of the tutorial.

Microsoft now refers to OLE objects as ActiveX objects. Microsoft defines ActiveX as "a set of technologies that allows software components to interact with one another in a networked environment, regardless of the language in which the components were created." While the focus of OLE 1.0 was the creation of compound documents, OLE 2.0 was not limited to compound documents, but rather extended the capabilities of OLE technology.

Next, you want to print a copy of the memo so that you can photocopy it and send it to all staff members. Before you print, you want to preview the memo and make sure it fits on one page so that you do not waste paper.

To preview, and then print the memo:

1. Click the **Print Preview** button 🔍 on the toolbar. WordPad displays a preview of the printed document. See Figure 5-28. Remember that because WordPad is not a full-featured word-processing application, your preview might not appear perfect. However, you should be able to tell if it can fit on one page.

   TROUBLE? If the memo does not fit on one page, click the Close button on the Print Preview toolbar (not the WordPad window's Close button), click File, and then click Page Setup. Change the margin settings, and then click OK to close the dialog box and save your changes. Preview your document again.

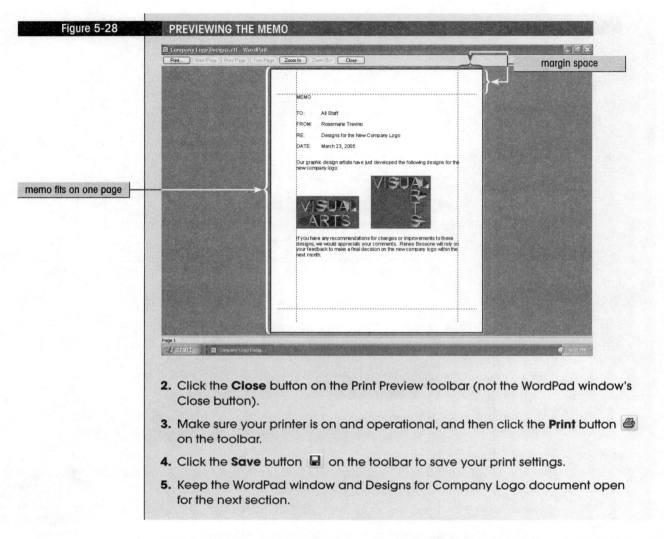

Figure 5-28   PREVIEWING THE MEMO

margin space

memo fits on one page

2. Click the **Close** button on the Print Preview toolbar (not the WordPad window's Close button).

3. Make sure your printer is on and operational, and then click the **Print** button 🖨 on the toolbar.

4. Click the **Save** button 💾 on the toolbar to save your print settings.

5. Keep the WordPad window and Designs for Company Logo document open for the next section.

With OLE 2.0 technology, creating and updating compound documents with linked and embedded objects is simple. Furthermore, your productivity increases because you can work more logically and efficiently.

In the next section of the tutorial, you create a special type of OLE object called scrap and insert it into a compound document. You examine properties of scrap before and after dragging the scrap into a document. You next look at how you can use OLE technology in the applications that you work with on a daily basis. You also examine how Windows XP uses and depends on OLE technology. Then you work with the OLE properties of the taskbar. Finally, you use link tracing to locate OLE objects on your computer.

Creating **and Using Scrap**

Another way to insert objects in a document is to create one or more "scrap objects" and place them on the desktop. **Scrap** is an object that Windows XP creates when you drag all or part of a file onto the desktop. The scrap object is stored in a file just like the original object from which you created the scrap. The scrap can consist of text, a graphic image, a sound clip, or any other type of data stored in a file. You can also create scrap from a linked or embedded object in a document. When you want to insert the scrap in a document, you open the document and then drag the scrap from the desktop (or wherever you stored it) into the document.

After evaluating staff feedback and reviewing the two designs for the new company logo, Renee Bessone, the president of Visual Arts, Inc. chooses the second of the two designs presented in the memo (the embedded logo). She asks Rosemarie to send another memo to employees, informing them of her decision. Rosemarie says this is a good opportunity for you to learn how to work with scrap, so she asks you to prepare the memo.

To create scrap using the embedded object in the WordPad memo:

1. If you closed the WordPad window and your memo, use your WordPad desktop shortcut to open WordPad, and then open Company Logo Designs.rtf.

2. Click the **Restore Down** button 🗗, move the WordPad window to the left side of the desktop, increase the height to fill the desktop, and adjust its width so that you can see the linked and embedded objects as well as the open area of your desktop on the right side of the screen. Use Figure 5-29 as a guideline to placing and adjusting the WordPad window.

Figure 5-29	ADJUSTING THE WORDPAD WINDOW AND DESKTOP VIEW

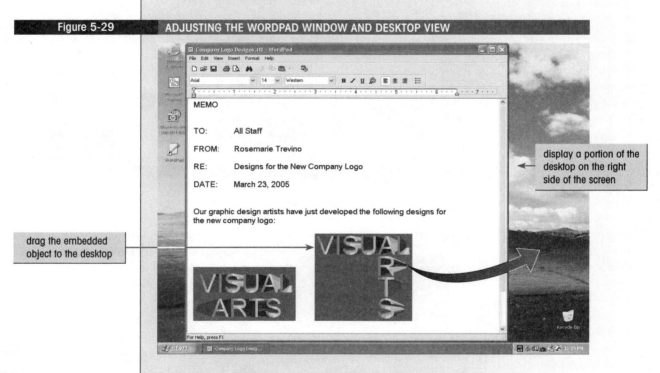

drag the embedded object to the desktop

display a portion of the desktop on the right side of the screen

Next, check the Auto Arrange setting for the desktop.

3. Right-click an empty area on the desktop, point to **Arrange Icons By** and, if you see a check mark next to the Auto Arrange option, click **Auto Arrange** to turn this feature off; otherwise, click the **desktop** again to close the shortcut menu. If this option is turned on when you create scrap, the scrap object might be hidden behind the WordPad window. When Auto Arrange is on, Windows XP arranges icons in columns from top to bottom and from left to right on the desktop. If Auto Arrange is off, Windows XP leaves icons wherever you put them on the desktop.

4. Click the **WordPad title bar**, drag the embedded object (the one on the right) from the document window to the desktop, release the left mouse button, and then click the desktop background to change the focus from the new object. Windows XP creates scrap (a file) that contains a copy of the embedded object. See Figure 5-30. You can now use this scrap as part of another document. Windows XP assigns the name Scrap to the first scrap object you create, Scrap (2) to the next, etc. Like any other type of file, you can rename the scrap object so that you know what type of data is contained in it.

| Figure 5-30 | SCRAP CREATED FROM THE EMBEDDED OBJECT |

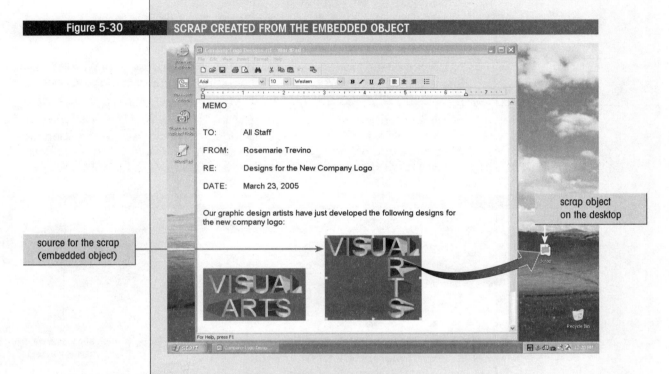

source for the scrap
(embedded object)

scrap object
on the desktop

5. Minimize the WordPad window.

POWER USERS TIP When you copy or move a set of objects, such as files or short-cuts, to the desktop or a folder window, you might not see all of the objects because they are positioned off screen. Right-click the desktop or folder window, point to Arrange By, and click Auto Arrange to display all of the objects on the desktop or within the window.

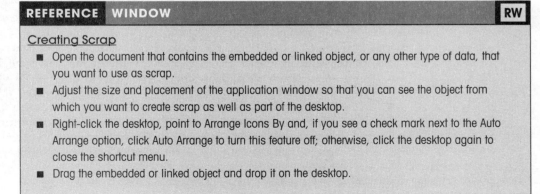

REFERENCE   WINDOW   **RW**

<u>Creating Scrap</u>
- Open the document that contains the embedded or linked object, or any other type of data, that you want to use as scrap.
- Adjust the size and placement of the application window so that you can see the object from which you want to create scrap as well as part of the desktop.
- Right-click the desktop, point to Arrange Icons By and, if you see a check mark next to the Auto Arrange option, click Auto Arrange to turn this feature off; otherwise, click the desktop again to close the shortcut menu.
- Drag the embedded or linked object and drop it on the desktop.

Scraps are a special type of OLE object produced from another OLE object, or from some other type of data, in a document.

Viewing the Contents of Scrap

When you create scrap, the scrap object contains information on the application that produced it or a link to an object in a file. You can open scrap by clicking the scrap object. If you open the scrap you just created, you will find that it contains the same image that you dragged from the WordPad document to the desktop.

> *To view the contents of scrap:*
>
> 1. Click the **Scrap** object on the desktop. Windows XP opens Paint and then opens the bitmap image in the scrap. See Figure 5-31. Notice the title on the title bar: Bitmap Image in Scrap - Paint. The scrap object looks identical to the embedded object in the WordPad document. Since this scrap object is a new object, you can change it without affecting the copy in the WordPad document.

Figure 5-31	OPENING SCRAP

bitmap image in scrap

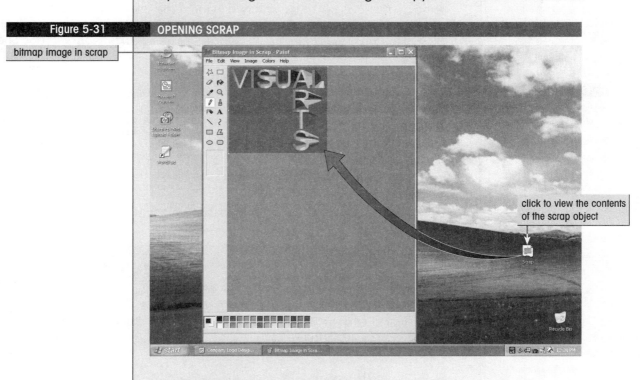

click to view the contents
of the scrap object

> 2. Close the Bitmap Image in Scrap - Paint window.

If you create scrap from a linked object, the scrap object also retains a link to the original object. When you click the scrap object, Windows XP opens the file with the original object in the application associated with that file type.

Viewing Properties of Scrap

Like any other type of object, you can view properties of scrap, including its file size. You will find that the scrap object is much larger than the original object used to create the scrap. This is because the scrap object must include all the information about the object so that you can edit it. It might also include a complete copy of the original file attached to the scrap object.

To view properties of a scrap object:

1. Right-click the **Scrap** object on the desktop, and then click **Properties** on the shortcut menu. Windows XP opens a Scrap Properties dialog box. The General property sheet identifies the type of object (Scrap object), the Windows XP component for opening scrap (Shell scrap object handler), the location of the scrap, its size (295 KB, or 302,592 bytes), the date it was created, accessed, and modified, and its attributes. See Figure 5-32. Notice that the size of the scrap object has more than doubled (from 144 KB to 295 KB), indicating that a copy of the original file (144 KB) is attached to the scrap object. The path for the location of the scrap, your file sizes, and the number of property sheets might differ. Although not shown, Windows XP assigns the file extension "shs" (for "Shell Scrap") to scrap objects.

Figure 5-32   **VIEWING PROPERTIES OF SCRAP**

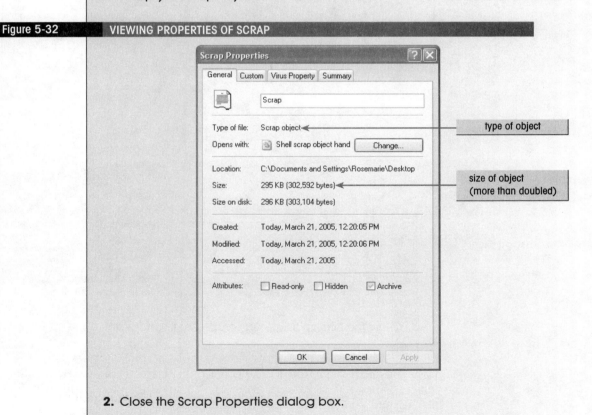

2. Close the Scrap Properties dialog box.

Once you create scrap, you can use it in other documents.

Inserting Scrap into a Document

Your next task for Rosemarie is to create a new memo about the final design chosen for the company logo. Since you want to include a copy of the embedded object in the memo, you can drag the desktop scrap with the logo into the new memo.

To create a new file:

1. Click the **Company Logo Designs.rtf - WordPad** taskbar button to restore the WordPad window.

2. Click the **New** button ⬚ on the toolbar. In the New dialog box, you can choose from one of three document types—Rich Text Document, Text Document, or Unicode Text Document.

3. Click the **Help** button ❓, and then click the **New document type** list box. As explained in the pop-up Help window, you can open and edit a Word 6 Document in Microsoft Word 6.0 or later. Although this document type is not one of the options listed in the list box, it was available in previous versions of Windows. See Figure 5-33. A **Rich Text Document** includes character formatting and tab codes that many types of word-processing applications recognize. A **Text Document** has unformatted text. A **Unicode Text Document** can include text from any of the world's writing systems.

Figure 5-33	VIEWING QUICK HELP ON DOCUMENT TYPES

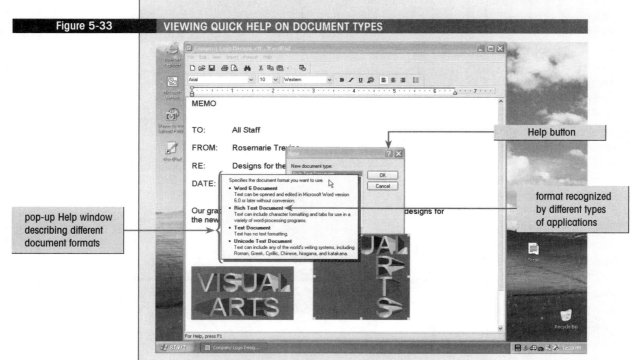

pop-up Help window describing different document formats

Help button

format recognized by different types of applications

4. Click the **pop-up Help** window to close it, click **Rich Text Document** in the New document type list box if it is not already selected, click the **OK** button, and if a WordPad dialog box opens asking whether you want to save changes to Designs for Company Logo.doc, click the **Yes** button to save and close the first memo, and then open a new file.

5. Click **File**, click **Page Setup**, and, if necessary, change the Left, Right, Top, and Bottom margins to **1** inch, and then click the **OK** button.

6. Click **View**, click **Options**, click the **Rich Text** tab, if necessary, click the **Wrap to ruler** option button (if necessary), and then click the **OK** button.

7. If WordPad is not using the Arial font, click the **Font** list arrow Arial, locate and click **Arial**, click the **Font Size** list arrow 10, and then click **14**.

8. Type the text shown in Figure 5-34. Use your name instead of Rosemarie Trevino's, use the current date, and leave three blank lines between the first and second paragraphs of the memo so that you can insert a copy of the new company logo.

| Figure 5-34 | CREATING A FOLLOW-UP MEMO TO STAFF |

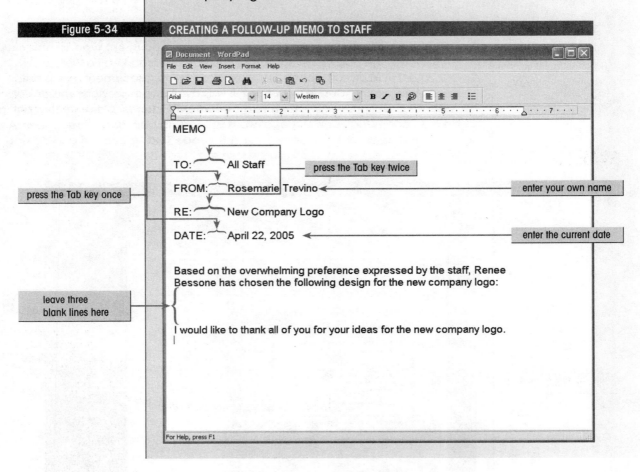

9. Click the **Save** button 🖫 on the Toolbar, and after the Save As dialog box opens, make sure the Save in list box shows that you are going to save your document in the Memos folder (otherwise, switch to that folder first), click **Document.rtf** in the File name text box, if necessary, type **New Company Logo**, and then click the **Save** button.

Now you are ready to insert a copy of the design for the new company logo in the memo.

To drag scrap into a file:

1. If necessary, move or adjust the size of the WordPad window so that you can see the scrap on the desktop.

2. If necessary, adjust your view in the WordPad window so that you can see the blank lines between the first and second paragraphs of the memo.

3. Drag the **Scrap** object from the desktop into the WordPad document, position the insertion point halfway between the first and second paragraphs, and then release the left mouse button. Windows XP embeds a copy of the contents of the scrap object in the WordPad document. See Figure 5-35.

| Figure 5-35 | INSERTING SCRAP INTO A DOCUMENT |

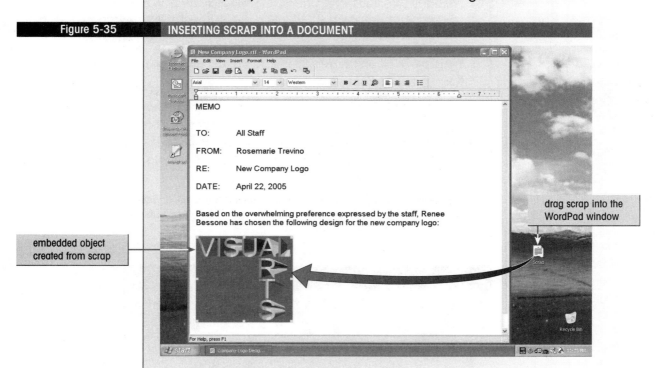

embedded object created from scrap

drag scrap into the WordPad window

4. With the embedded object still selected, click the **Center** button 🢒 on the Format Bar to center the object between the margins. You just edited the object with a tool of the current application.

5. Right-click the embedded object, and then click **Object Properties**. Notice that the object size dropped from 295 KB to 149 KB—the size of the image when Rosemarie first embedded it (149 KB). See Figure 5-36. Windows XP removed the copy of the file attached to the scrap object.

Figure 5-36 PROPERTIES OF AN EMBEDDED OBJECT CREATED FROM SCRAP

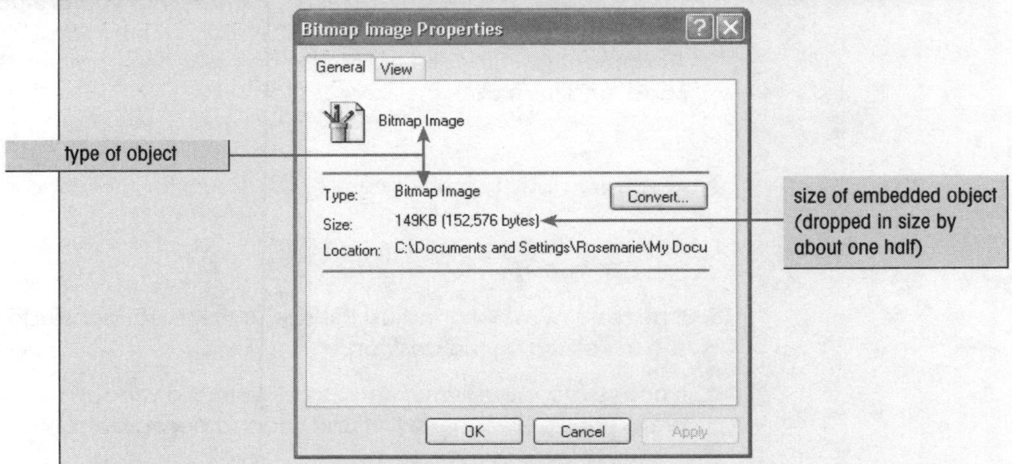

type of object

size of embedded object (dropped in size by about one half)

Bitmap Image Properties

General | View

Bitmap Image

Type: Bitmap Image   [Convert...]
Size: 149KB (152,576 bytes)
Location: C:\Documents and Settings\Rosemarie\My Docu

[OK] [Cancel] [Apply]

TROUBLE? If Windows XP (mis)reports the object size as Unknown, you have encountered a problem using OLE. Click the object once to select it (if it is not already selected), press the Delete key to delete the object, and then repeat the steps for dragging scrap into the document. If this approach does not resolve the problem, then you might need to close all applications and windows and restart your computer to clear memory. As noted earlier, other problems, such as problems with the file system, might affect the use of OLE.

6. Click the **path** to the right of location, and then press the **End** key. The object's location is now the document in which it is contained—not the scrap object. It is now an embedded object in the WordPad document.

7. Close the Bitmap Image Properties dialog box, click the **Save** button 💾 on the Toolbar, wait until the Save is complete, and then click the **Print** button 🖨 on the Toolbar to print your document.

8. Close the WordPad window and document and, if WordPad asks you if you want to save changes to the memo, click the **Yes** button.

REFERENCE WINDOW   RW

Inserting Scrap into a Document
- Open the document into which you want to insert the scrap.
- Adjust the size and placement of the application window so that you can see the scrap on the desktop.
- Drag the scrap from the desktop into the application window, and drop the scrap where you want it to appear in the document.
- Save your document.

Before you continue with the next section of the tutorial, you can remove the scrap from the desktop and the Visual Arts folder from the My Documents folder.

To clean up your computer:

1. Drag the **scrap object** to the Recycle Bin.

2. Open My Documents, adjust the size of the My Documents window so that you can see the desktop, and then drag the **Visual Arts** folder to the Recycle Bin.

3. If permitted by your lab use policy, empty the Recycle Bin.

You have just performed another type of OLE operation—dragging and dropping objects in the Recycle Bin.

Scrap objects are ideal for use as "boilerplate text" (like a company address), graphic images (like a company logo), and any other objects that you use in many different documents. Depending on the type of work that you do, you might create a library of commonly used scrap objects. For example, if you use the same opening and closing paragraphs in memos, you could insert each paragraph and your standard signature block from scrap.

Using OLE in Productivity Software

If you are working with an application like Microsoft Word or Excel, you can use the Object option on the Insert menu to create an object from a file, or insert and create a new object type. This option, however, uses the entire contents of the file. In many instances, you might want to use just a portion of a file. You can use two other methods to copy an object from one document and insert it as an object in another document: you can drag and drop, or you can copy and paste.

First, you can only use drag and drop for those applications that support this OLE 2.0 feature. For example, if you want to drag a chart from an Excel spreadsheet into a Word document, you open an Excel window with the Excel spreadsheet and a Word window with the Word document, then you tile the windows vertically so that you can see the contents of both windows at the same time. Next, you locate, select, and drag the chart from the Excel window to the Word window. Figure 5-37 illustrates this process. As you drag, you must hold down the Ctrl key so that Windows XP makes a *copy* of the original object. If you do not hold down the Ctrl key, Windows XP *moves* the chart from the Excel document to the Word document. When you drag and drop, Windows XP assumes you want to embed the object. Figure 5-38 shows the chart after it is copied to the Word memo. There is no option for creating a link using drag and drop. In the steps you performed earlier with WordPad and Paint, you could not have dragged the logo from the Paint window to the WordPad window because Paint does not support this feature.

Figure 5-37   USING DRAG AND DROP TO COPY AN EXCEL CHART INTO A WORD MEMO

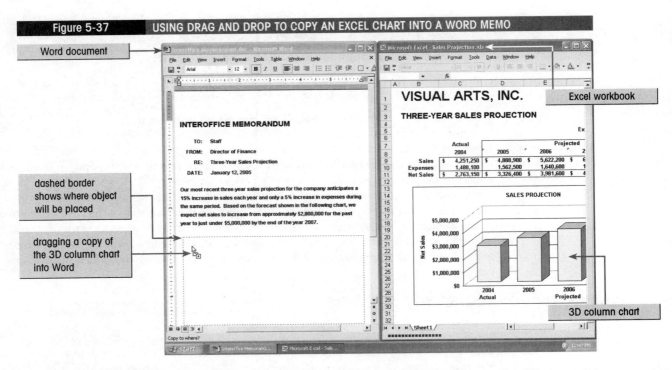

Word document

dashed border shows where object will be placed

dragging a copy of the 3D column chart into Word

Excel workbook

3D column chart

Figure 5-38   OBJECT COPIED TO WORD FROM EXCEL USING DRAG AND DROP

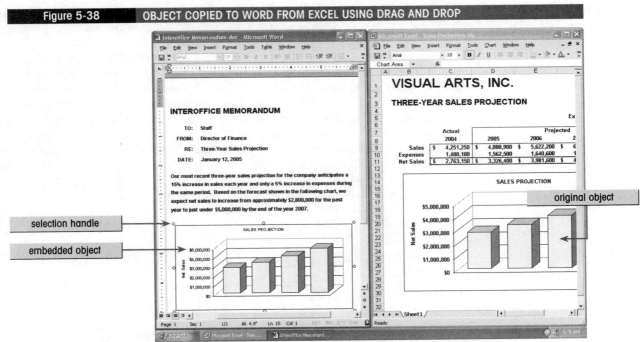

selection handle

embedded object

original object

If you find it difficult to use drag and drop, you can use copy and paste instead. You open the source document, select the object you want to copy, and then click the Copy button or choose Copy from the Edit menu, or you can just right-click the object, and choose Copy from its shortcut menu. If you are finished with the source document, you can close it. Next, you open the destination document. If you want to embed the object or create a link in the destination document, you choose Paste Special from the Edit menu. From the Paste

Special dialog box, you can embed the object or create a link to the object (paste link). Since the Paste Special dialog box lists different data formats for an object, you can also choose the data format that you want to use for the paste operation. Figure 5-39 illustrates the Paste Special dialog box for a copy-and-paste operation of a chart between Microsoft Excel and Word. Notice that you can paste an Excel chart into a Word document as a Microsoft Excel Chart Object or as a Picture (Enhanced Metafile). A **metafile** is a file that contains a list of commands that Windows XP can process to draw a graphic image. A **Windows metafile** (WMF) is a 16-bit metafile for displaying a picture under Windows 3.x and later versions of Windows. The dialog box would list this option as Picture (without the phrase Enhanced Metafile). An **enhanced metafile** is a 32-bit metafile with additional commands for creating images under Windows 95 and later versions of Windows. If all you need is the presentation data, you can chose the Picture or Picture (Enhanced Metafile) data format so that Windows XP renders the image better on screen and during printing. The Picture data format is the best for high-quality printers; it requires the least amount of storage space for the data and is displayed more quickly on screen. The Bitmap data format, if available, requires a lot of memory and disk storage space for the object data, but it matches exactly what you see on the screen.

Figure 5-39   CREATING AN EMBEDDED OBJECT WITH COPY AND PASTE

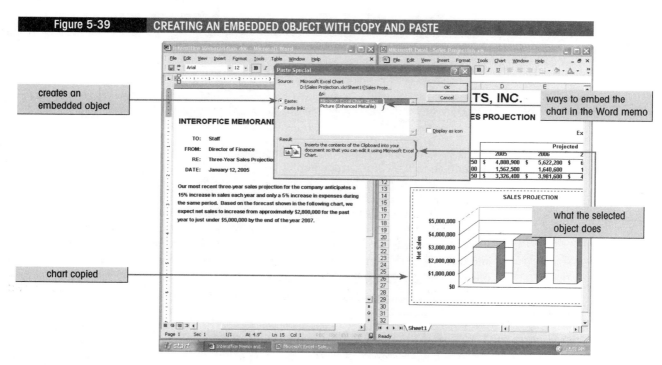

In the case of an embedded bitmap image, you can also convert a bitmap image to a Device Independent Bitmap. A **Device Independent Bitmap** (DIB) is another bitmap image format used by Windows to render images on the screen and printer. The colors in the file are represented in a format that is independent of the output device (monitor or printer). The device driver for the monitor translates the DIB color format into colors that the monitor can display.

If you choose the Paste Link option in the Paste Special dialog box, you see a list of options, or perhaps only one option, for pasting the object into the document and creating a link with the original object stored in another file. In Figure 5-40, there is one option for pasting a Microsoft Excel chart into the Word document, namely, as a Microsoft Excel Chart Object. If you edit the linked object later by double-clicking it, Windows XP opens Microsoft Excel and the spreadsheet that contains the chart so that you can update the spreadsheet, the chart, or both. Any changes that affect the chart are reflected also in the Word document.

| Figure 5-40 | CREATING A LINK USING COPY AND PASTE |

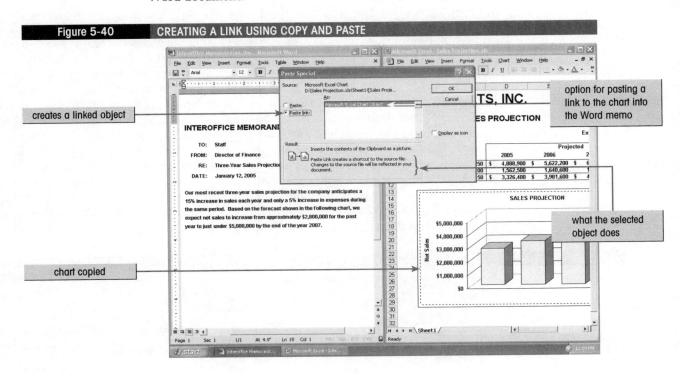

When you use Paste Special, the list of data formats vary, depending on what type of data you copied to the Clipboard, whether you choose to embed or link data, what type of application you are copying from, the version of that application (for example, whether you are working with Office XP or another version of Office), and even whether the application from which you copied the object is still open. In the case of embedding, if you leave the application open, more object types are available. For example, if you copy a worksheet from Microsoft Excel 2002 to Microsoft Word 2002 with the intent of embedding the data, and if you leave Microsoft Excel open during the paste operation, Windows XP displays the following data formats in the Paste Special dialog box:

- **Microsoft Excel Worksheet Object**. If you choose this option, Windows XP embeds the data as an object so that you can edit it with Microsoft Excel.

- **Formatted Text (RTF)**. If you choose this option, Windows XP pastes the data into Word with font and table formatting.

- **Unformatted Text**. If you choose this option, Windows XP pastes the data without any formatting. Actually, the data takes on the default format of data in the Word document, and therefore can be handy in those situations when you don't want to carry formatting over into your document.

- **Picture**, **Bitmap**, and **Picture (Enhanced Metafile)** (explained earlier)

- **HTML Format**

- **Unformatted Unicode Text**. **Unicode** is a coding scheme that can represent 65,536 character combinations, or all the characters within the alphabets of most of the world's languages.

With Formatted Text and Unformatted Text, you are limited to editing the data with Microsoft Word.

On the other hand, if you copy the object, and then close Microsoft Excel, the Paste Special dialog box only contains three data formats for embedding the data: Formatted Text (RTF), Unformatted Text, and Unformatted Unicode Text. So it pays to leave the source application open, because that application provides multiple data types to the Windows Clipboard. You also need to keep the application open if you want to paste a link. If you choose the option for a link, the object types listed in the Paste Special dialog box are slightly different from those for embedding an object. For example, if you choose to create a link to a Microsoft Excel worksheet, the object types include Microsoft Excel Worksheet Object, Formatted Text (RTF), Unformatted Text, Picture, Bitmap, Word Hyperlink, HTML Format, and Unformatted Unicode Text. If you paste a link as a Word Hyperlink, Word creates a link to the source file in your Word document.

When pasting data from one application into another application, you might discover that the data is pasted in HTML format, rather than in the format used by the original application. You might then need to undo the paste operation, and then use Paste Special to choose the format you want.

Try different options for pasting objects into a document or presentation to determine which option provides the best representation of the object.

If you perform a copy and paste, and then find that the Paste button or the Paste option on the Edit menu is dimmed and therefore unavailable, you have more than likely encountered a problem, such as not enough memory available for the OLE operation. After you exit an application, Windows XP is supposed to reclaim all of the memory that application used. However, this is not always the case, because software developers design their applications so that program code is left in memory. Their assumption is that you will open that same application again later, or that the next application you use will be one of that software developer's other software products. If this is the case, it is useful for part of the program code—the part shared by applications or the part previously used—to already be loaded and available in memory. This feature, however, can decrease the amount of RAM available for use with other applications. If your computer has a limited amount of RAM, and if you have used applications that leave some program code in memory, you may run into difficulties when trying to perform copy-and-paste operations. If you log off your computer and restart Windows XP, you clear the memory, and your OLE operations stand a better chance of working properly. However, if you copy an object and then restart your computer for some reason, anything stored in memory is lost, and you have to select and copy the object again.

OLE 2.0 supports many new features not available in OLE 1.0. You have already examined three of those features—visual editing, object conversion, and drag and drop. As you've learned, visual editing allows you to edit embedded objects in the current application using the tools of the original application. With object conversion, you can convert an object to another object type for another application, to another object type that is similar to the original object type, or to an object type that makes it simpler to render the object on screen and during printing. The drag-and-drop feature, as you've discovered, not only lets you drag an object from one application window to another application window (where supported), but also lets you drag an object to a system resource, such as the Recycle Bin.

If your application supports OLE 2.0, you can move the source document for a linked object to another folder on the same computer, and Windows XP updates the pointer for the link so it still refers to the same object. With OLE 2.0, but not OLE 1.0, you can create links over a network, an object can span more than one page, objects can break at a logical boundary within the object, and you can use the spelling checker to check the spelling of embedded objects.

OLE 2.0 is the standard today for applications, even for Office products used on the Macintosh platform. However, some applications, such as Notepad, do not support OLE. Notepad is a simple text editor for opening, examining, and editing simple text files, and there is no need to insert objects into a Notepad file.

How **Windows XP Uses OLE Technology**

OLE technology is a fundamental part of the Windows XP operating system. As you already know, Windows XP treats nearly everything as an object, and each object has properties and actions associated with it. The standard types of objects that you work with daily—such as folders and files—are OLE objects. For example, a file is an OLE object because it is associated with (or "contained in") another object—a folder. The folder is an OLE object because it is associated with (or "contained in") another folder or a drive. Like OLE objects within a document, you can change the associations of files and folders. For example, you can use drag and drop to move a file from one folder to another folder, or from a folder on one drive to a folder on another drive.

Here are some examples of OLE interactions and associations between Windows XP objects:

- **Opening a document by clicking or double-clicking the file icon for a document**. When you install software on your computer, the installation program defines associations between specific file extensions and the application that it installs. Later, when you click (in Web style) or double-click (in Classic style) a file icon associated with an application, Windows XP opens the application for that file type, and then opens the document inside the file. The document is an object contained with the file, and the file is an object contained within an application, and the application is an object contained in a file, folder, and drive on your computer. The document is associated with (or linked to) an application via its file extension, and Windows XP knows the full path (a link) to the application. To manage the interaction between objects, Windows XP uses the Windows Registry, which contains information on not only hardware and user settings, but also on file associations and the full path to each installed application.

- **Dragging a file to a folder**. When you drag a file and drop it onto a folder, Windows XP moves the file if the file and folder are on the same drive (or creates a copy if the file and folder are on different drives). The file then becomes associated with the new folder. The file's association with the folder changes after the drag and drop.

- **Dragging an object from one window to another window**. When you drag a folder or file from one folder window to another, Windows XP moves the object if the windows are on the same drive, or copies it if the windows are on different drives. Again, by using drag and drop, you are redefining the association between a file and a folder. Dragging and dropping from one window to another window, and from one location in a window to another location in the same window, is a part of the OLE technology built into Windows XP.

- **Dragging an object to the Recycle Bin**. When you drag an object, such as a file or folder, to the Recycle Bin, Windows XP moves the object to the Recycle Bin and marks it for deletion. The Recycle Bin is an OLE object. Again, you are changing the association of a file or folder when you delete the file or folder.

- **Creating and using shortcuts**. When you create a shortcut, Windows XP creates a file that is a direct link to a document or part of a document, hardware or software component on your computer (such as a drive, printer, or application), part of the file system (such as a folder or subfolder), to a window (such as a My Computer or Explorer window), a property sheet for an application or object, another computer or component of another computer on a network, or a Web site. Shortcuts, which you have worked with extensively, are OLE objects. Like linked objects, shortcuts contain the full path to the object so that Windows XP can open the original object when you click the shortcut (or link) to that object. It should be no surprise that the file extension for shortcuts is "lnk" (for "link").

■ **Using hyperlinks in Windows XP Help and Support Center**. When you open the Windows XP Help and Support Center, and then click a hyperlink that points to an object, Windows XP opens that object. For example, if you locate information on changing mouse pointer schemes, the Help page contains a hyperlink to the Mouse Properties dialog box. These hyperlinks are comparable to shortcuts. When you switch to Web style, drive, folder, and file icons (for example) become hyperlinks that point to objects on your computer.

■ **Creating new objects in a window or on the desktop**. If you right-click the background of a folder window or the desktop, you can use the New menu to create a new type of object, such as a folder, shortcut, or document, and associate it with an existing application on your computer.

■ **Creating compound documents**. As you've seen, Windows XP works with applications to create compound documents with embedded or linked objects.

■ **Creating document scraps**. Again, as you've seen, Windows XP creates an OLE object known as a scrap when you select part of a document and drag that object onto the desktop. You can then drag the scrap into another document.

OLE technology is intrinsic to Windows XP. Although you may have never created a compound document before, and therefore assumed you have never worked with OLE technology before, the desktop is a compound document. Also, everyone has used drag and drop, an OLE technology.

Using the OLE Properties of the Taskbar

Like every other type of object, the taskbar is an OLE object. In Tutorial 3, you dragged a desktop shortcut and dropped it on the Start button. That OLE operation added the desktop shortcut to the Start menu. Likewise, you can create associations with taskbar buttons for open windows by using drag and drop. For example, if you drag a folder or file and hold it above the taskbar button for a minimized window, the OLE interaction causes Windows XP to open the folder window so that you can drop the object in the window. This OLE feature is an example of another power user feature that simplifies the process of copying and moving folders and files.

Rosemarie just returned from a business trip. While she was away, she worked with the original designs of the company logo for the upcoming annual report. Now, she wants you to copy these files from her laptop computer to her desktop PC using a floppy disk.

First, you create a new folder on Rosemarie's desktop computer so that you can copy the files with the logo designs from a floppy disk to that folder.

To complete this part of the tutorial, you need your copy of Data Disk #3.

To copy files to a new folder using the taskbar OLE properties:

1. Open My Documents, maximize the folder window, click **Make a new folder** on the File and Folder Tasks dynamic menu, type **Logo Designs** for the new folder name, press the **Enter** key to assign the new name to the folder, and then press the **Enter** key again to open the folder. You can now copy the files with the logo designs from your disk to this new folder.

2. Minimize the Logo Designs folder window.

3. Open My Computer, maximize My Computer, open a window onto your 3½ Floppy (A:) drive (or other drive) with the Data Disk #3 files, click the **Visual Arts** folder icon, and then click the **Designs** folder icon. You can copy both files at the same time.

4. Click **Edit** on the menu bar, and then click **Select All**.

5. Drag one of the file icons to the **Logo Designs** taskbar button and hold the file icons over the taskbar button, *but do not release the left mouse button*. As a result of the OLE interaction, Windows XP opens the Logo Designs folder window.

6. While still holding the mouse button, drag the file icons into the Logo Designs window, as shown in Figure 5-41, and then release the left mouse button. Windows XP copies the files to the Logo Designs folder.

   POWER USER TIP If you want to move a set of files from one drive to another, hold down the Shift key while you drag the files

Figure 5-41	USING THE OLE PROPERTIES OF THE TASKBAR

Windows XP opens the Logo Designs folder using OLE interaction

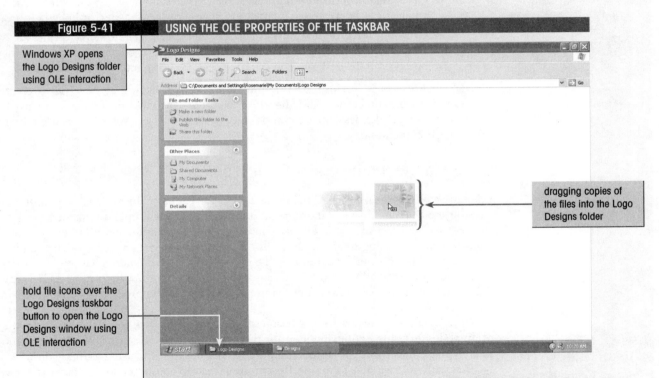

dragging copies of the files into the Logo Designs folder

hold file icons over the Logo Designs taskbar button to open the Logo Designs window using OLE interaction

7. Close the Logo Designs folder window, and then close the Designs folder window.

If you perform this same operation using two folders on the same drive, Windows XP moves your document files rather than copies them. Usually this is what you want, so that you do not end up with multiple copies of the same document files in different folders.

POWER USER TIP If you want to copy files from one folder to another on the same drive, hold down the Ctrl key as you drag the files.

REFERENCE **WINDOW**   **RW**

<u>Copying Files Using the OLE Properties of the Taskbar</u>

- Create or open the folder to which you want to copy or move files (the destination folder), and then minimize the folder window.
- Open a window onto the folder that contains the file(s) that you want to copy or move (the source folder).
- Select and drag the file or files to the taskbar button for the destination folder, and then hold the file or files over the taskbar button until Windows XP opens the folder window. If you want to copy rather than move files from one folder to another on the same drive, press and hold the Ctrl key. If you want to move rather than copy files from one drive to another drive, press and hold the Shift key.
- After Windows XP opens the folder window, drag the file(s) into the window, release the left mouse button, and then release the Ctrl or Shift Key, if necessary.
- Close the folder windows.

Rosemarie wants you to create another memo to the staff members who will be working on the annual report asking them for ideas about adapting a variation of the original design of the new company logo for use in the annual report.

To use the OLE properties of the taskbar to open an application window:

1. Open **WordPad**, choose Arial 14-point font (or one of your own choosing), and then enter the text shown in Figure 5-42. As before, use your name instead of Rosemarie Trevino's, use the current date, and add three blank lines at the end of the memo.

Figure 5-42   CREATING A MEMO TO THE ANNUAL REPORT STAFF

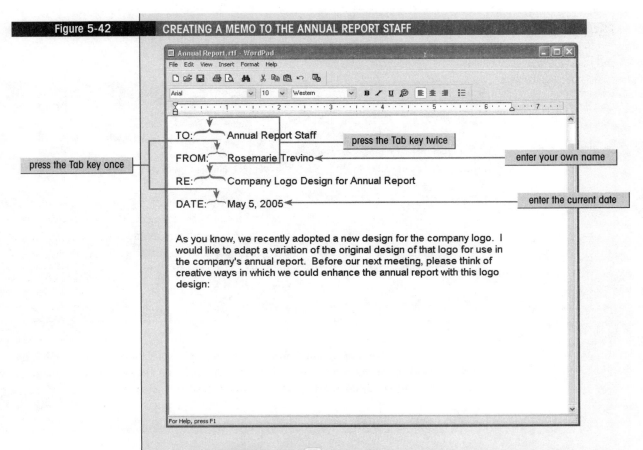

2. Click the **Save** button 🖫 on the Toolbar, and when the Save As dialog box opens, open the My Documents folder (if necessary), click the **Create New Folder** button 📄, type **Memos,** press the **Enter** key, press the **Enter** key again to open the Memos folder, type **Annual Report** in the File name box, and then click the **Save** button.

3. Minimize the WordPad window (*do not close it*).

4. Open My Documents, and then open the **Logo Designs** folder.

5. Drag the **Logo Design #2** file icon and hold it over the **Annual Report.rtf - WordPad** taskbar button, *but do not release the left mouse button*. As a result of the OLE interaction, Windows XP opens the WordPad application window.

   TROUBLE? If you accidentally hold the mouse pointer over the wrong application button, you open that application. Just move your mouse pointer to the correct taskbar button to open the application you want to use. You can close the other application later.

6. While still holding the mouse button, drag the file icon into the WordPad window and drop the file after the end of the first paragraph. Windows XP inserts the contents of the file as an embedded object in the memo. See Figure 5-43.

Figure 5-43   USING OLE PROPERTIES OF THE TASKBAR

Windows XP opens the WordPad window using OLE interaction

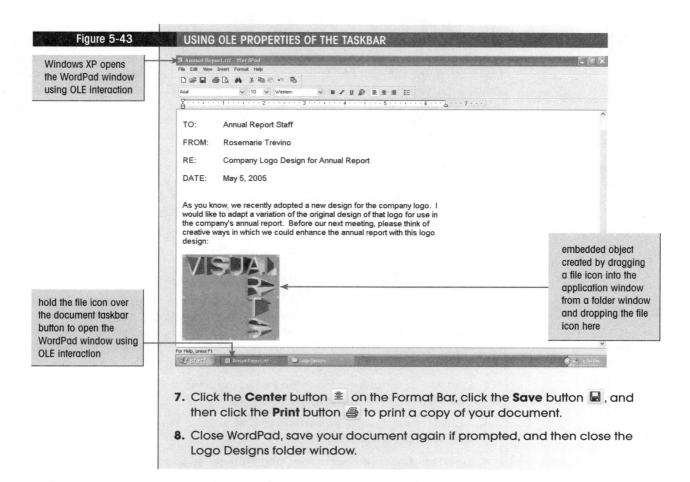

embedded object created by dragging a file icon into the application window from a folder window and dropping the file icon here

hold the file icon over the document taskbar button to open the WordPad window using OLE interaction

7. Click the **Center** button ≣ on the Format Bar, click the **Save** button 🖫 , and then click the **Print** button 🖨 to print a copy of your document.

8. Close WordPad, save your document again if prompted, and then close the Logo Designs folder window.

As noted earlier, when you drag and drop an object from one window to another, Windows XP creates an embedded object.

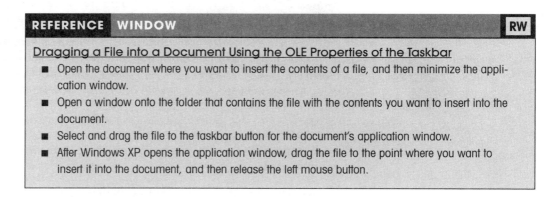

REFERENCE WINDOW   **RW**

Dragging a File into a Document Using the OLE Properties of the Taskbar
- Open the document where you want to insert the contents of a file, and then minimize the application window.
- Open a window onto the folder that contains the file with the contents you want to insert into the document.
- Select and drag the file to the taskbar button for the document's application window.
- After Windows XP opens the application window, drag the file to the point where you want to insert it into the document, and then release the left mouse button.

By using the OLE properties of the taskbar, you can drag and drop objects between two folder windows with only one window maximized at a time. You can also use this feature to drag a file into an application window and embed its contents into a document. Although the two types of operations appear different, they are in essence the same, and they depend on the OLE technology built into Windows XP.

Using Link Tracing

As you know, when you create a shortcut to an object, Windows XP stores the full path to that object in the shortcut file. If you change the name of the object to which the shortcut points, or if you move the object, the shortcut still works. In each case, Windows XP updates the full path so that the shortcut still points to the same object. It uses the object's name, type, and modification date and time to locate the object. This is called **link tracing**, and not surprisingly, it depends on OLE technology to work.

Rosemarie asks an intern at Visual Arts to make changes to the logo designs stored on her computer while she concentrates on another important project with a tight deadline. Because the intern is busy with another project, Rosemarie asks you to create a new folder for the intern to use. Once you copy her files with the logo designs to that folder, you can create a shortcut to the folder so that the intern can go directly to the files.

To create a new copy of the Logo Designs folder:

1. Open My Documents, and then change the name of the Logo Designs folder to **Annual Report** using the **F2** (Rename) key.

2. Point to and select the **Annual Report** folder, if necessary, click **Move this folder** on the File and Folder Tasks dynamic menu, and in the Move Items dialog box, click **Local Disk (C:)** or the name assigned to drive C, and then click the **Move** button.

3. Click **My Computer** on the Other Places dynamic menu, and then click **Local Disk (C:)** or the name assigned to drive C.

4. Right-click the **Annual Report** folder icon, point to **Send To**, and then click **Desktop (create shortcut)**.

5. Open the **Annual Report** folder, and then delete **Logo Design #1.bmp**.

6. Right-click **Logo Design #2.bmp** file icon, point to **Send To**, click **Desktop (create shortcut)**, and then close the Annual Report folder window.

7. Change the name for the "Shortcut to Annual Report" desktop shortcut to **Annual Report**, and then change the name of the "Shortcut to Logo Design #2.bmp" shortcut to **Logo Design** using the **F2** (Rename) key.

8. Right-click the **Logo Design** shortcut, and then click **Properties** on the shortcut menu. On the Shortcut property sheet, Windows XP shows the full path to the target file: "C:\Annual Report\Logo Design #2.bmp". See Figure 5-44.

Figure 5-44 ┃ **VIEWING THE FULL PATH FOR THE DESKTOP SHORTCUT**

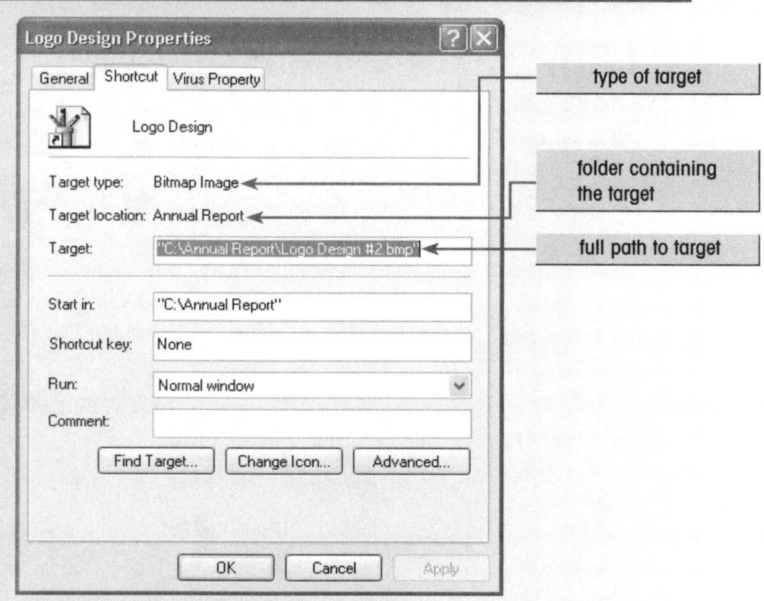

type of target

folder containing the target

full path to target

9. Close the Logo Design Properties dialog box, and then click the **Logo Design** shortcut. Windows XP opens the file that contains the second logo design in Windows Picture and Fax Viewer. The shortcut works; in other words, it finds its target.

TROUBLE? If Windows XP opens the file in another application, that's okay. The point is that the shortcut works.

10. Close the Windows Picture and Fax Viewer window.

Next, you decide that it might be a good idea to change the name of the file so that Rosemarie knows that this file is the one to use for the annual report.

To rename the target file:

1. Click the **Annual Report** shortcut, and then change the name of the Logo Design #2.bmp file to **Annual Report Logo.bmp** by using the **F2** (Rename) key.

2. Close the Annual Report folder window, and then click the **Logo Design** shortcut. Windows XP opens the Annual Report Logo.bmp file (see the filename on the title bar)—not the Logo Design #2.bmp file. See Figure 5-45. Even though you changed the name of the file, Windows XP found the file in a fraction of a second.

Figure 5-45   USING LINK TRACING TO LOCATE A RENAMED FILE

Windows XP found the file using the shortcut even though the file was renamed

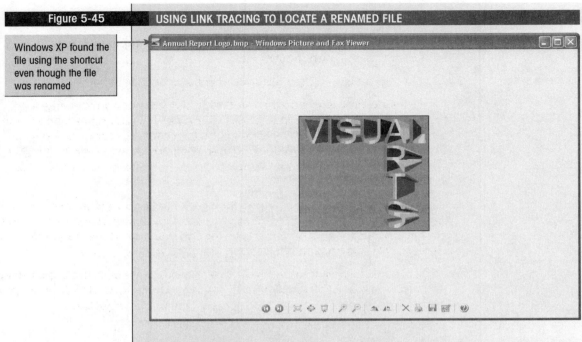

3. Close the Windows Picture and Fax Viewer window, right-click the **Logo Design** shortcut, and then click **Properties**. On the Shortcut property sheet, Windows XP shows the full path to the target file: "C:\Annual Report\Annual Report Logo.bmp". See Figure 5-46. Windows XP updated the path for the shortcut's target.

Figure 5-46   VIEWING THE UPDATED PATH FOR A SHORTCUT

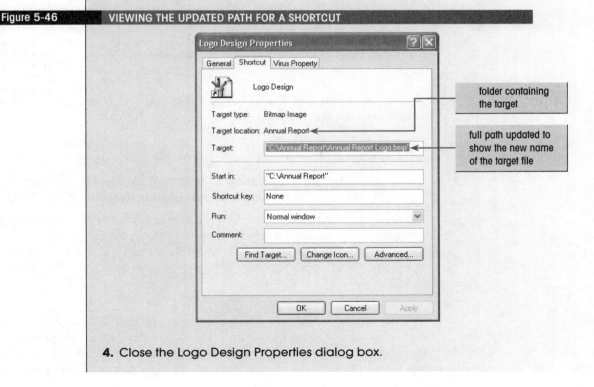

4. Close the Logo Design Properties dialog box.

You decide to move the file with the logo design for the annual report to another folder, so that Rosemarie's intern can use that folder instead to work on this file and other files.

To find a file with link tracing:

1. Click the **Annual Report** shortcut, right-click **Annual Report Logo.bmp**, and then click **Cut** on the shortcut menu.

2. Click the **Up** button 📂 on the Standard Buttons toolbar.

3. Click **Make a new folder** on the File and Folder Tasks dynamic menu, type **Logos** for the new folder name, press the **Enter** key to assign the name to the new folder, press the **Enter** key to open the Logos folder, right-click the white background of the Logos folder, and then click **Paste** on the shortcut menu. Windows XP moves the Annual Report Logo file from the Annual Report folder to the Logos folder.

4. Close the Logos folder window, and then click the **Logo Design** shortcut. Windows XP may briefly display a Missing Shortcut dialog box, and then open the Annual Report Logo.bmp file. Even though you moved the file, Windows XP found the file in a fraction of a second using link tracing.

5. Close the Windows Picture and Fax Viewer window, right-click the **Logo Design** shortcut, and then click **Properties** on the shortcut menu. On the Shortcut property sheet, Windows XP shows the updated path to the target file: "C:\Logos\Annual Report Logo.bmp". See Figure 5-47.

Figure 5-47   VIEWING THE UPDATED PATH FOR A SHORTCUT

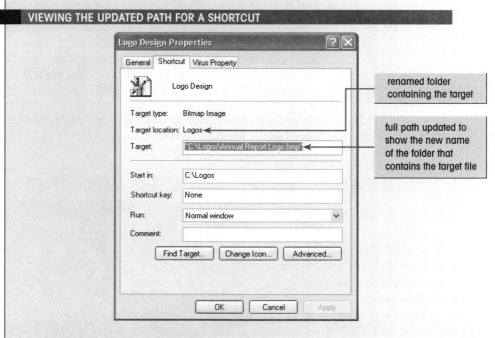

6. Close the Logo Design Properties dialog box.

If you delete the object to which a shortcut points, Windows XP searches your entire computer in a few seconds and finds the object that is the closest match to the object you deleted. It then asks you if you want to update the path for the shortcut to the new object. You can cancel the operation or, if you prefer, you can associate the shortcut with the object Windows XP found.

To find the closest match to an object using link tracing:

1. Open the Logos folder.

2. Right-click the **Annual Report Logo.bmp** file icon, and then click **Cut** on the shortcut menu.

3. Close the Logos folder window, click the **Annual Report** desktop shortcut, right-click the white background of the Annual Report folder window, and then click **Paste** on the shortcut menu. Windows XP moves the file back to the Annual Report folder.

   TROUBLE? If Windows XP switches to Filmstrip view, right-click the white background of the Filmstrip at the bottom of the Annual Report folder window, and then click Paste on the shortcut menu.

4. Right-click the **Annual Report Logo.bmp** file icon, click **Copy** on the shortcut menu, right-click the white background of the folder window, and then click **Paste** on the shortcut menu. Windows XP makes a copy of the Annual Report Logo.bmp file.

5. Point to the **Annual Report Logo.bmp** until Windows XP selects the file, press the **Delete** key, and then click the **Yes** button to confirm the file deletion.

6. Change the name of the Copy of Annual Report Logo.bmp to **Original Logo.bmp** using the **F2** (Rename) key.

7. Close the Annual Report folder window, click the **Logo Design** shortcut, and then wait. Windows XP displays a Missing Shortcut dialog box as it looks for the missing object. See Figure 5-48. Then it displays a Problem with Shortcut dialog box and informs you that the item "Annual Report Logo.bmp" that the shortcut points to has been changed or moved. The nearest match, based on size, date, and type is Original Logo.bmp in the Annual Report folder. Finally, it asks you if you want the shortcut to point to this item. See Figure 5-49. You have just seen link tracing in action.

| Figure 5-48 | USING LINK TRACING TO FIND THE TARGET OF THE SHORTCUT |

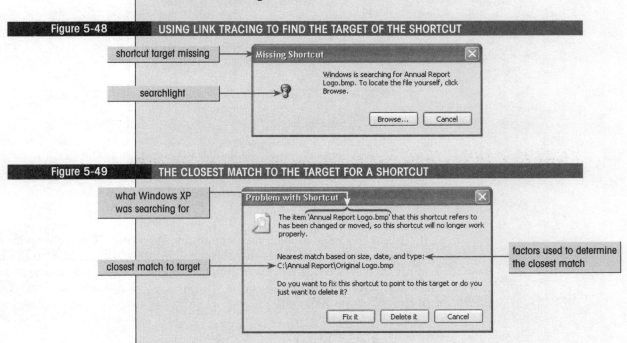

| Figure 5-49 | THE CLOSEST MATCH TO THE TARGET FOR A SHORTCUT |

8. Click the **Fix It** button to repair the problem with the Logo Design shortcut. Windows XP opens the Original Logo.bmp file, as shown in the title bar of the Windows Picture and Fax Viewer window.

9. Close the Windows Picture and Fax Viewer window, right-click the **Logo Design** shortcut, and then click **Properties** on the shortcut menu. On the Shortcut property sheet, Windows XP shows the updated path to the target file: "C:\Annual Report\Original Logo.bmp". See Figure 5-50.

Figure 5-50	VIEWING THE UPDATED PATH FOR A SHORTCUT

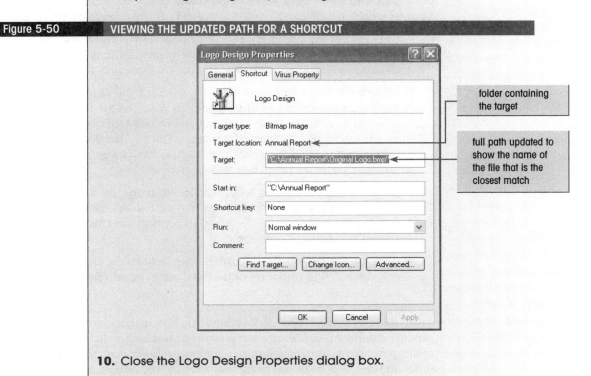

folder containing the target

full path updated to show the name of the file that is the closest match

10. Close the Logo Design Properties dialog box.

Each change that you made to the shortcut's target made it more difficult for Windows XP to locate the object; however, with link tracing, Windows XP was able to find the object in every instance. As you can see, the use of OLE technology increases the power and flexibility of shortcuts on your computer.

Restoring **Your Computer's Settings**

If you are working in a computer lab, or if you want to restore your desktop computer to the settings that existed prior to working on this tutorial, complete the following steps to remove folders, files, and shortcuts.

To remove folders, files, and shortcuts:

1. Open My Documents (or the drive you used), and then delete the **Annual Report**, **Logos**, and **Memos** folders.

2. Drag the **WordPad**, **Annual Report**, and **Logo Design** desktop shortcuts to the Recycle Bin.

3. If permitted by your lab use policy, empty the Recycle Bin.

You also need to restore your computer's settings.

To restore your computer's display settings:

1. If your computer was originally set for the Windows Classic style, right-click the **desktop**, click **Properties** on the shortcut menu, and after Windows XP opens the Display Properties dialog box, click the **Theme** list arrow on the Themes property sheet, click **Windows Classic**, and then click the **OK** button.

2. To switch to the Windows Classic Start menu style, right-click the **Start** button, click **Properties** on the shortcut menu, and after Windows XP opens the Taskbar and Start Menu Properties dialog box, click the **Classic Start menu** option button on the Start Menu property sheet, and then click the **OK** button.

3. To change Windows classic folders view, click the **Start** button, point to **Settings**, click **Control Panel**, and after Windows XP opens a Control Panel window, click **Tools** on the menu bar, click **Folder Options**, and after Windows XP opens the Folder Options dialog box, click the **Use Windows classic folders** option button, and then click the **Double-click to open an item** option button under "Click items as follows."

4. Click the **View** tab in the Folder Options dialog box. If necessary, restore the original settings for the "Display the full path in the address bar" check box, the "Do not show hidden files and folders" option, and the "Hide file extensions for known file types" check box.

5. Click the **OK** button to close the Folder Options dialog box and restore your original settings, and then close the Control Panel folder window.

By using Windows XP's OLE technology, Rosemarie and her staff can quickly and easily produce compound documents that contain embedded and linked objects derived from documents produced by other applications. They can also take advantage of the OLE properties of different types of objects, including shortcuts and the taskbar, to work more efficiently.

REVIEW ASSIGNMENTS

Rosemarie just hired a new person to work with her and the other graphic artists at Visual Arts. Although she plans to give him a tour and introduce him to other staff personally, she realizes that she might not be able to introduce him to everyone. So she wants you to prepare a short memo to send to all staff and announce his hiring. Since the company's new letterhead has not yet arrived, she advises you to use OLE technology to insert the new company logo in the memo.

To complete this Review Assignment, you need your copy of Data Disk #3. Because files with embedded objects take up storage space on disk, you need to copy these files to a disk with more storage capacity than is available on a floppy disk.

As you complete each step in these Review Assignments, record your answers to questions so that you can submit them to your instructor. Use a word-processing application such as Word or WordPad to prepare and then print your answers to these questions. Also, if you change any settings on the computer you are using, note the original settings so that you can restore them later.

1. Copy the Visual Arts folder from your copy of Data Disk #3 to either the My Documents folder or to drive C (or drive D).

2. Open the Visual Arts folder, open the Designs folder, and then view properties of the Logo Design #2.bmp file. What is the size of this file (in KB and bytes)? Close the Logo Design #2.bmp Properties dialog box and the Designs folder.

3. Open WordPad and change the page layout settings so that the top margin is 1.5 inches and all the other margins are 1 inch.

4. On the View menu, select Options, and in the Options dialog box, select the Rich Text tab. If necessary, under Word Wrap, select the Wrap to ruler option button, and then click the OK button.

5. Embed a copy of the Logo Design #2.bmp file in the WordPad document. View properties of the embedded object. What type of object is the embedded object? What is the size of the embedded object? What is the location of the embedded object? Close the Bitmap Image Properties dialog box.

6. While the embedded object is still selected, use the Align Right button on the Format bar to right-justify the embedded object.

7. Deselect the object by clicking to the right of the embedded object, press the Enter key, click the Align Left button, and then press the Enter key four more times to insert four more blank lines.

8. Change the font to Arial (or one of your own choosing), and change the point size to 14 (or a size close to 14). Use a legible font, and do not use a font size below 12, because the smaller sizes are more difficult to read.

9. Enter the text shown in Figure 5-51. Use your own name rather than Rosemarie Trevino's, and use the current date.

Figure 5-51

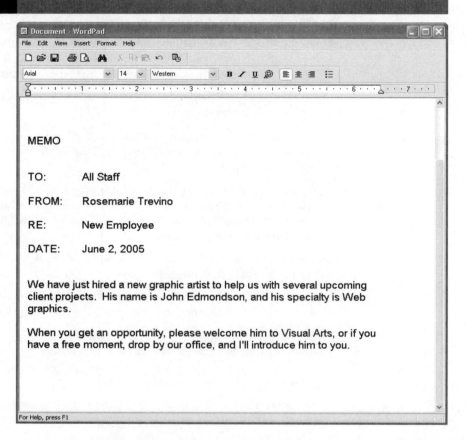

10. Save your document under the filename "New Employee" (without the quotation marks) in a folder named Memos under the Visual Arts folder on your hard disk.

11. Use visual editing to change the background color of the embedded object to a color of your choosing, and make any other changes you want, and then return to WordPad.

12. View properties of the embedded object again. Did any of the properties, such as the size, change after you edited the object? What is the location of the object?

    Note: To view the entire path, click the path, and press the End key.

13. Save your changes, and then print the memo.

14. Create scrap on the desktop from the embedded object.

15. Choose the option to start a new Rich Text Document, and then minimize the WordPad window.

16. Open the scrap object and check the title bar. What type of object is stored in scrap? Close the Paint window.

17. View properties of the scrap. What type of object is this file? Where is this object stored? What is the size of the object? Close the Scrap Properties dialog box.

18. Drag the scrap to the WordPad taskbar button and, after Windows XP opens the WordPad window, drop the scrap into the WordPad document, and then right-align the object. View properties of the object in your WordPad document. To what type of object did Windows XP convert the scrap object? How can you tell? What is the size of the object? Where is the object stored? If you wanted to convert this object to another type, what option or options are available? Close the Properties dialog box for this object.

19. Edit the object, and change the background color of the object.

20. Save the document with this logo under the filename "Letterhead Design" (without the quotation marks) in the Memos folder, and then close the document.

21. Create a desktop shortcut to the Memos folder, open the Memos folder, create a desktop shortcut to the Letterhead Design document, and then close the Memos folder.

22. Use the shortcut to open the Letterhead Design document. What application did Windows XP open on your computer? Close that application.

Explore 23. View the shortcut's properties, and then use the Find Target button to open the Memos folder with the Letterhead Design document.

24. Use the File and Folder Tasks dynamic menu or cut and paste to move **Letterhead Design.rtf** file to the My Documents folder. Close the Memos folder window.

25. Click the Letterhead Design shortcut. Was Windows XP able to find this document file after you moved it? If so, with what application does Windows XP open the document? Close that application.

26. View properties of the Letterhead Design shortcut. What is the full path to the file?

27. Open the Memos folder that contains the New Employee.rtf file. What is the size of this file? Minimize the Memos folder window.

28. Open WordPad, and then open the **New Employee.rtf** file.

Explore 29. View the Bitmap Image Properties dialog box for the embedded object, and choose the option to view the object as an icon instead of as editable information. Then close the Properties dialog box for this object. What does Windows XP display for the embedded object?

30. From the File menu, select Save As, and save the file under another name, "New Employee #2" (without the quotation marks).

31. Using your taskbar button, open the Memos folder that contains the New Employee #2.rtf file. What is the size of this file? By what percentage did Windows XP compress the file? Close the Memos folder.

32. Delete the Memos and Letterhead Design shortcuts from the desktop, delete the Scrap object, delete the **Letterhead Design.rtf** file in the My Documents folder, delete the Visual Arts folder under My Documents or on drive C (or drive D), and empty the Recycle Bin.

CASE PROBLEMS

Case 1. Creating a Cover Sheet for a Term Paper at Prescott Community College In addition to his full-time job as an editorial assistant for a local newspaper, James Wright is taking evening classes at his local community college. Currently, he is enrolled in a course where he has to prepare a term paper on different graphics file formats. James asks you to help him create a cover sheet that includes the title of his term paper and a graphics image.

As you complete each step in this case, record your answers to questions so that you can submit them to your instructor. Use a word-processing application such as Word or WordPad to prepare and then print your answers to these questions. Also, if you change any settings on the computer you are using, note the original settings so that you can restore them later.

Explore ▸ 1. On the Start menu, click Search to open the Search Companion, and then choose the option for searching for all files and folders. Click the "More advanced options" link, in the Type of file list box, click "Bitmap Image," in the Look in list box, click drive C, and then start your search. If necessary, choose the option for displaying thumbnails in the Search Results window. Locate a Bitmap Image that is 100-350 KB in size. If you point to and select an image, Windows XP reports the file size, or you can switch to Details view, and sort the files by size. Once you locate a bitmap image that you want to use, right-click the image, choose Copy, and then close the Search Results window. Open the My Documents window, create a folder named "Term Paper", open this folder, and then paste the bitmap image into the Term Paper folder.

2. On the shortcut menu for this image, choose the option to open the file with Paint.

3. Open WordPad, use Page Setup on the File menu to set the margins to 1 inch, choose the Arial 24-point font, and type and center the following term paper title: Graphics File Formats.

4. Choose the option for wrapping text to the ruler.

5. Two rows below the title, change the font size to 18-point font, and type the following with your name: Prepared by [Your Name]

6. Switch to the Paint window, click Select All from the Edit menu (or use Ctrl+A), click Copy from the Edit menu, and then switch back to the WordPad window.

Explore ▸ 7. Position the insertion point five rows below the subtitle, and then click Paste Special on the Edit menu. What options are available for pasting the bitmap image into the WordPad file? Select each of the options for pasting the image, and then examine the Result area in the Paste Special dialog box. Describe what each option does.

8. Paste the object into your document as a Bitmap Image, and view the properties of the object. *Note*: If the object extends beyond the right margin, point to a corner selection handle and reduce the size of the object in the same way you size a window. What is the object's size? Where is the bitmap image currently stored? Close the Bitmap Images Properties dialog box.

9. Double-click the embedded object. What happens, and what options are available to you?

10. Close the visual editing window.

11. Press the Delete key to delete the selected object from the WordPad document.

Explore ▸ 12. Using Paste Special again, paste the object as a Picture (Metafile). What is the size of this object? Can you edit this object by double-clicking it? Explain.

Explore ▸ 13. Delete the object, and paste the object as a Picture (Device Independent Bitmap). What is the size of this object? Can you edit this object by double-clicking it? Explain.

14. Save your memo under the name "Cover Sheet" (without the quotation marks) in the Term Paper folder, and then print a copy of your final memo. Close WordPad and Paint, and then delete the Term Paper folder.

15. What are the advantages or disadvantages of each of these different object formats?

16. What two other options do you have if you want to keep the document size smaller?

Case 2. Creating a Break-Even Analysis Memo at Stroud Investment Group Stroud Investment Group provides a broad range of investment services for its clients, and it also provides venture capital for new businesses. Recently, the president of International Enterprises, Inc. approached the Stroud Investment Group for venture capital for a new product line. The president of Stroud Investment Group asks you to prepare a break-even analysis for this new product line, and then summarize the results in a memo.

To complete this case problem, you need a copy of Data Disk #1. You also need to use Microsoft Word and Microsoft Excel to prepare the final memo.

1. Create a folder named "Stroud Investment Group" (without the quotation marks) in the My Documents folder or on one of the drives on your computer.

2. Using Data Disk #1, open the Company Projections folder, copy the **Break-Even Analysis.xls** file to the Stroud Investment Group folder, and then close the Company Projections folder.

3. Open Microsoft Word, use Page Setup on the File menu to change the margin settings to one inch, select the Arial 14-point font, create the memo shown in Figure 5-52, and then save it under the name "Break-Even Analysis Memo" (without the quotation marks) in the Stroud Investment Group folder.

Figure 5-52

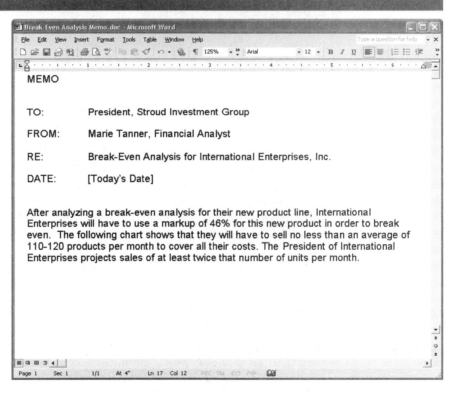

4. Open Microsoft Excel, open **Break-Even Analysis.xls** in the Stroud Investment Group folder, and then click the XY Chart #2 tab at the bottom of the Microsoft Excel window.

5. Tile the Microsoft Word and Microsoft Excel windows vertically.

6. In the Microsoft Excel window, click the white background of the Break-Even Analysis XY chart, and then copy the chart to the Windows Clipboard.

7. Switch to the Microsoft Word window, position the insertion point two or three lines below the paragraph in the memo, use Paste Special to paste a copy of the XY chart into the Word document as a Picture (Enhanced Metafile), save your work, and then close the Microsoft Excel window.

Explore   8. Double-click the XY chart in the memo. What happens? Judging from the title on the title bar of the dialog box that Word opened and the types of property sheets in this dialog box, what types of changes can you make to this object in Microsoft Word? Can you edit this object using Microsoft Excel? If so, how would you do it? If not, why not? Close the dialog box.

Explore   9. What are the advantages and disadvantages of pasting the XY chart in the memo as a Picture (Enhanced Metafile)?

10. Save the memo, close the Microsoft Word window, and then open the Stroud Investment Group folder. What is the size of the Microsoft Excel file (Break-Even Analysis.xls) with the XY chart? What is the size of the Microsoft Word file (Break-Even Analysis Memo)? After comparing these two file sizes, what would you conclude about the amount of space required to store the XY chart in the Microsoft Word memo as a Picture (Enhanced Metafile)?

11. Print a copy of your final memo, and then restore your computer by removing the Stroud Investment Group folder.

12. What ways might you use this type of OLE technology in the types of documents that you produce?

Case 3. Evaluating OLE Object Format Options at International Enterprises, Inc.
International Enterprises, Inc. sells designer products in markets all around the world. Javier Rojas, Finance Manager at International Enterprises, asks you to prepare a Microsoft Word document that summarizes the company's sales for last year. The document should contain a Microsoft Excel spreadsheet and chart, and Javier wants you to test the different options for pasting the spreadsheet and chart into the Microsoft Word document.

To complete this case problem, you need a copy of the Data Disk #1. You also need to use Microsoft Word and Microsoft Excel to prepare the final document.

As you complete each step in this case, record your answers to questions so that you can submit them to your instructor. Use a word-processing application such as Word or WordPad to prepare and then print your answers to these questions. Also, if you change any settings on the computer you are using, note the original settings so you can restore them later.

1. Create a folder named "International Enterprises" (without the quotation marks) in the My Documents folder or on one of the drives on your computer.

2. Using Data Disk #1, open the Company Projections folder, copy the **2004 Sales Summary.xls** file to the International Enterprises folder, and then close the Company Projections folder.

3. Open Microsoft Word, use Page Setup on the File menu to change the margin settings to one inch, select the Arial 12-point font, create the memo shown in Figure 5-53, and then save it under the name "Sales Summary Memo" (without the quotation marks) in the International Enterprises folder.

Figure 5-53

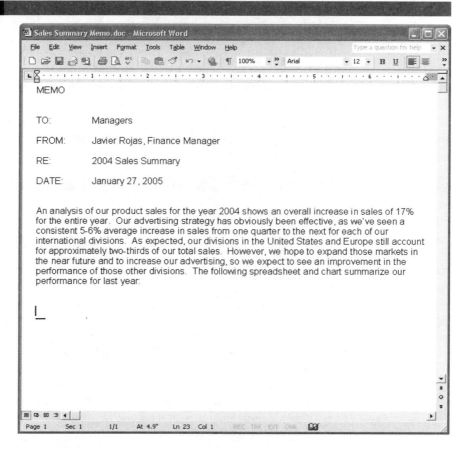

4. Open Microsoft Excel, and then open **2004 Sales Summary.xls** in the International Enterprises folder.

Explore   5. Starting in the upper-left corner of the spreadsheet, on the row containing the title "Sales Summary," drag and select rows 1 through 31, which include the spreadsheet and the 3D column chart.

6. Click Copy on the Edit menu.

Explore   7. Switch to the Microsoft Word window, position the insertion point three lines below the last paragraph in the memo, and then click Paste Special from the Edit menu. What format does Word automatically choose for pasting the object into the Word document? Try that format, and explain what happens. Is this format a useful format? Explain.

Explore   8. Click Undo Paste Special on the Edit menu to reverse your changes, try each of the other formats, and note how that option affects your ability to paste the spreadsheet and chart into the memo. Also note any advantages, or disadvantages to each format. Which formats are the best, and why?

9. Paste the spreadsheet and chart into the memo using the best format you found, save your work, print a copy of the document, and then close the Microsoft Excel window without saving. If a message appears asking you if you want to save the contents of the Clipboard, click the No button. Which format did you use for the final memo? Close the Microsoft Word window.

10. To restore your computer, remove the International Enterprises folder from your computer.

11. What ways might you use this type of OLE technology in the types of documents that you produce?

Case 4. Preparing Training Materials at PC Trainers, Inc. PC Trainers, Inc. specializes in workshops that focus on advanced Windows XP topics. Instructors, lab directors, technical support staff, and other contract trainers sign up for courses from PC Trainers to improve their own technical and job skills. May-Ling Chung, one of the staff trainers, asks you to prepare an overview of Object Linking and Embedding for her, so that she can develop a handout for an upcoming workshop on the use of OLE 2.0 in Windows XP.

1. Use your word-processing application or WordPad to prepare a document similar to the one shown in Figure 5-54. Your document does not have to exactly match that shown in the figure; however, you should organize your information in a table format like the one shown.

Figure 5-54

Object linking and embedding		
		OLE Technology
Under the Object Linking column and the Object Embedding Column, answer the following questions with Yes or No. If you feel the answer to a question may depend on another factor, explain your answer.	Object linking	Object embedding
1. Does Windows XP create a link to the object in the source document using this OLE technology?		
2. Is the object independent of the original object?		
3. If you change the object in the source document, does Windows XP update the object in the destination document?		
4. If you change the object in the destination document, does Windows XP update the object in the source document?		
5. Does this OLE technology support visual editing?		
6. Can you create scrap from an object created with this OLE technology?		
7. Can you create an object from part of the contents of a file using this OLE technology?		
8. Can you use drag and drop to create an object using this OLE technology?		
9. Can you use a simple copy and paste to create an object using this OLE technology?		
10. Can you use Paste Special to create an object using this OLE technology?		

2. In the table that you prepare, include your answer to each of the questions.

3. Preview your document, make any last minute changes to the page layout settings, save the document, and then print a copy of your document.

BACKING UP A HARD DISK

Developing a Backup Strategy at Multimedia Enterprises

CASE

Multimedia Enterprises, Inc.

Multimedia Enterprises, Inc. (MEI) is a large Boston corporation that produces Plug and Play multimedia kits with the latest DVD and CD technology, high-quality sound cards and speakers, multimedia games, and educational software.

Marci Bauman, a contracts specialist for Multimedia Enterprises, Inc., develops new contracts for joint ventures with other companies. Marci and her staff rely on her client records and documents for contract negotiations with current and new clients. When setting up contracts for a new client, Marci adapts copies of contracts prepared for other clients. To ensure that she always has copies of the documents she needs for contract negotiations, Marci periodically creates backups of her files. A **backup** is a copy of one or more files that you keep in reserve in the event of a problem that results in the loss of the original copies of those files. Most people utilize a backup strategy that ensures they have multiple backups of all their document files. If necessary, they can restore all the files, a select group of files, or even a single file from their backups. Because you are new to MEI, Marci offers to explain her backup strategy and show you how to back up a hard disk.

In this tutorial, you learn why it's important to back up files, and how to organize folders and files to simplify backups. You also examine how to integrate incremental and differential backups with full backups, and how to select the appropriate backup media. You look at how backup utilities use the Archive bit to determine which files to back up. You also examine other backup strategies, such as the use of online backups.

The Importance of Backing Up Files

Like many others who depend on their computers for their job, Marci understands the importance of regular backups. She explains to you that several years ago, she accidentally deleted some important client contract files while she was rushing to meet a deadline. Fortunately, she had developed the habit of performing regular backups, and was able to quickly restore the files with the client contracts from her backups so that she and her staff could complete negotiations on the new contract. If she had not had backup copies of those client files, she and her staff would have had to reconstruct all the contract documents from scratch using printed copies of those files.

Common causes for loss of data are:

- User errors, such as accidentally deleting folders and files
- Hardware failure, such as the failure of the hard disk
- Software problems, such as a failed installation of a new software product or a software upgrade
- Damage caused to a computer by a hacker
- Loss of a computer system and even backups from theft or vandalism
- Loss from some type of natural disaster, such as a fire, flood, or earthquake
- Damage caused by a computer virus

Today, hard disks store gigabytes of data, so the potential loss is greater if a problem occurs. Furthermore, if you do not back up your computer, the time required for restoring business documents increases substantially. If you operate a business and do not routinely back up important business and client records, and if a hard disk failure resulted in the loss of all your business and client records, you could easily be out of business.

Even though the reliability of hard disk drives has improved considerably, and the useful lifetime of a hard disk is estimated at five to seven years (depending on the age of the system), they are still susceptible to damage and failure. As noted, restoring the contents of a hard disk from scratch would be a formidable task—one that could cost you a lot of time and money. That's why it's important to regularly back up your hard disk. Think of a backup as an insurance policy that helps you protect your business assets.

Approaches for Backing Up Files

The method you use to back up files on your computer depends on how you work, how much data you store on your hard disk, and how important that data is. Three common approaches used by individuals are as follows:

- **Backing up files stored on a floppy disk**. If you work with a small set of files and prefer to store those files on floppy disks, you can use the Windows XP copy disk feature to back up the floppy disks that you work with daily. When you get ready to make your next backup copy of one of your working disks, you should use a brand new floppy disk rather than copy over your first backup. If this next disk copy fails, you still have your first backup. When you are ready to make the next backup copy of that same working disk, you should again use a brand new disk and keep your first two backups in reserve. After the backup is complete, you have a total of three backups. When you are ready to perform your next backup, you can reuse the disk with the oldest backup. By using this strategy, you always have your two most recent backups in the event a problem arises.

After you make a backup, you should write-protect each disk that contains a backup and keep them in a safe area away from your computer. You might even want to consider keeping a set off site. You could work out an arrangement with friends in which they store your backups and you store their backups. Write-protection serves two purposes. First, you cannot accidentally copy over a disk that has backup copies of your important files. Second, if your computer is infected with a computer virus, that virus cannot infect your backup copy if it is write-protected.

One obvious advantage of working with floppy disks is portability. You can take them with you wherever you go, and work on whatever computer is available to you. However, there are some disadvantages. First, the lifetime of floppy disks is much shorter (on the order of one or two years) than that of a hard disk. Second, since it takes much longer for your computer to access files stored on a floppy disk than a hard disk, you spend more time waiting for disk reads and writes. Third, file sizes are limited to the size of the floppy disk (1.44 MB), a size that is not practical for documents produced with certain applications, such as desktop publishing and graphics software. That's why computer users now rely on removable media, such as writable DVD, CD-R (recordable CDs), CD-RW (rewriteable CDs), and Zip and Jaz disks, for storing copies of their documents. The software for working with each type of these drives also permits you to make a duplicate copy of the disk. For example, you can use your CD burner to copy a CD, or use the Iomega removable disk copy option to make a duplicate copy of a Zip disk. Also, your Iomega software includes its own backup utility, Iomega Backup, with a 1-Step Backup.

■ **Copying files from a hard disk**. If you work with a group of files that are stored in one or more folders on your hard disk, you can use drag and drop or the Send To menu to copy the entire folder with all its files to one or more floppy disks, a removable disk (such as a DVD, CD, or Zip disk), a network drive, or a second hard disk drive. This backup approach is useful if you need to make a quick backup at the end of a busy day before you leave the office. As you learned in Tutorial 3, you can also use the Briefcase utility to simplify the process of updating and synchronizing files stored on your hard disk and removable media. If you are using a floppy disk, remember that you cannot copy a file that is larger than the capacity of the disk; however, you might be able to use a Compressed (zipped) folder to compress it so that it can fit on the disk.

■ **Using a backup utility**. If you work with a large number of files stored in many different folders on your hard disk, your best bet is to use a backup utility to back up those files onto some type of permanent, high-capacity storage medium such as tape or a removable disk. Backup utilities use storage space more efficiently than copying files to a disk, and can also compress files to reduce the amount of media needed for the backup. These utilities also let you back up to a variety of media, including floppy disks, removable disks or tape, network drives, and other hard disk drives. In the case of floppy disks, if you want to back up a file that's larger than the capacity of the disk, the backup utility can split the file over two or more floppy disks. If you need to restore a file or files from a backup that you made with a backup utility, you must use the restore features in the backup utility. You cannot open one of your files directly from the backup set.

You might discover that a combination of these approaches serves your needs best and allows you to conveniently fit backups into your schedule.

Organizing Folders and Files for Backups

Marci explains that when she first started working for Multimedia Enterprises, she discovered that her computer contained client contract files that were stored in many different document folders, including folders that were located below the folders of the application that produced the file. When she was ready to perform her first backup of client files on her hard disk, she was faced with the time-consuming task of trying to locate all the files for the backup. Furthermore, she could not be sure that she had even found all of the files she needed to include in the backup. Rather than run the risk of not backing up important client contract files, she immediately set aside time from her already busy schedule to evaluate the folder structure of her computer's hard disk, and reorganize the files so that backups were not only easier, but also included everything she needed.

Like Marci, if you store all or most of your files on your hard disk and work primarily from that disk, you should pay close attention to how you organize files. You can streamline your backups if files and folders are organized logically. For example, you might want to make sure that your software applications store all your document files in a central location on your hard disk, such as the My Documents folder (many applications today do in fact use that folder as the default folder for files). If you work with many files, you can organize them into subfolders within the My Documents folder. When you are ready to back up the files, all you have to do is select the My Documents folder, and then start the backup. Or you can set up your computer so that the hard disk is divided into two logical drives—a drive C and a drive D, for example—or you might install a second hard disk drive. You could then use drive C just for installed software, and store all your document files on drive D. When you are ready to back up your document files, you open your backup utility, select drive D, and then start the backup.

As an example, suppose you operate your own business and store all your client documents in a folder called Clients. Within that Clients folder, you could create folders for each client. Within each client folder, you could have folders for specific projects, as illustrated in Figure 6-1. When you are ready to back up your client records, you open your backup utility, select the Clients folder, and then start the backup.

Figure 6-1	ORGANIZING DOCUMENT FOLDERS FOR BACKUPS

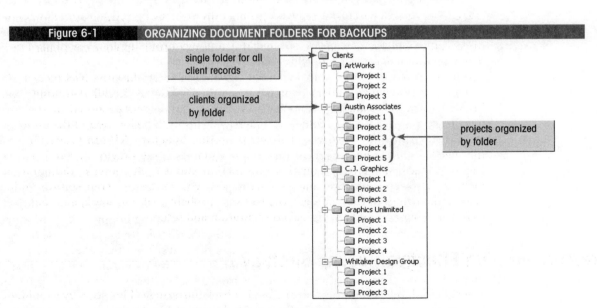

Or you might create a folder called Business, and within that folder, create a folder called Business Records that contains folders for specific types of business information, as shown in Figure 6-2. You could also move your Clients folder with all your client records to that same Business folder. When you are ready to back up all your documents, you simply open your backup utility, select the Business folder, and then start the backup.

Figure 6-2	ORGANIZING BUSINESS AND CLIENT RECORDS FOR BACKUPS

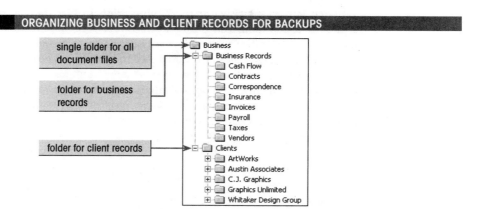

You do not need to back up installed software as frequently as you back up folders that contain your document files. Your document files change more frequently and, if lost, require the most time to reconstruct. If your computer crashes, you can always reinstall software from the original CDs, floppy disks, or software you originally downloaded from Web sites. However, you might want to back up certain installed software, especially if it takes less time to restore it from backups than to reinstall it. Another advantage of this approach is that the backup will contain settings that you specified and changed after originally installing the software. By installing from a backup, you do not have to spend time checking and changing settings so that the software application is set up the way in which you prefer to use it. However, in the case of an office suite such as Microsoft Office, which installs many different files in many different folders, including the Windows folder, it is easier to reinstall it from the original CD.

Before installing software or an upgrade to the operating system, you might want to make a full system backup. A **full system backup** includes everything stored on your hard disk. Your hard disk might be partitioned into only one drive, or it might contain several drives, all of which you want to back up. If you want to back up your entire hard disk, you will need to use tapes and a tape backup drive.

Although reorganizing your document folders can streamline the backup process, you should not reorganize folders containing installed software. Recall that when you first install a software product, it is copied to the folder or folders proposed by the Setup or installation program, or to a folder or folders you specify. The location of the installed software is stored in the Windows XP Registry so that Windows XP can locate the program files needed to start and run a software application. As noted previously, the Windows XP Registry is a database that contains information about a computer's configuration, and includes hardware, software, and user settings. If you reorganize your software folders or change the names of these folders, the software probably will not work, and then you have to restore your computer's original configuration and setup.

Developing **an Effective Backup Strategy**

You should develop and practice an effective backup strategy. This strategy should guarantee that you have copies of all your important document files so that you can restore them at any time. An effective backup strategy also reduces the amount of time, effort, and media required for each backup you perform.

Your backup strategy should always include a full backup at regular intervals, such as every week, month, quarter, or perhaps even every day. This interval of time is called the **backup cycle**, and it begins by backing up your whole system, or an important or major part of your computer, continues with backups of important files at shorter intervals of time within the backup cycle, and then ends with the next full backup. The first backup, a **normal backup** (or **full backup**) marks the start of a backup cycle and might include the entire contents of your hard disk. Or, to save time and effort and reduce the amount of media you need, you might want to limit your full backups to folders that contain just your document files. The length of your backup cycle depends on how important your files are to you, how frequently you change your files, and how heavily you use your computer system. For example, if you use your computer every day, and create and modify many files within a day, you might opt for a weekly or daily backup cycle.

Combining Differential Backups with a Normal Backup

If you perform a normal backup each month, you would perform either a differential or an incremental backup weekly; on the other hand, if you perform a normal backup each week, you would perform a differential or incremental backup every day.

A **differential backup** includes all new and modified files since your last normal or last full backup. Each additional differential backup that you perform within the same backup cycle includes all the files you backed up during previous differential backups. For example, assume you perform a full backup each month. After you perform a normal backup at the beginning of the month, or at the end of the previous month, you might then perform your first differential backup at the end of the first week. This backup would include all files that you created or modified during the first week, since the previous normal backup. Any file that did not change is not included in the differential backup. At the end of the second week, you perform your second differential backup. This backup includes all files that you created or modified during the first *and* second weeks, again since the normal backup. At the end of the third week, you perform your third and last differential backup. This backup will include all files that you created and modified during the first, second, *and* third weeks, again since the normal backup at the start of the backup cycle. At the end of the month, you perform a new normal backup that includes all files, and then you start a new backup cycle with a new set of tapes or disks.

Figure 6-3 illustrates an example of this use of differential backups. Assume you regularly back up two folders on your hard disk: a Clients folder and a Business Records folder. At the beginning of the backup cycle, you back up all your client and business records, including your business portfolios. During the first week, assume you change two of your business portfolios—Portfolio 1.doc and Portfolio 2.doc. When you do your first differential backup, that backup will include these two files. During the second week, assume you change Portfolio 3.doc and Portfolio 4.doc. Your second differential backup includes these two files plus the two you worked on during the first week; in other words, Portfolio 1.doc, Portfolio 2.doc, Portfolio 3.doc, and Portfolio 4.doc. During the third week, assume you change Portfolio 2.doc, create a new portfolio called Portfolio 5.doc, and revise your Portfolio Cover Letter. These three files, plus the others you worked on during the previous two weeks, are backed up when you perform your third differential backup. During the last week of the backup cycle, assume you revise Portfolio 1.doc again. At the end of that fourth week, you start a new backup cycle with a new normal backup that includes all the files in your Client and Business Records folder plus any new or modified files. After the first differential backup, you can think of each new differential backup as a "cumulative backup" because each one includes all files backed up in previous differential backups.

Figure 6-3	COMBINING A NORMAL BACKUP WITH DIFFERENTIAL BACKUPS

	NEW OR MODIFIED FILES	TYPE OF BACKUP	FILES BACKED UP
Beginning of Backup Cycle:		Normal Backup #1	All Folders & Files in Clients Folder
			All Folders & Files in Business Records Folder
By the end of Week 1:	Portfolio 1.doc Portfolio 2.doc	Differential Backup #1	Portfolio 1.doc Portfolio 2.doc
By the end of Week 2:		Differential Backup #2	Portfolio 1.doc Portfolio 2.doc
	Portfolio 3.doc Portfolio 4.doc		Portfolio 3.doc Portfolio 4.doc
By the end of Week 3:	Portfolio 2.doc	Differential Backup #3	Portfolio 1.doc Portfolio 2.doc Portfolio 3.doc Portfolio 4.doc
	Portfolio 5.doc Portfolio Cover Letter.doc		Portfolio 5.doc Portfolio Cover Letter.doc
By the end of Week 4: Start of a New Backup Cycle	Portfolio 1.doc	Normal Backup #2	All Folders & Files in Clients Folder All Folders & Files in Business Records Folder

After the first differential backup, subsequent differential backups take longer because you are backing up more files. Once you complete a differential backup, you do not need to keep the backup media with the previous differential backups in that same backup cycle (unless you want to play it safe). Differential backups are therefore designed to keep only the most recent version of files that you have worked on during the current backup cycle. (However, if you keep each of your differential backup sets, you might be able to find previous versions of some files on a differential backup set.) Another advantage of differential backups is that they are easy to restore. For example, if you need to restore all the files in your Clients and Business Records folders, you first restore all the files from your last normal backup, and then you restore all the files in the last differential backup for that backup cycle.

Combining Incremental Backups with a Normal Backup

Instead of using a differential backup strategy, you can combine a normal backup with incremental backups. An **incremental backup** includes only those files that you created or changed since your previous backup—whether it was a normal backup *or* an incremental backup. Assume that you've just started a new backup cycle, and that you've performed a normal backup. At the end of the first week, you perform your first incremental backup. This backup includes all files that you created or modified during the first week (and would therefore be identical to a differential backup). At the end of the second week, you perform your second incremental backup. This backup includes all files that you created or modified during the second week *only*. This is the point at which an incremental backup differs from a differential backup. Unlike a differential backup, this next incremental backup would not include files that you created or modified and backed up during the first incremental backup. At the end of the third week, you perform your third and last incremental backup. This backup includes all files you created or modified during the third week *only*. It does not include files you created or modified during the first week and the second week. At the end of the month, you perform a new normal backup that includes all files, and start a new backup cycle.

Figure 6-4 illustrates the use of incremental backups. Again, assume you regularly back up two folders on your hard disk—a Clients folder and a Business Records folder. At the beginning of the backup cycle, you back up all files in the Clients and Business Records folders. During the first week, you modify the Portfolio 1.doc and Portfolio 2.doc files. Your first incremental backup at the end of the first week includes those two files. During the second week, you modify Portfolio 3.doc and create Portfolio 4.doc. Your second incremental backup at the end of that week includes *only* Portfolio 3.doc and Portfolio 4.doc. It does not include Portfolio 1.doc and Portfolio 2.doc, which you worked on during the first week; rather, the backups for these files are contained in your first incremental backup. During the third week, you modify the Portfolio Cover Letter.doc and Portfolio 2.doc, and you create Portfolio 5.doc. Your third incremental backup at the end of that week includes *only* those three files. It does not include Portfolio 1.doc, Portfolio 3.doc, and Portfolio 4.doc from the first two weeks. The copy of Portfolio 2.doc in your third incremental backup is a more recent version of the copy of Portfolio 2.doc in your first incremental backup. So, you now have two versions of this file in your incremental backups (allowing you to return to an earlier version of the same file). In contrast, with a differential backup strategy, you would typically have only the most recent version of this file. During the last week of this backup cycle, you revise Portfolio 1.doc. At the end of the fourth week, you start a new backup cycle with a new normal backup that includes all the files in your Client and Business Records folders (including any new or modified files that you worked on during the last week of the backup cycle).

Figure 6-4	COMBINING A NORMAL BACKUP WITH INCREMENTAL BACKUPS		
	NEW OR MODIFIED FILES	**TYPE OF BACKUP**	**FILES BACKED UP**
Beginning of Backup Cycle:		Normal Backup #1	All Folders & Files in Clients Folder All Folders & Files in Business Records Folder
By the end of Week 1:	Portfolio 1.doc Portfolio 2.doc	Incremental Backup #1	Portfolio 1.doc Portfolio 2.doc
By the end of Week 2:	Portfolio 3.doc Portfolio 4.doc	Incremental Backup #2	Portfolio 3.doc Portfolio 4.doc
By the end of Week 3:	Portfolio Cover Letter.doc Portfolio 2.doc Portfolio 5.doc	Incremental Backup #3	Portfolio Cover Letter.doc Portfolio 2.doc Portfolio 5.doc
By the end of Week 4: Start of a New Backup Cycle	Portfolio 1.doc	Normal Backup #2	All Folders & Files in Clients Folder All Folders & Files in Business Records Folder

Incremental backups are faster than differential backups because your backup includes fewer files. Since they do not include files backed up during previous incremental backups, you do not need to use as much backup media. However, unlike a differential backup strategy, you need to keep all your incremental backups. Incremental backups take longer to restore. For example, if you need to restore all the files in your Clients and Business Records folders, you would first restore all the files from your previous normal backup, and then you would restore all the files in each of your incremental backup sets in the order in which you produced them during that backup cycle.

Why do you need to restore all the incremental backups? You might have created a new file during the second week of the backup cycle, and not worked on that file during the remainder of the backup cycle. The only copy of that file is in the second incremental backup. If you restore just the normal backup and the last incremental backup, you will not have that file, because it's not included in either the full or last incremental backups. If you use differential backups, that file would automatically be included in the last differential backup, so you would only need to restore the normal backup and the last differential backup.

Why not then use a differential background strategy rather than an incremental one? If you've worked on a document every day during a backup cycle, each incremental backup has a different version of the file that contains that document. Unlike a differential backup strategy, where you do not typically save previous differential backups, you can restore earlier versions of a file if you use an incremental backup strategy. You just choose the incremental backup that contains the version of the file you want to restore. Also, because incremental backups are faster and require fewer backup media, they are the most common types of backups that people and businesses make.

Windows XP supports two other types of backups—a copy backup and a daily backup. A **copy backup** backs up all the files you select without affecting other types of backups that you create during a backup cycle. For example, if you combine a normal backup with an incremental backup strategy, you can use a copy backup at any point during the backup cycle to back up files that you select. Any new or modified files that were included in the copy backup are also backed up in the next incremental backup. You might use a copy backup to make an extra backup within a backup cycle so that you can store the daily backup off site. A **daily backup** backs up all selected files that have been created or modified the day you perform the daily backup. Like the copy backup, a daily backup does not interfere with an incremental backup strategy. If you've had a particularly busy and productive day, and worked with and modified many files, you could make a daily backup before your next differential or incremental backup. If a problem occurs before your next differential or incremental backup, and you do not have a backup of the files you worked on that day, you would have to reconstruct those files from scratch.

It is a good habit to keep at least three of the most recent backup sets and alternate them. When you start the next backup cycle, you should use a new set of tapes or disks. If you attempt to restore files from your most recent backup, and find that that backup set is defective, then you can turn to the backup set from the previous backup cycle. The next month, you can use the backup tapes or disks that you used three months ago for the next backup cycle. By using this approach, you always have backup sets for at least the two most recent backup cycles held in reserve. Suppose you performed only one normal backup and decide to perform your next normal backup over the previous one. If the backup, drive, or computer fails, you have lost your only backup and you might also have lost everything on your hard disk.

If you are working with tape backups, you should adopt a scheme, such as Grandfather Father Son (GPS), for rotating the tapes. In a **Grandfather Father Son** rotation scheme, you create full backups once a week. Each daily backup is the Son. The last full backup of the week is the Father. Because you reuse the daily tapes after a week, they age only five days. The weekly tapes continue for a month and are reused the next month. The last full backup of the month is the monthly backup—the Grandfather. The Grandfather tapes become the oldest, and you retain them for a year before reusing them again. Rotation schemes like GPS require the fewest tapes for your backup cycle, and more importantly, save wear and tear on the tapes. You can also adapt this type of scheme to other media.

You should not rely on just one backup or even one backup strategy. You might, for example, want to back up important files on your computer to some type of removable storage (such as disk or tape), and also perform the same backup to a network drive or second hard disk drive so that you can restore the same set of files in one of two different ways. As part of your backup process, you should keep a log of what backups you have made—including the date of the backup, the backup utility (and version) you used, what's included in the backups, and where the backups are stored. Also, as noted earlier, it is also a good idea to store one set of backups off site. In fact, some insurance companies require you to store backups off site before they insure your data. Like insurance policies, backups are invaluable when you need them.

Selecting the Appropriate Backup Media

The most common type of media used for backups in businesses is tapes. In contrast, small businesses and individuals prefer removable high-capacity disks, such as DVDs, CDs, Zip disks, Jaz disks, and floppy disks. Floppy disks are inexpensive, and as noted earlier, are useful when you only need to back up a small folder, group of files, or a single file. However, if you want to back up most or all of your hard disk, floppy disks are not a viable backup medium. Not only would you need to purchase and format many floppy disks, you would also have to constantly insert and remove the floppy disks. This approach is time consuming and tedious. Furthermore, if one floppy disk out of 20 or 30 floppy disks in a backup set is bad, you cannot retrieve information from the bad disk and the disks that follow the bad one.

If you need to back up a large amount of data, you might want to purchase a tape drive and use tapes as your backup media. A **tape drive** is a unit in which you insert magnetic tapes that are similar in appearance and use to cassette tapes. Although you do have to purchase and install the tape drive unit, and although tapes are more expensive than most other types of disks, tape drives support large storage capacities—from 40 MB to 2.2 TB (terabytes), and cost the least per megabyte of data. Depending on the size of your hard disk and the storage capacity of the tapes you use in your tape drive, you might be able to store the entire contents of a hard disk on one tape. Tape drives typically come with backup software designed to work optimally with those units and to back up data more efficiently, so you would most likely use that backup utility rather than the Windows XP Backup utility. Businesses commonly rely on tape backup units for backing up hard disks on PCs because they are the most cost effective. It can cost as little as a penny to back up a megabyte of data using a tape backup strategy. Other types of backup media, such as removable disks, while more convenient, are more expensive.

Increasingly, CD-R and CD-RW drives are becoming popular with both businesses and home computer users for backing up data. The CD-R drives allow you to record to the CD only once, whereas the CD-RW drives allow you to record repeatedly to the same CD. You can record and store large quantities of data on CDs (approximately 600-700 MB), and you can quickly back up a large portion of your hard disk with a simple drag and drop operation. CDs are less expensive than other types of removable media such as Zip disks (100 or 250 MB) or Jaz disks (1 GB or 2 GB); however, if you want to archive and store data for longer than six years, you should use higher-quality (and more expensive) CDs that are rated by the manufacturer to have useful lifetimes of up to 100 or 200 years. Like any other type of storage media, the actual lifetime varies with the conditions and environment in which you store the CDs. Another advantage of CDs is that virtually any computer can read them. DVD drives are also a viable option for backups because they have much greater storage capacities (currently ranging from 9.4 or 17 GB).

You can even use a second hard disk drive for backups. Not only does this approach provide one of the fastest methods for backing up and recovering data, but you can also install a very large-capacity drive with gigabytes of storage. The cost of a second hard disk drive is approximately the same as other types of backup options (when you account for the cost of the tape or removable disk drive unit), plus you do not have to continue to purchase backup media. One disadvantage of using a second hard disk drive is that you cannot store that drive off site, and problems such as a computer virus infection might affect all the drives in the computer.

In some instances, you might even choose to back up data to a folder on your hard disk or to a network drive.

Since backup technology, like all other types of technology, is constantly evolving, you should check industry magazines, such as PC World and PC Magazine, to help you figure out the best backup approaches and devices to use. These magazines test and evaluate the performance, reliability, and costs of backup drive units and strategies, and publish information on the latest developments in backup technologies. As you compare backup media, calculate the cost per megabyte of storage space to arrive at a common denominator for evaluating the most cost-effective solution that meets your needs.

Media Maintenance, Care, and Storage

Because you rely on backups in the event of an emergency or disaster, you should take proper care of your backup devices and media. If you are using a tape backup unit, check the manual for that device and follow the instructions for periodically cleaning the media heads and properly maintaining the unit. You might need to clean the unit after every eight hours of use so that the tape unit performs reliably on subsequent backups. Tapes, like every other type of storage technology, have a useful lifetime, and must be replaced.

No matter what type of backup device or media you use, you should protect them from magnetic fields, dust, smoke, humidity, water, solvents, direct sunlight, and extreme temperatures. You might also want to consider other options for protecting backups, such as contracting with businesses that specialize in off-site storage facilities where the environment is carefully regulated and your backups are protected from natural disasters.

Always label your backup tapes or disks with the name of the utility that you used to produce the backup. You should also include that utility's software version number so that you can properly restore files from any backup set that you have made, if necessary (and if Windows XP supports those backup utilities). If your backup set includes two or more backup media, you should label each one with a sequential numbering scheme, such as "1 of n," "2 of n," etc., where n is the total number of backup media.

Understanding **the Importance of the Archive Attribute**

When you start a new backup cycle, you open your backup utility and select the option for performing a normal backup. You then select the drive(s), folder(s), and file(s) you want to include in the backup. If you select a drive, the backup utility includes all the files in all the folders on that drive in the backup. If you instead select only a folder, the backup utility selects all the files in that folder. If that folder has subfolders, the files in those subfolders are also included. When you are ready to perform a differential or an incremental backup, you open the backup utility and select the option for either a differential or an incremental backup. The backup utility then selects all new files as well as all files that you modified.

The obvious question is, "How does the backup utility know which files to select for differential and incremental backups?" When you create or modify a file, Windows XP turns on the Archive attribute for that file, and the Backup utility then uses that attribute to determine what to include in a backup. The Archive attribute is actually a bit that can be turned on or off, and, not surprisingly, it's also called the **Archive bit**. When you perform a normal backup, a backup utility (such as Backup) will back up all the files—whether the Archive bit is on or off. Once all the files are backed up, the backup utility turns off the Archive bit of any file that previously had the Archive bit turned on. The net result is that all the files that are backed up during a normal backup no longer have the Archive bit turned on once the backup is complete.

After the normal backup, if you open a file and change it, Windows XP turns on the Archive bit when you save the file. If you create and save a new file, Windows XP also turns on the Archive bit. If you then perform a differential backup, the backup utility selects all those files that have the Archive bit turned on (they are either new or modified files) and backs them up. The backup utility does not include files that have the Archive bit turned off (they have already been backed up). Unlike a normal backup, the backup utility does not change the Archive bit of the files that it backed up during your first differential backup. See Figure 6-5. When you perform your next differential backup, any newly created or modified files are backed up because their Archive bit is turned on. All previous files backed up in the previous differential backup are also included in the next differential backup because their Archive bits are still turned on. When you perform your next normal backup of those files, the backup utility turns off the Archive bits of all the files. As shown in Figure 6-5, the only time Archive bits are turned off with this backup strategy is when you do a normal backup. Therefore, differential backups do not change the Archive bit.

Figure 6-5	HOW DIFFERENTIAL BACKUPS AFFECT THE ARCHIVE BIT				
	NEW OR MODIFIED FILES	ARCHIVE BIT (BEFORE BACKUP)	TYPE OF BACKUP	FILES BACKED UP	ARCHIVE BIT (AFTER BACKUP)
Beginning of Backup Cycle:			Normal Backup #1	All Folders & Files in Clients Folder	Off
				All Folders & Files in Business Records Folder	Off
By the end of Week 1:	Portfolio 1.doc	On	Differential Backup #1	Portfolio 1.doc	On
	Portfolio 2.doc	On		Portfolio 2.doc	On
By the end of Week 2:			Differential Backup #2	Portfolio 1.doc	On
				Portfolio 2.doc	On
	Portfolio 3.doc			Portfolio 3.doc	On
	Portfolio 4.doc			Portfolio 4.doc	On
By the end of Week 3:	Portfolio 2.doc	On	Differential Backup #3	Portfolio 1.doc	On
				Portfolio 2.doc	On
				Portfolio 3.doc	On
				Portfolio 4.doc	On
	Portfolio 5.doc	On		Portfolio 5.doc	On
	Portfolio Cover Letter.doc	On		Portfolio Cover Letter.doc	On
By the end of Week 4: Start of a New Backup Cycle	Portfolio 1.doc	On	Normal Backup #2	All Folders & Files in Clients Folder	Off
				All Folders & Files in Business Records Folder	Off

What happens to the Archive bit during an incremental backup? As in the previous example, after you perform a normal backup, the Backup utility turns of all Archive bits. If you open a file and change it, Windows XP turns on the Archive bit when you save the file. If you create and save a new file, Windows XP also turns on its Archive bit. If you then perform an incremental backup, the backup utility selects all those files that have the Archive bit turned on and backs them up—just like what happens during a differential backup. However, after an incremental backup, the backup utility turns off the Archive bits of all the files that were backed up. See Figure 6-6. When you perform your next incremental backup, any newly created or modified files are backed up because their Archive bit is turned on. All previous files backed up are not included in the next incremental backup because their Archive bits were turned off. When you perform your next normal backup of all of those files, the backup utility turns off the Archive bits of all the files. As shown in Figure 6-6, Archive bits are turned off with this backup strategy after the normal backup and after each incremental backup.

Figure 6-6	HOW INCREMENTAL BACKUPS AFFECT THE ARCHIVE BIT				
	NEW OR MODIFIED FILES	ARCHIVE BIT (BEFORE BACKUP)	TYPE OF BACKUP	FILES BACKED UP	ARCHIVE BIT (AFTER BACKUP)
Beginning of Backup Cycle:			Normal Backup #1	All Folders & Files in Clients Folder	Off
				All Folders & Files in Business Records Folder	Off
By the end of Week 1:	Portfolio 1.doc	On	Incremental Backup #1	Portfolio 1.doc	Off
	Portfolio 2.doc	On		Portfolio 2.doc	Off
By the end of Week 2:	Portfolio 3.doc	On	Incremental Backup #2	Portfolio 3.doc	Off
	Portfolio 4.doc	On		Portfolio 4.doc	Off
By the end of Week 3:	Portfolio Cover Letter.doc	On	Incremental Backup #3	Portfolio Cover Letter.doc	Off
	Portfolio 2.doc	On		Portfolio 2.doc	Off
	Portfolio 5.doc	On		Portfolio 5.doc	Off
By the end of Week 4:	Portfolio 1.doc	On	Normal Backup #2	All Folders & Files in Clients Folder	Off
Start of a New Backup Cycle				All Folders & Files in Business Records Folder	Off

The copy backup and daily backup do not modify the Archive bit of files selected for the backup.

As you can tell, the Archive bit provides a simple, but powerful, technique for determining the status of a file for backup operations.

Getting Started

To complete this tutorial, you need to switch your computer to Web style, and you also need to turn on the options for showing file extensions and displaying the full path in the Address bar. As you complete these steps, you may discover that your computer is already set up for Web style, or that other settings are already in place, so you might only need to make a few changes to your computer's settings.

To set up your computer:

1. To change to the Windows XP theme, right-click the **desktop**, click **Properties** on the shortcut menu, and after Windows XP opens the Display Properties dialog box, click the **Theme** list arrow on the Themes property sheet, click **Windows XP**, and then click the **OK** button.

2. To switch to the Windows XP Start menu style, right-click the **Start** button, click **Properties** on the shortcut menu, and after Windows XP opens the Taskbar and Start Menu Properties dialog box, click the **Start menu** option button on the Start Menu property sheet, if necessary, and then click the **OK** button.

3. To change to a task-oriented view of folders and enable single-clicking, click the **Start** button, click **My Computer**, click **Tools** on the menu bar, click **Folder Options**, and after Windows XP opens the Folder Options dialog box, click the **Show common tasks in folders** option button if it is not already selected, click the **Single-click to open an item** option button if it is not already selected, and then click the **Underline icon titles only when I point at them** option button if it is not already selected.

4. Click the **View** tab, click the **Display the full path in the address bar** check box if it is not already selected, click the **Show hidden files and folders** option button if it is not already selected, and if there is a check mark in the "Hide extensions for known file types" check box, click that check box to remove the check mark, click the **OK** button to close the Folder Options dialog box, and then close My Computer.

5. Click the **Start** button to close the Start menu, if necessary.

Installing the Backup Utility in the Home Edition

If you are using Windows XP Home Edition, you probably need to install the Backup utility from the ValueAdd folder on your Windows XP CD; it is not installed when you or someone else installs Windows XP. However, since computer manufacturers set up computer systems in different ways, you can check the System Tools menu to determine whether you need to install the Backup utility.

The following steps apply only to users with Windows XP Home Edition installed on their computer.

To install the Backup utility for the Windows XP Home Edition:

1. Open the Start menu, point to **All Programs**, point to **Accessories**, point to **System Tools**, and then pause. If you do not see a Backup option on the System Tools menu, complete the remaining steps in this section. If you see a Backup option on the System Tools menu, Backup is already installed and you can skip the remainder of the steps in this section and continue with the next section entitled "Setting Up the MEI Folder."

2. Insert your Windows XP Home Edition CD into your CD drive. After the Welcome to Microsoft Windows window opens, click the **Perform additional tasks** button.

3. When prompted for what you want to do, click the **Browse the CD** button.

4. Click the **VALUEADD** folder, click the **MSFT** folder, and then click the **NTBACKUP** folder.

5. Click the **NTBACKUP.MSI** file icon, and after the wizard completes the installation of the Backup utility, click the **Finish** button in the Windows Backup Utility Installation dialog box.

6. Close the NTBACKUP window, close the Welcome to Microsoft Windows XP window, and then remove your Windows CD from the CD drive.

Setting Up the MEI Folder

Next, you need to create a new folder named "MEI" (for Multimedia Enterprises, Inc.) under the My Documents folder, or if you prefer, on another drive, such as drive C or D, and then copy the files for Data Disks #1, #2, and #3 to that folder so that you have enough files to do a representative backup with the Windows XP Backup utility. You also need to format at least two floppy disks for the backup.

If possible, set aside time to complete the tutorial in one session, especially if you are working in a computer lab; otherwise, another student might remove the MEI folder as well as your backup settings, or the computer that you used might restore its original settings when it reboots (including removing your backup settings and reports).

The tutorial steps assume you are using the My Documents folder. If you decide to create a folder on another drive, such as drive C or D, then you need to adapt the instructions for the use of that drive.

To set up the MEI folder:

1. Open the **My Documents** folder, and check the folder names to see if you already have a folder named MEI. If you find an MEI folder in the My Documents folder, and if you are working in a computer lab, another student probably stopped in the middle of this tutorial and left the MEI folder on the computer. If this is the case, point to and select the **MEI** folder icon, press the **Delete** key, and then click the **Yes** button to verify that you want to delete the folder and all its contents. If you are working on your own computer and if you have a folder named MEI, you can either rename that folder temporarily for this tutorial or, in the next step, you can create a folder with a different name.

2. On the File and Folder Tasks dynamic menu, click **Make a new folder** and, after Windows XP creates a new folder named New Folder, type **MEI**, press the **Enter** key to assign the name to the folder, and then press the **Enter** key again to open the MEI folder. If you are working on your own computer and already have a folder named MEI that you want to keep, either rename it temporarily or use a different name for the MEI folder (such as MEI Clients), and use that name for the rest of the tutorial steps.

3. From the Start menu, open **My Computer**, and then open a window onto the floppy disk or the network folder that contains the files for Data Disk #1, click the **MEI** taskbar button, right-click the **taskbar**, click **Tile Windows Vertically**, click the **title bar** or **background** of the window with the files for Data Disk #1, press and hold the **Ctrl** key while you point to and select each folder (select only the folders), and then drag the **selected folders** from the floppy drive window to the MEI folder window. Windows XP copies the Business Records, Company Documents, Company Projections, Personal Records, Presentations, and Resources folders to the MEI folder.

4. If you are using a floppy drive, remove your copy of Data Disk #1, insert Data Disk #2, click the **3½ Floppy (A:)** title bar, and then press the **F5** (Refresh) key to update your view onto this window and view the contents of Data Disk #2. If you are using a network drive, change to the folder that contains the files for Data Disk #2.

5. Open the **Delta Oil** folder, click **Edit** on the menu bar, click **Select All**, and then drag the **selected folders** from the floppy drive window to the MEI folder. Windows XP copies the Company Templates, Designs, Memos, Overhead Transparencies, and Training folders to the MEI folder.

6. Click the **3½ Floppy (A:) title bar**, and then click the **Up** button to return to the top-level folder of drive A, or to the network folder that contains the Delta Oil folder.

7. If you are using a floppy drive, remove your copy of Data Disk #2, insert Data Disk #3, and then press the **F5** (Refresh) key. If you are using a network drive, change to the folder that contains the files for Data Disk #3. Drag the **Visual Arts** folder from the floppy drive window to the MEI folder. Windows XP copies the Visual Arts folder and its contents to the MEI folder.

8. Remove the floppy disk from drive A, close the 3½ Floppy (A:) window or the network drive window, maximize the MEI folder window, click **View** on the menu bar, point to **Arrange Icons by**, and then click **Name** (even if it is already selected). The MEI folder should now contain the 12 folders shown in Figure 6-7. Your view might differ.

| Figure 6-7 | VIEWING THE CONTENTS OF THE MEI FOLDER |

9. If the contents of your MEI folder do not match what's shown in Figure 6-7, delete all the folders in the MEI folder, and repeat Steps 3 through 8.

This folder structure that you created using the contents of Data Disks #1, #2, and #3 mimics a folder structure that you might actually find or use on your own computer.

Estimating the Number of Disks for a Backup

Because you are going to back up files to floppy disks, you want to know how many disks you will need before starting the backup. If you back up files to tape, a Zip or Jaz disk, CD-RW disc, a high-capacity floppy disk, or even another folder on the same or a different hard disk, you need to know whether the backup media has the storage capacity to hold all your data.

 POWER USERS TIP To determine the amount of space for the folders and files you want to back up, you can view properties of a group of folders and files.

To check the size of the MEI folder:

1. Click the **Up** button on the Standard Buttons toolbar to change from the MEI folder to the My Documents folder, or to the folder located above the one that contains the MEI folder.

2. Right-click the **MEI folder**, and then click **Properties** on the shortcut menu. Windows XP opens the MEI Properties dialog box, and shows the size and contents of this folder on the General property sheet. See Figure 6-8. You are viewing the properties for 13 folders (including the MEI folder) with 68 files within its subfolders, all of which require 2.23 MB (or 2,343,718 bytes) of storage space. Your property sheets may differ.

   TROUBLE? If your property sheet shows a different number of files or folders, or if the storage capacity of the files is less than 2,343,718 bytes, you missed a set of files when you copied files from Data Disks #1, #2, and #3 to the MEI folder. Delete all the folders within the MEI folder, open the MEI folder, and repeat Steps 3 through 8 in the previous section for setting up the MEI folder.

Figure 6-8	VIEWING THE PROPERTIES OF THE MEI FOLDER

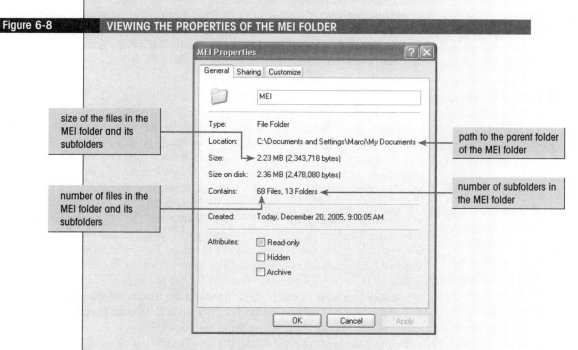

size of the files in the MEI folder and its subfolders

path to the parent folder of the MEI folder

number of files in the MEI folder and its subfolders

number of subfolders in the MEI folder

TROUBLE? If your drive uses NTFS, you do not see an Archive check box; instead, you see an Advanced button.

3. Close the MEI Properties dialog box, and then close the My Documents window.

Because a 3½-inch high-density disk stores 1.44 MB of data, that means you need two floppy disks (2.88 MB) to store the MEI folder and its contents. However, this estimate assumes you would be performing a simple file copy operation. If you use the Windows XP Backup utility, it combines all the files that you back up into one larger file so that disk space is used more efficiently. Recall that each file is allocated a certain number of clusters of storage space on a disk; however, the file may not use all the storage space within the last cluster. When Backup combines all the backup files into one larger file, each file you back up immediately follows another file you backed up, so no space is wasted and there is no slack.

Although Windows XP Backup does not support data compression for floppy disks, you can store even more data on your backup media if you use a utility that supports this feature. **Data compression** refers to the use of one or more techniques by a backup utility to store data so that it takes up less space on the backup media than it does on the hard disk. A backup utility can examine the data contained in each file and, if it finds repetitive patterns within the data, it can encode the data to reduce the overall file size. Certain files, such as bitmap images that contain repetitive colors, can be compressed up to 95% or more. Other files, such as programs, do not compress much. Using data compression, you can double the storage capacity of both Zip and Jaz disks as well as tapes and even floppy disks. Because of the large storage capacity of tapes, the actual cost for backups drops to a few cents or less per megabyte of backed-up data when you use data compression. With data compression, you can typically compress data to at least one half of its original size.

To determine the disk storage space used by the data you need to back up, view the properties of the folder, or the group properties of the folders that you want to back up. To determine the number of removable disks or media needed for the backup, divide the total storage space that these folders and files use by the storage capacity of the media you plan to use. Round up (rather than down) and build into your estimate a small amount of overhead for tracking information about the folders and files included in the backup set. If you are using floppy disks as your backup media, you should format the number of floppy disks that you think you need, and then, to be on the safe side, format one extra floppy disk.

Formatting Disks for a Backup

If you back up files to floppy disks, you should perform a full format of those disks on the computer you are going to use to make the backup.

Preformatted disks are usually formatted with an IBM DOS utility, which may not be compatible with a backup utility. Backup utilities check the boot sector—the first sector on the disk—to determine not only which operating system formatted the disk but also the version of that operating system. If the operating system or its version differs from what the backup utility expects, the backup utility might refuse to use the floppy disks or, worse yet, allow you to make a backup to the floppy disks, but then inform you that the floppy disks are incompatible when you attempt to restore files. By performing a full format of floppy disks, Windows XP writes a new copy of the boot sector to the disks and identifies itself and its version as the operating system that formatted the disks.

You should also do a full format to make sure that the floppy disks you use for a backup do not contain any bad sectors. Floppy disks with bad sectors more than likely will get worse with time, and you do not want to use them for backups. Backups are too important to take risks.

To continue with this tutorial, you need to format three floppy disks so that you can use them for a normal and an incremental backup.

To perform a full format:

1. Insert a new floppy disk in drive A, open **My Computer**, right-click the **3½ Floppy (A:)** drive icon, and then click **Format** on the shortcut menu.

2. In the Format 3½ Floppy (A:) dialog box, verify that the storage capacity in the Capacity list box matches the storage capacity of the disks you are going to use, make sure the Quick Format check box in the Format options section does not contain a check mark, click the **Start** button in the Format 3½ Floppy (A:) dialog box, click the **OK** button in the Format 3½ Floppy (A:) dialog box to format the disk, and after formatting is complete, click the **OK** button in the Formatting 3½ Floppy (A:) dialog box.

3. Repeat this process to format two more floppy disks, close the Format 3½ Floppy (A:) dialog box, and then close My Computer.

In the next section of the tutorial, you use Backup to perform a normal backup of a folder and its contents, restore a folder and its contents, perform an incremental backup, and restore a file from an incremental backup. As you perform these backups, you use the Backup and Restore Wizard and also look at how you select and specify settings for backups and restores. You also monitor the Archive bit before and after an incremental backup. Finally, you examine the use of online backup services.

Using **Backup**

The Backup utility allows you to back up or restore data. You can back up all or part of a hard disk onto some type of permanent storage medium, such as a tape, a local drive (a folder on drive C or drive D), a network drive, a floppy disk, or a removable disk such as a Zip or Jaz disk. You can also restore folders and files from a backup set. A **backup set** consists of one or more storage media for a specific type of backup.

You can use the Backup utility's Backup or Restore Wizard to step you through these backup and restore operations, or you can bypass the wizard and manually specify the settings you want to use for backup and restore operations. The wizard simplifies the backup process—which in turn encourages you to back up more frequently. Whether you use the wizard or select backup options manually, the process is similar.

If you specify settings manually, you can create, name, and save a backup job. That **backup job** contains default settings or settings you modify for a backup, and a list of the files and folders you selected for a specific type of backup. Once you define a backup job, you can use it again when you need to perform the same type of backup. When you open the backup job, Backup selects the specified files. You do not need to select them again.

In the remainder of the tutorial, you use the Backup or Restore Wizard to perform a full backup and restore, and you then perform an incremental backup and partial restore by specifying settings manually.

Marci explains that her backup cycle lasts one week. On Friday afternoon, she performs a normal backup and starts a new backup cycle. On Monday, Tuesday, Wednesday, and Thursday afternoons, she performs incremental backups. She chose incremental backups over differential backups because her clients often want to develop a new contract or proposal using an earlier version she developed with them. As noted earlier, incremental backups make it easier to restore a previous version of a document. Now that it's Friday afternoon, Marci is ready to show you how to perform the normal backup for her next backup cycle.

Marci uses the Backup utility included with Windows XP to make her backups. Backup can handle normal, incremental, differential, copy, and daily backups, so it provides Marci with the flexibility she needs.

Creating a Shortcut to Backup

You can create a desktop shortcut for Backup so that you can quickly access Backup as you perform daily backup and restore operations.

To create a shortcut to Backup:

1. Click the **Start** button, point to **All Programs**, point to **Accessories**, point to **System Tools**, right-click **Backup,** point to **Send To**, and then click **Desktop (create shortcut)**.

2. Click the **Start** button a second time or click the **desktop** to close the Start menu.

REFERENCE WINDOW   **RW**

Creating a Desktop Shortcut from the Start Menu

■ Click the Start button, point to All Programs, then, if necessary, point to the group folder that contains the program for which you want to create a shortcut, right-click the program's shortcut, point to Send To, and then click Desktop (create shortcut).

■ Click the Start button a second time or click the desktop to close the Start menu.

Another advantage of creating a desktop shortcut to Backup, or whatever backup utility you use, is that it serves as a useful reminder of the need to regularly perform backups.

Performing a Normal Backup

You are now ready to perform a normal backup of the MEI folder. The normal backup includes all files within all subfolders in the MEI folder.

After you open the Backup utility, the Backup or Restore Wizard starts by default. The wizard includes an option for switching to Advanced Mode so that you can change the settings of a backup or restore operation. In Advanced Mode, a Backup Utility window provides access to an advanced Backup Wizard, an advanced Restore Wizard, and the Automated System Recovery Wizard (which you examine in Tutorial 8). Your first task is to select the files in the MEI folder that you want to back up.

To select the files you want to back up:

1. Click the **Backup** shortcut on the desktop. Backup displays a Backup Utility dialog box and checks for backup devices, such as a tape device. In the Backup or Restore Wizard window, the Backup utility explains what the wizard does, and provides an Advanced Mode link to use an advanced wizard or to change the settings of a backup or restore operation. See Figure 6-9.

Figure 6-9   WELCOME TO THE BACKUP OR RESTORE WIZARD

what the Backup or Restore Wizard does

link to the Backup Utility window

2. Click the **Next** button. The next Backup or Restore Wizard dialog box asks whether you want to perform a backup or restore. See Figure 6-10.

Figure 6-10   CHOOSING BETWEEN A BACKUP AND A RESTORE

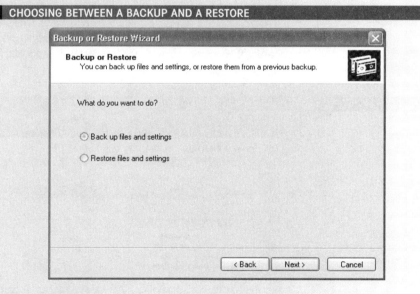

3. Make sure the "Back up files and settings" option is selected, and then click the **Next** button. The wizard now asks you what you want to back up. See Figure 6-11. You can back up your documents and settings, which includes your My Documents, Favorites, Desktop, and Cookies folders; everyone's documents and settings; or everything on your computer, including system settings on a system recovery disk, or you can pick what you want to back up.

Figure 6-11   CHOOSING WHAT TO BACK UP

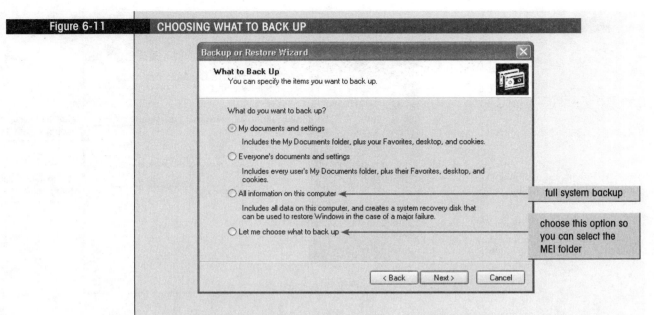

full system backup

choose this option so you can select the MEI folder

4. Click the **Let me choose what to back up** option button, and then click the **Next** button. The wizard now prompts you to select the items you want to back up. See Figure 6-12. As you can tell, the dialog box is similar to a view that you would see after you open Windows Explorer. In the "Items to back up" pane on the left, you select what you want to back up. This view is similar to that provided by the Folders Toolbar. The Contents pane on the right shows you the contents of whatever you select in the "Items to back up" pane. The items in your dialog box might differ.

Figure 6-12   EXPLORER-LIKE VIEW OF COMPUTER'S CONTENTS

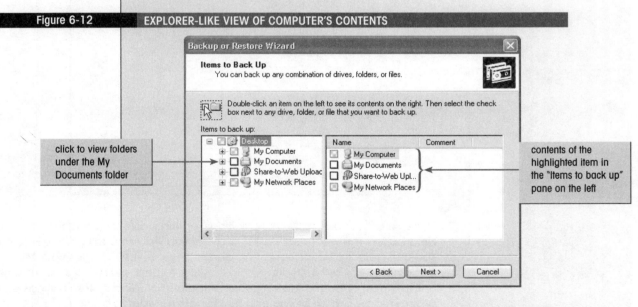

click to view folders under the My Documents folder

contents of the highlighted item in the "Items to back up" pane on the left

5. Click the **expand view** box ⊞ for My Documents (*do not click the empty check box for My Documents*), click the **MEI** folder check box, click ⊞ to the left of the MEI folder, and then use the right scroll arrow ❯ and left scroll arrow ❮ to adjust your view in the "Items to back up" pane. The wizard shows you

the folders below the MEI folder in alphabetical order—similar to the view you would see in Windows Explorer. See Figure 6-13. In the Contents pane, the gray check mark indicates that you selected part of the contents of the My Documents folder, not the entire folder.

| Figure 6-13 | CHOOSING THE MEI FOLDER |

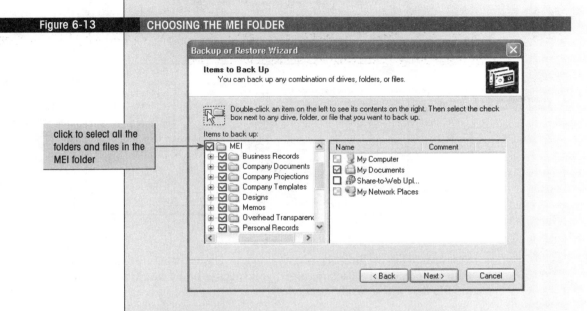

click to select all the folders and files in the MEI folder

If you did not want to back up one or more folders within the MEI folder, then you would click the check box for each folder in the "Items to back up" pane and remove the check mark from the MEI folder check box. Those folders are then not included in the backup.

6. In the "Items to back up" pane, click the **Company Projections** folder icon or folder name (do not click the Company Projections folder check box). The wizard updates the Contents pane to show you the files within the Company Projections folder that it will back up. See Figure 6-14. If you do not want to back up certain files in a folder, you click the check boxes for those files in the Contents pane and remove the check marks. Those files are then not included in the backup.

TROUBLE? If you clicked the Company Projections folder check box, you removed it from the backup selection. Click the Company Projections folder check box again to add a check mark to the check box, and then click the folder icon or folder name for the Company Projections folder.

Figure 6-14 | VIEWING THE FILES SELECTED FOR THE BACKUP

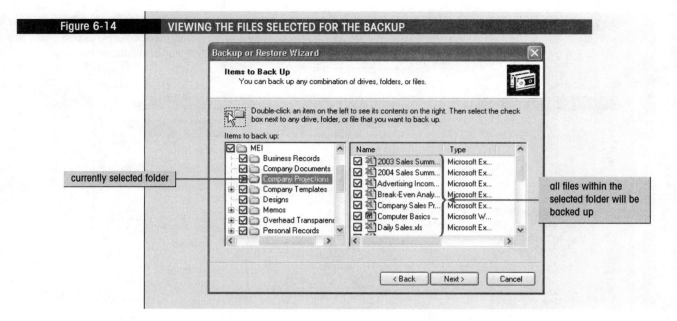

currently selected folder

all files within the selected folder will be backed up

During this preliminary phase, you can choose whatever drives, folders, and files you want to include in a backup. Next, you specify the backup type, destination, and name for the file that will store the backup.

To specify the destination and backup options:

1. Click the **Next** button. The wizard now prompts you for the backup type, destination, and name. See Figure 6-15. Since the computer used for this figure does not have a tape drive, the "Select the backup type" list box is dimmed. Any backup you perform is stored in a file; in other words, you're backing up to a file. You can choose the destination for your backup, or use the Browse button to locate the drive or folder to which you want to back up. If you have never used Backup before, the wizard proposes that the backup be stored in a file named "Backup" on drive A; otherwise, the name shown in the "Type a name for this backup" box is the last name you used for a backup.

Figure 6-15   CHOOSING THE DESTINATION FOR THE BACKUP

no tape drive; will
back up to file on
removable media

enter a descriptive
name for the backup

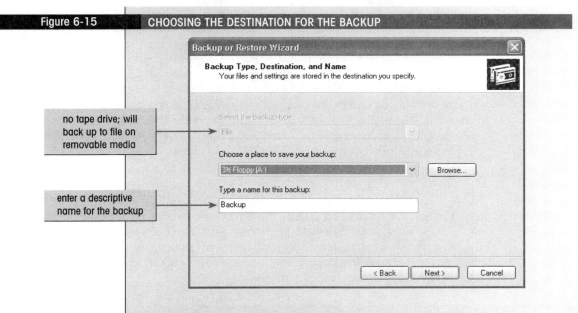

2. Make sure one of the floppy disks you formatted is in drive A.

3. In the "Type a name for this backup" box, type **MEI Normal Backup** (or edit the existing name), and then click the **Next** button. The last Backup or Restore Wizard dialog box summarizes your backup settings. See Figure 6-16. Next to Name, you see the full path to the file that stores the backup, namely, A:\MEI Normal Backup.bkf. Also, you are going to back up a set of selected files and folders to a file using a backup set created at a certain time on a certain date.

Figure 6-16   VIEWING THE BACKUP SETTINGS

backup path and
filename

click to check and
specify other backup
settings

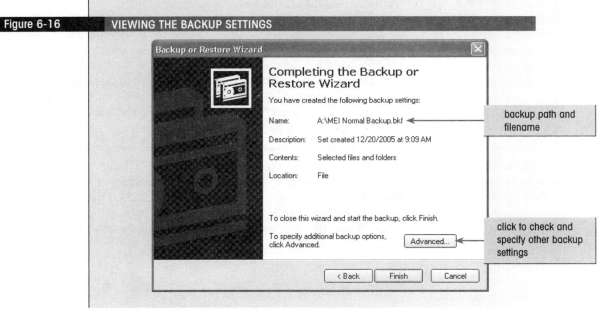

At this point, you can check and, if necessary, specify advanced options that give you greater control over the backup process. For example, you can choose to perform a Normal, Copy, Incremental, Differential, or Daily backup. You can also specify how you want to back up the files. To verify that the data was successfully backed up, Backup can compare the original and the backed up files at the end of the backup. Doing so takes additional time, though it is well worth it. The whole purpose of a backup is to guarantee that you can restore your computer should a problem or disaster occur. For drives that support compression, you can use hardware compression to increase the available storage space on your backup media. You can also disable or create a **volume shadow copy**, which allows Backup to back up files even if they are currently being used.

Another advanced option is to schedule the backup for now or later. If you choose the Later option, you enter your computer name, account name, and password for security, and then schedule the backup, such as for a time when the computer is idle. You can also schedule backups to occur at specific intervals, such as weekly or daily, or both. Windows XP then creates a scheduled task in the Scheduled Tasks folder.

To check and specify advanced backup settings:

1. Click the **Advanced** button. The wizard allows you to choose the type of backup you want. See Figure 6-17. By default, Normal is automatically selected. If necessary, you could use the "Select the type of backup" list box to choose a different backup type. The Description area explains what each option does after you select the option.

Figure 6-17	CHOOSING THE BACKUP TYPE

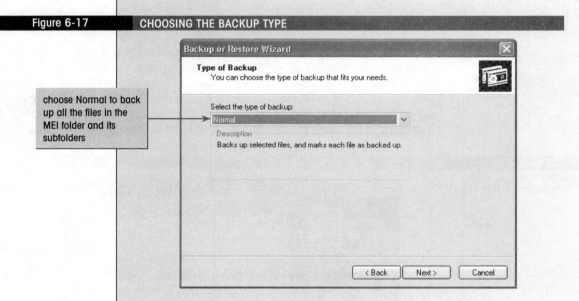

choose Normal to back up all the files in the MEI folder and its subfolders

2. If Normal is not selected, click the **Select the type of backup** list arrow, click **Normal**, and then click the **Next** button. You can now specify whether you want verification, hardware compression, and volume shadow copy options. See Figure 6-18. The hardware compression is dimmed because it is not available for floppy disks.

Figure 6-18   HOW TO BACK UP THE FOLDER

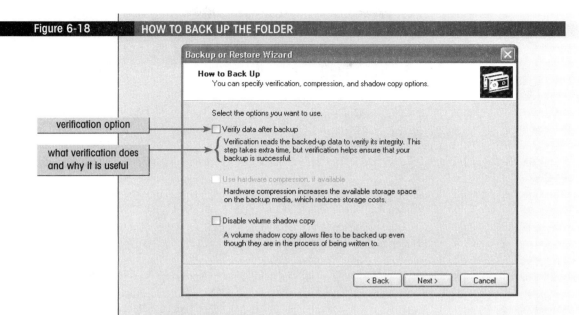

verification option

what verification does
and why it is useful

3. Click the **Verify data after backup** check box to add a check mark and
   select this option, and then click the **Next** button. In the next dialog box, the
   wizard asks you whether you want to append this backup to an existing
   backup, or whether you want to overwrite any existing backups on the backup
   media. See Figure 6-19. The Append option adds this backup to the backup set
   already on the storage media. If you are replacing the current backup contents on the backup media, you also have an option to allow only the owner of
   that data (you) or the Administrator access to the backups. If your backup
   media does not contain any backups, you can use either option.

Figure 6-19   BACKUP OPTIONS

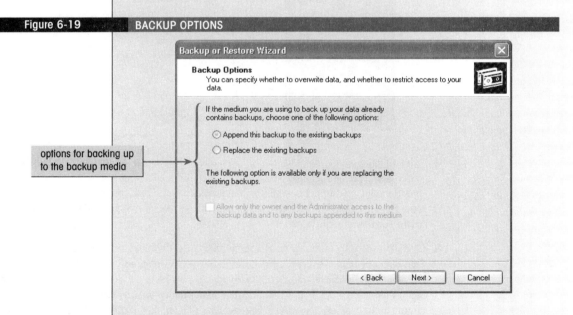

options for backing up
to the backup media

4. Click the **Replace the existing backups** option button, and then click the
   Next button. The wizard now asks you when you want to run the backup. See
   Figure 6-20. The default is to run the backup now; however, you can schedule it
   for later and give the backup job a name.

Figure 6-20   SCHEDULING THE BACKUP

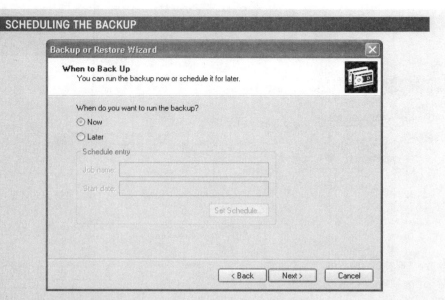

5. Make sure the **Now** option button is selected, and then click the **Next** button. You return to the dialog box that summarizes your backup settings. See Figure 6-21. Notice that verification is now on, and that you will be prompted to replace any data on the backup media.

Figure 6-21   UPDATED BACKUP SETTINGS

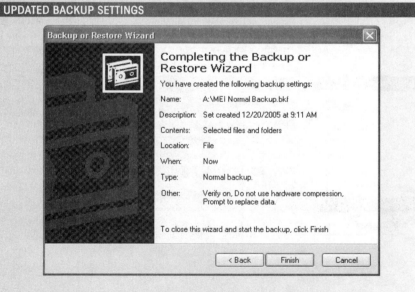

6. Click the **Finish** button. You briefly see a Selection Information dialog box as Backup selects the files, and then a Backup Progress window showing the device from which you are backing up (drive C), the name of the file that stores the backup, the status of the operation, which file it is processing at any given time, the elapsed and remaining time, estimated and processed number of files, and the estimated and processed number of bytes. See Figure 6-22. If Backup needs additional media, you see an Insert Media dialog box informing you that the tape is full and requesting that you insert the next tape.

See Figure 6-23. This dialog box refers to any backup media, not only tapes, but does emphasize the fact that tapes and tape backup drives have been a standard approach to backing up data on a hard disk for many years.

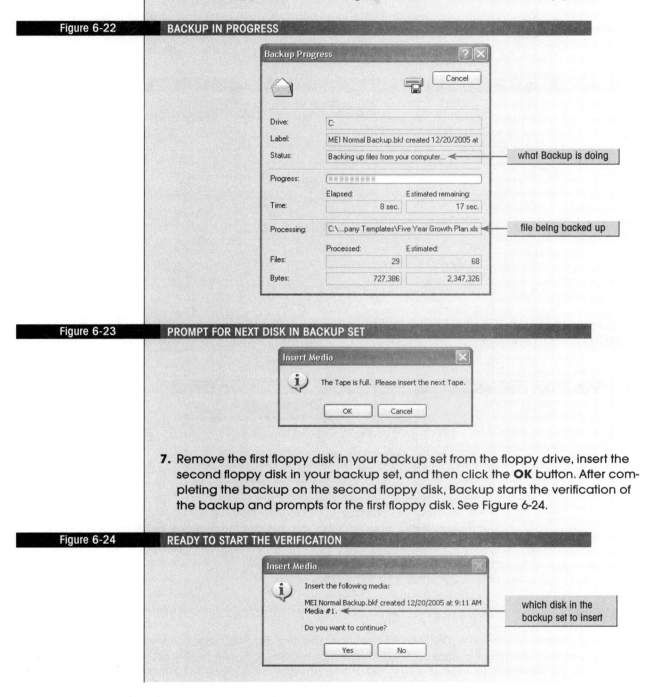

Figure 6-22 BACKUP IN PROGRESS

Backup Progress

Drive: C:
Label: MEI Normal Backup.bkf created 12/20/2005 at
Status: Backing up files from your computer... ← what Backup is doing

Progress: ▯▮▮▮▮▮▮▮▮

	Elapsed:	Estimated remaining:
Time:	8 sec.	17 sec.

Processing: C:\...pany Templates\Five Year Growth Plan.xls ← file being backed up

	Processed:	Estimated:
Files:	29	68
Bytes:	727,386	2,347,326

Figure 6-23 PROMPT FOR NEXT DISK IN BACKUP SET

Insert Media

ℹ The Tape is full. Please insert the next Tape.

OK   Cancel

7. Remove the first floppy disk in your backup set from the floppy drive, insert the second floppy disk in your backup set, and then click the **OK** button. After completing the backup on the second floppy disk, Backup starts the verification of the backup and prompts for the first floppy disk. See Figure 6-24.

Figure 6-24 READY TO START THE VERIFICATION

Insert Media

ℹ Insert the following media:

MEI Normal Backup.bkf created 12/20/2005 at 9:11 AM
Media #1. ← which disk in the backup set to insert

Do you want to continue?

Yes   No

Now you're ready to verify the backup.

To verify the backup:

1. Remove the second floppy disk in your backup set from drive A, insert the first floppy disk from your backup set, and then click the **Yes** button in the Insert Media dialog box. In the Verify Progress dialog box, Backup reports on the status of verifying the backup. See Figure 6-25. After it verifies the contents of the first disk in your backup set, it prompts for the next disk. See Figure 6-26.

| Figure 6-25 | VERIFYING THE BACKUP |

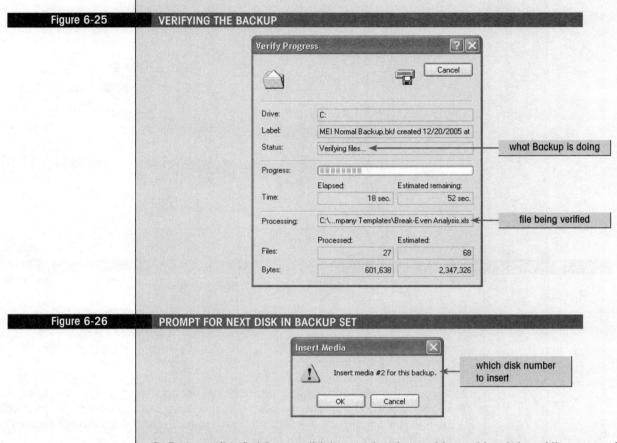

| Figure 6-26 | PROMPT FOR NEXT DISK IN BACKUP SET |

2. Remove the first floppy disk in your backup set from drive A, insert the second floppy disk from your backup set, and then click the **OK** button. After verifying that the data was successfully backed up, the Backup Progress dialog box informs you that the backup is complete. See Figure 6-27.

Figure 6-27   BACKUP COMPLETED

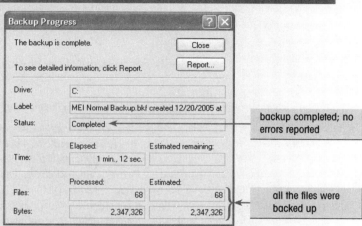

backup completed; no
errors reported

all the files were
backed up

If Backup reports errors during the backup, you should perform the backup
again and, if necessary, disable any background programs that might interfere with the operation of Backup, such as a screen saver, antivirus software, or
power management options. At this point, you have the option of viewing and
printing a report of the backup.

3. Click the **Report** button and, after Backup opens a Notepad window with the
   backup report, maximize the Notepad window. The backup report summarizes
   the backup and the verification. See Figure 6-28. Some details of your report
   will differ.

Figure 6-28   VIEWING THE BACKUP REPORT

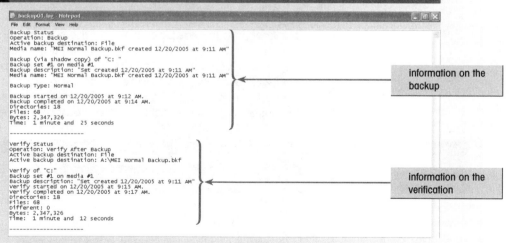

information on the
backup

information on the
verification

4. To print the report, click **File** on the menu bar, click **Print**, select the correct
   printer, and then click the **Print** button in the Print dialog box.

5. To save the report, click **File** on the Notepad menu bar, click **Save As**, click the
   Save in list arrow, click **My Documents**, click the **Create New Folder** button,
   type **My Backup Reports**, press the **Enter** key, press the **Enter** key a second
   time, type **MEI Normal Backup Report** in the File name box, and then click the
   Save button. You now have a copy of this report for your records.

6. Close Notepad.

7. Click the **Close** button to close the Backup Progress dialog box and Backup.

Next, check the contents of the destination disk.

To view the backup media:

1. Remove the second floppy disk in your backup set from drive A, insert the first floppy disk from your backup set into that drive, and then open a window onto drive A. There is only one file on the backup disk—the file named MEI Normal Backup.bkf, and it fills the entire disk (1,414 KB out of a possible 1,440 KB). See Figure 6-29. Your view might vary. The files that you backed up from drive C to this disk are all stored within this single file to efficiently use the storage space on the backup media. Notice also that Windows XP identifies the file type as a "Windows Backup File." In other words, the "bkf" file extension is associated with the Backup utility.

Figure 6-29   VIEWING THE CONTENTS OF THE FIRST BACKUP DISK

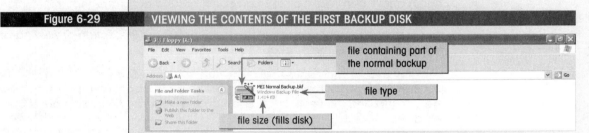

2. Remove the first floppy disk in your backup set from drive A, insert the second floppy disk from your backup set in drive A, and then press the **F5** key to refresh your view onto this floppy disk. Again, there is only one file on the backup disk, it has the same name as the file on the first floppy disk, and it uses only a portion of the storage space on the disk (967 KB out of a possible 1,440 KB, leaving about 473 KB of unused storage space). See Figure 6-30. Your view might vary. Since each floppy disk in a backup set has the same filename, you should sequentially label your disks in advance or as you perform the backup.

Figure 6-30   VIEWING THE CONTENTS OF THE SECOND BACKUP DISK

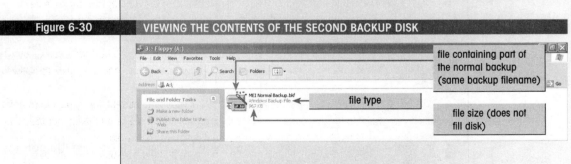

3. Close the drive A window.

REFERENCE WINDOW RW

<u>Using the Backup or Restore Wizard to Back Up Selected Folders on Drive C to Floppy Disks</u>

- Open My Documents (or the drive that contains the files you want to back up), select and right-click the folders and files you want to back up, and then click Properties. Check the size of the folders and files on the General property sheet, and divide that value by 1.44 to determine the total number of floppy disks you need. Round up, and add an additional floppy disk.
- Perform a full format of the floppy disks you need for the backup.
- Click the Start button, point to All Programs, point to Accessories, point to System Tools, and then click Backup, or if you have a Backup desktop shortcut, click that shortcut.
- After you read the Welcome information in the first Backup or Restore Wizard dialog box, click the Next button.
- In the next dialog box, make sure the "Back up files and settings" option button is selected, and then click the Next button.
- When prompted for what you want to back up, click the "Let me choose what to back up" option button, and then click the Next button.
- When prompted to select which files you want to back up, click the expand view box for My Documents or My Computer in the "Items to back up" pane, and if you selected a drive, click the expand view box for that drive (do not click the empty check box for the drive), and adjust your view within the "Items to back up" panel.
- Locate and click the check box for each folder you want to back up, and then click the Next button.
- Make sure one of the disks you formatted is in drive A.
- Select the destination for the backup in the "Choose a place to save your backup" or use the Browse button to locate the drive and folder to store the backup. In the "Type a name for this backup" box, type a name for the file that will contain the backup, and then click the Next button.
- In the dialog box that summarizes your backup settings, click the Advanced button to check or specify other backup settings.
- When prompted for the type of backup, make sure Normal is the selected backup type, and then click the Next button.
- When prompted about verification, hardware compression, and volume shadow copy options, click the "Verify data after backup" check box, and then click the Next button.
- When prompted about whether you want to append or overwrite data on the backup media, click the "Replace the existing backups" option button, and then click the Next button.
- When prompted as to when to run the backup, make sure the Now option button is selected, click Next, and when you return to the dialog box that summarizes your backup settings, click the Finish button.
- When Backup displays an Insert Media dialog box prompting for the next tape, remove the floppy disk from drive A, insert the next floppy disk from your backup set, and then click the OK button. Keep repeating this process until the backup is completed.
- When prompted for the first disk in the backup set, remove the current floppy disk from drive A, insert the first floppy disk in your backup set, and click Yes in the Insert Media dialog box to verify the backup. Continue to swap disks until the verification is completed.
- If you want to print and save the report on the backup after the backup and verification is complete, click the Report button and, after Backup opens a Notepad window with the backup report, click File on the menu bar, click Print, select the correct printer, and then click Print in the Print dialog box. To save the report, click File on the Notepad menu bar, click Save As, click the Save in list arrow, locate and click the folder where you want to store backup reports, type a name for the backup report in the File name box, and then click the Save button. Close Notepad.
- Click Close to close the Backup Progress dialog box and Backup.

You have successfully completed a normal backup. If you are backing up to floppy disks, it is a good idea to format, label, and number the disks in advance.

Restoring a Folder

Occasionally, working files on your hard disk can become corrupt, making it impossible to use those files. A **corrupted file** is a program or document file the contents of which have been altered as the result of a hardware, software, or power failure. If you encounter a corrupted file, or if you accidentally delete a folder or files within a folder, or if your hard disk fails, you can restore files from a backup set once you have resolved the problem that occurred with your computer. If your hard disk fails, you have to replace the drive and install Windows XP first. Then you can restore all the files that you lost. During a restore, the Backup utility rebuilds any folders so that it can restore files to their original locations.

If you perform a complete restore immediately after a file is corrupted, the restored files replace the ones that already exist on the hard disk. If you are concerned that restoring files from a backup might affect files currently stored in a folder on your hard disk, you can change the name of that folder, restore the original folder and its files from your backups, and then verify that you have what you need before you remove the renamed folder and its files.

To verify that the backup set is good, Marci suggests that you change the name of the MEI folder, restore the MEI folder and its contents from your backup set, and then verify that the restore worked properly.

To rename the MEI folder:

1. Open the My Documents folder or the drive and folder where you created the MEI folder.

2. Point to and select the **MEI** folder, press the **F2** key, type **MEI (Original)** for the new name, and then press the **Enter** key.

3. Minimize the My Documents or drive window.

Now you are ready to restore the MEI folder from your backup set. When you restore files, you start with the *last* floppy disk (or other media) in your backup set. The Backup utility needs to examine this disk first because it contains a directory with information on all the files included in the backup set. Then you select a catalog that you want to restore. A **catalog** identifies a backup and contains information on the folders and files that are included in a backup set.

To restore all the files from a normal backup:

1. If necessary, insert the second (or last) floppy disk from your backup set into drive A.

2. Click the **Backup** desktop shortcut, and after the Backup or Restore Wizard dialog box opens, click the **Next** button.

3. In the next Backup or Restore Wizard dialog box, click the **Restore files and settings** option button, and then click the **Next** button. The wizard now prompts you to choose the items you want to restore. See Figure 6-31. In the Contents pane on the right, the wizard lists the names of catalogs that you've created. You can use the Browse button to locate and catalog a backup file.

POWER USERS TIP You can delete catalogs you no longer need by right-clicking the catalog name, and then choosing the "Delete catalog" option.

Figure 6-31   CHOOSING THE BACKUP SET

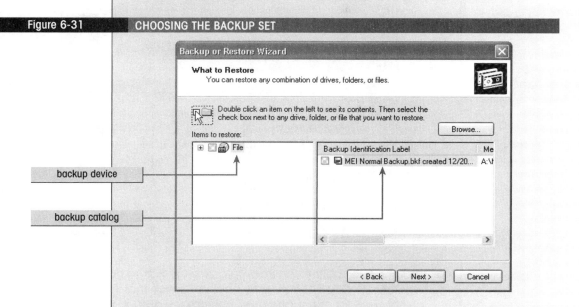

backup device

backup catalog

4. In the "Items to restore pane" on the left, click the **expand view** box ⊞ next to **File**, click ⊞ for the **MEI Normal Backup.bkf** backup set that you just created, click and select the **C:** folder, click the check box next to the **C:** folder icon to select all files on that drive which you backed up, click ⊞ for the **C:** folder, click ⊞ for the **Documents and Settings** folder, click ⊞ for your **user account** folder, adjust your view in the "Items to restore" pane as needed, click ⊞ for the **My Documents** folder, click ⊞ for the MEI folder, adjust your view in the "Items to restore" pane, and then click the **Company Projections** folder. You can now tell that the wizard selected all the folders and files you originally backed up when you clicked the C: folder check box. See Figure 6-32. If you do not want to restore specific folders, or specific files, you remove the check mark from the check boxes for those folders and files, thereby excluding them from the restore operation.

TROUBLE? If you stored the MEI folder on another drive, you see the drive name for that drive (for example, D:) instead of the drive name for drive C (C:). Adapt the step to the drive you used.

TROUBLE? If you clicked the Company Projections folder check box, you removed it from the restore selection. Click the Company Projections folder check box again to add a check mark to the check box, and then click the folder icon or folder name for the Company Projections folder.

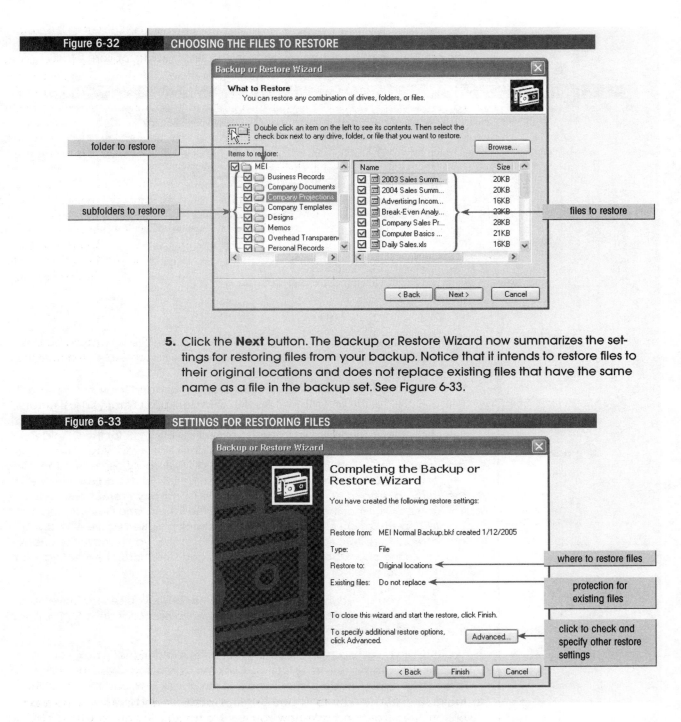

Figure 6-32   CHOOSING THE FILES TO RESTORE

Figure 6-33   SETTINGS FOR RESTORING FILES

5. Click the **Next** button. The Backup or Restore Wizard now summarizes the settings for restoring files from your backup. Notice that it intends to restore files to their original locations and does not replace existing files that have the same name as a file in the backup set. See Figure 6-33.

At this point, you can start the restore, or you can check and, if necessary, change other restore settings. For example, you can select where to restore the data—the original location, an alternate location, or a single folder. If you choose the original location, you restore the files to their original folders. If you choose an alternate location, you can restore files to another folder on your hard disk. The Backup utility then builds the same folder structure as previously existed below the folder you choose. If you choose the Single folder option, Backup restores all the files to a single folder that you choose and does not build the same folder structure below that folder.

You can also specify how you want to handle files on your hard disk that have the same names as files in your backup set. The recommended option is to leave your existing files (not overwrite them)—the assumption being that the files on your hard disk are more recent. This option is designed to protect files on your hard disk that have the same name as files that are being restored from the backup disk. You can also choose to replace the files on your computer only if the files on your computer are older, or you can choose to always replace the files. If you are restoring files to an existing folder, you might want to leave your existing files or replace older files to make sure you do not inadvertently lose an important file. Replace all the existing files when you know that you want to restore everything in a folder, such as when you know all the files are corrupted.

If you backed up data from a NTFS drive and are restoring it to an NTFS volume, you can restore security settings for each folder and file. You can restore junction points on your hard disk, but not the data that the junction point references. A **junction point** is a physical location on a hard disk that points to data found at another location on your hard disk or on a storage device. This feature is commonly used with mounted drives. A **mounted drive** (also known as a **volume mount point**) is a drive attached to an empty folder on an NTFS volume. Mounted drives are assigned a label or name instead of a drive letter for the drive name.

To check other restore settings:

1. Click the **Advanced** button. In the next Backup or Restore Wizard dialog box, you select where you want to restore the data. See Figure 6-34. The default is "Original location."

| Figure 6-34 | CHOOSING THE RESTORE LOCATION |

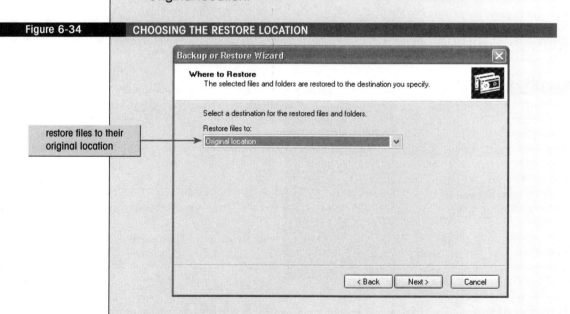

restore files to their original location

2. Make sure "Restore files to" shows **Original location**, and then click the **Next** button. The wizard now asks how you want to handle files on your hard disk that have the same names as files in your backup set. See Figure 6-35. You can leave the existing files, replace only older files, or replace all existing files. Because you renamed the MEI folder (and, as far as the operating system is concerned, there is no MEI folder), any of these options work.

Figure 6-35   HOW TO HANDLE FILES WITH THE SAME NAMES

protects existing files
from being overwritten

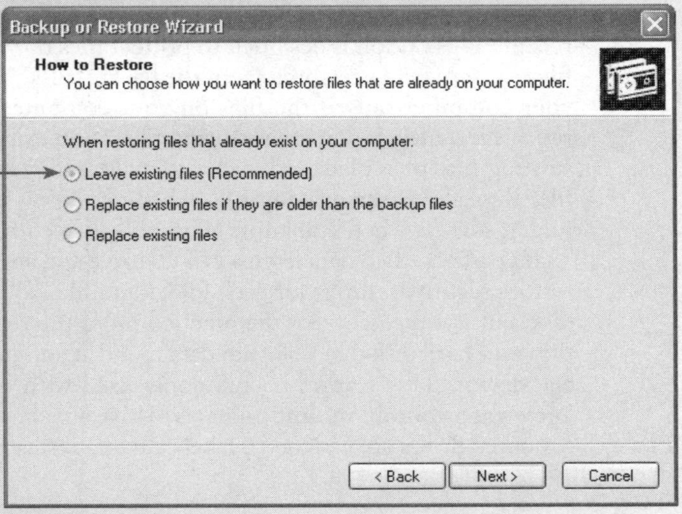

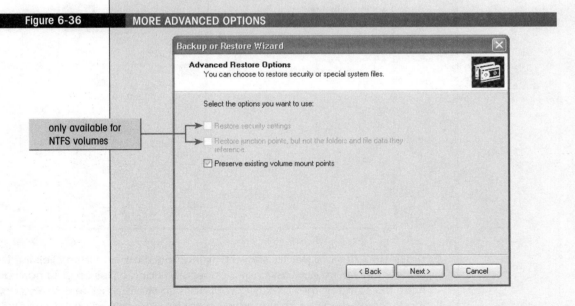

3. Make sure the "Leave existing files (Recommended)" option is selected, and then click the **Next** button. The next dialog box contains options for restoring security settings or junction points or for preserving existing volume mount points. See Figure 6-36. The Restore security settings option allows you to restore security settings for each folder and file, and is only available and enabled if you backed up data from a NTFS drive and are restoring it to an NTFS volume. Dimmed options are not available for the current restore.

Figure 6-36   MORE ADVANCED OPTIONS

only available for
NTFS volumes

4. Leave these options at their default settings, and then click the **Next** button. The wizard updates the dialog box that contains the summary of restore settings. See Figure 6-37.

Figure 6-37   FINAL SETTINGS FOR RESTORING FILES

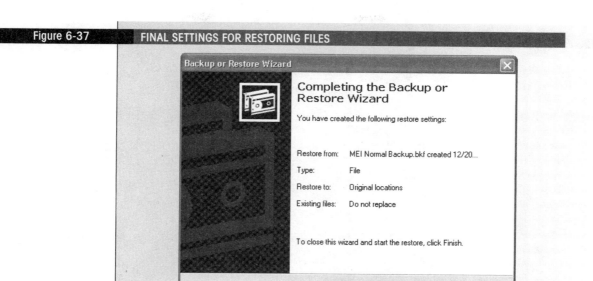

5. Click the **Finish** button. In the Restore Progress dialog box, the wizard notes that the wizard mounts the drive, creates a "System Restore checkpoint," and then prompts you to insert the first disk in the backup set. See Figure 6-38. As noted in Tutorial 1, the System Restore component of Windows XP monitors changes to the computer system, and creates restore points that consist of saved system settings and files so that you can roll back your computer to a previous state if a problem occurs.

Figure 6-38   PROMPT FOR BACKUP MEDIA

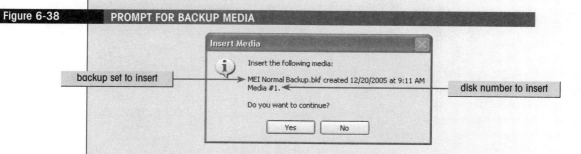

6. Remove the second floppy disk in your backup set from drive A, insert the first floppy disk in your backup set into drive A, and then click the **Yes** button. The Backup utility searches for the backup set, and then shows the device that you are restoring from (File), the media name (MEI Normal Media Backup.bkf), the status (of the operation), a progress indicator, the elapsed time, what file it is processing at any given time, the estimated and processed number of files, and the estimated and processed number of bytes. See Figure 6-39. Then it prompts you to insert the next disk in your backup set.

TROUBLE? If you are using the Windows XP Home Edition, remove the second floppy disk in your backup set from drive A, insert the first floppy disk in your backup set in drive A, and then click the OK button. After restoring files from the first floppy disk, the Insert Media dialog box opens, asking you for the next disk.

| Figure 6-39 | RESTORE IN PROGRESS |

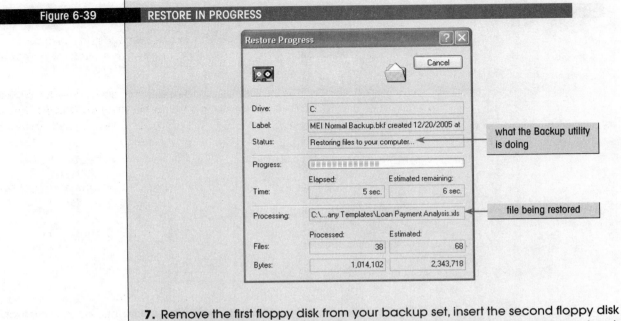

what the Backup utility is doing

file being restored

7. Remove the first floppy disk from your backup set, insert the second floppy disk from your backup set in drive, and then click the **OK** button. Once the restore is complete, you see a Backup dialog box that informs you the operation was completed (without errors). See Figure 6-40. Backup restored all 68 files.

| Figure 6-40 | RESTORE COMPLETED |

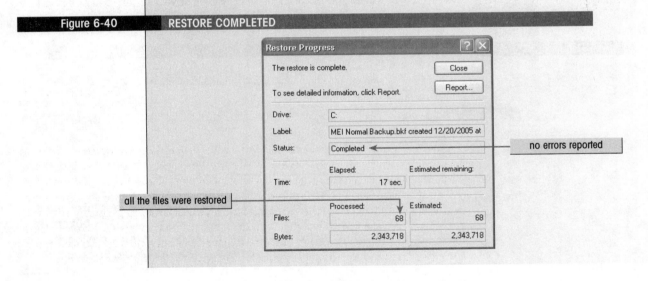

no errors reported

all the files were restored

You can now print a report of the results.

To print and save the report for the restore operation:

1. Click the **Report** button, read the information about the restore operation, click **File** on the menu bar, click **Print**, choose the correct printer, and then click the **Print** button.

2. To save the report, click **File** on the Notepad menu bar, click **Save As**, click the **Save in** list arrow, open **My Documents**, open the **My Backup Reports** folder, type **MEI Full Restore Report** in the File name box, and then click the **Save** button. You now have a copy of this report for your records.

3. Close Notepad.

4. Click the **Close** button to close the Restore Progress dialog box and Backup.

Now you can check the My Documents folder and verify the restore operation.

To verify the restore:

1. Click the **My Documents** taskbar button (or open the drive window that contains the MEI folder), press the **F5** (Refresh) key to arrange folders and files in order by name, and then locate the MEI folder. Notice that you still have the MEI (Original) folder. See Figure 6-41.

| Figure 6-41 | VIEWING THE CONTENTS OF THE MY DOCUMENTS FOLDER |

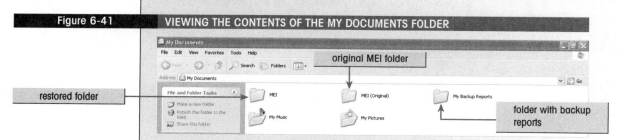

restored folder

original MEI folder

folder with backup reports

2. Right-click the **MEI** folder icon, and then click **Properties** on the shortcut menu. The General property sheet in the MEI Properties dialog box shows that the Backup utility restored 68 files in 13 folders that were 2.23 MB (or 2,343,768 bytes) in size. See Figure 6-42. The Backup utility rebuilt the entire folder structure and restored everything from the backup disk. If you check the property sheets of the 68 files, you will find that the Backup utility turned on the Archive attribute for all the restored files so that the MEI folder, its subfolders, and all the files are included in the next backup in your backup cycle. Your view might vary.

| Figure 6-42 | VIEWING PROPERTIES OF THE RESTORED FOLDER |

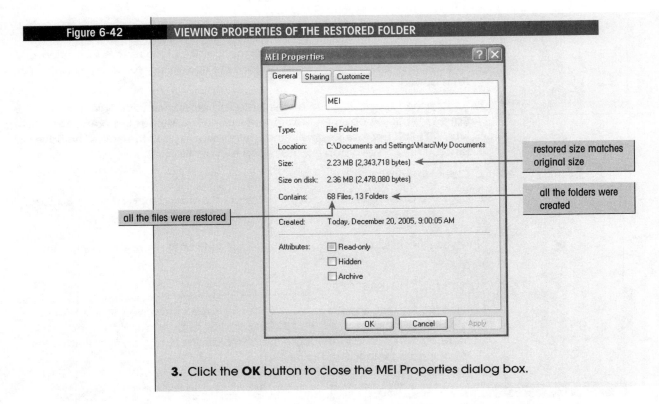

3. Click the **OK** button to close the MEI Properties dialog box.

You have successfully restored the entire MEI folder and its contents.

REFERENCE WINDOW   RW

Using the Backup or Restore Wizard to Restore Files from Floppy Disks

- Insert the last floppy disk from your backup set in drive A.
- Click the Start button, point to All Programs, point to Accessories, point to System Tools, and then click Backup, or if you have a Backup desktop shortcut, click the shortcut.
- In the first Backup or Restore Wizard dialog box, click the Next button.
- In the next Backup or Restore Wizard dialog box, click the Restore files and settings option button, and then click the Next button.
- In the "Items to restore pane" on the left, click the expand view box next to File, click the expand view box for the backup set that you just created, click the check box next to the C: folder icon to select all files on that drive which you backed up, and then click the Next button.
- In the next dialog box with a summary of your restore settings, click the Advanced button to check other restore settings.
- To restore files to their original locations, make sure "Restore files to" shows "Original location", and then click the Next button.
- To make sure you do not replace more recent files with files by the same name in your backup set, make sure the "Leave existing files (Recommended)" option is selected, and then click the Next button.
- When prompted to restore security settings, to restore junction points, and to preserve existing volume mount points, click the Next button to use the default settings for these options.
- In the dialog box that summarizes your restore settings, click the Finish button to start the restore.
- When prompted, remove the last disk in your backup set from drive A, insert the first disk in the backup set into drive A, and then click the Yes button.
- When prompted to insert the next disk in your backup set, remove the first disk from your backup set, insert the second disk in drive, and then click the OK button.
- If you want to print a summary of the restore operation, click Report in the Restore Progress dialog box, click File on the menu bar, and then click the Print button.
- To save the report, click File on the Notepad menu bar, click Save As, click the Save in list arrow, select the folder where you want to save the report, type a name for the report in the File name box, click Save, and then close Notepad.
- Click Close to close the Backup Progress dialog box and Backup.

If you inadvertently delete a subfolder within another folder, you can restore that subfolder and its files using a similar approach. If you accidentally delete an important file or set of files, you can restore the file or files from the same backup set, again using the same process. The only difference is what you select for the restore.

After you make a backup, you should test it. You should not automatically assume that the backup is going to work when you most need it. You want to verify that it works properly now. You do not want to discover later that the backup did not work properly, and then cannot restore files from your backup. As you did here, you can rename a folder, and do a test restore. You could also restore your backup to an alternate location, such as another drive.

Modifying Files After a Backup

After you make a normal backup of selected files, the Backup utility turns off the Archive bit for all the files. Once you modify and save changes to a file, Windows XP turns on the Archive bit. If you create a new file, Windows XP turns on its Archive bit. The next time you perform an incremental or differential backup, the Backup utility then knows which files to back up. All you have to specify is that you want an incremental or differential backup instead of another normal backup.

As the day progresses, Marci needs to update some of her client files in the MEI folder. She asks you to change a couple of files and then perform an incremental backup of selected files. She recommends that you examine the Archive attributes of these files before and after making changes.

Before you perform these operations, you delete the restored MEI folder, and then change the name of the MEI (Original) folder back to MEI. *These steps are critical.* Unlike the Backup utility in Windows 98, for example, the Windows XP Backup utility turned on the Archive bit for all the files in the restored MEI folder, and that change would affect your ability to perform an incremental backup if you used the restored MEI folder rather than the original MEI folder. The Archive bits for the original MEI folder are still all turned off.

To return to the original MEI folder:

1. From the My Documents or a drive window, point to and select the **MEI** folder, press the **Delete** key, and then click the **Yes** button to confirm the folder deletion.

2. Point to and select the **MEI (Original)** folder, press the **F2** (Rename) key, and change the name to **MEI**.

Now you're ready to make changes to selected files in the MEI folder. As you do, Windows XP turns on the Archive bit for those files you change, and then you can back them up using an incremental backup strategy.

To modify a file within the MEI folder:

1. Open the **MEI** folder, open the **Designs** folder, right-click **Company Logo Design.bmp**, and then click **Properties** on the shortcut menu. In the Attributes section on the General property sheet, Windows XP shows that the Archive bit for this file is turned off (in other words, there is no check mark in the Archive check box). See Figure 6-43.

TROUBLE? If the Archive check box contains a check mark, you did not delete the restored MEI folder and rename the MEI (Original) folder to MEI. Close the Company Logo Design.bmp Properties dialog box, and then complete the two steps prior to this step.

TROUBLE? If NTFS is the file system for your drive, you do not see an Archive check box. Click the Advanced button. The "File is ready for archiving" check box does not contain a check mark, indicating the Archive bit is turned off. If the "File is ready for archiving" check box contains a check box, you did not delete the restored MEI folder and rename the MEI (Original) folder to MEI. Close the Advanced Attributes dialog box, close Company Logo Design.bmp Properties dialog box, and then complete the two steps prior to this step.

Figure 6-43	VIEWING ATTRIBUTES OF A FILE BEFORE MODIFYING IT

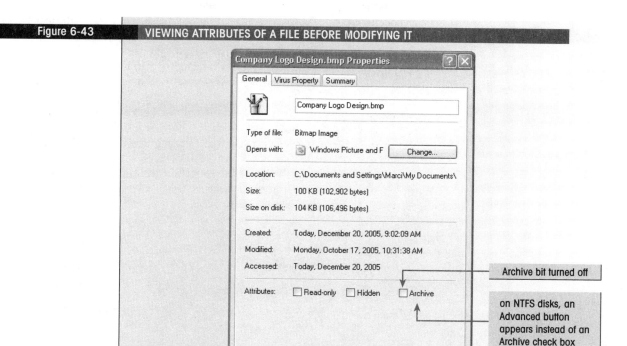

2. Close the Company Logo Design.bmp Properties dialog box without making any changes.

TROUBLE? If NTFS is the file system for your drive, close the Advanced Attributes dialog box, and then close the Company Logo Design.bmp Properties dialog box without making any changes.

3. Right-click the **Company Logo Design.bmp** thumbnail, point to **Open With**, and then click **Paint**.

4. Maximize the Paint window, if necessary, click the **Fill With Color** button 🖌 in the toolbox, click the reddish-brown color box (first row, third color box from left), and then click the dark blue background of the image. Paint changes the color of the background from a dark blue to reddish-brown.

5. Click **File** on the menu bar, click **Save**, and then close the Paint window.

6. Right-click the **Company Logo Design.bmp** thumbnail in the Designs window, and then click **Properties** on the shortcut menu. Notice that the Archive bit is now turned on (in other words, there is a check mark in the Archive check box). See Figure 6-44. You just changed the contents of the file, and during the file save, Windows XP updated the Archive bit.

Figure 6-44	VIEWING ATTRIBUTES OF A FILE AFTER MODIFYING IT

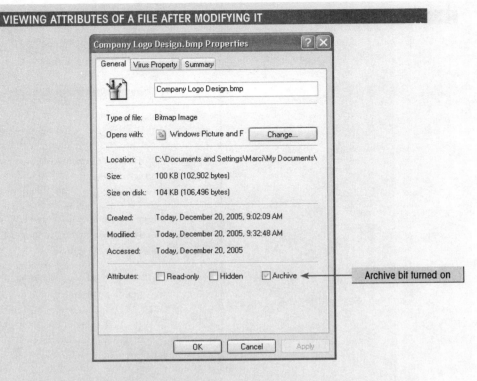

TROUBLE? If NTFS is the file system for your drive, you do not see an Archive check box. Click the Advanced button. The "File is ready for archiving" check box now contains a check mark, indicating the Archive bit is turned on.

7. Close the Company Logo Design.bmp Properties dialog box without making any changes.

TROUBLE? If NTFS is the file system for your drive, close the Advanced Attributes dialog box, and then close the Company Logo Design.bmp Properties dialog box without making any changes.

Next, modify another file in another folder.

To revise a memo:

1. Click the **Up** button 🔄 on the Standard Buttons toolbar to move up one folder level, and then click the **Memos** folder icon.

2. Right-click **Microsoft's Web Site.doc**, click **Properties**, notice that the Archive bit is turned off, and then close the Microsoft's Web Site.doc Properties dialog box without making any changes.

TROUBLE? If NTFS is the file system for your drive, click the Advanced button. The "File is ready for archiving" check box does not contain a check mark (the Archive bit is turned off). Close the Advanced Attributes dialog box, and then close the Microsoft's Web Site.doc Properties dialog box.

3. Click the **Microsoft Web Site.doc** icon. Windows XP opens this file in either Microsoft Word (if available) or WordPad, depending on which program it associates with the "doc" file extension.

4. Make a change to the contents of the file (such as entering the current date), click **File** on the menu bar, click **Save**, and, if the application asks if you want to update the document to another format, click the **No** button, and then close the application window.

5. Right-click **Microsoft's Web Site.doc**, click **Properties**, notice that the Archive bit is now turned on, and then close the Microsoft's Web Site.doc Properties dialog box without making any changes.

   TROUBLE? If NTFS is the file system for your drive, click the Advanced button. The "File is ready for archiving" check box now contains a check mark (the Archive bit is turned on). Close the Advanced Attributes dialog box, and then click the OK button to close the Microsoft's Web Site.doc Properties dialog box.

6. Click the **Up** button to return to the MEI folder.

Marci needs to create an outline for an upcoming workshop on advanced Excel features. To save time, she asks you to make a copy of the outline used for a workshop on Excel Basics, and then revise it to include advanced Excel topics.

To create a new file from an existing file:

1. Click the **Training** folder icon, right-click the **Excel Basics.doc** file icon, click **Properties**, notice that the Archive bit is turned off, and then close the Excel Basics.doc Properties dialog box without making any changes.

   TROUBLE? If NTFS is the file system for your drive, click the Advanced button. The "File is ready for archiving" check box does not contain a check mark (the Archive bit is turned off). Close the Advanced Attributes dialog box, and then close the Excel Basics.doc Properties dialog box.

2. If the Excel Basics.doc file is not already selected, point to and select **Excel Basics.doc**.

3. Click **Edit** on the menu bar, click **Copy** (do not click "Copy to Folder"), click **Edit** again, and then click **Paste**. Windows XP makes a copy of the Excel Basics.doc file and names it "Copy of Excel Basics.doc". No two files in the same folder can have the same name.

4. Point to and select the **Copy of Excel Basics.doc** file, press the **F2** (Rename) key, type **Advanced Excel.doc**, and then press the **Enter** key.

5. Right-click **Advanced Excel.doc**, click **Properties**, notice that Windows XP turned on the Archive bit of the new file, and then close the Advanced Excel.doc Properties dialog box.

> TROUBLE? If NTFS is the file system for your drive, click the Advanced button. The "File is ready for archiving" check box now contains a check mark (the Archive bit is turned on). Close the Advanced Attributes dialog box, and then close the Advanced Excel.doc Properties dialog box.
>
> **6.** Click the **Up** button 🔟, and then minimize the MEI folder window.

You have just made changes to three different files in three different folders. In each case, Windows XP turned on the Archive bit, and the files are now marked for your next backup.

Performing an Incremental Backup

Now that you have updated some files, you are ready to perform an incremental backup. This time, rather than use a wizard, you open the Backup Utility window and manually choose the settings you need for the incremental backup. For example, you can specify which files to exclude from the backup. You can specify which files to exclude either for all users (if you log on as Administrator or are a member of the Administrators group) or for your logon only. For example, your folder might contain backup files for a specific application, thumbnail database files, or other types of files that you do not need to back up. If this is the case, you can specify that you want to exclude them, rather than to manually go from folder to folder and deselect each file you do not want to back up.

You can also exclude registered file types and specify masks for custom file types. A **custom file type** is a file type that is not tracked by the system Registry. These files have file extensions that you create when you save the file rather than ones that are assigned by the application you're using, and the file type is then not associated with any application. You can exclude all files with a certain extension, or only those in a specific path starting at any location within the folder hierarchy on your disk, including all subfolders below that path.

Besides excluding files from the backup, you can set options that affect Removable Storage. **Removable Storage** is a Windows XP tool for tracking your removable storage media, such as tapes, and managing the corresponding hardware. This tool organizes all of your storage media into different media pools. A **media pool** is a collection of removable media with the same management policies. An **import media pool** is a collection of data storage media that has not yet been cataloged by Windows XP's Removable Storage Media tool. With the Removable Storage tool, multiple applications can share the same storage media.

The second disk in your backup set should have enough room for the incremental backup; if not, you need to use an additional formatted, but empty, floppy disk.

> *To perform an incremental backup:*
>
> **1.** Insert the last disk from your backup set into drive A, if necessary.
>
> **2.** Click the **Backup** desktop shortcut, and then click the **Advanced Mode** link. In the Backup Utility window, the Welcome sheet includes options for using the Backup Wizard, the Restore Wizard, and an Automated System Recovery Wizard (which you examine in Tutorial 8). See Figure 6-45.

Figure 6-45   USING THE BACKUP UTILITY'S ADVANCED MODE

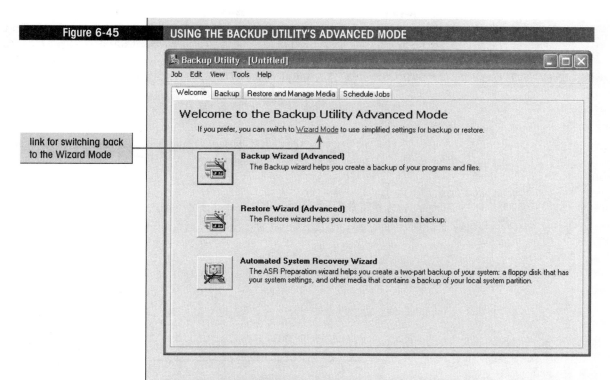

link for switching back
to the Wizard Mode

3. Click the **Backup** tab. From the Backup sheet, you can select the drive(s), folder(s), and file(s) you want to back up, you can specify the destination (in some cases), you can specify a file name for the backup media, and you can use the menu to specify Backup settings. See Figure 6-46.

Figure 6-46   SELECTING THE FOLDER FOR AN INCREMENTAL BACKUP

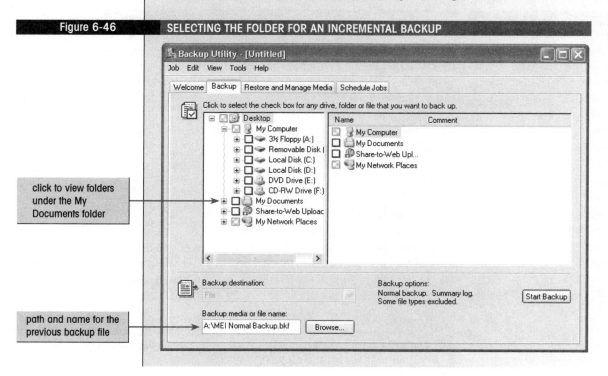

click to view folders
under the My
Documents folder

path and name for the
previous backup file

4. Click **Tools** on the menu bar, and then click **Options**. Backup opens the Options dialog box and displays the Backup Type property sheet. See Figure 6-47.

Figure 6-47   CHOOSING THE BACKUP TYPE

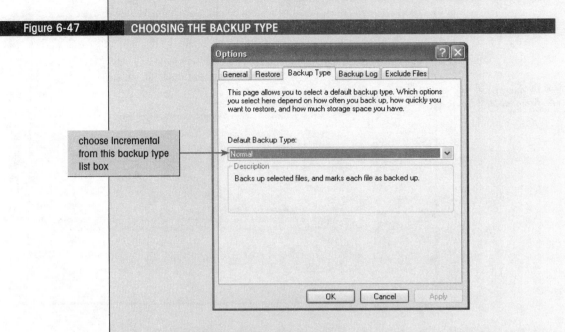

choose Incremental from this backup type list box

5. Click the **Default Backup Type** list arrow, click **Incremental**, and then click the **Backup Log** tab. You can create a detailed backup log (or report), a summary (the default), or not log backup operations. See Figure 6-48.

Figure 6-48   CHANGING THE BACKUP LOG OPTION

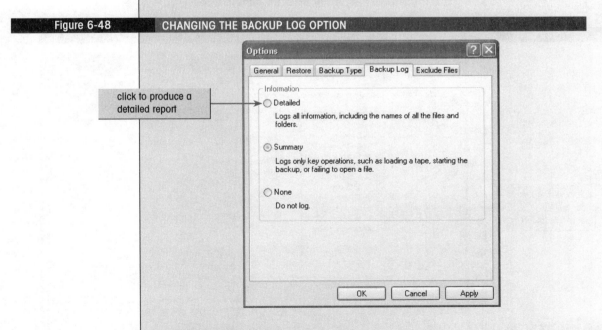

click to produce a detailed report

6. Click the **Detailed** option button, and then click the **Exclude Files** tab. On the Exclude Files sheet, Backup shows a list of files that are excluded for all users from backups. See Figure 6-49.

Figure 6-49   OPTIONS FOR EXCLUDING FILES

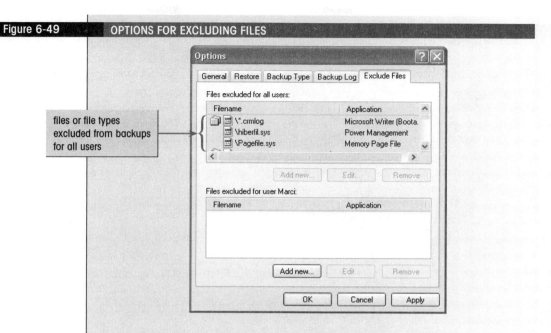

files or file types
excluded from backups
for all users

7. Click the **Add new** button under "Files excluded for user (your user account)."
In the Add Excluded Files dialog box, you can indicate which registered file
types and masks for custom file types you want to exclude from backups. See
Figure 6-50. You specify custom file types in the Custom file mask box by entering the file extension. You can also apply your selections to a specific path.

Figure 6-50   OPTIONS FOR EXCLUDING FILES AND FILE TYPES

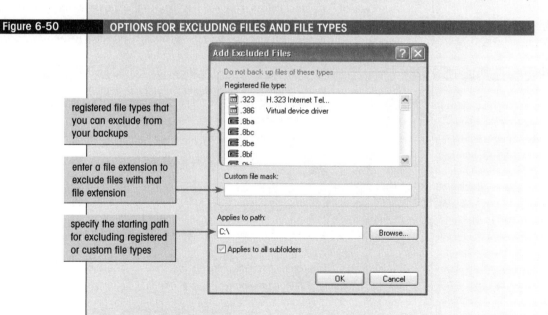

registered file types that
you can exclude from
your backups

enter a file extension to
exclude files with that
file extension

specify the starting path
for excluding registered
or custom file types

8. In the "Registered file type" box, locate and click the registered file type **.db**
(identified as a Data Base File), and then click the **OK** button. You have now
excluded files of this type from the backup for just your user logon. See
Figure 6-51. That means that the Backup utility will not include the Thumbs.db
file in the Designs folder in your backup, but only the three files you changed.

Figure 6-51   REGISTERED FILE TYPE EXCLUDED FROM BACKUPS

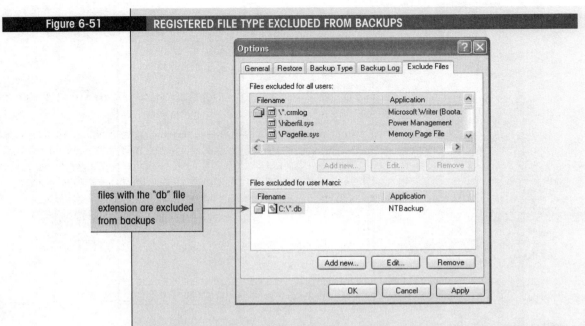

files with the "db" file extension are excluded from backups

9. Click the **General** tab. On this sheet, you have a variety of options that you can control. For example, you can compute selection information, use catalogs on your backup media (called **on-media catalogs**) to restore catalogs on your computer (called **on-disk catalogs**), and turn verification on or off. See Figure 6-52. The "Compute selection information" option estimates the number of files and bytes that will be backed up or restored. The Backup utility displays this information before a backup or restore begins. Several of the options on the General sheet affect Removable Storage.

Figure 6-52   GENERAL BACKUP AND RESTORE OPTIONS

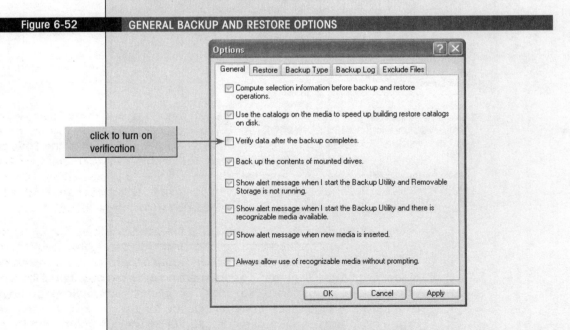

click to turn on verification

10. Click the **Verify data after the backup completes** check box, and then click the **OK** button to close the Options dialog box.

Next, select what you want to back up, enter a filename for the backup media, save your backup settings, and then start the backup.

To continue with the backup:

1. Click the **expand view** box ⊞ for My Documents, and then click the **MEI** folder check box.

2. In the "Backup media or file name" text box, change the backup media file-name to **A:\MEI Incremental #1 Backup.bkf** either by typing over the existing backup media filename, or by double-clicking **Normal** and then typing **Incremental #1** in its place. Figure 6-53 shows the selections you've made.

Figure 6-53	SELECTION FOR THE INCREMENTAL BACKUP

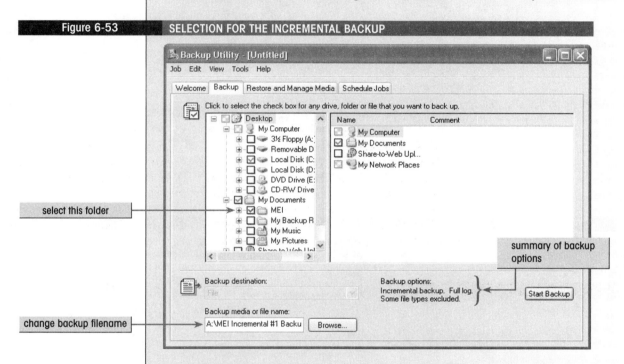

select this folder

change backup filename

3. Click **Job** on the menu bar, click **Save Selections**, and in the Save As dialog box, type **MEI Incremental** in the File name text box (notice that the file type is "Selection Scripts" with the "bks" file extension), and then click the **Save** button. If you need to perform this type of backup again, then you can open Backup, select Load Selections from the Job menu, pick the selection script file you want to use, and Backup automatically selects all the files that need to be backed up. (You need to change the backup filename, though.)

4. Click the **Start Backup** button, and after the Backup Job Information dialog box opens, modify the Backup description for identifying the media to read "MEI Incr #1 Set created...", as shown in Figure 6-54. You have a limited amount of space for the description, so you might have to use abbreviations.

Figure 6-54   SPECIFYING A BACKUP DESCRIPTION

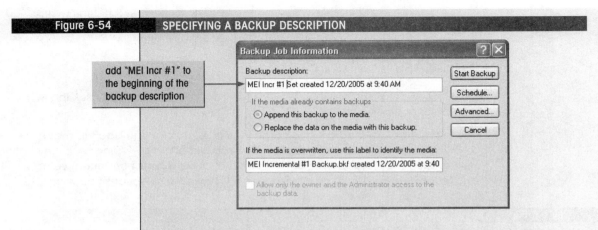

add "MEI Incr #1" to
the beginning of the
backup description

5. In the Backup Job Information dialog box, click the **Start Backup** button and, after the backup and verify are complete, note that the Backup utility only backed up three files. See Figure 6-55.

TROUBLE? The Backup utility might report that it backed up four files if you are using Windows XP Home Edition. If this is the case, the Backup Utility backed up the Thumbs.db file even though you specified that it exclude files with the "db" file extension. Continue with the remaining steps, but when you print the report in the next step, make a note on the report that you excluded files with the "db" file extension so that your instructor knows that you did not skip that step.

Figure 6-55   FIRST INCREMENTAL BACKUP COMPLETED

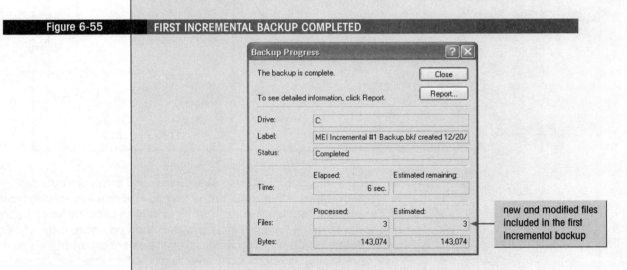

new and modified files
included in the first
incremental backup

6. Click the **Report** button, read the information about the backup operation, click **File** on the menu bar, click **Print**, choose the correct printer, and then click the **Print** button.

7. To save the report, click **File** on the Notepad menu bar, click **Save As**, click the **Save in** list arrow, open **My Documents**, open the **My Backup Reports** folder, type **MEI Incremental #1 Backup Report** in the File name box, and then click the **Save** button. You now have a copy of this report for your records.

8. Close Notepad, close the Backup Progress dialog box, and then close the Backup Utility window.

9. Open **My Computer**, and then open **3½ Floppy (A:)**. Your first incremental backup is now added to the backup media that contains part of the MEI Normal Backup. See Figure 6-56. Your view might vary, and your incremental backup size might differ.

Figure 6-56	VIEWING THE CONTENTS OF THE BACKUP DISK

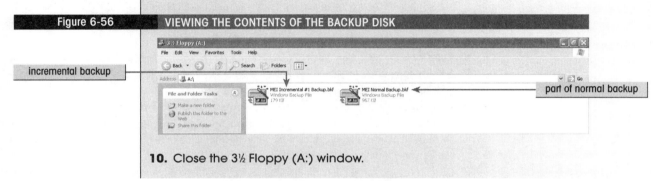

10. Close the 3½ Floppy (A:) window.

As you did here, you can add incremental or differential backups to the same media that contains the normal backup, assuming there is still space on the media. Since incremental and differential backups take less space, and assuming you are backing up to a medium other than floppy disks, you might be able to store all the backups for a backup cycle together on the same backup medium. Make sure that you use different names for your files so that you do not overwrite the existing (previous) backups.

You can save yourself time and effort by saving the settings for a backup as a "Selection Script." When you get ready to do the next incremental backup, you can open the backup job with the settings for the previous incremental backup and then perform your backup. You can also save the settings for the normal backup that you perform at the beginning of a backup cycle, so that you do not need to specify the save settings repeatedly.

<u>Performing an Incremental Backup of Selected Files to a Floppy Disk</u>

- If the last disk in your backup set has enough storage space for an incremental backup, insert that disk into drive A; otherwise, insert a new floppy disk.
- Click the Start button, point to All Programs, point to Accessories, point to System Tools, and then click Backup, or if you have a Backup shortcut on the desktop, click that shortcut.
- In the first Backup or Restore Wizard dialog box, click the Advanced Mode link to open the Backup Utility window.
- Click the Backup tab, click Tools on the menu bar, click Options, click the Default Backup Type list box on the Backup Type property sheet, and click Incremental.
- If you want a record of the names of the backed up files, click the Backup Log tab, and click the Detailed option button.
- If you want to exclude certain files from the backup, click the Exclude Files tab, click the Add new button under "Files excluded for user [*your user account*]," and in the Add Excluded Files dialog box, indicate which registered file types and custom file types you want to exclude from backups. Then click OK to close this dialog box.
- If you want to check other backup and restore settings, click the General tab, choose any options, such as computing selection information and using verification, that are appropriate for your backup, and then click OK to close the Options dialog box.
- In the Explorer-like pane on the left, click the expand view box next to the drive C icon or My Documents icon, and locate and click the check boxes for the folders you want to back up.
- In the Backup media or file name box, enter the path and name of the file for storing the backup (for example, A:\Incremental #1.bkf).
- Click Job on the menu bar, click Save Selections, and in the Save dialog box, enter a name for the file that contains your backup file settings (such as Incremental), and then click the Save button.
- Click the Start Backup button, and after the Backup Job Information dialog box opens, modify the Backup description for identifying the backup.
- Click the Start Backup button and, after the backup is complete, click the Report button if you want to view, print, and save the report, close Notepad, close the Backup Progress dialog box, and then close the Backup Utility window.

Instead of storing incremental and differential backups in separate backup sets on your backup media, you can append (or add) the backups to the normal backup set for the beginning of that backup cycle. Using this strategy, the Backup Utility then keeps all the backups for one backup cycle within one backup set and more efficiently uses storage space on your backup media.

Restoring a File from a Normal Backup

As Marci was working on her computer the following day, she accidentally deleted one of the files she backed up the previous afternoon, and then emptied the Recycle Bin. Later, she realized what had happened, and she asks you to restore a copy of that file from her backup set.

To simulate this common type of scenario that you might face, you will "accidentally" delete a file in the MEI folder, and then restore it from your backup.

To restore a file that you accidentally deleted:

1. Click the **MEI** taskbar button, open the **Designs** folder, select and delete **Company Logo Design.bmp**, and then minimize the Designs folder window.

2. Insert the first floppy disk from your backup set in drive A, click the **Backup** desktop shortcut, click the **Advanced Mode** link in the Backup or Restore Wizard dialog box, and then click the **Restore and Manage Media** tab in the Backup Utility window. In the Contents pane on the right, you see a list of backups that you have performed on your computer. See Figure 6-57.

Figure 6-57   VIEWING THE CATALOGS FOR RECENT BACKUPS

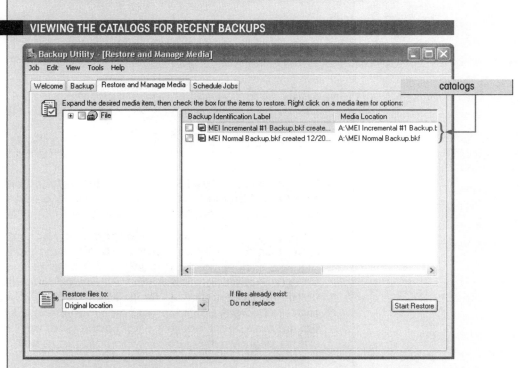

3. Click **Tools** on the menu bar, click **Options**, and on the Restore property sheet, verify that Backup is using the "Do not replace the file on my computer (recommended)" option (if not, click this option button). See Figure 6-58. Backup restores a file on your disk only if it does not exist on that disk. If there is a file with this name on your hard disk, Backup does not replace it with a copy from a backup set. You also can set Backup to replace the file only if the file on your computer is older, or to always replace the file. Because you just deleted the file you want to restore, any of these options would work.

Figure 6-58   REVIEWING RESTORE OPTIONS

protects existing files

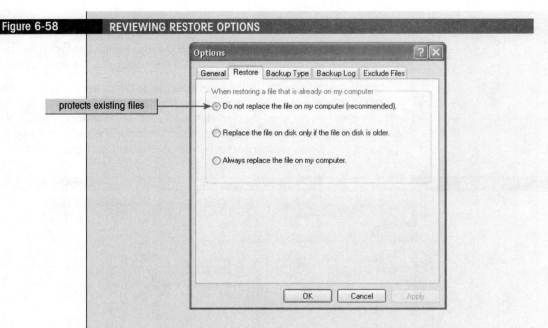

4. Click the **Backup Log** tab, make sure the **Detailed** option is selected, and then click the **OK** button. Even though this option is on a property sheet labeled "Backup," it also includes Restore operations.

5. In the pane on the left, click the **expand view** box ⊞ next to File, click ⊞ next to MEI Normal Backup.bkf, click the **C:** folder icon or name, click ⊞ for the C: folder, click ⊞ for the Documents and Settings folder, adjust your view in this pane (if necessary), click ⊞ for your user account folder, click ⊞ for the My Documents folder, click ⊞ for the MEI folder, adjust your view in this pane, click the **Designs** folder icon or name, and then click the **Company Logo Design.bmp** check box in the right pane (you might not see the entire file-name), as shown in Figure 6-59. You have just selected one file for the restore operation. Note also that the file will be restored to its original location.

Figure 6-59   CHOOSING A FILE TO RESTORE FROM A NORMAL BACKUP

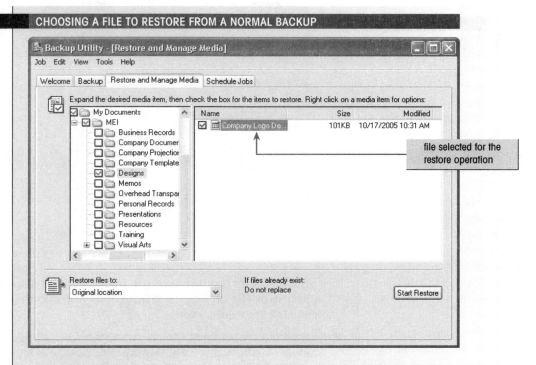

Because you've specified that the Backup utility should not replace files that already exist, you could have just clicked the C: check box without having to navigate the entire folder structure, but this step allows you to see how you would select a specific folder or file, or files, to restore from within a larger backup set.

6. Click the **Start Restore** button, click the **OK** button in the Confirm Restore dialog box, wait for Windows XP to create a System Restore checkpoint, and if prompted, insert the second floppy disk from your backup set, and then click the **OK** button. Backup eventually displays a Restore Progress dialog box and informs you that the restore is complete and that it restored one file. See Figure 6-60.

TROUBLE? If the Backup Utility displays a Check Backup File Location dialog box, verify that it has selected the correct backup file (or use the Browse button to locate and select it), and then click the OK button.

Figure 6-60 | **RESTORING FROM THE NORMAL BACKUP**

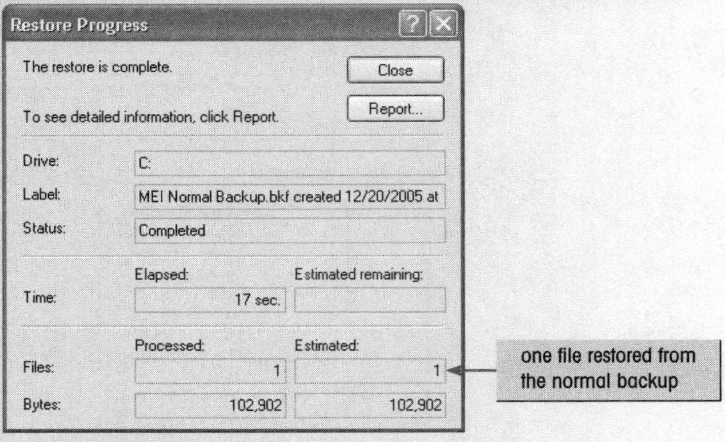

one file restored from the normal backup

7. If your instructor requests that you print a copy of this report, click the **Report** button, click **File** on the menu bar, click **Print**, choose the correct printer, and then click the **Print** button.

8. To save the report, click **File** on the Notepad menu bar, click **Save As**, click the **Save in** list arrow, open **My Documents**, open the **My Backup Reports** folder, type **MEI Partial Restore #1 Report** in the File name box, and then click the **Save** button.

9. Close Notepad.

10. Click the **Close** button to close the Backup Progress dialog box, and then close the Backup Utility window.

Next, check the Designs folder to see if Backup restored the correct file.

To verify the restore:

1. Click the **Designs** button on the taskbar to restore the Designs folder window. Notice that Backup restored the original copy of Company Logo Design.bmp to its original folder—the one with the dark blue background.

2. Minimize the Designs window.

By restoring this file from the MEI Normal backup, you restored the original version of the file, not the most recently modified version.

Restoring a File from an Incremental Backup

To restore the most recent version of a file, you would use the incremental backup that contained a copy of the revised file that you want to restore to your computer. If you restored all the files in a normal backup as you were rebuilding that folder on your computer, you would then restore files from each incremental backup in the order in which it was produced. If you discover that you need a previous version of a file, you can work your way back through the incremental backup sets.

After examining the restored file, Marci realized that she really wanted you to restore the more recent version of that file, not the original version. She notes that you have to use one of her incremental backups instead of her last normal backup.

To restore a file from an incremental backup:

1. Insert the floppy disk that contains your incremental backup into drive A (your second backup disk).

2. Click the **Backup** desktop shortcut, click the **Advanced Mode** link in the Backup or Restore Wizard dialog box, and then click the **Restore and Manage Media** tab.

3. Click **Tools** on the menu bar, click **Options**, and on the Restore property sheet, click the **Replace the file on disk only if the file on disk is older** option button.

4. Click the **Backup Log** tab, make sure that the **Detailed** option is selected, and then click the **OK** button.

5. In the pane on the left, click the **expand view** box ⊞ next to File, click ⊞ next to MEI Incremental #1 Backup.bkf, click the **C:** folder icon or name, click ⊞ for the C: folder, click ⊞ for the Documents and Settings folder, adjust your view in this pane (if necessary), click ⊞ for your user account folder, click ⊞ for the My Documents folder, click ⊞ for the MEI folder, adjust your view in this pane, click the **Designs** folder icon or name, and then click the **Company Logo Design.bmp** check box in the right pane (you might not see the entire filename).

6. Click the **Start Restore** button, click the **OK** button in the Confirm Restore dialog box, and wait for Windows XP to create a System Restore checkpoint. Backup then informs you that the restore is complete and that it restored one file. See Figure 6-61.

TROUBLE? If the Backup Utility displays a Check Backup File Location dialog box, verify that it has selected the correct backup file (or use the Browse button to locate and select it), and then click the OK button.

TROUBLE? If the Backup Utility did not restore the Company Logo Design.bmp file, but instead informs you that it skipped a file, close the Restore Progress dialog box, click Tools on the menu bar, click Options, click the Restore tab, click the "Always replace the file on my computer" option button, click the OK button to close the Options dialog box, click the Company Logo Design check box in the Contents pane, click the Start Restore button, click the OK button in the Confirm Restore dialog box, wait for Windows XP to create yet another System Restore checkpoint, and then wait for the Backup Utility to complete the restore operation.

Figure 6-61   FILE RESTORED FROM AN INCREMENTAL BACKUP

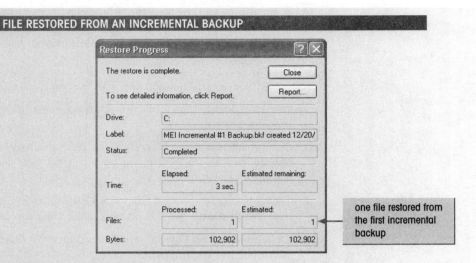

one file restored from the first incremental backup

7. If your instructor requests a printed copy of the restore report, click **Report**, click **File** on the menu bar, click **Print**, choose the correct printer, and then click the **Print** button.

8. To save the report, click **File** on the Notepad menu bar, click **Save As**, click the **Save in** list arrow, open **My Documents**, open the **My Backup Reports** folder, type **MEI Partial Restore #2 Report** in the File name box, and then click the **Save** button.

9. Close Notepad, close the Backup Progress dialog box, and then close the Backup Utility window.

Next, check to make sure Backup restored the most recent version of Company Logo Design.bmp

To verify the restore:

1. Click the **Designs** button on the taskbar. The Backup Utility restored the modified version of the Company Logo Design.bmp file—the one with the reddish-brown background.

2. Minimize the Designs folder window.

REFERENCE WINDOW   `RW`

Restoring a File From a Normal or Incremental Backup

- Insert the first floppy disk from your normal backup set in drive A.
- Click the Start button, point to All Programs, point to Accessories, point to System Tools, and then click Backup, or if you have a Backup shortcut on the desktop, click that shortcut.
- Click the Advanced Mode link in the Backup or Restore Wizard dialog box, and then click the Restore and Manage Media tab in the Backup Utility window.
- Click Tools on the menu bar, click Options, and on the Restore property sheet, verify that Backup is using the "Do not replace the file on my computer (recommended)" option (if not, click this option button).
- If you want a report with the names of restored files, click the Backup Log tab, make sure the Detailed option is selected, and then click the OK button.
- In the Explorer-like pane on the left, expand File and the backup that contains the file you want to restore, click the C: folder icon or name, expand the C: folder and the Documents and Settings folder, adjust your view in this pane (if necessary), expand your user account folder, the My Documents folder, and the folder that contains your files, keep repeating this process for each folder level, adjust your view in this pane, and then click the check box for the file you want to restore in the Content pane (you might not see the entire name).
- Click the Start Restore button, click OK in the Confirm Restore dialog box, wait for Windows XP to create a System Restore checkpoint, and then wait for Backup to display a Restore Progress dialog box and inform you that the restore is complete.
- If you want to print a report of the restore operation, click Report, click File on the menu bar, click Print, choose the correct printer, and then click the Print button.
- If you want to save the report, click File on the Notepad menu bar, click Save As, click the Save in list arrow, open My Documents, open the folder where you store your backup reports, type Partial Restore Report in the File name box, and then click the Save button.
- Close Notepad.
- Close the Backup Progress dialog box, and then close the Backup Utility window.

You have successfully performed a normal backup, restored a normal backup, performed an incremental backup of modified files, and restored a file from a normal backup and an incremental backup.

Using Saved Selections for an Incremental Backup

If you work on one or more other files after performing an incremental backup, you can perform your next incremental backup by using the backup job settings that you saved.

Since Marci performs a normal backup each week, and an incremental backup each Monday, Tuesday, Wednesday, and Thursday on the same set of files, she stores her backup settings in a Selection Scripts file called MEI Incremental.bks to save herself time and effort. It's now Tuesday, and Marci asks you to change one of her files, and then perform another incremental backup using her backup settings in the MEI Incremental.bks file.

The second disk in your backup set should have enough room for the incremental backup; if not, you need to use an additional formatted, but empty, floppy disk.

To change and then back up files:

1. Click the **Designs** taskbar button, right-click the **Company Logo Design.bmp** thumbnail, point to **Open With**, and then click **Paint**.

2. Change the background color of this image to a color of your own choosing, save your change to this file, close Paint, and then close the Designs folder window.

3. Click the **Backup** desktop shortcut, click the **Advanced Mode** link in the Backup or Restore Wizard dialog box, and then click the **Backup** tab. Notice that there are no files selected on drive C for a backup.

4. Click **Job** on the menu bar, click **Load Selections**, and in the Open dialog box, click **MEI Incremental.bks**. Backup uses the backup settings in this file to select files on drive C. Notice the light gray check mark in the drive C check box; this indicates only some of the files on the drive are selected for the backup.

5. Click the **expand view** box ⊞ for the My Documents folder, and then click ⊞ for the MEI folder. Notice that Backup selected all the folders in the MEI folder.

6. In the "Backup media or file name" text box, change the backup set filename to **A:\MEI Incremental #2.bkf**, and then click the **Start Backup** button.

7. In the Backup Job Information dialog box, add **MEI Incr #2** before the Backup description, make sure **Append this backup to the media** option button is selected, and then click the **Start Backup** button. After the backup is complete, Backup informs you that it backed up one file.

   TROUBLE? The Backup utility might report that it backed up two files if you are using Windows XP Home Edition. If this is the case, the Backup Utility backed up the Thumbs.db file even though you specified that it exclude files with the "db" file extension. Continue with the remaining steps, but when you print the report in the next step, make a note on the report that you excluded files with the "db" file extension so that your instructor knows that you did not skip that step.

8. If your instructor requests a printed copy of the restore report, click the **Report** button, click **File** on the menu bar, click **Print**, choose the correct printer, and then click the **Print** button.

9. To save the report, click **File** on the Notepad menu bar, click **Save As**, click the **Save in** list arrow, open **My Documents**, open the **My Backup Reports** folder, type **MEI Incremental #2 Backup Report** in the File name box, and then click the **Save** button.

10. Close Notepad, close the Backup Progress dialog box, and then close the Backup Utility window.

Next, check the floppy disk that contains the second incremental backup.

To view the disk with the second incremental backup:

1. Open a window onto drive A. Backup has added your second incremental backup to the same disk. See Figure 6-62. Your view might vary.

Figure 6-62   **VIEWING THE CONTENTS OF THE BACKUP MEDIA**

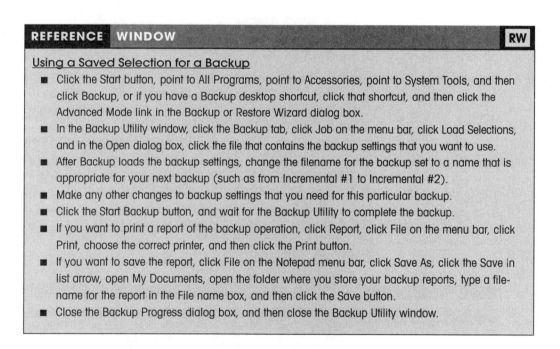

2. Close the 3½ Floppy (A:) window.

If you save each of your backup job settings, you can quickly open Backup, load the selections you need—whether for a normal backup or an incremental backup—change the name of the backup set, and then start the backup and append it to your backup media.

Scheduling **Backups**

If you want to schedule a backup job for a specific date or at specific intervals of time, you can open the Backup utility in Advanced Mode, select the Schedule Jobs tab, select a day of the week, and then click the Add Job button. The Backup Wizard steps you through the process of selecting files for the backup, specifying the destination and backup type for the backup, selecting backup options, scheduling when you want to run the backup, and specifying a password for the backup. Figure 6-63 shows Marci's scheduled backups for

December 2005. Normal backups are scheduled for every Friday (as shown by the blue letter "N" next to the backup icon), and incremental backups are scheduled for Monday, Tuesday, Wednesday, and Thursday (as shown by the light green letter "I" next to the backup icon).

Figure 6-63	MARCI'S SCHEDULED BACKUP JOBS

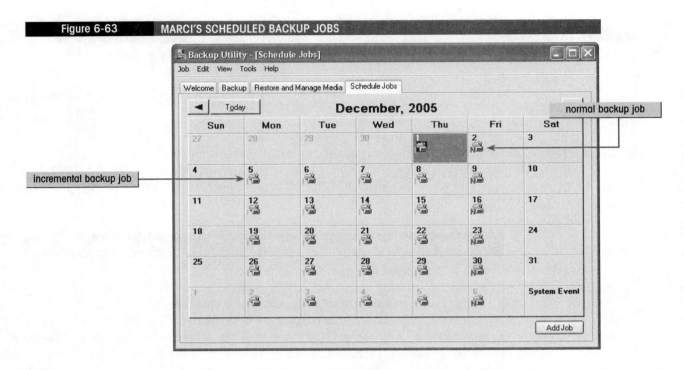

If you want to change the schedule for a backup job or delete a backup job, click the backup icon for a specific date on the Schedule Jobs sheet, and then change the properties and schedule of that backup, or delete it.

If you open the Scheduled Tasks folder using the Performance and Maintenance category link in the Control Panel, Windows XP displays a scheduled task for each type of backup, as shown in Figure 6-64.

Figure 6-64	VIEWING SCHEDULED TASKS

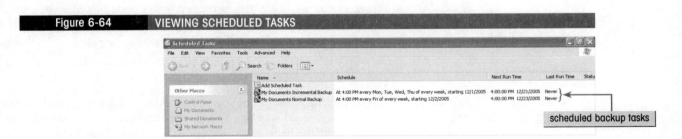

Notice that there is a normal backup scheduled for every Friday at 4:00 P.M., and incremental backups scheduled for every Monday, Tuesday, Wednesday, and Thursday, also at 4:00 P.M. Windows XP automatically runs the scheduled tasks on the designated days at the designated times.

By scheduling backups on a regular basis, you can focus on your work and let Windows XP open the Backup Utility at scheduled times so that you can back up your important files.

Using **Online Backup Services**

Online backup services, or Internet backup services, represent another option for backing up your computer. In fact, you might combine this option with other options to guarantee that you have at least two or more backup strategies. With an online backup service, you can back up the contents of your hard disk to a Web site using either backup software provided by that service or by using generic backup utilities to save data to FTP sites. These online backup services charge a fee based on the quantity of data that you store at their Web site. Figure 6-65 lists the names of some online backup services and their Web address.

Figure 6-65	ONLINE BACKUP SERVICES
COMPANY	**ADDRESS**
Ahsay Online Backup Services	www.ahsay.com/en/home
Amerivault Corp	www.amerivault.com
@Backup	www.backup.com
Back-It-Up Dot Com	www.back-it-up.com
BackupNet	www.backup.net
Compaq LiveVault	www.compaq.com/services/spotlight/index_livevault.html
Connected Jamcracker	www.jamcracker.com/solution/s2_20.shtml
NetMass SystemSafe	www.systemrestore.com
NOVaSTOR	services.online-backup.com
officesitebackupservices	www.offsitebackupservices.com
Online Internet Backup	www.onlinebackup.org
SwapDrive Backup	www.swapdrive.com
Virtual Backup	www.virtualbackup.com
XDrive Plus	www.xdrive.com

The first time you back up to an Internet server, you perform a normal backup. Thereafter, you are performing incremental backups that save only changes within modified files, not the entire file. To simplify the backup process, and to take advantage of those services that support drag and drop, organize the folders and files that you want to back up into a central folder. Some advantages of using an online backup service may include the following:

- **Free backup software** and, in some cases, free backups for a limited amount of data or for a trial period
- **Access 24 hours a day seven days a week** for backing up and for retrieving files from backups; if you are traveling or if you work in different locations, you can access your important files no matter where you are, and restore copies of them onto whatever computer you are using, so that you can work with those files. You can also back up a set of files on your current computer so that you can later restore those files to your office or home computer.

- **Off-site storage** to protect against damage to your primary site; if you experience a disaster in the region where you live and do business, you can still access and restore copies of your important business and personal records from the online backup service's vaults

- **Incremental backups** that save only changes within modified files, not the entire file

- **Data compression** for fast backups over the Internet and efficient use of storage space at the remote server (the server used by the online backup service)

- **Data encryption** to protect the security of your data during transmission over the Internet and while in long-term storage

- **Wizards** for simplifying the process of identifying files on your computer for backups

- **Drag-and-drop** support

- **Scheduling features** that let you schedule backups at times that suit your needs, or times that provide faster access to the service

- **Multiple sites and mirrored sites** for added security; some services provide multiple sites for backups. Some have mirrored sites, where one site is a mirror image of another. If you cannot access your data at one site, you try the other site.

- **Auxiliary power supplies** to handle power failures and power problems

- **Secure, guarded, fire-proof, flood-proof, temperature-controlled, and humidity-controlled vaults**; one service guarantees that their vaults can withstand direct hits from certain types of nuclear bombs

- **CD-ROM service** that provide next day delivery of a CD with your backups for a year

When evaluating online backup services, you should evaluate the type of user interface the service supports, and also determine how easy that interface is to use. Services, such as those that include wizards and that support features such as drag and drop, simplify the backup process. Other important concerns are the amount of storage space, the process for selecting files for backups and also for restoring files to your computer, the types of security and protection the service provides, and of course, the speed of the connection used for the backup.

These online backup services are relatively new, and features vary considerably. Furthermore, the services are constantly changing and improving. The best approach is to read reviews of online backup services in computer trade journals, use a Web search engine to locate information about online backup services, or visit the Web sites of the companies that offer this service, and evaluate the features, software, performance, and cost of their services.

Restoring **Other Types of Backups**

If you have upgraded your computer and your operating system over the years from MS-DOS to Windows 3.1 (or perhaps Windows 3.11), and then to Windows 95, Windows 98, Windows NT Workstation 4.0, Windows Me, or Windows 2000 before you then upgraded to Windows XP, you might have backups of files made with backup utilities designed for one or more of those operating systems. If you find that you need to restore files from those backups, you might need to use the same backup utility. You should therefore keep copies of the backup and restore utilities that you used, in the event that you need them. You also have to find out if you can install and use that backup utility under Windows XP. You might even want to consider dual or multiple boot configurations that provide access to different operating systems and that require different partitions on your hard disk that support different file systems.

Restoring **Your Computer's Settings**

If you are working in a computer lab, or if you want to restore your desktop computer to the settings that existed prior to working on this tutorial, complete the following steps to remove and restore Backup settings, to remove folders, files, and shortcuts, and to restore your computer system's settings.

To remove or restore Backup settings:

1. Click the **Backup** desktop shortcut, click the **Advanced Mode** link in the Backup or Restore Wizard dialog box, click the **Backup** tab, click **Job** on the menu bar, click **Load Selections**, and in the Open dialog box, right-click **MEI Incremental.bks**, click **Delete**, click the **Yes** button in the Confirm File Delete dialog box, and then click the **Cancel** button to close the Open dialog box.

2. Click **Tools** on the menu bar, click **Options**, click the **General** tab, and remove the check mark from the "Verify data after the backup completes" check box.

3. Click the **Restore** tab, and then click the **Do not replace the file on my computer (recommended)** option button.

4. Click the **Backup Type** tab, click the **Default Backup Type** list arrow, and then click **Normal**.

5. Click the **Backup Log** tab, and then click the **Summary** option button.

6. Click the **Exclude Files** tab, click **C:*.db** in the Files excluded for user (your user account name) section, click the **Remove** button, and then click the **OK** button.

7. Click the **Restore and Manage Media** tab, right-click the **MEI Normal Backup.bkf** Backup Identification Label, and then click **Delete catalog** on the shortcut menu. Repeat the same process for the MEI Incremental #1 Backup.bkf and MEI Incremental #2 Back.bkf Backup Identification Labels to delete these catalogs.

   POWER USER TIP If you want to select a group of catalogs to delete, and if the catalogs are adjacent to each other in the Backup Identification Label column, click the Backup Identification label for the first catalog (or backup job), hold down the **Shift** key, click the Backup Identification Label for the last catalog (or backup job), right-click the highlighted files, and then click Delete catalog.

8. Close the Backup Utility window.

Next, remove the folders, files, and shortcuts you no longer need.

To remove folders, files, and shortcuts:

1. Open My Documents, and then delete the **MEI** and **My Backup Reports** folders. Close the My Documents window.

2. Drag the **Backup** desktop shortcut to the Recycle Bin.

3. Empty the Recycle Bin.

You also need to restore your computer's settings.

To restore your computer's display settings:

1. If your computer was originally set for the Windows Classic style, right-click the **desktop**, click **Properties** on the shortcut menu, and after Windows XP opens the Display Properties dialog box, click the **Theme** list arrow on the Themes property sheet, click **Windows Classic**, and click the **OK** button.

2. To switch to the Windows Classic Start menu style, right-click the **Start** button, click **Properties** on the shortcut menu, and after Windows XP opens the Taskbar and Start Menu Properties dialog box, click the **Classic Start menu** option button on the Start Menu property sheet, and click then **OK** button.

3. To change Windows classic folders view, click the **Start** button, point to **Settings**, click **Control Panel**, and after Windows XP opens a Control Panel window, click **Tools** on the menu bar, click **Folder Options**, and after Windows XP opens the Folder Options dialog box, click the **Use Windows classic folders** option button, and then click the **Double-click to open an item** option button under "Click items as follows."

4. Click the **View** tab in the Folder Options dialog box. If necessary, restore the original settings for the "Display the full path in the address bar" check box, the "Do not show hidden files and folders" option, and the "Hide extensions for known file types" check box.

5. Click the **OK** button to close the Folder Options dialog box and restore your original settings, and then close the Control Panel folder window.

After reviewing and reevaluating her backup strategies and options, Marci decides to implement a combination of backup strategies so that she can restore important business files either from her on-site backups, her off-site backups, or from the Web site of her company's online backup service. The advantage of this plan is that she has a variety of sources from which to restore no matter what tragedy may befall her local hard disk. Plus, there is the added advantage that when she travels on business trips to meet with prospective clients, she can always access her online backup service to obtain copies of files should the necessity arise.

REVIEW ASSIGNMENT

Over the next week, Marci revises contracts and project proposals for two of MEI's largest clients. Now that a week has passed since her last backup, she wants you to make another normal backup of her MEI folder, and then do differential backups on a daily basis.

To complete this Review Assignment, you need copies of the files for Data Disk #1 and Data Disk #2, as well as two blank, formatted floppy disks that you can use for backups.

As you complete each step in this Review Assignment, record your answers to questions so that you can submit them to your instructor. Use a word-processing application such as Word or WordPad to prepare and then print your answers to these questions. Also, if you change any settings on the computer you are using, note what the original settings were so that you can restore them later.

1. Create a folder called MEI under the My Documents folder or on one of your drives. If a folder by that name already exists and if you are working in a computer lab, delete that folder.

2. Open the disk or folder containing the files for Data Disk #1, use the Ctrl key to select the Business Records, Company Documents, Company Projections, Presentations, and Resources folders, and then use the OLE properties of the taskbar to drag a copy of to the MEI folder. (*Do not copy the Personal Records folder or the two files to the MEI folder.*)

3. Open the disk or folder containing the files for Data Disk #2, open the Delta Oil folder, and then copy all the folders (Company Templates, Designs, Memos, Overhead Transparencies, and Training) to the MEI folder.

4. Examine the General property sheet for the MEI folder. How many folders does it contain? How many files are stored in those folders? What is the total size of those files? Close the MEI Properties dialog box, minimize the My Documents window, and close any other windows.

5. Open Backup and use the Backup or Restore Wizard to back up all the files in the MEI folder to a file named MEI Normal Backup on a floppy disk in drive A. Use the Advanced button to verify and change settings. Choose a Normal backup, include the option to verify data after the backup, choose the option to replace the data on the backup media with this backup, and then start the backup. How many files did the Backup utility back up? How many bytes were backed up? Were there any errors? Print a report that summarizes the backup, and then close the Backup Progress dialog box.

6. Check the backup set on your floppy disks. What is the name of the file with the normal backup on each disk? What is the file type? How large is the file that contains the normal backup on each disk? Close the 3½ Floppy (A:) window.

7. Open the MEI folder, open the Designs folder, open the Company Logo Design.bmp file with Paint, make a change to the image (you might, for example, use the Flip/Rotate option on the Image menu to rotate the image 270 degrees), save the changes, and then close Paint. Open the Training folder, open the Computer Basics Training Proposal.doc file in Word or WordPad, make a change to this file, and save the changes. Open the Memos folder, open the Microsoft's Web Site.doc in Word or WordPad, and use the Save As command on the File menu to save a copy of this document in a new file named Intel's Web Site in the Memos folder. Change the references to Microsoft in the memo to Intel, delete the second sentence in the first paragraph, and then save the updated document. Close any open windows.

Explore 8. Insert the last disk from your normal backup into drive A. Open Backup, and use the Backup Wizard to perform a differential backup. Select the MEI folder, change the backup media name to MEI Differential #1 Backup, and then use the Advanced button to specify other backup settings. Choose the options for a Differential backup option, for verifying data after the backup, for appending this backup to the backup media, and then start the backup. View and print a report of the differential backup. How many files were backed up? How many bytes of data were backed up? Close the Backup Progress dialog box.

9. Check the backup set on your floppy disk. What is the name of the file with the differential backup? How large is the file that contains the differential backup?

10. Delete the MEI folder to simulate an accidental deletion.

11. Use the Backup or Restore Wizard to restore the MEI folder. Make sure you use the correct backup set (and correct disk) for the restore. Use the Advanced button to choose the option to restore the folder to its original location. How many files were restored? How many bytes were restored? Were there any errors? Print a report that summarizes the restore, and then close the Restore Progress dialog box.

12. Open the MEI folder, and then the Designs folder. Which version of the Company Logo Design.bmp file did the Backup utility restore? Why did this occur?

Explore

13. Use the Backup or Restore Wizard to restore changes made to files in the MEI folder from your first differential backup. Make sure you use the correct backup set (and correct disk) for the restore. Use the Advanced button to restore the files to their original locations, and to replace existing files. How many files were restored? How many bytes were restored? Were there any errors? Print a report that summarizes the restore, and then close the Restore Progress dialog box.

14. Open the MEI folder, and then the Designs folder. Which version of the Company Logo Design.bmp file did the Backup utility restore? Why did this occur?

15. To restore the original settings to your Backup utility, open Backup, click the Advanced Mode link, click Tools on the menu bar, click Options, click the Restore tab, click the "Do not replace the file on my computer (recommended)" option button, if necessary click the Backup Type tab, click the Default Backup Type list arrow, click Normal, if necessary click the OK button to close the Options dialog box, click the Restore and Manage Media tab, select "MEI Differential #1.bkf" and "MEI Normal Backup.bkf" listed under Backup Identification Label, delete these catalogs, and then close Backup.

16. Delete the MEI folder, empty the Recycle Bin, and perform a quick format on each of your backup media to erase the backup sets on the disks.

CASE PROBLEMS

Case 1. Backing Up Files at First Mortgage Corporation First Mortgage Corporation (FMC) offers FHA, VA, and conventional home loans to prospective buyers in California. Allan Thompson works as a finance officer for one of First Mortgage Corporation's branches. Allan performs a normal backup of his files every week and performs incremental backups daily. It's Friday afternoon, and Allan is ready for his next normal backup. After he performs that backup, he wants to use Backup to restore a copy of the files in his backup set to his laptop computer that he uses while traveling on business trips.

As you complete each step in this case, record your answers to questions so that you can submit them to your instructor. Use a word-processing application such as Word or WordPad to prepare and then print your answers to these questions. Also, if you change any settings on the computer you are using, note what the original settings were so that you can restore them later.

To complete this case, you need copies of the folders and files on Data Disk #1 and Data Disk #2, as well as a blank, formatted floppy disk.

1. Open My Documents, create a new folder on drive C named FMC, open the drive or folder that contains the files for Data Disk #1, and then copy the Company Documents, Company Projections, and Resources folders to the FMC folder. From the drive or folder that contains the files for Data Disk #2, copy the Company Templates and Memos folders from the Delta Oil folder to the FMC folder.

2. View the properties of the FMC folder. How many folders are included in this folder? How many files are included in this folder? What is the size of this folder and its contents in MB and in bytes? How many disks do you estimate you would need for this backup?

3. Open Backup, switch to Advanced Mode, select the Backup sheet, select the FMC folder to include it in your backup, assign the name FMC Normal Backup to the backup media filename, set the backup type to Normal, and choose the options for verifying data after a backup and for a detailed backup log.

4. Save the backup selections as FMC Normal, make sure a blank, formatted floppy disk is in drive A, start the backup, and change the Backup description to include "FMC Normal" at the beginning of the label, and then complete the backup. View, and then print a copy of the backup report.

Explore   5. To simulate the process of restoring a folder from a backup set onto another computer, select the Restore and Manage Media sheet, delete the FMC Normal Backup.bkf catalog, and change the name of the FMC folder in the My Documents folder to First Mortgage Corporation. *Note*: If you were installing this backup set onto another computer, that computer would not have the backup catalog. Also, since you are going to restore your backup to the My Documents folder, which contains the FMC folder, you need to rename the FMC folder so that it does not interfere with your restore operation.

Explore   6. On the Tools menu, in the Backup utility window, click Catalog a backup file, and then use the Browse button, if necessary, to select the FMC Normal Backup.bkf file on the floppy disk used as your backup media, so that the Backup utility can rebuild the on-disk catalog from the on-media catalog.

Explore   7. Load the set list and set directory from the backup file by expanding File, FMC Normal Backup, and then C: in the left pane. Select the option for restoring everything on drive C, and then expand the folder structure to verify that the Backup utility will restore the FMC folder and its contents. Start the restore. After the restore is complete, view and then print the restore report.

8. Check the properties of the FMC folder. How many folders does the FMC folder contain? How many files are stored in these folders? What is the total size of the FMC folder and its contents in both megabytes and in bytes?

9. Compare your responses to the questions in Steps 2 and 8. Did the Backup utility restore the entire FMC folder structure and all the files?

10. To restore the original settings to the Backup utility and clean up your computer, open the Backup utility in Advanced Mode, select the Backup sheet, select Job on the menu bar, select Load Selections, and delete the FMC Normal.bks selection script, select the Restore and Manage Media sheet, delete the FMC Normal Backup.bkf catalog under Backup Identification Label, select Tools on the menu bar, select Options, remove the check mark from the "Verify data after the backup completes" check box on the General property sheet, select the Backup Log sheet, select the Summary option, and then close Backup. Delete the First Mortgage Corporation and FMC folders, and then empty the Recycle Bin.

Case 2. Backing Up and Restoring Files at Voice Mail Communications, Inc. Voice Mail Communications, Inc. (VMC) sells voice-messaging systems to businesses and corporations in the Midwest. Gloria McPherson, a manager at Voice Mail Communications, is exploring different options for backing up her important documents. Rather than use only one backup approach, backing up to tape, she wants to use three different backup approaches. In the event she is unable to restore her documents from one type of backup, she might be able to restore them from one of her other backup approaches. She decides to back up her document files to a folder on her hard disk, and then test the backup with a sample restore.

As you complete each step in this case, record your answers to questions so that you can submit them to your instructor. Use a word-processing application such as Word or WordPad to prepare and then print your answers to these questions. Also, if you change any settings on the computer you are using, note what the original settings were so that you can restore them later.

To complete this case, you need copies of the folders and files on Data Disk #1 and Data Disk #2.

1. Create a new folder named VMC under the My Documents folder or on one of your drives, and then open the VMC folder.

2. Copy the Business Records, Company Documents, and Company Projections folders from the folder or floppy disk that contains the files for Data Disk #1 to the VMC folder. Copy the Company Templates folder from the folder or floppy disk that contains the files for Data Disk #2 to the VMC folder.

3. View properties of the VMC folder. How many folders are included in this folder? How many files are included in this folder? What is the size of this folder and its contents in MB and in bytes?

4. Create another folder called VMC Backup in the My Documents folder or on one of your drives.

Explore   5. Open Backup in Advanced Mode, select the Backup sheet, and create a new backup job that includes the VMC folder. For the Backup media or file name, use the Browse button to locate the VMC Backup folder, and then specify VMC Normal Backup.bkf as the backup file name.

Explore   6. Set the backup type to Normal, choose the option for a detailed backup log, exclude the "db" (or Data Base File) registered file type for your user account, apply it to a path that starts at the VMC folder, choose the option to verify data after the backup, and then start the backup. Edit the Backup Job Information to include "VMC Normal" at the beginning of the Backup description, and then perform the backup. View and print a copy of the backup report, and then close Backup.

Explore   7. Open the VMC Backup folder. How large is the VMC Normal Backup.bkf file? Divide this value, expressed in KB, by 1,024 to determine the size in MB. How large is the VMC Normal Backup.bkf file in MB? How do your responses for this step compare with those for Step 3? Explain why one file is larger than another.

8. Delete the VMC folder, and then use the Backup Advanced Mode to restore the VMC folder and its contents from the backup you just created. After the restore is complete, view and print the summary report, and then close Backup.

9. View properties of the VMC folder. How many folders are included in this folder? How many files are included in this folder? What is the size of this folder and its contents in MB and in bytes? How do your responses in this step compare with those for Step 3?

10. To restore the original settings to the Backup utility and clean up your computer, open the Backup utility in Advanced Mode, select the Restore and Manage Media sheet, delete the VMC Normal Backup.bkf catalog under Backup Identification Label, select Tools on the menu bar, select Options, remove the check mark from the "Verify data after the backup completes" check box, select the Backup Log sheet, select the Summary option, select the Exclude Files sheet, and remove the excluded file for your user account (the "db" registered file type), and then close Backup. Delete the VMC and VMC Backup folders, and then empty the Recycle Bin.

11. How does backing up to drive C differ from backing up to a floppy disk in drive A?

Case 3. Developing a Backup Strategy for Redwood County Water Agency The Redwood County Water Agency recently hired Anthony Fenwick to use AutoCAD to prepare maps from aerial photos of the different habitats within the county. Since each map represents a major investment of time and resources for the water agency, Anthony wants to develop an effective backup strategy. The following list summarizes his approach to identify the best backup strategy to use:

- Anthony has partitioned his computer into two drives, and stores all the files with his maps in project subfolders under the Maps folder on drive D.
- Because maps require an extensive amount of time to produce, he wants to be able to restore previous versions of any map, in the event a map becomes corrupted. Then he can reconstruct the remainder of that map using the previous version.
- Anthony also needs to routinely retrieve an earlier version of a map from a backup set so that he can produce a new variation of the same map.

Using the factors in the preceding list, answer the following questions:

1. What types of backups should Anthony use as part of his overall backup strategy to ensure that he can restore the folders that contain his maps in the event of a major problem?

2. What settings should he specify when he performs a backup, and why?

3. How many copies of each backup set should Anthony keep, and where should he store those backup sets?

Explore

4. Using the factors in the preceding list, outline Anthony's backup schedule in a table similar to the one shown in Figure 6-66.

Figure 6-66   **BACKUP STRATEGY FOR REDWOOD COUNTY WATER AGENCY**

BACKUP SCHEDULE	TYPE OF BACKUP	FILES INCLUDED IN THE BACKUP
Start of Backup Cycle: Friday		
End of Day 1: Monday		
End of Day 2: Tuesday		
End of Day 3: Wednesday		
End of Day 4: Thursday		
Start of Next Backup Cycle: Friday		

Case 4. Developing a Backup Strategy for Ross and Bauer Ross and Bauer is a consulting firm that assists city and regional managers in long-range planning. Annabel Clayton works as a staff biologist who consults with city and regional planners on the impact that growth and development will have on the natural resources of a region. Annabel wants to develop a backup strategy that enables her to reconstruct her records should she experience problems with her computer. She asks you to analyze the following factors to help her develop a comprehensive backup strategy:

- Annabel wants to restore her entire system in the event her hard disk fails.
- She has organized her document folders on drive C by project, resource, and client.

- Because each project usually requires analysis and development of long-range proposals, she works on the same projects for one to two years. During this time, she works with the same set of files each day.
- During each backup cycle, she wants to keep backup copies of only the most recent versions of her files. Since each draft of a file is thoroughly reviewed before it is updated, Annabel does not need to restore earlier versions of her files.

Using the factors in the preceding list, answer the following questions:

1. What types of backups should Annabel use as part of her overall backup strategy to ensure that she can restore her entire system and the folders that contain her project files?

2. What settings should she specify when she performs a backup, and why?

Explore

3. Using the factors in the preceding list, outline Annabel's backup schedule in a table similar to the one shown in Figure 6-67.

Figure 6-67	BACKUP STRATEGY FOR ROSS AND BAUER

BACKUP SCHEDULE	TYPE OF BACKUP	FILES INCLUDED IN THE BACKUP
Start of Backup Cycle: Friday		
End of Day 1: Monday		
End of Day 2: Tuesday		
End of Day 3: Wednesday		
End of Day 4: Thursday		
Start of Next Backup Cycle: Friday		

OBJECTIVES

In this tutorial you will:

- Use the Disk Cleanup Wizard to remove files that you no longer need

- Use the Check Disk utility to check a FAT volume for errors

- Learn what causes file fragmentation

- Defragment a disk

- Use the Disk Management snap-in tool

- Learn how to set disk quotas for users

- Compress and uncompress a folder and its files

- Encrypt and decrypt a folder and its files

- Schedule a task to start automatically

OPTIMIZING DISKS

Optimizing the Storage of Files on Disks

CASE

Harris & Banche

Harris & Banche, a large advertising agency in Atlanta, handles product advertising, public relations, sales promotions, and direct marketing services for its corporate clients. Mark Ames works as a telecommunications specialist for Harris & Banche. As part of his management responsibilities, Mark oversees two microcomputer specialists who provide support to other employees. Mark recently discussed the value of implementing a regular disk optimization routine with his staff at Harris & Banche.

Disk optimization refers to checking for and correcting errors that interfere with the performance of your hard disk, reorganizing the storage space on a disk so that the operating system can quickly locate folders and files, and using other techniques that improve the performance, availability, and efficient use of storage space on a hard disk.

Mark asks you to show other employees how to use the Disk Cleanup Wizard, check the integrity of their hard disks, and optimize the performance of their hard disks. He wants you to encourage staff to periodically archive or delete files they no longer need so that they do not run into problems with nearly full hard disks. Mark also asks you to evaluate the use of disk quotas, folder and file compression, and folder and file encryption to determine how staff might best benefit from these technologies.

In the first part of this tutorial, you use the Disk Cleanup Wizard to check a hard disk for files that can safely be deleted. You also learn how to use Check Disk and the Error-checking reporting tool to examine a hard disk for errors, and how to use Disk Defragmenter to defragment a hard disk.

Getting Started

To complete this tutorial, you need to switch your computer to Web style, and turn on the options for displaying file extensions and displaying the full path in the Address bar. As you complete these steps, you may discover that your computer is already set up for Web style, or that other settings are already in place, so you might only need to make a few changes to your computer's settings.

To set up your computer:

1. To change to the Windows XP theme, right-click the **desktop**, click **Properties** on the shortcut menu, and after Windows XP opens the Display Properties dialog box, click the **Theme** list arrow on the Themes property sheet, click **Windows XP**, if necessary, and then click the **OK** button.

2. To switch to the Windows XP Start menu style, right-click the **Start** button, click **Properties** on the shortcut menu, and after Windows XP opens the Taskbar and Start Menu Properties dialog box, click the **Start menu** option button on the Start Menu property sheet, if necessary, and then click the **OK** button.

3. To change to a task-oriented view of folders and enable single-clicking, click the **Start** button, click **My Computer**, click **Tools** on the menu bar, click **Folder Options**, and after Windows XP opens the Folder Options dialog box, click the **Show common tasks in folders** option button if it is not already selected, click the **Single-click to open an item** option button if it is not already selected, and click the **Underline icon titles only when I point at them** option button if it is not already selected.

4. Click the **View** tab, click the **Display the full path in the address bar** check box if it is not already selected, click the **Show hidden files and folders** option button if it is not already selected, and if there is a check mark in the "Hide extensions for known file types" check box, click that check box to remove the check mark, click the **OK** button to close the Folder Options dialog box, and then close My Computer.

Now you're ready to look at different ways to optimize the performance of your computer.

Using the Disk Cleanup Wizard

The Disk Cleanup Wizard searches for and removes the following types of files and components:

- Downloaded program files
- Temporary Internet files
- Offline Web pages
- Old Chkdsk files
- Files in the Recycle Bin
- Setup log files
- Temporary files
- WebClient/Publisher temporary files

■ Catalog files for the Content Indexer

■ Old files it can compress

Downloaded program files consist of ActiveX controls and Java applets that Internet Explorer automatically downloads and stores in the Downloaded Program Files folder under the Windows folder. An **ActiveX control** is a small program, such as an animated counter, that Internet Explorer downloads from a Web site and runs locally on your computer. A **Java applet** is similar to an ActiveX control; however, the program is written in the Java programming language while ActiveX controls are typically written in Visual Basic or C++. Note that the Downloaded Program Files folder does not include files for programs that you deliberately download and then install on your computer. Nor does it include Web browser plug-ins, device drivers, or program updates (such as Real Player or Acrobat) that you download and install on your computer. You should store copies of these important downloaded files in a folder within the My Documents folder in case you need to reinstall the programs later. However, you can safely remove program files that your Web browser automatically downloaded to the Downloaded Program Files folder from Web sites.

Temporary Internet files are files that Internet Explorer downloads and stores in the Temporary Internet Files folder for your user account. Whenever you access a Web page, all of the components on the Web page—graphics, sounds, animations, the HTML code for the page itself, and many other types of files—are downloaded to the Temporary Internet Files folder. The Disk Cleanup Wizard can remove all of these files, but does not change personalized settings for Web pages. Over time, the number of files in this folder increases and consumes more storage space on your hard disk, which can impair the performance of your computer. These files constitute what is commonly known as your Internet cache. A **cache** (pronounced "cash") is a folder or area of memory where data is temporarily stored. If you visit the same Web sites repeatedly, Internet Explorer can display Web pages more quickly because it doesn't have to download them; instead, it accesses the files for those Web pages in the Temporary Internet Files folder and, if necessary, updates them if the content of the Web page you visit has changed. You therefore probably want to retain the contents of the Temporary Internet Files folder. If you do not frequently visit the same Web sites, you may want to periodically empty the Temporary Internet Files folder, reclaim valuable storage space, and improve the performance of your computer. Because the Disk Cleanup Wizard does not identify files cached by other browsers, such as Netscape Navigator, you must use your Web browser to remove the files downloaded and stored locally on your computer.

Offline Web pages are Web pages that are stored on your computer so that you can view them without being connected to the Internet.

If a drive contains file fragments recovered by the Check Disk utility (which you examine in the next section), the Disk Cleanup Wizard displays a category of files called Old Chkdsk files. In most cases, these files are unnecessary, and you can delete them.

You can also remove deleted files in the Recycle Bin, but then they are no longer available if you need to restore a file to a hard disk.

Setup log files are files that contain information about the installation of Windows XP or other software.

Temporary files are files that applications create when you are working with a document. The application uses these temporary files for processing data. When you close the file, the temporary files are deleted from disk. However, if a power failure or some other type of problem occurs, any open temporary files remain on disk. These files are stored in one of four folders: C:\Windows\Temp (used by all versions of Windows); C:\Documents and Settings\[*User Account*]\Local Settings\Temp (for an individual's user logon); and the current folder with the original file. You can even view the process of creating a temporary file. For example, Figure 7-1 shows a tiled view of a Microsoft Word window and the Harris & Banche folder window that contains a Microsoft Word file named Financial Performance.doc. After opening the file in Microsoft Word, Windows XP updates the view of the folder window to show a temporary file called ~$nancial Performance.doc. See Figure 7-2. After closing Microsoft Word, Windows XP again updates the folder window to show that the temporary file no longer exists. See Figure 7-3. If the power failed while you were working on this file, the temporary file would remain on disk, and you might be able to recover the document later by opening this file. Although you might still have the original copy of this file, the temporary file might contain changes that you did not have a chance to save under the original filename before the power failure occurred.

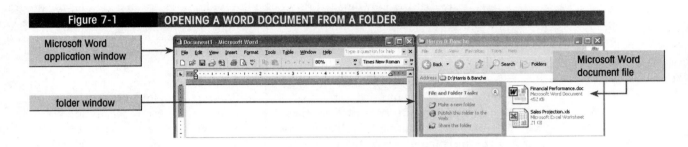

Figure 7-1   OPENING A WORD DOCUMENT FROM A FOLDER

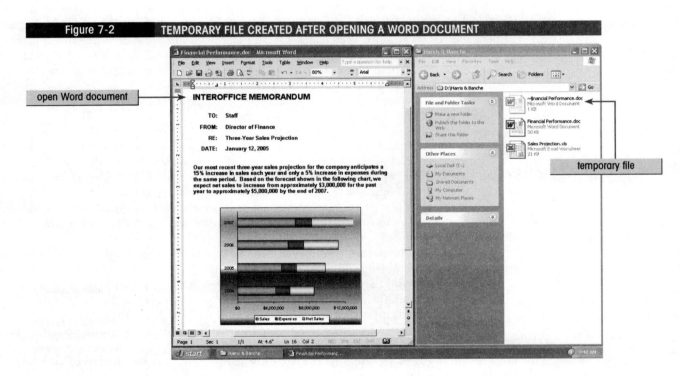

Figure 7-2   TEMPORARY FILE CREATED AFTER OPENING A WORD DOCUMENT

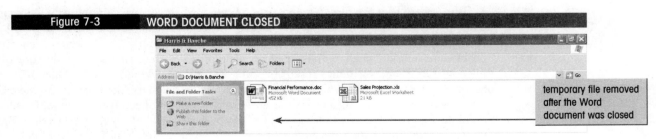

Figure 7-3   WORD DOCUMENT CLOSED

WebClient/Publisher is a service that maintains a cache of accessed files on your hard disk.

The Catalog files for the Content Indexer category includes index files created by the Indexing Service in Windows XP to speed up file searches. This service indexes the contents and properties of files on your local hard disk drive(s) and on shared network drives. The Disk Cleanup Wizard can delete files that remain from a previous indexing operation.

On an NTFS drive, the Disk Cleanup Wizard identifies files that you have not used for over 50 days, and you have the option of compressing those files to save valuable disk storage space. You still have access to the files.

The Disk Cleanup Wizard is only available for drives on your hard disk.

As part of a regular disk maintenance program, Mark asks you to show employees how to use the Disk Cleanup Wizard to remove files that they no longer need and that waste valuable storage space on their hard disks.

In the following steps, you determine how much storage space you can free up on your hard disk. If you are working in a computer lab, the technical support staff might use the Disk Cleanup Wizard on a regular basis and might prefer that you not make any changes to the computer without their permission. Ask your instructor or technical support staff whether you can use the Disk Cleanup Wizard.

To run the Disk Cleanup Wizard:

1. Open My Computer, right-click the icon for **drive C** (which might be labeled Local Disk (C:)), click **Properties** on the shortcut menu, and then click the **Disk Cleanup** button. After the Disk Cleanup Wizard examines drive C (which may take several minutes, depending upon the size of your hard disk, the speed of the processor, and the number of files to be reviewed), it reports on its findings. See Figure 7-4. The options shown in the Files to delete list box vary depending on how your computer is set up, which file system a drive uses, what the Disk Cleanup Wizard finds, and what it proposes to remove.

Figure 7-4	RUNNING THE DISK CLEANUP WIZARD ON A FAT VOLUME

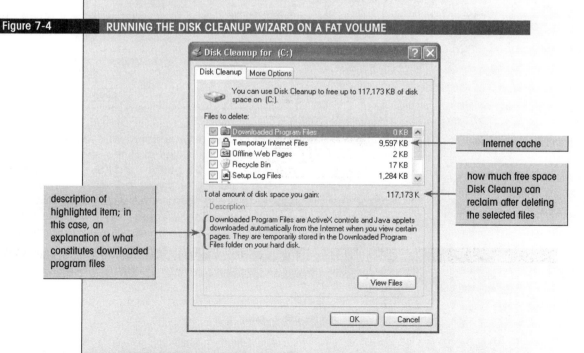

On the computer used for this figure, the Disk Cleanup Wizard reports that it can free up to 117,173 KB (or approximately 114.4 MB) of storage space on drive C by deleting specific files that are no longer needed. Most of those files are temporary files (103.8 MB) and Temporary Internet Files (9.4 MB). For some of the options listed in the Files to delete box, you can view the contents of the folder that contains a specific type of file. To do so, you first select an option, and then click the View Files button.

If you run Disk Cleanup on an NTFS volume, this dialog box includes a "Compress old files" check box. See Figure 7-5. As noted earlier, if you enable this option, Windows XP compresses files that you have not accessed in a while. The amount of space that you gain could be considerable. On the computer used for this figure, you could gain up to 3.6 GB (or 3,779,819 KB) of extra storage space by compressing unused files. If you select this option, and then click the Options button, you can specify how many days Windows XP should wait before it selects files as candidates for compression. The default is 50 days.

Figure 7-5	RUNNING THE DISK CLEANUP WIZARD ON AN NTFS VOLUME

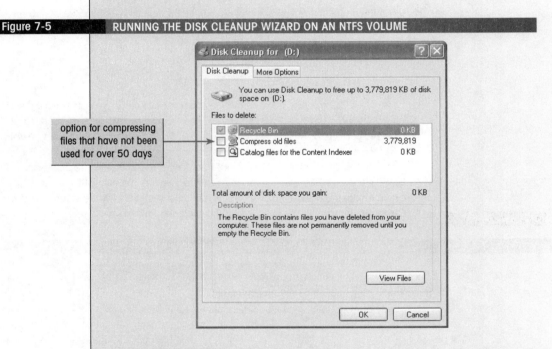

option for compressing files that have not been used for over 50 days

2. If you are working on your own computer and want to free storage space by removing one or more categories of files, click the check box for each type of file you want to remove, click the **OK** button, and then click the **Yes** button. If you are working in a computer lab, ask your instructor or technical support staff for permission to remove files from the hard disk. (The Disk Cleanup for (C:) dialog box charts your progress. The cleanup may take several moments depending upon how many files are to be removed or compressed.)

3. Close the Properties dialog box for drive C, and then close My Computer.

The Disk Cleanup Wizard is one simple way you can maintain your computer by removing files that are no longer needed.

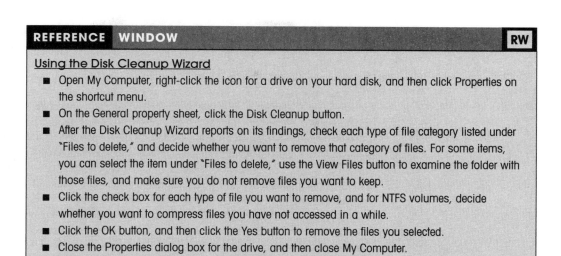

REFERENCE WINDOW   **RW**

Using the Disk Cleanup Wizard

- Open My Computer, right-click the icon for a drive on your hard disk, and then click Properties on the shortcut menu.
- On the General property sheet, click the Disk Cleanup button.
- After the Disk Cleanup Wizard reports on its findings, check each type of file category listed under "Files to delete," and decide whether you want to remove that category of files. For some items, you can select the item under "Files to delete," use the View Files button to examine the folder with those files, and make sure you do not remove files you want to keep.
- Click the check box for each type of file you want to remove, and for NTFS volumes, decide whether you want to compress files you have not accessed in a while.
- Click the OK button, and then click the Yes button to remove the files you selected.
- Close the Properties dialog box for the drive, and then close My Computer.

You can use another approach to delete downloaded program files and temporary Internet files. If you right-click the Internet Explorer desktop icon and select Properties, Windows XP opens an Internet Properties dialog box. See Figure 7-6. You can then use the Delete Files button under Temporary Internet files on the General property sheet to delete temporary Internet files stored in the Temporary Internet files folder for your user account and to delete downloaded program files stored in the Downloaded Program Files folder under the Windows folder. You also can delete cookies stored in the Cookies folder for your user account.

Figure 7-6   INTERNET EXPLORER OPTIONS FOR CLEARING THE INTERNET CACHE

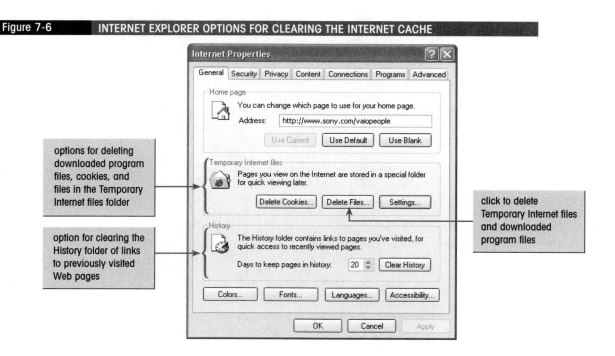

Under History on the General property sheet, you can clear the contents of the History folder for your user account. This folder contains links to Web pages that you've visited.

Windows XP also has a Desktop Cleanup Wizard for removing unused desktop icons. The Desktop Cleanup Wizard is automatically scheduled to run every 60 days so you can remove any desktop objects and shortcuts that have not been used for 60 days or more. When you first use the Desktop Cleanup Wizard, it creates an Unused Desktop Shortcuts folder on the desktop for any desktop shortcuts you choose to remove. If you want to run the Desktop Cleanup Wizard at any time, you can right-click the desktop, select Properties on the shortcut menu, select the Desktop tab in the Display Properties dialog box, click the Customize Desktop button, and after the Desktop Items dialog box opens, click the Clean Desktop Now button under Desktop cleanup on the General property sheet. The Desktop Cleanup Wizard displays a Welcome dialog box explaining its function, and then displays a list of desktop shortcuts that have not been used for 60 days or more, identifies the date they were last used, and lets you choose which ones you want to remove from the desktop. If you change your mind later, you can open the Unused Desktop Shortcuts folder, and drag a desktop shortcut back onto the desktop. If you do not want to use this feature, you can use the General property sheet in the Desktop Items dialog box to turn off the option for running the Desktop Cleanup Wizard every 60 days.

Understanding the Importance of the Check Disk Utility

The Check Disk utility is a disk analysis and repair utility that examines disks for errors and repairs errors when possible. It checks the **logical structure** (the file system), and it can also check the physical structure (the integrity of a disk's surface). Since the file systems of FAT volumes and NTFS volumes differ, the Check Disk utility examines different data structures important to tracking folders and files on each type of volume. If it finds bad sectors that contain data, the Check Disk utility attempts to move the data to another location and recover that data.

The Check Disk utility was originally introduced with the DOS operating system and is available in both the Windows 9x and Windows NT product lines. In contrast, the Windows 9x product line relies on the use of the ScanDisk utility, also introduced originally under MS-DOS. Both utilities are disk analysis and repair utilities that work in a similar way; however, ScanDisk is typically used in the Windows GUI in the Windows 9x product line, whereas Check Disk is used in command-line window in both product lines. The Windows 9x product line also has a command-line version of ScanDisk, and Windows 2000 and Windows XP have a GUI version of Check Disk called the Error-checking tool.

Using Check Disk on FAT Volumes

Although NTFS is the native file system for the Windows NT product line, including Windows XP, the FAT file system is still important for Windows XP users. DOS and the different versions of the Windows operating systems all support the FAT file system, and if you need to set up a dual-boot or multiple-boot configuration, you might need to use the FAT file system. Dual-boot and multiple-boot configurations are useful in training environments, including computer labs, where individuals might need to use different operating systems on the same computer. Increasingly, computer labs rely on computers with removable hard disks, and the technical support staff inserts hard disks containing the appropriate operating system prior to a workshop or training session. If you want the option of booting Windows XP with Windows ME, Windows 98, Windows 95, or MS-DOS and Windows 3.1, for example, you must have a FAT partition where you can install those other operating systems. Those other operating systems cannot recognize or access an NTFS volume; however, Windows XP can access the FAT volume. Likewise, if you create a dual-boot configuration with Windows XP and Windows NT Workstation 4.0, Microsoft recommends using the

FAT file system on the partition with Windows NT Workstation 4.0. Although Windows NT Workstation 4.0 also supports NTFS, it does not support the newer features of NTFS found in Windows XP, such as the ability to encrypt folders and files.

When it examines the file system on a FAT volume, the Check Disk utility checks the File Allocation Tables (FAT1 and FAT2), the directory table for the top-level folder (or root directory), the folder (or directory) structure, the integrity of files, and the validity of long filenames. Recall that the File Allocation Table contains information on cluster usage, and that the operating system keeps and updates two copies of that File Allocation Table (FAT1 and FAT2). When the Check Disk utility examines the File Allocation Tables, it traces the chain for each file and accounts for all clusters in use by each file. If the operating system cannot read the disk clusters that contain the first copy of the File Allocation Table (FAT1) for the information it needs, it reads the disk clusters that contain the second copy of the File Allocation Table (FAT2). If you notice that the latter occurs on your computer, you should back up your hard disk as soon as possible because it might be close to failure. Then you can try to reformat the drive to determine if it is still functional. If so, you would then reinstall the operating system, application software, and utilities, and restore your data files from backups.

The directory table for the top-level folder (or root directory) tracks information on the folders and files that are stored in the top-level folder of a disk, including the starting cluster for each file and its size. The Check Disk utility verifies that the size of each file matches the total amount of storage space assigned to clusters for each file in the File Allocation Table.

The folder or directory structure is also important because Windows XP must be able to navigate it to locate and store files on a disk. The Check Disk utility navigates up and down the entire directory structure of a disk to ensure that it is functional and intact.

Checking for Lost Clusters

When Check Disk verifies the integrity of files, it looks for lost clusters and cross-linked files. A **lost cluster** is a cluster on a disk that contains data that once belonged to a program, document, or another type of file, such as a temporary file. In the File Allocation Table, there is no pointer to the lost cluster; therefore, the lost cluster is not associated with any file and you cannot view the data in the lost cluster. The data is still allocated to the lost cluster, so the lost cluster wastes storage space. Lost data might develop when a power failure occurs, when you reboot a computer system after it locks up, when a brownout (a diminished supply of power) or a power surge occurs, or when you do not properly shut down Windows XP.

In these cases, lost clusters develop because Windows XP might not be able to record any remaining information it has on the location of all the clusters for a file in the File Allocation Table, or the information it has on the starting cluster of the file in the folder or directory file. Figure 7-7 illustrates this common problem.

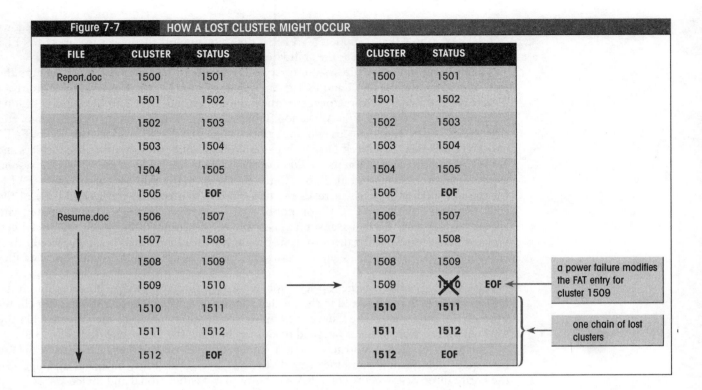

Figure 7-7 HOW A LOST CLUSTER MIGHT OCCUR

Assume you are looking at the part of the File Allocation Table where Windows XP tracks the usage of cluster numbers 1500 through 1512. In this example, assume clusters 1500 through 1505 are used by a file named Report.doc, and clusters 1506 through 1512 are used by another file named Resume.doc. Also assume that, as a result of a power failure, the pointer for cluster 1509 for Resume.doc changes to an end-of-file code (EOF). If you open Resume.doc in the application that produced it, Windows XP reads clusters 1506 through 1509 and then stops, because it finds an end-of-file code for cluster 1509. If you examine the end of this file (assuming you can open it at all), you not only discover that part of the file is missing, but you probably see uninterpretable characters. Clusters 1510 through 1512, which once belonged to Resume.doc, are now lost clusters. In fact, they constitute one **chain** of lost clusters because they are derived from a single file. The File Allocation Table shows those clusters as being in use; however, those clusters are not associated with any file on disk because there is no pointer to cluster 1510. The operating system cannot use the storage space occupied by these lost clusters, and since you cannot access these lost clusters, they waste valuable storage space on disk. Because lost clusters arise so easily, they are the most common type of problem encountered on hard disks.

If a power problem occurs near the end of a file save operation, you might end up with lost clusters on a disk. For example, Figure 7-8 shows a floppy disk that contains a 105-page file that is approximately 250 KB in size. Windows XP identifies the file as a Microsoft Word Document because of its file extension; however, Microsoft Word did not create the document in the file.

Figure 7-8	EXAMINING A FILE IN DETAILS VIEW

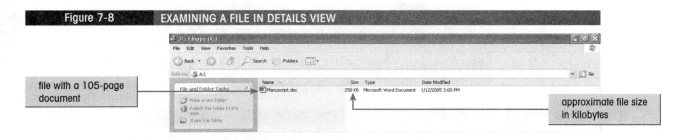

file with a 105-page document

approximate file size in kilobytes

If power was interrupted while you were saving this file to the disk, Windows XP might report the file size as 0 (zero), as it does in Figure 7-9. All of the clusters originally assigned to the file are now lost clusters.

Figure 7-9	POWER FAILURE INTERFERES WITH SAVING A FILE

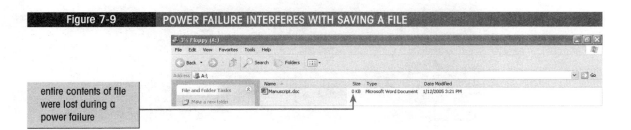

entire contents of file were lost during a power failure

When viewing a disk like the one used for these figures, you might first assume that all of the storage space (1.44 MB) on the disk is still available. However, the disk could have lost clusters that are not visible when viewing the contents of the disk. In this case, how would you know that there were lost clusters on the disk? If you examine the property sheet for this drive, you can compare the total storage space used by files on the disk with the group property sheet for all of the files in the drive window. If the totals don't match, you have lost clusters on the disk. If you check the property sheet for the floppy disk shown in Figure 7-9, Windows XP reports that 249 KB of storage space is in use on the disk, even though there is only one file with a file size of 0. See Figure 7-10. That 249 KB is the storage space used by the lost clusters.

Figure 7-10	VIEWING PROPERTIES OF THE 3½ FLOPPY DISK

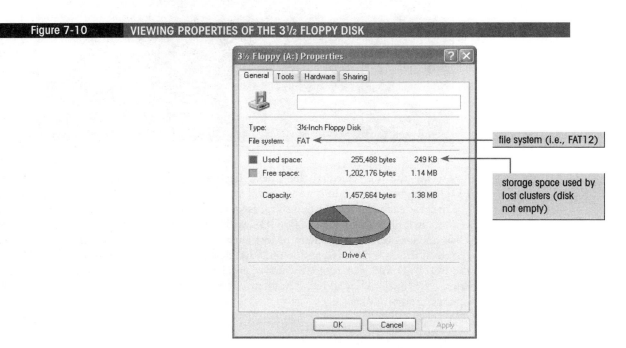

file system (i.e., FAT12)

storage space used by lost clusters (disk not empty)

If you open a Command Prompt window (covered later in this tutorial and in Tutorial 14) and use the Check Disk utility on this disk, it reports that it found errors on the disk, and asks if you want to convert the lost chains to files. See Figure 7-11. It also notes that 255,488 bytes of data are stored in one file that it can recover. A **lost chain** is a sequence of lost clusters that once belonged to a single file.

Figure 7-11	CHECKING A FAT VOLUME

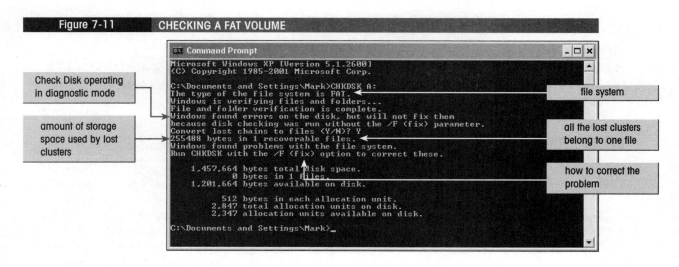

When used with the Fix switch (/F), the Check Disk utility recovers the lost clusters, as shown in Figure 7-12. A switch is an optional parameter that changes the way a program works.

Figure 7-12	RECOVERING LOST CLUSTERS FROM A DISK

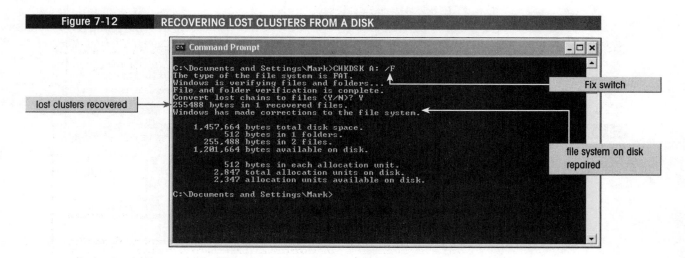

During the file recovery, the Check Disk utility creates a hidden system folder named FOUND.*nnn* (where nnn is a sequential number, starting with 000) in the top-level folder of the disk for each chain of lost clusters, as shown in Figure 7-13, and then stores the recovered clusters in a file named FILE0000.CHK within that folder, as shown in Figure 7-14. If Check Disk finds more than one chain of lost clusters, it names the second chain FILE0001.CHK, the third FILE0002.CHK, and so on. The file extension "chk" stands for Check Disk. To view the FOUND folder in a folder window, you have to open the Folder Options dialog box, and choose the options for showing hidden files and folders and for displaying hidden, protected operating system files.

Figure 7-13   FOLDER RECOVERED BY CHECK DISK

folder for recovered lost clusters

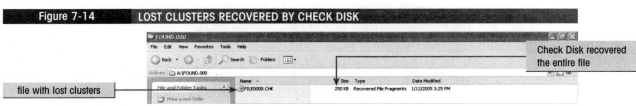

Figure 7-14   LOST CLUSTERS RECOVERED BY CHECK DISK

Check Disk recovered the entire file

file with lost clusters

At this point, you would open FILE0000.CHK, and attempt to determine if it had anything of value to you. For example, if you opened this file in WordPad (or perhaps Notepad), you might see something similar to what is shown in Figure 7-15. This copy of the original file, which was 105 pages long, contains text and uninterpretable characters that represent formatting codes inserted by the original application. Although you might assume that the file was a Microsoft Word document because of the "doc" file extension and the file icon, the "WPC" code at the beginning of this file indicates that WordPerfect was the application used to produce this file. The next step would be to close WordPad without saving, and then open this file in WordPerfect (or perhaps Microsoft Word) so that the application can interpret the formatting codes.

Figure 7-15   EXAMINING A FILE THAT CONTAINS RECOVERED LOST CLUSTERS

code indicating the document was created in WordPerfect

font used in the document

document formatted for this printer

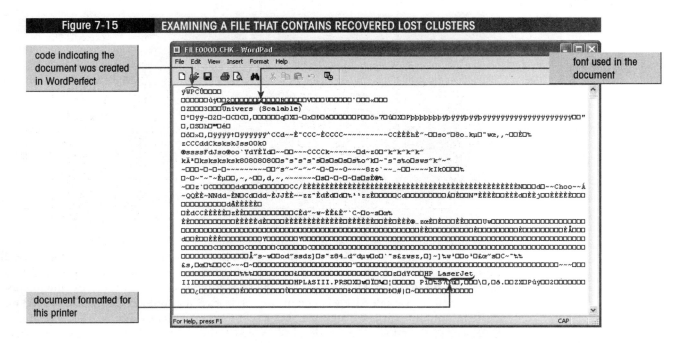

If the file contains useful information, and if you do not have a copy of that information elsewhere, you would insert the contents of the recovered file into another file, or use copy and paste to copy what you need from this file to another file. You could also rename and edit this file. If the file does not contain anything of value to you, or if you still cannot tell which application produced the file or what type of information was contained in the file, delete the file to recover the disk space used by the file. Later, if you discover that a program fails to operate properly or not at all, you would reinstall that program on your hard disk or restore it from a backup set. If you later discover that you are missing part of a data file, you would restore it from a backup set.

Over time, lost clusters can increase in number, waste more valuable disk space, lead to further disk errors, and affect the proper functioning of your computer. In most cases, you just delete the files that contain lost clusters and reclaim the storage space on your hard disk.

Checking for Cross-Linked Files

Another important but less common problem is cross-linked files. A **cross-linked file** is a file that contains at least one cluster that belongs to or is shared by two (or perhaps more) files. In most cases, one file is cross-linked with only one other file through just one cluster. In the File Allocation Table, Windows XP records the cross-linked cluster as the next available cluster for two different files. Figure 7-16 illustrates how cross-linked clusters might occur.

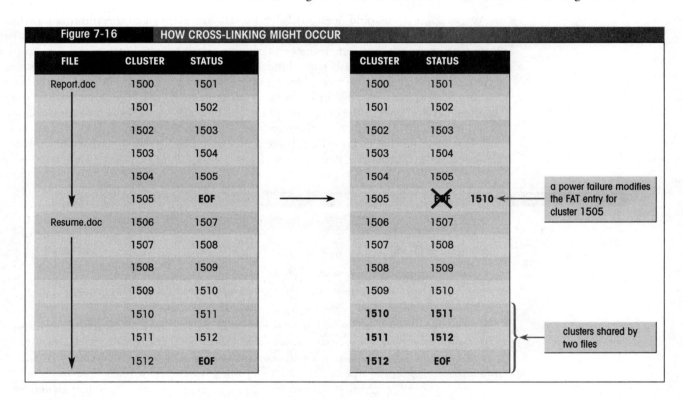

Figure 7-16 — HOW CROSS-LINKING MIGHT OCCUR

FILE	CLUSTER	STATUS		CLUSTER	STATUS	
Report.doc	1500	1501		1500	1501	
	1501	1502		1501	1502	
	1502	1503		1502	1503	
	1503	1504		1503	1504	
	1504	1505		1504	1505	
	1505	EOF		1505	~~EOF~~ 1510	a power failure modifies the FAT entry for cluster 1505
Resume.doc	1506	1507		1506	1507	
	1507	1508		1507	1508	
	1508	1509		1508	1509	
	1509	1510		1509	1510	
	1510	1511		1510	1511	clusters shared by two files
	1511	1512		1511	1512	
	1512	EOF		1512	EOF	

Again, assume you are looking at cluster usage in the File Allocation Table for the same two files you examined earlier. Also assume that as a result of a power problem, the end-of-file (EOF) code for the last cluster of the file Report.doc changes so that it points to a cluster used by the file Resume.doc. In this example, the end-of-file code for cluster 1505 now points to cluster 1510. If you open Report.doc in the application that produced it, Windows XP reads clusters 1500 through 1505, and then, because it finds a pointer to another cluster (and not an EOF code), Windows XP reads clusters 1510 through 1512 (which are also part of Resume.doc). Windows XP stops when it encounters the EOF code for cluster 1512. If you examine this file (assuming you can open it at all), you discover uninterpretable characters in the file where the cross-link occurs, and perhaps in other parts of the file as well. If you open

Resume.doc in the application that produced it, Windows XP reads clusters 1506 through 1512, the clusters originally assigned to this file before the cross-link occurred. Again, if you examine this file, you will discover uninterpretable characters and perhaps lost data where the cross-link occurs.

How do you repair cross-linked files? You can copy each file to a new location and remove the original files so that the files are no longer cross-linked. You then open both files (if possible), examine them, and edit the files to remove the uninterpretable characters and add any data that might have been lost.

Using Check Disk on an NTFS Volume

NTFS uses a **Master File Table (MFT)** to track every file on an NTFS volume, including the Master File Table itself. The MFT contains entries on all the information that Windows XP tracks on a file, including its size, date and time stamps, permissions, and data content.

When you use the Check Disk utility on an NTFS volume, it makes three passes of the volume and examines all the data used to keep track of everything about all of the folders and files on the volume. This data includes information on the allocation units assigned to the file for storing data, the available (or free) allocation units, and the allocation units that contain bad sectors.

During the first pass or phase, Check Disk verifies files. It examines each file record segment (FRS) in the volume's MFT for internal consistency, and identifies which file record segments and clusters are in use. The **file record segment** refers to a unique ID assigned to each folder and file in the MFT. At the completion of this phase, Check Disk compares the information it compiled to the same type of information that NTFS maintains on disk to find discrepancies or problems such as corrupted file record segments.

During the second pass or phase, Check Disk verifies **indexes**, or NTFS directories, on the volume. It examines each directory on the volume for internal consistency by making sure that every directory and file is referenced by at least one directory, and that the file record segment reference in the master file table is valid. During this pass, Check Disk also verifies time stamps and file sizes. From the information garnered during this phase, Check Disk can determine whether the volume contains any orphaned files. An **orphaned file** has a valid file record segment in the master file table, but is not listed in any directory. An orphaned file is comparable to a lost cluster. Check Disk can restore an orphaned file to its original directory if that directory still exists. If that directory does not exist, Check Disk creates a directory in the root directory for that file. If it finds a file record segment that is no longer in use or that does not correspond to the file in the directory, it removes the directory entry. This phase takes the most time.

In the third pass or phase, Check Disk verifies the integrity of security descriptors for each directory and file. A **security descriptor** contains information about the owner of the directory or file, permissions granted to users and groups for that directory or file, and information on security events to be audited for that directory or file.

If you want to perform a surface scan with Check Disk, you use the Repair switch (/R) to instruct Check Disk to locate bad sectors and, if possible, recover any data from the bad sector and record it elsewhere on the disk.

If you specify the Repair switch (/R), Check Disk includes two other phases that determine whether the OS can read from and write to sectors in a cluster. During the fourth phase, Check Disk verifies all used clusters, and in the fifth phase, it verifies all unused clusters.

If Check Disk detects a problem, it tries to fix the problem, but this is no substitute for backups.

Using the Check Disk Utility

Before you run the Check Disk utility, you should close all other programs that you are using, including applications and other utilities. For example, you might need to temporarily turn off your screen saver, power management features, and antivirus software. If you right-click the icons in the taskbar Notification area, the shortcut menu might include an Exit or Disable option that allows you to close or temporarily turn off the background programs represented by these icons, but remember that not all background programs place icons in the Notification area. If the Check Disk utility finds a defective cluster on the hard disk, it attempts to move the data in that bad cluster to another location on the same disk. If an open program is also using that same cluster, it interferes with Check Disk. If Check Disk cannot lock or prevent access to the drive, it offers to check the drive the next time you start the computer. If the drive you're checking is not the boot volume, Check Disk might be able to dismount the volume so that it has exclusive access to the volume. When a volume is dismounted, it is no longer available for use. The operating system must mount the volume later to make it available for use. If you do not want to dismount a volume, you can instead schedule the Check Disk for the next boot.

If you want to use Check Disk to examine your hard disk, but have never used Check Disk before, you should first back up the hard disk. If Check Disk detects and then repairs errors in the file system or the surface of the disk, you might lose important information. In fact, as you discovered in Tutorial 6, it is a good idea to back up on a regular basis anyway.

You should not use a Check Disk utility designed for DOS or Windows 3.1, because you can corrupt long filenames. If that occurs, you might discover that your programs do not work properly, or at all. Furthermore, you should use the Check Disk utility included with your version of Windows.

In the next set of steps, you start the Error-checking tool and check one of your floppy disks. Recall that the Error-checking tool is the GUI version of the Check Disk utility. Although you should check your hard disk, you can also check floppy disks. If you store your homework on floppy disks and carry those disks with you, they experience more wear and tear than a hard disk, so it's just as important to check those floppy disks to prevent the loss of an important file. If you rely on Zip disks rather than floppy disks, you should also check them frequently for disk errors.

To check drive C (or another drive on your hard disk), you must log on as Administrator or log on under an account with Administrator privileges.

Mark emphasizes the importance of using the Check Disk utility regularly to check and maintain the integrity of hard disks that contain important company documents. He points out that it is easier to repair problems while they are relatively minor, rather than wait until the problems become more serious and perhaps impossible to repair. To become familiar with Check Disk, Mark suggests you use it to check a floppy disk.

To start Check Disk:

1. If necessary, back up your document files, turn off your screen saver, adjust power management features (if necessary), close all open applications and utilities, and return to the desktop.

2. Insert a floppy disk with your copy of the files for Data Disk #2.

3. Open My Computer, right-click the **3½ Floppy (A:)** icon, click **Properties** on the shortcut menu, and then click the **Tools** tab in the 3½ Floppy (A:) Properties dialog box. See Figure 7-17.

Figure 7-17 **SELECTING THE WINDOWS XP ERROR-CHECKING TOOL**

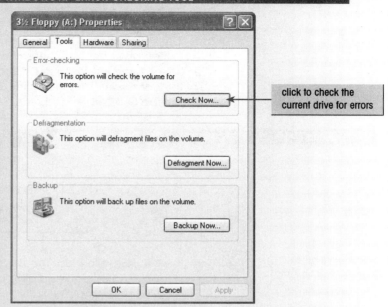

click to check the current drive for errors

4. Under Error-checking, click the **Check Now** button. The Check Disk 3½ Floppy (A:) dialog box contains two options. See Figure 7-18. The first option automatically fixes file system errors, and requires that all files be closed. The second option attempts to recover data from bad sectors on the disk. If you do not check either option, Check Disk runs in diagnostic mode, or read-only mode, and reports on potential problems, but does not repair them. If you select either option, you cannot perform other tasks on the drive while the Check Disk utility examines it.

Figure 7-18 **OPTIONS FOR CHECKING A DISK**

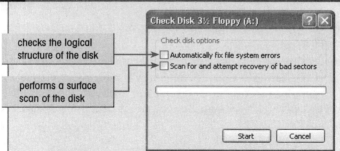

checks the logical structure of the disk

performs a surface scan of the disk

5. Click the **Automatically fix file system errors** check box, click the **Scan for and attempt recovery of bad sectors** check box, and then click the **Start** button in the Check Disk 3½ Floppy (A:) dialog box. The Checking Disk 3½ Floppy (A:) dialog box opens with a progress bar for each phase. After Check Disk completes its check of drive A, the Checking Disk 3½ Floppy (A:) dialog box informs you that the disk check is complete. See Figure 7-19.

TROUBLE? If your system hangs, or seems not to respond for a long time, right-click the taskbar, click Task Manager, click the Applications tab, select the non-responding task, and then click End Task. If you cannot shut down the Error-checking tool, and if your computer system does not respond, press the Reset button on your computer to restart it or shut the power off (if possible). After you restart your computer, open the Start menu, point to All Programs, point to Accessories, and then click Command Prompt. At the command prompt, type CHKDSK A: and press Enter to check your floppy disk.

| Figure 7-19 | COMPLETED CHECK DISK OPERATION |

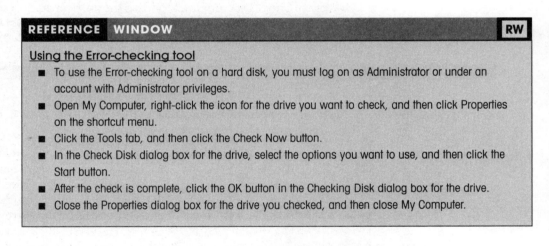

6. Click the **OK** button to close the Checking Disk 3½ Floppy (A:) dialog box, close the 3½ Floppy (A:) Properties dialog box, and then close My Computer.

As a follow-up to the Trouble in Step 5, if you need to check drive C with the Check Disk utility and its Fix switch (/F), Check Disk reports that it cannot lock the drive because another process (Windows XP) is using the drive. However, it gives you the option of running Check Disk at the next boot, and you should choose that option.

| REFERENCE WINDOW | RW |

Using the Error-checking tool

- To use the Error-checking tool on a hard disk, you must log on as Administrator or under an account with Administrator privileges.
- Open My Computer, right-click the icon for the drive you want to check, and then click Properties on the shortcut menu.
- Click the Tools tab, and then click the Check Now button.
- In the Check Disk dialog box for the drive, select the options you want to use, and then click the Start button.
- After the check is complete, click the OK button in the Checking Disk dialog box for the drive.
- Close the Properties dialog box for the drive you checked, and then close My Computer.

Using Check Disk from the Command Prompt Window

You can also open a Command Prompt window to run the Check Disk utility. If you are troubleshooting a problem on your computer, you might need to run Check Disk from the command line. Likewise, if you need to troubleshoot another version of Windows with a boot or startup disk designed for that version of Windows, you can run Check Disk from that disk in drive A. Windows XP and earlier versions of Windows NT also contain other of utilities that are commonly run from the Command Prompt window.

By default, Check Disk operates in **read-only mode**, a diagnostic mode in which Check Disk checks the drive and reports any errors it finds and simulates how it would correct the problem. After you see how Check Disk would correct the problem, you can decide what course of action you want to take. You can use the Check Disk **Fix switch** (**/F**) to repair certain types of problems. Check Disk can also check the physical structure of a disk if you use the **Repair switch** (**/R**). When you use this switch, Check Disk attempts to recover data stored in bad sectors before marking those sectors as unusable. Any recovered data is recorded in other unused, but good, sectors on the disk. As noted earlier, you must log on as Administrator or with Administrator privileges if you want to check your hard disk. Also, if you are checking a large disk volume or one that contains many files, Check Disk can take a long time, making the disk volume unavailable until the Check Disk utility completes its check of the disk.

If you select the Command Prompt option on the Accessories menu, Windows XP opens a Command Prompt window, as shown in Figure 7-20. In this window, Windows XP displays a **command prompt** (C:\>) to identify the current drive and directory. The backslash after the drive name refers to the root directory. You also see the version number of Windows XP you are running.

Figure 7-20	COMMAND PROMPT WINDOW

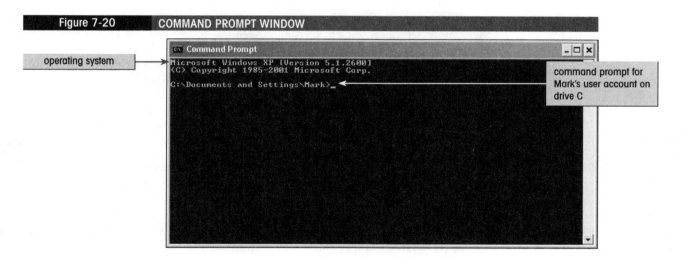

If you type the command CHKDSK (or CHKDSK C:) and then press Enter, Check Disk checks drive C. If you do not specify the drive to check, the utility assumes you want to check the current drive (shown in the command prompt). After checking the hard disk, Check Disk displays a three-section report on the results of its check, how storage space is used on the drive, and how storage space is allocated on the drive. See Figure 7-21. If there are errors on the disk, it first reports on those errors, as shown in the figure. Also, commands entered at the command prompt are not case sensitive.

Figure 7-21 | **DRIVE C CHECKED FOR ERRORS**

Command Prompt

```
Microsoft Windows XP [Version 5.1.2600]
(C) Copyright 1985-2001 Microsoft Corp.

C:\Documents and Settings\Mark>CHKDSK
The type of the file system is FAT32.
Volume Serial Number is 1052-B046
Windows is verifying files and folders...
Windows found errors on the disk, but will not fix them
because disk checking was run without the /F (fix) parameter.
\WINDOWS\Prefetch\CHKDSK.EXE-2CC4C59D.pf  first allocation unit is not valid. Th
e entry will be truncated.
File and folder verification is complete.
Convert lost chains to files (Y/N)? Y
8 KB in 1 recoverable files.
Windows found problems with the file system.
Run CHKDSK with the /F (fix) option to correct these.
  16,747,100 KB total disk space.
     571,760 KB in 1,561 hidden files.
      35,928 KB in 8,281 folders.
   8,951,932 KB in 98,683 files.
   7,187,464 KB are available.

       4,096 bytes in each allocation unit.
   4,186,775 total allocation units on disk.
   1,796,866 allocation units available on disk.

C:\Documents and Settings\Mark>_
```

Labels:
- Check Disk command
- file system
- a problem was found on the drive
- what happens if you correct this problem
- how storage space is used on the drive
- how to correct this problem
- how storage space is allocated on the drive

During this process, Check Disk identifies the file system used on drive C, and then shows the volume name for the drive (if there is one), the date and time the volume name was assigned, and its serial number. Then it verifies the integrity of the file system. In this instance, Check Disk found errors on drive C (a FAT32 volume), but noted that it did not fix them because it operated in diagnostic mode. It identifies a file, shows the path to that file, informs you that the first allocation unit for the file is not valid, and indicates the entry should be truncated. Next, it informs you that file and folder verification is complete, and then asks whether you want to convert lost chains to files. If you enter "Y" for "Yes," Check Disk informs you that it will recover 8 KB in one file, and again notes that it found problems with the file system. It then recommends that you run CHKDSK with the Fix switch to correct the problem. Before you use the Fix switch to correct a problem, you might want to back up your computer. In some cases, you might also need to use the /R switch (for Recover) for a more thorough but time-consuming check of your hard disk.

Ironically, the error reported by Check Disk in Figure 7-21 resulted from a problem with a file in the Prefetch folder that contains information about loading Check Disk during booting. Check Disk informed Mark that he should run Check Disk again, but with the Fix switch. When he used the Fix switch, Windows XP reported that it could not lock the drive, and asked if he wanted to schedule this check the next time the computer restarts. See Figure 7-22. After responding "Y" for "Yes," Mark restarted the computer used for these figures, and Check Disk checked drive C, but found no problem. After Mark logged onto his user account, he ran Check Disk again, and it reported the same problem with a file in the Prefetch folder. Mark corrected the problem by making a duplicate copy of the file in the same folder, and then deleted the original file and renamed the copy so that the new filename matched the original filename. Another check with Check Disk showed this solved the problem. Also, Microsoft reports that the Check Disk utility can identify errors that do not exist when you use the Check Disk utility in read-only, or diagnostic, mode.

Figure 7-22	SCHEDULING CHECK BOX DISK TO RUN AT THE NEXT BOOT

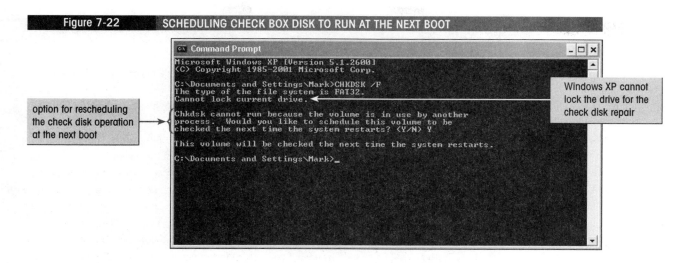

option for rescheduling the check disk operation at the next boot

Windows XP cannot lock the drive for the check disk repair

From the additional summary information Check Disk provides on the number of bytes in an allocation unit, you can determine the size of a cluster by dividing the number of bytes in each allocation unit (or cluster) by 512 (because there are 512 bytes per sector). For the drive used for this figure, this FAT32 volume has eight sectors per cluster.

If you use Check Disk without the Fix switch on an NTFS volume, as shown in Figure 7-23, it runs in a read-only mode as it did for the FAT32 volume. First, it identifies the file system as NTFS (this information might scroll off the screen), and then it shows the three stages of its check: the file verification, index verification, and security descriptor verification phases. On the computer used for this figure, Check Disk did not find any problems on this drive.

Figure 7-23	CHECKING AN NTFS VOLUME

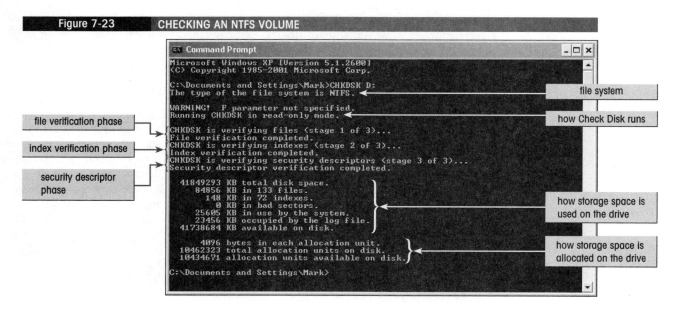

file verification phase

index verification phase

security descriptor phase

file system

how Check Disk runs

how storage space is used on the drive

how storage space is allocated on the drive

If Windows XP detects a problem with a disk during booting, it automatically runs Autochk.exe, a version of Check Disk that runs only before Windows XP starts. If you schedule a Check Disk for the next boot, Windows XP runs Autochk.exe at the next boot.

REFERENCE WINDOW   **RW**

Using Check Disk from a Command Prompt Window

- To use the Check Disk utility on a hard disk, you must log on as Administrator or under an account with Administrator privileges.
- Click the Start button, point to All Programs, point to Accessories, and then click Command Prompt.
- At the command prompt, type CHKDSK followed by a space and the drive name (such as A: or D:), and then press Enter. If you instruct Check Disk to check a hard disk and it then displays the message "Access denied," you did not log on under an account with Administrator privileges.
- If CHKDSK reports a problem, you might want to back up your computer before you use the command CHKDSK /F to fix the problem. You might also need to use the command CHKDSK /R to perform a more thorough and time-consuming check of your hard disk. If CHKDSK reports that it cannot lock the drive, choose the option to run Check Disk at the next boot, and after you close the Command Prompt window, restart your computer so that Autochk.exe can check the disk.
- Close the Command Prompt window.

The average useful lifetime of a hard disk is estimated to be five to seven years. The actual lifetime of a hard disk, however, might range anywhere from a few months to five or seven years, and depends on how well you take care of it and the demands you place on it. If you check your hard disk with the Error-checking tool or the Check Disk utility frequently, such as once a week or at least once a month, and eliminate small errors that might cause serious problems if left unresolved, you can extend the longevity of your hard disk (barring another type of disaster such as a natural disaster or computer virus infection). Windows XP also monitors the drives and, if necessary, automatically runs Check Disk during booting. Even with care, however, all hard disks eventually fail. This is why there is great emphasis placed on performing regular backups—as discussed in the previous tutorial.

Understanding **File Fragmentation**

As you create, modify, and save files to a hard disk, Zip disk, or floppy disk, Windows XP attempts to store the different parts of each file in **contiguous**, or adjacent, clusters. However, as you add, delete, and modify files, Windows XP might need to store different parts of the same file in **noncontiguous**, or nonadjacent, clusters that are scattered across the surface of a disk because the disk does not have enough space to store the file in contiguous clusters. In fact, Windows XP saves updates to a file on the largest continuous space on a disk, and that space is often in a different location than other parts of the file. The file is then called a **fragmented file**. As file fragmentation builds up on a disk, you need to use a defragmenting utility such as Disk Defragmenter to rearrange the files on the disk so that the different clusters for the same file are stored in consecutive clusters.

Each time you use a command to retrieve a file from a hard disk, the read/write heads that retrieve data from and record data on the surface of the disk must locate each cluster for a file and reassemble its contents so that the application you are using can work with some or all of the file. If the read/write heads attempt to retrieve a fragmented file from disk, it takes your drive longer to locate and read the different parts of that file. Likewise, when you issue a command to save a new or modified file to a disk, Windows XP must locate available clusters for that file on disk. If a file is stored in noncontiguous clusters, it takes the read/write heads longer to write the file to the disk. Obviously, the problem is compounded if all or most of the files on a disk are fragmented. As noted in Tutorial 3, because the access time of a hard disk is around 120,000 times slower than RAM, you spend more time waiting as the hard drive locates and reads file clusters into RAM. Furthermore, as fragmentation builds up on a disk, it results in more disk access, and that in turn causes increased wear and tear on the drive.

To give you a better understanding of how file fragmentation occurs, examine a simple example. Assume that over the last six months, you added files to a disk, and you deleted and modified files on the disk. Figure 7-24 shows a part of the disk that contains three files.

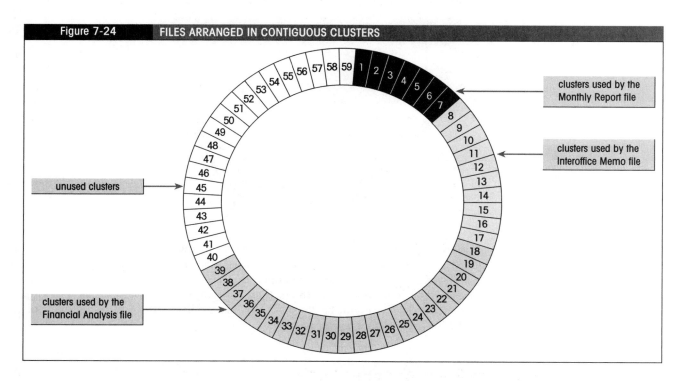

Figure 7-24 **FILES ARRANGED IN CONTIGUOUS CLUSTERS**

clusters used by the Monthly Report file

clusters used by the Interoffice Memo file

unused clusters

clusters used by the Financial Analysis file

The file with the Monthly Report occupies seven clusters, the file with the Interoffice Memo occupies the next ten clusters, the file with the Financial Analysis occupies the next 22 clusters, and the next 20 clusters are not used and are therefore available. You decide you no longer need the file with the Interoffice Memo, so you delete this file. By removing this file, you have freed ten clusters, as shown in Figure 7-25.

Figure 7-25   **CLUSTERS FREED AFTER A FILE DELETION**

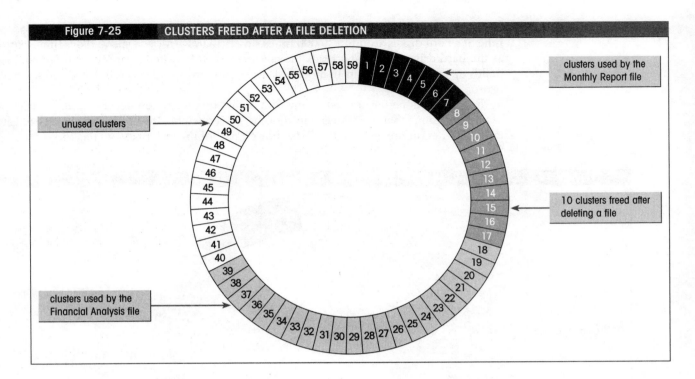

clusters used by the Monthly Report file

unused clusters

10 clusters freed after deleting a file

clusters used by the Financial Analysis file

Now you prepare a bid proposal and save it to the same disk. Assume that this file requires ten clusters and that Windows XP uses the clusters that were previously occupied by the letter. A short while later, you open the file again and add a new section to the bid proposal so that the final size is 28 clusters. When Windows XP saves the file to disk, the additional 18 clusters might be stored in the next available set of contiguous sectors, right after the Financial Analysis file, as shown in Figure 7-26.

Figure 7-26   **FRAGMENTED FILE STORED IN NONCONTIGUOUS CLUSTERS**

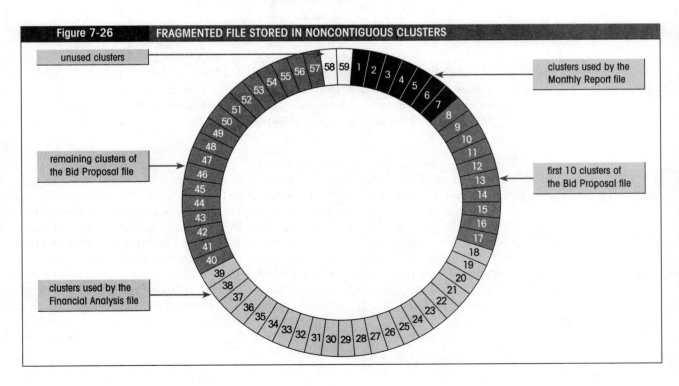

unused clusters

clusters used by the Monthly Report file

remaining clusters of the Bid Proposal file

first 10 clusters of the Bid Proposal file

clusters used by the Financial Analysis file

The file with the bid proposal is a fragmented file because it is stored in noncontiguous clusters. From this example, you can see that if you continue to reduce the size of files or delete files from a disk, you free clusters that Windows XP might use later for part of a different file. If you increase the size of files or add new files to a disk and the disk does not contain enough consecutive clusters to hold the entire file, Windows XP stores the files in noncontiguous clusters.

Disk Defragmenter can reorganize the clusters assigned to a file so that they are located one right after the other, rather than remaining scattered on the disk. It also records the clusters for one file right after the clusters for another file, and in the process, removes free space (or empty space) between files that would result in more fragmentation later. After using Disk Defragmenter on a disk, all or most of the files are stored in contiguous clusters starting from the outer edge of the disk, and as a result, all unused disk space is consolidated near the inner edge of the disk. If all of the clusters of a file are stored in adjacent clusters, the read/write heads can quickly retrieve the contents of that file, improving the response time and performance of your computer, and preventing deterioration of your hard disk. By using Disk Defragmenter periodically, you can eliminate or reduce both file fragmentation and free space fragmentation. **Free space fragmentation** occurs when the available free space is scattered around the disk, rather than consolidated in adjacent clusters in one part of the disk.

Before you run the Disk Defragmenter, you should close all other programs that you are using, including applications and other utilities, turn off your screen saver, and possibly disable your antivirus software and adjust power management settings. Because the primary function of the Disk Defragmenter is to rearrange data stored on disk, you do not want to have any open programs accessing data in clusters that the Disk Defragmenter needs to move to another location.

You should not use a Disk Defragmenter utility designed for DOS or a version of Windows before Windows 95 because you can corrupt long filenames. If that occurs, you might discover that your programs do not work properly, or at all. Furthermore, you should only use the Disk Defragmenter utility included with Windows XP, or one that is designed by another company only if that company specifies that you can use it with Windows XP.

If you periodically use both Check Disk and Disk Defragmenter to optimize your computer, you should run Check Disk before you run Disk Defragmenter so that it can repair errors in the file system that might interfere with Disk Defragmenter. Since file fragmentation does not build up as fast as errors to the file system (such as lost clusters), you probably need to use the Disk Defragmenter less frequently than Check Disk, perhaps only once every month or every few months.

Analyzing a Disk for Fragmentation

The time it takes to defragment a hard disk depends on the size of the hard disk, the number of folders and files on the disk, how much of the hard disk's storage space is used, the amount of fragmentation that already exists on the volume, the available system resources (such as memory), and how often you run Disk Defragmenter. The first time you optimize your hard disk with the Disk Defragmenter, it may take a long time to defragment the hard disk, but it is well worth it. If you run Disk Defragmenter frequently, it takes less time to defragment the disk because most of the disk is already optimized. If disk fragmentation builds up quickly, the amount of time required to defragment the disk increases.

Before you defragment a disk, Disk Defragmenter lets you analyze the disk to determine whether you need to defragment the disk and what you gain if you do. Disk Defragmenter recommends that you defragment your disk when fragmentation is 10% or greater, though you can still defragment the disk if fragmentation is less than 10%. When you analyze a disk, Disk Defragmenter shows you which areas include fragmented, contiguous, or unmovable files and which areas contain free space. Disk Defragmenter uses different colors to represent the status of different areas of the disk. Bright blue represents areas of the disk where most files are contiguous, red represents areas of the disk where most files are fragmented, bright green represents areas of the disk with unmovable files that cannot be defragmented, and white represents free space on the disk. Unmovable files include Windows XP operating system files, such as the paging file. The **paging file** is the system file on the hard disk that Windows XP uses as supplemental RAM (called virtual memory). In Tutorial 10, you examine virtual memory and the paging file in more detail.

The Disk Defragmenter in Windows XP does not operate on floppy disks, so in the next section of the tutorial, you use it to examine a hard disk drive or, if you prefer, a Zip disk. This process typically consists of two phases. First, you analyze a disk to determine the level of fragmentation, and then you defragment the disk if the fragmentation is high. The analysis is fairly quick; however, as noted earlier, defragmenting a hard disk can take time, so plan accordingly. For example, on the computer used for the steps in this section and the next section, it took 5.25 hours to defragment a 16 GB drive with 58% of the drive used to store files and with 8% file fragmentation. If you have a Zip drive, you might want to analyze and defragment a Zip disk instead of drive C to save time. Also, Disk Defragmenter requires that at least 15% of the drive contains free space for use to sort file fragments. If a drive has less than 15% free space, Disk Defragmenter only partially defragments the drive. If there is a problem with the file system on a drive, you must first use Check Disk or the Error-checking tool to correct the problem before you can use Disk Defragmenter.

Mark recommends that you show Harris & Banche employees how to analyze a disk for fragmentation and how to defragment the disk. He also says that, since defragmenting a disk can be a time-consuming process, employees should know in advance whether their disk really needs defragmentation. Then they can plan their time more effectively, and schedule the defragmentation when their schedule permits.

To complete the following tutorial steps, you must be logged on as Administrator or logged on under an account with Administrator privileges. If you are working in a computer lab, ask your instructor or technical support staff whether you have permission to analyze and defragment one of the hard disk drives. If you do not have permission to use the Disk Defragmenter, read the steps and examine the figures so that you are familiar with how Disk Defragmenter works, but do not keystroke the following steps.

To analyze disk defragmentation on drive C or a Zip disk:

1. Close any applications or other windows you may have open on your computer, and temporarily turn off your screen saver, power management options, and antivirus software so that they do not interfere with Disk Defragmenter.

2. Open My Computer, right-click the icon for a hard disk or Zip disk, click **Properties** on the shortcut menu, click the **Tools** tab, and then click the **Defragment Now** button. The Disk Defragmenter window lists the volumes available on your computer. See Figure 7-27. The computer used for this figure has two volumes—one volume (drive C) is a FAT32 volume while the other (drive D) is an NTFS volume. You have the option of analyzing a volume for fragmentation, as well as an option for defragmenting it. The areas labeled "Estimated disk usage before defragmentation" and "Estimated disk usage after defragmentation" are designed to show you the progress of analyzing or defragmenting the disk. The legend at the bottom of the window identifies the color codes used in these areas to represent the status of clusters on the disk. *Note*: You can also start Disk Defragmenter from the System Tools menu.

Figure 7-27   SELECTING THE DRIVE TO DEFRAGMENT

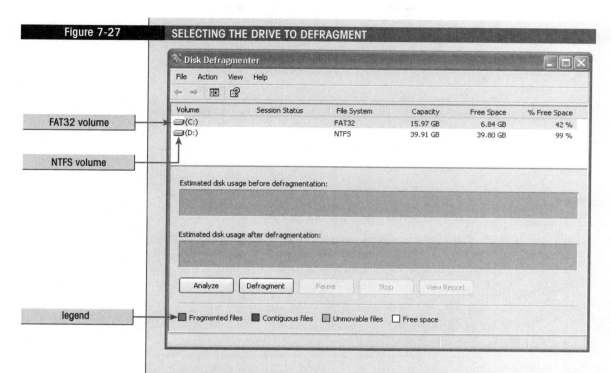

FAT32 volume

NTFS volume

legend

3. If you have more than two volumes, select the volume for drive C or, if you prefer, select the Zip drive.

4. Click the **Analyze** button. Disk Defragmenter analyzes the volume while you wait, periodically updates the Analysis display, and then displays its recommendation. See Figure 7-28. On the computer used for this figure, Disk Defragmenter recommends that this volume does not need defragmenting; however, the analysis in the "Estimated disk usage before defragmentation" display area indicates otherwise. On an optimized disk, with a minimum of file fragmentation, you would not see red bands and thin red vertical bars indicating regions of fragmented files. Also, you would not see free space scattered across the disk. Instead, you would see a continuous band of bright blue, which indicates that the majority of the files are not fragmented, and the free space would be consolidated on the right side of the disk analysis area. The bright blue bands would only be broken up by bright green areas denoting unmovable files. Note that your view actually consists of very thin vertical bars that are a pixel wide and that represent an average of thousands of clusters. If a thin vertical bar represents exactly 1,000 clusters, and if 501 of those clusters contain fragmented files, for example, the thin vertical bar is red. On FAT volumes, the unmovable areas represent the paging file, and on NTFS volumes, the unmovable areas represent space used by the NTFS Change Journal. The NTFS Change Journal keeps track of changes made to the files on a drive. Notice also that you have the option of viewing a report of its findings.

TROUBLE? If Windows XP displays a Disk Defragmenter dialog box and informs you that you must have Administrator privileges to defragment a volume, you are not logged on as an Administrator or you are not logged on under an account with Administrator's privileges. Click the OK button, close the Disk Defragmenter window, log off the computer, log on under an account with Administrator privileges, and then repeat these steps. Or, if you prefer to not log off, read the steps and examine the figures, but do not keystroke the remaining steps.

Figure 7-28   DISK DEFRAGMENTER RECOMMENDATION

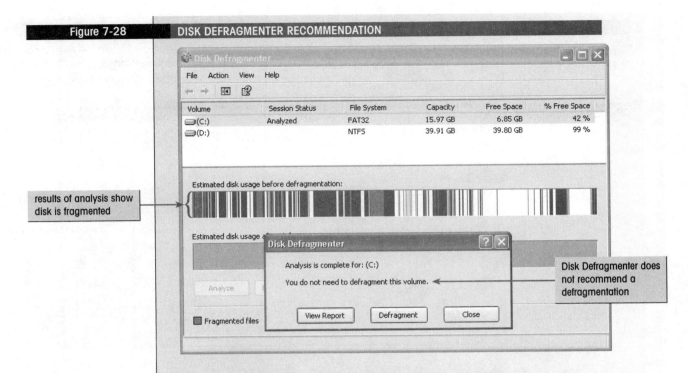

results of analysis show
disk is fragmented

Disk Defragmenter does
not recommend a
defragmentation

5. Click the **View Report** button. The Analysis Report dialog box displays information about the volume, file fragmentation, and free space fragmentation. See
   Figure 7-29. Under "Most fragmented files," Disk Defragmenter lists the path of
   each fragmented file, its file size, and the number of fragments. Notice that on
   the computer used for this figure, one of the files is broken into 517 fragments,
   indicating a heavily fragmented file. Your list will differ.

Figure 7-29   DISK DEFRAGMENTER ANALYSIS REPORT

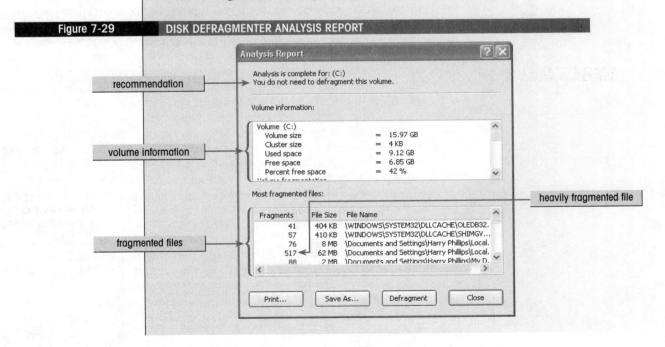

recommendation

volume information

fragmented files

heavily fragmented file

6. Adjust your view under Volume information so that you can see information on volume fragmentation. On the computer used for Figure 7-30, the total fragmentation is 8%, file fragmentation is 17%, and free space fragmentation is 0% (which differs from the impression the graphical view of the disk analysis presents).

Figure 7-30   **VOLUME FRAGMENTATION**

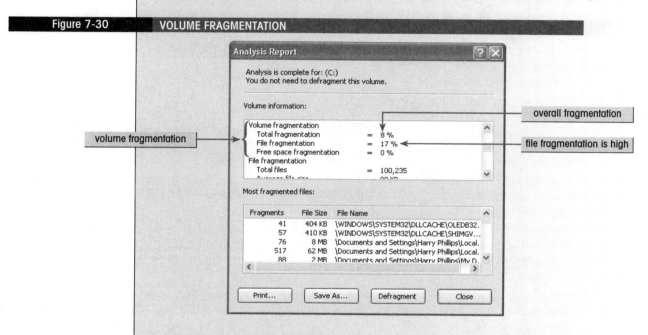

7. Adjust your view under Volume information so that you can see information on file fragmentation. The computer used for Figure 7-31 has 3,815 fragmented files out of a total of 100,235 files, and the average fragments per file is 1.08. A value of 1.00 indicates that all the files (or nearly all) are contiguous. If the value were 1.10, then 10% of the files, on average, are stored as two fragments. If the value were 1.20, then 20% of the files, on average, are stored as two fragments.

Figure 7-31   **FILE FRAGMENTATION**

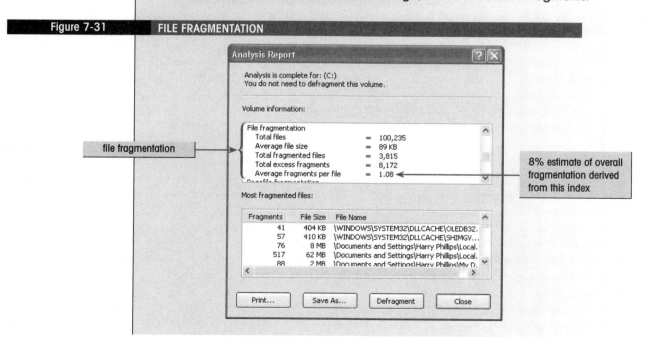

8. Adjust your view under Volume information so that you can see information on Pagefile and Folder (or directory) fragmentation. On the computer used for Figure 7-32, the Pagefile is fragmented into 22 pieces, and there are 169 fragmented folders.

Figure 7-32	PAGEFILE AND FOLDER FRAGMENTATION

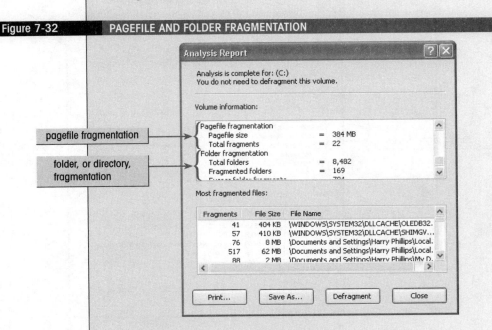

9. To print this report, click the **Print** button, make sure Windows XP is using the correct printer in the Print dialog box, click the **Print** button, and then click the **Close** button.

10. Click the **Save As** button, and in the My Documents folder, type **Volume C Analysis Report** (or an appropriate filename for the drive you checked) in the File name box, and then click the **Save** button.

While Disk Defragmenter optimizes the arrangement of files on a drive and reduces free space fragmentation, it does not consolidate all of the free space on the volume, but may leave some free space scattered around the volume.

Analyzing a Disk for Fragmentation

- Log on as Administrator or under an account with Administrator privileges.
- Open My Computer, right-click the drive you want to analyze, click Properties, click the Tools tab, and then click the Defragment Now button. Or click the Start button, point to All Programs, point to Accessories, point to System Tools, and then click Disk Defragmenter.
- If you have more than one volume, select the volume you want to analyze.
- Click the Analyze button in the Disk Defragmenter dialog box.
- After the analysis is complete, click the View Report button and examine the information on fragmentation in the Analysis Report dialog box so that you can decide whether to defragment the disk.
- If you want to print the report, click the Print button, make sure Windows XP is using the correct printer in the Print dialog box, click the Print button, and then click the Close button.
- If you want to save the report, click the Save As button, locate the folder where you want to save the report (if different than the default folder), decide whether you want to use a different name for the report, and then click the Save button.
- Close the Analysis Report dialog box, close the Disk Defragmenter dialog box, close the Properties dialog box for the drive you selected, and then close My Computer.

Rather than rely on the initial recommendation of Disk Defragmenter to determine whether to defragment a disk, you should rely on the more detailed information in the Analysis Report and your sense of the overall performance of your computer. However, if the total fragmentation or the file fragmentation is 10 percent or more, it's time to defragment the disk.

Defragmenting a Disk

When Disk Defragmenter optimizes a disk, it rearranges clusters on the disk so that all the clusters for a file are stored contiguous to each other (where possible), and it consolidates free space to reduce the rate at which file fragmentation builds up after the defragmentation.

Even if Disk Defragmenter informs you that you do not need to defragment your hard disk, you can still step through the process if you want, or you can read, but not keystroke, the following steps. If you already analyzed your hard disk, you might want to read, but not keystroke, the following steps because the defragmentation may literally take hours. Also, as noted earlier, you must be logged on as Administrator or logged on under an account with Administrator privileges. Your instructor will inform you whether you can perform these steps and, if so, how you should log on. If you do not have these privileges, read the steps and examine the figures so that you are familiar with how Disk Defragmenter works, but do not keystroke the following steps.

Also, you can interrupt or temporarily stop and then resume analysis or defragmentation of a volume with the Stop and Pause buttons. If you stop the defragmentation, your disk is only partially defragmented, but you might want to use this option if you realize that the defragmentation will take far longer than you anticipated, and you do not have the time to complete that defragmentation.

If you are working in a computer lab, make sure you have permission to use the Disk Defragmenter to defragment one of the hard disk drives.

Now that you have demonstrated to Mark's staff how to properly analyze a disk for fragmentation, Mark asks you to defragment the disk and then determine the effectiveness of the defragmentation.

To defragment drive C:

1. So that you have a general idea of how long it takes for Disk Defragmenter to defragment drive C, note the time you started the defragmentation.

2. In the Analysis Report dialog box, click the **Defragment** button, or if you have closed the Analysis Report dialog box, click the **Defragment** button in the Disk Defragmenter window, and then wait patiently. The Disk Defragmenter analyzes the disk again, and then starts the defragmentation. After the defragmentation is complete, notice the dramatic difference between the "Estimated disk usage before defragmentation" and the "Estimated disk usage after defragmentation" display areas. On the computer used for Figure 7-33, the Disk Defragmenter substantially reduced fragmentation, consolidated contiguous files, and consolidated free space. The left side of the two areas represents the outer edge of the disk, and the right side represents the inner surface of the disk. As you can see, files are laid down in contiguous clusters from the outer edge of the disk, and free space is consolidated near the inner surface of the disk.

Figure 7-33	DEFRAGMENTATION COMPLETED

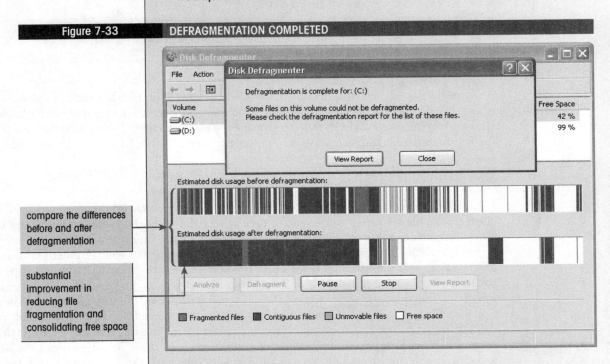

compare the differences before and after defragmentation

substantial improvement in reducing file fragmentation and consolidating free space

3. Click the **View Report** button, and then adjust your view to see the information on volume fragmentation. On the computer used for Figure 7-34, the Disk Defragmenter reports 1% total fragmentation, 3% file fragmentation, and 0% free space fragmentation. Although there are still some fragmented files, overall file fragmentation was substantially reduced. Your report will differ.

Figure 7-34   VOLUME DEFRAGMENTATION RESULTS

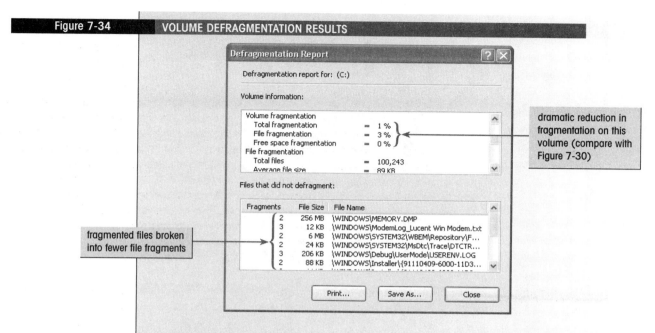

dramatic reduction in fragmentation on this volume (compare with Figure 7-30)

fragmented files broken into fewer file fragments

4. Adjust your view so that you can see information on File fragmentation under Volume information. On the computer used for Figure 7-35, Disk Defragmenter reports only 12 fragmented files (as compared to 3,815 prior to defragmentation), and an average of 1.00 fragments per file (almost perfect defragmentation for a volume this size). Yours will differ.

Figure 7-35   FILE DEFRAGMENTATION RESULTS

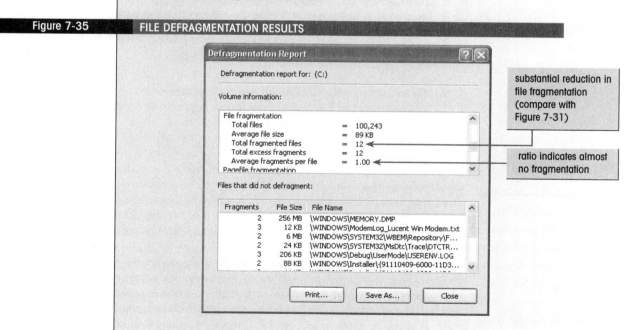

substantial reduction in file fragmentation (compare with Figure 7-31)

ratio indicates almost no fragmentation

5. Adjust your view in the Volume information area so that you can see information on Pagefile and Folder fragmentation. On the computer used for Figure 7-36, there was no change in pagefile fragmentation or folder fragmentation. Yours will differ. Windows XP must have access to the paging file at all times, so the Disk Defragmenter cannot defragment this file.

Figure 7-36   PAGEFILE AND FOLDER DEFRAGMENTATION RESULTS

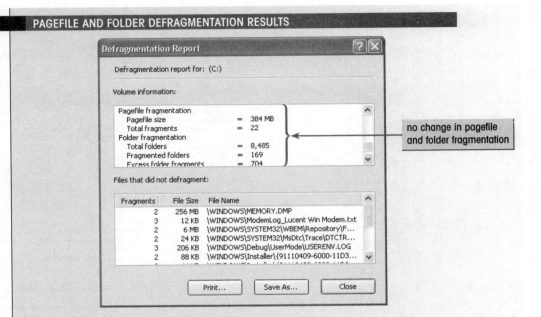

6. To print this report, click the **Print** button, make sure Windows XP is using the correct printer in the Print dialog box, click the **Print** button, and then click the **Close** button.

7. Click the **Save As** button, and in the My Documents folder, type **Volume C Defragmentation Report** (or an appropriate filename for the drive you checked) in the File name box, and then click the **Save** button.

8. Close the Defragmentation Report dialog box, close the Disk Defragmenter dialog box, close the Properties dialog box for drive C, and then close My Computer.

9. Note the time you completed the defragmentation, and compare it with the time you started the defragmentation. You can use this information to schedule future defragmentations of your hard disk.

If you now perform a few operations on your computer, such as opening, creating, modifying, and saving files, and then analyze the disk for defragmentation, you discover more fragmented files. Obviously, the number of fragmented files is lower than if you had not defragmented the disk, because there is more contiguous space available; therefore it is easier for the operating system to store all the clusters for one file together in contiguous clusters.

Certain operating system files, such as the paging file and the hibernation file, are excluded from the defragmentation, so you can never achieve 100% defragmentation. You can, however, purchase a defragmenting utility from another company, such as Executive Software International's Diskeeper, to provide more information about the organization of your disk, dramatically improve the amount of defragmentation, and substantially reduce the amount of time required to perform a defragmentation. The Windows XP Disk Defragmenter was also developed by Executive Software International.

Defragmenting a Disk

- Log on as Administrator or under an account with Administrator privileges.
- Open My Computer, right-click the drive you want to analyze, click Properties, click the Tools tab, and then click the Defragment Now button. Or click the Start button, point to All Programs, point to Accessories, point to System Tools, click Disk Defragmenter, and then click the Defragment button.
- If you have more than one volume, select the volume you want to analyze and defragment.
- Note your starting time.
- In the Disk Defragmenter dialog box, click the Analyze button.
- After the analysis is complete, click the View Report button and examine the information on fragmentation in the Analysis Report dialog box so that you can decide whether to defragment the disk.
- If you want to print the report, click the Print button, make sure Windows XP is using the correct printer in the Print dialog box, click the Print button, and then click the Close button.
- If you want to save the report, click the Save button, locate the folder where you want to save the report (if different than the default folder), decide whether you want to use a different name for the report, and then click the Save button.
- If you want to defragment the disk, click the Defragment button in the Analysis Report dialog box, or if you closed the Analysis Report dialog box, click the Defragment button in the Disk Defragmenter window.
- After the defragmentation is complete, click the View Report button and examine the information on fragmentation in the Analysis Report dialog box to determine the effectiveness of the defragmentation.
- If you want to print the report, click the Print button, make sure Windows XP is using the correct printer in the Print dialog box, click the Print button, and then click the Close button.
- If you want to save the report, click the Save button, locate the folder where you want to save the report (if different than the default folder), decide whether you want to use a different name for the report, and then click the Save button.
- Close the Defragmentation Report dialog box, close the Disk Defragmenter dialog box, close the Properties dialog box for the drive you selected, and then close My Computer.
- Note the time you finished, and compare it to the time you started so that you can plan future defragmentations.

You should optimize disks, especially your hard disk, on a regular basis, such as monthly or weekly. If you are working with graphics applications and creating and removing large graphic files, or if you work with a large number of files (creating, modifying, deleting, copying, and moving files) everyday, you should defragment your disk at least weekly. If you do not optimize your hard disk with the Disk Defragmenter, the disk's performance gradually declines. In fact, if you spend too much time waiting for applications and documents to load, that is a good sign you need to use the Disk Defragmenter. Also, as you use more of your hard disk's storage space, it becomes increasingly difficult for Disk Defragmenter to optimize your disk, because the disk contains only a limited area of storage space for rewriting clusters as it defragments the disk. As a result, the amount of time that Disk Defragmenter takes to optimize a disk increases substantially. You might have to temporarily remove files from the hard disk so that you can optimize the disk, and then copy those files back to the drive later. Before you "defrag" a disk, you should review which data files remain on disk and which can be deleted or archived (moved off the disk for long-term storage).

In the next half of the tutorial, you examine how to use the Disk Management snap-in tool, set disk quotas for users, compress folders and files, encrypt folders and files, and schedule a task (such as Disk Defragmenter or Disk Cleanup) so that Windows XP automatically runs the task on a regular basis. Finally, you develop a disk maintenance plan.

Using the Disk Management Snap-In Tool

The Disk Management snap-in tool provides information about the disks on your computer and the volumes on each disk. It also identifies the type of file system each volume uses, such as FAT32 or NTFS, and whether the volume is a primary partition or a logical drive on an extended partition. A **partition** is a subdivision of a physical hard disk that functions as if it were a separate physical disk. A **primary partition** is a partition on a **basic disk** (a physical disk) that contains the boot files for loading the operating system and is therefore designated as the active partition. Every hard disk has a primary partition; otherwise, you would not be able to start up your computer system. A basic disk can contain up to four primary partitions, or three primary partitions and one extended partition. An **extended partition** is a partition that contains one or more logical drives. Basic disks can be converted to dynamic disks using the Disk Management snap-in. A **dynamic disk** is a physical disk that only Windows XP and Windows 2000 can access, and that provides additional features not supported on basic disks, such as volumes that scan multiple disks. The Windows XP Home Edition supports the use of basic disks, but not dynamic disks. The Windows XP 64-Bit Edition supports the use of a new partition style called **GPT (Globally Unique Identifier Partition Table)**, which in turn supports 128 partitions per disk and partition sizes up to 18 exabytes (or 19,327,352,832 GB). An **exabyte** is equal to 2^{60} bytes, whereas a gigabyte is equal to 2^{30} bytes.

The **boot partition** is the partition that contains the Windows XP operating system files. The **system partition** is the partition that contains the hardware-specific files needed to load Windows XP—namely, NTLdr, Boot.ini, and Ntdetect.com. Although these are boot files, they are stored on the system partition (or system volume) rather than the boot partition (logically backwards). Likewise, the operating system files are stored on the boot partition (or boot volume), not the system partition (also logically backwards). The boot partition and system partition are usually the same, but they can be different.

To use the Disk Management snap-in tool, you must log on your computer as Administrator or under an account with Administrator privileges. To simplify access to the Disk Management snap-in, you can add the Administrative Tools menu to the All Programs menu.

If you are working in a computer lab, ask your instructor whether you have permission to use the Disk Management snap-in tool to view information about volumes on the disk. If you do not have permission to use the Disk Management snap-in tool, read the steps and examine the figures so that you are familiar with the use of this tool, but do not keystroke the following steps.

Mark asks you to show his staff how to use the Disk Management snap-in tool to examine information about the status of disks in a computer system. The staff also can use this tool to restructure and troubleshoot disks. Mark notes that they can also run Disk Defragmenter from the Disk Management snap-in tool.

To add the Administrative Tools menu to the All Programs menu:

1. Right-click the **Start** button, and then click **Properties** on the shortcut menu.

2. On the Start Menu property sheet of the Taskbar and Start Menu Properties dialog box, click the **Customize** button next to the start menu option button, and in the Customize Start Menu dialog box, click the **Advanced** tab.

3. Under "Start menu items," scroll to the bottom of this list box, and under "System Administrative Tools," click the **Display on the All Programs menu** option button, click the **OK** button to close the Customize Start Menu dialog box, and then click the **OK** button to close the Taskbar and Start Menu Properties dialog box.

Now you can open Computer Management, and examine disk information with the Disk Management snap-in.

To open the Disk Management snap-in:

1. From the Start menu, point to **All Programs**, point to **Administrative Tools**, click **Computer Management**, and then maximize the Computer Management window. Computer Management consists of a collection of administrative tools for managing a local or remote computer.

2. Under Storage in the console tree pane on the left, click **Disk Defragmenter**. The Details pane on the right provides you with the same view and access to the same resources as were available when you opened Disk Defragmenter from the System Tools menu. See Figure 7-37.

Figure 7-37	SELECTING DISK DEFRAGMENTER IN COMPUTER MANAGEMENT

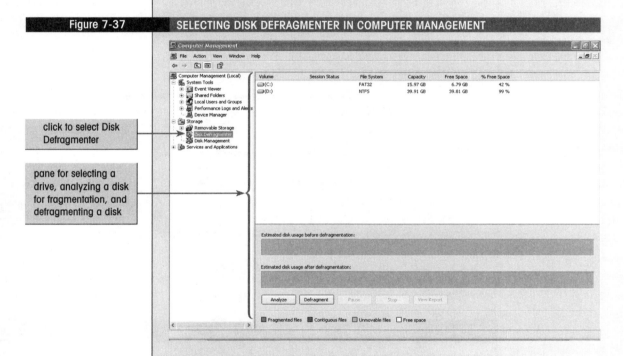

click to select Disk Defragmenter

pane for selecting a drive, analyzing a disk for fragmentation, and defragmenting a disk

3. Under Storage in the console tree pane on the left, click **Disk Management**. The Details pane on the right provides information about the different volumes and disks on your computer. See Figure 7-38. At the top of the Details pane is the Volume List area, and at the bottom is the Graphical View area. On the computer used for this figure, the Graphical View area shows that one hard disk (Disk 0, the disk name) with approximately 56 GB of storage capacity is divided into two volumes (drive C and drive D). Drive C is a FAT32 volume, while drive D is an NTFS volume. Drive C is a primary partition, and drive D is a logical drive on an extended partition (as shown by the color codes in the legend at the bottom of the window). In the Volume List area at the top, the Disk Management snap-in tool uses "Healthy" as a volume status description for the primary and extended partition to indicate that you can access these volumes, and that they have no identified problems. "System" is a volume substatus description that indicates the volume is the system volume.

TROUBLE? If Windows XP opens a Disk Management dialog box and informs you that you do not have access rights to Local Disk Manager on your computer, click the OK button, close the Computer Management window, log off the computer, and log on under an account with Administrator privileges, and then repeat these steps. Or if you prefer to not log off, read the steps and examine the figures, but do not keystroke the remaining steps.

| Figure 7-38 | VIEWING DISK INFORMATION WITH THE DISK MANAGEMENT TOOL |

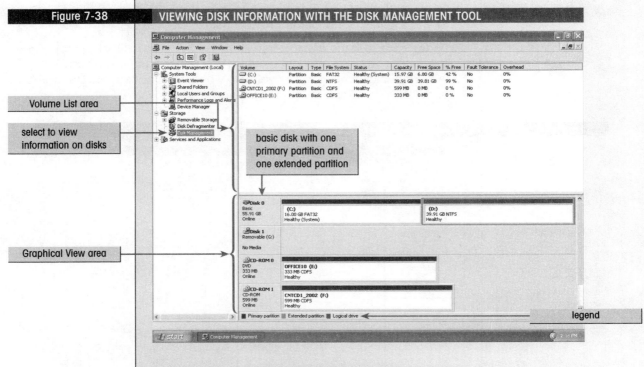

Volume List area

select to view information on disks

basic disk with one primary partition and one extended partition

Graphical View area

legend

4. Close the Computer Management window.

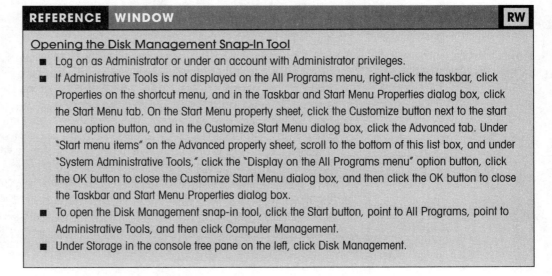

Opening the Disk Management Snap-In Tool

- Log on as Administrator or under an account with Administrator privileges.
- If Administrative Tools is not displayed on the All Programs menu, right-click the taskbar, click Properties on the shortcut menu, and in the Taskbar and Start Menu Properties dialog box, click the Start Menu tab. On the Start Menu property sheet, click the Customize button next to the start menu option button, and in the Customize Start Menu dialog box, click the Advanced tab. Under "Start menu items" on the Advanced property sheet, scroll to the bottom of this list box, and under "System Administrative Tools," click the "Display on the All Programs menu" option button, click the OK button to close the Customize Start Menu dialog box, and then click the OK button to close the Taskbar and Start Menu Properties dialog box.
- To open the Disk Management snap-in tool, click the Start button, point to All Programs, point to Administrative Tools, and then click Computer Management.
- Under Storage in the console tree pane on the left, click Disk Management.

You can use the Disk Management snap-in to create and format partitions and volumes; assign, reassign, or remove drive names; view drive properties; and troubleshoot disk problems. For example, from the shortcut menu for drive D on the computer used for Figure 7-39, you can open or explore this drive, change this drive's letter and paths, format the drive, delete this logical drive, view properties of this drive, or open the Disk Management Help.

Figure 7-39   **OPTIONS FOR WORKING WITH AN EXTENDED PARTITION**

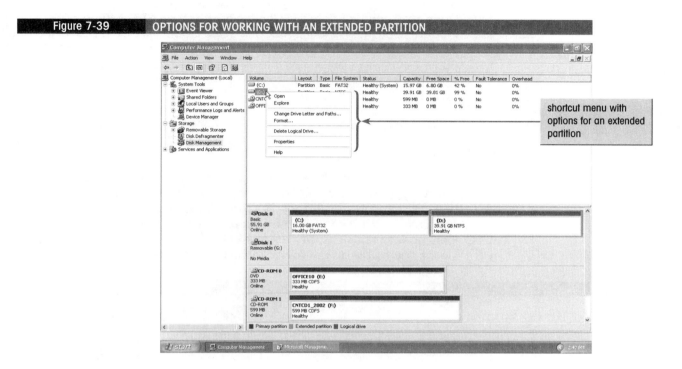

Setting Disk Quotas on NTFS Volumes

Like Windows 2000, Windows XP supports the use of **disk quotas** that enable Administrators or members of the Administrators group to control and track the usage of storage space on an NTFS volume. Disk quotas are therefore designed to limit the amount of hard disk storage space that is available to individual users. For example, in a business that runs three shifts with 10 computers and 30 employees (each of whom must use a computer), three employees working different shifts would share the same computer, and therefore the Administrator would need to set disk quotas for each user on each computer.

In addition to assigning a disk quota for each user, Administrators can prevent users from further access to a disk if they exceed their disk quota or permit users to exceed their disk quota. In either case, the Administrator can also choose to log the event so that they can monitor disk space usage. Not only can the Administrator set a disk quota for a user, but the Administrator can specify that a warning be issued when the user nears his or her quota limit. For example, an Administrator might set a user's disk quota to 1 GB, and then set the disk quota warning level to 950 MB. Disk quotas apply only to NTFS-formatted volumes that are shared.

The following steps require that you log on as Administrator, or log on under an account with Administrator privileges. If you do not have these privileges, read the steps and examine the figures, but do not keystroke the following steps. If you are working in a computer lab, ask your instructor or technical support staff whether you have permission to view and set quotas on an NTFS volume. If you do not have permission to view and set disk quotas on a volume, read the steps and examine the figures so that you are familiar with this process, but do not keystroke the steps. You must also work on a computer with an NTFS volume to complete these steps.

To allot a fair share of each computer's resources to users of those systems, Mark wants you to prepare for setting disk quotas for each user of his computer by examining the current disk quota settings on that computer.

To enable, set, and examine disk quotas:

1. Open My Computer, right-click the drive icon for an NTFS volume, click **Properties** on the shortcut menu, and in the Properties dialog box for the drive, click the **Quota** tab. Windows XP displays the Quota property sheet, shown in Figure 7-40. If disk quotas have not been enabled, the only option available on the property sheet is the Enable quota management check box. All other options are dimmed.

POWER USERS TIP If you are using the Disk Management snap-in, you can right-click the drive icon of an NTFS volume, choose Properties, and then select the Quota property sheet.

TROUBLE? If the drive Properties dialog box does not contain a Quota tab, you are not logged on under an account with Administrator privileges. Click the OK button to close the drive Properties dialog box, close My Computer, log off the computer, and log on under an account with Administrator privileges, and then repeat these steps. Or if you prefer to not log off, read the steps and examine the figures, but do not keystroke the following steps.

Figure 7-40 | **QUOTA PROPERTY SHEET**

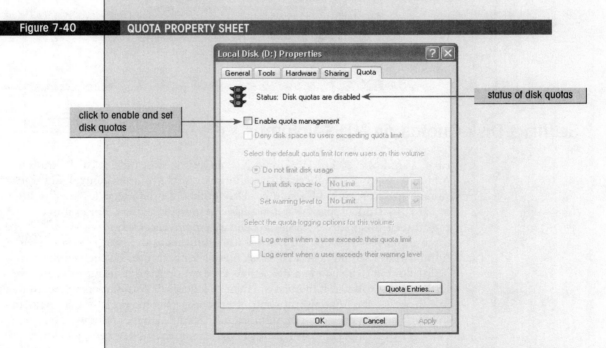

2. If you want to enable disk quotas, click the **Enable quota management** check box. All the other options on the Quota property sheet now become available.

3. Click the **Apply** button. The Disk Quota dialog box warns you that you should enable the quota system only if you intend to use disk quotas on the volume. See Figure 7-41. It also notes that it takes several minutes to update disk usage statistics before enabling the quota system.

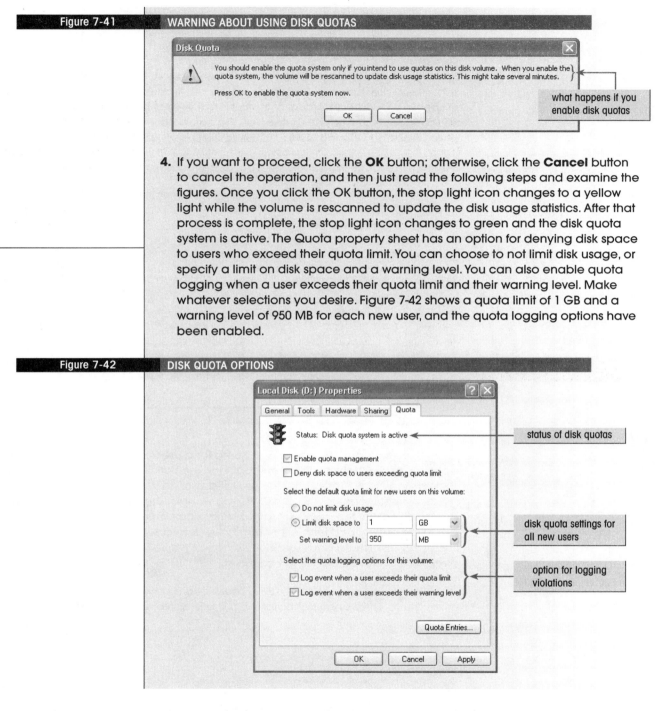

Figure 7-41   **WARNING ABOUT USING DISK QUOTAS**

4. If you want to proceed, click the **OK** button; otherwise, click the **Cancel** button to cancel the operation, and then just read the following steps and examine the figures. Once you click the OK button, the stop light icon changes to a yellow light while the volume is rescanned to update the disk usage statistics. After that process is complete, the stop light icon changes to green and the disk quota system is active. The Quota property sheet has an option for denying disk space to users who exceed their quota limit. You can choose to not limit disk usage, or specify a limit on disk space and a warning level. You can also enable quota logging when a user exceeds their quota limit and their warning level. Make whatever selections you desire. Figure 7-42 shows a quota limit of 1 GB and a warning level of 950 MB for each new user, and the quota logging options have been enabled.

Figure 7-42   **DISK QUOTA OPTIONS**

Before you apply these changes, you can specify or examine quota entries for all users and, if necessary, change a user quota limit or warning level.

To examine quota entries for all users:

1. Click the **Quota Entries** button. Windows XP displays the status for each user. (You may want to maximize this window to view the information more easily.) See Figure 7-43. Windows XP shows each user's logon, the amount of storage space they are currently using, their quota limit (if specified), their warning level (if specified), and the percent of their quota that they have used (if applicable). Because quotas were just enabled on the computer used for this figure, the quota limit and warning level for existing users is set as "No Limit."

Figure 7-43	QUOTA ENTRIES FOR USERS

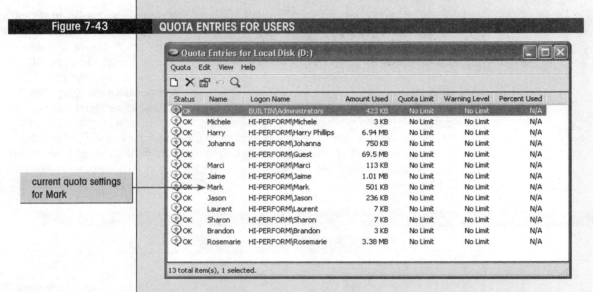

current quota settings for Mark

Quota Entries for Local Disk (D:)

Quota Edit View Help

Status	Name	Logon Name	Amount Used	Quota Limit	Warning Level	Percent Used
OK		BUILTIN\Administrators	423 KB	No Limit	No Limit	N/A
OK	Michele	HI-PERFORM\Michele	3 KB	No Limit	No Limit	N/A
OK	Harry	HI-PERFORM\Harry Phillips	6.94 MB	No Limit	No Limit	N/A
OK	Johanna	HI-PERFORM\Johanna	750 KB	No Limit	No Limit	N/A
OK		HI-PERFORM\Guest	69.5 MB	No Limit	No Limit	N/A
OK	Marci	HI-PERFORM\Marci	113 KB	No Limit	No Limit	N/A
OK	Jaime	HI-PERFORM\Jaime	1.01 MB	No Limit	No Limit	N/A
OK	Mark	HI-PERFORM\Mark	501 KB	No Limit	No Limit	N/A
OK	Jason	HI-PERFORM\Jason	236 KB	No Limit	No Limit	N/A
OK	Laurent	HI-PERFORM\Laurent	7 KB	No Limit	No Limit	N/A
OK	Sharon	HI-PERFORM\Sharon	7 KB	No Limit	No Limit	N/A
OK	Brandon	HI-PERFORM\Brandon	3 KB	No Limit	No Limit	N/A
OK	Rosemarie	HI-PERFORM\Rosemarie	3.38 MB	No Limit	No Limit	N/A

13 total item(s), 1 selected.

2. If you want to examine or specify a quota for a user, click the entry for that user account, click **Quota** on the menu bar, and then click **Properties**. Windows XP displays the Quota Settings for the selected user (in this example, Mark). See Figure 7-44. You can now set the limits you want for the user you selected. If the quota settings for the user is set to "No Limit," you can click the "Limit disk space to" option button, and then either retain the default settings you specified earlier for the disk quota and warning level, as shown in Figure 7-45, or you can customize those settings for this one user.

POWER USERS TIP You can also view a user's quota settings by double-clicking a user's quota entry, or by right-clicking a user's quota entry and then selecting Properties.

Figure 7-44	CHANGING QUOTA SETTINGS FOR A USER

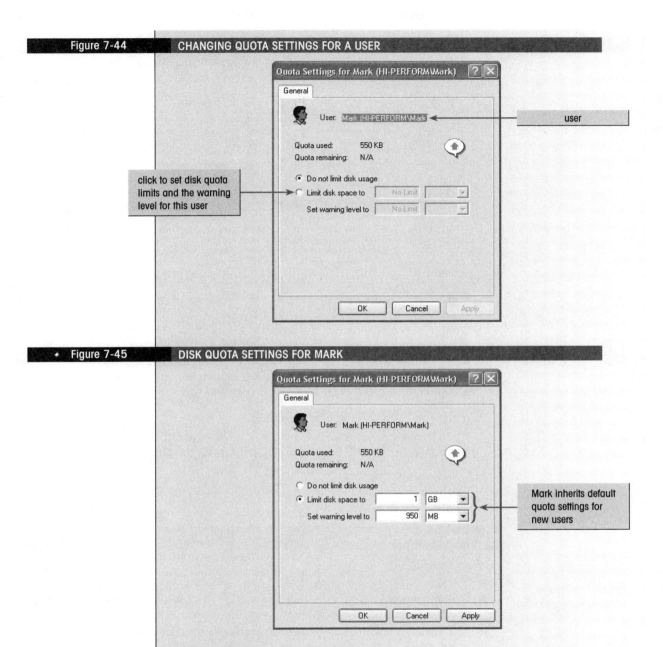

Figure 7-45	DISK QUOTA SETTINGS FOR MARK

3. If you changed a user's quota limit and warning, and want to apply those settings, click the **OK** button; otherwise, click the **Cancel** button to leave the settings unchanged. Figure 7-46 shows that you have changed Mark's limits to the default settings (in this example, 1 GB for the quota limit and 950 MB for the warning level).

Figure 7-46   **DISK QUOTA CHANGED FOR A USER**

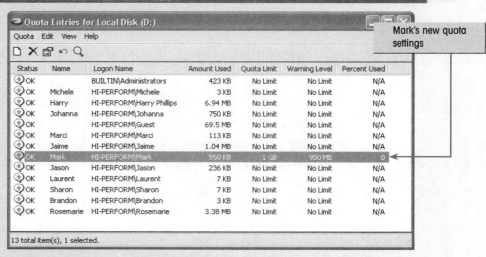

Mark's new quota settings

On the Quota menu, you can select the New Quota Entry option to locate quota information for a user or group of users by setting criteria, such as the user's display name, user name, or a computer's name. You can use the Import and Export option to import or export quota settings. You can use the Delete Quota Entry to remove an entry for a selected user.

4. Close the Quota Entries dialog box.

5. If you made changes you want to keep, click the **OK** button in the Properties dialog box for the NTFS volume; otherwise click the **Cancel** button.

6. Close My Computer.

REFERENCE WINDOW   **RW**

Setting Disk Quotas
- Log on as Administrator or under an account with Administrator privileges.
- Open My Computer, right-click the drive icon for an NTFS volume, click Properties on the shortcut menu, and in the Properties dialog box for the drive, click the Quota tab.
- If you want to enable disk quotas, click the "Enable quota management" check box, and then click the Apply button. Windows XP warns you that you should continue only if you want to enable disk quotas. If you want to proceed, click the OK button; otherwise, click the Cancel button to cancel the operation.
- Choose the disk quota options you want to apply to new users.
- Click the Quota Entries button, and then maximize the Quota Entries dialog box.
- Click the entry for the user you want to examine or change, click Quota on the menu bar, and then click Properties. (You also can double-click a user's quota entry or right-click a user's quota entry, and then click Properties.)
- Make whatever changes you need to make for that user, and then click the OK button; or click the Cancel button to close the Quota Settings dialog box.
- If you have made changes you want to keep, click the OK button in the Properties dialog box for the NTFS volume; otherwise click the Cancel button.
- Close My Computer.

By setting disk quotas for all Harris & Banche users, Mark has a mechanism for tracking disk usage by individual user and ensuring that all users have an equal share of the resources of the computer on which they work and share with other users.

Compressing and Uncompressing Folders and Files on NTFS Volumes

You can compress files, folders, or even an entire drive on an NTFS volume, but not on a FAT volume. Note that the NTFS file system already efficiently uses storage space, and has cluster sizes that are smaller than those for FAT32 and FAT16. The amount of additional space that you gain by enabling compression on an NTFS volume is not as dramatic as converting a FAT16 volume to FAT32 or NTFS.

In the following steps, you are going to create a folder on an NTFS volume, and then compress and uncompress that folder. If you are working in a computer lab, ask your instructor or technical support staff for permission to create a folder on an NTFS volume and for permission to compress and uncompress that folder. If you do not have permission to use the NTFS compression feature on a volume, read the steps and examine the figures so that you are familiar with this feature, but do not keystroke the following steps. Likewise, if you do not have an NTFS volume, you cannot complete the steps.

At his weekly staff meeting, Mark asks you to demonstrate how to compress a folder on an NTFS drive so that Harris & Banche employees can compress their folders and files, and thereby maximize the use of the storage space on their hard disks.

To set up a folder for Harris & Banche:

1. If your My Documents folder is located on an NTFS volume, open the My Documents folder; otherwise, open the top-level folder of an NTFS drive.

2. Click **Make a new folder** on the File and Folder Tasks dynamic menu, and after Windows XP creates a new folder named "New Folder," type **Harris & Banche**, press the **Enter** key to assign the name to the folder, and then press the **Enter** key again to open the Harris & Banche folder.

3. Open My Computer, and then open a window onto the floppy disk or the network folder that contains the files for Data Disk #2, click the **Harris & Banche** taskbar button, right-click the **taskbar**, click **Tile Windows Vertically**, click the **title bar** or **background** of the window with the files for Data Disk #2, open the **Delta Oil** folder, click **Edit** on the menu bar, click **Select All**, and then drag the **selected folders** from the 3½ Floppy (A:) window to the Harris & Banche folder window.

4. After the copy operation is complete, close the 3½ Floppy (A:) window, maximize the Harris & Banche folder window, and then click the **Up** button 📂.

Now you're ready to compress this folder, its subfolders, and files.

To compress a folder and its contents:

1. Right-click the **Harris & Banche** folder, and then click **Properties** on the shortcut menu. On the General property sheet in the Harris & Banche Properties dialog box, Windows XP reports that this folder and its subfolder and files are 0.98 MB (or 1,032,834 bytes) in size and use 1.04 MB (or 1,097,728 bytes) of storage space on the disk. See Figure 7-47. The Harris & Banche folder contains 33 files in five subfolders.

Figure 7-47 **HARRIS & BANCHE FOLDER PROPERTIES BEFORE COMPRESSION**

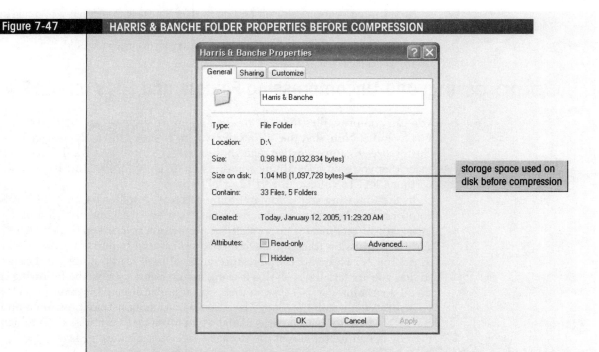

storage space used on disk before compression

2. Click the **Advanced** button. The Compress or Encrypt attributes section of the Advanced Attributes dialog box includes an option for compressing the contents of the folder to save disk space. See Figure 7-48.

Figure 7-48 **SELECTING THE OPTION FOR COMPRESSING A FOLDER**

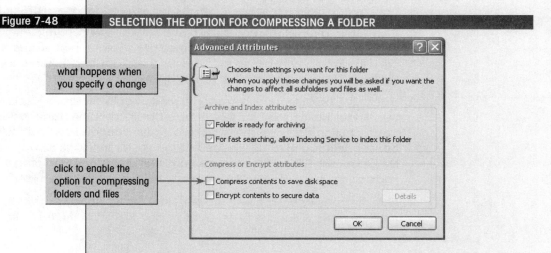

what happens when you specify a change

click to enable the option for compressing folders and files

3. Click the **Compress contents to save disk space** check box, click the **OK** button in the Advanced Attributes dialog box, and then click the **Apply** button in the Harris & Banche Properties dialog box. The Confirm Attribute Changes dialog box informs you that it will apply the Compress attribute. See Figure 7-49. You have the option of applying this change to only the Harris & Banche folder, or you can apply the change to the Harris & Banche folder and all its subfolders and files.

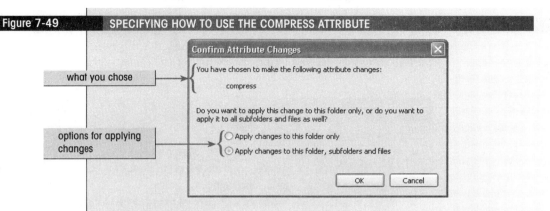

what you chose

options for applying
changes

4. Click the **Apply changes to this folder, subfolders and files** option button (if
necessary), and then click the **OK** button. On the General property sheet in the
Harris & Banche Properties dialog box, Windows XP reports that this folder and
its subfolder and files are still 0.98 MB (or 1,032,834 bytes) in size, but they now
use only 424 KB (or 434,176 bytes) of storage space on the disk rather than the
previously reported 1.04 MB (or 1,097,728 bytes). See Figure 7-50. That indicates
an average compression of approximately 60% per file. In other words, the files
now only take up 40% of the space they originally required.

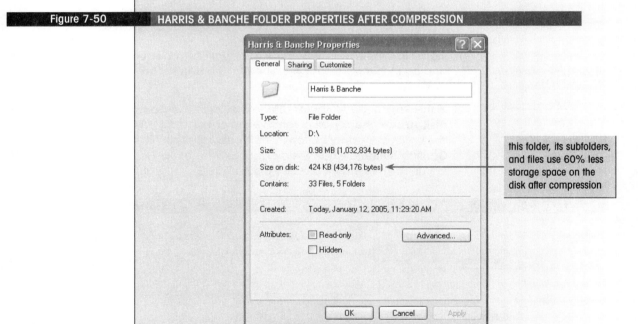

this folder, its subfolders,
and files use 60% less
storage space on the
disk after compression

5. Close the Harris & Banche Properties dialog box, click the **folder window background**, and notice that the Harris & Banche folder name is displayed in bright
blue to indicate that the folder's contents are compressed.

6. Open the Harris & Banche folder, notice that the subfolder names are also
shown in bright blue, open the Company Templates folder, and notice that all
the filenames are also displayed in bright blue.

7. Click the **Back** button ☺ ˙ on the Standard Buttons toolbar until you return to
the My Documents folder, or to the top-level folder of the drive you are using.

If you *copy* a file (compressed or uncompressed) to a folder, the file takes on the compression attribute of the folder (compressed or uncompressed). If you *move* a compressed or uncompressed file from one folder to another, the file remains as it originally was (compressed or uncompressed), no matter whether the folder is compressed or uncompressed.

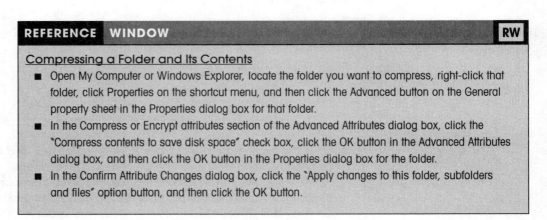

REFERENCE WINDOW   RW

Compressing a Folder and Its Contents

■ Open My Computer or Windows Explorer, locate the folder you want to compress, right-click that folder, click Properties on the shortcut menu, and then click the Advanced button on the General property sheet in the Properties dialog box for that folder.

■ In the Compress or Encrypt attributes section of the Advanced Attributes dialog box, click the "Compress contents to save disk space" check box, click the OK button in the Advanced Attributes dialog box, and then click the OK button in the Properties dialog box for the folder.

■ In the Confirm Attribute Changes dialog box, click the "Apply changes to this folder, subfolders and files" option button, and then click the OK button.

Next, you are going to reverse the compression process, and uncompress the Harris & Banche folder and its contents.

To uncompress a folder and its contents:

1. Right-click the **Harris & Banche** folder, click **Properties** on the shortcut menu, and on the General property sheet of the Harris & Banche Properties dialog box, click the **Advanced** button.

2. In the Advanced Attributes dialog box, click the **Compress contents to save disk space** check box to remove the check mark, click the **OK** button, and then click the **Apply** button in the Harris & Banche Properties dialog box. The Confirm Attribute Changes dialog box informs you that Windows XP will apply the Uncompress attribute. See Figure 7-51.

Figure 7-51   CHANGING THE COMPRESS ATTRIBUTE

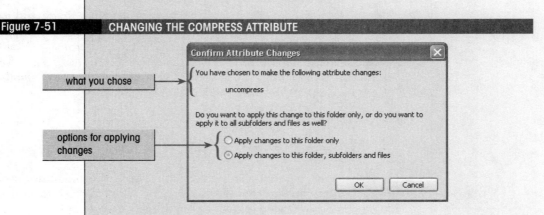

3. Click the **Apply changes to this folder, subfolders and files** option button (if necessary), and then click the **OK** button. On the General property sheet in the Harris & Banche Properties dialog box, Windows XP reports that this folder and its subfolder and files are still 0.98 MB (or 1,032,834 bytes) in size, but they now use 1.04 MB (or 1,097,728 bytes) of disk storage space instead of the previous compressed size of 424 KB (or 434,176 bytes). See Figure 7-52.

Figure 7-52   HARRIS & BANCHE FOLDER PROPERTIES AFTER REMOVING THE COMPRESSION

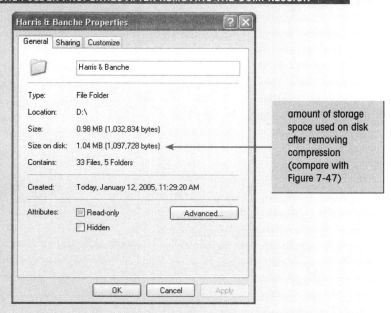

amount of storage space used on disk after removing compression (compare with Figure 7-47)

4. Close the Harris & Banche Properties dialog box, click the **folder window background**, and notice that the Harris & Banche folder name is now displayed in black to indicate that it is not compressed.

5. Open the Harris & Banche folder, notice that the subfolder names are also shown in black, open the Company Templates folder, and notice that all the filenames are also displayed in black.

6. Click the **Back** button ⊙ᐧ on the Standard Buttons toolbar until you return to the My Documents folder, or to the top-level folder of the drive you are using. Keep this window open for the next section of the tutorial.

You just successfully compressed and then uncompressed a folder and its contents. As noted earlier, you can compress an entire NTFS volume. Open My Computer, right-click the NTFS volume, and then choose Properties. The General property sheet for the NTFS volume includes a check box labeled "Compress drive to save disk space" for compressing the entire volume. See Figure 7-53. If your NTFS volume has a large number of files, the time required to compress the drive might be substantial.

Figure 7-53	OPTION FOR COMPRESSING AN ENTIRE NTFS VOLUME

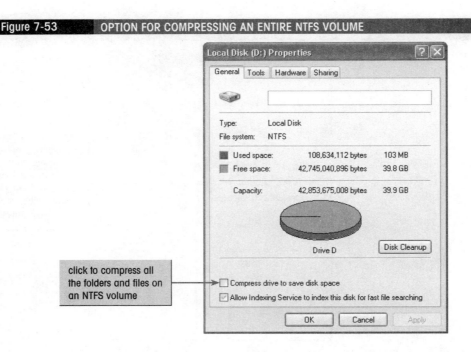

click to compress all the folders and files on an NTFS volume

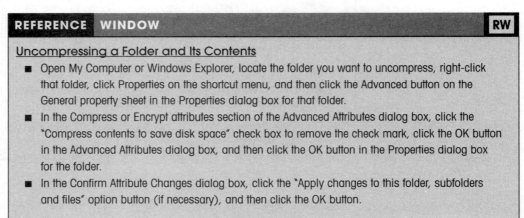

REFERENCE WINDOW   RW

Uncompressing a Folder and Its Contents

- Open My Computer or Windows Explorer, locate the folder you want to uncompress, right-click that folder, click Properties on the shortcut menu, and then click the Advanced button on the General property sheet in the Properties dialog box for that folder.
- In the Compress or Encrypt attributes section of the Advanced Attributes dialog box, click the "Compress contents to save disk space" check box to remove the check mark, click the OK button in the Advanced Attributes dialog box, and then click the OK button in the Properties dialog box for the folder.
- In the Confirm Attribute Changes dialog box, click the "Apply changes to this folder, subfolders and files" option button (if necessary), and then click the OK button.

If storage space is at a premium, or if your computer is shared by other users, using file compression on an NTFS volume might be an important factor in maximizing your use of storage space on that disk. Since the operating system must uncompress each file that you open, and then compress it again once you close the file, you may discover that compression slows down the performance of your computer slightly.

Encrypting and Decrypting Folders and Files on an NTFS Volume

The **Encrypting File Service** (**EFS**) allows you to encrypt and decrypt folders and files to protect your important documents. This protection is especially important if you share your computer with other users, use a portable computer, or connect your computer to a larger network, including the Internet. The Encrypting File Service is available in Windows XP Professional, but not in the Windows XP Home Edition. In Windows XP Professional, you can encrypt folders and files on an NTFS volume, but not a FAT volume. This service is part of the Windows XP security subsystem, and is automatically implemented by NTFS.

If you open an encrypted file, NTFS automatically decrypts the file. When you save a file to disk, NTFS automatically encrypts it. In other words, the process is transparent to you, and you can work with the contents of your files just as you would if they were not encrypted. Although you can encrypt files one by one, a more effective approach is to encrypt the folder that contains your files, and then all files stored in that folder are automatically encrypted.

You cannot encrypt system files with the System attribute or system files in the Systemroot folder (the folder with the Windows system files).

If you are working in a computer lab, ask your instructor or technical support staff for permission to create a folder on an NTFS volume (if necessary), and for permission to encrypt and decrypt that folder. If you do not have permission to use encryption on an NTFS volume, read the steps and examine the figures so that you are familiar with this feature, but do not keystroke the following steps. Likewise, if you do not have an NTFS volume, you cannot complete these steps.

With the increasing attention paid to security, Mark discusses with his staff the potential value of the Windows XP Encrypting File Service (EFS). He asks you to encrypt and decrypt the Harris & Banche folder so that you are familiar with this process.

To encrypt a folder and its contents:

1. Right-click the **Harris & Banche** folder, click **Properties** on the shortcut menu, and after Windows XP opens the Harris & Banche Properties dialog box, click the **Advanced** button on the General property sheet. The Advanced Attributes dialog box includes an option for encrypting the contents of this folder under "Compress or Encrypt attributes." See Figure 7-54.

   TROUBLE? If the "Encrypt contents to secure data" option is dimmed and if you are using Windows XP Home Edition, then you are not able to complete the following steps. Read these steps and examine the figures so that you are familiar with the process for encrypting a folder and its contents, but do not keystroke the steps.

Figure 7-54	SELECTING THE OPTION FOR ENCRYPTING A FOLDER

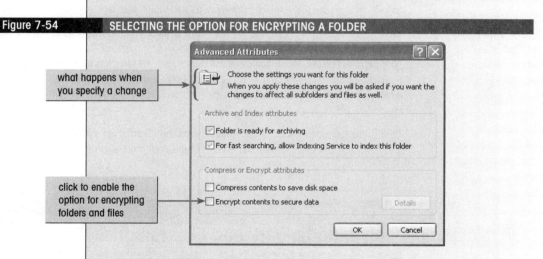

what happens when you specify a change

click to enable the option for encrypting folders and files

2. Click the **Encrypt contents to secure data** check box, click the **OK** button in the Advanced Attributes dialog box, and then click the **OK** button in the Harris & Banche Properties dialog box. The Confirm Attribute Changes dialog box informs you that Windows XP will apply the Encrypt attribute. See Figure 7-55. Similar to the Compress attribute, you have the option of applying this change to only the current folder, or you can apply it to not only the current folder, but also all subfolders and files within this folder.

| Figure 7-55 | SPECIFYING HOW TO USE THE ENCRYPT ATTRIBUTE |

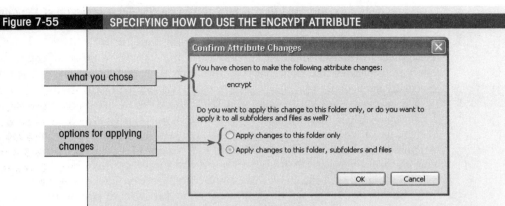

what you chose

options for applying changes

3. Click the **Apply changes to this folder, subfolders and files** option button (if necessary), and then click the **OK** button. Windows XP now displays an Applying Attributes dialog box, processes all the files within this folder, and enables the Encrypt attribute. See Figure 7-56.

| Figure 7-56 | APPLYING THE ENCRYPT ATTRIBUTE TO FILES |

file being encrypted

4. Click the **folder window background** and notice that the Harris & Banche folder name is displayed in green to indicate it is encrypted.

5. Open the Harris & Banche folder, notice that Windows XP displays these folder names in green to indicate that they are encrypted, open the Company Templates folder, and notice that Windows XP displays the filenames in green to indicate that they are encrypted. Notice also that you can work with these encrypted folders and files just as you would work with unencrypted folders and files.

6. Click the **Back** button ⊙ on the Standard Buttons toolbar until you return to the My Documents folder, or to the top-level folder of the drive you are using.

REFERENCE WINDOW | **RW**

Encrypting a Folder and Its Contents
- Open My Computer or Windows Explorer, locate the folder you want to encrypt, right-click that folder, click Properties on the shortcut menu, and then click the Advanced button on the General property sheet in the Properties dialog box for that folder.
- In the Compress or Encrypt attributes section of the Advanced Attributes dialog box, click the "Encrypt contents to secure data" check box, click the OK button in the Advanced Attributes dialog box, and then click the OK button in the Properties dialog box for the folder.
- In the Confirm Attributes dialog box, click the "Apply changes to this folder, subfolders and files" option button (if necessary), and then click the OK button.

Now you're going to reverse this process, and decrypt the Harris & Banche folder and its contents.

To decrypt a folder and its subfolders and files:

1. Right-click the **Harris & Banche** folder, click **Properties** on the shortcut menu, click the **Advanced** button on the General property sheet in the Harris & Banche Properties dialog box, click the **Encrypt contents to secure data** check box to remove the check mark, click the **OK** button in the Advanced Attributes dialog box, and then click the **OK** button in the Harris & Banche Properties dialog box. The Confirm Attribute Changes dialog box informs you that Windows XP will apply the decrypt attribute. See Figure 7-57.

   TROUBLE? If the "Encrypt contents to secure data" option is dimmed and if you are using Windows XP Home Edition, then you cannot complete the following steps. Read these steps and examine the figures so that you are familiar with the process for decrypting a folder and its contents, but do not keystroke the steps.

Figure 7-57	SPECIFYING HOW TO USE THE DECRYPT ATTRIBUTE

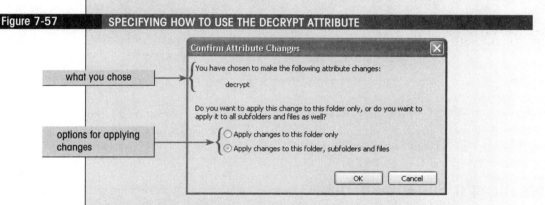

2. Click the **Apply changes to this folder, subfolders and files** option button, and then click the **OK** button. Windows XP now displays an Applying Attributes dialog box as it processes all the files on the drive.

3. Click the **folder window background**, and notice that the Harris & Banche folder name is now shown in black to indicate that it is no longer encrypted.

4. Open the Harris & Banche folder, notice that the folder names are now shown in black, open the Company Templates folder, and notice that the filenames are now shown in black. Windows XP has reversed the encryption that you applied earlier to the Harris & Banche folder and its contents.

5. Click the **Back** button ⊙⁻ on the Standard Buttons toolbar until you return to the My Documents folder, or to the top-level folder of the drive you are using.

6. Delete the Harris & Banche folder, and then close the My Documents or drive window.

In Windows XP Professional, the process for encrypting a folder or file is similar to that for compressing a folder or file. However, you can only apply either the Compress or the Encrypt attribute—you cannot apply both.

If you copy or move an unencrypted file to an encrypted folder, the unencrypted file is automatically encrypted. If you copy or move an encrypted file to an unencrypted folder, the file remains encrypted. If you copy an encrypted file to a volume that is not an NTFS volume, the file is no longer encrypted, because FAT volumes do not support encryption. If you e-mail an encrypted file, the file is no longer encrypted.

If a problem arises, the individual designated as the Data Recovery Agent (the Local Administrator or one or more other designated users) can recover encrypted files by decrypting them. On a stand-alone computer, you can designate a Data Recovery Agent using Local Security Policies on the Administrative Tools menu.

REFERENCE WINDOW   **RW**

Decrypting a Folder and Its Contents
- Open My Computer or Windows Explorer, locate the folder you want to decrypt, right-click that folder, click Properties on the shortcut menu, and then click the Advanced button on the General property sheet in the Properties dialog box for that folder.
- In the Compress or Encrypt attributes section of the Advanced Attributes dialog box, click the "Encrypt contents to secure data" check box to remove the check mark, click the OK button in the Advanced Attributes dialog box, and then click the OK button in the Properties dialog box for the folder.
- In the Confirm Attributes dialog box, click the "Apply changes to this folder, subfolders and files" option button (if necessary), and then click the OK button.

If you share a computer with other users, if you use a laptop, or if you want added security for a group of files, such as your tax records, you can encrypt the folders that contain your important documents.

Creating a Scheduled Task

You can use the Scheduled Task Wizard to set up a regular maintenance schedule for optimizing the performance of your computer. You might, for example, want to schedule the Disk Cleanup Wizard or Disk Defragmenter to run at a specific time each week to guarantee that you do not forget to clean your disk of unneeded files or to optimize your hard disk. Like other programs, the Disk Cleanup Wizard and Disk Defragmenter do not include a built-in scheduling feature, so you would use the Scheduled Task Wizard to set up a schedule for the Disk Cleanup Wizard or Disk Defragmenter.

If you are working in a computer lab, ask your instructor or technical support staff for permission to create a scheduled task. The lab staff might have already set up a regular maintenance schedule for each computer, and if that is the case, then do not change the tasks in the Scheduled Tasks folder. Instead, read the steps and examine the figures so that you are familiar with how to create and remove scheduled tasks, but do not keystroke the following steps.

To create a Scheduled Task:

1. On the Start menu, point to **All Programs**, point to **Accessories**, point to **System Tools**, and then click **Scheduled Tasks**. Windows XP opens the Scheduled Tasks folder. See Figure 7-58.

Figure 7-58 SCHEDULED TASKS FOLDER

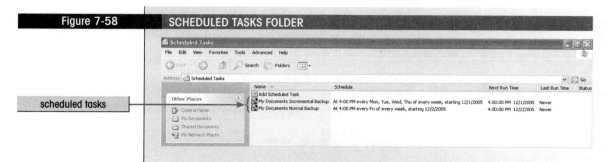

scheduled tasks

2. Click the **Add Scheduled Task** icon. The Scheduled Task Wizard dialog box opens, and the wizard informs you that you can select the program you want to run and then schedule it for a convenient time. See Figure 7-59.

Figure 7-59 HOW TO USE THE SCHEDULED TASK WIZARD

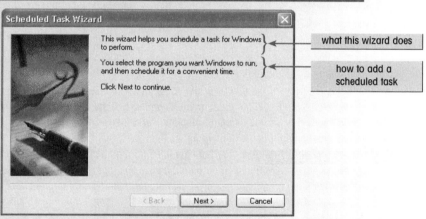

what this wizard does

how to add a scheduled task

3. Click the **Next** button. In the next Scheduled Task Wizard dialog box, you select the application you want to run. (This is a list of all installed programs on your computer, and for many of them, it would not make sense to run them on a scheduled basis.) See Figure 7-60.

Figure 7-60 CHOOSING THE PROGRAM FOR A SCHEDULED TASK

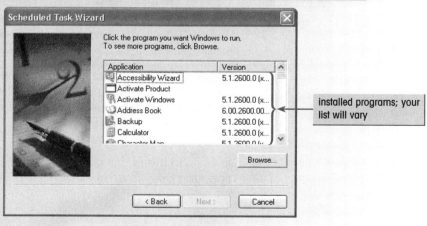

installed programs; your list will vary

4. In the Application column, locate and click **Disk Cleanup**, and then click the **Next** button. The wizard identifies the task name (which you can change if you like), and allows you to select when you want to perform this task. See Figure 7-61.

Figure 7-61 | **SPECIFYING WHEN TO PERFORM THE TASK**

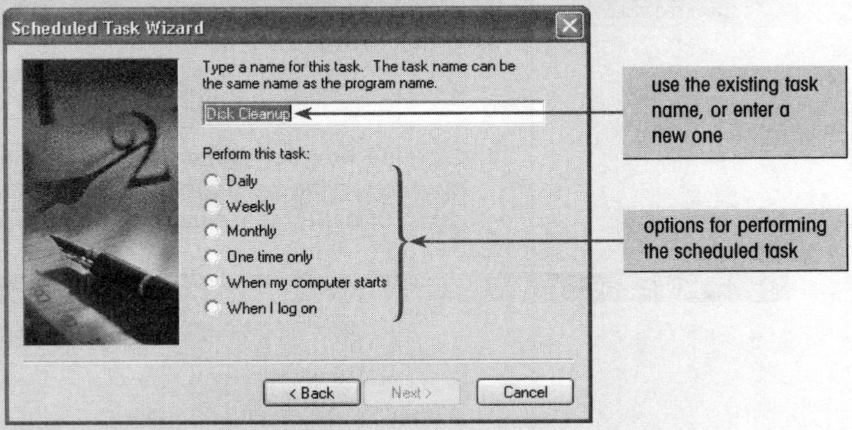

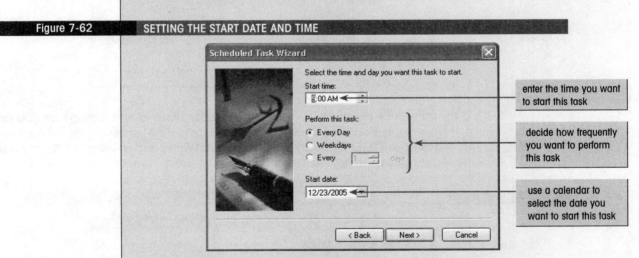

5. Click the **Daily** option button, and then click the **Next** button. In the next dialog box, the wizard prompts for the time and day to start this task, and displays the current date and time. See Figure 7-62.

Figure 7-62 | **SETTING THE START DATE AND TIME**

6. Change the time so that it is five minutes from now, and then click the **Next** button. For example, if the time is 11:00 A.M., set it to 11:05 A.M. so that you can test this feature. In the next dialog box, you specify the password for your logon. See Figure 7-63.

Figure 7-63 | SPECIFYING A PASSWORD FOR THE SCHEDULED TASK

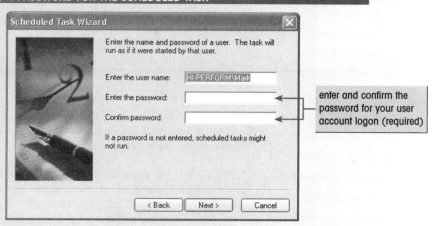

enter and confirm the password for your user account logon (required)

7. Enter the password for your logon account and confirm it, and then click the **Next** button. The password is required. If you do not have a password for your user account, the scheduled task does not run at its scheduled time. The Scheduled Task Wizard summarizes the settings for this task. See Figure 7-64. You also can open the advanced properties dialog box for this task after you finish it if you want to check or change task settings.

Figure 7-64 | SUMMARY OF SCHEDULED TASK

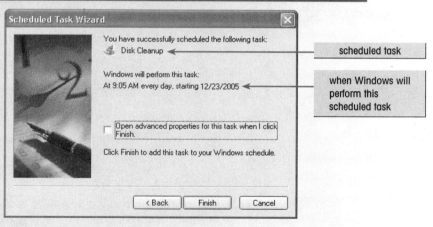

scheduled task

when Windows will perform this scheduled task

8. Click the **Finish** button, and if you do not see an icon for this scheduled task, click **View** on the menu bar, and then click **Refresh** (or press the **F5** key). Windows XP adds a scheduled task to the Scheduled Tasks folder. See Figure 7-65. The scheduled tasks are files with the "job" file extension (although Windows XP does not display the file extension by default).

Figure 7-65   NEW SCHEDULED TASK IN THE SCHEDULED TASKS FOLDER

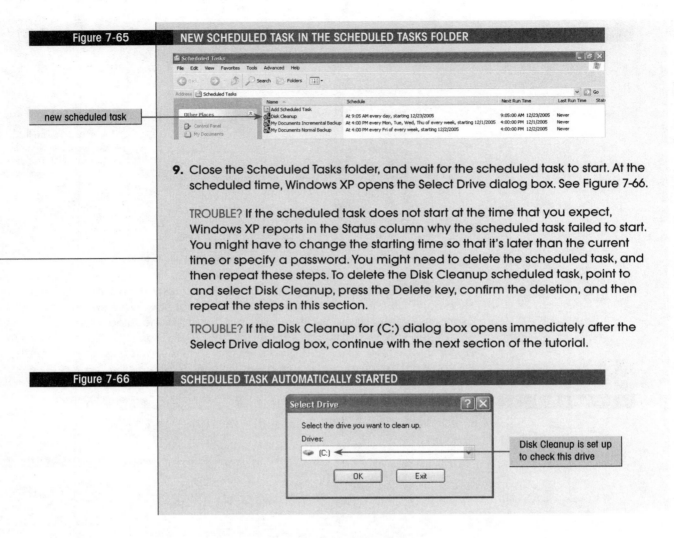

new scheduled task

9. Close the Scheduled Tasks folder, and wait for the scheduled task to start. At the scheduled time, Windows XP opens the Select Drive dialog box. See Figure 7-66.

TROUBLE? If the scheduled task does not start at the time that you expect, Windows XP reports in the Status column why the scheduled task failed to start. You might have to change the starting time so that it's later than the current time or specify a password. You might need to delete the scheduled task, and then repeat these steps. To delete the Disk Cleanup scheduled task, point to and select Disk Cleanup, press the Delete key, confirm the deletion, and then repeat the steps in this section.

TROUBLE? If the Disk Cleanup for (C:) dialog box opens immediately after the Select Drive dialog box, continue with the next section of the tutorial.

Figure 7-66   SCHEDULED TASK AUTOMATICALLY STARTED

Disk Cleanup is set up to check this drive

Now you're ready to run the scheduled task.

To run Disk Cleanup:

1. Click the **OK** button in the Select Drive dialog box, or if the Disk Cleanup for (C:) dialog box opened, continue with the next step. The Disk Cleanup Wizard checks drive C, and then displays the Disk Cleanup dialog box for that drive.

2. If you are working on your own computer and want to remove files from drive C, select those files, click the **OK** button, and then click the **Yes** button; if you are working in a computer lab, or if you do not want to make any changes to drive C on your computer, click the **Cancel** button.

Because you chose the default option of running this task every day, Windows XP starts this scheduled task at the same time each day.

REFERENCE WINDOW **RW**

Creating a Scheduled Task

- Click the Start button, point to All Programs, point to Accessories, point to System Tools, and then click Scheduled Tasks.
- After Windows XP opens the Scheduled Tasks folder, click the Add Scheduled Task icon.
- After the welcome dialog box opens for the Scheduled Task Wizard, click the Next button.
- In the Scheduled Task Wizard dialog box, locate and click the name of the application you want to run as a scheduled task, and then click the Next button.
- In the next dialog box, check and, if necessary, change the task name, select when you want to run the task, and then click the Next button.
- In the next dialog box, specify the starting date and time for the scheduled task.
- In the next dialog box, enter the password for your logon account (a password is required for the scheduled task to run), and then click the Next button.
- In the last dialog box, check the settings for this task.
- Click Finish, and then close the Scheduled Tasks folder.

If you choose the Browse button to look for the program file you want to use for a scheduled task, you have to know the location and name of the program file. For example, the Scheduled Task Wizard does not include Disk Defragmenter in its list of programs, so you have to browse for the program file, which is located in the System32 folder under the Windows folder. The program filename is dfrg.msc.

You can also view and change settings for a scheduled task.

To check settings for a scheduled task:

1. On the Start menu, point to **All Programs**, point to **Accessories**, point to **System Tools**, click **Scheduled Tasks**, and after the Scheduled Tasks folder opens, click **Disk Cleanup**. Windows XP opens a dialog box for the program that you've scheduled, as shown in Figure 7-67. On the Task property sheet, you can view the path and filename of the program you've scheduled, set the password for the scheduled task, or turn the task off by removing the check mark from the Enabled check box.

Figure 7-67   **VIEWING PROPERTIES OF A SCHEDULED TASK**

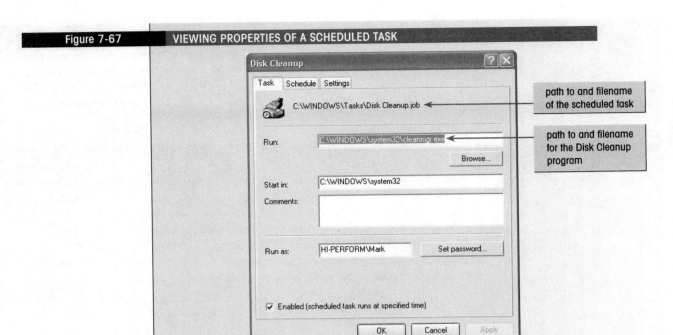

path to and filename of the scheduled task

path to and filename for the Disk Cleanup program

2. Click the **Schedule** tab. You can use the Schedule property sheet to verify or change the schedule for the task, specify multiple schedules, or use the Advanced button to specify an end date for the task and how frequently you want to repeat the task. See Figure 7-68.

Figure 7-68   **VIEWING THE SCHEDULE FOR A SCHEDULED TASK**

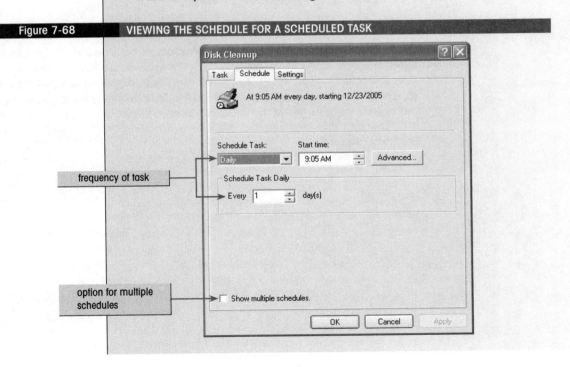

frequency of task

option for multiple schedules

3. Click the **Settings** tab. You can use the Settings property sheet to delete the task if it is not scheduled to run again, stop the task if it runs for a certain period of time, start the task only if the computer has been idle for a certain period of time, specify how long to retry the scheduled task, stop the task if you start to use the computer (and it is no longer idle), and specify power management settings. See Figure 7-69.

Figure 7-69   VIEWING SETTINGS FOR A SCHEDULED TASK

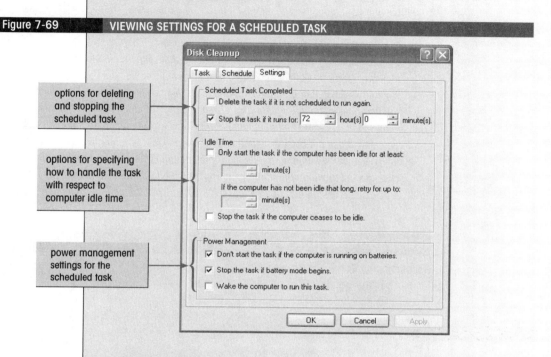

options for deleting and stopping the scheduled task

options for specifying how to handle the task with respect to computer idle time

power management settings for the scheduled task

4. Close the Disk Cleanup dialog box.

5. If you want to delete the Disk Cleanup scheduled task, point to and select **Disk Cleanup**, press the **Delete** key, and in the Confirm File Delete dialog box, click the **Yes** button.

6. Close the Scheduled Tasks folder, and then empty the Recycle Bin.

REFERENCE WINDOW **RW**

Checking Settings for a Scheduled Task
- Click the Start button, point to All Programs, point to Accessories, point to System Tools, and then click Scheduled Tasks.
- After Windows XP opens the Scheduled Tasks folder, click a scheduled task.
- Use the Task property sheet to view the path of the program you've scheduled, set the password for the scheduled task, or turn the task off by removing the check mark from the Enabled check box.
- Click the Schedule tab, and use the Schedule property sheet to verify or change the schedule for the task, specify multiple schedules, or use the Advanced button to specify an end date for the task and how frequently you want to repeat the task.
- Click the Settings tab, and use the Settings property sheet to delete the task if it is not scheduled to run again, stop the task if it runs for a certain period of time, start the task only if the computer has been idle for a certain period of time, specify how long to retry the scheduled task, stop the task if you start to use the computer (and it is no longer idle), and specify power management settings.
- When you are finished, close the Properties dialog box for the scheduled task and apply any changes you have made, and then close the Scheduled Tasks folder window.

REFERENCE WINDOW **RW**

Deleting a Scheduled Task
- Click the Start button, point to All Programs, point to Accessories, point to System Tools, and then click Scheduled Tasks.
- After Windows XP opens the Scheduled Tasks folder, point to and select the scheduled task you want to delete, press the Delete key, and confirm the deletion.
- Close the Scheduled Tasks folder.

You can use the Scheduled Task Wizard to schedule other common types of tasks, such as defragmenting your disk or starting a backup job, that are important to maintaining, protecting, and optimizing your computer.

Developing a Disk Maintenance Plan

Since the hard disk is one of the most important components of your computer, and since you store all your software and documents on that disk, it's a good idea to develop a disk maintenance plan. Now that you are familiar with the tools available for protecting and optimizing your hard disk, here are some guidelines and ideas for implementing a disk maintenance plan:

- **Implement disk quotas for users on shared computers.** If multiple users share the same computer, set disk quotas for each user, along with a warning level so that users know when they are approaching their limit on available disk space. Disk quotas also ensure that each person has access to the disk storage space that they need, and that they do not use storage space needed by other users.

- **Implement folder and file compression, or folder and file encryption.** To conserve disk storage space, you might want to compress your document folders and files, or if disk storage space is plentiful, you might want to encrypt your document folders and files for increased protection. Since these features are mutually exclusive in Windows XP Professional, you can only implement one.

- **Use the Disk Cleanup Wizard on a regular basis.** Before you back up your computer and run the Error-checking tool or Check Disk and Disk Defragmenter, remove any unneeded files on your hard disk first. If you run the Disk Cleanup Wizard before you perform a backup, you can remove unneeded files that might otherwise be included in the backup. However, if you want to avoid inadvertently deleting files that you actually want to back up, perform your backup first. If you use Disk Defragmenter to optimize your disk and then run the Disk Cleanup Wizard and delete unneeded files, you end up with empty clusters between existing files, which in turn leads to more file fragmentation, so it makes more sense to run the Disk Cleanup Wizard first, and then run Disk Defragmenter afterwards. Periodic use of the Disk Cleanup Wizard also improves the performance of your computer by emptying the Temporary Internet files folder and by removing temporary files that can accumulate quickly.

- **Back up your computer on a regular basis.** Develop an effective backup strategy that combines normal backups with a periodic incremental or differential backups. Your strategy should reflect the way you use your computer and the importance of your documents. As you saw in Tutorial 6, if you use Microsoft Backup, you can create and name backup jobs and schedule backups. Also, by organizing your document files within the My Documents folder, you can simplify the backup process.

- **Check your hard disks with the Error-checking tool or with the Check Disk utility on a regular basis.** Before you use Disk Defragmenter, first check and remove any errors in the file system of your hard disks. If you run Disk Defragmenter without running the Error-checking tool or Check Disk, and if the file system on the hard disk has problems, Disk Defragmenter stops and informs you that you have to check the disk for errors first and remove them. If possible, use the Error-checking tool or Check Disk once a week, or at least once a month, to locate and repair small errors before they become more serious errors and to increase the longevity of your hard disk.

- **Optimize your hard disk with Disk Defragmenter on a regular basis.** Since defragmentation can build up quickly on a hard disk drive, use Disk Defragmenter once a week, or at least once a month, to reduce file fragmentation and free space fragmentation, improve the performance and response time of your computer, and reduce wear and tear on your hard disk.

- **Use the Scheduled Task Wizard.** By creating scheduled tasks with the Scheduled Task Wizard, you improve your chances of implementing a regular disk maintenance schedule. For example, you can use the Scheduled Task Wizard to run the Disk Cleanup Wizard and Disk Defragmenter once a week. If you have noted the amount of time that it takes for each of these tasks, you can set up your scheduled tasks to run one right after the other on the same day after you perform your normal backup for the week. You might also want to consider scheduling other tasks that are important, such as a full scan of your computer by your antivirus software once a week. You might be able to schedule this operation within the antivirus software itself.

Whatever type of disk maintenance plan you develop, make sure you implement it regularly, or use tools such as the Scheduled Task Wizard to make sure you perform other tasks that are equally as important.

Restoring **Your Computer**

To restore a lab computer or your computer to its original state before you started the tutorial, complete the following steps.

To restore your computer's display settings:

1. If your computer was originally set for the Windows Classic style, right-click the **desktop**, click **Properties** on the shortcut menu, and after Windows XP opens the Display Properties dialog box, click the **Theme** list arrow on the Themes property sheet, click **Windows Classic**, and then click the **OK** button.

2. To switch to the Windows Classic Start menu style, right-click the **Start** button, click **Properties**, and after Windows XP opens the Taskbar and Start Menu Properties dialog box, click the **Classic Start menu** option button on the Start Menu property sheet, and then click the **OK** button.

3. To change to Windows classic folders view, click the **Start** button, point to **Settings**, click **Control Panel**, and after Windows XP opens a Control Panel window, click **Tools** on the menu bar, click **Folder Options**, and after Windows XP opens the Folder Options dialog box, click the **Use Windows classic folders** option button, and then click the **Double-click to open an item** option button under "Click items as follows."

4. Click the **View** tab in the Folder Options dialog box. If necessary, restore the original settings for the "Display the full path in the address bar" check box, the "Do not show hidden files and folders" option, and the "Hide extensions for known file types" check box.

5. Click the **OK** button to close the Folder Options dialog box and restore your original settings, and then close the Control Panel folder window.

Mark and the employees at Harris & Banche now have a valuable set of tools and strategies for periodically cleaning their computers' hard disk of files that are no longer needed, optimizing the performance of their computers, maximizing the use of storage space on their hard disks, ensuring that their important document files are secure, and scheduling commonly performed tasks.

REVIEW ASSIGNMENTS

Mark just hired a new staff member, Michael Everett, to assist him with his duties. He shows Mike his desk and his computer system, and asks you to show Mike how to perform a thorough check of his computer and customize it for his new job.

Try to use a computer that is different from the one that you used for the tutorial so that you can compare your results with those from the tutorial. Also, to perform some of these operations, you must log on as Administrator or under a user account with Administrator privileges.

As you complete each step in the Review Assignments, record your answers to questions so that you can submit them to your instructor. Use a word-processing application such as Word or WordPad to prepare and then print your answers to these questions. Also, if you change any settings on the computer you are using, note the original settings so that you can restore them later.

1. Open My Computer. Under Hard Disk Drives, how many drives does your computer have, and what are their names? Point to and select each drive icon. What file system does each drive use? What is the total storage capacity of each drive?

2. If you have one drive, select it; if you have two or more drives, select one drive that you did not use in the tutorial, right-click the drive icon, select Properties, and run the Disk Cleanup Wizard. How much storage space can the Disk Cleanup Wizard free on your hard disk drive? What types of files does it propose to remove? Are there any files that the Disk Cleanup Wizard did not identify—ones that you need to periodically remove from your hard disk? If so, which ones are they? After you finish using the Disk Cleanup Wizard, close it, and then close the Properties dialog box for the drive.

Explore

3. Examine the files from Data Disk #1. What type of file is File0000.chk, and how was it most likely created? If you want to find out whether the file contained anything useful, what would you do? What type of file is ~WRC0070.tmp, and how was it most likely created? Even if you did not know what is contained in these files, can you safely remove these files from the disk to free up storage space? Explain.

4. *(You need to log on using an account with Administrator privileges to complete this step.)* If you are working in a computer lab, ask your instructor or technical support staff for permission to run the Error-checking tool on one of the hard disks. If you are working on your own computer, decide whether you want to use the Error-checking tool on one of your hard disks. Open the Properties dialog box for one of the drives on your hard disk, select the Tools property sheet, and then run the Error-checking tool on this drive with its default settings. Did the Error-checking tool find any problems? If so, what were the problems? After you finish using the Error-checking tool, close the Checking Disk dialog box for the drive, close the Properties dialog box for the drive, and then close My Computer.

Explore

5. *(You need to log on using an account with Administrator privileges to complete this step.)* If you are working in a computer lab, ask your instructor or technical support staff for permission to run the Check Disk utility on one of the hard disks. If you are working on your own computer, decide whether you want to use Check Disk on one of your hard disks. Open Command Prompt from the Accessories menu, and use the Check Disk utility to check the same drive for errors in read-only, or diagnostic, mode (without making any changes to the hard disk), making sure you specify the drive name as it may be different from the default drive used by Windows XP in the Command Prompt window. For example, to check drive C, type CHKDSK C: and press Enter. Does Check Disk report any errors or problems? If so, what are they?

6. *(You need to log on using an account with Administrator privileges to complete this step.)* If you are working in a computer lab, ask your instructor or technical support staff for permission to run Disk Defragmenter on one of the hard disks. If you are working on your own computer, decide whether you want to use Disk Defragmenter on one of your hard disks. From the Accessories menu, point to System Tools, and then open the Disk Defragmenter and perform a disk analysis of one of the hard disks. What type of file system does the drive use? Does the Disk Defragmenter recommend that you defragment the drive? Is it obvious from the Disk Analysis area that the drive has recently been defragmented? How did you arrive at this conclusion? View, print, and save the Analysis Report. Next, decide whether you have time to defragment that drive (it might take hours). If you defragment the drive, view, print, and save the Defragmentation Report.

7. *(You need to log on using an account with Administrator privileges to complete this step.)* If Administrative Tools is not listed on the All Programs menu, view properties of the taskbar, select the Start Menu property sheet, choose the option to customize the Start menu, select the Advanced property sheet, and then choose the option to display System Administrative Tools on the All Programs menu. Using the Administrative Tools menu, open Computer Management, and then select the Disk Management snap-in tool. Using the information in the Volume List area, list the names of each volume, as well as the layout, type, file system, and status of each volume. Which drive is your system volume? Which drives have primary partitions? Which drives are extended partitions? Close the Computer Management window without making any changes.

8. *(You need to log on using an account with Administrator privileges to complete this step.)* If you are working in a computer lab, ask your instructor or technical support staff for permission to check the disk quotas on an NTFS volume. If you are working on your own computer, decide whether you want to set disk quotas on one of your hard disks that is an NTFS volume. Open My Computer, display the property sheets for an NTFS volume, and then examine disk quotas. Are disk quotas enabled on your computer? If so, what is the default disk quota for new users? What is your disk quota? Close both the window with the Quota Entries for the local disk and the Properties dialog box for the drive without making any changes to the quota settings.

9. *(If you are working in a computer lab, obtain permission from your instructor or technical support staff to compress and uncompress a folder on an NTFS volume.)* Create a folder named Harris & Banche on an NTFS volume, and then copy the folders and files from Data Disk #1 to the Harris & Banche folder. Step up one level in the folder hierarchy of the disk, and view properties of the Harris & Banche folder. What is the size of this folder and its contents? How much disk space does the folder and its contents use on the disk? How much of that storage space is slack? Is this folder and its files compressed? How can you tell? If the folder and its contents are not compressed, compress them; if the folder and its contents are already compressed, uncompress them. Did you compress or uncompress the folder and its contents? After the operation is complete, how much disk space does the folder and its contents now use? If you compressed the folder and its contents, reverse this process for the next step.

10. *Windows XP Professional only: (If you are working in a computer lab, obtain permission from your instructor or technical support staff to encrypt and decrypt a folder on an NTFS volume.)* Display the Properties dialog box for the Company Projections folder, and choose the option for viewing advanced attributes. Choose the option for encrypting this folder, and then apply the change to this folder and its contents. After the operation is complete, describe how this folder and its contents differ from the other folders and files on the disk. Reverse the encryption and decrypt the Company Projections folder and its contents.

Explore 11. *(If you are working in a computer lab, obtain permission from your instructor or technical support staff to use the Scheduled Task Wizard to schedule a task.)* Open the Scheduled Tasks folder from the System Tools menu, use the Scheduled Task Wizard to schedule Disk Cleanup when you log onto your computer, and choose the option to view the advanced properties dialog box for this task. What is the name of the program that Windows XP runs when it starts Disk Cleanup, and in what folder is this program stored? Select the Settings property sheet. If you had scheduled this task to run once a week at a specific time, what optional setting(s) could you use to schedule this task so that it does not automatically start while you are working with another application? If you wanted to temporarily turn off this scheduled task, how would you do it? Close the Disk Cleanup dialog box and the Scheduled Tasks folder. Log off your computer, and then log on again. Did Windows XP start the scheduled task? If you want to run the scheduled task, select the drive you want to clean up, and then click the OK button; otherwise, click the Exit button to close the Select Drive dialog box and skip the scheduled task.

12. (*If you are working in a computer lab, do not remove scheduled tasks from the Scheduled Tasks folder without permission.*) Restore your computer to its original state by deleting the Harris & Banche folder and removing the Disk Cleanup task you created from the Scheduled Tasks folder. Then empty the Recycle Bin.

13. Which of the techniques covered in this tutorial have you used in the last three months to optimize the storage of files on your hard disk or to optimize the performance of your computer? Are there any additional strategies or tasks that you want to implement in the future? Explain.

CASE PROBLEMS

Case 1. Scanning a Hard Disk at Sheshmani's Carpet Care Center Sheshmani's Carpet Care Center is a small business that sells, repairs, and cleans carpets, rugs, draperies, and office partitions. Patrick Sydow, a partner in the company, uses a computer to handle all customer transactions, schedule work crews, track cash flow, prepare tax statements, and prepare payroll. Since he maintains all his business records on this one computer, he optimizes the hard disk once a week. Because he is attending a convention this coming week, he asks you to check the hard disk for errors during his absence.

If you are working in a computer lab, make sure you have permission to use the Check Disk utility. Also, you need to log on under an account with Administrator privileges. Because running Check Disk might take time, run it at a time that works with your schedule.

As you complete each step in this case, record your answers to questions so that you can submit them to your instructor. Use a word-processing application such as Word or WordPad to prepare and then print your answers to these questions. Also, if you change any settings on the computer you are using, note the original settings so that you can restore them later.

1. What precautions, if any, should you take before you run the Check Disk utility?

2. Open the General property sheet for drive C. Is this drive an NTFS or FAT volume? Is this drive the system volume? What is the total storage capacity of this drive? How much storage space on the drive is already used? How much is available?

3. Note your starting time. Select the Tools property sheet for your hard disk, choose the option for running the Error-checking tool, and then choose the option for automatically fixing file system errors. Verify that you want to check the disk when you next restart Windows XP, close the Local Disk (C:) Properties dialog box, close My Computer (or Windows Explorer), close all other open applications and windows, and then restart your computer. Explain what happens when Windows XP checks the disk. Did it find any problems? If so, explain.

4. Note the ending time. How long did it take for the disk check? Based on this information, how frequently might you check this disk?

Explore 5. If your computer has an NTFS volume, open the Command Prompt from the Accessories menu, and then enter the CHKDSK command followed by a space, the drive name of the NTFS volume, and then the /V switch to display any cleanup messages. What command did you enter? What types of results did the Check Disk utility report? Is Check Disk running in read-only, or diagnostic, mode? If so, run the CHKDSK command again with the Fix switch. What command did you enter? Run Check Disk one more time in read-only mode to verify that any errors were corrected, and then close the Command Prompt window.

Case 2. Defragmenting a Hard Disk at the Westside Radiology Medical Lab The Computerized Tomography, Nuclear Medicine, Ultrasound Imaging, and Magnetic Resonance Imaging (MRI) units of the Westside Radiology Medical Lab conduct tests for physicians and hospitals that refer patients under their care. Marna Tennyson, a medical technician, uses one of the lab's computers to keep patient information and test results. Since patient information on this computer is constantly updated and changed, Marna uses the Disk Defragmenter once a week to eliminate file fragmentation and optimize the performance of the hard disk.

If you are working in a computer lab, make sure you have permission to use Disk Defragmenter on the hard disk of a computer. Also, you need to log on under an account with Administrator privileges. Since defragmenting might take time, run Disk Defragmenter at a time that works with your schedule.

As you complete each step in this case, record your answers to questions so that you can submit them to your instructor. Use a word-processing application such as Word or WordPad to prepare and then print your answers to these questions. Also, if you change any settings on the computer you are using, note the original settings so that you can restore them later.

1. What precautions, if any, should you take before you run Disk Defragmenter?

2. Open the General property sheet for a hard disk on your computer. Is this drive an NTFS or FAT volume? What is the total storage capacity of this drive? How much storage space on the drive is already used? How much is available?

3. Select the Tools property sheet for your hard disk, and then start Disk Defragmenter. What drive are you going to check? What is the percentage of free space on that drive?

4. Start by analyzing the drive for file fragmentation. Does the Disk Defragmenter recommend that you defragment the drive? Choose the option to view the Analysis Report. What is the total fragmentation? What is the file fragmentation? What is the free space fragmentation? What is the total number of fragmented files? What is the average number of fragments per file? How many fragmented folders are there? Save and print the Analysis Report. Close the Analysis Report dialog box.

5. Using the information in the legend, examine the "Estimated disk usage before defragmentation" area and compare the arrangement of fragmented files, contiguous files, and free space. If you had not seen the Analysis Report, would you conclude that the drive is fragmented or not fragmented? Explain how you arrived at this conclusion.

6. Notice the starting time, start the defragmentation, and note the ending time. How long did it take to defragment the drive? How many megabytes of disk space were defragmented per minute?

7. Choose the option to view the Defragmentation Report. What is the total fragmentation? What is the file fragmentation? What is the free space fragmentation? What is the total number of fragmented files? What is the average number of fragments per file? How many fragmented folders are there? Save and print the Defragmentation Report. In your estimation, how successful was the defragmentation? Close the Defragmentation Report dialog box.

8. Examine the Fragmentation display area. If you had not seen the Defragmentation Report, would you conclude that the defragmentation was successful? Explain how you arrived at this conclusion.

Case 3. Preparing a Hard Disk Maintenance Schedule for Data Recovery Services Customers Data Recovery Services (DRS) is a small business that specializes in recovering data from damaged hard disks. Many of its customers are small business and home users who need assistance in optimizing the performance of their computer and repairing damage to the hard disk. As a service to its customers, Justin Noakes, a data recovery specialist, wants to prepare a Hard Disk Maintenance & Optimization Schedule that he can provide to customers either in person or via e-mail.

Explore

1. Using Figure 7-70 as a guideline, prepare a table that lists information for six recommended tasks or features that customers should use as part of their regular disk maintenance schedule. Think about tasks you consider important and features that you learned about in previous tutorials. Identify the type of task, the name of the program or feature, how frequently the task should be performed, and what precautions customers should take. If you can think of more than six recommended tasks, include them as well. Assume that recommended tasks are ones that customers can perform using easily available tools within Windows XP without making a major change to the configuration of their computer.

Figure 7-70

HARD DISK MAINTENANCE & OPTIMIZATION SCHEDULE				
	Recommended Tasks	Utility or Feature	Frequency	Precautions
1				
2				
3				
4				
5				
6				

2. Print a copy of your recommended Hard Disk Maintenance & Optimization Schedule.

3. Describe how customers might automate these tasks.

Case 4. Compressing Client Files at Media Designs Company Media Designs Company (MDC) designs and customizes Web pages for corporate clients. Jennifer Thompson, a graphic artist working on a special project for one of the company's clients—Delta Oil Company—wants to optimize the disk storage space used by these client files on her computer. She also wants to compare Windows XP's new Compressed (zipped) Folder feature with the option for compressing folders and files.

As you complete each step in this case, record your answers to questions so that you can submit them to your instructor. Use a word-processing application such as Word or WordPad to prepare and then print your answers to these questions. Also, if you change any settings on the computer you are using, note the original settings so that you can restore them later.

1. Copy the files from Data Disk #2 to a floppy disk, if necessary.

2. Copy the Delta Oil folder from the floppy disk to an NTFS volume, open the Delta Oil folder on the NTFS volume, and delete the Overhead Transparencies and Training folders.

3. View properties of the Delta Oil folder on the NTFS volume. How many folders are contained within the Delta Oil folder? How many files are stored in this folder? What is the total size of these folders and files? How much space do they use on the disk?

4. Compress the Delta Oil folder, its subfolders, and files. How much storage space does this folder use now? What is the percentage of compression?

Explore ▶ 5. Using the File menu, create a new Compressed (zipped) Folder on the NTFS volume, and name it Delta Oil. How can you have two folders by the same name in the same folder?

6. Open the Delta Oil Compressed (zipped) Folder, and copy the Company Templates, Designs, and Memos folders within the Delta Oil folder on your floppy disk to the Delta Oil Compressed (zipped) Folder on the NTFS volume.

7. View the properties of the Delta Oil Compressed (zipped) folder. What is the size of the Delta Oil Compressed (zipped) folder and its contents? How much storage space does this folder use? What is the percentage of compression compared to the folder's original size of 680 KB (696,320 bytes)? How does this compare with applying the Compress attribute to the same folder? If you wanted to conserve disk storage space, which type of compression would you use?

Explore ▶ 8. List the advantages (if any) and disadvantages (if any) offered by these two approaches.

9. Open the compressed (not the zipped) Delta Oil folder, and copy the Invoice Form.wk4 from the Overhead Transparencies folder on your floppy disk to the Company Templates folder on the NTFS volume. Does Windows XP automatically compress this file? How can you tell?

10. Copy the Company Sales Projection.xls file from the Company Templates folder on the NTFS volume to the Overhead Transparencies folder on your floppy disk. Does Windows XP automatically uncompress this file? How can you tell?

11. To restore your computer, delete the Delta Oil folders (compressed and zipped) from the NTFS volume that you used for this case, and then empty the Recycle Bin.

OBJECTIVES

In this tutorial you will:

- Use the BIOS Setup utility to set the boot sequence

- Make and test an MS-DOS startup disk

- Learn how to make Windows XP Setup Disks

- Use System Restore to create a restore point, roll back your computer, and undo a restoration

- Examine how to use the Automated System Recovery Wizard to back up your computer's system state and system files

- Enable and specify settings for Internet Connection Firewall

- Examine the use of cookies and Web bugs

- Check Internet Explorer security and privacy settings

- Review safe computing guidelines

SAFEGUARDING YOUR COMPUTER

Safeguarding Computers at Grenfeld Publishing Company

CASE

Grenfeld Publishing Company

Grenfeld Publishing Company is a general trade book publisher located in St. Louis, Missouri. Grenfeld publishes a broad range of books, including biographies, science fiction, cookbooks, gardening guides, and children's books.

Lenore Ruhling, a tech support specialist at Grenfeld, and her staff train employees on the use of new hardware and software and provide troubleshooting assistance. As a member of her staff, you help other Grenfeld employees meet tight production and publication deadlines by customizing their computers and providing training in the use of new Windows XP features.

In this section of the tutorial, you check and change the boot setting on your computer, if necessary, so that your computer checks drive A first for a boot disk. You also create and test an MS-DOS startup disk, and examine how to make Windows XP Setup disks. Finally, you use System Restore to create a restore point, restore your computer to an earlier state, and undo a restoration.

Getting Started

To complete this tutorial, you need to switch your computer to Web style so that your screens match those shown in the figures, and you also need to turn on the options for showing file extensions, showing all folders and files, displaying protected operating system files that are hidden, and displaying the full path in the Address bar. As you complete these steps, you may discover that your computer is already set up for Web style, or that other settings are already in place, so you might only need to make a few changes to your computer's settings.

To set up your computer:

1. To change to the Windows XP theme, right-click the **desktop**, click **Properties** on the shortcut menu, and after Windows XP opens the Display Properties dialog box, click the **Theme** list arrow on the Themes property sheet, click **Windows XP**, if necessary, and then click the **OK** button.

2. To switch to the Windows XP Start menu style, right-click the **Start** button, click **Properties** on the shortcut menu, and after Windows XP opens the Taskbar and Start Menu Properties dialog box, click the **Start menu** option button on the Start Menu property sheet, if necessary, and then click the **OK** button.

3. To change to a task-oriented view of folders and enable single-clicking, click the **Start** button, click **My Computer**, click **Tools** on the menu bar, click **Folder Options**, and after Windows XP opens the Folder Options dialog box, click the **Show common tasks in folders** option button if it is not already selected, click the **Single-click to open an item** option button if it is not already selected, and click the **Underline icon titles only when I point at them** option button if it is not already selected.

4. Click the **View** tab, click the **Display the full path in the address bar** check box if it is not already selected, click the **Show hidden files and folders** option button if it is not already selected, and if there is a check mark in the "Hide extensions for known file types" check box, click that check box to remove the check mark.

5. Click the **Hide protected operating system files** check box to deselect it, click the **Yes** button in the Warning dialog box to display protected operating system files, click the **OK** button to close the Folder Options dialog box, and then close My Computer.

Now you're ready to examine how to use different types of tools, features, and techniques for safeguarding your computer.

Changing the Boot Sequence

CMOS, which stands for Complementary Metal Oxide Semiconductor, refers to a special type of computer chip, or integrated circuit, that requires less power and that, with the use of a battery backup, retains important BIOS computer settings after you turn off the power to your computer. The BIOS settings stored in CMOS identify the types and specifications of your disk drives, the system date and time, password options, the boot sequence or boot order, power management settings, and a number of other settings. To view and change the settings in CMOS, you must open a built-in Setup utility during booting by pressing a specific key, such as F2, F1, Del, F10, or perhaps a combination of keys, such as Ctrl+A, Ctrl+S, or Ctrl+F1. During the very early stages of booting, most computers (but not all) identify on the initial startup screen the key or keys to press to open the Setup utility.

The battery that provides power to CMOS so that it can retain settings usually runs down in five to seven years. When it does, you lose all of the CMOS settings, and you may not be able to boot your computer. Since the CMOS settings are very important, you should know how to open and use CMOS, and also print or document these settings on your computer. You can also download a DOS utility that backs up BIOS settings in CMOS memory to a floppy disk, so that you can restore those settings if necessary.

When you work with CMOS settings, you have to be extremely cautious. You do not want to accidentally change a setting that might affect the performance of your computer system or prevent your computer from booting.

To open the Setup utility, you have to reboot your computer or, if your computer is already off, power on your system, and identify the key or keys needed to open Setup. As your computer starts up, pay close attention to the information displayed on the monitor so that you know what you need to press to open the Setup utility. You must press the key or keys at that point, before booting continues. Otherwise, you have to let Windows XP boot to the desktop, restart Windows XP, and then try again.

If you are working in a computer lab, your technical support staff might have already password protected the Setup utility so that only the technical support staff can access and change these settings, or you might be able to open the Setup utility, but not make any changes to CMOS settings. If you are working in a computer lab, and if the Setup utility is not password protected, do not perform the following steps without the permission of your instructor or technical support staff. If you cannot or prefer not to open the Setup utility until you are more familiar with how it is organized and the BIOS settings it contains, read but do not keystroke the following steps.

Lenore and her staff have already configured the computers at Grenfeld so that they automatically boot from drive C first. This simple change guarantees that employees' computer systems do not attempt to boot from a floppy disk that is accidentally left in drive A— a disk that might contain a computer virus which could then gain access to their computer system. Lenore asks you to verify that her computer also boots from drive C first.

Read the following steps before you perform them, because you will not have enough time to read them and check the information displayed on the monitor at the same time.

To check the boot order:

1. If your computer is turned off, power on your computer. If you already logged on your computer, close all open applications and windows, and then click the **Start** button, click **Turn off computer** or **Shut Down**, select **Restart** in the Turn off computer or Shut Down Windows dialog box, and then click the **OK** button if necessary, or from the Start menu, click **Log Off**, click the **Log Off** button in the Log Off Windows dialog box, and on the Welcome screen, click **Turn off Windows XP System**, and in the Turn off computer dialog box, click the **Restart** button.

2. During booting or rebooting, watch the monitor for information on which key(s) to press, and then press the key or keys for opening the Setup utility. For example, you might see the message, "Press F2 to enter Setup."

> **TROUBLE?** If you see the Windows XP logo, you've passed the point at which you can open the Setup utility. Wait for Windows XP to boot to the desktop, restart your computer, and then try again. In some cases, booting is so quick that you might not be able to see any messages displayed on the monitor. However, if you press the Pause key, you can temporarily halt booting so that you can see what's displayed on the screen. To resume booting, press the Enter key. If you do not see a message on how to open Setup, try pressing F2, F1, or Del in the first few seconds of the boot process, check your computer documentation or the manufacturer's Web site for information on accessing the Setup utility.

Your view of BIOS settings varies depending on the type of computer you use because companies manufacture more than one type of BIOS with different settings. Although approximately ten companies write BIOS programs, three of them—American Megatrends (AMI), Award Software, and Phoenix Technologies—account for most of the BIOS business.

The opening screen that you see might contain a category of settings, or you might see a menu from which you can choose a category of settings. Figure 8-1 shows CMOS settings for a Pentium 4 computer, while Figure 8-2 shows CMOS settings for a Pentium III computer. Although your system might display some of the same settings, the screen layout, menu options, and help information might vary.

Figure 8-1   **MAIN CMOS MENU FOR A PENTIUM 4 COMPUTER (YOURS WILL DIFFER)**

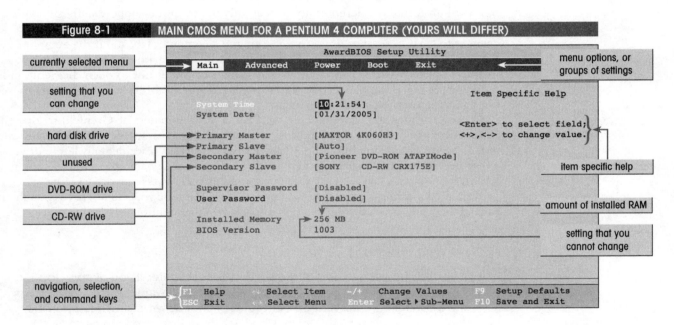

Figure 8-2   **MAIN CMOS MENU FOR A PENTIUM III COMPUTER (YOURS WILL DIFFER)**

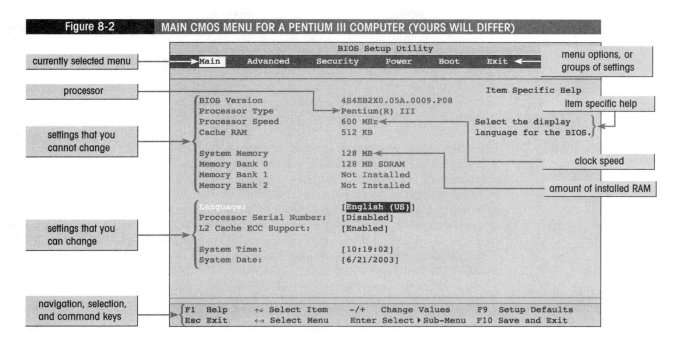

On the computer used for Figure 8-1, the opening screen shows the contents of the Main menu, namely, the system time, system date, and the default settings for the primary master, primary slave, secondary master, and secondary slave, as well as the amount of installed memory (256 MB) and the BIOS version. The primary master is the hard disk, the secondary master is a DVD-ROM drive, and the secondary slave is a CD-RW drive. There is no primary slave, so one more drive could be added to this computer. An Auto setting indicates that the Setup utility automatically detects and configures the device (if present). Since there is no primary slave, you can change the setting to None for a slightly faster boot.

At the bottom of the opening screen, you see information on how to get help, exit, select items and menus, change values, restore Setup defaults, and save and exit. Also, the area on the right displays Item Specific Help. When you select an item on a menu, this area briefly describes that option or explains how to select the contents of a field and how to change the value. For example, the System Time was automatically selected when the Setup utility opened on this computer, so the Item Specific Help area informs you that you can press the Enter key to select a field (the hour, minutes, or seconds), and you then use the key with the plus sign or the minus sign on the numeric keypad to increment or decrement the setting. Settings shown within square brackets are ones that you can select and change. Settings shown without square brackets, such as the amount of installed memory and the BIOS version, are those you cannot change. Your opening menu or screen might differ from that shown in the figure; in fact, you might not see any menus, and therefore all of the CMOS settings would appear on the opening screen.

On the computer used for Figure 8-2, the opening screen shows the BIOS version, processor type, processor speed, cache RAM, total system memory (128 MB of RAM), amount and type of system memory installed in each memory bank (or slot on the motherboard), the BIOS display language, the processor serial time setting (disabled), the L2 Cache ECC support setting (an error-checking feature—enabled), the system time, and the system date. An **L1 cache** is high-speed memory built into the processor, whereas an **L2 cache** is high-speed memory that resides on a separate chip or, on newer computers, is also built into the processor. These high-speed caches act as holding areas for data retrieved from RAM that is slower and used by the processor, in some cases, repeatedly.

If you select the Boot menu for the computer in Figure 8-1, Setup displays the current boot sequence. As shown in Figure 8-3, there are four possible boot devices, but only three drives are designated as such. In this case, the ROM-BIOS routine that examines drives for the operating system would first attempt to boot from the hard disk drive, and if a problem prevented the computer from booting from the hard disk drive, the ROM-BIOS routine then tries to boot from the floppy disk drive. If there is no disk in the floppy disk drive, the ROM-BIOS routine attempts to boot from a disc in the DVD-ROM drive. A **boot disk**, or **system disk**, is a floppy disk that contains the core operating system files for booting a computer from drive A. The number of boot devices available to you might vary from two to five.

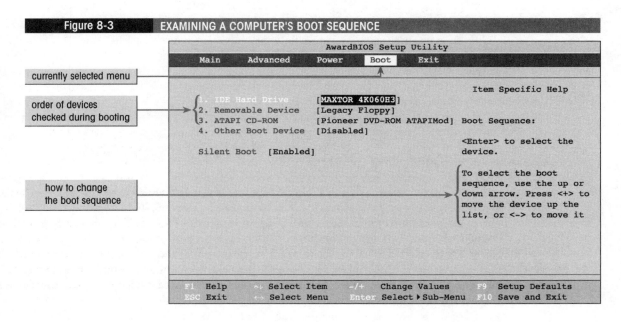

Figure 8-3   EXAMINING A COMPUTER'S BOOT SEQUENCE

In the past, PCs were typically configured so that the ROM-BIOS routine first checked drive A for the operating system, and then drive C. If drive A did not contain a disk, the ROM-BIOS routine then checked drive C for the operating system and, if found, booted the computer from drive C. If drive A contained a boot disk, the computer booted from that disk, and drive C was not checked. If drive A contained a disk that was not a boot disk (in other words, a data disk), the bootstrap loader program in the boot record would display the message, "Non-system disk or disk error," or "Invalid system disk."

Today, computers are typically configured so that they check drive C first, and then drive A. If there are no problems with drive C, the computer boots from that drive and loads the operating system. If the computer cannot boot from drive C, it checks drive A. If drive A contains a boot disk, the computer boots from that disk.

To change the order of the boot devices on this computer (as shown in the Item Specific Help area), you select a boot device, and use the plus sign (+) or minus sign (–) keys on the numeric keypad to move that device up or down the list.

After you check and, if necessary, change the setting for the boot sequence (or other settings), you then exit the Setup utility. The Exit menu, shown in Figure 8-4, includes an option for saving changes before you exit Setup. You can also press the Esc key to select the Exit menu, or you might be able to press the Esc key until you see a dialog box that asks you to confirm that you want to save (or discard) any configuration changes you might have made and exit. If you intentionally change the boot sequence, you need to save the new settings and exit so that your system uses them as it continues to boot.

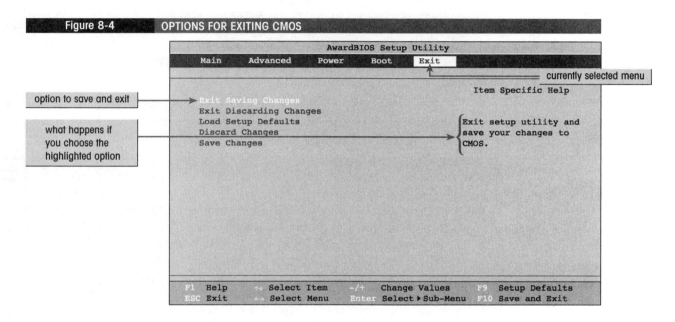

Figure 8-4   **OPTIONS FOR EXITING CMOS**

CMOS also has an option for loading default Setup settings in case you want to restore the original settings.

In the next section of the tutorial, you create an MS-DOS startup disk, a type of boot disk. You might need to change the boot sequence on your computer before you continue booting so you can test the use of this disk. It is also a good idea to document, or record, the current settings in CMOS before you make any changes. If your computer is connected to a local printer, you might be able to print a copy of your boot settings; if not, you must record them manually.

To document and then change the boot sequence:

1. Locate the screen that contains information about the boot sequence on the computer you are using.

2. If you are connected directly to a printer (a local printer, not a network printer), press the **Print Screen** key to "dump" the image of the screen with your boot settings and send it to the printer. You might also need to use the Form Feed button on the printer to advance the sheet of paper through the printer.

   TROUBLE? If you are not connected to a local printer, or cannot print these boot settings, go to the next step and record the settings manually.

3. If you are not directly connected to a printer, or did not print a copy of your boot settings in the previous step, manually record the computer's current boot sequence on paper so that you can restore the sequence later.

4. If you need to change the boot sequence, change the settings so that your computer boots first from drive A and then from drive C. If necessary, ask your instructor or technical support staff person for assistance.

5. While the Setup utility is open, you might also want to print or document other CMOS settings.

6. If you did not make any changes to CMOS, or want to exit without saving changes, choose the option to exit without saving changes, or the option to exit and discard changes. If you changed CMOS settings and want to use those new settings, choose the option to exit and save your changes. If necessary, ask your instructor or technical support staff person for assistance.

You might also find that you need to open the Setup utility to check or change other settings, troubleshoot problems, or reconfigure your computer for new hardware.

REFERENCE WINDOW **RW**

Changing the Boot Sequence

■ If your computer is turned off, power on your computer. If you have already started Windows XP and booted to the desktop, close all open applications and windows, and then restart Windows XP.

■ During the initial stages of booting, watch the monitor for information on which key(s) to press to enter Setup, or BIOS Setup (it goes by different names), and then press the key or keys shown on the monitor. For example, you might see the message, "Press F2 to enter Setup."

■ If you are connected directly to a printer (a local printer, not a network printer), press the Print Screen key to print a copy of the CMOS boot settings, and then use the Form Feed button on your printer to advance the sheet of paper through the printer. If you are connected to a network printer, or decide not to print (or cannot print) the CMOS boot settings, manually record the boot sequence on paper so that you can restore it later.

■ Select the Boot menu or Boot Options on the Main menu, and change the boot sequence to the order that you want to use.

■ Select the Exit menu, and then choose the option that allows you to save your changes and exit Setup.

Because BIOS settings are so important and because they affect the performance of your computer, you should check the materials that came with your computer to see if they contain any information on the options available on your computer. You can also search the Web for sites that contain information about BIOS settings and about troubleshooting problems using the BIOS Setup utility.

Making an MS-DOS Startup Disk

The Windows XP **MS-DOS startup disk** is a floppy disk that contains the core operating system files needed to boot your computer from drive A. The MS-DOS startup disk does not contain any additional troubleshooting utilities; however, you can add utilities or diagnostic programs to the disk so that you can use them after you boot your computer with this disk. You cannot use this disk to access the contents of NTFS volumes; however, you can use it to examine and navigate FAT volumes, or use troubleshooting utilities to diagnose problems on FAT volumes. In the unlikely event your computer has more than one floppy disk drive, you have to make the MS-DOS startup disk using drive A. You cannot use drive B because the BIOS (Basic Input/Output) routine that looks for the operating system files during the booting process checks drive A and drive C—not drive B—for a boot disk.

Also, if a disk contains defective sectors, do not use the disk as a MS-DOS startup disk, or for any other type of boot disk or system disk. You need as reliable a disk as possible should a problem develop later. A disk with defective sectors could prove to be unreliable. You can use the Error-checking tool or Check Disk utility (both of which you examined in Tutorial 7) to check for defective sectors on a newly formatted disk.

So that you are ready to handle any emergency or problem that might arise, Lenore asks you to make a Windows XP MS-DOS startup disk for your work computer.

To make an MS-DOS startup disk and then to check the disk:

1. Insert a floppy disk into drive A.

2. Open My Computer, right-click the **3½ Floppy (A:)** drive icon, click **Format** on the shortcut menu, and after Windows XP opens the Format 3½ Floppy (A:) dialog box, click the **Create an MS-DOS startup disk** check box, click the **Start** button in the Format 3½ Floppy (A:) dialog box (not the Start button on the taskbar), and then click the **OK** button in the Format 3½ Floppy (A:) dialog box warning you that formatting erases all data on the disk.

3. After formatting is complete, click the **OK** button in the Formatting 3½ Floppy (A:) dialog box, and then click the **Close** button in the Format 3½ Floppy (A:) dialog box.

4. Right-click the **3½ Floppy (A:)** drive icon, click **Properties** on the shortcut menu, click the **Tools** tab, click the **Check Now** button, and in the Check Disk 3½ Floppy (A:) dialog box, click the **Automatically fix file system errors** check box, click the **Scan for and attempt recovery of bad sectors** check box, click the **Start** button in the Check Disk 3½ Floppy (A:) dialog box (not the Start button on the taskbar). After the disk check is complete, click the **OK** button in the Checking Disk 3½ Floppy (A:) dialog box, and then click the **OK** button in the 3½ Floppy (A:) Properties dialog box.

5. Open a window onto the floppy disk. Figure 8-5 shows the contents of this disk. Your MS-DOS Startup Disk might also contain an Autoexec.bat file.

Figure 8-5	EXAMINING THE CONTENTS OF AN MS-DOS STARTUP DISK

program for displaying a command-line interface, interpreting commands, and locating and loading program

operating system file that first loads

The hidden protected operating system files on this disk are Io.sys, Msdos.sys, and Command.com. Io.sys is responsible for booting the computer from the MS-DOS startup disk. Msdos.sys contains a remark (;W98EBD) that identifies the disk as a (Windows 98) Emergency Boot Disk (EBD). Command.com is the **command interpreter**, and is responsible for displaying the command-line user interface (the operating system prompt, or command prompt) so you can interact with the operating system, for interpreting commands that you enter at the command prompt, and for locating and loading programs for those commands. The startup configuration files, Config.sys and Autoexec.bat (if available) are empty. However, under previous versions of Windows and under DOS, **directives**, or commands, included in Config.sys modified the operating system as it loaded into memory. For example, device drivers for hardware devices, such as a CD-ROM drive, might have loaded along with the operating system. Also, commands were included in Autoexec.bat for customizing a computer.

The other files with the "sys" and "cpi" (for "Code Page Information") file extensions are device drivers for the video display and keyboard. The different versions of these driver files provide support for different countries and regions. Mode.com is a multi-purpose program for configuring system devices, and Keyb.com allows you to set up a keyboard for use with another language. Both programs work with code page information files to specify a character set for use with a device.

After you create an MS-DOS startup disk, or any other type of boot disk or startup disk, you should test the disk to make sure that it's working properly. You do not want to wait until a problem arises, only to discover that the boot disk does not work.

To test the disk, you boot from the MS-DOS startup disk and wait for an operating system prompt (A:\>) that indicates the computer successfully booted and that the operating system is now using drive A as the default drive and the top-level folder, or root directory, (\ ) as the default directory. From the command prompt, you can use the **DIR (Directory)** command to display a **directory listing** of the folders and files stored on a disk so that you know what's available. You can also use switches to change the way the Directory command operates. The **Attribute** switch, /A, instructs the Directory command to display all folders and files, no matter what attributes are assigned to them. That means that hidden system files are also included in the directory listing. You can also use the Attribute switch with other parameters to display files with a specific attribute. For example, /AS displays files assigned the System attribute, /AH displays files assigned the Hidden attribute, /AR displays files assigned the Read-Only attribute, /AA displays files assigned the Archive attribute, and /AD displays files assigned the Directory attribute (displays only folders). You can use the **Order** switch , /O, to display a directory listing in alphabetical order, with folders listed first, followed by files, each group in alphabetical order. The **Pause** switch, /P, (also called the **Page** switch) displays one screen of the directory listing and then pauses, displaying the message "Press any key to continue." You can also combine switches to further customize the information the Directory command provides.

After you test the MS-DOS startup disk, reboot your computer to the desktop. To do so, you remove the MS-DOS startup disk from drive A, and then press the Reset button on the front of your system unit, or press Ctrl+Alt+Del. This type of boot is called a **warm boot**, or **system reset**, and differs from a **cold boot** where you power on the computer. The BIOS skips the Power-On Self-Test (POST) during a warm boot.

Before you test the MS-DOS startup disk, you need to know which file system drive C uses.

To test the MS-DOS startup disk.

1. Click the **Up** button 🕮, point to and select the **drive C** icon, examine the Details dynamic menu, note which file system drive C uses (NTFS, FAT32, or FAT), and then close My Computer.

2. Close any other open applications and windows.

3. From the Start menu, click **Turn off computer** or **Shut Down**, select the **Restart** in the Turn off computer or Shut Down Windows dialog box, and then click the **OK** button if necessary. After your computer restarts, your computer boots from the MS-DOS startup disk. See Figure 8-6. Command.com displays the operating system prompt (A:\>).

| Figure 8-6 | BOOTING A COMPUTER WITH AN MS-DOS STARTUP DISK |

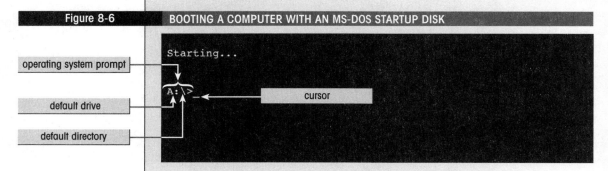

operating system prompt

default drive

default directory

Starting...

cursor

4. Type **VER** and press the **Enter** key. The Version (VER) command informs you that the operating system used for the MS-DOS startup disk is Windows Millennium (Version 4.90.3000).

5. Type DIR /A and press the **Enter** key. Windows Millennium displays the contents of the disk. See Figure 8-7. The directory listing shows the main part of the filename in the first column, the file extension (if any) in the second column, the file size in the third column, the file date in the fourth column, and the file time in the fifth column. The Directory (DIR) command also identifies the path for the directory listing, the total number of files and directories (folders) on the disk, the storage space used by files, and the total storage space. Your MS-DOS Startup Disk might also contain an Autoexec.bat file.

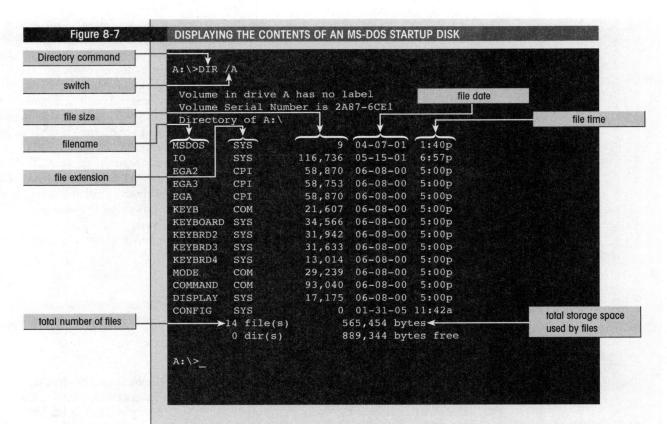

Figure 8-7   DISPLAYING THE CONTENTS OF AN MS-DOS STARTUP DISK

Directory command

switch

file size

filename

file extension

file date

file time

```
A:\>DIR /A

 Volume in drive A has no label
 Volume Serial Number is 2A87-6CE1
 Directory of A:\

MSDOS     SYS              9  04-07-01   1:40p
IO        SYS        116,736  05-15-01   6:57p
EGA2      CPI         58,870  06-08-00   5:00p
EGA3      CPI         58,753  06-08-00   5:00p
EGA       CPI         58,870  06-08-00   5:00p
KEYB      COM         21,607  06-08-00   5:00p
KEYBOARD  SYS         34,566  06-08-00   5:00p
KEYBRD2   SYS         31,942  06-08-00   5:00p
KEYBRD3   SYS         31,633  06-08-00   5:00p
KEYBRD4   SYS         13,014  06-08-00   5:00p
MODE      COM         29,239  06-08-00   5:00p
COMMAND   COM         93,040  06-08-00   5:00p
DISPLAY   SYS         17,175  06-08-00   5:00p
CONFIG    SYS              0  01-31-05  11:42a
        14 file(s)        565,454 bytes
         0 dir(s)         889,344 bytes free

A:\>_
```

total number of files

total storage space used by files

6. If drive C is a FAT or FAT32 volume, type `DIR C: /A /O /P` (the "O" is a letter of the alphabet, not the number 0) and press the **Enter** key; otherwise, if drive C is an NTFS volume, read but do not keystroke this step, and examine the figure. On the computer used for Figure 8-8, the Directory command displays a partial directory of drive C (a FAT32 volume). This time, you've modified the Directory command to indicate that you want to view the contents of another drive by including the drive's name (in this case, C:). Notice that Windows Millennium does not display long filenames; instead, you have to be familiar with aliases or short (MS-DOS) folder names and short (MS-DOS) filenames. Your list of folders and files will differ.

TROUBLE? If Windows Millennium displays the message "Invalid drive specification," the drive is an NTFS volume. Read the steps and examine the figures, but do not keystroke the steps.

TROUBLE? If your computer locks up, press the Reset button on the front of your system unit, or press Ctrl+Alt+Del (press and hold the Ctrl and Alt keys while you press and release the Del key, and then release the Ctrl and Alt keys). After your computer reboots, repeat this step.

Figure 8-8   VIEWING A DIRECTORY LISTING OF A FAT VOLUME

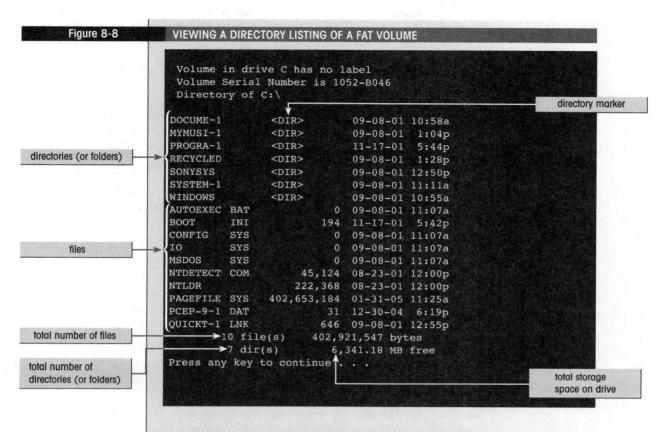

7. If necessary, keep pressing the **spacebar** to view each of the next screens of the directory listing unless Windows Millennium displays a command prompt again.

8. To reboot your computer to the desktop, remove the MS-DOS startup disk from drive A, press the Reset button on the front of your system unit, or press Ctrl+Alt+Del (press and hold the **Ctrl** and **Alt** keys while you press and release the **Del** key, and then release the **Ctrl** and **Alt** keys).

   TROUBLE? On some computers, Ctrl+Alt+Del does not work, so you must use the Reset button.

9. Log onto your computer under your user account.

After you make an MS-DOS Startup Disk, you should decide whether you want to add the following programs in the Windows System32 folder to the disk:

■ **Attrib.exe** for viewing and changing attributes of a file
■ **Chkdsk.exe** (the Check Disk utility) for examining a disk for errors
■ **Comp.exe** for comparing the contents of two files or sets of files
■ **Diskcomp.com** for comparing the contents of two floppy disks
■ **Diskcopy.com** for making a duplicate copy of a floppy disk
■ **Doskey.exe** for recalling and editing commands
■ **Edit.com** (the MS-DOS Editor), a simple text editor for viewing and changing configuration files
■ **Expand.exe** for extracting the contents of cabinet files
■ **Fc.exe** for comparing the contents of two files or sets of files and displaying the differences between the files

- **Find.exe** and **Findstr.exe** ("Find String") for searching for text in one or more text files
- **Format.com** for formatting disks
- **Label.exe** for assigning a volume label to a drive or removing a volume label
- **Mem.exe** for examining the contents of memory and for viewing the amount of used and free memory
- **More.com** for displaying output from commands one screen at a time
- **Print.exe** for printing text files
- **Recover.exe** for recovering data from damaged sectors on a disk
- **Replace.exe** for replacing or updating files on a disk
- **Tree.com** for displaying a graphical view of the directory structure of a drive or folder
- **Xcopy.exe** for copying files and the directory structure from one location to another

However, remember that you can only access drives that use FAT or FAT32. If one or more of your drives use NTFS, you cannot access those drives.

Finally, you should write-protect the MS-DOS Startup Disk so that a computer virus cannot gain access to the disk.

REFERENCE WINDOW   **RW**

Making, Checking, and Testing an MS-DOS Startup Disk

- If necessary, open the Setup utility during booting, and change the BIOS boot sequence so that your computer boots from drive A rather than from another drive.
- Exit the Setup utility, boot to the Windows XP Welcome screen or to the Log On to Windows dialog box, and log on under your user account.
- Insert a floppy disk into drive A.
- Open My Computer, right-click the 3½ Floppy (A:) drive icon, click Format, and after Windows XP opens the Format 3½ Floppy (A:) dialog box, click the "Create an MS-DOS startup disk" check box (and add a check mark), click the Start button in the Format 3½ Floppy (A:) dialog box, and click OK in the Format 3½ Floppy (A:) dialog box which warns you that formatting erases all data on the disk.
- After formatting is complete, click OK in the Formatting 3½ Floppy (A:) dialog box, and then close the Format 3½ Floppy (A:) dialog box.
- To check the disk for problems, right-click the 3½ Floppy (A:) drive icon, click Properties on the shortcut menu, click the Tools tab, click the Check Now button, and in the Check Disk 3½ Floppy (A:) dialog box, click the Automatically fix file system errors check box, click the Scan for and attempt recovery of bad sectors check box, and click the Start button in the Check Disk 3½ Floppy (A:) dialog box (not the Start button on the taskbar). After the disk check is complete, click the OK button in the Checking Disk 3½ Floppy (A:) dialog box, and then click the OK button in the 3½ Floppy (A:) Properties dialog box.
- Close all other open applications and windows.
- From the Start menu, click Turn off computer or Shut Down, select Restart in the Turn off computer or Shut Down Windows dialog box, and then, if necessary, click the OK button in the Shut Down Windows dialog box. When you see the A:\> operating system prompt, you have successfully booted with the MS-DOS Startup Disk.
- To reboot your computer to the desktop, remove the MS-DOS Startup Disk from drive A, press the Reset button on the front of your system unit, or press Ctrl+Alt+Del (press and hold the Ctrl and Alt keys while you press and release the Del key, then release the Ctrl and Alt keys).

The MS-DOS Startup Disk is designed for use with Windows XP. However, other versions of Windows allow you to create boot disks or system disks so that you can gain access to your computer, troubleshoot your computer, reinstall Windows, or rebuild your computer. With Windows 95 and Windows 98, you can create a generic boot disk similar to the Windows XP MS-DOS Startup Disk that contains the core operating system files needed to boot your computer from a floppy disk in drive A. As shown in Figure 8-9, the Windows 98 Format - 3½ Floppy (A:) dialog box contains two options for copying operating system files to a floppy disk. If the floppy disk is already formatted, you can choose the "Copy system files only" option under Format type to add operating system files to the disk. However, if you are performing a Quick or Full format, you must choose the "Copy system files" option under Other options and, after formatting is complete, Windows 98 (or Windows 95) copies operating system files to the disk. The core operating system files on a Windows 95 or Windows 98 generic boot disk include Io.sys, Msdos.sys, Command.com, and Drvspace.bin. Drvspace.bin is a device driver for accessing compressed hard disks; in other words, drives that have been compressed using Microsoft's DoubleSpace or DriveSpace disk compression utility, or a third-party disk compression utility. Similar to the Windows XP MS-DOS Startup Disk, you cannot access your CD drive, and this disk does not contain any troubleshooting utilities. You have to configure the disk to access your CD drive, and you have to add troubleshooting utilities to the disk.

Figure 8-9	WINDOWS 98 OPTION FOR CREATING A GENERIC BOOT DISK

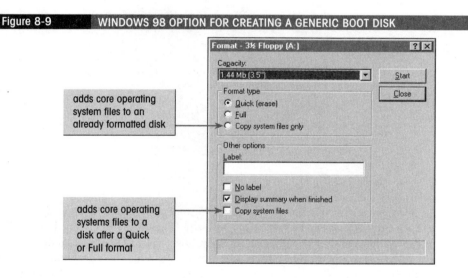

adds core operating system files to an already formatted disk

adds core operating systems files to a disk after a Quick or Full format

With Windows 95, Windows 98, and Windows Me, you can create a **Startup Disk** that not only contains the core operating system files for booting from a floppy disk in drive A, but also contains troubleshooting utilities. The Windows 98 and Windows Me Startup Disks also contain device drivers for accessing a CD drive. To make this type of disk, you open the Control Panel, click the Add/Remove Properties icon, and then, as shown in Figure 8-10, you click the Create Disk button on the Startup Disk property sheet in the Add/Remove Programs Properties dialog box. Windows 95, Windows 98, and Windows Me then copy the Startup Disk files from your Windows CD. After you boot your computer with a Windows 98 or Windows Me Startup Disk, you not only have access to your CD drive, but you also have access to a RAM drive with additional troubleshooting utilities. A **RAM drive** (also called a **virtual drive**) is a portion of RAM that acts and functions like a real disk drive. You can store files on a RAM drive, and you can create and navigate directories (or folders) on a RAM drive. RAM drives are faster than physical hard disk drives—over 120,000 times faster. On a Windows 98 or Windows Me Startup Disk, a RAM drive serves another important function. It provides more storage space than is available on a 1.44 MB 3½-inch high-density disk. By converting part of RAM into a drive, Windows 98 and Windows Me can extract and copy troubleshooting utilities from the compressed cabinet file named Ebd.cab (Emergency Boot Disk) on the Startup Disk to the RAM drive, giving you access to these utilities. A **cabinet file** is a file that contains all or part of some of the Windows program and supporting files stored in a compressed format. Cabinet files have the "cab" file extension. The Windows 95 Startup Disk does not provide access to your CD drive, and it does not contain the configuration and files needed to create a RAM drive.

Figure 8-10	WINDOWS 98 OPTION FOR CREATING A STARTUP DISK

how you can use a Startup Disk

In the original version of Windows 95 and also in Windows 95a, you could create an **Emergency Recovery Disk (ERD)** with the Emergency Recovery Utility (Eru.exe) located in the \Other\Misc\Eru folder on the Windows 95 CD. The Emergency Recovery Disk contained the core operating systems files needed to boot the computer from a floppy disk in drive A, plus copies of the Windows 95 startup configuration files (Config.sys, Autoexec.bat, Win.ini, and System.ini), the Windows 95 Registry, and an Emergency Recovery Disk program (Erd.exe) for restoring files from this disk to your computer, as well as a second copy of the Windows 95 core operating system files. This utility was not available in or supported by later versions of Windows.

Some computer vendors provide customers with a Restore or Recovery CD that allows customers to restore specific programs to their computer or to reformat the hard disk and perform a complete restore, so that the computer returns to the state it was in when it was shipped. However, to use a Restore or Recovery CD, you need access to your CD drive, so you would use it after booting to the desktop or after booting with a boot disk configured to provide you with access to the CD drive. This Restore or Recovery CD is different from a Windows CD. If you restore Windows from a Restore or Recovery CD, you still have to install Windows.

Boot disks have proven to be an effective tool for gaining access to a computer, troubleshooting problems, and rebuilding systems for more than 20 years.

Making **Windows XP Setup Disks**

Windows XP Setup Disks allow you to boot your computer from a set of floppy disks using drive A and to reinstall Windows, repair Windows, or restore your computer. During booting, all necessary components of the Windows XP operating system are loaded into memory, and after booting is complete, you have access to your CD drive so that you can reinstall Windows XP from the Windows XP CD. You can also use the Automated Recovery Wizard to rebuild your computer (covered later in the tutorial). You can create Windows XP Setup Disks from your Windows CD. Or you can download a Win32 Cabinet Self-Extractor file from Microsoft's Download Center (*www.microsoft.com/downloads*) to create Windows XP Setup Disks for either the Professional Edition or Home Edition of Windows XP. Figure 8-11 shows the Web site for downloading the Win32 Cabinet Self-Extractor for Windows XP Professional.

Figure 8-11	MICROSOFT'S DOWNLOAD CENTER

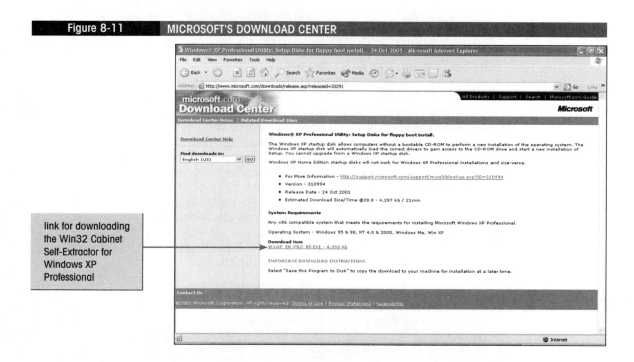

link for downloading the Win32 Cabinet Self-Extractor for Windows XP Professional

After you download this program, you need to format six floppy disks for use as setup disks and check the disks for errors before you use them. When you run the Win32 Cabinet Self-Extractor program (by clicking the file icon), it opens a Command Prompt window, runs a program called Makeboot.exe, and prompts you for each disk in turn. See Figure 8-12.

| Figure 8-12 | CREATING WINDOWS XP PROFESSIONAL SETUP DISKS |

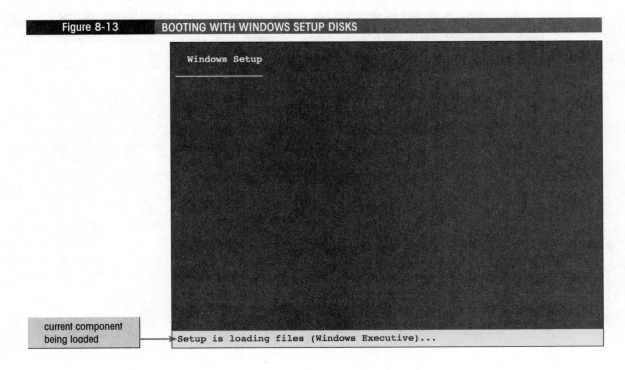

Each disk contains a file that identifies the order of the disk in the set; for example, the Windows XP Setup Boot Disk contains a file named DISK101, the Windows XP Setup Disk #2 contains a file named DISK102, etc. However, you should still label the disks in advance so that you do not have to examine each disk to know which is the first disk, second disk, etc.

If you need to use these setup disks, you insert the Windows XP Setup Boot Disk (the first disk) in drive A, and then restart Windows XP. If your computer is set up to boot from drive A instead of drive C, you first see a message informing you that Setup is inspecting your computer's configuration. After loading components from the first setup disk, the Setup program prompts you for each of the next disks and loads device drivers and other Windows XP components, including support for the different Windows XP file systems. As shown in Figure 8-13 for Windows Setup Disk #2, Setup displays information on which Windows XP components are being loaded in the status bar at the bottom of the screen. After loading the contents of the sixth disk, you see a Windows Setup screen like the one shown in Figure 8-14 from which you can install Windows XP, or repair your computer using the Recovery Console (covered in Tutorial 9).

| Figure 8-13 | BOOTING WITH WINDOWS SETUP DISKS |

Figure 8-14   **SETUP OPTIONS FOR REINSTALLING OR REPAIRING WINDOWS**

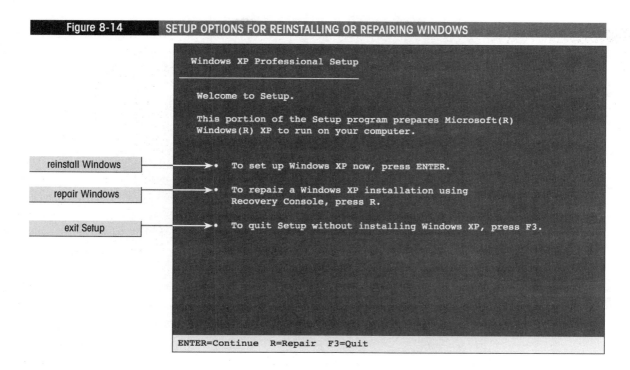

```
Windows XP Professional Setup
_____

Welcome to Setup.

This portion of the Setup program prepares Microsoft(R)
Windows(R) XP to run on your computer.

  •  To set up Windows XP now, press ENTER.

  •  To repair a Windows XP installation using
     Recovery Console, press R.

  •  To quit Setup without installing Windows XP, press F3.




  ENTER=Continue   R=Repair   F3=Quit
```

reinstall Windows

repair Windows

exit Setup

After you make Windows XP Setup Disks, you should write-protect them so that a computer virus cannot gain access to any of the disks.

Under Windows 2000, you can also create a set of Windows 2000 Setup Disks using the Makeboot.exe program; however, you only need four floppy disks. You can use the Windows 2000 Setup Disks with the Windows 2000 CD to reinstall Windows 2000, or with an **Emergency Repair Disk (ERD)** to repair problems with Windows 2000 system files (such as damaged or missing files), the Windows 2000 startup environment for dual-boot or multiple-boot systems, and the partition boot sector on the boot volume, and to also restore the Windows 2000 Registry. **System files** are files that Windows uses to load, configure, and run the operating system. The **startup environment** consists of configuration settings that specify which operating system to start, and how to start each operating system. To make an Emergency Repair Disk in Windows 2000, you open the Backup utility and use the Emergency Repair Disk button to create an ERD and back up the Windows 2000 Registry to the Repair folder. See Figure 8-15.

Figure 8-15   MAKING A WINDOWS 2000 EMERGENCY REPAIR DISK

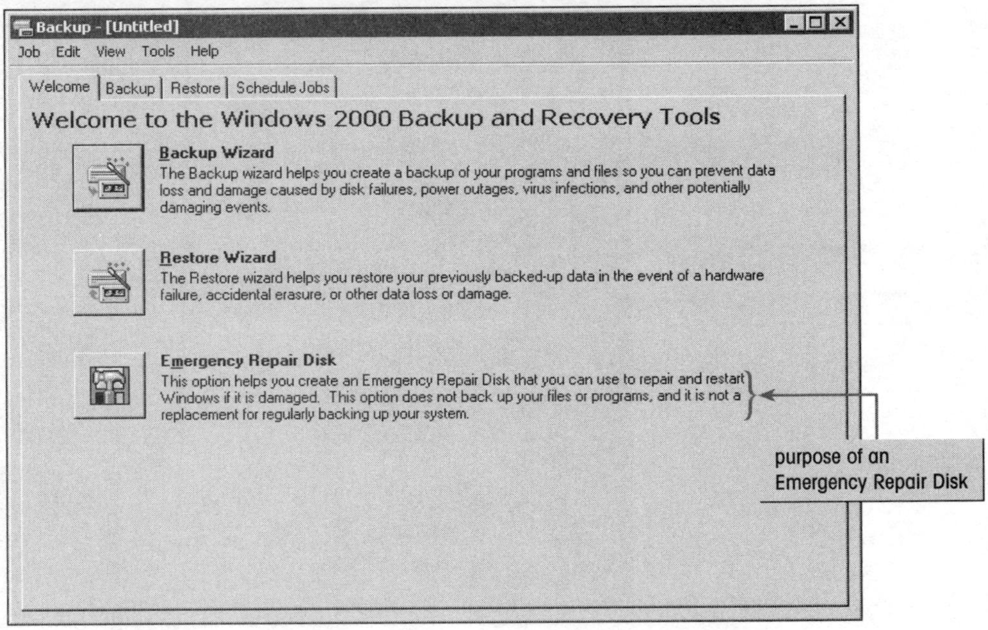

Backup - [Untitled]

Job Edit View Tools Help

Welcome | Backup | Restore | Schedule Jobs |

Welcome to the Windows 2000 Backup and Recovery Tools

Backup Wizard
The Backup wizard helps you create a backup of your programs and files so you can prevent data loss and damage caused by disk failures, power outages, virus infections, and other potentially damaging events.

Restore Wizard
The Restore wizard helps you restore your previously backed-up data in the event of a hardware failure, accidental erasure, or other data loss or damage.

Emergency Repair Disk
This option helps you create an Emergency Repair Disk that you can use to repair and restart Windows if it is damaged. This option does not back up your files or programs, and it is not a replacement for regularly backing up your system.

purpose of an
Emergency Repair Disk

Windows NT Workstation 4.0 and earlier versions of Windows NT included a program called Rdisk.exe (for Repair Disk) for making an Emergency Repair Disk (ERD); however, that program is not included in Windows 2000.

Even though the names are similar and the acronyms identical, the Windows 95 Emergency Recovery Disk (ERD) is different from the Windows NT Workstation 4.0 and Windows 2000 Emergency Repair Disk (ERD).

The options for creating boot disks, startup disks, setup disks, and emergency repair disks in the different versions of Windows emphasize one important point. If you experience a problem booting from drive C or with Windows, you might need some type of boot disk to boot your computer from a floppy disk in drive A so that you can troubleshoot, repair, restore, or rebuild your computer. You also need access to your CD drive to reinstall Windows or other software or to restore your computer.

Using System **Restore**

System Restore, first introduced in Windows Me (but not available in Windows 2000), is a Windows XP component that allows you to restore your computer to a previous working state if you encounter a problem after installing an operating system upgrade, installing or upgrading an application or utility, installing or upgrading a device driver for a hardware device, restoring files from a backup, experiencing damage caused by a virus infection or file corruption, or making changes to system settings. System Restore creates restore points periodically in response to system events (such as those just described), or at the request of the user. System Restore also creates a restore point every 24 hours, or when 24 hours have elapsed since the last restore point. Each **restore point** contains a snapshot of the Registry as well as information on the system state, and represents a "picture" of the state of your computer at a given point in time. The **System State** consists of the operating system components that define the current state of the operating system, and includes Registry settings for user accounts, applications, hardware, and software, as well as files in the top-level folder and Windows folder that Windows XP needs to boot the computer. These restore points do not include user files (such as those found in the My Documents folder), files with file extensions known to be common document file extensions (such as "doc"), shortcuts (such as Internet shortcuts found in the user's Favorites folder), e-mail, graphics files, passwords, or the Windows paging file.

System Restore creates the following types of restore points:

- **Initial system checkpoints**. System Restore creates a system checkpoint when you first start a new computer with Windows XP or after you upgrade a computer to Windows XP. A **system checkpoint** is a scheduled restore point that System Restore automatically creates.

- **System checkpoints**. System Restore creates a system checkpoint after every 24 hours of calendar time.

- **Program name installation restore points**. System Restore creates a restore point before you install a program using an installer such as InstallShield or Windows Installer. If you need to revert to this restore point, System Restore removes installed files and Registry settings for the newly installed program and restores programs and system files that were altered during the installation of the new program. If you roll back your computer to a state that existed before a program was installed, the program will not work after the roll back, and you will need to reinstall the program.

- **Automatic update restore points**. If you use the automatic update feature to download operating system updates, System Restore creates a restore point before you install any updates.

- **Unsigned device driver restore points**. If you install a device driver that has not been digitally signed or certified by Microsoft's Windows Hardware Quality Labs (WHQL), System Restore creates a restore point before installing the driver. If a problem arises after installing the updated device driver, you can use the restore point to roll back your computer and restore your previous device driver.

- **Microsoft Backup Utility restore points**. As you saw in Tutorial 6, if you restore files from a backup using the Microsoft Backup Utility, System Restore creates a restore point before the restore operation.

- **Restore operation restore points**. If you need to roll back your computer using a restore point, System Restore creates a new restore point first so that if a problem develops after the restore, you can roll your computer forward to its original state before the restore.

- **Manual restore points**. You can manually create restore points before you make changes to your computer. For example, before you manually make changes to Registry settings or other system settings, or before you install a downloaded program that does not use an InstallShield wizard or Windows XP Professional Installer, you can create a restore point in the event a problem develops later.

System Restore is enabled on all drives when you first power on a new computer or after you install Windows XP unless there is less than 200 MB of hard disk space available on the partition that contains the Windows operating system folder. You have to make sure that you do not run out of disk space, otherwise System Restore becomes inactive.

Using the information stored in Filelist.xml, System Restore monitors changes to operating system and application files, and either records changes to the original files or backs them up. Notice that the Filelist.xml file shown in Figure 8-16 lists files, directories, and file extensions that are either included or excluded from the restore checkpoints. On the computer used for this figure, the path to this file is: C:\Windows\System32\Restore\Filelist.xml.

Figure 8-16   VIEWING THE CONTENTS OF FILELIST.XML

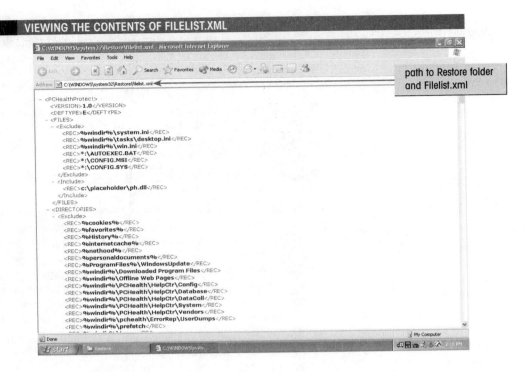

Examining System Restore Settings

Because System Restore is such an invaluable tool for troubleshooting problems on employees' computers, Lenore and her staff check the System Restore settings on all new computer systems with Windows XP and on all existing computers upgraded to Windows XP.

Before you create a restore point in the following steps, examine the System Restore settings on the computer you are using. You must log on your computer under an account with Administrator privileges. If you do not have Administrator privileges on the computer you are using, read the steps and examine the figures, but do not keystroke the steps.

To view System Restore settings:

1. Log on under an account with Administrator privileges.

2. From the Start menu, right-click **My Computer**, click **Properties** on the shortcut menu, and in the System Properties dialog box, click the **System Restore** tab. From the System Restore property sheet, shown in Figure 8-17, you can turn off the System Restore feature for all drives, or examine drive settings used by System Restore; however, if you do turn off this feature, System Restore deletes all existing restore points and you cannot track or undo changes to your computer. On the computer used for this figure, System Restore is currently monitoring drive C and drive D.

   TROUBLE? If you do not see a System Restore tab in the System Properties dialog box, you did not log on under an account with Administrator privileges. You must log out of the current account, and log on under another account with Administrator privileges.

Figure 8-17   VIEWING SYSTEM RESTORE PROPERTIES

option for turning
off System Restore

System Restore is
monitoring changes
to system files on
these drives

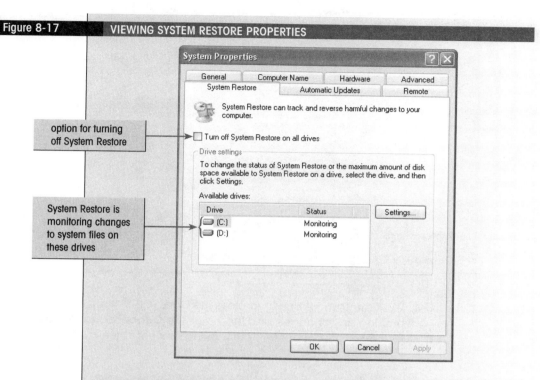

3. Under Available drives, click **(C:)**, and then click the **Settings** button. In the Drive (C:) Settings dialog box, Windows XP notes that you cannot turn off System Restore on this drive (the system volume) without turning it off on all drives. See Figure 8-18. If your computer has another disk drive, as is the case for the computer used for the figure, you can turn off System Restore for that volume. In the Disk space usage section, Windows XP automatically allocates approximately 12% of a volume over 4 GB for storing restore points. For the computer used for this figure, that translates into 1,962 MB, or approximately 1.9 GB of storage space. If you do not want to keep older restore points or if you need to conserve storage space on a drive, you can reduce the amount of disk space used for restore points, but if you decrease the available storage space, that reduces the number of restore points that System Restore can create and store on the disk.

TROUBLE? If you cannot click the icon for drive C, and if you do not have a Settings button, read this step and the next step and examine the figure.

Figure 8-18	VIEWING SYSTEM RESTORE DRIVE SETTINGS

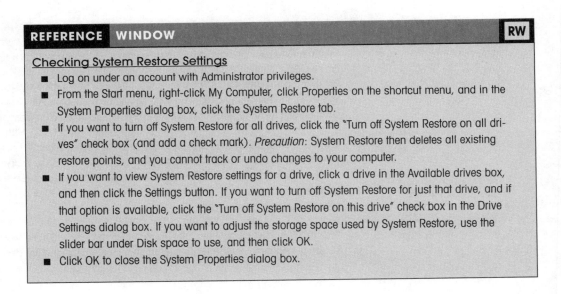

4. Click the **Cancel** button to close the Drive (C:) Settings dialog box without making any changes, and then click the **Cancel** button to close the System Properties dialog box without making any changes.

REFERENCE WINDOW **RW**

Checking System Restore Settings

- Log on under an account with Administrator privileges.
- From the Start menu, right-click My Computer, click Properties on the shortcut menu, and in the System Properties dialog box, click the System Restore tab.
- If you want to turn off System Restore for all drives, click the "Turn off System Restore on all drives" check box (and add a check mark). *Precaution*: System Restore then deletes all existing restore points, and you cannot track or undo changes to your computer.
- If you want to view System Restore settings for a drive, click a drive in the Available drives box, and then click the Settings button. If you want to turn off System Restore for just that drive, and if that option is available, click the "Turn off System Restore on this drive" check box in the Drive Settings dialog box. If you want to adjust the storage space used by System Restore, use the slider bar under Disk space to use, and then click OK.
- Click OK to close the System Properties dialog box.

Although System Restore is automatically enabled, you should check the System Restore settings to make sure it is functioning the way you expect.

Creating a Restore Point

In the next set of steps, you manually create a restore point, and then immediately use the restore point to restore your computer to a previous state that is identical to when you made the restore point. After that, you reverse the restoration. Outside of this tutorial, you would restore an earlier, or perhaps a later, restore point after you discovered or encountered a problem on your computer, and that could mean that some time elapsed since you created the restore point. Here, you must perform the restore immediately before System Restore creates other restore points and before you make any other changes to your computer. Also, if you select a restore point from a much earlier date, you might actually undo changes you have made to your computer, such as installing an application or upgrading the operating system.

If you are working in a computer lab, make sure you have permission from your instructor or technical support staff to use System Restore to create and restore a restore point, and then perform both operations before you stop working in the computer lab.

As you and Lenore upgrade computers for Windows XP and provide new computers to employees, you show each employee how to create a restore point before they make a change that might affect the use of their computer.

To create a restore point:

1. Make sure you are logged on under an account with Administrator privileges.

2. From the Start menu, point to **All Programs**, point to **Accessories**, point to **System Tools**, and then click **System Restore**. In the first System Restore dialog box, Windows XP explains the value of System Restore, the use of restore points, and notes that any changes you make to your computer with System Restore are completely reversible because System Restore creates a new restore point before restoring your computer to a previous state with a previously made restore point. See Figure 8-19. Windows XP also notes that before you change your system, you can manually create a restore point so that you can reverse any changes you make. If you decide to check or make changes to System Restore settings, you can also use the System Restore Settings link in this dialog box to open the System Properties dialog box and select the System Restore property sheet.

Figure 8-19	CHOOSING A SYSTEM RESTORE TASK

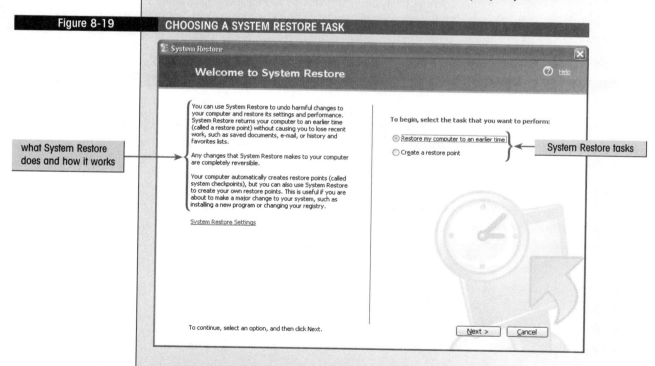

3. Click the **Create a restore point** option button, and then click the **Next** button. In the Create a Restore Point window, you can provide a description for this restore point. See Figure 8-20. A description is useful, so that you know why you manually created a specific restore point.

Figure 8-20   ENTERING A RESTORE POINT DESCRIPTION

enter a description for
this new restore point

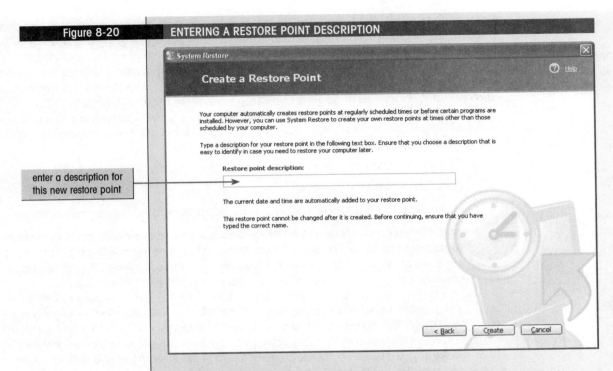

4. In the Restore point description box, type **RP** (for Restore Point), press the **spacebar**, type your last name (for example, Lenore Ruhling would type RP Ruhling), and then click the **Create** button. System Restore informs you that it has created a restore point, and it identifies the date, time, and name of the restore point. See Figure 8-21.

Figure 8-21   RESTORE POINT CREATED

information on the
restore point you
just created

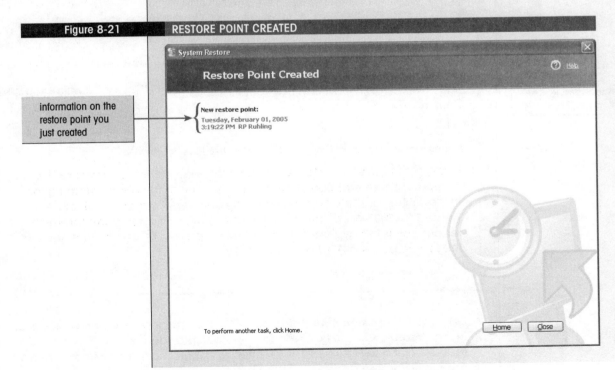

5. Click the **Home** button to return to the first System Restore dialog box, and leave the dialog box open for the next section of the tutorial.

REFERENCE WINDOW **RW**

Creating a Restore Point
- Log on under an account with Administrator privileges.
- From the Start menu, point to All Programs, point to Accessories, point to System Tools, and then click System Restore.
- Click the "Create a restore point" option button, and then click the Next button.
- When prompted to provide a description for this restore point, type the description in the "Restore point description" text box, and then click the Create button.
- Close the System Restore dialog box.

Because System Restore works in the background during computer idle time to create restore points when you make changes to your computer, such as installing or upgrading software and device drivers, you are free to work on your computer with the knowledge that you can roll it back to an earlier point in time if a problem should develop.

Using a Restore Point to Roll Back a Computer

To roll back your computer to a restore point, you select a date from a system calendar that includes all of the dates for which restore points are available. After you select a restore point, you restart your computer and Windows XP uses the system configuration from that previous date.

Next, you roll back your computer system using the restore point you just created. If you do not want to roll back your computer, or if you work in a computer lab which does not permit you to roll back a computer, close System Restore, and then examine the figures and read, but do not keystroke, the next set of steps.

Lenore asks you to step employees through the process of restoring their computer to an earlier operating state with a previously created restore point.

To use a restore point to roll back a computer:

1. If you want to use the restore point you just created, click the **Restore my computer to an earlier time** option button, and then click the **Next** button. In the Select a Restore Point window, you can select a restore point. See Figure 8-22. The system calendar displays in bold all of the dates for which restore points are available. If you select a date, the list on the right displays the restore points for that particular date.

Figure 8-22 SELECTING A RESTORE POINT

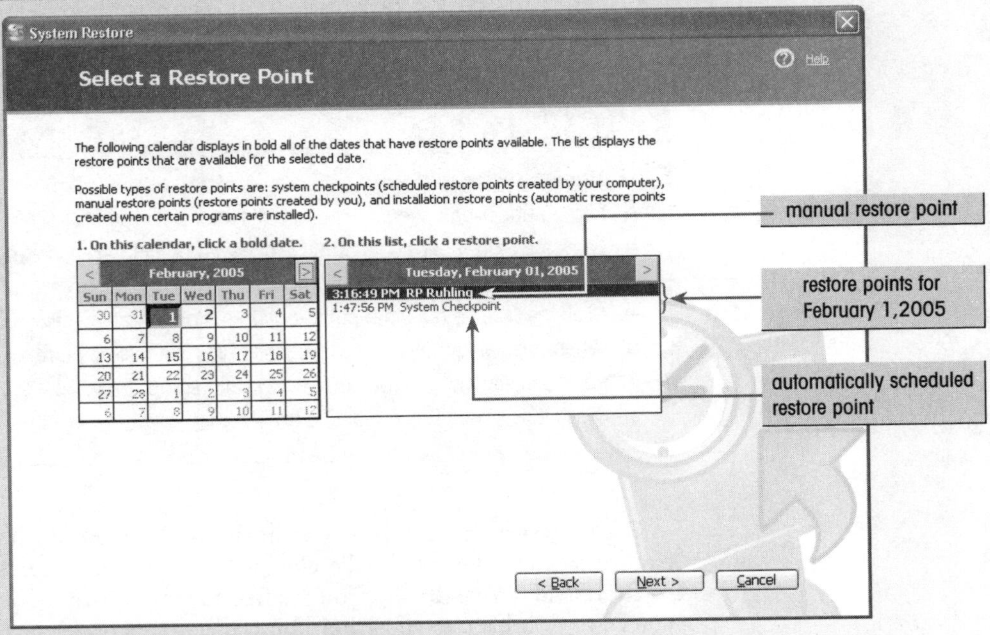

System Restore

Select a Restore Point

⑦ Help

The following calendar displays in bold all of the dates that have restore points available. The list displays the restore points that are available for the selected date.

Possible types of restore points are: system checkpoints (scheduled restore points created by your computer), manual restore points (restore points created by you), and installation restore points (automatic restore points created when certain programs are installed).

1. On this calendar, click a bold date.   2. On this list, click a restore point.

February, 2005						
Sun	Mon	Tue	Wed	Thu	Fri	Sat
30	31	1	2	3	4	5
6	7	8	9	10	11	12
13	14	15	16	17	18	19
20	21	22	23	24	25	26
27	28	1	2	3	4	5
6	7	8	9	10	11	12

Tuesday, February 01, 2005

3:16:49 PM RP Ruhling
1:47:56 PM System Checkpoint

— manual restore point

restore points for February 1, 2005

automatically scheduled restore point

< Back   Next >   Cancel

2. Select the month and day for which you created a restore point (if necessary), click the **restore point** that you want to use in the list on the right (make sure you select the one that you just created), and then click the **Next** button. You are now prompted to confirm the restore point. See Figure 8-23. The restore point you selected is displayed in red in the upper-left corner of the dialog box. System Restore shuts down Windows XP during the restoration, and then restarts using the settings from the restore point you just made.

TROUBLE? If the selected restore point is not the one that you just made, or is not the one that you want to use, click the Back button, select the correct restore point, click the Next button, and then verify that you have selected the correct restore point.

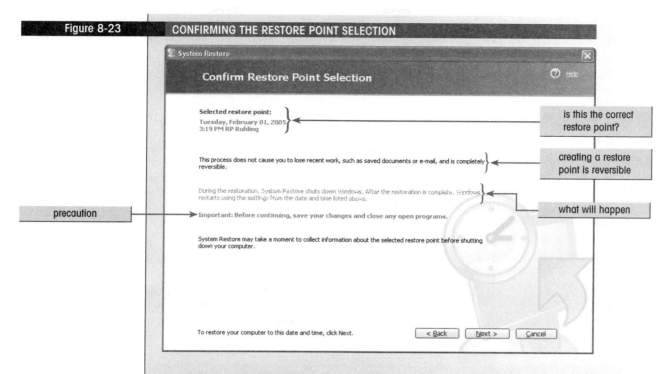

Figure 8-23 CONFIRMING THE RESTORE POINT SELECTION

3. Click the **Next** button. As your system shuts down, a System Restore dialog box appears with a progress indicator showing how far the restore process has progressed.

4. After your computer restarts, log on under your user account. System Restore then displays a System Restore dialog box verifying that the restoration is complete. It also notes that if the restoration did not correct the problem, you can choose another restore point, or undo this restoration.

5. In the System Restore dialog box, click the **OK** button to display the desktop.

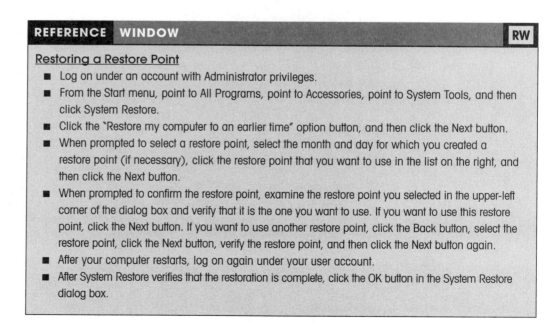

REFERENCE WINDOW RW

Restoring a Restore Point
- Log on under an account with Administrator privileges.
- From the Start menu, point to All Programs, point to Accessories, point to System Tools, and then click System Restore.
- Click the "Restore my computer to an earlier time" option button, and then click the Next button.
- When prompted to select a restore point, select the month and day for which you created a restore point (if necessary), click the restore point that you want to use in the list on the right, and then click the Next button.
- When prompted to confirm the restore point, examine the restore point you selected in the upper-left corner of the dialog box and verify that it is the one you want to use. If you want to use this restore point, click the Next button. If you want to use another restore point, click the Back button, select the restore point, click the Next button, verify the restore point, and then click the Next button again.
- After your computer restarts, log on again under your user account.
- After System Restore verifies that the restoration is complete, click the OK button in the System Restore dialog box.

After you roll back your computer using a restore point, you should examine your computer and the applications you use to make sure that everything is working properly and that you have access to the resources you need.

Undoing a Restoration

In the next set of steps, you undo the restoration you just performed. If you did not use the restore point to roll back your computer in the previous section, or if you are working in a computer lab where you are not permitted to use System Restore, examine the figures and read, but do not keystroke, the following steps.

When Lenore works with employees to restore a computer to an earlier operating system, she points out that they can reverse the restoration if they later encounter a problem that they did not anticipate. Lenore asks you to try undoing the restoration now on her computer.

To undo the restore point:

1. From the Start menu, point to **All Programs**, point to **Accessories**, point to **System Tools**, and then click **System Restore**. Notice that the System Restore dialog box lists an additional option to indicate that you can undo the last restoration. See Figure 8-24.

Figure 8-24   SYSTEM RESTORE TASK OPTIONS

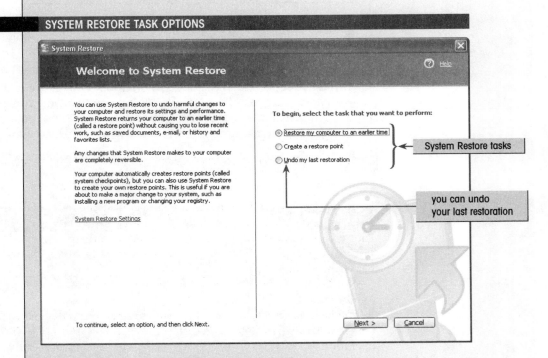

2. If you do not want to undo the last restoration, close the System Restore dialog box. If you want to undo the last restoration, click the **Undo my last restoration** option button, and then click the **Next** button. System Restore informs you that it will undo the restoration you just performed. See Figure 8-25.

Figure 8-25   CONFIRMING AN UNDO OF A SYSTEM RESTORATION

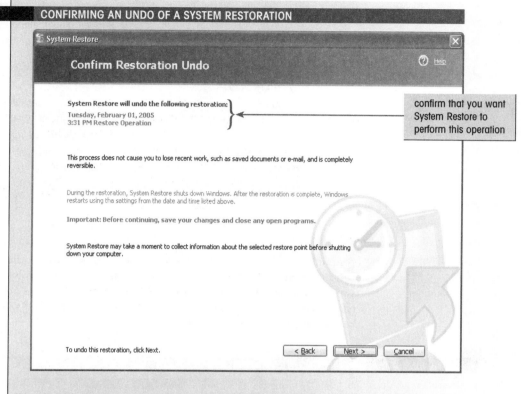

confirm that you want System Restore to perform this operation

3. Click the **Next** button. System Restore restores your files and settings, shuts down Windows XP, and then restarts the computer.

4. After your computer restarts, log on again under your user account. The System Restore dialog box opens, verifying that it has successfully reversed the previous restoration operation.

5. In the System Restore dialog box, click the **OK** button to display the desktop.

Suppose you open System Restore and choose the option for restoring your computer to an earlier date. Then you select the date for which you created a restore point, and roll back your computer to that restore point. If you undo the restoration, System Restore lists both restore operations along with your restore points for that date, so that you have a record of the changes you've made to your computer.

Note that you can roll back your computer to a previous state and also roll your computer forward.

You have successfully created a restore point, restored your computer system to the state that it was in when you created the restore point, and then you reversed the restoration operation.

REFERENCE WINDOW   **RW**

Undoing a Restoration with System Restore
- Log on under an account with Administrator privileges.
- From the Start menu, point to All Programs, point to Accessories, point to System Tools, and then click System Restore.
- Click the "Undo my last restoration" option button, and then click the Next button.
- When prompted to confirm the restoration undo, check the selected system restore operation shown in the upper-left corner of the System Restore dialog box, and then click the Next button.
- After your computer restarts, log back on under your user account.
- After System Restore displays a dialog box verifying that it has successfully reversed the previous restoration operation, click the OK button in the System Restore dialog box.

The hidden System Volume Information folder on your system volume (most likely drive C), contains a _Restore folder, which contains folders with different restore points for your computer. See Figure 8-26. These restore points are identified by the label RP followed by a number. System Restore periodically purges older restore points from this folder to make room for new restore points. Purging is on a first in, first out (**FIFO**) basis, and Fifo.log keeps track of this information.

Figure 8-26   **VIEWING THE CONTENTS OF THE _RESTORE FOLDER**

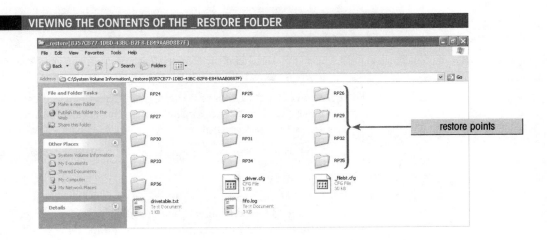

If you open the most recent restore point folder, you see a Snapshot folder that contains information on Registry settings, and you also see files with configuration settings (the ones with the "ini" file extension) as well as log, configuration, and ID files with information about the restore point. See Figure 8-27. Your files will differ from the ones shown in the figure.

| Figure 8-27 | VIEWING THE CONTENTS OF A RESTORE POINT FOLDER |

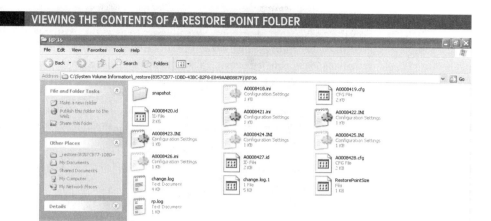

System Restore provides you with a powerful tool for reversing changes that affect the performance of your computer system. Although System Restore is designed to create restore points prior to operations that affect the use of your computer, such as installing new software, you can use System Restore to manually create restore points before you make changes to your computer. Furthermore, while System Restore is invaluable, it does not substitute for backups, so you still must back up your important documents on a regular basis.

In the next section of the tutorial, you examine how to use the Automated System Recovery Wizard to back up your computer's system state and system files. You also enable and specify settings for Internet Connection Firewall to protect your computer system. Finally, you examine the use of cookies and Web bugs, check Internet Explorer security and privacy settings, and review safe computing guidelines.

Using the Automated System Recovery Wizard

You can use the **Automated System Recovery (ASR) Wizard** to back up the system state, system services, and the system volume of your computer so that you have the system files and settings required to rebuild that computer. Recall from the section on System Restore that the system state consists of the operating system components that define the current state of the operating system, and includes Registry settings for user accounts, applications, hardware, and software, as well as files in the top-level folder and Windows folder that Windows XP needs to boot the computer. The system volume contains the hardware-specific files for loading Windows XP on x86-based computers with a BIOS. The system volume might be the same volume as the boot volume that contains the Windows operating system and its support files. **x86-based computers** are ones based on the architecture of the Intel 8086 processor.

The ASR Wizard backs up contents of your system volume to tape or hard disk, and your system settings are backed up to a floppy disk. If you experience a system failure, you should use the Automated System Recovery Wizard as a last resort after you have attempted to restart and troubleshoot your computer using other troubleshooting tools, such as System Restore. The Automated System Recovery Wizard is not available in the Home Edition of Windows XP.

To complete the following steps, you need a blank, formatted high-density disk and sufficient media to back up your system volume (i.e., drive C). That means that you need to back up to a tape backup drive or to another hard disk drive, but you cannot back up to a network drive. Because of the volume of data that's backed up, using other types of removable media, such as rewritable CDs or Zip disks, is impractical. Since the Automated System Recovery Wizard backs up the system volume (usually drive C), you also have to factor in the time required for a backup of that hard disk. For example, on the computer used for the following steps, the Automated System Recovery Wizard backed up approximately 8.3 GB of data in 45 minutes to another hard disk drive.

If you do not have sufficient media or time to perform this operation, or if you work in a computer lab that does not permit you to use the Automated System Recovery Wizard, examine the figures and read, but do not keystroke, the following steps so that you are familiar with this process. Also, your user account must include backup and restore privileges, and therefore, you must log on under an account with Administrator privileges or an account with backup and restore privileges.

If you are using Windows XP Home Edition, then you cannot complete the following steps. Read the steps and examine the figures, but do not keystroke the steps.

Your instructor and technical support staff can inform you whether it's even possible for you to use the Automated System Recovery Wizard on a lab computer and, if so, how you perform the backup.

Lenore and her staff have trained employees to use the Automated System Recovery (ASR) Wizard to prepare a disk that contains system settings for restoring a computer system in case of system failure and to back up system files. Employees now integrate this procedure into their general backup plan.

To use the Automated System Recovery Wizard:

1. Close all open applications and windows and, if necessary, log on under an account with Administrator privileges or with backup and restore privileges.

2. From the Start menu, point to **All Programs**, point to **Accessories**, point to **System Tools**, click **Backup**, and after the Backup or Restore Wizard dialog box opens, click the **Advanced Mode** link. You can start the Automated System Recovery Wizard from the Welcome sheet in the Backup Utility window. See Figure 8-28. Note that the ASR Preparation Wizard creates a two-part backup of your computer system: a floppy disk with your system settings, and then a backup of your local system partition on other media. Although the Windows XP Home Edition includes an Automated System Recovery Wizard button, the Automated System Recovery feature does not work.

| Figure 8-28 | STARTING THE AUTOMATED SYSTEM RECOVERY WIZARD |

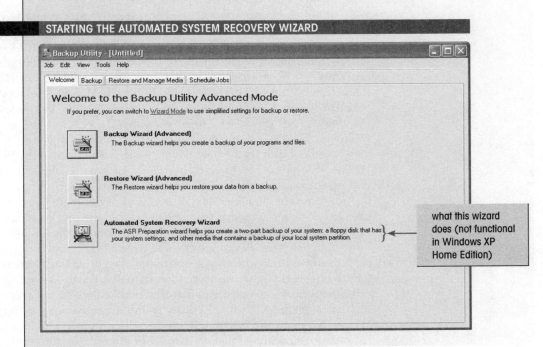

3. Click the **Automated System Recovery Wizard** button. The Automated System Recovery Preparation Wizard dialog box opens, explaining the importance of making an ASR disk and backup of system files in the event of a system failure. See Figure 8-29. The wizard also emphasizes the importance of backing up your data separately.

   TROUBLE? If you see a Backup Utility dialog box that informs you that you must log on under an account with backup and restore privileges, click the OK button, close the Backup Utility window, log off the account you are currently using, and log on again under an account with Administrator privileges or an account with backup and restore privileges.

| Figure 8-29 | ASR WIZARD WELCOME SCREEN |

what this wizard does

this procedure is no substitute for backing up your personal files

4. Click the **Next** button. In the Backup Destination dialog box, you specify the location and name of the file for storing the backup. See Figure 8-30. In the Backup media or file name box, it proposes to use the filename Backup.bkf (the default filename) or the filename of your last backup, and under the Backup media or file name box, the wizard informs you that it also needs a floppy disk to create a recovery disk.

Figure 8-30   SELECTING THE BACKUP MEDIA AND FILE

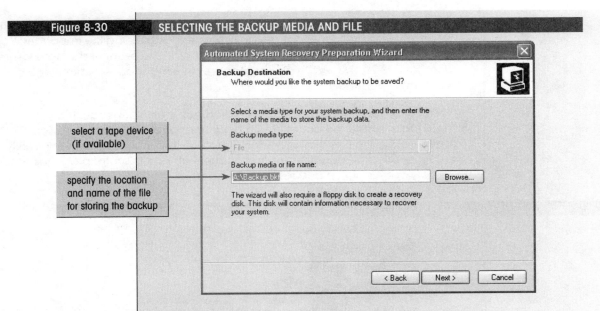

select a tape device (if available)

specify the location and name of the file for storing the backup

5. Click the **Browse** button, and in the Save as dialog box, locate the drive and folder where you want to store the backup, type **ASR Backup**, press the **spacebar**, and type the current date (in the format mm-dd-yyyy, such as 2-1-2005) in the File name box, click the **Save** button, and then click the **Next** button in the Automated System Recovery Preparation Wizard dialog box. The next, and last, Automated System Recovery Preparation Wizard dialog box informs you that the wizard will create a backup of your system files, and that you will be prompted to insert a floppy disk. See Figure 8-31.

Figure 8-31   COMPLETING THE PREPARATION FOR AN ASR BACKUP

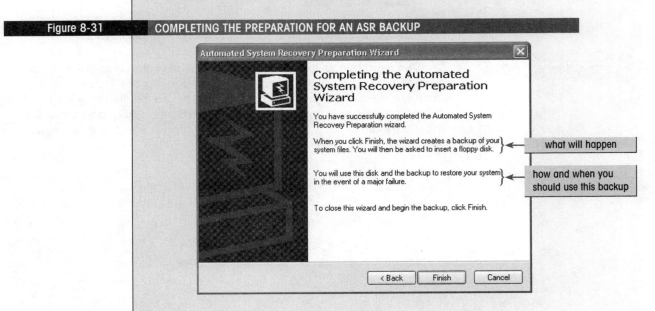

what will happen

how and when you should use this backup

6. Click the **Finish** button. After examining all the files on your computer, the Backup Progress dialog box displays the status of the backup. See Figure 8-32. On the computer used for this figure, the backup utility selected 8,927,167,284 bytes, or approximately 8.3 GB of data for the backup. The backup operation, initially estimated at close to 3 hours by the Backup Utility, actually took 45 minutes, because the data was backed up to another hard disk.

Figure 8-32	PROGRESS OF THE ASR BACKUP

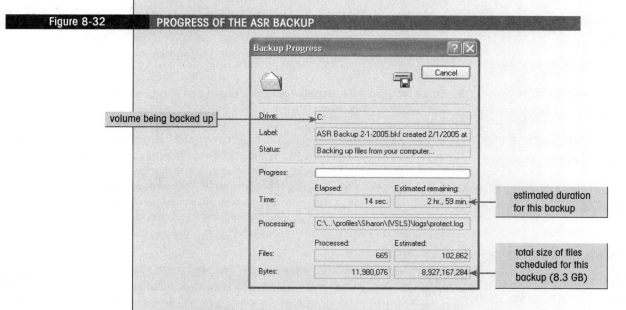

7. When prompted, insert a formatted floppy disk in the drive, and then click the **OK** button in the Backup Utility dialog box. After creating the ASR Disk, the Backup Utility asks you to remove the floppy disk, place a specific label on the disk to identify the backup set, and then keep it in a safe place. See Figure 8-33.

Figure 8-33	ASR DISK COMPLETED

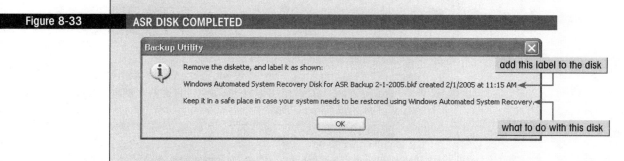

8. Click the **OK** button in the Backup Utility dialog box.

You can print and save a report that summarizes this operation:

To print, and save, a report of the backup operation:

1. Click the **Report** button, read the information about the restore operation, click **File** on the menu bar, click **Print**, choose the correct printer, and then click the **Print** button.

2. To save the report, click **File** on the menu bar, click **Save As**, click the **Save in** list arrow, open **My Documents**, use the backup name as a filename in the File name box, and then click the **Save** button. You now have a copy of this report for your records.

3. Close Notepad, close the Backup Progress dialog box, and then close the Backup Utility window.

Because system settings and the contents of the system volume change over time, you should develop a periodic schedule for updating the backup created by the Automated System Recovery Wizard. Because it is comparable to a normal backup in terms of the time and amount of media required, you might want to schedule it on as frequent a basis as you schedule a normal backup of your document files. After you download and install operating system updates, or reconfigure Windows XP, you must update your ASR backup.

REFERENCE WINDOW   **RW**

<u>Using the Automated System Recovery Wizard</u> (Windows XP Professional Only)

■ Log on under an account with Administrator privileges or backup and restore privileges.

■ From the Start menu, point to All Programs, point to Accessories, point to System Tools, click Backup, and after the Backup or Restore Wizard dialog box opens, click the Advanced Mode link.

■ Click the Automated System Recovery Wizard button.

■ After reading the explanation of the Automated System Recovery Preparation Wizard, click the Next button.

■ When prompted for the Backup Destination, click the Browse button, and in the Save as dialog box, locate the drive and folder where you want to store the backup, type a name for the ASR backup in the File name box, click Save, and then click the Next button.

■ In the next, and last, Automated System Recovery Preparation Wizard dialog box, which summarizes what will happen next, click the Finish button.

■ When prompted, insert a formatted floppy disk in the drive, and then click the OK button in the Backup Utility dialog box.

■ After creating the ASR Disk, the Backup Utility prompts you to remove the floppy disk, place a specific label on the disk to identify the backup set, and then keep it in a safe place.

■ Click the OK button in the Backup Utility dialog box.

■ If you want to print the report, click Report, read the information about the restore operation, click File on the menu bar, click Print, choose the correct printer, and then click the Print button.

■ If you want to save the report, click File on the menu bar, click Save As, click the Save in list arrow, open My Documents, use the backup name as a filename in the File name box, and then click the Save button.

■ Close Notepad, close the Backup Progress dialog box, and then close the Backup Utility window.

The contents of the backup media include the following files:

- A backup of files in the Documents and Settings, My Music, Program Files, Recycle Bin, System Volume Information, and Windows folders, as well as a backup of operating system files in the top-level folder of drive C. That means this backup also includes any files stored in your My Documents, My Pictures, and My Music folders, but also the corresponding folders for all other user accounts.

- A System State backup that includes boot files, the COM+ Class Registration Database, and the Registry. The **COM+ Class Registration Database** stores information about COM+ components, or operating system services for applications and components in a networking environment.

Next, view the contents of the ASR Disk.

To view the contents of the ASR Disk:

1. Open a window onto the floppy disk drive that contains the ASR Disk. See Figure 8-34. The files with the file extension "sif" (for Setup Installation File) are Windows NT Setup files. The Asr.sif file is the Microsoft Windows Automated System Recovery State Information File that contains information about the operating system, disks, partitions, and buses on your computer. The Setup.log file is a copy of the Setup.log file first created when Windows XP was installed on your computer, and it contains information on the location of Windows XP system files and settings.

| Figure 8-34 | VIEWING THE CONTENTS OF THE ASR DISK |

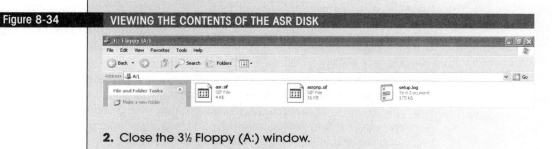

2. Close the 3½ Floppy (A:) window.

If your system fails and you must restore your computer using the Automated System Recovery tool, you need your most recent ASR Disk, your most recent ASR backup, and your Windows XP CD. After inserting your Windows CD into the bootable CD drive, restart your computer from the Windows XP CD or using the Windows XP Setup Disks. When you see the message "Press F2 to run Automated System Recovery," press F2, insert your ASR Disk and backup media to start the system recovery, and then follow the instructions for restoring your computer. You are then prompted for the name of the Windows folder, and after the system recovery is complete, you must restore your document files from your most recent backup sets because the Automated System Recovery formats the system partition during the restore process. As noted earlier, Microsoft has designed the Automated System Recovery as a last resort measure in case other troubleshooting methods do not resolve a problem.

The Automated System Recovery option in the Windows XP Microsoft Backup Utility replaces the option for creating an Emergency Repair Disk using Microsoft Windows 2000's Backup utility.

Setting Up Internet Connection Firewall

Internet Connection Firewall (ICF) tracks and stores information on all outbound communications from your computer in a table, and then compares that information with all inbound communications arriving to your computer from the Internet to determine whether it is safe for the data to pass. If the ICF table contains a matching entry, indicating that the communication is a response to a communication you originated, it allows the incoming data to reach your computer; otherwise, the incoming communication is silently discarded. The net effect is that you do not receive unsolicited communications, and ICF blocks hackers who use programs to probe the ports on your computer in an attempt to find and exploit a weakness in your computer.

Internet Connection Firewall provides this protection for a single computer whether you are connected to the Internet via a cable modem, DSL modem, or a dial-up modem. Internet Connection Firewall is available in both Windows XP Professional and Windows XP Home Edition, but not in the Windows XP 64-Bit Edition.

You can use Internet Connection Firewall with or without Internet Connection Sharing. With **Internet Connection Sharing (ICS)**, individuals who use different computers on a small home or office network can all connect to the Internet via one connection on one of the computers in the network. When Internet Connection Sharing is enabled on a computer, that computer becomes the ICS host for all other computers on the network. Internet Connection Sharing is also available in Windows 2000, Windows Me, and Windows 98 Second Edition, but it is not available in Windows XP 64-Bit Edition.

If the ICS host uses an external DSL or cable modem to connect to the Internet, you need to install two network adapters—one that connects to the DSL or cable modem and that provides the Internet connection, and one for communicating with the other computers in your home or small business network. If the ICS host has an internal modem, you only need one network adapter. You can use the Network Setup Wizard (covered in Tutorial 13) to set up and properly configure a home network with both Internet Connection Firewall and Internet Connection Sharing. To enable Internet Connection Firewall and check Internet Connection Firewall settings on a computer with a dedicated connection to the Internet, such as a dial-up modem, cable modem, ISDN, or DSL modem connection, you must log on your computer under an account with Administrator privileges.

In response to an increasing number of queries about Internet security, Lenore encourages home users to enable Internet Connection Firewall in Windows XP to protect their computer systems, or to purchase and install another type of firewall software product. She asks you to show interested employees how to enable Internet Connection Firewall.

To enable Internet Connection Firewall:

1. If necessary, log on under an account with Administrator privileges.

2. From the Start menu, click **Control Panel**, click the **Switch to Category view** link in the Control Panel dynamic menu if you are using Classic View, click **Network and Internet Connections** in the Control Panel window, click **Network Connections**, and after the Network Connections window opens, right-click your **dial-up connection** (such as MSN Explorer) or, if you do not have a dial-up connection, right-click **Local Area Connection**, click **Properties** on the shortcut menu, and then click the **Advanced** tab, if necessary. You might also have General and Authentication tabs. On the Advanced property sheet, you can enable or disable the use of Internet Connection Firewall. See Figure 8-35.

TROUBLE? If you have another type of LAN or High-Speed Internet connection, right-click that connection, and then click the Advanced tab (if necessary).

Figure 8-35   VIEWING INTERNET CONNECTION FIREWALL PROPERTIES

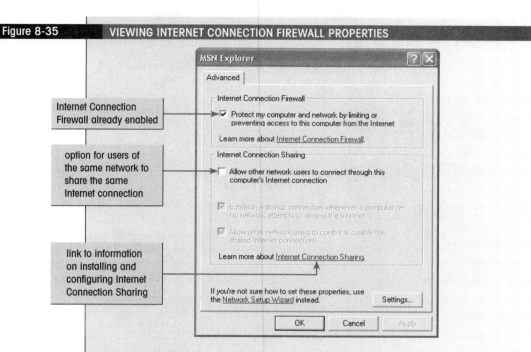

Internet Connection Firewall already enabled

option for users of the same network to share the same Internet connection

link to information on installing and configuring Internet Connection Sharing

3. If you want to enable Internet Connection Firewall, click the **Protect my computer and network** check box under Internet Connection Firewall (to add a check mark). If you choose to turn off this option (by removing the check mark), your computer is not protected and intruders can gain access to your computer.

4. Click the **Settings** button, and then click the **Security Logging** tab in the Advanced Settings dialog box. From this property sheet, you can enable the logging of actions performed by Internet Connection Firewall in a log file name Pfirewall.log in the Windows folder. See Figure 8-36. If you choose to log dropped packets (for inbound communications) and log successful connections (for outbound communications), Internet Connection Firewall records all unsuccessful and successful connections that originate from the Internet or your private network.

Figure 8-36   SETTING ICF LOGGING OPTIONS

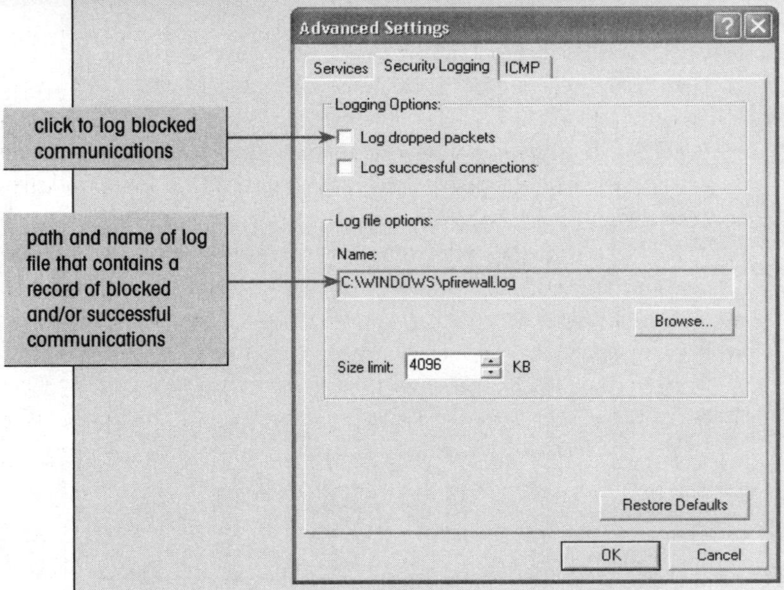

click to log blocked communications

path and name of log file that contains a record of blocked and/or successful communications

Advanced Settings

Services   Security Logging   ICMP

Logging Options:

☐ Log dropped packets

☐ Log successful connections

Log file options:

Name:

C:\WINDOWS\pfirewall.log

Browse...

Size limit: 4096 KB

Restore Defaults

OK   Cancel

5. If you want to enable logging options, click the **Log dropped packets** check box (to add a check mark) and the **Log successful connections** check mark (also adding a check mark). If the Pfirewall.log exceeds its maximum allowable size, the information in this log file is written to a new file named pfirewall.log.1 so that you have an ongoing record of unsuccessful and successful connections.

6. Click the **OK** button to close the Advanced Settings dialog box, click the **OK** button to close the dialog box for your Internet connection, and then close the Network Connections window.

On the Services property sheet in the Advanced Settings dialog box, you can select the services on your network that Internet users can access. For example, if you want someone to connect to your computer via the Internet and help you with your computer using Remote Desktop (covered in Tutorial 9), you would enable access to this service on your computer.

REFERENCE WINDOW   **RW**

Enabling Internet Connection Firewall

- Log on under an account with Administrator privileges.
- From the Start menu, click Control Panel, click the "Switch to Category view" link in the Control Panel dynamic menu if you are using Classic View, click Network and Internet Connections in the Control Panel window, click Network Connections, and after the Network Connections window opens, right-click your dial-up connection (such as MSN Explorer) or local area connection you want to protect, click Properties on the shortcut menu, and then click the Advanced tab.
- If you want to enable Internet Connection Firewall, click the "Protect my computer and network" check box under Internet Connection Firewall (add a check mark) on the Advanced property sheet.
- Click the Settings button, and then click the Security Logging tab in the Advanced Settings dialog box.
- If you want to enable the logging options, click the "Log dropped packets" check box (add a check mark) and the "Log successful connections" check box (also adding a check mark).
- Click OK to close the Advanced Settings dialog box, click OK to close the dialog box for your Internet connection, and then close the Network Connections window.

To protect the security of your computer system and to protect your private records, consider using firewall software to prevent unauthorized access to your computer system. You can combine the use of Internet Connection Firewall with another firewall software product that also monitors outbound communications to increase the protection of your system.

Internet Security and Privacy

In addition to protecting your computer system from intruders and hackers with the use of Internet Connection Firewall or another type of firewall, you face other security and privacy issues when working online. In Tutorial 1, you examined the concept and use of cookies that store information about your visits to a Web site. If you open the Cookies folder for your user account, open each cookie in Notepad, locate the URL for the Web site that placed the cookie on your computer, and then visit the Web site for each cookie, you might easily discover that half of the Web sites for which you have cookies are ones that you have never visited. However, a cookie from that Web site was still placed on your computer system. How does this happen? Besides using cookies, a Web site you visit may also use Web bugs.

Cookies, Web Bugs, and Online Profiling

A **Web bug**, also called a **clear GIF** or **Web beacon**, consists of an HTML tag on a Web page that you visit. The HTML tag contains the address of another Web site that supplies an image or banner advertising to the Web site that you visit. Following is a simple example of the HTML tag for a Web bug that provides an image:

    <img src="http://www.webbugsite.com" width=1 height=1 border=0>

The SRC attribute identifies the address of the Web site providing the image. (Webbugsite.com is not a real Web site.) The Width and Height attributes define the width and height of the image in pixels. The Border attribute determines the width of the border in pixels.

If an image is derived from another Web site, the Web bug is invisible on the Web page you visit because the image is one pixel wide by one pixel tall (called a **pixel tag**). By deriving content (the image or banner advertising) from another Web site, the other Web site can then place a cookie on your computer system even if you do not visit that Web site. In addition to knowing which Web site you visited and when you visited that site, the Web site referenced by the Web bug can also retrieve your IP address, identify your Web browser version and operating system, and associate the Web bug with a cookie on your computer.

Web bugs are commonly used to gather information such as statistics on the amount of traffic to a particular Web site and Web page at a specific Web site, and are also used to place cookies from another Web site on your computer. Along with cookies, Web bugs can provide online marketing firms with profiles of a user's personal interests, and that information can be used to deliver custom banner advertising. If you are part of an online community, and if you use their Web tools for designing a personal Web page at their Web site, those tools might already contain one or more Web bugs, and unknown to you, the Web bugs then become part of your personal Web page.

Web bugs can also be placed in e-mail messages, e-mail attachments, or documents that support HTML (such as Microsoft Word, Microsoft Excel, and Microsoft PowerPoint), as well as in HTML messages posted in newsgroups. A Web bug in an e-mail message can determine when and if an e-mail message (including junk mail) was read, follow an e-mail message from person to person in a company, and associate a cookie with a user's e-mail address. When placed in a document, a Web bug can be used to identify copyright infringements when someone copies a portion of the document to another file.

A high-tech company that specializes in Web security demonstrated the power of Web bugs before a Congressional panel in March 2001. In this demonstration, a Web bug on a Web page retrieved all 1,800 e-mail addresses from an address book, as well as a personal document, from a computer that accessed the company's Web site. The company that prepared this demonstration discovered that a Web bug could be used to retrieve all files from a computer, or retrieve selected personal files, and also place hidden files on a computer.

Like cookies, Web bugs are just another tool for **online profiling**, a process for identifying and accumulating information on users' preferences and interests. Firewalls and antivirus software do not protect your computer from Web bugs, and software designed to control cookies does not necessarily protect you from Web bugs. As you will see in the next section, Internet Explorer 6.0 allows you to specify security and privacy settings, as well as control cookie usage, but it does not protect your computer from Web bugs. You might want to consider a software product such as Web Washer (at *www.webwasher.com*) that not only filters cookies and Web bugs, but also provides a whole host of other features, such as controlling the display of banner advertising and pop-up windows.

Checking Web Browser Security and Privacy Settings

If you use the Microsoft Internet Explorer Web browser (or any other Web browser), you should examine its security settings and privacy options, and make sure it is properly configured for your needs. For example, you can view and specify security settings for Internet sites, Local intranet sites, Trusted sites, and Restricted sites. **Trusted sites** are Web sites that you trust not to damage your computer or its data. **Restricted sites** are Web sites that could potentially damage your computer or its data. **Local intranet sites** are Web sites that are part of your company's or organization's intranet. An **intranet** is a private network that relies on the use of Internet technologies and **protocols** (the rules and conventions for transmitting data over a network), and that is limited to a specific group of people, such as employees within a company. **Internet sites** are all Web sites that you have not placed in one of the other zones.

You can also set the security level for a Web content zone. If the security level is set at Medium (the default setting), Internet Explorer blocks cookies from third-party Web sites that do not have a **compact policy** (a privacy statement that you can read); it blocks cookies from third-party Web sites that use personally identifiable information (such as your name and e-mail address) without your implicit consent; and it deletes cookies from first-party Web sites that use personally identifiable information without your implicit consent after you close Internet Explorer. A **first-party Web site** is the Web page you are currently viewing, whereas a **third-party Web site** is another Web site that provides content to the Web site you're visiting.

You can also specify whether you want to accept **per-session cookies**—temporary cookies that expire and are deleted when you close Internet Explorer. In contrast, a **persistent cookie** is one that remains on your computer and that can be read by the Web site that created it when you next visit that Web site.

To protect the security of employees' computers and the privacy of company information, Lenore and her staff configure Internet Explorer on each computer, and work with employees on an ongoing basis to make sure their security and privacy settings meet their needs and the company's needs. Lenore asks you to examine and configure Internet Explorer settings on your computer.

To examine Internet Explorer settings:

1. Right-click the **Internet Explorer** desktop icon, and then click **Properties** on the shortcut menu, or open the Start menu, right-click the **Internet Explorer** icon in the pinned items list, and click **Internet Properties** on the shortcut menu, or open **Internet Explorer**, click **Tools** on the menu bar, and then click **Internet Options**. On the General property sheet of the Internet Properties dialog box, you can specify your home page, and specify settings for the Temporary Internet Files and History folders. See Figure 8-37. Under Temporary Internet files, you can delete the cookies or the files in this folder. The Delete Files button removes all files except for cookies. The Delete Cookies button is new to Internet Explorer 6.0. Using these buttons, you can empty the Temporary Internet Files folder (you can also use the Disk Cleanup Wizard covered in Tutorial 7). Likewise, you can use the Clear History button to remove shortcuts to previously visited Web sites from the History folder.

| Figure 8-37 | VIEWING GENERAL INTERNET EXPLORER SETTINGS |

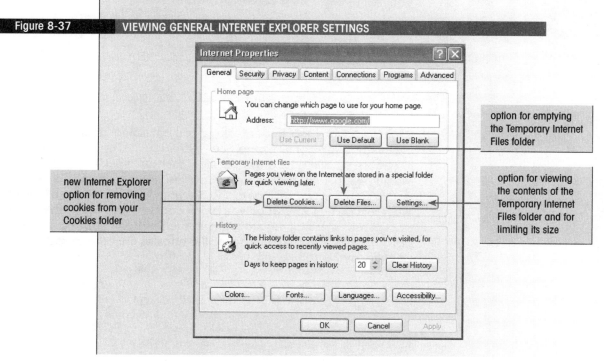

new Internet Explorer option for removing cookies from your Cookies folder

option for emptying the Temporary Internet Files folder

option for viewing the contents of the Temporary Internet Files folder and for limiting its size

The Settings button under Temporary Internet files allows you to set the amount of disk space to use for the Temporary Internet Files folder, view the contents of the Temporary Internet Files folder and Downloaded Program Files folder, and determine how (and if) Internet Explorer updates cached Web pages when you visit the same Web site again.

2. Click the **Security** tab. You can view and specify security settings for Internet sites, Local intranet sites, Trusted sites, and Restricted sites. See Figure 8-38. The "Security level for this zone" shows the security level for the Web content zone selected at the top of the property sheet. The default setting for Internet sites is Medium, but you can change that setting to High, Medium-Low, or Low by using the Custom Level button. If you select the Custom Level button, you can also customize each security setting for a Web content zone.

Figure 8-38	VIEWING INTERNET EXPLORER SECURITY SETTINGS

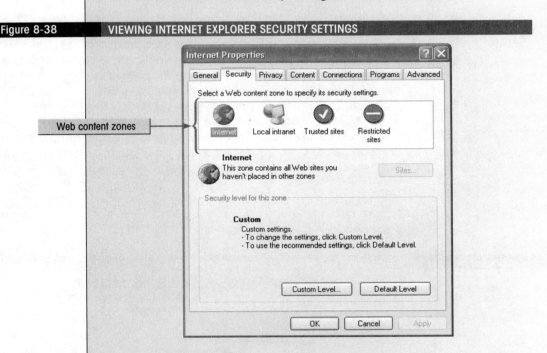

3. Click the **Privacy** tab. Under Settings, you can select a privacy setting for the Internet Web content zone. See Figure 8-39. You can drag the slider bar to choose an alternate privacy setting, such as "Block All Cookies," "High, Medium-High, Low," or "Accept All Cookies." You might want to examine and test different privacy settings to find out what works best for the types of Web sites that you typically visit. If you block cookies, you might not be able to access Web sites that require cookies, such as Hotmail. If you change these privacy settings, you should delete the cookies currently stored in your Cookies folder.

Figure 8-39   **VIEWING INTERNET EXPLORER PRIVACY SETTINGS**

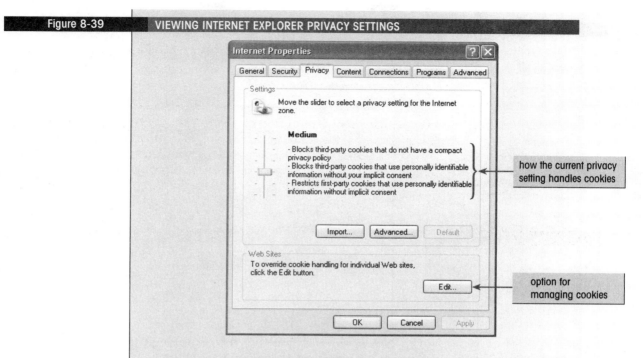

how the current privacy setting handles cookies

option for managing cookies

4. Click the **Advanced** button. In the Advanced Privacy Settings dialog box, you can override automatic cookie handling by Internet Explorer, and specify whether you want to accept or block first-party and third-party cookies, or whether you want to be prompted. See Figure 8-40. In the latter case, you can choose to accept, or reject, a cookie.

Figure 8-40   **EXAMINING OPTIONS FOR HANDLING COOKIES**

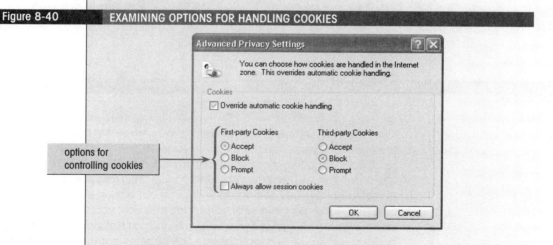

options for controlling cookies

5. If you want to save changes to cookie settings, click the **OK** button, otherwise click the **Cancel** button.

6. Click the **Edit** button on the Privacy property sheet. In the Per Site Privacy Actions dialog box, you can further customize the handling of cookies by identifying the Web sites from which you do accept and do not accept cookies. See Figure 8-41.

Figure 8-41   OPTIONS FOR BLOCKING OR ALLOWING COOKIES FROM WEB SITES

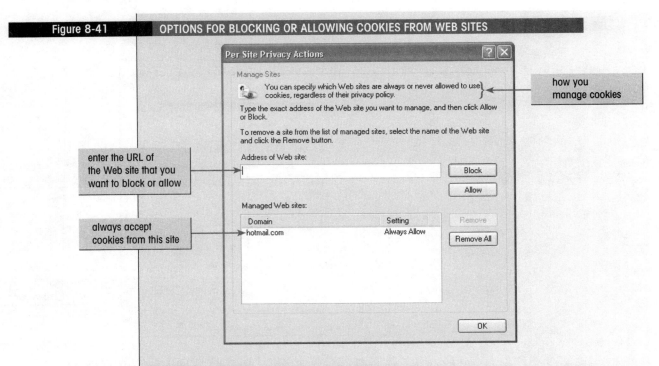

enter the URL of
the Web site that you
want to block or allow

always accept
cookies from this site

how you
manage cookies

7. Close the Per Site Privacy Actions dialog box, and then click the **Advanced** tab in the Internet Properties dialog box. The Settings box on the Advanced property sheet contains many settings that you should examine to determine whether they meet your needs. See Figure 8-42. For example, under Security (the last category), some options warn you if information you enter on a Web-based form is being transmitted to another Web site, and others warn you if you access a Web site that is secure when performing an online transaction, for example. You can use the Help button ? to display Help information on a specific setting.

Figure 8-42   VIEWING ADVANCED INTERNET EXPLORER SETTINGS

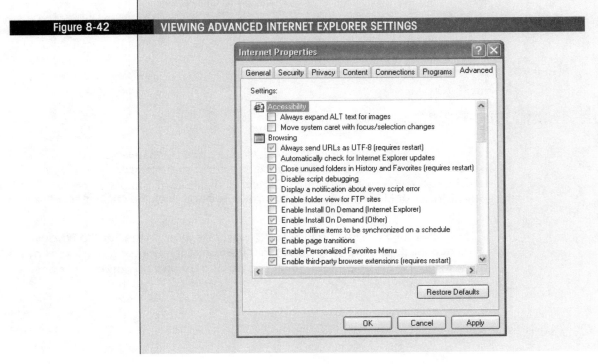

8. Close the Internet Properties dialog box.

REFERENCE WINDOW	RW

<u>Checking and Changing Internet Explorer Properties and Settings</u>

- Right-click the Internet Explorer desktop icon, and then click Properties on the shortcut menu, or open the Start menu, right-click the Internet Explorer icon in the pinned items list, and click Internet Properties on the shortcut menu, or open Internet Explorer, click Tools on the menu bar, and then click Internet Options.
- Use the General property sheet to specify your home page, specify settings for the Temporary Internet Files and History folders, delete cookies, delete the contents of the Temporary Internet Files folder, and clear the contents of the History folder. Use the Settings button under Temporary Internet files to set the amount of disk space to use for the Temporary Internet Files folder, view the contents of the Temporary Internet Files folder and Downloaded Program Files folder, and determine how (and if) Internet Explorer updates cached Web pages when you visit the same Web site again.
- Use the Security property sheet to view and specify security settings for Internet sites, Local intranet sites, Trusted sites, and Restricted sites. Use the Custom Level button on the Security property sheet to change the security level and individual security settings.
- Use the Privacy property sheet to select a privacy setting for an Internet Web content zone. Use the Advanced button to display the Advanced Privacy Settings dialog box, to override automatic cookie handling by Internet Explorer, and to specify whether you want to accept or block first-party and third-party cookies, or whether you want to be prompted. Use the Edit button on the Privacy property sheet to identify the Web sites from which you accept and do not accept cookies.
- Use the Advanced property sheet to view and change a wide variety of Internet Explorer settings, including security settings.
- Close the Internet Properties dialog box, and save your changes.

The privacy controls on the Privacy property sheet are new to Internet Explorer 6.0, and emphasize the increasing importance attached to security and privacy when working online. As noted earlier, it is a good idea to examine the settings on the different property sheets for Internet Explorer, or whatever browser you use, and make sure your Web browser is set up the way you prefer, rather than to rely on the default settings built into the Web browser.

Safe **Computing Guidelines**

Lenore recently developed and distributed a set of safe computing guidelines for the staff at Grenfeld Publishing. In her cover memo, she asked staff members to not only review the guidelines, but also to evaluate how they currently use their computer systems, so that they can effectively implement whatever safeguards they use.

Following are the safe computing guidelines that Lenore developed:

- **Document CMOS settings**. Print a copy of your original CMOS settings, and keep a record of changes that you make to CMOS settings. If you change CMOS settings, and then discover that you need to restore those settings to their previous values, you can use your records to restore the original settings. As noted earlier, you can also locate and download a DOS utility for backing up the contents of CMOS to a boot disk so that, should the need arise, you can restore CMOS settings using a utility on that boot disk.

- **Change the boot sequence in CMOS**. If your computer is set to boot from drive A first, change the boot order so that it boots from drive C first and bypasses drive A. If you accidentally leave a disk with a boot sector virus or a multipartite virus in drive A, that virus cannot gain access to your computer. A **boot sector virus** is one that infects the boot sector of a disk by replacing the boot record, or by moving the original boot record to another location on the disk and then overwriting the boot sector. If your computer attempts to boot from a disk in drive A, and if the disk contains a boot sector virus, the virus is loaded into memory after the boot sector is read, and the virus can then immediately infect the boot sector on drive C. If the boot sector virus moved the original boot record to another location on the disk, it redirects the ROM-BIOS routine to that copy of the boot record so that you are not aware of any problem. The infection occurs even if you see the "Invalid system disk," or "Non-system disk or error" message. A **multipartite virus** is one that can infect both the boot sector of a disk as well as program files, increasing its likelihood of being spread from one computer system to another.

- **Do not leave a floppy disk in drive A**. For the reasons mentioned in the last bullet, develop the habit of checking and removing floppy disks from drive A. As you work on different computers, which might be set to boot in different ways, this habit reduces the chances of infecting the hard disk with a boot sector virus or multipartite virus from a floppy disk.

- **Enable write-protection for the hard disk's boot sector**. On some computers, you can enable write-protection of the boot sector for the hard disk drive. Figure 8-43 shows the Boot Options screen in CMOS on a Pentium II MMX. Note that virus protection for the boot sector is enabled. This feature prevents any attempts to write to the Master Boot Record (MBR) on the hard disk. Recall that the Master Boot Record is the first sector on a hard disk, and it contains a Hard Disk Partition Table that contains a list of each of the partitions on the disk and their sizes. The MBR also contains a program that reads the boot sector of the partition that contains the operating system, so that your computer can boot from that partition. If a program attempts to write to the Master Boot Record, a message appears asking to verify that you want to allow this operation. This feature, while it does protect the Master Boot Record from a virus infection, also prevents other programs, such as the operating system, from writing to the MBR.

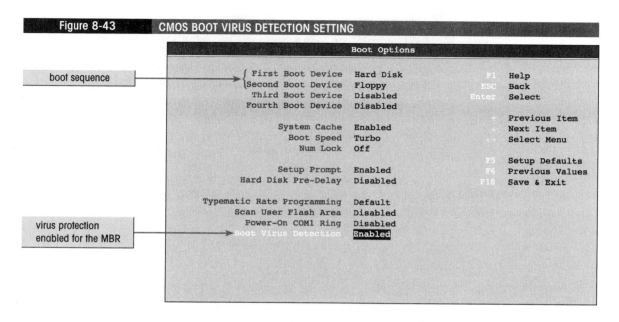

Figure 8-43 CMOS BOOT VIRUS DETECTION SETTING

- **Make and test an MS-DOS Startup Disk**. Prepare and test an MS-DOS Startup Disk in case you need to boot your computer from drive A to troubleshoot a FAT volume or rebuild your computer system. You should also add other utilities, such as the FDisk utility (Fdisk.exe) and Format utility (Format.com) for partitioning and formatting your hard disk from this boot disk in case you need to rebuild your computer. You might also need to configure the boot disk to provide you with access to the CD drive so you can reinstall Windows. Then write-protect this disk.

- **Create Windows XP Setup Disks**. If you are working on an older computer that does not support booting from a CD drive, create a set of Windows XP Setup Disks so that you can boot your computer from drive A and reinstall Windows XP or attempt to repair your system with the Recovery Console (covered in Tutorial 9).

- **Document hardware settings.** You can use Device Manager (covered in Tutorial 12) to print a full system summary of hardware configuration settings. Device Manager is a Windows XP component that contains information on the hardware configuration of your computer and is commonly used to identify and troubleshoot hardware problems.

- **Enable System Restore**. Enable System Restore for all your drives, and check System Restore settings so that you can use restore points to roll back your computer to an earlier functioning state if you encounter a problem.

- **Create manual restore points**. Before making a change to your computer that might affect its performance or integrity, such as changing the Registry or installing programs that do not use InstallShield or Windows Installer, manually create a restore point so that you can roll your computer back to the state it was in before you made the changes.

- **Encrypt important folders and files (Windows XP Professional only)**. Consider encrypting important document folders and files on your computer to prevent unauthorized access to those folders and files.

- **Back up your computer**. Organize all your important files in the My Documents folder so that nothing important is inadvertently left out when you back up your computer. Develop a backup strategy that works for you, and then follow that strategy and regularly back up important document files. Keep several generations of backups so that if you find that files in your most recent backup are infected with a computer virus, you can check the previous backup and, if necessary, the one before that and restore an uninfected version of a file or program.

- **Use Automated System Recovery (Windows XP Professional only)**. Back up your computer's system state and system files with the Automated System Recovery Wizard. If you experience a system failure, and are unable to restore your computer using other tools and features available in Windows XP Professional, you can use the Automated System Recovery Wizard to restore your system.

- **Use Internet Connection Firewall**. If you are working on a computer with a dial-up, cable modem, ISDN, or DSL connection, enable Internet Connection Firewall and check its settings so that you can protect your computer from intruders and hackers. If you prefer, you can download and install a firewall software product that monitors both outgoing and incoming communications and that offers additional features.

- **Check and adjust Web browser security settings**. Set the security level for different Web content zones, and check and change more advanced security settings, if necessary.

- **Check and adjust Web browser privacy settings**. Verify that your Web browser uses a privacy setting to verify a Web site's privacy policy, and that it protects you from potential harmful cookies that use personally identifiable information on your computer.

- **Download and install Web browser security upgrades**. No sooner does the company that makes your Web browser release a new version than someone has found and exploited a vulnerability in the software.

- **Conduct online transactions and purchases in secure mode**. If you are purchasing goods online, or if you are transmitting personal information, make sure your browser switches to Secure mode first; otherwise, think twice about completing the purchase or transaction.

- **Download files only from trusted sites**. If you are unfamiliar with a Web site, you should be cautious in downloading and opening files from that site. If you download files, save them to disk first, and then use your antivirus software to scan them before you open them.

- **Use caution in opening e-mail messages and e-mail attachments**. If you receive an e-mail message from someone you do not know, from e-mail addresses you do not recognize, or from an unfamiliar Web site, delete the e-mail message without opening it. Likewise, be cautious when opening e-mail attachments. Before you open an e-mail attachment, right-click the attachment and save it to disk. Then, scan the e-mail attachment with your antivirus software to make sure it is safe to open.

- **Use third-party software for filtering Web bugs and cookies**. Consider the use of other software, such as Web Washer, to protect your computer from Web bugs and cookies.

■ **Use antivirus software**. Purchase, install, and use one or more antivirus software products. Each antivirus software product detects and removes different types of viruses, so you might need to use more than one product. Periodically scan your computer. Use your antivirus software to scan all floppy disks, removable disks, and even CDs that are given or sent to you as well as Word documents and programs that you download from the Internet, e-mail attachments, compressed files, and preformatted disks. Because more computer viruses spread via e-mail attachments, you should save an e-mail attachment and use your antivirus software to scan that individual file for viruses before you open it. You might also want to set your antivirus software to scan e-mail messages and e-mail attachments.

■ **Download frequent updates to virus definitions**. Because new computer viruses appear daily, you should set up a regular schedule for downloading updates for your antivirus software. You might also need to download updates to the software itself, especially if the software employs new technologies for detecting computer viruses.

■ **Do not share floppy disks**. You can reduce your chances of a computer virus infection by not sharing floppy disks. If you do share floppy disks, scan each floppy disk with your antivirus software before you use the files on the disk and before you copy those files to your hard disk drive. Also, before you give a floppy disk to another person, scan the floppy disk for viruses.

■ **Do not use utilities designed for previous versions of Windows or for DOS**. These utilities might be designed for a different file system than the one used on your computer and, in some cases, they might damage folders and files with long filenames. For example, MS-DOS uses a Check Disk, ScanDisk, and Disk Defragmenter utility different from the ones found in the Windows 9.x and Windows NT product lines, and these utilities do not support long filenames.

■ **Carefully select and periodically change passwords**. You use passwords not only to gain access to your computer system via your user logon, but also to connect to your ISP and e-mail server as well as Web sites. Select passwords that are difficult to guess and that contain not only letters of the alphabet, but that also use a mix of uppercase and lowercase characters and contain numbers and symbols. Periodically change those passwords.

■ **Create a password reset disk** (covered in Tutorial 1). If you use a password that is difficult to remember, you should create a password reset disk so that you can create a new password for your account if you forget your current password. If you change the password for your account, create a new password reset disk.

■ **Develop a disaster recovery plan for your computer**. First, open the BIOS Setup utility and find out if the BIOS contains an option for booting your computer from your CD drive. If not, prepare Windows Setup Disks for either Windows XP Professional or Windows XP Home Edition so that you can use them with your Windows XP CD to reinstall windows or repair your computer. Periodically refresh the magnetic fields on these disks by repeating the process for making Setup Disks. You may also want to keep more than just one copy of these disks. If you have Windows XP Professional, use the Automated Recovery Wizard to back up your system volume. Also back up your document files, e-mail address book, and e-mail folders and messages separately. Keep a record of registration numbers for software products that you download and install on your computer.

Depending on the configuration and setup of your computer, the types of disks that you use, and the way you work, you should consider which guidelines you can implement to protect the integrity of your computer system or network. In later tutorials, you will learn about other features which you can add to your list of safe computing guidelines.

Restoring Your Computer

If you want to restore your computer to its original state before you started the tutorial, complete the following steps.

To restore your computer:

1. If your computer is turned off, power on your computer. If you are already logged on your computer, close all open applications and windows, click the **Start** button, click **Turn off computer** or **Shut Down**, select **Restart** in the Turn off computer or Shut Down Windows dialog box, and then click the **OK** button if necessary; or from the Start menu, click **Log Off**, click **Log Off** in the Log Off Windows dialog box, and at the Welcome screen, click **Turn off Windows XP System**, and in the Turn off computer dialog box, click the **Restart** button.

2. During booting or rebooting, watch the monitor for information on which key(s) to press, and then press the key or keys for opening the Setup utility. For example, you might see the message, "Press F2 to enter Setup."

3. If you changed the boot order, use the documentation you printed or recorded by hand to restore the original boot sequence using the Setup utility. If necessary, ask your instructor or technical support staff person for assistance.

4. Save your changes and exit the Setup utility. If necessary, ask your instructor or technical support staff person for assistance.

Now you are ready to restore your display settings.

To restore your computer's display settings:

1. If your computer was originally set for the Windows Classic style, right-click the **desktop**, click **Properties** on the shortcut menu, and after Windows XP opens the Display Properties dialog box, click the **Theme** list arrow on the Themes property sheet, click **Windows Classic**, and then click the **OK** button.

2. To switch to the Windows Classic Start menu style, right-click the **Start** button, click **Properties** on the shortcut menu, and after Windows XP opens the Taskbar and Start Menu Properties dialog box, click the **Classic Start menu** option button on the Start Menu property sheet, and then click the **OK** button.

3. To change Windows classic folders view, click the **Start** button, point to **Settings**, click **Control Panel**, and after Windows XP opens a Control Panel window, click **Tools** on the menu bar, click **Folder Options**, and after Windows XP opens the Folder Options dialog box, click the **Use Windows classic folders** option button, and then click the **Double-click to open an item** option button.

4. Click the **View** tab in the Folder Options dialog box. If necessary, restore the original settings for the "Display the full path in the address bar" check box, the "Do not show hidden files and folders" option button, and the "Hide extensions for known file types" check box.

5. Click the **OK** button to close the Folder Options dialog box and restore your original settings, and then close the Control Panel folder window.

By implementing the use of new Windows XP features, such as System Restore, Automated System Recovery, and Internet Connection Firewall, by preparing an MS-DOS startup disk and Windows XP Setup Disks, by properly configuring their Web browsers and specifying privacy settings, and by implementing safe computing guidelines, Lenore and the other employees at Grenfeld Publishing can reduce the chances of serious computer problems. If problems do occur, they have the tools they need to repair, restore, or rebuild their computers.

REVIEW ASSIGNMENTS

Lenore asks you to check the boot sequence on her new intern's computer, prepare and test an MS-DOS startup disk, customize and set up his computer system, check Internet Connection Firewall settings, check Internet Explorer security and privacy settings, and then use System Restore to create a restore point.

If you are working in a computer lab and if the lab restricts access to the BIOS settings stored in CMOS, you might not be able to complete all the steps.

As you complete each step in the Review Assignments, record your answers to questions so that you can submit them to your instructor. Use a word-processing application such as Word or WordPad to prepare and then print your answers to these questions. Also, if you change any settings on the computer you are using, note the original settings so that you can restore them later.

1. Insert a blank, formatted floppy disk in drive A, if necessary.

2. Open My Computer, right-click the 3½ Floppy (A:) disk drive icon, click Format, click the "Create an MS-DOS Startup disk" check box, click the Start button, click the OK button in the Format 3½ Floppy (A:) dialog box to confirm that you want to format the disk, and after the format is complete, click the OK button to close each of the Formatting 3½ Floppy (A:) dialog boxes.

3. Right-click the 3½ Floppy (A:) disk drive icon, and then click Properties on the shortcut menu. Enter "MS-DOS DISK" (without the quotation marks) in the Volume label box. How much storage space is used on the disk, and how much storage space is available? How might you use the additional available storage space? Close the 3½ Floppy (A:) Properties dialog box.

4. Point to and select each icon for the drives on your hard disk (you may only have one), identify which file system is used on each drive, and then close My Computer. Can you use the MS-DOS startup disk with the drives on your hard disk? Explain.

5. From the Start menu, point to All Programs, point to Accessories, and then click Command Prompt.

6. In the Command Prompt window, type CHKDSK A: /F /R and then press the Enter key. *Note*: Recall that the Fix switch (/F) repairs file system problems, and the Repair switch (/R) identifies bad sectors and attempts to recover data from bad sectors. Is your MS-DOS startup disk free of errors? Why is this important to check? Close the Command Prompt window.

7. Restart your computer, and if necessary, open the Setup utility during booting and change the boot sequence so that your computer boots from the MS-DOS startup disk in drive A. What key(s) did you press to open Setup and access the CMOS settings on your computer? After checking and changing the boot sequence (if necessary), exit CMOS, save your changes, and resume booting.

8. At the command prompt, type VER and press the Enter key. What version of Windows booted your computer from the MS-DOS startup disk? What type of user interface are you now using?

Explore 9. Type CLS and press the Enter key. What happens?

10. Type DIR and press the Enter key. How many files are on the MS-DOS startup disk, and how much storage space do they require? How do the filenames on the MS-DOS startup disk differ from the typical type of filenames you work with on a daily basis?

Explore 11. Type CLS, type DIR /A and then press the Enter key. How many files are on the MS-DOS startup disk, and how much storage space do they require? What is the difference between the command that you entered in the previous step and the command that you entered in this step? Why would using the Attribute switch be important if you were troubleshooting your computer?

12. Remove the MS-DOS startup disk, press the Reset button on the front of the system unit, or press the Ctrl+Alt+Del keys. What happens?

13. If your computer does not contain an option for booting from a CD drive, and if you experienced a problem that required you to restart your computer from a floppy disk in drive A and reinstall Windows XP, what type of disks would you need to complete the reinstall?

14. Log on your computer under an account with Administrator privileges.

15. From the Start menu, point to Connect To, and then click "Show all connections." What happens?

16. Right-click the dial-up connection for your ISP account or, if you do not have a dial-up connection, right-click your Local Area Connection (or other type of LAN or High-Speed Internet connection), click Properties on the shortcut menu, and then click the Advanced tab (if necessary). Is Internet Connection Firewall enabled on your computer? Why or why not?

17. Click the Settings button on the Advanced property sheet for your dial-up connection, and then click the Security Logging tab. If you want to adjust Internet Connection Firewall settings so that it creates a record of connections that it blocked, what changes would you make on this property sheet? Which file does Internet Connection Firewall use to store this information, and what folder is it contained in? Close the Advanced Settings dialog box.

18. Can you use Internet Connection Sharing on your computer, and what advantages does it offer? Explain. *Note*: If you want more information on Internet Connection Sharing, click the Internet Connection Sharing link on the Advanced property sheet, or open the Help and Support Center.

19. Close the dialog box for your dial-up connection, Local Area Connection, or other type of connection, and then close the Network Connections window.

Explore   20. Right-click the Internet Explorer desktop icon, click Properties on the shortcut menu, (or open Internet Explorer, click Tools on the menu bar, and then click Internet Options) and then click the Settings button under Temporary Internet Files on the General property sheet of the Internet Properties dialog box. How is Internet Explorer set up on your computer to check for newer versions of stored Web pages? How much disk space is set aside for the Temporary Internet Files folder on your computer? What is the path to the Temporary Internet Files folder for your user logon? What advantage might there be to moving this folder to another drive on a computer? Close the Settings dialog box.

Explore   21. Click the Security tab, select Internet under Web content zone (if it is not already selected), and then click the Custom Level button. What is the security level set at on your computer for the Internet Web content zone? How does this security setting affect your ability to download files? Close the Security Settings dialog box.

Explore   22. Click the Privacy tab. What privacy setting is used on your computer? How does this setting affect the use of cookies on your computer? Drag the slider bar to High (if it is not already set to High). How does the High security setting differ from the one that you use?

23. Click the Edit button under Web sites. How might you use the Per Site Privacy Actions option for managing Web sites that you frequently visit? Close the Per Site Privacy Actions dialog box, and then close the Internet Properties dialog box.

24. From the Start menu, click Help and Support, and under "Pick a task," click the "Undo changes to your computer with System Restore." What tasks can you perform with System Restore?

25. Click the "Create a restore point" option button, click Next, type RP followed by a space and your last name in the "Restore point description" text box, click the Create button, close the System Restore dialog box, and then close the Help and Support Center window.

26. How might you use the Automated System Recovery Wizard on a computer? What type of backup media would you use? How frequently would you use the Automated System Recovery Wizard? How might you integrate it in a backup strategy?

27. If you are working in a computer lab and changed the boot sequence in CMOS, or if you want to restore your computer's original boot sequence, restart your computer, open the Setup utility, restore the boot sequence, and then exit and save the changes that you made to CMOS.

CASE PROBLEMS

Case 1. Specifying CMOS Settings at EcoSystems, Inc. Jonathan Covington works as a microcomputer support specialist for a local environmental nonprofit company called EcoSystems, Inc. Because he just acquired a new work computer, he wants to examine its CMOS settings, and make sure that his computer is properly configured for his needs. He also wants to document the information stored in CMOS using a table he has prepared in Microsoft Word.

As you complete each step in this case, record your answers to questions so that you can submit them to your instructor. Use a word-processing application such as Word or WordPad to prepare and then print your answers to these questions. Also, if you change any settings on the computer you are using, note the original settings so that you can restore them later.

1. Reboot your computer, and open the CMOS Setup utility. What key(s) did you use to open Setup? How did you find this information?

2. What menus are available in your Setup utility?

3. Prepare a table similar to the one shown in Figure 8-44, and document CMOS settings for each of the options listed. If your Setup utility does not contain a specific type of setting, such as an option for a fifth boot drive, leave the second column blank.

Explore

4. *Optional*: If you want to use this exercise as an opportunity to more thoroughly document your computer, use other features of your computer or Windows XP tools to locate information that you did not find in CMOS. To distinguish that information from the information you found in CMOS, you can enclose it in square brackets, as follows: [Pentium 4]

5. After examining your current CMOS settings, are there any that you might change? If so, explain.

6. After you prepare a table documenting your CMOS settings, print a copy to submit with your assignment. Also, include answers to the questions in the case problem.

| Figure 8-44 | DOCUMENTING CMOS SETTINGS |

BIOS Manufacturer	
BIOS Version	
Processor Type	
Cache RAM	
CPU Speed	
Primary Master	
Cylinders	
Heads	
Sectors	
Primary Slave	
Secondary Master	
Secondary Slave	
Video Mode	
Installed Memory, System Memory, or Base Memory + Extended Memory	
Memory Bank 0	
Memory Bank 1	
Memory Bank 2	
Memory Bank 3	
Boot Sequence	
First Boot Drive	
Second Boot Drive	
Third Boot Drive	
Fourth Boot Drive	
Fifth Boot Drive	
Boot Virus Protection	

Case 2. *Preparing a Reference Table of Windows Tools at Computer Troubleshooters Unlimited*   Employees at Computer Troubleshooters Unlimited tackle a wide array of problems encountered by its corporate and home user customers. Miles Biehler, a specialist at rebuilding and repairing computer systems and at troubleshooting computer virus infections, works with customers either at their site or over the telephone to identify and resolve problems. He relies on the use of different types of boot disks, and Windows features, so that he can gain access to a computer and then repair, restore, or rebuild that computer. Because his customers work with different versions of Windows, he decides to prepare a reference tool for his assistants and interns.

Use a word-processing application such as Word or WordPad to prepare and then print your reference table. Also, if you change any settings on the computer you are using, note the original settings so that you can restore them later.

1. Using what you've learned in this tutorial, prepare a reference table similar to the one shown in Figure 8-45 that identifies which types of disks, tools, and features are available in the different versions of Windows. Use a check mark (√) to indicate that a feature is available in a particular version of Windows.

Explore

2. Following the table, prepare a list of concise footnotes that contain important information about the use of the different types of disks, tools, and features in different versions of Windows. When preparing the footnotes, consider the following questions:

   ■ What should a prospective user know about using a specific disk, tool, or feature?
   ■ If a type of disk is available in different versions of Windows, does the disk contain the same types of files or support different types of uses?
   ■ Is the same type of disk prepared in different ways in different versions of Windows?
   ■ Does a feature apply to only certain releases within a version of Windows?
   ■ Are there any other important distinctions between the use of different disks, tools, and features in different versions of Windows?

3. After you complete your reference table, print a copy to submit with your assignment.

| Figure 8-45 | WINDOWS TOOLS |

	Windows Versions						
	Win95	Win98	Me	NT 4.0	2000	XP Home	XP Pro
Generic or Basic Boot Disk							
Startup Disk							
Emergency Recovery Disk (ERD)							
Setup Disks							
Emergency Repair Disk (ERD)							
System Restore							
Automated System Recovery							
Internet Connection Firewall							
Internet Connection Sharing							
Internet Explorer Privacy Features							

Footnotes
1.
2.
3.
4.
5.
6.
7.
8.

Case 3. Analyzing Cookies at Centaur Graphics Marcee Zimmerman works as a Web design artist at Centaur Graphics. Recently, she discovered the Cookies folder on her computer, and was surprised at the number of cookies that different Web sites had placed on her computer. She wants to recommend to her supervisor that the company purchase software to control not only the use of cookies, but also Web bugs. To present a strong case for purchasing this type of software, she decides to analyze and document cookie usage on her computer.

To complete this case, you must work on a computer that contains cookies in the Cookies folder for your user account.

As you complete each step in this case, record your answers to questions so that you can submit them to your instructor. Use a word-processing application such as Word or WordPad to prepare and then print your answers to these questions. Also, if you change any settings on the computer you are using, note the original settings so that you can restore them later.

1. Open My Computer, open the Documents and Settings folder, open the folder for your user account, and then open the Cookies folder.

2. Change your view of this folder to List view. How many cookies are contained in this folder?

Explore

3. Select 10-15 cookies for Web sites that you do not recognize (enough to have a representative sample), open each of the cookies in Notepad, and using the table format shown in Figure 8-46, list the name of each cookie and the URL of the Web site that put the cookie on your computer.

Explore

4. Visit each of the Web sites, and use the About, About Us, or Company Info link to identify the nature of the company (if it's not already obvious), and list that in your table. Figure 8-46 lists one site Lenore visited as an example of the type of information you record in the table. In some cases, you might be redirected to another site; if so, type an equal sign after the URL and then list the URL of the site to which you were redirected. Some sites might be down for maintenance; in other cases, you might not be able to find the site of the company that placed the cookie on your computer. A search engine might help in this case. Also realize that as you visit these Web sites, they will place one or more additional cookies on your computer.

5. After you compile your table, examine the types of Web sites. Is there a common thread? In other words, do these Web sites offer similar types of services?

6. Have you ever visited these Web sites before you compiled this table? If not, how did the cookies get on your computer system?

7. Print a copy of this table to submit to your instructor. Also, include answers to the questions in the case problem.

Figure 8-46   **ANALYZING COOKIES**

	Cookie Name	URL	Type of Web Site
1	lenore@doubleclick[1].txt	doubleclick.net	Online, e-mail, and direct marketing service
2			
3			
4			
5			
6			
7			
8			
9			
10			
11			
12			
13			
14			
15			

Case 4. Evaluating Firewall Software at International Investments, Inc. The investment officers at International Investments, Inc. (3I) frequently travel on company business and invariably work at home in the evenings and on the weekends on their own computers. Because these employees work on computers with different versions of Windows, Kim Davis, one of 3I's technical support staff, decides to analyze different firewall software products so that these employees can protect their home computers and laptops.

Hint: The Home PC Firewall Guide Web site (*http://firewallguide.com*) contains information on personal firewall, antivirus, antitrojan, and privacy software, and might be a good first site to check for this case problem.

Use a word-processing application such as Word or WordPad to prepare and then print a table that summarizes information about firewall software. Also, if you change any settings on the computer you are using, note the original settings so that you can restore them later.

Explore

1. Using resources on the Internet and your favorite search engine, locate information on at least three different firewall software products, and prepare a table that concisely summarizes the following information (using Figure 8-47 as an example):

   ■ Product name
   ■ Company that produces the software, and their URL
   ■ Major features of each product (consider features such as effectiveness at controlling incoming and outbound traffic, ease of installation and use, level of intruder detection, back traces to identify hackers, network use, and other features, such as how it handles mail)
   ■ Limitations of the product
   ■ Operating systems supported by the product
   ■ Intended audience (business, home user, small business, etc.)
   ■ Cost

2. After the table, list at least three references that you used to compile information on firewall software.

3. Print a copy of the table you prepared to submit with your lab assignment.

Figure 8-47	EVALUATING FIREWALL SOFTWARE PRODUCTS

Product		
Company		
URL		
Features		
Limitations		
Operating Systems		
Audience		
Cost		

References (for first product):
-
-
-

References (for second product):
-
-
-

References (for third product):
-
-
-

OBJECTIVES

In this tutorial you will:

- Develop a strategy for troubleshooting problems

- Examine Windows XP boot options

- Use the System Configuration Utility to control the loading of programs during booting

- Install and use the Recovery Console

- Shut down a program with Windows Task Manager

- Use Help and Support Center tools and the Printing Troubleshooter

- Use the System Information utility to examine information about your computer

- Search for information using Microsoft's Knowledge Base

- Examine the use of Remote Desktop and Remote Assistance

USING TROUBLESHOOTING TOOLS

Using Diagnostic Tools at Yellow Brick Road Child Care

CASE

Yellow Brick Road Child Care Services

Yellow Brick Road Child Care Services relies on income from tuition fees and grants, as well as funding from both private and public programs, to provide child care services for working parents with limited incomes. Recently, it received corporate donations of six state-of-the-art computers loaded with Windows XP, plus a high-quality laser printer, and various software applications. The administrative staff now uses these computers to produce a range of documents, including financial and program reports, grant applications, budgets, an annual report, and employee manuals.

You assist Deshi Chiu, the office manager, who works with five full-time and part-time staff members in the administrative offices. One of his job responsibilities is to provide technical computer support to other staff members. Yellow Brick Road also relies on a committed core of volunteers to provide expertise in different areas. Deshi often consults with Stephanie Williamson, a troubleshooting specialist who volunteers eight hours a month to assist with hardware and software problems. Stephanie has assisted Deshi and the other staff members in setting up a small office network, configuring and customizing their computers, installing software applications, and troubleshooting network and printer problems.

In the first section of this tutorial, you will examine strategies, preventive measures, and resources that you can use to troubleshoot problems on your computer. Then you will explore different options for booting your computer, including the use of Safe Mode. You will use the System Configuration Utility to explore other boot options and learn how to select which programs load during booting. You will install and use the Recovery Console, a command-line troubleshooting tool. You will use the System Information utility to examine information on your computer's configuration. You will also learn how to use Windows Task Manager to shut down unresponsive programs.

9.01

Developing a Troubleshooting Strategy

So that staff can resolve problems they encounter on their computers, Deshi asks Stephanie to present a morning workshop that provides an overview of how to troubleshoot a computer problem. At the beginning of her presentation, Stephanie emphasizes to employees that they can use the resources that come with the Windows XP operating system along with their prior experience with Windows 2000 and Windows 98. She suggests that they use the following techniques when they need to troubleshoot a problem:

- **Define the problem**. First, make sure you know the exact nature of the problem. For example, if a printer is not working properly, ask questions that provide you with the information you need to troubleshoot the problem. Can you print at all? If so, is there a problem with the quality of the printed document? Does Windows XP report any error messages? If so, do the messages provide clues for troubleshooting the problem? Is this the first time you've encountered this problem? When were you last able to print a document without any problems? Did you or anyone else change the configuration of the computer or printer?

- **Analyze the problem**. Next, analyze the problem by evaluating your responses to the questions you ask. For example, if you recently changed the configuration on your computer, such as installing a new printer driver, and find that you are then unable to print, could the problem be caused by that change in your computer's configuration? Or might some other type of error be causing the problem, such as a loose cable, a hardware problem, or a change in a software setting?

- **Devise ways to test the possible cause of the problem**. To provide you with more information about the nature of a problem, devise other tests that help you identify the cause of the problem. For example, if you cannot print a document created in Microsoft Word, open another application and try printing a document produced with that application. If you now can print, the problem is probably not with the printer, but with the print settings for the first application. If you cannot print in either application, try to print a test page using your printer and then Windows XP. If you can print these test pages, check the configuration of the printer.

- **Check hardware and software settings**. If any hardware or software settings have been changed, restore them to their original values. To restore these settings, you should periodically document the hardware and software settings on your computer, especially before you install new hardware or software or change their settings. As you will discover in Tutorial 12, you can use Device Manager to print a summary of the hardware settings on your computer.

- **Draw on all the resources you have to resolve the problem**. Check the Windows XP Help and Support Center, online support, and Help provided within applications. The Help information you examine might provide you with additional ideas and direction, or with access to special troubleshooting tools, such as System Restore. Check Readme files provided with software and hardware that you install on your computer. A **Readme** file is a text file (often named Readme.doc, Readme.txt, or Readme.1st) that contains more up-to-date information, including troubleshooting information, for newly installed hardware and software. In some cases, the group folder on the All Programs menu for the software product includes a shortcut to a Readme file. Check any reference manuals provided with your hardware or software. If the manufacturer of the product you purchased has a technical support line, call and talk to a technical support person about the problem. That person might know the answer immediately, or might be able to replicate the problem and then determine how to resolve it. Many companies provide assistance via their Web sites, publish answers to frequently asked questions (FAQs), and post updates, such as device drivers, that users can download. The Microsoft Help and Support Center and Knowledge Base (*support.microsoft.com*) is another valuable source for information on Windows XP, other versions of the Windows operating system, Internet Explorer, Office applications, and other software products.

■ **Consider other alternatives**. If you attempt to troubleshoot a problem and cannot resolve it, consider other possible causes. For example, if you cannot print a document that you printed a few days ago, a computer virus might have infected your computer. Have you used your antivirus software recently to check your computer? Have you downloaded updates for your antivirus software recently? Did you turn off and then forget to turn on your antivirus software? Have you tried another antivirus software package?

If your field of specialty is technical support and troubleshooting, you should develop a system for reporting problems that includes the following:

■ **A database of problems and solutions to those problems**. You can create a database of problems that users have already encountered or are likely to encounter, identify the operating systems and applications for each problem and solution, include specific steps for resolving each problem, and also include warnings. You could design the database for yourself and other technical support staff who need to quickly consult this resource, and you can prepare an online version of this database for users so that they can search for solutions and resolve common problems that do not require major changes to the configuration of a computer, such as modifying the Registry.

■ **Online form for reporting problems**. Rather than relying on recording information via the telephone, you can create an online form for reporting problems that gathers all of the necessary information, provides the detail you need, and standardizes the reporting process.

■ **Remote control of user's screen**. You might also want to use a software tool, such as Remote Assistance, NetMeeting, or Symantec's PC Anywhere to control the user's screen from a remote location, and troubleshoot the problem experienced by that user.

After Stephanie completes her presentation on troubleshooting strategies, you and Deshi meet and discuss some of the other important troubleshooting options and tools available in Windows XP.

Getting Started

To complete this tutorial, you need to switch your computer to Web style so that your screens match those shown in the figures, and you also need to turn on the options for showing all folders and files, and for displaying protected operating system files, file extensions, and the full path in the Address bar. As you complete these steps, you may discover that your computer is already set up for Web style, or that other settings are already in place, so you might only need to make a few changes to your computer's settings.

To set up your computer:

1. To change to the Windows XP theme, right-click the **desktop**, click **Properties** on the shortcut menu, and after Windows XP opens the Display Properties dialog box, click the **Theme** list arrow on the Themes property sheet, click **Windows XP**, if necessary, and then click the **OK** button.

2. To switch to the Windows XP Start menu style, right-click the **Start** button, click **Properties** on the shortcut menu, and after Windows XP opens the Taskbar and Start Menu Properties dialog box, click the **Start menu** option button on the Start Menu property sheet, if necessary, and then click the **OK** button.

3. To change to a task-oriented view of folders and enable single-clicking, click the **Start** button, click **My Computer**, click **Tools** on the menu bar, click **Folder Options**, and after Windows XP opens the Folder Options dialog box, click the **Show common tasks in folders** option button if it is not already selected, click the **Single-click to open an item** option button if it is not already selected, and click the **Underline icon titles only when I point at them** option button if it is not already selected.

4. Click the **View** tab, click the **Display the full path in the address bar** check box if it is not already selected, click the **Show hidden files and folders** option button if it is not already selected, and if there is a check mark in the **Hide extensions for known file types** check box, click that check box to remove the check mark.

5. Click the **Hide protected operating system files** check box, click the **Yes** button in the Warning dialog box to display protected operating system files, click the **OK** button to close the Folder Options dialog box, and then close My Computer.

Now you're ready to examine different types of boot options and the Recovery Console in case you experience problems starting Windows XP or problems booting from your hard disk.

The **Booting Process**

As you have already learned, when you turn on an Intel-based computer system, the processor locates and executes startup routines, or programs, stored in the Basic Input/Output System (BIOS) to identify and enable devices, perform a Power-On Self Test (POST), and then locate and load the operating system. The BIOS is especially important because its startup routines work no matter which operating system is installed on a computer.

The BIOS also contains instructions for communicating with hardware devices. If your computer has a Plug and Play BIOS, the first routine identifies, enables, and configures Plug and Play devices. If your computer has a legacy BIOS, the BIOS simply enables devices. As noted in Tutorial 1, Plug and Play refers to a set of specifications for new hardware that enable Windows XP to detect and configure hardware so that you can use it immediately after Windows XP has loaded. The term **legacy** refers to devices that do not support the Plug and Play standards defined by Microsoft in conjunction with other hardware manufacturers, and that invariably require you to manually configure the device by using jumpers or dip switches.

The POST checks for hardware errors, including memory errors. If you hear a single beep after the boot process, that signal means that the hardware components passed the POST. If the POST detects a problem or failure with a hardware component needed to boot the computer, your computer emits a series of beeps to identify the nature of the first problem that POST discovered. For example, if you hear one long and one short beep, the system board, video display adapter, or power supply might have a problem. The use of audible beeps is important, because the problem might reside with the video display adapter, which in turn would prevent a message from being displayed on the screen to indicate the nature of the problem. If the video display adapter is functioning, the POST reports subsequent problems with an error code on the screen and perhaps a brief message. For example, an error code of 100 through 199 indicates a problem with the system board. To find a list of the problems identified by a series of beeps and the POST error codes, you would need to consult a reference manual designed specifically for this purpose, or locate a Web site with a list of POST error codes. If POST reports a memory error, you might have a malfunctioning RAM chip, and should replace it. If POST reports problems for other hardware components, such as the keyboard, make sure all cables are properly attached, and then boot the computer again.

After the POST, another routine uses the boot sequence in CMOS to determine which disk drive to check first for the operating system. As noted in Tutorial 8, today's computers typically boot first from the hard disk rather than from drive A; however, depending on your needs, you can change the boot sequence. When booting from the hard disk, the BIOS locates the Master Boot Record (MBR)—the first sector on the hard disk, and reads the MBR into memory. A boot loader program in the MBR locates the boot partition and then starts loading the operating system from that partition. This program locates and loads NTLdr (for "NT Loader"), a hidden system file in the top-level folder or root directory of the boot drive, and it switches the processor from real mode (DOS mode) to protected mode, which uses extended memory (all memory above 1 MB). NTLdr also contains the program code needed for Windows XP to work with NTFS and FAT volumes. Figure 9-1 shows NTLdr and other system files in the top-level folder of drive C. To display these files and their file extensions, you must turn on the option for showing hidden folders and files, turn off the option for hiding protected operating system files, and turn off the option for hiding extensions for known file types.

| Figure 9-1 | VIEWING SYSTEM FILES ON THE BOOT VOLUME |

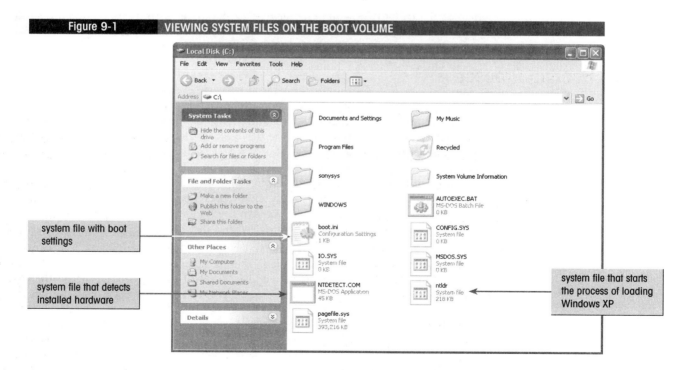

NTLdr uses boot settings in Boot.ini (another hidden system file), shown in Figure 9-2. The [boot loader] section of this file identifies the location of the default operating system to load, and the [operating systems] section identifies which operating systems are installed on the computer and available during booting. The timeout value (30 seconds) under [boot loader] specifies how long to display the OS Choices before loading the default operating system. The default value under [boot loader] identifies the path to the default operating system.

Only one operating system is installed on the computer used for Figure 9-2, namely Windows XP Professional. The multi(0)disk(0)rdisk(0)partition(1)\WINDOWS is an Advanced RISC Computing (ARC) path that identifies the location of the Windows XP installation.

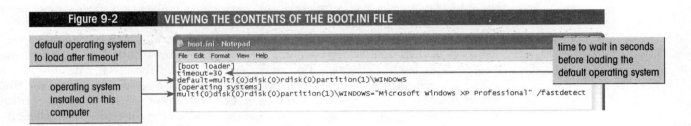

Figure 9-2   VIEWING THE CONTENTS OF THE BOOT.INI FILE

The components of the ARC path are as follows:

- multi(0) is the number of the drive controller. The multi() parameter also indicates that the system BIOS routines are responsible for loading the system files.
- disk(0) is always 0 if the ARC path uses the multi() parameter.
- rdisk(0) specifies that the first physical disk is attached to the controller.
- partition(1) specifies the partition number on the disk.
- \WINDOWS is the relative path of the folder with the Windows operating system files.
- "Microsoft Windows XP Professional" identifies the installed operating system on the OS Choices boot menu.

Figure 9-3 shows Boot.ini for a computer with a dual-boot configuration between Windows XP Home Edition and Windows 98 Second Edition. If you examine the [operating systems] section, note that it contains the ARC path for Windows XP Home Edition and the path to the root directory of the drive for Windows 98 Second Edition—namely, C:\. A Windows 98 installation does not use an ARC path. The partition(2) part of the ARC path indicates that Windows XP Home Edition is installed on the second partition on the hard disk. Windows 98 Second Edition is installed on the first partition. Because two operating systems are installed on this computer, an OS Choices menu lists both operating systems, so that you can pick the one you want to use.

Figure 9-3   BOOT.INI FOR A DUAL-BOOT COMPUTER

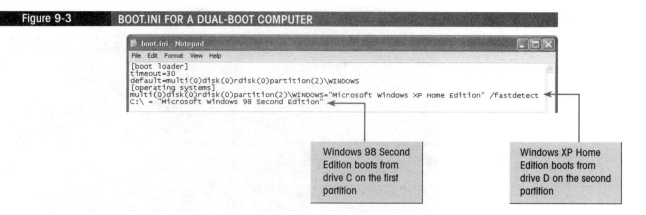

Windows 98 Second Edition boots from drive C on the first partition

Windows XP Home Edition boots from drive D on the second partition

NTLdr loads and runs NTDetect.com (another hidden system file identified as an MS-DOS application), which checks the hardware in the computer so that Windows XP can properly configure the computer. Then core components of the Windows XP operating system, such as the Windows XP kernel (NTOSKrnl.exe) and Hardware Abstraction Layer (HAL.dll), are loaded into memory along with the device drivers for the hardware on the computer. The kernel starts Session Manager, which performs a variety of tasks, including switching Windows from text mode to graphics mode and starting the Logon Manager. These two system files are located in the System32 folder, which is within your Windows folder. The **kernel** is the portion of the Windows XP operating system that resides in memory at all times and that provides services for applications. The **Hardware Abstraction Layer (HAL)** contains the machine-specific program code for a particular type of processor. NTLdr also processes hardware-specific information in the Windows Registry, so that it knows which hardware device drivers to load. If you boot your computer and enable boot logging (covered in the next section), Windows XP produces a boot log, called NTBtLog.txt, in the Windows folder that documents the boot operations.

Performing an Interactive Boot

In further discussions with you, Deshi emphasizes that Windows XP, like its Windows NT predecessors, is a stable operating system, and therefore you are not likely to experience problems booting your computer. However, if Windows XP cannot boot to the desktop, or if Windows XP reports a problem during booting, you can try to boot the computer using the Windows Advanced Options Menu.

This menu, shown in Figure 9-4, contains a list of booting options that provide alternate approaches for booting a computer. To display the Windows Advanced Options Menu, you press the F8 function key after the POST and before Windows displays the desktop.

Figure 9-4	WINDOWS ADVANCED OPTIONS MENU

```
Windows Advanced Options Menu
Please select an option:

    Safe Mode
    Safe Mode with Networking
    Safe Mode with Command Prompt

    Enable Boot Logging
    Enable VGA Mode
    Last Known Good Configuration (your most recent settings that worked)
    Directory Services Restore Mode (Windows domain controllers only)
    Debugging Mode

    Start Windows Normally
    Reboot
    Return to OS Choices Menu

Use the up and down arrow keys to move the highlight to your choice.
```

Safe mode options

option for logging boot operations

option for using VGA mode to boot

how to select an option

option for using last known good configuration

option for a normal boot (the default)

Using the Start Windows Normally and Enabling Boot Logging Options

The **Start Windows Normally** option is the default boot option. If you choose this option from the Windows Advanced Options Menu, Windows XP performs a full boot and starts Windows XP in what is called **standard mode**. The **Enable Boot Logging** option is identical to the Start Windows Normally option, except Windows XP creates a special startup log called NTBtLog.txt in the Windows folder during booting, and logs all the drivers and services that it loads (or fails to load). By examining the drivers and services that failed to load, you might be able to identify the exact cause of a problem and also eliminate the possible cause of the problem you're experiencing. Figure 9-5 shows part of NTBtLog.txt.

Figure 9-5	VIEWING THE CONTENTS OF NTBTLOG.TXT

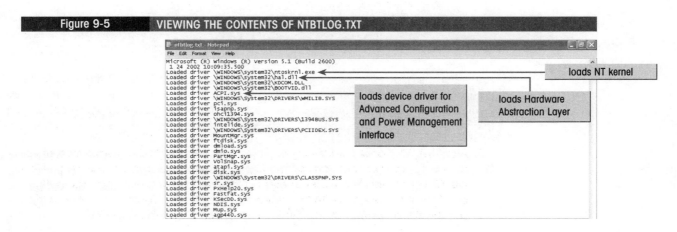

loads NT kernel

loads device driver for Advanced Configuration and Power Management interface

loads Hardware Abstraction Layer

Using the Last Known Good Configuration

The **Last Known Good Configuration** boot option starts Windows XP using the configuration saved by the operating system from the last successful boot. Because this boot option restores previously used device drivers and the previous set of Registry settings from the last successful boot, you could lose any changes to the configuration of your computer that you recently made. You would use this option if your computer stops responding, if it restarts unexpectedly, or if Windows XP automatically shuts down. The problem that caused the system interruption might be due to a recent change to the hardware or software configuration of your computer. However, the Last Known Good Configuration does not help if there is a problem with the hardware itself.

Using the Safe Mode and Enabling VGA Mode Boot Options

The **Safe Mode** boot option starts Windows XP, but only loads the minimum set of drivers for the mouse, monitor, keyboard, mass storage, and video, as well as default system services. This basic set of drivers gets your computer up and running so that you can then attempt to troubleshoot the source of the problem or problems you were experiencing. For example, you might use Safe Mode to troubleshoot an upgrade to Windows XP or to device drivers, or to change settings for newly installed software (or remove the software), and then restart your computer to see if it boots properly. If the problem that caused you to choose the Safe Mode boot option does not appear in Safe Mode, the basic device drivers and settings loaded by Windows XP during Safe Mode are not the source of the problem. Rather, the problem is more likely to lie with a new device that you've added to your computer, or to a change in device drivers for a hardware component.

When you boot in Safe Mode, you might not have access to all of the hardware devices on your computer. Also, if your computer is on a network, you cannot access or browse the network. In Safe Mode, Windows XP does not load the Network Interface Card (NIC) driver. If you right-click the taskbar, choose the option to open Task Manager, and then choose the Networking tab, Windows XP reports that it did not find any active network adapters.

The first thing you might want to try after rebooting in Safe Mode is to restart Windows XP to determine if it can rebuild damaged files and reconfigure itself.

So that you are familiar with Safe Mode in case you need to troubleshoot a problem, Deshi recommends that you use the Windows XP Advanced Options Menu to boot in this mode.

When you reboot your computer, you need to press the F8 key after the POST (or press and release the F8 key several times during this phase of booting) and before you see the Starting Windows screen with the progress indicator. If you pass this point, Windows XP boots to the desktop. Also, when you switch from one operating mode to another, Windows XP boots more slowly, so you must be patient.

To boot in Safe Mode:

1. From the Start menu, choose the option to turn off or shut down your computer, and then choose the option to restart it.

2. After the POST and the screen with information about the configuration of your computer, and before you see the Starting Windows screen, press and release the **F8** key (several times, if necessary), or if you have a dual-boot or multiple configuration, press the **F8** key when you see the OS Choices menu. You then see the Windows Advanced Options Menu, as shown in Figure 9-6.

Figure 9-6 | WINDOWS ADVANCED OPTIONS MENU

click to start in
Safe Mode

```
Windows Advanced Options Menu
Please select an option:

    Safe Mode
    Safe Mode with Networking
    Safe Mode with Command Prompt

    Enable Boot Logging
    Enable VGA Mode
    Last Known Good Configuration (your most recent settings that worked)
    Directory Services Restore Mode (Windows domain controllers only)
    Debugging Mode

    Start Windows Normally
    Reboot
    Return to OS Choices Menu

Use the up and down arrow keys to move the highlight to your choice.
```

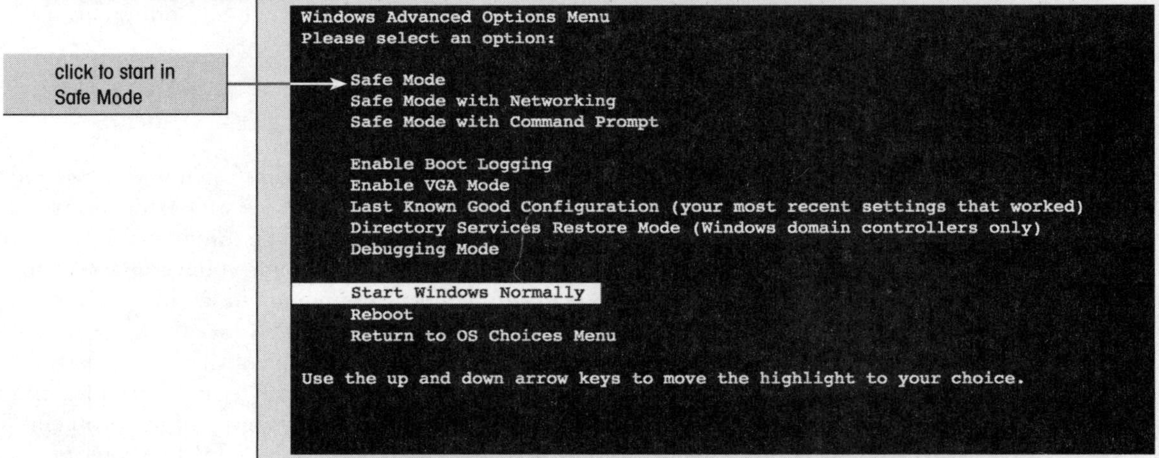

3. Use ↑ to highlight the **Safe Mode** menu option, and then press the **Enter** key. You are now prompted for the operating system to start, as shown in Figure 9-7.

   TROUBLE? If the directional arrow keys on the numeric keypad do not allow you to highlight the Safe Mode menu option, press the Num Lock key to switch the keys from a numeric keypad to a directional keypad.

Figure 9-7 | SELECTING AN OPERATING SYSTEM

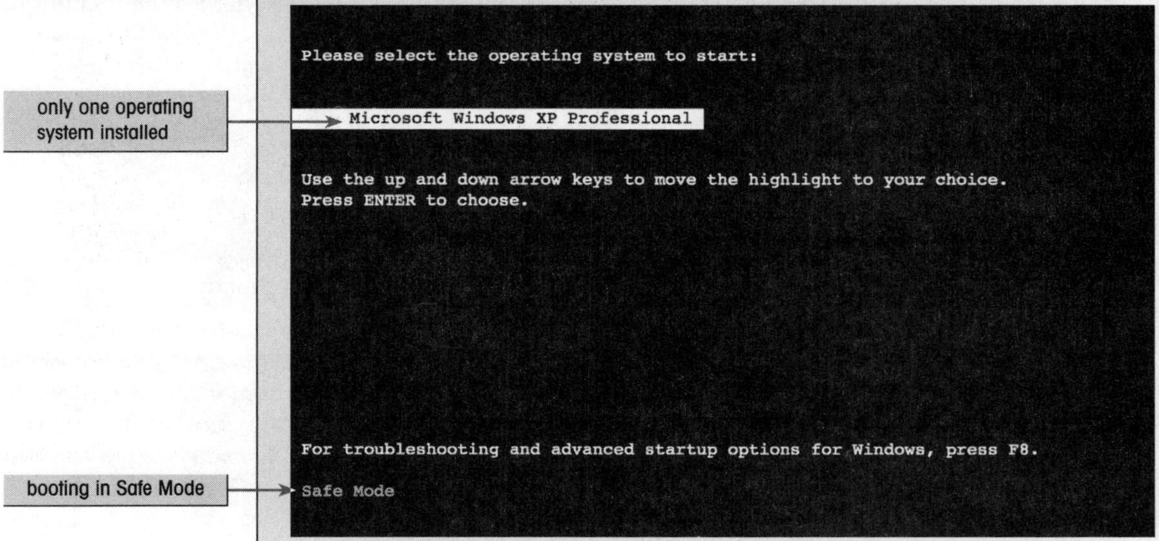

only one operating
system installed

```
Please select the operating system to start:

    Microsoft Windows XP Professional

Use the up and down arrow keys to move the highlight to your choice.
Press ENTER to choose.




For troubleshooting and advanced startup options for Windows, press F8.
```

booting in Safe Mode → Safe Mode

4. Select the version of the Windows XP operating system installed on your computer (if it is not already selected), and then press the **Enter** key. Various components of the Windows XP operating system are loaded, and then listed on a line-by-line basis. Next, you are prompted to select your user name and enter your password.

5. Log onto your computer under your user account if it is an account with Administrator privileges or log under the Administrator account. Before Windows XP displays the contents of the desktop, the Desktop dialog box explains that Safe Mode is a special diagnostic mode for troubleshooting Windows XP problems. See Figure 9-8. Windows XP notes that the problems you have encountered might be caused by your network or hardware settings. It suggests that you open the Control Panel to check and, if necessary, change settings, and then restart Windows XP. It also warns you that not all devices are available while you are using Safe Mode. You also have the option of using System Restore to restore your computer to a previous state. While you are in Safe Mode, System Restore does not create any restore points. That means that you cannot undo a restore.

Figure 9-8	WARNING ABOUT THE USE OF SAFE MODE

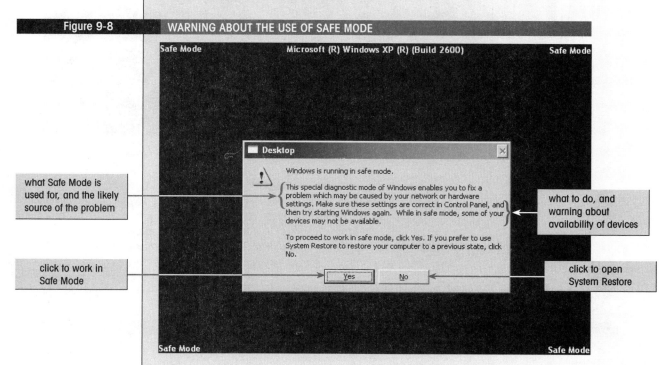

what Safe Mode is used for, and the likely source of the problem

what to do, and warning about availability of devices

click to work in Safe Mode

click to open System Restore

6. In the Desktop dialog box, click the **Yes** button. In the four corners of the screen, Windows XP displays the message "Safe Mode." See Figure 9-9. At this point, you can open the Control Panel, check, and if necessary change, system settings, and then restart Windows XP. You can also open the Help and Support Center, and use a Help troubleshooter (discussed later in this tutorial) to identify, and if possible, resolve a problem.

Figure 9-9 | VIEWING THE DESKTOP IN SAFE MODE

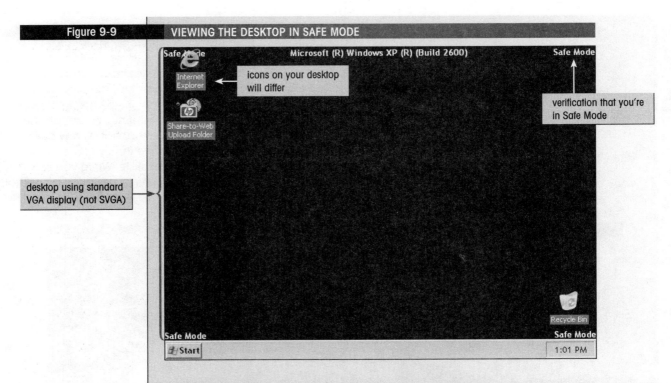

icons on your desktop will differ

verification that you're in Safe Mode

desktop using standard VGA display (not SVGA)

7. Right-click the **desktop**, click **Properties** on the shortcut menu, and in the Display Properties dialog box, click the **Settings** tab. As shown on the Settings property sheet, Windows XP is configured for a (Default Monitor), and the Screen resolution is 640 by 480 pixels. See Figure 9-10. These standard display settings enable Windows XP to boot the computer so that you can see an image on the monitor. Note that you still have access to your Color quality setting (which may differ from that shown in the figure). You can use the Troubleshoot button to open the Video Display Troubleshooter if you need to resolve a problem with the video display.

Figure 9-10 | VIEWING SAFE MODE DISPLAY SETTINGS

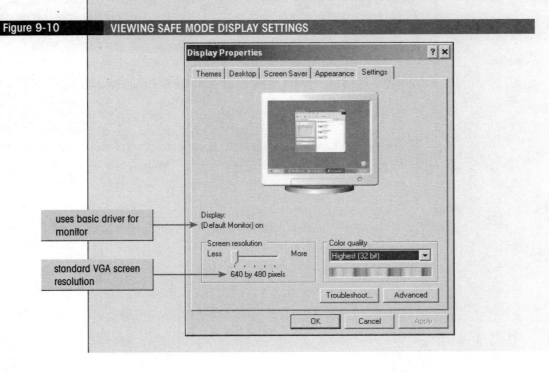

uses basic driver for monitor

standard VGA screen resolution

8. Click the **Cancel** button to close this dialog box.

9. Choose the option to restart your computer, and after Windows XP boots to the desktop, log on your computer under your user account.

In Safe Mode, you can also reinstall Windows XP, or reinstall a Windows XP service pack upgrade.

REFERENCE WINDOW   **RW**

Booting in Safe Mode

- Open the Start menu and choose the option to restart your computer.
- After the POST and the screen with information about the configuration of your computer but before you see the Starting Windows screen, press and release the F8 key (several times, if necessary).
- After Windows XP displays the Windows Advanced Options Menu, use the up arrow key to highlight the Safe Mode menu option, and then press the Enter key.
- When prompted for the operating system to start, select the version of the Windows XP operating system installed on your computer (if it is not already selected), and then press the Enter key.
- Log onto your computer under your Administrator account.
- In the Desktop dialog box that describes the use of Safe Mode, click the Yes button.
- After you've booted into Safe Mode, check and, if necessary, change settings; use troubleshooting tools at your disposal, such as the Windows Help Troubleshooters, to identify and resolve a problem; or simply reboot your computer to see if Windows XP can automatically resolve the problem.
- After you have finished working in Safe Mode, choose the option to restart your computer, and after Windows XP boots to the desktop, log on your computer under your user account.

The **Safe Mode with Networking** option is similar to the Safe Mode option, except that Windows XP establishes network connections so that you can troubleshoot a problem that requires network access. If you are connected to a network, Windows XP loads network drivers. This option is useful when the Safe Mode option does not work.

The **Safe Mode with Command Prompt** option is similar to Safe Mode, but Windows XP boots to a command prompt instead of booting to the desktop so that you can use a command-line operating environment to troubleshoot system problems. After selecting this boot option, you are prompted first for the operating system to load, and then you log on as Administrator. Figure 9-11 shows the command-line environment after choosing the Safe Mode with Command Prompt boot option. You do not have access to your network.

Figure 9-11	SAFE MODE WITH COMMAND PROMPT

command prompt

Safe Mode

program displaying
Command Prompt
window

The **Enable VGA Mode** starts Windows XP with the basic VGA device driver. All of
the Safe Mode options also use the same basic video driver. If you install a new device driver
for your video card, or if a problem develops with your current video display driver, and you
discover that Windows XP does not start properly, you can start your computer with the
Enable VGA Mode boot option and its basic VGA device driver and troubleshoot the problem. The currently installed video driver might be corrupt or incompatible. For example,
you might need to change the device configuration, and therefore the device driver used for
the video adapter, or update the device driver. One advantage of Enable VGA Mode over
Safe Mode is that it changes the use of only one driver (the video driver) during booting. On
the Settings property sheet in the Display Properties dialog box, Windows XP usually identifies your monitor and video display adapter by brand name (unlike Safe Mode). Windows XP
also uses a screen resolution of 640 by 480 pixels and a Low (8 bit) Color quality setting, the latter of which is not available to you during a full boot. Also unlike Safe Mode, network drivers
are loaded, so you have access to your network.

The Directory Service Restore Mode (Windows XP domain controllers only) boot
option is only for server-based operating systems. An Administrator would use this option
to restore the SYSVOL (system volume) directory and the Active Directory service on a
domain controller. **SYSVOL** is a shared directory that stores the server copy of the
domain's public files. A **domain** is a group of computers that are part of a network and share
a common directory database. A **domain controller** is a computer that uses Active
Directory to manage access to a network—including logging on and authenticating users
and providing access to the directory and shared resources. **Active Directory** tracks information about objects on a network, supports a single logon process for network users so that
they can access resources anywhere on the network for which they have permission, and
allows network administrators to administer all network objects using a hierarchical view of
the network. The Debugging Mode option sends debug information through a serial cable
to another computer as Windows XP starts.

You now know how to work with the Windows Advanced Options Menu. If you need to troubleshoot a problem on the telephone with Stephanie or another technical support person, you now have a better idea of how they might want you to start and diagnose your computer.

Using the System Configuration Utility

The System Configuration Utility allows you to control the startup process by deciding which startup configuration files, services, and programs to process or load during booting. If you suspect that a particular program is the source of a problem you're experiencing on your computer, you temporarily turn off the use of that program with the System Configuration Utility, so that it is not loaded during the next boot. If the problem does not reoccur, you've identified the source of the problem. If the problem remains, the program that you turned off is not the source of the problem. You can restart your computer, turn on the option to load that program again, and then repeat the process with another program, service, or startup configuration file. Using this strategy, you can identify and isolate the source of a problem.

You must be logged on under an account with Administrator privileges to change settings in the System Configuration Utility. However, you do not need to log on under an account with Administrator privileges to examine the settings.

Because staff members periodically run into problems with specific background programs, Deshi sets aside some time to show you how to use the System Configuration Utility to troubleshoot programs that cause problems.

To examine your computer's startup options:

1. From the Start menu, open the Help and Support Center, and under "Pick a task," click **Use Tools to view your computer information and diagnose problems**. Under Tools are links to various system tools as well as to resources that provide information on how to use these and other tools. See Figure 9-12. Notice that there are links for opening Disk Cleanup, Disk Defragmenter, and Backup from the Help and Support Center. If you are using Windows XP Home Edition, you do not see the options for Offer Remote Assistance, Backup, Command-line reference A-Z, New command-line tools, Command shell overview, Windows Support tools, and Resource Kit tools. Also, because the manufacturer of this computer customized the Help and Support Center, you might notice slight differences between this figure and later figures for the Help and Support Center and the view onto your Help and Support Center.

Figure 9-12	TROUBLESHOOTING TOOLS

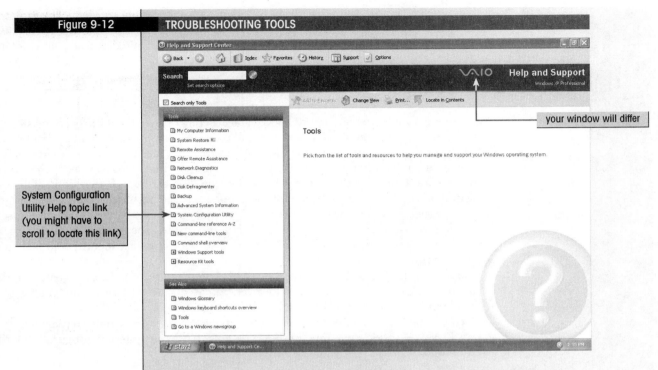

System Configuration
Utility Help topic link
(you might have to
scroll to locate this link)

your window will differ

2. Under Tools, locate and click the **System Configuration Utility** link, and then click the **Open System Configuration Utility** link. Windows XP opens the System Configuration Utility dialog box. See Figure 9-13. Under Startup Selection on the General property sheet, Normal Startup is automatically selected as the default option for starting your computer unless you have a dual-boot or multiple-boot configuration in which Boot.ini has been modified, or have already used the System Configuration Utility to modify the startup process on your computer. Normal Startup loads all device drivers and Windows XP services. If you choose Diagnostic Startup, Windows XP boots in Safe Mode, and loads only basic devices and services. If you choose this option, you do not have access to certain Control Panel or Computer Management tools. You may also experience a problem and have to acti-vate your version of Windows again (see the following Trouble). Selective Startup allows you to pick which system files, services, and startup programs are processed during booting. You can open System Restore from this sheet if you are logged on under an account with Administrator privileges.

POWER USERS TIP A faster way to open the System Configuration Utility is to select Run on the Start menu, type MSCONFIG (case does not matter), and press the Enter key.

TROUBLE? If you enable the Diagnostic Startup option, reboot your computer, and attempt to log on, a Windows Product Activation dialog box may inform you that a problem has prevented Windows from accurately checking the sta-tus of the license for your computer. It also claims that before you can proceed, you must activate your copy of Windows with Microsoft, and then it asks if you want to activate Windows now. If you click the No button, Windows XP saves your settings and prompts you to log on again. In other words, you cannot log on unless you activate your copy of Windows. Log on your computer, click the Yes button in the Windows Product Activation dialog box, and activate Windows XP. Repeat Steps 1 and 2 to open the System Configuration Utility.

Figure 9-13   **OPTIONS FOR STARTING UP WINDOWS XP**

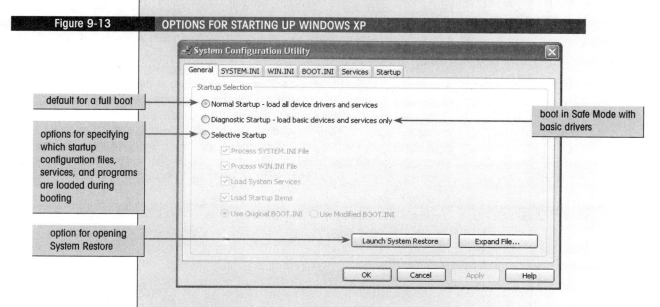

3. Click the **Selective Startup** option button. After you select this option, you can turn off the processing of the System.ini and Win.ini startup configuration files, the loading of system services and startup items, and either the original or a modified version of the Boot.ini file (if available). See Figure 9-14. System.ini and Win.ini contain settings for applications designed for early versions of Windows (pre-Windows 95) that stored settings in these files rather than in the Windows Registry. Windows XP does not need these files to boot your computer.

Figure 9-14   **SELECTIVE STARTUP OPTIONS**

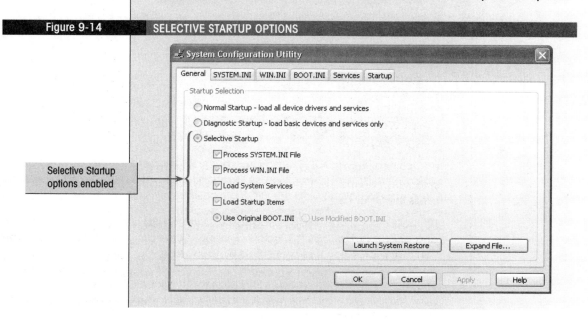

4. Click the **SYSTEM.INI** tab, examine the categories of options available within this configuration file, and then click the **WIN.INI** tab. On the SYSTEM.INI and WIN.INI sheets, you can modify an individual setting within one of these files, but still process the remainder of the file if you are troubleshooting a program, driver, service, or setting loaded from one of these files. In other words, you can edit the contents of these files without opening them in Notepad. The "for 16-bit app support" comment at the beginning of each file documents the fact that the settings in these files are for use with 16-bit applications (pre-Windows 95 applications), not 32-bit applications (applications designed for Windows 95 and later). Figure 9-15 shows the [Collage Capture] section of WIN.INI on the computer used for this figure. This computer uses Collage Complete, an application designed for versions of Windows before Windows 95. Almost all of the screen captures in this book were taken with this screen capture program. This section identifies the location of the file that contains the settings for the screen capture program, and other settings used by this program.

Figure 9-15	VIEWING PART OF THE WIN.INI FILE

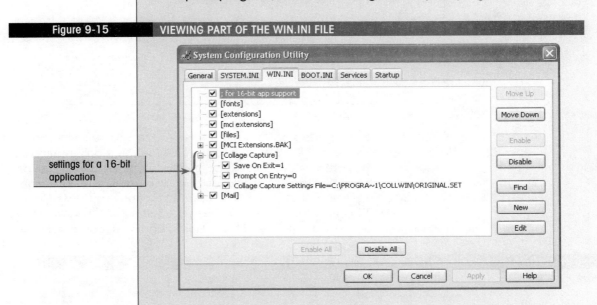

settings for a 16-bit application

5. Click the **BOOT.INI** tab. This sheet shows you the contents of your BOOT.INI file. See Figure 9-16. Yours may differ. Like System.ini and Win.ini, you can edit this file without opening it in Notepad. Under Boot Options, you can change the way Windows XP boots. The /SAFEBOOT option forces Windows XP to start in Safe Mode, the /NOGUIBOOT parameter turns off the display of the progress bar during booting, the /BOOTLOG parameter enables boot logging, the /BASEVIDEO switch instructs Windows XP to use standard VGA mode (640 by 480 screen resolution and 16 colors), and the /SOS parameter instructs Windows XP to display each device driver that it loads during booting. You have to be careful when you make changes to Boot.ini. A mistake might mean that you cannot boot your computer. If your computer boots from a FAT volume, you might want to copy Boot.ini onto an MS-DOS startup disk before you start making changes to Boot.ini. You should also make sure you can boot your computer from your Windows XP CD. If not, you should make Windows XP Setup Disks. You can also use the Recovery Console (covered later in the tutorial) to rebuild Boot.ini.

Figure 9-16	VIEWING THE CONTENTS OF THE BOOT.INI FILE

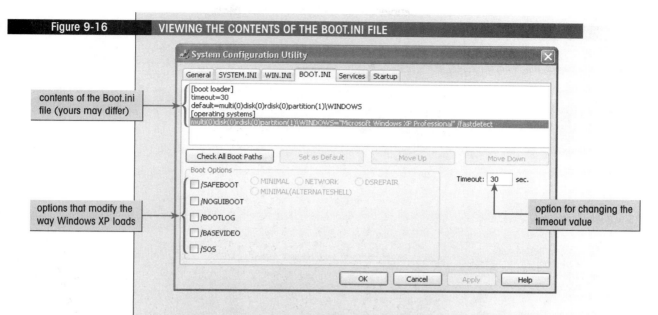

contents of the Boot.ini file (yours may differ)

options that modify the way Windows XP loads

option for changing the timeout value

6. Click the **Services** tab. This sheet lists all the services that are loaded during booting. See Figure 9-17. You can turn off, or turn on, specific services as part of your troubleshooting strategy. There might easily be 90 different services and, of course, you need to know not only what each service does, but also what happens if you turn off the service.

Figure 9-17	SERVICES LOADED DURING BOOTING

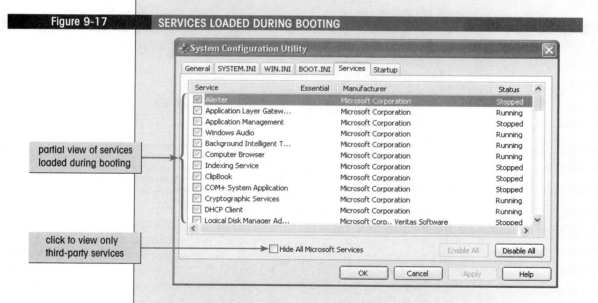

partial view of services loaded during booting

click to view only third-party services

7. Click the **Hide All Microsoft Services** check box. Now you only see a list of third-party services. See Figure 9-18. Yours may differ. When troubleshooting system startup problems, seriously consider the possibility of a problem caused by a third-party service or a program (such as antivirus software) that loads as a service.

Figure 9-18 | HIDING MICROSOFT SERVICES

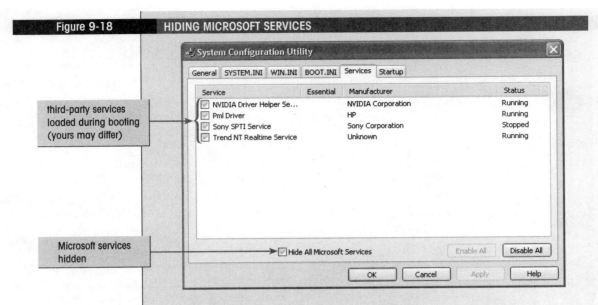

third-party services
loaded during booting
(yours may differ)

Microsoft services
hidden

8. Click the **Startup** tab. The Startup sheet lists programs that are loaded during booting. Icons for some of these programs may appear in the Notification area, but here is where you find a more complete accounting of these programs. See Figure 9-19. Yours may differ. The programs with locations (or paths) that start with HKLM are programs that are loaded from the Registry.

Figure 9-19 | PROGRAMS LOADED DURING BOOTING (YOURS MAY DIFFER)

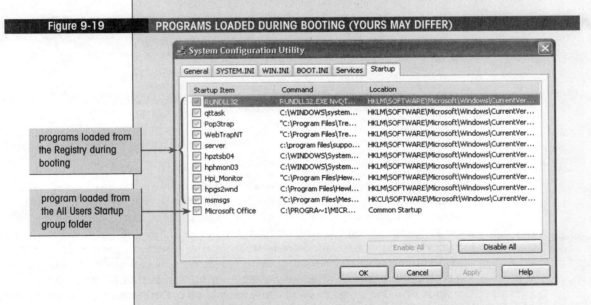

programs loaded from
the Registry during
booting

program loaded from
the All Users Startup
group folder

9. Click the **Cancel** button to close the System Configuration Utility without making any changes, and then close the Help and Support Center.

REFERENCE WINDOW   **RW**

Using the System Configuration Utility

- From the Start menu, open the Help and Support Center, and under "Pick a task," click "Use Tools to view your computer information and diagnose problems," or from the Start menu, click Run, type MSCONFIG, and then press the Enter key.
- Under Tools, click the System Configuration Utility Help topic link, and then click the "Open System Configuration Utility" link.
- On the General property sheet of the System Configuration Utility dialog box, select the type of Startup Selection you want to use. Use Diagnostic Startup to boot in Safe Mode and load only basic devices and services. Use Selective Startup to pick which system files, services, and startup programs you want processed or loaded during booting. Use Normal Startup to restore your original settings. You can also open System Restore from this sheet if you are logged on under an account with Administrator privileges.
- Use the SYSTEM.INI and WIN.INI sheets to modify an individual setting within one of these files, but still process the remainder of the file if you are troubleshooting a program, driver, service, or setting loaded from one of these files.
- Use the BOOT.INI sheet to edit this file, and specify Boot Options. Before you change Boot.ini and run the risk of not being able to boot your computer, copy Boot.ini to an MS-DOS startup disk, and make sure you can boot your computer from your Windows CD (if not, make Windows XP Setup Disks).
- Use the Services sheet to turn off, or turn on, specific services as part of your troubleshooting strategy. Click the "Hide All Microsoft Services" check box to view a list of third-party services.
- Use the Startup sheet to turn off, or turn on, those programs you want to load during booting so that you can identify and isolate the program that is the source of the problem.
- Close the System Configuration Utility, and restart your computer to apply the changes, or if you did not make any changes, close the Help and Support Center.

If you are experiencing a problem with your computer, and you suspect that one of the background programs loaded during booting might be the source of that problem, you can turn off the loading of that program on the Startup sheet. An error message as you log on may give you a clue as to which program to test first.

 POWER USERS TIP If you do not know which program might be the source of the problem, and if you do not want to test each program separately (which requires a reboot), you can reduce the amount of time that it takes to locate the program that is the source of the problem by choosing to not load half of them, and then restarting your computer. If the problem remains, you've eliminated the startup programs you just turned off prior to booting. If the problem no longer appears, you know that the problem program is one that was not loaded. You can open the System Configuration Utility, and then continue to test half of the remaining programs using the same approach until you locate the one that is the source of the problem.

If you need to restore the loading of all startup configuration files, services, and programs, choose Normal Startup on the General property sheet and reboot your computer.

Installing **and Using the Recovery Console**

The Recovery Console is a command-line version of the Windows XP operating system, and it is designed for advanced users who are familiar with how to work with commands and directories in a command-line environment. You can use the Recovery Console to start and stop services, read and write to any local disk even if the disks use different file systems, format drives, and copy files from a floppy disk or CD to the hard disk drive. You can also use the Recovery Console to manually repair individual Registry files or replace the entire Registry.

You can start the Recovery Console from the Windows XP Setup CD, or you can install it on your computer so that you can choose the Recovery Console from the OS Choices menu during booting. The latter is the preferred method if you are unable to start Windows XP. If you decide to start the Recovery Console from the Windows XP Setup CD, you must change the boot sequence in CMOS so that your computer examines the CD drive first. As noted previously, if your computer does not support booting from a CD drive, you must make Windows XP Professional or Windows XP Home Edition Setup Disks to boot from drive A and to access the Windows CD in your CD drive. To install and use the Recovery Console, you must log on your computer as Administrator or as a member of the Administrators group.

During her next scheduled visits to Yellow Brick Road Child Care Services, Stephanie shows you and Deshi how to install the Recovery Console. She explains that you might use the Recovery Console if Safe Mode or other startup options do not work.

In the next set of steps, you have the option of installing and using the Recovery Console on your computer. If you prefer not to make any changes to your computer, do not complete the next set of steps. Instead, examine the figures and read, but do not keystroke, the following steps so that you are familiar with the process for installing and using the Recovery Console.

To install the Recovery Console:

1. Log on under an account with Administrator privileges so that you can install the Recovery Console.

2. Connect to your Internet service provider (ISP), start your browser, if necessary, and then minimize your browser window. Windows Setup needs to check Microsoft's Web site for updates to the operating system.

3. Insert your Windows XP Setup CD in your CD or DVD drive.

4. Open My Computer, and verify the drive name of the CD or DVD drive that contains the Windows XP Setup CD, and then close My Computer.

5. From the Start menu, click **Run**, and after the Run dialog box opens, type the following command in the Open box, as shown in Figure 9-20, and then press the **Enter** key (Remember to use the name of your CD or DVD drive in place of E: (if it is different) in the following command): **E:\i386\winnt32.exe   /cmdcons** Note that /cmdcons is an optional switch. You must type the forward slash before "cmdcons." After you enter the command for installing the Recovery Console, Windows Setup displays a dialog box and explains that you can install the Windows Recovery Console as a startup option, and that you can use it to help you gain access to your system and replace damaged files, or turn off or turn on services. See Figure 9-21. It also notes that you can run the Recovery Console from the Windows XP Setup CD if you cannot start the Recovery Console from your computer's hard disk. To install the Recovery Console, you need approximately 7 MB of storage space on your hard disk.

TROUBLE? If the Run dialog box opens and informs you that it cannot find the location defined in the path, click the OK button to close the Run (error) dialog box, and then click the Cancel button to close the Run dialog box with the command you typed. From the Start menu, click Search, choose the option to search for all files and folders, type winnt32.exe in the "All or part of the file name" box, select the drive with your Windows XP CD in the Look in list box, and then click the Search button. If necessary, switch to Details view using the View menu in the Search Results window, note the path to the folder that contains the Winnt32.exe program file, close the Search Results window, and then repeat this step using the correct path to Winnt32.exe for your Windows XP CD.

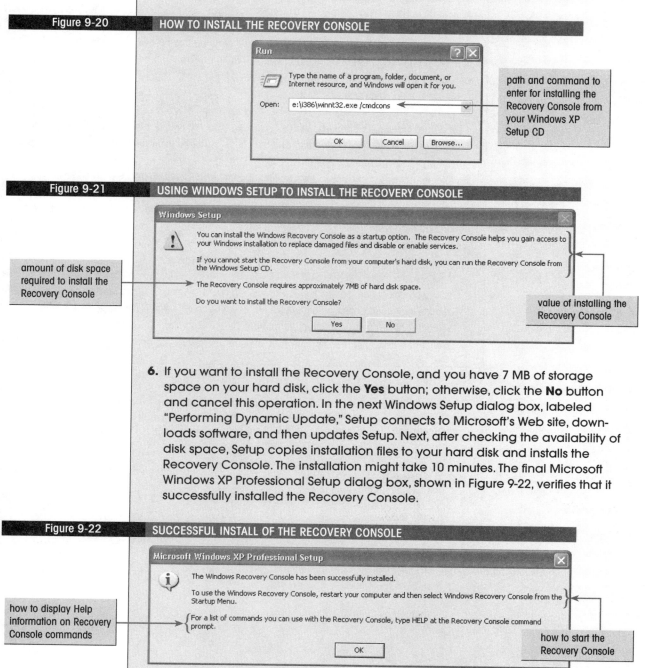

| Figure 9-20 | HOW TO INSTALL THE RECOVERY CONSOLE |

path and command to enter for installing the Recovery Console from your Windows XP Setup CD

| Figure 9-21 | USING WINDOWS SETUP TO INSTALL THE RECOVERY CONSOLE |

amount of disk space required to install the Recovery Console

value of installing the Recovery Console

6. If you want to install the Recovery Console, and you have 7 MB of storage space on your hard disk, click the **Yes** button; otherwise, click the **No** button and cancel this operation. In the next Windows Setup dialog box, labeled "Performing Dynamic Update," Setup connects to Microsoft's Web site, downloads software, and then updates Setup. Next, after checking the availability of disk space, Setup copies installation files to your hard disk and installs the Recovery Console. The installation might take 10 minutes. The final Microsoft Windows XP Professional Setup dialog box, shown in Figure 9-22, verifies that it successfully installed the Recovery Console.

| Figure 9-22 | SUCCESSFUL INSTALL OF THE RECOVERY CONSOLE |

how to display Help information on Recovery Console commands

how to start the Recovery Console

7. Click the **OK** button to close the Microsoft Windows XP Professional Setup dialog box.

8. Disconnect from your ISP, remove your Windows XP Setup CD, and place it back in safe storage.

REFERENCE WINDOW | RW

Installing the Recovery Console

- Log on under an account with Administrator privileges, so that you can install the Recovery Console.
- Because Windows Setup needs to check Microsoft's Web site for updates to the operating system, connect to your Internet service provider, and then minimize your browser window.
- Insert your Windows XP Setup CD in your CD or DVD drive.
- Open My Computer, and verify the drive name of the CD or DVD drive that contains the Windows XP Setup CD, and then close My Computer.
- From the Start menu, click Run, and after the Run dialog box opens, type the following command in the Open box, and then press the Enter key (Remember to use the drive name of your CD or DVD drive in place of E: (if it is different) and the correct path (if it is different) in the following command): E:\i386\winnt32.exe /cmdcons
- After you enter the command for installing the Recovery Console, Windows Setup displays a dialog box and explains that you can install the Windows Recovery Console as a startup option, and that you can use it to help you gain access to your system and replace damaged files, or turn off and on services.
- If you want to install the Recovery Console, and if you have 7 MB of storage space on your hard disk, click Yes; otherwise, click No and cancel this operation.
- After Setup connects to Microsoft's Web site, downloads software, updates itself, checks the availability of disk space, copies installation files to your hard disk, installs the Recovery Console, and verifies that it successfully installed the Recovery Console, click OK to close the Microsoft Windows XP Professional Setup dialog box.
- Disconnect from your ISP, remove your Windows XP Setup CD, and place it back in safe storage.

To use the Recovery Console, you have to restart your computer and select it from the OS Choices menu (also called the Startup Menu). You must also have an Administrator's password.

To open the Recovery Console.

1. Restart your computer. Windows XP displays the OS Choices menu. See Figure 9-23.

Figure 9-23   SELECTING THE RECOVERY CONSOLE FROM THE OS CHOICES MENU

select to open the
Recovery Console

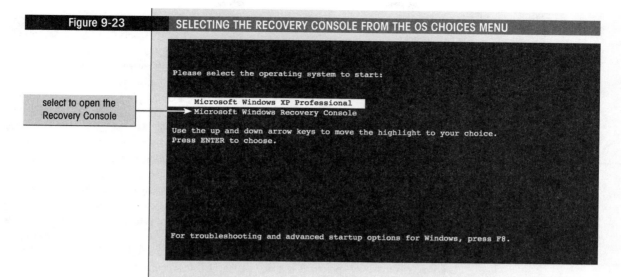

```
Please select the operating system to start:

    Microsoft Windows XP Professional
    Microsoft Windows Recovery Console

Use the up and down arrow keys to move the highlight to your choice.
Press ENTER to choose.




For troubleshooting and advanced startup options for Windows, press F8.
```

2. Press an arrow key to highlight **Microsoft Windows Recovery Console**, and then press the **Enter** key. NTDetect.com detects hardware, and then you see the message "Starting Windows Recovery Console" along with a progress indicator. On the next screen, you see an explanation of the use of the Recovery Console, and you are informed that you must type EXIT if you want to quit the Recovery Console and restart your computer. See Figure 9-24. Then, you are prompted to select which Windows installation you want to log onto. The Windows installations are shown directly above the prompt. On the computer used for this figure, there is only one installation.

Figure 9-24   SELECTING THE WINDOWS INSTALLATION

value of using the
Recovery Console

how to exit the
Recovery Console

type the number of the
Windows installation
you want to install

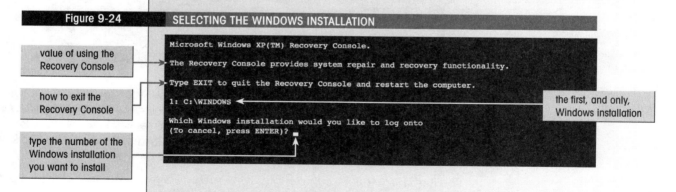

```
Microsoft Windows XP(TM) Recovery Console.

The Recovery Console provides system repair and recovery functionality.

Type EXIT to quit the Recovery Console and restart the computer.

1: C:\WINDOWS

Which Windows installation would you like to log onto
(To cancel, press ENTER)? _
```

the first, and only,
Windows installation

3. Type the number of the installation you want to log onto, press the **Enter** key, and when prompted for your Administrator password, type that password, and then press the **Enter** key. The Windows Recovery Console displays a command line prompt. See Figure 9-25. The default directory is the Windows directory—C:\WINDOWS on the computer used for this figure. The name of your Windows directory and its path may differ. If you have a dual-boot or multiple-boot configuration, the path to the Windows directory shows the drive where Windows XP is installed.

TROUBLE? If you accidentally press the Enter key without specifying which installation to use, Windows XP restarts. Select "Microsoft Windows Recovery Console" from the OS Choices menu, press the Enter key, and then repeat this step.

TROUBLE? If the Recovery Console informs you that your Administrator password is not valid (and if you entered it correctly), press the Ctrl+Alt+Del keys (or press the Enter key after trying your password three times) to reboot your computer to the desktop (choose Windows XP from the OS Choices menu), log on under an account with Administrator privileges, click the Start button, point to All Programs, point to Administrative Tools, click Local Security Policy, click the expand view button ⊞ to the left of Local Policies, click Security Options, locate and double-click the Policy setting identified as "Recovery Console: Allow automatic administrative logon", click the Enabled option button in the Recovery Console dialog box, click the OK button, close the Local Security Settings window, restart your computer, and then try this step again. This problem is described in the "Using the Knowledge Base" section later in the tutorial. (If Administrative Tools is not displayed on the All Programs menu, right-click the taskbar, click Properties, click the Start menu tab in the Taskbar and Start Menu properties dialog box, click the Customize button, click the Advanced tab in the Customize Start menu dialog box, locate "System Administrative Tools" in the Start menu items box, click the "Display on the All Programs menu" option button, click the OK button to close the Customize Start Menu dialog box, and then click the OK button to close the Taskbar and Start Menu Properties dialog box.)

| Figure 9-25 | LOGGING ONTO THE RECOVERY CONSOLE |

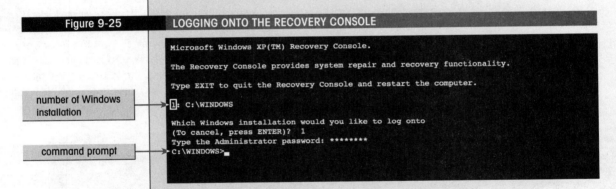

number of Windows installation

command prompt

```
Microsoft Windows XP(TM) Recovery Console.

The Recovery Console provides system repair and recovery functionality.

Type EXIT to quit the Recovery Console and restart the computer.

1: C:\WINDOWS

Which Windows installation would you like to log onto
(To cancel, press ENTER)?  1
Type the Administrator password: ********
C:\WINDOWS>_
```

4. Type **HELP** (you can also use lowercase) and press the **Enter** key. Windows XP displays a list of Recovery Console commands, and then pauses. See Figure 9-26. As shown on the bottom of the screen, you can use the Enter key to scroll and display the next line, the spacebar to scroll and display the next page, or the Esc key to cancel the operation and redisplay the command prompt.

The term **page** refers to the length of the screen (or the remainder of the output to be displayed), and is a logical concept rather than a physical concept.

Figure 9-26   VIEWING A LIST OF COMMANDS FOR WHICH HELP IS AVAILABLE

how to display Help for a command

CHKDSK command

options for continuing the paused command

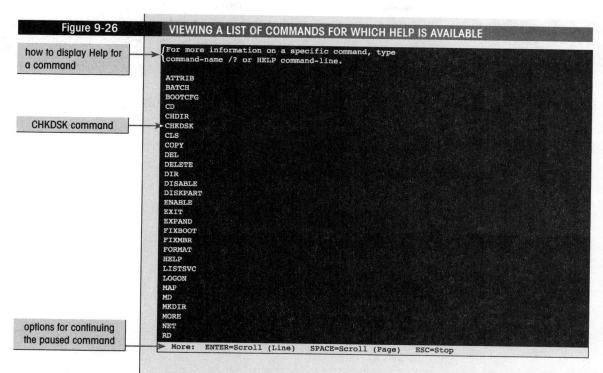

```
For more information on a specific command, type
command-name /? or HELP command-line.

ATTRIB
BATCH
BOOTCFG
CD
CHDIR
CHKDSK
CLS
COPY
DEL
DELETE
DIR
DISABLE
DISKPART
ENABLE
EXIT
EXPAND
FIXBOOT
FIXMBR
FORMAT
HELP
LISTSVC
LOGON
MAP
MD
MKDIR
MORE
NET
RD
More:   ENTER=Scroll (Line)    SPACE=Scroll (Page)    ESC=Stop
```

5. Press the **spacebar**. Windows XP displays the remainder of the commands, and then displays the command prompt. Figure 9-27 lists all the Recovery Console commands and their use.

Figure 9-27   RECOVERY CONSOLE COMMANDS

COMMAND	USE
ATTRIB	Displays or changes attributes assigned to a folder or file
BATCH	Executes commands stored in a text file
BOOTCFG	Configures the boot process, or recovers a Windows installation
CD or CHDIR	Changes to another directory, or displays the name of the current directory
CHKDSK	Checks a disk and displays a status report, locates bad sectors and attempts to recover data
CLS	Clears the screen of previously displayed output, and places the command prompt in the upper-left corner of the screen
COPY	Copies a file to another location
DEL or DELETE	Deletes a file
DIR	Displays a directory listing of subdirectories and files within a directory
DISABLE	Disables a Windows system service or device driver
DISKPART	Creates or deletes a disk partition
ENABLE	Enables a Windows system service or device driver
EXIT	Closes the Recovery Console and restarts the computer
EXPAND	Extracts the contents of a compressed file

Figure 9-27	RECOVERY CONSOLE COMMANDS (CONTINUED)
COMMAND	**USE**
FIXBOOT	Writes a new boot sector on the system partition
FIXMBR	Repairs the Master Boot Record (MBR) on the boot partition
FORMAT	Formats a disk
HELP	Displays Help information for a command
LISTSVC	Lists all available services and drivers on a computer
LOGON	Logs onto a Windows installation
MAP	Displays the drive letter mappings
MD or MKDIR	Creates a directory
MORE	Displays the contents of a text file on the screen
NET	Maps a network share point to a drive letter
RD or RMDIR	Removes a directory
REN or RENAME	Renames a single file
SYSTEMROOT	Sets the current directory to the SystemRoot
TYPE	Displays the contents of a text file on the screen

You will recognize one command—the CHKDSK command (which you used in Tutorial 7). If you have used the DOS operating system or worked with Windows commands in a Command Prompt window, you may recognize most of these commands. However, note that some of these commands do not support all the options or features available under the DOS operating system or when using a Windows Command Prompt window.

You can type the command HELP followed by a space and then a specific command to display Help for just that command. For example, if you type HELP CD and then press the Enter key, you see Help information extracted from the program file itself. CD is the command for "Change Directory." First, the Help information explains what the command does. Then the Help information lists the syntax for the command. **Syntax** refers to the proper format for entering the command. The items displayed in square brackets, such as [path], are optional parameters that you can use with the command. If these parameters are not enclosed within square brackets, they are required parameters. After the syntax, the Help information includes notes about the use of the command.

When you work in the Recovery Console, you can only change to a directory within the Windows system directory, the Recovery Console folder (named Cmdcons), the root directory (top-level folder) of the hard disk drive(s), and to removable media (such as a floppy disk, CD, or DVD drive). If you need access to all folders on all drives, you can change the setting for one of the Recovery Console's environment variables; however, you have to first enable the command for performing this operation within the Microsoft Management Console before you reboot your computer, and then log onto the Recovery Console.

To navigate your computer:

1. Type **CLS** and press the **Enter** key. CLS (for "Clear Screen") clears the screen of any previously displayed output, and places the command prompt and cursor in the upper-left corner of the screen.

2. Type **HELP CD** and press the **Enter** key. The HELP command displays Help information about the use of the CHDIR and CD commands, both of which perform the same function. See Figure 9-28. These commands display the name of the current directory or switch to a new directory (that you specify). Then Help lists the syntax for both the CHDIR and CD commands.

POWER USERS TIP You can also use the Help switch (/?) after a command to display the same type of command-specific Help. For example, CD /? produces the same result.

Figure 9-28 DISPLAYING HELP FOR THE CD COMMAND

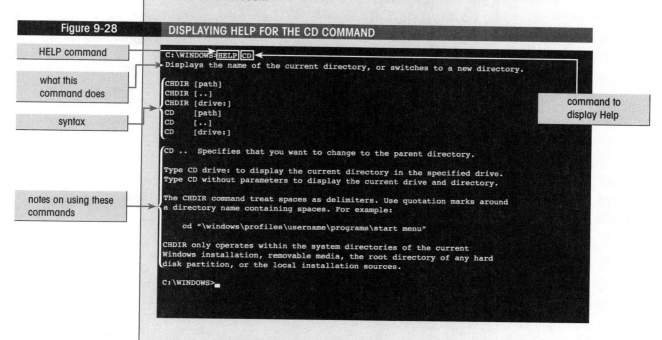

HELP command

what this command does

syntax

notes on using these commands

command to display Help

```
C:\WINDOWS>HELP CD
Displays the name of the current directory, or switches to a new directory.

CHDIR [path]
CHDIR [..]
CHDIR [drive:]
CD    [path]
CD    [..]
CD    [drive:]

CD ..  Specifies that you want to change to the parent directory.

Type CD drive: to display the current directory in the specified drive.
Type CD without parameters to display the current drive and directory.

The CHDIR command treat spaces as delimiters. Use quotation marks around
a directory name containing spaces. For example:

    cd "\windows\profiles\username\programs\start menu"

CHDIR only operates within the system directories of the current
Windows installation, removable media, the root directory of any hard
disk partition, or the local installation sources.

C:\WINDOWS>
```

3. Type **CLS** and press the **Enter** key. Then type **CD ** and press the **Enter** key. After CLS clears the screen, the Change Directory command switches to the root directory (or top-level folder) of drive C. See Figure 9-29.

TROUBLE? If the Recovery Console displays a message warning you that the command is not recognized, you did not use the proper syntax for the command. In this instance, you need to leave a space between the CD command and the backslash character that represents the root directory.

Figure 9-29 CHANGING DIRECTORIES

Change Directory command

command prompt updated to show current directory

root directory

```
C:\WINDOWS>CD \

C:\>
```

4. Type **CLS** and press the **Enter** key. Then type **DIR** and press the **Enter** key. The Directory command displays a directory listing for the root directory of the current drive (usually drive C). See Figure 9-30. Your directory listing may differ.

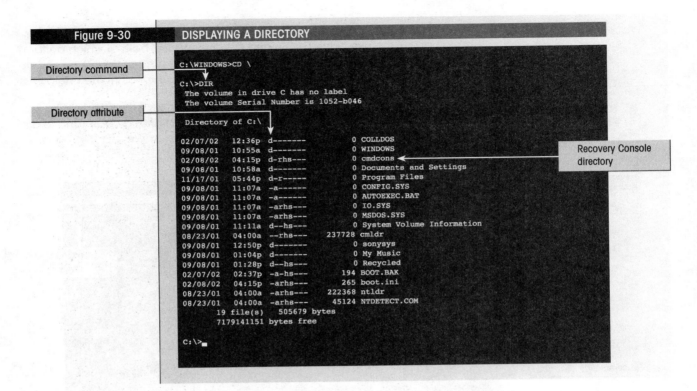

Figure 9-30   DISPLAYING A DIRECTORY

Directory command

Directory attribute

Recovery Console directory

```
C:\WINDOWS>CD \

C:\>DIR
 The volume in drive C has no label
 The volume Serial Number is 1052-b046

 Directory of C:\

02/07/02  12:36p  d-------        0 COLLDOS
09/08/01  10:55a  d-------        0 WINDOWS
02/08/02  04:15p  d-rhs---        0 cmdcons
09/08/01  10:58a  d-------        0 Documents and Settings
11/17/01  05:44p  d-r-----        0 Program Files
09/08/01  11:07a  -a------        0 CONFIG.SYS
09/08/01  11:07a  -a------        0 AUTOEXEC.BAT
09/08/01  11:07a  -arhs---        0 IO.SYS
09/08/01  11:07a  -arhs---        0 MSDOS.SYS
09/08/01  11:11a  d--hs---        0 System Volume Information
08/23/01  04:00a  --rhs---   237728 cmldr
09/08/01  12:50p  d-------        0 sonysys
09/08/01  01:04p  d-------        0 My Music
09/08/01  01:28p  d--hs---        0 Recycled
02/07/02  02:37p  -a-hs---      194 BOOT.BAK
02/08/02  04:15p  -arhs---      265 boot.ini
08/23/01  04:00a  -arhs---   222368 ntldr
08/23/01  04:00a  -arhs---    45124 NTDETECT.COM
         19 file(s)    505679 bytes
      7179141151 bytes free

C:\>_
```

The first column of the directory listing displays the date a directory (same as a folder) or file was created or modified, the second column displays the time the directory or file was created or modified, the third column identifies the attributes assigned to a directory or file, the fourth column displays the directory or file size in bytes, and the fifth column displays the directory or filename. Notice that the Directory command displays long filenames in the Recovery Console. Those items that are assigned the "d" attribute for "Directory" are directories (or folders), and their file sizes are noted as zero bytes. An "r" indicates the Read-Only attribute is enabled (or turned on) for a directory or file, "h" indicates the Hidden attribute is enabled for a directory or file, "s" indicates the System attribute is enabled for a directory or file, and "a" indicates the Archive attribute is enabled for a directory or file. Some directories and files have multiple attributes enabled. The directory named "cmdcons" is the Recovery Console folder.

If you have a dual-boot or multiple-boot configuration, and if Windows XP is not installed on drive C, then you can find Cmdcons, Cmldr, NTLdr, NTdetect.com, Boot.ini (and perhaps also Boot.bak), Io.sys, Msdos.sys, Config.sys, and Autoexec.bat on drive C.

To examine other features of the Recovery Console:

1. Type **CLS** and press the **Enter** key. Then type **CD "Program Files"** and press the **Enter** key. Recovery Console displays the message "Access is denied." As noted earlier, Recovery Console restricts which directories you can access.

2. Type **CLS** and press the **Enter** key. Then type **CHKDSK /?** and press the **Enter** key. The syntax for this version of CHKDSK indicates that you can use the /P switch to check a drive not flagged as **dirty**, in other words, one that has problems with the file system. See Figure 9-31. When used with the Repair switch (/R), CHKDSK locates bad sectors and attempt to recover the data. The notes

explain that this command requires AUTOCHK.EXE, the version of CHKDSK that runs during booting. However, you can use CHKDSK in the Recovery Console without rebooting first.

Figure 9-31	DISPLAYING HELP FOR CHKDSK

command to display Help

what this command does

syntax

notes on using this command

Help switch

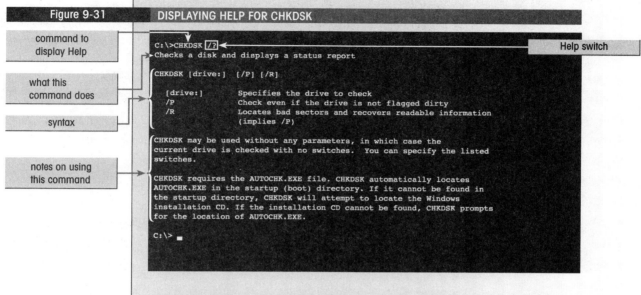

```
C:\>CHKDSK /?
Checks a disk and displays a status report

CHKDSK [drive:] [/P] [/R]

  [drive:]        Specifies the drive to check
  /P              Check even if the drive is not flagged dirty
  /R              Locates bad sectors and recovers readable information
                  (implies /P)

CHKDSK may be used without any parameters, in which case the
current drive is checked with no switches.  You can specify the listed
switches.

CHKDSK requires the AUTOCHK.EXE file. CHKDSK automatically locates
AUTOCHK.EXE in the startup (boot) directory. If it cannot be found in
the startup directory, CHKDSK will attempt to locate the Windows
installation CD. If the installation CD cannot be found, CHKDSK prompts
for the location of AUTOCHK.EXE.

C:\> _
```

3. Type **CLS** and press the **Enter** key. Then type **CHKDSK** and press the **Enter** key. CHKDSK informs you that the volume appears to be in good condition and was not checked. See Figure 9-32. If you want to check the volume anyway, you need to use the /P switch. Then CHKDSK reports on disk storage space, and how that storage space is allocated on this disk. Yours will differ. If you run CHKDSK with the /P switch on a Pentium 4 to check a disk volume with a size of 17 GB, it takes three minutes.

Figure 9-32	USING CHKDSK ON THE CURRENT VOLUME

command assumes current drive

status of volume

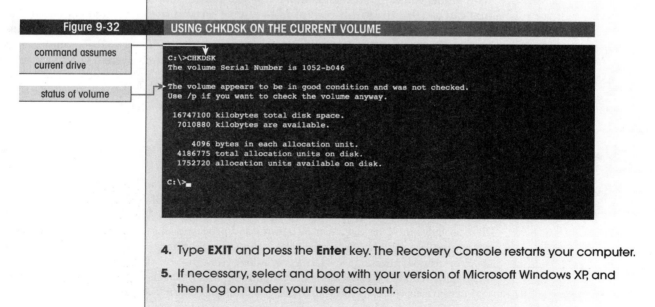

```
C:\>CHKDSK
The volume Serial Number is 1052-b046

The volume appears to be in good condition and was not checked.
Use /p if you want to check the volume anyway.

 16747100 kilobytes total disk space.
  7010880 kilobytes are available.

     4096 bytes in each allocation unit.
  4186775 total allocation units on disk.
  1752720 allocation units available on disk.

C:\>_
```

4. Type **EXIT** and press the **Enter** key. The Recovery Console restarts your computer.

5. If necessary, select and boot with your version of Microsoft Windows XP, and then log on under your user account.

REFERENCE WINDOW **RW**

Opening and Using the Recovery Console

- Restart your computer, and after Windows XP displays the OS Choices menu, use an arrow key to highlight Microsoft Windows Recovery Console, and then press the Enter key.
- When prompted to select which Windows installation you want to log onto (shown directly above the prompt), type the number of the installation you want to log onto, press the Enter key, and when prompted for your Administrator password, type that password, and press the Enter key.
- After the Windows Recovery Console displays a command-line prompt (usually C:\WINDOWS>), type HELP and press the Enter key to display a list of Recovery Console commands. Press the spacebar to view the remainder of the Recovery Console commands.
- To view Help for a specific command, type HELP, press the spacebar, type the command for which you want help, and press the Enter key. Or, type the command for which you want help, press the spacebar, type /? and press the Enter key.
- If you want to clear the screen at any point, type CLS and press the Enter key.
- If you want to view a directory of the subdirectories and files under the current directory, type DIR and press the Enter key.
- If you want to change to another directory, type CD, press the spacebar, type the path to the directory, and then press the Enter key. If you want to change to the root directory, type CD, press the spacebar, type \ and then press the Enter key.
- If you want to check the current drive for errors, type CHKDSK and press the Enter key.
- When you are ready to exit the Recovery Console, type EXIT and press the Enter key. Then, after Windows XP displays the OS Choices menu, select the version of Microsoft Windows XP that you want to start, press the Enter key, and then log on under your user account.

As noted earlier, if you cannot start your computer in Normal mode (default boot) or in Safe Mode, you can start the Recovery Console and attempt to troubleshoot your computer. You can use the DISABLE command to disable services or device drivers that you suspect might be the cause for a Windows startup problem. If the MBR is damaged, perhaps as a result of a computer virus infection, then you can use the FIXMBR command in the Recovery Console to repair the MBR. If the boot sector on the system volume is damaged, you can use the FIXBOOT command to overwrite the existing boot sector with a new version. You can also replace damaged or missing system files, such as NTLdr or NTDetect.com, by copying new versions from the Windows XP Setup CD.

Using **Windows Task Manager**

If you are using an application that stops responding, or responds very slowly, first try to shut down the application rather than shut down the entire system. To do so, you can use Windows Task Manager to shut down the nonresponding application. Windows Task Manager is a tool that provides information about programs and processes that are open and running on your computer. You can also use it to display common performance measures for processes.

From the Windows Task Manager window, you can view a list of running applications and determine whether a program is not responding. If so, you can instruct Windows XP to shut it down so that you can continue to use your computer. Windows Task Manager also shows all running processes. A **process** is an executable program, such as Explorer, Microsoft Word, and Windows Task Manager itself; a service, such as the Print Spooler service which handles the printing of files in the background; or a subsystem, such as the one for Windows XP applications. A **service** is a program, routine, or process that provides support to other programs.

In addition to the name of the process, Task Manager also displays the User Name, the CPU Usage, and Memory Usage.

To see how Windows Task Manager works, you can open a couple of programs, such as WordPad and Paint, open Windows Task Manager, and then examine the options available to you. Obviously, you do not want to just shut down your computer if it's not necessary. When possible, you should always shut down your computer properly so that Windows XP has an opportunity to save settings.

You mention to Deshi that you occasionally notice that an application you are using stops responding, or responds very slowly. In some cases, after unreasonably long waits, you press the Reset button or shut the power off, and then restart the computer. You then ask Deshi if there is any other way to handle this type of problem. Deshi tells you to use Windows Task Manager to shut down the application rather than shut down the entire system. So that you know how to use Windows Task Manager, Deshi suggests that you open a couple of applications, open Windows Task Manager, and then shut down one of the applications.

To use Windows Task Manager to shut down an application:

1. Using the Start menu, open **Paint**, and then open **WordPad**.

2. Right-click the **taskbar**, click **Task Manager** on the shortcut menu, and then click the **Applications** tab (if necessary). Windows XP opens the Windows Task Manager window. See Figure 9-33. On the Applications sheet of the Windows Task Manager window, Windows XP displays a list of running applications—in this case, WordPad and Paint. In the Status column, Windows XP shows whether a process is running, or whether it is not responding. If it is not responding, you can select that process in the Task box, click the End Task button, and let Windows XP shut it down so that you can continue to use your computer. In this example, and in most cases, all tasks displayed in this dialog box are ones that are running, but Windows Task Manager sometimes identifies a task that's not responding. You can end one of these programs, switch to one of these programs, or use the New Task button to start a program. If you end a task, you lose any changes that you made to a document you were working on with that program.

Figure 9-33	VIEWING RUNNING TASKS IN TASK MANAGER

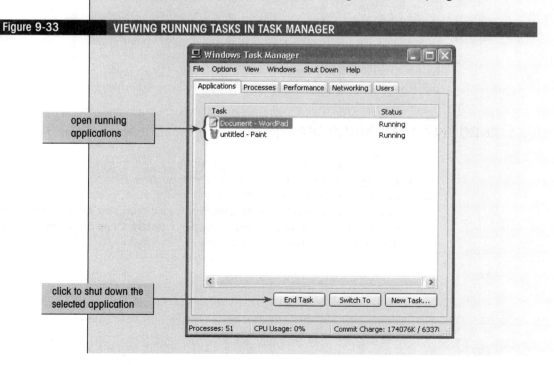

open running applications

click to shut down the selected application

At the bottom of the dialog box, Windows XP lists information about the number of Processes, the percent CPU Usage, and the Commit Charge. You will examine this information in more detail in Tutorial 10.

On most, but not all, computers, you can also open Task Manager by using Ctrl+Alt+Del. However, if you press and then hold down these keys for too long, you might completely shut down your computer and lose important work. To ensure that this doesn't happen, you can press and hold the Ctrl and the Alt keys, quickly press and release the Del key, and then release the Ctrl and Alt keys. As you can tell, right-clicking the taskbar is easier.

3. Select the **untitled - Paint** task in the Task column, and then click the **End Task** button. If a program is not responding, Windows XP may display an End Program dialog box for this task informing you that the program is waiting for a response from you. If it does, you have the option of returning to Windows XP and checking the program, or ending the program now. If the program is running and responding normally, you do not see this dialog box—Windows XP simply shuts down the program. Windows XP closes Paint, and it is no longer listed in the Windows Task Manager dialog box as a running application. See Figure 9-34. Although you would normally switch to an open task and close it without shutting it down, you are now familiar with how to shut down a task should it stop responding and tie up the resources of your computer.

| Figure 9-34 | PROGRAM SHUT DOWN |

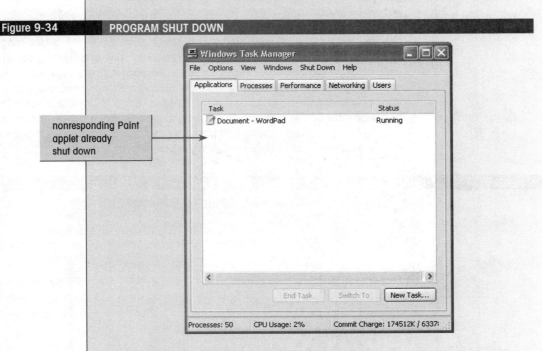

nonresponding Paint applet already shut down

4. Click the **Processes** tab. Windows XP shows all running processes. See Figure 9-35. Your list of processes will differ; however, wordpad.exe appears in this list because WordPad is still open.

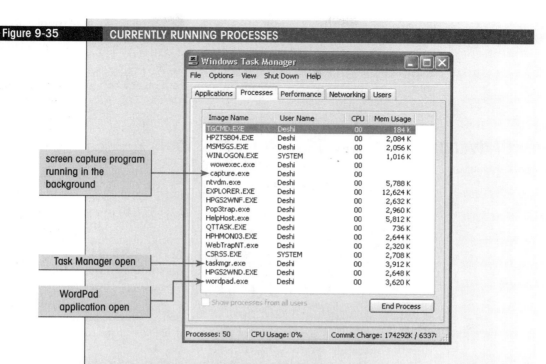

Figure 9-35 CURRENTLY RUNNING PROCESSES

screen capture program running in the background

Task Manager open

WordPad application open

From the Shut Down menu, you can switch your computer to standby or hibernation mode (if available and enabled), turn off or restart your computer, log off, or switch users. The Users tab displays users who are currently logged on the computer, and is only available on computers with Fast User Switching enabled.

5. Close the Windows Task Manager dialog box, and then close WordPad.

In Tutorial 10, you will examine how you can monitor the performance of your computer with the Task Manager Performance sheet.

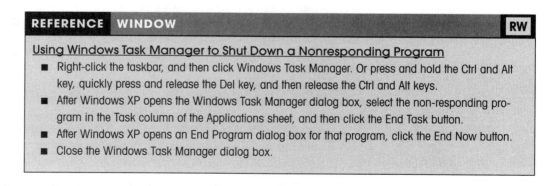

REFERENCE WINDOW RW

Using Windows Task Manager to Shut Down a Nonresponding Program
- Right-click the taskbar, and then click Windows Task Manager. Or press and hold the Ctrl and Alt key, quickly press and release the Del key, and then release the Ctrl and Alt keys.
- After Windows XP opens the Windows Task Manager dialog box, select the non-responding program in the Task column of the Applications sheet, and then click the End Task button.
- After Windows XP opens an End Program dialog box for that program, click the End Now button.
- Close the Windows Task Manager dialog box.

Although you might only use this option occasionally, remember that it is available. It lets you shut down an unresponsive or a slowly responding program that is tying up your computer system without affecting any other open programs, and without losing valuable documents or data in other windows. A complete shutdown clears all memory, so it's better to try Windows Task Manager first.

In the next section of the tutorial, you will examine Help and Support Center tools, including the use of My Computer Information and the System Information utility to view information about your computer, and the use of the Printing Troubleshooter to identify and resolve printing problems. You will search for information on a Recovery Console problem using Microsoft's Knowledge Base. Finally, you will examine the use of two remote assistance tools, Remote Desktop and Remote Assistance, which allow you to connect to another computer and either troubleshoot problems or collaborate with another user on a project.

Using Advanced Help and Support Center Tools

You can use more advanced Help and Support Center tools to generate online reports about your computer. If you select the My Computer Information tool, you can display general information about your computer, such as the specific model of the computer you are using and its BIOS version (which can be important if you need to update the BIOS); details on the version of the operating system you are using, including whether you have installed a service pack upgrade or hot fix; the total amount of installed RAM; details on the processor, including its operating speed; general computer information, including the system name, the name of the domain to which the computer belongs, the type of connection, and the IP address of the computer; and information about the hard disk, including its total storage capacity and whether the hard disk is partitioned. A **service pack** consists of a set of updates for an operating system. A **hot fix** consists of one or more files used to correct a problem with the operating system software.

If you choose the option to view the status of your system hardware and software, Windows XP displays a Status report that lists any obsolete applications and device drivers; provides details on system software (your version of Windows and your BIOS) and a link for updating Windows XP; information on whether specific hardware components are supported, whether an update is required, and a link to a Help troubleshooter for troubleshooting each hardware component; the amount of storage space used on each disk partition; and the amount of installed RAM, as well as the minimum required for your version of Windows.

If you choose the option to view a list of Microsoft software installed on your computer, Windows XP displays a Software report that lists registered Microsoft software on your computer, software loaded from the Startup Program Group and its install date, and information about Windows Watson Crash Information. **Dr. Watson** is a system component that automatically starts and compiles information when an application error occurs. It stores the information it collects in a log file named Drwtsn32.log. That information might be useful to a Microsoft technical support person who is assisting you with a problem on your computer. This information includes application errors related to the **Microsoft Management Console**, a Windows component that supports the use of administrative tools called consoles. A **console** might consist of tools, folders, Web pages, or other items displayed in a console tree pane (like an Explorer folders toolbar or pane).

Deshi recommends that you use My Computer Information to display General, Status, and Software reports with information about your computer.

To examine information about your computer system:

1. From the Start menu, open the Help and Support Center, and under "Pick a task," click the **Use Tools to view your computer information and diagnose problems** Help link.

2. Under Tools, click the **My Computer Information** Help topic link, and then click the **View general system information about this computer** Help link. Windows XP compiles information about your computer, and displays a General Report with this information in the details pane on the right. See Figure 9-36. On the

computer used for this figure, Windows XP identifies the computer model and reports that the BIOS is an ACPI BIOS, indicating that it supports the Advanced Configuration and Power Interface (ACPI); in other words, it supports Plug and Play hardware detection and configuration, and power management. The report also provides information about the installed operating system, memory, the processor, the role of this computer in this home network, and the hard disk. Your General Report will differ.

 Figure 9-36   **VIEWING GENERAL INFORMATION ABOUT YOUR COMPUTER (YOURS WILL DIFFER)**

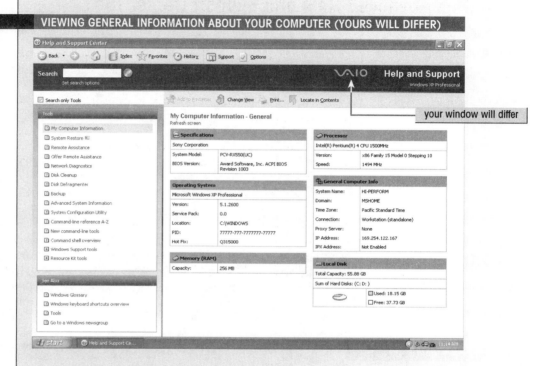

3. Click the **Print** button to print the general information about your computer.

4. Click the **Back** button , and if you are logged on under an account with Administrator privileges, click the **View the status of my system hardware and software link**. This Help option notes whether this feature is available to local administrators only. The My Computer Information – Status report appears. See Figure 9-37.

Figure 9-37   VIEWING INFORMATION ON THE STATUS OF HARDWARE AND SOFTWARE

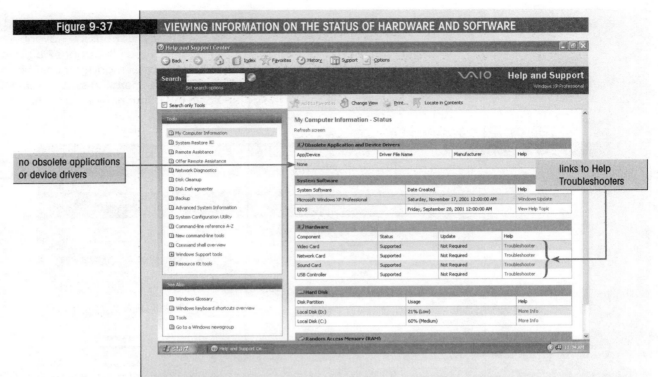

no obsolete applications or device drivers

links to Help Troubleshooters

5. Click [image], and then click the **View a list of Microsoft software installed on this computer** link. In the Software report, Windows XP identifies Microsoft registered software on this computer, programs in the Startup Program Group that are loaded during booting, and Dr. Watson Crash information. See Figure 9-38. Your Software report will differ.

Figure 9-38   VIEWING INFORMATION ON INSTALLED SOFTWARE

6. Scroll down to view information about Windows Watson Crash Information. On the computer shown in Figure 9-39, Dr. Watson has recorded information on four applications errors—one with the Windows Backup Utility (ntbackup.exe), two for the Microsoft Management Console (mmc.exe), and one with Windows Explorer itself.

Figure 9-39   **VIEWING INFORMATION ON APPLICATION ERRORS**

application errors tracked by Dr. Watson

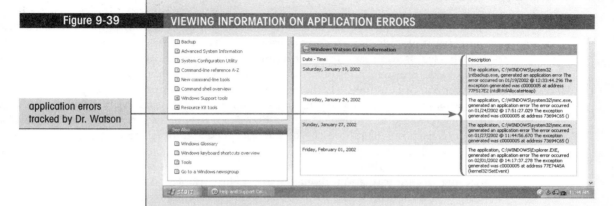

7. Click ⊙·, and then leave the Help and Support Center window open for the next section of the tutorial.

REFERENCE   WINDOW   RW

Viewing Information About Your Computer

- From the Start menu, open the Help and Support Center, and under "Pick a task," click the "Use Tools to view your computer information and diagnose problems" Help link.
- Under Tools, click the "My Computer Information" Help topic link.
- To view information about your computer model, the BIOS, the operating system, the amount of installed RAM, the processor, the role of your computer in a network, and the hard disks, click the "View general system information about this computer" Help link.
- If you want to print the information (or any other information) compiled by Windows XP, click the Print button.
- To view information about obsolete applications and device drivers, installed system software, memory, specific hardware components and whether an update is required, and hard disk partitions click the Back button, and if you are logged on under an account with Administrator privileges, click the "View the status of my system hardware and software" Help link.
- If you want to view information about adapters, cards, and other hardware installed on your computer, click the Back button, and then click the "Find information about the hardware installed on this computer" Help link.
- If you want to view information about Microsoft software installed on your computer, software loaded from the Startup Program Group, and Windows Watson Crash Information, click the Back button, and then click the "View a list of Microsoft software installed on this computer" Help link.
- If you want to view advanced system information and information about errors that occur on your computer, click the Back button, click the "View Advanced System Information" Help link (or the Advanced System Information Help topic link under Tools), and then click the Help link for the type of advanced system information you want to view.
- Close the Help and Support Center.

Microsoft has expanded the role of the Help system in Windows XP so that it provides you with easy access to information about your computer as well as troubleshooting tools and resources.

Using **the System Information Utility**

Another useful utility is the System Information utility. In addition to a detailed System Summary, it provides information on the use of hardware resources, hardware components, the software environment, Internet settings, and Office settings (if installed). After you open the System Information utility, it displays a System Summary that lists information about your version of Windows XP, the type of system and microprocessor in your computer, the BIOS manufacturer and version, and other information, such as how Windows XP uses memory (covered in Tutorial 10). The Hardware Resources category includes information on hardware problems, shared hardware resources, and forced hardware configurations that might provide useful information when troubleshooting hardware conflicts (covered in Tutorial 12). The Software Environment category includes an Environment Variables category that lists information about environment variables. An **environment variable** is a string of text that contains information about the computer system, such as the name of the operating system—namely, Windows_NT for Windows XP). The setting for an environment variable is assigned to a symbolic name (such as "OS") that acts as a pointer to the information about the operating system. Environment variables and their settings are stored in an area of memory known as the **Windows environment** (previously known as the DOS environment under the DOS operating system). Windows XP, applications, and utilities check the Windows environment for information that they need.

Deshi recommends that you also become familiar with the System Information utility, so that you can examine the status and configuration of staff computer systems and identify and troubleshoot problems. He also points out that if a Microsoft technical support representative asks you to look up information about your computer so that she can help you troubleshoot a problem, she might want you to use the My Computer Information tool in the Help and Support Center, the System Information utility, and Device Manager (which you will examine in Tutorial 12). After you open the System Information utility, you can then access other useful utilities.

To open the System Information utility:

1. Under "My Computer Information", click the **View Advanced System Information** Help link, click the **View detailed system information (Msinfo32.exe)** Help link, and then maximize the System Information window. See Figure 9-40. Windows XP compiled and displayed some of this information when you selected "My Computer Information" in the Help and Support Center. You can also open the System Information utility from the System Tools menu.

Figure 9-40   **USING SYSTEM INFORMATION TO VIEW A SYSTEM SUMMARY**

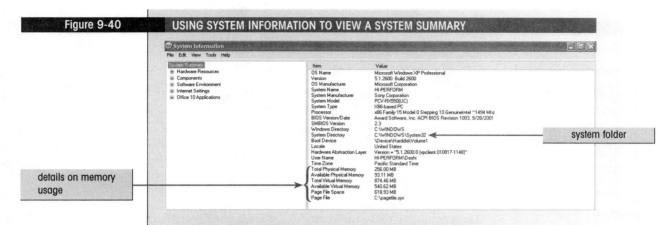

details on memory usage

system folder

2. Click the **expand view** box ⊞ to the left of the Hardware Resources category in the category pane on the left. The System Information utility expands this category to show you the types of information it can display on hardware-specific settings. The Conflicts/Sharing category is particularly useful because it lists hardware devices (if any) that share resources, or that are in conflict with each other. The Forced Hardware category identifies user changes to resources allocated to hardware devices, and is useful for troubleshooting Plug and Play problems.

3. Click ⊞ to the left of the Components category. From the Components category, you can display information about the configuration of various components on your computer. The Problem Devices category identifies hardware devices (if any) that are not properly configured. You can use the information in the Components category, for example, to find out what type of video display adapter your computer uses (it might be different from the information on the invoice for your computer if Windows XP uses a compatible device driver), whether you have any infrared devices in your system, the name of your modem port, the model or brand of your network adapter card, and whether you have any USB devices.

4. Click ⊞ to the left of the Software Environment category node. The Software Environment category provides detailed information on the software currently loaded in the computer's memory, such as drivers, running tasks, and loaded modules, as well as information on print jobs.

5. Under Software Environment, click the **Environment Variables** node and then double-click the borders between columns in the details pane on the right if you cannot view all the information. You can also drag the border between the category and details panes to the left so that you can view more of the details pane. The details pane lists environment variables and their corresponding values. See Figure 9-41. Your settings might differ from those shown in the figure (and described below).

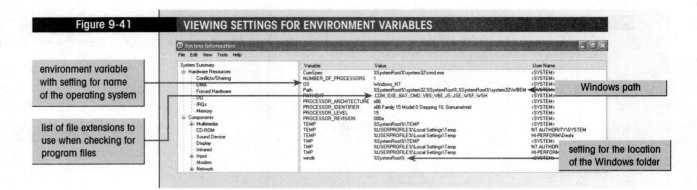

Figure 9-41   VIEWING SETTINGS FOR ENVIRONMENT VARIABLES

environment variable with setting for name of the operating system

list of file extensions to use when checking for program files

Windows path

setting for the location of the Windows folder

Understanding these environment variables gives you a better sense of how Windows XP works. The windir environment variable is assigned the value %SystemRoot%. SystemRoot refers to the directory or folder that contains Windows XP. During booting, Windows XP replaces SystemRoot with the path to the Windows folder. On this computer, that path is: C:\Windows

The ComSpec variable (a holdover from the DOS operating system) identifies the path of the command interpreter. If you open a Command Prompt window, or if you boot in Safe Mode with Command Prompt, Windows XP automatically starts this program. On the computer used for this figure, the path is: C:\Windows\system32\cmd.exe (because %SystemRoot% is replaced with its corresponding value, namely C:\Windows).

The Path variable (a holdover from the DOS operating system) identifies a sequence of directories (or folders) that contain program files that Windows XP searches to locate and load a program from disk. On the computer used for this figure, C:\Windows is substituted for %SystemRoot% in each part of the path, so that the final path used by Windows XP to locate programs is:

C:\Windows\system32;C:\Windows;C:\Windows\system32\WBEM

Note that the path for each directory is separated from the previous one by a semicolon. If you issue a command to use a specific program, Windows XP searches the current directory first to see if the program file is contained in that directory. If it finds the program file, it loads the program into memory. If it does not find the program file, it checks the path defined by the Path variable. When checking the path shown previously for a program file, Windows XP first checks the System32 folder (C:\Window\system32) because it is listed first in the path. If the program is not found in the System32 folder, then it checks the Windows directory next (in this case, C:\Windows). If the program is not found in the Windows directory, then it checks the Wbem folder (C:\Windows\system32\WBEM). These three directories contain program files for the Windows XP operating system.

The PATHEXT variable identifies a set of file extensions that are used to locate a program file, and is used with the Path variable. For example, if you want to open a Command Prompt window using Run on the Start menu, you can type CMD in the Run Open box and the press the Enter key. The command you type is actually the main part of the filename for the program file (for example, the program file for the CMD command is named CMD.EXE). Windows XP then checks the current directory and each of the directories listed in the path, in the order in which they are listed, for the program file. However, since program files can have different file extensions, Windows XP looks for that program file using the command you type and different possible file extensions. For example, in each directory it checks, it looks for a program using the first file extension in the PATHEXT variable (in this case, COM), and searches for a file named CMD.COM. If it finds a program by that name, it loads the program into memory so that you can use it. If it does not find a program by this name, then it looks for a program using the next file extension in the PATHEXT variable (in this case, EXE), and then searches for a file named CMD.EXE. As it turns out, CMD.EXE is the name of the program for opening a Command Prompt window, so it finds and loads this program from the System32 directory (or folder), the first directory it checks in the path. If this directory did not contain a program by this name, then it would repeat the same process on a directory-by-directory basis—using the Path environment variable and each of the file extensions contained within the PATHEXT environment variable.

If you are more specific and type CMD.EXE in the Run Open box, Windows XP searches for a file by that filename and file extension using the directories listed in the Path variable. Since it's common practice to first check for a program file with the COM file extension before checking for one with the EXE file extension, some computer viruses create a program file with the same name as a legitimate program on your computer, but use the COM file extension. When you specify the command for that program (without specifying the file extension), the contents of the file with the COM file extension (namely, the computer virus) is loaded into memory first, and then the computer virus passes control to the file with the EXE file extension so that it also loads. You are not even aware that a computer virus has been loaded into memory, and that it now has access to your entire system.

Figure 9-42 identifies the file extensions used in the PATHEXT variable. The DOS operating system used the same technique for locating program files; however, it looked only for files with the COM, EXE, and BAT file extensions (in that order). Those program file extensions were carried over to Windows, and additional file extensions were added.

Figure 9-42	FILE EXTENSIONS STORED IN THE PATHEXT ENVIRONMENT VARIABLE

EXTENSION	MEANING
COM	Command
EXE	Executable
BAT	Batch
CMD	Command
VBS	Visual Basic Script
VBE	VBScript Encoded Script File
JS	JScript
JSE	JScript Encoded Script File
WSF	Windows Script File
WSH	Windows Script Host

The System Information utility also includes a Startup Programs category that displays the name of each program or process loaded during startup, the filename or the full path for the command used to start the program or process, for which user (or users) it's loaded, and from where it's loaded—for example, Startup, Common Startup, or the Registry. From this information, you can identify what the loaded tasks represent. For example, you can associate the name of a loaded task (such as qttask) with the name of the program (namely, Quick Time Task). You can also use this information to verify whether a program is in fact loaded, from where it's loaded, and what command-line parameters (or switches) were used to load the program (if any). This information might be useful if you are attempting to identify a program that is affecting the performance of your computer or interfering with the use of another program.

In the Internet Settings category, you can view a summary of information about Internet Explorer (such as which version you are using, whether its cipher strength is 128-bit encryption, and whether Content Advisor is enabled), what files and file versions it uses, connectivity (LAN settings, ISP settings, modem settings, and network protocols), a summary or list of objects in the Internet cache, information about Content settings and certificates (which you can also obtain by examining the Content property sheet and Content Advisor in the Internet Explorer Properties dialog box), and security settings. A **cipher** refers to a method for encrypting data, and therefore **cipher strength** refers to the level of encoding which provides the greatest amount of security for the cipher. 128-bit encryption, which refers to the size of the key used to encrypt the message, is considered very secure. **Key** refers to the length of a variable value applied by an algorithm to a string or block of unencrypted data. A **certificate** is a digital document used to authenticate and guarantee the secure exchange of data over the Internet or an intranet.

Deshi asks you to examine several other categories before you export a copy of all the system settings to a file on disk. That file then provides a record of the system settings at that time.

To continue viewing information, and then export system settings to a file:

1. Under Software Environment, click **Startup Programs**, and then, if necessary, adjust the size of the category and details panes so that you can view as much information as possible. The System Information utility displays information about each program or process loaded during startup. See Figure 9-43. Note that in the Location column, items that begin with "HK" followed by a path are Registry keys, indicating that the program loads from the Registry during booting. Also note that, in some cases, the path listed in the Command column uses MS-DOS short filenames (such as the one for Microsoft Office).

Figure 9-43	VIEWING STARTUP PROGRAMS

2. Under the Software Environment category, click **Windows Error Reporting**. System Information reports on errors and problems that have occurred on the computer you are using (if any). See Figure 9-44. If you are trying to troubleshoot a problem with an application, you might want to examine this information to see any previous errors.

Figure 9-44	VIEWING APPLICATION ERRORS

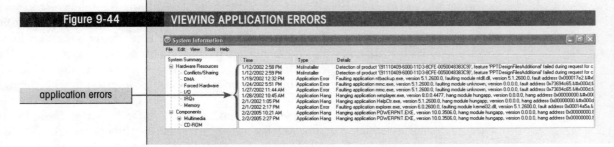

3. Click the **collapse view** boxes ⊟ to the left of the Hardware Resources, Components, and Software Environment categories, click the **expand view** box ⊞ to the left of the Internet Settings and the Internet Explorer categories, and then click **Summary** to view a summary of information about Internet Explorer, a list of objects in the Internet cache, information about Content settings and certificates, and security settings for your computer.

4. Click ⊞ to the left of the Applications category. Under this category, you find subcategories for each Microsoft application installed on your computer, and within each of those subcategories, System Information displays configuration information on the installed application.

TROUBLE? If you have installed Office XP on your computer, the Applications category is called Office 10 Applications.

5. Insert a blank, formatted floppy disk in drive A.

6. Click **System Summary** (at the top of the category pane), click **File** on the menu bar, click **Export**, and in the Export As dialog box, select **3½ Floppy (A:)** in the Save in list box, type **System Settings** followed by the current date (for example, System Settings 01-24-2005), and then click the **Save** button. A System Information dialog box shows you the progress of saving all system information in the file you specified.

7. Close the System Information window. If you want to take a break, also close the Help and Support Center; otherwise, if you intend to continue with the tutorial, leave the Help and Support Center open.

If you choose Save on the File menu instead of Export, the system settings are saved in a System Information File (with the file extension "nfo")—a file format that System Information can read. If you use the View menu to switch from "Current System Information" to "System History," you can choose to view a history of all changes to Hardware Resources, Components, and the Software Environment.

By exporting all system settings to a text file, you have a record of those settings on disk, and you can use that information to troubleshoot problems, or you can forward that information to a technical support representative who is assisting you. If you select System Summary in the category pane first, the report includes all the information found in all the categories. You can also select a specific category, and just save the information for that category. This information is important because, if you are forced to boot your computer in Safe Mode, the System Information utility only reports on system components and the software environment, and you do not have access to hardware information.

Using the System Information Utility

- Open the Help and Support Center, click the "Use Tools to view your computer information and diagnose problems" Help link under "Pick a task," click the "Advanced System Information" Help topic link under Tools, and then click the "View detailed system information (Msinfo32.exe)" Help link. Or from the Start menu, point to All Programs, point to Accessories, point to System Tools, and then click System Information.
- In the category pane on the left side of the System Information window, click the expand view box next to a category to view options under that category, and then select the category that contains the information you want to view. Repeat this process for each category you want to examine.
- If you want to export all the system settings to a text file, click "System Summary" at the top of the category pane on the left, click File on the menu bar, click Export, and in the Export As dialog box, select the drive and folder where you want to store the file, enter a name for the file, and then click Save. If you want to export settings for a specific category only, select that category first.
- After you find the information you need, close the System Information window.

You can access a variety of other utilities from the System Information utility. Once you have opened the System Information utility, select the Tools menu, and then select the utility you want to use. These additional utilities include:

- **Net Diagnostics.** You can use Network Diagnostics to scan your computer system and compile information about your hardware, software, and network connections. You can specify what actions you want this tool to perform, and for which categories you want information.

- **System Restore.** As you learned in Tutorial 8, System Restore allows you to restore your computer to a previous working state if you encounter a problem after an installation or upgrade.

- **File Signature Verification Tool.** This utility, shown in Figure 9-45, checks the system files on your computer to make sure that they have the correct digital signatures (if not, the files have been changed). When you install new software on your computer, that software might attempt to replace existing system files with new files that are unsigned or incompatible with Windows XP. The original files provided with Windows XP therefore all have a Microsoft digital signature. The **digital signature** is an encoded tag that verifies the authenticity of the originating party by binding information about that party to the file. This utility verifies the digital signatures of those files and reports on any changes to those files. If you run this utility, and it does not find any problems, it displays a SIGVERIF dialog box and informs, you that "Your files have been scanned and verified as digitally signed." If it finds files that have not been digitally signed, it lists the name, location (folder path), modified date, file type, and version (if known) for each file. If you want to view the log file, you click the Advanced button to open the Advanced File Signature Verification Settings dialog box, click the Logging tab, and then click the View Log button. The results are logged to a text file named Sigverif.txt, shown in Figure 9-46, in the Windows folder. It lists the total number of files scanned and not scanned (the latter are files that are not installed), the number of signed and unsigned files and, for each file, the filename, date of modification, version, status (for example, signed), catalog, and what entity provided the digital signature (for example, Microsoft Windows XP Publisher). You can also use the Search sheet in the

Advanced File Signature Verification Settings dialog box to look for other nonsystem files on your computer that are not digitally signed.

Figure 9-45	FILE SIGNATURE VERIFICATION UTILITY

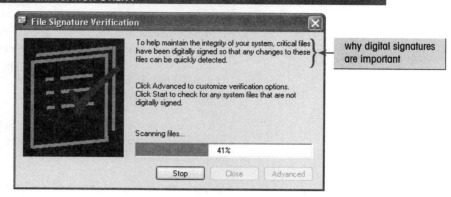

why digital signatures are important

Figure 9-46	VIEWING RESULTS OF SCANNING FOR DIGITAL SIGNATURES

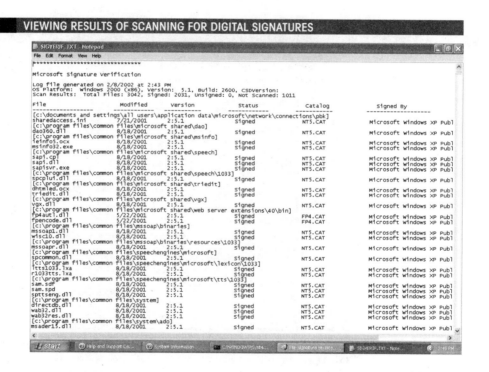

- **DirectX Diagnostic Tool**. This utility, shown in Figure 9-47, reports detailed information about the DirectX components and drivers installed on your computer system. **DirectX** is a Windows technology that enables games and programs to use the capabilities of your computer's multimedia hardware devices. You can use this utility to determine functionality, troubleshoot problems, and optimize your system's configuration. Each sheet contains detailed information about specific components, and the DirectX Diagnostic Tool reports which drivers are used with each component, and whether they are certified. Uncertified drivers are ones that have not been tested for compatibility with the versions of DirectX components used on your computer. In the Notes box at the bottom of the property sheets for different components, this tool lists problems that it finds, such as incorrect versions of

DirectX components, uncertified drivers, lack of hardware acceleration (indicating the need to upgrade the hardware), and devices that are not connected to the computer, as well as whether the DirectX components are working properly. If you upgraded your DirectX drivers, the More Help sheet contains a Restore button that allows you to open DirectX Setup and restore older versions of audio and display drivers.

The Display, Sound, Music, and Network sheets include options for testing specific components on your computer (assuming they've available). For example, if you click the Test DirectSound button on the Sound sheet, the DirectX Diagnostic Tool plays a series of sounds using different audio formats, and then asks you if you heard each sound. You might want to check these property sheets and make sure that Windows XP has access to all of the features that you thought were provided with the hardware in your computer (such as your video display adapter) and, if they are not available, then you can find out why that support is not available, and whether you need to download and install device drivers. If you use the DirectX Diagnostic Tool for your video display, your video display might blank out for a few seconds before it displays an image used as part of the test this tool performs.

Figure 9-47	DIRECTX DIAGNOSTIC TOOL

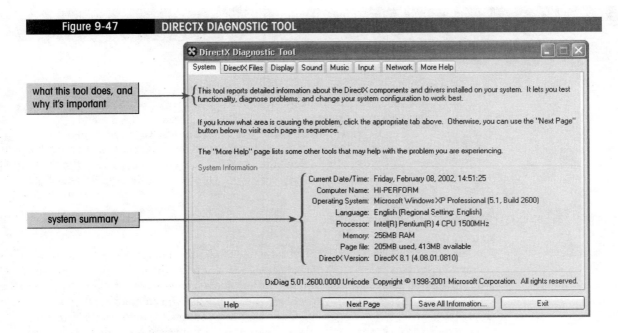

Dr. Watson. You can use this utility, shown in Figure 9-48, to record information about a problem on your computer, so that you can forward this information to a technical support person who can then evaluate the problem. The Dr. Watson utility logs information to a text file by the name of Drwtsn32.log. If a program error (called an **application exception**) occurs, Dr. Watson starts and logs information about the problem to the log file. The log file contains sections on the program error (which program caused the error, the date and time the error occurred, and the type of error), system information (computer name, user name, number of processors, processor type, and Windows version), a list of tasks running on the computer when the error occurred, a list of modules that the program loaded, and finally more detailed and more technical information about the actual problem that occurred and its effect on the system. If you experience a problem with an application, you can attach the Dr. Watson log to a problem report, and transmit the information to a Microsoft support technician via e-mail.

Figure 9-48   DR. WATSON

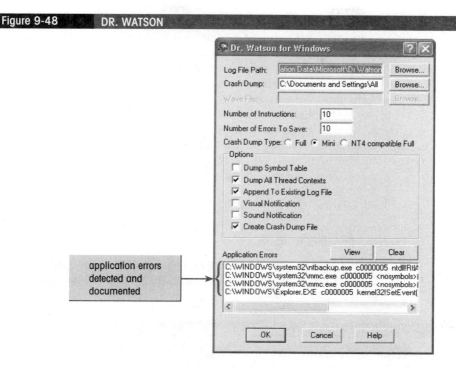

application errors detected and documented

Windows XP provides you with an assortment of tools and support (via the Help and Support Center) for examining, diagnosing, and configuring your system, as well as troubleshooting computer problems.

In the next section of the tutorial, you will examine how to use a Windows XP Help Troubleshooter to troubleshoot a problem. You will learn how to use Microsoft's Knowledge Base to locate troubleshooting information not available within Windows XP Help and Support Center. You will also examine the Remote Desktop and Remote Assistance features.

Using **Help Troubleshooters**

Windows XP Help Troubleshooters are designed to identify and resolve common problems by guiding you through the process of analyzing and identifying the source of a hardware or software problem. At each step, the troubleshooter explains what to do and asks you a question. Depending on your response, the troubleshooter might ask you another question in an attempt to more precisely define the problem. Or it might ask you to check and change settings, or perform a test. Two of the primary advantages of using troubleshooters is that they provide you with a starting point for solving a problem and a logical approach to troubleshooting.

For example, if you are having a problem with your printer, you can use the Printing Troubleshooter. Printer problems are quite common because applications have a wide variety of printing options that you can combine in different ways. These applications also must work on different types of computer systems that use different types of printers. Furthermore, individuals work with a wide range of documents—from short, simple letters or memos to complex, desktop publishing documents that combine an array of fonts and graphics.

As you step through the use of the Printing Troubleshooter, take into account that each computer uses a different type of printer, and that the Printing Troubleshooter in the next upgrade to Windows XP might have a different sequence of steps. That means you might have to adapt the instructions in the following steps. The primary purpose of these steps is to familiarize you with the use of one of the Windows XP Help Troubleshooters, and to examine common printing problems and solutions for resolving these problems.

You have just tried unsuccessfully to print a staff manual that you produced with a desktop publishing program. During Stephanie's workshop on troubleshooting computer problems, she told the staff that they can use the Windows XP Help Troubleshooters to solve problems with both hardware and software components. After further discussion with Deshi about the value of these troubleshooters, you decide to use the Printing Troubleshooter to see if it can help you solve this problem.

If Windows XP displays an Internet Explorer Script Error dialog box after any of the following steps, informing you that an error has occurred in the script on this page and asking if you want to continue running scripts on this page, click the No button, and continue with the steps.

To open the Printing Troubleshooter:

1. If necessary, open the Help and Support Center, click the **Home** button 🏠 , and then maximize its window.

2. Under "Pick a Help topic," click the **Fixing a problem** Help link. Under "Fixing a problem," Windows XP displays Help links for troubleshooting different types of problems. See Figure 9-49.

Figure 9-49   **VIEWING OPTIONS FOR FIXING PROBLEMS**

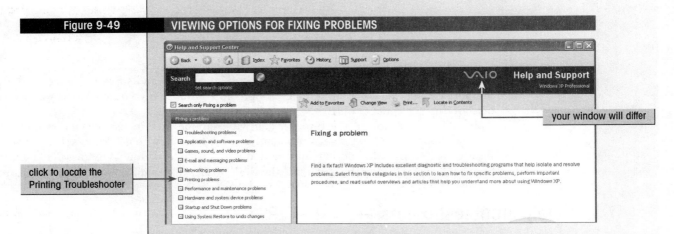

click to locate the
Printing Troubleshooter

your window will differ

3. Click the **Printing problems** Help link. In the details pane on the right, you can open the Printing Troubleshooter, fix a print problem, fix a connection problem, install new or updated printer drivers, print a test page, change a print setting so that complex pages print properly, cancel the printing of all documents, pause or resume printing of a document, get Help with printing, and examine print settings. See Figure 9-50.

TROUBLE? Windows XP Home Edition does not include a link for the Printing Troubleshooter or for printing a test page.

Figure 9-50   **ACCESSING HELP ON TROUBLESHOOTING PRINTING PROBLEMS**

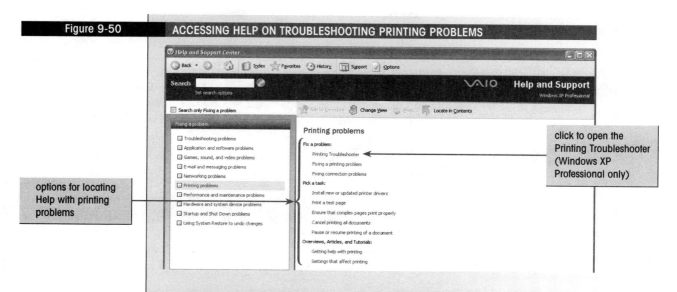

options for locating Help with printing problems

click to open the Printing Troubleshooter (Windows XP Professional only)

4. If you are using Windows XP Professional, click the **Printing Troubleshooter** Help link. If you are using Windows XP Home Edition, click the **Fixing a printing problem** Help link, click the **expand view** box ➕ to the left of Using the Printing Troubleshooter, and then click the **Step-by-step procedure** Help link. The Printing Troubleshooter asks you to identify the type of problem you are having, and it provides options for troubleshooting nine common printing problems. See Figure 9-51.

Figure 9-51   **IDENTIFYING YOUR PRINTING PROBLEM**

identify the type of printing problem you're facing

5. Click the **My document doesn't print at all** option button, and then click the **Next** button. The Printing Troubleshooter asks you if you can print other documents from the same program, and if you can print from Notepad. See Figure 9-52. It proposes that you create a new document in the program you are using, and then try to print the document. It notes that if you can print other documents, the original document is damaged in some way. If you are unable to print other documents in the same program, it recommends that you next try to print a document with Notepad or WordPad. Then it lists the

steps for printing a test page. Finally, it asks what happens when you try to print a test document. The choice you select affects what the Printing Troubleshooter proposes next. Assume you still cannot print any documents.

TROUBLE? If Windows XP displays an Internet Explorer Script Error dialog box, informing you that an error has occurred in the script on this page and asking if you want to continue running scripts on this page, click the No button.

Figure 9-52   TRY PRINTING A TEST DOCUMENT

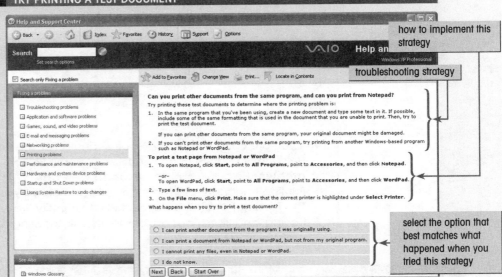

6. Click the **I cannot print any files, even in Notepad or WordPad** option button, and then click the **Next** button. The Printing Troubleshooter asks if you are printing to a network printer or a local printer. See Figure 9-53. If you click the Investigate button, the troubleshooter locates this information for you. Assume that you are trying to print to a new printer attached directly to the computer you are using.

Figure 9-53   ARE YOU USING A NETWORK OR LOCAL PRINTER?

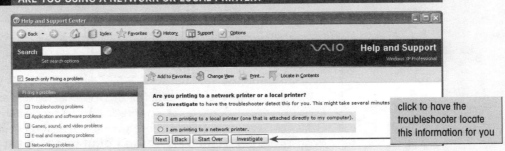

7. Click the **I am printing to a local printer (one that is attached directly to my computer)** option button, and then click the **Next** button. The Printing Troubleshooter now asks if you can print from a command prompt (a time-honored way of testing a printer connection). The Printing Troubleshooter explains that this option can determine whether there is a connection between your computer and printer. To complete this step, you need to determine to which port your printer is connected, and whether your printer is a Postscript or

non-Postscript printer. **PostScript** is a page-description language that defines how a document is to be printed. Assume you have a PostScript printer.

8. Click the **expand view** boxes ⊞ next to "To determine which port your printer is connected to" and "To print from a command prompt with a PostScript printer." The Printing Troubleshooter displays instructions for the steps you need to complete. See Figure 9-54.

Figure 9-54   **TRYING TO PRINT FROM A COMMAND PROMPT**

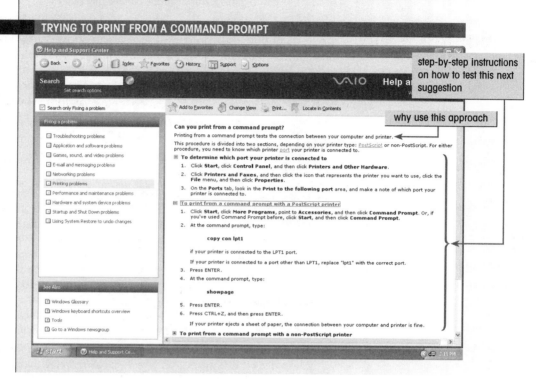

The first set of steps, determining your printer port, is straightforward; however, the option for printing from a command prompt with a Postscript or non-Postscript printer assumes you are familiar with the process of working in a Command Prompt window and that you are familiar with commands unique to that environment.

You decide to examine other possible options using the Printing Troubleshooter.

To continue with the Printing Troubleshooter:

1. Scroll further down the details pane, click the **I want to skip this step and try something else** option button, and then click the **Next** button. The Printing Troubleshooter asks if your printer is turned on and if it is online. Assume your printer cable is plugged into a power outlet, the printer's power switch is on, and your printer is online.

2. Click the **No, my printer is on and set to online, but I still have a problem** option button, and then click the **Next** button. The Printing Troubleshooter asks if you have installed your printer. You can use the Investigate button or manually open the Printers and Faxes folder, check for a printer icon for your printer, and verify that it is set as the default printer. Assume you have already verified that the printer is installed.

3. Click the **No, my printer is installed and set as the default printer, but I still have a problem** option button, and then click the **Next** button. The Printing Troubleshooter asks if your printer needs to be reset. Here, you are asked to turn your printer off and then on to clear the printer's memory. If you had clicked the Investigate button, and if the Printing Troubleshooter had detected an installed printer, the troubleshooter would have displayed this same screen. Assume that you tried this option, and it did not help.

4. Click the **No, this does not solve the problem** option button, and then click the **Next** button. The Printing Troubleshooter now asks you to restart your computer and, if possible, view this troubleshooter on another computer while you use the troubleshooter. Because most people have only one computer on a desk, this is not a reasonable expectation. Assume you have booted and examined this Help topic on the same computer several times.

5. Click the **No, I still cannot print** option button, and then click the **Next** button. The Printing Troubleshooter asks if printing is paused. It recommends you open the Printers and Faxes folder, right-click your printer icon, click either "Resume Printing" or "Use Printer Online" if they appear in the menu, and then try to print again.

6. Click the **No, this does not solve the problem. Or, these commands don't appear in the menu for any printer.** option button, and then click the **Next** button. You are now asked if the printer port is set correctly. If you view the instructions for verifying your local printer port, the Printing Troubleshooter asks you to open the Printers and Faxes folder, right-click the printer, select Properties, click the Ports tab, and check the port designated for your printer (which you might already have done when asked to print from a command prompt). It informs you that the most common printer port is LPT1 (for "Line Printer 1"), but that some printers require a different port, and recommends you check your printer documentation. Assume that you have checked and verified the printer port.

7. Click the **No, I am printing to the correct port or network path, but I still have a problem** option button, and then click the **Next** button. The Printing Troubleshooter now asks if you have at least 120 MB of free space on your hard disk. Windows XP needs storage space on the hard disk for spool files.

As noted in Tutorial 1, a spool file is a temporary file that contains a processed print job request, complete with printer formatting codes. If storage space on the hard disk is limited, this could be the source of the printing problem. To check this option, you can use the Investigate button, or you can open My Computer, right-click the icon for the disk where Windows XP is installed, and then view its properties.

The Printing Troubleshooter also provides information about making more space available. You can empty the Recycle Bin, use the Disk Cleanup tool, delete any documents or data files you do not need (or move them to another drive), or uninstall programs you do not need.

Like many other users, you are working on a computer where storage space is not a limiting factor yet.

To continue troubleshooting:

1. Click the **No, I have enough disk space, but I still have a problem** option button, and then click the **Next** button. The Printing Troubleshooter asks if there is a problem with your printer driver. It explains that a corrupted or outdated

printer driver might be the source of your printing problems. It includes instructions for deleting and then reinstalling your printer and printer driver, for finding and downloading an updated driver, and for installing an updated driver. To delete and reinstall your printer and printer driver, you open the Printers and Faxes folder, select and delete your printer icon, and then use the Add Printer wizard to reinstall support for your printer. To search for, and download, an updated driver, you use Windows Update on the All Programs menu. To install an updated driver, you open the Printers and Faxes folder, view properties of your printer, and on the Advanced property sheet, use the New Driver button to install support for your printer. During this process, you specify the manufacturer's name and printer model, and then indicate the location of the disk or folder that contains the updated driver. Assume you have downloaded and installed an updated device driver from the printer manufacturer's Web site, and that your printer now works.

2. Click the **Yes, this solves the problem** option button, and then click the **Next** button. After this, Windows XP thanks you for using the Printing Troubleshooter.

3. Click the **Start Over** button.

If you had continued to troubleshoot the problem using the Printing Troubleshooter, it would have asked you the following questions:

- **Is your printer supplied with paper, toner, and any other required supplies?** The Printing Troubleshooter asks you to verify that the printer has enough paper, is free of paper jams, and has sufficient toner or a fresh ink cartridge.

- **Do you need to change your spooler settings?** The Printing Troubleshooter explains that, if you are low on disk space, you can turn off printing spooling to increase printing speed. However, you must wait for a document to be printed before you can perform any other tasks on your computer. Although you might do this temporarily, you would be better off to increase the amount of available storage space on your hard disk, or install a new hard disk with greater storage capacity.

- **Is there a resource conflict for your port?** The Printing Troubleshooter asks you to open Device Manager and check for conflicts with other hardware devices. If you discover a hardware conflict, it recommends that you switch to the Hardware Troubleshooter. You will examine hardware conflicts in Tutorial 12.

- **Is your cable working correctly?** The Printing Troubleshooter asks you to verify that the printer cable is plugged in properly (you did this earlier), that there is not a problem with the cable itself, and, if you have a print switching device (so you can switch between two printers), that you connect the printer directly to the computer and bypass the print switching device to see if it's the source of the problem.

- **Is your port working?** The Printing Troubleshooter asks if the port itself is faulty. You can have it test the port for you with the Investigate button, or you can remove your printer port, restart your computer, and let Windows XP reinstall support for that printer port. It also recommends that you try connecting the printer to another port, and then try to print a document, to determine if the port is in fact the source of the problem.

■ **Can your printer perform a self-test?** The Printing Troubleshooter asks you to verify that the printer itself is working properly by printing a self-test directly from the printer. You might need to check your printer documentation for instructions on how to perform a self-test. Like checking to see if your printer is on, this is logically one of the first things you would test.

If you make it this far through the Printing Troubleshooter, and then decide to see what it recommends next, the troubleshooter informs you that it was unable to solve your problem. See Figure 9-55. It recommends you check the documentation for the program that you are using to print a document, or go to Microsoft's Web site and use troubleshooters for specific Microsoft programs, such as Microsoft Word and Microsoft Excel.

Figure 9-55	UNSOLVABLE PROBLEM

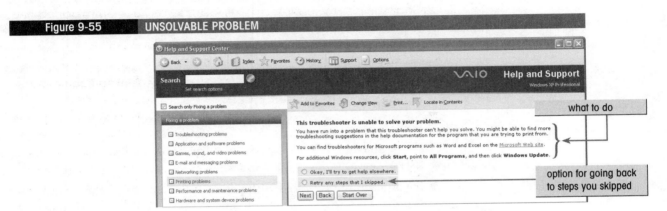

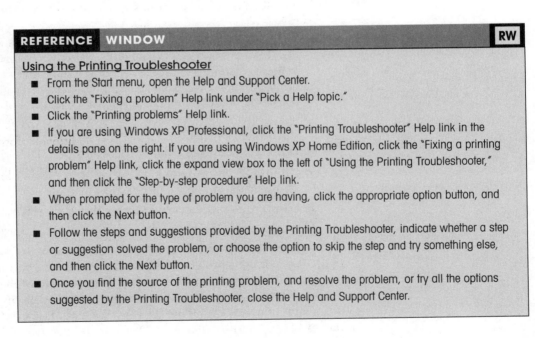

REFERENCE WINDOW **RW**

Using the Printing Troubleshooter

■ From the Start menu, open the Help and Support Center.

■ Click the "Fixing a problem" Help link under "Pick a Help topic."

■ Click the "Printing problems" Help link.

■ If you are using Windows XP Professional, click the "Printing Troubleshooter" Help link in the details pane on the right. If you are using Windows XP Home Edition, click the "Fixing a printing problem" Help link, click the expand view box to the left of "Using the Printing Troubleshooter," and then click the "Step-by-step procedure" Help link.

■ When prompted for the type of problem you are having, click the appropriate option button, and then click the Next button.

■ Follow the steps and suggestions provided by the Printing Troubleshooter, indicate whether a step or suggestion solved the problem, or choose the option to skip the step and try something else, and then click the Next button.

■ Once you find the source of the printing problem, and resolve the problem, or try all the options suggested by the Printing Troubleshooter, close the Help and Support Center.

Keep in mind that when you use a troubleshooter to help you solve a problem, your responses to each step in the troubleshooting process may determine what type of information the troubleshooter displays next and what suggestions it offers. In some cases, the troubleshooter might not find a solution to your problem. If this occurs, start over or back up, follow another set of options, and find out where they lead. In fact, you might want to play it safe and explore various options proposed by the troubleshooter by selecting and then reading them before you take action to solve the problem.

Help Troubleshooters also recommend that you refer to your hardware or software manuals, contact the hardware or software vendor or manufacturer, or check the support they provide at their Web site.

Using **Microsoft's Knowledge Base**

After installing the Recovery Console on his computer, Deshi was not able to log onto the Recovery Console using his Administrator password. He asks you to search the Microsoft Knowledge Base to see if you can find the information he needs to resolve this problem.

If you cannot find the information you need in the Windows XP Help and Support Center, you can try Microsoft's Knowledge Base. The Knowledge Base has hundreds of thousands of articles that provide you with information on how to use features and troubleshoot problems in Microsoft software. Depending on the nature of the information you need, a Knowledge Base article may contain one or more of the following sections:

- **Windows version(s)**. Each Knowledge Base article identifies the versions of Windows for which the information in the article applies.
- **Summary**. For articles that provide an overview of a Windows tool, such as Remote Assistance, or a process, such as troubleshooting printing problems, this section summarizes the contents of the article.
- **Symptoms**. This section identifies the type of problem you are likely to experience and the conditions under which the problem occurs, so that you can verify that you have located the appropriate article.
- **Cause**. This section explains why the problem occurred.
- **Resolution**. This section provides one or more ways to resolve the problem and includes links to other Web sites with further information, links for downloading an update, and links to other Knowledge Base Articles with related information.
- **Workaround**. In some cases, the Knowledge Base article might also describe workarounds for a particular problem.
- **More Information**. This section describes a process, such as how to install the Recovery Console, and provides additional information and warnings about the use of a specific feature.
- **Additional Information**. This section might have links to other Knowledge Base articles with more specific information.
- **Status**. This section includes a note that Microsoft has confirmed this problem.
- **Comments**? You might also have the option of providing comments to Microsoft on an article.

To locate the Web page for searching the Knowledge Base, you go to Microsoft's home page (*www.microsoft.com*), click Support at the upper-right of the Web page, and then click Knowledge Base. To use the Knowledge Base Search, you specify the product for which you want to locate information, and the keyword or keywords (a word or phrase) you want to use for the search.

The Search options that are available at this Web site also let you specify how the search engine uses your keywords (all of the words you enter, any of the words you enter, the exact phrase you enter, or a Boolean expression), whether to search the full text (the default) of an article, just the title of an article, or the Article ID. You can also indicate the length of time to use for the search (for example, anytime, or a time period ranging from three days to one year), and how many results to display at a time. A **Boolean expression** consists of one or more keywords that uses qualifiers such as AND or OR to specify multiple conditions and more precisely define what you want to locate. For example, you might use the Boolean expression "Recovery Console AND password" to locate all articles that include both terms in the text of the articles. Or you might use the Boolean expression "Remote Assistance OR Remote Desktop" to display a list of articles that discuss either Remote Assistance or Remote Desktop.

To resolve Deshi's problem, you can search the Knowledge Base using the phrase "Administrator password". The search results include an article titled "Cannot Log On To Recovery Console After Running Sysprep in Windows XP (Q308402)" that describes this problem. See Figure 9-56.

Figure 9-56   ARTICLE DESCRIBING A RECOVERY CONSOLE PROBLEM

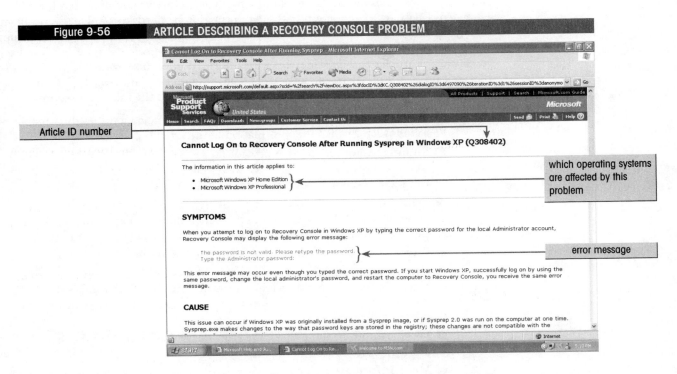

At the beginning of the article, Microsoft notes that the information in this article applies to Microsoft Windows XP Home Edition and Microsoft XP Professional. When looking for a solution to a problem, make sure that the Help you obtain from the Knowledge Base applies to the version of Windows you are using.

The Symptoms section of the article describes what you see when you encounter this problem. In this example, Microsoft notes that when you attempt to log onto the Recovery Console, the Recovery Console might display an error message indicating that your password is not valid. You are then prompted to retype the Administrator password. The article further notes that this error message might occur even if you enter the correct Administrator password. Even if you reboot, log on as Administrator, and change the Administrator password, you might still experience this problem. When examining the Symptoms section, make sure that the symptoms match what you experienced, and that any error messages match what is shown in the Knowledge Base article.

The Cause section explains the possible cause of the problem you're experiencing. In this example, the article explains that this problem can occur if Windows XP was originally installed using the System Preparation Tool (Sysprep) image, or if Sysprep 2.0 was run on the computer. Sysprep, in turn, changes the way password keys are stored in the Registry, and these changes are not compatible with the Recovery Console. Sysprep allows someone to create a disk image of one computer, and then copy that disk image to other computers. This process is obviously designed to save time and effort in deploying Windows XP on many computers, because the user of this tool does not need to install the operating system on each computer, install software applications on each computer, and configure each computer separately. However, as is evident from this article, such disk imaging tools can pose problems for you, and require Microsoft to develop a hot fix.

The Resolution section explains how to resolve the problem. The article notes that Microsoft provides a fix, but that it is intended only for computer systems that have this problem. The article further notes that Microsoft recommends you wait for the next Windows XP service pack upgrade to fix this problem. If you need to resolve the problem immediately, the article recommends you contact Microsoft to obtain a hot fix. Alternatively, you can download one of two files to create floppy disks that allow you to make repairs using the Recovery Console. These floppy disks are the Windows XP Setup Disks that you examined in the previous tutorial. The article further notes that this hot fix updates the Cmdcons folder if you have already installed the Recovery Console.

The Status section verifies that Microsoft has confirmed this as a problem in the products listed at the beginning of the article. The "More Information" section explains that if you reinstall the Recovery Console, you also need to reinstall the hot fix. If you choose, you can also provide comments to Microsoft about this article.

In addition to the Knowledge Base, another valuable resource is the Microsoft Windows XP Professional Resource Kit, which is approximately 1,700 pages long and contains information on the deployment of Windows, desktop management, security, networking, interoperability, and troubleshooting.

In Tutorials 10, 11, 12, and 13, you will examine other resources and strategies for optimizing and troubleshooting the use of memory on your computer, installing and troubleshooting software and hardware, and for customizing your system with the Windows XP Registry.

Using **Remote Desktop**

Remote Desktop is a new feature available in Windows XP Professional, but not Windows XP Home Edition. Using Remote Desktop, you can access a computer running Windows XP Professional (called the remote computer) from another computer that has any version of Windows (called the client computer). For example, you could connect to your work computer from home or while traveling as long as your work computer is running Windows XP Professional. You can also use Remote Desktop to connect to another computer and troubleshoot problems on that other computer. The computer to which you connect must have Remote Desktop Connection installed on it.

You can establish the remote connection via a dial-up, ISDN, DSL, or virtual private network connection, via the Internet or using a local area network (LAN) or wide area network (WAN). A **virtual private network (VPN)** is an extension of a private network to include public or shared networks, such as the Internet. Once you make the connection to another computer, that computer is locked, and any operations you perform on the other computer are not visible on that computer's monitor. Plus, no one can use the keyboard or mouse on the computer to which you've connected. Once the Remote Desktop connection is established, you have access to the remote computer's file system, software, and hardware; you can use applications from the remote computer on your computer; and you can redirect video, audio, and print jobs to your computer.

Before you can set up a Remote Desktop connection, you must complete the following tasks:

- **Enable Remote Desktop on the computer with Windows XP Professional**. After logging on as Administrator, right-click My Computer on the Start menu, select Properties, and in the System Properties dialog box, select the Remote tab, shown in Figure 9-57. Then you can enable Remote Desktop by selecting the "Allow users to connect remotely to this computer" check box.

Figure 9-57   ENABLING REMOTE DESKTOP

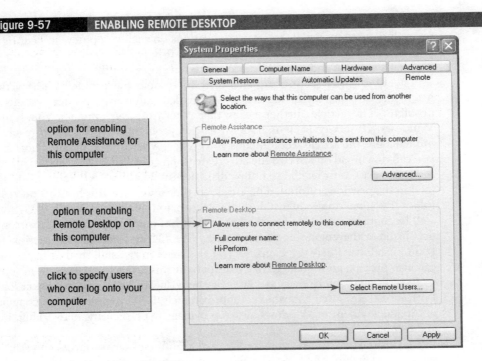

option for enabling Remote Assistance for this computer

option for enabling Remote Desktop on this computer

click to specify users who can log onto your computer

■ **Select the remote users you want to allow to connect to your computer**. From the Remote property sheet, you click the Select Remote Users button and, in the Remote Desktop Users dialog box shown in Figure 9-58, you use the Add button to select the users. The users you select must have an account with a password. Any member of the Administrators group can connect even if they are not listed here.

Figure 9-58   SELECTING REMOTE DESKTOP USERS

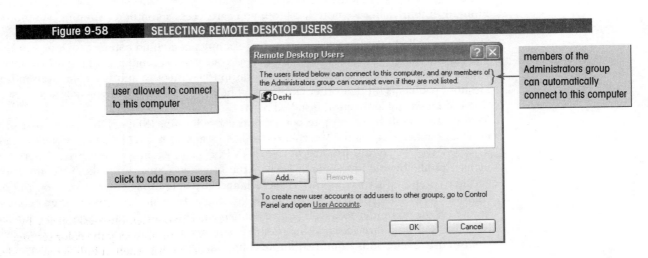

user allowed to connect to this computer

click to add more users

members of the Administrators group can automatically connect to this computer

■ **Install Remote Desktop Connection on the client computer**. The client computer is the computer you use to remotely connect to your Windows XP Professional computer. To install Remote Desktop Connection on a computer with Windows 2000, Windows NT 4.0, Windows 98, or Windows 95, insert your Windows XP Professional CD into the CD drive on that computer, and when the Welcome to Microsoft Windows XP window opens, choose the "Perform Additional Tasks" option, and then choose "Set up Remote Desktop Connection." A Remote Desktop Connection shortcut is then added to the Communications menu (under the Accessories menu).

After completing these tasks, you're ready to establish a Remote Desktop connection with another computer. The following steps provide an overview of a Remote Desktop session:

- To create a connection, open Remote Desktop Connection on the client computer by selecting Remote Desktop Connection from the Communications menu.

- Once the Remote Desktop Connection dialog box opens, click the Options button to expand the dialog box. See Figure 9-59. Under Logon settings, you enter the computer name or IP address in the Computer box (or browse for the computer), and then enter your user name, password, and domain (if required). You can save (or open) Remote Desktop connection settings you specify in a Remote Desktop File with the ".rdp" file extension for each particular Remote Desktop connection.

Figure 9-59   **CREATING A REMOTE DESKTOP CONNECTION**

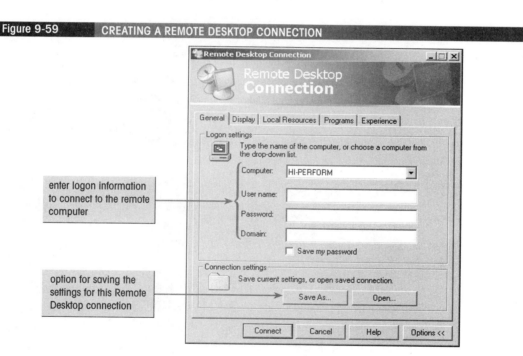

enter logon information to connect to the remote computer

option for saving the settings for this Remote Desktop connection

- On the Display property sheet, you can specify the Remote Desktop size by choosing Full Screen or a specific screen resolution, specify the color setting, and choose the option to display the connection bar when in Full Screen mode.

On the Local Resources property sheet, you can choose the option for bringing the remote computer's sound to your computer, use Windows key combinations, and automatically connect to disk drives, printers, and serial ports on the remote computer. On the Programs property sheet, you can specify the name and path of a program to start once the Remote Desktop connection is made. On the Experience property sheet, you can choose your connection speed (modem, broadband, LAN, or custom) to optimize performance, and you can choose whether to show the desktop background, display the contents of windows when dragging, display menu and window animation, display themes, and use bitmap caching. **Bitmap caching** optimizes the connection by storing frequently used images from the remote computer on your hard disk.

■ After you set up your computer, you click the Connect button. If you've chosen Full Screen mode, the desktop of the remote computer appears above your desktop and fills the entire screen, and the user on the remote computer is logged out. See Figure 9-60. You also see a connection bar (which is not visible in the captured screen shot) at the top of the screen, and it identifies the computer to which you've connected. If you click the Restore button on the connection bar, the remote computer's desktop appears within a window on your desktop. See Figure 9-61.

| Figure 9-60 | DESKTOP OF REMOTE COMPUTER |

a connection bar appears at the top center of the desktop for controlling the window on the remote computer

Figure 9-61 REMOTE DESKTOP WINDOW

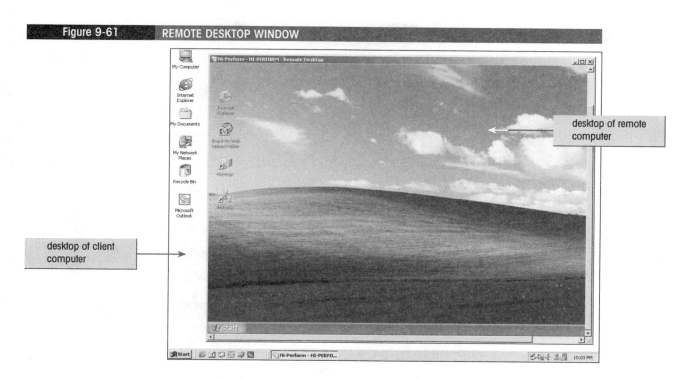

desktop of remote computer

desktop of client computer

■ As shown in Figure 9-62, you can open the Start menu on the remote computer, and as shown in Figure 9-63, you can open the Start menu on your computer. As you can see from the Start menu, the client computer is the one with Windows 2000. Figure 9-63 also shows the System Properties dialog box from the remote computer with Windows XP Professional.

Figure 9-62 OPENING ANOTHER USER'S START MENU

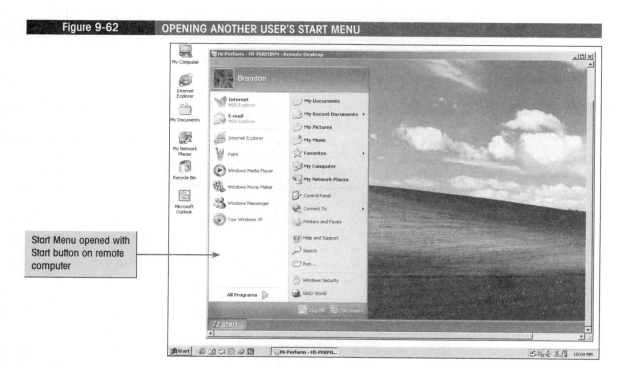

Start Menu opened with Start button on remote computer

Figure 9-63	WORKING ON TWO DIFFERENT DESKTOPS

Windows XP System Properties dialog box for the remote computer

Windows 2000 Professional Start Menu on the client computer

- You can now troubleshoot that user's computer system, or you can assist with some other type of task, such as creating a presentation or a spreadsheet.
- When you're ready to disconnect from the remote computer, click the Close button on the connection bar, or close the desktop window onto the remote computer. The Disconnect Windows dialog box opens so that you can verify the operation. It also informs you that your programs on the remote computer are still running, and that you can reconnect to that remote computer later. The remote computer user must log back onto his computer after you are finished.

Another valuable remote assistance tool is Remote Assistance.

Using **Remote Assistance**

Remote Assistance is a new feature in Windows XP Professional and also Windows XP Home Edition. You can use Remote Assistance to allow another person to connect to your computer system remotely, and help you with a problem you're experiencing. Likewise, you can connect to another person's computer and help that person. Both computers must be running a version of Windows XP. Also, both individuals must be present at their computers and must work with each other. You can establish the remote connection via the Internet or using a local area network (LAN). The connection still works even if one or both individuals work on a computer with a firewall.

If you want someone to examine your computer, you contact that person and provide the password you intend to use for the Remote Assistance session. You are referred to as the **novice**, the one who extends the invitation, and the other person is referred to as the **expert**, the one accepting the invitation. The following steps provide an overview of a Remote Assistance session:

- To start a Remote Assistance session, the novice opens the Help and Support Center, and clicks the "Invite a friend to connect to your computer with Remote Assistance" link or button. The novice can choose to invite someone to help him or view the status of invitations that he has already extended. After choosing the option for inviting someone to help, the novice can use Windows Messenger or e-mail to extend the invitation. The novice can also save the invitation to a file in a shared folder on a network. In the invitation, the novice provides his name, specifies when the invitation expires (such as in one hour), specifies a password for access to the Remote Assistance session, and then saves the invitation to a file on disk. The expiration time and password are important for protecting the security of the novice's computer. If the invitation is saved to disk, the file has an "msrcincident" file extension and Windows XP identifies the file type as a "Microsoft Remote Assistance Incident" file.

■ After receiving the invitation, or after opening the file with the invitation, the expert enters the password, and then chooses the option for connecting to the novice's computer. See Figure 9-64. On the computer used for this figure, the expert opened an invitation from a shared folder on a network.

Figure 9-64	EXPERT RESPONDING TO A NOVICE'S INVITATION

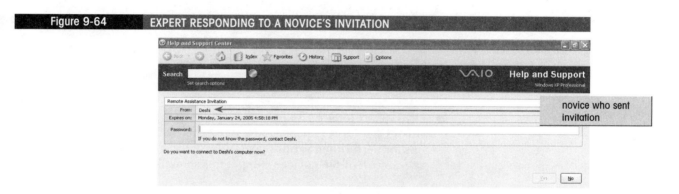

■ The novice receives a message indicating that the expert has accepted his invitation, and is then asked if he wants the expert to view his screen and chat with him. See Figure 9-65.

Figure 9-65	NOVICE NOTIFIED THAT THE EXPERT ACCEPTED HIS INVITATION

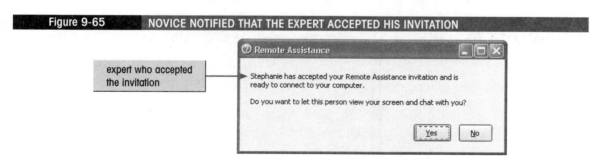

■ After he clicks the Yes button, the novice's Remote Assistance includes Chat History, Message Entry, and Connection Status panes, and buttons for taking control away from the expert (if necessary), sending a file, starting a conversation via a microphone, specifying settings, disconnecting, and viewing Help. See Figure 9-66.

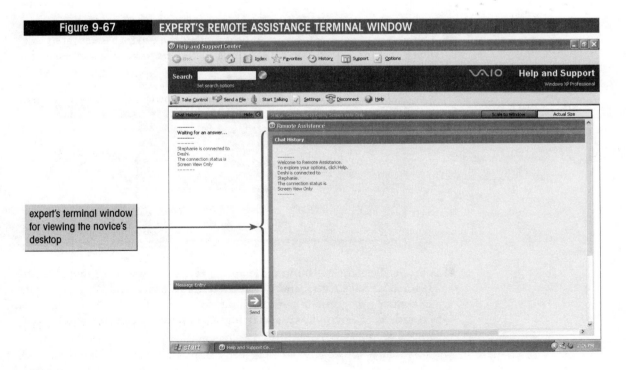

Figure 9-66   NOVICE'S REMOTE ASSISTANCE WINDOW

- expert
- click to talk over the Internet
- type a message
- click to send message

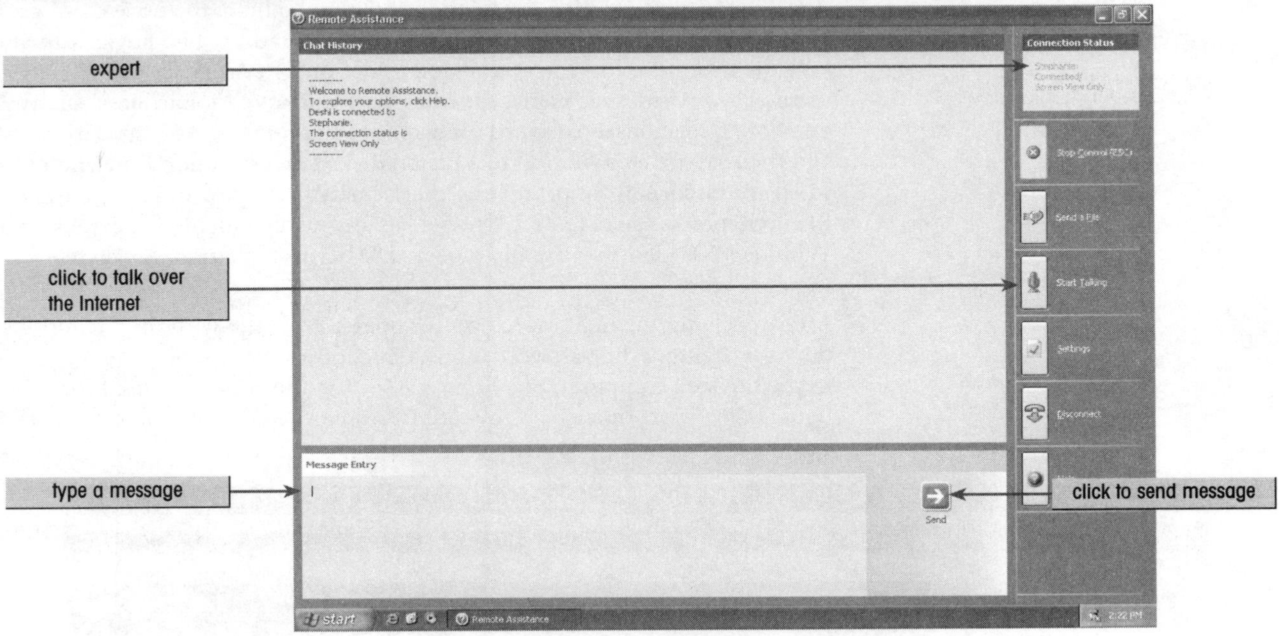

- The expert's Remote Assistance window consists of a terminal window with a Chat History pane, a Message Entry pane, and the same set of buttons for performing various operations, except for one. The expert can take control of the novice's computer system. See Figure 9-67.

Figure 9-67   EXPERT'S REMOTE ASSISTANCE TERMINAL WINDOW

- expert's terminal window for viewing the novice's desktop

■ The novice can use the Chat feature to enter and send a message that explains the problem to the expert. See Figure 9-68.

Figure 9-68   NOVICE'S MESSAGE SENT VIA CHAT

■ When the expert clicks her Take Control button, a Remote Assistance — Web Page Dialog box on both the novice's and expert's systems explains that the expert wants to share control of the novice's computer to help him solve his problem. The Remote Assistance dialog box also recommends that they should not use the mouse at the same time. Also, it notes that the novice can press the Esc key to take control away from the expert. See Figure 9-69.

Figure 9-69   EXPERT REQUESTS CONTROL OF A NOVICE'S COMPUTER

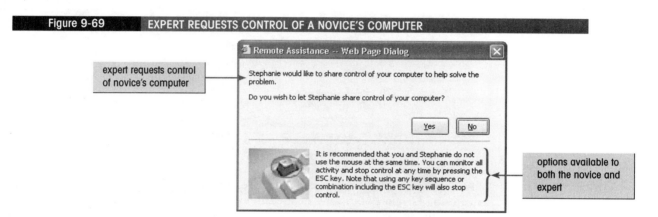

■ Once the novice agrees, a Remote Assistance dialog box on the expert's computer explains that the expert is now sharing control of the novice's computer. See Figure 9-70.

Figure 9-70   EXPERT AND NOVICE SHARE CONTROL OF NOVICE'S COMPUTER

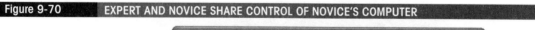
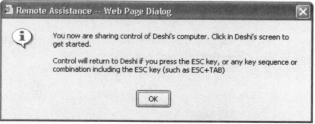

■ The expert can click the Scale to Window button to show the novice's desktop within the expert's terminal window on the right. In Figure 9-71, the expert has already opened the novice's Printers and Faxes folder, right-clicked the installed network printer, selected Properties on the printer's shortcut menu, and then clicked the Ports property sheet to view the network printer connection to see if that is the source of the problem. When the expert resolves the problem or gathers more information about the problem, the expert can disconnect from the novice's computer.

| Figure 9-71 | EXPERT ANALYZING A PROBLEM ON A NOVICE'S COMPUTER |

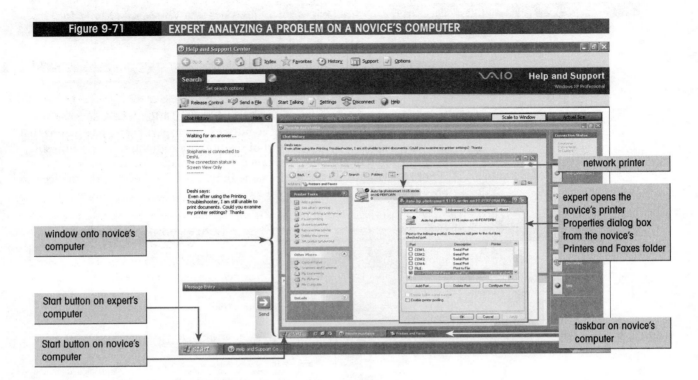

An expert with Administrator privileges can enable the option for offering remote assistance using Group Policy, so that she can extend an offer of assistance directly to another person without receiving an invitation. **Group Policy** is a Microsoft Management Console snap-in that an Administrator can use to specify a wide variety of policy settings, including system, network, and security settings.

If you discover that you have an aptitude for troubleshooting computer problems, and if you have Windows XP Professional, then you can use both Remote Desktop and Remote Assistance to assist your clients and build a home-based business.

Restoring Your Computer

If you want to restore your computer to its original state before you started the tutorial, complete the following steps.

To restore your computer's display settings:

1. If your computer was originally set for the Windows Classic style, right-click the **desktop**, click **Properties** on the shortcut menu, and after Windows XP opens the Display Properties dialog box, click the **Theme** list arrow on the Themes property sheet, click **Windows Classic**, and then click the **OK** button.

2. To switch to the Windows Classic Start menu style, right-click the **Start** button, click **Properties** on the shortcut menu, and after Windows XP opens the Taskbar and Start Menu Properties dialog box, click the **Classic Start menu** option button on the Start Menu property sheet, and then click the **OK** button.

3. To change to Windows classic folders view, click the **Start** button, point to **Settings**, click **Control Panel**, and after Windows XP opens a Control Panel window, click **Tools** on the menu bar, click **Folder Options**, and after Windows XP opens the Folder Options dialog box, click the **Use Windows classic folders** option button, and then click the **Double-click to open an item** option button under "Click items as follows".

4. Click the **View** tab in the Folder Options dialog box. If necessary, restore the original settings for the "Display the full path in the address bar" check box, the "Do not show hidden files and folders" option, the "Hide extensions for known file types" check box, and the "Hide protected operating system files" check box.

5. Click the **OK** button to close the Folder Options dialog box and restore your original settings, and then close the Control Panel folder window.

Thanks to your efforts and the assistance of Stephanie and Deshi, staff members at Yellow Brick Child Care Services now know how to troubleshoot their computer systems by using the best possible troubleshooting strategy and a rich assortment of Windows XP tools and utilities. Furthermore, Stephanie can use Remote Desktop and Remote Assistance from her work or home computer to assist you and other staff members when you encounter a difficult problem that can be handled with these remote assistance tools.

REVIEW ASSIGNMENTS

Jessica Thompson, one of Deshi's coworkers, has experienced printing problems with Microsoft Word documents that contain graphic images. She also mentions that the printer sometimes displays a message indicating that there is an overflow. You offer to help her troubleshoot these problems.

As you complete each step in these Review Assignments, record your answers to questions so that you can submit them to your instructor. Use a word-processing application such as Word or WordPad to prepare and then print your answers to these questions. Also, if you change any settings on the computer you are using, note the original settings so that you can restore them later.

To complete some of these steps, you might need to log on your computer under an account with Administrator privileges.

1. What troubleshooting strategy can you use to help Jessica solve her problem? Briefly outline the steps you might take prior to actually troubleshooting the problem described above.

2. Open the Windows XP Help and Support Center, click the "Printing and faxing" link under "Pick a Help topic," click the "Fixing a printing problem" link under "Printing and faxing," and then use the Printing Troubleshooter to assist you with this problem. After considering the questions posed by the Printing Troubleshooter, what do you think is the most likely cause of this problem? Explain how you arrived at this conclusion.

3. What does the Printing Troubleshooter recommend that you try?

4. What Windows XP features can you use to provide you with more information about the likely cause of this problem?

5. If you follow the recommendations of the Printing Troubleshooter, test what you think is the most likely cause of the problem, and then discover that the problem remains, what other possible causes might you investigate?

6. Close the Printing Troubleshooter.

   After resolving this problem, another coworker complains that his monitor flickers, and occasionally his desktop view is garbled. After talking with him, you learn that he recently changed display settings on his computer. You decide to step the coworker through the use of the Display Troubleshooter, and show him how to use a troubleshooter to check his display settings.

7. Click the "Go to the Help and Support home page" button 🔘 , click the Hardware link under "Pick a Help topic," click the "Fixing a hardware problem" link under Hardware, click the Display Troubleshooter link under "Fixing a hardware problem," choose the "My display flickers or is garbled" option when asked what problem you are having, and then click the Next button.

8. When asked if you have a redraw problem, click the "I don't know" option, and then click the Next button to locate the Help topic "Are your display settings appropriate for your hardware?"

Explore 9. What does the Display Troubleshooter recommend that you do if you do not see anything on the computer screen?

Explore 10. How do you change your display settings? What specific options does the Display Troubleshooter recommend that you adjust? Does the Display Troubleshooter provide any warnings? If so, what are they?

11. Return to the Help and Support Center's home page, click the "Use Tools to view your computer information and diagnose problems" link, click the "My Computer Information" link, and then click the "View the status of my system hardware and software" link. Can this feature of the Help and Support Center provide any useful information? Explain.

12. Click the Advanced System Information Help topic link under Tools, and then click the "View detailed system information (MsInfo32.exe)" link. Are there any categories under Hardware Resources, Components, Software Environment, Internet Settings, or Applications that might provide you with information to troubleshoot this problem? Explain.

Explore 13. Click Tools on the menu bar, click DirectX Diagnostic Tool, and then click the Display tab. Would there be any value to checking the information provided by this tool when troubleshooting this problem? Explain.

14. Close the DirectX Diagnostic Tool, and then close the System Information window.

15. Are there any other sources that you could check for more information on this problem? If so, list those sources.

16. Are there any other tools that you might consider using to troubleshoot the problem? If so, list those tools.

CASE PROBLEMS

Case 1. Troubleshooting a Modem at Muelrath & Harbaugh Dental Group The Muelrath & Harbaugh Dental Group provides regular, restorative, and cosmetic dentistry services. Shelby Harwick, the office manager, just encountered a problem with her external modem when she was trying to connect to the Internet. For some reason, Windows XP did not detect her modem. Also, prior to this problem, she noticed that the transmission speed of the modem was well below the rated speed of 56K. She wants to find out why this is the case.

As you complete each step in this case, record your answers to questions so that you can submit them to your instructor. Use a word-processing application such as Word or WordPad to prepare and then print your answers to these questions. Also, if you change any settings on the computer you are using, note the original settings so that you can restore them later.

1. Open the Help and Support Center, choose the option for using the Modem Troubleshooter, and select the option that corresponds to the type of problem that Shelby observed on her computer. Which option did you select?

Explore

2. Using Figure 9-72 as a guideline, prepare a list of each possible type of problem that the Modem Troubleshooter identifies, and describe how you would test that option. Identify any Windows XP tools or features required for each troubleshooting option. Do not attempt to list all the information provided by the Modem Troubleshooter; instead, be concise in listing the possible causes, and solutions. An example is shown in the table for one of the possible causes reported by the Modem Troubleshooter. Print the list of guidelines that you prepare.

Explore

3. Open the System Information utility and locate information on your modem. What is the brand name of your modem? Is it an internal, or external modem? To what port is the modem attached? What is the name of the modem's "inf" file?

4. Check the Conflicts/Sharing, Forced Hardware, and Problem Devices nodes. Is the modem listed in any of these categories? If so, which categories?

5. Search the Help and Support Center for information on modem speed, and then locate information on attaining fast speed with a 56 Kbps modem. Answer the following questions:

   - What three requirements must a modem connection meet to support a 56 Kbps connection?
   - What happens if a modem connection does not meet these requirements?
   - Are there other factors that might affect modem transmission speeds? Explain.
   - What is the maximum allowed modem transmission speed over public phone systems?
   - What is the average modem transmission speed over public phone systems?

| Figure 9-72 | COMPILING TROUBLESHOOTING INFORMATION FOR A MODEM |

	Possible Cause	What to do
1		•
2	Modem disabled	• Use Device Manager to verify that the device is enabled
3		•
4		•
5		•
6		•
7		•
8		•

Case 2. Troubleshooting a Shutdown Problem at JFM Systems Using the Microsoft Knowledge Base JFM Systems installs fiber-optic cable, components, equipment, and systems for its clients in Philadelphia. Elsie Simmons, a technical representative, installed Windows XP on her computer system at home. Periodically, Windows XP displays a "Wait, End Task, or Cancel" dialog box when she shuts down her computer. Since she uses her computer at home to prepare documentation for clients of JFM Systems, she wants her computer to function as reliably as possible. At work the next day, she uses her desktop computer to look for Help information on Windows XP shutdown problems in the Microsoft Support Knowledge Base.

As you complete each step in this case, record your answers to questions so that you can submit them to your instructor. Use a word-processing application such as Word or WordPad to prepare and then print your answers to these questions. Also, if you change any settings on the computer you are using, note the original settings so that you can restore them later.

1. Connect to Microsoft's Web site (*www.microsoft.com*), and then choose the option for using the Knowledge Base from the Support menu.

2. Use the search string "shutdown problems" to search for articles on Windows XP shutdown problems.

3. Locate and open the article entitled "HOW TO: Increase Shutdown Time So That Processes Can Quit Properly in Windows XP (Q305788)".

4. To what operating systems does the information in this article apply?

5. What important warning does Microsoft include at the beginning of this article?

Explore 6. Explain what happens when Windows shuts down.

7. What is the next warning provided by Microsoft?

Explore 8. How can you prolong the time-out period during shutdown?

9. Are there any other precautions that Microsoft warns you about?

Case 3. Using the DirectX Diagnostic Tool at A&E Construction Company A&E Construction Company provides general construction services to commercial businesses and residential properties. Zhou Qiao, an administrative assistant, wants to check his computer system to determine if it supports DirectX.

As you complete each step in this case, record your answers to questions so that you can submit them to your instructor. Use a word-processing application such as Word or WordPad to prepare and then print your answers to these questions. Also, if you change any settings on the computer you are using, note the original settings so that you can restore them later.

1. Open the System Information utility, and then open the DirectX Diagnostic Tool.

2. Using the information provided on the System sheet, list the name and version of the operating system, the processor type and speed, the amount of RAM, and the DirectX Version on your computer.

3. Check the Notes box on the DirectX Files, Display, Sound, Music, Input, and Network sheets, and list any problems, such as missing files, found by this diagnostic tool.

4. Select the Display property sheet.

5. Using the information on this sheet, list the name of your video display card, amount of video RAM (approximate total memory), current display mode, and refresh frequency (expressed in Hz) on your computer.

Explore 6. In the DirectX Features section, list which features are enabled and which are not available. If the DirectDraw Acceleration option is enabled, use the Test DirectDraw button to test this feature on your computer. If the Direct3D Acceleration option is enabled, use the Test Direct3D button to test this feature on your computer. What information does the DirectX Diagnostic Tool report about the use of DirectDraw and Direct3D functionality in the Notes box after you complete these tests?

Explore 7. If the computer you are using has speakers, turn on your speakers (if necessary), select the Sound sheet, and use the Test DirectSound button to test different audio formats, and then summarize the results.

Explore 8. If the computer you are using has speakers, select the Music sheet, and use the Test DirectMusic button to test the functionality of this feature. Test different ports by selecting each one from the "Test using this port" list box. Summarize the results of the tests you performed.

9. At the conclusion of your tests, use the Save All Information button to save a copy of the information in a file named DxDiag.txt on a floppy disk or, if you prefer, in a folder that contains documentation for your computer.

10. Close the DirectX Diagnostic Tool, and then close the System Information utility.

Case 4. Using the Recovery Console at Morrisey & Dubois Law Offices Morrisey & Dubois Law Offices specialize in the preparation of bond documents for major state reconstruction projects. Since the lawyers and their staff work under very tight deadlines to prepare documents that are hundreds of pages in length, they cannot afford any computer downtime, and therefore they rely on Suzanne Johnson, their computer support specialist, to perform regular maintenance checks on their computer systems and to troubleshoot problems that arise. Anticipating the possibility that she might need to use the Recovery Console to troubleshoot a serious computer problem, she decides to check and, if necessary, change Recovery Console settings, and to become more familiar with using commands in the Recovery Console.

To complete this case problem, you must use a computer that already has the Recovery Console installed on it, or you must install the Recovery Console on your computer. Also, you need to log on under an account with Administrator privileges to check and change Recovery Console settings and to use the Recovery Console.

As you complete each step in this case, record your answers to questions so that you can submit them to your instructor. Use a word-processing application such as Word or WordPad to prepare and then print your answers to these questions. Also, if you change any settings on the computer you are using, note the original settings so that you can restore them later.

1. Log onto your computer under an account with Administrator privileges.

2. Open Local Security Policy from the Administrative Tools menu. *Note*: If Administrative Tools is not listed on the All Programs menu, open the Taskbar and Start Menu properties dialog box, and choose the option to display System Administrative Tools on the All Programs menu.

3. Select Security Options under Local Policies, double-click the border between Policy (settings) and Security Setting, and locate the two policy settings for the Recovery Console. Double-click the "Recovery console: Allow floppy copy and access to all drives and all folders" policy setting, and enable this setting (if necessary). What advantages might there be to enabling this setting?

Explore　　4. What is the other Recovery Console policy setting, and under what condition might you want to use it? Can you foresee any problems by enabling this other Recovery Console policy setting? Explain.

5. Close the Local Security Settings window, restart your computer, and log into the Recovery Console.

Explore　　6. Display Help for the SET command. What does this command do? List the environment variables supported by this command, and explain their purpose. If you wanted to change the setting for one of these environment variables, how would you do it? Which environment variables would you prefer to have enabled?

Explore　　7. At the command prompt, type SET and press the Enter key. List the default (or current) settings for each of the environment variables.

8. Display Help for the MAP command. What does this command do?

Explore　　9. Try the MAP command. List the information that it reports about your computer system. From the information provided for this command, how many hard disks do you have in your computer? If you only have one hard disk, how many partitions does it have?

10. Use the Change Directory (CD) command to change to the root directory of drive C. What command did you enter?

11. Display Help for the SYSTEMROOT command. What does this command do?

Explore　　12. Try the SYSTEMROOT command. Explain what happens.

13. If you have a second drive, type the name of that drive to change to that drive. What does the command prompt now display? Try the SYSTEMROOT command. Explain what happens.

14. Type EXIT to close the Recovery Console and restart your computer.

15. After logging on your computer, open the Help and Support Center and locate Help information on the Recovery Console.

16. If you want to remove the Recovery Console from your computer, what do you need to do?

17. To restore the original setting for the Recovery Console, open Local Security Policy from the Administrative Tools menu, select Security Options under Local Policies, double-click the "Recovery console: Allow floppy copy and access to all drives and all folders" policy setting, and restore the original setting (if necessary).

In this tutorial you will:

- Examine the importance of RAM, virtual memory, and the paging file

- Use Windows Task Manager to obtain information on system performance

- Use System Monitor to track performance changes on your computer

- Analyze system performance

- Understand other memory performance factors

- Determine when and how to upgrade memory

- Examine settings for printer properties and printing preferences

- Use the print queue to manage printing

EVALUATING SYSTEM PERFORMANCE

Optimizing System and Printer Performance

CASE

Landmark Associates, Inc.

Landmark Associates is a St. Louis firm that produces maps for federal, state, county, and local governments, as well as for corporations and businesses. Its employees rely on high-performance and resource-intensive mapping software to develop and produce maps for clients. Olivia Serrano, a tech specialist at Landmark Associates, has offered to show you how to measure and optimize the performance of your computer system. Then you can work with other Landmark employees and clients to optimize their computers.

In the first part of this tutorial, you examine the importance of RAM, virtual memory, and the paging file. Next, you examine how Windows XP uses virtual memory to provide applications with the resources they need to function properly. You open Windows Task Manager and examine information on processor and memory usage. Then you use System Monitor to track allocated memory and virtual memory as you work on your computer. Lastly, you examine performance settings for your computer and learn what options are available for improving the way your computer operates.

Understanding the Importance of RAM and Virtual Memory

Other than the capabilities of the processor, the two most important factors that affect the performance of a computer system are the amount of installed memory (RAM) and the storage capacity of the hard disk. Because computers now typically come with high-capacity hard disks with gigabytes of storage space, the primary limiting factor on the performance of a system still remains the amount of installed RAM.

If Windows XP does not have enough RAM for the applications that you use on your computer, it must create more memory than actually exists on the computer, just so you can open and use those applications. To accomplish this, Windows XP creates a special system file on your hard disk called a **paging file** (or **swap file**) that it uses as supplemental RAM. The installed physical RAM and the paging file constitute what is called **virtual memory**. For example, assume you open Microsoft Word and work on a report for a while, and then you decide to check your e-mail before working with an Excel spreadsheet. Windows XP can temporarily swap part of Word and the report to the paging file on the hard disk to free up memory for the other tasks you want to perform. If you decide to switch back to Word and the report, Windows XP can swap part of Excel and the spreadsheet to the paging file on disk, and then swap Word and the report from the paging file to RAM.

The segments of memory that Windows XP swaps to disk are called **pages**; hence the name of the paging file. A page is usually 4 KB (or 4,096 bytes). The paging file, which is named Pagefile.sys, is stored in the top-level folder of the volume where Windows is installed (usually drive C); however, you can specify that Windows XP store it on another volume. The default size of the paging file is 1.5 times the amount of RAM installed in your computer. Windows XP dynamically increases the size of this paging file when more virtual memory is needed, or reduces its size when less virtual memory is needed. This process is therefore transparent to the user, and provides Windows XP with whatever memory it needs to work with the applications and documents on your computer. When you start your computer, Windows XP automatically creates the paging file, even if it is not needed.

Although the use of storage space on a hard disk as supplemental RAM provides the memory that you may need, it does pose a problem. Virtual memory slows down the performance of a computer. Swapping data to and from disk is slow compared to the speed with which data is accessed in RAM. If your computer does not have enough RAM, it functions more slowly as the operating system swaps pages to and from RAM to the paging file on disk, and from the paging file back into RAM. As noted in Tutorial 3, in a computer with RAM that has an access time of 50 nanoseconds (50 billionths of a second, or 0.00000005 seconds) and a hard disk that has an access time of 6 milliseconds (6 thousands of a second, or 0.006 seconds), the RAM would be 120,000 times faster than the hard disk. The more RAM you have, the less you have to rely on virtual memory. The less your computer has to rely on virtual memory, the faster it runs.

When you buy a computer, you should have some idea of the amount of memory required by the different types of programs you intend to use. These programs include not only the ones you use on an everyday basis, such as a Web browser, e-mail software, and word-processing, spreadsheet, graphics, and database applications, but also the Windows XP operating system and other programs that operate in the background, such as antivirus software. Furthermore, when you multitask and open and use more than one application at the same time, Windows XP must allocate memory to each application.

It's easy to underestimate the amount of RAM your computer needs to operate properly. To illustrate how Windows XP and various applications use memory, examine Figure 10-1 and Figure 10-2. The three-dimensional bar chart shows memory usage on a Pentium 4 computer with 256 MB of RAM as the system boots and as the user opens several applications. The table in Figure 10-2 shows the actual memory measurements used for the three-dimensional bar chart in Figure 10-1. As shown in Figure 10-2, Windows XP uses 111.3 MB of memory after booting and creates a 384 MB paging file on the hard disk (256 MB RAM × 1.5 = 384 MB). Because each computer is configured differently, Windows XP can have different memory requirements and use memory differently.

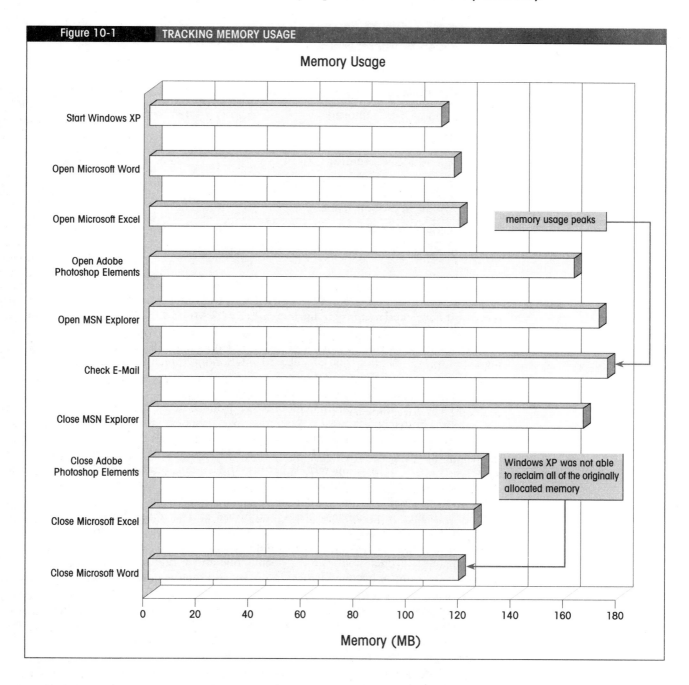

Figure 10-1   TRACKING MEMORY USAGE

| Figure 10-2 | TRACKING ALLOCATED MEMORY AND PAGING FILE SIZE |

Operation	Allocated Memory (MB)	Paging File Size (MB)
Start Windows XP	111.3	384.0
Open Microsoft Word	116.1	384.0
Open Microsoft Excel	118.4	384.0
Open Adobe Photoshop Elements	162.0	384.0
Open MSN Explorer	171.5	384.0
Check E-Mail	174.8	384.0
Close MSN Explorer	165.6	384.0
Close Adobe Photoshop Elements	126.9	384.0
Close Microsoft Excel	124.1	384.0
Close Microsoft Word	118.2	384.0

After this computer boots to the desktop and the user logs on, the user opens Microsoft Word. Memory usage increases by 4.8 MB to a total of 116.1 MB. The user then opens Microsoft Excel, and memory usage increases by 2.3 MB to 118.4 MB. Next, the user opens Adobe Photoshop Elements, and memory usage increases by 43.6 MB to 162.0 MB. Next, after connecting to the World Wide Web and opening MSN Explorer, memory usage increased by 9.5 MB to a total of 171.5 MB. Checking e-mail increased memory usage by 3.3 MB, for a total of 174.8 MB. Overall, memory usage increased by 63.5 MB over the initial amount used by Windows XP after booting, a 57% increase.

After closing MSN Explorer, memory usage dropped by 9.2 MB to 165.6 MB. After closing Adobe Photoshop Elements, memory usage dropped 38.7 MB to 126.9 MB. After closing Microsoft Excel, memory usage dropped by 2.8 MB to 124.1 MB. After closing Microsoft Word, memory usage dropped by 5.9 MB to 118.2 MB. The paging file remained at 384 MB for all of these operations because the amount of available RAM was sufficient for all these operations. If Windows XP needed more than 384 MB of memory, it would have increased the size of the paging file.

Judging from how memory was used in this case, and assuming this is a typical usage pattern, where a user opens and works with multiple applications and documents, it would make sense to have at least 256 MB of RAM installed on this particular computer. If this user continues to open applications, documents, and windows, allocated memory might exceed the amount of installed RAM (256 MB), and then Windows XP would be forced to rely on virtual memory.

After closing all the applications on this computer, memory usage drops to 118.2 MB, but does not return to the original level of 111.3 MB. That means 6.9 MB of RAM was still in use, and was therefore not available for use by other applications. If the user rebooted this computer, memory usage would once again be close to 111.3 MB.

The operating system not only allocates memory to applications that you need to use, but it is also supposed to reclaim memory after you close an application. Some applications have this feature, which lets them open more quickly. If this is the case, the applications you start open more quickly. However, if you don't open those applications again, that memory is tied up and unavailable. This phenomenon, where allocated memory is not reclaimed by the operating system, but rather tied up by previously open applications or processes, is referred to as a **memory leak**. When you reboot, everything in memory is erased, so the amount of memory available to the operating system and applications returns to the level you would expect. This example illustrates some basic features of memory usage on a computer system, namely:

- Windows XP allocates memory to itself and to background programs loaded during booting. The amount of memory allocated after booting is completed varies with the configuration of your computer system, but you should know what Windows XP requires just to boot your computer. In fact, the bulk of memory allocated on the computer used for Figure 10-1 and Figure 10-2 is used simply to boot the computer. When you examine memory usage on your computer, you might discover that Windows XP needs more memory than is provided by the installed RAM. That means Windows XP needs virtual memory just to boot your computer.

- Each time you open a program, Windows XP allocates memory to that program. That same principle applies to opening windows, such as the My Computer or My Documents folder windows.

- Some programs require more memory than other programs. If you rely on resource-intensive applications such as Adobe Photoshop or Macromedia Dreamweaver, and if you multitask with those applications, you should have enough installed RAM to support those applications.

- Multitasking requires more memory than single-tasking because you have more open programs.

- Each time you close a program, Windows XP reclaims memory allocated to that program. This same principle applies to closing windows, such as the My Computer or Documents folder windows.

- After you close all open programs, memory usage may not return to the original level from which you started after booting your computer because Windows XP may not be able to reclaim all the originally allocated memory.

This example also illustrates the importance of having a sufficient amount of RAM in your computer for the way you work on that computer. Furthermore, it illustrates how Windows XP can adapt to changes in the way you work and provide additional memory if needed. If you increase the amount of installed RAM on your computer, you see a marked improvement in the performance and speed of your computer, particularly when you are multitasking and have more than one application open at a time, or when you use resource-intensive applications. Note that other factors, such as the speed of the processor, might also affect the performance of a computer. If a computer has an older, and therefore slower processor, increasing the amount of RAM in that computer might not improve its performance significantly.

For virtual memory to work, there must be storage space available on the hard disk. If your hard disk is nearly full, Windows XP does not have the necessary space for creating or enlarging the paging file. You might then have trouble opening and using applications, and Windows XP might report out-of-memory errors. If for example, you only have 50-100 MB of storage space left on a computer's hard disk, Windows XP might not be able to provide an application with additional memory, multitasking might be slower, or you might not even be able to load an application. You should keep at least 1.5 times the installed RAM of free space on your hard disk drive for use by Windows XP as virtual memory. You also need additional storage space above that amount for temporary files, spool files, and the Internet cache. All of these operations and files affect the performance of your computer if your available storage space is limited.

Getting Started

To complete this tutorial, you need to switch your computer to Web style so that your screens match those shown in the figures, and you also need to turn on the options for showing all folders and files, displaying protected operating system files, displaying file extensions, and displaying the full path in the Address bar. As you complete these steps, you may discover that your computer is already set up for Web style, or that other settings are already in place, so you might only need to make a few changes to your computer's settings.

To set up your computer:

1. To change to the Windows XP theme, right-click the **desktop**, click **Properties** on the shortcut menu, and after Windows XP opens the Display Properties dialog box, click the **Theme** list arrow on the Themes property sheet, click **Windows XP** (if necessary), and then click the **OK** button.

2. To switch to the Windows XP Start menu style, right-click the **Start** button, click **Properties** on the shortcut menu, and after Windows XP opens the Taskbar and Start Menu Properties dialog box, click the **Start menu** option button on the Start Menu property sheet (if necessary), and then click the **OK** button.

3. To change to a task-oriented view of folders and enable single-clicking, click the **Start** button, click **My Computer**, click **Tools** on the menu bar, click **Folder Options**, and after Windows XP opens the Folder Options dialog box, click the **Show common tasks in folders** option button if it is not already selected, click the **Single-click to open an item** option button if it is not already selected, and click the **Underline icon titles only when I point at them** option button if it is not already selected.

4. Click the **View** tab, click the **Display the full path in the address bar** check box if it does not contain a check mark, click the **Show hidden files and folders** option button if it is not already selected, and if there is a check mark in the "Hide extensions for known file types" check box, click that check box to remove the check mark.

5. Click the **Hide protected operating system files** check box, click the **Yes** button in the Warning dialog box to display protected operating system files, click the **OK** button to close the Folder Options dialog box, and then close My Computer.

Now you're ready to view the Windows XP paging file and use two different approaches for monitoring memory on your computer.

Viewing the Paging File

The paging file is one of many hidden system files that Windows XP does not display in a folder window in order to protect the file. However, you can view the paging file if you choose the options for showing hidden files and folders, and for displaying hidden protected operating system files.

To view the paging file:

1. Open My Computer, open a window onto the drive where Windows XP is installed (usually drive C), and examine the files in the top-level folder of that drive. The file named pagefile.sys is the paging file, or swap file. See Figure 10-3. On the computer used for this figure, the pagefile.sys is 393,216 KB, or 384 MB (393,216 KB ÷ 1,024 KB/MB = 384 MB).

   TROUBLE? If you do not see pagefile.sys in the top-level folder of drive C, it might be located on another drive.

Figure 10-3	VIEWING FILES ON THE BOOT VOLUME

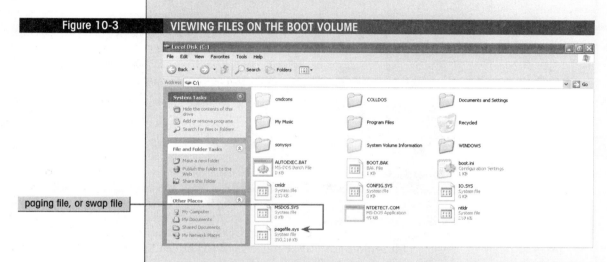

paging file, or swap file

2. Point to and select the **pagefile.sys** file icon, and then click the **Details dynamic menu** button ⊗ (if necessary) to expand the Details dynamic menu and display information about the paging file. See Figure 10-4. Pagefile.sys is a system file assigned the Hidden and System attributes. The date for this file should be the current date (or the date when this computer was last restarted). Note that the size is reported in MB rather than KB.

Figure 10-4   VIEWING INFORMATION ON THE PAGING FILE

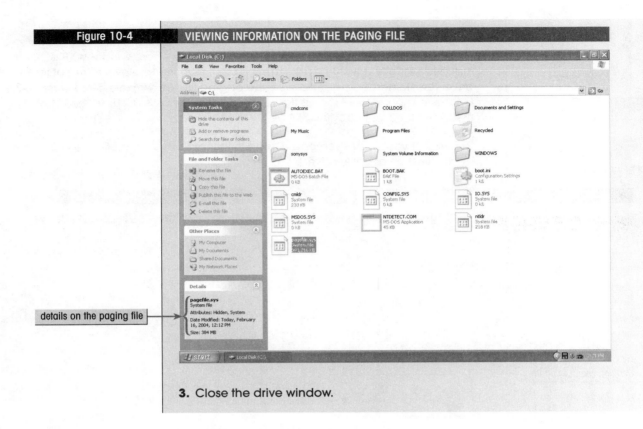

details on the paging file

3. Close the drive window.

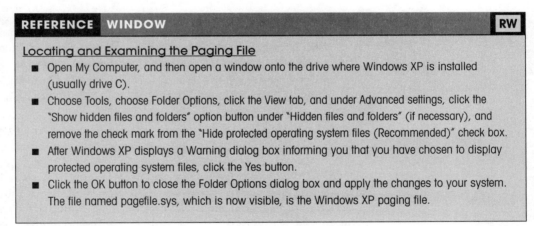

Locating and Examining the Paging File

■ Open My Computer, and then open a window onto the drive where Windows XP is installed (usually drive C).

■ Choose Tools, choose Folder Options, click the View tab, and under Advanced settings, click the "Show hidden files and folders" option button under "Hidden files and folders" (if necessary), and remove the check mark from the "Hide protected operating system files (Recommended)" check box.

■ After Windows XP displays a Warning dialog box informing you that you have chosen to display protected operating system files, click the Yes button.

■ Click the OK button to close the Folder Options dialog box and apply the changes to your system. The file named pagefile.sys, which is now visible, is the Windows XP paging file.

It is easier to understand the concept and use of virtual memory if you can associate it with something physical on your computer, such as installed RAM and the paging file.

Using Windows Task Manager to Track System Performance

With Windows Task Manager, you can view and track changes in processes occurring on your computer system. For example, you can monitor changes to allocated memory and to the size of the paging file and view changes in the activity of the processor. Although you examined how you could use Windows Task Manager to shut down nonresponding programs in Tutorial 9, this utility is also useful for examining the performance of your system.

Olivia offers to show you how to use Windows Task Manager to track memory usage on your computer, and thereby monitor the performance of your system.

To view your system's performance:

1. Right-click the **taskbar**, click **Task Manager**, and then click the **Performance** tab. Windows Task Manager is tracking CPU Usage and PF Usage (for Page File usage). See Figure 10-5. On the computer used for this figure, Windows Task Manager reports that CPU Usage is 0% (though it fluctuates), and Page File Usage is 91.6 MB. Because each computer is configured differently, and because the information shown on the Performance property sheet changes as you use your computer, your details will differ.

   TROUBLE? If you logged on under an account without Administrator privileges, you do not see a Shut Down menu option and the Users tab.

Figure 10-5	USING TASK MANAGER TO MONITOR PERFORMANCE

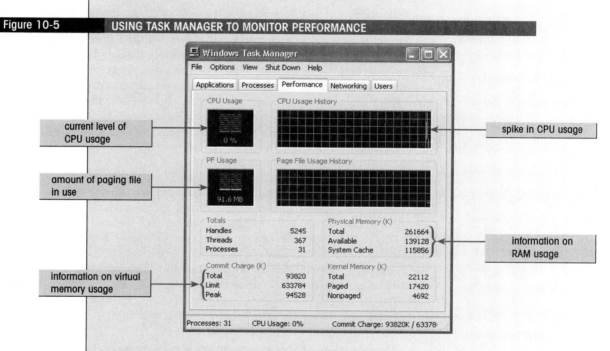

2. Leave Windows Task Manager open for the next set of steps.

The CPU Usage monitors the activity of the processor. If you use Windows Task Manager on a regular basis, you will find that CPU Usage is low, unless you are performing an operation, such as clicking the Start button, opening My Computer, loading an application, or connecting to the Internet; then it peaks momentarily before it drops again. If the value for CPU Usage remains high, some process (or program) might be unduly burdening the CPU with requests for processing, and the performance of your computer slows down. You might be able to identify that rogue program with the use of the System Configuration Utility, which you examined in Tutorial 9. As you may recall, you can use the General and Startup sheet in the System Configuration utility to change which startup configuration files are processed and which programs load during booting. By following the process described in Tutorial 9, you might be able to identify the program or service adversely affecting the performance of your computer. Once you locate that program, you can prevent it from loading, remove it from your computer, or replace it with another program that does not adversely affect your computer.

In this figure, the CPU Usage of 0% indicates that the computer is currently idle. In the graphical plot of CPU Usage History, the peak in CPU usage occurs right after opening the

Windows Task Manager window. By default, sampling is taken every two seconds; however, you can adjust the sampling rate using the Update Speed option on the View menu.

Under Physical Memory (K), Windows Task Manager lists the total amount of installed RAM in KB; on this computer, the amount of installed RAM is 261,664 KB, or 255.5 MB (just shy of the total installed 256 MB). Of that RAM, 139,128 KB (or 135.9 MB) is still available for use. The System Cache is the amount of RAM used to map pages of open files. Commit Charge (K) refers to the memory allocated to the operating system and open programs. The Total value shown represents total memory usage (for this computer, 93,820 KB, or 91.6 MB), and is represented by the plot shown under PF Usage. Memory usage peaked at 94,528 KB, or 92.3 MB. The value reported for Limit is the total amount of memory available in RAM and in the paging file (633,784 KB, or 618.9 MB). For this computer, the theoretical total available would be 256 MB (RAM) plus 384 MB (paging file), or 640 MB.

Under Totals, Task Manager reports 31 open processes, 367 threads, and 5,245 handles on the computer shown in the figure. As you may recall, a **process** is an executable program, a service, or a subsystem. A **thread** is an object within a process that executes instructions within a program. Windows XP supports multiple threads for each program so that it can execute instructions for different parts of the same program at the same time, or execute multiple instructions for the same part of the same program at the same time (called multi-threading). On a computer with more than one processor, these different parts of the same program can run concurrently on different processors. If a program creates threads and does not release those threads when you close it, you have found the source of a memory leak. A **handle** is a value that uniquely identifies a resource, such as a file or Registry setting, so that a program can access that resource.

Kernel memory refers to the memory used by core components of the operating system and by device drivers. Nonpaged kernel memory is available only to the operating system and cannot be paged to disk. Paged kernel memory is memory that can be paged, or swapped, to disk so that other programs can use that memory.

As you work on your computer, you can use Windows Task Manager to monitor changes in your system so that you have a better idea of what resources your system uses and needs. For example, after you open an application, you can watch the change in CPU Usage and memory usage and review the detailed statistics that Task Manager provides.

To monitor changes in your system:

1. Click **Options** on the Windows Task Manager menu bar, and if the Always on Top option does not have a check mark next to it, click **Always On Top**; otherwise, click **Options** a second time to close the menu. The Windows Task Manager window opens on top of any other open window.

2. Click **Options** on the Windows Task Manager menu bar, and if the Minimize on Use option has a check mark next to it, click **Minimize on Use**; otherwise, click **Options** a second time to close the menu. This option keeps Windows XP from minimizing Windows Task Manager when you open an application.

3. If you have Microsoft Word installed on your computer, open that application; otherwise, open another application that you commonly use. The percent CPU Usage jumps momentarily. See Figure 10-6. Memory usage also increases. On the computer shown in this figure, memory usage increased from 93,820 KB, or 91.6 MB (as shown in Figure 10-5), to 101,400 KB, or 99.0 MB, an increase of 7.4 MB when opening Microsoft Word 2002. Available memory decreased, and the number of processes, threads, and handles increased. Again, the details of these changes will differ for your computer.

Figure 10-6   **CHANGE IN MEMORY USAGE AFTER OPENING MICROSOFT WORD**

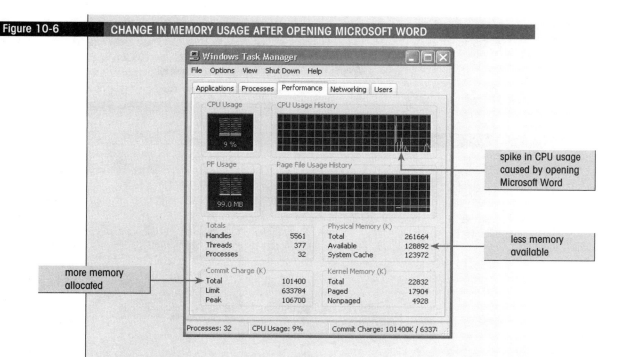

more memory allocated

spike in CPU usage caused by opening Microsoft Word

less memory available

4. If you have Microsoft Excel installed on your computer, open that application; otherwise, open yet another application installed on your computer. CPU Usage spikes momentarily, and Memory usage again increases. See Figure 10-7. On the computer shown in this figure, memory usage increased from 101,400 KB, or 99.0 MB (as seen in Figure 10-6) to 105,668 KB, or 103.2 MB, (105,668 KB ÷ 1,024 KB/MB = 103.2 MB) an increase of 4.2 MB when opening Microsoft Excel 2002. As before, the number of processes, threads, and handles increased. The details of these changes will differ for your computer. Also, the calculated value shown under PF Usage will differ slightly from that shown for the Commit Charge Total (K) because of the way Windows Task Manager rounds off values.

Figure 10-7   **CHANGE IN MEMORY USAGE AFTER OPENING MICROSOFT EXCEL**

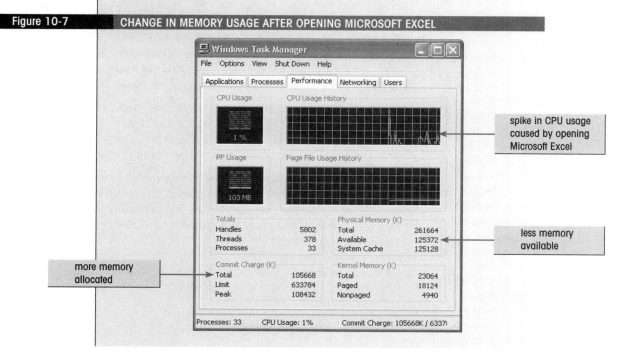

more memory allocated

spike in CPU usage caused by opening Microsoft Excel

less memory available

5. Close Microsoft Excel or the application that you opened in the last step. Memory usage drops. See Figure 10-8. On the computer used for this figure, memory usage dropped from 105,668 KB, or 103.2 MB, (as shown in Figure 10-7) to 104,348 KB, or 101.9 MB, a decrease of 1.3 MB when closing Microsoft Excel 2002. Available memory increased, and the number of processes, threads, and handles decreased. The details of these changes will differ for your computer.

Figure 10-8   CHANGE IN MEMORY USAGE AFTER CLOSING MICROSOFT EXCEL

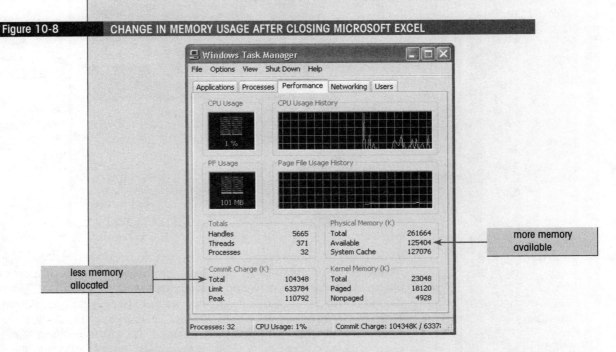

6. Close Microsoft Word or the first application that you opened. Memory usage drops again. See Figure 10-9. On the computer used for this figure, memory usage dropped from 104,348 KB, or 101.9 MB, (as seen in Figure 10-8) to 98,700 KB, or 96.4 MB, a decrease of 5.5 MB when closing Microsoft Word 2002. Available memory increased, and the number of processes, threads, and handles decreased. The details of these changes will differ for your computer.

Figure 10-9 CHANGE IN MEMORY USAGE AFTER CLOSING MICROSOFT WORD

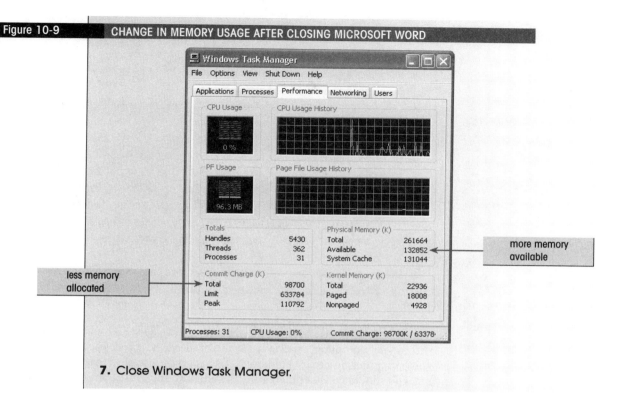

7. Close Windows Task Manager.

If you compare the total amount of memory allocated after opening these two applications and the amount of memory reclaimed after closing these applications, you more than likely find that Windows XP did not reclaim all of the originally allocated memory. On the computer used for these figures, memory usage increased from 93,820 KB, or 91.6 MB (as shown in Figure 10-5), to 105,668 KB, or 103.2 MB (as shown in Figure 10-7), an overall increase of 11.6 MB when opening Microsoft Word 2002 and Microsoft Excel 2002. Memory usage dropped to 98,700 KB, or 96.4 MB (as shown in Figure 10-9), after closing both applications. Windows XP reclaimed 6.8 MB, or approximately 60%, of the 11.6 MB originally allocated to these two applications. The difference, 4.8 MB, means that program code from these applications still remains in memory. This is an example of a memory leak. If you wait and do not use your computer for a short while, Windows XP might reclaim some of that still-used memory. However, you can always reclaim all of that memory by rebooting your computer.

Windows Task Manager itself uses very little memory, so it is a useful tool for monitoring memory.

Using Windows Task Manager to Monitor Performance

- Right-click the taskbar, click Task Manager, and then click the Performance tab in the Windows Task Manager window.
- Click Options on the Windows Task Manager menu bar, and if the Always on Top option does not have a check mark next to it, click Always On Top; otherwise, click Options a second time to close the menu.
- Click Options on the Windows Task Manager menu bar, and if the Minimize on Use option has a check mark next to it, click Minimize on Use; otherwise, click Options a second time to close the menu.
- As you open and close applications or windows, check the CPU Usage, CPU Usage History, and Total Commit Charge indicators on the Windows Task Manager Performance property sheet for changes in processor activity and memory usage on your computer. Compare initial values for Total Commit Charge and Threads with those after a work session to determine whether a memory leak occurred.
- When you have finished monitoring your system's performance, close Task Manager.

As you can see, Windows Task Manager can be a useful tool for monitoring basic processes within your computer, especially the use of memory. If you discover that memory is limited on your computer, and that Windows XP relies on the use of virtual memory, especially after booting, you should consider increasing the amount of installed physical RAM on your computer.

Using System Monitor to Evaluate System Performance

In contrast to Windows Task Manager, System Monitor can track information on a variety of performance objects, such as memory, disk activity, processes, printer, and network activity. A **performance object** is a logical collection of performance counters associated with a resource or service that you can monitor, such as Memory. A **performance counter** is an item of data associated with a specific performance object, such as Available Bytes for the Memory performance object. For some performance counters, you can also select an instance. An **instance** allows you to sample a performance counter in different ways. For example, under the Process performance object, you can monitor the % Processor Time (a performance counter) either for all programs, or for one specific program. If you want to measure % Processor Time for all programs, you would select the _Total instance. If you want to measure % Processor Time for a specific program, such as Microsoft Word, you would select that program's name (for example, for Microsoft Word, select WINWORD).

To open System Monitor, you select Performance on the Administrative Tools menu. Windows XP then opens the Microsoft Management Console and displays a Performance window. The **Microsoft Management Console (MMC)** is a Windows XP tool that allows you to open, use, create, and save **consoles**, or administrative snap-ins, for managing the hardware, software, and network components on your computer system. A **snap-in** is a management tool or plug-in provided by Microsoft or another software vendor. You can use the Microsoft Management Console in what is called **user mode**, where you use an existing MMC console, or you can work in **author mode** and create new consoles or modify existing consoles.

Olivia relies on System Monitor to track changes in processor and memory resources, two components that significantly affect the performance of computer systems. She encourages you to open System Monitor and track performance objects on your computer so that you can determine whether your computer's memory meets your needs.

Before you can open System Monitor, display the Administrative Tools menu on the Start menu or All Programs menu and the My Recent Documents menu on the Start menu. If you have already added the Administrative Tools menu to the Start menu, All Programs menu, or both, and if you have already added the My Recent Documents menu to the Start menu, you can skip the next set of steps and continue with the steps labeled "To specify performance counters."

To display Administrative Tools:

1. Right-click the **taskbar**, click **Properties** on the shortcut menu, and after the Taskbar and Start Menu Properties dialog box opens, click the **Start Menu** tab.

2. On the Start Menu property sheet, click the **Customize** button.

3. In the Customize Start Menu dialog box, click the **Advanced** tab, and under "Start menu items," locate "System Administrative Tools," and then click the **Display on the All Programs menu and the Start menu** option button.

4. Under Recent documents, click the **List my most recently opened documents** check box if it does not contain a check mark.

5. Click the **OK** button to close the Customize Start Menu dialog box, and then click the **OK** button to close the Taskbar and Start Menu Properties dialog box.

REFERENCE WINDOW   **RW**

Adding Administrative Tools to the Start and All Programs Menus

- Right-click the taskbar, click Properties on the shortcut menu, and after the Taskbar and Start Menu Properties dialog box opens, click the Start Menu tab.
- On the Start Menu property sheet, click the Customize button.
- In the Customize Start Menu dialog box, click the Advanced tab, and under "Start menu items," locate "System Administrative Tools," and then click the "Display on the All Programs menu and the Start menu" option button.
- Click the OK button to close the Customize Start Menu dialog box, and then click the OK button to close the Taskbar and Start Menu Properties dialog box.

Now you are ready to open System Monitor and specify the performance objects you want to track.

To specify performance counters:

1. On the Start menu, point to **Administrative Tools**, click **Performance**, and after the Performance window opens, maximize the window.

2. If the System Monitor console is not selected in the Console tree pane on the left side of the Performance window, click **System Monitor**. See Figure 10-10.

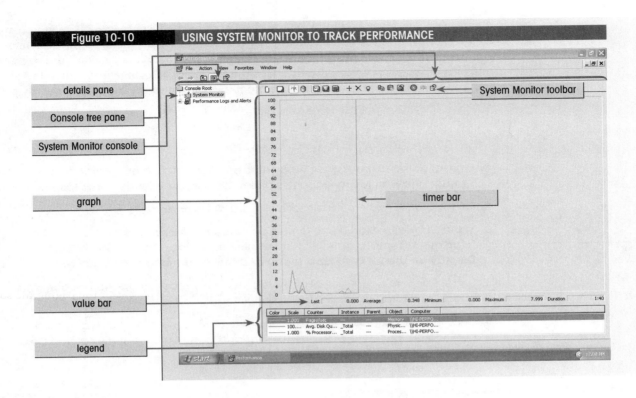

Figure 10-10   USING SYSTEM MONITOR TO TRACK PERFORMANCE

The **Console tree pane** displays the consoles from which you can choose; you have the option of adding other administrative snap-ins or consoles to this pane. The pane on the right is the details pane where the console displays information related to its function.

As you can see, System Monitor is already charting values for performance counters in the graph. By default, System Monitor displays Pages/sec, Avg. Disk Queue Length, and % Processor Time performance counter data for the local computer you're using. In the **legend** at the bottom of the details pane, System Monitor identifies the names of the performance counters currently being measured (such as Pages/sec), the instance (if any, such as _Total), the type of performance object (such as Memory), the computer to which these performance counters apply, the color codes for the corresponding lines which represent plotted values in the graph, and the scale used for different performance counters. The **value bar** above the legend and below the graph lists the last value, average value, minimum value, maximum value, and duration for the counter selected in the legend. The **timer bar** is the red vertical bar that slowly moves to the right as values are sampled, plotted on the graph, and added to the value bar. Samples are taken every second (by default), and System Monitor always plots 100 samples for each counter on the graph (by default).

Pages/sec measures the number of pages read from or written to disk for hard page faults, and therefore is useful for monitoring paging activity. A **hard page fault** occurs when a process requires program code or data that is not in its working set or elsewhere in physical memory, and therefore must be retrieved from the paging file on disk. A **working set** is the physical memory allocated to and used by a process. A **page fault error (PFE)**, or **invalid page fault**, occurs when Windows XP is unable to find data in the paging file. Possible causes for this type of problem include an insufficient amount of RAM, an insufficient amount of available disk storage space, a memory conflict between two applications where one attempts to access data used by the other, a problem in translating virtual memory addresses to physical memory addresses, or some other type of corruption or problem in virtual memory. This counter can help you determine whether these hard page faults affect the performance of a computer. If this performance counter is 20 or more, there might be a low-memory problem, and you need to monitor paging activity in more detail.

The **Avg. Disk Queue Length** is the average number of read and write requests for the selected disk. If this value is high, and if Pages/sec is low, there might be a disk bottleneck. If the Avg. Disk Queue Length increases, and there is no corresponding decrease in Pages/sec, you do not have enough memory.

The **% Processor Time** performance counter measures the demands placed on the processor by a process or operation, such as loading a program or saving a file to disk. If the value for this performance counter is high, you have to evaluate whether this activity represents heavy demands placed on the processor by the types of tasks you are performing, by the types of applications that you are using, by the ways in which you work (for example, multitasking), or whether it represents an excessive demand by one program. You might be working with too many programs open at the same time, or a newer application designed for a higher-performance computer might be affecting the performance of the computer. If this value starts high and remains high, you might need a faster processor to keep up with the demands of your system. Or it may mean that you have to open your system unit and remove the dust that blocks air intake and circulation.

Olivia suggests that you remove the Avg. Disk Queue Length counter, and then add counters for Available Bytes to measure available memory, Committed Bytes to measure allocated memory, and Page File Bytes to measure changes in the size of the paging file so that you can examine potential bottlenecks in memory and processor usage.

You need a floppy disk to save your performance data.

To specify performance counters for memory and processor usage:

1. In the legend, click the **Avg. Disk Queue Length** for the PhysicalDisk performance object to select this counter, and then click the **Delete** button ✕ on the System Monitor toolbar. System Monitor removes this performance counter.

2. Click the **Add** button ➕ on the System Monitor toolbar. In the Add Counters dialog box, you specify which counters you want to track for specific performance objects. See Figure 10-11. You can use local computer counters or counters from a specific computer on a network (as is the case for the computer used in the figure).

Figure 10-11   SELECTING A PERFORMANCE COUNTER

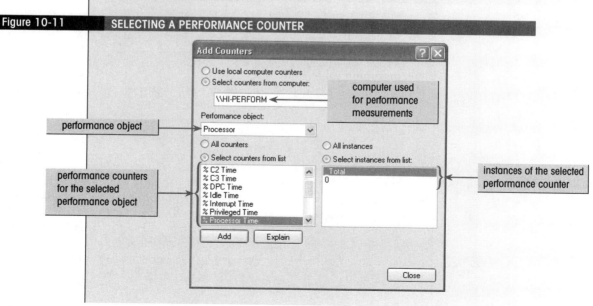

3. Click the **Performance object** list arrow, and then locate and click **Memory**. System Monitor now displays counters for this specific performance object. See Figure 10-12.

| Figure 10-12 | SELECTING A MEMORY PERFORMANCE COUNTER |

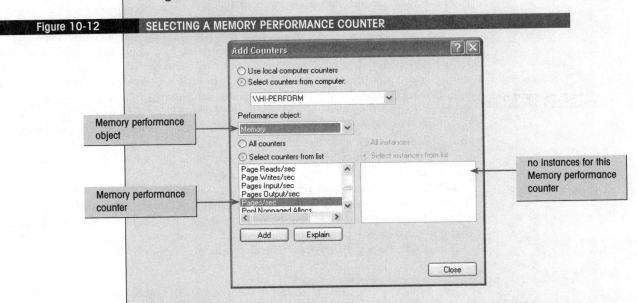

Memory performance object

Memory performance counter

no instances for this Memory performance counter

4. In the "Select counters from list" box, locate and click **Available Bytes**, click the **Add** button in the Add Counters dialog box to track this performance counter for the Memory performance object, and then click the **Explain** button. In the Explain Text dialog box (shown in Figure 10-13), System Monitor explains that Available Bytes is the amount of physical memory available to processes. Then it discusses how this value is derived. If Available Bytes is 4 MB or less, there might not be enough RAM or a program might not be releasing memory, so that memory is not available to other processes.

| Figure 10-13 | VIEWING AN EXPLANATION OF AVAILABLE BYTES |

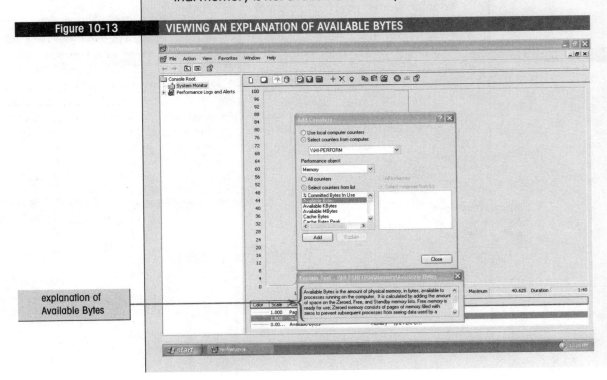

explanation of Available Bytes

5. In the "Select counters from list" box, locate and click **Committed Bytes**, and then click the **Add** button to track this performance counter for the Memory performance object. In the Explain Text dialog box (shown in Figure 10-14), System Monitor explains that Committed Bytes is the amount of committed virtual memory, measured in bytes. Then it explains that **committed memory** is physical memory for which space has been reserved in the paging file (or paging files) in case it's needed. It further notes that each physical disk can have one or more paging files.

Figure 10-14	VIEWING AN EXPLANATION OF COMMITTED BYTES

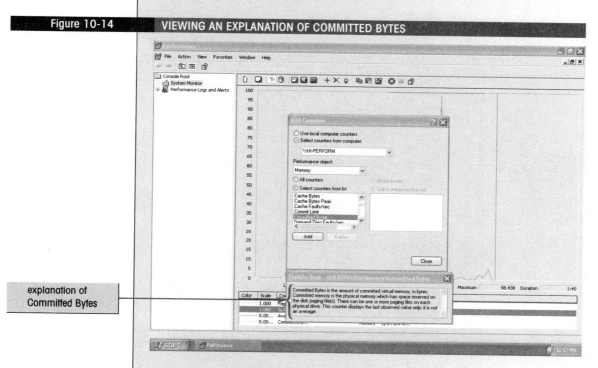

explanation of Committed Bytes

6. In the Performance object list box, locate and click **Process**, locate and click **Page File Bytes** in the "Select counters from list" box, and make sure the **_Total** instance is selected in the "Select instances from list" box. In the Explain Text dialog box, System Monitor notes that this counter measures the number of bytes a process uses in the paging file. See Figure 10-15. It also notes that all processes share the paging file, and an insufficient amount of space in a paging file can interfere with the performance of other processes and their use of memory.

Figure 10-15 | **VIEWING AN EXPLANATION OF PAGE FILE BYTES**

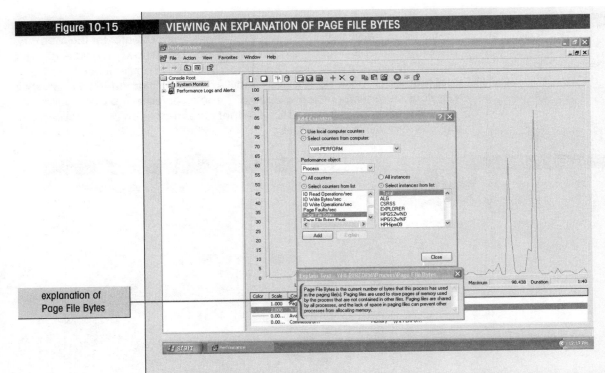

explanation of
Page File Bytes

7. Click the **Add** button in the Add Counters dialog box, close the **Explain Text** dialog box, and click the **Close** button to close the Add Counters dialog box.

POWER USERS TIP You can also add performance counters by right-clicking the chart, and then selecting Add Counters on the shortcut menu.

8. Click the **Clear Display** button 🖵 on the System Monitor toolbar, click the **Counter** column button in the legend to sort the counters in alphabetical order by counter name, and if you cannot see the entire entry within a column in the legend, drag the column border between that column and the next column to the right to manually adjust your view of each column. You should now see the names of five counters: % Processor Time, Available Bytes, Committed Bytes, Page File Bytes, and Pages/sec. See Figure 10-16.

TROUBLE? If you are missing one of the five performance counters just described, use the Add button + to locate and add that performance counter to the set of performance counters that you are measuring, and then click the Counter button to sort them in alphabetical order by Counter name.

TROUBLE? If the same performance counter is listed twice, select one of the two performance counters, and then click the Delete button ✕ . You might obtain a spurious reading with two of the same counters.

| Figure 10-16 | EXAMINING PERFORMANCE COUNTERS |

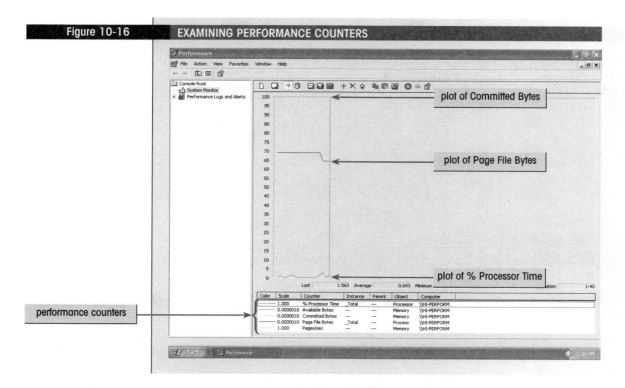

Next, examine the values for each of the counters, starting with the % Processor Time.

To examine information on a specific counter:

1. On the System Monitor toolbar, click the **Freeze Display** button ⊗ . This button pauses the plotting of performance data so that you can analyze the data, select different performance counters in the legend, and examine the details of each measurement in the value bar.

2. Under Counter in the legend, click **% Processor Time**, and then click the **Highlight** button ♀ . System Monitor highlights the measurement of processor activity. See Figure 10-17. Your plot will differ in appearance. As shown on the computer used for this figure, the percentage of processor activity is low (or should be low) whenever the computer is idle. However, if you perform an operation, you see a momentary spike in processor activity. The Highlight button ♀ is useful not only in separating a single performance measurement from all others, but it also displays plotted values that are represented by lines with a light color (such as light blue) that are otherwise difficult to see.

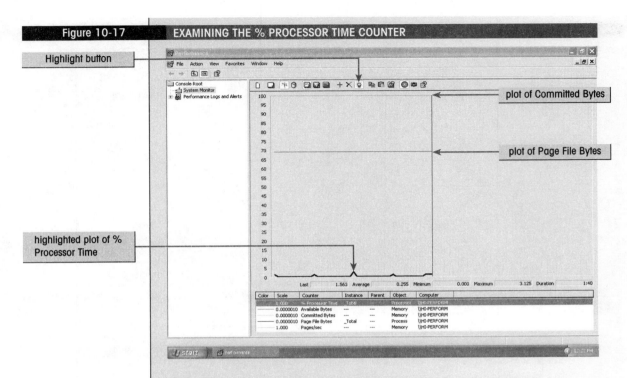

Figure 10-17   EXAMINING THE % PROCESSOR TIME COUNTER

Highlight button

plot of Committed Bytes

plot of Page File Bytes

highlighted plot of %
Processor Time

3. Click the **Highlight** button 💡 to turn off the highlight of the plot of %
   Processor Time.

4. Click the **Available Bytes** counter in the legend. System Monitor has scaled
   these values so that they appear as a flat line on the graph; however, if you
   examine the value bar, System Monitor shows detailed information for this
   counter. See Figure 10-18. If you examine the Last measured value on the computer used for this figure, there is a total of 141,000,704 bytes, or 134.5 MB
   (141,000,704 divided by 1,024 twice), of memory still available for processes on
   this computer. Your details will differ.

Figure 10-18 VIEWING VALUES FOR THE AVAILABLE BYTES COUNTER

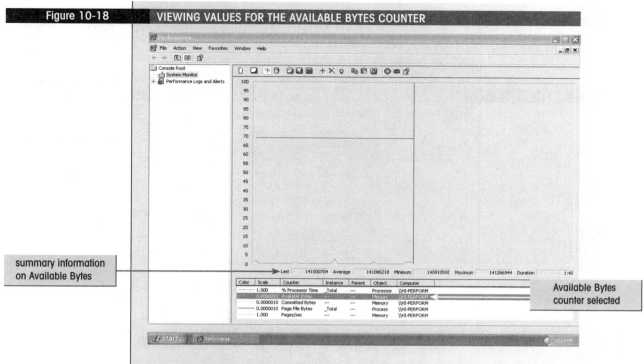

summary information on Available Bytes

Available Bytes counter selected

5. Click the **Committed Bytes** counter in the legend. In the value bar, System Monitor reports on how much memory is committed to processes, and therefore is currently in use. See Figure 10-19. Like Available Bytes, the values for this counter are plotted as a flat line. However, if you examine the Last measured value on the computer used for this figure, Windows XP uses a total of 111,067,136 bytes, or 105.9 MB (111,067,136 divided by 1,024 twice). Your details will differ.

Figure 10-19 VIEWING VALUES FOR THE COMMITTED BYTES COUNTER

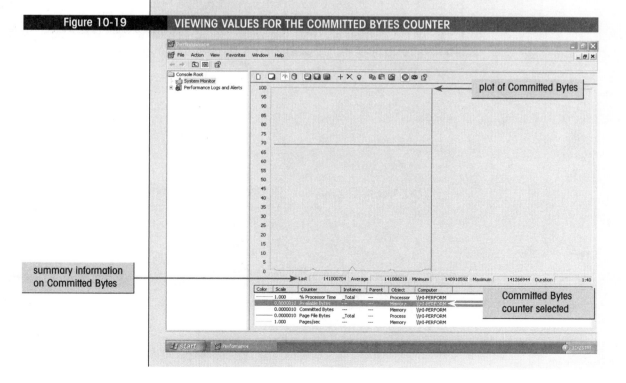

summary information on Committed Bytes

plot of Committed Bytes

Committed Bytes counter selected

6. Click the **Page File Bytes** counter in the legend. On the computer used for Figure 10-20, System Monitor reports the Last measured value as 69,476,352 bytes, or 62.4 MB, the amount of storage space used in the paging file for all processes. Your measurement will differ.

Figure 10-20	VIEWING DETAILS ON THE PAGE FILE BYTES COUNTER

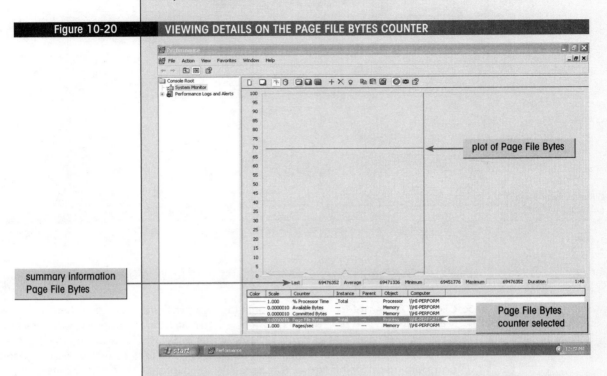

summary information
Page File Bytes

plot of Page File Bytes

Page File Bytes
counter selected

7. Click the **Pages/sec** counter in the legend area. System Monitor now reports on the values for this counter in the value bar. See Figure 10-21. The values range from 0.000 to 0.000 Pages/sec on the computer used for this figure. Because the computer is idle, this value indicates that no pages are being written to or read from the paging file at the moment. Your results may differ.

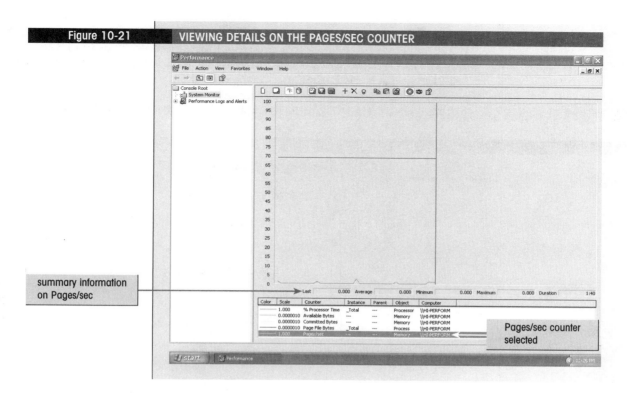

Figure 10-21   VIEWING DETAILS ON THE PAGES/SEC COUNTER

summary information on Pages/sec

Pages/sec counter selected

These measurements give you baseline values from which to start after you have booted your computer, opened System Monitor, selected the performance counters you want to use, and then waited for activity to quiet down to the background level you currently observe. Now you can start a process, such as opening an application, and observe how that activity affects these performance counters.

To measure activity while opening and then closing an application:

1. Click the **Freeze Display** button ⊗ again to resume plotting of performance data, and then click the **Clear Display** button 🗋 to remove previously plotted data.

2. Wait a few seconds, open Microsoft Word or another application on your computer (preferably one you depend on), click the **Performance** taskbar button, click ⊗ , and if a performance counter is plotted with a color that is difficult to see in the graph (such as Pages/sec on the computer used for this figure), click that **performance counter** in the legend, and then click the **Highlight** button ♀ . System Monitor now shows how the loading of this application affected the counters for the different performance objects. See Figure 10-22.

On the computer used for this figure, the % Processor Time spiked momentarily to indicate that the processor was busy with the loading of Microsoft Word. This spike is higher the first time you open an application, and then smaller when you reopen it later, indicating that some of the program was already cached (or stored) in memory. The spike in the measurement of the Pages/sec counter indicates that the operating system was reading program code from files on the hard disk. Page File Bytes also increased, and then leveled off, indicating the use of more storage space in the paging file.

The amount of used memory increased from 111,067,136 bytes, or 105.9 MB to 115,302,400 bytes, or 110.0 MB (a gain of 4.1 MB); the amount of available memory decreased from 141,000,704 bytes, or 134.5 MB to 134,373,376 bytes, or 128.1 MB (a decrease of 6.4 MB); and the amount of used storage space in the paging file increased from 69,476,352 bytes, or 62.4 MB, to 73,408,512 bytes, or 70.0 MB (a gain of 7.6 MB). Yours will differ.

Figure 10-22   **CHANGES IN PERFORMANCE COUNTERS AFTER OPENING MICROSOFT WORD**

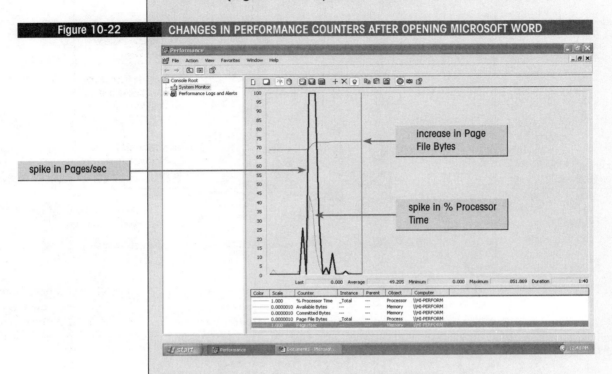

3. If necessary, click 💡 again to turn off this feature.

4. Click ⊗ again to resume plotting, pause for a few seconds, click the **taskbar button** for Microsoft Word (or the application you opened), close Microsoft Word or the application you just opened, wait for a few more seconds so that System Monitor can plot the changes that just occurred, and then click ⊗. On the computer used in Figure 10-23, % Processor Time showed a much smaller spike in processor activity than what happened when opening the application. Pages/sec spiked twice when switching tasks and closing the program. The amount of used memory decreased from 115,302,400 bytes, or 110.0 MB, to 110,776,320 bytes, or 105.6 MB (a decrease of 4.4 MB); the amount of available memory increased from 134,373,376 bytes, or 128.1 MB, to 140,472,320 bytes, or 140 MB (a gain of 11.9 MB); and the amount of used storage space in the paging file decreased from 73,408,512 bytes, or 70.0 MB, to 69,296,128 bytes, or 66.1 MB (a decrease of 3.9 MB). In this instance, Windows XP reclaimed the memory originally allocated to opening this application. Your details will differ.

Figure 10-23 | **CHANGES IN PERFORMANCE COUNTERS AFTER CLOSING MICROSOFT WORD**

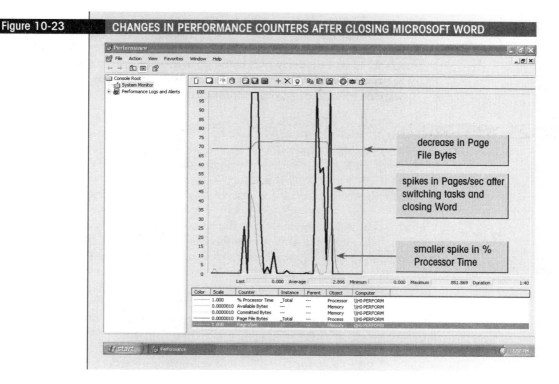

Other useful options on the System Monitor toolbar are the following:

- The default view is Chart View, but you can use the View Histogram button ![icon] to display the magnitude of results (relative to each other) by the height of vertical bars. Also, you can use the View Report button ![icon] to display the current values for performance counters.

- You can use the New Counter Set button ![icon] to remove all the performance counters so that you can select new ones.

- You can use the Properties button ![icon] to open the System Monitor Properties dialog box where you can specify which elements (such as the legend, value bar, or toolbar) you want to display, what you want to report for histogram and report data (current value, average value, minimum value, or maximum value), how frequently the update occurs (in seconds), whether you want to log this data to a file, adjust the vertical scale axis in the graph area, specify the use of vertical and horizontal gridlines, label the graph and the vertical axis, specify colors for the graph area, and choose fonts.

- You can use the Help button ![icon] to open System Monitor Help if you want an overview of System Monitor, or to view information on best practices for monitoring performance, setting up a monitoring configuration, analyzing performance data, resolving performance problems, evaluating trends, finding bottlenecks in your computer or network, or to view a quick reference to System Monitor settings.

Point to a button to see a ScreenTip that identifies the button.

Olivia suggests that you save the results of these performance measurements as a Web page so that you can examine them later.

To save performance measurements:

1. Insert a floppy disk in drive A, right-click the **graph**, click **Save As** on the shortcut menu, click **3½ Floppy (A:)** in the Save in list box, type **Performance Measurements** in the File name box, select **Web Page (*.htm, *.html)** in the Save as type list box (if it is not already selected), and then click the **Save** button.

2. Close the Performance window.

As noted earlier, Committed Bytes is the amount of memory your computer is using at any given time. By monitoring this value, you can determine how much memory Windows XP needs after booting, and you can observe the demands on memory by the types of applications that you use and by the way you work (multitasking vs. single-tasking). This information gives you a baseline value (or values) for the amount of memory that Windows XP needs as you work on your computer. You can use this baseline value to decide whether to add more RAM to your computer, to estimate how much you might need to meet the most demanding applications that you use, and to handle multitasking of those resource-intensive applications.

If System Monitor continually reports a value of 20 or higher for the Pages/sec performance counter, a bottleneck is probably degrading the performance of your computer. You can close application and folder windows you no longer use, turn off features that you use in applications (such as optional add-ins), or move the paging file to another disk with more space, less disk activity, and/or a faster speed. Since all processes share the paging file, Windows XP might not be able to allocate memory to other processes if the paging file lacks space. You might need to add more physical memory (more RAM) to your computer to reduce the amount of paging that occurs—paging that also makes excessive demands of your hard disk.

You can use the Page File Bytes performance counter to determine how much paging different applications or components require. Again, if the amount of RAM for paging is limited (either by the amount of RAM that is installed, or by the amount of RAM that is used for components that require nonpaging memory), Windows XP might not be able to allocate memory to these applications.

You should monitor the performance of your computer so that you know how resources are allocated from one session to the next, and from one way of working to another (such as multitasking vs. single-tasking), so that if problems develop, you can monitor the performance of your computer and compare it to times when those problems did not occur.

REFERENCE	WINDOW	RW

Using System Monitor to Track Performance

- Open the Start menu, point to Administrative Tools, and then click Performance.
- If you want to remove any existing performance counters, select each of those performance counters in the legend, and then click the Delete button on the System Monitor toolbar.
- If you want to add performance counters, click the Add button on the System Monitor toolbar to open the Add Counters dialog box, or right-click the graph, and click Add Counters.
- Select the option to use either local computer counters, or counters from a specific computer on your network.
- Click the Performance object list arrow, and select the performance object you want to measure.
- Locate and select the counter you want to measure from the "Select counters from list" box.
- If necessary, select the instance you want to measure from the "Select instances from list" box.
- To view Help information about the counter, click the Explain button.
- Click the Add button to add the performance counter to the chart.
- Repeat this process for each counter you want to use for the performance objects you're measuring, and then close the Explain Text and Add Counters dialog boxes.
- To display the performance measurements in the value bar for a specific counter, select that counter in the legend area or by double clicking on its line in the graph area.
- If you want to highlight a specific performance counter in the graph, click the performance counter in the legend, and then click the Highlight button. Click this button a second time if you want to turn off the highlight.
- If you want to clear the display, click the Clear Display button.
- If you want to save the graph as a Web page, click the Freeze Display button, right-click the graph, click Save As on the shortcut menu, select the drive and folder where you want to save the performance information from the Save in list box, type a filename in the File name box, select Web Page (*.htm, *.html) in the Save as type list box (if necessary), and then click Save.
- Click the Freeze Display button again to view further updates to the graph.
- When you have finished your performance measurements, close the Performance window.

Next, Olivia wants you to view and then print the Web page with the performance measurements for your computer. If your default Web browser is not Internet Explorer, you might need to adapt the following steps to your browser.

To print the Web page with the performance measurements:

1. Open the Start menu, point to **My Recent Documents**, and then click **Performance Measurements.htm** on the Documents menu. Windows XP opens Internet Explorer and then opens Performance Measurements.htm. See Figure 10-24. This Web page shows performance counter measurements before you saved these measurements.

TROUBLE? If Performance Measurements.htm is not listed in your My Recent Documents window, open Internet Explorer, click File on the menu bar, click Open, click the Browse button in the Open dialog box, locate and open the folder where you saved this Web page, click Performance Measurements.htm, and then click the OK button in the Open dialog box. Or open a window onto the drive and folder where the Web page is stored, and then click the file to open it in your Web browser.

Figure 10-24 | VIEWING THE HTML DOCUMENT WITH PERFORMANCE MEASUREMENTS

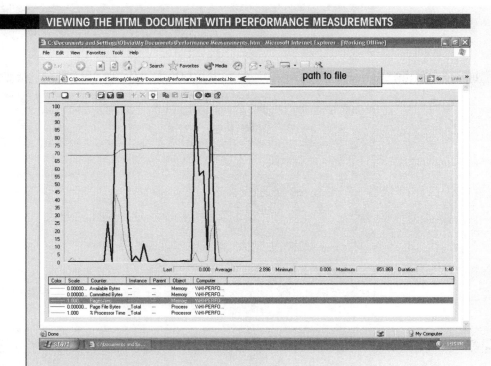

2. Click **File** on the menu bar, click **Page Setup**, click the **Landscape** option button under Orientation in the Page Setup dialog box, and then click the **OK** button.

3. Click the **Print** button on the Standard Buttons toolbar. Internet Explorer prints the contents of the Performance Measurements file.

4. Close Internet Explorer.

If you are an Administrator, you can use System Monitor to track hardware and system service usage on local or remote computers. Whether you need to monitor other computers as an Administrator or your own computer, you can use System Monitor to identify bottlenecks that affect the performance of your computer system.

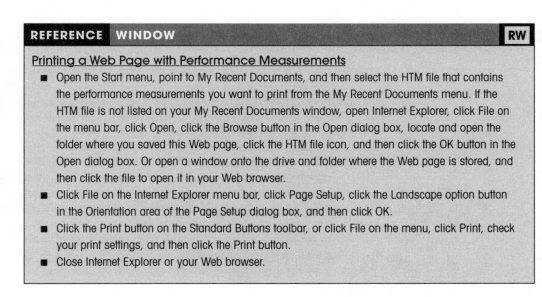

REFERENCE WINDOW | RW

Printing a Web Page with Performance Measurements

■ Open the Start menu, point to My Recent Documents, and then select the HTM file that contains the performance measurements you want to print from the My Recent Documents menu. If the HTM file is not listed on your My Recent Documents window, open Internet Explorer, click File on the menu bar, click Open, click the Browse button in the Open dialog box, locate and open the folder where you saved this Web page, click the HTM file icon, and then click the OK button in the Open dialog box. Or open a window onto the drive and folder where the Web page is stored, and then click the file to open it in your Web browser.

■ Click File on the Internet Explorer menu bar, click Page Setup, click the Landscape option button in the Orientation area of the Page Setup dialog box, and then click OK.

■ Click the Print button on the Standard Buttons toolbar, or click File on the menu, click Print, check your print settings, and then click the Print button.

■ Close Internet Explorer or your Web browser.

If you open System Monitor Help (from the System Monitor toolbar, not the MMC Standard toolbar), you can find information on identifying bottlenecks in your computer using System Monitor. See Figure 10-25.

Figure 10-25 | **USING HELP TO IDENTIFY PERFORMANCE BOTTLENECKS**

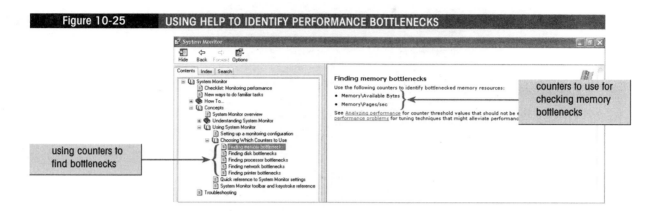

using counters to find bottlenecks

counters to use for checking memory bottlenecks

System Monitor Help also includes information on determining acceptable values for counters so that you can evaluate your computer's performance, as shown in Figure 10-26.

Figure 10-26 | **USING HELP TO DETERMINE ACCEPTABLE VALUES FOR COUNTERS**

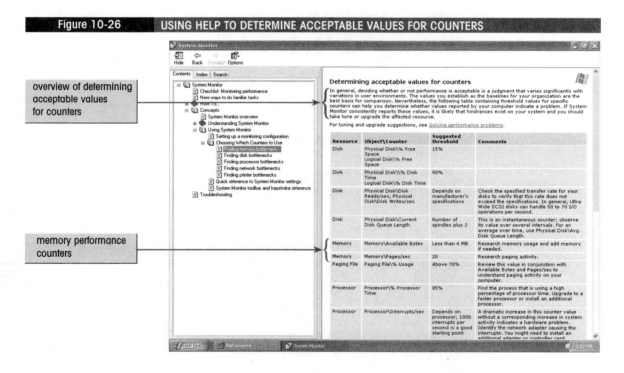

overview of determining acceptable values for counters

memory performance counters

It also provides practical guidelines on solving performance problems, as shown in Figure 10-27.

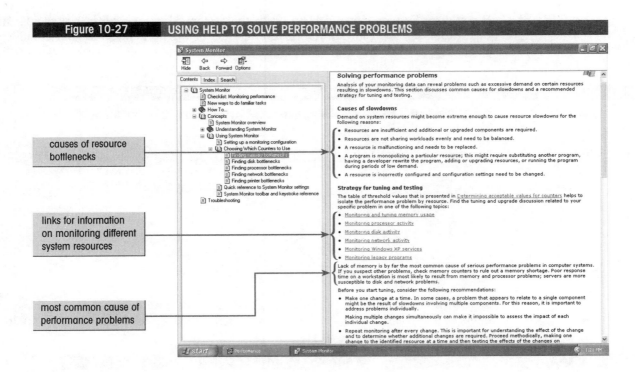

Figure 10-27   USING HELP TO SOLVE PERFORMANCE PROBLEMS

causes of resource bottlenecks

links for information on monitoring different system resources

most common cause of performance problems

Notice that Microsoft identifies five reasons for bottlenecks:

- **Insufficient resources**—such as amount of installed RAM, amount of available disk storage space, processor speed, and heavy demands made on CPU time

- **Unbalanced resources**—such as exceeding the transfer rate for a disk (number of I/O operations per second), excessive paging, and server activities

- **Malfunctioning resources**—such as a problem with a hardware device (for example, a network adapter)

- **Monopolizing resources**—such as using most of RAM for nonpaged activities

- **Incorrectly configured resources**—such as an incorrectly configured network adapter

Note also that in System Monitor Help, Microsoft states that lack of memory is the major cause of serious performance problems in computer systems, and Microsoft recommends that you check memory counters first to ascertain if a memory bottleneck is the source of a problem you're experiencing. Microsoft also recommends an important strategy that troubleshooters and technical support staff commonly employ in troubleshooting performance problems. Namely, make one change in your system at a time, and address problems one at a time as you attempt to isolate, identify, and resolve a performance problem (or any other type of problem). Microsoft then lists tips you can follow for tuning up the performance of your system, for example, adding more RAM, creating multiple paging files, adjusting the size of the paging file(s), and properly configuring memory. Since most performance problems result from too little RAM, the best way to improve the performance of your computer is to install more RAM.

If you are an Administrator or have Administrator privileges, you can use the Performance Logs and Alerts console in the Performance window to create performance logs that track performance counters for a set period of time. You can use this information to establish the baseline performance of your computer and to troubleshoot problems that occur as you make changes to your computer and network.

By frequently using the System Monitor, you can develop a sense of what's happening behind the scenes on your computer. You might discover that the information System Monitor provides you is useful when you need to understand how your computer works, when you need to justify a computer upgrade, or when you need to troubleshoot your computer's performance. And as noted earlier, System Monitor can also be a useful diagnostic tool for network administrators who need to monitor the performance of the network, as well as individual computers on the network.

Examining Memory Performance Options for Applications

You can adjust other performance settings, such as those for visual effects, processor scheduling, memory usage, and virtual memory, all of which in turn affect the speed and performance of your computer. For example, if you notice that your computer responds slowly to basic types of operations, such as dragging a window or a dialog box, or moving the mouse, you can find out which visual settings are enabled on your computer, turn off specific visual settings, or turn off each one, one at a time, and then determine whether the performance of your computer improves.

You also can specify whether Windows XP provides more processor resources to the foreground program over background programs. The **foreground program** is the program that you are currently using in the active or selected window and is the one that responds to commands. A **background program** is a program that you opened, but which is not currently in the active or selected window. These programs are performing tasks in the background as you work with the foreground program. If you set Windows XP to provide more processor resources to the foreground program, it performs more smoothly and faster. You can also set Windows XP to provide all programs an equal amount of processor resources. That means a program operating in the background, such as a Backup utility, performs faster, but the response time of the foreground application may not be as smooth or as fast.

Another way to manage memory performance is to examine which drives Windows XP uses for paging files. If your computer has more than one drive, but Windows XP maintains a paging file on only one drive, such as drive C, you can use the Properties dialog box for your computer to find out whether another drive on your computer has more storage space. If that drive is accessed less frequently than drive C, is a faster drive, and has more storage space, it might make more sense to use that drive for the paging file, and thereby free up valuable storage space on drive C for installed applications and the operating system and also reduce disk access. Microsoft recommends that you do not put a paging file on the same drive as the system files, and it also recommends that you do not put multiple paging files on different partitions of the same physical hard disk. Although you can specify no paging file, Microsoft recommends against that option. Unless you have enough physical memory, or RAM, you need at least one paging file on one of the drives. If you specify no paging file, you might not be able to boot your computer.

For an upcoming professional development day for employees, Olivia asks you to show the staff how to view and analyze additional information about the performance of applications on their computers, environment variable settings, and startup and recovery options.

To view performance information for applications:

1. On the Start menu, right-click **My Computer**, click **Properties** on the shortcut menu, and then click the **Advanced** tab. The Advanced property sheet provides access to information about performance, user profiles, startup and recovery, environment variables, and error reporting. See Figure 10-28.

Figure 10-28   ADVANCED SYSTEM OPTIONS

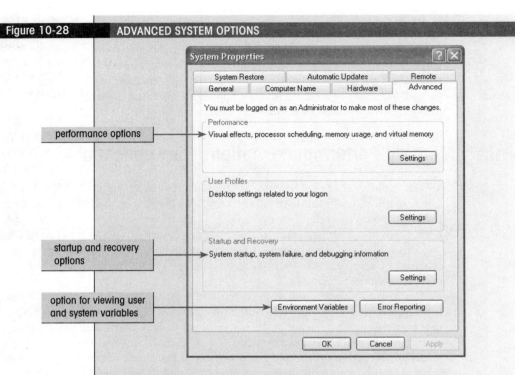

performance options

startup and recovery options

option for viewing user and system variables

2. Under Performance, click the **Settings** button. On the Visual Effects property sheet, you can let Windows XP select the best settings for your computer. You can also adjust settings on your computer for either the best appearance or the best performance, or you can choose which settings you want in the Custom box. See Figure 10-29. Since the settings that Windows XP automatically selects vary with different computer systems and their capabilities, your settings may differ.

Figure 10-29   VIEWING VISUAL EFFECTS SETTINGS

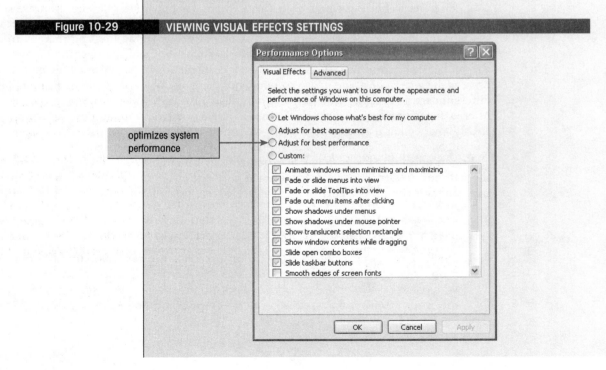

optimizes system performance

3. Click the **Advanced** tab. Windows XP shows the size of the paging file in the Virtual memory section. See Figure 10-30. Windows XP allows individuals with Administrator privileges to optimize processor scheduling and memory usage for programs or background services and change the size of the paging file used for virtual memory. If you do not have Administrator privileges, the options in this area are dimmed so that you cannot change them.

If the Programs option button is selected under Processor scheduling, Windows XP provides more processor resources to the foreground program than background programs, and your foreground program performs more smoothly and faster. If you select the Background services option under Processor scheduling, all programs receive an equal amount of processor resources.

Figure 10-30 VIEWING ADVANCED PERFORMANCE SETTINGS

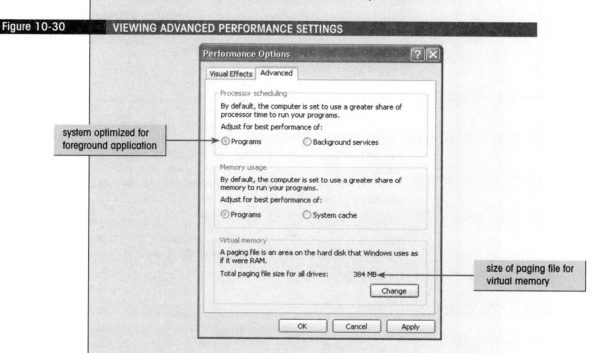

system optimized for foreground application

size of paging file for virtual memory

If you choose Programs under Memory usage, your programs work faster, and the size of the system cache is set at a default size. This option is the best for a workstation. In contrast, you would choose the System cache option if your programs require a large system cache, or the computer functions as a server.

4. Under Virtual memory, click the **Change** button. In the Virtual Memory dialog box, Windows XP shows information about the use of virtual memory and the paging file for each drive. See Figure 10-31. The computer used for this figure has three drives. Only drive C has a paging file. The initial size of the paging file is set at 384 MB, but Windows XP can increase it to a maximum of 768 MB (double the initial amount) if needed. In the "Total paging file size for all drives," the minimum allowed size of the paging file is 2 MB, the recommended size is 382 MB, and the current allocated size is 384 MB. Your settings may differ.

Figure 10-31   VIRTUAL MEMORY SETTINGS

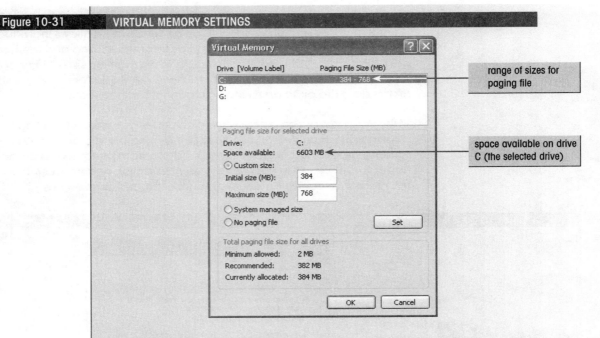

You can select the drive in the Drive box, and under "Paging file size for selected drive," Windows XP reports whether that drive has more storage space. To change the size of the virtual memory paging file, you must be logged on as a member of the Administrators group.

5. Click the **Cancel** button to close the Virtual Memory dialog box without making changes, and then click the **Cancel** button to close the Performance Options dialog box without making changes and return to the System Properties dialog box.

As you change the way you work with your computer, you can adjust these performance settings and optimize the use of paging files on multiple volumes if you have Administrator privileges. Microsoft recommends that you not reduce the size of the paging file to less than its recommended size (1.5 times the amount of RAM installed on your computer) if you want optimal performance. However, if you move the paging file from one drive to another, you obviously have to create a paging file on the new drive, and then reduce the size of the paging file on the other drive to zero to eliminate it. If you routinely use programs that demand a lot of memory, you can increase the size of the paging file to provide extra memory and thereby optimize performance.

REFERENCE WINDOW **RW**

Viewing and Changing Performance Options for Applications

- On the Start menu, right-click My Computer, click Properties on the shortcut menu, and then click the Advanced tab in the System Properties dialog box.
- If you want to change Performance settings, and if you have Administrator privileges, click the Settings button under Performance. On the Visual Effects property sheet, choose how you want Windows XP to handle visual settings, or choose the ones you want to use in the Custom box. On the Advanced property sheet, you can change the Processor scheduling setting and choose the Programs option so that the foreground application receives more processor resources than background applications, or you can choose the Background services option so that all applications receive the same equal share of resources.
- Under Memory usage, you can choose the Programs option so that your programs work faster with a default system cache size, or you can choose System cache if your programs require a larger system cache.
- If you want to view or change virtual memory settings, click the Change button under Virtual memory. If you have Administrator privileges, you can change the initial or maximum size of the paging file, move the paging file from one drive to another, or specify multiple paging files.
- If you want to save changes to virtual memory, click the OK button; otherwise, if you are just viewing settings, click the Cancel button to close the Virtual Memory dialog box without applying changes to your system.
- If you want to save changes to Performance Options settings, click the OK button; otherwise, if you are just viewing settings, click the Cancel button to close the Performance Options dialog box without applying changes to your system.
- If you want to save changes to any System Property settings, click the OK button; otherwise, if you are just viewing information on settings, click the Cancel button to close the System Properties dialog box without applying changes to your system.

In Tutorial 9, "Using Troubleshooting Tools," you examined settings for environment variables using the System Information utility. That utility lists all the environment variables for the system and for all users. The Environment Variables section of the System Properties dialog box lists system variables as well as user variables for the current user logon. The information on environment variables is more specific than that provided by the System Information utility. For example, the System Information utility might report that the value for the windir variable is %SystemRoot%, a generic reference. If you choose to view environment variables from the System Properties dialog box, Windows XP reports the setting for the windir variable as C:\Windows (or the path to your Windows folder), the actual location of the system files.

You can also define settings for new environment variables, change settings, and delete environment variables just for your logon. For example, if you developed batch programs (covered in Tutorial 14) to customize your computer or automate operations, you could define new variables for those programs to process. Only individuals with Administrator privileges can create, modify, or delete system variables. An Administrator could, for example, change the Path system variable to change the list of folders identified in the Windows path.

To view environment variable settings for your logon:

1. Click the **Environment Variables** button. In the Environment Variables dialog box, Windows XP lists the settings for the TEMP and TMP user variables for Olivia's logon. See Figure 10-32. In the System variables area, Windows XP lists the settings for variables required for the proper functioning of Windows XP. These system variables are defined by Windows XP and are the same for all user logons. Your settings will differ. If your user account does not have Administrator privileges, the New, Edit, and Delete buttons under System variables on this property sheet are dimmed so that you cannot change these settings.

Figure 10-32	ENVIRONMENT VARIABLES SETTINGS

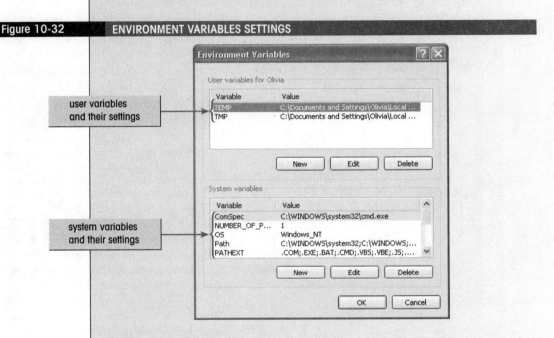

2. Click the **Cancel** button to close the Environment Variables dialog box without making changes to any settings on your computer.

If you need to find out what a particular setting is for your logon, change a user variable, or add a new user variable, you can examine the user and system variables in the Environment Variables dialog box.

REFERENCE WINDOW   **RW**

Viewing User and System Environment Variable Settings

- On the Start menu, right-click My Computer, click Properties on the shortcut menu, click the Advanced tab in the System Properties dialog box, and then click the Environment Variables button.
- Check the user variable settings for your user logon in the User variables box, and system variable settings for all users in the System variables box.
- Use the New, Edit, or Delete buttons to create new user variables, modify variable settings, or delete environment variables for your logon.
- If you have Administrator privileges, you can create, modify, or delete system variables.
- If you want to save changes to Environment Variables settings, click the OK button; otherwise, if you are just viewing settings, click the Cancel button to close the Environment Variables dialog box without applying changes to your system.
- If you want to save changes to any System Property settings, click the OK button; otherwise, if you are just viewing information on settings, click the Cancel button to close the System Properties dialog box without applying changes to your system.

If you view System Startup and Recovery settings, Windows XP displays important information from Boot.ini about how your system starts, and also explains what to do if an error causes the computer to stop. For example, if your computer has more than one operating system installed, and if you log on as an Administrator, you can choose which operating system to use to start your computer. If necessary, you can adjust the amount of time that Windows XP displays the OS Choices menu so that you can select an operating system or the Recovery Console before the default operating system loads. You can also open Boot.ini in Notepad to edit the contents of the startup settings file; however, be very cautious about making changes to Boot.ini, or you might not be able to boot your computer.

A user with Administrator privileges can also use the System Startup and Recovery dialog box to specify what happens if there is a system failure. If a system failure occurs, Windows XP displays a STOP error screen and message with details on the nature of the problem. **STOP errors** can result from problems with software or hardware, such as invalid program instructions, poorly designed device drivers, incompatible hardware, failing hardware, or incorrectly configured hardware. Windows XP can then write an event to the system log and thereby document the problem, send an alert to the Administrator, automatically restart the computer, or dump the contents of system memory to a file called a **memory dump file** that Administrators or Microsoft tech support can use for resolving the problem. An **event** is a significant occurrence in the system or an application that requires Windows XP to notify users of the event and to log the event. You can specify whether you want a Small Memory Dump (a small set of data that identifies why the system stopped), a Kernel Memory Dump (data on just the kernel memory), or a Complete Memory Dump (the entire contents of system memory). These options also affect the amount of storage space required on disk, including the size of the paging file. The latter is important, because Windows XP writes data to the paging file when an error occurs, and during the next successful boot, uses that data to create the memory dump file. This is one more reason why a paging file is important. If you need to contact a Microsoft support technician, that person may need the system memory dump to help resolve the problem.

To examine startup and recovery settings:

1. Under Startup and Recovery, click the **Settings** button. The Startup and Recovery dialog box lists the default operating system used to start your computer. See Figure 10-33. This information is derived from Boot.ini (which you examined in Tutorial 9). Yours may differ.

Figure 10-33 STARTUP AND RECOVERY OPTIONS

default operating system for booting computer

option for adjusting the amount of time for displaying a list of operating systems to choose from during booting

opens Boot.ini in Notepad for editing

options for handling STOP errors

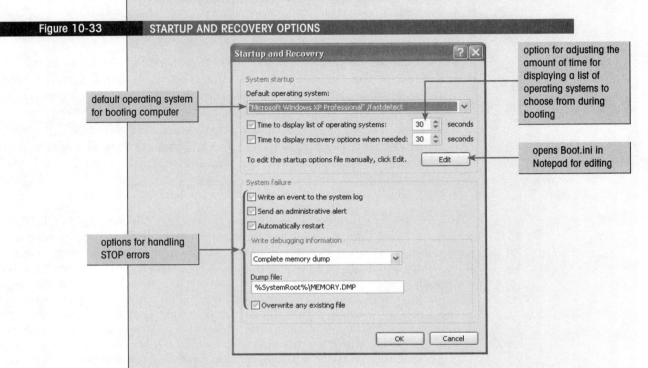

In the System Failure section, an individual with Administrator privileges can specify what happens if there is a system failure. In the "Write debugging information" list box, you can also specify the type and amount of information written to the memory dump file. If your user account does not have Administrator privileges, all of the settings on this property sheet are dimmed except those for setting the time to display a list of operating systems on the OS Choices menu and for specifying the Dump file.

2. Click the **Cancel** button to close the Startup and Recovery dialog box, and then click the **Cancel** button to close the System Properties dialog box without making changes to any system settings.

REFERENCE WINDOW `RW`

Viewing or Changing Startup and Recovery Settings

- On the Start menu, right-click My Computer, click Properties on the shortcut menu, click the Advanced tab in the System Properties dialog box, and then click the Settings button under Startup and Recovery.
- In the System startup section, examine or select the default operating system used to start the computer, and examine or change whether you want to see a list of operating systems during booting, and for how long.
- If you have Administrator privileges, you can specify that Windows XP write an event to the system log, send an alert to Administrators, automatically restart the computer, or dump the contents of RAM to a file on disk if there is a system failure so that technical support can help you resolve the problem. You can also specify the type and amount of information written to the memory dump file in the "Write debugging information" list box.
- If you want to save changes to Startup and Recovery settings, click the OK button; otherwise, if you are just viewing settings, click the Cancel button to close the Startup and Recovery dialog box without applying changes to your system.
- If you want to save changes to any System Property settings, click the OK button; otherwise, if you are just viewing information on settings, click the Cancel button to close the System Properties dialog box without applying changes to your system.

As you can tell from the information in the first part of this tutorial, the Windows XP operating system is rich in resources and tools for evaluating, configuring, and optimizing the performance of your computer. Later, if you need to locate any of this information or modify these settings, you now know where to look.

Upgrading **Memory**

If you intend to upgrade the RAM in your computer, consider using the following strategy before you make a purchase:

- **Examine the documentation for your computer**. You need to find out the type of RAM, type of memory module, storage capacities, speed, and parity (or lack thereof) of the memory required for your computer. A **memory module** is a circuit board that contains memory chips (or RAM chips) and plugs into a socket on the motherboard. **SDRAM (Synchronous Dynamic Random Access Memory)**, a common type of memory, supports data transfer speeds of up to 1.1 GB/sec, while DDR SDRAM (Double Data Rate SDRAM), a newer type of memory technology, supports data transfer speeds of up to 2.1 GB/sec.

  The most common types of memory modules are the DIMM (Dual In-line Memory Module) for use in desktop computers, and the SO DIMM (Small Outline DIMM) for use in notebooks or laptops. Older computers used the SIMM (Single In-line Memory Module).SIMM (Single In-line Memory Module).

  Depending on the type of computer you have, you might be able to simply install additional RAM, even if the memory modules have different capacities (such as 8 MB, 16 MB, 32 MB, 64 MB, etc.). You might have to add memory modules in pairs or replace the existing memory module with a new one that has a greater storage capacity.

You have to make sure your memory modules operate at the same speed. Over the years, the speed of memory chips has been rated in **nanoseconds (ns)**, or billionths of a second, and speeds of 50 to 70 ns were common. Memory speeds have also been rated in MHz (such as 100 or 133 MHz) so that they can be compared to CPU bus speeds. The **CPU bus** refers to the wiring that provides a high-speed direct connection to the processor. The **clock speed** is the speed at which a processor executes instructions, and is measured in **Megahertz (MHz)**, or millions of cycles per second. DDR SDRAM is rated based on its throughput (or bandwidth), such as PC2100 DDR with a throughput of 2.1 GB/sec.

You also have to make sure the metal used for the connector (the edge of the memory module that plugs into the socket on the motherboard) is the same as the one used for the socket itself to prevent corrosion. The metal is either gold or tin (which has a silvery color). Gold conducts electricity better, creates a thinner and more uniform layer, is more resistant to corrosion, and lasts longer than tin; however, it's also more expensive than tin.

■ **Examine the motherboard.** Open the system unit and locate and verify how many memory modules are connected to the system board, how many slots (if any) are available for inserting additional memory modules, and whether the slots are gold or tin.

■ **Decide how much memory you want to add to your computer.** The amount of RAM that you can add to your computer depends on the maximum amount of RAM supported by your computer, the number of slots on your motherboard, the amount of RAM that is already installed on your computer, and whether you must add memory modules with the same amount of RAM as the existing modules or whether you can add memory modules with different memory capacities. If you want to add more RAM to your computer, you should be careful how you go about that upgrade. For example, suppose your motherboard has three slots and suppose one of those slots has a 64 MB memory module. You could save money and buy two 32 MB memory modules to increase the amount of RAM in your computer to 128 MB. But, what happens when you discover later that you need even more memory and you no longer have any empty slots? You might need to throw away one or more of the 32 MB memory modules to make room for one or more memory modules with more RAM. Your computer manual more than likely contains information about what upgrades are supported and how to install memory modules.

■ **Visit the Web site of your computer manufacturer.** You can find additional information about the type of RAM needed for your computer model or series and verify that the information that you have collected thus far is correct.

■ **Check the type of memory sold by your supplier.** If you are going to purchase RAM from a retail outlet, find out which company supplies the memory modules sold in that store, and also make a note of the exact type of memory, its speed, its storage capacity, and whether your system uses parity or nonparity memory chips.

■ **Visit the Web site of the memory module supplier.** You might find information about the type of RAM needed for your computer model or series, and verify that the memory sold by your supplier is the right type to use in your computer.

It's a good idea to purchase the memory you need for your computer when you first acquire that computer so that you don't encounter performance problems. The longer you wait to add more memory, the less available and the more expensive it becomes. Also, you do not want to install more RAM than you might ever need or use. Anticipate how long you intend to keep your computer and evaluate your use of that computer before deciding how much RAM you need.

To make an educated decision about purchasing memory with a new computer or upgrading memory, you also need to understand the demands made by the operating system and applications on memory usage and, in the case of an upgrade, monitor how your current computer's operating system and applications use memory. New software products, including operating systems, invariably include information on their specific memory requirements.

In the next section of the tutorial, you examine the property settings for the printer installed on your computer, verify that the settings are correct, and examine how to optimize your printer. You also examine printing preferences for your computer so that you can take full advantage of its capabilities.

Optimizing **Printer Performance**

For most people, the quality and performance of their printer is an important aspect of using a computer, even though printers have always been considered optional computer components. For that reason, you should understand how to configure printers properly and troubleshoot printer problems.

As you discovered in Tutorial 9, the Printers and Faxes folder includes an option for installing support for a printer, as well as specifying configuration settings. If you connect a new printer to your computer, you should also check the printer's property sheets and verify that the settings are correct so that you obtain the optimum performance from Windows XP and your printer.

From the Printer and Faxes window, you can open the Properties dialog box for a printer installed on your computer. Using the General property sheet for your printer, you can change the name of the printer (which Windows assigns when you install the printer), and you can enter comments with important information, such as the location of the printer (building, floor, etc.) and changes made to the printer. For example, you might note the date when you last installed a new toner cartridge. If multiple users have access to the same printer on a network, any such comments are visible to all users.

The General property sheet for your printer may also provide you with information on whether your printer supports color and double-sided printing (also referred to as **duplex** printing), whether it can staple sheets together, and its speed and print resolution (if known). The printer speed is the maximum speed, measured in pages per minute, and the actual speed is lower for documents with graphics and color (if your printer supports color printing). The resolution is measured in **dots per inch (dpi)**, and varies depending on the capabilities of the printer. A higher value, such as 2400 x 1200 dpi, produces a better quality image but takes longer to print, in contrast to a lower value, such as 150 dpi, which renders a printed document at a lower quality in a shorter period of time.

From the General property sheet, you can also print a test page, which not only verifies that your printer is working properly, but also provides information about your installed printer. Among other things, the test page shows the printer model, filename of your printer driver, the driver version, the name of the printer port, the data format used for printing, and additional files used by the printer driver.

The Sharing property sheet shows whether a printer is shared with other users on a network, and, if so, the share name for the printer (such as HP PhotoSmart Printer). If you want to share a printer with other users on a network, you can choose the "Share this printer" option, and then enter a name for the shared device. Be sure to use a name that distinguishes this printer from other printers that might be available on the network; don't use the default name of "Printer."

For shared printers, Windows XP notes that you should install additional drivers for the printer if other network users work on computers that have another installed version of Windows. You can select and install drivers from a list for other versions of Windows operating on the same platform (Intel-based, or x86-based computers) or another platform

(Alpha or IA64 platforms). **Alpha** refers to a family of 64-bit RISC processors from Digital Corporation. **RISC (Reduced Instruction Set Computing)** refers to a processor design that uses a small set of simple instructions for processing data, in contrast to **CISC (Complex Instruction Set Computing)**, which relies on many complex instructions. IA64 refers to the new Intel Itanium processor.

The Ports property sheet identifies the port to which a printer is connected. For example, Windows XP might show that a printer is connected to an IEEE 1394 port. Figure 10-34 shows transmission speeds for different types of ports.

Figure 10-34	PORT TYPES, PORT SPEEDS, AND SUPPORTED CONNECTIONS

Type of Port	Data Speed	Connections Supported
Parallel	150 Kbps	1
Enhanced Parallel Port (EPP)	500 Kbps	1
Serial	56 Kbps	1
ISDN	128 Kbps	1
IrDA (InfraRed) (Wireless)	4,000 Kbps	1
USB (Universal Serial Bus)	12,000 Kbps	127
IEEE 1394 (FireWire)	400,000 Kbps	63
Next Generation:		
USB 2	480,000 Kbps	127
IEEE 1394b	800,000-3,200,000 Kbps	63

Notes:
- USB also supports a slower speed of 1,500 Kbps
- IEEE 1394 also supports slower speeds of 100,000 Kbps and 2000 Kbps

Kbps = Kilobits per second

Universal Serial Bus (USB) and IEEE 1394 ports are expected to replace the use of the standard parallel and serial ports on computers in the future because they support higher transmission speeds required for digital video, digital audio, digital animation, and digital graphics. With USB and IEEE 1394, you can also connect more than one device to the same port, and since these devices are Plug and Play devices, Windows XP automatically detects and configures them. Furthermore, these devices support **hot swapping** (also called **hot plugging** and **hot insertion-and-removal**); in other words, you can connect the devices when your computer is up and running. You do not have to power down your computer first.

Most computers have one LPT port (called LPT1 for the first Line Printer port), and two serial or com ports (called COM1 and COM2 for the first and second communications ports). Parallel ports support **parallel transmission**, which means that a computer can transmit 8 bits (for each byte of data) simultaneously down eight different lines in the printer cable to the printer. In contrast, serial ports support **serial transmission**, which means that a computer can transmit only one bit at a time down one line in the printer cable to the printer. Parallel cables are typically limited to no more than 15 feet in length, so the device to which they are connected must be close to the computer. In contrast, serial cables can be up to 500 feet in length, so the device can be located at a further distance from the computer.

From the Ports property sheet, you can add a port to your computer's configuration by selecting a port type, such as a Local Port, LPR Port, or Standard TCP/IP port. An **LPR Port** (Line Printer Remote) is used on servers that communicate with host computers, such as UNIX computers, using RFC 1179 (Line Printer Daemon Protocol). A **daemon** (pronounced "demon" and derived from Greek mythology for "guardian spirit") is an operating system process, such as a print spooler, that waits for and handles requests for a service. A **Standard TCP/IP port** is one that supports the TCP/IP protocol and that can be used to connect remote printers. **TCP/IP (Transmission Control Protocol/Internet Protocol)** is a set of networking protocols that determine how computers communicate, how they connect to networks, and how they route data.

For some printers, you also can specify whether to enable **bidirectional support**, which supports the flow of information to and from the printer so that the printer can report a problem, such as a paper jam, low toner, or an out-of-paper error condition. Otherwise, if Windows XP reports a problem with the printer, you have to manually check all the possibilities to determine the source of the problem. For some printers, you can enable **printer pooling**, which supports printing to two or more identical physical printers that act as if they were a single printer. A print job is then sent to the first available printer in the pool.

In addition to the General, Sharing, and Ports property sheets, your printer Properties dialog box also includes other property sheets for more advanced settings or for settings specific to your printer model and its manufacturer.

As a support tech, Olivia finds that she spends a fair amount of time helping other staff members configure, use, and troubleshoot problems with their printers. Most of the staff members use three types of printers—laser printers for high-quality documents, inkjet printers for documents with graphics, and plotters for producing maps. When you assist staff, Olivia wants you to show employees how to test their printer connections, set default printer settings, and specify graphics settings.

The following steps describe settings for an HP PhotoSmart printer (an inkjet printer). As you examine your own printer properties, remember that, unless you are using the same model, your printer settings will differ from those shown in the figures. If your printer does not have the same property sheets described in the next section, examine the other property sheets to see if some or all of the settings are available from another property sheet, or if they include similar options that you can examine. Complete the steps that are appropriate for your printer and its configuration. If certain options are not available, read the information and then continue with the next step. Your access privileges also determine what options are available to you. Also, remember that the details on the different options and settings that are available for your printer are in your printer manual—not Windows XP's Help and Support Center. Even if you do not have the specific type of printer described in this section, you might discover valuable information which can assist you in the future when you decide to purchase a new printer.

To check printer properties:

1. On the Start menu, click **Printers and Faxes**. Windows XP opens the Printers and Faxes folder. See Figure 10-35. The Printers and Faxes window for the computer used for this figure contains two printer configurations—one for an HP LaserJet III, and one for an HP PhotoSmart 1115 Series. As evidenced from the icon for the HP LaserJet printer, this is a network printer. The ✓ icon identifies the HP PhotoSmart printer as the default printer, and it is directly connected to this Windows XP Professional workstation. The contents of your Printers and

Faxes folder will differ. Also, the Printer Tasks dynamic menu includes an option for adding a new printer configuration. This option starts the Add Printer Wizard, which steps you through the process of installing a printer.

TROUBLE? If the Start menu does not contain a Printers and Faxes menu option, right-click the taskbar, click Properties on the shortcut menu, click the Start Menu tab in the Taskbar and Start Menu Properties dialog box, click the Customize button, click the Advanced tab in the Customize Start Menu dialog box, locate and click the Printers and Faxes check box under "Start menu items," click the OK button to close the Customize Start Menu dialog box, click the OK button to close the Taskbar and Start Menu Properties dialog box, and then try this step again.

Figure 10-35	VIEWING INSTALLED PRINTERS

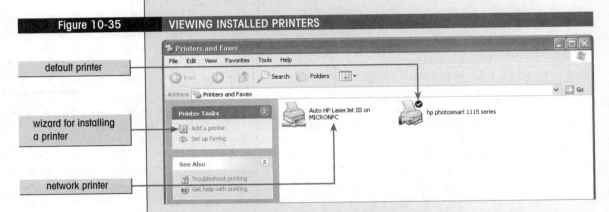

default printer

wizard for installing a printer

network printer

2. Right-click the icon for your installed printer or for the default printer, and then click **Properties** on the shortcut menu. The General property sheet in your Properties dialog box shows the name of your installed printer in the box to the right of the printer icon. See Figure 10-36. You can enter comments in the Location and Comment text boxes, if you like. The Features section for the printer used for this configuration summarizes some features of this installed printer (where known). Notice that you also have an option for examining printing preferences and for printing a test page.

TROUBLE? If there are no installed printers for the computer you are using, examine the figures and read, but do not keystroke, the steps in this section so that you are familiar with how to locate and specify printer settings.

TROUBLE? Your Properties dialog box might differ from the one shown in Figure 10-36. The number and types of property sheets, as well as the settings on each property sheet, in the Properties dialog box depend on the type of printer you're using. For example, a Postscript property sheet is included for a Postscript printer.

Figure 10-36   GENERAL PRINTER PROPERTIES

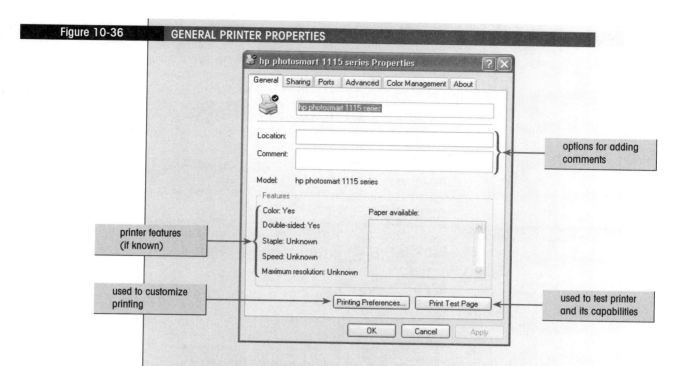

options for adding comments

printer features (if known)

used to customize printing

used to test printer and its capabilities

If you click the Print Test Page button, Windows XP displays a dialog box for your printer, asking if the test page printed correctly. See Figure 10-37. As noted, Windows XP tests your printer's ability to print both graphics and text, and provides information about your printer driver and port settings.

Figure 10-37   PRINTING A TEST PAGE

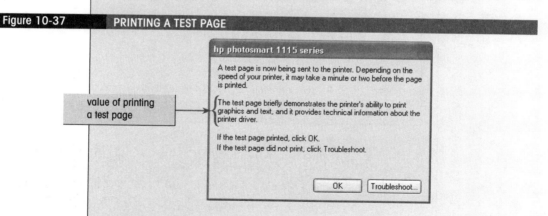

value of printing a test page

Figure 10-38 shows the Printer Test Page for a HP PhotoSmart printer. Assuming you encountered no problems, you would click the OK button; otherwise, you can click the Troubleshooting button to open the Printing Troubleshooter that you used in Tutorial 9.

Figure 10-38	PRINTER TEST PAGE

graphic

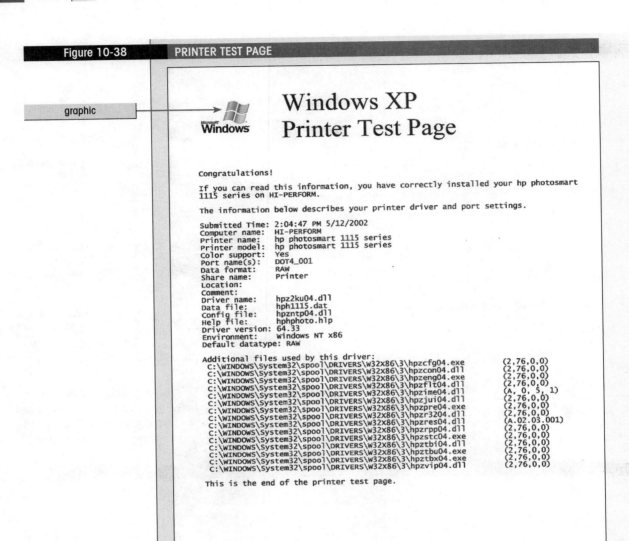

3. Click the **Sharing** tab (if available). On the Sharing property sheet, Windows XP shows whether the printer is shared with other users on your network, and, if so, the share name for the printer. See Figure 10-39. If your user account does not have Administrator privileges, the settings on this property sheet are dimmed.

TROUBLE? If prompted to run the Network Setup Wizard, click the Cancel button so you do not make any changes to your computer.

TROUBLE? Network security restrictions might prevent access to the features typically available on this property sheet.

Figure 10-39   VIEWING NETWORK SHARING SETTINGS

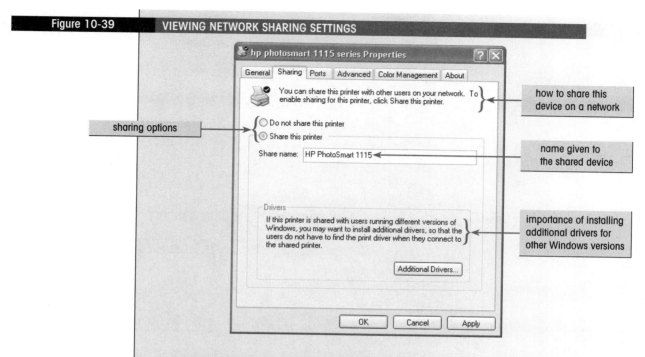

sharing options

how to share this device on a network

name given to the shared device

importance of installing additional drivers for other Windows versions

If available, you can use the Additional Drivers button to install additional drivers needed by users who work with other versions of Windows on the same platform (Intel-based, or x86-based computers) or another platform (Alpha or IA64 platforms). See Figure 10-40.

Figure 10-40   OPTIONS FOR INSTALLING DIFFERENT DRIVERS

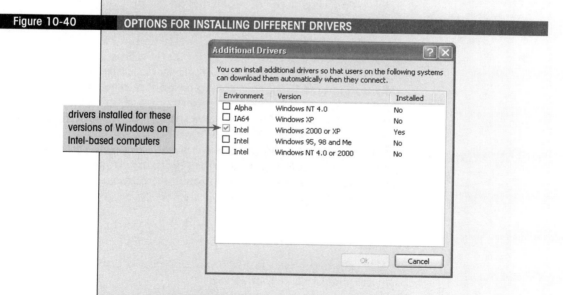

drivers installed for these versions of Windows on Intel-based computers

4. Click the **Ports** tab. The Ports property sheet identifies the printer port by name, includes a description for the port, and identifies the printer name. See Figure 10-41. The HP PhotoSmart 1115 printer on the computer used for this figure is connected to a port identified as DOT4_001, which is a USB port with an IEEE 1284.4 compatible driver.

Figure 10-41	VIEWING PORT SETTINGS

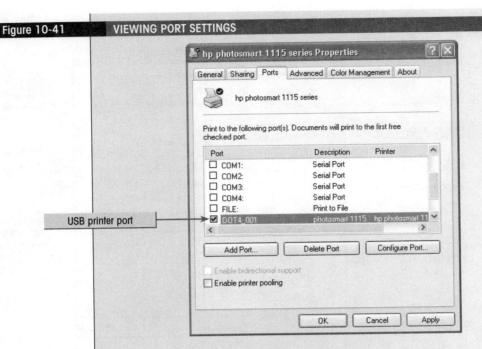

USB printer port

As noted earlier, you can enable bidirectional support (if available) and printer pooling (if available). You can also use the Add Port button to select a port type and add a new port to your computer's configuration. If your user account does not have Administrator privileges, the Add Port, Delete Port, and Configure Port, as well as some settings on this property sheet, are dimmed.

5. Click the **Advanced** tab (if available). On the Advanced tab of the printer used for Figure 10-42, the user can specify whether the printer is always available, or whether it's only available for a certain time period. You can increase the priority setting if you want higher-priority documents to print before lower-priority documents. The lowest setting for print priority (default) is 1 and the highest setting is 99. You can only change this setting if you have the Manage Documents permission. The Driver box shows the driver for the printer (identified by the printer name). The New Driver button allows you to start the Add Printer Driver Wizard if you want to install another driver. You can also specify print spooling and other print settings. If your user account does not have Administrator privileges, the settings on this property sheet are dimmed.

Figure 10-42 | VIEWING ADVANCED PRINTER SETTINGS

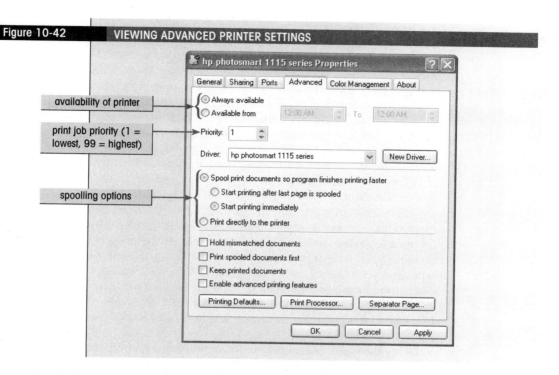

availability of printer

print job priority (1 = lowest, 99 = highest)

spoolling options

By default, Windows XP spools print jobs by creating a temporary spool file on disk to store the processed print job. You can then continue working with the current application or another application while the contents of the temporary spool file are transmitted to the printer in the background. For this to work properly, there must be space on your hard disk for Windows XP to store the temporary spool files. Once a print job is complete, the spool files are deleted. On the Advanced property sheet shown in Figure 10-42, the user can specify spool settings that control how Windows XP manages print jobs. Under the default "Spool print jobs so program finishes printing faster" option, the user can choose to start printing after the last page or after the first page is spooled to disk. If you use the "Start printing immediately" option (the default), Windows XP starts printing a document as soon as it spools the first page to disk, and then continues to spool other pages in the document to disk. Your document prints faster with this option. If you choose to start printing after the last page is spooled, printing is delayed until all pages within the document are spooled to the temporary file on disk. Although this option delays printing somewhat, it is useful because Windows XP does not have to both spool and print at the same time, and the application is made available to you sooner. However, you cannot use the application until spooling is completed.

The "Print spooled documents first" option prints documents that have completed spooling, even if the documents have a lower priority setting than documents that are still spooling. If you disable this option, documents are printed in order of priority. The use of this option maximizes the efficiency of printer use.

Normally, spooled documents are deleted after printing is complete; however, the "Keep printed documents" option, if enabled, retains the spooled documents so that they can be resubmitted to the printer from the printer queue. However, this option uses valuable storage space on the hard disk. The "Hold mismatched documents" option compares the printer setup with the document setup, and if they do not match, the document is held in the print queue and not printed. Other documents still continue to print.

The "Print directly to the printer" option turns off spooling. Your document is sent to the printer, and you do not have access to your application until Windows XP transmits the entire print job to the printer's buffer. Like your computer, the printer has RAM, and part of this RAM (the **printer buffer**) holds the document currently being printed. If you are having trouble printing, you might want to turn off spooling, and see if it eliminates the problem.

The "Enable advanced printing features" option turns on features that you examine later, such as page order, booklet printing, and pages per sheet. The Printing Defaults button displays property sheets in which you can specify printing preferences.

The Separator Page button lets you specify whether you want to insert a page between each document that prints. A **separator page,** or **banner page**, is a page that identifies who sent the document to the printer, and the date and time of printing. Since the separator page prints before each document, this feature can be useful in a networked environment where users share the same printer, and need to quickly identify and retrieve their print job. Windows XP has standard separator page files (with the "sep" file extension) in the System32 folder, or you can create your own separator pages. Sysprint.sep switches the printer to Postscript printing and prints a separator page before each document. Recall that **Postscript** is a page description language that provides information to a printer on how to lay out a page on a sheet of paper. Pscript.sep switches the printer to Postscript printing, but does not print a separator page. Pcl.sep switches the printer to PCL printing, and prints a separator page before each document. **PCL**, for Printer Control Language, is a page description language developed by Hewlett Packard for their laser and inkjet printers. This last option might not work if a printer does not also support PJL (Printer Job Language). **PJL** is a printer command language developed by Hewlett Packard that controls printers at the print-job level.

Using the Color Management property sheet, a graphics artist or desktop publisher with a user account that has Administrator privileges can associate a specific color profile with a printer, and thereby control the color of the final image. A **color profile** consists of data about specific colors, **hue** (the position of a color in the color spectrum), **saturation** (the amount of gray in the color, and therefore a determinant of the purity of a color), and brightness.

As shown in Figure 10-43, you might have a Device Settings property sheet in which you can specify device settings, such as the amount of printer memory. If you install additional memory in your printer, you need to change the amount of memory shown here. For example, if your printer came with 1 MB of memory and you then installed a circuit board with another 4 MB of memory, you would need to change this setting to 5 MB. If you receive out-of-memory error messages when printing, check this setting to make sure it is set properly. If you do not know how much memory your printer has, have your printer perform a self-test; it might provide memory information on the self-test printout.

Figure 10-43   SPECIFYING PRINTER MEMORY

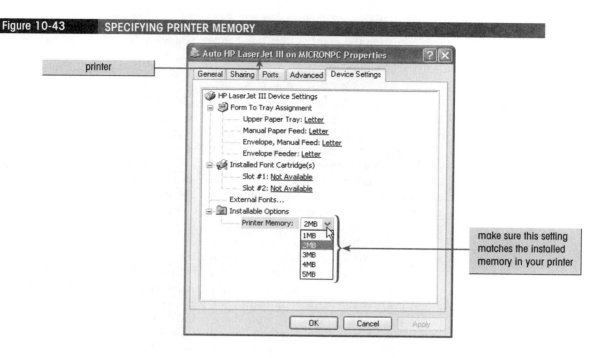

Next, you're going to examine settings for printing preferences. One preference you can set is print quality, which you might be able to specify as Draft, Normal, or Best. The Draft option uses less ink and prints faster, but the print quality is the lowest. The Normal option produces letter-quality documents, and is the recommended option for both speed and quality. The Best option produces the highest level of quality, no matter what type of paper is used, but printing is slower. Best is the preferred option for printing color photos and graphics. If you primarily print graphics and photos, choose Best and override the default setting of Normal, for the highest-quality printouts.

Depending on the capabilities of your printer, you might be able to select different paper types, such as plain paper, Inkjet papers, Photo Papers, Transparency Films, Special Papers, Greeting Cards, and Brochure Papers. You might also be able to specify the optimum combination of print speed and quality for certain paper types. Paper sizes may include the standard Letter (8½" × 11"), Legal (8½" × 14"), and Executive (7½" × 10½"), as well as Envelope #10 (4½" × 9½"). A4 (210 × 297 mm), A5 (148 × 210 mm), and B5 (182 × 257 mm) are European paper sizes, and there are European envelope sizes as well.

Depending on your printer, you might be able to select such features as page orientation and two-sided printing. For orientation, you can select the standard Portrait mode (where the page is taller than it is wide) or Landscape mode (where the printing is rotated 90 degrees), and you might be able to select a mirror image option (which reverses your image or document by flipping it horizontally). Mirror image is useful if you want to print iron-on transfers or presentation slides. The Rotate 180 degrees option, if available for printing envelopes, is useful if your printer smudges return addresses. When printing on both sides of a page, you might have a Book option, which assumes pages are bound in a way similar to that found in books, a Tablet option, which assumes pages are bound at the top of the page (such as when used for a calendar), or an Automatic option, for duplex printing on plain paper. For Book and Tablet printing, you have to follow the on-screen instructions for manually reinserting the paper in the paper tray after the printer prints the first side. If your printer can print multiple pages per sheet, you can also set how many pages you want to include on a sheet of paper. You might also be able to print a document as a poster, and thereby magnify an image or document.

Other settings you might be able to specify include printing a document in reverse order and indicating the number of printed copies you want of each document.

If you are using a color printer, you can set color options that let you print in black and white. If available, you can use a Print in Grayscale option to print colors as shades of gray. Printing is not only faster, but drafts save color ink on a color printer until you need it for the final printed document. If you choose the Print in Grayscale option, you might then be able to select a Black Only option to use just the black print cartridge, a High Quality option to use the color print cartridge for high-quality grayscale, or an Optimize for Photocopy or Fax option for documents that you photocopy or fax in black and white.

Other color options allow you to control saturation, brightness, and color tone. You can use a Saturation option to adjust the purity of printed colors. If the color of your printed document or image seems too dull, you can set the color so that it's more vibrant. If the color appears too dense, you can mute the color. You can use a Brightness option to adjust the relative lightness or darkness of the document or image. If the document or image seems too dark, you can choose a lighter setting; likewise, if it seems too light, you can choose a darker setting. A Color Tone option adjusts the relative warmth or coolness of colors.

For some printers, you can adjust the amount of ink used for a printed document or image. The less ink you use, the faster the ink on the printed document or image dries. You might also be able to specify extra time for drying a printed document or image if you increase the Ink Volume setting. Many printers also let you set a Low Memory Mode option, which is useful if your computer does not have enough RAM or disk space to print a complex document or a document with high-resolution images.

As noted earlier, if your printer does not have the same property sheets described in the next section, examine the other property sheets to see if some or all of the settings are available from another property sheet, or to see if there are similar options that you can examine.

To examine printing preferences:

1. Click the **General** tab, and then click the **Printing Preferences** button (if available). The Setup property sheet for the HP PhotoSmart printer contains options for specifying the print quality and paper settings. See Figure 10-44. Under Print Quality, you can choose the Draft (for faster printing, lower ink usage, but also lower quality), Normal (for letter-quality documents), or Best (for color photos and graphics) option.

   TROUBLE? If your printer does not have a Setup property sheet, or any of the other property sheets shown in Figure 10-44 and discussed in later steps, examine the other property sheets in the Printing Preferences dialog box to see if some or all of the settings are available from some other sheet or to see if there are similar options that you can examine. You might discover new features of your printer.

Figure 10-44 | **VIEWING PRINTING PREFERENCES**

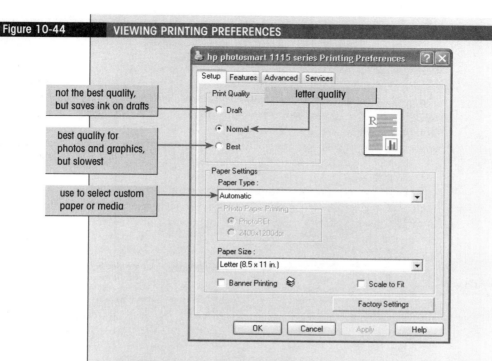

In the Paper Type list box under Paper Settings, you can select the type of paper that best matches your needs. See Figure 10-45. Some paper types provide additional settings. For example, if Photo Papers is selected from the Paper Type list box for this particular type of HP PhotoSmart printer, the options in the Photo Paper Printing section become available. You can then choose PhotoREt, which selects the best combination of speed and quality, or 2400 x 1200 dpi, which prints high-resolution images more slowly and requires a large amount of disk storage space.

The Banner Printing option prints a document or documents over multiple sheets as a banner. The Scale To Fit option reduces an image to fit on whatever size of paper you have chosen. The Factory Settings button restores the default settings for this printer.

Figure 10-45   CHOOSING A PAPER TYPE

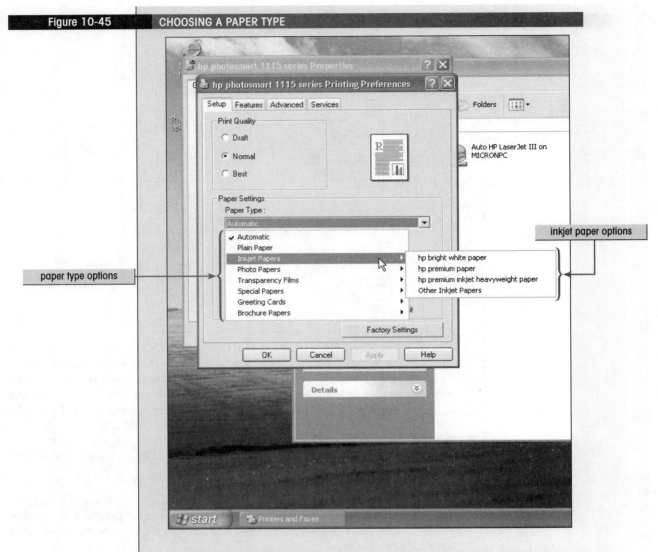

paper type options

inkjet paper options

In the Paper Size list box, you can select the size or type of media you want to use for printing. See Figure 10-46. In addition to options for the standard paper sizes, this printer provides options for printing on index cards of various sizes, and Photo 4 x 6 in. (with tear-off tab).

Figure 10-46   SPECIFYING THE PAPER SIZE

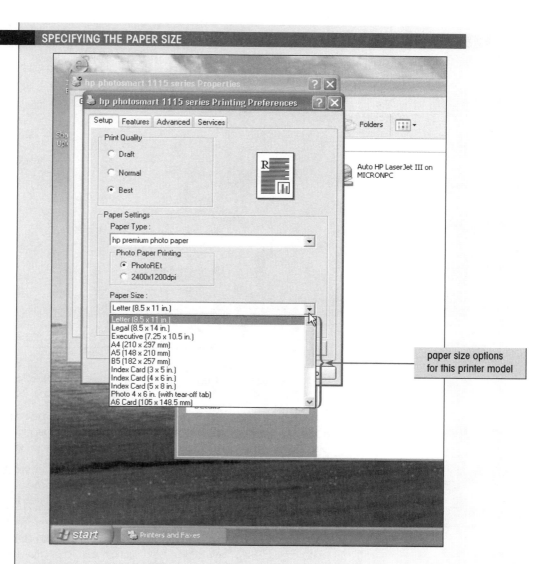

paper size options
for this printer model

2. Click the **Features** tab (if available). On the Features property sheet for the
   HP PhotoSmart printer, you can specify the page orientation, whether you want
   duplex or two-sided printing, how many pages you want to print per sheet of
   paper, and how you want to print posters. See Figure 10-47.

Figure 10-47 | SPECIFYING PRINTER FEATURES

options for orienting printed page

preview of selected printer features

automatic preview prior to printing

stack order

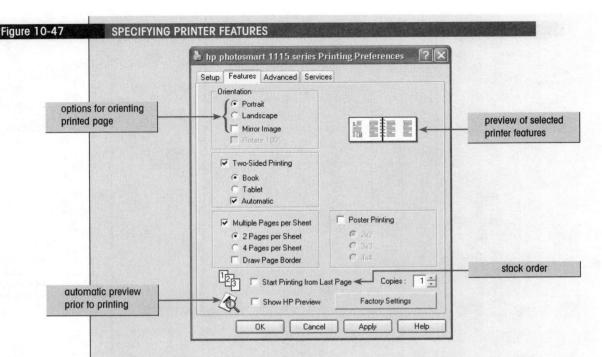

Under Two-Sided Printing, you can choose the Book, Tablet, or Automatic option to define how you want to print on both sides of the page.

The Multiple Pages per Sheet option prints multiple pages on a single sheet of paper by reducing the image of each page. On this printer, you can specify 2 or 4 pages per sheet, and you can include a page border around each page image.

The Poster Printing option prints an image or document as if it were a poster over as many pages as you specify and, in the process, magnifies the image or document. Once completed, you tape the pages together to form a poster.

The Start Printing from Last Page option prints in reverse order, and guarantees that the order of pages in the output tray is correct (from the first page to the last page). The Show HP Preview option displays a preview of the document before it prints so that you can correct any last minute problems that you notice. You can also use the Copies box to specify the number of printed copies you want of each document.

3. Click the **Advanced** tab (if available). See Figure 10-48. Under Color, the Print in Grayscale option allows you to print colors as shades of gray with a High Quality (using only the black print cartridge), High Quality (using the color print cartridge), and Optimize for Photocopy or Fax (in black and white) options.

Figure 10-48   **ADVANCED PRINTING PREFERENCES**

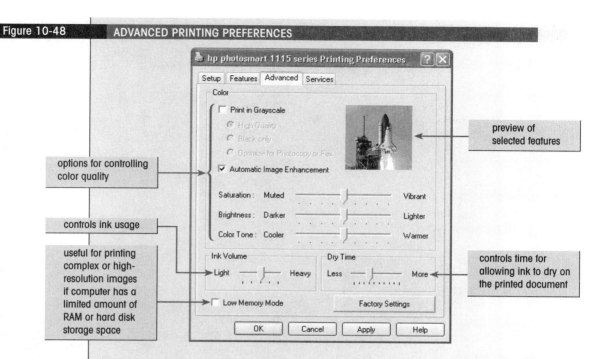

options for controlling color quality

controls ink usage

useful for printing complex or high-resolution images if computer has a limited amount of RAM or hard disk storage space

preview of selected features

controls time for allowing ink to dry on the printed document

The Automatic Image Enhancement allows you to control Saturation (by muting an image or making it more vibrant), Brightness (by making it darker or lighter), and Color Tone (by making it cooler or warmer). Under Ink Volume, you can adjust the amount of ink used for a printed document or image. Under Dry Time, you can specify extra time for drying a printed document or image if you increased the Ink Volume setting. You can also select the Low Memory Mode option if your computer does not have enough memory or disk space to process the print job or if you are printing documents with complex or high-resolution images. Do not use this option for text, or text with line art, because the quality of the output will be poor.

The Services property sheet for the PhotoSmart printer provides access to different device services, such as the User's Guide, and options for calibrating the printer to obtain the best possible print quality or correcting a misalignment problem, cleaning the print cartridges, printing a test page, printing a diagnostic page that shows how the nozzles on the device's print cartridges are working, and calibrating the photo tray so that images are correctly positioned on a page. See Figure 10-49.

Figure 10-49   PRINTER SPECIFIC SERVICES

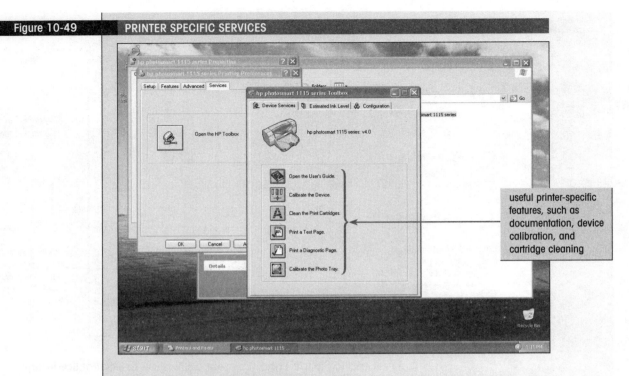

useful printer-specific features, such as documentation, device calibration, and cartridge cleaning

The Estimated Ink Level property sheet, shown in Figure 10-50, provides you valuable information on how much ink is available in each cartridge, the part number for each cartridge, and information for ordering new cartridges. The Configuration property sheet for this type of printer allows you to specify printing accessories, configure the display of messages regarding print settings, and specify port settings (if applicable).

Figure 10-50   PRINTER CARTRIDGE STATUS

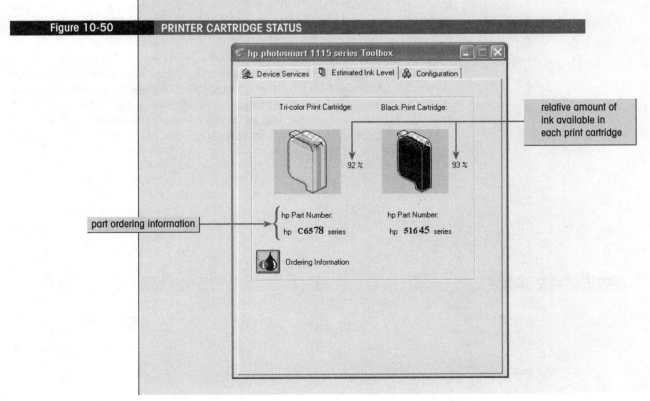

relative amount of ink available in each print cartridge

part ordering information

4. Click the **OK** button if you want to save changes to the printing preferences for your printer; otherwise, click the **Cancel** button.

5. Leave the Printers and Faxes folder open for the next section of the tutorial.

REFERENCE WINDOW   **RW**

<u>Checking or Changing Printer Settings and Printing Preferences</u>

- From the Start menu, click Printers and Faxes.
- After the Printers and Faxes folder window opens, right-click the icon for an installed printer, and then click Properties on the shortcut menu.
- Examine the settings on each property sheet, verify that your printer is properly configured, and, if necessary, make any changes you need to your printer settings. Use the Help button to display information on printer-specific settings.
- To change printing preferences, click the General tab, and then click the Printing Preferences button. (Or right-click the icon for an installed printer configuration in the Printers and Faxes window, and then click Printing Preferences.)
- Examine the settings on each property sheet, verify that your printer is using the printing preferences you want, and, if necessary, make any changes you need to the settings for your printing preferences. Use the Help button to display information on printer-specific settings.
- Click the OK button to close the Printing Preferences dialog box, and then (if necessary) click the OK button to close the Properties dialog box for your computer.
- Close the Printers and Faxes folder.

You can definitely benefit from reading your printer manual and learning more about the capabilities of your printer.

Managing Print Jobs in the Print Queue

When you print a document, that document is sent to the print queue, and Windows XP displays a printer icon in the Notification area of the taskbar. You can double-click the printer icon to view the contents of the print queue and, if necessary, change the print job. You can also open the print queue by first opening the Printers and Faxes folder, and then clicking the printer icon. The **print queue** contains a list of all the documents that are scheduled to print, and it also contains information about each print job, including the document name, the status of the document, the owner (or user name of the person who submitted the print job), the number of pages that have printed and the total number of pages, the document size (in kilobytes), the time and date the print job was submitted, and the port used by the printer. Figure 10-51 shows the print queue after a print job was sent to the printer. The Status column identifies the current status of the print job (such as whether it's spooling, printing, or paused).

Figure 10-51   VIEWING THE STATUS OF A PRINT JOB IN THE PRINT QUEUE

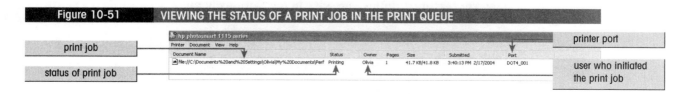

If you select a print job in the print queue, you can use the Document menu to pause the print job, resume a print job, restart a print job (from the beginning), cancel a print job, or change its properties (such as its priority or time restriction). Figure 10-52 shows the Properties dialog box for the document shown in the print queue of the previous figure. To change the print job's priority, you drag the slider bar under Priority (1 being the lowest, 99 the highest). Under Schedule, you can schedule a print job so that it's processed during a certain time period. The latter is useful if you need to print a long or complex document during a period of the day when the printer is not as busy. From this dialog box, you can also change your printing preferences.

Figure 10-52   **VIEWING PROPERTIES OF A PRINT JOB**

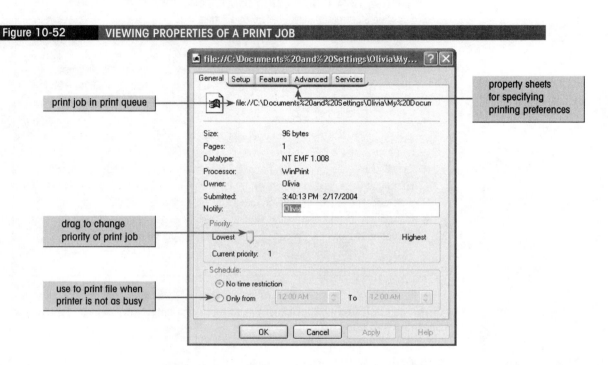

print job in print queue

property sheets for specifying printing preferences

drag to change priority of print job

use to print file when printer is not as busy

If you choose the Pause Printing option from the Printer menu, you suspend printing of all jobs on the printer, not just an individual job or selected jobs. To resume printing, you remove the check mark before the Pause Printing option on the Printer menu. If you choose the option to pause or cancel a print job, the document might be printed before that request is completed because the printer's buffer might be able to store an entire document. Once you send a document to the printer, you cannot use the print queue to change printer settings and printing preferences

If you need to select multiple print jobs in the print queue, hold down the Ctrl key while you click each job, and then you can change the settings for all the print jobs at the same time.

If a problem occurs when you try to print, Windows XP displays a balloon tip from the printer icon in the Notification area informing you that the document failed to print. See Figure 10-53. You can click that balloon tip to open the print queue. In the print queue, you see the "Error - Printing" message in the Status column.

Figure 10-53   NOTIFICATION OF A PRINTING PROBLEM

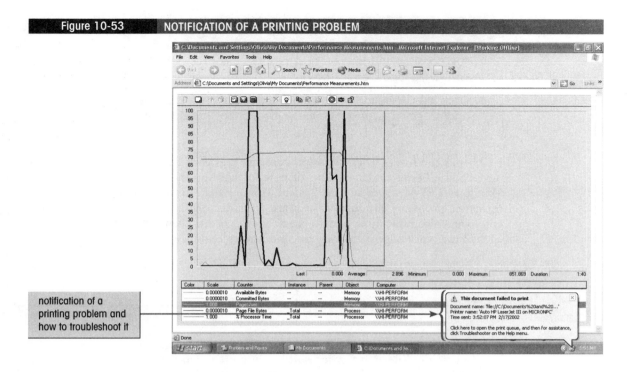

notification of a printing problem and how to troubleshoot it

You can only control your own print jobs, not those of other users, unless you are assigned the Manage Documents permission.

Restoring Your Computer

If you want to restore your computer to its original state before you started the tutorial, complete the following steps.

To restore your computer's display settings:

1. If your computer was originally set for the Windows Classic style, right-click the **desktop**, click **Properties** on the shortcut menu, and after Windows XP opens the Display Properties dialog box, click the **Theme** list arrow on the Themes property sheet, click **Windows Classic**, and then click the **OK** button.

2. To switch to the Windows Classic Start menu style, right-click the **Start** button, click **Properties** on the shortcut menu, and after Windows XP opens the Taskbar and Start Menu Properties dialog box, click the **Classic Start menu** option button on the Start Menu property sheet, and then click the **OK** button.

3. To change to Windows classic folders view, click the **Start** button, point to **Settings**, click **Control Panel**, and after Windows XP opens a Control Panel window, click **Tools** on the menu bar, click **Folder Options**, and after Windows XP opens the Folder Options dialog box, click the **Use Windows classic folders** option button, and then click the **Double-click to open an item** option button under "Click items as follows."

4. Click the **View** tab in the Folder Options dialog box. If necessary, restore the original settings for the "Display the full path in the address bar" check box, the "Do not show hidden files and folders" option, and the "Hide extensions for known file types" check box.

5. Click the **OK** button to close the Folder Options dialog box and restore your original settings, and then close the Control Panel folder window.

Thanks to Olivia's workshops and guidance and your help, Landmark's employees have developed a better understanding of how to monitor and interpret memory usage using Windows Task Manager and the System Monitor snap-in tool so that they can identify performance problems and justify hardware upgrades. With assistance from you and Olivia, employees also now know how to check and set print settings and printing preferences on each of the types of printers they use, and how to optimize printing.

REVIEW ASSIGNMENTS

Landmark Associates just hired Eileen Sanger, a new financial analyst, to assist with long-range planning. Eileen uses Microsoft Excel to prepare financial analyses and forecasts and Microsoft Word to prepare detailed reports summarizing her findings and recommendations. Although she does not need a computer that has as much memory as the ones used by staff members who produce maps, Olivia wants you to make sure that the 256 MB of memory in the computer Eileen uses meets her needs.

As you complete each step in these Review Assignments, record your answers to questions so that you can submit them to your instructor. Use a word-processing application such as Word or WordPad to prepare and then print your answers to these questions. Also, if you change any settings on the computer you are using, note the original settings so that you can restore them later.

1. From the Start menu, right-click My Computer, click Properties on the shortcut menu, and examine the information on the General property sheet. What version of Windows XP are you using? How much RAM is installed in the computer you are using? Close the System Properties dialog box.

2. From the Start menu, open My Computer, open the drive that contains the Windows XP paging file, and then examine information on the paging file using the Details dynamic menu. What is the name of the paging file? What is the file type for this file? How large is the paging file in KB and MB? What attributes are assigned to this file? Close the drive window.

3. Right-click the taskbar, select the option for opening Task Manager, and then select its Performance sheet. What is the total physical memory on your computer? How much of that memory is available? What is the Commit Charge Total? How many processes and threads are open? Have you been working on this computer for a while, or did you just power on this computer? If you had just booted your computer, would you expect the Commit Charge Total to be lower or higher? Explain.

4. Open a resource-intensive application, such as Internet Explorer, Netscape Navigator, Microsoft Access, Microsoft Outlook, Dreamweaver, or Adobe Pagemaker. If you do not have any of these applications installed on your computer, open another application instead (preferably one other than Microsoft Word that you used in the tutorial). What application did you open? What changes occurred in CPU Usage and Page File Usage

when you opened that application? What is the Commit Charge Total now? What is the Commit Peak? How much RAM is available? How many processes and threads are open? Briefly summarize what happened when you opened this application.

5. Close the application you just opened. What changes occurred in CPU Usage and Page File Usage when you opened that application? What is the Commit Charge Total now? How much RAM is available? How many processes and threads are open? Briefly summarize what happened when you closed this application. Close Windows Task Manager.

6. From the Start menu, point to Administrative Tools, select Performance, and after the Performance window opens, maximize that window.

7. Select the Avg. Disk Queue Length performance counter in the legend, and then use the Delete button to remove this performance counter.

8. Use the Add button to open the Add Counters dialog box, select Memory from the Performance object list box, and select and add the Available Bytes and Committed Bytes performance counters. Explain what each of these performance counters measures. After selecting and adding these two performance counters, close the Add Counters dialog box.

9. Click the Counter column button to sort the performance counters in alphabetical order, and then adjust the width of the Counter column so that you can see the counter names.

10. Click the Freeze Display button.

Explore
11. List each of the performance counters in the legend, along with their Last measured value.

12. Click the Freeze Display button to continue plotting performance counters.

13. Open the same application that you opened earlier when you were using Windows Task Manager, switch back to the Performance window, and after a few seconds, use the Freeze Display button to temporarily halt the plotting of performance counters. What application did you open? List each of the performance counters in the legend, along with their Last measured value. Compare these values to those that you observed in Step 11, examine the plotted values on your graph, and then describe what changed when you opened an application.

14. Click the Freeze Display button to resume the plotting of performance counters, close the application you opened, and, after a few seconds, use the Freeze Display button again to temporarily halt the plotting of performance counters. Use the Highlight button to highlight the % Processor Time and Pages/sec performance counters, and then explain what happened when you closed the application.

15. Click the Highlight button again to turn this feature off, right-click the graph, save your performance measurements as an HTML document, and then print a copy of that document using Landscape orientation.

16. Based on your observations of what happened when you opened and then closed an application, what would you expect to happen if you open and then later close a different application on your computer?

17. Close System Monitor.

18. Open the System Properties dialog box, select the Advanced property sheet, select the Settings button under Performance, and in the Performance Options dialog box, select the Advanced property sheet. Use the Change button under Virtual memory to examine (*but not change*) your virtual memory settings. On what drive is the paging file located?

What is the total space available on that drive? What are the initial and maximum sizes of the paging file? Use the Cancel button to close the Virtual Memory and Performance Options dialog box without making changes to your computer.

19. Click the Environment Variables button. What is the setting for the OS and windir system variables on your computer? Use the Cancel button to close the Environment Variables dialog box without making changes to your computer.

20. Use the Settings button under Startup and Recovery to view information on system startup settings. What operating systems can you choose from during booting? Use the Cancel button to close the Startup and Recovery and System Properties dialog boxes without making changes to your computer.

21. From the Start menu, open the Printers and Faxes folder, right-click the icon for your installed (or default) printer, and then choose Properties on the shortcut menu. What type of printer is attached to the computer you are using? What is the speed and maximum resolution of this printer? Does it have any special features, such as support for color printing and duplex printing? If so, what are they?

22. Select the Sharing property sheet. Is this printer shared on the network and, if so, what is its share name?

23. Select the Ports property sheet. What is the name of your printer port?

24. Select the Advanced property sheet. Does Windows XP spool print jobs, and, if so, how does it spool documents?

25. Use the Cancel button to close the Printer Properties dialog box without making any changes, and then close the Printers and Faxes folder.

CASE PROBLEMS

Case 1. Monitoring System Performance at Global Networking, Inc. Michael Kelsey works as a technical writer for Global Networking, Inc., a multinational corporation that develops customized communications software for its clients around the world. As Michael works on a technical manual, he uses five or more applications at a time, and has multiple documents open as well. As a result, he needs a high-performance computer that is optimally configured. He decides to more closely examine the performance of his computer to make sure it can meet his needs on upcoming projects.

To complete this assignment, you need to have Microsoft Office installed on your computer, or have four major software applications that you can open.

As you complete each step in this case, record your answers to questions so that you can submit them to your instructor. Use a word-processing application such as Word or WordPad to prepare and then print your answers to these questions. Also, if you change any settings on the computer you are using, note the original settings so that you can restore them later.

1. Open System Properties. What version of Windows XP are you using? What type of computer are using, and what is its operating speed? How much memory does your computer have?

2. Open System Monitor, remove any performance counters automatically included by System Monitor, and add performance counters for tracking allocated memory, available memory, the number of bytes used by a process in the paging file, and the number of system processes. Which performance objects and counters did you choose?

Explore

3. Click the Properties button on the System Monitor toolbar, click the Graph tab in the System Monitor Properties dialog box, and under Vertical scale, adjust the Maximum value so that you can see all performance counters on the graph. *Note*: Increment the value by 100 until the uppermost performance counter is plotted below the highest value on the vertical scale, and then adjust this value in smaller increments (such as 50) up or down so that all performance counters fit within the graph and you can distinguish one performance counter from another. As you open applications in the subsequent steps, you must adjust this setting if you want to distinguish one performance counter from another.

4. As you perform an operation in each of the following steps, use the Freeze Display button to temporarily halt the plotting of values on the graph shortly after performing an operation, record the Last reported value for each performance counter, use the Freeze Display button to continue plotting values, and then perform the next operation.

5. Record the current settings for your performance counters in a table, save the results to an HTML document, and then print that document using Landscape orientation. Use the format shown in Figure 10-54 for your table, and replace the headings [*Counter #1*], etc. with the actual names of the performance counters you selected and observed. Identify the names of the applications you used if they are different than those shown in the figure.

Figure 10-54 | **MONITORING PERFORMANCE**

Performance Measurements	[*Counter #1*]	[*Counter #2*]	[*Counter #3*]	[*Counter #4*]
After opening System Monitor				
After opening Microsoft Word				
After opening Microsoft Excel				
After opening Microsoft PowerPoint				
After opening Microsoft Access				
After closing all applications				

6. Open Microsoft Word (or another major application), and then record the current settings for your performance counters in your table (including the name of the application).

7. Open Microsoft Excel (or another major application), and then record the current settings for your performance counters in your table (including the name of the application).

8. Open Microsoft PowerPoint (or another major application), and then record the current settings for your performance counters in your table (including the name of the application).

9. Open Microsoft Access (or another major application), record the current settings for your performance counters in your table (including the name of the application), save the results to an HTML document, and then print that document using Landscape orientation.

10. Close all of the open applications. Record the current settings for your performance counters in your table, save the results to an HTML document, and then print that document using Landscape orientation.

Explore

11. Examine the performance results that you tracked. What conclusions can you draw about the effects of opening and closing multiple applications on your computer? Does your computer have enough installed RAM to support multitasking of major applications? Explain. Did Windows XP reclaim all of the memory it originally allocated to these processes? Explain.

Case 2. Evaluating Memory Usage on Your Computer Use System Monitor to track changes in memory usage on your computer during a typical day so that you can evaluate the performance of your computer. Before starting, read through the entire case problem so that you have a general idea of what you need to do in advance of using your computer.

As you complete each step in this case, record your answers to questions so that you can submit them to your instructor. Use a word-processing application such as Word or WordPad to prepare and then print your answers to these questions. Also, if you change any settings on the computer you are using, note the original settings so that you can restore them later.

1. Record your starting time so that you have an idea of how long you typically work at your computer.

2. If necessary, reboot your computer to clear memory.

3. Open System Properties. What version of Windows XP are you using? What type of computer are you using, and what is its operating speed? How much memory does your computer have?

Explore

4. Open System Monitor, add the following performance counters, and then sort the legend in alphabetical order by performance counter:
   - Available Bytes for the Memory performance object
   - Committed Bytes for the Memory performance object
   - Pages/sec for the Memory performance object
   - Page File Bytes Peak for the Process performance object
   - Virtual Bytes Peak for the Process performance object
   - % Processor Time for the Processor performance object

5. After adding these performance counters, record the current settings shown for the last value of each of these performance counters in a table format. List each activity you perform in the first column, and in each of the subsequent columns, list the performance measurements for each performance counter.

6. For the remainder of your work session, use your computer as you typically would, but note the basic types of tasks that you perform, such as checking e-mail, using an application, opening a document, opening a folder, searching the Web, or playing a game, etc. After you open an application or perform an action (such as emptying the Recycle Bin), freeze the display, update the table of measurements that you are tracking, and then unfreeze the display to continue plotting performance counters. For each performance counter, record the Last measured value. Remember to also briefly describe the action you performed.

7. After you complete your workday, record your ending time. How many hours and minutes did you work?

Explore 8. What conclusions would you draw about the impact of different types of operations (such as opening or closing applications, utilities, folders, and files, etc.) on the resources available in your computer? Were there any bottlenecks or problems? If so, what are they? Are there any ways in which you might be able to improve the performance of your computer? Was Windows XP able to reclaim all of the memory it allocated during your work session? Explain.

9. Print the table that contains your performance measurements.

Case 3. *Troubleshooting Memory Usage Problems at Peninsula Bank* Janet Abrams works as a computer support specialist and trainer for Peninsula Bank's main branch and, when needed, provides telephone support and training for employees at other branch offices. As she was developing a new set of training materials with her presentation graphics software, Windows XP reported an out-of-memory error.

Use a word-processing application such as Word or WordPad to prepare and then print your answers to these questions.

1. Using what you have learned in this tutorial, identify at least 10 possible causes for this problem and describe how you might resolve the problem. Compile your results in a table that includes three columns: Rank, Possible Causes, and Strategy or Tool. In the Rank column, identify the order in which you would troubleshoot the problem (for example, 1, 2, 3, etc.). In the Possible Causes column, list the possible causes for this memory problem. In the Strategy or Tool column, briefly describe how you would troubleshoot the problem and identify any Windows XP tools you would use.

2. Print your troubleshooting analysis and strategy.

Case 4. *Troubleshooting a Printing Problem at Gannon Associates* Gannon Associates is an accounting firm in the Los Angeles metropolitan area. In addition to managing the company's telephone system and equipment, Javier Eseguia provides computer technical support to the staff. Recently, one of the staff members working on the company's annual report experienced difficulties printing a cover page with a graphics design. Javier offers to help him troubleshoot the problem. Since this employee has not experienced any other printing problems, Javier assumes that the problem might result from insufficient memory or from an incorrectly configured printer.

As you complete each step in this case, record your answers to questions so that you can submit them to your instructor. Use a word-processing application such as Word or WordPad to prepare and then print your answers to these questions. Also, if you change any settings on the computer you are using, note the original settings so that you can restore them later.

1. If you were Javier, what other questions would you ask this employee about the nature of the printing problem that he experienced? List at least six other questions you might ask this employee.

2. Using what you have learned in this tutorial, identify at least eight possible causes for this printing problem and describe how you might resolve this problem. Compile your results in a table that includes three columns: Rank, Possible Causes, and Strategy or Tool. In the Rank column, identify the order in which you would troubleshoot the problem (for example, 1, 2, 3, etc.). In the Possible Causes column, list the possible causes for this printer problem. In the Strategy or Tool column, briefly describe how you would troubleshoot the problem and identify any Windows XP tools you would use.

3. Print your troubleshooting analysis and strategy.

OBJECTIVES

In this tutorial you will:

- Learn how to prepare your computer for an upgrade of its operating system and software applications

- Examine the process for upgrading to Windows XP, performing a clean installation, and setting up a dual-boot or multiple-boot configuration

- Examine how to use the Files and Settings Transfer Wizard to migrate settings from one computer to another

- Learn about Windows File Protection and System File Checker

- Compare how you install and uninstall Win32, Win16, and DOS applications

- Examine the process for installing and uninstalling a Win32 application

- Learn about Windows Installer and the Program Compatibility Wizard

- Examine how you install and uninstall Windows XP components

- Download and install updates with Windows Update and then view your installation history

INSTALLING SOFTWARE

Upgrading Software at SolarWinds, Inc.

CASE

SolarWinds, Inc.

Phoenix-based SolarWinds, Inc. specializes in using renewable energy resources such as solar power, wind, and geothermal heat. Its long-range goal is to become one of the leading environment-friendly energy suppliers in the southwestern United States over the next five to ten years.

In anticipation of its rapid growth and its desire to take advantage of new operating systems and software applications, the management at SolarWinds has decided to upgrade its employees' computer systems to Windows XP Professional. Yamakoa Takao, a computer support technician, has been assigned the responsibility for supervising these upgrades and for providing technical assistance to staff members so that the changeover occurs as smoothly as possible. You work with Takao to prepare for the upgrades.

In the first part of this tutorial, you learn how to prepare your computer for an operating system installation or upgrade. Then you examine the procedure for upgrading to Windows XP Professional and Windows XP Home Edition. You also learn how to perform a clean installation, and how to set up a dual-boot or multiple-boot configuration on your computer. You examine how you can use the Files and Settings Transfer Wizard to migrate files and settings from one computer to another. Finally, you learn about the importance of Windows File Protection, and how to use the System File Checker to check the integrity of system files.

Preparing for an Operating System Upgrade

Before upgrading the operating system on other employees' computer systems at the SolarWinds headquarters, Takao decides to install Windows XP Professional on his computer first so that he is familiar with the installation process and can identify potential problems that might arise when he and his staff install Windows XP Professional on employees' computers.

Because of the many changes Microsoft implemented in Windows XP, upgrading to the Windows XP operating system represents a significant change, not only in the way that you use your computer, but also to the configuration of your computer. Before you install Windows XP or any other operating system, you should take certain steps to protect your work and the integrity of your computer system. These steps also improve the chances that Windows XP installs properly. Once you complete these preparatory steps, you can start the Windows XP Setup program and let the Setup Wizard guide you through the installation process. You should perform the following steps before installing a new operating system or an operating system upgrade:

1. **Check system requirements**. Operating systems, as well as software applications and utilities, have specific requirements that you should check before attempting an upgrade. One important resource is the Microsoft Windows XP Professional Resource Kit, which includes extensive information on deploying and installing Windows XP (including customizing and automating installations). The Microsoft Web site also provides information about upgrading to Windows XP Professional or Windows XP Home Edition. See Figure 11-1 for the Windows XP Professional Upgrade Center Web site (*www.microsoft.com/windowsxp/pro/howtobuy/upgrading/default.asp*), and Figure 11-2 for the Windows XP Home Edition Upgrade Center Web site (*www.microsoft.com/windowsxp/home/howtobuy/upgrading/default.asp*).

Figure 11-1	WEB SITE FOR WINDOWS XP PROFESSIONAL UPGRADE CENTER

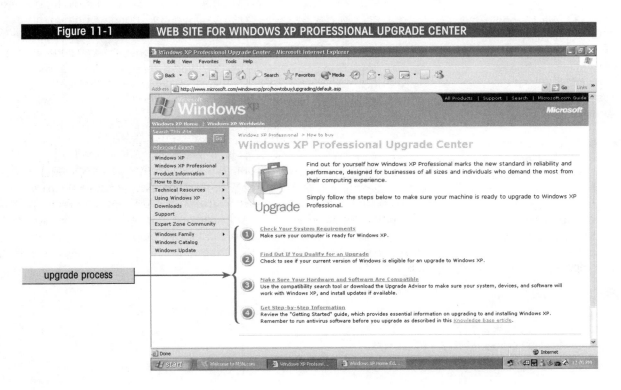

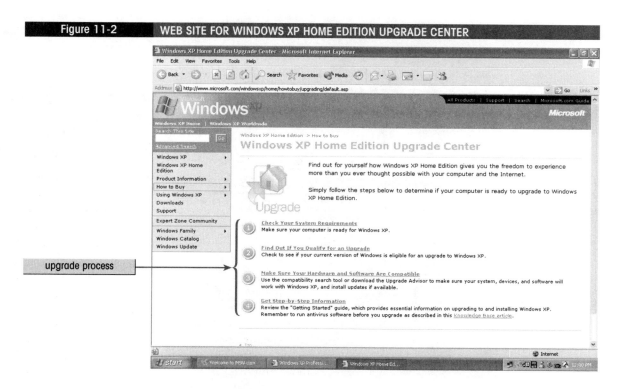

Figure 11-2   WEB SITE FOR WINDOWS XP HOME EDITION UPGRADE CENTER

■ **Type of processor.** As shown in Figure 11-3 and Figure 11-4, Microsoft recommends that you have a processor in the Intel Pentium or Celeron family, the AMD (Advanced Micro Devices) K6, Athlon, or Duron family, or a compatible processor that operates at 300 MHz or higher for either Windows XP Professional or Windows XP Home Edition. Microsoft also notes that 233 MHz is the minimum operating speed, or clock speed. Also, Windows XP Professional can be used on computers that have one or two processors. Although a software manufacturer might state that you need a specific type of processor, you have to evaluate whether you can expect reasonable performance with your current processor and its operating speed. Typically, software manufacturers state the minimum requirements for their software product. If your computer has more than enough RAM, but has an older and slower microprocessor, the processor might act as a bottleneck and affect the overall performance of your computer. At the release time of Windows XP, Intel P4 computers had operating speeds of 1 to 1.5 GHz. Note that the basic requirements for Windows XP Professional and Windows XP Home Edition are the same.

Figure 11-3   SYSTEM REQUIREMENTS FOR WINDOWS XP PROFESSIONAL

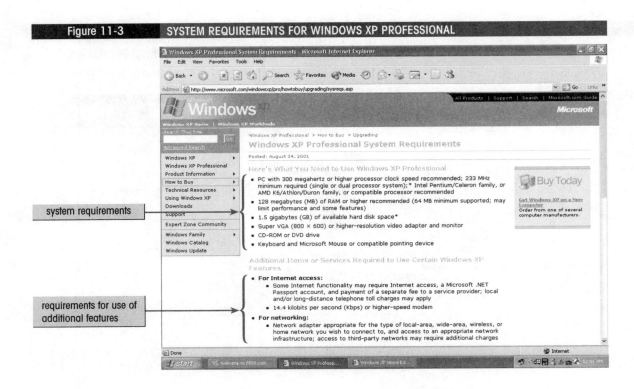

system requirements

requirements for use of additional features

Figure 11-4   SYSTEM REQUIREMENTS FOR WINDOWS XP HOME EDITION

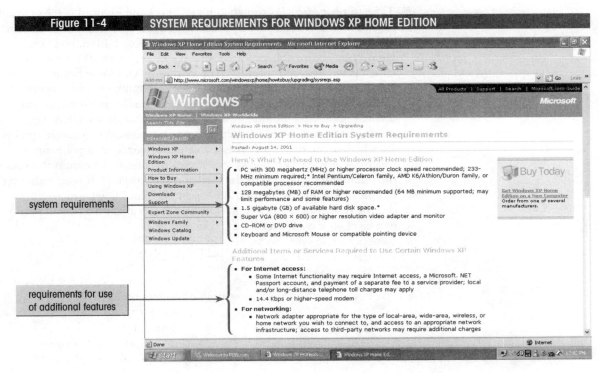

system requirements

requirements for use of additional features

■ **RAM**. Microsoft recommends that you have at least 128 MB of RAM for either Windows XP Professional or Windows XP Home Edition. It also notes that both products support 64 MB of RAM; however, 64 MB of RAM might limit the performance of Windows and the use of some features. Invariably, you need more RAM than the recommended minimum in order to ensure optimal performance of Windows XP and the software on your computer. In fact, you should have no less than 256 MB for Windows XP to function efficiently. Furthermore, as you discovered in Tutorial 10, if you multitask and use several software applications at the same time, you must account for the memory needs of each software product separately as well as the needs of the operating system. Without sufficient memory, Windows XP must rely on the use of virtual memory, which is far slower than RAM. If you have a computer with less than 128 MB of RAM, you need to add more RAM or consider purchasing a new computer with a faster microprocessor and more RAM. When Windows XP was released, computers typically had 256 to 512 MB of RAM.

■ **Hard disk storage space and file system**. To accommodate the demands of users and rapidly emerging hardware technologies, operating systems require an ever increasing amount of hard disk storage space. Microsoft recommends that you have at least 1.5 GB of free space on your hard disk for both Windows XP Professional and Windows XP Home Edition. In a footnote, it also adds that, if you are installing Windows XP Professional or Windows XP Home Edition over a network, you need additional free space on your hard disk. Another related consideration is the file system used for the boot drive. If you are using FAT16 for the boot drive, the maximum supported size of the hard disk or volume is 2 GB. That means that you need to use either FAT32 or NTFS as the file system for your boot volume.

■ **Other components**. Microsoft recommends that you have a Super VGA (SVGA) or higher resolution video adapter and monitor that supports a resolution of 800 x 600, a CD-ROM or DVD drive (to install software), a keyboard, and a Microsoft mouse or compatible pointing device for both Windows XP Professional and Windows XP Home Edition. For both products, Microsoft also lists information about additional components or features which affect system requirements. For example, Microsoft recommends a modem that operates at 14.4 Kbps or higher for Internet access. When Windows XP was released, computers typically included a 56K modem (even if it did not operate at the rated speed). If your computer is part of a network, you also need a network adapter.

2. **Qualifying for an upgrade**. Microsoft also provides information on whether your current version of Windows qualifies for an upgrade. As shown in Figure 11-5, you cannot upgrade from Windows 3.1, an evaluation version of Windows, a server version of Windows, Windows 95, or Windows NT Workstation 3.51 to either Windows XP Professional or Windows XP Home Edition. However, you can upgrade from either version of Windows 98 or Windows Me to Windows XP Professional or Windows XP Home Edition. You cannot upgrade to Windows XP Home Edition from Windows NT Workstation 4.0, Windows 2000 Professional, or Windows XP Professional. However, you can upgrade to Windows XP Professional from Windows NT Workstation 4.0 (Service Pack 6 or later), Windows 2000 Professional, or Windows XP Home Edition.

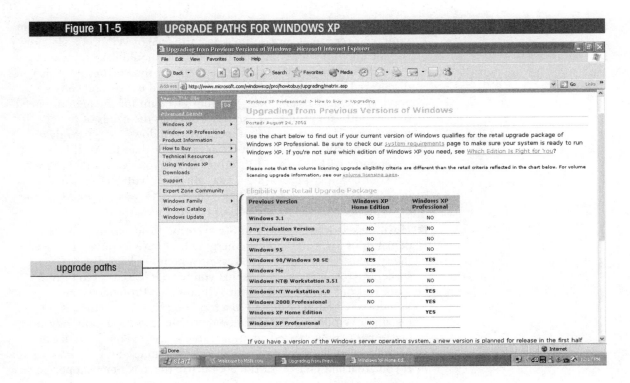

Figure 11-5   UPGRADE PATHS FOR WINDOWS XP

upgrade paths

3. **Check hardware and software compatibility**. As shown in Figure 11-6, Microsoft recommends that you use one of two options for checking hardware and software compatibility before upgrading to Windows XP. You can search the Windows Catalog or use the Upgrade Advisor. The Windows Catalog lists products that are compatible with Windows XP. Microsoft recommends that you use the Windows Catalog if you already have Windows XP and want to check a product's compatibility before you purchase it for your computer. You should also use the Windows Catalog if you are upgrading your computer to Windows XP and need to check the compatibility of your current hardware and software. The Learn More note explains that Microsoft or the product manufacturer is responsible for determining whether a product is compatible with Windows XP and that, in turn, is the minimum requirement for being listed in the Windows Catalog. It further notes that if a product has the "Designed for Windows XP" logo, that product takes advantage of the new features in Windows XP and is likely to cause you fewer problems.

Figure 11-6   CHECKING COMPATIBILITY

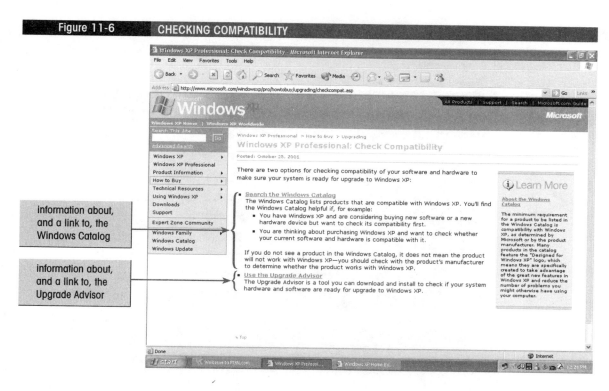

information about, and a link to, the Windows Catalog

information about, and a link to, the Upgrade Advisor

If you click the "Search the Windows Catalog" link, you can then enter the manufacturer name or product type or model to check for compatibility with Windows XP. See Figure 11-7. *Note*: You can also open Windows Catalog by choosing it from the All Programs menu.

Figure 11-7   SEARCHING THE WINDOWS CATALOG

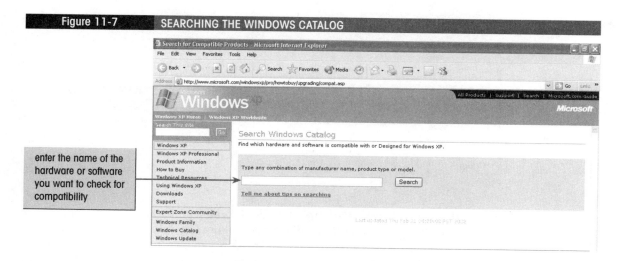

enter the name of the hardware or software you want to check for compatibility

After searching for a SONY PCV RX-550 (the computer used for the next figure), the Windows Catalog reported a listing of 456 products. An examination of the listing shows that this particular computer is not only supported, but it also has the "Designed for Windows XP" logo. See Figure 11-8.

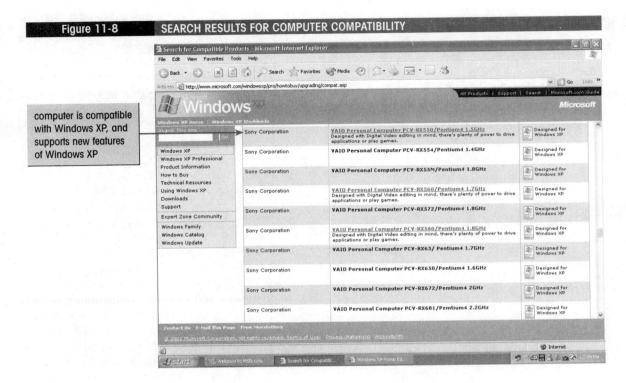

Figure 11-8   SEARCH RESULTS FOR COMPUTER COMPATIBILITY

computer is compatible with Windows XP, and supports new features of Windows XP

Another search for Micron Millennia (a computer for which an upgrade is contemplated) shows that the computer is "Compatible with Windows XP" (the minimal requirement for being listed), indicating that it might not support all the new features in Windows XP. See Figure 11-9.

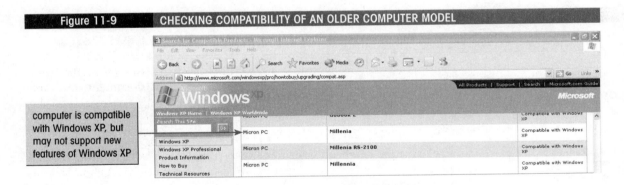

Figure 11-9   CHECKING COMPATIBILITY OF AN OLDER COMPUTER MODEL

computer is compatible with Windows XP, but may not support new features of Windows XP

If you search for a hardware or software product on your computer and do not find a listing for that product in the Windows Catalog, you might need to change the way you search for information, or you might need to examine the Web site for the manufacturer of that product to determine whether it is compatible with Windows XP.

Your other option for determining whether your computer and its hardware and software are compatible with Windows XP is to download and run the Upgrade Advisor. The Upgrade Advisor uses 50 MB, and you need a high-speed Internet connection to download the Upgrade Advisor. Also, it only determines upgrade eligibility for Windows XP Professional.

You can also visit the Web site for the Microsoft Windows Hardware Compatibility List (*www.microsoft.com/hcl/default.asp*) and search for information on a specific product. You specify the product name and category, the search results show the degree of compatibility (for example, fully compatible or compatible) for Windows XP, Windows 2000, Windows Me, Windows XP 64-Bit, Windows NT 4.0, and Windows 98. You can also download a plain text version of the HCL. The HCL document changes as Microsoft tests new hardware devices.

4. **Read the documentation on your Windows XP CD**. If you have already purchased Windows XP Professional or Windows XP Home Edition, you can open Windows Explorer and then examine the documentation on the CD. Read1st.txt contains information on system requirements and preinstallation notes, such as Windows Product Activation (WPA). Microsoft recommends that you defer activation until after you have upgraded your computer's hardware and device drivers that affect activation of Windows XP. Pro.txt (in the Docs folder) contains release notes on installing Windows XP on a single computer and using the Windows XP Setup Wizard. It includes information on hardware requirements, checking hardware and software compatibility, obtaining network information, backing up your files, and upgrading versus installing a new copy of Windows XP. It also explains how to run Windows XP Setup for a clean install (covered later) or an upgrade, how to automate setup using Unattended Setup Mode (which uses an answer file that provides information you've specified in advance for prompts made by the Setup program), and how to log on to Windows XP and create a user account. Relnotes.htm (in the Docs folder) provides technical information on file systems, Windows XP software components, hardware, network communications, software applications, storage, and even Windows XP 64-Bit Edition. If you click the Readme.htm file in the top-level folder of your Windows XP CD, you can then open Read1st.txt, Pro.txt, and Relnotes.htm from Readme.htm.

5. **Document settings**. It is a good idea to collect or compile information about your computer. You can use Device Manager (as you will see in Tutorial 12) to document hardware settings on your computer, and the My Computer Information and System Information Utility (both accessible from the Help and Support Center, and both covered in Tutorial 9) to document hardware, software, and system settings. If your computer is part of a network, you should know your computer name, your workgroup or domain name, and your IP address, unless it is automatically assigned.

6. **Free storage space on your hard disk**. Make sure you have enough storage space on the drive where you intend to install Windows XP. As noted earlier, both versions of Windows XP need at least 1.5 GB of storage space on the hard disk. If you are installing over a network, it needs even more storage space. Also make sure that this drive contains enough storage space for installing periodic service pack upgrades and other important updates, which all increase the amount of disk space used by Windows XP. Take into account the storage space required for the virtual memory paging file, the Internet cache, printer spool files, and temporary files. As noted in Tutorial 10, your drive should have 1.5 times the amount of installed RAM for the paging file.

To free storage space, you can perform the following tasks:

- **Empty the Internet cache**. Use a Web browser such as Internet Explorer or Netscape Navigator to empty the contents of the folder used to cache files downloaded from the World Wide Web. You can use the Disk Cleanup Wizard to help you find these and other files (covered in Tutorial 7).

■ **Delete temporary files, backup files, and files with lost clusters**. If storage space is limited, you can use the Disk Cleanup Wizard to locate and delete any temporary files stored in the Temp folder under your Windows folder and recovered files from the top-level folder of a drive. If your applications create backup files, consider removing any of these files that you no longer need.

■ **Archive document files**. If your computer contains document files that you no longer use or need, consider archiving them. Make sure you have backup copies of these files, and then move them off your hard disk onto a permanent storage medium, such as a Zip disk. If you want to keep them on your hard disk, you can create and store them in a Compressed (zipped) folder.

■ **Uninstall unneeded software applications and utilities**. Examine the software installed on your computer and decide whether you still need certain installed applications, utilities, and games. If not, uninstall them.

■ **Uninstall Windows accessories and components**. Examine the installed accessories and components on your computer, and then uninstall those you no longer use or need.

7. **Scan for computer viruses**. Even if you've installed antivirus software to monitor your computer for computer viruses, Microsoft recommends that you perform a full scan of your computer prior installing a new operating system.

8. **Back up important files on your hard disk**. There are two types of backups you should consider prior to installing or upgrading software:

■ **Document files backup**. If you do not have recent normal and incremental, or differential, backups of your document files prior to upgrading your operating system, it's time to do that backup. Remember to also back up the files with your e-mail and address book, as well as your Internet Explorer Favorites folder or Netscape bookmarks.

■ **Full system backup**. Although you might back up your document files on a regular basis, you should perform a full backup of your computer system in the event the upgrade fails or you need to restore your current system for some other reason. A full system backup includes the entire contents of your computer: the operating system, all of the associated configuration files, the installed software applications and utilities, and all your document files. If time and cost is an important factor, and if you already have backups of the document files on your computer, you can limit the full system backup to just the operating system, software applications and utilities, and configuration files. Although you can reinstall your previous operating system and software from either CD-ROM or floppy disks, the process is more time consuming than restoring the software from a backup. Furthermore, many people often forget that they also configure and customize installed software to meet their specific needs, and they also frequently download and install upgrades. Restoring a computer to its original state from a backup is much easier and more reliable than reinstalling the software and all of its upgrades, and then trying to recall how you might have previously configured and customized that software. Although you typically back up your computer to a permanent storage medium outside of your computer, you can also perform a full system backup to a folder on your hard disk or to a second drive, provided that you have sufficient space for that backup and for the new operating system software you intend to install. Backing up to a folder on your hard drive is relatively fast, and it represents one more option for protecting the integrity of your computer system. However, you should not rely only on this type of backup because it assumes you always have access to your hard disk. If the drive fails, and if the folder on your hard drive contains the only backup you have, you are obviously in trouble. You can also back up to a network drive on another computer.

9. **Check the hard disk for errors**. Before you install or upgrade a new operating system, application, or utility, use a disk analysis and repair utility, such as the Microsoft ScanDisk or Check Disk utilities or a third party utility, to verify the integrity of the file system and, if necessary, repair errors in the file system.

10. **Optimize hard disk storage space**. Use a defragmenter utility, such as the Microsoft Disk Defragmenter or a third-party utility, and perform a full optimization of the storage space on your hard disk.

11. **Make a boot disk**. If you are upgrading from Windows 98 or Windows Me, make sure you have a Startup Disk so that you can boot your computer from drive A if you need to troubleshoot problems. If you already have a Startup Disk, you might want to update your copy first, and make a second copy as a precautionary measure. If you do not have a Startup Disk, make two copies before you install Windows XP. If you are upgrading from Windows NT Workstation 4.0, you can make a generic boot disk with the files necessary to boot your computer from a floppy disk in drive A. If you decide to make your own boot disk, make sure it contains the device driver for your CD drive, Mscdex.exe (a program for configuring the CD drive during booting), and startup configuration files (Config.sys and Autoexec.bat) for configuring the CD drive during booting. Make sure you have configured these disks so that the startup configuration files look for device drivers and programs on your boot disk, not your hard disk. If you are upgrading from Windows 2000 Professional or if you are reinstalling Windows XP, you can prepare Windows 2000 Setup Disks or Windows XP Setup Disks first.

12. **Turn off background programs**. Programs, such as antivirus software or a screen saver, that operate in the background can interfere with the installation of an operating system or a software application. Because one of the functions of an antivirus program is to alert you to attempts to modify or replace system files or the contents of the boot sector, it might interfere with the installation of an operating system, as well as other types of software products that update system files. If your antivirus software places an icon in the system tray, you can right-click this icon and close the program. If there is a directive in Config.sys or a command in Autoexec.bat that loads your antivirus software, you can use the REM command to "remark out" that directive or command (that is, add a REM statement before the command).

13. **Remove the virus protection feature for the boot sector on the hard disk**. As you learned in Tutorial 8, some computers have a built-in CMOS virus protection feature that prevents modification of the boot sector on the hard disk. When you install an operating system, it invariably needs to update the boot sector, so you may need to open your computer's Setup utility, and if necessary, turn off the write-protection for the boot sector. After you complete the installation, you can then turn the virus protection feature back on.

14. **Reboot your computer**. Prior to installing or upgrading an operating system or major software product, close all open applications, utilities, and windows, and then reboot your computer to clear memory.

The Config.sys and Autoexec.bat startup configuration files are retained for backward compatibility with earlier versions of Windows before Windows 98. These files are usually empty because Io.sys and the Windows Registry now provide settings for configuring your computer during booting. If your startup configuration files contain directives or commands, they are processed during booting. If any directives or commands specify settings that are of a greater value than what is specified by Io.sys or stored in the Registry, these settings override those of Io.sys or the Registry; otherwise, the commands are ignored.

Although it takes time to prepare your computer for an operating system upgrade, it's even more time-consuming to rebuild your computer from scratch. Follow the preceding steps, examine the information posted at Microsoft's Web site on upgrading to Windows XP, review the information in the Windows XP Resource Kit on deploying and installing Windows XP, and examine your computer's hardware and software documentation to ensure a reliable and problem-free installation of Windows XP Professional or Windows XP Home Edition.

Installing **Windows XP**

Takao has installed and used almost every version of Windows since Windows 95 either on a work computer or his home computer. In each version of Windows, he has discovered that Microsoft has simplified and automated the process for installing Windows.

The simplest way to install Windows XP is to insert the Windows XP CD in your CD drive. An Autorun.inf (Setup information file) on the CD automatically opens the Setup program for installing Windows XP. Once the Windows XP Setup program starts from the Windows XP CD, you can select the option for installing Windows XP, performing additional tasks, or checking your system's compatibility. See Figure 11-10. If you're reinstalling Windows XP, you will see an additional option on the menu: Install optional Windows components.

| Figure 11-10 | SETUP PROGRAM FOR WINDOWS XP |

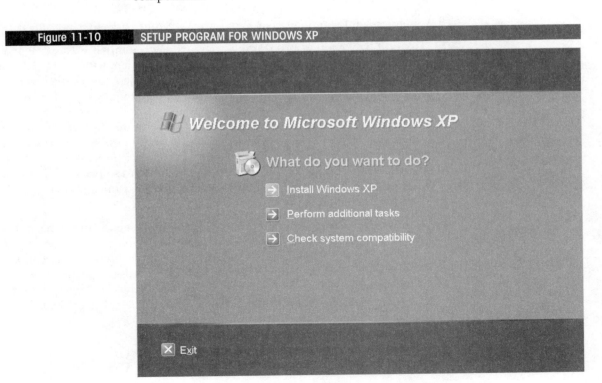

If you choose the option for performing additional tasks, you can set up a Remote Desktop connection, set up a home or small office network, transfer files and settings, browse the CD, or examine the release notes for this version of Windows. See Figure 11-11.

| Figure 11-11 | LIST OF ADDITIONAL TASKS |

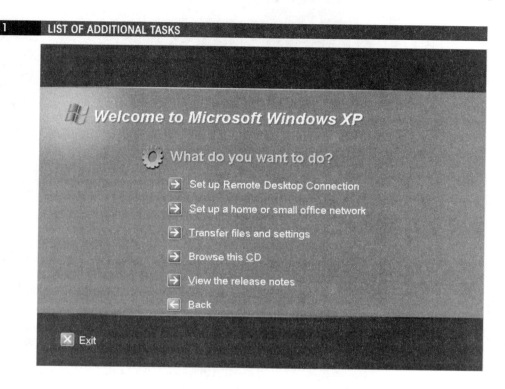

If you choose the option for checking system compatibility, you can run the system check, or you can visit the Microsoft compatibility Web site (the home page for Windows Catalog). See Figure 11-12.

Figure 11-12	SYSTEM COMPATIBILITY MENU OPTIONS

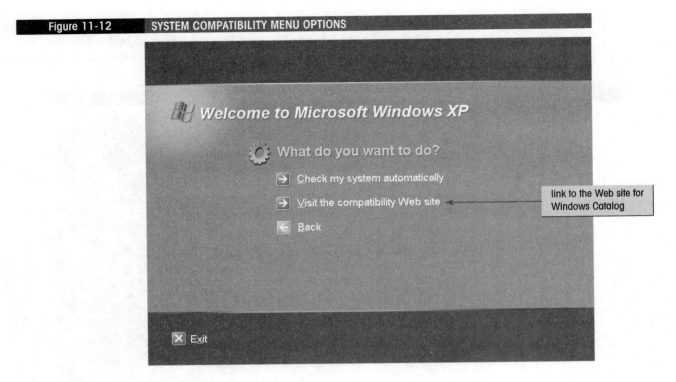

If you choose the option for checking system compatibility, Setup displays a Report System Compatibility dialog box that lists items that are incompatible with Windows XP, as well as other problems that affect the intended upgrade. See Figure 11-13. You have to resolve these problems before you can install Windows XP. On the Windows 2000 computer used for this figure, the Upgrade Advisor reports problems with one of the network drivers, a Symantec Utility device driver, and the lack of available space on the hard disk. As you can tell from the icon for the last identified problem, the lack of available disk space is the most serious of the three problems.

Figure 11-13	UPGRADE ADVISOR'S REPORT ON A WINDOWS 2000 SYSTEM

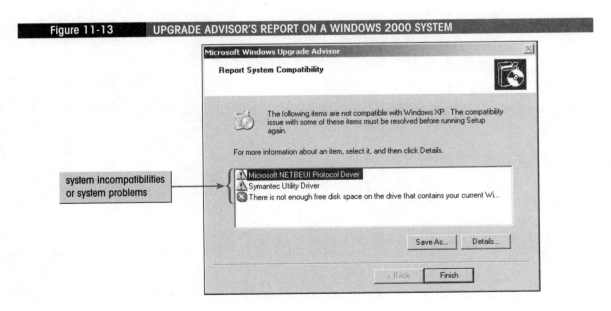

If you click the Details button for the first identified incompatibility (already selected), the Microsoft Windows Upgrade Advisor opens a Compatibility Details window using Microsoft Internet Explorer and informs you that the driver for this specific network protocol is incompatible with Windows XP, and will be removed during installation. See Figure 11-14.

| Figure 11-14 | COMPATIBILITY DETAILS FOR A NETWORK DRIVER |

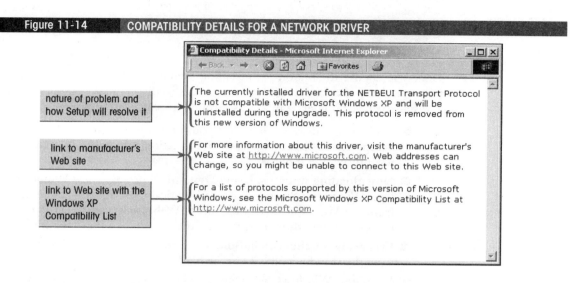

If you view details on the driver problem, the Microsoft Windows Upgrade Advisor informs you in another Compatibility Details window that an installed driver is causing stability problems with this computer. See Figure 11-15. It also notes that Setup disables this driver during installation, and it recommends that you contact the manufacturer of this driver to obtain an update for use with Windows XP. Before running Setup and installing Windows XP, you should obtain and install any device driver updates.

| Figure 11-15 | COMPATIBILITY DETAILS FOR A DEVICE DRIVER |

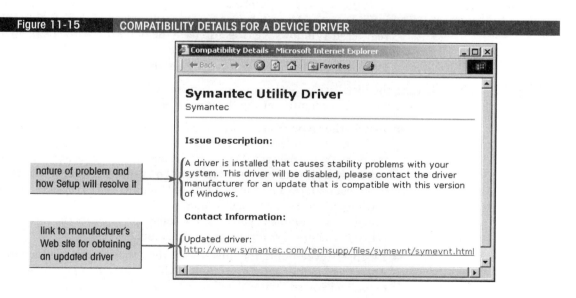

If you view details on the availability of disk storage space problem, the Microsoft Windows Upgrade Advisor informs you of the amount of additional storage space you need on your hard disk for upgrading to Windows XP. See Figure 11-16.

Figure 11-16   NOT ENOUGH FREE DISK SPACE FOR INSTALLING WINDOWS XP

Once you choose the option for installing Windows XP, either an upgrade or a clean installation, Setup checks the disk and copies files to the Windows installation folders, and then restarts your computer. It proceeds through five installation phases:

- **Collecting information about your computer system.** The Windows XP Setup Wizard either gathers the information automatically or prompts you for information it needs.

- **Downloading updates.** Using **Dynamic Update**, a new Windows XP feature, Windows XP Setup downloads critical fixes, updates, and device drivers from the Microsoft Dynamic Update Web site (if you so choose), so that it can incorporate those updates into the Windows XP installation.

- **Preparing for the installation.** The Setup Wizard copies installation files from the Windows XP CD to the hard drive, and then restarts the computer.

- **Installing Windows.** This phase includes installing support for devices, installing network support, configuring your computer, deleting files, copying files, completing the installation, installing Start menu items, registering components, and saving settings.

- **Finalizing the installation.** Windows XP removes temporary files and then reboots. A Welcome screen asks whether you want to want to set up your Internet connection, activate Windows XP, and register online. If so, it collects the registration information, connects to the Internet, transfers the information to Microsoft, and finally verifies that you have activated and registered Windows XP. You also have the opportunity to create up to five user accounts. After setting up your computer, Windows XP displays the Welcome screen so that you can log on under a user account.

During the installation, Setup prompts you for certain types of information, depending on your computer's configuration and the type of installation you choose:

- **Installation type.** You are prompted for the type of installation you want to perform—Upgrade or New Installation. If you are upgrading to Windows XP, the Setup Wizard installs Windows XP, but keeps your existing settings and applications. If your computer contains an unsupported version of Windows, you must perform a new installation of Windows XP to replace your existing version of Windows or install Windows XP on a new disk or partition. After installation is complete, you must reinstall your applications. If your hard disk is blank, you must perform a new installation.

- **License Agreement.** You must accept the conditions of the License Agreement before you can continue. This contract is a legally binding agreement, and you should read and understand all its components before you accept the agreement.

- **Product Key.** The back cover of the package for your Windows XP CD should have a sticker with the Product Key.

- **Get updated setup files**. Windows XP proposes to use Dynamic Update to get updated setup files from the Microsoft Windows Update Web site. If you prefer, you can continue without obtaining updated setup files.

- **Special Options**. For a new installation of Windows XP, you can customize the installation, language, and accessibility settings.

- **File system**. Windows XP can convert partitions on your hard disk to NTFS or you can choose to keep your existing file systems. If you are upgrading, the Setup Wizard keeps your current file system.

- **Regional and language options**. Verify or select the language you want to use, such as English (US), and the location, such as the United States. Setup identifies the default text input language and method, such as the US Keyboard Layout, but you have the option of entering text in a different language.

- **Information on personalizing your software**. Enter your name and organization so that Windows XP can use this information to personalize your software applications.

- **Computer's name and Administrator password**. Enter a name up to 15 characters to identify your computer. The Setup Wizard automatically creates an Administrator account, and you can provide a password for that account.

- **Date and time settings**. Check and, if necessary, change the date, time, and time zone, and specify whether you want Windows XP to automatically adjust your computer for daylight saving time.

- **Networking settings**. Setup also installs Windows XP networking components and asks you about network settings. You can choose the Typical settings option for an automated installation or the Custom settings option so that you can specify network settings.

- **Workgroup or computer domain**. You must choose to join either a workgroup or a domain. A **workgroup** consists of one or more computers with the same workgroup name—such as a peer-to-peer network. A **domain** consists of a group of computers defined by and managed by a network Administrator. To join a domain, you must already have a user account in the domain.

- **Identify network users**. A Network Identification Wizard prompts you to identify other users who will also work on this computer. You can enter user names for up to five accounts. Each of these accounts automatically are designated as an Administrator account. If you indicate that you are the only user, you are automatically assigned Administrator rights.

If you are installing Windows XP on a computer with an operating system already installed on one partition, it identifies the existing partitions and any unpartitioned space, formats a partition (if necessary) and sets up a FAT32 or NTFS file system on the partition.

Performing a Clean Installation

If you decide to rebuild your system from scratch before installing Windows XP, you can boot your computer from a MS-DOS boot disk, or a Windows 95, Windows 98, or Windows Me Startup Disk, and use the FDisk utility to partition the hard disk. Since the FDisk utility is not included in Windows 2000 Professional and Windows XP, this process is illustrated in the next set of figures for Windows 98. When you open FDisk, it asks if you want to enable large disk support. See Figure 11-17. If you choose to enable large disk support, you are indicating that you want to use a FAT32 file system. If you do not choose this option, you are indicating that you want to use the FAT16 file system. As noted in earlier tutorials, FAT32 uses storage space more efficiently on your computer than FAT16. Windows 95B, Windows 95c, Windows 98, Windows Me, Windows 2000 Professional, and Windows XP support this file system. MS-DOS, Windows 95 (the original version), Windows 95a, and Windows NT Workstation 4.0 do not support FAT32, and if you are setting up a dual-boot computer with Windows XP, the primary partition must be FAT16. All of these operating systems, however, do support FAT16. Also, FDisk notes that utilities which were not designed for FAT32 do not work on a FAT32 volume.

Figure 11-17	USING THE FDISK UTILITY

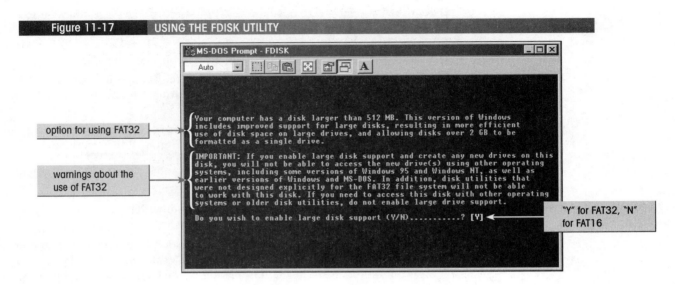

option for using FAT32

warnings about the use of FAT32

"Y" for FAT32, "N" for FAT16

Next, you use the FDisk menu, shown in Figure 11-18, to delete the primary DOS partition, and then redefine a new primary DOS partition and (if necessary) mark it as the active partition (the boot drive). After that step, you exit FDisk and use the Format utility and its System switch (/S) to format drive C, create file allocation tables that support either FAT32 (or FAT16), and copy the operating system files onto the drive. The command line that you enter is the following: FORMAT C: /S

Figure 11-18	FDISK MAIN MENU

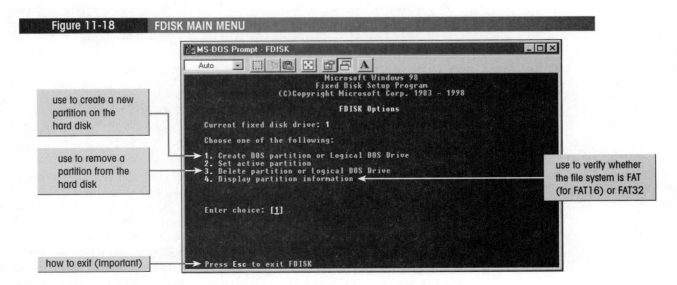

use to create a new partition on the hard disk

use to remove a partition from the hard disk

use to verify whether the file system is FAT (for FAT16) or FAT32

how to exit (important)

After you format the disk, you can open FDisk and view partition information to verify that you are in fact using FAT32 (or FAT16). See Figure 11-19. After you install Windows XP, you can convert the FAT16 or FAT32 partition to NTFS.

Figure 11-19	CHECKING A PARTITION'S FILE SYSTEM

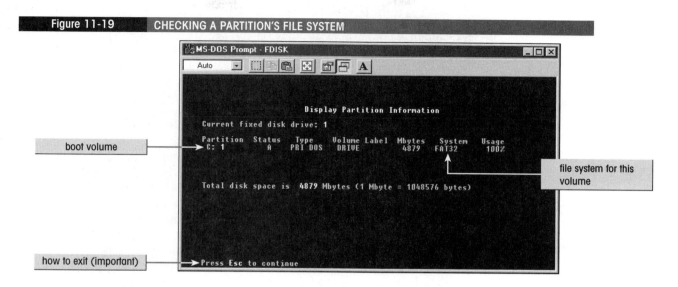

If you create other logical drives on your hard disk (such as drive D) with the FDisk utility, you also need to use the Format utility (without the System switch) to format each of those drives. If you experience problems with Windows FDisk (such as not being able to delete a partition), or if you want access to more features than provided in FDisk, you can use another utility, such as Norton's GDisk. Since you cannot recover information from a hard disk after you partition it with FDisk, you do not want to use the FDisk and Format utilities unless you absolutely need to rebuild the system from scratch.

If the boot disk or Startup Disk does not provide you with access to your CD-ROM drive, you must also create a Config.sys and an Autoexec.bat file to load the device driver for your CD-ROM drive and assign a drive letter to it. If you cannot identify the device driver for your CD-ROM drive using this approach, you must use a DOS utility to install support for the CD-ROM drive. Once you have access to your CD-ROM drive, you enter the command D:\SETUP.EXE at the command prompt. (D: assumes that the CD drive is drive D; if not, you must use the appropriate drive name.)

Another option available to you is to boot from your Windows XP CD and install Windows XP Professional or Windows XP Home Edition directly from the CD. As noted in Tutorial 9, most computer systems provide an option for booting from a CD-ROM drive. You must open the BIOS Setup utility, and change the boot sequence so that the BIOS checks the CD drive before checking drive C. During booting, a prompt might appear on the screen, prompting you to press a key if you want to boot from the CD. If this is the case, and you do not press a key, the computer boots from the next available drive in the boot sequence. If necessary, Windows XP partitions the hard disk and then formats the boot drive using FAT32 or NTFS before it installs itself. This option is useful if you've just installed a new hard disk in your computer prior to installing Windows XP.

If your computer does not have a bootable CD-ROM drive and if you cannot boot from the hard disk, you must make and use a boot disk that provides you with access to your CD-ROM drive.

Using the FDisk utility is also helpful if you want to create a dual-boot or multiple-boot configuration on your computer. For example, if you want to dual-boot Windows 98 and Windows XP, you can use FDisk to partition your computer into two drives, and then you can format each drive with the Format utility. First you would install Windows 98 on drive C, then you install Windows XP on the other drive. Windows XP must be installed last because it updates the boot sector.

Setting Up a Multiple-Boot Configuration

Because employees often work at home on company projects, and because their computers might have another version of Windows, such as Windows 2000 Professional, Windows Me, or Windows 98, Takao has created a multiple-boot configuration on his computer so that he can help employees with questions they have about the use of these different versions of Windows.

If you need to work with more than one operating system on your computer, you can create a dual-boot or a multiple boot configuration with Windows XP Professional or Windows XP Home Edition. For example, you might want to configure a computer so that you can boot with Windows XP and Windows 2000, or perhaps with Windows XP and Windows 98. Or you might want to create a multiple-boot configuration that includes Windows XP Professional, Windows 2000, and Windows 98.

You can create dual-boot or multiple-boot configurations with Windows XP Professional, Windows XP Home Edition, Windows 2000 Professional, Windows NT Workstation 4.0, Windows Me, Windows 98, Windows 95, and MS-DOS.

To create a dual-boot or multiple-boot configuration with Windows XP, each operating system must be installed on a different partition. You can create up to four partitions on a hard disk, each functioning as a logical drive with a different drive letter and each supporting a different operating system. For example, you could create a multiple-boot configuration with Windows XP Professional, Windows XP Home Edition, Windows 2000, and Windows 98 or Windows 95. You can create partitions with the FDisk utility described earlier, or you can use Advanced Options during Setup while installing Windows XP.

Each partition can use a different file system. Obviously, the operating system that you install might dictate the file system you use for a partition. For example, MS-DOS, Windows 95 (original version), and Windows 95a can only be installed on a FAT16 partition. Windows 95B and Windows 95c must be installed on a FAT32 partition. Windows 98 and Windows Me can be installed on a FAT16 or FAT32 partition. If you are creating a multiple-boot configuration with Windows XP and an operating system that uses FAT16 or FAT32, you should install the other operating system on the system partition (the first partition, drive C), and you should use FAT16 or FAT32 on that partition. Even with Windows NT Workstation 4.0, which supports NTFS, Microsoft recommends that the system partition use the FAT file system.

By installing each operating system on a different partition, you do not run the risk of one operating system overwriting files needed by another operating system. However, if you intend to use the same application with different operating systems, you must boot with each operating system and install that application on each partition.

You also have to install the operating systems in a specific order. For example, if you want to create a dual-boot between Windows XP and Windows 2000 Professional, you would install Windows 2000 Professional first, and then install Windows XP. If you want to create a multiple-boot configuration with Windows XP, Windows 2000 Professional, and Windows 98, you would install Windows 98 first, then install Windows 2000 Professional, and finally install Windows XP.

If you are considering a dual-boot or multiple-boot configuration, you should examine the Resource Kit Documentation for Microsoft Windows XP Professional, or visit the Microsoft Web site and examine the information it provides on multiple-boot configurations. The process for creating a multiple-boot configuration can be complex and varies with the types of operating systems included in the multiple-boot configuration, the partition used to install a specific operating system, the file system used on each partition, the file system used on the system partition (usually the first partition), and the implementation of more advanced Windows XP features, such as dynamic disks.

You can also use a third-party software product such as Partition Magic to partition your hard disk and set up a multiple-boot configuration while, at the same time, retaining all your files and settings.

Using the Files and Settings Transfer Wizard

As SolarWinds replaces its employees' computer with new computers, Takao uses the Files and Settings Transfer Wizard to transfer copies of an employee's current computer's settings and files from the employee's old computer to the new computer. This not only saves Takao valuable time and effort, but employees are ready to work on their new computers within a short period of time with the same settings they used on their old computers.

You can use the Files and Settings Transfer Wizard to copy your personal settings and files from a computer that you have been using to a new computer, so that you do not have to reconfigure the new computer. The settings include your desktop settings, display properties, mouse and keyboard settings, taskbar settings, Internet browser settings, dial-up connection settings, mail settings, application settings, network settings, and settings for registered files. As part of the migration process, the Files and Settings Transfer Wizard copies the Desktop, Fonts, My Documents, My Pictures, Shared Desktop, and Shared Documents folders.

Before you can use the Files and Settings Transfer Wizard on your older computer, you must either create a Wizard Disk using the Files and Settings Transfer Wizard on your new Windows XP computer, or use your Windows XP CD to start the Files and Settings Transfer Wizard on your older computer.

After you open the Files and Settings Transfer Wizard on your older computer, either from the Windows XPCD, System Tools menu, or Help and Support Center, the wizard recommends that you use either a direct cable connection (meaning a serial cable connection) or a network interface connection for the transfer. See Figure 11-20.

Figure 11-20	USING THE FILES AND SETTINGS TRANSFER WIZARD

Then the wizard asks whether the computer you are using is your new one or your old one. It notes that the old computer might be one that uses Windows 95, Windows 98, Windows 98SE, Windows Me, Windows NT Workstation 4.0, Windows 2000, or Windows XP as the operating system. See Figure 11-21.

Figure 11-21 **IDENTIFYING THE COMPUTER YOU'RE USING**

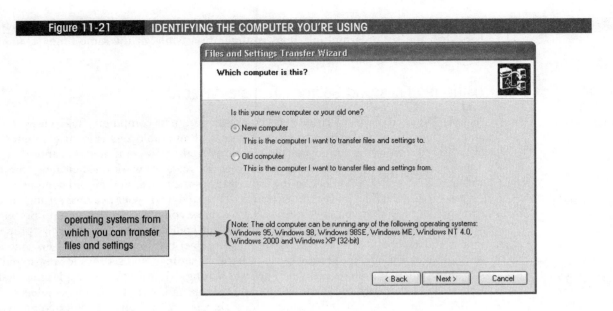

operating systems from which you can transfer files and settings

If you indicate that the current computer is your old computer, you are prompted for the transfer method. See Figure 11-22. You can transfer the data via direct cable, a home or small office network, a floppy disk drive or other removable media, a removable drive, a network drive, or any disk drive or folder on your computer.

Figure 11-22 **CHOOSING A TRANSFER METHOD**

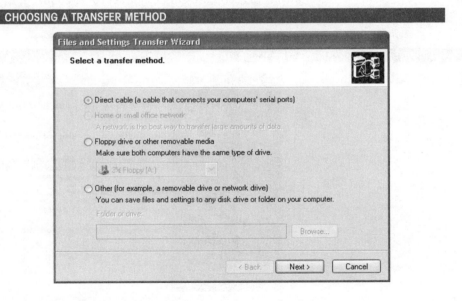

After you specify the method for transferring the data, you are asked to identify what you want to transfer. See Figure 11-23. You can transfer just settings, just files, or both files and settings. You also have the option of selecting files and settings from a list. The Files and Settings Transfer Wizard also lists the types of settings that are transferred.

Figure 11-23   CHOOSING WHAT TO TRANSFER

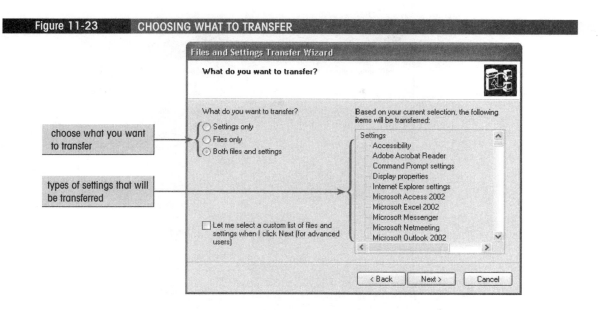

In the next step, the Files and Settings Transfer Wizard lists applications that you must install on the new computer. See Figure 11-24. Because settings for these applications are also transferred to the new computer, you must install the corresponding applications.

Figure 11-24   INSTALL THESE PROGRAMS ON THE NEW COMPUTER

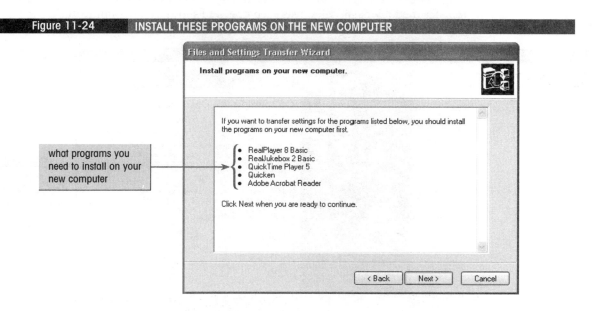

Then the wizard collects your files and settings. See Figure 11-25. If you chose the option for including files, this process takes time and consumes storage space on the media you selected earlier, because the Files and Settings Transfer Wizard copies everything in the My Documents and Shared Documents folders not only for your user account, but also for all other user accounts. If you have an additional volume (such as a drive D), it copies all the files on that volume. To conserve space, these files are compressed. However, if you intend to repartition your hard disk before installing Windows XP, you should instruct the Files and Settings Transfer Wizard to save the settings and files it collects to a folder on your desktop or elsewhere on your hard disk so that you can then copy the folder to a Zip disk or CD.

Figure 11-25   COLLECTING FILES AND SETTINGS FROM A COMPUTER

After collecting the files and settings, the wizard instructs you to go to your new computer and then run the Files and Settings Transfer Wizard on that computer to transfer the files and settings you collected. See Figure 11-26. The Files and Settings Transfer Wizard might note that it could not save some of your folders and files. It then asks you to manually transfer the folders and files, lists each one, and shows you the full path.

Figure 11-26   COLLECTION PHASE COMPLETED

After you start the Files and Settings Transfer Wizard on your new computer, and identify that computer as your new computer, the wizard asks if you have a Windows XP CD. See Figure 11-27. It also informs you that you need to run this wizard on your old computer (if you have not already done so) by either creating a wizard disk or by using the wizard from the Windows XP CD.

Figure 11-27	OPTION FOR CREATING A WIZARD DISK

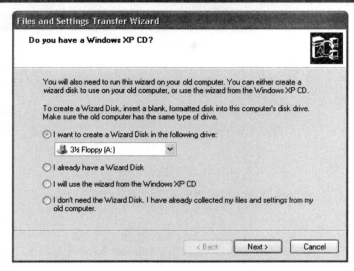

The Files and Settings Transfer Wizard then asks you for the location of the files and settings. See Figure 11-28.

Figure 11-28	IDENTIFYING THE LOCATION OF THE FILES AND SETTINGS

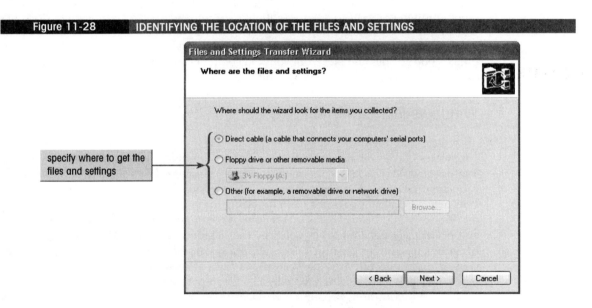

specify where to get the files and settings

After you identify the location of the files and settings, the wizard organizes and then transfers and applies the settings to your new computer. During this time, you cannot use your computer. See Figure 11-29.

Figure 11-29   **TRANSFERRING FILES AND SETTINGS**

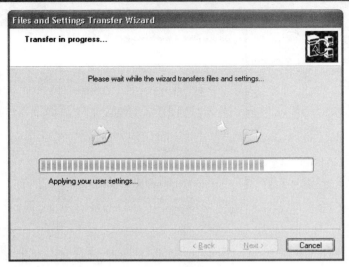

Then it informs you that it has successfully completed the transfer. After you click the Finish button, the wizard informs you that you need to log off for the changes to take effect.

The Files and Settings Transfer Wizard automates the process for upgrading from an older computer system to a new computer system, and saves you time and effort; however, you should also be careful and think about which settings are copied from your old computer to a new computer. For example, if the Files and Settings Transfer Wizard copies your Office 2000 settings and files from your old computer to your new computer with Office 2002, how does this migration of settings and files affect Office 2002?

Windows File Protection and System Checker

To reduce potential problems that might arise from installing new software on their home computers, Takao recommends that employees upgrade their computers to Windows 2000 Professional, Windows XP Home Edition, or Windows XP Professional, if their computers can support these operating systems. Then the Windows File Protection service can prevent newly installed programs from replacing important system files.

Windows File Protection is a Windows XP component that operates in the background and protects all system files installed by the Windows Setup program from newly installed programs that might attempt to overwrite a system file and replace it with a different version of that same file. If a newly installed file replaces an existing system file, and if that newly installed file does not have a digital signature that identifies it as the correct Microsoft version, Windows File Protection replaces the newly installed file with a backup copy of that file stored in the Dllcache folder or, if necessary, from the Windows XP CD. Without the use of Windows File Protection, which is always enabled, the stability of the Windows XP operating system could be jeopardized.

System File Checker, another component available in both Windows XP Professional and Windows XP Home Edition, is a command-line tool that you can use to scan and verify protected operating system files. To use this tool, your account must have Administrator privileges. To use System File Checker, you can issue the command SFC /SCANNOW in a Command Prompt window or by using the Run option on the Start menu. System File Checker then checks protected system files, as shown in Figure 11-30, and if it detects that a system file has been overwritten, it retrieves the correct version from the Dllcache folder or the Windows XP CD. In this figure, System File Checker is checking system files against the original copies on the Windows XP CD. If the Dllcache folder is corrupt or unusable, System File Checker can repair the folder if you use the proper switches. As shown in the figure, if you type SFC at the prompt in a Command Prompt window, the System File Checker displays information on the syntax for using the command.

Figure 11-30	USING SYSTEM FILE CHECKER

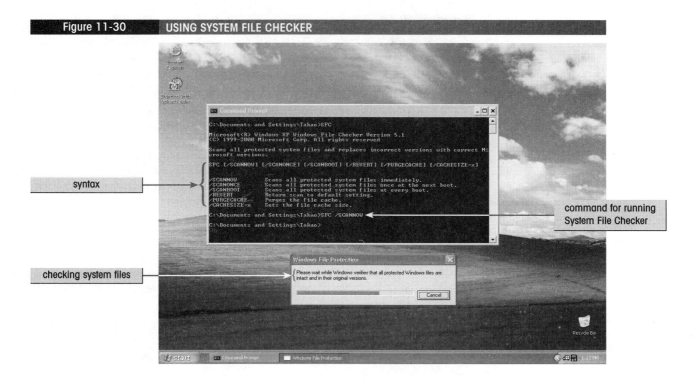

In the next section of the tutorial, you examine the use of Win32, Win16, and DOS applications under Windows XP, how you install and uninstall each type of applications, and how to prepare your computer for a software application upgrade. You examine the process for installing and uninstalling a Win32 application, learn about the importance of Windows Installer, and examine the use of the Program Compatibility Wizard to resolve problems with using older programs under Windows XP. You also step through the process for installing and uninstalling Windows XP components. Finally, you use Windows Update to download and install updates, and to view your installation history.

Getting **Started**

To complete this tutorial, you must switch your computer to Web style so that your screens match those shown in the figures, and you must also turn on the options for showing all folders and files, displaying protected operating system files, displaying file extensions, and displaying the full path in the Address bar. As you complete these steps, you may discover that your computer is already set up for Web style, or that other settings are already in place, so you might only need to make a few changes to your computer's settings.

To set up your computer:

1. To change to the Windows XP theme, right-click the **desktop**, click **Properties** on the shortcut menu, and after Windows XP opens the Display Properties dialog box, click the **Theme** list arrow on the Themes property sheet, click **Windows XP** if it is not already selected, and then click the **OK** button.

2. To switch to the Windows XP Start menu style, right-click the **Start** button, click **Properties** on the shortcut menu, and after Windows XP opens the Taskbar and Start Menu Properties dialog box, click the **Start menu** option button on the Start Menu property sheet if it is not already selected, and then click the **OK** button.

3. To change to a task-oriented view of folders and enable single-clicking, click the **Start** button, click **My Computer**, click **Tools** on the menu bar, click **Folder Options**, and after Windows XP opens the Folder Options dialog box, click the **Show common tasks in folders** option button if it is not already selected, click the **Single-click to open an item** option button if it is not already selected, and click the **Underline icon titles only when I point at them** option button if it is not already selected.

4. Click the **View** tab, click the **Display the full path in the address bar** check box if it is not already selected, click the **Show hidden files and folders** option button if it is not already selected, and if there is a check mark in the "Hide extensions for known file types" check box, click that check box to remove the check mark.

5. Click the **Hide protected operating system files** check box to deselect it, click the **Yes** button in the Warning dialog box to display protected operating system files, click the **OK** button to close the Folder Options dialog box, and then close My Computer.

Now you're ready to examine the process for installing and uninstalling applications, and Windows components.

Working **with Applications**

After installing Windows XP Professional on his computer, Takao asks you to check his hardware configuration settings and verify that the installation worked properly. Next, he wants you to install the newest version of Microsoft Office on his computer.

Although software manufacturers try to simplify and automate the process for installing or upgrading a software application, today's operating systems and applications are more complex, offer more features and options, and are installed on different computers with different configurations. You should understand what happens when you install software.

There are three types of applications that you can install and use under Windows XP:

- **Win32 applications.** Win32 applications are Windows XP, Windows 2000, Windows Me, Windows 98, Windows NT Workstation 4.0, and Windows 95 applications that are designed for a 32-bit operating system and operating environment. Adobe Photoshop 6.0 and Macromedia Dreamweaver 4, as well as the applications found in Office 2002, Office 2000, Office 97, Office 95, Microsoft Works 6.0, Corel WordPerfect Office 2002, and StarOffice 5.2 are all examples of Win32 applications.

- **Win16 applications**. Win16 applications, such as dBase III Plus and Lotus 1-2-3 Release 4.0 for Windows, are 16-bit Windows 3.x applications. The applications in Office 4.3 are also examples of Win16 applications designed for the Windows 3.x operating environment, but which function just as well in the Windows XP operating environment. All of the figures in this book were captured with a Win16 application called Collage Complete for Windows.

- **DOS applications**. Like Win16 applications, DOS applications and games are designed for a 16-bit operating environment. Support for these applications varies in the different versions of Windows; however, Microsoft has made every effort to improve support for them in Windows XP.

These three types of applications differ in how they function in the Windows XP operating environment. Win32 applications run in an operating environment called the Win32 subsystem, which supports a type of multitasking referred to as preemptive multitasking. In contrast, Windows XP runs Win16 applications originally designed for Windows 3.x in a VDM (Virtual DOS Machine) under the WOW subsystem (a Win32 process). A **Virtual DOS Machine (VDM)** is an operating environment for DOS applications that emulates the type of environment found under the DOS operating system. The **WOW (Win16 on Win32) subsystem** emulates 16-bit Windows. Windows XP creates an NTVDM (NT Virtual DOS Machine), a Win32 process, for DOS applications.

As you already know, multitasking is an operating system or operating environment feature that supports multiple tasks, or what Microsoft calls multiple processes, by allocating a share of the system resources to each system process or each application that you open. Although each application or task does not run at exactly the same time (unless you have two processors), the operating system handles each process so that each application or task thinks it is the only process that is running. Depending on the type of system you use, this sharing of the microprocessor and other system resources might happen so fast that you have the impression that the tasks are actually running simultaneously.

Windows 3.x supported cooperative multitasking, while Windows XP supports both cooperative and preemptive multitasking. In the Windows 3.x **cooperative multitasking** environment, the currently running application periodically relinquishes control of system resources so that the operating environment can permit another application access to those same system resources. Once the currently running application yields control to the operating system, you can then switch to and use another running application. This approach obviously has its disadvantages. You and the operating system must wait until the running application completes a task and yields control to the operating system so that a task from another application can start. For example, you might have to wait for a spreadsheet application to calculate values for a complex loan analysis table before you can use your communications software to connect to your ISP and download your e-mail. While one process runs, you wait for the mouse pointer hourglass to change so that you can then perform some other function or switch to another application. Another disadvantage of working in a cooperative multitasking environment is that the entire system might crash if the running application crashes.

In the Windows XP **preemptive multitasking** environment, the Windows XP operating system assigns and then removes access to system resources for each application. This approach provides a more stable and reliable operating environment because Windows XP, not the applications, controls access to system resources. If you are using Win32 applications, you can switch to your communications software, for example, connect to an ISP, and download e-mail while your spreadsheet application calculates values for a complex loan analysis table. Preemptive multitasking not only works with Win32-based applications, but also with NTVDMs designed for Win16 and DOS applications. To provide backward compatibility with applications designed for Windows 3.x, Windows XP cooperatively multitasks those applications.

Another important feature of preemptive multitasking is that Win32 applications can use multithreading. As noted earlier, multithreading is the ability of an operating system to execute more than one sequence of program code within the same application program at the same time. When you run an application that supports multithreading, the operating system manages a single task or process. Within that process, the operating system supports the execution of one or more threads, or units of program code, for that application. Windows XP can manage multiple threads for the current application, as well as multiple threads for background processes. The net effect is that multithreading improves the speed of the applications that you run. For example, in a spreadsheet application, one thread might be recalculating a complex table of values while another thread updates a three-dimensional chart produced from those calculations. Not surprisingly, Windows XP itself uses multithreading.

Because one of the primary functions of Windows XP is to protect the security and stability of a computer system, Windows XP does not support the use of all Win16 and all DOS applications. You might need to check the Microsoft Windows Catalog Web site to determine whether Windows XP supports the use of a particular application that you might want to use on your computer—particularly older (pre-1990) applications. If your program is not listed, you can install it and determine whether it works under Windows XP. If not, you might be able to use Program Compatibility Mode (described later in the tutorial) to simulate the operating environment of an earlier version of Windows in which the program worked.

Preparing for a Software Installation or Upgrade

Takao has discovered that the guidelines that apply for preparing for an operating system upgrade also apply when installing new software applications on a computer. He asks you to review the preparatory steps that he takes to insure that few or no problems arise during the installation process for a software product.

Before you install a Win32, Win16, or DOS application under Windows XP, you should prepare your computer system using the guidelines described earlier for installing or upgrading an operating system. As noted earlier, it is wise to back up your document files and, perhaps, your installed software before installing a new application or an upgrade to an existing application. It also helps if you use Check Disk to check for file system problems and Disk Defragmenter to optimize storage space on the hard disk before installing another application. Clear memory by restarting Windows XP, and then install the application by using the Add/Remove Programs Wizard in the Control Panel.

If you are installing a Win16 application on your computer, the software manual or instructions on the installation disk will probably tell you to open Program Manager, select File, select Run, and then type the command for the Setup program. Instead of using the Run option on the Start menu, open the Control Panel, start the Add/Remove Programs Wizard, let it locate the Setup file for that application, and then you can install the Win16 application.

Likewise, use the Add/Remove Programs Wizard if you are installing a DOS application. Although the instructions for your DOS application or game usually tell you to enter a command, such as A:\Install.bat, A:\Install.exe, or A:\Setup.exe at a command prompt to start the installation, use the Add/Remove Programs Wizard to install the software instead. Windows XP then monitors the installation of the Win16 or DOS application and, if a problem arises, Windows XP can attempt to recover the installation program. In the case of Win16 applications, Windows XP copies configuration settings to the Windows Registry.

When you install a Win32 application, the Setup program performs the following types of operations:

■ **Installs the application**. The Setup program creates a folder for the application on the hard disk and creates any subfolders needed for installing program files and supporting files. You can use the default folder name that the Setup program proposes, or you can choose your own folder name. Most Setup programs install the software in a folder under the Program Files folder. If the

Setup program indicates that it will install the software product elsewhere, you can override this option, and designate the Program Files folder.

- **Installs shared files**. The Setup program copies shared program files, such as DLLs (program files that one or more applications might use) to the Windows folder. As noted earlier, the Windows File Protection (WFP) service monitors this process to prevent the replacement of protected system files that do not have the proper digital signature.

- **Updates the Registry**. The Setup program copies application settings and other information, such as the full path for program files and registration information, to the Windows Registry. Win32 applications do not modify the Windows 3.x configuration files Win.ini and System.ini.

- **Creates a group folder and shortcuts**. The Setup program adds a group folder to the All Programs menu, and within the group folder, creates shortcuts to the application, as well as to other programs included with that software product (such as an Uninstall program), and to Help and Readme files that contain documentation on using the software product.

- **Installs an Uninstall program**. Win32 applications install an Uninstall program that allows you to remove that application from your computer system. In fact, as just noted, the Uninstall program might be one of the options in the application's group folder on the Start or All Programs menu.

The Setup programs for Win16 applications perform most of the same functions as a Setup program for a Win32 application, *except* they do not update the Registry and they do not usually include an Uninstall program. Instead, the Setup program updates the Windows 3.x configuration files (Win.ini and System.ini). Then, when you run the Win16 application, it checks these configuration files for the settings that it needs. During the installation of the Win16 application, Windows XP copies the configuration settings entered by the Win16 installation program in Win.ini and System.ini to the Windows Registry. Unlike Win32 applications, the Setup program does not create a folder for the software product under the Program Files folder unless you specifically designate it.

One of the primary problems faced by users of Win16 applications is that, more often than not, the programs do not come with an Uninstall program, so the user invariably encounters problems when attempting to remove a Win16 application. Later in this tutorial, you look at how to uninstall or remove different types of applications.

When you install a DOS application, you usually run an Install program that performs the following types of operations:

- **Installs the application**. Like a Win32 or Win16 Setup program, the Install program (which might be named Install.bat) creates a folder for the application on the hard disk, and creates any subfolders needed for installing program files and supporting files. You can use the default folder name that the Install program proposes, or you can choose your own name. Like the Setup program for Win16 applications, the Install program does not create a folder for the software product under the Program Files folder unless you specifically designate it.

- **Updates the MS-DOS configuration files**. The Install program might examine the Config.sys and Autoexec.bat startup files and either make changes to those files or propose that it, or you, make the changes needed for that application to work properly.

The Install program for a DOS application does not install shared files, and it does not change the Windows Registry or the Windows 3.x configuration files. Also, since the Install program does not create a group folder or shortcuts on the All Programs menu for the DOS application, you have to create them after the installation. You can add a shortcut for the application to the desktop, to the All Programs menu, or both. Like Win16 applications, DOS applications typically do not come with an Uninstall program; however, as you see later, uninstalling a DOS application is easier than uninstalling a Win16 application.

Installing a Win32 Application

Next, Takao wants you to download and install an evaluation copy of the most recent version of PolyView, a graphics application developed by Polybytes.

You can install a Win32 application in one of several ways:

- **Insert the CD for the software product.** Windows XP automatically starts the Setup program on the CD, and you can then install the software product.
- **Use the Add or Remove Programs Wizard.** If you open the Control Panel, click Add or Remove Programs, and then click the Add New Programs button in the Add or Remove Programs window, you can use the CD or Floppy button to install a program from a CD-ROM or floppy disk, or you can use the Windows Update button to download new Windows XP features, updates, and device drivers from Microsoft's Windows Update Web site. See Figure 11-31.

| Figure 11-31 | USING ADD OR REMOVE PROGRAMS |

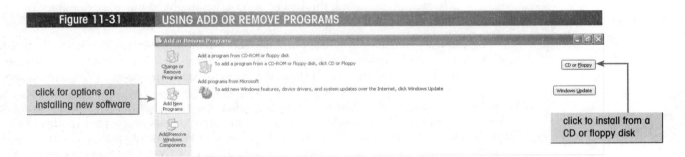

If you click the CD or Floppy button, Windows XP displays an Install Program from Floppy Disk or CD-ROM dialog box that prompts you to insert the product's first installation floppy disk or CD-ROM. See Figure 11-32.

| Figure 11-32 | PROMPT TO INSERT THE FIRST INSTALLATION DISK |

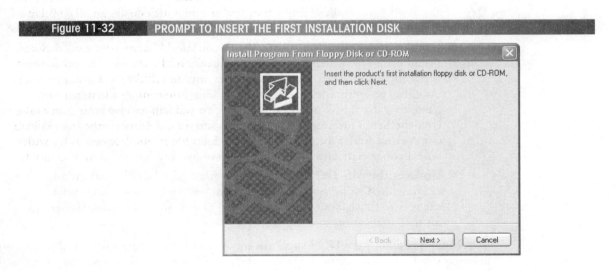

Windows XP then checks the drives, in drive order, and locates the Setup.exe program. In the next dialog box, it asks you to verify its selection. See Figure 11-33. You can use the Browse button to locate the installation program by drive or by folder.

Figure 11-33	SELECTING THE SETUP PROGRAM

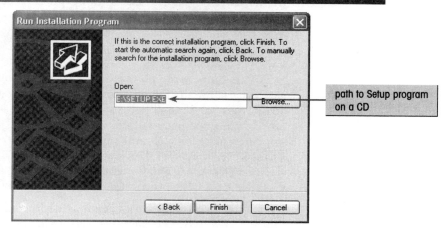

After you click the Finish button, Windows XP opens the Setup program for the Win32 application, and then you can install the software product.

■ **Use a self-extracting executable file.** When you download a program from a Web site, the downloaded program might be stored in a self-extracting executable file with the "exe" file extension. A **self-extracting executable file** is a file that contains one or more files stored in a compressed format, plus a program for extracting the contents of the self-extracting executable file itself. When you click (or double-click) the self-extracting executable file, a program within the downloaded file extracts the contents of this downloaded file, and then starts the Setup program for installing the software product. If the downloaded file has the "zip" file extension, it is a zip file that contains one or more files stored in a compressed format. This file format is commonly used for compressing files that are downloaded from the Internet or a Web site, or for compressing files that are then included as an attachment to an e-mail message.

Under previous versions of Windows, you would have to use a utility like WinZip or PKUnzip to extract the contents of the zip file. Then you would click (or double-click) the Setup.exe file, and install the software. However, Windows XP treats a file with the "zip" file extension as a Compressed (zipped) folder. You can open the Compressed (zipped) folder like any other folder and work directly with the files. You do not need a utility like WinZip or PKUnzip. However, if you transfer a zip file to another computer with another version of Windows, you need to use WinZip or another utility to extract and uncompress the file.

The remainder of this section of the tutorial illustrates how to download and install PolyView, a graphics application, from a Web site. Downloading software from Web sites is becoming increasingly more common. In fact, you usually obtain software updates by downloading self-extracting executable files.

Before you install a software product on your computer, you should make sure that Windows XP supports that software product. As illustrated earlier, you can search the Windows Catalog, or you can check the Web site of the company that makes the software you want to download to determine which versions of Windows support that product, and if it is supported by more than one version of Windows, to make sure that you download the correct version.

Although there are no tutorial steps for downloading and installing this software product, you can use the following overview of downloading and installing this software product to download and install PolyView or another software product on your computer. If you are working in a computer lab and want to download and install this software product, first ask your instructor or technical support staff for permission. Remember also that Web sites change over time, and the views shown in the figures may differ from what you see if you decide to download and install this software product.

Here is the basic process for downloading and installing a program:

- **Log on under an account with Administrator privileges**. To install a software product, you need to log on under an account with Administrator privileges.

- **Create a restore point**. Use System Restore (covered in Tutorial 8) to create a manual restore point before downloading and installing software.

- **Locate the Web site for the program you want to download**. After you connect to your ISP and load your Web browser, you can use a search engine to locate the Web site for the software product you want to download. If you know the name of the company or the product, you might be able to locate it more quickly by specifying the company or product name in the URL. For example, to locate the Web site for PolyView, you could search for PolyView using a search engine such as Google.com. Or you could enter *www.polyview.com* or *www.polybytes.com* in the Address bar, and then press the Enter key. Both URLs locate the home page for Polybytes Software. See Figure 11-34. The Web page invites you to look around and download anything that appeals to you; it also provides information about Polybytes, and then provides information on several of its products. Polybytes explains that PolyView is a fast and powerful image viewer, conversion, and printing utility for 32-bit Windows. After you locate the Web site for a software product, you want to verify that the product you are downloading works with Windows XP. Notice that PolyView works with Windows 95, Windows 98, Windows Me, Windows NT, Windows 2000, and Windows XP.

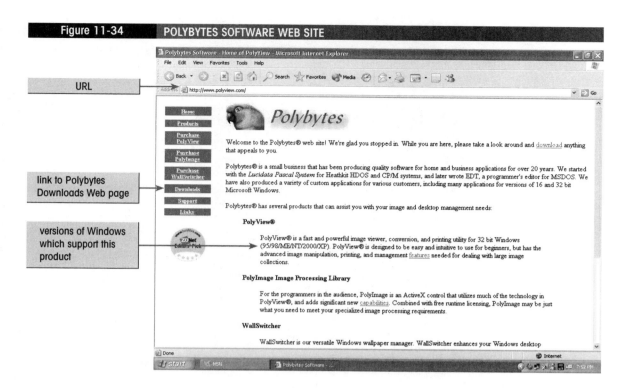

| Figure 11-34 | POLYBYTES SOFTWARE WEB SITE |

URL

link to Polybytes
Downloads Web page

versions of Windows
which support this
product

■ **Download the software product**. On the Polybytes Software home page, there is a Downloads link from which you can download PolyView. After you click the Downloads link, links provide you with different ways for acquiring this software product. See Figure 11-35. The notes for the second link, PolyView 3.70 Setup Program, explain that you should use this link for a complete installation setup program. The notes also explain that, after you download the polyview3.70.exe program, you run the program to install PolyView 3.70.

Figure 11-35	WEB PAGE FOR DOWNLOADING AN EVALUATION VERSION

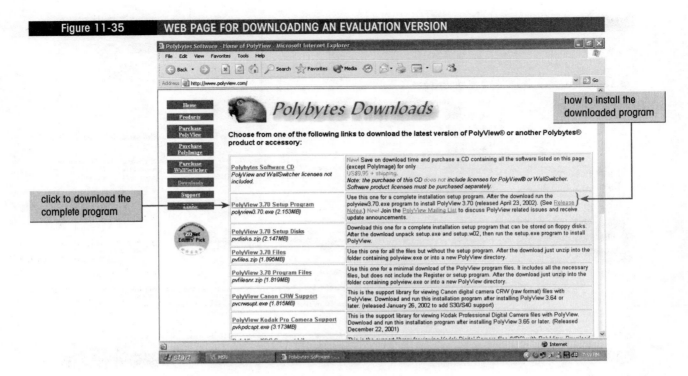

After you click the PolyView 3.70 Setup Program link, you are prompted in a File Download dialog box whether you want to open this program or save it on your computer. See Figure 11-36. By saving the downloaded file to your hard disk, you can scan it for computer viruses before you install the software. Also, you should keep a copy of this downloaded file in a folder on your hard disk so that you can reinstall the software product later if the need should arise.

Figure 11-36	OPTION FOR OPENING OR SAVING THE DOWNLOADED FILE TO DISK

The next dialog box shows the progress of the download. See Figure 11-37. Notice that this file is 2.10 MB in size and probably takes close to 10 minutes using a 56K modem operating at 36.0 Kbps. After the download is complete, you close the Download complete dialog box if it does not automatically close by itself. You can then close your Web browser and disconnect from your ISP.

Figure 11-37 — DOWNLOADING POLYVIEW

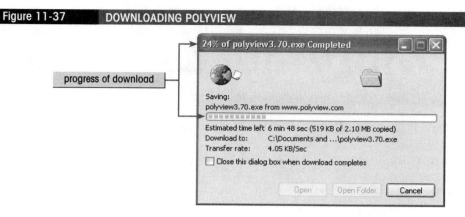

progress of download

■ **Scan the downloaded file for computer viruses**. After right-clicking the file icon, and selecting the option for scanning the downloaded file with PC-cillin (Takao's antivirus software), Trend PC-cillin reports that no viruses were detected. See Figure 11-38. Notice that the self-extracting executable file was downloaded to a folder named Polyview Evaluation under Takao's My Documents folder.

Figure 11-38 — SCANNING THE DOWNLOADED FILE FOR VIRUSES

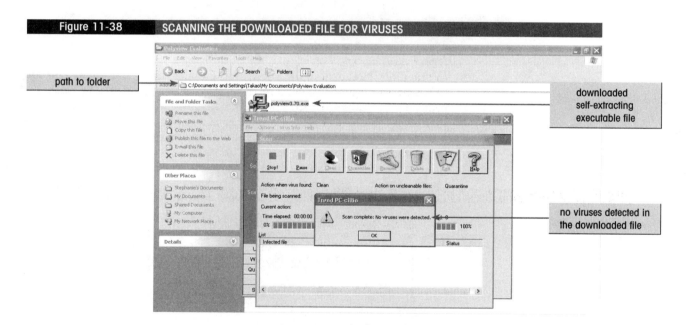

path to folder

downloaded self-extracting executable file

no viruses detected in the downloaded file

■ **Install the software product**. If the file is a self-extracting executable file with the "exe" file extension, you can install the software product by clicking (or double-clicking) the file icon. If the downloaded file has a "zip" file extension, you would open the Compressed (zipped) folder, and locate and click the Setup.exe program file to install the software product.

After you click the self-extracting executable file, a PolyView Installation dialog box informs you that it is starting the Wise Installation Wizard which then examines your computer for a previous installation of PolyView.

The first PolyView 3.70 Installation dialog box explains what this installation program does. See Figure 11-39.

Figure 11-39	READY TO INSTALL POLYVIEW

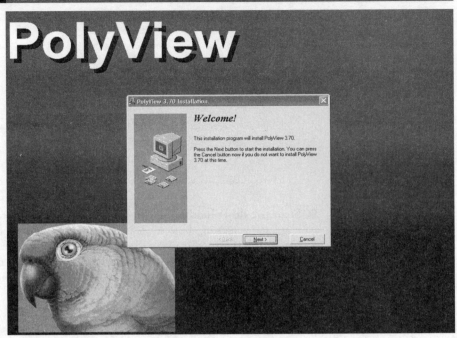

After you click the Next button, the next dialog box asks you to select the Destination Directory, in other words, the folder where you want to install PolyView. See Figure 11-40. The installation program proposes to install PolyView in a folder named PolyView, which will be under a folder named Polybytes located under the Program Files folder. Microsoft encourages software manufacturers to install their software in the Program Files folder rather than in the Windows folder or another location. You can use the path proposed by the installation program, or you can use the Browse button to locate another folder for the software product. The installation program also shows the available disk space before and after the product is installed.

Figure 11-40	OPTION FOR SELECTING THE DESTINATION DIRECTORY

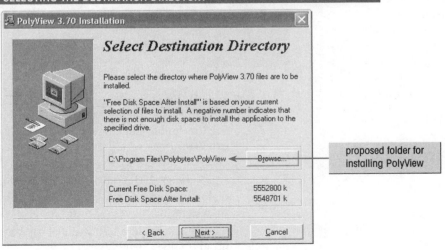

proposed folder for installing PolyView

If you accept the directory proposed by the installation program and then click the Next button, the installation program asks if you want to back up files that it replaces during the installation. See Figure 11-41. This feature is particularly useful if you encounter a problem later.

Figure 11-41	OPTION FOR BACKING UP REPLACED FILES

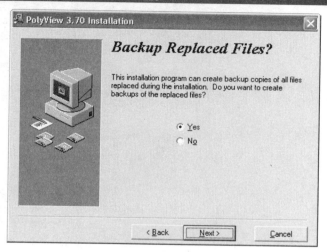

If you keep the default Yes option, and then click the Next button, the installation program asks you to select the backup directory (or folder). See Figure 11-42. Any replaced files are stored in a folder named BACKUP under the PolyView folder.

Figure 11-42	SELECTING THE BACKUP DIRECTORY

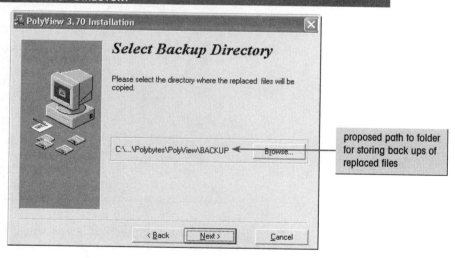

proposed path to folder for storing back ups of replaced files

After you click the Next button, the installation program prompts you for a name for the group folder which will appear on the All Programs menu and contain shortcuts for this software product. See Figure 11-43. Note that the installation program keeps the convention used under Windows 3.1 and refers to the group folder as a Program Manager group. The installation program proposes to use the name PolyView, which is fine, and it also shows you the names of some of the existing group folders on the All Programs menu.

| Figure 11-43 | SPECIFYING THE GROUP FOLDER ON THE ALL PROGRAMS MENU |

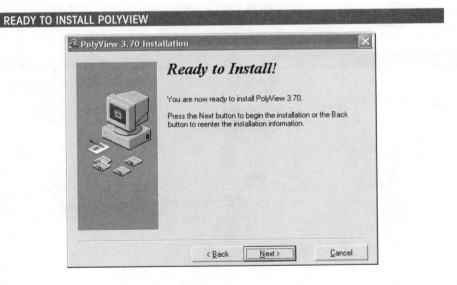

Next, the install program informs you that it is ready to install the software product. See Figure 11-44.

| Figure 11-44 | READY TO INSTALL POLYVIEW |

After you click the Next button, the installation program installs PolyView and then displays a dialog box informing you that the installation was successful. See Figure 11-45.

Figure 11-45 INSTALLATION COMPLETED

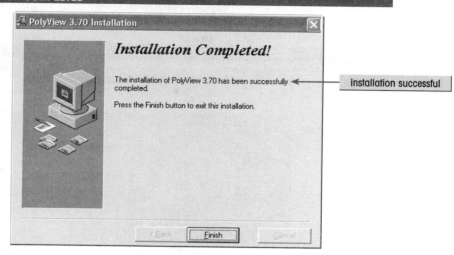

installation successful

After you click the Finish button, the installation program closes and you return to the folder with the self-extracting executable file. If you examine the All Programs menu, you find a PolyView group folder. See Figure 11-46. In addition to a shortcut for opening PolyView, there are shortcuts to a ReadMe file and Polyview Help.

Figure 11-46 SELECTING THE POLYVIEW GROUP FOLDER

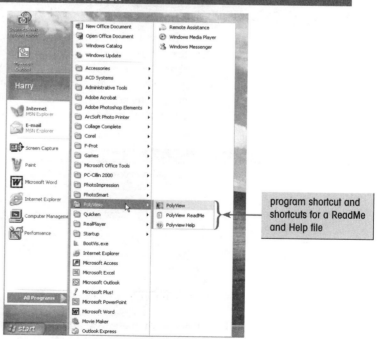

program shortcut and shortcuts for a ReadMe and Help file

■ **Open the program and a file**. After you install a downloaded program, open that program and a file appropriate to that program so that you can verify that the program is working properly. When you open PolyView, you see an Unregistered logo before you see the application window. Figure 11-47 shows the PolyView application window and one of the images included with Microsoft Plus!

| Figure 11-47 | POLYVIEW APPLICATION WINDOW |

After you close PolyView, an Unregistered PolyView dialog box thanks you for trying out this product, and explains that you can use it for 30 days so that you can evaluate the product and its features. See Figure 11-48. After 30 days, you are obligated to either purchase a license or remove it from your computer. At this point, you can also enter your license number, purchase the product online or offline, or purchase it later.

| Figure 11-48 | USAGE POLICY FOR THE EVALUATION VERSION OF POLYVIEW |

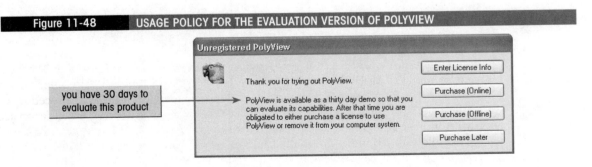

you have 30 days to evaluate this product

The process for installing any other Win32 or Win16 application is very similar to that shown for PolyView, though, in the case of an office suite such as Microsoft Office, you might be installing multiple software applications, and also choosing specific components within each application to install.

The Importance of Windows Installer

The network administrator at SolarWinds has customized the use of Windows Installer so that it permits employees to install additional software components when needed.

Windows Installer is a Windows XP service that manages and standardizes the installation of software. One of its main features is its ability to provide "on-demand" installation of components of a software product that were not originally installed. These on-demand features include, for example, Microsoft Office Document Imaging for scanning and optical character recognition (OCR), or the Microsoft Excel Text to Speech component for reading aloud the data in a spreadsheet. If you initially do not need these features, there is no reason to install them and waste valuable storage space on your hard disk.

If you access a feature that is not currently installed, Windows Installer automatically prompts you for the CD and installs that component (a process called **advertising**). The primary problem with on-demand installation of software is that the CD must always be available and therefore must be left in the CD or DVD drive. You can also set up Windows Installer so that it removes components that are not used within a specified period.

When you install a software application, Windows Installer keeps track of all the changes made to your computer so that it can restore your computer to its original state (called a **rollback**) in the event a problem develops during the installation. Windows Installer can also repair an application that has a missing or corrupted file by copying that file to your computer from the CD for that software product.

Windows Installer also makes sure that a DLL file required for one application does not replace the DLL file (with the same name) required for another application. It stores the two DLLs in separate folders.

If you have an account with Administrator privileges, you can configure Windows Installer using the Group Policy snap-in within the Microsoft Management Console.

Uninstalling a Win32 Application

So that he can easily uninstall applications he no longer needs on his computer, Takao has upgraded his Win16 applications, and now works primarily with Win32 applications.

If you find that you no longer need an application, you can uninstall or remove it. How you uninstall depends on the type of application. If the application is a Win32 application, you can use the Add/Remove Programs Wizard to uninstall the application because Win32 applications come with an Uninstall component. There might also be an Uninstall option in the All Programs menu group folder for that application.

To illustrate the advantage of using Win32 applications that come with an Uninstall component, you examine the process for removing an installed copy of an evaluation version of the PolyView application described earlier. If you are working on your computer and want to uninstall the evaluation version of PolyView, or if you want to uninstall another Win32 application that you no longer need, you can adapt the following procedure to that application. To uninstall applications, you must log on as Administrator or under an account with Administrator privileges. If you are working in a computer lab, you more than likely are not allowed to remove an installed application. *If the computer you are using has a registered version of PolyView, do not uninstall it.*

Here is the basic process for uninstalling a Win32 application:

1. **Open Add or Remove Programs**. From the Start menu, open Control Panel, and then click Add or Remove Programs. After Windows XP lists the currently installed programs, you locate the program you want to uninstall. See Figure 11-49. Windows XP identifies the amount of storage space that program uses on the disk, describes how frequently the program is used, and identifies the date the program was last used. You can use the Change/Remove

button to either add or remove components included with this program, or to completely remove the program from your computer system.

Figure 11-49   CURRENTLY INSTALLED PROGRAMS

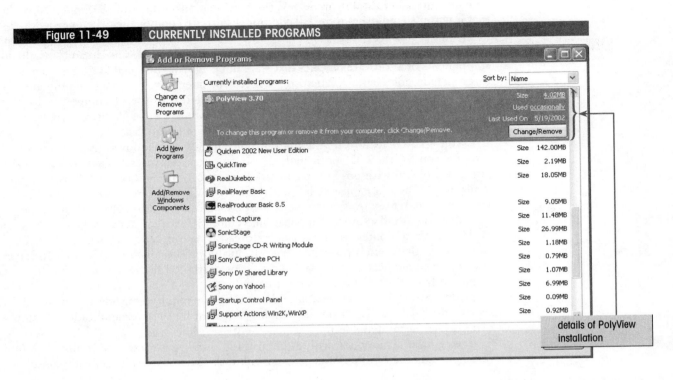

2. **Remove the program**. After you click the Change/Remove button, the Wise Installation System Uninstaller starts, and the Select Uninstall Method dialog box prompts you to select the method for uninstalling this application. See Figure 11-50. You can use the default Automatic option, which is the fastest and requires the least interaction with you, or you can use the Custom button to specify what the uninstall program modifies. Even if you do not want to specify the modifications, you can still use the Custom button so that you know what changes occur when you uninstall a program.

Figure 11-50   SELECTING AN UNINSTALL METHOD

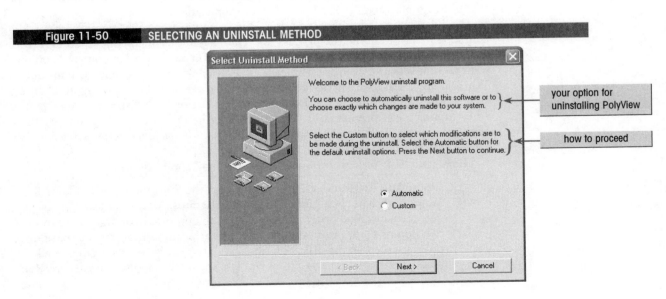

After you select the Custom option, the Select Private Files to Remove dialog box lists the files that the uninstall program will remove. See Figure 11-51. You can select all of them or only the individual files you want to remove.

| Figure 11-51 | SELECTING THE FILES TO REMOVE |

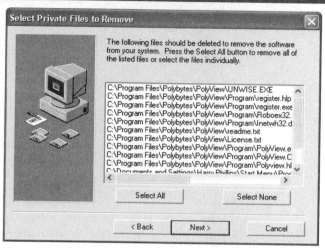

After you select all the files, the Select Directories to Remove dialog box identifies the directories (or folders) that were created when you installed PolyView. See Figure 11-52. You can select all of the directories, or select only the ones you want to remove. If you select a directory, all directories and files within that directory are also removed.

| Figure 11-52 | SELECTING THE DIRECTORIES TO REMOVE |

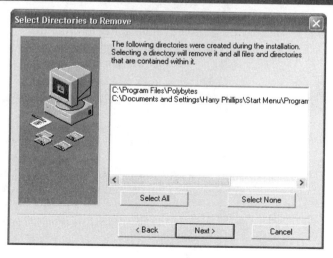

After you select all the directories, the Select Registry Keys to Remove dialog box shows the Registration Database Keys that the install program created in the Windows Registry. See Figure 11-53. Again, you can select all of the keys, or select only those keys that you want to remove.

Figure 11-53   SELECTING THE REGISTRY KEYS TO REMOVE

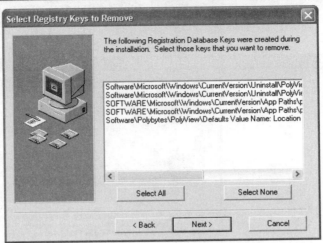

After you select all the keys, the Select Registry Trees to Remove dialog box shows you Registry keys created during the installation of this program. See Figure 11-54. You can remove all of them, or only individual keys.

Figure 11-54   SELECTING THE REGISTRY TREES TO REMOVE

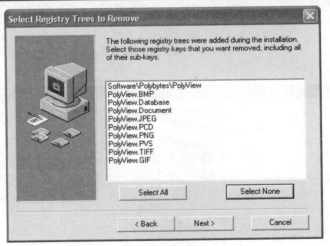

After selecting all the keys, the Perform Uninstall dialog box informs you that you are now ready to uninstall this software product. See Figure 11-55.

Figure 11-55	READY TO UNINSTALL

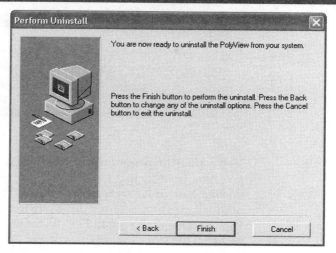

After you click the Finish button, the Remove Shared Component dialog box opens, explaining that one file it removes is a shared file that is no longer used by any programs. See Figure 11-56. The dialog box warns you that if you remove this file, which might still be used by other programs, those other programs may not function properly. You can leave this file on your computer without harming your system; however, these types of files waste valuable storage space on your disk and may not be used by any other program. The dialog box indicates that if you are not sure what to do, you should select the No to All button. If you do remove the shared file and then discover that another program needed it, you would have to reinstall that other program.

Figure 11-56	OPTION TO REMOVE A SHARED FILE

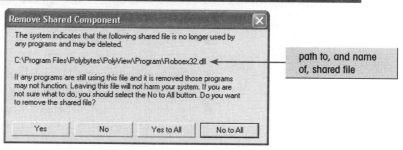

path to, and name of, shared file

After indicating that you want to remove this shared file, the uninstall program removes PolyView. The Add or Remove Programs window shows that PolyView is no longer listed as an installed program. See Figure 11-57.

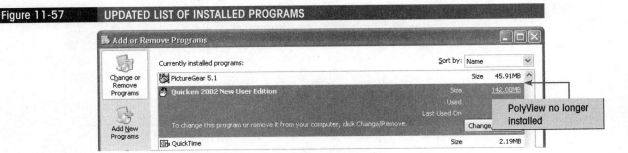

Figure 11-57 | UPDATED LIST OF INSTALLED PROGRAMS

3. **Verify that the program was completely uninstalled**. After uninstalling a program, to verify that no program components remain to waste storage space on your hard disk, you can check the All Programs menu to make sure the uninstall program removed the group folder for the software product, and then you can open the Program Files folder to make sure the uninstall program removed the folder where the software product was installed.

If Windows XP reports during the next boot that it cannot find a file or files, the uninstall program did not fully uninstall the software product. You might need to check the Registry and remove Registry keys manually. Although changes to the Registry can prevent your computer from booting and therefore is risky, you can search the Registry for the name of the company and the name of the software product that you installed to help you find the Registry keys that must be removed. Make sure you back up your computer first. You might be able to use System Restore to roll back your computer to an earlier functioning state—the point before you installed the software product. However, any other configuration changes you have made to your computer are also affected, so carefully weigh this option before implementing it. If you do not use Add or Remove Programs to uninstall a program, but rather simply delete the folder with the software product, you more than likely must edit the Registry as just described or use System Restore to roll back your computer.

If you want to remove a Win16 application, you cannot use Add or Remove Programs to uninstall it because it is not listed as an installed program in the Add or Remove Programs window. You have three options for removing the application:

- If the application is one of those few Win16 applications that have an Uninstall program, you can run that program to remove the application.

- If there is no separate Uninstall program, open the application's Setup program, and check for an option for uninstalling the application.

- If there is no Uninstall program, and no option available in Setup for uninstalling the application, you have to manually remove the application by deleting the folder and subfolders that contain the program files, supporting files, and any shortcuts that refer to the program. However, this approach is problematic, because the application might have put components in the Windows folder and its subfolders, and locating and removing these components is just about impossible.

If the Setup program for the Win16 application modified Win.ini, System.ini, Config.sys, or Autoexec.bat, and if there is no built-in uninstall program to remove or edit changes made to these files when you installed the Win16 application, you have to open each of these files and manually remove or modify the directives and commands associated with the application you removed. In some cases, the reference to a particular program is obvious because the command includes the program's path and name. If you create a backup or printed copies of these files before you install a program and immediately after you install a program, you can compare the two versions of each file and determine what changes you need to make to restore your computer.

If you want to uninstall a DOS application, you delete the folder and subfolders that contain the installed software. You might want to first check for an uninstall program or batch program (a user-defined program file) included with the software for accomplishing this task. If the DOS application modified Config.sys and Autoexec.bat, you must open each file and remark out those directives or commands by placing REM at the beginning of the command line to remove or modify the directives and commands. Again, this is not an easy task, especially if you are unfamiliar with these startup configuration files or if you do not know the changes the application's Install program (or batch program) originally made. As noted before, some command references might be easy to figure out when you examine these files. Also, if you back up or print a copy of these configuration files before and after you install a DOS application, such as by copying Config.sys to Config.bak, you can compare the current version of one of these files with the previous version.

To protect your computer, consider purchasing and using an uninstaller, such as Norton CleanSweep (*www.symantec.com*), Ontrack EasyUninstall (*www.ontrack.com*), and Ultra WinCleaner (*www.wincleaner.com*). An **uninstaller** is a software product that monitors the installation of a program installation so that you can more fully uninstall that program later. Uninstallers can safely remove unwanted programs, back up and restore installed programs, make copies of programs you uninstall so you can reinstall them later, and clean your Windows Registry. McAfee.com (*www.mcafee.com*) has an online uninstaller subscription (fee-based) service where you can use its Application Remover to locate and remove files for a software product and then store them in a compressed format in case you need them later.

One advantage of upgrading to and using Win32 applications is that the process for uninstalling these applications is easy.

Adding or Removing Microsoft Office Components

People who use the Microsoft Office suite often find that they do not have access to all the features and components included in the software suite because they choose the default install option. However, you can open Setup, examine what's installed, and add or remove individual components.

In the next section of the tutorial, you are going to open Microsoft Office Setup and examine installed components. You will need your Microsoft Office CD. If you do not have a Microsoft Office CD, or if you are working on a computer in a computer lab which does not permit you to install or remove software, read the steps and examine the figures, but do not keystroke the following steps, so that you are familiar with how to add and remove program components. The following steps illustrate the use of Microsoft Office XP Professional. If you have a different version, you will notice differences in the availability of features.

When installing software on employees' computers, Takao typically performs a full installation so that employees have access to any of the features available in a software product. However, employees who carry work home do not always have access to the same features, because they perform a typical installation, which does not always include all the components available with that software product. This is invariably the case with Microsoft Office, because it contains so many different features. Takao asks you to examine the Microsoft Office components so that you can inform other staff members of what's available within this software suite.

To examine installable Microsoft Office components:

1. Insert your Microsoft Office CD into your DVD or CD drive, close that drive, and if the Setup program does not automatically open, open a window onto the CD drive (if necessary), and then click **Setup.exe**. The Microsoft Office XP Setup dialog box provides access to Maintenance Mode options—including options for adding or removing features, repairing Office and restoring it to its original state, and for uninstalling Office. See Figure 11-58.

   TROUBLE? If Windows XP displays an Install Program as Other User dialog box and informs you that some programs do not install correctly if you do not have Administrator privileges on the computer you're using, and if you know the password for the Administrator account, enter that password, and then click the OK button. If you do not know the Administrator password, click the Cancel button, log off, and then log on under an account with Administrator privileges.

Figure 11-58	MAINTENANCE MODE OPTIONS

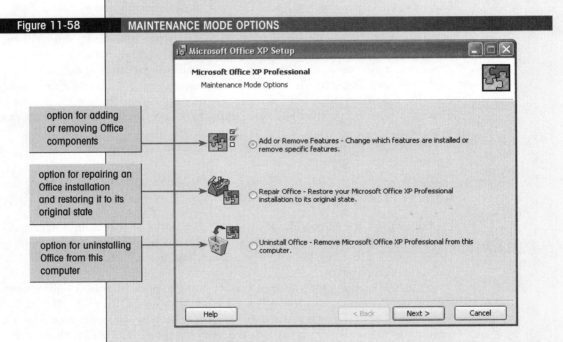

option for adding or removing Office components

option for repairing an Office installation and restoring it to its original state

option for uninstalling Office from this computer

2. Make sure the **Add or Remove Features** option button is selected, and then click the **Next** button. You can now choose installation options for your version of Office. See Figure 11-59. Note that the features are divided into categories for each application, and also include shared features and Office tools.

Figure 11-59   **OFFICE COMPONENTS**

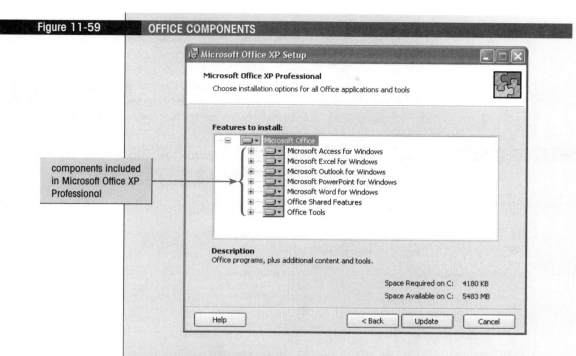

components included
in Microsoft Office XP
Professional

3. Click the **expand view** box ➕ to the left of the Office Tools icon. Microsoft
Office XP Setup displays the tools provided with this version of Office. See Figure
11-60. Notice that this version includes Microsoft Photo Editor. The Not Available
icon ✖ indicates that the component is not installed. The Installed on First Use
icon 📭 indicates that Windows Installer will install the component when you
first need to use it. The Setup program then prompts you for the CD, or needs
access to the network server to install the feature.

Figure 11-60   **OFFICE TOOLS COMPONENTS**

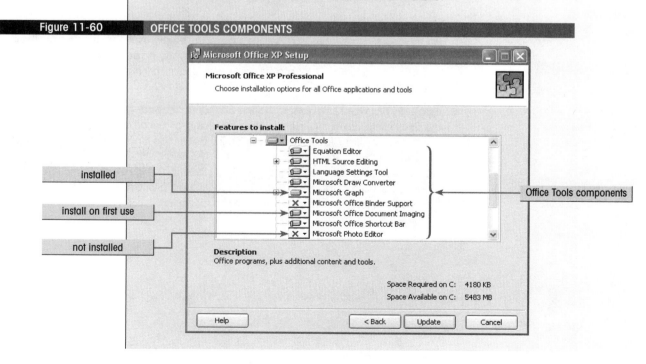

installed

install on first use

not installed

Office Tools components

4. Click the **Microsoft Photo Editor** button. As shown in Figure 11-61, Microsoft Office XP Setup displays a menu that allows you to choose whether you want to install that component and, if so, how you want to install it. You can install the component on your hard disk (Run from My Computer), install the feature and all its components on your hard disk (Run all from My Computer); choose to install the component on First Use–in other words, when first needed (Installed on First Use); or not install the component by making it Not Available (Not Available).

| Figure 11-61 | OPTIONS FOR INSTALLING MICROSOFT PHOTO EDITOR |

options for installing Microsoft Photo Editor

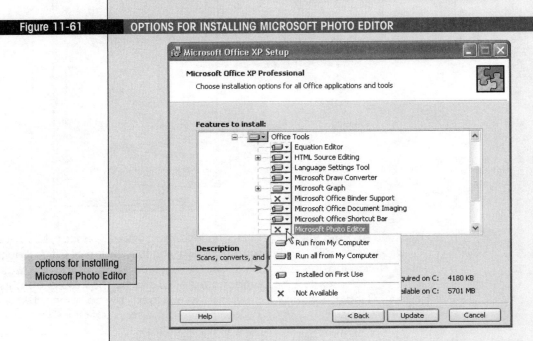

If disk space is limited on your computer, or if you prefer to keep as much of your hard disk as free as possible, you can review these features and their components to determine the ones you actually need. Then only install the ones that you will be using and save disk space by not installing components you'll never use.

5. If you do not want to change the installation option for Microsoft Photo Editor, press the **Esc** key to close the menu, examine each of the other options, change the installation options for components you want to use and for those you do not want to use, and then click the **Update** button. The Microsoft Office XP Professional window opens to show the progress of the installation. See Figure 11-62. After the installation is complete, the Microsoft Office XP dialog box opens to verify that the installation of this software product was successful.

| Figure 11-62 | OFFICE CURRENTLY BEING UPDATED |

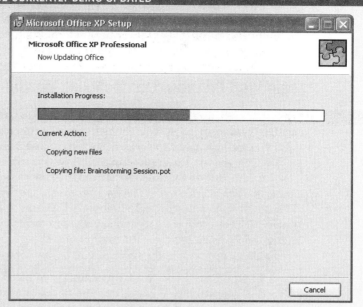

6. Click the **OK** button to close the Microsoft Office XP Professional dialog box, or if you did not make and apply any changes in the last step, click the **Cancel** button, click the **Yes** button in the Office XP Setup dialog box to verify that you want to cancel Office Setup, click the **OK** button in the next Office XP Setup dialog box, and then close the window onto the Office CD.

REFERENCE WINDOW **RW**

Adding or Removing Microsoft Office Components

■ Insert your Microsoft Office CD into your DVD or CD drive, close that drive, and if the Setup program does not automatically open, open a window onto the CD drive (if necessary), and then click Setup.exe.
■ After the Microsoft Office XP Setup dialog box opens, and displays Maintenance Mode options, make sure the Add or Remove Features option button is selected, and then click the Next button.
■ Click the expand view box to the left of one of the main Office components categories.
■ Click the drop-down menu button next to the component you want to add or remove, and then choose Run from My Computer to install the component on your computer, Run all from My Computer to install the feature and all its components on your hard disk, Installed on First Use to install the component on First Use—in other words, when first needed, or Not Available to uninstall the component.
■ Click the Update button.
■ After Microsoft Office XP Setup displays a Microsoft Office XP Professional dialog box verifying that the installation of this software product was successful, click the OK button to close the Microsoft Office XP Professional dialog box.

You have successfully updated the installation of a Win32 application. If your computer comes with installed software, or if you or someone else opted for a standard, typical, or default installation of a software product on your computer, you might want to open the Setup program for that software product, examine the list of installed and uninstalled components, and change your setup so that you have the tools you need for your work.

Using the Program Compatibility Wizard

In a few rare instances, Takao has discovered that the Program Compatibility Wizard has enabled him to adapt an older, but still useful, program for use with Windows XP. He encourages you to learn about this wizard so you can use it to troubleshoot installation problems.

You can use the Program Compatibility Wizard, a new Windows XP feature, to test and resolve compatibility problems that you are experiencing with an older program that worked under earlier versions of Windows. You can specify that Windows XP use Windows 95, Windows 98, Windows Me, Windows NT Workstation 4.0, or Windows 2000 compatibility mode for that program. If you have a video display problem with a program, you can also adjust video display settings for that program.

To check program compatibility, you follow these steps:

1. **Open the Program Compatibility Wizard**. After you choose Program Compatibility Wizard from the Accessories menu on the All Programs menu, Windows XP opens the Program Compatibility Wizard in the Help and Support Center. See Figure 11-63. The introduction notes that if you are experiencing problems with a program that worked correctly with an earlier version of Windows, the Program Compatibility Wizard helps you select and test compatibility settings so that the program works properly under Windows XP. The Caution emphasizes that you should not use this wizard for older antivirus software, backup programs, and system utilities. The same precaution applies to disk utilities, firewall software, and software for burning CDs.

Figure 11-63	USING THE PROGRAM COMPATIBILITY WIZARD

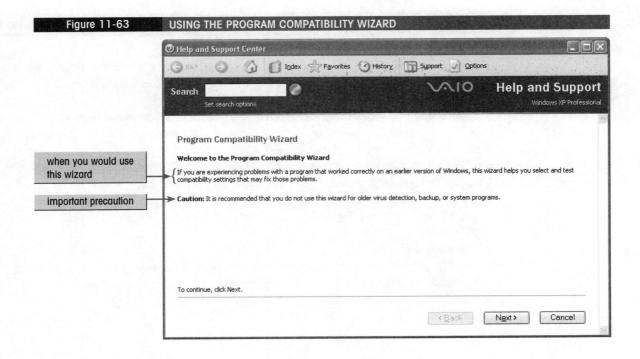

2. **Locate the program for which you want to specify compatibility settings**. In the next step, you specify the location of the program that does not function properly under Windows XP. See Figure 11-64. You can choose the program from a list of programs that the wizard then compiles, specify that it use a program in your CD drive, or locate the program manually. If you choose the last option, you can browse for that program.

Figure 11-64	CHOOSE THE WAY IN WHICH YOU WANT TO LOCATE THE PROGRAM

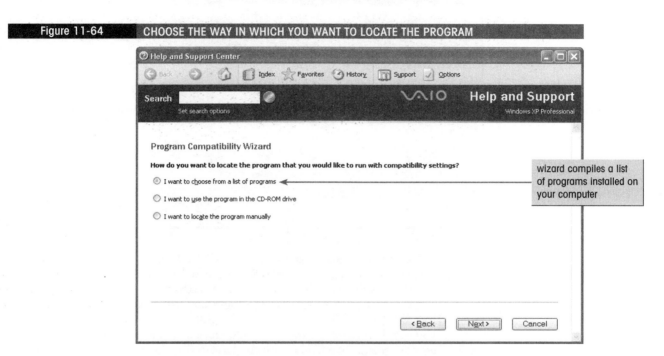

3. **Select a compatibility mode for the program**. After you specify the location and select the program, you choose the operating system recommended for this program, or the operating system under which this program functioned properly. See Figure 11-65. For this example, the Program Compatibility Wizard tests a program named Spider, a hidden URL inspector. Spider worked under Windows 2000, but support with Windows XP is unknown, so Microsoft Windows 2000 compatibility mode was selected.

Figure 11-65   SELECTING THE COMPATIBILITY MODE

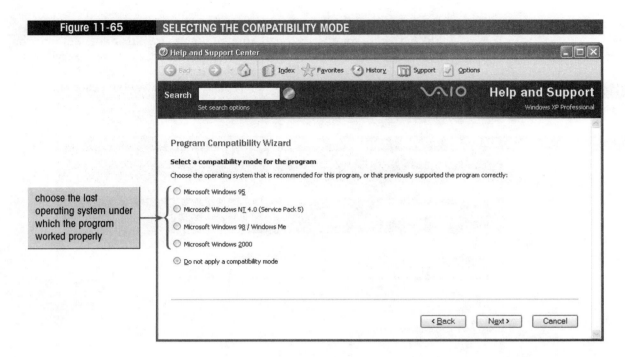

choose the last operating system under which the program worked properly

4. **Select display settings for the program**. In the next step, the wizard asks you to select the settings recommended for the program, or settings that worked previously with the program under an earlier version of Windows. See Figure 11-66. You can choose the setting for 256 colors and 640 by 480 screen resolution, and turn off the use of visual themes. If this program causes a video display problem, you should turn off the use of visual themes first, and see if that simple change corrects the problem. The note emphasizes that these options apply mainly to games and educational programs.

Figure 11-66   SPECIFYING DISPLAY SETTINGS FOR A PROGRAM

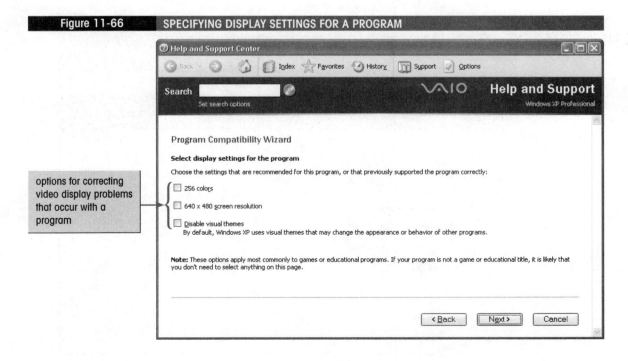

options for correcting video display problems that occur with a program

5. **Test your compatibility settings**. The Program Compatibility Wizard now summarizes your compatibility settings, and explains how to test these settings with the program you specified earlier. See Figure 11-67.

| Figure 11-67 | SUMMARY OF COMPATIBILITY SETTINGS |

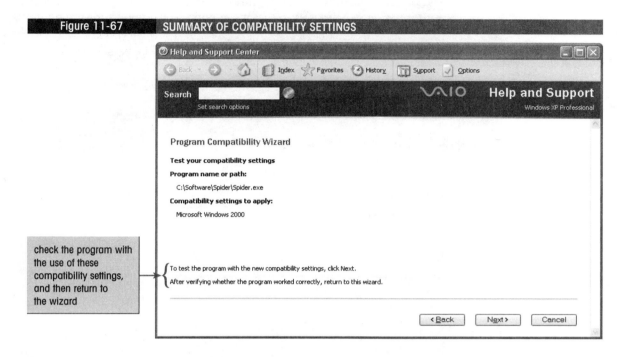

check the program with the use of these compatibility settings, and then return to the wizard

6. **Evaluate the results of testing compatibility settings**. The Program Compatibility Wizard opens the program so that you can test the program. Then it asks you if the program works correctly. See Figure 11-68. If so, you can set this program so that it always uses the compatibility settings you selected. If not, you can try other compatibility settings.

| Figure 11-68 | DID THE PROGRAM WORK WITH THE COMPATIBILITY SETTINGS? |

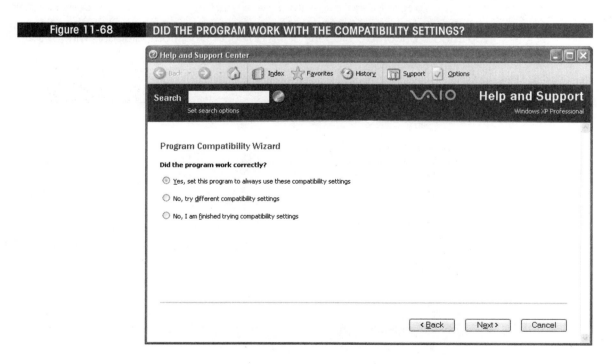

7. **Send program compatibility data to Microsoft**. Next, the Program Compatibility Wizard notes that it has created temporary files that contain information about the compatibility settings you tested, and whether those settings corrected the problem. See Figure 11-69. You have the option of sending the information to Microsoft so that it can improve its support for programs.

| Figure 11-69 | OPTION FOR SENDING MICROSOFT THE PROGRAM COMPATIBILITY DATA |

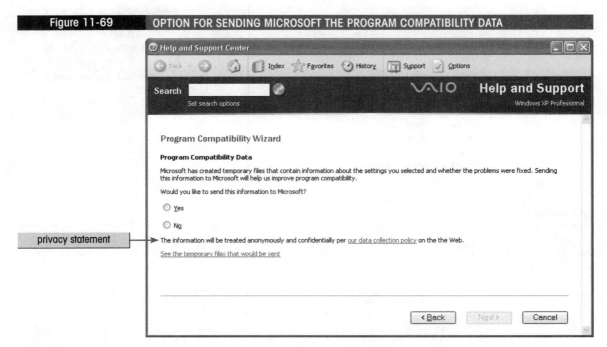

privacy statement

POWER USERS TIP You can use an alternate approach to specify compatibility settings. If you open the folder that contains the program for which you want to specify compatibility settings, right-click the program file, and then choose Properties, a Properties dialog box opens for that program. If you select the Compatibility property sheet, you can specify compatibility mode and display settings. See Figure 11-70. The settings you choose become a property of this object on your computer, and Windows XP uses these settings when you open the program.

Figure 11-70 | SETTING COMPATIBILITY OPTIONS FOR A PROGRAM

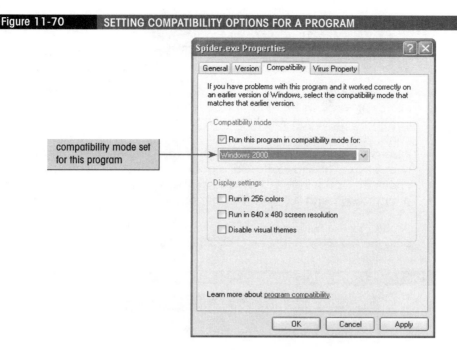

compatibility mode set
for this program

You use the Program Compatibility Wizard if a program indicates that it requires a certain version of Windows, if it does not open under Windows XP, if it produces an error when you attempt to open the program, or if it opens, but does not operate properly.

If the Program Compatibility Wizard does not correct the problem, check the Web site of the manufacturer of the software to determine if there is an update that enables the program to work properly under Windows XP, check the Windows Update Web site (covered later in the tutorial) for an update to the program, or upgrade to a program that does work under Windows XP.

Installing a Windows XP Component

Windows XP includes a Fax Services component that is not installed during Windows Setup; if you need to use this component, you must use the Windows Components Wizard to install it from your Windows XP CD. You can use the Fax services component to send and receive faxes, monitor fax activity, and access archived faxes. You can send and receive faxes using a fax device attached to your local computer, or you can use a remote fax device on a network.

In the next set of steps, you examine the process for installing a Windows XP component. If you are working in a computer lab, you need permission to install Windows XP components. If you are not allowed to make changes to the installed software on computers in your lab, read the following steps and examine the figures, but do not keystroke the steps. If you are working on your own computer, and if Fax Services is already installed, read, but do not keystroke the following steps.

Before you can install a Windows XP component, you must log on as Administrator or use a logon that has Administrator privileges. You also need a copy of the Windows XP CD.

Takao asks you to install Fax Services on your computer system so that you can send and receive faxes with this Windows XP component.

To install the Fax Services component:

1. If necessary, log on your computer as Administrator or log on under an account with Administrator privileges.

2. Insert your Windows XP CD in a DVD or CD drive, and after the Welcome to Microsoft Windows XP window opens, click the **Install optional Windows components** button. After Windows XP Setup searches for installed components, you see a list of Windows XP components in the Windows Components Wizard dialog box. See Figure 11-71. A component with a check mark in the check box is already installed, a component without a check mark in its check box is not installed, and a component with a check mark against a gray background is a category of components, some of which are installed.

   TROUBLE? If the Setup program does not open automatically, open a window onto the CD drive, and then click Setup.exe.

Figure 11-71	WINDOWS COMPONENTS WIZARD

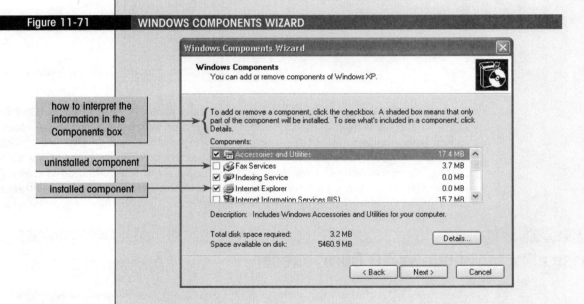

3. If Fax Services is not installed on your computer, and if you want to install the Fax Services component, click the **Fax Services** check box to add a check mark in this check box, and then click the **Next** button. The Windows Components Wizard dialog box displays information about the status of copying and configuring this Windows XP component. See Figure 11-72. Then the Windows Components Wizard verifies that you have successfully installed the Windows XP component.

Figure 11-72   INSTALLING AND CONFIGURING FAX SERVICES

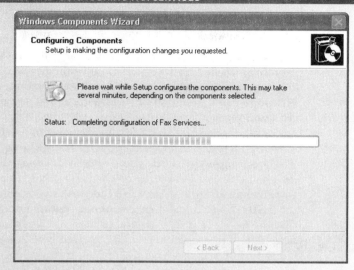

4. Click the **Finish** button, and then close the Welcome to Microsoft Windows XP window.

5. Click the **Start** button, point to **All Programs**, point to **Accessories**, point to **Communications**, and then point to **Fax**. The Fax menu includes the Fax Console, Fax Cover Page Editor, and Send a Fax options. See Figure 11-73. The Fax Console displays incoming and outgoing faxes so that you can view and manage faxes, while the Fax Cover Page Editor allows you to create and edit cover pages used with faxes. You have just successfully installed a Windows XP component.

Figure 11-73   FAX MENU

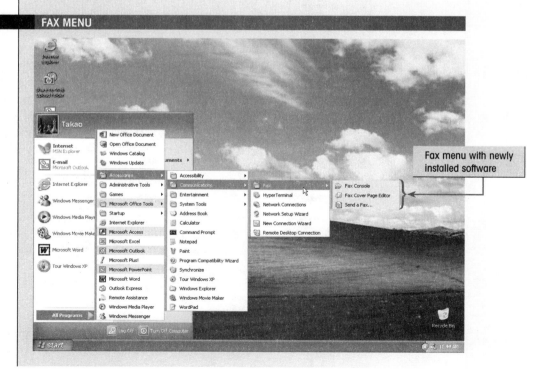

Fax menu with newly installed software

6. Click the **Start** button to close the Start menu.

If you choose Fax Console from the Fax menu, the Fax Configuration Wizard steps you through the process for configuring your computer to send and receive faxes. You are first prompted for Sender Information, including your name, fax number, e-mail address, title, company, office location, department, home phone, work phone, address, and billing code. Next, the Fax Configuration Wizard prompts you to select the device you want to use to send and receive faxes (for example, your modem). You can enable the Send and Receive options, and you can specify a manual answer or an automatic answer after a certain number of rings. Then the wizard asks for your Transmitting Subscriber Identification (TSID). The TSID is transmitted when you send a fax, and usually consists of a fax number and a business name that is limited to 20 characters. Next, you are asked for the Called Subscriber Identification (CSID). The CSID identifies your computer to a fax sender, and is similar to the TSID. The wizard then asks about routing options for incoming faxes. You can specify that the fax be sent to a specific printer and also that a copy be stored in a folder that you designate. The wizard notes that received faxes are stored in the Inbox archive of the Fax Console, but you also have the option of storing an additional copy in a folder. That completes the Fax Configuration Wizard. The Fax Console, shown in Figure 11-74, is similar to Microsoft Outlook or Outlook Express. From the File menu or toolbar, you can send, receive, view, print, save, mail, and import faxes, or pause, resume, restart, and delete a fax.

Figure 11-74	FAX CONSOLE

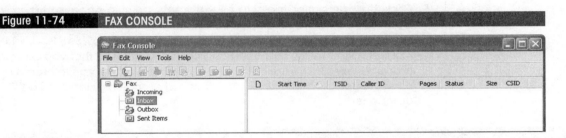

The Send Fax option on the Fax menu starts the Send Fax Wizard, which steps you through the process of sending a fax. You first specify information about the recipient of the fax, including the name of the individual (either by entering the name, or by picking the name out of your Address Book), their location, and their fax number. You can also specify multiple recipients. Then the wizard helps you prepare the cover page. You can select a cover page template, and then enter a subject line and a note. Next, you specify the schedule for the fax (send now, send when discount rates apply, or specify a specific time) and set the fax priority. In the last step, you can preview your fax before you send it.

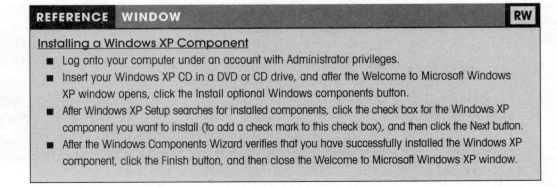

REFERENCE WINDOW   RW

Installing a Windows XP Component

- Log onto your computer under an account with Administrator privileges.
- Insert your Windows XP CD in a DVD or CD drive, and after the Welcome to Microsoft Windows XP window opens, click the Install optional Windows components button.
- After Windows XP Setup searches for installed components, click the check box for the Windows XP component you want to install (to add a check mark to this check box), and then click the Next button.
- After the Windows Components Wizard verifies that you have successfully installed the Windows XP component, click the Finish button, and then close the Welcome to Microsoft Windows XP window.

To install Windows XP components, you can also open the Control Panel, select Add or Remove Programs, and then click the Add/Remove Windows Components button.

Some of the components listed in the Windows Components list box represent categories of related components. When you select a component, such as Accessories and Utilities, by clicking the component label (not the component check box), you can then click the Details button to view a list of the components within that category. You might, for example, want to only install certain components instead of all components, or you might want to find out what other components are available that are not installed. If you click the check box for that component category, you are selecting all components within that category automatically. You might then end up installing more components than you need, wasting valuable disk storage space.

You should examine each category of Windows XP components to determine whether you need to install any additional components that might prove useful to you, and to also identify components that you do not need and do not use, so that you can uninstall them and free up storage space on your hard disk.

Uninstalling a Windows XP Component

When employees report that they are running low on hard disk storage space, Takao recommends that the employees examine which Windows XP components are installed on their computer, and then remove any components that they do not need or do not use. Because you have not used the Fax Services component yet, Takao recommends you uninstall this component so that you are familiar with this process. You can then reinstall it later.

In the next set of steps, you uninstall the Fax Services that you just installed. If you want to keep Fax Services on your computer, examine the figures and read, but do not keystroke the following steps so that you are familiar with how to uninstall a Windows XP component.

To uninstall Fax Services:

1. If necessary, log onto your computer as Administrator or log on with an account that has Administrator privileges

2. From the Start menu, click **Control Panel**, click the **Add or Remove Programs** icon, and after the Add or Remove Programs window opens, click the **Add/Remove Windows Components** button.

3. In the Windows Components Wizard dialog box, click the **Fax Services** check box to remove the check mark, and then click the **Next** button. You see the same Windows Components Wizard dialog box that you saw earlier when you installed Fax Services (one that displays the progress of removing this component), and then you see another Windows Components Wizard dialog box that indicates that you have successfully uninstalled the component.

4. Click the **Finish** button to close the Windows Components Wizard dialog box, and if prompted to restart your computer so that the new settings take effect, click the **No** button to update your computer at the next boot.

5. Close the Add or Remove Programs window, and then close Control Panel.

You have just successfully uninstalled a Windows XP component.

Recall that you might need to select a component, such as Accessories and Utilities, by clicking the component label (not the component check box), and then clicking the Details button to view a list of the components within that category so that you can select just those components you want to uninstall. Clicking the check box for that component category indicates that you want to remove all components within that category, and you might end up uninstalling components that you need.

When installing and uninstalling Accessories, keep in mind that you only need to select the component or components you want to install or uninstall. You do not need to change the status of any of the other installed components. You can also install and uninstall several components at the same time, in a single operation.

Using **Windows Update**

The Windows Update Wizard is a tool that updates software on your computer using the Microsoft Windows Update Web site. The wizard examines your computer system, lists software updates for your system, and then installs the updates you select. Some updates are critical, such as security updates, and others are optional.

You have to log on your computer under an account with Administrator privileges to use Windows Update. If you are working in a computer lab, you probably cannot use the Windows Update Wizard, because the computer's configuration would be altered as system files are updated. If your lab does not permit you to use Windows Update, read the following steps and examine the figures, but do not keystroke the steps. If you are working in a corporate environment, you might not be able to use the Windows Update Wizard, because different users could implement the use of this tool in different ways; this would complicate a company's ability to provide technical support for their employees. For this reason, you might not find a Windows Update option on the All Programs menu if you are working on a computer in a college lab or on your work computer. Likewise, if you do not want to make any changes to your computer, read, but do not keystroke, the following steps.

Because Microsoft frequently updates its Web sites and changes its Web pages, you might need to adapt the instructions in the following steps. The process and logic, however, are the same.

Takao relies on Microsoft's Windows Update Web site to upgrade and maintain his computer system. He recommends that you also use the Windows Update Wizard to check your computer for updates.

To open Windows Update:

1. If necessary, log onto your computer under an account with Administrator privileges, and then connect to your ISP.

2. From the Start menu, point to **All programs**, and then click **Windows Update**. On the Microsoft Windows Update Web page, you can use the Scan for updates button to check your computer for needed updates, and then display a list of those updates so that you can pick which ones you want to install. See Figure 11-75. In the Windows Update frame, you can pick updates to install, you can review and install updates, you can view your installation history, you can personalize Windows Update, you can view information about Windows Update, and you can view support information.

Figure 11-75	WINDOWS UPDATE WEB SITE

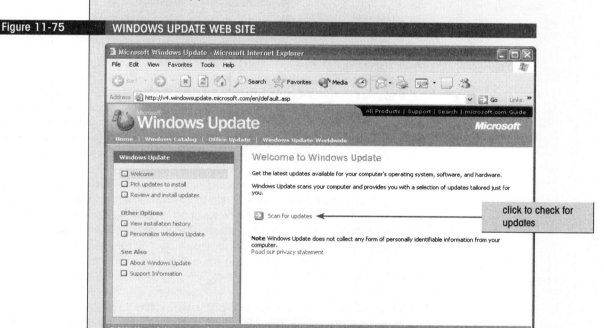

3. Click the **Scan for updates** button or link. On the computer used for this figure, which has deliberately not been updated since installing Windows XP, Windows Update locates four critical updates. See Figure 11-76. Windows Update also notes that it found other updates. Under Windows Update, the updates are organized into three categories—critical updates, Windows XP updates, and driver updates. Your results will differ.

| Figure 11-76 | RESULTS OF WINDOWS UPDATE CHECKING A COMPUTER |

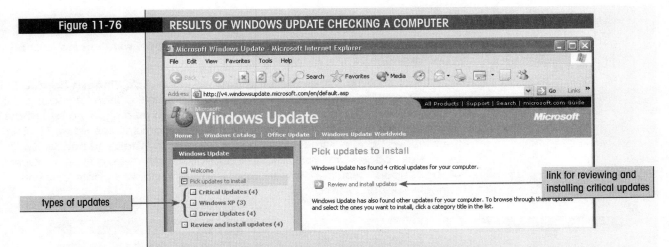

types of updates

link for reviewing and installing critical updates

4. If Windows Update identified critical updates for your computer, click the **Review and install updates** button or link, and then maximize the Internet Explorer window. On the computer used for this figure, Windows Update lists four Security Updates (three of which are visible). See Figure 11-77. Two updates apply to Internet Explorer, and the other two apply to Windows XP. Briefly, these security updates correct problems that would allow an attacker to run code on this computer, launch a denial of service (DoS) attack, and read files on this computer. A **denial of service (DoS)** is a type of attack that exploits a weakness in the software at the Web site and denies users access to one or more Web site services, or that sends more traffic to the Web site than the site can handle. You can click the "Read more" link for each update if you want more information on that update before installing it. In this example, the total download size is 3.8 MB, and the estimated time for the downloads is 19 minutes. The Install Now button installs all the updates. You can use the Remove button to eliminate an update from this list if you don't want to download and install it on your computer. Your list of options will vary, since they depend on what updates are available at the time you use Windows Update and also on what updates you've previously downloaded and installed; however, the preceding examples give you an idea of what types of updates to expect from Windows Update.

Figure 11-77 | CRITICAL SECURITY UPDATES

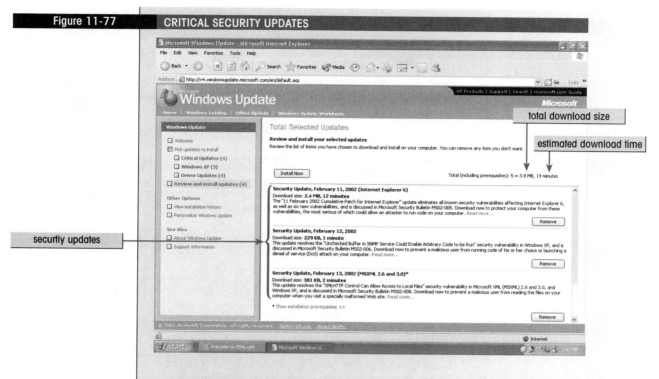

securtiy updates

total download size

estimated download time

5. *Read this step before you choose an action:* If you want to download and install the updates identified for your computer, click the **Install Now** button. If you want to download and install only certain updates, click the **Remove** button for those updates you do *not* want to install, and then click the **Install Now** button. If you do not want to install any updates, read the remainder of this step and the next step. After you click the Install Now button, the Microsoft Windows Update - - Web Page Dialog box lists the updates, asks you to read the terms of the license agreement for these updates, and then choose the Accept or Don't Accept button. See Figure 11-78. To install these updates, you have to accept the license agreement. If you choose "Don't Accept," the updates are not installed.

Figure 11-78 | LICENSE AGREEMENT FOR CRITICAL UPDATES

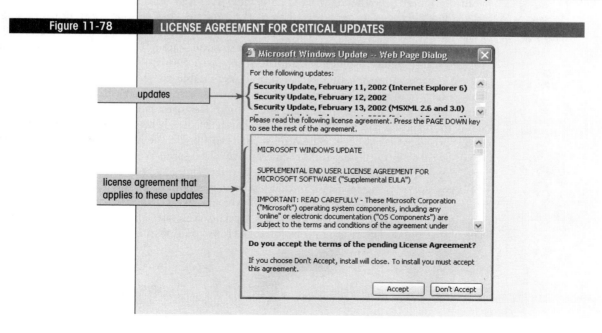

updates

license agreement that applies to these updates

6. If you accept the license agreement and want to install the updates, click the **Accept** button; otherwise, if you do not accept the license agreement, click the **Don't Accept** button. If you accept the license agreement, the Windows Update - - Web Page Dialog box shows you the progress of the download and the install. See Figure 11-79. Then a Microsoft Internet Explorer dialog box opens, informing you that you must restart your computer to finish installing the updates. If you want to restart later, or close other programs before restarting, you can click the Cancel button, and then restart your computer manually.

| Figure 11-79 | STATUS OF DOWNLOADING UPDATES |

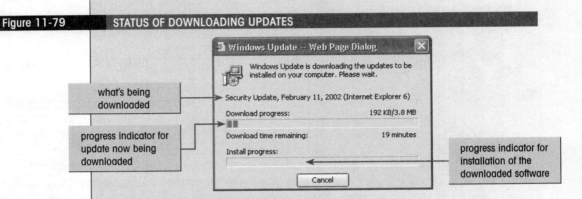

7. Click the **OK** button, wait for your computer to reboot, and then log back on under an account with Administrator privileges.

If Windows Update identified other updates for your system, you can reconnect to your ISP, examine those updates, decide whether to download and install them, and then install any additional updates using the same process that you completed in the preceding steps. On the computer used for the previous steps, there were three Windows XP updates: Euro Conversion Tool, Windows Messenger 4.6 (which allows you to make a phone call from your computer to a phone almost anywhere in the world for a very low rate using the service provider you choose), and an update that fixes a computer failure problem that occurs when your computer is connected to a UPS device. The four driver updates included drivers for the video display, the network adapter, the modem, and sound. After downloading and installing all these updates on the computer used for these figures, problems occurred with the device drivers for the video display, modem, and sound. The image on the monitor was distorted, the video display's resolution dropped to 640 by 480 (resulting in a low-quality image on the monitor), Internet Explorer was unable to access Windows Update or this computer's mail server after the modem connected to this user's ISP, and the sound level from the speakers dropped dramatically. System Restore restored the computer to its state prior to installing the updates, and immediately resolved the modem, sound, and all of the video problems except one. The monitor controls had to be used to remove the screen distortion. Internet Explorer could then connect to the same Web sites without problems, and the sound level from the speakers returned to its original state.

If you are working on a system that has been customized by the manufacturer, check that manufacturer's Web site first for device driver updates. Also, it is a good idea to download one update at a time from the Windows Update Web site, and then use your computer to verify that the update caused no problems before you download and install another update.

REFERENCE WINDOW   **RW**

Using Windows Update

- If necessary, log onto your computer under an account with Administrator privileges, and then connect to your ISP.
- From the Start menu, point to All programs, and then click Windows Update.
- On the Microsoft Windows Update Web page, click the "Scan for updates" button or link.
- If Windows Update identifies updates for your computer, click the Review and install updates button or link, examine the information on the proposed updates, and, if necessary, click the "Read more" link for each update if you want more information on that update before installing it.
- If you want to download and install the updates identified for your computer, click the Install Now button. If you want to download and install only certain updates, click the Remove button for those updates you do not want to install, or click the Add button for those updates that you do want to download and install, and then click the Install Now button.
- In the Microsoft Windows Update -- Web Page dialog box that lists the updates, read the terms of the license agreement for these updates, and then click the Accept button if you want to install the updates and if you accept the license agreement, or if you do not accept the license agreement, click the Don't Accept button.
- After the updates are downloaded and installed, click the OK button in the next Microsoft Windows Update -- Web Page dialog box when informed that you must restart your computer to complete the installation of the updates. If the updates do not require a reboot and if you are finished downloading and installing updates, close Internet Explorer, and then disconnect from your ISP.

Because software technology changes so rapidly and security problems that require updates are constantly being discovered, you should use the Windows Update feature periodically to check and update your computer.

Checking Your Installation History

Takao asks you to take a moment to use Windows Update to display and review a history of updates made to your computer.

To view your installation history:

1. If necessary, log onto your computer under an account with Administrator privileges, and then connect to your ISP.

2. From the Start menu, point to **All programs**, click **Windows Update**, and then maximize the Internet Explorer window.

3. Under Windows Update and Other Options, click **View installation history**. Windows Update shows you a history of updates for your computer system. See Figure 11-80. The Installation History lists the dates and times for each component that you installed, and whether the installation succeeded or failed.

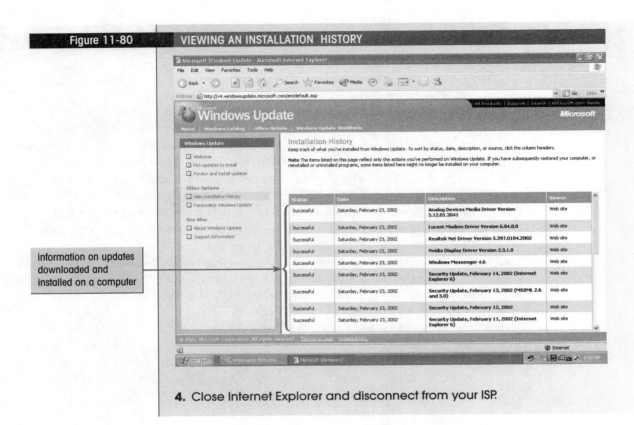

Figure 11-80   VIEWING AN INSTALLATION HISTORY

information on updates
downloaded and
installed on a computer

4. Close Internet Explorer and disconnect from your ISP.

You might need to check this installation history later if you have any questions about what you have installed on your computer.

Restoring Your Computer

If you want to restore your computer or a lab computer to its original state before you started the tutorial, complete the following steps.

To restore your computer's display settings:

1. If your computer was originally set for the Windows Classic style, right-click the **desktop**, click **Properties** on the shortcut menu, and after Windows XP opens the Display Properties dialog box, click the **Theme** list box arrow on the Themes property sheet, click **Windows Classic**, and then click the **OK** button.

2. To switch to the Windows Classic Start menu style, right-click the **Start** button, click **Properties** on the shortcut menu, and after Windows XP opens the Taskbar and Start Menu Properties dialog box, click the **Classic Start menu** option button on the Start Menu property sheet, and then click the **OK** button.

3. To change Windows classic folders view, click the **Start** button, point to **Settings**, click **Control Panel**, and after Windows XP opens the Control Panel window, click **Tools** on the menu bar, click **Folder Options**, and after Windows XP opens the Folder Options dialog box, click the **Use Windows classic folders** option button, and click the **Double-click to open an item** option button under "Click items as follows".

4. Click the **View** tab in the Folder Options dialog box. If necessary, restore the original settings for the "Display the full path in the address bar" check box, the "Do not show hidden files and folders" option, and the "Hide extensions for known file types" check box.

5. Click the **OK** button to close the Folder Options dialog box and restore your original settings, and then close the Control Panel folder window.

You and Takao have successfully upgraded to Windows XP, updated Microsoft Office on your computers, installed additional Windows XP components, and downloaded and installed updates using Windows Update. Now you are ready to turn your efforts to assisting your coworkers in upgrading the software on their computer systems.

REVIEW ASSIGNMENTS

Takao wants you to upgrade a computer with Windows 98 to Windows XP Professional, install Windows XP Professional components, and then download and install a graphics application from the Web.

Read each step completely before you perform it so that you know what is expected and so that you do not accidentally omit or skip any part of the step. Some of the optional steps require that you use your Windows XP CD or Microsoft Office CD.

As you complete each step in these Review Assignments, record your answers to questions so that you can submit them to your instructor. Use a word-processing application such as Word or WordPad to prepare and then print your answers to these questions. Also, if you change any settings on the computer you are using, note the original settings so that you can restore them later.

1. Log on your computer under an account with Administrator privileges.

2. Can Takao upgrade a computer that is currently running Windows 98 to Windows XP Professional? If so, what basic requirements would the system need to meet? What tool(s) could he use to check his computer's hardware and software for compatibility before attempting an upgrade?

3. Assuming he can install Windows XP Professional on this computer, outline the steps that Takao should take prior to installing Windows XP Professional. Include any steps Takao should take to improve the chances of a successful installation or upgrade and, if necessary, to restore the computer to its original state.

4. What does Takao need to assemble and have on hand before installing Windows XP Professional?

5. Can Takao create a dual-boot configuration with Windows 98 and Windows XP Professional on this computer? If so, explain what factors Takao should take into account, identify what changes he should make to this computer, and explain how he would install these two operating systems.

6. Assume Takao upgraded the system to Windows XP Professional, and now wants to find out if there are any updates for Windows XP Professional. Open Windows Update and connect to Microsoft's Windows Update Web site. Are there any additional updates that are not installed on your computer that you might want to install? If so, which ones? If

you are logged on your own computer, and want to download and install those updates, do so. If you are working in a computer lab, do not attempt to download and install any updates.

7. If you have used Windows Update previously, view and then print a copy of the installation history. If you are unsure whether the computer you are using has been updated with Windows Update, open Windows Update, and check the installation history.

Explore ▸ 8. *Optional*: Insert your Windows XP CD into a DVD or CD drive, and in the Welcome to Microsoft Windows XP window, select the option for installing optional Windows components. After the Windows Components Wizard lists the available Windows Components, make sure Accessories and Utilities is selected in the Components box, and then click the Details button. How much storage space on your computer does the Accessories subcomponent use? How much storage space does the Games subcomponent use? Make sure Accessories is selected in the Accessories and Utilities dialog box, and then click the Details button. Examine the list of Subcomponents of Accessories. Are there any accessories that you do not use and could remove to free up storage space on your computer? If so, list their names and how much space you would gain. If you want to remove, or install, accessories on your computer, click the OK button; otherwise, click the Cancel button to close the Accessories dialog box. If you are working in a computer lab, do not attempt to uninstall any Windows XP components on a lab computer. Select Games in the Accessories and Utilities dialog box, and then click the Details button. Are there any games that you do not use, and could remove to free up storage space on your computer? If so, list their names, and how much space you would gain. If you want to remove, or install, games on your computer, click the OK button; otherwise, click the Cancel button to close the Games dialog box. If you want to install or remove any Windows XP components, click the OK button to close the Accessories dialog box and then the Windows Components Wizard dialog box; otherwise, click the Cancel button to close the Accessories and Utilities dialog box and then the Windows Components Wizard dialog box without making any changes to your computer. Close the Welcome to Microsoft Windows XP window.

Explore ▸ 9. *Optional*: To examine the installed software on your computer, make sure you are logged on with Administrator privileges, open Add or Remove Programs in the Control Panel, and click the Change or Remove Programs button (if necessary). What types of applications does Windows XP list in the Add or Remove Programs window—Win32, Win16, or DOS applications? Which applications do you frequently use? Choose the option to sort the currently installed programs by size. List the five applications that require the most space on your hard disk and list their sizes. Are there any software products that you do not need and might want to remove from your computer? If so, list the names of those software products and the amount of space you would gain by removing them.

Explore ▸ 10. *Optional*: If Microsoft Office is installed on your computer, insert your Microsoft Office CD in a DVD or CD drive. If Windows XP does not open a Microsoft Office Setup dialog box, open a window onto your Office CD, and then click Setup.exe. In the Microsoft Office Setup dialog box, choose the option for adding or removing features or components, and then go to the next step. Expand the category for the Office component that you use the most (such as Microsoft Word or Microsoft Excel). What version of Microsoft Office do you have? Which Office application did you select? Which components under that Office application are already installed? Which components would be installed on first use? Which components under this Office application include subcomponents, some of which are installed, set to be installed on first use, or are not installed? Which components are not installed? Which components are you likely not to use and therefore would keep as installed on first use, or not installed at all? If you are working on your own computer, and want to update your Office installation, click the Update button; otherwise, if you want to exit without making any changes, click the Cancel button, and then close the Office window.

Explore 11. If Takao wants to transfer settings and files for an employee from a slightly older computer with Windows XP Professional to a new computer also with Windows XP Professional, what is the easiest way to accomplish this task? Explain how he would accomplish this task.

12. If there are SolarWinds employees who need to work with older DOS or Win16 programs that might not be compatible with Windows XP Professional, is there anything that Takao can do so that these employees can use these older programs? If so, explain.

CASE PROBLEMS

Case 1. Documenting Your Computer Before you make any further changes to your computer, you decide it's time to document how your system is currently used. Then, you will be in a better position to decide whether to download and install additional software and updates, and you will also have a better idea of how your system might perform afterwards.

As you complete each step in this case, record your answers to questions so that you can submit them to your instructor. Use a word-processing application such as Word or WordPad to prepare and then print your answers to these questions. Also, if you change any settings on the computer you are using, note what the original settings are so that you can restore them later.

1. What version of Windows are you using on your computer? List not only the popular name, but also the version number.

2. What type of processor does your computer use, and what is the operating speed of your processor?

3. How much RAM is installed on your computer?

4. Judging from the size of the paging file, how much virtual memory does Windows XP set aside after you start your computer?

5. What is the storage capacity of your hard disk(s)? If you have multiple drives, identify each drive by name and list each drive's storage capacity. How much storage space is used on each drive? How much storage space is available on each drive?

6. What file system is used on each drive?

7. How much storage space could you reclaim from drive C by removing unneeded files, such as downloaded program files, temporary Internet files, offline Web pages, and temporary files?

8. On what drive is Windows XP installed? What is the name of the folder with the installed version of Windows XP?

Explore 9. What is the size of your Windows folder, and how much storage space does it use?

Explore 10. What is the size of the Program Files folder and its contents, and how much storage space does it use?

Explore 11. If Microsoft Office is installed on your computer, what is the size and storage space used by the program and supporting files in the Microsoft Office folder?

12. Based on the information you have collected, and on your perception of your computer's performance, is there any one factor or multiple factors that limit its overall performance? If so, what are they? Are there any changes you can make to improve the performance of

your computer? Do you think that it would be a good idea to purchase a newer, higher-performance computer, or would you upgrade your current computer? If you decided to upgrade it, what would you change?

Case 2. Preparing for a Windows XP Professional Upgrade at McKenzie Community College After a thorough evaluation of current operating system technologies, Julie Evans, the Director of Computing Services at McKenzie Community College in North Dakota, has decided to upgrade as many computers as possible on campus to Windows XP Professional. Since the college has a mix of computer systems—some older, some newer—she asks you to prepare a list of which computers can and cannot be upgraded to Windows XP Professional. She also asks her assistant to evaluate the installed copy of Windows XP Professional on your computer.

As you complete each step in this case, record your answers to questions so that you can submit them to your instructor. Use a word-processing application such as Word or WordPad to prepare and then print your answers to these questions. Also, if you change any settings on the computer you are using, note the original settings so that you can restore them later.

1. What factors should you use in evaluating whether a computer can support Windows XP Professional?

Explore 2. Several departments on campus use Intel Pentiums that operate at 90 MHz, 233 MHz, and 266 MHz. Can you install and use Windows XP on these computers? If so, which ones? Another department uses Intel Pentium IIs that operate at 266 MHz or faster, and that have 64 MB or 128 MB of RAM. Can these systems be upgraded to support Windows XP? If so, what would need to be done to upgrade them, and is it worth it in your opinion?

3. What hardware, software, and compatibility issues must you evaluate in determining which systems to upgrade?

4. For those computers that support an upgrade to Windows XP Professional, prepare a checklist of the steps (in the order that you would perform them) for employees to follow before upgrading their computers to Windows XP Professional, and before upgrading Win16 applications to Win32 applications.

Case 3. Updating Microsoft Office at Prescott Associates Prescott Associates is a Web marketing research firm that works with clients around the world. Its employees rely on the most recent version of Microsoft Office and its extensive Web support to meet the needs of its clients. Benjy Lukas, an employee who works in technical support, assists other staff members with software upgrades and updates. Since Microsoft has recently introduced several important updates for Microsoft Office, he wants you to download and install these updates on your computer, and evaluate them before you assist other employees with updates.

This case problem requires that Microsoft Office is installed on your computer. You must also log on under an account with Administrator privileges.

As you complete each step in this case, record your answers to questions so that you can submit them to your instructor. Use a word-processing application such as Word or WordPad to prepare and then print your answers to these questions. Also, if you change any settings on the computer you are using, note the original settings so that you can restore them later.

Explore 1. Before you download and install an update for Microsoft Office, what steps should you take to prepare your computer for the update? What precautions might you also take to restore your computer if a problem develops?

2. Open Microsoft Word, click Help on the menu bar, and then click About Microsoft Word. What version of Microsoft Office is installed on your computer? Close this dialog box.

Explore

3. If necessary, connect to your ISP, open Windows Update, and at the Microsoft Windows Update Web site, select the Office Update link. At the Microsoft Office Update Web site, select the option for automatically detecting the updates your computer needs. What important updates are available for your version of Office? Which updates would benefit you?

Explore

4. If there is a Service Pack release, click the name link for obtaining detailed information about that Service Pack release update, and then examine the information for that Office update. What is the name of that Service Pack update? What is the size of this update, and how long would it take to download this update? Why might you want to download and install this service pack update? What precautions do you need to take before downloading and installing this update?

Explore

5. Return to the Product Updates Web page, and click the link for obtaining detailed information about one of the other updates that you might be interested in, and examine the information on that update. Which update did you examine? Briefly explain how you might benefit from this update.

6. Return to the Product Updates Web page.

7. Have you used the Office Update Web site previously? If not, do you see any benefit in using it in the future? Explain.

Case 4. *Checking Computer, Hardware, and Software Compatibility Prior to Upgrading to Windows XP Professional* Heather Malone operates a small contract business providing project management, editorial, copyediting, and indexing services for publishers around the country. She has three networked computers on which she and her two employees rely to meet project deadlines. So that she and her staff can take advantage of the new technologies available in Windows XP, she wants to upgrade these systems. One of the computers uses Windows 2000, and the other two computers use the Second Edition of Windows 98. She wants to evaluate the feasibility of upgrading each of these systems to Windows XP Professional.

As you complete each step in this case, record your answers to questions so that you can submit them to your instructor. Use a word-processing application such as Word or WordPad to prepare and then print your answers to these questions. Also, if you change any settings on the computer you are using, note the original settings so that you can restore them later.

1. Connect to your ISP, and then connect to the Microsoft Windows XP Professional Web site.

2. Under How to Buy, select the link for Upgrading.

Explore

3. At the Windows XP Professional Upgrade Center, select the link for checking the compatibility of your hardware and software, and then select the link for searching the Windows Catalog.

Explore

4. Search for the type of computer system you are currently using. What type of computer system do you have? Does Windows XP Professional support the use of this system? If your computer is not listed or not supported, where would you go to find more information about upgrading that computer?

5. Use this same search feature to determine whether Windows XP Professional supports the specific type of printer and modem that you use on your computer. Which of these hardware devices does Windows XP Professional support (if any), and which ones are not supported (if any)? Did you discover any other useful information about these hardware products? If a hardware device is not listed or not supported, where would you recommend Heather go to find more information about upgrading the device drivers for a hardware device?

Explore

6. Assume that Heather wants you to check software compatibility for Photoshop, Dreamweaver, and Norton AntiVirus. Perform a search for these three products. Also check a software application on the computer you are using. List which versions of these products, if any, are supported under Windows XP Professional, and also note the degree of compatibility with Windows XP (shown in the Status column). If you have any of these software products, is the version you have supported under Windows XP? If a software product is not supported, where would Heather go to find more information about upgrading that software?

7. Before Heather upgrades her work computers, is there any other tool that you could download and use to check the compatibility of her computer? If so, identify the tool, and explain what information it provides.

INSTALLING AND TROUBLESHOOTING HARDWARE

Optimizing Hardware at North Coast Broadcasting

North Coast Broadcasting, Inc.

North Coast Broadcasting (NCB) provides cable TV services to residents of northern California. To meet the needs of its customers, and to foster an efficient, productive working environment for employees, NCB wants to take advantage of the newest hardware and software technologies available in Windows XP Professional. Kate Evans works as a technical support specialist at the company's headquarters in San Rafael, California. She is responsible for assisting employees in evaluating, installing, and troubleshooting hardware and software. She also helps employees set up network connections on their computers. You have offered to help her at NCB so you can learn more about optimizing hardware.

In this section of the tutorial, you examine the difference between Plug and Play and legacy hardware, and discover the advantages that Plug and Play computer systems offer. You also examine Windows XP support for newer types of hardware devices. Then you open Device Manager, examine your computer's hardware configuration, and document those hardware settings.

Types of Hardware Devices

The president of North Coast Broadcasting (NCB) has asked Kate to supervise a group of technical staff and managers in developing long-range plans for identifying and implementing new hardware technologies that will be critical to the company's growth in the twenty-first century. Kate tells you that her 15 years of experience in the computer industry has helped her realize the importance of choosing hardware technologies that are reliable, stable, easy to install and use, and designed to meet the future needs of her company.

One of the major problems computer users faced in the past was the overly complex process for installing and configuring new hardware devices. To reduce the problems and support costs that often resulted from installing new components, hardware manufacturers now design their devices using a set of standards called Plug and Play. Using Plug and Play (PnP), an operating system can automatically detect a hardware device, install device drivers for that device, and configure the device during booting. The goal of Plug and Play is simple: you plug in the device, turn on your computer, the operating system detects and installs support for the device, and you are ready to play with the device. Although Plug and Play hardware has been standard on Macintosh computers since their introduction in 1984, the technology only became available on PCs with Windows 95 in 1995.

Hardware devices that do not support Plug and Play are called **legacy devices**, or **non-Plug and Play** devices, and require manual installation. Even though Windows XP might be able to detect non-Plug and Play hardware (such as a legacy modem), it might only be able to configure the hardware as a generic device (for example, as a standard modem). Although this configuration might work, you do not have access to all the features for that particular model. If you manually configure the device by specifying the manufacturer, model, and make, Windows XP installs the proper device drivers, and you have access to all the features of the device.

To manually configure a non-Plug and Play device, you must perform one or more of the following tasks:

- **Read the documentation**. You must read the documentation provided with a legacy device so that you know not only how to properly install the device, but also how to properly configure it. Unfortunately, hardware documentation for legacy devices is either difficult to understand, not logically organized and presented, or very limited in its scope and accuracy.

- **Set switches and jumpers**. You might have to set one or more switches, such as DIP switches or jumpers, on an adapter or add-in card. You usually find the instructions for configuring a device with DIP switches or jumpers in the documentation for the hardware device.

- **Install software and device drivers**. When you purchase a hardware device, the product also includes a CD or floppy disk with software and device drivers that you more than likely need to install. For older hardware devices, you might need to contact the manufacturer for a copy of a device driver for Windows XP. Also, you might be able to download an updated Windows XP device driver from the company's Web site or from the Microsoft Windows Update Web site.

- **Assign resources using Device Manager**. As you see later in this tutorial, Device Manager is a Windows XP tool that contains information about hardware configuration settings for Plug and Play and legacy devices. You might need to use Device Manager to assign or change resources assigned to a hardware device by Windows XP to properly configure that device.

- **Troubleshoot hardware configuration problems and conflicts**. You might need to use Device Manager or one of the Help Troubleshooters to address a problem with the configuration of a legacy hardware device.

Under Windows XP (and Windows 2000), you can use a Plug and Play driver for a legacy device, and thereby improve Windows support for that device.

Each time you boot your computer, Windows XP checks for any new hardware. If Windows XP detects a new hardware component that supports Plug and Play, it automatically installs and loads the device drivers for that component and then configures the device to work properly. If Windows XP does not have a device driver for that Plug and Play component, it prompts you to insert a disk with the software that includes the device driver(s).

Although most new computer systems are billed as Plug and Play, a *bona fide* Plug and Play system has the following features:

- **ACPI BIOS**. In addition to performing a power-on self test and locating and loading the operating system from disk, the BIOS also enables the devices needed to boot your computer, and handles I/O (Input/Output). A legacy BIOS enables devices, but does not identify and initially configure them. In contrast, both a Plug and Play BIOS and ACPI BIOS identify and activate hardware devices, determine their resource requirements, create a nonconflicting hardware configuration, load device drivers, pass configuration information to the operating system, and notify it of any configuration changes. An ACPI BIOS also determines the power management capabilities of hardware devices. The Windows XP operating system, not the BIOS, is now responsible for configuring the system and managing power. The Windows XP Plug and Play Manager performs the same types of operations as a Plug and Play BIOS during boot. Windows XP supports Plug and Play using the Advanced Configuration and Power Interface (ACPI), which is part of the OnNow initiative for managing power in your computer. **OnNow** is the term Microsoft uses for a PC that is always on, but appears off and responds immediately to user or other requests.

- **Plug and Play hardware devices and device drivers**. For a hardware device to be automatically detected and configured with the proper device drivers, it must be a Plug and Play device. When you purchase a Plug and Play device, check the product labeling; if it identifies the product as Plug and Play compatible, ask if the device is really Plug and Play, and find out if you have to manually adjust a jumper so that Windows XP treats it as a Plug and Play device. For Windows XP to support a Plug and Play hardware device, a Plug and Play device driver must be available for it. Because a wide range of devices fully support the Plug and Play standards, there is no reason to purchase a Plug-and-Play compatible or non-Plug and Play device.

- **Plug and Play operating system**. Windows XP Professional and Windows XP Home Edition are Plug and Play operating systems. Like previous versions of Windows, Windows XP stores configuration information on Plug and Play devices in its Registry. When you install a new Plug and Play device, it checks the resources used by other Plug and Play devices in the Registry, and configures the new device without introducing conflicts between hardware devices.

PCs might include a mix of Plug and Play and legacy components. For example, a computer might have some legacy hardware devices, a Plug and Play operating system, and some Plug and Play hardware components. Or, a computer might have an ACPI BIOS with a Plug and Play operating system, and both Plug and Play and legacy hardware. When you purchase a computer, find out if it provides support for ACPI, and determine which hardware components are Plug and Play and which, if any, are legacy. If you are replacing or adding new hardware components, it's best to purchase Plug and Play devices. An ACPI computer with a Plug and Play operating system and Plug and Play hardware devices provides the best performance.

Windows XP also uses **Universal Plug and Play (UPnP)** for the automatic detection and configuration of devices in a networking environment, for consumer electronics equipment such as home entertainment systems and appliances, and for Internet gateways. A **gateway** consists of hardware and software that provide an access point to another network. UPnP relies on Internet and Web protocols (TCP/IP, HTTP, and XML) to enable devices to configure themselves, announce themselves on the network, discover or locate other devices on the network, communicate directly with other devices, and direct the operation of other devices. **TCP/IP (Transmission Control Protocol/Internet Protocol)** is a standard protocol for transferring data in packets with a source and destination address over the Internet or a private network. **HTTP (HyperText Transfer Protocol)** is a standard protocol for transferring files from a Web server to your browser so that you can view the contents of a Web page over the World Wide Web. Like HTML (Hypertext Markup Language), **XML (Extensible Markup Language)** describes the layout of a Web page and your ability to interact with that content, but unlike HTML, XML can also describe data to support the transfer and sharing of information. UPnP is part of the Networking Services component, and is automatically installed with Windows XP. Windows XP displays UPnP devices in the My Network Places folder.

Increased Hardware Support in Windows XP

For North Coast Broadcasting, the increased support that Windows XP Professional provides for new hardware technologies is one of its most important features. Not only do employees benefit from the expanded computer capabilities, NCB's customers benefit from hardware technologies that support digital broadcasting.

In addition to supporting many of the hardware technologies introduced in earlier versions of Windows, Windows XP provides enhanced support for the following technologies:

- **Human Interface Devices (HID)**. HID consists of a broad category of devices for interacting with and controlling computers. HID devices include not only the standard types of devices that people use on their computers, such as the keyboard, mouse, trackball, joystick, and wireless pointing devices for presentations, they also include devices used to control home entertainment systems, smart appliances, and virtual reality simulations (for example, head-mounted displays).

- **Multiple monitors and DualView**. Under Windows XP, you can connect up to 10 monitors to the same computer, view different documents in different applications on different monitors (such as a Microsoft Word document on one monitor, and your e-mail Inbox on the other monitor), view the same document over multiple monitors (such as a wide Excel spreadsheet), use different desktop settings on each monitor, designate which monitor is the primary monitor (for booting), designate the orientation of the monitors as right to left or top to bottom, and drag and drop objects across virtual space from one monitor to the next.

  To use this feature, each monitor must connect to a PCI or AGP video adapter. A **PCI (Peripheral Component Interconnect)** is an older local bus technology that supports data transfer rates of 133 MBps. MBps, with an uppercase "B," refers to megabytes per second whereas Mbps, with a lowercase "b," refers to megabits per second. A **bus** is a path on the motherboard for transferring data between computer components. ISA (Industry Standard Architecture, or AT bus), EISA (Enhanced ISA), and VESA Local Bus are even older bus technologies. A **local bus** has a direct connection to the processor for the high-speed transfer of data. The **AGP (Accelerated Graphics Port)** bus supports data transfer rates of 266 and 533 MBps and

1.07 GBps (gigabytes per second), thus providing a high-speed pathway for the transfer of graphics between the AGP graphics controller (or video card), the processor, and memory.

If your computer has a video card with two video ports, and if you have a monitor attached to each port, you can use a feature called **DualView** to expand your display to the second monitor.

- **Scanners and cameras**. Windows XP includes a Scanner and Camera Wizard for acquiring, viewing, modifying, and processing images derived from a scanner or digital camera.

- **Universal Serial Bus (USB)**. The Universal Serial Bus is an external, bidirectional, Plug and Play bus for connecting up to 127 high-speed serial devices via just one port on your computer. In the past, each type of device required a separate port, which meant that you had to install adapters for each device, and then figure out how to assign resources to each device; to complicate matters, resources were limited. With USB and IEEE 1394 devices, you no longer need to deal with DIP switches, jumpers, and limited resources such as IRQ settings, DMA channels, and I/O addresses (covered later in the tutorial). Because most USB devices receive power via the USB port, you do not need extra power cables.

  The USB bus supports two data speeds: full speed at 12 Mbps (12 megabits per second, or 12 million bits/second) for devices that require large amounts of bandwidth, such as devices that process video and audio, and a lower speed of 1.5 Mbps for devices such as keyboards and mice. **Bandwidth** refers to the amount of data that can be transmitted over a device in a fixed amount of time; digital devices measure bandwidth in bits per second or bytes per second. USB devices that support the next generation of USB standards, namely USB 2.0, have data transfer speeds of 480 Mbps.

  Not surprisingly, USB supports Plug and Play, power management, and **hot swapping** (also called **hot plugging** or **hot insertion and removal**), which means that you can connect or disconnect a USB device while the computer is still running. You do not need to power down your computer before adding or removing the USB device; however, because this technology is relatively new, it is a good idea to check your hardware manual to verify its ability to support hot swapping.

  Intel has built USB support into its newer microprocessor chips, starting with the Pentium MMX microprocessor. Intel and other industry leaders such as Microsoft defined the USB standard. USB plays an important role in the use of multimedia, gaming, digital imaging, and telephony. The next generation of hardware devices will have one or more USB ports, including keyboards, mice, monitors, joysticks, speakers, CD and DVD drives, modems, printers, hard disk drives, scanners, digital cameras, tape drives, audio players, telephones, telephone networks (PBXs), and ISDN adapters.

  If you want to take advantage of the newest types of hardware technologies, or if you want to upgrade the hardware on your computer, purchase USB devices for easy installation, automatic configuration, speed, and support for a greater number of devices.

- **IEEE 1394**. IEEE 1394 (for Institute of Electrical and Electronics Engineers) is another high-speed, Plug and Play bus with data transfer rates of 100, 200, and 400 Mbps. Apple originally developed this technology and called it FireWire. IEEE 1394 supports the connection of up to 63 devices via one bus. Furthermore, you can link 1,023 buses to create a network of approximately 64,000 IEEE 1394 devices. Each IEEE 1394 device can support up to 256 TB (terabytes) of memory. IEEE 1394 supports high-bandwidth devices and plays an important role in digital imaging, video teleconferencing, and can act as a bridge for connecting consumer electronics such as VCRs to computers. Digital VCRs, camcorders, and satellite receivers are now available with IEEE 1394 ports. Like USB, IEEE 1394 supports Plug and Play, power management, and hot swapping. USB and IEEE 1394 are expected to eventually replace the use of parallel and serial ports. IEEE 1394b, the next generation of IEEE 1394 devices, will support data transfer rates of 800 Mbps to 3.2 Gbps (gigabits per second).

■ **Digital Video Disc** or **Digital Versatile Disc (DVD)**. DVD is a high-capacity, optical storage technology for the storage and playback of audio and video, as well as other types of data. DVD technology supports higher video display resolutions, such as those found in HDTV (high-definition television), and CD-quality sound. By using one of two compression technologies, DVD drives can store and play back full-length feature movies in one of eight different languages. A DVD disc supports storage capacities in the range of 4.7 GB to 17 GB, with access speeds of 600 KBps to 1.3 MBps. In contrast, a 32X speed CD-ROM has a maximum data transfer rate of 4.8 Mbps, and a storage capacity of approximately 700 MB. Furthermore, DVD drives can read multiple data streams concurrently. Because DVD drives are backward-compatible and support earlier hardware technology, they can read CD-ROM discs and audio CDs.

■ **Smart Cards**. A smart card is made of plastic and is about the size of a credit card. It includes an embedded microchip for use with applications and for storing data, such as credentials used to authenticate a user, personal information, and cash balances.

While you may wonder how you might use and benefit from these new technologies, consider that CD-ROM drives were novelties when they were first introduced. Within a few years after their appearance in the marketplace, CD-ROM drives were standard components on new computers, and became the primary medium for installing software. Now DVD drives are replacing CD-ROM drives and are automatically installed in new computers. Within a few years these new hardware technologies will become indispensable to the way you work and play.

Getting Started

You need to switch your computer to Web style to continue with the tutorial. You also need to turn on the options for showing all folders and files, for displaying protected operating system files, for displaying file extensions, and for displaying the full path in the Address bar. As you complete these steps, you may discover that your computer is already set up for Web style, or that other settings are already in place. If so, you might only need to make a few changes to your computer's settings.

To set up your computer:

1. To change to the Windows XP theme, right-click the desktop and then click **Properties** on the shortcut menu. After Windows XP opens the Display Properties dialog box, click the **Theme** list arrow in the Themes property sheet, click **Windows XP** (if necessary), and then click the **OK** button.

2. To switch to the Windows XP Start menu style, right-click the **Start** button and then click **Properties** on the shortcut menu. After Windows XP opens the Taskbar and Start Menu Properties dialog box, click the **Start menu** option button on the Start Menu property sheet (if necessary), and then click the **OK** button.

3. To change to a task-oriented view of folders and enable single-clicking, click the **Start** button, click **My Computer**, click **Tools** on the menu bar, and then click **Folder Options**. After Windows XP opens the Folder Options dialog box, click the **Show common tasks in folders** option button (if necessary), click the **Single-click to open an item** option button (if necessary), and click the **Underline icon titles only when I point at them** option button (if necessary).

4. Click the **View** tab, click the **Display the full path in the address bar** check box if it is not already selected, and click the **Show hidden files and folders** option button if it is not already selected. If there is a check mark in the "Hide extensions for known file types" check box, click the check box to remove the check mark.

5. Click the **Hide protected operating system files** check box (if necessary), click **Yes** in the Warning dialog box to display protected operating system files, click the **OK** button to close the Folder Options dialog box, and then close My Computer.

Now you're ready to examine information about the hardware on your computer and document your hardware settings.

Using **Device Manager**

Device Manager provides an important source of information about the hardware components on a computer, and shows the configuration settings that Windows XP uses for both Plug and Play and legacy devices. You can use Device Manager to document hardware settings, verify the installation of a hardware device, check for hardware conflicts, troubleshoot hardware problems, change the configuration of a hardware device, and update device drivers for a hardware device.

Before you make changes to the configuration settings in Device Manager, make sure that you use Device Manager to print a record of your computer's current configuration settings, and that you understand how changes to your computer's configuration affect your computer's operation. Changing a configuration setting in Device Manager could create a conflict with another hardware device. A **hardware conflict**, **device conflict**, or **resource conflict** occurs when two hardware devices attempt to share the same resource. When a hardware conflict exists, one or both devices might not work properly or at all. Worse yet, the computer might become unstable or not function at all.

The instructions in the tutorial steps request that you view, but not change, hardware configuration settings in Device Manager. Only users with expert knowledge of computer hardware and hardware configuration settings should change resource settings for hardware devices. Also, you must log on as Administrator or as a member of the Administrators group before you can make changes to resource settings in Device Manager.

You can open Device Manager by viewing properties of My Computer, by using the System tool in the Control Panel, or via a Help Troubleshooter.

Because employees at North Coast Broadcasting work on a variety of computer systems that are configured with different types of hardware and software, Kate decides to present a one-day workshop on Device Manager to help employees better understand their computer's hardware. She asks you to help her prepare for the workshop by exploring Device Manager.

To open Device Manager:

1. Log on under an account with printing and Administrator privileges.

2. From the Start menu, right-click **My Computer** and then click **Properties** on the shortcut menu. After Windows XP opens the System Properties dialog box, click the **Hardware** tab. The Hardware property sheet provides access to Device Manager and several other options. See Figure 12-1.

Figure 12-1	OPENING DEVICE MANAGER

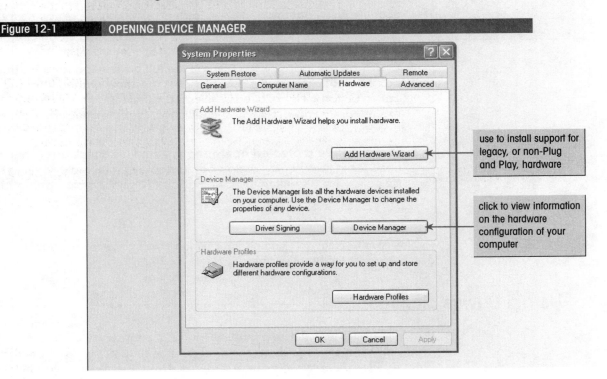

use to install support for legacy, or non-Plug and Play, hardware

click to view information on the hardware configuration of your computer

The other options include:

- An Add Hardware Wizard button for installing hardware and troubleshooting hardware problems.

- A Driver Signing button for specifying what Windows XP should do when installing hardware if it detects a device driver that has not been digitally signed. Unsigned device drivers have not been tested for compatibility with Windows XP, and therefore are not recommended for use with it. The default action is to warn you each time it detects an unsigned device driver so that you can decide whether to continue installing the device driver.

- A Hardware Profiles button for selecting a hardware profile during booting. Each **hardware profile** consists of different hardware devices and therefore different hardware configurations. By default, you have one hardware profile called "Profile 1 (Current)."

To view the hardware tree:

1. Click the **Device Manager** button. If necessary, adjust the height of the Device Manager window to display all the information in it. Windows XP displays a **hardware tree** that identifies categories of hardware components installed on your computer, as shown in Figure 12-2. This view is referred to as "Devices by type." The hardware devices include the computer itself, peripherals (external hardware devices), adapters and controllers connected to the system board, ports, and components on the system board itself. The expand view box ⊞ next to each device category indicates that the category contains one or more devices. Some of your hardware categories will differ.

   TROUBLE? If you open the Device Manager dialog box and see a warning that you do not have sufficient privileges to uninstall devices or change device properties and drivers, click the **OK** button. You did not log on under an account with Administrator privileges. Although you cannot make any changes, you can still view the information in Device Manager.

Figure 12-2   **VIEWING THE HARDWARE TREE**

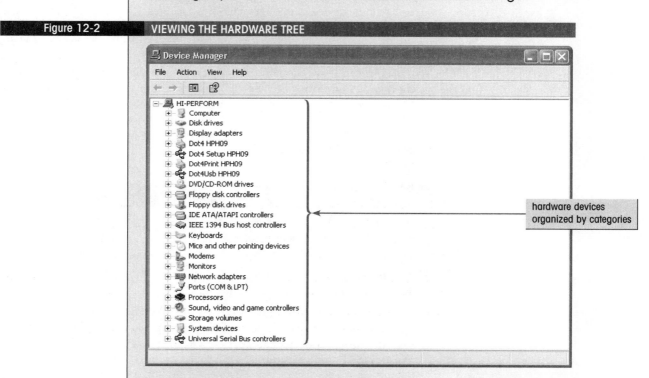

2. Leave Device Manager open for the next section of the tutorial.

Almost every computer system's hardware tree includes categories for standard components, such as Disk drives, Display adapters, DVD/CD-ROM drives, Floppy disk controllers, Floppy disk drives, controllers for the hard disk, Keyboards, Mice and other pointing devices, Modems, Monitors, Ports (COM & LPT), Processors, Sound, video and game controllers, and System devices. Most of these categories identify the model of each of the installed hardware components listed under the category. For example, on the computer used in Figure 12-2, the Dot4 categories identify a USB printer and its connection via a USB port.

In the hardware categories for Floppy disk controllers, hard disk controllers, IEEE 1394 Bus host controllers, Universal Serial Bus controllers, Sound, video, and game controllers, Windows XP lists information on the types of adapters or controllers in your computer. An **adapter** is a circuit board or card that connects one system component with another, and that enables the components to work together. A **controller** is a circuit board or card that controls a peripheral device, such as a hard disk or floppy disk. Adapter and controller cards are connected to the **motherboard**, or main system board, within the system unit of the computer. The **system unit** houses the main system board with the processor, RAM, and electronic circuitry, as well as any circuit boards attached to the motherboard, the power supply, and the drives.

The controllers for the hard disk are listed as IDE ATA/ATAPI controllers on the computer used in Figure 12-2. **IDE (Integrated Driver Electronics)** is a hard disk drive interface in which the electronics for the controller are included in the drive itself so that there is no need for a separate adapter. **ATA (AT Attachment)** refers to one of five different techniques for integrating the controller electronics on the drive itself; IDE is just one approach. **ATAPI (AT Attachment Packet Interface)** is an extension to EIDE that supports CD-ROM players and tape drives. **EIDE (Enhanced IDE)** is an improvement in IDE technology that supports larger storage devices and offers data transfer rates that are three to four times faster than IDE. **SCSI (Small Computer System Interface)** (pronounced "scuzzy") is a parallel interface standard used by Macintosh Computers, PCs, and UNIX systems for attaching peripheral devices to computers.

The System devices category contains information about the system board and components on the system board. The Ports (COM & LPT) identify the serial and parallel ports in your computer that may be used by your modem, mouse, printer, and other peripheral devices. You see a category for Network adapters if your computer contains a network interface card (NIC). The Computer category identifies whether your processor is ACPI compliant, and whether it is a **uniprocessor** (a single processor).

REFERENCE WINDOW   **RW**

Viewing the Hardware Tree in Device Manager
- Log on under an account with Administrator privileges.
- From the Start menu, right-click My Computer and then click Properties on the shortcut menu.
- Click the Hardware tab and then click the Device Manager button.

When you need to verify the installation of a device, view information on a hardware device, or troubleshoot a device problem, Device Manager is the logical tool to use.

Documenting Hardware Settings

It's especially important that you have a printed copy of your computer's hardware settings before you attempt to change the configuration of hardware in Device Manager. If you inadvertently make a change that causes a problem, you might be able to use your documentation to restore the original settings. You can produce three types of Resource Summary reports from Device Manager:

- **System summary**. This report summarizes information about the devices installed on your computer, or on the remote computer you are managing. The report includes a system summary, disk drive information, and a summary of resources assigned to devices by the operating system. Figure 12-3 shows the first page of this type of report.

Figure 12-3   FIRST PAGE OF A SYSTEM SUMMARY REPORT

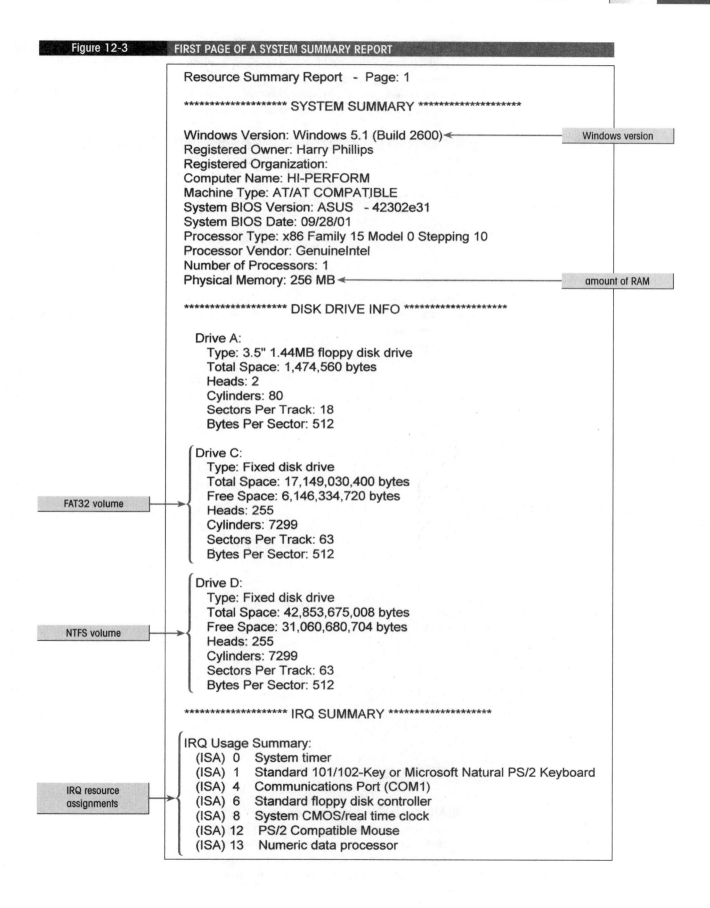

Resource Summary Report   -   Page: 1

********************* SYSTEM SUMMARY *********************

Windows Version: Windows 5.1 (Build 2600) ◄──────────────── Windows version
Registered Owner: Harry Phillips
Registered Organization:
Computer Name: HI-PERFORM
Machine Type: AT/AT COMPATIBLE
System BIOS Version: ASUS   - 42302e31
System BIOS Date: 09/28/01
Processor Type: x86 Family 15 Model 0 Stepping 10
Processor Vendor: GenuineIntel
Number of Processors: 1
Physical Memory: 256 MB ◄──────────────────────────────── amount of RAM

********************* DISK DRIVE INFO *********************

   Drive A:
     Type: 3.5" 1.44MB floppy disk drive
     Total Space: 1,474,560 bytes
     Heads: 2
     Cylinders: 80
     Sectors Per Track: 18
     Bytes Per Sector: 512

FAT32 volume ──►
   Drive C:
     Type: Fixed disk drive
     Total Space: 17,149,030,400 bytes
     Free Space: 6,146,334,720 bytes
     Heads: 255
     Cylinders: 7299
     Sectors Per Track: 63
     Bytes Per Sector: 512

NTFS volume ──►
   Drive D:
     Type: Fixed disk drive
     Total Space: 42,853,675,008 bytes
     Free Space: 31,060,680,704 bytes
     Heads: 255
     Cylinders: 7299
     Sectors Per Track: 63
     Bytes Per Sector: 512

********************* IRQ SUMMARY *********************

IRQ resource assignments ──►
IRQ Usage Summary:
  (ISA) 0   System timer
  (ISA) 1   Standard 101/102-Key or Microsoft Natural PS/2 Keyboard
  (ISA) 4   Communications Port (COM1)
  (ISA) 6   Standard floppy disk controller
  (ISA) 8   System CMOS/real time clock
  (ISA) 12   PS/2 Compatible Mouse
  (ISA) 13   Numeric data processor

■ **Selected class or device**. The Selected class or device report lists the resources and device drivers used for a category of hardware devices or for a specific hardware device. Figure 12-4 shows a report on devices in the Disk drives category. Before you can produce this type of report, you must first select the hardware category or hardware device; otherwise, this option is not available.

Figure 12-4	SYSTEM DEVICE CLASS REPORT

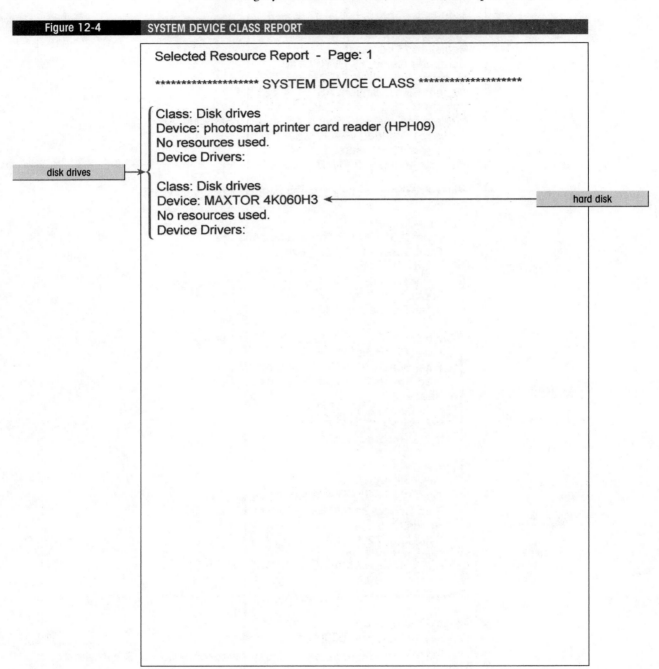

Selected Resource Report - Page: 1

******************** SYSTEM DEVICE CLASS ********************

Class: Disk drives
Device: photosmart printer card reader (HPH09)
No resources used.
Device Drivers:

Class: Disk drives
Device: MAXTOR 4K060H3
No resources used.
Device Drivers:

disk drives

hard disk

■ **All devices and system summary**. This report includes the information you find on the system summary report plus a system device information section that contains a list of all resources used by all hardware devices. Figure 12-5 shows a page from this type of report. Although this report might easily be 15 to 40 pages long, it is the most thorough and most useful.

Figure 12-5   **PAGE FOUR OF A SYSTEM RESOURCE REPORT**

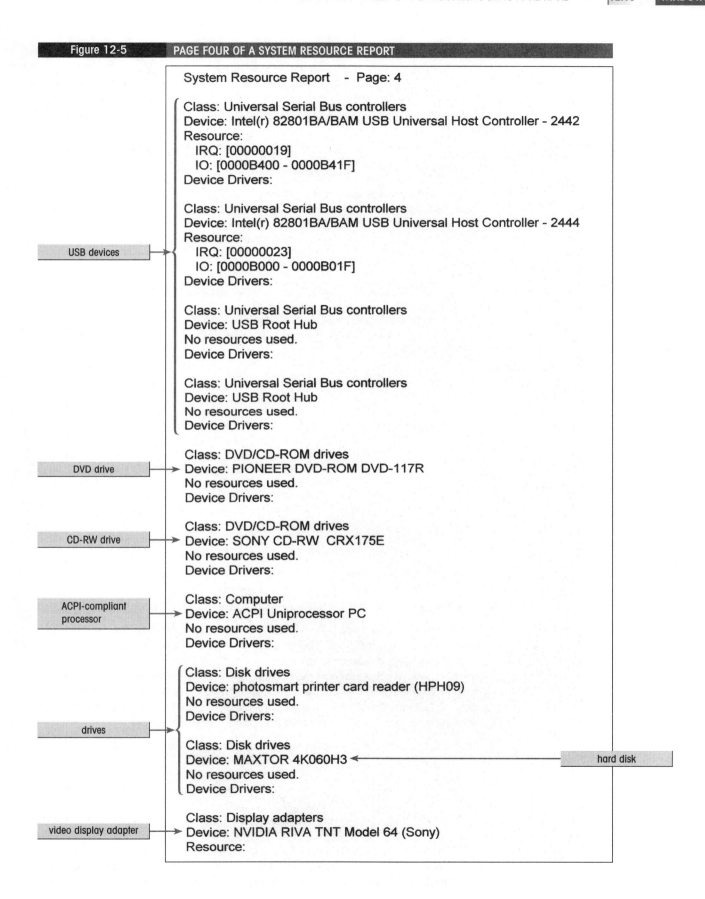

System Resource Report   - Page: 4

Class: Universal Serial Bus controllers
Device: Intel(r) 82801BA/BAM USB Universal Host Controller - 2442
Resource:
  IRQ: [00000019]
  IO: [0000B400 - 0000B41F]
Device Drivers:

Class: Universal Serial Bus controllers
Device: Intel(r) 82801BA/BAM USB Universal Host Controller - 2444
Resource:
  IRQ: [00000023]
  IO: [0000B000 - 0000B01F]
Device Drivers:

Class: Universal Serial Bus controllers
Device: USB Root Hub
No resources used.
Device Drivers:

Class: Universal Serial Bus controllers
Device: USB Root Hub
No resources used.
Device Drivers:

USB devices

Class: DVD/CD-ROM drives
Device: PIONEER DVD-ROM DVD-117R
No resources used.
Device Drivers:

DVD drive

Class: DVD/CD-ROM drives
Device: SONY CD-RW CRX175E
No resources used.
Device Drivers:

CD-RW drive

Class: Computer
Device: ACPI Uniprocessor PC
No resources used.
Device Drivers:

ACPI-compliant processor

Class: Disk drives
Device: photosmart printer card reader (HPH09)
No resources used.
Device Drivers:

Class: Disk drives
Device: MAXTOR 4K060H3
No resources used.
Device Drivers:

drives

hard disk

Class: Display adapters
Device: NVIDIA RIVA TNT Model 64 (Sony)
Resource:

video display adapter

This documentation is critical information that you need to have. You should print an "All devices and system summary" when you first acquire a computer or after it is properly configured and working.

Kate strongly recommends that all of her employees document their computer hardware settings in case they need to refer to those settings later. She asks you to do this on your own computer.

To document your hardware configuration settings:

1. Click the **computer name** at the top of the Device Manager hardware tree, click **Action** on the menu bar, and then click **Print**. The Print dialog box opens, where you can select a printer and specify the report type. See Figure 12-6. The Report type section shows the three types of reports you can print from Device Manager.

Figure 12-6	OPTIONS FOR DOCUMENTING HARDWARE SETTINGS

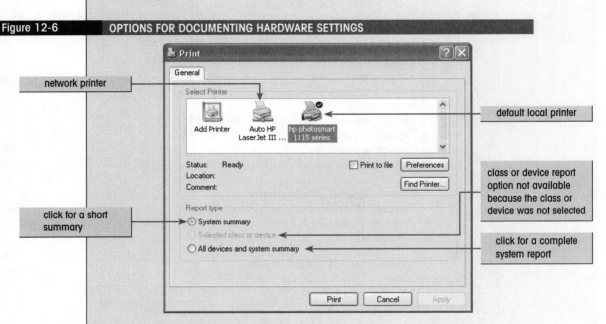

2. If necessary, select the printer you want to use for the report.

3. Because computer labs have strict printing policies that limit the number of pages you can print, do not print an "All devices and system summary" report in a computer lab. If you are working in a computer lab or on your own computer and only want a system summary, click the **System summary** option button (if necessary), and then click the **Print** button. If you are working on your own computer and want a complete system report, click the **All devices and system summary** option button, and then click the **Print** button.

4. Leave Device Manager open for the next section of the tutorial.

REFERENCE WINDOW   **RW**

Documenting Hardware Settings

- Log on your computer under an account with Administrator privileges.
- From the Start menu, right-click My Computer, click Properties on the shortcut menu, click the Hardware tab, and then click the Device Manager button.
- If you want to print a report for a specific class or device, select the class category or device first; otherwise, click the computer name at the top of the Device Manager hardware tree.
- Click Action on the menu bar, and then click Print to open the Print dialog box.
- If necessary, select the printer you want to use in the Select Printer box.
- In the Report type section, click the option button for the type of report you want to print, and then click the Print button.
- Close Device Manager.

Each of the report types serves a purpose. The "Selected class or device" report is useful if you need to document what happens as you test different resource settings for a specific hardware device.

Checking Resource Assignments

Windows XP can allocate four types of resources to hardware devices that require them:

- **Interrupt request (IRQ) resources**. An **interrupt** is a signal transmitted by hardware or software to the processor or operating system for some type of service. Hardware devices and software constantly interrupt the processor and operating system with requests for specific services. An interrupt request might require the processor to perform a function, handle an error condition, or move data. For example, when you press a key on the keyboard, you generate a **hardware interrupt**, and the operating system interprets the scan code generated by the keystroke. When you issue a command to save a document, the software application you are using generates a **software interrupt** for recording the contents of the file on disk.

  An interrupt request from a hardware device is transmitted to the processor via an IRQ line. Today's computers have 24 IRQ lines (starting with 0 and ending with 23), while slightly older computers have 16 IRQ lines (from 0 through 15), and very old computers only have 8 IRQ lines (from 0 through 7). Some interrupt request lines are dedicated to specific functions or devices, such as the keyboard controller (IRQ 1). Each hardware device that requires an IRQ line is assigned its own line, though it is possible for two devices to share the same IRQ if they are not being used at the same time. Because there are a limited number of IRQs, and because some of them are already pre-assigned to system devices, such as the system timer and the real time clock (RTC), they invariably become a limited resource. You might have more hardware devices that you want to add to your computer than you have IRQ lines to support them. That's why it's becoming increasingly important to purchase computers with USB and IEEE 1394 ports and devices, because they bypass this limitation.

- **Input/Output (I/O) resources**. Each hardware device that handles I/O, such as ports and disk drives, must have a unique address in memory, a resource that is called its **I/O address**. This I/O address uniquely identifies a hardware device and serves as a channel for communicating with the device.

■ **Direct Memory Access (DMA) resources.** **Direct Memory Access** is a channel for transferring data between two devices without the intervention of the processor. For example, by using a DMA channel, your computer can transfer data from a hard disk drive, floppy disk drive, or tape drive into main memory (RAM) without the processor. If the processor handles the data transfer, the overall process is much slower than a direct transfer to memory. DMA channels are obviously important in the transfer of video, audio, and graphics data. Today's computers have four or eight DMA channels that are identified by number from 0 to 7.

■ **Memory resources.** Memory resources refer to specific regions of memory allocated to a hardware device. For example, one or more regions of memory might be designated for the video display adapter that generates the image you see on the monitor. These memory resources are identified as a range of memory addresses assigned to a device.

Next, you view the resources Windows XP has allocated to hardware devices on your computer. Because each computer contains different types of hardware manufactured by different companies, and because each computer's configuration is different, the information you see for hardware resource assignments might differ from that shown in this section of the tutorial.

After you install Windows XP Professional on new staff computers, Kate asks you to show each employee how to open Device Manager, examine the computer's hardware configuration and resource requirements, and document their computer's hardware settings.

To view resource assignments:

1. Click **View** on the Device Manager menu bar. From this menu, you can choose to view devices by type or connection, or view resources by type or connection. See Figure 12-7. You can also display hidden devices (non-Plug and Play devices) and customize your view in Device Manager. The "Devices by connection" option lists devices under the hardware to which they are connected.

Figure 12-7	OPTIONS ON THE VIEW MENU

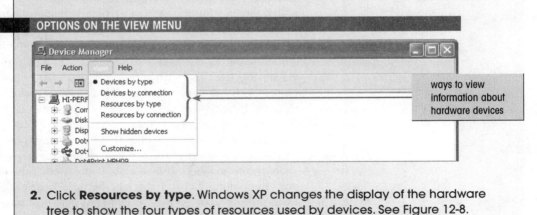

2. Click **Resources by type**. Windows XP changes the display of the hardware tree to show the four types of resources used by devices. See Figure 12-8.

Figure 12-8 SWITCHING TO A VIEW OF RESOURCE TYPES

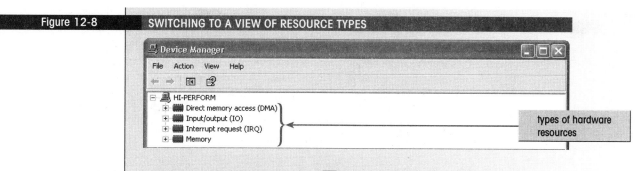

types of hardware resources

3. Click the **expand view** box ⊞ next to the Interrupt request (IRQ) category. Windows XP displays IRQ assignments on your computer. See Figure 12-9. If you examine the IRQ resource assignments on your computer, you might find IRQ lines that are not assigned to any hardware device yet; in other words, nothing is displayed for those IRQ numbers. On the computer used for this figure, IRQs 2, 3, 5, 7, 9, 10, 11, and 20 are free, and several devices share IRQ 23. (PCI) next to IRQ 23 refers to a PCI bus; Windows XP can dynamically allocate shared IRQs to devices on a PCI bus.

Figure 12-9 VEWING IRQ RESOURCE ASSIGNMENTS

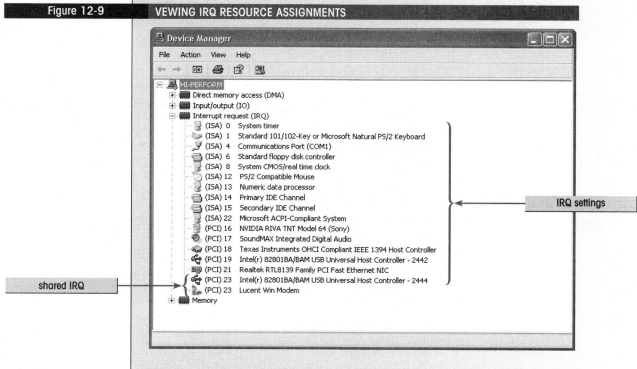

shared IRQ

IRQ settings

4. Click the **collapse view** box ⊟ next to the Interrupt request (IRQ) category, click ⊞ next to the Input/output (IO) category, and then maximize the Device Manager window. When you examine this list of I/O address assignments, you find that many different devices require an I/O address. These I/O addresses, also known as **port addresses**, consist of memory addresses assigned to memory banks on peripheral devices. On the computer used for Figure 12-10, the video display adapter (NVIDIA RIVA TNT Model 64) is assigned more than one I/O address. In contrast, the LPT1 parallel port and COM1 communications port are each assigned only one I/O address.

Figure 12-10   VIEWING I/O RESOURCE ASSIGNMENTS

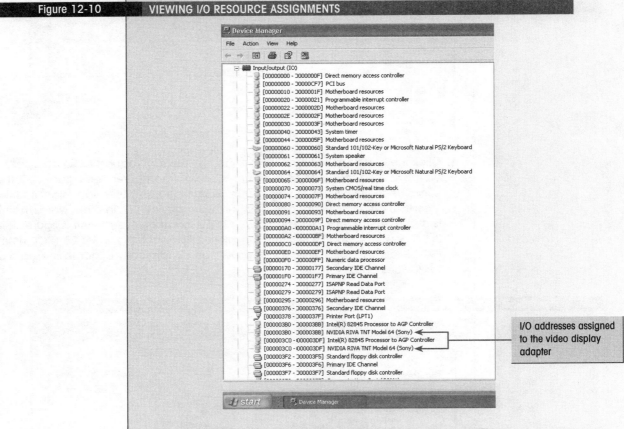

I/O addresses assigned to the video display adapter

5. Click ⊟ next to the Input/output (IO) category, click ⊞ next to the Direct memory access (DMA) category, and then restore your window to its original size. As shown in Figure 12-11, you should see a DMA assignment for your floppy disk controller and the direct memory access controller.

Figure 12-11   VIEWING DMA RESOURCE ASSIGNMENTS

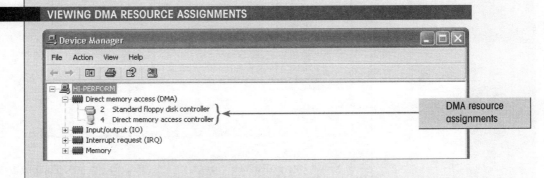

DMA resource assignments

6. Click ⊞ next to the Memory category and examine memory allocated to specific hardware devices. On the computer used for Figure 12-12, notice that Windows XP has allocated memory to the video display adapter (NVIDIA RIVA TNT Model 64) and the Lucent Win Modem.

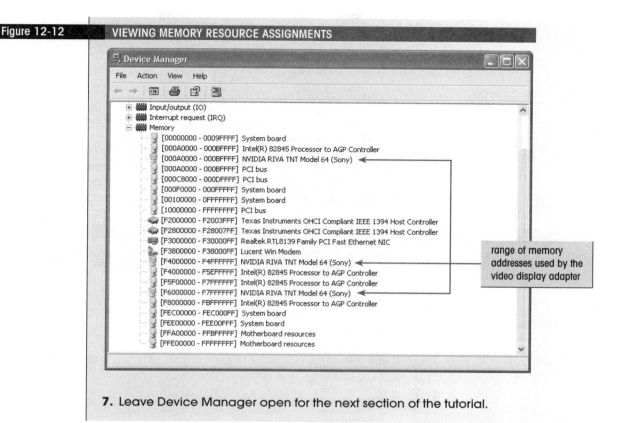

Figure 12-12   VIEWING MEMORY RESOURCE ASSIGNMENTS

range of memory addresses used by the video display adapter

7. Leave Device Manager open for the next section of the tutorial.

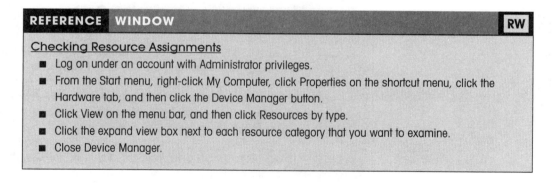

REFERENCE WINDOW   **RW**

Checking Resource Assignments

- Log on under an account with Administrator privileges.
- From the Start menu, right-click My Computer, click Properties on the shortcut menu, click the Hardware tab, and then click the Device Manager button.
- Click View on the menu bar, and then click Resources by type.
- Click the expand view box next to each resource category that you want to examine.
- Close Device Manager.

As you will see later when you examine how to troubleshoot hardware conflicts, resources are a precious commodity, and Windows XP attempts to assign resources without creating hardware conflicts. The limited number of IRQs has been the primary source of problems for PC users who want to add more hardware devices than their computer can support. As noted earlier, the Windows XP support for new hardware technologies overcomes these limitations.

Viewing Properties of a Hardware Device

When you view properties of a hardware device, Device Manager reports on the status of the device and provides detailed information about the device's resources. Because the keyboard is still a standard hardware component, and because its properties illustrate the most common types of settings for a hardware device, you check its properties.

As you help employees with their computers, Kate asks you to show them how to view properties of a specific hardware device with Device Manager. Employees can then determine whether the device is functioning properly.

To view properties of the keyboard:

1. Click **View** on the menu bar, click **Devices by type**, and click the **expand view** box ⊞ next to the Keyboards category. Windows XP expands the category to show the keyboard used on your computer. See Figure 12-13. Notice that Windows XP identifies this keyboard as a "Standard 101/102-Key or Microsoft Natural PS/2 Keyboard." The documentation for this Sony VAIO Smart keyboard identifies it as a PS/2 keyboard with programmable shortcut buttons.

| Figure 12-13 | SELECTING THE INSTALLED KEYBOARD |

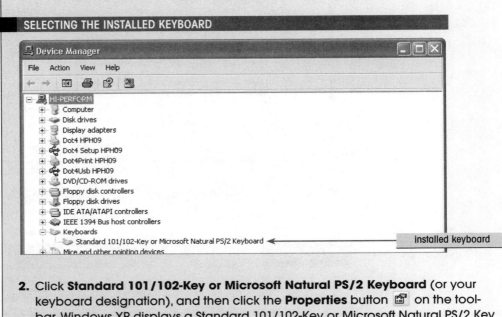

2. Click **Standard 101/102-Key or Microsoft Natural PS/2 Keyboard** (or your keyboard designation), and then click the **Properties** button 🖻 on the toolbar. Windows XP displays a Standard 101/102-Key or Microsoft Natural PS/2 Key Properties dialog box (although the word Properties may not be visible). See Figure 12-14. Your Keyboard Properties dialog box might not include a Power Management tab.

POWER USERS TIP You can double-click a device to view its property sheets.

Each hardware device has one or more property sheets. The General property sheet, common to all hardware devices, identifies the device type, the manufacturer (if known), and the location of the device. The most important information on this property sheet is shown in the Device status section. Assuming there are no hardware problems, Device Manager reports that "This device is working properly." If there is a hardware problem or conflict, Device Manager briefly describes the problem, displays a problem code, and suggests a solution. The problem code is used by Microsoft technical support to help troubleshoot your hardware problem. You can also click the Troubleshoot button to open the appropriate Help Troubleshooter and try to solve the problem yourself. The Troubleshoot button and the Device usage list box are available if you log on with Administrator privileges. The keyboard's Device usage list box is unavailable because it's a required device.

Figure 12-14   GENERAL KEYBOARD PROPERTIES

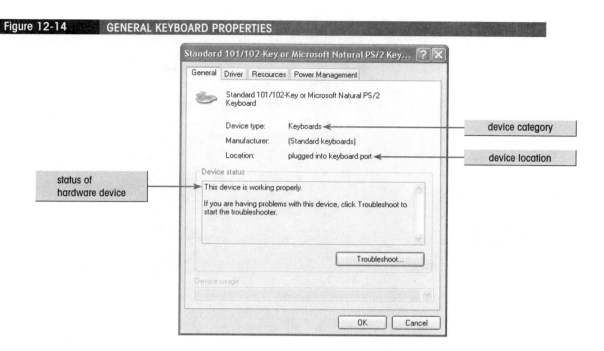

When available, the Device usage section indicates whether a device is enabled for a hardware profile. If the Device usage list box displays "Use this device (enable)," then the device is used as part of the current configuration. If you select "Do not use this device (disable)" in the Device usage list box, you are excluding the device from the hardware configuration.

To examine other keyboard properties:

1. Click the **Driver** tab. Device Manager provides information about the driver used for this port, including whether or not the driver is digitally signed. See Figure 12-15. You can click the Driver Details button to view information about the device drivers for this hardware device. The Update Driver button opens the Hardware Upgrade Wizard, which steps you through the process of checking for an upgrade to the device driver. You can click the Roll Back Driver button to restore the previously used device driver if you install a new driver and then discover that it doesn't work. You can click the Uninstall button to uninstall the device driver.

Figure 12-15   DRIVER PROPERTY SHEET

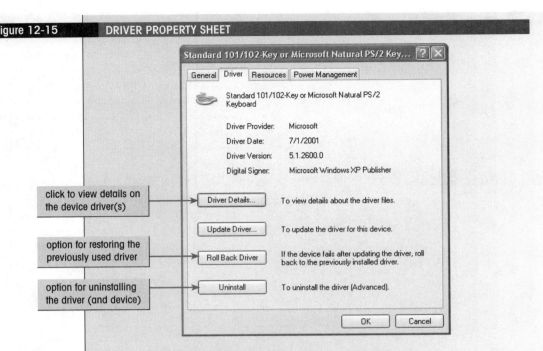

click to view details on
the device driver(s)

option for restoring the
previously used driver

option for uninstalling
the driver (and device)

2. Click the **Driver Details** button. In the Driver File Details dialog box, Windows XP displays the name of the driver files used for this hardware device. See Figure 12-16. Note that the drivers are stored in the Drivers folder, and that they have the "sys" file extension.

Figure 12-16   KEYBOARD DEVICE DRIVERS

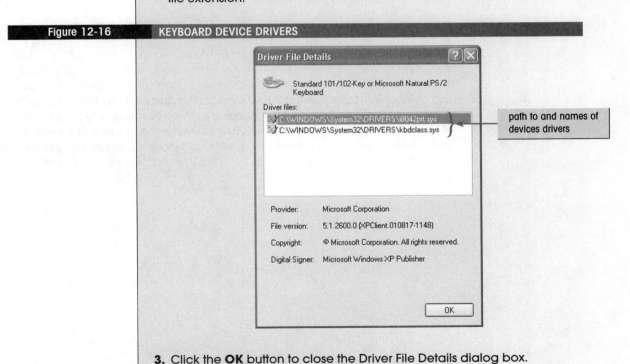

path to and names of
devices drivers

3. Click the **OK** button to close the Driver File Details dialog box.

4. Click the **Resources** tab. Under Resource settings in the Resources property sheet, Windows XP lists the types of resources assigned to a specific hardware device. See Figure 12-17. Windows XP has assigned the keyboard two I/O ranges and an IRQ. A check mark in the "Use automatic settings" check box indicates that Windows XP automatically assigns resource settings to this hardware device. The most important information in the Resources property sheet is in the Conflicting device list. Device Manager either reports no conflicts with other hardware devices, or it identifies the devices and the resource for the hardware conflict.

Figure 12-17   **VIEWING RESOURCE ASSIGNMENTS**

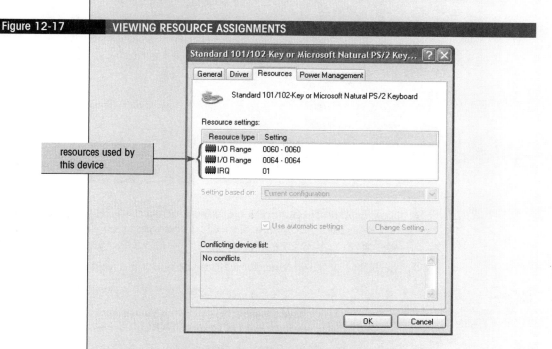

resources used by this device

5. Click the **Power Management** tab (if available). Windows XP displays power management options for a particular device on the Power Management property sheet. See Figure 12-18. For the keyboard used in this figure, there is only one option. You can designate whether the use of this device brings the computer out of standby.

| Figure 12-18 | POWER MANAGEMENT PROPERTY SHEET |

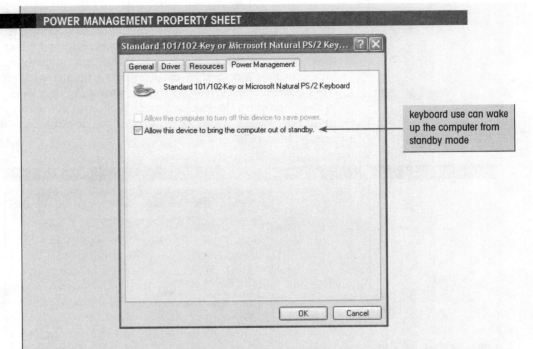

keyboard use can wake
up the computer from
standby mode

6. Click the **Cancel** button to close the Standard 101/102-Key or Microsoft Natural PS/2 Key dialog box without making changes to your hardware configuration settings.

7. Leave the Device Manager window open for the next section of the tutorial.

Some devices do not have a Resources or Power Management property sheet. Other devices, such as the hard disks, modem, and DVD and CD-ROM drives, have different property sheets.

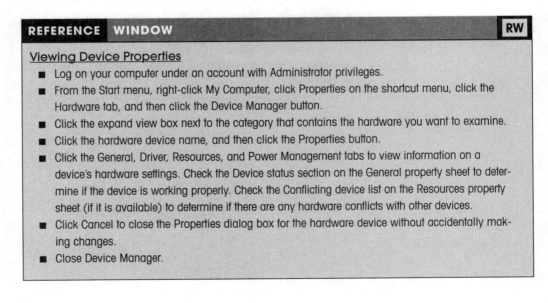

REFERENCE WINDOW | **RW**

Viewing Device Properties

- Log on your computer under an account with Administrator privileges.
- From the Start menu, right-click My Computer, click Properties on the shortcut menu, click the Hardware tab, and then click the Device Manager button.
- Click the expand view box next to the category that contains the hardware you want to examine.
- Click the hardware device name, and then click the Properties button.
- Click the General, Driver, Resources, and Power Management tabs to view information on a device's hardware settings. Check the Device status section on the General property sheet to determine if the device is working properly. Check the Conflicting device list on the Resources property sheet (if it is available) to determine if there are any hardware conflicts with other devices.
- Click Cancel to close the Properties dialog box for the hardware device without accidentally making changes.
- Close Device Manager.

You can use the Device status section on the General property sheet and the Conflicting device list on the Resources property sheet to verify that a hardware device is working properly and that there are no conflicts with other hardware devices. As you will see later, you might also use this information to help you troubleshoot hardware problems.

In the next section of the tutorial, you examine how to use Device Manager to evaluate and troubleshoot hardware configuration problems. You also open the System Information utility and compare the information it provides with information in Device Manager. Plus, you check for devices that share resources, devices in conflict with other devices, forced hardware configuration changes, and problem devices. Finally, you examine the Windows XP networking capabilities, the use of wizards for setting up a network, creating network connections, and adding network shortcuts to the My Network Places folders. You also examine network settings, the process for accessing other computers on a computer, the process for sharing a folder and other resources, and the use of network bridges.

Troubleshooting Hardware Problems

Kate relies on Device Manager to help her troubleshoot hardware configuration problems and reconfigure devices so they do not conflict with each other. At your next meeting with her, she describes how to recognize and troubleshoot hardware conflicts with Device Manager.

If there is a problem with the configuration of a hardware device, Windows XP automatically expands the hardware tree category with the problem, shows the configured hardware devices within this category, and displays an icon over the device icon to identify the type of problem.

Troubleshooting a Disabled Device

Figure 12-19 illustrates one type of hardware problem. Windows XP displays **X** through the icon for the Printer Port (LPT1) to indicate that the hardware device has been disabled for some reason. Even though Windows XP detected the presence of an LPT1 (line printer) port that uses resources within the computer, it is not included in the configuration of the computer. If a device were connected to this port, you would be unable to use the device. Also, your LPT1 port might be identified by a different name, such as ECP Printer Port (LPT1).

Figure 12-19   HARDWARE CONFIGURATION PROBLEM

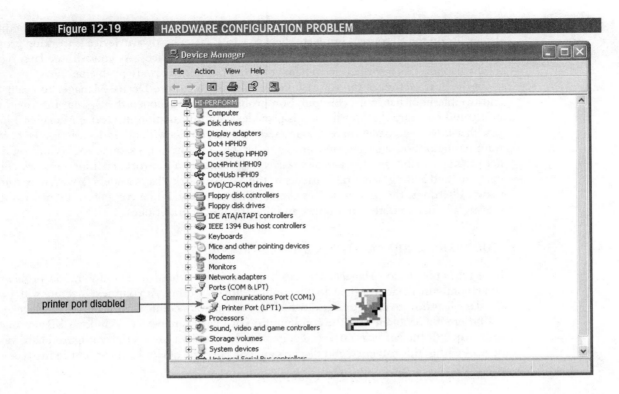

printer port disabled

To correct this problem, open Device Manager, click Printer Port (LPT1), click the Properties button 🖼 , and then check the Device status section on the General property sheet for information about the problem. See Figure 12-20. Windows XP reports that the device is disabled, and includes a hardware code (Code 22) for Microsoft support technicians to use in troubleshooting the problem. You can provide this information directly if you call Microsoft technical support, or you can send them an e-mail message with an attachment that includes an image captured with Alt+Print Scrn.

Figure 12-20   DISABLED LPT1 PORT

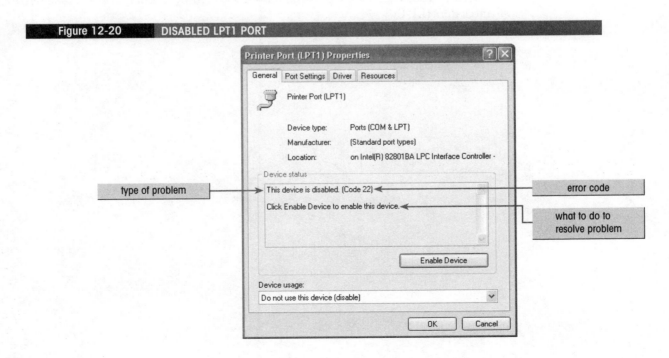

type of problem

error code

what to do to resolve problem

Windows XP also tells you to click the Enable Device button if you want to include the device as part of the system's configuration. You must be logged on as an Administrator or as a member of the Administrators group to make this change. Notice that the Device usage list box displays "Do not use this device (disable)," further verifying that the device is not included in the hardware configuration.

If you click the Enable Device button, Windows XP opens the Device Problems Troubleshooting Wizard, which explains why a device might be disabled. See Figure 12-21. The device might not be working properly, or it might be causing a resource conflict.

Figure 12-21   ENABLING A DEVICE

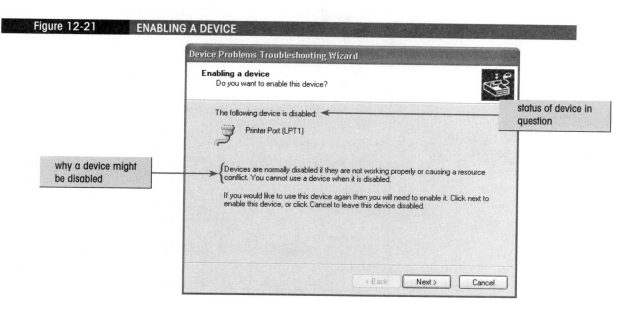

If you click the Next button, the Device Problems Troubleshooting Wizard tells you that it successfully enabled the device, as shown in Figure 12- 22.

Figure 12-22   DEVICE ENABLED

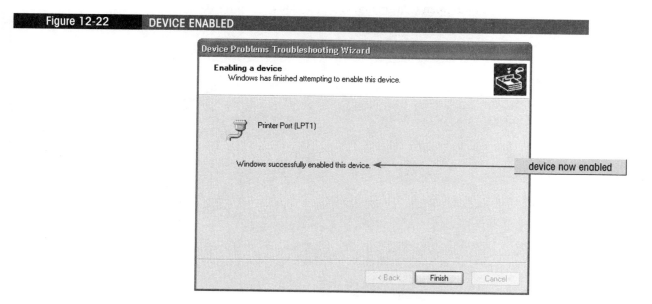

After you click the Finish button, Windows XP closes the Device Problems Troubleshooting Wizard and returns you to the Printer Port (LPT1) Properties dialog box. Notice that the Device usage list box now displays "Use this device (enable)," as shown in Figure 12-23. You could have just as easily corrected the problem by selecting this option from the Device usage list box.

Figure 12-23   LPT1 ENABLED

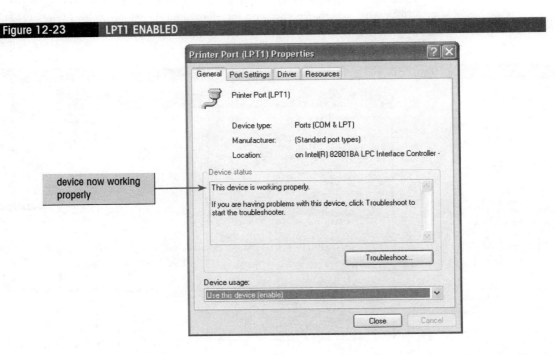

device now working properly

After you close the Printer Port (LPT1) Properties dialog box, Windows XP updates Device Manager and removes the ✖ icon that indicated a problem with the Printer Port (LPT1). See Figure 12-24. If you discover that you are still unable to print to this port, you should open CMOS and enable the use of this port.

Figure 12-24 | **LPT1 NO LONGER DISABLED**

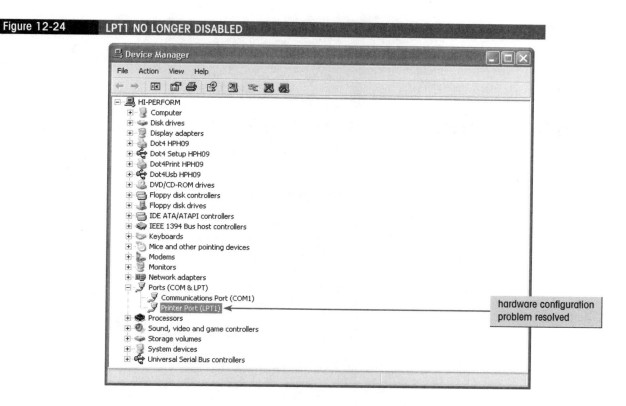

Troubleshooting a Resource Conflict

Another type of problem that you might encounter is a resource conflict—one in which two hardware devices use the same resource, such as the same IRQ or I/O address. If you view the Resources property sheet for one of these hardware devices, Device Manager identifies the names of the devices and the resources that are causing the conflict in the Conflicting device list. See Figure 12-25. On the computer used for this figure, Device Manager reports that Printer Port (LPT1) uses the same I/O Range as the ISAPNP Read Data Port (ISAPNP for ISA Plug and Play). In the Resource settings list box, there is a 🚫 icon over the I/O Range icon.

| Figure 12-25 | VIEWING A RESOURCE CONFLICT |

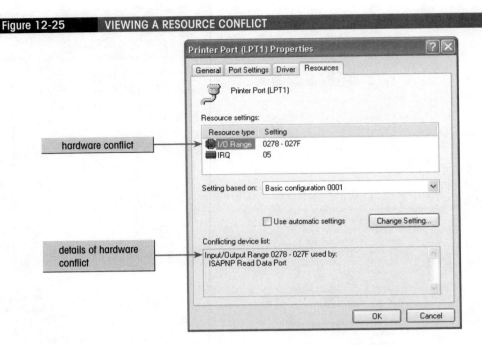

hardware conflict

details of hardware conflict

As noted earlier, a check mark in the "Use automatic settings" check box means that Windows XP chooses resource settings for the hardware device. If you remove the check mark, you can manually configure the device by choosing another combination of resource settings from the "Setting based on" list box. As shown in Figure 12-26, there are different groups of configuration settings for this hardware device, such as Current configuration (the original configuration), Basic configuration 0000, Basic configuration 0001, and Basic configuration 0002. These basic configurations are combinations of resource settings that work for this particular hardware device. Other devices have different combinations of configuration settings.

| Figure 12-26 | CHOOSING ANOTHER BASIC CONFIGURATION |

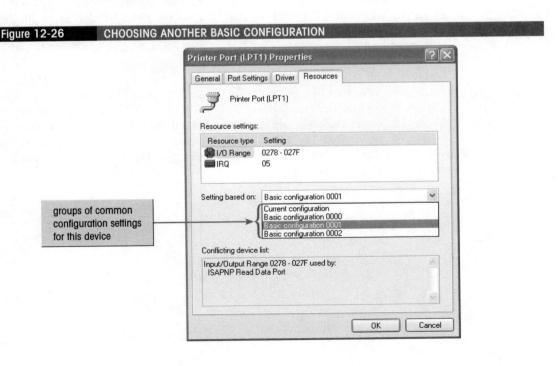

groups of common configuration settings for this device

Another combination of configuration settings might resolve the conflict. In this case, if you change from Basic configuration 0001 to Basic configuration 0002, Device Manager reports that the new configuration creates no conflicts; however, you would have to specify a setting for an IRQ resource. See Figure 12-27. You might find more than one combination of configuration settings that creates no conflicts; in rare cases, you might find that all of the Basic configuration settings create one or more conflicts with other hardware devices. In these cases, you examine the other hardware device to determine if you can find a combination of configuration settings for it that solve the problem. For some older hardware devices, you might first need to manually change DIP switch or jumper settings to support an alternate configuration that works with your computer system.

Figure 12-27   **ANOTHER CONFIGURATION RESOLVES THE CONFLICT**

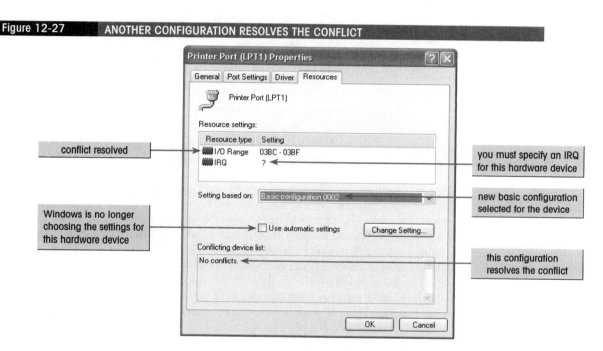

If you need to specify a setting for a specific resource, you select the resource in the Resource settings box, and then click the Change Setting button. Next, you see an Edit dialog box for the resource setting (if Windows XP permits you to change the setting), similar to the one shown in Figure 12-28. In this figure, you are examining an Edit Interrupt Request dialog box for Printer Port (LPT1). Windows XP prompts you to enter an IRQ for this device. You can select a value from the Value box either by using the up or down arrows or by typing a setting. The Conflict information box shows any conflicts with the setting you've chosen. Once you find a setting that creates no conflicts with other hardware devices, you can apply it to the computer.

Figure 12-28	EDITING A HARDWARE RESOURCE SETTING

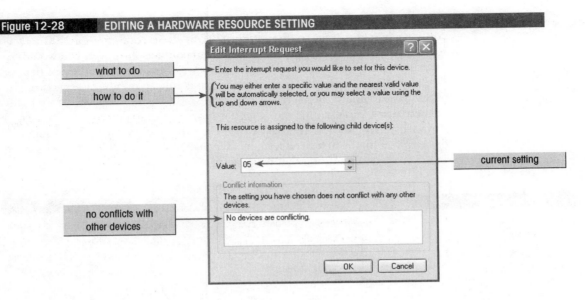

what to do

how to do it

current setting

no conflicts with other devices

If two hardware devices conflict and you cannot find another basic configuration for one of the hardware devices that eliminates the conflict, you can attempt to change the resource setting that causes the conflict. After you remove the check mark from the "Use automatic settings" check box, select a Basic configuration setting, select the resource in the Resource settings box, and click the Change Setting button. In the Edit dialog box for the resource setting you selected, enter or locate a resource setting that does not conflict with another hardware device, and then apply it to the computer. If you cannot find a resource setting that works, you might have to reset two or three other devices so as not to conflict with this device. If you select a Basic configuration setting, change a resource setting, and then click the OK button, Windows XP displays a Creating a Forced Configuration dialog box, warns that you are manually changing resources for a device, and then asks if you want to continue. See Figure 12-29. If you choose to continue, the changes are applied to your computer. When you change a resource assignment for a Plug and Play device and create what's called a **forced hardware configuration**, Windows XP has less flexibility in assigning resources to other devices that you might later add to your computer.

Figure 12-29	CREATING A FORCED CONFIGURATION

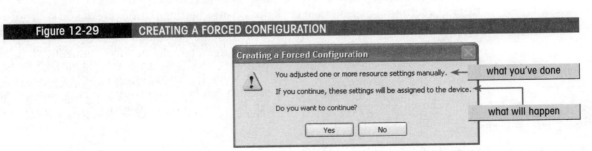

what you've done

what will happen

One other option at your disposal is a Help Troubleshooter, which you can start from the General property sheet for a hardware device or from the Windows XP Help and Support Center.

It's important to emphasize again that you must be careful in making changes to the hardware configuration settings on your computer. Before you manually make a change and create a forced hardware configuration, make sure you document the settings first, and then try the Help Troubleshooter to see if Windows XP can identify and correct the problem.

REFERENCE WINDOW   **RW**

Troubleshooting Hardware Problems with Device Manager

- Log on your computer under an account with Administrator privileges.
- From the Start menu, right-click My Computer, click Properties on the shortcut menu, click the Hardware tab, and then click the Device Manager button.
- Examine the hardware tree for hardware configuration problems. Windows XP automatically expands a category if one of the devices is not configured properly.
- Select the device with a hardware configuration problem, and then click the Properties button on the toolbar.
- Examine the Device status section on the General property sheet for information about the hardware problem, such as a disabled device, a resource conflict in which two devices share the same resource, lack of available resources, or no device drivers installed for the hardware device. In the case of a resource conflict, click the Resources tab and examine the information in the Conflicting device list. The list identifies the resource and which devices are attempting to share it.
- Check the Device status area of the General property sheet and follow the recommendation for enabling a device, reinstalling, installing, or updating device drivers, freeing up resources for use by a device, or starting a Troubleshooter. If you have to manually reconfigure resource assignments and create a forced hardware configuration, click the Resources tab, remove the check mark from the "Use automatic settings" check box, choose a different Basic configuration from the "Setting based on" list box, and check the Conflicting device list for possible conflicts. Repeat this process until you find a configuration that does not create a conflict. If none of the Basic configurations work, select one of the Basic configuration settings, click the resource with the hardware conflict in the Resource settings box, click the Change Setting button, specify or select a different resource in the Edit dialog box for that resource type, and then click the OK button to close the Edit dialog box.
- Click the OK button to close the Properties dialog box for the hardware device and apply the changes you made.
- Click the OK button to close the System Properties dialog box.
- If Windows XP recommends that you restart your computer, click the OK button.

You can use Device Manager in yet another way. Before you buy a computer in a store, open Device Manager on the computer and check the hardware configuration. If Windows XP reports a hardware conflict, don't buy that computer. If you do purchase it, you might find it difficult to resolve the problem, or your computer might not perform optimally. Make sure the computer contains devices that are supported by Windows XP. You might have to do some research and determine whether Windows XP supports other hardware devices you want to use in that computer, but the effort saves you time later and reduces troubleshooting problems. As noted earlier, it is a good idea to purchase Plug and Play rather than legacy devices.

Using the System Information Utility

You can use the System Information utility to verify and supplement the information shown in Device Manager. You might be able to pick up additional clues to help you troubleshoot problems on your computer or enhance your understanding of its configuration.

In addition to Device Manager, Kate suggests you use the System Information utility to provide more detailed information on hardware devices in your computer.

To view information on hardware configuration settings:

1. From the Start menu, point to **All Programs**, point to **Accessories**, point to **System Tools**, click **System Information**, and then maximize the System Information window. Windows XP displays summary information about your computer.

POWER USERS TIP To open System Information more quickly, click the Start button, click Run, type MSINFO32 in the Open box, and then press the Enter key.

TROUBLE? If Windows XP opens the Help and Support Center instead of opening the System Information utility, you must reinstall Windows XP.

2. Click the **expand view** box ☐ next to the Hardware Resources node (or category), and then click **Conflicts/Sharing**. The System Information utility shows which devices share specific types of resources or conflict with other devices. See Figure 12-30. Note that on the computer used for this figure, devices share I/O ports, memory addresses, and IRQ 23. Your computer will differ. The sharing of resources does not necessarily indicate a problem. If Device Manager does indicate a problem with a device, and if that device shares a resource with another device, the resource sharing might be the problem. Notice that you can also view DMA, Forced Hardware, I/O, IRQs, and Memory resource settings with the System Information utility.

| Figure 12-30 | VIEWING HARDWARE CONFLICTS AND SHARING |

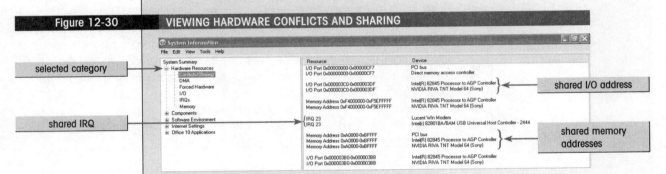

From the File menu, you can print all of the system data (which might be extensive), a selected category and its subcategories, or even a range of pages of the system data. You can save system data for the entire system or for a category, and you can save the data to a text file or to a system information file (with the "nfo" file extension). You can also use the Export option to save system data in a text file.

3. Click the **Forced Hardware** category. Here, the System Information utility lists any manually configured devices. If you need to troubleshoot Plug and Play resource conflicts, you check this category to see what other devices are manually configured. When you manually configure a device, even a Plug and Play device, you assign specific resources to it; as a result, Windows XP has less flexibility in finding the right mix of resource assignments that work for all your hardware devices.

4. Click the **DMA** category to display the DMA channels assigned to devices and view their status. See Figure 12-31. If Windows XP reports a problem in the Status column, you can use Device Manager to locate and troubleshoot the problem. You might also need to obtain an updated device driver from the manufacturer, and perhaps even open the BIOS Setup utility to check and change CMOS settings.

Figure 12-31   **VIEWING THE STATUS OF DMA RESOURCE ASSIGNMENTS**

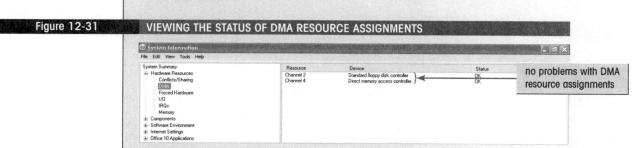

5. Click the **I/O** category to display the I/O resources assigned to devices and view their status. See Figure 12-32. Note that they are all listed as "OK." Again, if there is a sharing conflict, you would turn to Device Manager.

Figure 12-32   **VIEWING THE STATUS OF I/O RESOURCE ASSIGNMENTS**

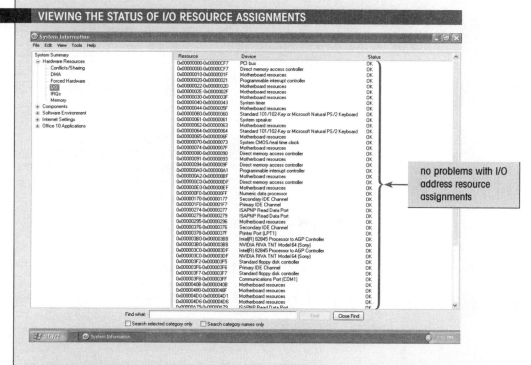

6. Click the **IRQs** category to display the IRQ resource assignments and view their status. See Figure 12-33.

Figure 12-33 | **VIEWING THE STATUS OF IRQ RESOURCE ASSIGNMENTS**

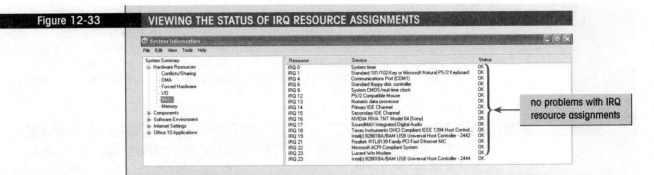

7. Click the **Memory** category to display the memory resources assigned to devices and view their status. See Figure 12-34. If two devices are configured to use the same memory address range, you use Device Manager to identify and troubleshoot the problem.

Figure 12-34 | **VIEWING THE STATUS OF MEMORY RESOURCE ASSIGNMENTS**

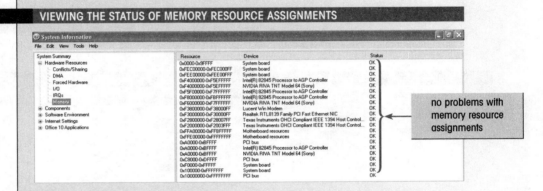

8. Click ➕ next to the Components category, and then click **Problem Devices**. The System Information utility provides information on any devices that are not properly configured, including their error codes. If a problem exists, you would attempt to resolve it with Device Manager.

9. Close the System Information window.

Although Device Manager is the tool you are most likely to use when troubleshooting hardware, the Microsoft System Information utility can provide more details about your computer configuration and verify the status of resource assignments.

The System Information utility not only provides a broad spectrum of information about your computer system, it identifies shared devices, hardware conflicts, forced hardware configurations, and problem devices. When troubleshooting a hardware problem, you can use both Device Manager and the System Information utility to provide the data you need to analyze and resolve the problem.

Using Windows XP's Networking Capabilities

Over the last several months, North Coast Broadcasting has hired additional technical support staff to keep up with its rapid growth and its customers' needs. Kate and her staff work with these new employees to set up network connections on their computers so they can perform their jobs.

Many users need a networked computer to access important applications and documents required for their work, as well as hardware devices such as printers and modems. Furthermore, users commonly access the Internet and World Wide Web through their company networks. In the future, more and more people will set up networks at home so they can interface with consumer electronics devices (such as VCRs) in the home itself.

If you are connected to a network, it is either a server-based network or a peer-to-peer network. In a server-based network, the **server** is the computer that manages the network and provides shared resources to network users within the domain. A **domain** consists of a group of networked computers that share a common directory database and security information on network resources. Your user account gives you access to all of the domain resources, such as printers, for which you also have permissions.

In contrast, a **peer-to-peer network**, or **workgroup**, is a network in which each computer is an equal; there is no server that manages network resources and provides network users access to those resources. Instead, computers communicate directly with each other. Users decide which resources to share with other users on the network. Peer-to-peer networks are typically home or small office networks with two to 10 computers, along with shared devices such as printers and scanners. Windows XP Professional and Windows XP Home Edition support a maximum of 10 computers in a peer-to-peer network.

The remainder of this tutorial focuses on peer-to-peer networks, or workgroups, that include Windows XP Professional, Windows XP Home Edition, or both. Also, because network configurations and settings vary considerably, and because restrictions are frequently placed on accessing network settings and network resources, the remainder of this tutorial does not include any tutorial steps. Instead, it describes the basic process for working on a peer-to-peer network, and for locating network information and network resources. If you examine network settings on your own computer network, make sure you document settings that you intend to change so that you can restore them later if a problem develops. Also, remember that you can click the Cancel button to close dialog boxes without inadvertently saving your changes.

Viewing Your Computer's Name

Each computer in a workgroup has a name that uniquely identifies the computer on the network. You can use the Network Setup Wizard to set up a home network, name your computer, and also set up Internet Connection Firewall and Internet Connection Sharing.

To locate your computer's name, open the Start menu, right-click My Computer, click Properties, and click the Computer Name tab. As shown in Figure 12-35, Windows XP displays the description you've provided for the computer, the full computer name, and the workgroup or domain to which the computer belongs. The description is important, because it determines how Windows XP identifies a computer when you are viewing network connections, and therefore makes it easier for you to locate a specific computer on a network. If available, you can click the Network ID button to start the Network Identification Wizard, which allows you to join a domain and create a local user account.

Figure 12-35 **VIEWING A COMPUTER'S NAME AND WORKGROUP AFFILIATION**

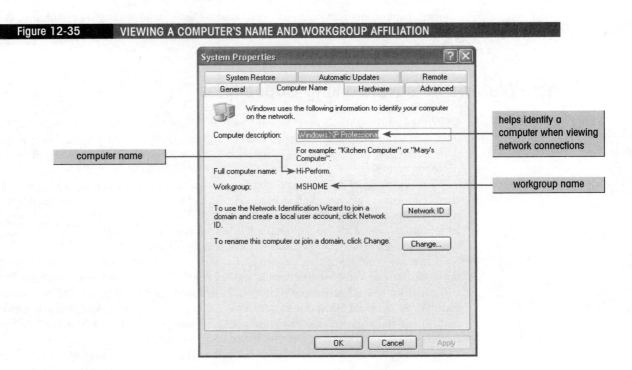

You can click the Change button on the Computer Name property sheet to change the name of your computer and identify the domain in which you already have an account. See Figure 12-36. If you have a peer-to-peer network at home, each computer should use the same workgroup name so you can easily access other computers on your home network. If you make changes on this property sheet, they may affect your access to network resources. You must restart your computer so Windows XP can apply the changes.

Figure 12-36   OPTION FOR CHANGING A COMPUTER'S NAME

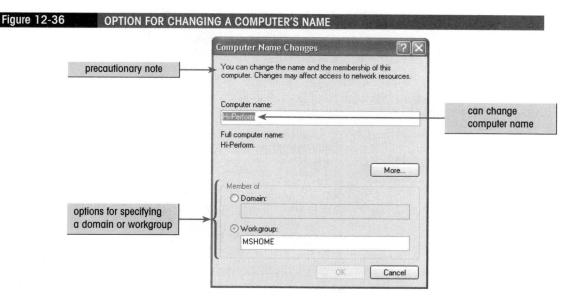

When you name a computer, you might want to use a standard naming convention, such as Sales-RM201-12, to identify the location of a computer. If you set up a dual-boot configuration with another version of Windows, you should use a different computer name for the same computer under each version of Windows.

Viewing Network Connection Settings

If you open My Network Places, click the "View network connections" link in the Network Tasks dynamic menu, point to and select Local Area Connection in the Network Connections window, and then click "Change settings of this connection" in the Network Tasks dynamic menu, Windows XP opens a Local Area Connection Properties dialog box. See Figure 12-37. Windows XP identifies the network adapter card in the "Connect using" box and lists the services that it installed during setup (your services and settings may differ):

- Client for Microsoft Networks is **client software** that you need to access resources on a Microsoft network.

- File and Printer Sharing for Microsoft Networks is **service software** that enables users of other computers within the same network to access your files and printer.

- QoS (Quality of Service) Packet Scheduler is a component that controls network traffic, including rate-of-flow and prioritization services.

- Internet Protocol (TCP/IP) is a commonly used network protocol that enables computers to communicate with each other over diverse networks.

Figure 12-37   VIEWING LOCAL AREA CONNECTION PROPERTIES

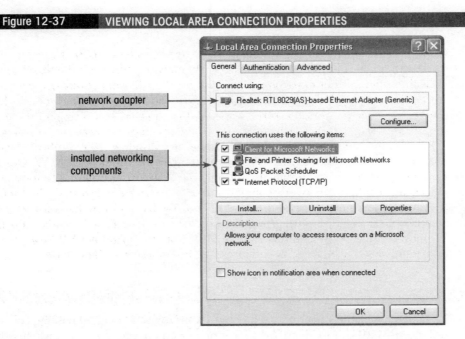

If you open My Network Places, choose "View network connections" in the Network Tasks dynamic menu, and then click (rather than select) Local Area Connection in the Network Connections window, Windows XP opens a Local Area Connection Status dialog box and provides information on the network connection and network activity. See Figure 12-38. Depending on your network adapter, the speed might be listed as 10.0 or 100.0 Mbps (megabits per second). In the Activity area, Windows XP lists the number of packets sent and received. A **packet** consists of a set of data (such as part of a file), as well as a source address and destination address, sent from one location to another over the Internet or other network. The Support property sheet lists information about the Internet Protocol (TCP/IP).

Figure 12-38   VIEWING NETWORK ACTIVITY

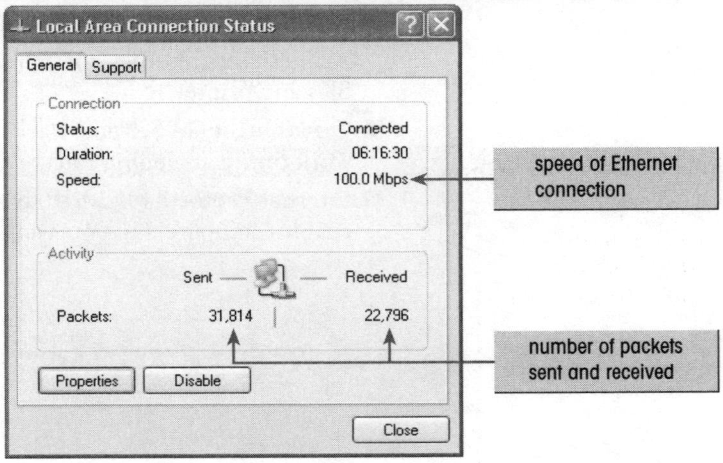

Viewing Computers in a Workgroup

On a peer-to-peer network, you can access shared resources on other computers within the same workgroup. For example, if you click My Network Places on the Start menu, and then click the "View workgroup computers" link on the Network Tasks dynamic menu in the workgroup window, Windows XP displays information about your network. In Figure 12-39 the peer-to-peer network has three networked computers, each using a different operating system: Windows XP Professional on the computer named Hi-Perform, Windows XP Home Edition on the computer named WinXPHome, and Windows 2000 Professional on the computer named MicronPC. This figure was captured on the computer with Windows XP Home Edition right after it was installed. Not only did Windows XP Home Edition automatically detect and configure network components, it automatically detected all three computers within the same network workgroup. The Address bar and title bar show that these three computers belong to a workgroup named Mshome (the default workgroup name under Windows XP). If you access this same window from the Windows XP Professional workstation, your view is identical. These figures and other figures use Tiles view.

| Figure 12-39 | VIEWING COMPUTERS IN THE SAME WORKGROUP |

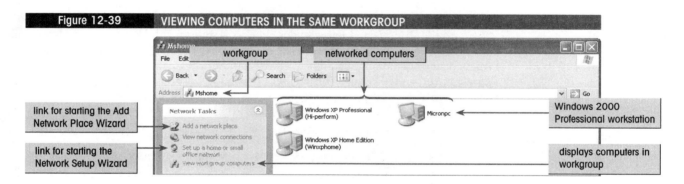

If you click the icon for the Windows XP Professional computer, Windows XP Home Edition opens a window that displays shared resources for that workstation—Drive D, SharedDocs, My Documents, Printer (the local printer on the workstation), and Printers and Faxes. See Figure 12-40. The Address bar shows the UNC path for the Windows XP Professional networked computer; the path is *Hi-perform* in this example. The **UNC (Universal Naming Convention) path** identifies the location of a shared resource on a network. When identifying a computer, the UNC path consists of two backslashes followed by the computer name. Unlike URLs, which use forward slashes, the UNC path uses backslashes.

| Figure 12-40 | VIEWING SHARED DEVICES ON ANOTHER COMPUTER IN THE NETWORK |

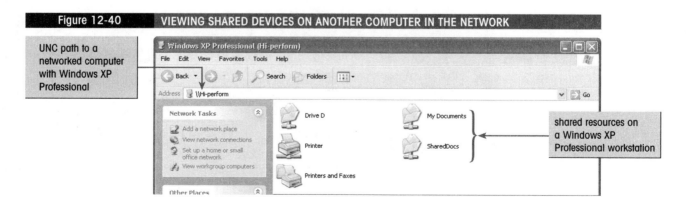

If you click the SharedDocs folder icon, Windows XP Home Edition opens a window that displays the contents of this folder on the other computer. See Figure 12-41. The Address bar now shows the UNC path to the folder that was accessed: \\Hi-perform\SharedDocs.

Figure 12-41   VIEWING THE CONTENTS OF A SHARED FOLDER ON ANOTHER COMPUTER

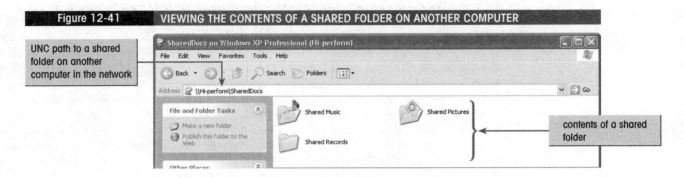

UNC path to a shared folder on another computer in the network

contents of a shared folder

Figure 12-42 shows the workstation with Windows XP Home Edition as viewed from the computer with Windows XP Professional. The two shared resources are the SharedDocs folder and the Printers and Faxes folder. The workstation with Windows XP Home Edition does not have a local printer; instead, it has access to the printer on the Windows XP Professional workstation. Shared printers are another advantage of having a network. You can also enhance printer security on an NTFS volume by granting permissions to users and groups, such as permission to print, manage printers, and manage documents.

Figure 12-42   VIEWING SHARED RESOURCES ON ANOTHER COMPUTER

UNC path to a computer in the network with Windows XP Home Edition

shared resources on a Windows XP Home Edition workstation

If you click the "View network connections" link on the Network Tasks dynamic menu, Windows XP identifies the type of network connection(s) on a computer. In Figure 12-43, the network connection is a Local Area Connection on a LAN (Local Area Network). During installation, or when you use the Network Setup Wizard, Windows XP automatically creates a Local Area Connection if it detects a network adapter.

Figure 12-43   VIEWING THE LOCAL AREA CONNECTION ON A COMPUTER

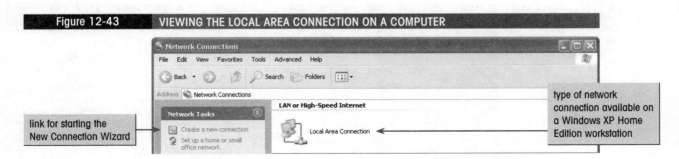

link for starting the New Connection Wizard

type of network connection available on a Windows XP Home Edition workstation

Sharing Folders

If you log onto the workstation with Windows XP Home Edition and then view the folder that contains the shared resources for the Windows XP Home Edition, Windows XP displays three shared resources: SharedDocs, Printers and Faxes, and Scheduled Tasks. See Figure 12-44.

Figure 12-44	VIEWING SHARED DEVICES ON A COMPUTER

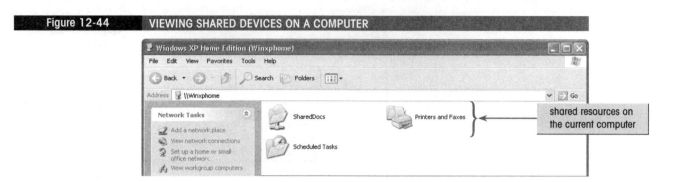

If you then open My Computer on the computer with Windows XP Home Edition, you would see the Shared Documents folder, which appears as SharedDocs in the window that shows shared resources for this workstation. See Figure 12-45. The hand included with the icon for the Shared Documents folder identifies it as a shared folder on a network. Notice that there are My Documents folders for three users of this computer. Also, this dual-boot computer has Windows 98 SE installed on drive C and Windows XP Home Edition installed on drive D. If you boot this computer with Windows 98 SE instead of Windows XP Home Edition, you can access the same networked computers, but this computer would be identified on the network under a different computer name.

Figure 12-45	VIEWING SHARED AND UNSHARED FOLDERS ON THE CURRENT DRIVE

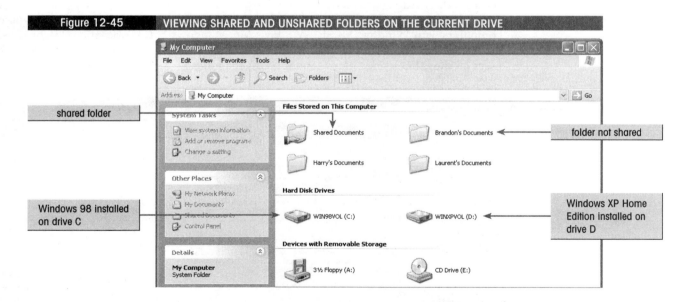

If the current user (in this case, Brandon) wanted to share his My Documents folder with other users on the network, he would right-click his My Documents folder (identified as Brandon's Documents) and then click Properties on the shortcut menu. After the My Documents Properties dialog box opens, he would click the Sharing tab. See Figure 12-46. Under "Local sharing and security," Brandon can share this folder with other users on the same computer by dragging the folder to the Shared Documents folder. Under "Network sharing and security," Brandon can also share the folder over the network. If Windows XP displays a message indicating that it has disabled remote access to your computer as a security measure, do not make any changes to your network settings and do not run the Network Setup Wizard without permission from the Administrator of your network.

Figure 12-46	CHOOSING THE OPTION TO SHARE A FOLDER

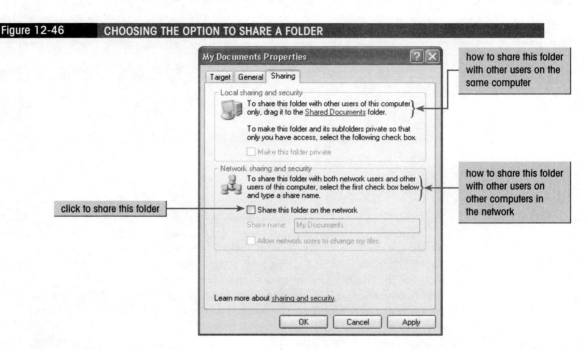

If Brandon adds a check mark to the "Share this folder on the network" check box, he can specify a share name (automatically set as "My Documents"), and then decide whether other network users can make changes to his files. See Figure 12-47. If there are other networked computers with Windows 98 SE, Windows Me, Windows NT Workstation 4.0, or earlier operating systems, Brandon needs to limit the share name to 12 characters; otherwise, the users on the other workstations cannot access the folder.

Figure 12-47	SHARING A FOLDER

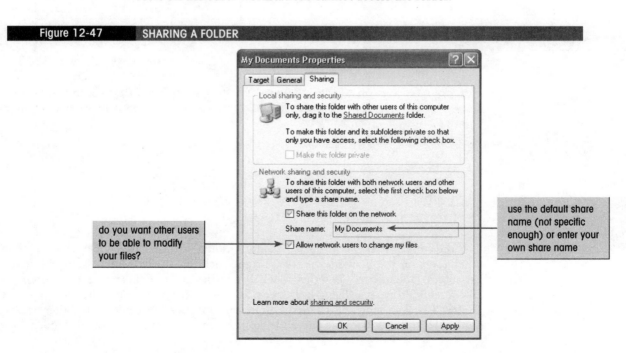

After sharing the computer, notice that Windows XP updates the icon for the Brandon's Documents folder to show that it's a shared resource. See Figure 12-48.

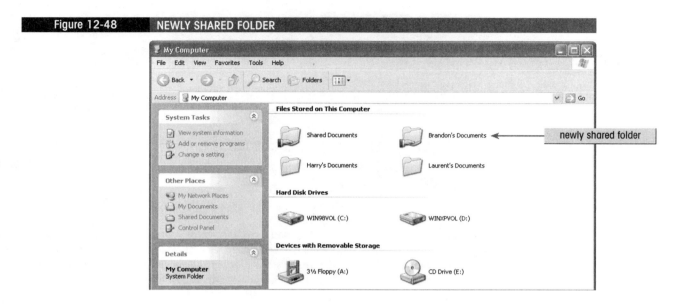

Figure 12-48   NEWLY SHARED FOLDER

If Brandon then examines the folder that contains shared resources for this computer on the network, Windows XP displays the new shared resource (BrandonsDocs). See Figure 12-49.

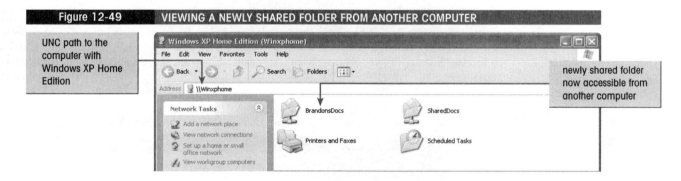

Figure 12-49   VIEWING A NEWLY SHARED FOLDER FROM ANOTHER COMPUTER

If Brandon logs on to the Windows XP Professional workstation and then opens My Network Places, he sees all of the shared resources on all three networked computers. See Figure 12-50.

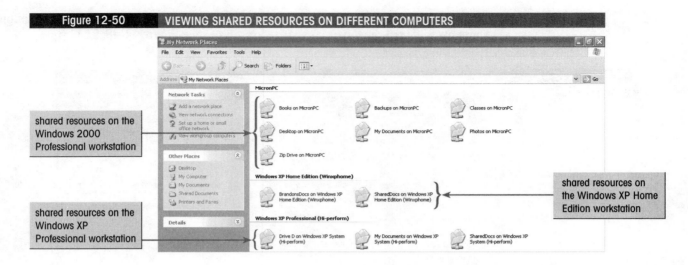

Figure 12-50 | VIEWING SHARED RESOURCES ON DIFFERENT COMPUTERS

To protect your computer from unauthorized access, you should not share the top-level (or root) folder on a drive. However, if your hard disk drive is divided into two drives to separate document files from operating system files, or if your computer contains two hard disk drives, you can share the drive that does not contain the operating system.

Using the Network Setup Wizard

You can use the Network Setup Wizard to set up a network for your computer. As noted earlier, Windows XP can automatically perform this operation when you install it.

After you open My Network Places, you can click the "Set up a home or small office network" option in the Network Tasks dynamic menu to set up your network. As shown in the Network Setup Wizard's Welcome dialog box in Figure 12-51, you can share an Internet connection, set up Internet Connection Firewall, share files and folders, and share a printer.

Figure 12-51 | OPENING THE NETWORK SETUP WIZARD

Network Setup Wizard

Welcome to the Network Setup Wizard

This wizard will help you set up this computer to run on your network. With a network you can:

- Share an Internet connection
- Set up Internet Connection Firewall
- Share files and folders
- Share a printer

what you can do with this wizard

To continue, click Next.

< Back | Next > | Cancel

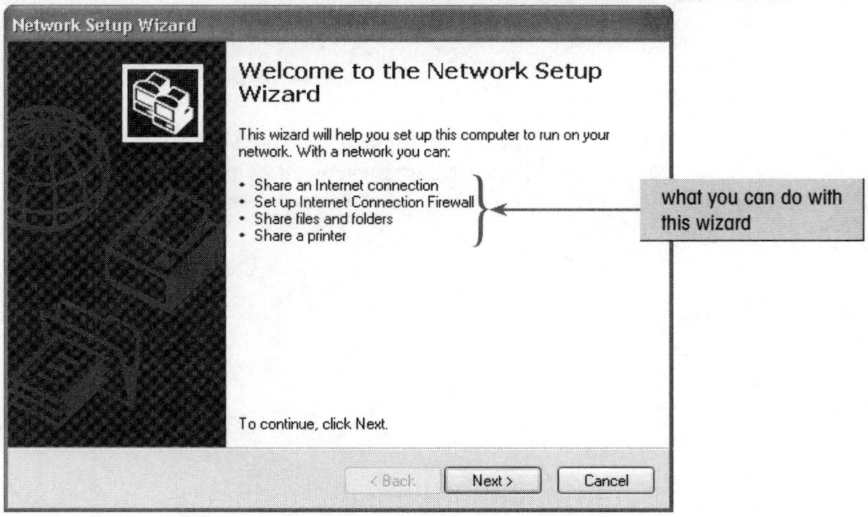

In the next step, the wizard recommends that you install network cards, modems, and cables. Before you continue, turn on all computers, printers, and external modems, and connect to the Internet. See Figure 12-52.

Figure 12-52   **WHAT YOU SHOULD DO BEFORE YOU PROCEED**

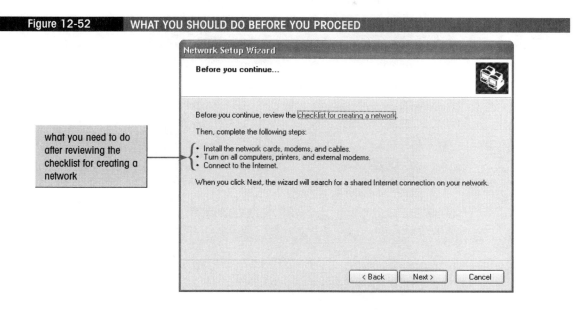

what you need to do after reviewing the checklist for creating a network

In the next step, the wizard asks you to select a connection method. See Figure 12-53. Identify whether your computer and other networked computers connect directly to the Internet through the computer you are currently using, or whether your computer connects to the Internet through another computer on your network or through a residential gateway. A **residential gateway** is a hardware device that connects your home or small office network to the Internet so that networked computers can share a single cable modem or DSL Internet connection. Links for the first two options allow you to view diagrams of the respective setups. If neither of these selections describes your computer, choose Other.

Figure 12-53   **CHOOSING A CONNECTION METHOD**

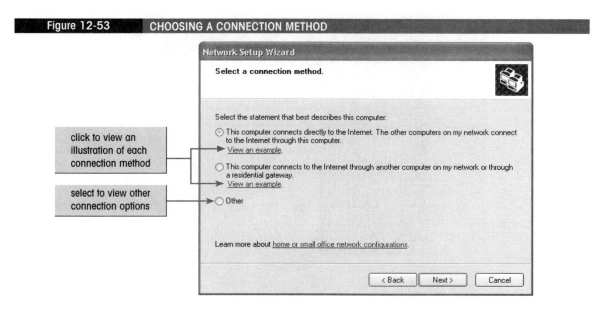

click to view an illustration of each connection method

select to view other connection options

If you choose Other, you can specify whether your computer connects directly to the Internet or through a network hub, whether your computer connects directly to the Internet without being on a network, and whether your computer belongs to a network that does not yet have an Internet connection. See Figure 12-54. You can also view diagrams for each option.

| Figure 12-54 | OTHER INTERNET CONNECTION METHODS |

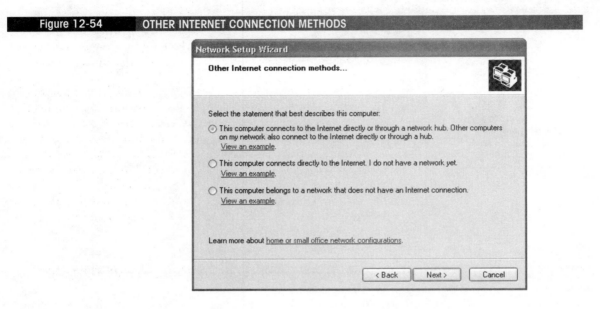

The option that you choose determines what type of information the Network Setup Wizard prompts you for, what recommendations it makes, and how it sets up and configures the type of connection you have chosen. If you examine the Help and Support Center for information on setting up a home or small office network, you find a checklist to follow. See Figure 12-55.

| Figure 12-55 | HELP AND SUPPORT CENTER CHECKLIST FOR SETTING UP A NETWORK |

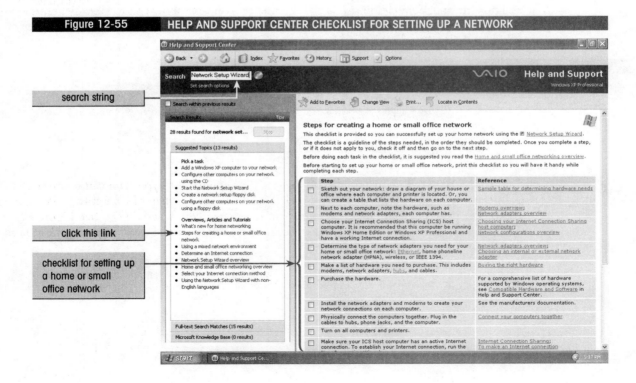

After using the Network Setup Wizard on a Windows XP computer in your network, use your Windows XP CD or a Network Setup floppy disk to run the Network Setup Wizard on all other computers in your network that use Windows 98, Windows 98 SE, or Windows Me. This completes the setup and configuration of your network.

Using the New Connection Wizard

The Windows XP New Connection Wizard replaces the Internet Connection Wizard found in earlier versions of Windows, and allows you to set up a network connection using different network configurations.

After you open My Network Places and click the "View network connections" link in the Network Tasks dynamic menu, you can click the "Create a new connection" link under Network Tasks to start the New Connection Wizard. See Figure 12-56. As noted on the Welcome screen, this wizard helps you connect to the Internet if you did not already set up the connection when you installed Windows XP. You can also use the wizard to connect to a private network (such as your office network), and set up a home or small office network. (If Windows XP also displays a Location Information dialog box and prompts you for information before it can set up a phone or modem connection, and if you want to create a new connection, enter the information requested and then click the OK button; otherwise, click the Cancel button.)

Figure 12-56   OPENING THE NEW CONNECTION WIZARD

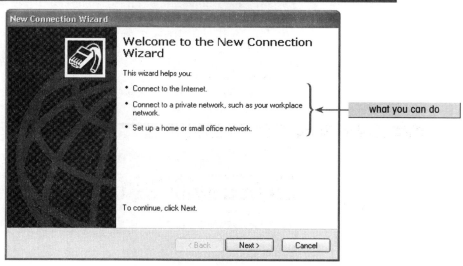

In the next step, you can choose the network connection type. You can connect to the Internet, connect to your office network, set up a home or small office network, or set up a direct connection using your computer's infrared, parallel, or serial port. See Figure 12-57. The option for connecting to your office network might prove useful if you work at home or travel on company business.

Figure 12-57   CHOOSING THE NETWORK CONNECTION TYPE

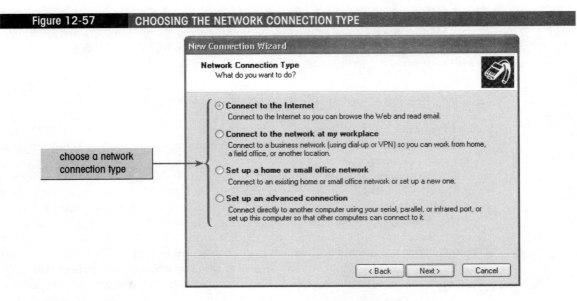

choose a network
connection type

If you choose to connect to the Internet, you can then choose from a list of ISPs, set up your connection manually, or use the CD from your ISP. If you choose to connect to your office network, you can then choose either to create a dial-up connection using a modem and a regular phone line or an ISDN line, or create a Virtual Private Network (VPN) connection. **ISDN (Integrated Services Digital Network)** lines are high-speed communication lines with data transfer rates of 64 Kbps, 128 Kbps, or 1.5 Mbps. A **Virtual Private Network (VPN)** connection allows you to connect to a remote access server through the Internet or another network. The VPN consists of the public and private networks used to make the connection.

If you choose the Advanced Connection options, you can set up your computer to accept incoming connections via the Internet, a phone line, or a direct cable connection. You can also connect directly to another computer using an infrared, parallel, or serial port.

Using the Add Network Place Wizard to Create an FTP Connection

You can use the Add Network Place Wizard to create a shortcut to a Web site, an FTP site, or some other network location. **FTP (File Transfer Protocol)** is a standard Internet protocol for transferring files between computers on the Internet and as such, is commonly used to download programs and other types of files from Internet servers to your computer. When you connect to an FTP server on the Internet, you are connecting to a file server instead of a Web server for the express purpose of uploading or downloading files. If you open My Network Places and click the "Add a network place" link in the Network Tasks dynamic menu, Windows XP opens the Add Network Place Wizard. See Figure 12-58. Note that you can also use the wizard to sign up for a service that offers online storage space (such as for backups).

Figure 12-58   OPENING THE ADD NETWORK PLACE WIZARD

how you can use
this wizard

In the next step, you are asked where you want to create this network place. See Figure 12-59. The wizard asks you to select a service provider; if necessary, it helps you create an account with that provider. (MSN Communities might be selected on your computer.)

Figure 12-59   CHOOSING THE NETWORK LOCATION

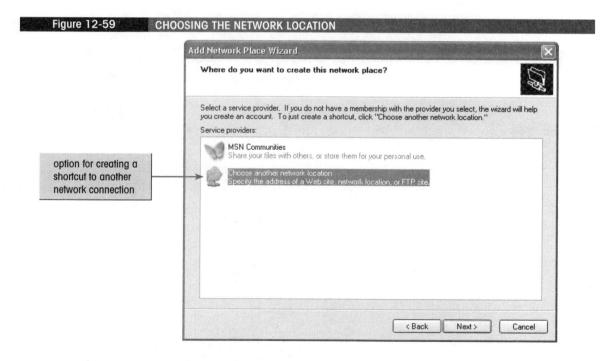

option for creating a
shortcut to another
network connection

If you select the option for choosing another network location, the wizard prompts you for the address of the network. See Figure 12-60. You can use the "View some examples" link to view the proper format for specifying the Internet or network address. You can specify a shared folder on a server or Web site, and you can specify an FTP site.

Figure 12-60   SPECIFYING THE ADDRESS OF A NETWORK LOCATION

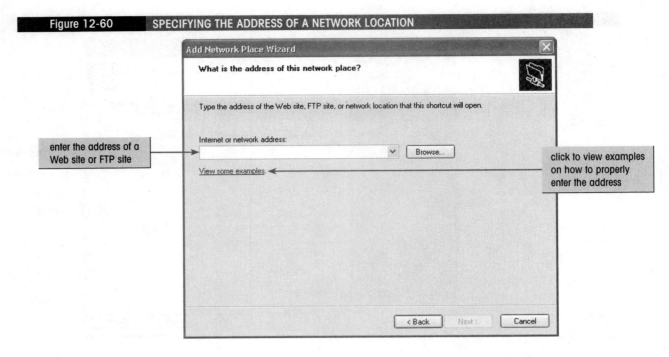

enter the address of a
Web site or FTP site

click to view examples
on how to properly
enter the address

If you specify an FTP site, the wizard prompts you for your user name and password. See Figure 12-61. The wizard notes that most FTP servers allow users to log on anonymously, but with limited access to the server. If you want to enter a user name, remove the check mark from the "Log on anonymously" check box and then enter the user name. You are prompted for the password when you connect to the FTP server.

Figure 12-61   SPECIFYING YOUR LOGON NAME

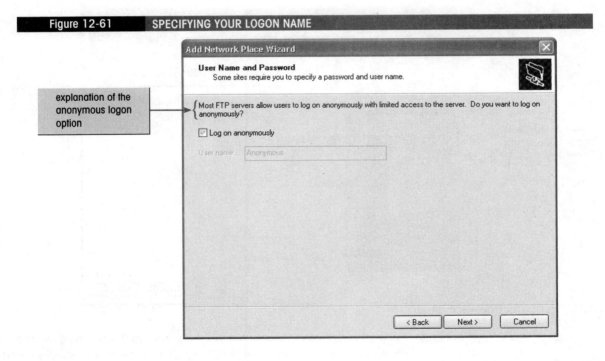

explanation of the
anonymous logon
option

In the next step, the wizard asks you to enter a name for this shortcut. By default, it shows you the address of the FTP site you entered earlier. See Figure 12-62.

Figure 12-62	NAMING THE NETWORK LOCATION SHORTCUT

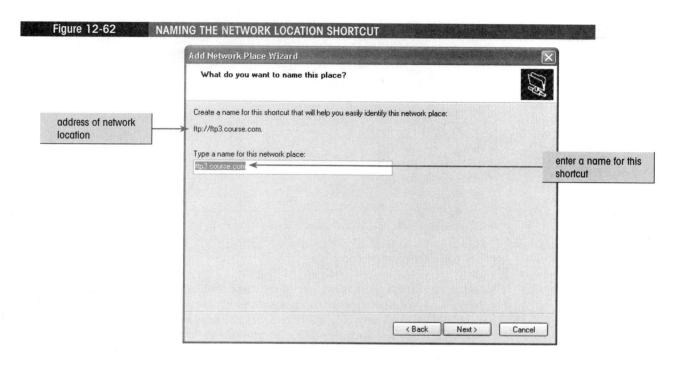

Once you specify a name for the shortcut and go to the next step, the wizard informs you that the shortcut will appear in My Network Places, and then it automatically opens this network place. See Figure 12-63.

Figure 12-63	COMPLETING THE PROCESS FOR ADDING A NETWORK LOCATION

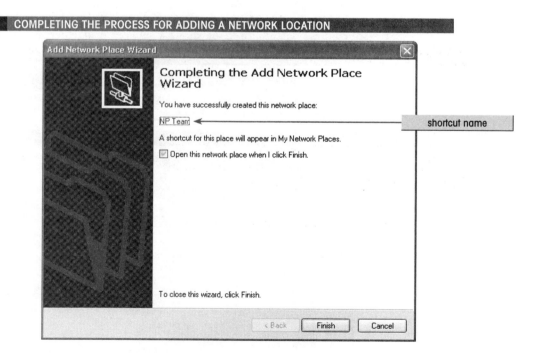

If you open My Network Places, you see the new FTP connection listed under Internet. See Figure 12-64. You also see shared resources on this network for the current user's logon. (If the contents of your My Network Places window is not grouped in categories by network location, click View on the menu bar, point to Arrange Icons by, click Network Location if it is not already selected, and click the Show in Groups option if it does not have a check mark.)

Figure 12-64	SHORTCUT TO AN FTP SITE

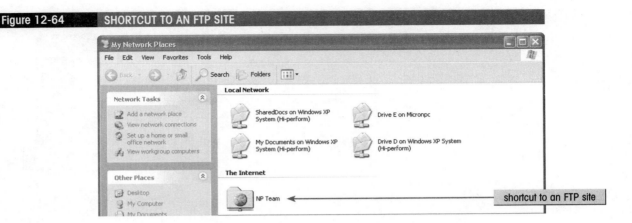

Using Network Bridges

Windows XP also supports the use of network bridges. A **network bridge** enables you to create a network that consists of connections between computers using different types of network adapters. A network bridge replaces the need for special equipment, and simplifies the process of setting up and configuring a network. Although you can create only one network bridge on a computer, that bridge can support any number of network connections. To create a network bridge, you open My Network Places, click the "View network connections" link in the Network Tasks dynamic menu, point to and select the connections under LAN or High-Speed Internet that you want to include in the network bridge, right-click the selected connections, and then click Bridge Connections on the shortcut menu. The connections then appear under Network Bridge. The Network Setup Wizard automatically creates a bridge when it finds two or more different network adapters on a computer with Windows XP. Figure 12-65 shows a network bridge between two connections—a Local Area Connection that uses an Ethernet adapter, and a 1394 Connection that uses an IEEE 1394 network adapter—on a Windows XP Professional workstation. The cables from Ethernet adapters connect to a central hub, a device with multiple ports that copies data to each port, so that all computers on the network have access to the same data.

Figure 12-65	VIEWING THE NETWORK BRIDGE SETUP ON A COMPUTER

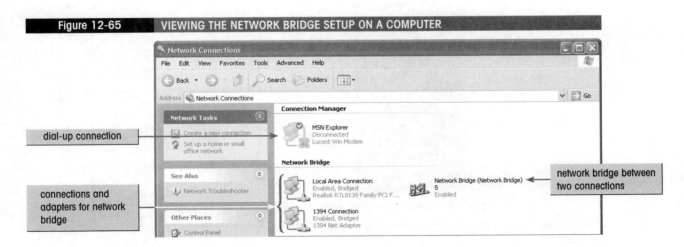

A network bridge can also include a wireless network adapter (for example, in a laptop) and a **Home Phoneline Network Adapter (HPNA)**. Wireless network adapters use radio frequencies to transmit data to and from your computer. An HPNA use the phone lines in your home to create a wireless network that eliminates the need for running network cables to different locations in a home. The cable from the network adapter is plugged into phone jacks using telephone cables. Because this technology uses a different band of frequencies than that used for regular telephone calls, it does not interfere with the use of voice or fax data on a telephone line. The Home Phoneline Networking Alliance, or HomePNA, developed this home networking standard.

Network Bridge is also available in Windows XP Home Edition, but not in Windows XP 64-Bit Edition.

As noted earlier, networks are indispensable to companies and businesses; small businesses and home users now implement simpler types of networks, such as peer-to-peer networks. The extensive networking support in Windows XP automates and simplifies the process of setting up a network.

With the availability of Plug and Play hardware, utilities such as Device Manager and System Information, and enhanced support for networking in Windows XP, Kate and the staff of North Coast Broadcasting find that their computers deliver better performance and reliability, and allow them to focus on the tasks they need to accomplish.

REVIEW ASSIGNMENTS

Kate periodically travels to North Coast Broadcasting's regional offices to help staff set up and troubleshoot their computers. Because some of these regional offices rely on slightly older computers, employees invariably encounter problems with their hardware configuration. On her next visit to NCB's regional office in Eureka, California, she wants to check the status of each computer and resolve any hardware problems if necessary.

As you complete each step in these Review Assignments, record your answers so you can submit them to your instructor. Use a word-processing application such as Word or WordPad to prepare and then print your answers to these questions. To save time in reporting or recording information, use Alt+Print Scrn to capture images of property sheets and print them with WordPad. Also, if you change any settings on the computer you are using, note the original settings so you can restore them later.

1. From the Start menu, right-click My Computer, click Properties, click the Hardware tab, and then click the Device Manager button.

Explore
2. Does Device Manager report that your computer includes newer hardware technologies, such as the USB and IEEE 1394? If so, what are they? How do you use these devices?

3. Click View on the menu bar, and then click Resources by type. How many IRQs does your computer have?

4. What device, if any, is assigned IRQ 6? Is there any other way you could locate this same information? If so, what is it?

5. Are any IRQs shared? If so, what is the IRQ number, and what devices share that IRQ?

Explore
6. Click View on the menu bar, and then click Devices by type. Expand the Computer category. How does Device Manager identify your computer? Is it ACPI compliant?

Explore
7. Expand the Processors category. What type of processor does your computer have?

Explore
8. Expand the Network adapters category. What type, or types, of adapter(s) does your computer have?

Explore

9. Expand the Display adapters category, select your display adapter, and then click the Properties button. What is the name of the display adapter? What is the location of the display adapter? Is the device working properly, or is there a hardware problem? If there is a problem, what information does Windows XP provide about the problem?

10. What types of resources does this display adapter use? What is the IRQ assignment for the adapter? Are there any conflicts with other hardware devices?

11. Close the Properties dialog box for the display adapter without making any changes to the configuration of your computer.

12. Locate and expand the System devices hardware category. Does Windows XP report that your computer has a Microsoft ACPI-Compliant System?

13. Close Device Manager without making any changes to the configuration of your computer.

14. From the Start menu, point to All Programs, point to Accessories, point to System Tools, and then click System Information.

Explore

15. Under System Summary, expand the Hardware Resources category and select IRQs. What IRQ is assigned to your display adapter? Are there any devices that share an IRQ? If so, identify the devices and the IRQ that they share.

16. Under Hardware Resources, select Conflicts/Sharing. What types of resources, if any, are shared on your computer? (You do not need to list all the details; just identify the type of resource.)

17. Under Hardware Resources, select Forced Hardware. Does the System Information utility report any problems? If so, what are they, and what information does this utility provide?

18. Under System Summary, expand the Components category and then select Problem Devices. Does the System Information utility report any hardware configuration problems on your computer? If so, list each device, the code that identifies the type of problem, and any other information that System Information provides.

Explore

19. Select the USB category. Does your computer have any USB devices? If so, what are they? Select the Infrared category. Does your computer have any Infrared devices? If so, what are they?

20. Close the System Information utility.

CASE PROBLEMS

Case 1. Troubleshooting a Hardware Configuration Problem at Holmberg's Auto Truck Repair & Fleet Maintenance Josh Holmberg works for his father's business, Holmberg's Auto Truck Repair & Fleet Maintenance. His job responsibilities include installing and configuring new software on the office computers and troubleshooting hardware problems. Josh asks you to help one of the other employees resolve a problem on her computer. You use Device Manager to quickly identify the problem, as shown in Figure 12-66.

As you complete each step in this case, record your answers so you can submit them to your instructor. Use a word-processing application such as Word or WordPad to prepare and then print your answers to these questions. Also, if you change any settings on the computer you are using, note the original settings so you can restore them later.

1. Which device does Device Manager identify as the one with a problem?

2. What type of hardware configuration problem is this?

3. What is the most likely cause of this hardware problem?

4. What three tools are available for troubleshooting this problem?

5. Describe how you would find out more information about this problem using Device Manager.

6. List the steps you would take to attempt to resolve the problem.

7. What other options would you try if you were unable to resolve the problem using the approach you described in the last step?

Figure 12-66

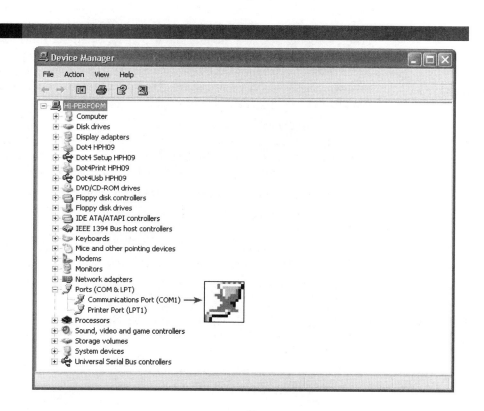

Case 2. Configuring Hardware at Quick Stop Copy In addition to high-speed copy machines, Quick Stop Copy provides a variety of other services for its customers, such as desktop publishing, binding, laminating, folding, cutting, and fax services. The store has PCs and Macs that its customers can use to prepare and print documents on high-quality color printers. Michelle Eagans, the owner, wants to replace the internal modem on one of the computers with an external modem.

As you complete each step in this case, record your answers so you can submit them to your instructor. Use a word-processing application such as Word or WordPad to prepare and then print your answers to these questions. Also, if you change any settings on the computer you are using, note the original settings so you can restore them later.

1. After Michelle connects the external modem and powers on her computer, Windows XP automatically detects the modem and then starts installing software to support the modem. What type of hardware device did she purchase?

2. After Windows XP boots to the desktop, Michelle tests the modem and discovers that it does not work. She automatically assumes that the most likely cause is a hardware configuration problem. Is this a reasonable assumption? If so, explain. If not, what is the most likely cause of the problem?

3. What tools are available for troubleshooting this problem?

4. What should Michelle do next? Describe what steps Michelle should take to resolve the problem.

5. What other options could Michelle try if she was unable to resolve the problem using the approach described in the last step?

Case 3. Troubleshooting Hardware Configuration Problems at McKinlay Flooring & Interiors, Inc. Timothy McKinlay operates a small home-improvement business that sells floor and wall products. He relies on his business computer for a variety of purposes: tracking business income and expenses, client accounts and projects, inventories, order processing, preparing advertising and promotional materials, and tax preparation. After installing Windows XP on his computer, he notices a hardware configuration problem, as shown in Figure 12-67. He wants to figure out the best way to troubleshoot the problem.

As you complete each step in this case, record your answers so you can submit them to your instructor. Use a word-processing application such as Word or WordPad to prepare and then print your answers to these questions. Also, if you change any settings on the computer you are using, note the original settings so you can restore them later.

1. What type of hardware configuration problem is this?

2. What is the nature of this hardware problem?

3. What tools are available for troubleshooting this problem?

4. Describe how you would find out more information about this problem.

5. List the steps you would take to attempt to resolve the problem.

6. What other options could Timothy try if he was unable to resolve the problem using the approach described in the last step?

Figure 12-67

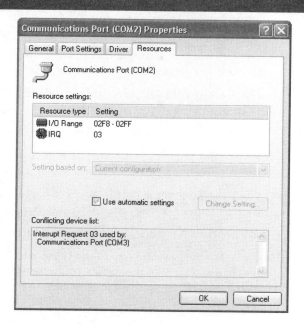

Case 4. *Using the Windows XP Net Diagnostics Tool at Maestri Desktop Publishing, Inc.*
Maestri Desktop Publishing has grown rapidly over the last three years, and it now handles
a variety of large business accounts in New York state. Carolyn Maestri, the owner, asks you
to use the new Windows XP Net Diagnostics tool to examine the Maestri office network.

As you complete each step in this case, record your answers so you can submit them to
your instructor. Use a word-processing application such as Word or WordPad to prepare
and then print your answers to these questions. Also, if you change any settings on the
computer you are using, note the original settings so you can restore them later.

Explore

1. Open System Information and, from the Tools menu, open Net Diagnostics.

2. Click the "Tell me about Network Diagnostics" link, and then read the summary information about this tool.

3. What does Network Diagnostics do? What does Network Diagnostics look for when it
   scans your system?

4. Close the Network Diagnostics — Web Page Dialog box.

Explore

5. Select the option for setting scanning options. Under Actions, click the Verbose check
   box (if it is not already selected). Under Categories, select any options that are not
   already included as options to check, and then click the Save Options button.

6. Click the link for scanning your system.

7. Expand the Computer System category, and then locate and list the information
   for the following settings: Description, Domain, InfraredSupported, Model,
   NetworkServerModeEnabled, NumberOfProcessors, PartOfDomain, Roles,
   SystemStartupOptions, SystemType, and TotalPhysicalMemory.

8. Expand the Operating System category, and then locate and list the information
   for the following settings: BootDevice, EncryptionLevel, FreePhysicalMemory,
   FreeSpaceInPagingFiles, FreeVirtualMemory, SystemDevice, SystemDirectory,
   SystemDrive, TotalVirtualMemorySize, and WindowsDirectory.

9. Expand the Modems category, list each modem, and for each modem, also list the modem port (AttachedTo) and the device type (DeviceType). If you do not have a modem, list N/A (for Not Applicable).

10. Did you discover that you had an additional modem that you did not know about, and that was not reported in Device Manager? If so, which one?

Explore ▷ 11. For the Network Adapters category, identify the component that passed the Net Diagnostics test.

12. For the IP Address category, identify the IP Address.

13. Right-click the background of the report. What options are available to you on the shortcut menu? Click the background to close the shortcut menu.

14. Click the Save to file button near the beginning of the report, and save the results, and then be patient, as the save takes time. *Note*: The file size might easily be 4-5 MB.

15. Where does Network Diagnostics save the file, and what type of file is it?

Explore ▷ 16. Open this file, expand one of the categories (by clicking the plus sign), and notice that you can access all of the results you were able to view in the Help and Support Center. What program does this file open in?

17. After closing Network Diagnostics and the System Information utility, you might want to move the file to a folder where you store documentation about your computer. If you are working on a lab computer and want to keep this file, move the file to a Zip disk or some other type of high-capacity removable disk.

18. Describe how you might use the Net Diagnostics tool on the computer network where you work, or on your own computer network.

EXPLORING THE WINDOWS REGISTRY

Customizing Systems at DGL Communications Group

CASE

DGL Communications Group

DGL Communications Group provides a variety of telecommunications services to its customers in northern Virginia, southeastern Maryland, and Washington, D.C. DGL's consulting services include network design, installation, troubleshooting, upgrades, repairs, and training, as well as integrating Internet technologies into a company's business strategies.

Eric Brenner works as a microcomputer specialist in DGL's Information Systems Department. You work with Eric to provide training and troubleshooting support to staff on the use of application software, hardware, networks, and Internet technologies. Eric offers to show you how to use the Windows Registry to customize the operating environment of desktop workstations, as well as portable computers used by staff working off site.

In the first section of the tutorial, you examine the role and importance of the Windows Registry. You back up the Registry, create a restore point, and then open the Registry and export Registry settings so that you have three backups of the Registry. After backing up the Registry, you examine the structure of the Registry, trace information on a registered file type, and examine the use of Class Identifiers.

The Role of the Windows Registry

Windows XP stores your computer's hardware, software, security, user settings or profiles, and property settings for objects such as folders and programs in a database known as the **Registry**. When you perform a normal boot of your computer, Windows XP processes the information in the Registry to properly configure your computer. For example, the Registry contains information on hardware devices and resources (such as IRQs, I/O addresses, and DMA channels) assigned to both Plug and Play and legacy devices. During booting, Windows XP uses this information to identify and configure hardware devices, reconfigure hardware devices (if necessary), and update the Registry.

When you open Device Manager, you are viewing the current hardware settings in the Registry. If you change your system's hardware configuration in Device Manager, you are updating the Registry. Also, when you log onto your computer, Windows XP uses your user profile settings stored in the Registry to customize your display of the desktop. If you change the display and desktop settings using options in the Control Panel, you are updating the Registry.

Microsoft recommends that you use tools, such as Device Manager, the Control Panel, and property sheets, to make configuration changes whenever possible, rather than opening and editing the Registry. If you open the Registry, and make a mistake while you are changing a Registry setting, you might not even be able to use your computer, or you might introduce errors in its hardware and software configuration so that you cannot boot your computer. Also, Windows XP does not warn you if the change you made is incorrect either at the time you make that change or when you close the Registry. Instead, Windows XP applies the change immediately. Furthermore, there is no Undo feature, so any changes you make are final.

The Windows Registry database consists of a set of files named Default, Sam, Security, Software, and System. Each of these files, and their associated log file (Default.log, Sam.log, Security.log, Software.log, and System.log), is called a **hive**. The log file has a list of changes made to the keys and values of a hive. All of these hives are stored in the %Systemroot%\System32\Config folder, where %Systemroot% is the path to your Windows XP folder. Because the log files are hidden files, you have to open the Folder Options dialog box from the Control Panel or a folder window, and on the View property sheet, choose the option for showing hidden files and folders. Figure 13-1 lists the names of the Registry files and the types of information stored in each Registry file.

Figure 13-1	REGISTRY FILES
REGISTRY FILE	**CONTENTS**
Default	Default system settings
SAM (Security Account Manager)	Information on user and group accounts
Security	Security information, such as user rights, password policy, and local group membership
Software	Software configuration settings
System	Hardware and startup configuration settings

Because these files are critical to the operation of Windows XP and your computer system, Windows XP stores backup copies of all or some of the hives. The backup copies have the same filename, but use "sav" as the file extension. For example, the backup copy of the Software hive is Software.sav. Figure 13-2 shows the hives on Eric's computer in Details view and in order by File Type. Note that these hives are stored in the Config folder, and the path to that folder is C:\Windows\System32\Config (assuming your Windows folder is named "Windows"). Because the log files are hidden files, you must choose the option for showing all folders and files. In addition to the backup copies of the Registry that Windows XP keeps, you should also back up the Registry so that you can restore your system in the event of an operating system boot failure.

Figure 13-2   **VIEWING THE CONTENTS OF THE CONFIG FOLDER**

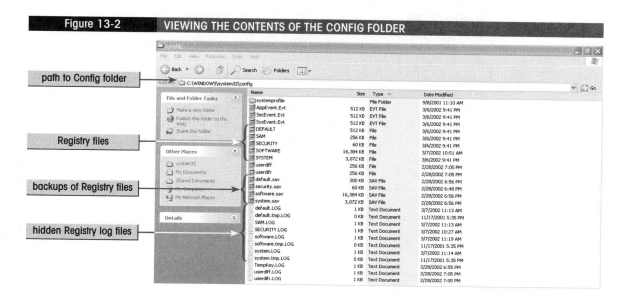

The default user profile is stored in a hidden file named NTUser.dat in the hidden Default User folder under the Documents and Settings folder. Also, each user's profile is stored in the corresponding user account folder, and consists of the files named NTUser.dat, NTUser.dat.log, NTUser.ini, and NTUser.pol. Figure 13-3 shows the files in Tiles view for Eric's user profile in his user account folder under the Documents and Settings folder. This folder also contains system folders, such as the Desktop, Start Menu, and SendTo folders, which Eric can customize for his user account.

Figure 13-3   **VIEWING ERIC'S USER ACCOUNT FOLDER**

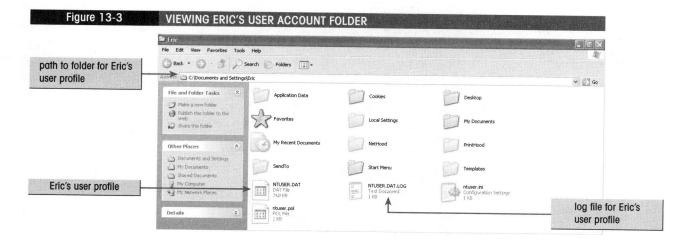

When you boot a computer, Windows XP loads and processes the contents of the Registry so that it can manage all the processes within your computer. For example, Windows XP uses the Registry to locate and load the device drivers needed for the specific types of hardware in your computer.

To support the object-oriented features of Windows XP, the Registry contains information on file associations and Object Linking and Embedding (OLE). If, for example, you double-click a file icon in My Computer or Windows Explorer, or if you select a document name from the Documents menu, Windows XP uses the Registry to locate the application associated with the file extension of the file that you selected. Then it loads that application and opens the document in the file. Using file associations with the Registry allows you to work in a docucentric environment.

When you create a shortcut, you are in effect creating a special type of OLE object that points to a system resource (such as a drive), a folder, an application, or a file. The Windows XP Registry contains information that permits Windows XP to support the use of OLE technology for shortcuts. It also enables you to build compound documents that use objects from documents produced by more than one application.

Windows XP updates the contents of the Registry when you change settings on your computer, such as when you customize your desktop with the Display Properties dialog box, when you install Plug and Play hardware or other new hardware with the Add Hardware Wizard, when you install or remove software with the Add or Remove Programs Wizard, when you change settings using the Control Panel and Device Manager, when you modify file associations on the File Types property sheet, and when you define user accounts and groups and specify user rights and audit policies. The Registry is constantly changing and it gradually increases in size as it tracks all system and user settings.

When you install Win32 software, the Setup program adds information about the application in the Windows XP Registry, including, for example, which file types (and therefore which file extensions) it supports. When you install Win16 software with the Add or Remove Programs Wizard, Windows XP monitors the process and copies settings that the Setup program adds to System.ini or Win.ini to the Registry.

Windows 98 and Windows 95 have a Registry that is similar, but not identical, to the Windows XP Registry. The Windows 98 and Windows 95 Registry consists of two hidden database files, System.dat and User.dat, that contain hardware, software, and user settings stored in the folder which contains the installed version of Windows 98 or Windows 95. Windows 95 keeps a backup copy of each file, and Windows 98 keeps multiple backups. After a successful boot, Windows 95 copies the settings in each of these two database files to System.da0 and User.da0, and Windows 98 stores copies of the Registry from the five most recent successful boots as cabinet files in the Windows Sysbckup folder. As you may recall, a cabinet file (with the file extension "cab") is a compressed file that contains operating system files. Windows 98 and Windows 95 also keep one other important file, named System.1st, in the top-level folder (C:\) of your hard disk. System.1st contains all the hardware settings detected by the Windows 98 or Windows 95 Setup program when Windows XP was installed on the computer. If you install Windows XP on your computer so that you have the option of dual booting with Windows 98 or Windows 95, you then have a copy of both the Windows XP Registry and the Registry for Windows 98 or Windows 95.

The Windows Me Registry, on the other hand, consists of three hidden files—User.dat, System.dat, and Classes.dat. System.dat contains hardware configuration settings, User.dat contains user settings or user profiles, and Classes.dat contains software settings, OLE settings, and GUI settings. The Windows 2000 Registry files are similar to those of Windows XP.

Although you generally make changes to your computer's hardware configuration and installed software as well as user settings and preferences using Windows tools, such as the Control Panel and property sheets, you may need to periodically open the Registry to view, change, add, or troubleshoot settings. Therefore, it's important to become familiar with the structure of the Registry and its use.

Backing Up the Windows Registry

Eric emphasizes to you the importance of backing up the Windows Registry before making any changes to the Registry. Since the Windows Registry is critical to the booting and functioning of your computer, the backup strategies that you develop for your computer system should also take into account the Registry. There are several ways in which you can back up the Registry:

- **Back up the System State**. You can back up the System State by using the Windows Backup utility. As noted in Tutorial 6, the System State includes the Windows Registry, the COM Class Registration database, and the system boot files.

- **Use System Restore**. As you discovered in Tutorial 8, you can use the Windows XP System Restore feature to create a restore point for a fixed point in time, and then you can roll back your computer to that point should a problem arise later. In fact, it's a good idea to create a restore point before editing the Windows Registry.

- **Automated System Recovery**. As you also learned in Tutorial 8, you can use the Automated System Recovery Wizard in Windows XP Professional to back up system settings to a floppy disk and system files to backup media such as tape. Later, if you encounter problems with your computer, such as a boot failure, you can use the ASR floppy disk and backup, along with your Windows XP CD and your ASR backup and your regular backups, to restore your computer system.

- **Export the Registry**. You can also open the Registry Editor, a utility for viewing the contents of and making changes to the Registry, and then export (or transfer) a copy of the Registry to a registration file (with the "reg" file extension) on disk. If you have a problem, you can import the contents of this registration file into the Registry if you need to restore it.

Since your Windows XP settings change over time (as you upgrade Windows XP, install new hardware and software, and reconfigure your system), you must make sure you perform regular backups of the Windows Registry.

If you need to restore Registry settings on your computer, or parts of the Registry, you also have other options available to you:

- **Use the Last Known Good Configuration**. If you experience a problem starting Windows XP, use the Last Known Good Configuration to restart your computer. Whenever Windows XP successfully loads all its startup drivers and a user logs onto a computer, it copies these startup settings, now known as the Last Known Good Configuration, to the Registry. If a problem occurs after installing a new device driver or application, you can reboot your computer, press the F8 key during the initial stages of booting to display the Windows Advanced Options menu, and then choose the Last Known Good Configuration from that menu. If you are unable to boot your computer, one or more of the hive files might be physically damaged, and you must replace them with a previous copy of the Registry. Remember that when you choose the Last Known Good Configuration, you lose all of your other configuration changes since you last successfully booted your computer, and you might need to further update your computer system.

- **Use the Recovery Console**. If you are unable to start Windows XP, you can boot your computer with the Recovery Console and copy backups of the System and Software Registry files from the Repair folder (C:\Windows\Repair) to the Config folder (C:\Windows\System32\Config) (covered in Tutorial 9). The backups in the Repair folder are created by the Backup utility when you choose the option for saving the System State from the Backup sheet. The most recent versions of these files might be corrupted, and by replacing them with backups, you might then be able to start your computer. If you use this approach, replace only one of these files at a time, and then try to boot your computer. If the problem is a hardware problem, replace the System file first; if the problem is a software problem, replace the Software file first. Also, remember that the backups of these files stored in the Repair folder are older versions of the Registry. Once you restart Windows XP, you might need to reinstall device drivers, service pack upgrades, and any other software that you've installed since the date of the System or Software file in the Repair folder.

If you have not already done so, you should install the Recovery Console on your computer so that if you experience a problem booting your computer with Windows XP Professional or Windows XP Home Edition, you can open the Recovery Console and attempt to repair the problem. Tutorial 9 describes how to install the Recovery Console.

It is a good idea to develop a consistent strategy for working with the Windows Registry, including backing up the Registry and documenting any changes made to the Registry, so that you can effectively troubleshoot problems that might arise later.

Getting Started

So that the tutorial steps and figures match what you do and then observe in the figures, you need to switch your computer to Web style, and you also need to turn on the options for showing all folders and files, displaying protected operating system files, displaying file extensions, and displaying the full path in the Address bar. As you complete these steps, you may discover that your computer is already set up for Web style, or that other settings are already in place, so you might only need to make a few changes to your computer's settings.

To set up your computer:

1. To change to the Windows XP theme, right-click the **desktop**, click **Properties** on the shortcut menu, and after Windows XP opens the Display Properties dialog box, click the **Theme** list arrow on the Themes property sheet, click **Windows XP** (if necessary), and then click the **OK** button.

2. To switch to the Windows XP Start menu style, right-click the **Start** button, click **Properties** on the shortcut menu, and after Windows XP opens the Taskbar and Start Menu Properties dialog box, click the **Start menu** option button on the Start Menu property sheet (if necessary), and then click the **OK** button.

3. To change to a task-oriented view of folders and enable single-clicking, click the **Start** button, click **My Computer**, click **Tools** on the menu bar, click **Folder Options**, and after Windows XP opens the Folder Options dialog box, click the **Show common tasks in folders** option button if it is not already selected, click the **Single-click to open an item** option button if it is not already selected, and click the **Underline icon titles only when I point at them** option button if it is not already selected.

4. Click the **View** tab, click the **Display the full path in the address bar** check box if it is not already selected, click the **Show hidden files and folders** option button if it is not already selected, and if there is a check mark in the "Hide extensions for known file types" check box, click that check box to remove the check mark.

5. Click the **Hide protected operating system files** check box to remove the check mark (if necessary), click the **Yes** button in the Warning dialog box to display protected operating system files (if necessary), click the **OK** button to close the Folder Options dialog box, and then close My Computer.

Now you're ready to back up the Registry.

Backing up the System State

As noted earlier, you can use the Backup utility to back up just the System State on your computer, and that backup includes a copy of the Windows Registry.

If you are using a computer that has Windows XP Home Edition, and if the Backup utility is not installed on that computer, you must install this utility by completing the steps in the section entitled "Installing the Backup Utility in the Home Edition" in Tutorial 6. Then you can back up the System State.

To complete this portion of the tutorial, you need sufficient backup media to store the backup of the System State. For example, on the computer used for the following figures, the backup required approximately 329 MB of storage space, and took slightly over four minutes. If you do not have sufficient backup media, but yet want to practice the process of backing up the System State, you can back up the System State to the My Documents folder, or you can read the following steps and examine the figures (but not keystroke the steps) so that you are familiar with this procedure.

You and Eric decide to examine the Registry on his computer so that he can point out some important features of the Registry. Eric suggests that you create three backups of his Windows Registry. He recommends that you back up the System State first, create a restore point, and then export the Windows Registry to a registration file. Eric also reminds you of the importance of having a recent backup of the System State in the event you need to restore your computer.

To back up the System State:

1. Log on under an account with Administrator privileges.

2. From the Start menu, point to **All Programs**, point to **Accessories**, point to **System Tools**, and then click **Backup**. Windows XP opens the Backup or Restore Wizard dialog box. See Figure 13-4.

Figure 13-4   OPENING THE BACKUP OR RESTORE WIZARD

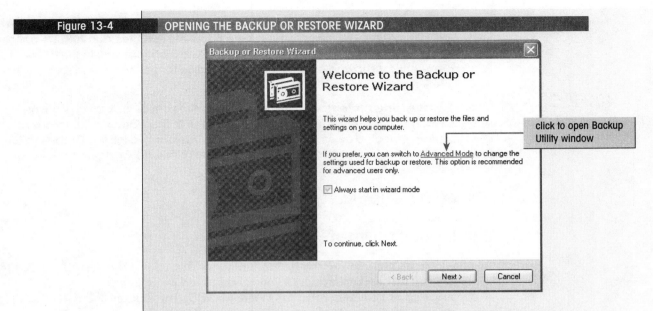

click to open Backup Utility window

3. Click the **Advanced Mode** link, and after the Backup Utility window opens, click the **Backup** tab. Under Desktop, you have the option of backing up the System State. See Figure 13-5.

Figure 13-5   SELECTING THE OPTION FOR BACKING UP THE SYSTEM STATE

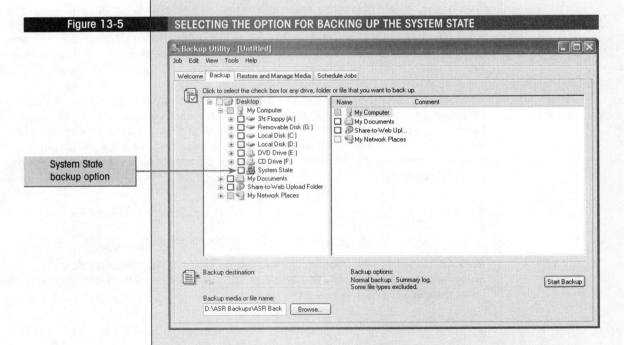

System State backup option

4. Click the **System State** check box, click the **Browse** button under Backup destination to select the My Documents folder, type **System State (current date)** in the File name text box, and then click the **Save** button.

5. Click **Tools** on the menu bar, click **Options**, click the **Backup Log** tab, click the **Detailed** option button under Information, and then click the **OK** button.

6. Click the **Start Backup** button, type **System State** before the text in the Backup description box, and then click the **Start Backup** button. After the backup is complete, the Backup Progress dialog box shows the amount of data included in the System State backup. See Figure 13-6.

Figure 13-6	BACKING UP THE SYSTEM STATE

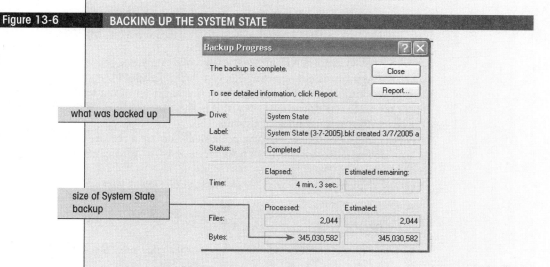

7. Click the **Report** button, and after the Notepad window opens with the backup log, click **File** on the menu bar, click **Save As**, select the drive or folder where you stored the backup, type **System State** *(current date)* in the File name text box, and then click the **Save** button.

8. Close the Notepad window, close the Backup Progress dialog box, and then close the Backup Utility window.

You have successfully created the first of three backups of the Windows Registry.

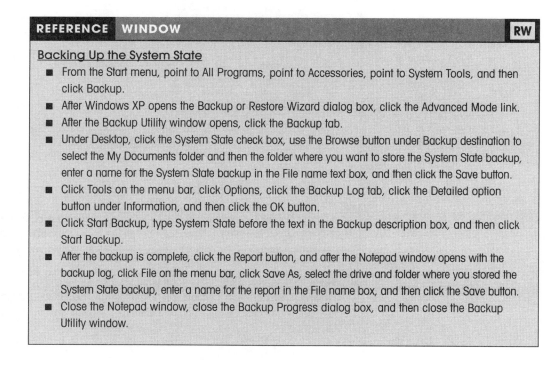

REFERENCE WINDOW   **RW**

Backing Up the System State

- From the Start menu, point to All Programs, point to Accessories, point to System Tools, and then click Backup.
- After Windows XP opens the Backup or Restore Wizard dialog box, click the Advanced Mode link.
- After the Backup Utility window opens, click the Backup tab.
- Under Desktop, click the System State check box, use the Browse button under Backup destination to select the My Documents folder and then the folder where you want to store the System State backup, enter a name for the System State backup in the File name text box, and then click the Save button.
- Click Tools on the menu bar, click Options, click the Backup Log tab, click the Detailed option button under Information, and then click the OK button.
- Click Start Backup, type System State before the text in the Backup description box, and then click Start Backup.
- After the backup is complete, click the Report button, and after the Notepad window opens with the backup log, click File on the menu bar, click Save As, select the drive and folder where you stored the System State backup, enter a name for the report in the File name box, and then click the Save button.
- Close the Notepad window, close the Backup Progress dialog box, and then close the Backup Utility window.

If you need to restore the System State from a System State backup, log on under an account with Administrator or backup and restore privileges, open the Backup Utility, click the Advanced Mode link, click the Restore and Manage Media tab, expand the backup media item containing your most recent System State backup, click the System State check box, and then click the Start Restore button.

Creating a Restore Point for the Windows Registry

Even though Windows XP automatically creates restore points on a periodic basis, or when you make significant changes to your system, you should create a restore point before opening and working with the Registry. Also, if you have not made a recent backup copy of your computer and your document files, this is the time to do it. Make these backups before you proceed with the remainder of this tutorial.

Next, Eric recommends that you manually create a restore point.

You also need to log on under an account with Administrator privileges to use System Restore.

Do not skip the following steps, as they are an important part of working with the Registry.

To create a restore point:

1. Log on under an account with Administrator privileges.

2. From the Start menu, point to **All Programs**, point to **Accessories**, point to **System Tools**, and then click **System Restore**. Windows XP opens the System Restore dialog box. See Figure 13-7. Your System Restore dialog box may not include the "Undo my last restoration" option shown in the figure.

Figure 13-7	CREATING A RESTORE POINT

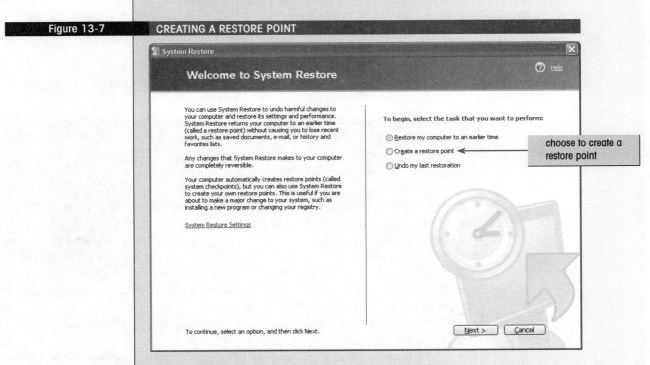

3. Under "To begin, select the task that you want to perform," click the **Create a restore point** option button, and then click the **Next** button. System Restore now prompts for a Restore point description, as shown in Figure 13-8.

Figure 13-8 PROMPT FOR RESTORE POINT DESCRIPTION

enter a restore point description

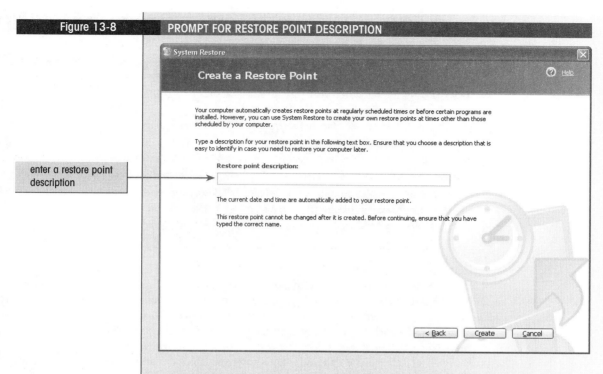

4. In the Restore point description text box, type **Registry Restore Point** and then click the **Create** button. After creating the restore point, System Restore verifies the new restore point. See Figure 13-9.

Figure 13-9 RESTORE POINT CREATED

new restore point

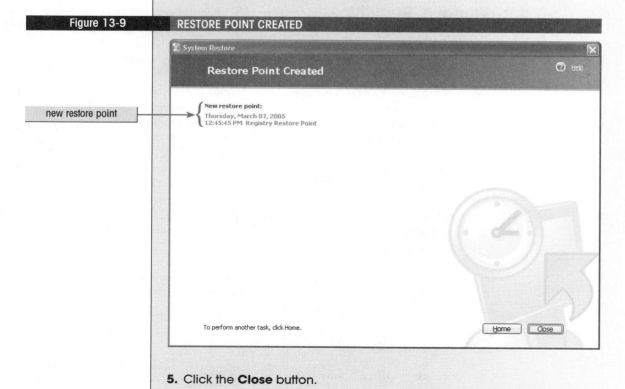

5. Click the **Close** button.

You have now successfully completed the second of three backups of the Windows Registry.

If you need to restore your computer to an earlier configuration using a restore point, click the Start button, point to All Programs, point to Accessories, point to System Tools, and then click System Restore. In the System Restore dialog box, click the "Restore my computer to an earlier time" option button, and then click the Next button. In the next System Restore dialog box, select the restore point that you want to use from a system calendar by first selecting a calendar day shown in boldface and then by selecting a restore point for that particular day. Click the Next button, verify that you have chosen the correct restore point, and then click the Next button to restore your computer.

Opening the Windows Registry

If you want to view the contents of the Registry, or make changes to the Registry either to customize your computer or troubleshoot problems, you can use a Windows XP tool called the Registry Editor.

Since there is no option on the Start menu for opening the Registry Editor, you can either create a desktop shortcut to one of the Registry Editor programs (C:\Windows\Regedit.exe), or use the Run option on the Start menu to enter the command for opening the Registry Editor. Once you open the Registry, you should immediately export Registry settings to a file on disk, so that you have an additional, alternate backup. You can then examine the structure and contents of the Registry and, if necessary, add new settings or modify existing settings in the Registry. Remember that all accidental or deliberate edits are final and that the Registry Editor and Windows XP do not warn you that changes have been made.

The other versions of Windows also contain a Registry Editor. Windows XP and Windows 2000 actually have two Registry Editors, Regedit.exe (C:\Windows\Regedit.exe) and Regedt32.exe (C:\Windows\System32\Regedt32.exe). Microsoft recommends that you use Regedit.exe only to search for information, and that you use Regedt32.exe to modify the Registry. Regedit.exe is safer because you can view and edit certain types of data stored in the Windows XP and Windows 2000 Registry, but you cannot work with Registry security settings with this version of the Registry Editor.

Exporting Registry Settings

If you open the Registry Editor and then export Registry settings, the Registry Editor creates a text file called a registration file with the "reg" file extension that contains a copy of all the Registry settings. If necessary, you can restore the Registry from a registration file. This type of backup is the easiest and fastest to make.

The Registry Editor is designed for the more advanced user, not a casual or inexperienced user. You must exercise *caution* as you use the Registry Editor, closely follow any instructions you might have for navigating, viewing, and modifying the Registry, double-check and triple-check changes you make, and be prepared to restore your computer and its Registry if you run into a problem. The well known adage "Measure twice, cut once" applies to many different situations, including the use of the Registry. If you want to create or modify a Registry setting, check your new setting twice before you apply it. If you want to delete a Registry setting, check twice to make sure you have selected the correct setting before you delete it.

Eric recommends that you start by opening the Registry with the Registry Editor, and then export Registry settings to a registration file on disk so that you have the last of the three backups you want to make.

If your computer lab does not permit you to use the Registry Editor, or if you prefer to not use it on your computer until you better understand how it works, read the remainder of the steps in this tutorial and examine the figures, but do not keystroke the steps.

In the next set of steps, you open and export the Registry to a file on disk. Because of the large size of this file, it does not fit on a floppy disk. You must store the file on some other type of removable media such as a Zip disk, or in the My Documents folder on the hard disk of the computer you are using. If you are working in a computer lab and intend to save the file to the hard disk, obtain permission from your instructor or technical support staff.

To open the Registry Editor:

1. From the Start menu, click **Run**, type **regedit**, and then press the **Enter** key (or click the **OK** button). After the Registry Editor opens, you see an Explorer-like pane with the Registry tree. See Figure 13-10. The information in the Registry tree is organized by **subtrees**, or branches, each of which is represented by a folder icon, and each of which stores a group of related settings in groups called **keys**. A key may have one or more subkeys. When you work directly with a subkey, you refer to it as a key. As you can tell, even though the Registry consists of separate files, the Registry Editor combines the contents of those files into a single unified view.

POWER USERS TIP If the Registry Editors (regedit.exe and regedt32.exe) are stored on an NTFS volume, and if you are logged on under an Administrator account, you can display the Properties dialog box for these program files, select the Security property sheet, and then restrict which groups and users have full control of modify, read and execute, read, and write permissions for using these programs.

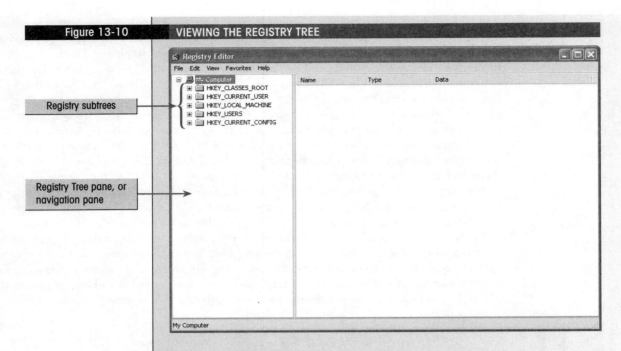

Figure 13-10   VIEWING THE REGISTRY TREE

Registry subtrees

Registry Tree pane, or navigation pane

2. Click **My Computer** in the Registry Tree pane, or navigation pane, on the left to select it, if necessary. By selecting My Computer first, you are guaranteeing that the Registry Editor exports all the Registry settings to a registration file. If you select a specific subtree or key, rather than My Computer, the Registry Editor exports only that portion of the Registry that falls under the subtree or key.

3. Click **File** on the menu bar, and then click **Export**. Windows XP opens the Export Registry File dialog box, and automatically selects the My Documents folder. See Figure 13-11. The Save as type box identifies the file type as Registration Files (*.reg). Under Export range, the Registry Editor is automatically set to export the entire range, not just a selected branch.

Figure 13-11 EXPORTING THE REGISTRY

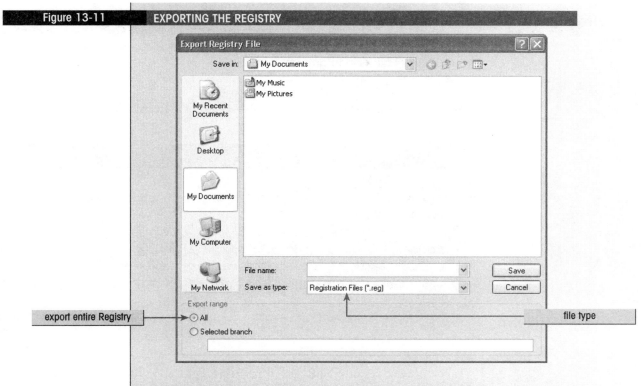

export entire Registry

file type

4. Use the Save in list box to select the drive and folder where you want to store the registration file, click the **Create New Folder** button, type **Registry Backup**, press the **Enter** key, and then press the **Enter** key a second time to open the new Registry Backup folder.

5. In the File name box, type **Registry Backup for *(current date)*** (using the current date in the format yyyy-mm-dd), click the **Save** button, and wait until the process is complete.

6. From the Start menu, open My Computer (or My Documents), and select the drive and folder where you created the Registry Backup folder, open the Registry Backup folder icon, click **View** on the menu bar, click **Details** (if necessary), and then double-click the border between the Name and Size column buttons. On the computer used for this figure, the registration file is 36,549 KB (yours will differ). See Figure 13-12. If you open this file in Microsoft Word, which is possible because it's a text file, you would find that the registration file is 7,848 pages.

Figure 13-12 VIEWING DETAILS ON THE REGISTRATION FILE

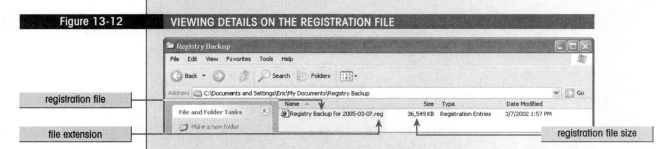

registration file

file extension

registration file size

7. Close the Registry Backup folder window.

8. If you are going to continue with the tutorial, leave the Registry Editor window open for the next section of the tutorial; otherwise, if you are going to continue the tutorial later, close the Registry Editor window. You should never leave the Registry Editor open and unattended.

You have just successfully created another backup of the Registry by creating a registration file.

REFERENCE WINDOW   RW

Exporting Registry Settings
- From the Start menu, select Run, type REGEDIT in the Open text box, and then press the Enter key (or click the OK button).
- Click My Computer in the Registry Tree pane.
- Click File on the menu bar, and then click Export.
- In the Export Registry File dialog box, locate the drive and folder where you want to store the exported Registry settings; in the File name box, type a name for your registration file and click the OK button.
- Close the Registry Editor.

If you need to restore the Registry from this registration file, you open the Registry and use the Import command on the File menu. In the Import Registry File dialog box, you select the registration file to import. The Import Registry File dialog box then shows a progress indicator. If the Registry Editor is unable to import all of the data to the Registry, it displays a Registry Editor dialog box explaining that some keys are open by the system or by other processes. You can also open the folder that contains the registration file, and then click (or double-click) it to restore the Registry (because of the association of the "reg" file extension with the Registry Editor).

Like other types of backups, you have to periodically make new backups of the System State and the Registry. If you restore the Registry from a System State backup or a registration file that is not recent, any configuration changes made since the date of the backup or the registration file are no longer in the Registry.

Examining the Structure of the Registry

The Registry consists of five major subtrees, whose names start with HKEY. The "H" in HKEY stands for "Handle," meaning each subtree is a handle for a specific group of settings. Within each subtree are sets of keys that contain groups of related settings. Under each key, there may be subkeys that break down the settings into smaller groups. In other words, Registry keys and settings are organized using a hierarchical approach.

Before you examine specific keys, Eric suggests that you first examine the Registry subtrees.

To view the contents of the subtrees:

1. If necessary, open the Registry Editor, and then maximize the Registry Editor window.

2. Click the **expand view** box ⊞ to the left of the HKEY_CLASSES_ROOT subtree. As you can immediately tell, this subtree contains a key for each registered file type. See Figure 13-13. Your keys will differ from those shown in the figure because the types of keys found under this subtree depend on what file types are available on your computer system. This key also contains information on registered objects, such as My Computer and the Recycle Bin, and OLE objects. The same information is stored under the HKEY_LOCAL_MACHINE\Software key.

Figure 13-13   VIEWING THE HKEY_CLASSES_ROOT SUBTREE

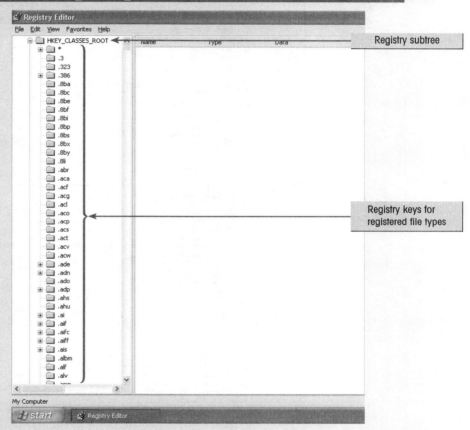

As you saw in Tutorial 3, you can view information about and change these file types by opening a My Computer or folder window, choosing the Tools menu, choosing Folder Options, selecting the File Types property sheet, and then choosing the file type you want to examine or change.

3. Click the **collapse view** box ⊟ to the left of the HKEY_CLASSES_ROOT key.

4. Click ⊞ to the left of the HKEY_CURRENT_USER folder icon, and then click ⊞ to the left of the Control Panel key. The HKEY_CURRENT_USER subtree, its keys and subkeys, such as the Mouse key, contain the user profile or user settings for the current user logged onto the computer. See Figure 13-14. The information for this subtree and its key and subkeys are derived from the Security ID (SID) for the current user under the HKEY_USERS subtree. That means each time a different user logs onto the computer, Windows XP creates a new HKEY_CURRENT_USER subtree with that user's settings and personal preferences. Every user, group, and computer account on a network is issued a unique Security ID, or Security Identifier, when the account is first created. Windows XP processes rely on an account's SID rather than the account's name because the account name could change. If you create an account, delete it, and then create an account with the same user name, the new account does not have the rights or permissions previously granted to the previous account because the accounts have different Security ID numbers.

Figure 13-14	VIEWING THE HKEY_CURRENT_USER SUBTREE

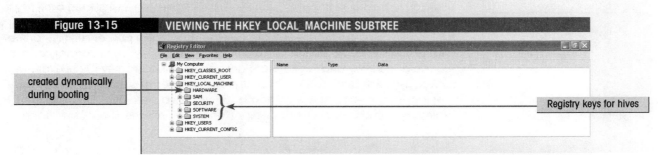

5. Click ▬ to the left of the HKEY_CURRENT_USER folder icon, and then click ✚ to the left of the HKEY_LOCAL_MACHINE folder icon. The HKEY_LOCAL_MACHINE subtree contains configuration settings for the local computer system. See Figure 13-15. Notice that there is a key for each of the Registry hives. The Hardware key is automatically created during booting, and contains information about the hardware configuration of the computer.

Figure 13-15	VIEWING THE HKEY_LOCAL_MACHINE SUBTREE

6. If you are going to continue with the tutorial, leave the Registry Editor window open for the next section of the tutorial; otherwise, if you are going to continue the tutorial later, close the Registry Editor window.

The HKEY_USERS subtree contains user profile settings for all users as well as a default profile. The HKEY_CURRENT_CONFIG subtree contains configuration settings for the currently used hardware profile. Like the HKEY_CURRENT_USER subtree, this subtree does not actually contain any data, but instead points to data stored in another location of the Registry, namely, in the Current subkey under HKEY_LOCAL_MACHINE. The Registry path to this key is HKEY_LOCAL_MACHINE\SYSTEM\CurrentControlSet\Hardware Profiles\Current. You can view and change these Registry settings from either location in the Registry. The **Registry path** specifies the subtree, key, and sequence of subkeys for a particular group of settings within the Registry.

Tracing Registered File Types

By examining information on registered files in the Windows Registry, you can gain a better understanding of the organization of the Registry, how to work with the Registry, and also improve your understanding of how Windows XP functions by drawing on the information in the Registry.

When you select a key in the Registry Editor, Windows XP displays the **value entries** associated with that key if there are any. Each value entry has three parts: a **name**, **data type**, and the **value** itself. For example, in the next set of steps you are going to examine the .bmp key. The first value entry in the .bmp key has the name (Default), and the value for the (Default) value entry is Paint.Picture. Its data type is REG_SZ, which identifies the value (Paint.Picture) as a fixed-length text string. A **string** is a nonnumeric value that is treated exactly as it is typed or shown.

Eric suggests that you next view information on file associations and registered file types, so that you become familiar with the process of navigating the Registry.

To view information on registered file types:

1. If necessary, open the Registry Editor, and then maximize the Registry Editor window.

2. Click the **expand view** box ⊞ to the left of the HKEY_CLASSES_ROOT key in the Registry Tree pane, or navigation pane.

3. Locate and double-click the **.bmp** key in the navigation pane. Not only do you select this key and see its associated values in the topic pane on the right, but the Registry Editor also expands this part of the Registry tree in the navigation pane, and displays the subkeys located below the .bmp key. See Figure 13-16. The settings shown in the topic pane on the right are the value entries. As noted earlier, the value for the (Default) value entry is Paint.Picture. This value entry points to another key—a class definition key—by the same name (Paint.Picture). The Paint.Picture Class Definition key contains additional information about this file association. Notice also that the path to the current key, shown on the status bar, is My Computer\HKEY_CLASSES_ROOT\.bmp.

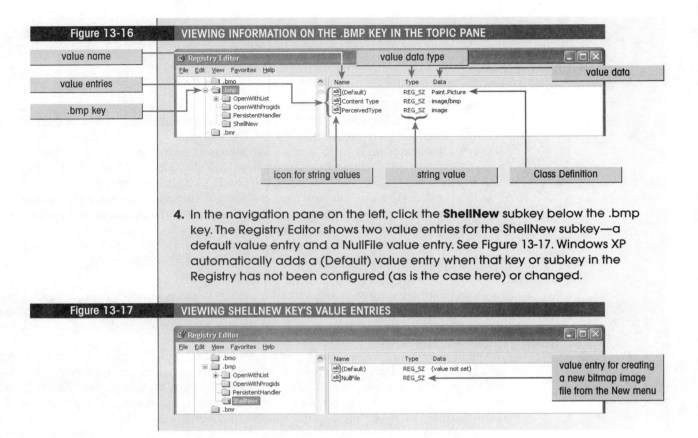

Figure 13-16 — VIEWING INFORMATION ON THE .BMP KEY IN THE TOPIC PANE

value name
value entries
.bmp key
value data type
value data
icon for string values
string value
Class Definition

4. In the navigation pane on the left, click the **ShellNew** subkey below the .bmp key. The Registry Editor shows two value entries for the ShellNew subkey—a default value entry and a NullFile value entry. See Figure 13-17. Windows XP automatically adds a (Default) value entry when that key or subkey in the Registry has not been configured (as is the case here) or changed.

Figure 13-17 — VIEWING SHELLNEW KEY'S VALUE ENTRIES

value entry for creating a new bitmap image file from the New menu

When you right-click the desktop or the background of a folder window, point to New, and then click Bitmap Image, Windows XP uses the information in the .bmp key's ShellNew subkey to create a new, empty bitmap image file that has no associated template (called a NullFile or null file). The **null file** is a file that is zero bytes in size. You can then open the file and create a new document using the application associated with this registered file type. Each menu option on the New menu has a corresponding ShellNew key in the Registry below that registered file type.

Shell refers to the interface provided by a program, so that the user can communicate with the program. In the case of Windows XP, the graphical user interface is the shell with which the user interacts to communicate user requests or commands into actions performed by the operating system.

Next, you and Eric decide to locate the Paint.Picture key. Although you could scroll through the Registry, it is faster to use Find to search for the key.

To locate Paint.Picture:

1. Click **Edit** on the menu bar, and then click **Find**. In the Find dialog box, you can not only enter a search string, but also specify what components of the Registry to examine—keys, values, or data. See Figure 13-18.

Figure 13-18   **USING THE REGISTRY FIND FEATURE**

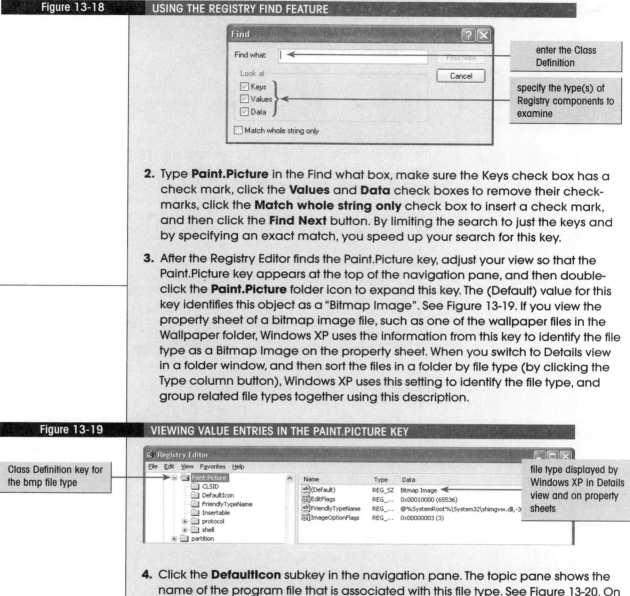

enter the Class Definition

specify the type(s) of Registry components to examine

2. Type **Paint.Picture** in the Find what box, make sure the Keys check box has a check mark, click the **Values** and **Data** check boxes to remove their check-marks, click the **Match whole string only** check box to insert a check mark, and then click the **Find Next** button. By limiting the search to just the keys and by specifying an exact match, you speed up your search for this key.

3. After the Registry Editor finds the Paint.Picture key, adjust your view so that the Paint.Picture key appears at the top of the navigation pane, and then double-click the **Paint.Picture** folder icon to expand this key. The (Default) value for this key identifies this object as a "Bitmap Image". See Figure 13-19. If you view the property sheet of a bitmap image file, such as one of the wallpaper files in the Wallpaper folder, Windows XP uses the information from this key to identify the file type as a Bitmap Image on the property sheet. When you switch to Details view in a folder window, and then sort the files in a folder by file type (by clicking the Type column button), Windows XP uses this setting to identify the file type, and group related file types together using this description.

Figure 13-19   **VIEWING VALUE ENTRIES IN THE PAINT.PICTURE KEY**

Class Definition key for the bmp file type

file type displayed by Windows XP in Details view and on property sheets

4. Click the **DefaultIcon** subkey in the navigation pane. The topic pane shows the name of the program file that is associated with this file type. See Figure 13-20. On the computer used for this figure, the icon for the "bmp" file type is drawn from a dynamic link library file named Shimgvw.dll. The "1" after the filename indicates that the file icon Windows XP uses for a Bitmap Image file is the second icon in Shimgvw.dll. (Since computers count by starting with the number 0 instead of the number 1, the first icon is 0, the second icon is 1, etc.) In previous versions of Windows, the icon for this file type was drawn from the Mspaint.exe program file.

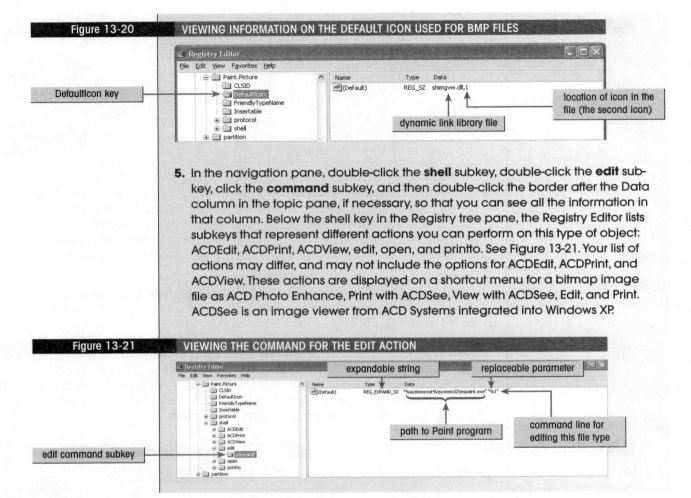

Figure 13-20   VIEWING INFORMATION ON THE DEFAULT ICON USED FOR BMP FILES

DefaultIcon key

location of icon in the file (the second icon)

dynamic link library file

5. In the navigation pane, double-click the **shell** subkey, double-click the **edit** sub-key, click the **command** subkey, and then double-click the border after the Data column in the topic pane, if necessary, so that you can see all the information in that column. Below the shell key in the Registry tree pane, the Registry Editor lists subkeys that represent different actions you can perform on this type of object: ACDEdit, ACDPrint, ACDView, edit, open, and printto. See Figure 13-21. Your list of actions may differ, and may not include the options for ACDEdit, ACDPrint, and ACDView. These actions are displayed on a shortcut menu for a bitmap image file as ACD Photo Enhance, Print with ACDSee, View with ACDSee, Edit, and Print. ACDSee is an image viewer from ACD Systems integrated into Windows XP.

Figure 13-21   VIEWING THE COMMAND FOR THE EDIT ACTION

expandable string

replaceable parameter

edit command subkey

path to Paint program

command line for editing this file type

The string for the Default value in the topic pane for the command subkey is the command Windows XP uses to edit this file type. On the computer used for this figure, the value for the edit action is:

"%systemroot%\system32\mspaint.exe" "%1"

Your path might differ. The REG_EXPAND_SZ type is another string format called an expandable string. Like a string, an **expandable string** contains text, but it also contains a reference to a variable value, such as %systemroot%—the environment variable with the path to the Windows folder. If Windows XP is installed in the Windows folder on drive C, Windows XP expands this string to include the path to the Windows folder: "C:\Windows\system32\mspaint.exe"

As you learned in Tutorial 3, the "%1" after the path to a program file is a replaceable parameter. When you right-click a bitmap image file and then click Edit on the shortcut menu, Windows XP replaces %1 with the filename of the bitmap image file and then opens that file. For example, if you right-click a bitmap image file named Bliss.bmp (the default Windows XP wallpaper) and choose Edit on the shortcut menu, this command becomes "C:\Windows\system32\mspaint.exe" "Bliss.bmp"

The quotation marks are included around the path in the event the value for the %systemroot% environment variable is a long folder name with one or more spaces. Likewise, the replaceable parameter is enclosed with quotation marks in case the file in question has a long filename with one or more spaces.

To continue your examination of the Paint.Picture key:

1. In the navigation pane, double-click the **ACDPrint** subkey folder icon, and then click the **command** subkey folder icon below the ACDPrint subkey. The value assigned to the ACDPrint action is "C:\PROGRA~1\ACDSYS~1\ACDSEE\ACDSEE.EXE" /p "%1". See Figure 13-22. Your path might differ. As you learned in Tutorial 3, this command is similar to the one for opening a Bitmap Image file, except the "/p" switch instructs the ACDSee program to print the contents of the file (rather than open it). In this path, Windows XP uses short folder and file names, or aliases, derived from the original long folder and file names. If translated into long file-names, the program path would read "C:\Program Files\ACD Systems\ACDSee\ ACDSee.exe" /p "%1"

   TROUBLE? If ACDPrint is not listed as a subkey under the Shell key, read this step for the explanatory information and examine the figure, but do not keystroke the step.

Figure 13-22	VIEWING THE COMMAND FOR THE ACDPRINT ACTION

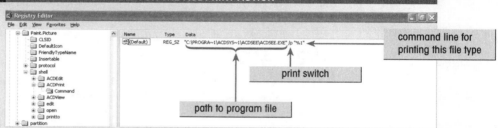

2. Click the **CLSID** (for Class ID, or Class Identifier) subkey folder icon and, if necessary, double-click the border to the right of the Data column to show the entire contents of this column. The Registry Editor shows the CLSID for Paint.Picture—in this case, {D3E34B21-9D75-101A-8C3D-00AA001A1652}. See Figure 13-23. The CLSID is a unique code that identifies an object or component as a Windows XP object that supports OLE.

Figure 13-23	EXAMINING THE CLSID KEY FOR THE BMP FILE TYPE

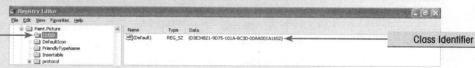

3. If you are going to continue with the tutorial, leave the Registry Editor window open for the next section of the tutorial; otherwise, if you are going to continue the tutorial later, close the Registry Editor window.

You can use the same strategy and approach to locate similar types of information on other types of registered files.

Tracing Information on Registered File Types

- From the Start menu, select Run, type REGEDIT in the Open box, and then click the OK button.
- Use Find on the Edit menu to locate the key for the file extension of a specific type of file (such as .bmp), and then view the name of the Class Definition subkey for the (Default) value in the topic pane.
- Use Find on the Edit menu to locate the key with the same name as the Class Definition subkey, and then double-click that key to view information on the type of object and its subkeys.
- Close the Registry Editor.

As you saw in Tutorial 3, when you open the Folder Options dialog box and select the File Types property sheet, Windows XP lists the names of all registered file types, and provides the same type of information as shown in the Registry keys for registered file types. That means you might be able to make whatever changes you want to make to registered file types from the File Types property sheet rather than from the Registry. It is a safer to use a Windows tool rather than the Registry.

Using CLSIDs

Windows XP assigns CLSIDs, or Class Identifiers, to system objects, such as My Computer, Network Neighborhood, and the Recycle Bin. You can find the CLSIDs for these objects in the Registry's HKEY_CLASSES_ROOT subtree. If you need to view or change the properties of these objects, you need to know how to work with CLSIDs in the Registry. In some cases, the only way to change a property of a system object might be via the Registry.

To search for an object's CLSID, you can search for the object name (such as Recycle Bin). However, in some cases, you might need to know the 16-character hexadecimal code for the object to locate the CLSID key for that object. After the next set of tutorials steps is a figure with a list of the CLSIDs for system components, such as the Recycle Bin.

So that you are familiar with the use of CLSIDs, Eric wants you to locate the CLSID for the Recycle Bin.

To locate the CLSID key for the Recycle Bin:

1. If necessary, open the Registry Editor, and then maximize the Registry Editor window.

2. Press the **Home** key to go back to the top of the Registry tree, and if My Computer is not highlighted, click **My Computer**. Your search now starts from this point in the Registry.

   TROUBLE? If you changed the focus from the navigation pane to the topic pane (perhaps by clicking on the background of the topic pane), you have to click a key in the navigation pane, and then press the Home key.

3. Click **Edit**, click **Find**, type **645FF** in the Find what text box, make sure the Keys check box has a check mark, click the **Values** and **Data** check boxes to remove their check marks (if necessary), click the **Match whole string only** check box to remove the check mark (if necessary), click the **Find Next** button, adjust your view so that the selected CLSID is at the top of the navigation

pane, drag the split bar between the two frames so that you can see the entire CLSID in the navigation pane, and then double-click the border between the Name and Type columns, the Type and Data columns, and after the Data column in the topic pane, if necessary, for a best fit. The Registry Editor finds the key for the Recycle Bin, {645FF040-5081-101B-9F08-00AA002F954E}, and in the topic pane, the Registry Editor identifies this key as the CLSID for the Recycle Bin (see the (Default) value). See Figure 13-24.

Figure 13-24   EXAMINING VALUE ENTRIES FOR THE RECYCLE BIN CLSID

CLSID for the Recycle Bin

object name

4. Double-click the **{645FF040-5081-101B-9F08-00AA002F954E}** key in the navigation pane (the one with the open folder icon), and then click the **DefaultIcon** subkey in the navigation pane. On the computer used for this figure, the Empty value name identifies the full path and name of the file that contains the icon that Windows XP uses for the Recycle Bin when it is empty, and also identifies the location of the icon within that program file. See Figure 13-25. In this case, the icon is icon 31 (the thirty-second icon) in the shell32.dll file in the System32 folder. As noted previously, %SystemRoot% is an environment variable that represents the path of the Windows folder (C:\Windows on this computer) determined during booting. The full path on this computer is therefore: C:\Windows\System32\shell32.dll,31

Figure 13-25   EXAMINING VALUE ENTRIES FOR RECYCLE BIN STATES

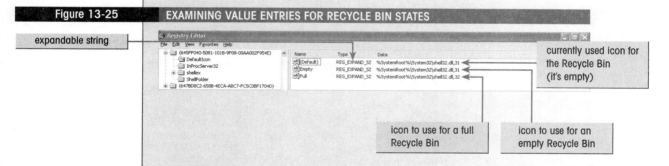

expandable string

currently used icon for the Recycle Bin (it's empty)

icon to use for a full Recycle Bin

icon to use for an empty Recycle Bin

The Full value name identifies the full path and name of the file that contains the icon that Windows XP uses for the Recycle Bin when it contains deleted files. Note that this icon is also derived from the same dynamic link library, shell32.dll, but the icon is icon 32 (the thirty-third one in the file). The (Default) value identifies the full path and name of the file that contains the icon that Windows XP uses to represent the current status of the Recycle Bin. On the computer used for this figure, the Recycle Bin is currently empty, so Windows XP uses the icon specified by the Empty value.

5. To close the Registry Editor, click **File** on the menu bar, and then click **Exit**.

You have just examined a minute amount of the information stored in the Registry, but the information you've examined provides a glimpse into how Windows XP uses Registry settings to support your use of registered file types.

REFERENCE WINDOW	RW

Locating Information on CLSIDs

- From the Start menu, select Run, type REGEDIT in the Open box, and then click the OK button.
- Click Edit on the menu bar, click Find, type part of the CLSID for the object you want to find (you might be able to search by object name, such as Recycle Bin, or you might have to know the CLSID), add a check mark to the Keys check box, remove the check marks from the Values, Data, and "Match whole string only" check boxes, and then click the Find Next button.

Figure 13-26 lists the CLSIDs for objects commonly found on a Windows XP computer. You can use these CLSIDs to locate the key in the Registry for an object so that you can customize your computer or correct an error condition. Although you could search for some objects by name, not all objects (including My Computer) are identified by name, so you might have to examine different CLSIDs until you find the one you need.

Figure 13-26   CLSIDS FOR COMMON SYSTEM OBJECTS

OBJECT	CLASSID
ActiveDesktop	{75048700-EF1F-11D0-9888-006097DEACF9}
Briefcase	{85BBD920-42A0-1069-A2E4-08002B30309D}
Control Panel*	{21EC2020-3AEA-1069-A2DD-08002B30309D}
Desktop	{00021400-0000-0000-C000-000000000046}
Help and Support	{2559a1f1-21d7-11d4-bdaf-00c04f60b9f0}
Internet Explorer*	{871C5380-42A0-1069-A2EA-08002B30309D}
My Computer	{20D04FE0-3AEA-1069-A2D8-08002B30309D}
My Documents Folder*	{450D8FBA-AD25-11D0-98A8-0800361B1103}
My Network Places	{208D2C60-3AEA-1069-A2D7-08002B30309D}
Printers and Faxes	{2227A280-3AEA-1069-A2DE-08002B30309D}
Recycle Bin	{645FF040-5081-101B-9F08-00AA002F954E}
Scheduled Tasks	{D6277990-4C6A-11CF-8D87-00AA0060F5BF}
Shortcut	{00021401-0000-0000-C000-000000000046}
Start Menu	{4622AD11-FF23-11d0-8D34-00A0C90F2719}
SysTray	{35CEC8A3-2BE6-11D2-8773-92E220524153}
Taskbar and Start Menu	{0DF44EAA-FF21-4412-828E-260A8728E7F1}
The Internet	{3DC7A020-0ACD-11CF-A9BB-00AA004AE837}
*Name not listed in Registry	

As you select and examine keys for registered file types and objects, you discover that you are already familiar with some or many of the settings, because you access and work with these settings using Windows XP tools, property sheets, and dialog boxes.

In the next section of the tutorial, you are going to examine the process for editing the Registry. You examine how to enter a new Registry key as well as how to change the value for a Registry key.

Editing the Registry

Computer trade magazines, professional and personal Web sites, and even the Microsoft Knowledge Base abound with tips that allow you to customize your computer, improve its performance, increase security, improve network connectivity, enhance hardware and software support, and troubleshoot problems by making changes to the Registry. In every instance, these sources for Registry tips also warn you to be especially cautious when you make changes to the Windows Registry, as errors might result in an unstable system or prevent you from even booting your computer. However, in certain cases, you might want and need to make changes to your system that require you to edit the Registry because you have no other option for making that change.

For example, Windows XP displays balloon tips that are designed to be helpful and to provide you with information that you might need to know (such as the availability of Windows updates). However, those balloon tips can interfere with the productivity of experienced and power users. Likewise, though these balloon tips might be initially useful to a novice, after a while even a novice knows how to work with basic Windows XP features. Is it really necessary for Windows XP to display a balloon tip like the one shown in Figure 13-27 every time you log on, just to remind you that it is hiding your inactive notification icons, and informing you that you can click the Show Hidden Icons button 🔘 to display your hidden icons in the notification area? You can just point to 🔘 , and Windows XP displays a ToolTip (identified as an InfoTip in the Registry) with the label "Show hidden icons." Or is it really necessary for Windows XP to display a balloon tip on the Start menu to inform you that new software has just been installed but, in the process, the balloon tip obscures the Start menu command that you're trying to use?

Figure 13-27	VIEWING A BALLOON TIP

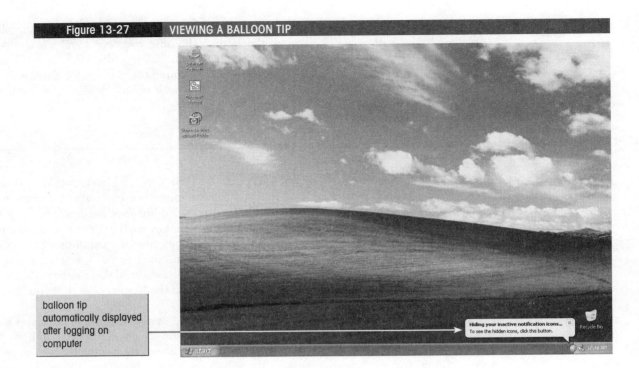

balloon tip automatically displayed after logging on computer

Once you become familiar with the Windows XP operating environment, features, and tools, you can edit a setting in the Registry to turn off the display of these balloon tips so that you can be more productive. To make this change, you have to first locate the correct subkey in the Registry, edit the existing value of that value entry, and then restart your computer.

Because you are now familiar with Windows XP, Eric encourages you to modify the Registry, and turn off the display of balloon tips. At your request, Eric guides you through this process.

Because changes to the Registry can adversely affect the performance of a computer, the next section of the tutorial does not include "hands-on" steps, but rather describes the process and illustrates it with figures. If you are working in a computer lab, the network administrator and technical support staff more than likely limit access to the Registry so that someone cannot accidentally or deliberately modify configuration settings that in turn might adversely affect the performance of that computer and the network.

Before you attempt to make this change on your own computer, you might want to read the following section so that you are familiar with the process for changing a setting in the Registry. Make sure you have the necessary backups you might need if you need to restore your computer, including recent backups of the Registry. Even Microsoft cannot guarantee that changes you make with the Registry Editor can be resolved if a problem occurs.

Locating the Correct Registry Key

After opening the Registry, the first step is to locate the correct key. Before you can edit the Registry, you must know the path to and name of the correct key. You also have to know the name of the value stored in the Registry and, if it's not present, you need to know how to add it to the Registry. You obviously also have to know the setting that you are going to assign to this value. As noted earlier, articles in computer magazines, Web sites that specialize in Registry tips, and reference books on Windows XP, as well as the Microsoft Online

Support Web site, provide you with step-by-step details on how to make a change to the Registry, so that you can customize or troubleshoot your computer. Also, as previously noted, these sources for Registry tips also always include a disclaimer warning you that making changes to the Registry might adversely affect the performance of your computer.

The Registry path to the correct Explorer key for disabling balloon tips is as follows:

My Computer\HKEY_CURRENT_USER\Software\Microsoft\Windows\CurrentVersion\Explorer\Advanced

To locate this key, you can open each key and subkey in the Registry path, or you can use the Find feature to search for the Advanced key (also use the option "Match whole string only"). Once you locate the Advanced key, you can check the path on the status bar to verify that you have found the correct key. Figure 13-28 shows the Advanced key, its current values, and the path to this key on the status bar. This key contains a number of settings that you can customize. Your list may differ from that shown for the computer used for this figure.

Figure 13-28	VIEWING VALUE ENTRIES IN THE EXPLORER ADVANCED KEY

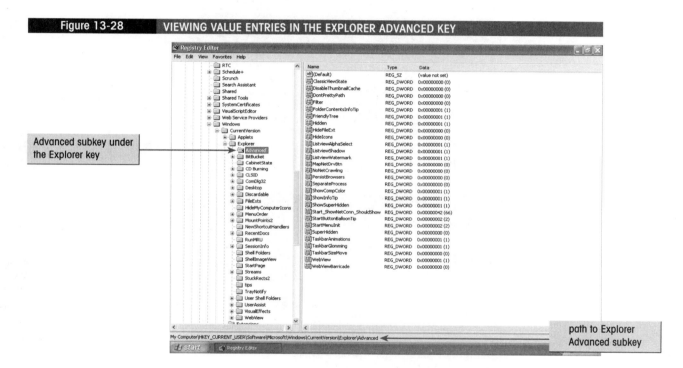

The value entry for controlling the display of balloon tips is called EnableBalloonTips (with no spaces). Since there is no EnableBalloonTips value entry for this key on the computer used for Figure 13-28, the next step is to add that value entry to the Advanced key.

Adding a Registry Key Location to the Favorites Menu

If you want to quickly return to a specific key in the Registry, which as you know is quite extensive, you can use the Favorites menu option (a new feature) to bookmark that Registry key. If you select the Favorites menu, it contains an "Add to Favorites" and a "Remove Favorite" option. If you choose the "Add to Favorites" option for the Advanced key, the Registry Editor displays an Add to Favorites dialog box and prompts you for the Favorite name you want to use for this key. As shown in Figure 13-29, the Favorites menu now identifies this Registry location as "Explorer Advanced."

Figure 13-29   BOOKMARK ADDED TO FAVORITES MENU

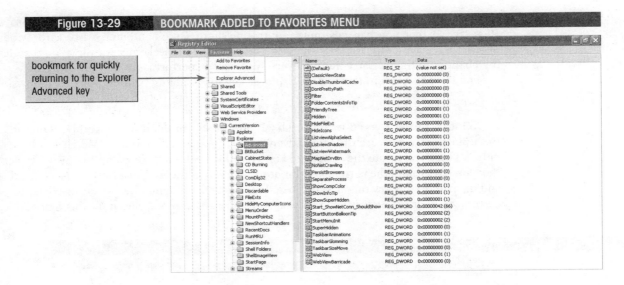

bookmark for quickly returning to the Explorer Advanced key

Adding a New Value Entry to a Registry Subkey

The New option on the Registry Editor Edit menu allows you to add a new key, or if you know the data type of the new value entry, you can add one of five types of values: a string value, a binary value, a DWORD (Double Word) value, a multi-string value, or an expandable string value. See Figure 13-30.

Figure 13-30   OPTIONS FOR ADDING NEW KEYS

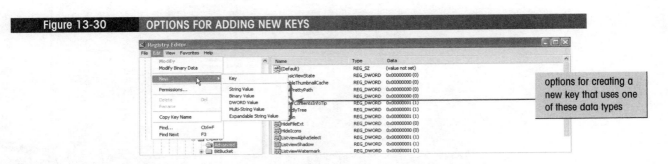

options for creating a new key that uses one of these data types

As noted earlier, a string value is a text entry, such as Paint.Picture (a Class Definition), Bitmap Image (an object type), shimgvw.dll,1 (a dynamic link library filename that also identifies the position of an icon within the program file to display for a file type), "Displays your e-mail, calendar, contacts, and other important personal information" (the ScreenTip text for Microsoft Outlook, but without the quotation marks). String values are identified using the REG_SZ (text string), REG_EXPAND_SZ (a variable-length text string), or REG_MULTI_SZ (a multiple-line text string) data types. Earlier, you examined the Registry value entry for editing a file with a bitmap image, namely "%systemroot%\system32\mspaint.exe" "%1", with a REG_EXPAND_SZ data type.

A **binary value** is identified as REG_BINARY, and the value data is represented using a hexadecimal code (a base-16 number system that uses the digits 0 through 9 and the uppercase and lowercase letters A through F to encode data). Examples of binary values are 00 00 00 00, the value data for the link value entry under the Explorer key, and b0 4a d0 66 50 ec c1 01, the value data for the Last used time value entry under the CleanupWiz key (for the Desktop Cleanup Wizard). The link value entry determines whether Windows XP adds the phrase "Shortcut to" at the beginning of shortcut names.

A DWORD value, identified by the REG_DWORD data type, is a four-byte number displayed in binary, hexadecimal, or decimal format. For example, the DWORD value 0x000000001 (1) for the WebView value entry under the Explorer key indicates that Web style is enabled. The value in parentheses is the decimal equivalent (the standard base-10 number system) of the DWORD value.

EnableBalloonTips requires a DWORD value, so from the Edit menu, you point to New, and then click DWORD Value. After you select this command, the Registry Editor inserts a new DWORD value, assigns it the name "New Value #1", and waits for you to specify a new name, as shown in Figure 13-31. The value in parentheses (0) for the DWORD value 0x00000000 (0) is the decimal equivalent of the value assigned to EnableBalloonTips. This default setting 0 (for "disabled") instructs Windows XP to not display balloon tips. If you change this value to 1 (for "enabled"), you are instructing Windows XP to display balloon tips.

Figure 13-31   CREATING A NEW VALUE ENTRY

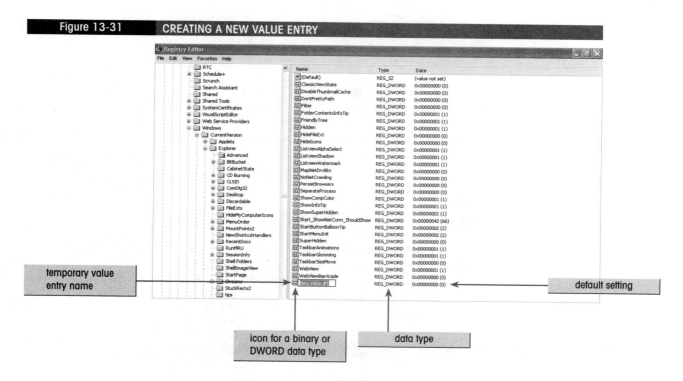

Next, you type EnableBalloonTips and press the Enter key, as shown in Figure 13-32.

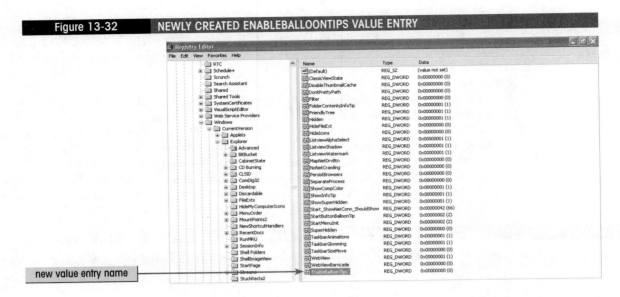

Figure 13-32   NEWLY CREATED ENABLEBALLOONTIPS VALUE ENTRY

new value entry name

The Registry Editor then updates the value entry's name. The next time you log on your computer, Windows XP does not display balloon tips. In some cases, Windows XP applies a setting immediately; in other instances, you have to restart your computer before it applies the setting.

Changing a Value

If you later want to change the setting for the EnableBalloonTips value entry for a new user, you can open the Registry, search for and locate the EnableBalloonTips value name, and then either double-click the value entry's name, or you can single-click the value entry's name, select the Edit menu, and then select Modify. The Registry Editor then displays an Edit DWORD Value dialog box, as shown in Figure 13-33. The dialog box shows the value entry's name (EnableBalloonTips), the value data (0), and the base (how you want to represent the value).

Figure 13-33   EDITING A DWORD VALUE

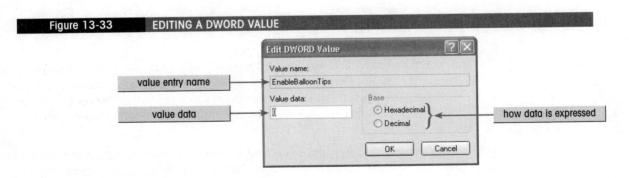

value entry name

value data

how data is expressed

The value data 0 is already highlighted, as shown in Figure 13-33, so all you need to do is to type 1 (*the number one, not a lowercase "L"*) to replace the current value, as shown in Figure 13-34.

Figure 13-34   CHANGING A DWORD VALUE

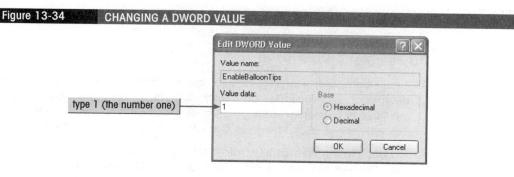

After you click the OK button, the Registry Editor shows the updated DWORD value in the topic pane. See Figure 13-35.

Figure 13-35   NEW REGISTRY VALUE

This change applies only to the current user's account; it does not apply to other accounts on the same computer.

Restoring Your Computer

If you are working in a computer lab, or if you want to restore your computer, you need to delete the Registry Backup folder and registration file, the System State backup, and the System State report. If you decide that you want to keep the Registry folder and registration file, The System State backup, and the System State report on your computer, you can skip this section.

> ### To restore your computer:
>
> **1.** If you do not want to keep, or no longer need, the registration file you created at the beginning of this tutorial, open the My Documents folder (or the folder that contains the registration file), and then select and delete the Registry Backup folder.
>
> **2.** If you do not want to keep, or no longer need, the System State backup and the System State report, open the My Documents folder (or the folder that contains these files), and then select and delete them.
>
> **3.** Empty the Recycle Bin.

If you also want to restore your computer's display settings, complete the following steps.

To restore your computer's display settings:

1. If your computer was originally set for the Windows Classic style, right-click the **desktop**, click **Properties** on the shortcut menu, and after Windows XP opens the Display Properties dialog box, click the **Theme** list arrow on the Themes property sheet, click **Windows Classic**, and then click the **OK** button.

2. To switch to the Windows Classic Start menu style, right-click the **Start** button, click **Properties** on the shortcut menu, and after Windows XP opens the Taskbar and Start Menu Properties dialog box, click the **Classic Start menu** option button on the Start Menu property sheet, and then click the **OK** button.

3. To change to Windows classic folders view, click the **Start** button, point to **Settings**, click **Control Panel**, and after Windows XP opens a Control Panel window, click **Tools** on the menu bar, click **Folder Options**, and after Windows XP opens the Folder Options dialog box, click the **Use Windows classic folders** option button, and click the **Double-click to open an item** option button under "Click items as follows".

4. Click the **View** tab in the Folder Options dialog box. If necessary, restore the original settings for the "Display the full path in the address bar" check box, the "Do not show hidden files and folders" option, and the "Hide extensions for known file types" check box.

5. Click the **OK** button to close the Folder Options dialog box and restore your original settings, and then close the Control Panel folder window.

Now you can periodically use the Registry Editor to check system settings, to customize computers in ways that would not otherwise be possible, and to troubleshoot computer systems for employees at DGL Communications Group. Before you use the Registry Editor, always create a restore point, make sure they you a recent copy of the System State, and export Registry settings to a registration file, in the event you need to restore the Registry.

REVIEW ASSIGNMENTS

During your first week on the job, Eric mentions that staff members frequently encounter problems when they open files with the "doc" file extension. In certain cases, Windows XP opens WordPad documents with Microsoft Word. Since Microsoft Word is the most commonly used word-processing application at DGL Communications Group, Eric recommends that you open the Registry and examine information on the "doc" file association, using the same approach that you used earlier for "bmp" file extensions.

As you complete each step in these Review Assignments, record your answers to questions so that you can submit them to your instructor. Use a word-processing application such as Word or WordPad to prepare and then print your answers to these questions. Also, if you change any settings on the computer you are using, note the original settings so that you can restore them later.

1. From the Start menu, point to All Programs, point to Accessories, point to System Tools, and then open System Restore. In the System Restore dialog box, choose the option for creating a restore point, and then go to the next step. When prompted for a Restore point description, type Registry Restore Point and then choose the option to create a restore point. After System Restore reports that it created a new restore point, close the System Restore dialog box.

2. Open the My Documents folder, and create a Registry Backup folder. If you prefer, you can create this folder on a Zip disk or other type of removable media.

3. From the Start menu, select Run, type REGEDIT and then press the Enter key. If My Computer is not selected in the Registry Tree pane, press the Home key.

4. Select File on the menu bar, select Export, open the Registry Backup folder you created earlier, and then export all of the Registry settings to a file named Registry Backup for *[current date]* (using the current date in the format yyyy-mm-dd). Examine the registration file in the Registry Backup folder. What is its file size? Close the Registry Backup folder window.

5. In the Registry Editor window, select Edit on the menu bar, select Find, and then search for the following key: .doc

6. Under what subtree is the .doc key? What is the default Class Definition for this file type? Is this value a string, binary, or DWORD value?

7. Select the Class Definition subkey below the .doc subkey (the one with the same name as the Class Definition), and then open the ShellNew subkey. What is the name of the template (or document file type) that Windows XP opens when you create a new "doc" file? In other words, what is the value assigned to the FileName value entry?

8. Use the Registry Editor's Find feature to locate the default Class Definition subkey that you identified in Step 6 for the .doc key (not the subkey with the same name under the .doc key). What is the default string value that Windows XP uses to identify this type of file on a property sheet or in a folder listing?

9. Expand the key you just found, and then expand the Shell subkey. What types of actions can you perform on this file type?

10. Open the key for creating a new document of this type, and then examine the (Default) value entry. What is the command for creating a new document of this type?

11. Close the Registry Editor, open My Computer, choose Tools on the menu bar, select Folder Options, and after the Folder Options dialog box opens, select the File Types tab.

12. Locate and select the DOC file extension under Registered file types. What description does Windows XP use for this file type? What application does it automatically open for this file type?

Explore

13. Select the Advanced button, and in the Edit File Type dialog box, choose the New action, and then click the Edit button. What is the command line for the application used to perform this action?

14. Click the Cancel button to close the Editing action for type dialog box, click the Cancel button to close the Edit File Type dialog box, click the Cancel button to close the Folder Options dialog box, and then close My Computer.

Explore

15. What would be the safest way to make a change to a registered file type? Explain.

16. If you do not want to keep, or no longer need, the registration file you created at the beginning of this Review Assignment, open the My Documents folder (or the folder that contains the registration file), and then select and delete the Registry Backup folder.

CASE PROBLEMS

Case 1. *Using the Registry to Document Registered File Types at Valley Community
College* The Office of Contract Education at Valley Community College near Phoenix,
Arizona, has asked one of the college's computer instructors, Nina O'Brien, to prepare an
intermediate to advanced level training workshop for the college's technical support staff.
Nina wants to prepare a variety of handouts that summarize the different features and concepts that she will cover during the workshop. One of these handouts will list file types
using the information on file associations in the Windows XP Registry.

As you complete each step in this case, record your answers to questions so that you can
submit them to your instructor. Use a word processing application such as Word or
WordPad to prepare and then print your answers to these questions. Also, if you change
any settings on the computer you are using, note the original settings so that you can
restore them later.

1. Use System Restore to create a restore point. Why should you perform this operation
   before using the Registry?

2. Open the Registry Editor, and with My Computer selected, export the contents of the
   Registry to a registration file on disk. Why should you perform this operation before
   using the Registry?

Explore

3. Using the information in the HKEY_CLASSES_ROOT key, prepare a table similar to that
   shown in Figure 13-36, which identifies the file type for each of the Class-Definitions listed.
   For example, the (Default) value entry for the Class-Definition "batfile" is "MS-DOS Batch
   File." *Note*: You can use the Find feature to quickly locate keys.

Figure 13-36	IDENTIFYING FILE TYPES FOR CLASS DEFINITIONS

CLASS DEFINITION	DATA VALUE (DESCRIPTION OF FILE TYPE)
anifile	
avifile	
batfile	MS-DOS Batch File
chkfile	
cmdfile	
comfile	
cplfile	
Directory	
dllfile	
DocShortcut	
drvfile	
dunfile	
exefile	
fndfile	
fonfile	

Figure 13-36	IDENTIFYING FILE TYPES FOR CLASS DEFINITIONS (CONTINUED)

CLASS DEFINITION	DATA VALUE (DESCRIPTION OF FILE TYPE)
giffile	
hlpfile	
icofile	
inffile	
inifile	
jpegfile	
lnkfile	
mpegfile	
MSCFile	
ocxfile	
otffile	
piffile	
RDP.File	
regfile	
rtffile	
scrfile	
sysfile	
ttffile	
txtfile	
vxdfile	
zapfile	

4. Print a copy of the table you prepared.

5. Is there any other way you might have found this same information? Explain.

6. Name at least three other places where you have seen some of the descriptions for these different file types.

7. Close the Registry Editor.

8. If you do not want to keep, or no longer need, the registration file you created at the beginning of this case problem, open the My Documents folder (or the folder that contains the registration file), and then select and delete the Registry Backup folder.

Case 2. Using the Registry to Prevent the Automatic Loading of Windows Messenger at Pirolle Custom Computers Pirolle Custom Computers is a computer consulting firm in East Lansing, Michigan. Adrian Pirolle, the owner, wants you to modify the Registry so that Windows XP does not automatically open Windows Messenger and display a Welcome to MSN Explorer dialog box informing him that no one is set up to use MSN Explorer, as shown in Figure 13-37. These dialog boxes either appear periodically, or in some cases, every few seconds, and he has to close both dialog boxes each time.

This case calls for you to delete a value entry for a Registry subkey. Prior to performing this operation, back up this subkey so that you can restore it later. If your computer lab does not allow you to use the Registry Editor, or allow you to make changes to a computer with the Registry Editor, you cannot complete this case problem.

As you complete each step in this case, record your answers to questions so that you can submit them to your instructor. Use a word-processing application such as Word or WordPad to prepare and then print your answers to these questions. Also, if you change any settings on the computer you are using, note the original settings so that you can restore them later.

Figure 13-37	WINDOWS XP AUTOMATICALLY OPENS WINDOWS MESSENGER

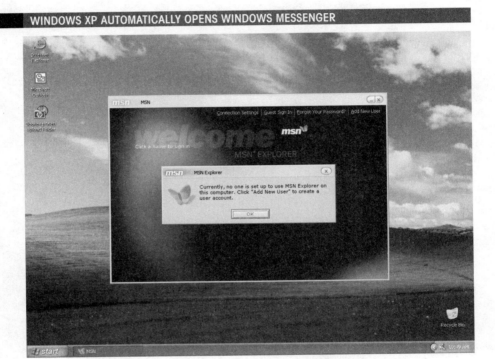

1. Use System Restore to create a restore point. Why should you perform this operation before using the Registry?

Explore

2. Right-click the taskbar, and then select Task Manager. In the Windows Task Manager dialog box, select the Processes tab (if necessary), and then click the Image Name column button to sort programs in alphabetical order by name. Is there a program named MSMSGS.EXE listed in the Image Name column in lowercase? If so, what user name is associated with this program? Close Windows Task Manager without making any changes to your computer.

3. Open the Registry Editor and then locate and select the following key: My Computer\HKEY_CURRENT_USER\Software\Microsoft\Windows\CurrentVersion\Run

4. Is there a value entry named MSMSGS? If so, what is its data type, and what setting is assigned to this value entry?

5. With the Run key selected, select File on the menu bar, select Export, and export the contents of this one Registry key to a registration file on disk. Why should you perform this operation before changing the Registry?

Explore

6. Select the MSMSGS value entry, select Edit on the menu bar, and then select Delete. When asked to verify that you want to delete this value, click Yes.

7. Close the Registry Editor.

8. Log off your computer, and then log back on.

9. Open Task Manager, and then sort the program filenames on the Processes sheet in alphabetical order. Did Windows XP load MSMSGS.EXE?

10. Close Windows Task Manager without making any changes to your computer.

11. To restore your Registry to its original setting, open the Registry Editor, and locate the subkey, the path of which is shown in Step 3. (The Registry Editor automatically displays the last key you examined.)

Explore

12. From the File menu, select Import, locate and select the registration file that contains a backup of the Run subkey, click the Open button in the Import Registry File dialog box to restore the original Registry settings for this key, and then click the OK button in the Registry Editor dialog box once the operation is complete.

13. Examine the value entries for the Run key and verify that the Registry Editor restored the MSMSGS key.

14. Close the Registry Editor.

15. If you do not want to keep, or no longer need, the registration file you created at the beginning of this case problem, open the My Documents folder (or the folder that contains the registration file), and then select and delete the Registry Backup folder.

Case 3. Using the Registry to Customize Shortcut Names at Network Data Recovery

Network Data Recovery (NDR) is a network consulting firm that assists clients in the Los Angeles area with the recovery of data that's lost because of network, hardware, and software problems. Neil Golden, a troubleshooting specialist at NDR, relies on the use of shortcuts. He wants you to modify the Registry on his office computer so that Windows XP no longer adds the prefix "Shortcut to" at the beginning of the names of newly created shortcuts.

This case calls for you to delete a value entry for a Registry subkey, and then create a new value entry by the same name, but with a different setting. Prior to performing this operation, you back up this subkey so that you can restore it later. If your computer lab does not allow you to use the Registry Editor or allow you to make changes to a computer with the Registry Editor, you cannot complete this case problem.

As you complete each step in this case, record your answers to questions so that you can submit them to your instructor. Use a word-processing application such as Word or WordPad to prepare and then print your answers to these questions. Also, if you change any settings on the computer you are using, note the original settings so that you can restore them later.

1. Use System Restore to create a restore point. Why should you perform this operation before using the Registry?

2. Open My Computer, and drag one of the drives to the desktop. What is the full name of the desktop shortcut? Drag the shortcut to the Recycle Bin, and then close My Computer.

3. Open the Registry Editor, and locate and select the following key:
   My Computer\HKEY_CURRENT_USER\Software\Microsoft\Windows\CurrentVersion\Explorer

4. Is there a value entry named "link"? If so, what is its data type, and what setting is assigned to this value entry?

5. With the Explorer key selected, select File on the menu bar, select Export, and export the contents of this one Registry key to a registration file on disk. Why should you perform this operation before changing the Registry?

Explore 6. Right-click the link value entry, select Delete on the shortcut menu, and then verify that you want to delete this value entry.

Explore 7. From the Edit menu, point to New, and then choose Binary Value. Type link for the new value entry name, and then press the Enter key twice to assign the name and then to open the Edit Binary Value dialog box. In the Value data box (which already has the first part of this value entry's data, namely 0000), type 00 00 00 00 (with spaces between each set of two zeroes), and then press the Enter key or click the OK button. Verify that the Type for this value entry is REG_BINARY and that the setting listed in the Data column for this value entry is 00 00 00 00 (If not, repeat the previous step and this step.)

8. Close the Registry Editor window.

9. Restart your computer and log on under your user account.

10. Open My Computer, and drag the icon for the same drive you used in the first step to the desktop. What is the full name of the desktop shortcut? Drag the shortcut to the Recycle Bin, and then close My Computer.

11. To restore your Registry, right-click the link value entry, select Delete on the shortcut menu, and then verify that you want to delete the link value entry. From the Edit menu, point to New, and then choose Binary Value. Type link for the new value entry name, and then press the Enter key twice to assign the name and then to open the Edit Binary Value dialog box. In the Value data box (which already has the first part of this value entry's data, namely 0000), type the original setting from your answer to the question in Step 4, and then press the Enter key or click the OK button. Verify that the Type for this value entry is REG_BINARY and that the setting listed in the Data column for this value entry is the original setting in your answer to Step 4. (If not, repeat this step.) Then, close the Registry Editor, restart your computer, and log on under your user account.

12. If you do not want to keep, or no longer need, the registration file you created at the beginning of this case problem, open the My Documents folder (or the folder that contains the registration file), and then select and delete the Registry Backup folder.

Case 4. Searching for Personal and Product Registration Information in the Registry
You recently upgraded the software on your computer to take advantage of the features of Win32 applications. Now you want to check the Registry for information on your installed software, including registration and personal information, to make sure it does not contain a reference to previously installed software.

As you complete each step in this case, record your answers to questions so that you can submit them to your instructor. Use a word-processing application such as Word or WordPad to prepare and then print your answers to these questions. Also, if you change any settings on the computer you are using, note the original settings so that you can restore them later.

1. Use System Restore to create a restore point. Why should you perform this operation before using the Registry?

2. Open the Registry Editor, and with My Computer selected, export the contents of the Registry to a registration file on disk. Why should you perform this operation before using the Registry?

3. Make sure My Computer is selected in the Registry Tree pane, and then use Find to search for the value entry RegisteredOwner (one word with no spaces). To save time, specify that you only want to search for Values.

Explore   4. After the Registry Editor locates the RegisteredOwner value entry, what is the path to the subkey that contains this value entry? What is the data type for the RegisteredOwner value entry? Who is the RegisteredOwner?

Explore   5. Examine the other settings in this subkey, and list the settings for the CurrentBuildNumber, CurrentType, CurrentVersion, ProductName, RegisteredOrganization, and SystemRoot value entries.

Explore   6. If your name or the registered organization were incorrectly spelled, could you correct that information here, and if so, how would you make this change?

    7. Return to My Computer at the top of the Registry Tree pane.

Explore   8. Use Find to search for your last name, and to save time, specify that you only want to search for Data. After Find locates the first instance of where your name is used, you can press the F3 key to continue the search from that point. List the types of information (including the value entry) that identify you by name. Because the amount of information is extensive, you might want to limit your list to 15 items.

Explore   9. *Optional*: The Registry might also contain other personal information, such as your day of birth (birthdayDay value entry), month of birth (birthdayMonth value entry), year of birth (birthdayYear value entry), your telephone number (phone value entry), and whether or not you are a male (male value entry). You might want to search the Registry for this information.

    10. Close the Registry Editor.

    11. If you do not want to keep, or no longer need, the registration file you created at the beginning of this case problem, open the My Documents folder (or the folder that contains the registration file), and then select and delete the Registry Backup folder.

In this tutorial you will:

- Learn about the importance of the command-line environment

- Examine the difference between internal and external commands

- Customize a command-line window

- Obtain Help on the use of a specific command

- Use commands to examine the status of your computer and its directory structure

- View directory listings, change drives, change directories, and create directories

- Format a disk, view file attributes, and copy files to a disk

- Use wildcards to streamline command operations

- View the Windows environment, and create an environment variable

THE WINDOWS XP COMMAND-LINE ENVIRONMENT

Working in a Command-Line Environment at The Travis Foundation

CASE

The Travis Foundation

The Travis Foundation is a philanthropic foundation that derives its income primarily from corporate giving programs and from its own business investments. Each year graduating high school students compete for hundreds of scholarships offered by the Travis Foundation. These scholarships support students for four years while they pursue interdisciplinary programs of study at universities and colleges overseas.

Terri Blackburn manages the foundation's computer network, and like other skilled computer professionals, she relies on the use of the Windows XP command-line environment when troubleshooting problems. Recently, Terri hired you as her new part-time assistant to help her provide support and troubleshooting assistance to the foundation's employees and volunteers. Since these skills are critical to providing staff support, Terri's first task is to show you how to work within the Windows XP command-line environment.

In the first section of the tutorial, you examine the importance of the command-line environment and command-line skills. You open a Command Prompt window, examine the use of internal and external commands, and use commands to customize the Command Prompt window, examine the status of your computer, format a floppy disk, and view the contents of text files. You also examine how to obtain Help on the use of commands. Once you complete this part of the tutorial, you will be ready to work with directories.

Understanding **the Importance of Command-Line Skills**

After the introduction of Windows 95, there has been a gradual, but dramatic, shift from working in a command-line environment, as typified by the DOS operating system, to operating systems like Windows that rely primarily on a graphical user interface. However, command-line skills are still essential today, especially for those who provide technical support and troubleshooting. Furthermore, concepts and features incorporated into the DOS operating system are important for understanding the Windows operating system and how it works. For example, when working with the DOS operating system, you had to know how to navigate your way through a computer system by specifying the MS-DOS path to drives and directories (or folders). The DOS operating system also relied on the path for locating and loading applications and other programs stored in different directories. Likewise, Windows XP and all previous versions of Windows rely on the path to locate and load applications and other programs. As you saw in Tutorial 13, the Windows Registry stores the paths of programs for registered file types, so that when you click (or double-click) a file icon, Windows XP can open the associated application as well as the document. As you saw in Tutorial 4, desktop shortcuts to drives, folders, files, applications, and system objects on your local computer rely on the use of a path to locate and open the target of the shortcut. Network shortcuts, which rely on the UNC path, and Internet shortcuts, which rely on a Web site's URL, use similar techniques.

As covered in Tutorial 12, the UNC (Universal Naming Convention) path identifies the location of a shared resource on a network, such as a computer, printer, drive, or folder. For example, *Hi-Perform\My Documents* is the UNC path for the My Documents folder on a computer named Hi-Perform. Two backslashes appear at the beginning of a UNC path and shared resources (such as Hi-Perform and My Documents) are separated by a single backslash. In contrast, Internet shortcuts rely on a URL (Uniform Resource Locator) to locate a Web site. You might, for example, have an Internet shortcut for a search engine, such as Google.com, with a target URL of *http://www.google.com*.

If you are a network administrator, specialist, or technician, you need to know command-line skills and concepts because you may need to use them to set up, configure, and troubleshoot a network. These same skills and concepts might also be important if you need to troubleshoot operating system, hardware, and software problems on your own computer. If Windows XP is unable to boot to the desktop, or if you experience a problem with your hard disk drive, you can boot your computer into Safe Mode with Command Prompt from the Windows Advanced Options Menu. Then you can attempt to troubleshoot problems, make backups, and restore important Windows XP system files. Or, as you saw in Tutorial 9, you might need to start the Recovery Console, a command-line tool, to troubleshoot problems or restore your computer to a working state. If you have to rebuild a computer system from scratch, you might need to know how to work in a command-line environment. In certain cases, if your computer is infected with a computer virus, you might have to work from a command-line prompt after using your antivirus software to complete the task of cleaning up your computer system. If you contact technical support to help you with a problem, you might be asked to open, examine, and perhaps change the contents of configuration files, and work with commands from a command-line environment.

Windows XP (and previous versions of Windows) include an option for working in a command-line environment to provide background compatibility, where possible, with DOS applications, utilities, and games. DOS programs require an operating environment that mimics the command-line environment found under the DOS operating system.

To acquire professional certifications in certain specialties, such as networking, you have to prove competency in the use of command-line skills. At many colleges, a command-line class is a requirement for networking courses that lead to certification in a specific area and that provide skills for a particular type of job. Other professions, such as trainers, can also benefit from a knowledge of command-line skills, as those skills may prove valuable when trying to resolve a problem, or when trying to illustrate a concept or feature.

Opening a Command Prompt Window

In Tutorial 7, you examined how to use the Check Disk utility from a Command Prompt window, and in Tutorial 9, you learned how to boot your computer to a command prompt with the Windows Advanced Options menu. In that same tutorial, you looked at how to work with the Recovery Console command-line tool. Therefore, you are already familiar with the use of specific Windows XP features that require a command-line environment.

To work in a command-line environment under Windows XP, you open a Command Prompt window from the Accessories menu or by using the Run command on the Start menu. In both cases, Windows XP uses the cmd.exe program in the System32 directory to open a Command Prompt window. Cmd.exe is the Windows XP command interpreter. A **command interpreter** is a program that interprets commands entered at the command prompt, locates and (if necessary) loads the appropriate program from memory or disk, and then executes the program. The command interpreter is also responsible for displaying the command prompt.

After your initial orientation, you and Terri decide it would be a good idea to spend a couple of hours each afternoon during your first week of work to review the basics of working with the Windows XP command-line environment. Terri wants to start by showing you how to open a command-line session, enter and use some basic Windows XP commands, navigate the directory structure of your computer, and customize system settings.

In the following steps, you are going to examine two approaches for opening a command-line session.

To open a Command Prompt window:

1. From the Start menu, point to **All Programs**, point to **Accessories**, and then click **Command Prompt**. Windows XP opens a Command Prompt window on the desktop, and displays a command prompt or operating system prompt that identifies the default drive (in this case, drive C) and default directory used by Windows XP. See Figure 14-1. On Terri's computer, the command prompt shows the full path to the directory for Terri's user profile. Note that the Command Prompt window also identifies the operating system (Microsoft Windows XP), and the version of Windows (Version 5.1.2600, the original version of Windows XP on the computer used for this figure). As you may recall, when you work in the graphical user interface, you use the terms "folder" and "subfolder" to describe the file system components for tracking files. However, when working in a command-line environment, you use the comparable terms "directory" and "subdirectory" instead.

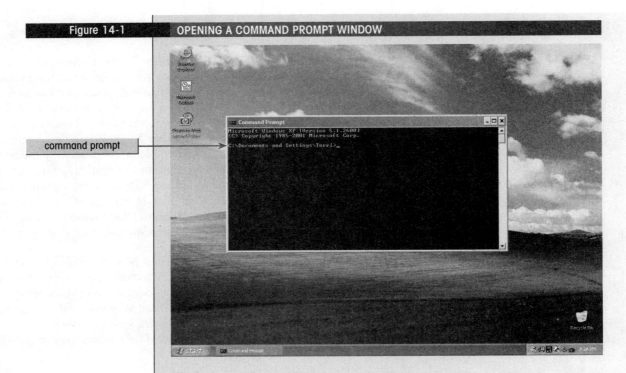

Figure 14-1 | OPENING A COMMAND PROMPT WINDOW

command prompt

2. Type **exit** and then press the **Enter** key. Windows XP closes the Command Prompt window. When entering commands in a Command Prompt window, you can use uppercase, lowercase, or mixed case. After you enter a command at the command prompt, you must press the Enter key; otherwise, nothing happens. The Enter key acts as a signal to the operating system to execute the command.

3. From the Start menu, click **Run**. Then, in the Open text box, type **cmd** and press the **Enter** key (as you would in a command-line environment). Windows XP opens a Command Prompt window, but instead of displaying the label "Command Prompt" in the title bar, it displays the path to the program that it opened, namely, cmd.exe from the System32 directory. See Figure 14-2.

Figure 14-2   OPENING THE COMMAND INTERPRETER

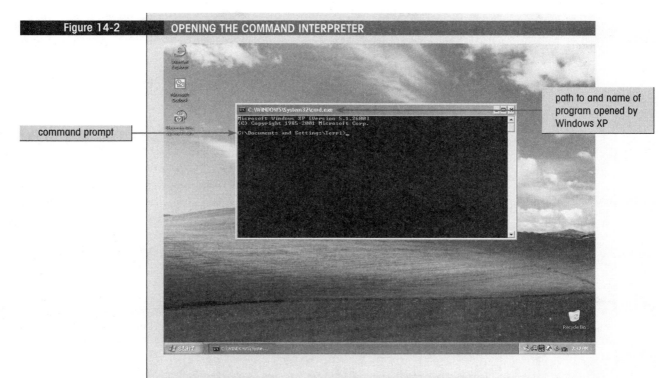

command prompt

path to and name of program opened by Windows XP

4. Press and hold the **Alt** key, press and release the **Enter** key, and then release the **Alt** key. Windows XP switches to full-screen view. See Figure 14-3. If you boot a computer with DOS, and assuming that the system has not been customized, a full-screen view similar to the one shown in the figure is the type of view in which you work. Note that full-screen view is different from a maximized window because you do not have a title bar with buttons for minimizing, restoring, or closing the window.

Figure 14-3   WORKING IN FULL SCREEN VIEW

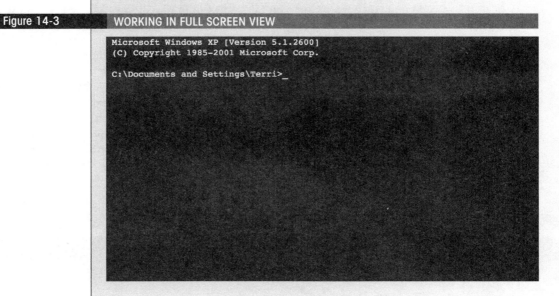

```
Microsoft Windows XP [Version 5.1.2600]
(C) Copyright 1985-2001 Microsoft Corp.

C:\Documents and Settings\Terri>_
```

5. Press **Alt+Enter** again to switch back to windowed view. The Alt+Enter shortcut key combination lets you quickly switch from a windowed view to a full-screen view, and vice versa.

6. Leave the Command Prompt window open for the next section of the tutorial.

REFERENCE WINDOW   **RW**

Opening and Closing a Command Prompt Window
- Click the Start button, click Run, and type CMD in the Open box, and then press the Enter key. Or click the Start button, point to All Programs, point to Accessories, and then click Command Prompt.
- To switch to full-screen view, press and hold the Alt key, press and release the Enter key, and then release the Alt key. To switch back to a windowed view, press Alt+Enter again.
- To close the Command Prompt window, type EXIT and then press the Enter key.

As you can see, using Run from the Start menu is a faster way to open a Command Prompt window. When you use the Run option, you are in effect working in a miniature command-line window.

Using Internal and External Commands

Once you open a Command Prompt window, you can enter commands at the command prompt to perform specific operations. These commands fall into two groups: internal commands and external commands. Internal commands are usually commands for common and important types of operations, such as creating a directory (or folder). The program code for an **internal command** is stored in the file Cmd.exe. After loading Cmd.exe into memory, you do not need a disk to load and open programs for internal commands.

When you open a Command Prompt window, Windows XP loads Cmd.exe into memory. Then Cmd.exe performs specific functions, such as displaying a user interface with a command prompt and interpreting commands that you enter. Once Cmd.exe loads into memory, you can access the program code for any of the internal commands it contains within itself. Because the operating system does not have to go back to disk to locate and load the program code for an internal command (it's already in memory), internal commands execute more quickly. Figure 14-4 lists some examples of internal commands and their usage. Commands are shown in uppercase; however, as noted earlier, you can use lowercase when you enter a command. Items shown in italics within brackets, such as [*drive:*] and [*path*], are optional parameters or items of data. If the drive and path are not specified for those commands that use them, Windows XP uses the current drive and directory. Items shown in italics without brackets, such as *filename* and *drive:* are required parameters; you must enter them.

Figure 14-4	INTERNAL COMMANDS
INTERNAL COMMAND	**USE**
ASSOC	Displays file types for file extensions, or changes the file type for a file extension
CD .. CHDIR ..	Changes to the parent directory of the current subdirectory
CD [*drive:*]*path* CHDIR [*drive:*]*path*	Changes from the current directory to another directory

Figure 14-4	INTERNAL COMMANDS (CONTINUED)

INTERNAL COMMAND	USE
CD \ CHDIR \	Changes from the current directory to the root directory
CLS	Clears the Command Prompt window, or the screen in full-screen view
COLOR [*attr*]	Sets foreground and background colors in a Command Prompt window
command /?	Displays Help information on the command you specify
COPY *directory1 directory2*	Copies all the files in the source directory (*directory1*) to another directory (*directory2*)
COPY *filename directory*	Copies a file to another directory (using the same filename)
COPY *filename drive:*	Copies a file to another drive (using the same filename)
COPY *filename1 filename2*	Copies a file to the current directory, and creates a new file with a new name
DATE	Displays or sets the system date
DEL [*drive:*][*path*]*filespec* [*/p*] ERASE [*drive:*][*path*]*filespec* [*/p*]	Deletes a file, or a group of files (if wildcards are used), with an option to prompt for verification (/p)
DIR	Displays a directory listing of the current subdirectory on the current drive
DIR *directory*	Displays a directory listing for a specific subdirectory
DIR *drive:*	Displays a directory listing of the current directory on a specific drive
DIR *filespec*	Displays a directory listing for a specific group of files (if wildcards are used), or for a single file
EXIT	Closes the Command Prompt window
MD [*drive:*]*path* MKDIR [*drive:*]*path*	Creates a subdirectory
MOVE [*drive:*][*path*]*filespec destination*	Moves one or more files to another drive, directory, or drive and directory
MOVE *directory1 directory2*	Renames a directory
PATH	Displays the Windows path
PATH [*drive:*]*path1;*[*drive:*]*path2;...*	Changes the current Windows path to a new path that includes the paths of directories and subdirectories listed after the Path command
POPD	Changes to the directory stored by PUSHD
PROMPT PG	Displays the full path in the command prompt, followed by a greater-than symbol
PROMPT [*text*]	Customizes the appearance of the command prompt
PUSHD	Stores the current directory for use by POPD, and then changes to that directory
RD [*drive:*]*path* [*/s*] RMDIR [*drive:*]*path* [*/s*]	Removes an empty subdirectory from the directory structure of a disk; when used with the Subdirectory switch (/s), removes a subdirectory and all its contents
REN [*drive:*][*path*]*filename1 filename2* RENAME [*drive:*][*path*]*filename1 filename2*	Changes the name of a file, or if wildcards are used with a file specification, changes the name of a group of files
SET	Displays, sets, or removes environment variables and their settings
START *filespec*	Opens a file and its associated Windows application from a command prompt
START *program*	Opens a Windows application from a command prompt
TIME	Displays or sets the system time
TITLE [*string*]	Sets the window title for a Command Prompt window

Figure 14-4	INTERNAL COMMANDS (CONTINUED)
INTERNAL COMMAND	**USE**
TYPE [*drive:*][*path*]*filename*	Displays the contents of a text file
VER	Displays the Windows version
VERIFY [*ON*] or [*OFF*]	Displays the verify status, or instructs Cmd.exe whether or not to verify that files are correctly written to disk
VOL [*drive:*]	Displays the volume label for a drive

When you create an MS-DOS startup disk, Windows XP copies Command.com, another command interpreter, to this type of boot disk. When you boot your computer with that MS-DOS startup disk, Command.com loads into memory. That means that all the programs contained with Command.com are also loaded into memory and are available to you. You can then use most of the internal commands shown in Figure 14-4. Command.com is the command interpreter used by the DOS operating system.

In contrast to internal commands, external commands are ones that you use less frequently, or perhaps not at all. The program code for an **external command** resides in a specific file on disk. When you enter an external command in a Command Prompt window, you are in effect typing the first part of the filename—the part before the file extension—as the actual command. The operating system locates the file on disk, and then loads the program into memory so that it can perform its intended function. Windows XP looks for files that have the name you specify and that have a specific file extension, such as "com," "exe," or "bat". Because the program code must be located and loaded from disk, external commands are slower than internal commands. Figure 14-5 lists examples of some external commands and their usage. Some of the external commands are not available in Windows XP Home Edition. The external commands are stored in the System32 directory under the Windows directory.

It is important to know which commands are external commands, because you must have the program file to use the external command. If you are troubleshooting a problem in a command-line environment and do not have the program file for an external command (such as FDisk for partitioning the hard disk) because you forgot to copy the program file to your boot disk, you cannot use that program. Instead, you have to locate a copy of the program file before you can use it. When you create a boot disk such as a Windows XP MS-DOS startup disk, you should anticipate what you might need later and copy the program files for specific external commands to the boot disk.

Figure 14-5	EXTERNAL COMMANDS
EXTERNAL COMMAND	**USE**
ATTRIB [*drive:*][*path*][*filename*]	Displays file attributes
ATTRIB *filespec* ± [*attribute*]	Assigns or removes a file attribute
BOOTCFG	Configures, queries, or changes Boot.ini file settings (Windows XP Professional)
CHKDSK [*drive:*] [*/f*]	Examines the status of a disk, checks for errors, produces a report on disk space usage, and when used with /F, converts lost clusters to files
CHKDSK *filespec*	Displays information on whether files on a FAT or FAT32 volume are contiguous (not fragmented) or noncontiguous (fragmented)
CHKNTFS volume	Displays or modifies the checking of a disk during booting
CIPHER	Displays or changes the encryption of directories and files on an NTFS volume (Windows XP Professional)

Figure 14-5	EXTERNAL COMMANDS (CONTINUED)

EXTERNAL COMMAND	USE
CMD	Runs the Windows XP command interpreter, and opens a Command Prompt window
command /?	Displays Help information on a command you specify
COMP filename1 filename2	Compares the contents of two files
COMPACT [filename]	Displays or changes the compression of files on an NTFS volume
CONVERT volume	Converts a FAT volume to an NTFS volume
DEFRAG volume	Analyses a volume for fragmentation, or defragments a volume
DISKCOMP drive1: drive2:	Compares the contents of two floppy disks
DISKCOPY drive1: drive2:	Copies the contents of one diskette to another diskette using the same drive or different drives and produces an identical sector-by-sector copy of the original disk
DOSKEY	Edits and recalls commands entered at the command prompt
DRIVERQUERY	Displays a list of drivers by module name, display name, driver type, and link date, for a local or remote computer (Windows XP Professional)
EXPAND source.cab	Expands one or more compressed files from a cabinet file
FC filename1 filename2	Compares two files and displays information on differences in the contents of the files
FIND "string" filespec	Searches for a text string (set of characters) in a file or group of files
FINDSTR [strings] [filespec]	Searches for strings in files
FORMAT drive:	Formats a disk in a drive to the maximum capacity of that drive
FTYPE	Displays file types with defined open commands, or assigns a command to a file type
HELP [command]	Displays Help information on a command
IPCONFIG [/all]	Displays the IP address, subnet mask, and default gateway for each network adapter bound to TCP/IP, and displays full configuration information with the All switch (/all)
LABEL [drive:]	Displays, creates, changes, or removes a disk's volume label
LPR	Sends a print job to a network printer
MMC	Opens Microsoft Management Console from a Command Prompt window
MODE	Configures system devices, including serial and parallel ports, the video display, and keyboard; redirects output from a parallel port to a serial port
MORE	Produces paged output when used with another command and the pipe operator (	)
NTBACKUP	Opens the Backup or Restore Wizard, and the Backup Utility, from a Command Prompt window
OPENFILES	Lists or disconnects files and folders opened on a computer system (Windows XP Professional)
PENTNT	Indicates whether a computer exhibits the Pentium floating point division error
PRINT filespec	Prints a text file
RECOVER drive	Recovers data from defective sectors on a disk
REG	Command-line tool for working with the Registry
REPLACE source destination	Replaces (or updates) files, and adds new files
SCHTASKS	Displays a list of scheduled tasks on a computer, along with the next run time (Windows XP Professional)

Figure 14-5	EXTERNAL COMMANDS (CONTINUED)
EXTERNAL COMMAND	**USE**
SORT	Sorts output when used with another command and the pipe operator (I)
SUBST *drive:* /d	Removes a virtual drive
SUBST *drive:* [*drive:*]*path*	Assigns a drive name to a directory to create a virtual drive
SYSTEMINFO	Compiles information about the configuration of a computer system (Windows XP Professional only)
TASKKILL	Ends one or more processes using the Process ID (PID) or image name (Windows XP Professional)
TASKLIST	Lists the image name, PID (Process ID), session name, session number, and memory usage for open processes and applications on a local or remote computer (Windows XP Professional)
TREE *[drive:][path]*	Graphically displays the directory structure of a drive or path
XCOPY *source destination* *[/s]*	Copies all the files in a directory, or a group of files, or a single file, to another disk and, when used with the Subdirectory switch (/s), also copies the subdirectory structure to that disk

To use internal and external commands, you must not only know what they are, but you also must know the syntax for entering the command. **Syntax** (pronounced "sin tax") refers to the proper format for entering a command, including how to spell the command (some are abbreviated, such as CHKDSK for "Check Disk"), how to use required parameters (such as specifying a drive when formatting a disk with the Format command), and optional parameters (such as a switch), as well as the spacing between the command, required parameters, and optional parameters. A **switch** is an optional parameter that you use with a command to change the way in which the command works. As you will learn from experience in this tutorial, the command-line interface is syntax sensitive. You must type the command exactly as specified or shown, or the command interpreter displays an error message. Even the use of spaces (by pressing the spacebar) count when entering commands, and if you forget a required space, the command interpreter displays an error message.

Many of the internal and external commands shown in Figure 14-4 and Figure 14-5 can be used in different ways. If you need to locate Help information about the use of a particular internal or external command, you can use the Help switch (/?) or the Help command. You examine both in the next two sections to extract Help information from the program code for a command.

Because the process for working in a command-line environment is different from that used when working in a graphical user interface, and because this process relies on the precise use and entry of commands, with the correct syntax and spacing, the following conventions are used for this tutorial only:

- Commands are displayed in lowercase and in boldface. You can use uppercase, lowercase, or mixed case when entering commands.

- Punctuation, such as a comma, is not used after commands (even though it might be grammatically correct), because you might conclude that the punctuation is part of the command, and enter it with the command. That in turn would result in an error.

- If a command contains multiple parts, each part is separated from the part that preceded it and the part that follows it by two spaces, so that you know that you should use a space and so that you do not inadvertently run two parts of a command together. That in turn would result in an error.

- Commands that include the number 0 or 1 are identified as such (namely, zero, or the number one), so that you do not interpret the 0 or 1 as the uppercase letter "O" or the lowercase letter "L" (which look similar).

■ Commands listed in Reference Windows, which are designed to summarize operations you just completed, are displayed in all uppercase. If the command consists of multiple parts, each part is separated by two spaces. In the tutorial steps, commands are shown in boldface, which helps you spot and distinguish the command from the surrounding text; however, this is not the case in the Reference Windows, so uppercase serves the same purpose.

■ Switches are displayed in uppercase in explanatory text, so that they are consistent with how they are presented when viewing Help on a command. When entering the actual command with the switch, you can use lowercase.

Although you might have some flexibility in entering commands in some cases, such as whether you include a space between a command and a switch (an optional parameter illustrated in more detail later), it is good practice to be consistent in the way you work to reduce the chances of accidentally entering a command in a format that the command interpreter cannot interpret. This is particularly important when working in a command-line environment such as the Recovery Console.

Also, when entering commands from the keyboard, it's not uncommon to press the wrong key or keys and make mistakes. If you inadvertently mistype a command in the Command Prompt window, you might see the following type of message: '*Command*' is not recognized as an internal or external command, operable program or batch file.

Command is the actual command you typed. If this occurs, retype the command with the correct syntax and spacing. If you type the command itself correctly, but make a mistake with the use of an optional parameter, you more than likely will see the following type of message:

ERROR: Invalid syntax

Type "*command /*?" for usage.

Again, *command* is the actual command you typed. If this occurs, retype the command with the correct syntax and spacing, or use the Help information to find out how to properly enter the command. You examine the Help feature in the next section of the tutorial.

Specifying Console Colors

The default background color for the console is black, and the default foreground color is white. In other words, when working in a Command Prompt window, Windows XP displays white text against a black background. Prior to Windows and the use of color monitors, people used the DOS operating system with monochrome monitors. A **monochrome monitor** can only display one foreground color and one background color, and usually that means displaying white text on a black background. (Some monochrome monitors display amber or green text against a black background, or black text on a white background.) The term **console** refers to the keyboard and monitor, which are used for input and output. Although it is possible to use a mouse in a Command Prompt window, your primary input device is the keyboard.

In Windows XP and Windows 2000, you can use the Color command, an internal command, to change the background and foreground colors so that it is easier to work in a Command Prompt window.

Terri suggests that you use the Color command to customize the Command Prompt window to best suit your needs. So that she knows what options are available to her, Terri recommends that you use the Help switch (/?).

To view Help information on the use of the Color command:

1. Maximize the Command Prompt window. The Command Prompt window does not maximize in the same way as an application window such as Microsoft Word; however, the increased height of the Command Prompt window permits you to view more output from commands.

   TROUBLE? If a portion of the Command Prompt window appears behind the taskbar, and if you want to see the entire window and its borders, you can right-click the taskbar, click "Lock the taskbar" on the shortcut menu (to remove the check mark and turn off this feature), and then drag the taskbar and dock it on the right side of the screen.

2. Type **color /?** and then press the **Enter** key. Windows XP displays Help information on the use of the Color command. See Figure 14-6. After completing the command, the command interpreter redisplays the command prompt, so that you can enter another command.

Figure 14-6	VIEWING HELP INFORMATION ON THE COLOR COMMAND

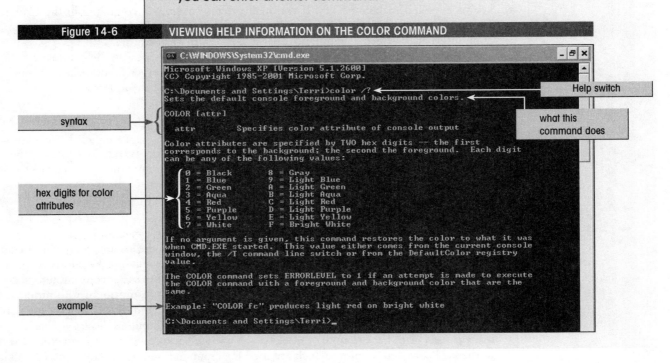

Right after the command you entered, Windows XP explains the purpose of the Color command. As noted, you can use this command to change the default console foreground and background colors. Then the Help information shows the syntax for the Color command: COLOR [attr].

That means that you type the command COLOR (using uppercase, lowercase, or mixed case) with or without the optional parameter "attr", which specifies the color attribute of the console output. If you use the optional parameter and specify a color attribute, you must include a space between the command and the optional parameter.

As shown in the Help explanation for the use of this command, you use two hex digits to specify the color attribute. A **hex digit** is a digit in the hexadecimal number system (0 through 9, and A through F). The first hex digit is the color attribute for the background color, and the second hex digit is the color attribute for the foreground color. Help also lists the hex digits and their corresponding color assignments.

If you use the Color command without the optional parameter (also called an **argument**), the command restores the default background and foreground colors that were used when you first opened the Command Prompt window. As noted, the default settings it uses can derive from three sources—the current console window, the use of the /T switch with the Cmd command, or from a setting stored in the Registry under the DefaultColor Registry value entry under the Command Processor key (described in more detail at the end of this section).

The Help information also includes an example. If you enter the command "COLOR fc" without the quotation marks, the Color command changes the foreground and background colors so that text is displayed in light red (the color attribute "c") against a bright white background (the color attribute "f"). The default console colors (white text on a black background) would be represented by the color attribute "07".

The Help switch works with almost every command. Because it's a switch, it modifies the way in which the command works.

REFERENCE WINDOW   **RW**

Using the Help Switch to Display Help for a Command

- Open the Start menu, click Run, type CMD in the Open box, and then press the Enter key. Or open the Start menu, point to All Programs, point to Accessories, and then click Command Prompt.
- Type the command for which you want to view Help, press the spacebar, type /? (the Help switch), and then press the Enter key.

Terri recommends that you first try black text against a bright white background, and then try bright white text against a light blue background.

To change the console colors:

1. Type **color f0** (the letter "f" followed by a zero), and then press the **Enter** key. The Color command applies the new color attribute. See Figure 14-7. If you are working in a Command Prompt window, and if that image is projected onto a screen by an overhead display panel, this color attribute makes it easier for everyone in the audience to see what you are doing in the Command Prompt window.

Figure 14-7 | CONSOLE COLORS CHANGED

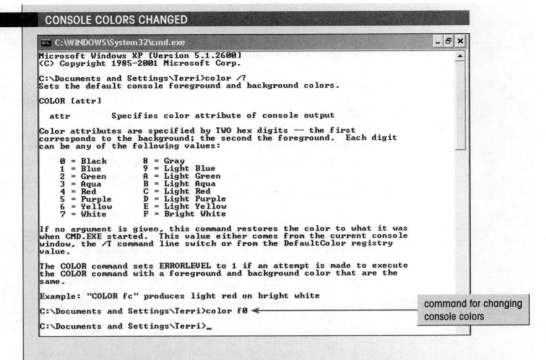

2. Type **color 9f** and then press the **Enter** key. The Color command changes the foreground color to bright white, and the background color to light blue. If you are working on your own computer in a Command Prompt window for an extended period of time, this combination of colors is easier on the eyes than the default colors.

You can change the console colors at any point. If you close the Command Prompt window, and then open it again, you find Windows XP has reverted to the default console colors. If you want to change the console colors permanently, you can open the Windows Registry and locate the Command Processor key using the following Registry path:

My Computer\HKEY_CURRENT_USER\Software\Microsoft\Command Processor

After you locate this key, locate and double-click the DefaultColor value entry, and in the Edit DWORD Value dialog box, verify that you are using the correct value name (DefaultColor), type the hex digits for the color attribute that you want to use (for example f0), and then press the Enter key (or click the OK button).

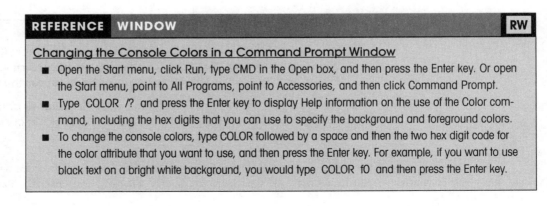

REFERENCE WINDOW | RW

Changing the Console Colors in a Command Prompt Window

- Open the Start menu, click Run, type CMD in the Open box, and then press the Enter key. Or open the Start menu, point to All Programs, point to Accessories, and then click Command Prompt.
- Type COLOR /? and press the Enter key to display Help information on the use of the Color command, including the hex digits that you can use to specify the background and foreground colors.
- To change the console colors, type COLOR followed by a space and then the two hex digit code for the color attribute that you want to use, and then press the Enter key. For example, if you want to use black text on a bright white background, you would type COLOR f0 and then press the Enter key.

When working in a Command Prompt window, you can recall previously entered commands by using the Up Arrow key, and you can use the F7 function key to display a command history. The **command history** is an area of memory which stores commands that you previously entered.

> ### To recall previously entered commands, and to view a command history:
>
> 1. Press ↑ once. Windows XP recalls the previously used command: color 9f
>
>   POWER USERS TIP You can use the F3 key to recall the last command.
>
> 2. Press ↑ again. Windows XP recalls the command used before the "color 9f" command, namely: color f0
>
> 3. Press the **Enter** key. The Color command changes the console colors.
>
> 4. Press the **F7** function key. Windows XP displays a command history. See Figure 14-8.

Figure 14-8	VIEWING THE COMMAND HISTORY

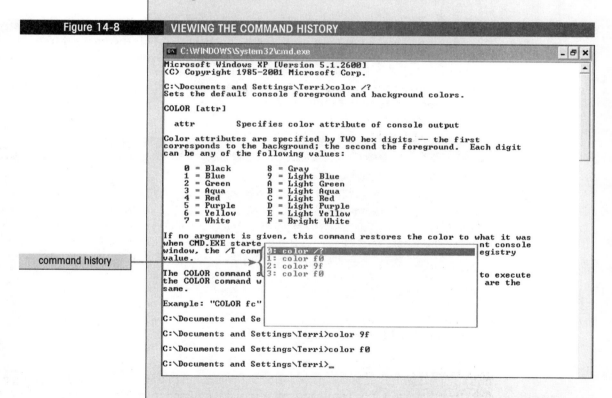

> 5. Press ↓ to select the **color 9f** command, and then press the **Enter** key. Windows XP uses the previously entered command that you selected from the command history, and the Color command changes the console colors.
>
> 6. Press the **F7** function key, press ↓ to select the **color f0** command, and then press the **Enter** key. The Color command changes the console colors again.

As you have just seen, when you work in a Command Prompt window, you have access to editing features that simplify the use of selecting and entering commands. After you enter or recall a command, you can also edit the command. If you make a mistake, or if you want to change the parameters of a command, and if you have not pressed the Enter key, you can use ← and → to move one character to the left or right on the command line. If you then type a character, it's automatically inserted, because insert mode is the default mode when editing a command line. If you want to type over one or more characters, you first press the Insert key to switch to overtype mode, and then start typing. The Insert key is a toggle key, so you can press the Insert key again to switch back to insert mode. A **toggle key** alternates between two related uses each time you press the key. You can use the Delete key to delete part of a command, one character at a time. You can also press the Home key to move the cursor to the beginning of a command line, and the End key to move the cursor to the end of the command line. If you recall a command and then decide you do not want to use it, you can press the Esc key to clear the command line.

Windows XP displays the last ten commands in the command history. You can use ↑ and ↓ to scroll through the commands—even going back past the last ten that are displayed. You can also use Alt+F7 to clear the command history, and the Esc key to close the command history. Another advantage of using the command history is that you can recall long or complicated commands, and then edit them without having to retype the entire command. When you close the Command Prompt window, all of the commands stored in the command history are erased.

Under DOS, you had to use the DOSKEY command, an external command, if you wanted to recall and edit previously entered commands and use a command history; however, under Windows XP, these features are available as soon as you open a Command Prompt window. The DOSKEY utility is also available under Windows XP so that you have access to more advanced features, such as the ability to set the size of the buffer (or area of memory) used for the command history.

REFERENCE WINDOW   **RW**

Recalling Commands from the Command History

- To recall the previously entered command in a Command Prompt window, press the Up Arrow key or press the F3 key.
- To step back through the command history one command at a time, press the Up Arrow key repeatedly.
- To display the command history, press the F7 function key, use the Up Arrow key or Down Arrow key to select the command you want to use, and then press the Enter key.

Formatting a Floppy Disk

You can use the Format command, an external command, to format a disk in a command-line environment. Before you use the Format command or any other command, you can use the Clear Screen (CLS) command, an internal command, to clear the Command Prompt window of the output of any previous command. Before each step in each section of the tutorial, you are asked to use this command so that you can clear the Command Prompt window and focus on the output of the next command. This also makes it easier for you to compare your output with that shown in the figures.

So that you can compare the use of a command with a comparable operation you might perform in the Windows XP graphical user interface, Terri suggests that you use the Format command to prepare a floppy disk for use with the operating system. She also recommends you use the Help command first to display information on how to use the Format command.

In the next set of steps, you need an empty, high-density floppy disk for drive A. If you have a floppy disk that contains files you no longer need, you can use that disk instead.

To view Help information on how to format a disk:

1. Type **cls** and then press the **Enter** key. The Clear Screen command (CLS) clears the window (or screen if operating in full-screen view) of any output, and displays the command prompt in the upper-left corner of the window or screen. Although you do not need to enter this command before you enter another command, this command does allow you to focus on the current command and its output without also viewing output of the previous command.

2. Insert a floppy disk into drive A.

3. Type **help format** and then press the **Enter** key. The Help command displays Help information on the Format command. See Figure 14-9.

| Figure 14-9 | VIEWING HELP ON THE FORMAT COMMAND |

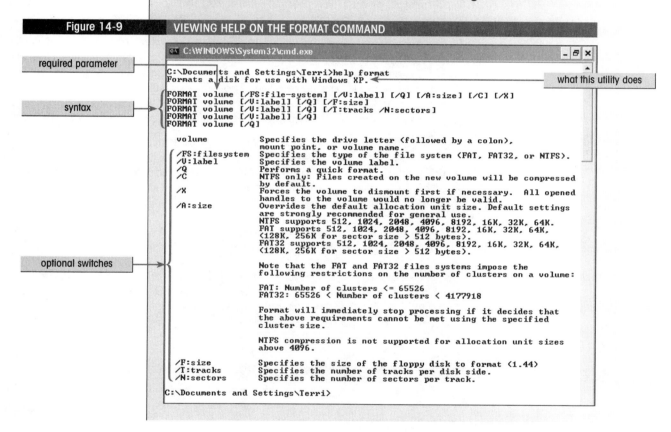

The Help information explains that the Format utility formats a disk for use with Windows XP. Then the Help information displays five different ways for entering this command. No matter which approach you use, you type the command FORMAT followed by a space and then the name of the volume (or drive) you want to format. The command and volume name (or drive name) are required; that's why they are not shown within square brackets. The space is required to distinguish the command from the volume name. The volume name is an example of a required parameter. You can no longer use the Format command without the volume name (as you could under the first versions of DOS).

Next, you choose which, if any, optional switches you want to use. Below the syntax for the command, the Help information explains each of the switches. The /FS switch allows you to specify the type of file system (FAT, FAT32, or NTFS) you want to use for the disk you format. As you learned in Tutorial 3, you can only format floppy disks with the FAT file system. To format a hard disk, where you might want to specify the file system, you must have Administrator privileges. With the Volume switch (/V), you can specify a **volume label**, or electronic label, for the disk to identify the purpose of the disk or its ownership. You can use the Quick switch (/Q) to perform a quick format of an already formatted diskette. The DOS operating system and other versions of Windows have a System switch (/S) for copying the core operating system files to a floppy disk so that you could create a generic boot disk. That option is not available in Windows XP.

To clear the screen, and then format the floppy disk:

1. Type **cls** and then press the **Enter** key to clear the screen.

2. Type **format a:** and then press the **Enter** key. The Format utility prompts you to insert a new disk into drive A.

3. Press the **Enter** key. Next, the utility identifies the file system as FAT (the default for floppy disks), indicates that it is verifying the 1.44 MB format capacity of the disk, shows the percentage complete, initializes the File Allocation Table (FAT), and then prompts you for a volume label. See Figure 14-10. Although the volume name is limited to 11 characters, you can use a space, but not a period. If you press the Enter key, the Format utility does not assign a volume label to the disk.

   If you are working in a computer lab, it's a good idea to enter your last name as a volume label, because individuals frequently leave their floppy disks in the disk drives. Disks from the same class have the same set of files; however, if you've added a volume label to your disk, you can identify the disk by examining its properties or by using the VOL command.

   TROUBLE? If Windows XP displays a message informing you that the Format utility cannot run because the volume is in use by another process and asks if you want to dismount the volume first, type N for No, press the Enter key, close any applications that are accessing files on drive A, switch from drive A to drive C (or the drive where Windows is installed) if necessary, close any other windows onto drive A, and then repeat this step. If you still cannot format a disk, read the remainder of this section and examine the figures, but do not keystroke the steps.

Figure 14-10	FORMATTING A FLOPPY DISK

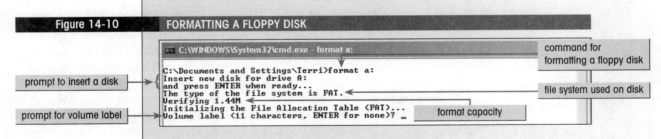

4. Type your **last name** (or an abbreviated version of your last name if your last name is more than 11 characters), and then press the **Enter** key. After reporting that the format is complete, the Format utility reports the total amount of space on the disk, and the amount available for you to use. See Figure 14-11. If the total disk space (in bytes) matches the total bytes available on the disk, there are no defective sectors on the disk. Finally, it asks if you want to format another disk.

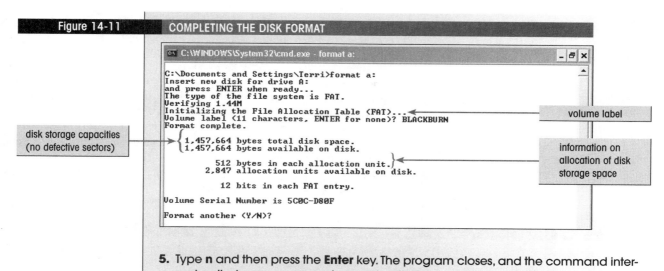

Figure 14-11 COMPLETING THE DISK FORMAT

disk storage capacities (no defective sectors)

volume label

information on allocation of disk storage space

5. Type **n** and then press the **Enter** key. The program closes, and the command interpreter displays a command prompt so that you can enter another command.

The output of the Format utility also displays the size of each allocation unit or cluster (note that one cluster contains one sector), and the total number of allocation units or clusters. As discussed in Tutorial 3, the size of an allocation unit or cluster depends on the type of disk, the storage capacity of the disk, and the file system on the disk (FAT12, FAT16, FAT32, or NTFS) and that, in turn, affects how efficiently the operating system allocates and uses storage space on the disk. The Format utility also reports the number of bits used for each FAT entry—for a floppy disk, it uses 12 bits (hence, FAT12), or one-and-a-half bytes. Then the Format utility assigns a unique serial number to the disk using the system date and time.

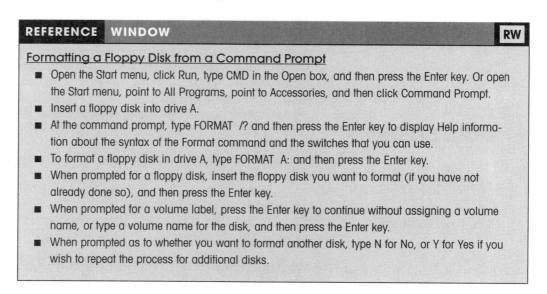

REFERENCE WINDOW **RW**

Formatting a Floppy Disk from a Command Prompt
- Open the Start menu, click Run, type CMD in the Open box, and then press the Enter key. Or open the Start menu, point to All Programs, point to Accessories, and then click Command Prompt.
- Insert a floppy disk into drive A.
- At the command prompt, type FORMAT /? and then press the Enter key to display Help information about the syntax of the Format command and the switches that you can use.
- To format a floppy disk in drive A, type FORMAT A: and then press the Enter key.
- When prompted for a floppy disk, insert the floppy disk you want to format (if you have not already done so), and then press the Enter key.
- When prompted for a volume label, press the Enter key to continue without assigning a volume name, or type a volume name for the disk, and then press the Enter key.
- When prompted as to whether you want to format another disk, type N for No, or Y for Yes if you wish to repeat the process for additional disks.

You have successfully formatted a floppy disk by using a command in a command-line window. The operation is comparable to that which you performed in Tutorial 3 from the graphical user interface. If you press F8 during booting to display the Windows Advanced Options menu, and then choose the option for booting with Safe Mode with Command Prompt, you can format a floppy disk using the same techniques.

Displaying a Command Reference List

With each new version of Windows, Microsoft has increased the support for working in a command-line environment under Windows, including the availability of newer types of commands. If you open the Help and Support Center in Windows XP Professional, search using the phrase "command-line reference", and then click the "Command-line reference A-Z" link, Windows XP displays a glossary with links to each command that you can use in a command-line environment. See Figure 14-12. To locate the command-line reference in Windows XP Home Edition, search using the phrase "command-line", click the "Managing System Information from the command line" Help link, and then click the "Command-line reference A-Z" Help link. You can also display a comparable list of commands from the Command Prompt window by using the Help command.

Figure 14-12	WINDOWS XP PROFESSIONAL COMMAND-LINE REFERENCE

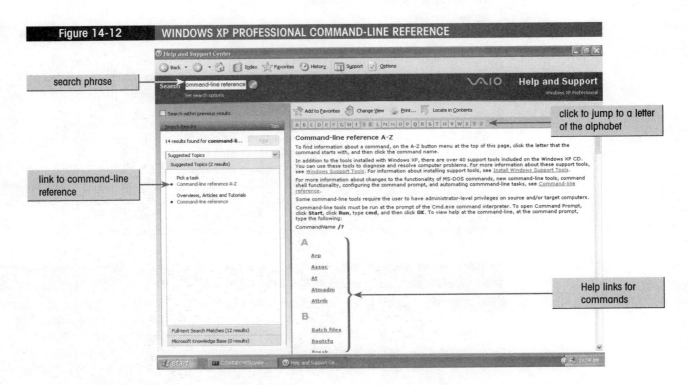

To view the commands for which Help is available, Terri suggests you use the Help command by itself.

> **To display a command reference list:**
>
> 1. Type **cls** and press the **Enter** key to clear the screen.
>
> 2. Type **help** and then press the **Enter** key. The Help command lists commands in alphabetical order, and provides a brief description of the use of each command. See Figure 14-13. However, because the window is not large enough to display all the commands, the initially displayed commands scrolled off screen.

Figure 14-13   USING THE HELP COMMAND TO DISPLAY A LIST OF COMMANDS

```
C:\WINDOWS\System32\cmd.exe                                              _  □  ×
DEL        Deletes one or more files.
DIR        Displays a list of files and subdirectories in a directory.
DISKCOMP   Compares the contents of two floppy disks.
DISKCOPY   Copies the contents of one floppy disk to another.
DOSKEY     Edits command lines, recalls Windows commands, and creates macros.
ECHO       Displays messages, or turns command echoing on or off.
ENDLOCAL   Ends localization of environment changes in a batch file.
ERASE      Deletes one or more files.
EXIT       Quits the CMD.EXE program (command interpreter).
FC         Compares two files or sets of files, and displays the differences
           between them.
FIND       Searches for a text string in a file or files.
FINDSTR    Searches for strings in files.
FOR        Runs a specified command for each file in a set of files.
FORMAT     Formats a disk for use with Windows.
FTYPE      Displays or modifies file types used in file extension associations.
GOTO       Directs the Windows command interpreter to a labeled line in a
           batch program.
GRAFTABL   Enables Windows to display an extended character set in graphics
           mode.
HELP       Provides Help information for Windows commands.
IF         Performs conditional processing in batch programs.
LABEL      Creates, changes, or deletes the volume label of a disk.
MD         Creates a directory.
MKDIR      Creates a directory.
MODE       Configures a system device.
MORE       Displays output one screen at a time.
MOVE       Moves one or more files from one directory to another directory.
PATH       Displays or sets a search path for executable files.
PAUSE      Suspends processing of a batch file and displays a message.
POPD       Restores the previous value of the current directory saved by PUSHD.
PRINT      Prints a text file.
PROMPT     Changes the Windows command prompt.
PUSHD      Saves the current directory then changes it.
RD         Removes a directory.
RECOVER    Recovers readable information from a bad or defective disk.
REM        Records comments (remarks) in batch files or CONFIG.SYS.
REN        Renames a file or files.
RENAME     Renames a file or files.
REPLACE    Replaces files.
RMDIR      Removes a directory.
SET        Displays, sets, or removes Windows environment variables.
SETLOCAL   Begins localization of environment changes in a batch file.
SHIFT      Shifts the position of replaceable parameters in batch files.
SORT       Sorts input.
START      Starts a separate window to run a specified program or command.
SUBST      Associates a path with a drive letter.
TIME       Displays or sets the system time.
TITLE      Sets the window title for a CMD.EXE session.
TREE       Graphically displays the directory structure of a drive or path.
TYPE       Displays the contents of a text file.
VER        Displays the Windows version.
VERIFY     Tells Windows whether to verify that your files are written
           correctly to a disk.
VOL        Displays a disk volume label and serial number.
XCOPY      Copies files and directory trees.
C:\Documents and Settings\Terri>_
```

3. Press ↑ to recall the help command you previously entered, press the **spacebar**, type **|** (a vertical bar found as the uppercase character on the key with the backslash character), press the **spacebar** again, type **more** and then press the **Enter** key (Your final command is: help | more.). In the Command Prompt window, you can now see the first page of commands, followed by a More prompt at the bottom of the window. See Figure 14-14.

TROUBLE? Although the vertical bar appears as a single vertical bar in a document, it appears as a vertical bar with two separate smaller bars in a Command Prompt window. The key on your keyboard might show a single vertical bar or two separate smaller bars.

Figure 14-14 | **OUTPUT PIPED TO THE MORE FILTER**

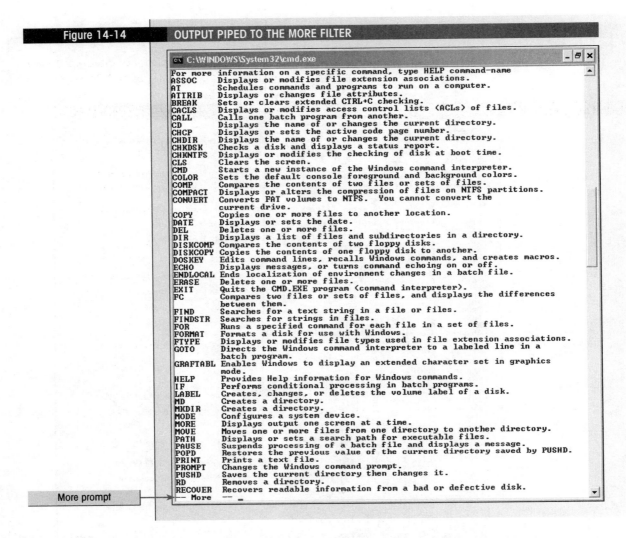

```
C:\WINDOWS\System32\cmd.exe                                          _ □ ×

For more information on a specific command, type HELP command-name
ASSOC     Displays or modifies file extension associations.
AT        Schedules commands and programs to run on a computer.
ATTRIB    Displays or changes file attributes.
BREAK     Sets or clears extended CTRL+C checking.
CACLS     Displays or modifies access control lists (ACLs) of files.
CALL      Calls one batch program from another.
CD        Displays the name of or changes the current directory.
CHCP      Displays or sets the active code page number.
CHDIR     Displays the name of or changes the current directory.
CHKDSK    Checks a disk and displays a status report.
CHKNTFS   Displays or modifies the checking of disk at boot time.
CLS       Clears the screen.
CMD       Starts a new instance of the Windows command interpreter.
COLOR     Sets the default console foreground and background colors.
COMP      Compares the contents of two files or sets of files.
COMPACT   Displays or alters the compression of files on NTFS partitions.
CONVERT   Converts FAT volumes to NTFS.  You cannot convert the
          current drive.
COPY      Copies one or more files to another location.
DATE      Displays or sets the date.
DEL       Deletes one or more files.
DIR       Displays a list of files and subdirectories in a directory.
DISKCOMP  Compares the contents of two floppy disks.
DISKCOPY  Copies the contents of one floppy disk to another.
DOSKEY    Edits command lines, recalls Windows commands, and creates macros.
ECHO      Displays messages, or turns command echoing on or off.
ENDLOCAL  Ends localization of environment changes in a batch file.
ERASE     Deletes one or more files.
EXIT      Quits the CMD.EXE program (command interpreter).
FC        Compares two files or sets of files, and displays the differences
          between them.
FIND      Searches for a text string in a file or files.
FINDSTR   Searches for strings in files.
FOR       Runs a specified command for each file in a set of files.
FORMAT    Formats a disk for use with Windows.
FTYPE     Displays or modifies file types used in file extension associations.
GOTO      Directs the Windows command interpreter to a labeled line in a
          batch program.
GRAFTABL  Enables Windows to display an extended character set in graphics
          mode.
HELP      Provides Help information for Windows commands.
IF        Performs conditional processing in batch programs.
LABEL     Creates, changes, or deletes the volume label of a disk.
MD        Creates a directory.
MKDIR     Creates a directory.
MODE      Configures a system device.
MORE      Displays output one screen at a time.
MOVE      Moves one or more files from one directory to another directory.
PATH      Displays or sets a search path for executable files.
PAUSE     Suspends processing of a batch file and displays a message.
POPD      Restores the previous value of the current directory saved by PUSHD.
PRINT     Prints a text file.
PROMPT    Changes the Windows command prompt.
PUSHD     Saves the current directory then changes it.
RD        Removes a directory.
RECOVER   Recovers readable information from a bad or defective disk.
-- More -- _
```

More prompt

This last command relies on some important concepts and techniques. The command was:

HELP | MORE

The vertical bar is called the **pipe operator**, and it combines the use of the Help command with the More filter to pipe the output of the Help command to the More filter. When you **pipe** output, you are using the output of one command as the input for another command. In this case, the Help command outputs a list of commands for which Help is available, along with a brief description of the use of each command. That output is then passed to the More filter. The More filter then produces **paged output**; in other words, it displays one window, or one screen (if you are working in full-screen view), of output at a time. After each page of output, the More filter displays the prompt "— More —" so that you know there is more output to view. The More utility is called a **filter** because it modifies the output of another command. The entire command is called a **pipeline**. These techniques enable you to modify the use of one command with another command, so that it is easier to work within a command-line environment. Some commands include a Pause or Page switch (/p) for producing paged output, so you do not need to use this technique with those commands (one of which you examine later).

To view the remainder of the output:

1. Press the **spacebar**. The More filter displays the remainder of the output, and then the command interpreter displays the command prompt. See Figure 14-15.

| Figure 14-15 | VIEWING THE NEXT PAGE OF OUTPUT |

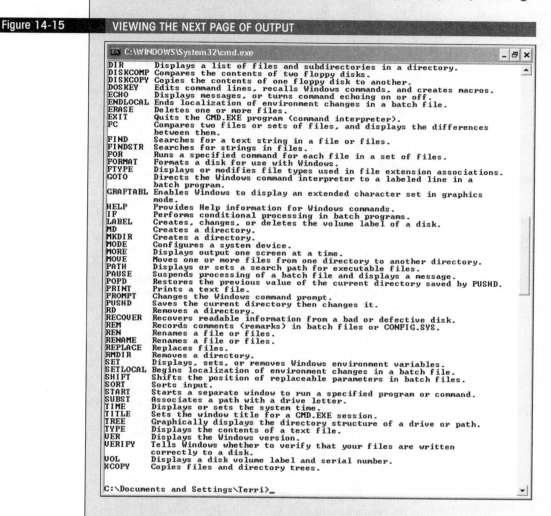

```
DIR        Displays a list of files and subdirectories in a directory.
DISKCOMP   Compares the contents of two floppy disks.
DISKCOPY   Copies the contents of one floppy disk to another.
DOSKEY     Edits command lines, recalls Windows commands, and creates macros.
ECHO       Displays messages, or turns command echoing on or off.
ENDLOCAL   Ends localization of environment changes in a batch file.
ERASE      Deletes one or more files.
EXIT       Quits the CMD.EXE program (command interpreter).
FC         Compares two files or sets of files, and displays the differences
           between them.
FIND       Searches for a text string in a file or files.
FINDSTR    Searches for strings in files.
FOR        Runs a specified command for each file in a set of files.
FORMAT     Formats a disk for use with Windows.
FTYPE      Displays or modifies file types used in file extension associations.
GOTO       Directs the Windows command interpreter to a labeled line in a
           batch program.
GRAFTABL   Enables Windows to display an extended character set in graphics
           mode.
HELP       Provides Help information for Windows commands.
IF         Performs conditional processing in batch programs.
LABEL      Creates, changes, or deletes the volume label of a disk.
MD         Creates a directory.
MKDIR      Creates a directory.
MODE       Configures a system device.
MORE       Displays output one screen at a time.
MOVE       Moves one or more files from one directory to another directory.
PATH       Displays or sets a search path for executable files.
PAUSE      Suspends processing of a batch file and displays a message.
POPD       Restores the previous value of the current directory saved by PUSHD.
PRINT      Prints a text file.
PROMPT     Changes the Windows command prompt.
PUSHD      Saves the current directory then changes it.
RD         Removes a directory.
RECOVER    Recovers readable information from a bad or defective disk.
REM        Records comments (remarks) in batch files or CONFIG.SYS.
REN        Renames a file or files.
RENAME     Renames a file or files.
REPLACE    Replaces files.
RMDIR      Removes a directory.
SET        Displays, sets, or removes Windows environment variables.
SETLOCAL   Begins localization of environment changes in a batch file.
SHIFT      Shifts the position of replaceable parameters in batch files.
SORT       Sorts input.
START      Starts a separate window to run a specified program or command.
SUBST      Associates a path with a drive letter.
TIME       Displays or sets the system time.
TITLE      Sets the window title for a CMD.EXE session.
TREE       Graphically displays the directory structure of a drive or path.
TYPE       Displays the contents of a text file.
VER        Displays the Windows version.
VERIFY     Tells Windows whether to verify that your files are written
           correctly to a disk.
VOL        Displays a disk volume label and serial number.
XCOPY      Copies files and directory trees.

C:\Documents and Settings\Terri>_
```

2. Leave the Command Prompt window open for the next section of the tutorial.

By default the command interpreter displays command output on the monitor. If you have a local printer connected to a local port (such as LPT1, a parallel port), you can redirect output of a command to the printer using the **output redirection operator (>)**. For example, if you want to print information about the subdirectories and files within a directory to document a directory's contents or help you troubleshoot a problem, you can redirect the output of the Directory (DIR) command, which you examine later, to your printer as follows:

DIR > LPT1

When you use this command, no output appears on the monitor. Instead, the printer prints that output. As you saw in Tutorial 9 on troubleshooting printer problems, this technique is a time-honored method for testing a printer connection.

<u>Displaying a Command Reference List from the Command Prompt</u>

- Open the Start menu, click Run, type CMD in the Open box, and then press the Enter key. Or open the Start menu, point to All Programs, point to Accessories, and then click Command Prompt.
- To display a list of commands for which Help is available, type HELP | MORE and press the Enter key. After you examine the first page of output, press the spacebar to view each of the next pages until the command interpreter displays a command prompt.
- If you want to view Help information on a specific command, type the command, press the spacebar, type /? and then press the Enter key. Or type HELP followed by a space, type the command for which you want help, and then press the Enter key. For example, if you want Help on the Format command, type FORMAT /? and then press the Enter key, or type HELP FORMAT and then press the Enter key.

Although you cannot use the Help utility with commands other than those shown in the command reference list that it produces, you can use the Help switch (/?) with almost all commands.

Unfortunately, this command reference list does not include all the commands available within the Windows XP command-line environment, but only the commands previously used with DOS. The Help and Support Center, on the other hand, covers the use of all available commands. If you are troubleshooting a problem with a command-line environment, you do not have access to the Help and Support Center, so you need to use the Help command and Help switch (/?) if you need information on the use of a command.

Using the SystemInfo Command

SystemInfo, an external command, is a new Windows XP Professional command-line tool that displays configuration information about your computer and the operating system. You can use it to examine information about your computer or a remote computer. You can also use the command with another user's account permissions and password. This program is not available in Windows XP Home Edition.

So that you are familiar with how to check employees' computers for information about the configuration of their systems and operating systems, Terri suggests that you use the SystemInfo command to check her computer system and then pipe the output of the command to the More filter.

If you are using Windows XP Home Edition, you cannot complete the following tutorial steps. Instead, read the steps and examine the figures so that you are familiar with this utility, but do not keystroke the steps.

To view system information about a computer:

1. Clear the screen.

2. Type **systeminfo | more** and then press the **Enter** key. The SystemInfo utility compiles information for your computer, and the More filter displays the first page of output. See Figure 14-16. The details of your output will differ.

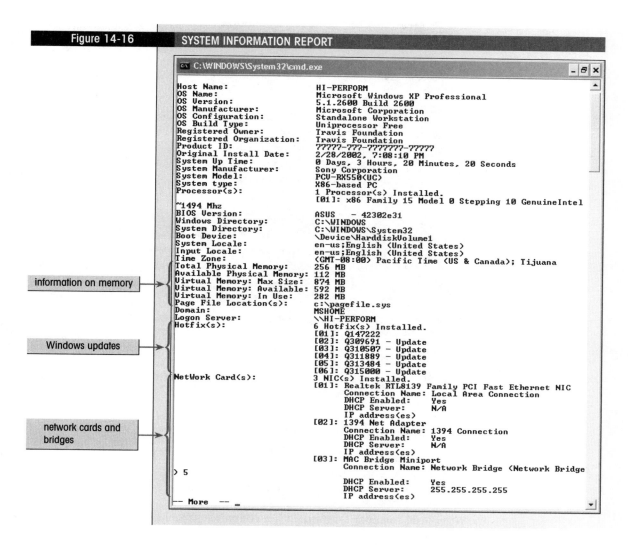

Figure 14-16   SYSTEM INFORMATION REPORT

The Host Name identifies the name of the computer. You can use this name to distinguish this computer from other computers on a network. Domain (further down the list) identifies the name of the workgroup or domain to which a networked computer belongs. The OS Name and OS Version identify the version of Windows XP used on a computer. Another piece of information that might prove helpful in analyzing a computer is the Original Install Date, especially if you are checking dates and times on system files while troubleshooting a problem. System Model identifies the specific model of your computer, and Processor(s) provides you with the exact operating speed of your computer.

The SystemInfo command identifies the paths for the Windows Directory, System Directory, and Boot Device. It provides information on memory usage, including the total RAM (Available Physical Memory), and details on virtual memory availability and usage. Hotfix(s) identifies how many updates, or hot fixes, have been applied to this computer, and more importantly, it identifies the Microsoft Knowledge Base Article Number that identifies each hot fix. If you have a question about an update, you can use Microsoft's Knowledge Base to locate the article by the Article ID number, and then examine information about the hot fix. The SystemInfo utility also provides information about network cards, and network bridges (if available).

To view the remainder of the output:

1. Press the **spacebar**. The More filter displays the remainder of the output.

2. Leave the Command Prompt window open for the next section of the tutorial.

Instead of using the More filter with this command, you could also have adjusted your view by using the mouse and the vertical bar in the Command Prompt window. However, the mouse may not always be available, or if you are skilled in the use of a command-line environment, you may prefer to use the keyboard.

REFERENCE WINDOW   **RW**

Displaying System Information from a Command Prompt (Windows XP Professional)

- Open the Start menu, click Run, type CMD in the Open box, and then press the Enter key. Or open the Start menu, point to All Programs, point to Accessories, and then click Command Prompt.
- Type SYSTEMINFO | HELP and then press the Enter key.
- After examining the first page of output, press the spacebar to view each of the next pages.

If you want to examine other ways in which to use the SystemInfo utility, you can use the Command Line Reference in the Help and Support Center or the Help switch.

Using BootCfg to Query Boot.ini

BootCfg, an external command, is another new Windows XP Professional command-line tool that you can use to configure, query, or change settings in Boot.ini, the startup boot configuration file used by Windows XP. This program is not available in Windows XP Home Edition.

Terri asks you to check Boot.ini on her computer so you know how Windows XP boots her computer.

If you are using Windows XP Home Edition, you cannot complete the following tutorial steps. Instead, read the steps and examine the figures so that you are familiar with this utility, but do not keystroke the steps.

To view information about the Boot.ini file:

1. Clear the screen.

2. Type **bootcfg /query** and then press the **Enter** key. The BootCfg command displays information on Boot Loader Settings and Boot Entries in the Boot.ini startup configuration file. See Figure 14-17. The details of your output will differ.

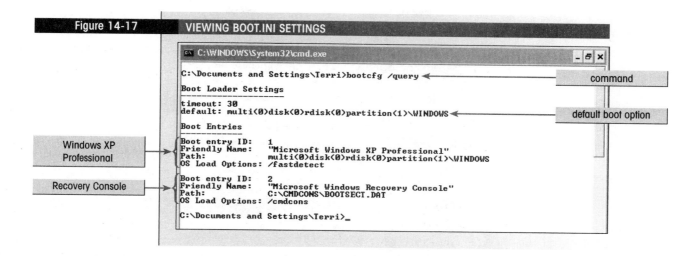

Figure 14-17 VIEWING BOOT.INI SETTINGS

Microsoft Windows XP Professional and Microsoft Windows Recovery Console are installed on the computer used for this figure, so both are listed under Boot Entries. Each has a unique Boot entry ID, and a friendly name that appears on the OS Choices menu during booting so that you can choose the one you want to use. The path identifies the location of the boot partition for Windows XP Professional (in this example), and the file with the boot sector data for loading the Recovery Console. The OS Load Options are switches used for loading the operating system or the Recovery Console.

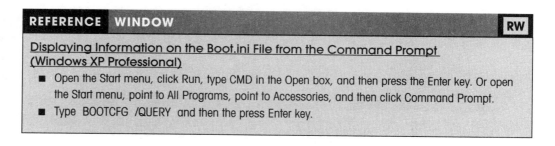

REFERENCE WINDOW RW

Displaying Information on the Boot.ini File from the Command Prompt (Windows XP Professional)
- Open the Start menu, click Run, type CMD in the Open box, and then press the Enter key. Or open the Start menu, point to All Programs, point to Accessories, and then click Command Prompt.
- Type BOOTCFG /QUERY and then the press Enter key.

Although you can obtain the same information by opening the Boot.ini file with Notepad, Boot.ini is a hidden file.

Using the Type Command to View the Contents of Text Files

If you want to examine a configuration file that is also a text file, such as Boot.ini, or a Setup Information File with the "inf" file extension, you can use the Type command. A **Setup Information File** is a file that contains settings Windows XP uses to install support for a hardware device or for software.

Terri recommends that you compare the use of the Type command, an internal command that can be used with any text file, with the more specific BootCfg command.

To view the contents of the Boot.ini file:

1. Type **type boot.ini** and then press the **Enter** key. Windows XP displays an error message, indicating that it cannot find the file. See Figure 14-18. This problem occurred because the Type command assumed that the file was located in the current directory. The current directory is the one that you are currently using; in this case, the directory for your user account. The Boot.ini is not in this directory. Instead, it's in the root directory, and to locate Boot.ini, you have to specify the path to the file in your command.

Figure 14-18	USING THE TYPE COMMAND

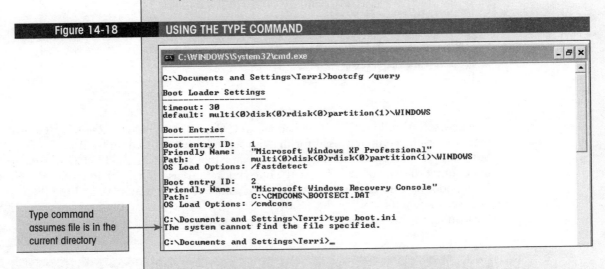

Type command assumes file is in the current directory

2. Press the **F3** function key. As shown in Figure 14-19, pressing the F3 function key recalls the last command you entered. You could also have recalled this command by pressing ↑ once.

Figure 14-19	RECALLING A COMMAND

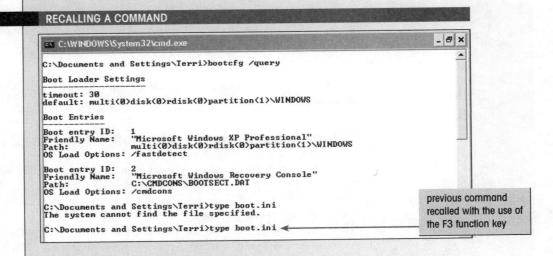

previous command recalled with the use of the F3 function key

3. Press ← until the cursor is positioned on the "b" in "boot.ini," as shown in Figure 14-20.

Figure 14-20   POSITIONING THE CURSOR ON A COMMAND LINE

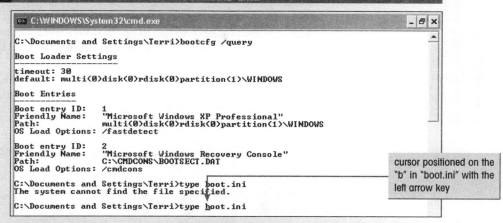

cursor positioned on the "b" in "boot.ini" with the left arrow key

4. Type **** (a backslash) for the root directory of the drive, and then press the **Enter** key. The command interpreter executes the revised command, and the Type command displays the contents of the Boot.ini file. See Figure 14-21. If you compare the contents of Boot.ini with the BootCfg command you used earlier, you can see that the BootCfg compiled the information in the Boot.ini file in a format that is easier to use.

TROUBLE? If the command interpreter still reports that the system cannot find the specified file, and if you are using a dual-boot or multiple-boot computer, you must edit the command to include the name of drive C and then try this step again. Your revised command should be: type c:\boot.ini

Figure 14-21   VIEWING THE CONTENTS OF BOOT.INI

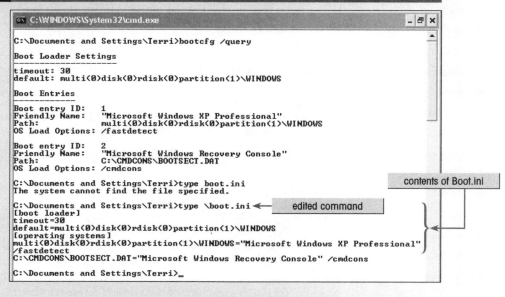

contents of Boot.ini

edited command

5. Leave the Command Prompt window open for the next section of the tutorial.

You just recalled and edited a command so that you did not have to retype it again with the correct syntax.

These steps also illustrate the importance of the path to Windows XP. In a command-line environment, you have to use the path if you need to identify a directory or file located in another directory. If you need to reference a directory or file on another drive, you must precede the path with the drive name.

If you want to view the contents of a text file, such as Win.ini or System.ini, that produces more than one page of output, you can redirect the output to the More filter with the pipe operator using the following syntax:

TYPE [drive:][path]filename | MORE

In this syntax, *drive:* and *path* are optional parameters, and *filename* is a required parameter.

REFERENCE WINDOW | **RW**

Using the Type Command to View the Contents of a Text File
- Open the Start menu, click Run, type CMD in the Open box, and then press the Enter key. Or open the Start menu, point to All Programs, point to Accessories, and then click Command Prompt.
- If the text file is in the current directory, type TYPE, press the spacebar, type the full filename (with the file extension), and press the Enter key.
- If the text file is located in another directory or on another drive, type TYPE, press the spacebar, type the full path and the full filename (with the file extension), and then press the Enter key.

In the next section of the tutorial, you work with directories and files. You view the directory structure of drive C, display different types of directory listings, change drives, change directories, and create a new directory. You then view file attributes and copy files to a floppy disk. You also use wildcards to streamline copy operations. Finally, you examine the Windows environment, the use of the Windows path, and step through the process for creating and using an environment variable.

Working **with Directories and Files**

To effectively work with directories and files in a command-line environment, you must understand the directory structure of your computer and how to specify the path. Like previous versions of Windows, Windows XP includes internal and external commands that provide you with the information you need.

Displaying a Directory Tree

When you work in the Windows XP graphical user interface, you can use My Computer or Windows Explorer to view the folders at any folder level within the hierarchy of your computer system, and also to navigate from one folder level to another or one drive to another. If you want to view the directory structure in a command-line environment, you can use the Tree command, an external command. The Tree command (without any parameters) displays the directory structure of the current directory and its subdirectories.

To find out what directories are under the one for your logon account, Terri encourages you to use the Tree command on her computer.

To view a directory tree for the current directory:

1. Clear the screen.

2. Type **tree** and then press the **Enter** key. The Tree command produces a diagrammatic view of the directory structure under the current directory. See Figure 14-22. The details of your output will differ, and it might be more extensive than that shown in the figure.

Figure 14-22	DISPLAYING A DIRECTORY TREE

command

directory tree

current directory

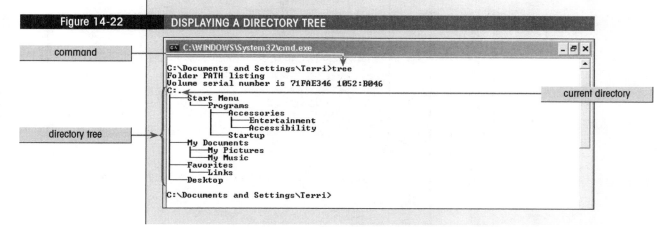

As shown in this figure, the Tree command identifies the output as a "Folder PATH listing." Under the serial number, the notation C:. (called "C colon dot") marks the top of the directory tree; the period (called a "dot") after C: is a special notation used to denote the current directory. So, you would interpret C:. as meaning the current drive on drive C. The Start Menu, My Documents, Favorites, and Desktop directories are located under the current directory. The My Pictures and My Music directories are located one step further down in the directory structure under the My Documents directory. If you want to store this directory tree in a file on disk, you would use the output redirection operator (>) to redirect the output to a file using the following syntax:

tree > [*drive:*][*path*]*filename*

You can also view a directory tree of your entire disk drive; however, because the tree might be extensive and exceed one page of output, you should pipe output to the More filter.

To view a directory tree of the current drive:

1. Clear the screen.

2. Type **tree \ | more** and press the **Enter** key. As shown in Figure 14-23, the Tree command shows a directory tree for drive C of the computer used for this figure. The details of your output will differ. The notation C:\ at the top of the directory tree indicates that the directory tree starts with the root directory (as represented by the backslash) of drive C. In your command, you used the backslash to represent the root directory and, since you did not specify the drive, the Tree command assumed you wanted to view the directory structure of the current drive.

If Windows XP is installed on another drive, your directory tree starts with the root directory of that drive.

| Figure 14-23 | DISPLAYING A DIRECTORY TREE OF DRIVE C |

current directory (the root directory) from which the directory tree starts

3. Press the **spacebar**. The More filter displays the next page of output produced by the Tree command. Because the directory structure of a disk drive is extensive, your output could comprise many pages.

4. Press and hold the **Ctrl** key while you press **C** on the keyboard, release **C**, and then release the **Ctrl** key. The command interpreter interrupts the output of the command, displays ^C after the output (for Ctrl+C), and then displays a command prompt. See Figure 14-24.

Figure 14-24 INTERRUPTING AND CANCELING A COMMAND

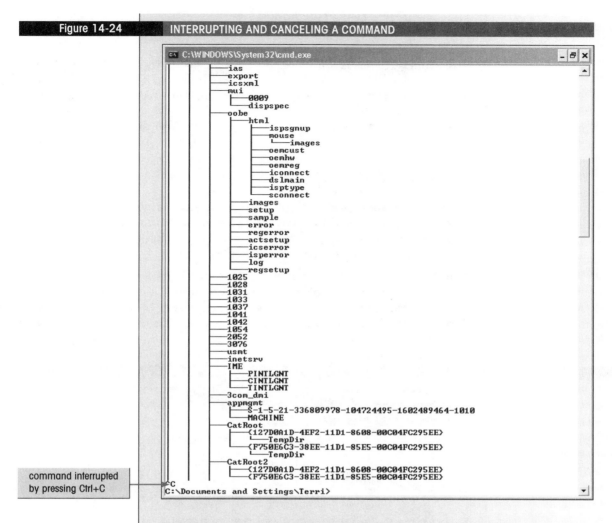

command interrupted by pressing Ctrl+C

5. Leave the Command Prompt window open for the next section of the tutorial.

Ctrl+C is called the interrupt command, or cancel command. You can also use Ctrl+Break to accomplish the same result.

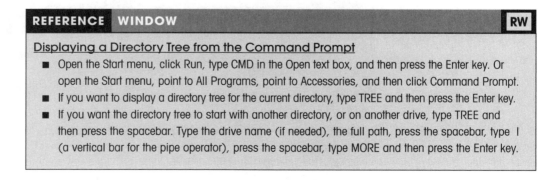

REFERENCE WINDOW RW

Displaying a Directory Tree from the Command Prompt
- Open the Start menu, click Run, type CMD in the Open text box, and then press the Enter key. Or open the Start menu, point to All Programs, point to Accessories, and then click Command Prompt.
- If you want to display a directory tree for the current directory, type TREE and then press the Enter key.
- If you want the directory tree to start with another directory, or on another drive, type TREE and then press the spacebar. Type the drive name (if needed), the full path, press the spacebar, type | (a vertical bar for the pipe operator), press the spacebar, type MORE and then press the Enter key.

Changing to the Root Directory

To navigate from directory to directory in a command-line environment, you use the Change Directory (CD) command, an internal command. When you use this command, you also include the path to the directory to which you want to switch. If you want to switch to the root directory of the current drive, you specify the path for that directory, which is represented by a backslash (\).

Terri suggests that you change to the root directory, so that you can then examine the contents of that directory.

To change to the root directory:

1. Clear the screen. From the path shown in the command prompt, you can tell that you are currently in the directory for your user account, and that you are on drive C (or if you are using a dual-boot or multiple-boot computer, you are on the drive where Windows is installed).

2. Type **cd ** (a backslash), and then press the **Enter** key. As shown by the path in the command prompt, you just changed from the directory for your user account to the root directory of drive C. See Figure 14-25. No matter where you are located in the directory structure of the disk, this command automatically switches you to the root directory.

Figure 14-25	CHANGING TO THE ROOT DIRECTORY

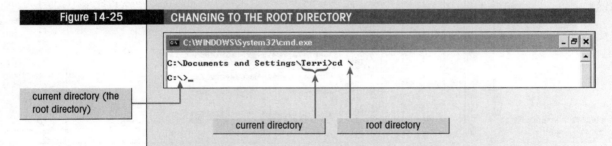

current directory (the root directory)

current directory   root directory

3. Leave the Command Prompt window open for the next section of the tutorial.

Later, you examine other ways in which to use the CD command to change directories.

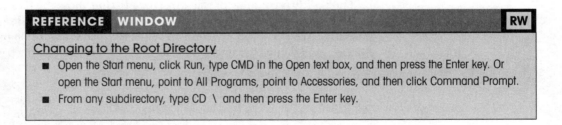

REFERENCE WINDOW   **RW**

Changing to the Root Directory
- Open the Start menu, click Run, type CMD in the Open text box, and then press the Enter key. Or open the Start menu, point to All Programs, point to Accessories, and then click Command Prompt.
- From any subdirectory, type CD \ and then press the Enter key.

Once you switch to another directory, you usually want to know what's stored in that directory.

Viewing the Contents of a Directory

You can use the Directory command (DIR), an internal command, to display a list of subdirectories and files within a directory, along with information about the contents of the directory. In fact, the Directory command is one of the most commonly used commands, and if used with switches, it is also a very versatile command.

Terri points out to you that you should become familiar with the contents of the root directory, and also with the different ways in which you can use the Directory command to view information about files on a disk.

To view the contents of the current directory:

1. Clear the screen.

2. At the command prompt, type **dir** and then press the **Enter** key. The Directory command displays the contents of the current directory—the root directory of the current drive (such as drive C). See Figure 14-26. After the directory listing, the Directory command reports that there are two files and seven directories in the root directory. The contents of your root directory will differ from that shown in this figure. Note that the Directory command does not display the contents of each subdirectory under the root directory.

| Figure 14-26 | DISPLAYING A DIRECTORY LISTING |

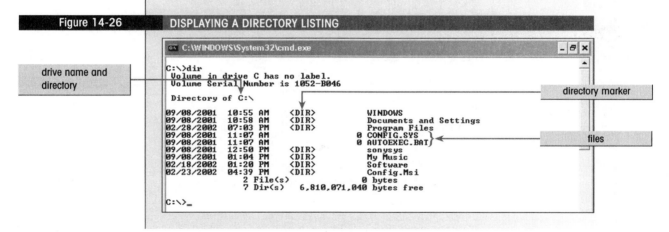

drive name and directory

directory marker

files

The first two columns of this **directory listing** show the date and time that each subdirectory or file was last modified, the third column identifies subdirectories with the use of the **directory marker** <DIR>, the fourth column displays file sizes in bytes (but not subdirectory sizes because they are so small), and the fifth column displays the name of the subdirectory or file. The Directory command also reports on the amount of space used by files, and the amount of available space on the drive. Note that the listing is not in alphabetical order; instead, the directory listing is in the default disk order—the order in which each directory or file was created on the disk. The two files, Config.sys and Autoexec.bat, are DOS startup configuration files. On this computer, these files are zero bytes in size, indicating that they are empty. Windows XP keeps these files for backward compatibility with older programs.

The Directory listing does not show hidden directories and hidden files. To view all subdirectories and files within a directory, you use the Attribute switch (/A) with the Directory command. So that the directory listing is easier to read, you can also use the Sort Order switch (/O), which lists subdirectories first in alphabetical order by directory name, and then files in alphabetical order by filename. Note that the "O" in the Sort Order switch (/O) is the uppercase letter "O", not the number 0 (zero).

To view all subdirectories and files within the root directory:

1. Clear the screen.

2. Type **dir /a /o** and then press the **Enter** key. The Directory command displays a directory listing in alphabetical order, first by subdirectory, then by files. See Figure 14-27. Now the Directory command reports that there are nine files (seven of which are hidden files) and 11 directories (four of which are hidden directories) in the root directory. The contents of your root directory will differ from that shown in this figure.

Figure 14-27	SORTED DIRECTORY LISTING OF ALL DIRECTORIES AND FILES

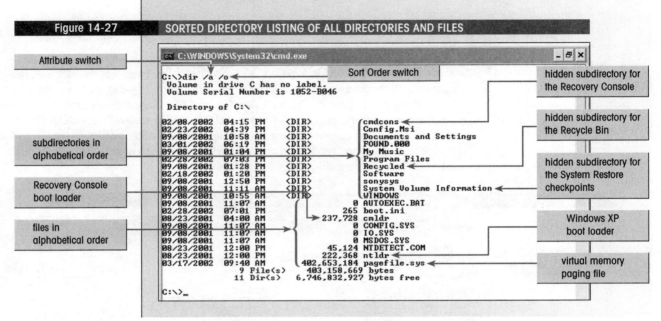

The Attribute switch (/A) instructs the Directory command to list all subdirectories and files, no matter what attributes are assigned to the subdirectories and files. If it makes it easier to remember, you can think of /A as meaning "all files." Also, the order in which you list switches in this command does not affect the output.

The hidden cmdcons subdirectory on the computer used for this figure contains the software for the Recovery Console, which you examined in Tutorial 9. The Documents and Settings subdirectory contains the directories for each user account, which in turn store information about each user's profile. The hidden FOUND.000 directory was created by the Check Disk utility, which you examined in Tutorial 7, and contains files with lost clusters. The Program Files subdirectory contains directories for operating system components (such as Internet Explorer), and directories for different software products installed on your computer. The hidden Recycled folder contains the deleted files stored in the Recycle Bin. The hidden System Volume Information subdirectory contains system restore checkpoints created by System Restore, which you examined in Tutorial 8. The Windows directory contains the bulk of the installed software for the operating system.

You examined the hidden startup configuration file Boot.ini in Tutorial 9 and also earlier in this tutorial. The hidden cmldr file is the boot loader for the Recovery Console. The hidden Io.sys and Msdos.sys files are DOS startup operating system files kept for backward compatibility with older programs. The hidden Ntdetect.com file is an operating system file that checks for installed hardware during booting. The hidden ntldr file is the boot loader for the Windows XP operating system. The hidden file pagefile.sys, which you examined in Tutorial 10, is the Windows XP paging file, or swap file, used for virtual memory.

Terri suggests that you examine the Windows folder next, and because the Windows folder contains many different directories and files, she also suggests that you use the Page or Pause switch (/P) to display one screen of output at a time. Because different computers might use different names for the Windows directory, she recommends you use the Directory command to check the name of the Windows directory on her computer.

To view a directory listing for the Windows folder:

1. Clear the screen.

2. Type **dir** and then press the **Enter** key. Check the directory listing for the name of your Windows directory. This directory might be named Windows or Winnt. You need to use this directory name in subsequent steps.

3. Type **dir windows /a /o /p** (replacing "windows" with the name of your Windows directory, if necessary) and then press the **Enter** key. Since you specified the path to the Windows directory, you are now viewing its contents. See Figure 14-28. You also specified the Page switch, so the Directory command produces paged output, and then displays the prompt "Press any key to continue…" The contents of your Windows directory will differ from that shown in this figure. Since this command has its own switch for producing paged output, you do not need to use the pipe operator and the More filter (though they work).

| Figure 14-28 | VIEWING THE CONTENTS OF THE WINDOWS SUBDIRECTORY |

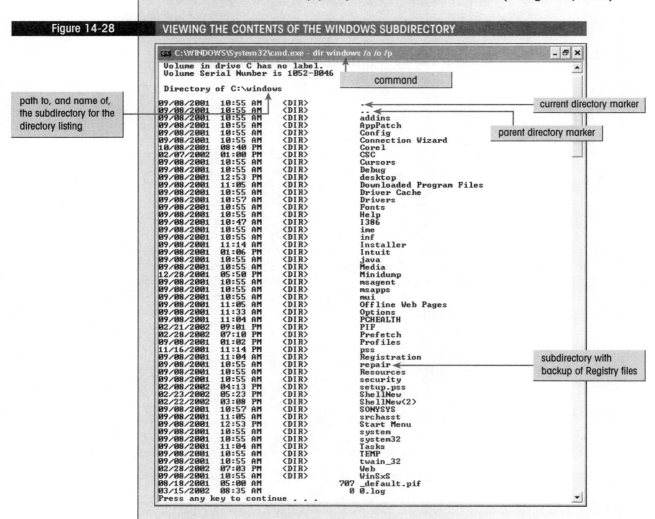

The single period (called "dot") in the column to the right of the first directory marker (<DIR>) refers to the current directory—the one for which you are viewing a directory listing (in this case, Windows). The two periods (called "dot dot") next to the right of the second directory marker refers to the parent directory of the current directory. The **parent directory** is the directory located one level above the current one. In this case, the parent directory of the Windows subdirectory is the root directory of drive C—in other words, C:\. Windows XP (and DOS) both use these directory markers to keep track of where they are in the directory structure of a disk and to navigate the directory structure. Every subdirectory has a "dot" and a "dot dot" entry.

To view the next page of the directory listing:

1. Press the **spacebar**. The next part of the directory listing for the computer used for this figure shows the names of files stored in the Windows folder, listed in alphabetical order. See Figure 14-29. The contents of your Windows directory will differ from that shown in this figure.

Figure 14-29 | VIEWING FILES IN THE WINDOWS SUBDIRECTORY

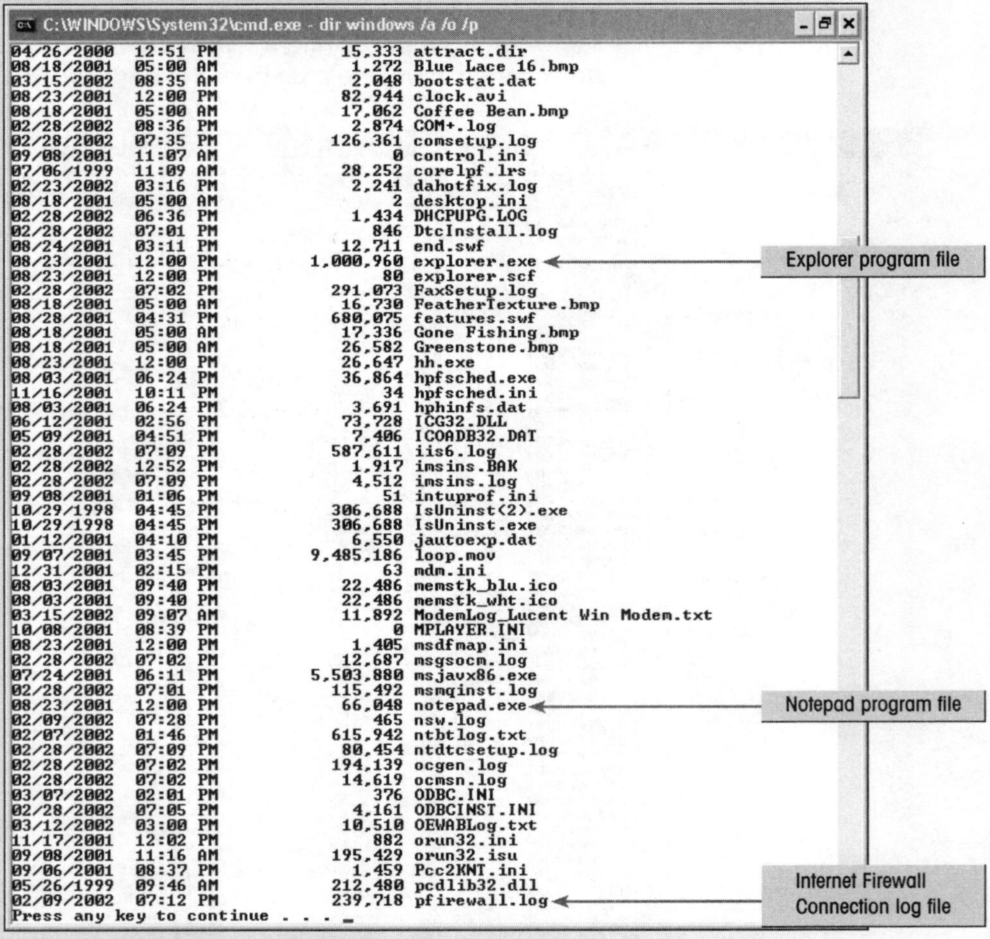

2. Keep pressing the **spacebar** to view the remainder of the output.

3. At the next command prompt, clear the screen.

4. Type **cd windows** (replacing "windows" with the name of your Windows directory, if necessary) and then press the **Enter** key. The Change Directory command switches to the Windows directory. See Figure 14-30. The command interpreter updates the command prompt to show the path to the current directory—now the Windows directory.

Figure 14-30	CHANGING TO THE WINDOWS SUBDIRECTORY

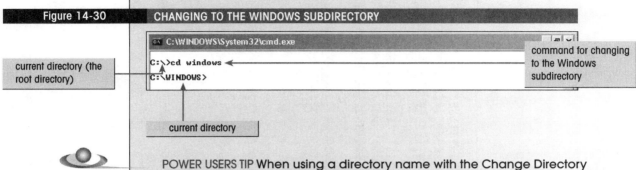

current directory (the root directory)

command for changing to the Windows subdirectory

current directory

POWER USERS TIP When using a directory name with the Change Directory command, you can type part of the directory name (enough to distinguish it from other directories whose names are similar). For example, if no other directory name starts with the letter "W", you can type CD W* and then press the Enter key to change to the Windows (or Winnt) directory. The asterisk is a wildcard (covered later) that you can use with directory names and filenames. If another directory name does start with "W" and the second character is a character other than "I", you could type CD WI* and then press the Enter key to change to the Windows (or Winnt) directory. This feature is particularly useful when working with very long directory names. For example, to change to the "Documents and Settings" directory from the root directory, you could type CD D* and then press the Enter key to change to this directory, instead of typing "CD Documents and Settings".

5. Type **dir /ad /o /p** and then press the **Enter** key. The Directory command displays only the subdirectories under the Windows directory. See Figure 14-31. By adding the "d" parameter for "directory" to the Attribute switch (/A), you changed the way in which it operates, and specified that the Directory command only show directories. You can use this technique to view and concentrate on subdirectories within a directory.

Figure 14-31   DISPLAYING AN ALPHABETICAL LIST OF SUBDIRECTORIES ONLY

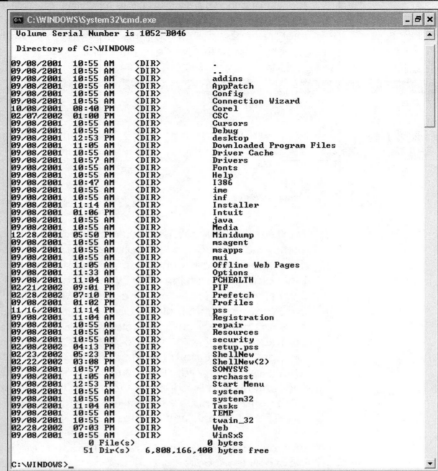

```
C:\WINDOWS\System32\cmd.exe                                    _ 8 x
Volume Serial Number is 1052-B046

Directory of C:\WINDOWS

09/08/2001  10:55 AM    <DIR>          .
09/08/2001  10:55 AM    <DIR>          ..
09/08/2001  10:55 AM    <DIR>          addins
09/08/2001  10:55 AM    <DIR>          AppPatch
09/08/2001  10:55 AM    <DIR>          Config
09/08/2001  10:55 AM    <DIR>          Connection Wizard
10/08/2001  08:40 PM    <DIR>          Corel
02/07/2002  01:00 PM    <DIR>          CSC
09/08/2001  10:55 AM    <DIR>          Cursors
09/08/2001  10:55 AM    <DIR>          Debug
09/08/2001  12:53 PM    <DIR>          desktop
09/08/2001  11:05 AM    <DIR>          Downloaded Program Files
09/08/2001  10:55 AM    <DIR>          Driver Cache
09/08/2001  10:57 AM    <DIR>          Drivers
09/08/2001  10:55 AM    <DIR>          Fonts
09/08/2001  10:55 AM    <DIR>          Help
09/08/2001  10:47 AM    <DIR>          I386
09/08/2001  10:55 AM    <DIR>          ime
09/08/2001  10:55 AM    <DIR>          inf
09/08/2001  11:14 AM    <DIR>          Installer
09/08/2001  01:06 PM    <DIR>          Intuit
09/08/2001  10:55 AM    <DIR>          java
09/08/2001  10:55 AM    <DIR>          Media
12/28/2001  05:50 PM    <DIR>          Minidump
09/08/2001  10:55 AM    <DIR>          msagent
09/08/2001  10:55 AM    <DIR>          msapps
09/08/2001  10:55 AM    <DIR>          mui
09/08/2001  11:05 AM    <DIR>          Offline Web Pages
09/08/2001  11:33 AM    <DIR>          Options
09/08/2001  11:04 AM    <DIR>          PCHEALTH
02/21/2002  09:01 PM    <DIR>          PIF
02/28/2002  07:10 PM    <DIR>          Prefetch
09/08/2001  01:02 PM    <DIR>          Profiles
11/16/2001  11:14 PM    <DIR>          pss
09/08/2001  11:04 AM    <DIR>          Registration
09/08/2001  10:55 AM    <DIR>          repair
09/08/2001  10:55 AM    <DIR>          Resources
09/08/2001  10:55 AM    <DIR>          security
02/08/2002  04:13 PM    <DIR>          setup.pss
02/23/2002  05:23 PM    <DIR>          ShellNew
02/22/2002  03:08 PM    <DIR>          ShellNew(2)
09/08/2001  10:57 AM    <DIR>          SONYSYS
09/08/2001  11:05 AM    <DIR>          srchasst
09/08/2001  12:53 PM    <DIR>          Start Menu
09/08/2001  10:55 AM    <DIR>          system
09/08/2001  10:55 AM    <DIR>          system32
09/08/2001  11:04 AM    <DIR>          Tasks
09/08/2001  10:55 AM    <DIR>          TEMP
09/08/2001  10:55 AM    <DIR>          twain_32
02/28/2002  07:03 PM    <DIR>          Web
09/08/2001  10:55 AM    <DIR>          WinSxS
               0 File(s)              0 bytes
              51 Dir(s)   6,808,166,400 bytes free

C:\WINDOWS>_
```

6. Type **dir /a-d /o /p** and then press the **Enter** key. The Directory command now displays only the files in the Windows directory. See Figure 14-32. By modifying the Attribute switch again, you changed the way in which it operates. If you place a minus sign before a parameter in a switch, you reverse its effect. /a-d instructs the Directory command to exclude directories. You can use this technique to view and concentrate on files within a directory.

POWER USERS TIP Because this command is a variation of the previous command, you could have used ↑ or the F3 key to recall the previous command, and then edited it by positioning the cursor on the "d" in "/ad", typing a minus sign, and then pressing the Enter key.

| Figure 14-32 | DISPLAYING AN ALPHABETICAL LIST OF FILES ONLY |

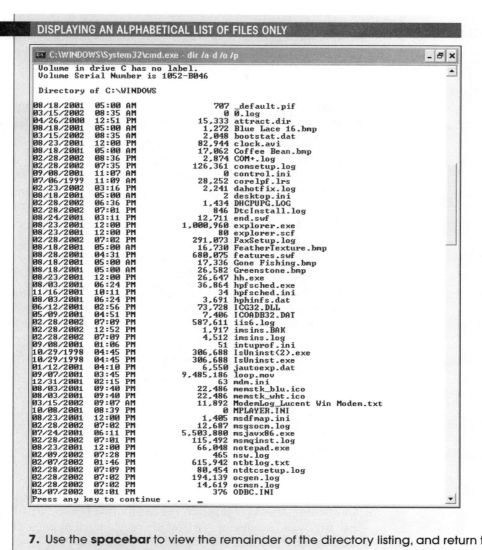

7. Use the **spacebar** to view the remainder of the directory listing, and return to the command prompt.

8. Leave the Command Prompt window open for the next section of the tutorial.

When using the Directory command, you can specify the path to the directory you want to examine, or you can use the Change Directory command to first switch to that subdirectory, and then use the Directory command to view its contents.

| REFERENCE | WINDOW | RW |

Changing Directories

- Open the Start menu, click Run, type CMD in the Open text box, and then press the Enter key. Or open the Start menu, point to All Programs, point to Accessories, and then click Command Prompt.
- Type CD, press the spacebar, type the path and name of the directory or subdirectory that you want to switch to, and then press the Enter key.

Since the Directory command has an extensive list of switches, and since the switches can be combined and used in different ways, you can use the Help switch (/?) with the Directory command to refresh your memory about the types and uses of the Directory command's switches.

REFERENCE WINDOW   **RW**

Displaying a Directory Listing

- Open the Start menu, click Run, type CMD in the Open text box, and then press the Enter key. Or open the Start menu, point to All Programs, point to Accessories, and then click Command Prompt.
- If you want to view Help information on the Directory command and its switches, type DIR /? and then press the Enter key.
- If you want to view a directory listing of the current directory or subdirectory, type DIR and then press the Enter key. Type DIR /A and press the Enter key to view a directory listing of all directories and files, no matter what attributes are assigned to them. Type DIR /O /P and press the Enter key to display a list of directories and files in alphabetical order by subdirectory and file-name, one screen at a time. Type DIR /A /O /P and press the Enter key to display a directory listing of all directories and files (including hidden and system files) in alphabetical order by file-name, one screen at a time. Type DIR /AD /O /P and press the Enter key to view an alphabetical directory listing of just subdirectories, one screen at a time. Type DIR /A-D /O /P and press the Enter key to view an alphabetical directory listing of just files, one screen at a time.

As you can tell, the Directory command is quite versatile, and also quite important, because it provides you with the information you need about the contents of a disk and directory.

Viewing File Attributes

Another important command is the Attribute command (Attrib), an external command that lists attributes assigned to files by the operating system (or by you, or someone else). You can also use this command to change file attributes. For example, if you need to edit a system file, and if that file is assigned the Read-Only attribute, you first need to turn off the Read-Only attribute so that you can make and save the change. Then you need to turn on the Read-Only attribute again to protect the file from further modification.

Terri suggests that you return to the root directory, and examine the attributes of the files, most of which are system files. Terri also suggests you use another variation of the Change Directory command to return to the root directory.

To change to the root directory, and then view attributes of directories and files:

1. Clear the screen.

2. Type **cd ..** (dot dot) and then press the **Enter** key. The Change Directory command switches to the parent directory of the current directory, as shown in the command prompt (C:\). See Figure 14-33. The current directory is the Windows directory, and its parent directory is the root directory. This command allows you to step up one directory level in the directory structure of a disk. Since you were one directory below the root directory, it has the same effect as the CD \ command in this instance.

Figure 14-33 | STEPPING UP ONE DIRECTORY LEVEL

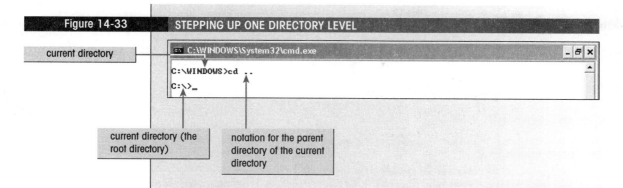

current directory

current directory (the root directory)

notation for the parent directory of the current directory

3. Type **attrib** and press the **Enter** key. The Attribute command lists all the attributes of all the files in the root directory. See Figure 14-34. Note that all of the files, except Config.sys and Autoexec.bat, are assigned the System attribute—identified by the code "S", indicating that they are operating system files. All of the files, except Config.sys and Autoexec.bat, are also assigned the Hidden attribute—identified by the code "H", indicating that they are hidden files, and therefore not displayed in a directory listing, unless you specify otherwise. All of the files, except pagefile.sys, Config.sys, and Autoexec.bat, are assigned the Read-Only attribute—identified by the code "R", indicating that you cannot modify, or delete the file. Windows XP needs to write to pagefile.sys to use virtual memory—so this file cannot be Read-only. All of the files, except cmldr and boot.ini, are assigned the Archive attribute—identified by the code "A", indicating that they have been modified, and not backed up.

Figure 14-34 | VIEWING FILE ATTRIBUTES

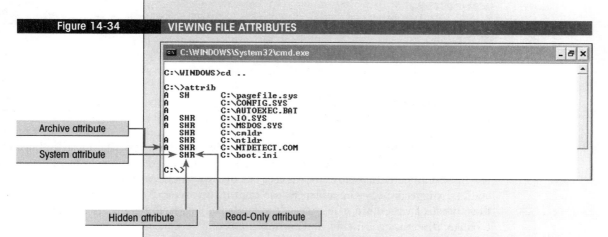

Archive attribute

System attribute

Hidden attribute

Read-Only attribute

4. Type **attrib /?** and then press the **Enter** key. The Help information shows how to turn on, and turn off, an attribute. See Figure 14-35. Note that you can also use the Subdirectory switch (/S) to view information or change attributes in the current directory, as well as all subdirectories under the current directory. The Directory switch (/D) also includes directories in the operation.

Figure 14-35 | VIEWING HELP ON THE ATTRIBUTE COMMAND

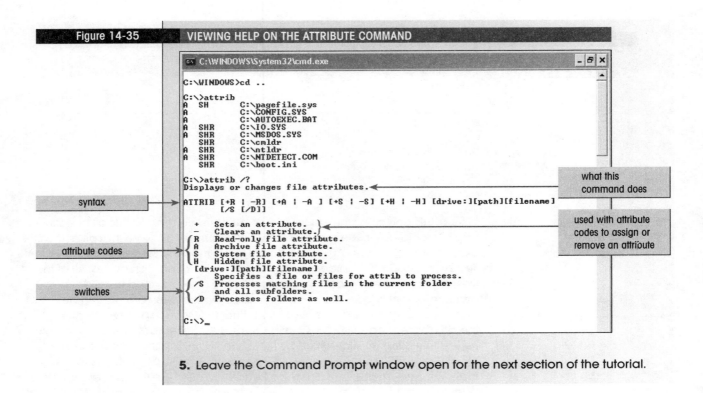

5. Leave the Command Prompt window open for the next section of the tutorial.

REFERENCE WINDOW | **RW**

Changing to the Parent Directory of the Current Subdirectory

- Open the Start menu, click Run, type CMD in the Open box, and then press the Enter key. Or open the Start menu, point to All Programs, point to Accessories, and then click Command Prompt.
- Type CD .. (dot dot) and then press the Enter key.

To use the Attribute command to change attributes, you type ATTRIB followed by a space and the filename (or file specification if you are selecting a group of files), and then you specify which attributes you want to turn on or off. If you place a plus sign before the code for an attribute, you enable, or turn on, that attribute. If you place a minus sign before the code for an attribute, you remove, or turn off, that attribute.

If you need to edit Boot.ini, and assuming you are in the root directory, you would first need to turn off the System, Hidden, and Read-only attributes before you open the file, as follows:

ATTRIB BOOT.INI -S -H -R

The spaces between the attribute codes are required. You would then make your changes to this file, save those changes, and then use the Attribute command to reassign the System, Hidden, and Read-only attributes, as follows:

ATTRIB BOOT.INI +S +H +R

If you need to edit a text file, such as Boot.ini, in a command-line environment, you can use the MS-DOS Editor, a simple text editor similar to Notepad. To start the MS-DOS Editor, you just type the command Edit, an external command, at the command prompt. If you want to start the MS-DOS Editor, and open a file at the same time, you type Edit followed by a space, and then the name of the file. You can also use Notepad, just by typing the command Notepad at the command prompt, followed by a space, and then the filename. In other words, you can open Windows applications from a Command Prompt window, if you know the name of the program file. If you are not able to boot your computer to the Windows desktop, but instead can only boot to a command-line environment, you cannot use Notepad, but you can use the MS-DOS Editor.

REFERENCE WINDOW **RW**

Viewing File Attributes from the Command Prompt

- Open the Start menu, click Run, type CMD in the Open text box, and then press the Enter key. Or open the Start menu, point to All Programs, point to Accessories, and then click Command Prompt.
- If you want to view Help information on the Attribute command, type ATTRIB /? and then press the Enter key.
- If you want to view attributes of files within a directory, change to that directory first (just to make it simpler), type ATTRIB and then press the Enter key.

The Attribute command is often used with the Directory command when troubleshooting problems in a command-line environment.

Creating a Subdirectory

You can use the Make Directory (MD) command, an internal command, to create subdirectories on a disk. When you use the Make Directory command, you specify the name of the subdirectory and, if you want the subdirectory created on another drive, you must also specify the drive name.

If you are entering a command in the Command Prompt window, and need to also include a reference to a long subdirectory name or filename that contains one or more spaces, you might also need to enclose the subdirectory name or filename within quotation marks (it depends on the command you're using). Otherwise, Windows XP might treat the spaces as delimiters (like the backslash (\) in a full path), and think that each space separates two different parameters within the command. For example, if you want to create a subdirectory called Performance Measurements on drive D, and assuming you were already at the root directory of drive D, you would enter this command:

MD "Performance Measurements"

If you did not use the quotation marks, the Make Directory creates two subdirectories— one called Performance and the other called Measurements. It does not create a subdirectory by the name of Performance Measurements.

If you want to create that same subdirectory on a floppy disk in drive A from drive C, you would enter one of the following commands:

MD "A:\Performance Measurements"

MD A:\"Performance Measurements"

If you do not use quotation marks, the Make Directory command creates a subdirectory on drive A called Performance, and another subdirectory *on drive C* called Measurements. (That also tells you that you can use the Make Directory command to create multiple directories at the same time.) For other commands, such as the Change Directory command, which you examined earlier, you do not need to use quotation marks around long subdirectory name or filenames with one or more spaces.

If a long subdirectory name or filename does not contain spaces, you do not need to use quotation marks, even if the name is longer than eight characters. For example, to create a subdirectory named Performance on drive D, and assuming you were already at the root directory of drive D, you would enter this command:

MD Performance

Terri encourages you to copy some of the important configuration files used on your computer to a floppy disk so that you have an additional backup of these files. If for some reason you cannot boot Windows XP, you must boot to the command prompt, and then you might need to copy files to the hard disk from your backup.

To create a subdirectory on a floppy disk:

1. If necessary, insert the floppy disk that you formatted earlier into drive A, and then clear the screen.

2. Type **dir a:** and then press the **Enter** key. If the disk is a newly formatted one without files, the Directory command displays the message "File Not Found." This is a way to quickly check a disk's contents before you start copying files to the disk. See Figure 14-36.

Figure 14-36	VIEWING THE CONTENTS OF A FLOPPY DISK

floppy disk does not contain any files

displays the contents of the default directory on drive A (usually the root directory)

3. Type **md "a:\System Files"** (you must type the quotation marks because of the space in the long subdirectory name, and if you want the subdirectory name to use mixed case, with uppercase characters for the first character in each word, you must type it as shown), and then press the **Enter** key.

4. Press ↑ *twice* to recall the command from two steps ago (dir a:), and then press the **Enter** key. Your floppy disk now contains a subdirectory named System Files. See Figure 14-37.

Figure 14-37	CREATING A SUBDIRECTORY

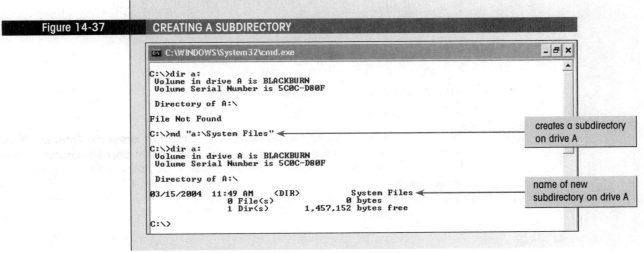

creates a subdirectory on drive A

name of new subdirectory on drive A

> **5.** Leave the Command Prompt window open for the next section of the tutorial.

After you create a subdirectory, the subdirectory is empty (except for the dot and "dot dot" directory markers). You can then add subdirectories and files to that directory.

REFERENCE WINDOW **RW**

Creating a Subdirectory from the Command Prompt
- Open the Start menu, click Run, type CMD in the Open text box, and then press the Enter key. Or open the Start menu, point to All Programs, point to Accessories, and then click Command Prompt.
- Use the CD command followed by a space and a directory name to switch to the directory where you want to create a subdirectory.
- Type MD, press the spacebar, type the name of the new subdirectory you want to create, and then press the Enter key. If you are using long subdirectory names that include one or more spaces, include the drive name and path of the new subdirectory within quotation marks. If you are working from another drive and directory, you must type the drive name, as well as the full path to, and name of, the new subdirectory you want to create.

If you want to remove a subdirectory, you can use the Remove Directory (RD) command. The syntax is similar to that of the Make Directory (MD) command. If the subdirectory that you want to use contains other subdirectories and/or files, you must use the Subdirectory (/S) switch with the Remove Directory (RD) command.

Copying Files

You can use the Copy command, an internal command, to copy files from one location to another. The general syntax for the Copy command is as follows:

COPY *source destination*

The **source** is the subdirectory, files, or file you want to copy. If you want to copy files from another drive, you have to also specify the drive that contains the files you want to copy. The **destination** is the drive or subdirectory where you want to copy the files. When you use this command, you can specify the full path of the source and destination so that Windows XP knows exactly what to copy and where to copy it to.

Terri recommends that you copy the Config.sys, Autoexec.bat, Win.ini, and System.ini configuration files to the System Files directory on your floppy disk, so that you have another backup copy of these configuration files.

To copy files:

1. Clear the screen.

2. Type **copy config.sys "a:\System Files"** and then press the **Enter** key. If the operation is successful, you see the message "1 file(s) copied," as shown in Figure 14-38.

TROUBLE? If you see the message "The system cannot find the file specified," use the F3 key (or ↑) to recall the command you just entered, check to make sure your command is entered correctly, edit the command (if necessary), and then try again.

TROUBLE? If Windows XP is installed on another partition (for example, drive D or drive E), edit the command to include the drive name before config.sys (for example, d:\config.sys or e:\config.sys).

| Figure 14-38 | COPYING A FILE TO A SUBDIRECTORY ON DRIVE A |

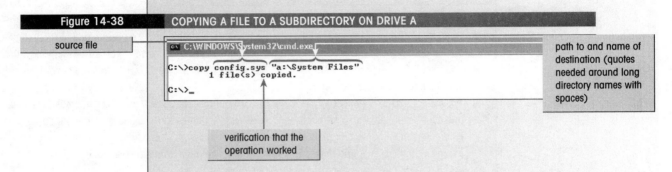

source file

path to and name of destination (quotes needed around long directory names with spaces)

verification that the operation worked

TROUBLE? If you entered the command correctly and are still unable to copy the file, the file is probably assigned the Hidden attribute. Type the following command: ATTRIB CONFIG.SYS –H (including the drive name before CONFIG.SYS, if necessary), press the Enter key, and then try the copy command in this step again (including the drive name before config.sys, if necessary). After you copy config.sys, restore the Hidden attribute by typing the following command: ATTRIB CONFIG.SYS +H (including the drive name before CONFIG.SYS, if necessary), and then press the Enter key.

3. Use the F3 key or ↑ to recall the previous command, and edit it so that the command reads **copy autoexec.bat "a:\System Files"** and then press the **Enter** key. You can use the Delete key to delete "config.sys" in the command you recall, and then type "autoexec.bat". Or you can use the Insert key to switch to overtype mode, type a portion of the new filename over "config.sys", press the Insert key to switch back to insert mode, and then type the remainder of the filename.

TROUBLE? If Windows XP is installed on another partition (for example, drive D or drive E), edit the command to include the drive name before autoexec.bat (for example, d:\autoexec.bat or e:\autoexec.bat).

TROUBLE? If you entered the command correctly and are still unable to copy the file, the file is probably assigned the Hidden attribute. Type the following command: ATTRIB AUTOEXEC.BAT –H (including the drive name before AUTOEXEC.BAT, if necessary), press the Enter key, and then try the copy command in this step again (including the drive name before autoexec.bat, if necessary). After you copy autoexec.bat, restore the Hidden attribute by typing the following command: ATTRIB AUTOEXEC.BAT +H (including the drive name before AUTOEXEC.BAT, if necessary), and then press the Enter key.

4. Use the **F3** key or ↑ to recall the previous command, and edit it so that it reads **copy windows\win.ini "a:\System Files"** (replacing "windows" with the name of your Windows directory, if necessary), and then press the **Enter**

key. Since Win.ini is stored in the Windows directory, you have to specify the path to that file. You could also have used the path "C:\Windows\Win.ini"; however, the Copy command assumes that you want to copy a file from the current drive (drive C), and also that the Windows directory is under the root directory of the current drive (drive C). In this case, both assumptions are correct.

TROUBLE? If Windows XP is installed on another partition (for example, drive D or drive E), edit the command to include the drive name before windows\win.ini (for example, d:\windows\win.ini or e:\windows\win.ini).

POWER USERS TIP Like all other commands that use a path, if you don't specify a drive, the command uses the current drive. If you don't specify a directory, the command assumes you want to use the current directory.

5. Use the **F3** key or ↑ to recall the previous command, and edit it so that it reads **copy windows\system.ini "a:\System Files"** (replacing "windows" with the name of your Windows directory, if necessary), and then press the **Enter** key.

TROUBLE? If Windows XP is installed on another partition (for example, drive D or drive E), edit the command to include the drive name before windows\system.ini (for example, d:\windows\system.ini or e:\windows\system.ini).

6. To verify that the files are copied to the correct directory (always a good idea), type **dir "a:\System Files"** and then press the **Enter** key. The System Files directory on your floppy disk now has a copy of these four configuration files. See Figure 14-39. If Config.sys and Autoexec.bat are empty, you might wonder why you would need to copy them. Namely, so that you have a record that, at one point in time, they did not contain any commands for configuring and customizing your system. Then, you don't have to keep all this information in your head.

Figure 14-39	VIEWING FILES COPIED TO THE SYSTEM FILES SUBDIRECTORY

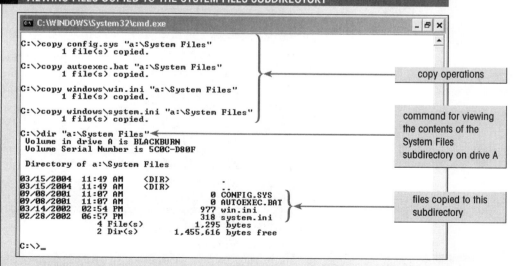

7. Leave the Command Prompt window open for the next section of the tutorial.

You can also copy all the files in a subdirectory at once by specifying the path and name of the subdirectory as the source. For example, assume you are in the subdirectory for your user account (under C:\Documents and Settings), and you want to copy all the Internet shortcuts in the Favorites directory to a floppy disk so that you can carry your Internet shortcuts with you somewhere else. Because the Favorites directory is under your user account directory, you can use the following command:

COPY Favorites A:

This command then copies the Internet shortcuts from the Favorites directory to the root directory of the target disk.

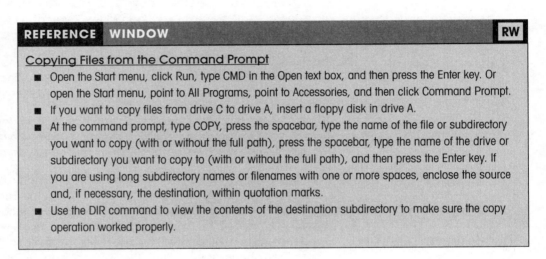

REFERENCE WINDOW | RW

Copying Files from the Command Prompt
- Open the Start menu, click Run, type CMD in the Open text box, and then press the Enter key. Or open the Start menu, point to All Programs, point to Accessories, and then click Command Prompt.
- If you want to copy files from drive C to drive A, insert a floppy disk in drive A.
- At the command prompt, type COPY, press the spacebar, type the name of the file or subdirectory you want to copy (with or without the full path), press the spacebar, type the name of the drive or subdirectory you want to copy to (with or without the full path), and then press the Enter key. If you are using long subdirectory names or filenames with one or more spaces, enclose the source and, if necessary, the destination, within quotation marks.
- Use the DIR command to view the contents of the destination subdirectory to make sure the copy operation worked properly.

The Copy command only copies files within a single subdirectory. If you need to copy files in several subdirectories at once, and also create the same directory structure on a target disk, you would use the XCopy command (for Extended Copy).

Changing Drives

Another simple, but important, operation is changing from one drive to another drive. To perform this operation, you just type the drive name after the command prompt and press the **Enter** key. Drive names consist of a letter of the alphabet followed by a colon. You must use the colon when typing a drive name.

Terri wants you to switch to drive A, and then open the System Files directory.

To change drives, and open a directory:

1. Clear the screen.

2. Type **a:** and press the **Enter** key. Windows XP changes to drive A, and updates the command prompt. See Figure 14-40.

Figure 14-40 | CHANGING DRIVES

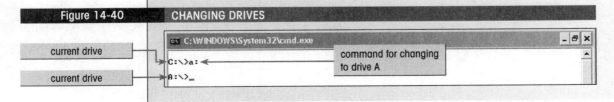

current drive

current drive

command for changing to drive A

3. Type **cd System Files** (you do not need to use quotation marks, though they work as well), and then press the **Enter** key. Windows XP changes to the System Files subdirectory, and updates the command prompt to show your exact location. See Figure 14-41. You do not need to specify drive A for the path to this subdirectory, because Windows XP assumes the subdirectory is on the current drive—drive A.

Figure 14-41	CHANGING DIRECTORIES

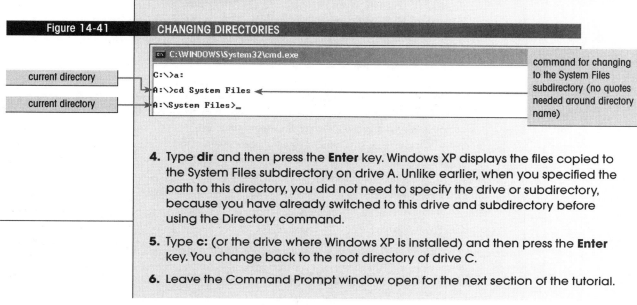

4. Type **dir** and then press the **Enter** key. Windows XP displays the files copied to the System Files subdirectory on drive A. Unlike earlier, when you specified the path to this directory, you did not need to specify the drive or subdirectory, because you have already switched to this drive and subdirectory before using the Directory command.

5. Type **c:** (or the drive where Windows XP is installed) and then press the **Enter** key. You change back to the root directory of drive C.

6. Leave the Command Prompt window open for the next section of the tutorial.

You cannot use CD to change from one drive to another. For example, if you enter the command:

CD A:

The Change Directory command does not change drives. You remain on drive C. However, the Change Directory command does show you which subdirectory is the current directory on drive A. However, you can use this command to change the current directory on another drive to another subdirectory on that drive. That subdirectory then becomes the current directory on that drive. Then, if you want to copy files to that subdirectory, you do not need to specify the subdirectory's path (you just specify the drive name) as the target.

REFERENCE WINDOW   **RW**

Changing Drives from the Command Prompt
- Open the Start menu, click Run, type CMD in the Open text box, and then press the Enter key. Or open the Start menu, point to All Programs, point to Accessories, and then click Command Prompt.
- If you need to change to another drive, type the drive name (including the colon) at the command prompt, and then press the Enter key.

Since drive names are device names, and since device names are **reserved names** that cannot be used as filenames, you cannot create a subdirectory or file that has the same name as a device. Also, you cannot use the colon in a subdirectory name or filename.

Using Wildcards in File Specifications

When you perform certain types of operations, such as copying multiple files, you can stream-line the process with the use of wildcards if the filenames have a feature in common, such as the same file extension. A **wildcard** is a symbol used in a file specification to select a group of files. There are two wildcards. The **asterisk wildcard (*)** substitutes for all or part of a file-name, and the **question mark wildcard (?)** substitutes for a single character in a filename.

For example, if you want to copy all the files in the Windows directory with the "ini" file extension to a floppy disk, you can use the following command:

COPY C:\WINDOWS*.INI A:

The file specification for the source is "*.INI". The asterisk wildcard before the file exten-sion substitutes for any filename; however, because you also specified that the file extension must be "ini", Windows XP only copies files with this extension. Using this approach, you can copy them as a group, rather than having to copy each "ini" file separately by specifying each full filename. Using wildcards, you can save yourself considerable time and effort.

If you have a set of budget files for different fiscal years, such as budget reports and finan-cial projections, each with different file extensions, you could copy all the files for a specific fiscal year by using the asterisk wildcard if all the filenames start with the same set of char-acters. For example:

COPY FY2004* A:

The file specification for the source, FY2004*, selects all files that have the same first six characters in the filename, no matter what the remainder of the filename is and no matter what the file extension is. The Copy command would then, for example, copy the files named FY2004 Budget Report.doc and FY2004 Budget Projection.xls.

If you want to copy all the files in a directory, such as the Favorites directory, and assum-ing you had already switched to that directory first, you can use the following command to copy the Internet shortcuts to a floppy disk:

COPY *.* A:

The file specification for the source is "*.*" (called "star dot star"). The asterisk wildcard before the period selects all files, no matter what the main part of the filename is, and the asterisk wildcard after the period selects all files, no matter what the file extension is. In other words, this file specification (*.*) selects all files.

 POWER USERS TIP If you are already in the directory that contains the files you want to copy, you can also use this command:

COPY . A:

The file specification for the source is represented by a period, the directory marker for the current directory, and the Copy command therefore copies all files in the cur-rent directory. This Power Tip simplifies copying.

Although the asterisk wildcard is commonly used because of its power, you might also find instances where you can use the question mark wildcard. Assume, for example, you have five different versions of your resume stored in files with the filenames Resume #1.doc, Resume #2.doc, Resume #3.doc, Resume #4.doc, and Resume #5.doc. To copy these files to a floppy disk, you could use the following command:

COPY "Resume #?.doc" A:

The question mark wildcard substitutes for a single character at this exact position in the filename (in this case, the ninth position), and the Copy command copies Resume #1.doc, Resume #2.doc, Resume #3.doc, Resume #4.doc, and Resume #5.doc. If you also had a draft of Resume #1.doc named Resume #1a.doc, the Copy command does not copy that file (which you might prefer).

Terri asks you to add two other important Windows XP configuration files to your floppy disk.

To copy files using a wildcard:

1. Clear the screen.

2. Type **copy windows\system32*.nt "a:\System Files"** (replacing "windows" with the name of your Windows directory, if necessary), and then press the **Enter** key, (or recall a previous Copy command from the command history, and then edit it). The Copy command copies two files in the Windows System32 directory that match the file specification for the source. See Figure 14-42. These two files are the Windows XP MS-DOS startup files. Windows XP uses these files instead of the traditional Config.sys and Autoexe.bat files to initialize the MS-DOS environment for DOS programs.

Figure 14-42	COPYING FILES WITH WILDCARDS

asterisk wildcard used in file specification

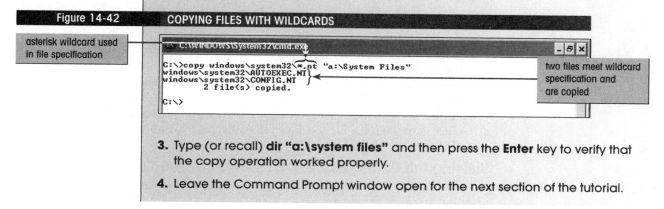

```
C:\>copy windows\system32\*.nt "a:\System Files"
windows\system32\AUTOEXEC.NT
windows\system32\CONFIG.NT
        2 file(s) copied.

C:\>
```

two files meet wildcard specification and are copied

3. Type (or recall) **dir "a:\system files"** and then press the **Enter** key to verify that the copy operation worked properly.

4. Leave the Command Prompt window open for the next section of the tutorial.

Many commands use a file specification with or without wildcards to select one or more files for an operation. A **file specification**, therefore, can refer to a specific subdirectory or file, or to a group of files selected with the use of wildcards.

You can also use wildcards with directory names. For example, if you want to change to the My Documents directory from your user account directory, you can type CD My* and then press the Enter key.

REFERENCE WINDOW	RW

Copying Files from the Command Prompt Using Wildcards

- Open the Start menu, click Run, type CMD in the Open text box, and then press the Enter key. Or open the Start menu, point to All Programs, point to Accessories, and then click Command Prompt.
- Use the Change Directory (CD) command to change to the subdirectory that contains the files you want to copy.
- If you want to copy all the files in the directory to a floppy disk (for example), type COPY *.* A: and then press the Enter key (or type COPY . A: and then press the Enter key).
- If you want to copy all files with a certain file extension, such as "doc" (for example), type COPY *.DOC A: and then press the Enter key.
- If you want to copy all files that begin with the same set of characters in the filename, such as "Resume" (for example), type COPY RESUME*.DOC A: and then press the Enter key. If the source files are long filenames with one or more spaces, include the file specification for the source within quotation marks.
- If you want to copy files with identical filenames, except for one character, such as Resume #1.doc, Resume #2.doc, etc. (for example), type COPY "Resume #?.doc" A: and then press the Enter key. If the source files are long filenames with one or more spaces, include the file specification for the source within quotation marks.

You have to be careful with the use of wildcards, because you might end up selecting far more files than you would have otherwise expected for an operation, such as a copy or delete operation. A safe strategy is to test wildcard file specifications first by using them with the Directory command. This approach selects the files based on the wildcard file specification you use, and you can then check to make sure the correct set of files are selected before then using that same wildcard file specification with another command.

Viewing the Contents of the Windows Environment

In Tutorial 9, you examined the environment variables stored in the Windows environment and their settings. If you need to check settings for environment variables, you can also examine the Windows environment in a command-line environment. One particularly important setting is the one for the PATH environment variable. Windows XP uses this setting, called the Windows path, to locate the program files for external commands.

Terri explains the importance of the Windows environment and path to you so that you can become more familiar with how Windows XP uses system settings, and so that you can more effectively troubleshoot problems that might arise. Terri also notes that you can create new environment variables to simplify the use of commands in a command-line environment. She recommends that you examine the Windows environment with the Set command, and that you customize the Directory command with an environment variable.

To view the contents of the Windows environment:

1. Clear the screen.

2. Type **set** and then press the **Enter** key. The Set command, an internal command, displays the contents of the Windows environment (which used to be called the DOS environment). See Figure 14-43. Some of your settings will differ.

Figure 14-43 — **VIEWING THE WINDOWS ENVIRONMENT**

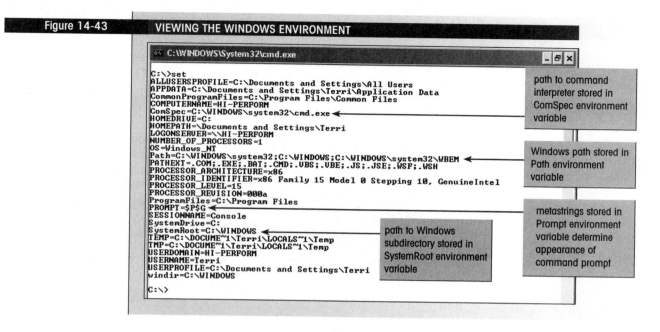

The setting for the ComSpec environment variable is the full path of the program for opening a Command Prompt window. If Windows XP needs to find Cmd.exe so that it can load it from disk, it checks the Windows environment for the ComSpec environment variable to determine the location and name of this program.

The Prompt environment variable determines how the command prompt appears in a command-line window. PG is a **metastring**, or code, that tells Cmd.exe how to display the Windows prompt. $P (for "path") instructs Cmd.exe to first display the full path of the current drive and directory (in this case, C:\). $G (for "greater than") instructs Cmd.exe to next display the greater than symbol (>) after the full path. The greater than symbol (>) separates the path of the current drive and directory from the command you enter. You can actually use the Prompt command to design your own custom command prompts.

The Path environment variable lists the names of subdirectories for Windows XP to search if it needs to locate a program file. As shown in the figure, the setting includes the path to three subdirectories—the System32 subdirectory, the Windows subdirectory, and the WBEM subdirectory (for Windows-Based Enterprise Management).

Notice that the SystemRoot environment variable is assigned the path to your Windows XP subdirectory, and the SystemDrive environment variable stores the setting for the drive where Windows XP is installed.

If you want to view just the setting for the Path environment variable only, you can use the Path command.

To view just the path:

1. Clear the screen.

2. Type **path** and then press the **Enter** key. The Path command, an internal command, displays the Windows path. See Figure 14-44.

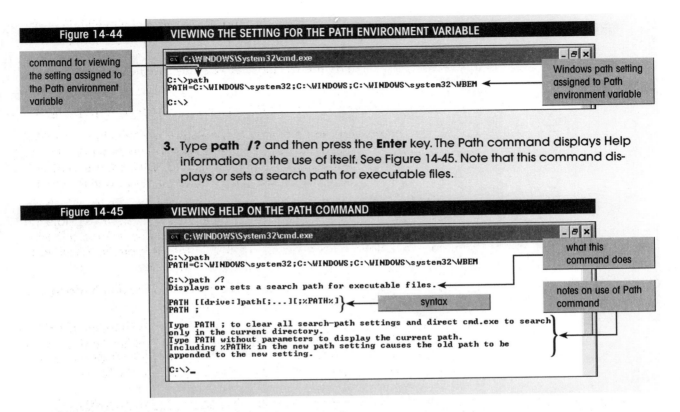

Figure 14-44   **VIEWING THE SETTING FOR THE PATH ENVIRONMENT VARIABLE**

command for viewing the setting assigned to the Path environment variable

Windows path setting assigned to Path environment variable

```
C:\>path
PATH=C:\WINDOWS\system32;C:\WINDOWS;C:\WINDOWS\system32\WBEM
C:\>
```

3. Type **path /?** and then press the **Enter** key. The Path command displays Help information on the use of itself. See Figure 14-45. Note that this command displays or sets a search path for executable files.

Figure 14-45   **VIEWING HELP ON THE PATH COMMAND**

```
C:\>path
PATH=C:\WINDOWS\system32;C:\WINDOWS;C:\WINDOWS\system32\WBEM

C:\>path /?
Displays or sets a search path for executable files.

PATH [[drive:]path[;...][;%PATH%]
PATH ;

Type PATH ; to clear all search-path settings and direct cmd.exe to search
only in the current directory.
Type PATH without parameters to display the current path.
Including %PATH% in the new path setting causes the old path to be
appended to the new setting.

C:\>_
```

what this command does

syntax

notes on use of Path command

If you want to change the path to include additional directories, to change the order of directories, or to exclude directories, you can type the Path command followed by the sequence of directories you want to use. For each directory, you specify the full path (including the drive) so that there is no ambiguity as to where to search for executable files. You separate each directory path from the previous one by a semicolon. You do not include a space after the semicolon. If you want to remove the setting for the path, you type the Path command followed by a space and then a semicolon. That then limits Cmd.exe to program files stored in the current directory.

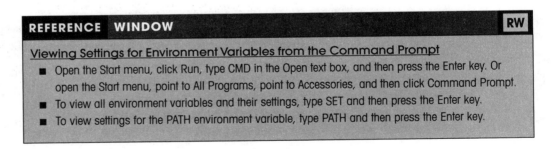

REFERENCE WINDOW   **RW**

Viewing Settings for Environment Variables from the Command Prompt

- Open the Start menu, click Run, type CMD in the Open text box, and then press the Enter key. Or open the Start menu, point to All Programs, point to Accessories, and then click Command Prompt.
- To view all environment variables and their settings, type SET and then press the Enter key.
- To view settings for the PATH environment variable, type PATH and then press the Enter key.

You can also add settings to the Windows environment. For example, when you first used the Directory command without any switches, it displayed directories and files in disk order. You altered that by using the Sort Order switch (/O), so that directories and files were listed in alphabetical order, and so that directories are listed first, followed by files. You also used the Page or Pause switch (/P) to display the directory listing one screen at a time. If you frequently use certain switches for the Directory command, such as the Attribute, Sort Order, and Page switches, you can assign them to the DIRCMD environment variable in the Windows environment. Then, when you use the Directory command, you do not have to type the switches every time you use the command.

Terri encourages you to try this technique of assigning switches.

To assign switches to the DIRCMD environment variable:

1. Clear the screen, type **set** and then press the **Enter** key. Note that there is no DIRCMD environment variable listed in the Windows environment (unless of course, you or someone else have already added it). If there is a DIRCMD environment variable, make a note of its setting so that you can restore it later.

2. Clear the screen, type **dir windows** (replacing "windows" with the name of your Windows directory, if necessary), and then press the **Enter** key. Note that the directory listing is not in alphabetical order by directory name and filename, directories are not grouped together, hidden files are not displayed, and the directory listing does not pause after one screen.

3. Clear the screen, type **set dircmd=/a /o /p** (do not include a space between dircmd and =) and then press the **Enter** key.

4. From the command history, recall the **set** command, and then press the **Enter** key. The Set command in the previous step created a new environment variable called dircmd (case does not matter), and assigns the Directory command's /a, /o, and /p switches to that variable. See Figure 14-46.

| Figure 14-46 | VIEWING A NEW ENVIRONMENT VARIABLE |

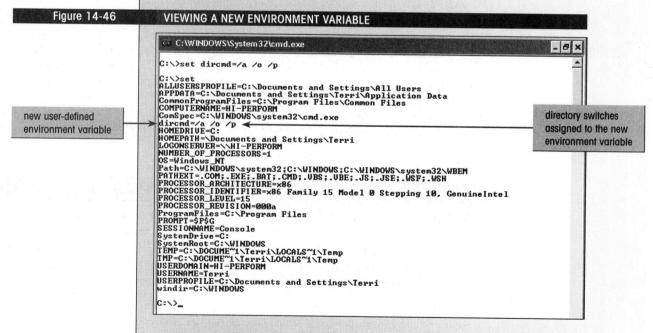

```
C:\>set dircmd=/a /o /p

C:\>set
ALLUSERSPROFILE=C:\Documents and Settings\All Users
APPDATA=C:\Documents and Settings\Terri\Application Data
CommonProgramFiles=C:\Program Files\Common Files
COMPUTERNAME=HI-PERFORM
ComSpec=C:\WINDOWS\system32\cmd.exe
dircmd=/a /o /p
HOMEDRIVE=C:
HOMEPATH=\Documents and Settings\Terri
LOGONSERUER=\\HI-PERFORM
NUMBER_OF_PROCESSORS=1
OS=Windows_NT
Path=C:\WINDOWS\system32;C:\WINDOWS;C:\WINDOWS\system32\WBEM
PATHEXT=.COM;.EXE;.BAT;.CMD;.UBS;.UBE;.JS;.JSE;.WSF;.WSH
PROCESSOR_ARCHITECTURE=x86
PROCESSOR_IDENTIFIER=x86 Family 15 Model 0 Stepping 10, GenuineIntel
PROCESSOR_LEUEL=15
PROCESSOR_REUISION=000a
ProgramFiles=C:\Program Files
PROMPT=$P$G
SESSIONNAME=Console
SystemDrive=C:
SystemRoot=C:\WINDOWS
TEMP=C:\DOCUME~1\Terri\LOCALS~1\Temp
TMP=C:\DOCUME~1\Terri\LOCALS~1\Temp
USERDOMAIN=HI-PERFORM
USERNAME=Terri
USERPROFILE=C:\Documents and Settings\Terri
windir=C:\WINDOWS

C:\>_
```

new user-defined environment variable

directory switches assigned to the new environment variable

5. Clear the screen, type (or recall) **dir windows** (replacing "windows" with the name of your Windows directory, if necessary), and then press the **Enter** key. Note that the directory listing is now in alphabetical order by directory name and filename, directories are grouped together, files are grouped together, hidden files are displayed, and the directory listing pauses after the first screen. You did not have to type the three switches to produce this type of directory listing; instead, the Directory command automatically used the switches assigned to the dircmd environment variable.

TROUBLE? If the Directory command did not display a directory listing as described, repeat Step 3, and make sure you do not include a space before or after the equal sign. Then continue with Step 4.

6. Use the **spacebar** to view the remainder of the directory listing.

7. To close the Command Prompt window, type **exit** and then press the **Enter** key. When you next open a Command Prompt window, you need to specify a setting for the DIRCMD environment variable again because it is only retained for the current Command Prompt session.

8. Keep the floppy disk for use with the Review Assignments.

If you want to update the settings stored in the Windows environment for the DIRCMD variable, just use the SET command to assign a new set of switches to the DIRCMD environment variable (it automatically overwrites the existing setting). If you want to remove this environment variable and its setting from the Windows environment, just type SET DIRCMD= followed by nothing (not even a space), and then press the Enter key. By assigning "nothing" to the environment variable, you remove it from the Windows environment. If you press the spacebar after the equal sign, you assign a space to the DIRCMD environment variable.

REFERENCE WINDOW | **RW**

Creating a DIRCMD Environment Variable from the Command Prompt
- Open the Start menu, click Run, type CMD in the Open text box, and then press the Enter key. Or open the Start menu, point to All Programs, point to Accessories, and then click Command Prompt.
- To assign switches to a DIRCMD environment variable, such as the switches /a /o /p (for example), type SET DIRCMD=/A /O /P and then press the Enter key.
- To view the current setting for the DIRCMD environment variable, type SET and then press the Enter key.
- To verify the new setting for the DIRCMD environment variable, type SET and then press the Enter key.
- To remove the DIRCMD environment variable from the Windows environment, type SET DIRCMD= followed by nothing (not even a space), and then press the Enter key.

When you work in a command-line environment, you might need to execute specific programs to troubleshoot a problem. You can switch to the subdirectory that contains those additional programs, or you can change the setting for the PATH environment variable to include that subdirectory. That's why you should know how to check the settings in the Windows environment so that you can verify, modify, or replace those settings. Without the correct path, Windows XP (like DOS) cannot find and load programs—unless the directory is included in the Windows path, or unless you just happen to be in the subdirectory where the program is stored. You can speed up a search for a program by listing the subdirectories in the order you want Windows XP to search them (for example, the most frequently used, or most important, directory is listed first, and then less frequently used, or the least important, directory is listed last).

Before you change the path, you can record the current path in a file on disk by using the output redirection operator (>), using the following approach:

PATH > OriginalPath.bat

The new file, OriginalPath.bat, is a batch program that you can then use later to restore the original path during the same command-line session. All you have to do is to type the command OriginalPath and press Enter. (In essence, you've created a simple program.)

A **batch program** is a user-defined program file with the "bat" file extension that contains a list of executable commands that the command interpreter can process one right after the other. Simple batch programs allow users to automate common types of operations. Since batch programs are text files, you can open them, or create them, with Notepad or the MS-DOS Editor, and you can view their contents with the Type command.

If you close the Command Prompt window, and then open it later, you find that Windows XP uses the original path setting (not the one you specified for the last command-line session).

Terri is pleased with the progress you have made during your first week on the job. You have picked up enough information so that you can work independently and help employees configure and customize their computers, as well as troubleshoot problems on their computers, both from the Windows desktop and from a command-line environment.

REVIEW ASSIGNMENTS

After working with Terri, you decide to update your backup floppy disk, which currently contains a copy of some of your system files, and add the output of the SystemInfo and BootCfg commands as well as a copy of Setuplog.txt.

As you complete each step in this Review Assignment, record your answers to questions so that you can submit them to your instructor. Use a word-processing application such as Word or WordPad to prepare and then print your answers to these questions. Also, if you change any settings on the computer you are using, note the original settings so that you can restore them later.

To complete these Review Assignments, you need to use the same floppy disk that you used in the tutorial. If you are using Windows XP Home Edition, you cannot complete those steps that require the SystemInfo and Bootcfg commands.

1. Are you using Windows XP Professional or Windows XP Home Edition?

2. From the Start menu, select Run, enter the CMD and then press the Enter key. What is the name of the program file that Windows XP uses to open a Command Prompt window? What is the path to that program file? What are its functions? What is the current drive? What is the current directory? If you wanted to switch to full-screen view, what command would you enter?

3. Maximize the Command Prompt window, type HELP COLOR and then press the Enter key. If you want to change the console colors so that the Command Prompt window uses a light aqua background and a blue foreground, what command would you enter at the command prompt? If you wanted to return to the default console colors without specifying hex digits for the color attribute, what command would you enter? Customize the Command Prompt window using console colors of your own preference. What command did you enter? What are your foreground and background colors now?

Explore 4. Type CLS and then press the Enter key to clear the screen. Type TREE C:\ | MORE and then press the Enter key. Explain what happens. Press Ctrl+C to interrupt the command and return to the command prompt.

5. Clear the screen, type FORMAT /? and then press the Enter key. Using the Help information provided on the Format command, what command would you enter to perform a quick format of a floppy disk in drive A and also, at the same time, add a volume label of your own choosing? Give an example of an actual command you might enter. Do you need to specify a file system for a floppy disk? If so, explain how you would do it. If not, explain why not. How many clusters are supported by the FAT file system?

6. Insert the formatted floppy disk that you used in this tutorial into drive A.

Explore 7. *For Windows XP Professional only*: At the command prompt, type SYSTEMINFO > A:\SystemInfo.txt and then press the Enter key. Then type DIR A: and press the Enter key. Explain what happened when you used the first command (the SystemInfo command). If you had not specified the path for the SystemInfo.txt file, what would have happened?

Explore 8. *For Windows XP Professional only*: At the command prompt, type TYPE A:\SystemInfo.txt | MORE and then press the Enter key. Explain what happens. What type of file is SystemInfo.txt? Use the spacebar to view the remainder of SystemInfo.txt, and return to the command prompt.

Explore 9. *For Windows XP Professional only*: At the command prompt, type BOOTCFG /QUERY > A:\Bootfile.txt and then press the Enter key. Then type DIR A: and press the Enter key. Explain what happened when you used the first command (the BootCfg command).

10. *For Windows XP Professional only*: At the command prompt, type TYPE A:\Bootfile.txt and then press the Enter key. Explain what happens. What type of file is Bootfile.txt?

11. List the path to the current directory.

12. Type CD \ and then press the Enter key. Explain what happens.

13. If you wanted to return to the directory from which you just switched, what command would you enter at the command prompt? Test that command to make sure it works properly.

14. Type A: and press the Enter key. Explain what happens. What is the current directory?

15. Type DIR and press the Enter key. Explain what happens.

16. What directories and files are contained on your floppy disk? How can you distinguish a subdirectory from a file in a directory listing?

17. Type CD System Files and then press the Enter key. Explain what happens.

18. Type DIR and then press the Enter key. What files are contained in the System Files directory? What do the dot and "dot dot" entries in the directory listing represent?

19. Type DIR /O and then press the Enter key. How does the directory listing change? If you did not want to type this switch every time you entered the Directory command, what could you do so that the Directory command always used this switch during this command-line session?

20. Type DIR \ and then press the Enter key. Explain what happens.

21. Type ATTRIB and then press the Enter key. Explain what happens. What do all the files have in common?

22. Type CD \ and then press the Enter key.

23. Type COPY C:\WINDOWS\SETUPLOG.TXT (replacing C: with the name of the drive where Windows XP is installed and "WINDOWS" with the name of your

Windows directory, if necessary), and then press the Enter key. Type DIR and then press the Enter key. Describe what happens.

24. Type DIR and then press the Enter key. Type MD Documentation and then press the Enter key. Type DIR and then press the Enter key. Explain how the directory listing changed?

Explore 25. Type MOVE *.* Documentation and then press the Enter key.

26. Type DIR and then press the Enter key. What files are listed in the root directory?

27. Type DIR Documentation and then press the Enter key. What files are listed in the Documentation directory?

28. Type PATH and then press the Enter key. What is the setting for the Windows path? Why is the path important, and how does Windows XP use it?

CASE PROBLEMS

Case 1. **Using Directory Command Switches at Telco Bonding Corp** Telco Bonding Corp provides a professional bonding service for counties, municipalities, developers, and individuals. Cory Childers, a computer specialist with strong command-line skills, provides troubleshooting support for employees experiencing problems with their computers. Cory is ready to show you, his new part-time assistant, how to work in a command-line environment. He wants you to become familiar with the use of the various Directory command switches, as well as wildcards, so that you can assist him with troubleshooting.

As you complete each step in this case problem, record your answers to questions so that you can submit them to your instructor. Use a word-processing application such as Word or WordPad to prepare and then print your answers to these questions. Also, if you change any settings on the computer you are using, note the original settings so that you can restore them later.

1. Open a Command Prompt window, and then change to the Windows directory. What command did you use?

2. Display Help on the use of the Directory command. What command did you enter?

3. Use the Help information to answer the remaining questions.

4. What command would you use to display a list of just files (excluding directories), one screen or page at a time? Use the command to display a directory listing. What is the first file in the directory listing, and what is its file size? View the remainder of the directory listing.

5. What command would you use to display folders and files in order by size, one page at a time? Use the command to display a directory listing. What is the first file in the directory listing? View the remainder of the directory listing.

6. What command would you use to display a list of just files (excluding directories) in order by file size, one page at a time? (*Hint*: Since there are three criteria, you need to specify three switches.) Use the command to display a directory listing. What is the first file in the directory listing, and what is its file size? View the remainder of the directory listing.

7. What command would you use to display a list of just files (excluding directories) in reverse order by file size, one page at a time? Use the command to display a directory listing. What is the first file in the directory listing, and what is its file size? View the remainder of the directory listing.

8. What command would you use to display a list of just files (excluding directories) in reverse order by date and time, one page at a time? Use the command to display a directory listing. What is the first file in the directory listing, and what is its file date? View the remainder of the directory listing.

9. What command would you use to display a list of just files (excluding directories) in order by file extension, one page at a time? Use the command to display a directory listing. What is the first file in the directory listing? View the remainder of the directory listing.

10. What command would you use to display an alphabetical list of files and directories with the System attribute, one page at a time? Use the command to display a directory listing. What is the first file in the directory listing? View the remainder of the directory listing.

11. What command would you use to display an alphabetical list of hidden directories and hidden files, one page at a time? Use the command to display a directory listing. What is the first file in the directory listing? View the remainder of the directory listing.

Explore 12. What command would you use to display an alphabetical directory listing in lowercase characters, one page at a time?

Explore 13. What command would you use to display an alphabetical directory listing of all files with the "log" file extension, one page at a time?

Explore 14. What command would you use to display an alphabetical directory listing of all setup files with a filename that starts with the characters SETUP, one page at a time?

Explore 15. What command would you use to display an alphabetical directory listing of all files with a filename that starts with the character Q and that have a file extension of "log" (in other words, log files with information on installed updates to Windows XP), one page at a time?

16. Switch to the subdirectory for your user account under the Documents and Settings subdirectory.

17. Enter the command DIR /O /P /S and view the first page of output. How does the Subdirectory switch (/S) affect the appearance of the directory listing? View the next several screens (if necessary), and then press Ctrl+C to interrupt the Directory command.

18. Close the Command Prompt window.

Case 2. Using Environment Variables at Bytes, Bits, & Nibbles Bytes, Bits, & Nibbles is a computer dealership that sells PCs, peripherals, software, and books. This dealership also has a service department for repairing PCs. Antonio Hernandez, one of the dealership's employees, sells computers and assists customers in customizing their new systems. During a quiet afternoon, he decides to share some power tips with his coworkers, and show them how to quickly navigate the directory structure of a computer using environment variables.

As you complete each step in this case problem, record your answers to questions so that you can submit them to your instructor. Use a word-processing application such as Word or WordPad to prepare and then print your answers to these questions. Also, if you change any settings on the computer you are using, note the original settings so that you can restore them later.

1. Open a Command Prompt window, and change to the root directory in one step. What command did you use? What is the path of the current directory?

2. Display the contents of the Windows environment. What command did you use? What settings are assigned to the USERPROFILE, SystemRoot, HOMEPATH, ProgramFiles, and TEMP environment variables?

Explore   3. Enter the following command: CD %USERPROFILE% (you must type the percentage symbols) and then press the Enter key. What subdirectory did the Change Directory command switch to? Explain why this happened.

Explore   4. Try the Change Directory command with the SystemRoot, HOMEPATH, ProgramFiles, and TEMP environment variables. (*Hint*: Remember to use the percentage symbols around the variable name.) List each command you entered, and to what directory you switched.

5. Are there any advantages to using these environment variables over specifying the path? Explain.

Explore   6. Insert your floppy disk in drive A, switch to drive A, and then use the Change Directory command with the USERPROFILE and HOMEPATH environment variables. What advantage does the USERPROFILE environment variable have over the HOMEPATH environment variable?

7. Switch back to drive C (or the drive where Windows XP is installed), and then use the USERPROFILE environment variable to change to the subdirectory for your user account (if necessary).

Explore   8. Use the SET command to create a new environment variable named MyDocs, and assign the path to your My Documents subdirectory (under your user account directory) to this environment variable. What command did you enter?

9. Change to the root directory, and then change to your My Documents subdirectory using the MyDocs environment variable. (*Hint*: Remember to use the percentage symbols around the variable name.)What command did you enter to change to your My Documents subdirectory?

10. Use the SET command to replace the setting for the MyDocs environment with the following setting: %USERPROFILE%\My Documents   What command did you use?

11. Change to the root directory, and then change to your My Documents subdirectory using the MyDocs environment variable. What command did you enter to change to your My Documents subdirectory?

12. What advantage is there to using the USERPROFILE environment variable in the setting for the MyDocs environment variable?

13. View the contents of the Windows environment. What is the setting for the MyDocs environment variable?

Explore   14. To restore your computer, remove the MyDocs environment variable from the Windows environment, and then verify this operation. What command did you use?

Case 3. *Documenting a Computer System at Rottiers Enterprises* Rottiers Enterprises uses AutoCAD to prepare engineering blueprints, topographic maps, and surveys for contractors, builders, landscape services, and county agencies. Mirielle Rottiers and her staff periodically customize computer system settings, and install updates to the operating system. Before she makes changes to your computer, she asks you to assist her by documenting the current structure of your computer system.

As you complete each step in this case problem, record your answers to questions so that you can submit them to your instructor. Use a word-processing application such as Word or WordPad to prepare and then print your answers to these questions. Also, if you change any settings on the computer you are using, note the original settings so that you can restore them later.

1. Open a Command Prompt window, and change to the root directory of drive C (or the drive where Windows XP is installed).

2. Insert a formatted but blank floppy disk into drive A.

3. Create a subdirectory named Documentation on your floppy disk. What command did you use?

4. Display an alphabetical listing of all directories and files in the root directory of drive C one screen at a time. What command did you use?

5. Recall the previous command from the command history, remove the switch for displaying directories and files one screen at a time, and then modify the command so that it redirects its output to a file named RootDir.txt in the Documentation directory on your floppy disk. What command did you use?

6. Display a list of attributes assigned to all files in the root directory. What command did you use?

7. Recall the previous command from the command history, and then modify it so that the command redirects the output to a file named RootAttributes.txt in the Documentation directory on your floppy disk. What command did you use?

8. Display an alphabetical listing of all directories and files in the Windows directory one screen at a time. What command did you use?

9. Recall the previous command from the command history, remove the switch for displaying directories and files one screen at a time, and then modify the command so that it redirects its output to a file named WinDir.txt in the Documentation directory on your floppy disk. What command did you use?

10. Change to the subdirectory for your user account under the Documents and Settings directory. What command did you use?

Explore ▶ 11. Display Help information on the use of the Tree command. What command did you use? What does the /F (for Filename) switch do? *Note*: The ASCII switch (/A) replaces the graphical lines in a directory tree with text characters.

12. Display a directory tree (not a directory listing) of this directory and its subdirectories. What command did you use?

Explore ▶ 13. Recall the previous command from the command history, and then modify it so that the command uses the ASCII switch (/A) and so that it redirects the output to a file named MyTree.txt in the Documentation directory on your floppy disk. What command did you use?

Explore ▶ 14. Use the Tree command with the Filename switch (/F) and the ASCII Switch (/A) to display a directory tree of the current directory and its subdirectories. What command did you use? How does the directory tree differ?

15. Recall the previous command from the command history, and then modify it so that the command redirects the output to a file named MyFileTree.txt in the Documentation directory on your floppy disk. What command did you use?

16. Use Notepad to print a copy of each file in the Documentation directory on your floppy disk or, if your instructor prefers, provide your instructor with a copy of the floppy disk with these files, or send an e-mail message to your instructor with the files as attachments.

Case 4. Analyzing a Volume for Fragmentation at Amalgamated Insurance

Amalgamated Insurance is a large firm that offers its customers health and dental insurance, life and liability insurance, and retirement plans. Nancy Zheng, a microcomputer specialist who provides technical support to the staff, recently learned that Windows XP includes a command-line version of the Disk Defragmenter tool. So that she is familiar with its use in case her staff needs it for troubleshooting, she asks you to examine the documentation for this utility, and then try it on your computer.

As you complete each step in this case problem, record your answers to questions so that you can submit them to your instructor. Use a word-processing application such as Word or WordPad to prepare and then print your answers to these questions. Also, if you change any settings on the computer you are using, note the original settings so that you can restore them later.

To complete this case problem, you must log on under an account with Administrator privileges. Also, you have the option of defragmenting drive C; however, the process could take time (on the order of an hour per 16 GB on a computer with a Pentium 4 processor). If you are working in a computer lab where restrictions are placed on the use of the computers, you might not be able to use the Defrag command-line tool.

1. Log onto a computer under an account with Administrator privileges.

2. Open the Help and Support Center, and use the search feature to locate information on the "Command-line reference." Then locate the Help information on the Defrag command. What does this command do?

Explore ▶ 3. If you want to just analyze a volume, which switch would you use?

Explore ▶ 4. If you want to defrag a volume, and view the analysis and defragmentation reports, which switch would you use?

5. In order to completely and adequately defragment a volume, how much free space must it have?

Explore ▶ 6. Close the Help and Support Center, open a Command Prompt window, and then display Help on the Defrag command. What command did you use?

7. If you need to locate documentation on the use of a command, would you use the Help and Support Center, or command-line Help? Explain.

8. Use the Defrag command and the Analyze switch to report on the fragmentation of drive C. What is the total storage capacity of the drive? How much of the drive is free? How much of the drive is fragmented? What is the percentage of file fragmentation on the drive?

Explore ▶ 9. *Optional*: If you want to defragment drive C with the Defrag command, use the Verbose output switch (-V) to display an Analysis and a Defragmentation Report so that you can measure the effectiveness of the defragmentation. After the defragmentation is complete, how much of the drive is fragmented? What is the percentage of file fragmentation on the drive? What is the percentage of free space fragmentation? How many fragmented files are there? What is the average number of fragments per file (1.00 being near perfect)? How many fragments does the Pagefile have? How many fragmented folders are there? How would you judge the effectiveness of the defragmentation?

% Processor Time

A System Monitor performance counter that measures the demands placed on the processor by a process or operation, such as loading a program or saving a file to disk, and therefore is a measure of processor activity

* (asterisk wildcard)

A symbol used as part of a file specification to substitute for any and all characters in the filename or file extension, starting from the position of the asterisk

. ("dot")

The directory marker denoting the current directory in a directory listing

. . ("dot dot")

The directory marker denoting the parent directory in a directory listing

? (question mark wildcard)

A symbol used as part of a file specification to substitute for a single character in the filename or file extension

\ (backslash)

(1) The symbol for the root directory; (2) a delimiter that separates two directory names, or a directory name and filename, in a path or file specification

8.3 filename

(1) A filename that follows the DOS conventions for naming files; (2) a filename that consists of up to eight characters for the main part of the filename, a separator (a period), and then up to three characters for the file extension

A

A:

The drive name, or device name, assigned to the first floppy disk drive in a computer system

absolute path

A path that spells out the full path for a folder or file (including the drive name), and therefore makes no assumptions about the location of a folder or file

access time

The amount of time it takes for a device to locate an item of data from disk or memory and make it available to the rest of the computer system

actions

Operations you can perform on an object

active content

Dynamic links to constantly-changing content on a Web page, such as a weather map or news

Active Desktop

A Windows technology that integrates the look and feel of the Web into the user interface and that enables you to work on your local computer and network in the same way in which you browse the Web

Active Directory

A Windows XP component that tracks information about objects on a network, supports a single logon process for network users so that they can access resources anywhere on the network for which they have permission, and provides network administrators with a mechanism for administering all network objects using a hierarchical view of the network

ActiveX

A set of technologies that allows software components to interact with one another in a networked environment, regardless of the language in which the components were created

ActiveX control

A small program, such as an animated counter, that is downloaded from a Web site and run locally on your computer

adapter or adapter card

A circuit board or card that connects one system component with another and enables those components to work together

add-in card

A circuit board that is inserted in the system unit and connected to the main system board so that the computer system can work with a hardware component

Address Bar

A toolbar that identifies your current location on your local computer or your network, and in which you can also enter an address for some other location on your local computer or network or a URL for a Web site

Administrators

A type of network domain user group in which the members have full access to the computer and can install an operating system, update or upgrade the operating system, configure and troubleshoot the operating system, manage the security of the computer system, and back up and restore the computer system

Advanced Configuration and Power Interface (ACPI)

A set of power-management specifications developed by Microsoft, Intel, and Toshiba that allows the Windows XP operating system to control the amount of power that each device receives

advanced user

One who knows and understands the effects of different system settings, understands how a change in one setting might affect other settings on a computer, and knows how to restore settings on a system if a change in a setting adversely affects system performance

advertising

The process by which Windows Installer prompts you for a software application CD if you access a feature within that application that is not currently installed, and then automatically installs the feature

AGP (Accelerated Graphics Port)

A bus technology that supports data transfer rates of 266 and 533 MBps and 1.07 GBps (gigabytes per second), thus providing a high-speed pathway for the transfer of graphics between the AGP graphics controller (or video card), the processor, and memory

algorithm

A formula or procedure used by a program for solving a problem or accomplishing a task, such as determining an alias or MS-DOS short filename from a long name

alias

An MS-DOS filename (also called a short filename) that follows the rules and conventions for 8.3 filenames—names that allow 8 characters and then a 3-character extension, only one period, and no spaces—and that is formulated and assigned by Windows XP to folders and files to provide backward compatibility with pre-Windows applications that do not recognize long filenames

allocation unit

(1) One or more sectors used by an operating system as the minimum storage space for a file or part of a file on a disk; (2) a cluster

Alpha

A family of 64-bit RISC processors from Digital Corporation

animated cursor

A mouse pointer shape that plays back a short animation

animated GIF

A GIF file format that contains multiple images through which a Web browser can cycle

antivirus software

A software product that scans a disk for computer viruses and, where possible, removes computer viruses and that monitors the use of other software and floppy disks for computer viruses

append output redirection operator (>>)

An operator that redirects and appends output to an existing text file

application exception

A program error

application-oriented

An operating mode in which you open the software application you want to use, then you locate and

open the document you want to use within that application

Archive attribute

An attribute assigned to a file by the operating system to indicate a newly created file or modified file, so that a backup utility can identify which files should be backed up

Archive bit

A bit that Windows XP turns on when it assigns the Archive attribute to a newly-created or a newly-modified file, and that determines whether or not a file is included in certain types of backups by a backup utility

argument

An optional or required parameter used with a command

asterisk wildcard (*)

A symbol used as part of a file specification to substitute for any and all characters in the filename or file extension, starting from the position of the asterisk

ATA (AT Attachment)

One of five different techniques for integrating the controller electronics on the drive itself—IDE being one approach

ATAPI (AT Attachment Packet Interface)

An extension to EIDE (Enhanced IDE) that supports CD-ROM players and tape drives

attribute

A special characteristic, such as System, Hidden, Read-Only, Archive, Directory, Compress, Encrypt, or Index assigned to a folder or file by the operating system

author mode

Creating new consoles, or modifying existing consoles, in the Microsoft Management Console (MMC)

Automated System Recovery (ASR)

A component of the Windows XP Professional operating system used to create an ASR backup of an operating system's system state, services, and disks, and used to

restore a computer in case of a system failure that cannot be resolved by using other troubleshooting tools, such as the Last Known Good Configuration or Safe Mode

Avg. Disk Queue Length

A System Monitor performance counter that measures the average number of read and write requests for a selected disk. If this value is high, and if Pages/sec is low, there might be a disk bottleneck

B:

The drive name, or device name, assigned to the second floppy disk drive (if present) in a computer system

background program

A program which you opened, but which is not available in the active or selected window

background wallpaper

An image that you display on the desktop background (a bitmap, JPEG, GIF, DIB, PNG, or HTML file)

backup

A copy of one or more files that you keep in reserve in the event of a problem that results in the loss of the original copies of those files

backup cycle

A periodic cycle which you use to back up files on a hard disk and which starts with a full backup, includes additional backups of selected files, and then ends with the next full backup

backup job

A file that contains backup settings and a list of the files and folders selected for a backup

Backup Operators

A type of network domain user group in which the members can back up and restore files on the computer, but who cannot change security settings

backup set

One or more storage media for a specific type of backup

backward compatibility

The ability of an operating system to handle hardware and software designed for earlier types of computers, microprocessors, and operating systems

bad sector

A defective area on a hard disk or floppy disk

bandwidth

The amount of data that can be transmitted over a device in a fixed amount of time (measured in bits per second, or bytes per second)

banner page or **separator page**

A page that is printed before each print job, and that identifies who sent the document to the printer, and the date and time of printing

basic disk

A physical disk that Windows XP can access

batch program or **batch file**

A user-defined program file with the file extension "bat" that contains a list of executable commands that the command interpreter can process one right after the other. Batch programs are often used to automate common types of operations

baud rate

The transmission speed of a modem, usually expressed as bits per second (bps)

bidirectional

Support for the flow of information to and from a device, such as a printer so that the device can report a problem, such as a paper jam, low toner, or an out-of-paper error condition

binary value

A Registry value, identified by the REG_BINARY data type, which consists of a hexadecimal code (a base-16 number system that uses the digits 0 through 9 and the uppercase and lowercase letters A through F to encode data)

bitmap caching

A process by which Windows stores frequently used images from a remote computer on your hard disk when you are connected to that computer with Remote Desktop

bitmapped graphic

An image represented by a pattern of pixels or picture elements

Boolean expression

One or more keywords used with an AND or OR qualifier to specify multiple conditions and more precisely define what you want to locate when searching for information

boot disk

A floppy disk that contains the core operating system files for booting a computer from drive A

boot record or **boot sector**

A hidden table in the system area of a disk that contains information about the version of the operating system used to format the disk and the physical characteristics of the disk, such as the number of bytes per sector, sectors per cluster, maximum number of files per disk, total number of sectors, and sectors per track

boot sector virus

A class of computer viruses that infect the boot sector of a disk by replacing the boot record, or by moving the original boot record to another location on the disk and then overwriting the boot sector

boot volume

The partition that contains the Windows XP operating system files

booting

The process of powering on a computer system and loading the operating system into memory so that it can configure the computer system and manage the basic processes of the computer, including providing support for applications

bootstrap loader

A program in the boot record that locates and loads the operating system or that displays an "Invalid

system disk" error message, or comparable error message, if your computer attempts to boot from a non-bootable floppy disk in drive A

Briefcase

A special Windows XP folder that contains a copy of files stored on another computer and that is capable of synchronizing and updating the two sets of files after changes are made to one or both sets of files

bus

The electronic pathways or channels on the motherboard for transmitting data using address and data lines between two or more devices

byte

(1) The storage space required on disk or in memory for one character; (2) A combination of eight binary digits, or bits, used to encode commonly used characters, including letters of the alphabet, numbers, and symbols

C prompt

The operating system prompt, or command prompt, (C:\>) displayed in a Command Prompt window

C:

The drive name, or device name, assigned to the first partition on the first hard disk drive in a computer system

cabinet file

A file with the "cab" file extension that contains all or part of one or more of the Windows program and supporting files stored in a compressed format

cache (pronounced "cash")

A folder on disk or an area of memory where data is temporarily stored

Carpal Tunnel Syndrome

A common form of repetitive stress injury (RSI) that starts with numbness and burning in the fingers and wrists, and that can eventually cause permanent and irreversible nerve damage

catalog

A feature of backup software that identifies a specific backup and that includes a list of the names of the folders and files that are included in a backup set

Category view

A new view in the Windows XP Control Panel that provides links to common tasks for customizing and configuring your computer

CDFS (Compact Disc File System)

The file system originally designed for CD drives

certificate

A digital document used to authenticate and guarantee the secure exchange of data over the Internet or an intranet

chain

A sequence of lost clusters that once belonged to a single file

channel

A dynamic (updateable) connection to active content on a Web site

cipher

A method of encrypting text

cipher strength

The level of encoding which provides the greatest amount of security for a cipher

CISC (Complex Instruction Set Computing)

A processor design that relies on many complex instructions for processing data. Compare with RISC

Classic view or **Classic style**

A Windows user interface and operating environment similar to that found in Windows 95

clean install

A process whereby you repartition your hard disk drive, format the drive, and then install (or reinstall) an operating system and all your applications, and restore your documents from backups

clear GIF

An object, such as an image or banner advertising, embedded on a Web page, and created by an

HTML tag that references another Web site from which part of the content of the Web page you are viewing is derived. The third-party Web site can then place a cookie on your computer even though you never visited that site

client

A computer in a network that requests and uses services provided by another computer called a server

client application

The application that contains data (or an object) embedded in a compound document, or that contains a link to the data (or object) in another document

client software

The software that you need to access resources on a Microsoft network

client/server network

A type of network in which a central computer provides file, printer, and communication support to other computers on the network

clock speed

The speed at which a processor executes instructions, measured in megahertz (MHz) or millions of cycles per second

CLSID (Class ID)

A unique code that identifies an object or component as a Windows XP object that supports OLE, such as {645FF040-5081-101B-9F08-00AA002F954E} for the Recycle Bin

cluster

(1) One or more sectors used by an operating system as the minimum storage space for a file or part of a file on a disk; (2) An allocation unit

CMOS (Complementary Metal Oxide Semiconductor)

A special type of computer chip, or integrated circuit, that requires less power and that, with the use of a battery backup, retains important BIOS computer settings after you turn off the power to your computer

cold boot

A full boot of your computer, starting from the moment you power on your computer, and including the Power-On Self-Test (POST)

collection

A group of objects that are not located adjacent to each other in a window or on the desktop

color depth

The number of colors displayed in the color palette

color palette

A set of colors used by either an application or by the operating system

color profile

Data about the specific colors—hue (the position of a color in the color spectrum), saturation (the amount of gray in the color, and therefore a determinant of the purity of a color), and brightness—that can be used with a specific printer

color scheme

A combination of settings that include different colors, fonts, sizes, and display formats for elements of the graphical user interface

COM+ Registration Database

A database that stores information about COM+ components, or operating system services for applications and components in a networking environment

COM1:, COM2:, COM3:, and COM4:

The device names for the first, second, third, and fourth communications ports, or serial ports, in a computer system

command history

An area of memory where Windows keeps track of the commands that you have entered in a Command Prompt window

command interpreter

A program such as Cmd.exe, which displays a command prompt, interprets commands entered at the command prompt, locates and loads the appropriate program from memory or disk, and then executes the program

command line interface

A text or character-based user interface with an operating system prompt at which you type commands in order to interact with the operating system and specify that it perform a task

command prompt

The operating system prompt (such as C:\>) displayed in a Command Prompt window or command-line environment to identify the current drive and directory and to provide an interface for interacting with the operating system

Committed Bytes

A System Monitor performance counter that measures the amount of committed virtual memory

committed memory

Physical memory for which space has been reserved in the paging file (or paging files) in case it's needed

compact policy

A Web site's privacy statement that you can read

compound document

A document produced with OLE technology that contains objects, such as graphics, tables, or text, drawn from other documents produced with other applications

compress attribute

An attribute available on an NTFS volume that, when enabled, allows NTFS to compress folder(s) and file(s) so that they use less disk space

Compressed (zipped) Folder

A new type of Windows XP folder that compresses folders and files within the folder on FAT16, FAT32, and NTFS volumes

Computer Administrator

A type of workgroup or stand-alone user account that allows members to make changes to the computer system, including, for example, creating and removing other user accounts as well as installing software

computer virus

A program that gains access to your computer, makes copies of itself, and often adversely affects the use or performance of a computer system, or damages the computer

configure

The process by which the operating system loads and installs software that it needs to operate with the hardware and software on your computer

console

(1) An administrative snap-in for managing the hardware, software, and network components of your computer system; (2) A set of tools, folders, Web pages, or other items displayed in the console tree pane in the Microsoft Management Console; (3) The combination of the keyboard and monitor, which are used for input and output

Console tree pane

A Windows Explorer-like panel in the Microsoft Management Console (MMC) that starts with the Console Root folder and that includes consoles like System Monitor

context menu

A menu that opens when you right-click an object, that displays menu options or actions appropriate to that object, and that provides access to the actions and properties of an object

contiguous clusters

Clusters of a file located adjacent to each other (one after the other) on a disk

controller

A circuit board or card that controls a peripheral device, such as a hard disk or floppy disk

cookie

A text file placed on your computer by a Web server and that contains information about your visit to that Web site

cooperative multitasking

An operating mode found in the Windows 3.x operating environment, and supported in later versions of Windows, in which the currently running application periodically relinquishes control of system resources, so that the operating system can permit another application access to those same system resources

copy backup

A type of backup that includes all the files you select and that does not affect other types of backups that you perform during a backup cycle. Backup utilities do *not* change the Archive bit of the backed-up files after the backup is complete

corrupted file

A program or document file whose contents have been altered as the result of a hardware, software, or power failure

CPU bus

The wiring that provides a high-speed direct connection to the processor

cross-linked file

A file that contains at least one cluster which belongs to, or is shared by, two (or perhaps more) files

current directory

The directory or subdirectory that is currently in use on a given drive

current folder

The folder or subfolder that is currently open and in use

custom file type

A file type that is not tracked by the system registry

customize

To set up a computer system to meet a specific set of user needs, such as loading antivirus software during booting

cylinder

A combination of tracks on different sides of the same platter and on different platters on a hard disk that are treated as a logical unit

D

daemon

(pronounced "demon" and derived from Greek mythology for "guardian spirit") An operating system process, such as a print spooler, that waits for and handles requests for a service

daily backup

A type of backup that includes selected files that have been created or modified the day you perform the backup and that does not affect other types of backups that you perform during a backup cycle. Backup utilities do *not* change the Archive bit of the backed-up files after the backup is complete

data compression

The use of one or more techniques by a backup utility to store data on backup media so that the data take up less space than they do on the hard disk

default

The setting or reference point a program uses until you specify another setting or reference point

defragmenting utility

A program that rearranges files on a disk so that all clusters for each file are stored consecutively (or in adjacent clusters), removes empty space between files, and, in the process, optimizes the loading of software applications

delimiter

(1) The backslash symbol (\) which serves to separate one folder or directory name from another folder or directory name, or a folder or directory name from a filename, in the full path; (2) A period in a filename that separates the main part of the filename from the file extension

denial of service (DoS)

A situation in which users of a Web site are denied access to one or more services at the Web site as the result of an attack that exploits a weakness in the software at the

Web site, or that sends more traffic to the Web site than can be handled

desktop

(1) The background of the graphical user interface on which Windows displays icons, the taskbar, menus, windows, and dialog boxes; (2) The Windows folder that contains desktop shortcuts

destination

The drive or subdirectory you want to copy to

destination disk

The floppy disk that receives a duplicate copy of the contents of another floppy disk

destination document

A compound document that contains data or an object copied from another document and inserted as an embedded or linked object

device

A hardware component within a computer system, such as a keyboard, mouse, system unit, monitor (or video display unit), disk drive, or printer

device conflict, hardware conflict, or resource conflict

A problem that results when two hardware devices attempt to share the same resource, such as the same IRQ (interrupt request line)

device driver

A file with program code that enables the operating system to communicate with, manage, and control the operation of a hardware or software component

Device Independent Bitmap (DIB)

A device-independent, bitmap image format used by Windows XP to render images on the screen and printer. The colors in the file are represented in a format that is independent of the output device (monitor or printer). The device driver for the monitor translates the DIB color format into colors that the monitor can display

device name

A name assigned to a device or hardware component by the operating system

dialog box

A component of the graphical user interface that displays information, lists object properties and settings, and provides options from which to choose as you complete a command operation

differential backup

A type of backup performed during a backup cycle that includes all new or modified files since the last normal or last full backup. Backup utilities do *not* turn off the Archive bit of backed-up files after the backup is complete

digital signature

An encoded tag that verifies the authenticity of the originating party by binding information about that party to the file

DIP (Dual In-Line Package) switch

A set of toggle switches that are mounted on a chip, which is in turn mounted on an add-in board, and that is used to specify the configuration for a hardware device

Direct Memory Access (DMA)

A channel or pathway for transferring data between two devices, such as a hard disk drive, floppy disk drive, or tape drive and main memory (RAM), without the intervention of the processor

directives

Commands included in Config.sys and used to modify the operating system as it loaded into memory during the booting process

directory

The command-line or DOS term for a folder

Directory attribute

An attribute assigned by the operating system to a file to designate it as a folder or directory that keeps track of information on a set of files

directory listing

A list of information about the names of subdirectories and files on a disk, produced by the Directory (DIR) command in a command-line environment, which includes the name of each subdirectory and file, the file extension of each file, the file size, and the date and time of each subdirectory and time

directory marker

The <DIR> notation in a directory listing that identifies the file as a directory (or subdirectory)

directory space

The storage space available in a directory table for tracking information about files on a disk

directory table

A table or file in the system area of a FAT volume that keeps track of the folders and files stored in the top-level folder or root directory

DirectX

A Windows technology that enables games and programs to use the capabilities of your computer's multimedia hardware devices

DirectX Diagnostic Tool

A utility for reporting detailed information about the DirectX components and drivers installed on a computer system

dirty

A drive that has problems with its file system

disk

A physical storage device, such as a hard disk, DVD, CD, or floppy disk

disk optimization

The steps you take to check for and correct errors that interfere with the performance of your hard disk. These include reorganizing the storage space on a disk so that the operating system can efficiently and quickly locate folders and files, and the use of other techniques that improve the performance, availability, and efficient use of storage space on a hard disk

disk quota

A Windows XP and Windows 2000 feature that enables Administrators to control, allocate, and track the usage of storage space on a disk by users

display adapter

A circuit board inside the system unit that controls the image displayed on the monitor

document-oriented

An operating mode in which you locate and open the document you want to use, and then the operating system opens the application that originally produced the document or the application currently associated with that type of file

domain

A group of computers on a network that share a common directory database

domain controller

A computer that uses Active Directory to manage access to a network—including logging on and authenticating users and providing access to the directory and shared resources

DoS (denial of service)

A situation in which users of a Web site are denied access to one or more services at the Web site as the result of an attack that exploits a weakness in the software at the Web site, or that sends more traffic to the Web site than can be handled

DOS (Disk Operating System)

(1) The Microsoft command-line operating system introduced and used on the first IBM PC, (2) A generic name for three related operating systems: MS-DOS, PC-DOS, and IBM-DOS

DOS application

An application, such as WordPerfect 5.1 or Lotus 1-2-3 Release 2.4, originally designed for use with the 16-bit DOS operating system

DOS prompt

The operating system prompt, or command prompt, (such as

C:\>) displayed in a Command Prompt window

dots per inch (DPI)

A measurement of the resolution of a printer

Dr. Watson

A Windows XP system component that automatically starts and compiles information when an application error occurs

drive

A name (such as C: and A:) assigned by the operating system to all or part of the storage space on a physical disk, such as a hard disk, a floppy disk, CD-ROM disc, Zip disk, or a virtual disk (a RAM drive)

drive name

A device name that consists of a letter of the alphabet and a colon (such as C: for drive C) and that is assigned to a disk drive by the operating system

dual-boot configuration

A computer with two installed operating systems, one of which you choose to load during booting

DualView

A Windows XP feature that enables you to expand your display to a second monitor if your computer has a video card with two video ports, and if you have a monitor attached to each port

duplex printing

Double-sided printing (printing on both sides of a sheet of paper)

DWORD

A Registry value, identified by the REG_DWORD data type, which consists of a four-byte number displayed in binary, hexadecimal, or decimal format, for example, the DWORD value 0x000000001 (1) for the WebView value entry

dynamic disk

A physical disk that only Windows XP Professional, Windows XP 64-Bit Edition, and Windows 2000 Professional can access, and that provides additional features not supported on basic disks, such as volumes that scan multiple disks

dynamic link library

A file with a "dll" file extension that contains executable program code which provides support to one or more programs

dynamic menus

Menus in folder windows that display options for common types of operations and that provide links to other places on your computer where you are likely to work

Dynamic Update

A new Windows XP feature that downloads critical fixes or updates, and device drivers, from Microsoft's Dynamic Update Web site, so that the Windows XP Setup Wizard can incorporate those updates into a Windows XP installation

E

EFS (Encrypting File Service)

A Windows XP Professional service that allows you to encrypt and decrypt folders and files on NTFS volumes, and thereby provides increased protection for your important files

EIDE (Enhanced IDE)

An improvement in IDE technology that supports larger storage devices and data transfer rates that are three to four times faster than IDE

Emergency Recovery Disk (ERD)

A disk that you can create with the Windows 95 or Windows 95a Emergency Recovery Utility (ERU) that contains the core operating system files needed to boot the computer from a floppy disk in drive A, copies of the Windows 95 startup configuration files (Config.sys, Autoexec.bat, Win.ini, and System.ini), the Windows 95 Registry, an Emergency Recovery Disk program (Erd.exe) for restoring files from this disk to your computer, and a second copy of the Windows 95 core operating system files

Emergency Repair Disk (ERD)

(1) A disk that you can create with the Windows 2000 Backup utility to repair problems that arise with Windows 2000 system files (such as damaged or missing files), the Windows 2000 startup environment for dual-boot or multiple-boot systems, and the partition boot sector on the boot volume, and to also restore the Windows 2000 Registry; (2) A disk that you can create with the Windows NT Workstation 4.0 Repair Disk utility (Rdisk.exe) to repair problems that arise with the Windows NT Workstation 4.0 operating system

Enable Boot Logging

A boot option that is identical to the Start Windows Normally option, except that Windows XP logs boot operations in a special startup log called NTBtLog.txt in the Windows folder during booting

Enable VGA Mode

A boot option in which Windows XP boots with the basic VGA device driver

encrypt attribute

An attribute available on an NTFS volume that, when enabled, prevents access to a folder or file by any person other than the Administrator and the user who encrypted the folder or file

end-of-file code (EOF) or end-of-file marker

The code in the File Allocation Table that identifies a cluster as the last cluster in use by a specific file

enhanced metafile

A 32-bit metafile with additional commands for creating images under Windows 95 and later versions of Windows

environment variable

A setting stored in the Windows environment that contains information about the computer system (such as the name of the operating system), and that is assigned to a symbolic name (such as "OS")

event

A significant occurrence in the system or application that requires Windows XP to notify users of the event and to log the event

exabyte

2^{60} bytes

executable or executable file

A file that contains program code which Windows XP can load into memory and run, that has the file extension "exe"

expandable string

A type of string value that contains a reference to a variable value, such as %systemroot%— the environment variable for the path to the Windows folder

expert

The individual who accepts an invitation from another person for a Remote Assistance session

extended partition

A partition on a disk that does not contain operating system files, but which can be divided into additional logical drives

external command

A command whose program code is stored in a file on disk

F

FAT12

The file system used for floppy disks

FAT16

An MS-DOS and Windows file system for hard disks with less than 2 GB of storage

FAT32

A variation of the FAT16 file system that more efficiently uses storage space on a disk by working with small cluster sizes and thereby reduces slack, that supports the use of more clusters on a disk than FAT16, that keeps a backup of critical data structures in the boot record, and that supports larger volume sizes (up to 32 GB)

FIFO

first-in, first-out

file

(1) A collection of data, such as a program or document, stored in a folder on disk; (2) a certain amount of storage space on a disk that is set aside for the contents of a program, document, or data file

File Allocation Table (FAT)

A file in the system area of a FAT volume that indicates whether each allocation unit or cluster is available, in use, defective (i.e., contains a bad sector), or reserved for use by the operating system

file extension

The characters that follow the main part of a filename and separator (a period) and which identify the type of application that produced the file or the type of data in the file

file record segment (FRS)

A unique ID assigned to each folder and file in the Master File Table on an NTFS volume

File Signature Verification Tool

A utility for checking system files on a computer to make sure that they have the correct digital signatures (if not, the files have been changed)

file system

The operating system components and data structures which the operating system uses for naming, organizing, storing, and keeping track of folders and files on disks

filename

A name assigned to a program, document, or data file to identify the file's contents and distinguish the file from all other files

files area

The area of a disk that follows the system area and that contains any folders and files created or copied onto the disk

Filmstrip view

A new Windows XP view available in the My Pictures folder for displaying thumbnail views of images contained within files

filter

A utility that modifies the output of another command in a command-line environment

first-party Web site

One whose Web page you are currently viewing

folder

A file that keeps track of a group of related objects, such as files and other folders

Folders pane

A toolbar within a folder window that shows the relationships between objects on your computer

font

A design style for a set of characters

forced hardware configuration

A configuration created by manually changing the resource assignment for a Plug and Play device

foreground program

The program that you are currently using in the active or selected window, and which is the one that responds to commands

format capacity

The storage capacity of a drive or disk

fragmented file

A file stored in two or more non-contiguous, or non-adjacent, clusters on a disk

free space fragmentation

A condition in which the available free space is scattered around the disk, rather than consolidated in adjacent clusters in one part of the disk

FTP (File Transfer Protocol)

A standard Internet protocol for transferring files between computers on the Internet and as such, is commonly used to download programs and other types of files from Internet servers to your computer

full backup

A type of backup that marks the start of a backup cycle and that includes all or part of the contents of a hard disk (in other words, all selected files). Backup utilities turn off the Archive bit of backed-up files after the backup is complete

full format

A type of format used on new or formatted disks to define the tracks and sectors on a disk; create a boot sector, new File Allocation Tables, and a new directory table; and perform a surface scan for defective sectors

full path (also called the **MS-DOS path**)

A notation that identifies the exact location of a file or folder on a disk by including a reference to the drive and folders that lead to the folder or file and, if necessary, a file's name

full system backup

A backup that includes all the files stored on your computer system, including operating system, application software, and document files

gateway

The hardware and software that provide an access point to another network

GIF (Graphics Interchange Format)

A graphics file format that stores a bitmapped image at a compression of 1.5:1 to 2:1 without any loss of detail in the image. The standard types of GIF files are limited to a palette of 256 colors or less

gigabyte (GB, G, or gig)

1,024 megabytes, or approximately one billion bytes, of storage space on disk or memory

GPT (Globally Unique Identifier Partition Table)

A new partition style supported by Windows XP 64-Bit Edition which supports 128 partitions per disk and partition sizes up to 18 exabytes

Grandfather Father Son (GFS)

A tape rotation scheme that requires the least number of tapes and that reduces wear and tear on tapes. Full backups are done once a week. Each daily backup is the Son. The last full backup of the week is the Father. Because the daily tapes are reused after a week, they age only five days. The weekly tapes continue for a month and are reused the next month. The last full backup of the month is the monthly backup—the Grandfather. The Grandfather tapes become the oldest, and you retain them for a year before reusing them again

graphical user interface (GUI)

An interface that provides a more visual method for interacting with the operating system through the use of icons, windows, menus with task-related lists, dialog boxes, colors, fonts, and shading

graphics mode

A video display mode for displaying graphic images as well as text in a variety of fonts and colors

group

A set of users, computers, contacts, or perhaps even other groups in a network domain

Group Policy

A Microsoft Management Console snap-in that an Administrator can use to specify a wide variety of policy settings, including system, network, and security settings

Guest

A type of workgroup or stand-alone user group that allows users who do not have a user account to log onto and use a computer

Guests

A type of network domain user group that allows users who do not have a user account to log onto and use a computer

GUI (graphical user interface)

(pronounced "gooey")

An interface that provides a more visual method for interacting with the operating system through the use of icons, windows, menus with task-related lists, dialog boxes, colors, fonts, and shading

H

handle

A value that uniquely identifies a resource, such as a file or Registry setting, so that a program can access that resource

hard disk controller

A board or card that controls access to the hard disk

Hard Disk Partition Table

A table within the Master Boot Record of a hard disk that contains information that identifies where each partition starts and which partition on the hard disk is the boot drive

hard page fault

A situation in which a process requires program code or data that is neither in its working set nor elsewhere in its physical memory, and therefore must be retrieved from the paging file on disk

Hardware Abstraction Layer (HAL)

The component of the Windows XP operating system that contains the machine-specific program code for a particular type of processor

hardware conflict, device conflict, or resource conflict

A problem that results when two hardware devices attempt to share the same resource, such as the same IRQ (interrupt request line)

hardware interrupt

A signal transmitted from a hardware device to the processor when the device is ready to send or accept data

hardware profile

A combination of hardware settings that Windows XP can use to boot your computer

hardware tree

The Device Manager view that lists categories of hardware components installed on your computer

head

A side of a disk or platter in a hard disk drive

Help switch

An optional parameter (/?) which, when used with the command for a program in a command-line environment, displays Help information about the use of that program

Help Troubleshooter

A Help and Support Center tool for identifying and resolving common hardware and software problems by guiding you through the process of analyzing and identifying the source of the problem

hex digit

A digit in the hexadecimal number system (0 through 9, and A through F) used with the Color command to customize the background and foreground colors of a Command Prompt window

Hibernation or Hibernation mode

A power savings mode in which Windows XP turns off the monitor and hard disk, saves everything in memory to a file named Hiberfil.sys in the top-level folder of the drive where Windows is installed, and turns off the computer. When you power on your computer, Windows XP restores your computer to its previous state

Hidden attribute

An attribute assigned to a folder or file to indicate that the icon and filename of a folder or file should not be displayed in a folder window (unless specified otherwise), or that the filename of a file should not be displayed in a directory listing in a command-line environment

hidden file

A file that does not appear in a folder or directory listing because its Hidden attribute is turned on

High Color

A color setting for a video display adapter that allows it to display 2^{16} or 65,536 colors or, in some cases, 2^{15} or 32,768 colors

hive

A Registry database file (Default, SAM, Security, Software, and System) and its associated log file (Default.log, SAM.log, Security.log, Software.log, and System.log)

home directory

The folder that contains the user profile for the currently logged on user

Home Phoneline Network Adapter (HPNA)

An adapter that uses the phone lines in your home to create a wireless network and that eliminates the need for running network cables to different locations in a home

hot fix

One or more files used to correct a problem with the operating system software

hot swapping, hot plugging, or hot insertion and removal

Inserting or removing a hardware device or card while the computer is running

hover

To select an object in Web style by letting the mouse pointer rest over the object's icon

HTML document

A file that contains HTML (HyperText Markup Language) code for determining the layout and appearance of a Web page

HTTP (HyperText Transfer Protocol)

A standard protocol for transferring files from a Web server to your browser so that you can view the contents of a Web page over the World Wide Web

hue

The position of a color in the color spectrum

Human Interface Devices (HID)

A broad category of devices for interacting with and controlling computers—such as the keyboard, mouse, trackball, joystick, and wireless pointing devices for

presentations as well as devices used to control home entertainment systems, smart appliances, and virtual reality simulations (for example, head-mounted displays)

hyperlink

A link between one object and another on your local computer, network, or the Web

I/O address or port address

A unique memory address for a hardware device, such as a port or disk drive, that handles I/O (input/output)

IBM-compatible

A personal computer that adheres to standards set forth by IBM for the IBM-PC, that contains similar or identical hardware, that functions like an IBM-PC, and that provides support for the same applications

icon

An image or picture displayed on the screen to represent hardware and software resources (such as drives, disks, applications, and files) as well as system tools on your computer that you can open and use

IDE (Integrated Drive Electronics)

A hard disk drive interface in which the electronics for the controller are included in the drive itself so that there is no need for a separate adapter

import media pool

A collection of data storage media that has not yet been catalogued by Windows XP's Removable Storage Media tool

incremental backup

A type of backup performed during a backup cycle that includes only those files that you created or changed since your last normal backup or last incremental backup. Backup utilities turn off the Archive bit of all backed-up files after the backup is complete

index attribute

An attribute that indexes the content of a file and its properties so that you can search for text within a file or folder as well as search for properties of the folder or file

index entry

A word or phrase found in a Help file and used by Windows XP to locate Help information on a specific topic

indexes

NTFS directories

in-place editing or visual editing

The process of editing an object in a compound document within the current application's application window using the menus and tools of the application that produced the original object

input focus indicator

The dotted rectangle that appears around the currently selected object

instance

An option for sampling a performance counter in a different way; for example, under the Process performance object, you can monitor the % Processor Time (a performance counter) used by all programs, or by one specific program

internal command

A command whose program code is contained in the file Cmd.exe and therefore is available once Cmd.exe loads into memory

Internet Connection Firewall (ICF)

A component of the Windows XP operating system that monitors and compares incoming communications with outgoing communications in an effort to block potentially harmful Internet access to your computer, such as intruder or hacker attacks

Internet Connection Sharing (ICS)

A component of the Windows XP operating system that enables computers on a small home or office network to connect to the Internet using a shared dial-up connection via one of the computers within a network

Internet Service Provider (ISP)

A business that provides a connection to the Internet, as well as other services such as e-mail, chat rooms, and software and multimedia libraries, for a set fee or for free

Internet sites

All Web sites that you have not placed in one of the other Web content security zones

interrupt

A signal transmitted by hardware or software to the processor or operating system for some type of service

Interrupt Request Line or IRQ

A hardware interrupt request line used for transmitting signals from a hardware device to the processor

intranet

A private network that relies on the use of Internet technologies and protocols and that is limited to a specific group of people, such as employees within a company

invalid page fault

An error condition that occurs when Windows XP is not able to find data in the paging file

ISDN (Integrated Services Digital Network)

High-speed communication lines with data transfer rates of 64 Kbps, 128 Kbps, or 1.5 Mbps

Itanium processor

A new Intel processor that is capable of performing 20 instructions simultaneously and that can preload data into virtual memory for faster access and processing

Java applet

A small program, such as an animated counter, that is written in the Java programming language and that is downloaded from a Web site and run locally on your computer

JPG or JPEG (Joint Photographics Expert Group)

A graphics file format that achieves higher compression

ratios of 10:1 or 20:1 by removing some of the detail in an image (changes that the human eye cannot detect)

jumper

A small metal block that you use to complete a circuit for two pins on a circuit board and, in the process, specify a configuration

junction point

A physical location on a hard disk that points to data found at another location on the hard disk or on a storage device

kernel

That portion of the Windows XP operating system that resides in memory at all times and that provides services for applications

kernel memory

Memory used by the core components of the operating system and by device drivers

key

(1) The length of a variable value applied by an algorithm to a string or block of unencrypted text; (2) A group of related Registry settings, such as the .bmp key, that contains information on the Bitmap Image file type

keyboard shortcut

A key or combination of keys used to accomplish a task that you might otherwise accomplish with a mouse

kilobyte (KB or K)

1,024 bytes, or approximately 1,000 bytes of storage space on disk or in memory

L

L1 Cache

High-speed memory built into the processor

L2 cache

High-speed memory that resides on a separate chip or, on newer computers, is built into the processor

Last Known Good Configuration

A boot option in which Windows XP boots with the configuration saved by the operating system from the last successful boot

legacy device or non-Plug and Play device

A hardware device that does not support the Plug and Play standards defined by Microsoft Corporation and hardware manufacturers and that requires manual installation, including in many cases, setting jumpers or DIP switches

legend

The area at the bottom of the System Monitor pane for displaying the names of performance counters currently being measured, the instance, the type of performance object, the computer to which these performance counters apply, the color codes for the corresponding lines which represent plotted values in the graph, and the scale used for different performance counters

Limited

A type of workgroup or standalone user account in which a member cannot install hardware or software or change his or her account name or account type

link tracing

The use of an object's name, its type, and the date and time the object was modified by Windows XP to locate the object

linked object

A type of OLE object that contains a pointer (full path) to the file with the original object and that uses the object's presentation data to display the contents of the object

loading

Copying programs, documents, or data into a computer's memory

local bus

A bus that has a direct connection to the processor for the high-speed transfer of data

Local intranet sites

Web sites that are part of your company's or organization's intranet

local user

An individual who uses a computer that is not connected to a network

logical drive

A drive name, such as C: and D:, assigned to all or part of the storage space on a hard disk

logical structure

The file system used on a disk

long filename

A folder or file name that is up to 255 characters in length, or that may contain spaces and more than one period

lossless compression

A type of compression used for graphics files that reduces the size of the file without any loss of detail in the image

lossy compression

A type of compression used for graphics file that reduces the size of the file by removing some of the detail of the image

lost chain

A sequence of lost clusters that once belonged to a single file

lost cluster

A cluster on a disk that contains data that once belonged to a program, document, or some other type of file, such as a temporary file, but which is no longer associated with that file

LPR Port (Line Printer Remote)

A type of port used on servers that communicate with host servers, such as UNIX computers, using RFC 1179 (Line Printer Daemon Protocol)

LPT1:, LPT2:, and LPT3:

The device names for the first, second, and third parallel ports in a computer system

M

MAPI (Messaging Application Program Interface)

A programming interface for sending e-mail using a Windows application and for attaching a document to the e-mail message

Master Boot Record (MBR)

The first sector on a hard disk that contains a Hard Disk Partition Table with information on the partitions on a disk

Master File Table (MFT)

A table that tracks information about folders and files on an NTFS volume or disk, as well as the volume itself

media descriptor

A byte in the File Allocation Table that identifies the type of disk

media pool

A collection of removable media with the same management policies

megabyte (MB, M, or meg)

1,024 kilobytes, or approximately one million bytes of storage space on a disk or in memory

memory

A set of storage locations where instructions and data are stored while you use a microcomputer

memory dump file

A file that contains the contents of system memory, that is derived from the paging file after a system failure, and which is used for troubleshooting the problem that occurred

memory leak

A gradual decrease in available memory caused by program code that remains in memory after you exit an application and that ties up that memory so the operating system and other applications cannot use it

memory module

A circuit board that contains memory chips (or RAM chips) and that plugs into a socket on the motherboard

memory resources

Specific regions of memory allocated to a hardware device

menu

A list of choices or options that represent different types of command operations from which you can choose

menu bar

A component of a graphical user interface with a list of choices or options that represent different types of command operations from which you can choose

metafile

A file that contains a list of commands that Windows XP can process to draw a graphic image

metastring

A code, such as PG, which, when used with the Prompt command, instructs Cmd.exe how to display the command prompt

MHz (MegaHertz)

Millions of cycles per second

Microsoft Management Console (MMC)

A Windows XP tool that allows you to open, use, create, and save consoles, or administrative snap-ins, for managing the hardware, software, and network components of your computer system

Microsoft's Knowledge Base

A Microsoft Web site that has hundreds of thousands of articles which provide you with information on how to use features and troubleshoot problems with Microsoft software

monochrome monitor

A monitor that can only display one foreground color and one background color, such as white, amber, or green text on a black background, or black text on a white background

most frequently used programs list

An area located on the lower left side of the Start menu that contains a list of your most frequently used programs

motherboard

The main board, or system board, located within the system unit and that contains the processor, memory modules, expansion slots, and electronic circuitry

mounted drive (or volume mount point)

A drive that is attached to an empty folder on an NTFS volume

MS-DOS (Microsoft Disk Operating System)

The brand of DOS used on IBM-compatibles

MS-DOS path (also called **full path**)

A notation that identifies the exact location of a file or folder on a disk by including a reference to the drive and folders that lead to the folder or file and, if necessary, a file's name

MS-DOS startup disk

A Windows XP floppy disk that contains the core operating system files for booting a computer from drive A

MSN (The Microsoft Network)

Microsoft's online service, or ISP

multimedia

The integration of video, audio, animation, graphics, and text

multipartite virus

A class of computer viruses that can infect both the boot sector of a disk as well as program files

multiple-boot configuration

A computer that has multiple operating systems installed on it, and during booting, you can choose which of the operating systems to load and use

multitasking

The simultaneous or concurrent use of more than one application

multithreading

The execution of multiple units of program code within the same application

N

nanosecond (ns)

Billionths of a second

native data

The original copy of an object embedded in a document, plus the data needed to edit and maintain the object

network bridge

A Windows XP feature that enables you to create a network which consists of connections

between computers using different types of network adapters

Network Diagnostics

A utility for scanning your computer system and compiling information about your network

node

A device that is connected to a network and that can communicate with other network devices

non-contiguous clusters

Clusters of a file scattered across the surface of a disk (and therefore not stored adjacent to each other)

non-Plug and Play device or **legacy device**

A hardware device that does not support the Plug and Play standards defined by Microsoft Corporation and hardware manufacturers and that requires manual installation, including in many cases, setting jumpers or DIP switches

normal backup

A type of backup that marks the start of a backup cycle and that includes all or part of the contents of a hard disk (in other words, all selected files). Backup utilities turn off the Archive bit of all backed-up files after the backup is complete

notification area

(1) The area of the taskbar that displays the current time as well as icons for open programs loaded during booting; (2) The area on the taskbar once known as the system tray

novice

The individual who extends an invitation to another person for a Remote Assistance session

NTFS (NT File System)

The native file system for Windows XP and for the Windows NT product line that uses a Master File Table (MFT) to track information about folders and files on disk, that supports larger storage media than FAT16 or FAT32 (up to 2 TB), that supports long filenames and object-oriented

applications that treat objects with user-defined and system-defined properties, that supports disk compression, encryption, and indexing, and that supports the use of security permissions for folders and files

null file

A file that is zero bytes in size and that is used by Windows XP to create a specific type of file (such as a bitmap image)

object

A component of the graphical user interface and your computer system, such as a hardware device, software application, folder, file, document, or part of a document

object embedding

The process of copying data or an object from a document in one application to another document produced by another application and retaining information on the application that originally produced the object

object linking

The process of copying an object from the document of an application to a document produced by another application and maintaining a reference to the original object

Object Linking and Embedding (OLE)

A technology that enables you to use data from a document produced by one application in a document produced by another application, and retain either a link to the original data or a reference to the application that produced the original data

object-oriented operating system

An operating system that treats each component of the computer as an object and that manages all the actions and properties associated with an object

Offline Web page

A Web page that is stored locally on your computer so that you can view the Web page without being connected to the Internet

OLE server (or **server application**)

The application that provides the data (or object) when embedding or creating a link in a compound document

on-disk catalog

A catalog stored on your hard disk drive

online profiling

A process for identifying and accumulating information on users' preferences and interests with the use of cookies, Web bugs, and other surveillance tools

online service

A business or company that provides fee-based, dial-up access to information stored on its computer system(s) as well as Internet access

on-media catalog

A catalog stored on backup media

OnNow

The term Microsoft uses for "a PC that is always on but appears off and responds immediately to user or other requests"

OpenType font

(1) An outline font that relies on the use of commands to draw lines and curves, (2) A scalable font technology that is an extension of the TrueType font technology

operating environment

A software product that performs the same functions as an operating system, except for configuring and customizing a computer system and handling the storage and retrieval of data in files on a disk

operating system

A software product that manages the basic processes that occur within a computer, coordinates the interaction of hardware and software so that each component

works together, and provides support for the use of other software, such as application software

operating system prompt

A set of characters displayed on the monitor in a command-line environment to provide an interface for interacting with the computer

orphaned file

A file that has a valid file record segment in the Master File Table, but which is not listed in any directory

output redirection operator (>)

An operator that redirects output to another device, such as a port or a .txt file, instead of to the monitor

packet

A set of data (such as part of a file), as well as a source address and destination address, sent from one location to another over the Internet or other network

page

(1) A segment of memory 4 KB in size that can be swapped to disk by Windows XP; (2) Output displayed on the monitor or within a window (a logical concept rather than a physical concept)

page fault error (PFE)

An error condition that occurs when Windows XP is not able to find data in the paging file

paged output

Output displayed one window or one screen at a time (hence, a page)

Pages/sec

A System Monitor performance counter that measures the number of pages read from, or written to, disk for hard page faults, and therefore is useful for monitoring paging activity

paging file

A hidden system file (Pagefile.sys) created on a hard disk by Windows XP for use as supplemental RAM (called virtual memory)

palette

A set of colors used by either an application or by the operating system

parallel port

A port or connection for transmitting data between the processor and another component eight bits, or one byte, at a time

parallel transmission

The simultaneous transmission of eight bits down eight separate data lines in a cable. Compare with serial transmission

parameter

An optional or required item of data for a command in a command-line environment

parent directory

The directory located one level above the current directory

partition

(1) All or part of the physical hard disk that is set aside for a drive or set of logical drives; (2) A subdivision of a physical disk that functions as if it were a separate physical disk; (3) To subdivide a hard disk into one or more logical drives, either for storing different types of files or for installing different operating systems

path

A notation used to identify the location of a folder or file. For example, C:\Windows is the path for the Windows folder on drive C, and C:\Windows\Explorer.exe is the path for the Explorer program file

PCI (Peripheral Component Interconnect)

An older local bus technology that supports bus clock speeds of 33 or 66 MHz and data transfer speeds of 133 MBps

PCL (Printer Control Language)

A page description language developed by Hewlett Packard for their laser and inkjet printers

peer-to-peer network or **workgroup**

A simple type of network in which each computer is equal and can access other computers to which it is connected and share hardware, such as the same printer(s), hard disk drives, removable storage devices (such as CD-ROM, Zip, and DVD drives) and other drives as well as software, folders, and files (there is no server that manages network resources and provides network users access to those resources)

performance counter

An item of data associated with a performance object, such as Available Bytes for the Memory performance object

performance object

A logical collection of performance counters associated with a resource or service that you can monitor, such as memory

permission

A rule that determines which users can access an object and how they can access that object

per-session cookie

A temporary cookie that expires and that is deleted when you close Internet Explorer

persistent cookie

A cookie that remains on your computer, and that can be read by the Web site that created it when you next visit that Web site

pinned items list

An area located in the upper left corner of the Start menu that contains a list of programs that always remain on the Start menu

pipe operator

A symbol (|) used between two commands in a command-line environment to indicate that the output of the first command is to be used as the input for the second command

pipe or **piping**

To use the output of one command as the input for another command in a command-line environment

pipeline

A command that uses a pipe operator to transfer the output of one command so that it becomes the input for another command in a command-line environment

pixel or **pel** (picture element)

One or more dots, or points, which are treated as one unit on the monitor

pixel tag

An image that is created by an HTML tag, that is one pixel wide by one pixel tall on a Web page, and that defines the position of a Web bug on the Web page

PJL (Printer Job Language)

A printer command language developed by Hewlett Packard to control printers at the print-job level

platform

A microprocessor architecture, or system that relies on a specific operating system

platter

A disk within a hard disk drive that is made of aluminum or glass and that provides all or part of the storage capacity of the entire hard disk drive

Plug and Play (PnP)

A set of specifications for designing hardware so that an operating system can automatically detect and configure the device either during booting or (in some cases) when the computer is already on, with little or no intervention on your part

PNG

A graphics file format similar to the GIF file format, but which achieves a slightly greater compression, and which may eventually replace the GIF file format since it improves on the GIF file format in several ways, and is patent-free, therefore requiring no license for its use

point size

The height of characters in a font, measured in ½nds of an inch

pointer

The full path of the file with the original object referenced by a link in a compound document

port

(1) A connection for attaching a cable from a peripheral device, such as a monitor, printer, or modem, to circuit boards connected to the main system board; (2) An electronic pathway or connection for passing data between the computer's processor and its peripherals

port address or **I/O address**

A unique memory address for a hardware device, such as a port or disk drive, that handles I/O (input/output)

Postscript

A page description language that provides information to a printer on how to lay out a page on a sheet of paper

power scheme

A combination of settings that Windows XP uses to manage power usage on your computer

power user

A more advanced user who is familiar with different strategies for using a computer system and its software, and more often than not, chooses the more direct approach

Power Users

A type of network domain user group where the members can install software that does not modify the operating system, customize or make changes to some system settings and system resources (such as power options), and create and manage local user accounts and groups

preemptive multitasking

An operating mode in which the Windows operating system assigns priorities to the processes that it manages, and decides at any given point in time whether to take control away from, or give control to, a process

presentation data

The data needed to display and print an embedded or linked object

preview area

An area on a property sheet that displays the effects of the current settings or changes to the current settings

primary mouse button

The mouse button that you use to select, click, and drag objects as well as position an insertion point marker or cursor in a document (left mouse button for right-handed individuals)

primary partition

A partition on a basic disk (a physical disk) that contains the boot files for loading the operating system and that is therefore designated as the active partition

print queue

A list of all print jobs or documents that are scheduled to print, along with information about each print job, such as the document name, the status of the document, the owner (or user name of the person who submitted the print job), the number of pages that have printed and the total number of pages, the document size (in kilobytes), the time and date the print job was submitted, and the port used by the printer

printer buffer

The RAM in a printer that holds the document currently being printed

Printer Control Language (PCL)

A page description language developed by Hewlett Packard for their laser and inkjet prints

Printer Job Language (PJL)

A printer command language developed by Hewlett Packard to control printers at the print-job level

printer pooling

An option for printing to two or more identical physical printers that act as if they were a single printer (print jobs are sent to the first available printer in the pool)

process

An executable program, such as Explorer, Microsoft Word, and Task Manager itself; a service, such as the Print Spooler service which handles the printing of files in the background; or a subsystem, such as the one for Windows XP applications

property

A characteristic or setting of an object

property sheet

A group of related settings displayed on a sheet in a dialog box

protected mode

A processor operating mode in which the processor can address more than 1 MB of memory, support the use of virtual memory (a technique for supplementing memory by using unused storage space on a hard disk as memory), provide memory protection features for applications (so that one application does not attempt to use the memory space allocated to another application), use 32-bit (rather than 16-bit) processing, and support multitasking

protocols

The rules and conventions for transmitting data over a network

Q

question mark wildcard (?)

A symbol used as part of a file specification to substitute for a single character in the filename or file extension

Quick format

A type of format in which the formatting program erases the contents of the File Allocation Tables and directory file on a floppy disk, thereby erasing any reference to the files stored on the disk, but that does not lay down new tracks and sectors and that does not verify the integrity of each sector on a previously formatted disk

R

RAM drive or **virtual disk**

A portion of memory, or RAM, that acts and functions like a real disk drive

Random-Access Memory (RAM)

(1) The predominant type of memory within a computer; (2) Temporary, or volatile, computer memory used to store program instructions, input, processing, and output; (3) Work space for working with software and documents

Readme file

A text file (often named Readme.doc, Readme.txt, or Readme.1st) that contains more up-to-date information, including troubleshooting information, for newly installed hardware and software

Read-Only attribute

An attribute assigned to a file by the operating system to indicate that you can read from, but not write to, the file

Read-Only file

A file that you can read from, but not write to

Read-Only Memory (ROM)

Permanent memory which includes instructions for starting the computer system, for testing the system components at startup (the POST, or Power-On Self-Test), and for locating and transferring the operating system software from disk into memory

read-only mode

A diagnostic mode of operation in which the command-line Check Disk utility checks a drive and, if it finds errors, reports the presence of these errors and simulates how it would correct the problem

Recovery Console

A command-line tool designed for advanced users who need to troubleshoot problems with booting, the Registry, Windows XP, or the hard disk

refresh rate

The number of times that the image on the screen is redrawn by the video card

registered file or **registered file type**

A file that is associated with an application on your computer via its file extension

registration file

A file with the file extension "reg" that contains a backup of the entire Registry, or a specific subtree or key within the Registry

Registry

A database that consists of a set of files where Windows XP stores your computer's hardware, software, network, security, OLE information, user settings or profiles, and property settings for folders and programs

Registry path

The path leading to a specific key in the Windows Registry, such as My Computer \HKEY_CURRENT_USER\ Software\Microsoft\Windows\ CurrentVersion\Explorer\ Advanced

relative path

A path that makes assumptions about the location of a folder or file relative to where you are working, such as the current drive or the current folder

Remote Assistance

A tool that permits an expert using Windows XP Professional or Windows XP Home Edition to access another computer using Windows XP Professional or Windows XP Home Edition and provide a novice with troubleshooting support or assistance with a project

Remote Desktop

A remote assistance tool for accessing a computer running Windows XP Professional (called the remote computer) from another computer that has any version of Windows (called the client computer) so that you can

troubleshoot problems or assist someone with a project

Removable Storage

A Windows XP tool for tracking removable storage media, such as tapes, and for managing the corresponding hardware

replaceable parameter

A symbol, such as %1, that acts as a placeholder and identifies where Windows XP should substitute the name of the current file (or another piece of information) to complete a command

Replicator

A type of network domain user group in which the members can replicate files across a network domain

reserved names

Drive names or device names that cannot be used as directory names or filenames

reserved symbols

Symbols that have special meaning to the operating system and that cannot be used as part of a filename

residential gateway

A hardware device that connects your home or small office network to the Internet so that the networked computers can share a single cable modem or DSL Internet connection

resizing buttons

(1) Buttons on the right side of a title bar for minimizing, maximizing, restoring, and closing a window; (2) Buttons on the right side of a menu bar or document window for minimizing, maximizing, restoring, and closing a document window

resource conflict, hardware conflict or **device conflict**

A problem that results when two hardware devices attempt to share the same resource, such as the same IRQ (interrupt request line)

Resource Kit

A Windows XP Professional reference book (published by

Microsoft) which contains information on the deployment of Windows, desktop management, security, networking, interoperability, and troubleshooting

restore

To copy files and rebuild folders (if necessary) on a hard disk using a backup set

restore point

A snapshot of the Registry as well as information on the system state created by System Restore (essentially, a "picture" of the state of your computer at a given point in time)

Restricted sites

Web sites that could potentially damage your computer or its data

Restricted User

A user who is part of the Users Group and who cannot install software or change system settings

Rich Text Document

A document format that includes character formatting and tab codes that many types of word processing applications recognize

right

A task that a user is permitted to perform on a computer or within a domain

RISC (Reduced Instruction Set Computing)

A processor design that uses a small set of simple instructions for processing data. Compare with CISC

robustness

The stability associated with an operating system and the system resources that it manages and protects

rollback

The process by which Windows Installer keeps track of all the changes made to your computer when you install an application so that it can restore your computer to its original state in the event a problem develops

ROM-BIOS (Read Only Memory Basic Input Output System)

A computer chip that contains the program routines for the

Power-On Self Test, for identifying and configuring Plug and Play devices, for communicating with peripheral devices, and for locating and loading the operating system

root directory

(1) The first directory created on a disk during the formatting of the disk; (2) The command-line or DOS name for the top-level folder on a disk

root folder

The folder at the top of the folder hierarchy in the Folders toolbar

routine

A program executed during the booting process to check the availability and functioning of hardware components or to locate and load the operating system from disk

Run-Length Encoding (RLE)

A compressed bitmapped file format

S

Safe Mode

A boot option in which Windows XP loads the minimum set of files and drivers needed for the mouse, monitor, keyboard, mass storage, and video as well as default system services

Safe Mode with Command Prompt

A boot option that is similar to Safe Mode, except that Windows XP boots to a command prompt instead of booting to the desktop so that you can use a command-line operating environment to troubleshoot system problems

Safe Mode with Networking

A boot option that is similar to Safe Mode, except that Windows XP establishes network connections so that you can troubleshoot a problem that requires network access

saturation

The amount of gray in the color, and therefore a determinant of the purity of a color

scan code

A code that is produced from pressing a key on the keyboard and that is used by the operating system to determine the character to display on the monitor

scheduled task

A task stored in the Scheduled Tasks folder that identifies a program scheduled to run at a specified date and time or under a specific condition, such as at booting

scrap

A file with an OLE object that Windows XP automatically creates when you drag all or part of a file onto the desktop

screen font

A typeface designed for display on a computer monitor's screen

screen resolution

The sharpness and distinctness of an image on the screen determined by the number of pixels displayed horizontally across the monitor and vertically down the monitor by the video display card

screen saver

A program that Windows XP automatically starts if you have not used the mouse or keyboard for a certain period of time, and that usually displays some type of moving image on the monitor

SCSI (Small Computer System Interface) (pronounced "scuzzy")

A parallel interface standard used by Macintosh Computers, PCs, and Unix systems for attaching peripheral devices to computers

SDRAM (Synchronous Dynamic Random Access Memory)

A common type of memory technology that synchronizes itself with and supports higher CPU bus speeds of up to 100 to 133 MHz

secondary mouse button

The mouse that you use to right-click an object (right mouse button for right-handed individuals)

sector

(1) An equal subdivision of a track that provides storage space for data; (2) The basic unit of storage space on a floppy disk or hard disk that can hold 512 bytes of data

security descriptor

Information attached to an object about the owner of a directory or file, permissions granted to users and groups for that directory or file, and information on security events to be audited for that directory or file

selection script

A type of file that contains settings for a backup job

self-extracting executable file

A file that contains one or more files stored in a compressed format, plus a program for extracting the contents of the self-extracting executable file itself

separator

A period in a filename that separates the main part of the filename from the file extension

separator page or **banner page**

A page that is printed before each print job, and that identifies who sent the document to the printer, and the date and time of printing

serial port

A port or connection for sending information between the processor and another device one bit at a time

serial transmission

The process of transmitting only one bit (out of 8 bits for each byte of data) at a time down one line in a cable. Compare with parallel transmission

server

A high-performance computer that manages a computer network with the use of network operating system software, and that provides access to shared resources, such as hardware, software, and files on the network

server application (or OLE server)

The application that provides the data (or object) when embedding or creating a link in a compound document

service

A program, routine, or process that provides support to other programs

service pack

A set of updates for an operating system

service software

Software that provides file and print sharing on Microsoft networks

Setup Disks

(1) A set of six Windows XP disks that allow you to boot your computer from drive A and either install Windows XP, repair your computer by using the Recovery Console, or restore your computer using Automated System Recovery (Windows XP Professional only); (2) A set of four Windows 2000 disks that allow you to boot your computer from drive A and install Windows 2000, or repair your computer by using an Emergency Repair Disk to restore Windows 2000 settings

Setup Information File

A file that contains settings Windows XP uses to install support for a hardware device or for software

Setup log file

A file that contains information about the installation of Windows XP or other software

shell

The interface provided by a program so that the user can communicate with the program. In the case of Windows XP, the graphical user interface is the shell that the user interacts with so as to communicate user requests or commands into actions performed by the operating system

shortcut

(1) A special type of file that acts as a direct link to another object on your local computer, a network computer, or the Web using the full path or address for that object; (2) A feature that allows you to quickly access an object within your computer; (3) A file that points to an object, application, or document

shortcut menu

A menu that opens when you right-click an object, that displays menu options or actions appropriate to that object, and that provides access to the properties of an object

skin

A design scheme for changing the look of Windows Media Player

slack

Part of a cluster allocated to a file, but not used to store data, and therefore, wasted space

smart card

A plastic card about the size of a credit card which includes an embedded microchip for use with applications and for storing data, such as credentials used to authenticate a user, personal information, and cash balances

snap-in

A management tool or plug-in provided by Microsoft or some other software vendor

software interrupt

A signal from an application to the operating system to assist with an operation, such as saving a file to disk

source

The subdirectory, files, or file you want to copy

source application

The application that provides the data (or object) when embedding or creating a link in a compound document

source disk

The floppy disk that contains data you want to copy

source document

The document that contains the data or object that you want to copy to another document

spool

To store print jobs on disk until the printer is ready to process the print request

spool file

A temporary file that contains a processed print job request, complete with printer formatting codes

spooling

The process of storing a document processed for printing in a temporary file on disk and transferring the document to the printer in the background

stairstep effect

An effect in which a diagonal or curved line in a character looks uneven

Standard Buttons toolbar

A toolbar that is found in folder windows and that contains buttons for performing common tasks

Standard TCP/IP port

A port that supports the TCP/IP protocol, and that is used to connect remote printers

Standard User

A user who is part of the Power Users Group and who can modify computer settings and install software

standard VGA display mode

A resolution of 640x480 (a low resolution mode)

Standby mode

A state in which hardware devices, such as the monitor and hard disk, are turned off and the computer is placed in a low-power state

Start Windows Normally

A full boot (the default boot option)

Startup Disk

A Windows 95, Windows 98, and Windows Me boot disk that contains the core Windows operating system files for booting from a floppy disk in drive A, and contains troubleshooting utilities. The Windows 98 and Windows Me Startup Disk also contains device drivers for accessing a CD drive and for creating a RAM drive

startup environment

Configuration settings that specify which operating system to start and how to start each operating system

static cursor

A mouse pointer shape that does not change in appearance

STOP error

An error that can result from a problem with software or hardware, such as invalid program instructions, poorly designed device drivers, incompatible hardware, failing hardware, or incorrectly configured hardware

string

(1) A sequence of characters; (2) A non-numeric value that is treated exactly as it is typed or shown

subdirectory

(1) A directory that is subordinate to the root directory or to another subdirectory; (2) The command-line or DOS term for a subfolder

subfolder

(1) A folder contained within another folder; (2) A subdirectory

subtree

A branch of the Registry tree represented by a folder icon, and used to store a group of related Registry settings, such as the HKEY_CLASSES_ROOT subtree that contains information on registered file types

surface scan

(1) A part of the formatting process in which the formatting program records dummy data onto each sector of a disk and reads it back to determine the reliability of each sector; (2) The phase during which the operating system examines the surface of a disk for defects and, if necessary, mark clusters with defective sectors as unusable

swap file

A hidden system file (Pagefile.sys) created on a hard disk by Windows XP for use as supplemental RAM

switch

An optional parameter or item of data that is used with a command to modify the way in which a program operates

symmetric multiprocessing

A computer that supports the simultaneous processing of programs or tasks by multiple microprocessors

syntax

The proper format for entering a command, including how to spell the command, how to use required parameters (such as a drive) and optional parameters (such as a switch), and the spacing between the command, required parameters, and optional parameters

Sysprep

A utility for creating a disk image of one computer, and then copying that disk image to other computers

system architecture

The internal design and coding of an operating system

system area

The area of a disk that contains the boot sector, File Allocation Tables, and directory table on a FAT volume

System attribute

An attribute assigned by the operating system to a folder or file to identify the folder or file as an operating system folder or file

system board

The main board, or motherboard, with the microprocessor, memory modules, expansion slots, and electronic circuitry

system bus

The network of electronic circuitry (data, address, and control lines) responsible for transmitting data and signals between the processor and various components as well as storing information on the location of instructions and data in memory

system checkpoint

A point in time when the System Restore feature of Windows ME and Windows XP saves changes to system files, device drivers, and system settings on your computer system so that if you run into a problem later, you can "roll back" the computer system and restore it to an earlier working state

System Configuration Utility

A tool for deciding which startup configuration files, services, and programs to process or load during booting

system disk

A floppy disk that contains the core operating system files for booting a computer from drive A

system files

Files that Windows uses to load, configure, and run the operating system

system reset

A type of boot in which you press your computer's Reset button on the front of the system unit, or press Ctrl+Alt+Del, to restart your computer and, in the process, skip the Power-On Self-Test (POST)

System Restore

A Windows XP and Windows Me component that monitors changes to a computer system, that creates a restore point with information on the current system state and settings and changes to system files either automatically or when changes are made to your computer (such as updating the operating system, or installing new software), and that can roll back a computer to an earlier (or later) functioning state

System State

The operating system components that define the current state of the operating system, including Registry settings for user accounts, applications, hardware, and software, as well as files in the top-level folder and Windows folder that Windows XP needs to boot the computer

system unit

The unit that houses the main system board with the processor, memory modules, expansion slots, and electronic circuitry as well as circuit boards attached to the motherboard, disk drives, and the power supply

system volume

The partition that contains the hardware-specific files needed to load Windows XP—namely, NTLdr, Boot.ini, and Ntdetect.com

SYSVOL

A shared directory that stores the server copy of a domain's public files

T

tape drive

A backup drive unit in which you can insert high-capacity tapes that are similar in appearance and use to cassette tapes

Targa or **TGA**

A bitmap file format for 24-bit and 32-bit color images

target disk

The floppy disk that receives a duplicate copy of the contents of another floppy disk

taskbar

A component of the desktop that displays a Start button for starting programs or opening documents, that supports the use of toolbars, that displays buttons for currently open software applications, documents, and folder windows, and that contains a notification area with the current time and icons for programs loaded into memory during booting

taskbar grouping

A new Windows XP feature for providing access to all open documents of a certain type (such as Word documents) under one taskbar button

task-oriented view

A Windows XP view that uses dynamic menus to display links to common tasks and to other locations on your computer

task-switching

The ability to switch from one open task, or process, in one window to another task in another window

TCP/IP (Transmission Control Protocol/Internet Protocol)

A set of networking protocols that determine how computers communicate, how they connect to networks, and how they route data

template

A file that contains the structure, formatting, and some of the actual contents of a specific type of document, such as a spreadsheet for analyzing a company's performance and projected growth

temporary file

A file used by the operating system, an application, or a utility to store a copy of the data that it is currently processing until it completes the operation

Temporary Internet files

(1) Files downloaded from Web sites by Internet Explorer and stored in the Temporary Internet Files folder for your user account, (2) Internet cache

terabyte (TB)

1,024 gigabytes, or approximately one trillion bytes of storage space on a disk or in memory

Text Document

A document format that contains unformatted text

text mode

A simple and fast video display mode for displaying text, including letters, numbers, symbols, and a small set of graphics characters using (usually) white characters on a black background

theme

A set of visual elements that are designed to provide a unified look for your desktop and user interface

third-party Web site

Another Web site that provides content to the Web site you're visiting

thrashing

Excessive paging

thread

A segment or unit of program code within an application that Windows can execute at the same time it is executing the same segment or other segments of program code within the same program

Tiles view

A new Windows XP folder view that organizes the contents of a folder in groups by file type

timer bar

The red vertical bar in the System Monitor pane that slowly moves to the right as values are sampled, plotted on the graph, and added to the value bar

title bar

The bar at the top of a window that identifies the name of the window, or the name of an open application (and perhaps also includes a document name)

toggle key

A key that alternates between two related uses each time you press the key

top-level folder

(1) The first folder created on a disk by an operating system or a formatting utility; (2) The root directory

track

A concentric recording band on a hard disk or floppy disk for storing data

Trojan horses

Programs that appear to be bona fide programs, but which are designed to retrieve information from your computer, such as user names and passwords, and then transmit that information to others who can then later access your computer via an Internet connection

True Color

A color setting of a video display adapter that allows it to display 2^{24} or 16,777,216 colors, or that uses 32 bits to display 16,777,216 colors with a transparency feature

TrueType

A scalable font technology developed by Apple and later adapted by Microsoft for use with Windows

Trusted sites

Web sites that you trust not to damage your computer or its data

typeface

The design style of the characters that constitute a font

UDF (Universal Disk Format)

The file system which is used for DVD and CD drives and which provides support for long file names (greater than 64 characters) and a multi-tiered folder structure

UNC (Universal Naming Convention) path

A convention and notation that identifies a server, computer (such as \\Windows XP System), printer, or other shared resource on a network

Unicode

A coding scheme that can represent 65,536 character combinations, or all the characters within the alphabets of most of the world's languages

Unicode Text Document

A document format that includes text from any of the world's writing systems

Uniform Resource Locator (URL)

The address of a specific site on the World Wide Web and a page

or document at the Web site. For example, www.microsoft.com is the URL, or Web address, for Microsoft Corporation

uninstaller

A software product that monitors the installation of a program so that you can more fully uninstall that program later

Uninterruptible Power Supply (UPS)

A device that relies on a battery backup to provide power to a computer for a short interval of time (such as a few minutes) so that you can save your work and shut down your computer. The UPS device can signal the operating system about a critical power event, such as a power failure

uniprocessor

A computer with a single processor

universal serial bus (USB)

A high-speed communications port

unregistered file

A file that is not associated with a specific application

user interface

The combination of hardware and software that lets you interact with a computer

user mode

Working in the Microsoft Management Console (MMC) with an existing console

Users

A type of group user who cannot modify the operating system, its settings, or data belonging to other users

utility

A program included with operating system software for performing common types of tasks, such as searching the hard disk for files that can be safely deleted, or for monitoring or optimizing the performance of your computer and its hard disk

value bar

The area in the System Monitor pane (above the legend and below the graph) that lists the last value, average value, minimum value, and maximum value for the performance counter selected in the legend

value entry

An entry in the Registry that consists of a **value name** (a name assigned to a setting), its data type, and its **value data** (the setting itself)

VFAT (Virtual File Allocation Table)

A Windows adaptation of the DOS File Allocation Table that allows for faster disk access and that also supports the use of long filenames

VGA

Video graphics array

video card or **video adapter**

A video display card within the system unit that controls the display of the image on the monitor

virtual device driver

A special type of device driver that Windows uses when it operates in protected mode and exploits the full capabilities of 80386 and later processors to address memory above 1 MB, provide memory protection features, and support multitasking. See VxD

virtual disk or **RAM drive**

A portion of memory, or RAM, that acts and functions like a real disk drive

Virtual DOS Machine (VDM)

A Windows operating environment for DOS applications that emulates the type of environment found under the DOS operating system

virtual drive

(1) A portion of RAM that acts and functions like a real disk drive; (2) A logical storage device created by assigning a drive name to a folder (such as a network drive)

virtual memory

(1) Space on a hard disk that an operating system uses as extra memory to supplement the memory available in RAM; (2) The combination of RAM and the paging file used to provide memory for programs

Virtual Private Network (VPN)

The use of public and private networks to connect to a remote access server through the Internet or another network

visual editing or **in-place editing**

The process of editing an object in a compound document within the current application's application window using the menus and tools of the application that produced the original object

visual editing window

The window in a compound document that contains an embedded object which you can edit with tools of the original application that produced the object

volatile

Dependent on the availability of power, and therefore temporary (such as RAM)

volume

A logical storage device that consists of all or part of a hard disk, that uses its own file system, that is assigned a drive name, and that can span multiple disks

volume label or **volume name**

A name or electronic label assigned to a disk, such as a hard disk, DVD, CD, or floppy disk

volume mount point or **mounted drive**

A drive that is attached to an empty folder on an NTFS volume

volume shadow copy

A feature that enables a Backup utility to back up files even if Windows XP is currently writing to them

VRAM (Video RAM)

Memory on the video display card

VxD

A virtual device driver for managing a hardware or software resource for more than one application

W

wallpaper

A graphic image that appears on, or overlays, the desktop

warm boot

A type of boot in which you press your computer's Reset button on the front of the system, or simultaneously press Ctrl+Alt+Del, to restart your computer and, in the process, skip the Power-On Self-Test (POST)

Web bug or **Web beacon**

An object, such as an image or banner advertising, embedded on a Web page, and created by an HTML tag that references another Web site from which part of the content of the Web page you are viewing is derived. The third-party Web site can then place a cookie on your computer even though you never visited that site

Web view or **Web style**

(1) A Windows user interface and operating environment that allows you to work on your local computer in the same way that you work on the Web and that treats objects on your local computer like hyperlinks on a Web page; (2) A Web browser view

wildcard

A symbol used in a file specification to select a group of files

Win16 application

An application, such as dBASE III Plus, Lotus 1-2-3 Release 4.0 for Windows, and Office 4.3,

originally designed for use with Windows 3.x with a 16-bit operating system

Win32 application

A Windows XP, Windows 2000, Windows Me, Windows 98, Windows NT Workstation 4.0, or Windows 95 application, such as Office XP, Office 2000, Office 97, Office 95, and Microsoft Works 6.0 that are designed for a 32-bit operating system

window

A work area on the screen defined by borders and designed to organize your view of applications, documents, drives, folders, and files

Windows environment

An area of memory that stores environment variables and their settings and that Windows XP, applications, and utilities check for settings

Windows metafile (WMF)

A 16-bit metafile with GDI (graphics device interface) drawing commands for producing graphical objects, such as circles and lines, under Windows 3.x and later versions of Windows

Windows Task Manager

A tool for shutting down non-responding programs, viewing loading processes, monitoring the performance of a computer, and providing information about network performance

wizard

A program tool that asks you a series of questions about what you want to do and the settings you want to use, then completes the operation or task for you

workgroup or **peer-to-peer network**

A simple type of network in which each computer is equal and can access other computers to which it is connected and share hardware, such as the same printer(s), hard disk drives, removable storage devices (such as CD-ROM, Zip, and DVD drives), and other drives as well as software, folders, and files (there is no server that manages network resources and provides network users access to those resources)

working set

The physical memory allocated to and used by a process

WOW (Win16 on Win32) subsystem

A component of Windows XP that emulates a 16-bit Windows operating environment so that Win16 applications originally designed for Windows 3.x can run as a Win32 process in a VDM (Virtual DOS Machine)

X

x86-based computer

A computer based on the architecture of the Intel 8086 processor

XML (Extensible Markup Language)

A language that describes the layout of a Web page and your ability to interact with that content, and also can describe data to support the transfer and sharing of information

INDEX

TASK	PAGE #	RECOMMENDED METHOD
Administrative Tools, add to the Start menu and All Programs menu the option for using	10.15	See Reference Window "Adding Administrative Tools to the Start and All Programs Menus"
All Programs menu, create a group folder on	4.39	See Reference Window "Creating a Group Folder on the Programs Menu"
All Programs menu, delete a group folder or application shortcut from	4.58	Right-click the group folder or application shortcut, click Delete
Application, create a shortcut to	4.27	See Reference Window "Creating a Shortcut to an Application"
Attribute command, use	14.45	See Reference Window "Viewing File Attributes from the Command Prompt"
Automated System Recovery Wizard, use the Windows XP Professional	8.38	See Reference Window "Using the Automated System Recovery Wizard"
Boot sequence, change	8.08	See Reference Window "Changing the Boot Sequence"
Boot.ini file, display information on	14.27	See Reference Window "Displaying Information on the Boot.ini File from the Command Prompt (Windows XP Professional Only)"
BootCfg command, use the Windows XP Professional	14.27	See Reference Window "Displaying Information on the Boot.ini File from the Command Prompt (Windows XP Professional Only)"
Briefcase action, change	4.55	Right-click the Update Briefcase action arrow, click Replace or Skip
Briefcase, copy a folder to	4.50	See Reference Window "Copying a Folder to a Briefcase"
Briefcase, create a new	4.48	Right-click desktop or folder window background, point to New, click Briefcase
Briefcase, modify a file in	4.49	See Reference Window "Modifying a File in a Briefcase"
Briefcase, update files in	4.57	See Reference Window "Updating Files in a Briefcase"
Change Directory command, use	14.41	See Reference Window "Changing Directories"
Check Disk command, use	7.22	See Reference Window "Using Check Disk from a Command Prompt Window"
Classic style, change to	1.37	See Reference Window "Changing to Windows Classic Style"
Clipboard, copy an image of the desktop, active window, or dialog box to	1.75	See Reference Window "Copying and Pasting the Image of a Window or Dialog Box into a Document"

TASK	PAGE #	RECOMMENDED METHOD
Clipboard, paste an image of the desktop, active window, or dialog box from	1.75	See Reference Window "Copying and Pasting the Image of a Window or Dialog Box into a Document"
CLSIDs, locate information in the Registry on	13.26	See Reference Window "Locating Information on CLSIDs"
CMOS, open	8.03	During booting, press the key or keys for opening the Setup utility
Collection of drives, folders, files, or shortcuts, select	4.38	Press and hold down the Ctrl key while you point to and select each object
Color command, use	14.14	See Reference Window "Changing the Console Colors in a Command Prompt Window"
Color depth setting, change	2.55	See Reference Window "Changing the Color Depth Setting"
Command history, display	14.16	See Reference Window "Recalling Commands from the Command History"
Command in a Command Prompt window, repeat or recall	14.16	See Reference Window "Recalling Commands from the Command History"
Command Prompt window or screen, clear	14.17	Type CLS and press the Enter key
Command Prompt window, close	14.06	See Reference Window "Opening and Closing a Command Prompt Window"
Command Prompt window, open	14.06	See Reference Window "Opening and Closing a Command Prompt Window"
Command reference list, display	14.24	See Reference Window "Displaying a Command Reference List from the Command Prompt"
Computer, navigate	1.72	See Reference Window "Navigating Your Computer"
Computer, view information about	9.39	See Reference Window "Viewing Information About Your Computer"
Computer, view properties of	1.73	Click Start button, right-click My Computer, click Properties
Console colors, change the Command Prompt window's	14.14	See Reference Window "Changing the Console Colors in a Command Prompt Window"
Copy command, use	14.50	See Reference Window "Copying Files from the Command Prompt"
Desktop, copy and paste an image of	1.75	See Reference Window "Copying and Pasting the Image of a Window or Dialog Box into a Document"
Details view, change to	1.65	Click View, click Details

TASK	PAGE #	RECOMMENDED METHOD
Device Manager, view the hardware tree in	12.10	See Reference Window "Viewing the Hardware Tree in Device Manager"
Device properties, view	12.24	See Reference Window "Viewing Device Properties"
Dialog box, copy and paste an image of the active	1.75	See Reference Window "Copying and Pasting the Image of a Window or Dialog Box into a Document"
DIRCMD environment variable, create	14.57	See Reference Window "Creating a DIRCMD Environment Variable from the Command Prompt"
Directories, change	14.41	See Reference Window "Changing Directories"
Directory command switches, use	14.42	See Reference Window "Displaying a Directory Listing"
Directory command, use	14.42	See Reference Window "Displaying a Directory Listing"
Directory listing, display	14.42	See Reference Window "Displaying a Directory Listing"
Directory tree, display	14.33	See Reference Window "Displaying a Directory Tree from the Command Prompt"
Disk Cleanup Wizard, run	7.07	See Reference Window "Using the Disk Cleanup Wizard"
Disk Defragmenter, use	7.35	See Reference Window "Defragmenting a Disk"
Disk Management snap-in tool, open	7.38	See Reference Window "Opening the Disk Management Snap-In Tool
Disk quotas, set	7.44	See Reference Window "Setting Disk Quotas"
Disk, defragment	7.35	See Reference Window "Defragmenting a Disk"
Document, drag a file into	5.51	See Reference Window "Dragging a File into a Document Using the OLE Properties of the Taskbar"
Document, select a program for opening	4.54	Right-click file icon, point to Open With, click program
Drive, create a shortcut to	4.08	See Reference Window "Creating a Shortcut to a Drive"
Drives, change	14.51	See Reference Window "Changing Drives from the Command Prompt"
Embedded object, create or insert	5.25	See Reference Window "Inserting an Embedded Object in a Document"
Embedded object, edit	5.30	See Reference Window "Editing an Embedded Object"
Embedded object, view properties of	5.26	See Reference Window "Viewing Properties of an Embedded Object in WordPad"
Environment variables, use a Command Prompt window to view settings for	14.56	See Reference Window "Viewing Settings for Environment Variables from the Command Prompt"

TASK	PAGE #	RECOMMENDED METHOD
Environment variables, view settings for	10.39	See Reference Window "Viewing User and System Environment Variable Settings"
Error-checking tool, use	7.18	See Reference Window "Using the Error-Checking Tool"
File system, identify a drive's	3.28	See Reference Window "Identifying a Drive's File System"
File, create a shortcut to	4.23	See Reference Window "Creating a Shortcut to a File"
File, save	5.13	See Reference Window "Saving a File in a New or Existing Folder"
File, use a normal backup to restore	6.64	See Reference Window "Restoring a File from a Normal Backup or Incremental Backup"
File, use an incremental backup to restore	6.64	See Reference Window "Restoring a File from a Normal Backup or Incremental Backup"
File, use the Send To menu to copy	4.43	See Reference Window "Copying a File to a Folder Using the Send To Menu"
File, view attributes of	14.45	See Reference Window "Viewing File Attributes from the Command Prompt"
File, view properties of	3.43	See Reference Window "Viewing Properties of a Folder or File, or a Group of Folders or Files"
Files and folders, back up	6.33	See Reference Window "Using the Back or Restore Wizard to Back Up Selected Folders on Drive C to Floppy Disks"
Files and folders, restore	6.43	See Reference Window "Using the Backup or Restore Wizard to Restore Files from Floppy Disks"
Files, use OLE properties of the taskbar to copy	5.49	See Reference Window "Copying Files Using the OLE Properties of the Taskbar"
Files, use the Copy command to copy	14.50	See Reference Window "Copying Files from the Command Prompt"
Files, use wildcards to copy	14.54	See Reference Window "Copying Files from the Command Prompt Using Wildcards"
Floppy disk, copy	3.33	See Reference Window "Copying a Floppy Disk"
Floppy disk, format	3.31	See Reference Window "Formatting a Floppy Disk"
Floppy disk, use the Format utility to format	14.19	See Reference Window "Formatting a Floppy Disk from a Command Prompt"
Folder and its files, compress	7.48	See Reference Window "Compressing a Folder and Its Contents"
Folder and its files, copy	4.19	See Reference Window "Copying a Folder from Drive A to Drive C"
Folder and its files, decrypt	7.54	See Reference Window "Decrypting a Folder and Its Contents"
Folder and its files, encrypt	7.52	See Reference Window "Encrypting a Folder and Its Contents"

TASK	PAGE #	RECOMMENDED METHOD
Folder and its files, uncompress	7.51	See Reference Window "Uncompressing a Folder and Its Contents"
Folder properties, view	3.43	See Reference Window "Viewing Properties of a Folder or File, or a Group of Folders or Files"
Folder shortcut, use Windows Explorer to customize	4.31	See Reference Window "Customizing a Folder Shortcut for Windows Explorer"
Folder, create a shortcut to	4.17	See Reference Window "Creating a Shortcut to a Folder"
Folders and files, back up	6.33	See Reference Window "Using the Backup or Restore Wizard to Back Up Selected Folders on Drive C to Floppy Disks"
Folders and files, restore	6.43	See Reference Window "Using the Backup or Restore Wizard to Restore Files from Floppy Disks"
Folders toolbar, display	1.68	Click the Folders 📂 button
Format command, use	14.19	See Reference Window "Formatting a Floppy Disk from a Command Prompt"
Fragmentation, analyze a disk for	7.31	See Reference Window "Analyzing a Disk for Fragmentation"
Full-screen view, switch to from a command prompt	14.05	Press Alt+Enter
Group folder on the All Programs menu, create	4.39	See Reference Window "Creating a Group Folder on the All Programs Menu"
Group of files, view properties of	3.43	See Reference Window "Viewing Properties of a Folder or File, or a Group of Folders or Files"
Hardware configuration problems, use the System Information utility to identify	12.37	See Reference Window "Using the System Information Utility to Identify Hardware Configuration Problems"
Hardware problems, use Device Manager to troubleshoot	12.33	See Reference Window "Troubleshooting Hardware Problems with Device Manager"
Hardware settings, document	12.15	See Reference Window "Documenting Hardware Settings"
Help and Support Center, use	1.53	See Reference Window "Using the Help and Support Center"
Help button, use	4.09	Click Help ❓ button, then click dialog box option
Help command, use	14.24	See Reference Window "Displaying a Command Reference List from the Command Prompt"
Help for a command, display	14.13	See Reference Window "Using the Help Switch to Display Help for a Command"

TASK	PAGE #	RECOMMENDED METHOD
Help switch, use	14.13	See Reference Window "Using the Help Switch to Display Help for a Command"
Incremental backup, perform	6.56	See Reference Window "Performing an Incremental Backup of Selected Files to a Floppy Disk"
Internet Connection Firewall, enable	8.43	See Reference Window "Enabling Internet Connection Firewall"
Internet Explorer properties and settings, check and change	8.49	See Reference Window "Checking and Changing Internet Explorer Properties and Settings"
Internet Explorer security settings, check and change	8.49	See Reference Window "Checking and Changing Internet Explorer Properties and Settings"
Internet shortcut, create	4.33	See Reference Window "Creating an Internet Shortcut to a Web Site"
Linked object, create or insert	5.16	See Reference Window "Creating a Linked Object from a File"
Linked object, edit	5.23	See Reference Window "Editing a Linked Object"
Linked object, view properties of	5.20	See Reference Window "Viewing Properties of a Linked Object in WordPad"
Local reboot, perform	9.35	See Reference Window "Using Windows Task Manager to Shut Down a Non-Responding Program"
Make Directory command, use	14.47	See Reference Window "Creating a Subdirectory from the Command Prompt"
Microsoft Office components, add or remove	11.53	See Reference Window "Adding or Removing Microsoft Office Components"
Mouse pointer shapes or schemes, choose	2.34	See Reference Window "Choosing Mouse Pointer Shapes and Schemes"
Mouse properties, change	2.28	See Reference Window "Changing Mouse Properties"
MS-DOS startup disk, make, check, and test	8.14	See Reference Window "Making, Checking, and Testing an MS-DOS Startup Disk"
My Computer icon on the desktop, display	2.05	See Reference Window "Displaying My Documents and My Computer on the Desktop"
My Documents icon on the desktop, display	2.05	See Reference Window "Displaying My Documents and My Computer on the Desktop"
My Documents to the Quick Launch toolbar, add	2.15	Drag the My Documents icon onto the Quick Launch toolbar
Nonresponding program, shut down	9.35	See Reference Window "Using Windows Task Manager to Shut Down a Nonresponding Program"

TASK	PAGE #	RECOMMENDED METHOD
Paging file, locate and examine	10.08	See Reference Window "Locating and Examining the Paging File"
Parent directory, change to	14.44	See Reference Window "Changing to the Parent Directory of the Current Subdirectory"
Path command, use	14.56	See Reference Window "Viewing Settings for Environment Variables from the Command Prompt"
Performance Measurements, print	10.30	See Reference Window "Printing a Web Page with Performance Measurements"
Performance options for applications, view and change	10.37	See Reference Window "Viewing and Changing Performance Options for Applications"
Performance, use System Monitor to track	10.29	See Reference Window "Using System Monitor to Track Performance"
Performance, use Windows Task Manager to track	10.14	See Reference Window "Using Window Task Manager to Monitor Performance"
Pinned items list, remove an item from	4.58	Right-click the item in the pinned items list, click Remove from This List
Power management settings, check	2.72	See Reference Window "Checking Power Management Settings"
Printer problem, troubleshoot	9.55	See Reference Window "Using the Printing Troubleshooter"
Printer settings, check or change	10.61	See Reference Window "Checking or Changing Printer Settings and Printing Preferences"
Printing preferences, check or change	10.61	See Reference Window "Checking or Changing Printer Settings and Printing Preferences"
Printing Troubleshooter, use	9.55	See Reference Window "Using the Printing Troubleshooter"
Privacy settings, check and change	8.49	See Reference Window "Checking and Changing Internet Explorer Properties and Settings"
Programs menu, sort	4.40	Right-click the Programs menu, click Sort by Name
Properties of a group of folders or files, view	3.43	See Reference Window "Viewing Properties of a Folder or File, or a Group of Folders or Files"
Quick Launch toolbar, display and customize	2.17	See Reference Window "Displaying and Customizing the Quick Launch toolbar
RAM in your computer, find the total amount of	1.73	Click Start button, right-click My Computer, click Properties
Recovery Console, install	9.24	See Reference Window "Installing the Recovery Console"

TASK	PAGE #	RECOMMENDED METHOD
Recovery Console, open and use	9.31	See Reference Window "Opening and Using the Recovery Console"
Registered file type, view information on	3.60	See Reference Window "Viewing Information on a Registered File Type"
Registered file types, trace information in the Registry on	13.24	See Reference Window "Tracing Information on Registered File Types"
Registry Editors, open one of	13.16	See Reference Window "Exporting Registry Settings"
Registry settings, export	13.16	See Reference Window "Exporting Registry Settings"
Resolution, change the screen	2.52	See Reference Window "Changing the Screen Resolution"
Resource assignments, view	12.19	See Reference Window "Checking Resource Assignments"
Restoration, use System Restore to undo	8.32	See Reference Window "Undoing a Restoration with System Restore"
Restore point before using the Windows Registry, use System Restore to create	13.12	See Reference Window "Creating a Restore Point Before Using the Windows Registry"
Restore point, create	8.27	See Reference Window "Creating a Restore Point"
Restore point, restore	8.29	See Reference Window "Restoring a Restore Point"
Root directory, change to	14.34	See Reference Window "Changing to the Root Directory"
Safe Mode, boot in	9.13	See Reference Window "Booting in Safe Mode"
Scheduled task, create	7.59	See Reference Window "Creating a Scheduled Task"
Scheduled task, delete	7.62	See Reference Window "Deleting a Scheduled Task"
Scheduled task, view and change settings for	7.62	See Reference Window "Checking Settings for a Scheduled Task"
Scrap in a document, insert	5.40	See Reference Window "Inserting Scrap in a Document"
Scrap, create	5.34	See Reference Window "Creating Scrap"
Scrap, view properties of	5.36	Right-click scrap object, click Properties
Scrap, view the contents of	5.35	Click (or double-click) the scrap object
Screen saver, choose and customize	2.63	See Reference Window "Choosing and Customizing a Screen Saver"
Selection, use a saved backup	6.66	See Reference Window "Using a Saved Selection for a Backup"

TASK	PAGE #	RECOMMENDED METHOD
Send To menu, copy files to a floppy disk using	4.47	See Reference Window "Copying Files to a Floppy Disk Using the Send To Menu"
SendTo folder, copy shortcuts to	4.45	See Reference Window "Copying Shortcuts to the SendTo Folder"
Set command, use	14.56	See Reference Window "Viewing Settings for Environment Variables from the Command Prompt"
Shortcut, rename	4.06	Hover over and select a shortcut, press F2, type or edit name, press Enter
Shortcut, use the Start Menu to create a desktop	6.20	See Reference Window "Creating a Desktop Shortcut from the Start Menu"
Shortcut, view properties of	4.12	See Reference Window "Viewing Properties of a Shortcut"
Slide show screen saver, use your own pictures to create	2.66	See Reference Window "Creating a Slide Show Screen Saver Using Your Own Pictures"
Start menu, add a desktop shortcut to the	4.36	Drag the desktop shortcut and drop it on the Start button
Start Menu, customize the	2.09	See Reference Window "Customizing the Start Menu"
Start menu, use a shortcut key to close the	1.43	Press the Esc key
Start menu, use a shortcut key to open the	1.43	Press Ctrl+Esc
Startup and recovery settings, view or change	10.41	See Reference Window "Viewing or Changing Startup and Recovery Settings"
Subdirectory, create	14.47	See Reference Window "Creating a Subdirectory from the Command Prompt"
Subdirectory, view the contents of	14.42	See Reference Window "Displaying a Directory Listing"
System Configuration Utility, use	9.21	See Reference Window "Using the System Configuration Utility"
System Information utility, use	9.45	See Reference Window "Using the System Information Utility"
System information, display	14.26	See Reference Window "Displaying System Information from a Command Prompt (Windows XP Professional)"
System Monitor, track performance with	10.29	See Reference Window "Using System Monitor to Track Performance"
System Restore settings, check	8.24	See Reference Window "Checking System Restore Settings"
System State, back up	13.09	See Reference Window "Backing Up the System State"

TASK	PAGE #	RECOMMENDED METHOD
SystemInfo command, use the Windows XP Professional	14.26	See Reference Window "Displaying System Information from a Command Prompt (Windows XP Professional)"
Taskbar, customize	2.13	See Reference Window "Customizing the Taskbar"
Text file, view the contents of	14.30	See Reference Window "Using the Type Command to View the Contents of a Text File"
Theme, choose a desktop	2.37	See Reference Window "Choosing a Desktop Theme"
Toolbar, create a new desktop	2.23	See Reference Window "Creating a New Desktop Toolbar"
Tree command, use	14.33	See Reference Window "Displaying a Directory Tree from the Command Prompt"
Type command, use	14.30	See Reference Window "Using the Type Command to View the Contents of a Text File"
User interface elements, customize	2.45	See Reference Window "Customizing Elements of the User Interface"
Video display settings, check	2.59	See Reference Window "Checking Video Display Settings"
Visual effects, choose special	2.48	See Reference Window "Choosing Special Visual Effects"
Wallpaper, choose background	2.42	See Reference Window "Choosing Background Wallpaper"
Web style, change to	1.39	See Reference Window "Changing to Web Style"
Wildcards, create file specifications that use	14.54	See Reference Window "Copying Files from the Command Prompt Using Wildcards"
Window, copy and paste an image of the active	1.75	See Reference Window "Copying and Pasting the Image of a Window or Dialog Box into a Document"
Windowed view from a command prompt, switch to	14.06	Press Alt+Enter
Windows Advanced Options menu, display	9.09	During booting, press F8 before the Starting Windows progress indicator
Windows Classic style, change to	1.37	See Reference Window "Changing to Windows Classic Style"
Windows environment, use a Command Prompt window to view	14.56	See Reference Window "Viewing Settings for Environment Variables from the Command Prompt"

TASK	PAGE #	RECOMMENDED METHOD
Windows environment, use a Command Prompt window to view	14.56	See Reference Window "Viewing Settings for Environment Variables from the Command Prompt"
Windows Task Manager, use	10.14	See Reference Window "Using Task Manager to Monitor Performance"
Windows Update, use	11.69	See Reference Window "Using Windows Update"
Windows version, find your	1.73	Click Start button, right-click My Computer, click Properties
Windows XP component, install	11.62	See Reference Window "Installing a Windows XP Component"
Windows XP component, uninstall	11.64	See Reference Window "Uninstalling a Windows XP Component"
Windows, vertically tile	4.48	Right-click the taskbar, click Tile Windows Vertically

File Finder

Location in Tutorial	Name and Location of Data File	Student Creates New File
Tutorial 1	Drive C: (top-level folder)	
	Autoexec.bat	
	Boot.ini	
	Config.sys	
	Io.sys	
	Msdos.sys	
	Ntdetect.com	
	Ntldr	
	Pagefile.sys	
	Documents and Settings (folder)	
	[User Account Folder]	
	Ntuser.dat	
	Ntuser.dat.log	
	Ntuser.ini	
	Ntuser.pol	
	Cookies (folder)	
	Index.dat	
	[Any cookie text file]	
	Windows (folder)	
	Fonts (folder)	
	Arial.ttf	
	Times New Roman.ttf	
		System Properties Dialog Box.rtf
Review Assignments	My Pictures (folder)	
	Sample Pictures (folder)	
	Blue hills.jpg	Copy of Blue hills.jpg, or
	Desktop.ini	
	Sunset.jpg	Copy of Sunset.jpg, or
	Thumbs.db	
	Water lilies.jpg	Copy of Water lilies.jpg, or
	Winter.jpg	Copy of Winter.jpg
	My Music (folder)	
	Sample Music (folder)	
	Beethoven's Symphony No. 9 (Scherzo).wma	
	Desktop.ini	
	New Stories (Highway Blues).wma	
Case 1		Upgrading Computers at Townsend & Sumner Publishing.doc
Case 2		Upgrading Hardware at Stratton Graphics.doc
Case 4		Fast User Switching.doc
Extra Case		Providing Customer Support at Data Specialists.doc
Tutorial 2	Windows folder	Display Properties Dialog box.rtf
	Cursors folder	
	Horse.ani	
	Web folder	
	Wallpaper folder	
Case 1		Using Taskbar and Desktop Toolbars.rtf
Case 3		Desktop Design #1 (Before).doc
		Desktop Design #1 (After).doc
		Preparing a Desktop Design for a Home Computer.rtf

File Finder

Location in Tutorial	Name and Location of Data File	Student Creates New File

Tutorial 3	Data Disk #1
	  ~WRC0070.tmp
	  File0000.chk
	  Company Projections (folder)
	    2003 Sales Summary.xls
	    2004 Sales Summary.xls
	    Advertising Income.xls
	    Break-Even Analysis.xls
	    Company Sales Projection.xls
	    Computer Basics Training Proposal.doc
	    Daily Sales.xls
	    Five Year Growth Plan.xls
	    Five Year Plan Template.xls
	    Product List.xls
	    Product Sales Summary.xls
	    Projected Growth Memo.doc
	    Regional Sales Projection.xls
	    Sale Projection Models.xls
	    Sales.wk4
	    ShowCase Enterprises Balance Sheet.xls
	    VAI Three Year Sales Projection.xls
	    Visual Arts Budget.xls
	  Presentations (folder)
	    Example of a Memory Leak.ppt	

Review Assignments	Data Disk #1
	  Business Records (folder)
	    Contract Jobs.xls
	    Customer Accounts.xls
	    Invoice Form.wk4
	    Sales Commissions.xls
	    Personal Records (folder)
	    Resources (folder)
	    Presentations (folder)
	      File Systems.pps	

Case 2	Data Disk #1	Cases (folder)
		  Case 0001 (folder)
		  Case 0002 (folder)
		  Case 0005 (folder)
		  Case 0012 (folder)

Tutorial 4		Drive A (shortcut) Drive C (shortcut) Windows (shortcut)

	Data Disk #2
	  Delta Oil (folder)
	    Designs (folder)
	      Company Logo Design.bmp
		Delta Oil (shortcut)
		
		Company Logo Design (shortcut)
		WordPad (shortcut)
		Microsoft (Internet shortcut)
		Delta Oil (shortcut)
		Shortcuts (folder) [in Programs folder]
		  Company Logo Design (shortcut)
		  Delta Oil (shortcut)
		  Drive A (shortcut)
		  Drive C (shortcut)
		  Microsoft (Internet shortcut)
		  Windows (shortcut)
		  WordPad (shortcut)
		Shortcuts (folder) [in My
		Documents folder]

File Finder

Location in Tutorial	Name and Location of Data File	Student Creates New File
		Company Logo Design (shortcut)
		Delta Oil (shortcut)
		Drive A (shortcut)
		Drive C (shortcut)
		Microsoft (Internet shortcut)
		Windows (shortcut)
		WordPad (shortcut)
	Delta Oil (folder) [second copy on drive A]	Delta Oil (folder) [second copy on drive A]
	on drive A]	
	Overhead Transparencies (folder)	Delta Oil (shortcut) [in SendTo folder]
	Drive C (shortcut) [in SendTo folder]	
	Windows (shortcut) [in SendTo folder]	
	WordPad (shortcut) [in SendTo folder]	
	Delta Oil (folder)	
	Designs (folder)	
	Company Logo Design.bmp	
	Briefcase (folder)	Briefcase (folder)
	Delta Oil (folder)	Delta Oil (folder)
	Memos (folder)	
	Microsoft's Web Site.doc	
	Delta Oil (folder) [in My Documents folder]	
	Memos (folder)	
	Microsoft's Web Site.doc	
	Designs (folder)	
	Company Logo Design.bmp	
	Overhead Transparencies (folder)	
	Sales.wk4	
	Briefcase (folder)	
	Delta Oil (folder)	
	Memos (folder)	
	Microsoft's Web Site.doc	
	Overhead Transparencies (folder)	
	Designs (folder)	
	Company Logo Design.bmp	
Review Assignments	Data Disk #2	[Removable drive shortcut]
	Delta Oil (folder)	Control Panel (shortcut)
	Training (folder)	Training (folder shortcut)
	Designs (folder)	Company Logo Design (shortcut)
	Company Logo Design.bmp	Paint (shortcut)
	Windows	Windows (shortcut)
	Web	Intel (Internet shortcut)
	Wallpaper	Windows (shortcut) [on Start Menu]
	JPG File	Training Resources (group folder)
	Briefcase	Training (shortcut)
	Training (folder)	Training (shortcut) [in SendTo folder]
	Excel Basics.doc	Paint (shortcut) [in SendTo folder]
	JPG File	Windows (shortcut) [in SendTo folder]
		JPG File [in Training folder]
		Training Briefcase
		Training (folder)
Case 1	Program Files (folder)	Program Files (shortcut)
	Printers and Faxes (folder)	Printers and Faxes (shortcut)
	Accessibility Options (folder)	Accessibility Options (shortcut)
		Resources (folder)
		Resources (shortcut)

File Finder

Location in Tutorial	Name and Location of Data File	Student Creates New File

Case 2	Start Menu (folder)
	  Programs (folder)
	    Accessories (folder)
	  System Tools (folder)
	  System Utilities (folder)
	Control Panel
	
	Data Disk #2
		System Utilities (folder)
		  Control Panel
		    Display (shortcut)
		    Folder Options (shortcut)
		    Power Options (shortcut)
		    Scheduled Tasks (shortcut)
		    System (shortcut)
		    Mouse (shortcut)
		    Printers and Faxes (shortcut)
		    Date and Time (shortcut)
		    Regional and Language Options
		      (shortcut)
		System Utilities (folder) [duplicate]
		System Utilities (folder) [triplicate]

Case 3	Data Disk #2
	  Delta Oil (folder) [now O'Donnell Associates]
	    Overhead Transparencies (folder)
	    Training (folder)
	    Memos (folder)
	    Company Templates (folder)
	    Designs (folder)
		My Documents (shortcut)
		3½ Floppy (A:) (shortcut)
		O'Donnell Associates (folder)
		O'Donnell Associates (shortcut)
		Stafford Client Files (shortcut)
		Stafford Designs (shortcut)
		Microsoft Word (shortcut)
		Microsoft Excel (shortcut)
		Internet shortcut (landscaping firm)
		O'Donnell Shortcuts (folder)
		  My Documents (shortcut)
		  3½ Floppy (A:) (shortcut)
		  O'Donnell Associates (shortcut)
		  Stafford Client Files (shortcut)
		  Stafford Designs (shortcut)
		  Microsoft Word (shortcut)
		  Microsoft Excel (shortcut)
		  Internet shortcut (landscaping firm)
		O'Donnell Shortcuts (shortcut)

Case 4	Data Disk #2
	  Delta Oil (folder) [now Nolan Associates]
	  Training (folder)
	  Company Templates (folder)
	  Overhead Transparencies (folder)
	  Business Spreadsheets (folder)
	    Break-Even Analysis.xls
	    Daily Sales.xls
	    Loan Payment Analysis.xls
	    Product List.xls
	    Regional Sales Projection.xls
	    Savings Plan.xls
	    Software Quotes.xls
	    Visual Arts Employees.xls
	    ShowCase Enterprises Balance Sheet.xls
	    VAI Three Year Sales Projection.xls
	    Visual Arts Budget.xls
	  Presentations (folder)
	    Invoice Form.wk4
	    Sales.wk4
	  Memos (folder)
	    Microsoft's Web Site.doc
		My Documents (shortcut)
		3½ Floppy (A:) (shortcut)
		Nolan Associates Briefcase
		  Nolan Associates (folder)
		    Advertising (folder)
		    Projections (folder)
		Business Plan.doc

Location in Tutorial	Name and Location of Data File	Student Creates New File

	Nolan Associates Briefcase
	  Nolan Associates (folder)
	    Business Spreadsheets (folder)
	      Advertising Income.xls
	      Company Sales Projection.xls
	      Five Year Growth Plan.xls
	      Five Year Plan Template.xls
	      Nolan Associates Three Year Sales
	       Projection.xls
	      Sales Projection Models.xls
	
	    Memos (folder)
	      Business Plan.doc
	  Nolan Associates (folder) [on drive C]
	    Memos
	      Business Plan.doc	

Extra Case	Data Disk #2
	  Delta Oil (folder) [now Class Files]
	Class Files.zip [on drive C]
	  Company Templates (folder)
	Class Files.zip [on drive A]
		Class Files.zip [on drive C]
		Class Files.zip [on floppy disk]

Tutorial 5	Data Disk #3
	  Visual Arts (folder)
	    Designs (folder)
	      Logo Design #1.bmp
	      Logo Design #2.bmp
		Visual Arts (folder)
		  Memos
		    Company Logo Designs.rtf
		    New Company Logo.rtf
		    Annual Report.rtf
		  Scrap
		  Annual Report (folder)
		  Annual Report (shortcut)
		  Logo Design (shortcut)
		  Annual Report Logo.bmp
		  Logos (folder)
		  Original Logo.bmp

Review Assignments	Data Disk #3
	  Designs (folder)
	    Logo Design #2.bmp
		Visual Arts (folder)
		  Memos (folder)
		    New Employee.rtf
		    Scrap
		    Letterhead Design.rtf
		    New Employee #2.rtf

Case 1		Term Paper (folder)
		  Bitmap Image (file of their own
		  choosing)
		  Cover Sheet.rtf

Case 2	Data Disk #1	Stroud Investment Group (folder)
		  Break-Even Analysis.xls
		  Break-Even Analysis Memo.doc

Case 3	Data Disk #1	International Enterprises (folder)
		  2004 Sales Summary.xls
		  Sale Summary Memo.doc

Extra Case		Reichman's Nursery (folder)
		  Correspondence (folder)
		    Catalog Requests.rtf
		    Letter to [Customer Name]
		  Correspondence Library (folder)
		    Company Address
		    Catalog Request
		    Signature

File Finder

Location in Tutorial	Name and Location of Data File	Student Creates New File

Tutorial 6	Data Disk #1
	  Business Records (folder)
	  Company Documents (folder)
	  Company Projections (folder)
	  Personal Records (folder)
	  Presentations (folder)
	  Resources (folder)
	Data Disk #2
	  Delta Oil (folder)
	    Company Templates (folder)
	    Designs (folder)
	    Memos (folder)
	    Overhead Transparencies (folder)
	    Training (folder)
	Data Disk #3
	  Visual Arts (folder)
	MEI (folder)
	  Designs (folder)
	    Company Logo Design.bmp
	  Memos (folder)
	    Microsoft's Web Site.doc
	  Training (folder)
	    Excel Basics.doc
		MEI (folder)
		  Business Records (folder)
		  Company Documents (folder)
		  Company Projections (folder)
		  Personal Records (folder)
		  Presentations (folder)
		  Resources (folder)
		  Company Templates (folder)
		  Designs (folder)
		  Memos (folder)
		  Overhead Transparencies (folder)
		  Training (folder)
		  Visual Arts (folder)
		MEI Normal Backup.bkf
		My Backup Reports (folder)
		MEI Normal Backup Report.txt
		MEI (Original) (folder) [renamed]
		MEI (folder) [second copy]
		MEI Full Restore Report.txt
		Copy of Excel Basics.doc
		Advanced Excel. doc [renamed]
		MEI Incremental #1 Backup.bkf
		MEI Incremental.bks
		MEI Incremental #1 Backup Report.txt
		Company Logo Design.bmp [restored]
		MEI Partial Restore #1 Report.txt
		MEI Partial Restore #2 Report.txt
		MEI Incremental #2 Backup.bkf
		MEI Incremental #2 Backup Report.txt

Review Assignments	Data Disk #1
	  Business Records (folder)
	  Company Documents (folder)
	  Company Projections (folder)
	  Presentations (folder)
	  Resources (folder)
	Data Disk #2
	  Delta Oil (folder)
	    Company Templates (folder)
	    Designs (folder)
	    Memos (folder)
	    Overhead Transparencies (folder)
	    Training (folder)
		MEI (folder)
		  Business Records (folder)
		  Company Documents (folder)
		  Company Projections (folder)
		  Presentations (folder)
		  Resources (folder)
		  Company Templates (folder)
		  Designs (folder)
		  Memos (folder)
		  Overhead Transparencies (folder)
		Training (folder)
		MEI Normal Backup.bkf
		MEI Normal Backup Report.txt
		Intel's Web Site.rtf (or Intel's Web Site.doc)
		MEI Differential #1 Backup.bkf
		MEI Differential #1 Backup Report.txt
		MEI (folder) [restored]
		MEI Full Restore Report.txt
		MEI Partial Restore Report.txt

Case 1	Data Disk #1
	  Company Documents (folder)
	  Company Projections (folder)
	  Resources (folder)
	Data Disk #2
	  Company Templates (folder)
	  Memos (folder)
		FMC (folder)
		  Company Documents (folder)
		  Company Projections (folder)
		  Resources (folder)
		  Company Templates (folder)
		  Memos (folder)
		FMC Normal Backup.bkf
		FMC Normal Backup Report.txt
		First Mortgage Corporation (folder) [renamed]
		FMC (folder) [restored]
		FMC Full Restore Report.txt

File Finder

Location in Tutorial	Name and Location of Data File	Student Creates New File

Case 2	Data Disk #1
	  Business Records (folder)
	  Company Documents (folder)
	  Company Projections (folder)
	Data Disk #2
	  Delta Oil (folder)
	    Company Templates (folder)
		VMC (folder)
		  Business Records (folder)
		  Company Documents (folder)
		  Company Projections (folder)
		  Company Templates (folder)
		VMC Backup (folder)
		VMC Normal Backup.bkf
		VMC Normal Backup Report.txt
		VMC (folder) [restored]
		VMC Full Restore Report.txt

Case 3		Backup Schedule.doc
Case 4		Backup Schedule.doc
Extra Case		Evaluating an Online Backup Service.doc
Tutorial 7	Data Disk #2 Harris & Banche (folder) Company Templates (folder)	Volume C Analysis Report.txt Volume C Defragmentation Report.txt Harris & Banche (folder) Disk Cleanup (Scheduled Task)

Review Assignments	Data Disk #1
	  File0000.chk
	  ~WRC0070.tmp
	Harris & Banche (folder)
	  Company Projections (folder)
		Harris & Banche (folder)
		Disk Cleanup (Scheduled Task)

Case 2		Volume C Analysis Report.txt Volume C Defragmentation Report.txt
Case 3		Hard Disk Maintenance & Optimization Schedule.doc

Case 4	Data Disk #2
	Delta Oil (folder)
	  Overhead Transparencies (folder)
	  Training (folder)
	  Company Templates (folder)
	    Company Sales Projection.xls
	  Designs (folder)
	  Memos (folder)
	Invoice.wk4
		Delta Oil (folder)
		Delta Oil.zip
		Company Templates (folder)
		Invoice.wk4
		Designs (folder)
		Memos (folder)

Extra Case		Disk Defragmenter (Scheduled Task)
Tutorial 9		System Settings 01-24-2005.txt
Case 3		DxDiag.txt
Tutorial 10		Performance Measurements.htm
Review Assignments		Performance Measurements.htm
Case 1		Performance Measurements (Step 5).htm Performance Measurements (Step 9).htm Performance Measurements (Step 10).htm

File Finder		
Location in Tutorial	**Name and Location of Data File**	**Student Creates New File**
Case 2		Performance Measurements.doc
Case 3		Troubleshooting Strategy.doc
Case 4		Troubleshooting Strategy.doc
Tutorial 12		
Case 4		Netdiag.htm
Tutorial 13		Registry Backup (folder) Registry Backup for 2005-03-07.reg
Review Assignments		Registry Backup (folder) Registry Backup for 2005-03-08.reg
Case 1		Registry Backup (folder) Registry Backup for 2005-03-08.reg Class Definitions.doc
Case 2		Registry Backup (folder) Run MSMSGS.reg
Case 3		Registry Backup (folder) Explorer Link.reg
Case 4		Registry Backup (folder) Registry Backup for 2005-03-08.reg
Extra Case		Registry Backup (folder) Command Processor.reg

Tutorial 14		System Files (directory)
		  Config.sys
		  Autoexec.bat
		  Win.ini
		  System.ini
		  Autoexec.nt
		  Config.nt

Review Assignments		SystemInfo.txt (Windows XP Professional) Bootfile.txt (Windows XP Professional) Setuplog.txt Documentation (directory)
Case 3		Documentation (directory) RootDir.txt RootAttributes.txt WinDir.txt MyTree.txt MyFileTree.txt
Extra Case		Network Information.doc